FIND WHAT YOU
BELIEVE

AN ULTIMATE
A to Z
RESOURCE

THOMAS NELSON
Since 1798

NASHVILLE   DALLAS   MEXICO CITY   RIO DE JANEIRO

© 2013 by Thomas Nelson, Inc.

Published in Nashville, Tennessee, by Thomas Nelson, Inc.

Typesetting by Kevin A. Wilson, Upper Case Textual Services, Lawrence, MA.

ISBN: 978-1-4016-7784-8

Previous published as *Nelson's Biblical Cyclopedic Index*, ISBN 978-1-4185-4374-7.

Printed in the United States of America

13 14 15 16 17 18 [RRD] 6 5 4 3 2 1

How to Use *Find What You Believe*

Find What You Believe is a special kind of subject index that combines the best features of a concordance, a topical index, the usable study features of a syllabus, and other related study aids into one unique, quick, easy-to-use form. This index offers advantages for personal Bible study that not even a combination of the above study helps would provide. With 300 Word Studies and over 8,000 subjects, names, places, things, concepts, events, and doctrines of the Bible, *Find What You Believe* is truly a valuable key to Bible study.

Find What You Believe is arranged alphabetically giving the book, chapter, and verse where every reference in this index is found.

The example below will illustrate how to use *Find What You Believe*. Suppose you need to prepare or study a lesson on "The Peace of Jesus." Follow three easy steps.

1. Look up the subject heading Peace.

2. Next, find the subheading "Of Christ."

3. Now you see the various Scripture references dealing with the Peace of Jesus.

Find What You Believe has provided two important sources of information for you. First, you have the scriptural material needed to prepare or study your lesson. Second, you have this material in order as it appears in the Bible, so you have a ready-made outline for your personal use.

Peace
A. Kinds of:
    International . . . . .1 Sam. 7:14
    National . . . . .1 Kin. 4:24
    Civil . . . . .Rom. 14:19
    Domestic. . . . . 1 Cor. 7:15
    Individual. . . . . .Luke 8:48
    False. . . . . 1 Thess. 5:3
    Hypocritical. . . . . James 2:16
    Spiritual . . . . .Rom. 5:1
B. Source of:
    God . . . . Phil. 4:7
    Christ. . . . . .John 14:27
    Holy Spirit . . . . Gal. 5:22
C. Of Christ:
    Predicted . . . . Is. 9:6, 7
    Promised. . . . . Hag. 2:9
    Announced. . . . . Is. 52:7
D. Lord's relation to, He:
    Reveals . . . . Jer. 33:6
    Gives . . . . .Ps. 29:11
    Establishes . . . . Is. 26:12

Look for these word studies positioned alphabetically within the book:

head, *rosh*

heal, *rapha'*

healing, *marpe'*

healthy, be; be sound, *hugiainō*

heart, *leb*

heaven (expanse above earth), *shamayim*

helper, *paraklētos*

heresy, faction, *hairesis*

holy (set aside for holy purpose), *qadosh*

holy, *hagios*

honor, *hadar*

horn, *qeren*

hour, time, *hōra*

house, *bayith*

humble, *shaphel*

humility, *tapeinophrosunē*

hypocrisy, *hupokrisis*

hypocrite, *hupokritēs*

inheritance, *cheleq*

inheritance, *nachalah*

iniquity (crooked direction, warped deed), *'avon*

intercession, make, *paga'*

Jesus, *Iesous*

join, *proskollaō*

joy (laud, cheering in triumph), *rinnah*

joyful, *sameach*

judge, *shaphat*

judge, *krinō*

judgment, justice, *mishpat*

judgment, *krisis*

justify, *dikaioō*

keep a feast, *chagag*

keep under guard, *phroureō*

kind, good, *chrēstos*

kindness, *philanthrōpia*

know, *yada'*

know, *ginōskō*

know completely, *epiginōskō*

land, *'eretz*

laugh, *tsachaq*

law, *torah*

life, *zōē*

lift up, exalt, *hupsoō*

light, *phōs*

listen, *shama'*

little child, *teknion*

lord, master, *despotēs*

lord, master, *kurios*

love, *agapē*

lust, *epithumia*

majesty, *hod*

majesty, magnificence, *megaleiotēs*

man, *'adam*

man, *'ish*

manifest, reveal, *emphanizō*

mature, complete, perfect, *teleios*

meditate, *hagah*

memorial, *zikron*

mercy, *eleos*

messiah, *mashiach*

Messiah, *Messias*

minister, *sharat*

mortal, *'enosh*

mystery, *mustērion*

name, *shem*

name, *onoma*

natural, unspiritual, *psuchikos*

new, *kainos*

obey, *hupakouō*

one, *'echad*

one accord, of, *homothumadon*

open, *patach*

partial, one who is, *prosōpolēptēs*

partiality, *prosōpolēpsia*

partner, share in (partaker), *metochos*

pay, reward, *misthos*

peace, *eirēnē*

perdition, destruction, *apōleia*

perfect, make; complete, *teleioō*

physician, *iatros*

poor, *'ani*

possession, *'achuzzah*

power, *koach*

power, *dunamis*

praise, *halal*

praise, *shabach*

praise Yah, *allēlouia*

pray, *sha'al*

precept, *piqud*

preserve, *shamar*

priest, *cohen*

proclaim, *kērussō*

promise, *epaggelia*

prophecy, *prophēteia*

prophet, *nabi'*

propitiation, expiation, *hilasmos*

proud, arrogant, *huperēphanos*

proverb, *mashal*

psalm, *mizmor*

psalm, *psalmos*

purchase, buy, *agorazō*

ransom, *lutron*

reconcile, *katallassō*

redeem, *padah*

redeem, *ga'al*

redemption, *apolutrōsis*

reign, *malak*

repent, *metanoeō*

rest, *shabat*

rest, *anapauō*

rest, give, *nuach*

reveal, make known, *phaneroō*

revelation, *apokalupsis*

rock, *petra*

sabaoth, hosts, *sabaōth*

salt, *halas*

salvation, *sōtēria*

sanctification, *hagiasmos*

Satan, *satan*

save, *yashaʿ*

save, *sōzō*

save now, *hōsanna*

seer, *roʾeh*

self-control, *egkrateia*

send, *apostellō*

seraphim, *seraphim*

serve, *ʿabad*

serve, *douleuō*

service, *leitourgia*

set free, liberate, *eleutheroō*

Shiloh, *shiloh*

shout, *teruʿah*

sign, *ʾot*

sign, portent, *sēmeion*

sin, *hamartia*

snatch, seize, *harpazō*

son, only, *yachid*

son, *ben*

sorcery, magic, *pharmakeia*

soul, life, *psuchē*

soul, person, *nephesh*

spirit, *ruach*

spiritual, *pneumatikos*

spitefully treat, *hubrizō*

statute, *choq*

sustain, *kul*

swear, *shabaʿ*

take up, lift up, *airō*

taste, *taʿam*

teach, *yarah*

teach, disciple, *mathēteuō*

tempt, *nasah*

tempt, test, *peirazō*

testimony, proof, *marturion*

thank, *yadah*

thanks, give, *eucharisteō*

thanksgiving, *todah*

thought, opinion, *dialogismos*

time (quality of), *kairos*

time (quantity of, that is, lapse, span), *chronos*

trance, amazement, *ekstasis*

transgression, *peshaʿ*

transgression, *parabasis*

tribe, *matteh*

tribulation, affliction, *thlipsis*

trouble, *ʿamal*

trouble, disturb, *tarassō*

truth, *ʾemet*

unclean, *tameʾ*

understand, *bin*

understanding, *sunesis*

useless, worthless, *mataios*

utterance, oracle, *massaʾ*

virgin, *betulah*

virgin, *parthenos*

virtue, *aretē*

vision, *chazon*

wait, *qavah*

way, *derek*

wealth, *mammōnas*

wicked, *rashaʿ*

wind, spirit, *pneuma*

wipe away, erase, *exaleiphō*

wisdom, *chokmah*

wisdom, *sophia*

wonder, *teras*

wondrous thing, do a, *palaʾ*

word, *ʾimrah*

word, *dabar*

word, *logos*

work, be at, *energeō*

world, order, *kosmos*

worship, *shachah*

worship, *proskuneō*

wrath, *thumos*

write, *katab*

Yah, *Yah*

You have forsaken me, *sabachthani*

zeal, jealousy, *zēlos*

zealous, be, *qanaʾ*

A

Aaron—*bright*

A. Ancestry and family of:

Descendant of Levi .... Ex. 6:16–20
Son of Amram and Jochebed............Ex. 6:20
Moses' older brother ....Ex. 7:1, 7
Brother of Miriam ....Ex. 15:20
Husband of Elisheba ....Ex. 6:23
Father of Nadab, Abihu, Eleazar,
    and Ithamar ....Ex. 6:23

B. Position of:

Moses' helper......................Ex. 4:13–31
Becomes "prophet" to Moses...........Ex. 7:1, 2
God inspired ....Ex. 12:1
Commissioned, with Moses to deliver Israelites
    from Egypt ....Ex. 6:13, 26; Josh. 24:5
Inferior to that of Melchizedek ..... Heb. 7:11–19

C. Special privileges of:

Appears before Pharaoh............... Ex. 5:1–4
Performs miracles .... Ex. 7:9, 10, 19, 20
Supports Moses' hands............. Ex. 17:10–12
Ascends Mt. Sinai.............. Ex. 19:24; 24:1, 9
Sees God's glory .... Ex. 24:9, 10
Judges Israel in Moses' absence.........Ex. 24:14
Allowed inside the veil ....Lev. 16:15
Blesses the people.....................Lev. 9:22
Intercedes for Miriam...........Num. 12:10–12

D. Sins of:

Tolerates idolatry................... Ex. 32:1–4
Permits evil ....Ex. 32:21–25
Conspires against Moses ....Num. 12:1–16
With Moses, fails at Meribah .. Num. 20:1–13, 24

E. Character of:

A good speaker ....Ex. 4:14
Weak in crises ....Ex. 32:1–24
Subject to jealousy .... Num. 12:1, 2
Conscious of guilt .... Num. 12:11
Submissive ....Lev. 10:1–7
A saint..............................Ps. 106:16

F. Priesthood of:

Chosen by God ....Ex. 28:1
Sons, in office .... Lev. 8:1–36
Anointed with oil.................. Ex. 30:25, 30
Duties given....................... Ex. 30:7–10
Garments prescribed................ Ex. 39:1–31
Ordained to teach ....Lev. 10:8, 11
Set apart to offer sacrifices ....Lev. 9:1–24;
    Heb. 5:1–4
Alone enters within the holy place......Ex. 30:10;
    Heb. 9:7, 25
Intercedes for others .... Num. 16:46–48
Confirmed by God.......Num. 17:8–10; Heb. 9:4
Hereditary .... Num. 20:23–28
For lifetime .... Heb. 7:23
Inferior to Melchizedek's.......... Heb. 7:11–19

G. Death and successor of:

Lives 123 years .... Num. 33:39
Death........................ Num. 20:23–29

Eleazar, son of, successor ....Num. 20:25–28;
    Deut. 10:6

Aaronites—*descendants of Aaron*

Fight with David..................... 1 Chr. 12:27
Under Zadok .... 1 Chr. 27:17

Ab—*fifth month of the Jewish year*

Aaron died in...................... Num. 33:38
See Jewish calendar

Ab—*father*

A part of many Hebrew names (e.g., Abinadab,
    Abner, Abijah) ....1 Sam. 7:1

Abaddon—*a Hebrew word translated "destruction"*

Designates ruin in ....Job 31:12
Parallel with Sheol in................. Job 26:6
Refers to death .... Job 28:22
Personified..........................Rev. 9:11

Abagtha

A eunuch under King Ahasuerus....... Esth. 1:10

Abanah—*a river flowing through Damascus*

Spoken of highly by Naaman .... 2 Kin. 5:12

Abandon—*desert*

A. Required for:

Safety.............Gen. 19:12–26; Acts 27:41–44
Salvation.......................... Phil. 3:7–10
Service..........................Matt. 10:37–39
Sanctification ....2 Cor. 6:14–18
Spiritual success .... Heb. 11:24–27

B. Aspects of:

Land, commanded.................Gen. 12:1–5
Idolatry, admonished .... Ex. 32:1–10
One's ministry, rebuked .... 1 Kin. 19:3–18
Family, regretted .... 1 Sam. 30:1–6
The tabernacle, remembered............Jer. 7:12
Jerusalem, lamented .... Matt. 23:37, 38

C. Of people to judgment because of:

Sin.................................Gen. 6:5–7
Rebellion ....1 Sam. 15:16–26
Unbelief ....Matt. 23:37–39
Rejecting God..................... Rom. 1:21–32
Sexual immorality ....1 Cor. 5:1–5
Apostasy....................... Heb. 10:26–29

Abarim—*regions beyond*

Moses sees the Promised Land from .. Num. 27:12

Abasement—*degradation; humiliation*

A. As a judgment for:

Stubbornness.................... 2 Kin. 14:8–14
Defaming God .... 2 Chr. 32:1–22
Pride ....Is. 14:12–17
Haman's prejudice .... Esth. 7:4–10
Arrogance.......... Dan. 4:33, 37; Acts 12:20–23

B. As a virtue, seen in:

Nineveh's repentance ....Jon. 3:1–10; Matt. 12:41
A tax collector's unworthiness .....Luke 18:13, 14
Paul's life .... 1 Cor. 9:19–23
Christ's humiliation................Phil. 2:5–8

C. Rewards of, seen in:

Healing..........................2 Kin. 5:11–14
Elevation........................... Matt. 23:12
Restoration.......................Luke 15:11–24
Renewed service ....1 Cor. 15:9, 10

Abate—*diminish, desist*

Floodwaters....................... Gen. 8:8, 11
Moses' natural force not............. Deut. 34:7
Anger of Ephraim.....................Judg. 8:3

Abba—*an Aramaic word meaning "father"*

Used by Christ..................... Mark 14:36
Expressive of sonship.................Rom. 8:15

Abda—*servant (of God)*

1. The father of Adoniram................ 1 Kin. 4:6
2. A Levite, son of Shammua.............Neh. 11:17
Called Obadiah...................... 1 Chr. 9:16

Abdeel—*servant of God*

The father of Shelemiah.............. Jer. 36:26

Abdi—*servant of Yahweh*

1. The grandfather of Ethan .... 1 Chr. 6:44
2. A Levite .... 2 Chr. 29:12
3. One who divorced his foreign wife ......Ezra 10:26

Abdiel—*servant of God*

A Gadite residing in Gilead........1 Chr. 5:15, 16

Abdon—*servile*

1. A minor judge ....Judg. 12:13–15
2. A Benjamite living in Jerusalem..... 1 Chr. 8:23, 28
3. A son of Jeiel .... 1 Chr. 8:30; 9:36
4. A courtier of King Josiah............. 2 Chr. 34:20
5. A Levitical city .... Josh. 21:30; 1 Chr. 6:74

Abed-Nego—*servant of Nego*

Name given to Azariah, a Hebrew
captive .... Dan. 1:7
Appointed by Nebuchadnezzar ....Dan. 2:49
Accused of disobedience ....Dan. 3:12
Cast into furnace but delivered .... Dan. 3:13–27
Promoted by Nebuchadnezzar ..... Dan. 3:28–30

Abel—*breath*

Adam's second son..................... Gen. 4:2
The first shepherd .... Gen. 4:2
Offering of, accepted.................... Gen. 4:4
Hated and slain by Cain................. Gen. 4:8
Christ's blood superior to............Heb. 12:24
Place of, filled by Seth................. Gen. 4:25
First martyr .... Matt. 23:35
Righteous........................... Matt. 23:35
Offered sacrifice to God by faith .... Heb. 11:4

Abel—*meadow*

1. A city involved in Sheba's
rebellion.................. 2 Sam. 20:14, 15, 18
2. Translated as "large stone of Abel" in .. 1 Sam. 6:18
3. Elsewhere in place-names (see below)

Abel Acacia Grove—*meadow of acacias*

A place in Moab .... Num. 33:49

Abel Beth Maachah—*meadow of the house of oppression*

A town in North Palestine ...... 2 Sam. 20:14, 15;
1 Kin. 15:20
Captured by Tiglath-Pileser ....2 Kin. 15:29
Refuge of Sheba; saved from
destruction ....2 Sam. 20:14–22
Seized by Ben-Hadad ....1 Kin. 15:20

Abel Maim—*meadow of waters*

Another name for Abel Beth
Maachah ....2 Chr. 16:4

Abel Meholah—*meadow of dancing*

Midianites flee to....................Judg. 7:22
A few miles east of Jabesh Gilead...... 1 Kin. 4:12
Elisha's native city ....1 Kin. 19:16

Abel Mizraim—*meadow of Egypt*

A place, east of Jordan, where Israelites mourned
for Jacob.....................Gen. 50:10, 11

Abez—*whiteness*

A town of Issachar ....Josh. 19:20

Abhor—*to detest, loathe, hate*

A. Descriptive of:

Disliking God's laws ....Lev. 26:15
Prejudice toward non-Israelites .... Deut. 23:7
Right attitude toward idolatry ..... Deut. 7:25, 26
Self-rejection .... Job 42:6
Israel abhorred by Rezon .... 1 Kin. 11:23–25
Israel's rejection by God............. Ps. 89:38, 39
Rejection by former friends............Job 19:19
Loss of appetite...................... Job 33:20
Rejecting false description...........Prov. 24:24

B. Expressive of God's loathing of:

Israel's idolatry ....Ps. 78:58, 59
Customs of other nations.............Lev. 20:23
Men of bloodshed...................... Ps. 5:6

C. Expressive of Israel's rejection of God's:

Judgments ....Lev. 26:15
Statutes............................ Lev. 26:43
Ceremonies ....1 Sam. 2:17

D. Expressive of the believer's hatred of:

Lying ....Ps. 119:163
Evil................................Rom. 12:9

Abi—*an old form of father of*

King Hezekiah's mother ....2 Kin. 18:2
Also called Abijah ....2 Chr. 29:1

Abi-Albon

An Arbathite...................... 2 Sam. 23:31
See Abiel

Abiasaph—*the father gathers*

A descendant of Levi through Korah .....Ex. 6:24
Called Ebiasaph .... 1 Chr. 6:23, 37
Descendants of, act as doorkeepers.... 1 Chr. 9:19

Abiathar—*father of preeminence*

A priest who escapes Saul
at Nob.................... 1 Sam. 22:20–23
Becomes high priest under David ....1 Sam. 23:6,
9–12

Shares high priesthood with Zadok...2 Sam. 19:11
Remains faithful to David.......2 Sam. 15:24–29
Informs David about
    Ahithophel ....2 Sam. 15:34–36
Supports Adonijah's usurpation...1 Kin. 1:7, 9, 25
Deposed by Solomon......... 1 Kin. 2:26, 27, 35
Eli's line ends.................... 1 Sam. 2:31–35
Referred to by Christ................ Mark 2:26

Abib—*an ear of corn*
First month in Hebrew year...........Ex. 12:1, 2
Commemorative of the Passover ..... Ex. 12:1–28
Called Nisan in postexilic times........ Neh. 2:1

Abida, Abidah—*the father knows*
A son of Midian; grandson of Abraham
    and Keturah .... Gen. 25:4

Abidan—*the father is judge*
Represents tribe of Benjamin .... Num. 1:11
Brings offering ....Num. 7:60, 65
Leads Benjamites ....Num. 10:24

Abide, abiding—*continuing in a permanent state*
A. Applied to:
    Earth's existence......................Ps. 119:90
    Three graces .... 1 Cor. 13:13
    God's Word .... 1 Pet. 1:23
    Believer's eternity....................1 John 2:17
B. Sphere of, in the Christian's life:
    Christ.............................John 15:4–6
    Christ's words .... John 15:7
    Christ's love .... John 15:10
    Christ's doctrine.......................2 John 9
    The Holy Spirit.....................John 14:16
    God's Word .... 1 John 2:14, 24
    The truth ....2 John 2
C. Descriptive of the believer's:
    Protection............................. Ps. 91:1
    Fruitfulness ....John 15:4, 5
    Prayer life .... John 15:7
    Assurance......................... 1 John 2:28

Abiel—*God is father*
1. The grandfather of Saul and Abner.... 1 Sam. 9:1, 2
2. One of David's mighty men .... 1 Chr. 11:32
    Also called Abi-Albon.............. 2 Sam. 23:31

Abiezer—*the father is help*
1. A descendant of Joseph................Josh. 17:1, 2
    Called Jeezer ....Num. 26:30
    Family settles at Ophrah ....Judg. 6:24
    Gideon belongs to ....Judg. 6:11, 12
    Family rallies to Gideon's call.........Judg. 6:34
2. A mighty man and commander in
    David's army....................2 Sam. 23:27

Abiezrite
A member of the family of
    Abiezer................... Judg. 6:11, 24, 34

Abigail—*the father is joyful*
1. Nabal's beautiful and wise wife .... 1 Sam. 25:3
    Appeases David's anger ....1 Sam. 25:14–35
    Becomes David's wife .... 1 Sam. 25:36–42

Captured and rescued........... 1 Sam. 30:5, 18
Mother of Chileab ....2 Sam. 3:3
2. A stepsister of David............... 1 Chr. 2:16, 17

Abihail—*the father is might*
1. A Levite head of the house of Merari ....Num. 3:35
2. Abishur's wife .... 1 Chr. 2:29
3. A Gadite chief in Bashan .... 1 Chr. 5:14
4. Wife of King Rehoboam .... 2 Chr. 11:18
5. Father of Queen Esther .... Esth. 2:15

Abihu—*he is father*
Second of Aaron's four sons.............Ex. 6:23
Ascends Mt. Sinai....................Ex. 24:1, 9
Chosen as priest ....Ex. 28:1
Offers, with Nadab, strange fire......Lev. 10:1–7
Dies in the presence of the Lord....... Num. 3:4
Dies without heirs ....1 Chr. 24:2

Abihud—*the father is majesty*
A Benjamite........................ 1 Chr. 8:3

Abijah—*Yahweh is Father*
1. Wife of Hezron...................... 1 Chr. 2:24
2. Son of Becher ....1 Chr. 7:8
3. Samuel's second son; follows corrupt
    ways............................1 Sam. 8:2, 3
4. Descendant of Aaron; head of an office
    of priests.......................1 Chr. 24:3, 10
    Zacharias belongs to .... Luke 1:5
5. Son of Jeroboam I.................. 1 Kin. 14:1–18
6. Another name for King Abijam....... 2 Chr. 11:20
7. The mother of Hezekiah .... 2 Chr. 29:1
    Called Abi ....2 Kin. 18:2
8. A priest who signs the document........Neh. 10:7
9. A priest returning from Babylon with
    Zerubbabel .... Neh. 12:1, 4, 17

Abijam—*another form of Abijah*
King of Judah ....1 Kin. 14:31
Son and successor of King Rehoboam ..... 1 Kin.
    15:1–7
Follows in his father's sins ....1 Kin. 15:3, 4
Wars against King Jeroboam ....1 Kin. 15:6, 7
Also called Abijah .... 1 Chr. 3:10
Slays 500,000 Israelites......... 2 Chr. 13:13–20
Fathers 38 children by 14 wives ......2 Chr. 13:21

Abilene—*grassy place*
A province or tetrarchy of Syria .... Luke 3:1

Ability—*power to perform*
A. Descriptive of:
    Material prosperity .... Deut. 16:17
    Emotional strength .... Num. 11:14
    Military power ....Num. 13:31; 1 Kin. 9:21
    Physical strength .... Ex. 18:18, 23
    Mental power........................ Gen. 15:5
    Moral power......................... 1 Cor. 3:2
    Spiritual power .... James 3:2
    Divine power ....Rom. 4:21
B. Of God's power to:
    Deliver............................1 Cor. 10:13
    Humble men .... Dan. 4:37

Create life............................Matt. 3:9
Destroy .... Matt. 10:28
Preserve believers....................John 10:28
Keep His promise....................Rom. 4:21
Establish us .... Rom. 16:25
Supply grace......................... 2 Cor. 9:8
Exceed our petitions .... Eph. 3:20
Supply ability........................1 Pet. 4:11
Comfort others...................... 2 Cor. 1:4
Keep what we have committed
     to Him ....2 Tim. 1:12
Save from death .... Heb. 5:7
Resurrect men....................... Heb. 11:19
Keep from stumbling ....Jude 24, 25
C. Of Christ's power to:
Heal........................... Matt. 9:28, 29
Subdue all things .... Phil. 3:21
Help His own........................ Heb. 2:18
Have compassion ....Heb. 4:15, 16
Save completely...................... Heb. 7:25
D. Of the Christian's power to:
Speak for the Lord .... Luke 21:15
Admonish..........................Rom. 15:14
Survive testings...................1 Cor. 3:13–15
Withstand Satan.................... Eph. 6:11, 13
Convict opposition ....Titus 1:9
Bridle the whole body .... James 3:2

Abimael—*God is Father*
A son of Joktan .... Gen. 10:28

Abimelech—*the father is king*
1. A Philistine king of Gerar .... Gen. 20:1–18
     Makes treaty with Abraham ...... Gen. 21:22–34
2. A second king of Gerar.............. Gen. 26:1–11
     Tells Isaac to go home........... Gen. 26:12–16
     Makes a treaty with Isaac concerning
         certain wells ....Gen. 26:17–33
3. A son of Gideon by a concubine........ Judg. 8:31
     Conspires to become king ....Judg. 9:1–4
     Slays his 70 brothers....................Judg. 9:5
     Made king of Shechem ....Judg. 9:6
     Rebuked by Jotham, lone survivor.... Judg. 9:7–21
     Conspired against by Gaal.........Judg. 9:22–29
     Captures Shechem and Thebez..... Judg. 9:41–50
     Death of .... Judg. 9:51–57
4. A son of Abiathar the priest .... 1 Chr. 18:16
     Also called Ahimelech ....1 Chr. 24:6

Abinadab—*the father is generous*
1. A man of Kirjath Jearim whose house
     tabernacles the ark of the Lord..... 1 Sam. 7:1, 2
2. The second of Jesse's eight sons........ 1 Sam. 16:8
     A soldier in Saul's army........... 1 Sam. 17:13
3. A son of Saul slain at Mt. Gilboa .....1 Sam. 31:1–8
     Bones of, buried by men of Jabesh . 1 Chr. 10:1–12

Abinoam—*the father is pleasantness*
Father of Barak......................Judg. 4:6

Abiram—*the father is exalted*
1. Reubenite who conspired against
     Moses .... Num. 16:1–50

2. The firstborn son of Hiel...Josh. 6:26; 1 Kin. 16:34

Abishag—*the father wanders*
A Shunammite employed as David's
     nurse .... 1 Kin. 1:1–4, 15
Witnessed David's choice of Solomon
     as successor...................1 Kin. 1:15–31
Adonijah slain for desiring to marry
     her .... 1 Kin. 2:13–25

Abishai—*father of a gift*
A son of Zeruiah, David's sister ....2 Sam. 2:18
Brother of Joab and Asahel ....1 Chr. 2:16
Rebuked by David ....1 Sam. 26:5–9
Serves under Joab in David's
     army .... 2 Sam. 2:17, 18
Joins Joab in blood-revenge against
     Abner ....2 Sam. 2:18–24
Cocommander of David's army ... 2 Sam. 10:9, 10
Loyal to David during Absalom's
     uprising ....2 Sam. 16:9–12
Sternly rebuked by David........2 Sam. 19:21–23
Loyal to David during Sheba's
     rebellion...................2 Sam. 20:1–6, 10
Slays 300 Philistines .... 2 Sam. 23:18
Slays 18,000 Edomites.......... 1 Chr. 18:12, 13
Saves David by killing a giant.... 2 Sam. 21:16, 17

Abishalom—*father of peace*
A variant form of Absalom ....1 Kin. 15:2, 10

Abishua—*the father is salvation*
1. A Benjamite......................... 1 Chr. 8:3, 4
2. Phinehas's son....................1 Chr. 6:4, 5, 50

Abishur—*the father is a wall*
A Jerahmeelite................... 1 Chr. 2:28, 29

Abital—*the father is dew*
Wife of David .... 2 Sam. 3:2, 4

Abitub—*the father is goodness*
A Benjamite......................1 Chr. 8:8–11

Abiud—*Greek form of Abihud*
Ancestor of Jesus ....Matt. 1:13

Ablution—*ceremonial washing*
Of priests .... Ex. 30:18–21; 40:30, 31
Of ceremonially unclean ....Lev. 14:7–9; 15:5–10
Of a house...........................Lev. 14:52
By Pharisees........................ Mark 7:1–5

Abner—*the father is a lamp*
Commands Saul's army .... 1 Sam. 14:50, 51
Introduces David to Saul .... 1 Sam. 17:55–58
Rebuked by David ....1 Sam. 26:5, 14–16
Saul's cousin.................... 1 Sam. 14:50, 51
Supports Ishbosheth as Saul's
     successor .... 2 Sam. 2:8–10
Defeated by David's men .... 2 Sam. 2:12–17
Kills Asahel in self-defense .... 2 Sam. 2:18–23
Pursued by Joab ....2 Sam. 2:24–32
Slain by Joab ....2 Sam. 3:8–27
Death of, condemned by David ...2 Sam. 3:28–39

Abolish—*to do away with*

A. Of evil things:

Idolatry.................................Is. 2:18

Man-made ordinances ....Col. 2:20–22

Death.............................1 Cor. 15:26

Evil works..........................Ezek. 6:6

Enmity............................. Eph. 2:15

B. Of things good for a while:

Old covenant........................2 Cor. 3:13

Present world......................Heb. 1:10–12

Temporal rule ....1 Cor. 15:24

Partial things.......................1 Cor. 13:10

C. Of things not to be abolished:

God's righteousness......................Is. 51:6

God's Word ....Matt. 5:18

Abominations—*things utterly repulsive*

A. Descriptive of:

Undesirable social relations.. Gen. 43:32; Ex. 8:26

Spiritist practices ....Deut. 18:9–12

Heathen idolatry ....Deut. 7:25, 26

Child-sacrifice...................... Deut. 12:31

Pagan gods..........................2 Kin. 23:13

B. Applied to perverse sexual relations:

Unnatural acts.................... Lev. 18:19–29

Wrong clothing...................... Deut. 22:5

Prostitution and sodomy .... Deut. 23:17, 18

Reclaiming a defiled woman......... Deut. 24:4

Racial intermarriage .... Ezra 9:1–14

C. In ceremonial matters, applied to:

Unclean animals.......... Lev. 11:10–23, 41–43

Deformed animals....................Deut. 17:1

Heathen practices in God's house ....2 Chr. 36:14

D. Sinfulness of, seen in:

Being enticed.......................1 Kin. 11:5, 7

Delighting in........................... Is. 66:3

Rejecting admonitions against........ Jer. 44:4, 5

Polluting God's house..................Jer. 7:30

Being defiled ....Ezek. 20:7, 30–32

E. Judgments upon, manifested in:

Stoning to death .... Deut. 17:2–5

Destroying a city....................Deut. 13:13–17

Diminishing of, by God's

vengeance .... Ezek. 5:11–13

Experiencing God's fury............ Ezek. 20:7, 8

F. Things especially classed as:

Silver or gold from graven images ..... Deut. 7:25

Perverse man........................Prov. 3:32

Seven sins .... Prov. 6:16–19

False balance ....Prov. 11:1

Lying lips ....Prov. 12:22

Sacrifices of the wicked ....Prov. 15:8, 9

Proud in heart.......................Prov. 16:5

Justifying the wicked.................. Prov. 17:15

Scoffer.............................Prov. 24:9

Prayer of one who turns away his ear ...Prov. 28:9

False worship...........................Is. 1:13

Scant measures .... Mic. 6:10

Self-righteousness ....Luke 16:15

Abomination of desolation

Predicted by Daniel.......Dan. 9:27; 11:31; 12:11

Cited by Christ .... Matt. 24:15

Abortion—*accidental or planned miscarriage*

Laws concerning................... Ex. 21:22–25

Pronounced as a judgment............ Hos. 9:14

Sought to relieve misery.................Job 3:16

Of animals, by thunder...................Ps. 29:9

Figurative of abrupt conversion .... 1 Cor. 15:8

Abound—*to increase greatly*

A. Of good things:

God's grace...................... Rom. 5:15, 20

Hope ....Rom. 15:13

God's work ....1 Cor. 15:58

Suffering of Christ.....................2 Cor. 1:5

Joy in suffering ....2 Cor. 8:2

Gracious works ....2 Cor. 8:7

Good works ....2 Cor. 9:8

Love............................... Phil. 1:9

Fruitfulness .... Phil. 4:17, 18

Faith...............................Col. 2:7

Pleasing God .... 1 Thess. 4:1

Christian qualities .... 2 Pet. 1:5–8

Blessings ....Prov. 28:20

B. Source of, in good things:

From God............................ 2 Cor. 9:8

From Christian generosity...........2 Cor. 8:2, 3

Faithfulness.......................Prov. 28:20

Generosity ....Phil. 4:14–18

C. Of evil things:

Transgressions ....Prov. 29:22

Lawlessness .... Matt. 24:12

Increasing sins.......................Rom. 5:20

Abraham—*the father of a multitude*

A. Ancestry and family:

Descendant of Shem .... 1 Chr. 1:24–27

Son of Terah.......................... Gen. 11:26

First named Abram .... Gen. 11:27

A native of Ur ....Gen. 11:28, 31

Pagan ancestors ....Josh. 24:2

Weds Sarai .... Gen. 11:29

B. Wanderings of:

Goes to Haran...................... Gen. 11:31

Receives God's call.......Gen. 12:1–3; Acts 7:2–4

Prompted by faith .... Heb. 11:8

Enters Canaan...................... Gen. 12:4–6

Canaan promised to, by God........ Gen. 12:1, 7

Pitched his tent near Bethel........... Gen. 12:8

Famine sends him to Egypt........... Gen. 12:10

Calls Sarai his sister...............Gen. 12:11–20

Returns to Canaan enriched.........Gen. 13:1–5

Chooses Hebron rather than

strife .... Gen. 13:6–12

C. Testing and victory of:

Separates from Lot.................Gen. 13:8–12

Rescues captured Lot ....Gen. 14:14–16

Receives Melchizedek's blessing... Gen. 14:18–20

Covenant renewed; a son
    promised to . . . . Gen. 15:1–21
Justified by faith . . . . Gen. 15:6; Rom. 4:3
Takes Hagar as concubine . . . . Gen. 16:1–4
Ishmael born . . . . Gen. 16:5–16
Covenant renewed; named
    Abraham . . . . Gen. 17:1–8
Household of,
    circumcised . . . . Gen. 17:9–14, 23–27
Promised a son . . . . Gen. 17:15–19
Covenant in Isaac, not Ishmael . . . . Gen. 17:20–22;
    Gal. 4:22–31
Receives messengers . . . . Gen. 18:1–15
Intercedes concerning Sodom . . . . . . Gen. 18:16–33
Witnesses Sodom's doom . . . . Gen. 19:27, 28
His intercession saves Lot . . . . Gen. 19:29
Sojourns at Gerar; deceives
    Abimelech . . . . Gen. 20:1–18
Isaac born to, and circumcised . . . . Gen. 21:1–8
Sends Hagar and Ishmael away . . . . . Gen. 21:9–21
Makes covenant with Abimelech . . Gen. 21:22–34
Testing of, in offering Isaac . . . . Gen. 22:1–19
Receives news about Nahor . . . . Gen. 22:20–24
Buys burial place for Sarah . . . . Gen. 23:1–20
Obtains wife for Isaac . . . . Gen. 24:1–67
Marries Keturah; fathers other
    children; dies . . . . Gen. 25:1–10
D. Characteristics of:
    Friend of God . . . . 2 Chr. 20:7
    Obedient . . . . Gen. 22:1–18
    Giving . . . . Gen. 14:20; Heb. 7:1, 2, 4
    Generous . . . . Gen. 13:8, 9
    Courageous . . . . Gen. 14:13–16
    Independent . . . . Gen. 14:21–23
    Man of prayer . . . . Gen. 18:23–33
    Man of faith . . . . Gen. 15:6
    Rich man . . . . Gen. 13:2
    Mighty prince . . . . Gen. 23:5, 6
    Good provider . . . . Gen. 25:5, 6
E. References to, in the New Testament:
    Ancestor of Jesus . . . . Matt. 1:1
    In the line of faith . . . . Heb. 11:8–10
    Christ the true Seed of . . . . Gal. 3:16
    Foresees Christ's day . . . . John 8:56
    Hears the gospel preached . . . . Gal. 3:8
    Justified by faith . . . . Rom. 4:1–12
    Faith of, seen in works . . . . James 2:21–23
    Father of true believers . . . . Matt. 8:11;
    Rom. 4:11–25; Gal. 3:7, 29
    Sees the eternal city . . . . Heb. 11:8–10, 13–16
    Covenant with, still valid . . . . Luke 1:73; Acts 3:25
    Sons of, illustrate covenants . . . . Gal. 4:22–31
    Tithing of, has deeper meaning . . . . . . Heb. 7:9, 10
    Headship of, in marriage . . . . 1 Pet. 3:5–7
    Eternal home of, in heaven . . . . Luke 16:19–25

Abraham's bosom
    Expressive of heavenly status . . . . . Luke 16:22, 23

Abram (see Abraham)

Abronah—*passage*
    Israelite encampment . . . . Num. 33:34

Absalom—*the father of peace*
    Son of David . . . . 2 Sam. 3:3
    A handsome man . . . . 2 Sam. 14:25
    Receives Tamar after her rape by
    Amnon . . . . 2 Sam. 13:20
    Slays Amnon for raping Tamar . . . 2 Sam. 13:22–33
    Flees from David . . . . 2 Sam. 13:34–39
    Returns through Joab's intrigue . . . 2 Sam. 14:1–24
    Fathers children . . . . 2 Sam. 14:27
    Reconciled to David . . . . 2 Sam. 14:28–33
    Alienates the people from David . . . 2 Sam. 15:1–6
    Conspires against David . . . . 2 Sam. 15:7–12
    Forces David from Jerusalem . . . . 2 Sam. 15:13–29
    Receives Hushai . . . . 2 Sam. 15:31–37
    Hears Ahithophel's counsel . . . . . . 2 Sam. 16:20–23
    Prefers Hushai's counsel . . . . 2 Sam. 17:5–14
    Strategy of, revealed to David . . . . 2 Sam. 17:15–22
    Masses his army against David . . . 2 Sam. 17:24–26
    Caught and slain by Joab . . . . 2 Sam. 18:9–18
    Death of, brings sorrow
    to David . . . . 2 Sam. 18:19–33
    Joab rebukes David for mourning
    over . . . . 2 Sam. 19:1–8
    Death of, unites Israel again
    to David . . . . 2 Sam. 19:9–15

Absence
A. Of physical relations:
    A child from its father . . . . Gen. 37:32–35
    Israel's ark . . . . 1 Sam. 4:21, 22
    Israel from her land . . . . 2 Chr. 36:17–21
    Believers from one another . . . . Phil. 1:25–27
    Believers from Christ . . . . 2 Cor. 5:6–9
B. Of God's Spirit as:
    Judgment on the world . . . . Gen. 6:3
    Judgment on an individual . . . . 1 Sam. 16:14
    Unable to flee . . . . Ps. 139:7–12
C. Of graces:
    Holy Spirit . . . . Jude 19
    Faith . . . . 2 Thess. 3:2
    Love . . . . 2 Tim. 3:2
    Holiness . . . . Rev. 22:11
    Righteousness . . . . Rev. 22:11

Absenteeism—*habitual absence from*
    Work, condemned . . . . 2 Thess. 3:6–14
    Church, rebuked . . . . Heb. 10:25

Abstain—*to refrain from*
A. From moral evil:
    Vindictiveness . . . . 2 Sam. 16:5–14
    Idolatry . . . . Acts 15:20, 29
    Sexual immorality . . . . Acts 15:20
    Sexual sins . . . . 1 Thess. 4:3
    Fleshly lusts . . . . 1 Pet. 2:11
    Every form of evil . . . . 1 Thess. 5:22
B. From things:
    Food . . . . 2 Sam. 12:16, 23

Married relations . . . . .Ex. 19:15; 1 Cor. 7:5
Meats. . . . . .Rom. 14:1–23; 1 Cor. 8:1–13
C. From unauthorized commands:
Forbidding to marry . . . . 1 Tim. 4:3
Requiring man-made ceremonies . . . Col. 2:20–23
Abstaining from foods . . . . 1 Tim. 4:3

Abstinence—*to refrain from*
Blood. . . . . Acts 15:20
Evil. . . . . .1 Thess. 5:22
Eating . . . . Acts 27:21
Sexual immorality . . . . Acts 15:20; 1 Thess. 4:3
Idolatry. . . . . Acts 15:20
Intoxicants. . . . . .Prov. 23:31
Lust . . . . .1 Pet. 2:11
Things offered to idols . . . . Acts 15:29
Meats contaminated . . . . Acts 15:20

Abstinence—*to refrain from strong drink*
A. Required of:
Priests . . . . .Lev. 10:9
Kings. . . . . Prov. 31:4
Nazirites . . . . Num. 6:1–4
B. Failure of, a cause of:
Sudden death. . . . . .1 Sam. 25:36–38
Delirium tremens. . . . . Prov. 23:31–35
Insensibility to justice. . . . . Is. 5:11, 12, 22, 23
Error in judgment. . . . . Is. 28:7
Moral callousness. Is. 56:12
Revelry . . . . .Dan. 5:2–4
Debauchery .Hab. 2:15, 16
A weaker brother's stumble . . . . Rom. 14:20, 21
Excess . . . . .Eph. 5:18
C. Examples of:
Manoah's wife. . . . . Judg. 13:3, 4, 7
Samson . . . . .Judg. 16:17
Hannah. . . . . .1 Sam. 1:15
Rechabites . . . . Jer. 35:1–19
Daniel . . . . Dan. 1:8
John the Baptist . . . . .Luke 1:13–15

Abundance—*plentiful supply*
A. Of material things:
Spices. . . . . .1 Kin. 10:10
Rain. . . . . .1 Kin. 18:41
Metals . . . . .1 Chr. 22:3, 14
Trees . . . . .1 Chr. 22:4; Neh. 9:25
Sacrifices. . . . . .1 Chr. 29:21
Camels. . . . . .2 Chr. 14:15
Great numbers . . . . .2 Chr. 15:9
Flocks and herds. . . . . .2 Chr. 18:2; 32:29
Money. . . . . .2 Chr. 24:11
Weapons. . . . . .2 Chr. 32:5
Riches . . . . .Ps. 52:7
Milk. . . . . Is. 7:22
Wine . . . . Is. 56:12
Horses. . . . . .Ezek. 26:10
Labors. . . . . .2 Cor. 11:23
B. Of God's spiritual blessings:
Goodness . . . . .Ex. 34:6
Pardon. . . . . Is. 55:7

Peace and truth. .Jer. 33:6
Answers to our prayers . . . . Eph. 3:20
Grace. . . . . .1 Tim. 1:14
Mercy. . . . . .1 Pet. 1:3
C. Of spiritual things:
Predicted for gospel times . . . . Is. 35:2
Realized in the Messiah . . . . .Ps. 72:7
Given to the gentle. . . . . Ps. 37:11
Through Christ. . . . . Rom. 5:17, 18, 20
By grace. . . . . .Eph. 1:3–6
D. Of good things for Christians:
Greater usefulness . . . . .Matt. 13:11–13
Greater reward . . . . Matt. 25:29
Spiritual life. . . . . John 10:10
Grace. . . . . .Rom. 5:17
Christian service . . . . 1 Cor. 15:10
Joy. . . . . .2 Cor. 8:2
Thanksgiving . . . . .2 Cor. 4:15; 9:12
Rejoicing. . . . . Phil. 1:26
Holy Spirit . . . . .Titus 3:5, 6
Entrance in God's kingdom. . . . . .2 Pet. 1:11
E. Of undesirable things:
Witchcraft . . . . Is. 47:9
Idleness. . . . . Ezek. 16:49
F. Characteristics of:
Given to the obedient . . . . Lev. 26:3–13
Useful in God's work. . . . . .2 Chr. 24:11
Cannot satisfy fully . . . . .Eccl. 5:10–12
Not to be trusted. . . . . Ps. 52:7
Subject to conditions. . . . . Mal. 3:10–12;
Matt. 6:32, 33
Can be taken away . . . . Luke 12:13–21
Not a sign of real worth . . . . .Luke 12:15
G. Obtained by:
Putting away sin . . . . .2 Chr. 15:8, 9
Following God's commands . . . . .2 Chr. 17:3–5
Given by God. . . . . Job 36:31
Through Christ. . . . . John 10:10

Abuse—*application to a wrong purpose*
A. Of physical things:
Sexual perversions . . . . Gen. 19:5–9, 31–38
Torture . . . . .Judg. 16:21
B. Of spiritual things:
Misuse of authority. . . Num. 20:10–13; 1 Cor. 9:18
Using the world wrongly. . . . . 1 Cor. 7:31
Perverting the truth. . . . . .2 Pet. 2:10–22
Corrupting. . . . . 1 Sam. 2:12–17
God's ordinances . . . . .1 Cor. 11:17–22
C. Manifested by:
Unbelieving. . . . . .Mark 15:29–32

Abyss
Translated:
"Bottomless pit" . . . . Rev. 9:1, 2, 11; 17:8

Acacia Grove
1. Israel's last camp before crossing the
Jordan. . . . . .Josh. 3:1
Scene of Baalam's attempted curse . . . Num. 22–24
Sin of Baal of Peor here. . . . . .Num. 25:1–18

WORD STUDY

ACCOUNT, *chashab* (khaw-shahv), *Chashab* is a verb occurring throughout the OT, meaning "think," "account," "plan," or "devise." The word can refer either to God or humans and how they view others, as in Job 19:11 where Job says God *counts* him as one of His enemies. In Gen. 15:6 God *accounts* Abraham's belief "to him for righteousness." The word can also be used to describe the action of planning something either for or against someone. See Jer. 18:18, which records that the people of Jerusalem "devised plans" against Jeremiah for saying that the priests and prophets were corrupt. (Strong's #2803)

Accountability—*responsibility for own acts*
A. Kinds of:
　　Universal............................Rom. 14:12
　　Personal .... 2 Sam. 12:1–15
　　Personal and family.................Josh. 7:1–26
　　Personal and national .... 2 Sam. 24:1–17
　　Delayed but exacted.............. 2 Sam. 21:1–14
　　Final......................... Rom. 2:1–12
B. Determined by:
　　Federal headship......Gen. 3:1–24; Rom. 5:12–21
　　Personal responsibility .... Ezek. 18:1–32
　　Faithfulness.....................Matt. 25:14–30
　　Knowledge.......................Luke 12:47, 48
　　Conscience...................... Rom. 2:12–16
　　Greater light .... Rom. 2:17–29
　　Maturity of judgment ....1 Cor. 8:1–13

> **WORD STUDY**　**ACCURSED,** *anathema* (an-*ath*-cm-ah). Although this noun originally designated a thing "devoted to the divinity," like "a votive offering" (as in Luke 21:5), most NT occurrences of the word refer to the object of a curse. In Acts 23:14 conspirators bind themselves with an oath that they should be "accursed" if they fail to kill Paul. In Paul's letters this word has a negative meaning (Rom. 9:3; 1 Cor. 12:3), especially with reference to someone who preaches another gospel (Gal. 1:8, 9) or who "does not love the Lord Jesus Christ" (1 Cor. 16:22). (Strong's #331)

Accursed—*under a curse; doomed*
A. Caused by:
　　Hanging on a tree................... Deut. 21:23
　　Sin among God's people............... Josh. 7:12
　　Possessing a banned thing............. Josh. 6:18
　　Preaching contrary to the gospel ....Gal. 1:8, 9
　　Blaspheming Christ.................1 Cor. 12:3
B. Objects of being:
　　A city............................... Josh. 6:17
　　A forbidden thing....................Josh. 22:20
　　An elderly sinner .... Is. 65:20
　　Christ haters or nonbelievers ....1 Cor. 16:22
　　Paul (for the sake of Israel) ....Rom. 9:3

Accusations—*to charge; speak against*
A. Kinds of:
　　Pagan................................. Dan. 3:8
　　Personal ....Dan. 6:24
　　Public.............................. John 18:29
B. Sources of, in:
　　The devil.............. Job 1:6–12; Rev. 12:9, 10
　　Enemies................................Ezra 4:6
　　Hearer's conscience .... John 8:9
　　God's Word .... John 5:45

Hypocritical.....................John 8:6, 10, 11
The last days .... 2 Tim. 3:1, 3
Apostates .... 2 Pet. 2:10, 11
C. Forbidden:
　　Against servants.....................Prov. 30:10
　　False.............................. Luke 3:14
　　Among slanderers......................Titus 2:3
D. False, examples of, against:
　　Jacob .... Gen. 31:26–30
　　Joseph .... Gen. 39:10–21
　　Ahimelech .... 1 Sam. 22:11–16
　　David............................. 2 Sam. 10:3
　　Job .... Job 2:3–5
　　Jeremiah .... Jer. 26:8–11
　　Amos .... Amos 7:10, 11
　　Joshua .... Zech. 3:1–5
　　Christ......................... Matt. 26:59–66
　　Stephen .... Acts 6:11–14
　　Paul and Silas.................... Acts 16:19–21
　　Paul .... Acts 21:27–29
　　Christians.......................... 1 Pet. 2:12

Achaia—*a region of Greece*
　　Visited by Paul .... Acts 18:1, 12
　　Gallio proconsul................... Acts 18:12
　　Apollos preaches in ....Acts 18:24–28
　　Christians of, very generous .... Rom. 15:26
　　Saints in all of .... 2 Cor. 1:1
　　Paul commends Christians of........ 2 Cor. 11:10
　　Gospel proclaimed throughout .... 1 Thess. 1:7, 8

Achaicus—*belonging to Achaia*
　　A Corinthian Christian who visited
　　　　Paul........................1 Cor. 16:17, 18

Achan, Achar—*trouble*
　　A son of Carmi .... Josh. 7:1
　　Sin of, caused Israel's defeat .... Josh. 7:1–15
　　Stoned to death....................Josh. 7:16–25
　　Sin of, recalled....................Josh. 22:20
　　Called Achar .... 1 Chr. 2:7

Achbor—*mouse*
1. Father of Edomite king............. Gen. 36:36, 38
2. A courtier under Josiah ....2 Kin. 22:12, 14
　　Called Abdon ....2 Chr. 34:20

Achim—*short form of Jehoiachim*
　　Ancestor of Jesus ....Matt. 1:14

Achish—*serpent charmer*
　　A king of Gath.................. 1 Sam. 21:10–15
　　David seeks refuge............... 1 Sam. 27:1–12
　　Forced to expel David by Philistine
　　　　lords .... 1 Sam. 29:1–11
　　Receives Shimei's servants....... 1 Kin. 2:39, 40

Achmetha—*capital of Media (same as Ecbatana)*
　　Site of Persian archives ....Ezra 6:2

Achor, Valley of—*trouble*
　　Site of Achan's stoning .... Josh. 7:24–26
　　On Judah's boundary .... Josh. 15:7
　　Promises concerning .... Is. 65:10

Achsah—*anklet*
   A daughter of Caleb..................1 Chr. 2:49
   Given to Othniel.................Josh. 15:16–19
   Given springs of water .... Judg. 1:12–15

Achshaph—*dedicated*
   A royal city of Canaan................ Josh. 11:1
   Captured by Joshua ....Josh. 12:7, 20
   Assigned to Asher...............Josh. 19:24, 25

Achzib—*a lie*
   1. City of Judah...................... Josh. 15:44
     Also called Chezib .... Gen. 38:5
   2. Town of Asher .... Josh. 19:29

Acknowledge—*to recognize*
   A. Evil objects of:
     Sin.....................................Ps. 32:5
     Transgressions .... Ps. 51:3
     Iniquity...............................Jer. 3:13
     Wickedness .... Jer. 14:20
   B. Good objects of:
     God .... Prov. 3:6
     God's might.......................... Is. 33:13
     God's people ....Is. 61:9
     God's mystery.........................Col. 2:2
     God's truth........................ 2 Tim. 2:25
     The apostles......................1 Cor. 14:37
     Christian leaders .... 1 Cor. 16:18

Acquaintance—*personal knowledge*
   With God, gives peace .... Job 22:21
   Of God, with human ways.............Ps. 139:3

Acquaintances
   Deserted by .... Ps. 31:11
   Made an abomination...............Ps. 88:8, 18
   Jesus sought among ....Luke 2:44
   Stand afar off from Christ ....Luke 23:49

Acquit—*to declare to be innocent; pardon*
   Not possible with the wicked .... Nah. 1:3
   Sought by the righteous ....Job 7:21
   Difficulty of obtaining.............Job 9:28–31

Acre—*a land measurement*
   Plowing of, by a yoke of oxen........ 1 Sam. 14:14
   Descriptive of barrenness................Is. 5:10

Acrostic
   A literary device using the Hebrew alphabet;
     illustrated best in (Hebrew) .....Ps. 119:1–176

> **WORD STUDY**   **ACT OF SIN,** *hamartēma* (ham-ar-tay-mah). A noun derived from the verb *hamartanō* (literally, "to miss the mark," usually with the sense "to transgress, to sin"), *hamartēma* stresses that a specific act (such as blasphemy; see Mark 3:28) goes against, or transgresses, the religious or moral law of God. Another noun, *hamartia* ("sin"), is derived from the same verb and occurs far more frequently in the NT. Although nearly synonymous, *hamartēma* usually refers to a concrete act as a "sin," while *hamartia* is commonly used as an abstract noun to denote the action of transgression. (Strong's #265)

Acts of the Apostles—*a book of the New Testament*
   Written by Luke .... Luke 1:1–4; Acts 1:1, 2
   Parts of, written by eyewitness .... Acts 27:1, 2

Adadah—*holiday*
   A city of Judah......................Josh. 15:22

Adah—*ornament*
   1. One of Lamech's wives ....Gen. 4:19
   2. One of Esau's wives ....Gen. 36:2, 4, 10, 12
     Also called Basemath ....Gen. 26:34

Adaiah—*Yahweh has adorned*
   1. The maternal grandfather of Josiah .... 2 Kin. 22:1
   2. A Levite ....1 Chr. 6:41
   3. Son of Shimhi ....1 Chr. 8:21
     Called Shema.......................1 Chr. 8:13
   4. Aaronite priest .... 1 Chr. 9:10–12
   5. The father of Maaseiah .... 2 Chr. 23:1
   6. A son of Bani......................Ezra 10:29
   7. Another of a different family
     of Bani...................... Ezra 10:34, 39
   8. A descendant of Judah ....Neh. 11:4, 5

Adalia
   Haman's son ....Esth. 9:8, 10

Adam—*red earth*
   A. Creation of:
     In God's image ....Gen. 1:26, 27
     By God's breath...................... Gen. 2:7
     A living soul......................1 Cor. 15:45
     From dust........................... Gen. 2:7
     Before Eve......................... 1 Tim. 2:13
     Upright .... Eccl. 7:29
     Intelligent being ....Gen. 2:19, 20
   B. Position of, first:
     Worker ....Gen. 2:8, 15
     To receive God's law .... Gen. 2:16, 17
     Husband.........................Gen. 2:18–25
     Man to sin ....Gen. 3:6–12
     To receive promise of the Messiah...... Gen. 3:15
     Father .... Gen. 4:1
     Head of race...................... Rom. 5:12–14
   C. Sin of:
     Instigated by Satan ....Gen. 3:1–5
     Prompted by Eve...................... Gen. 3:6
     Done knowingly....................1 Tim. 2:14
     Resulted in broken fellowship........... Gen. 3:8
     Brought God's curse ....Gen. 3:14–19
   D. Descendants of, are all:
     Sinners.............................Rom. 5:12
     Subject to death .... Rom. 5:12–14
     Scattered over the earth .... Deut. 32:8
     In need of salvation .... John 3:16

Adam—*a city near Zaretan*
   Site of backing up Jordan's waters to let
     Israel pass over.................... Josh. 3:16

Adamah—*red ground*
   City of Naphtali ....Josh. 19:35, 36

Adami Nekeb—*earthy*
   In Naphtali........................ Josh. 19:33

Adam, Last—*an attribution of Christ*
Prefigured in Adam....................Rom. 5:14
Gift of, abound to many...............Rom. 5:15
A life-giving spirit ....1 Cor. 15:20–24, 45
Spiritual and heavenly...........1 Cor. 15:46–48

Adar—*dark or cloudy*
A town of Judah ....Josh. 15:1, 3

Adar—*the twelfth month of the Hebrew year*
Date set by Haman for massacre of
    Jews...........................Esth. 3:7, 13
Date adopted for Purim .....Esth. 9:19, 21, 26–28
Date of completion of temple ....Ezra 6:15

Adbeel—*disciplined of God*
A son of Ishmael.....................Gen. 25:13

Add—*to increase the sum of*
A. Of material things:
    Another child ....Gen. 30:24
    A population ....2 Sam. 24:3
    Heavy burdens ....1 Kin. 12:11, 14
    Years to life ....Prov. 3:2
    Kingly majesty ....Dan. 4:36
    Stature............................Matt. 6:27
B. Of good things:
    No sorrow.........................Prov. 10:22
    Inspired words ....Jer. 36:32
    Learning...........................Prov. 16:23
    Spiritual blessings....................Matt. 6:33
    Converts to Christ ....Acts 2:41, 47
    A covenant...........................Gal. 3:15
    The Law ....Gal. 3:19
C. Of evil things:
    Additions to God's Word..............Deut. 4:2
    National sins ....1 Sam. 12:19
    Iniquity............................Ps. 69:27
    Sin to sin............................Is. 30:1
    Grief to sorrow ....Jer. 45:3
    Personal sin ....Luke 3:19, 20
    Afflictions ....Phil. 1:16

Addan—*strong*
A place in Babylonia whose returnees
    fail to prove Israelite ancestry ......Ezra 2:59

Addar—*wide, open place*
A Benjamite..........................1 Chr. 8:3
Also called Ard ....Num. 26:40

Addi—*my witness*
Ancestor of Jesus ....Luke 3:23, 28

Additions to the church
A. Manner and number of:
    "The Lord added" ....Acts 2:47
    "Believers added to the Lord"...........Acts 5:14
    "Disciples multiplied"...................Acts 6:1
    "A great many of the priests"............Acts 6:7
    "Churches were multiplied" ....Acts 9:31
    "A great number believed"...........Acts 11:21
    "Many people were added" ....Acts 11:24
    "Churches increased in number" ....Acts 16:5

B. By means of:
    Word preached ....Acts 2:14–41
    The Spirit's convicting power ....John 16:7–11
    The gospel as God's power............Rom. 1:16
    Responding faith ....Acts 14:1

Addon (see Addan)

Address—*a public message*
A. In Old Testament:
    Moses' expository...............Deut. 1:1–4:40
    Moses' second ....Deut. 4:44–26:19
    Moses' third..................Deut. 27:1–30:20
    Moses' fourth ....Deut. 32:1–43
    Moses' final ....Deut. 33:1–29
    Joshua's exhortation ....Josh. 23:2–16
    Joshua's farewell ....Josh. 24:1–25
    Solomon's to God..................1 Kin. 3:6–9
    Ezra's expository....................Neh. 8:1–8
    Jeremiah's temple sermon ....Jer. 7:1–10:25
B. Of Paul:
    First ....Acts 9:20–22
    Second.........................Acts 13:16–41
    To Peter.........................Gal. 2:14–21
    To women...........................Acts 16:13
    With Silas.........................Acts 16:29–32
    At Athens ....Acts 17:22–31
    At Troas ....Acts 20:6, 7
    To elders ....Acts 20:17–35
    To the crowd ....Acts 22:1–21
    Before Felix ....Acts 24:10–21
    Before Agrippa ....Acts 26:1–29
    On the ship.......................Acts 27:21–26
    Final recorded ....Acts 28:25–28
C. Of Peter:
    In upper room ....Acts 1:13–22
    Pentecost ....Acts 2:14–40
    At temple ....Acts 3:12–26
    Before Sanhedrin ....Acts 4:8–12, 19, 20
    In house of Cornelius ....Acts 10:34–43
    At Jerusalem council ....Acts 15:7–11
D. Of Others:
    Gamaliel.........................Acts 5:34–39
    Stephen...........................Acts 7:2–60
    Herod ....Acts 12:21, 22
    James.............................Acts 15:13–21
    Tertullus.........................Acts 24:1–8

Adiel—*ornament of God*
1. A Simeonite prince ....1 Chr. 4:24, 36
2. Aaronite priest ....1 Chr. 9:12, 13
3. Father of Azmaveth..................1 Chr. 27:25

Adin—*effeminate*
1. A man whose descendants return with
    Zerubbabel ....Ezra 2:2, 15
2. A man whose descendants return
    with Ezra ....Ezra 8:1, 6
3. Sealer of the covenant..............Neh. 10:1, 16

Adina—*delicate*
A Reubenite captain under David ....1 Chr. 11:42

Adino—*slender*
- Sound doctrine . . . . Titus 2:1–6
- A mighty man under David . . . . 2 Sam. 23:8
- Compare parallel passage in . . . . 1 Chr. 11:11

Adithaim—*double ornaments*
- A city of Judah . . . . Josh. 15:21, 36

Adjuration—*earnest advising; to charge as if under an oath*
- Joshua's, to Jericho . . . . Josh. 6:26
- Saul's, to those breaking a fast . . . 1 Sam. 14:24–28
- Ahab's, to the prophet Micaiah . . . . . . 1 Kin. 22:16
- Caiaphas's, by God . . . . Matt. 26:63
- Demon's, by God . . . . Mark 5:7
- Exorcists', by Jesus . . . . Acts 19:13
- Paul's charge, by the Lord . . . . 1 Thess. 5:27

Adlai—*Yahweh is just*
- Father of Shaphat . . . . 1 Chr. 27:29

Admah—*red earth*
- A city near Sodom . . . . Gen. 10:19
- Joins other cities against
  Chedorlaomer . . . . Gen. 14:1–4, 8
- Destroyed with Sodom and
  Gomorrah . . . . Gen. 19:24–28

Admatha—*God-given*
- One of Ahasuerus's chamberlains . . . Esth. 1:13–15

Administer—*serve; execute; manage*
Applied to:
- Judgment . . . . 1 Kin. 3:28
- Vengeance . . . . Jer. 21:12
- Justice . . . . 2 Sam. 8:15

Administration—*the management or disposition of affairs*
- Of gifts to Jerusalem saints . . . . 2 Cor. 8:19, 20
- Of spiritual gifts . . . . 1 Cor. 12:5; 2 Cor. 9:12

Admiration—*exceptional esteem*
- Reserved for saints . . . . 2 Thess. 1:10
- Flattering, shown by false teachers . . . . Jude 16

Admonition—*wise words spoken against evil acts; warning*
A. Performed by:
- God . . . . Heb. 8:5
- Earthly fathers . . . . Eph. 6:4
- Leaders . . . . 1 Thess. 5:12
- Christians . . . . Rom. 15:14
B. Directed against:
- A remnant . . . . Jer. 42:19
- Elders . . . . Acts 20:28–35
- Those who will not work . . . . 2 Thess. 3:10, 15
- Divisive individual . . . . Titus 3:10
C. Sources of in:
- Scriptures . . . . 1 Cor. 10:11
- Wise words . . . . Eccl. 12:11, 12
- Spiritual knowledge . . . . Col. 3:16

Adna—*pleasure*
1. One who divorced his foreign wife . . . Ezra 10:18, 30
2. Postexilic priest . . . . Neh. 12:12, 15

Adnah—*pleasure*
1. Captain of Saul . . . . 1 Chr. 12:20

2. Chief captain of Jehoshaphat . . . . 2 Chr. 17:14

Adonai—*Lord*
The Hebrew title for God (translated "Lord") expressing lordship (found in the following five compound words)

Adoni-Bezek—*lord of Bezek*
- A king of Bezek . . . . Judg. 1:3–7

Adonijah—*my Lord is Yahweh*
1. David's fourth son . . . . 2 Sam. 3:2, 4
- Attempts to usurp throne . . . . 1 Kin. 1:5–53
- Desires Abishag as wife . . . . 1 Kin. 2:13–18
- Executed by Solomon . . . . 1 Kin. 2:19–25
2. A teacher . . . . 2 Chr. 17:8, 9
3. A Jew who signed the document . . . Neh. 9:38; 10:16
- Probably the same as Adonikam in . . . . . Ezra 2:13

Adonikam—*my Lord has risen*
- Descendants of, return from exile . . . . . . Ezra 2:13

Adoniram, Adoram—*my Lord is exalted*
- A son of Abda . . . . 1 Kin. 4:6
- Official under David, Solomon, and
  Rehoboam . . . . 2 Sam. 20:24; 1 Kin. 5:14; 12:18
- Stoned by angry Israelites . . . . 1 Kin. 12:18
- Called Hadoram . . . . 2 Chr. 10:18

Adoni-Zedek—*my Lord is righteous*
- An Amorite king of Jerusalem . . . . Josh. 10:1–5
- Defeated and slain by Joshua . . . . Josh. 10:6–27

WORD STUDY   **ADOPTION,** *huiothesia* (hwee-oth-es-*ee*-ah). This compound noun (from *huios,* "son," and *thesis,* "a placing") is a legal term that refers to a father's declaration that his natural child was officially his child and thus entitled to all the attendant rights and privileges. In the NT *huiothesia* can only be found in the letters of Paul, who uses it metaphorically to indicate: that God accepts believers as His children (Gal. 4:5; Eph. 1:5; cf. Rom. 9:4), that by receiving the "Spirit of adoption" believers can call God "Abba, Father" (Rom. 8:15), and that their "adoption" includes the future redemption of the body (8:23). (Strong's #5206)

Adoption—*the legal act of investing with sonship*
A. Used naturally of:
- Eliezer under Abraham . . . . Gen. 15:2–4
- Joseph's sons under Jacob . . . . Gen. 48:5, 14, 16
- Moses under Pharaoh's daughter . . . Ex. 2:10; Acts 7:21
- Esther under Mordecai . . . . Esth. 2:7
B. Used spiritually of Israel as:
- Elected by God . . . . . . Deut. 14:1, 2; Rom. 11:1–32
- Blessed by God . . . . Rom. 9:4
- Realized in history . . . . Ex. 4:22, 23
C. Used spiritually of the Gentiles as:
- Predicted in the prophets . . . . Is. 65:1
- Confirmed by faith . . . . Rom. 10:20
- Realized in the new covenant . . . . Eph. 2:12; 3:1–6
D. The time of:
- Past, predestined to . . . . Rom. 8:29

Present, regarded as sons . . . .John 1:12, 13; 3:1–11
Future, glorified as sons . . . . .Rom. 8:19, 23;
1 John 3:2
E. The source of:
By God's grace. . . . . Rom. 4:16, 17
By faith . . . . .Gal. 3:7, 26
Through Christ. . . . . .Gal. 4:4, 5
F. Assurances of, by:
Spirit's witness. . . . . .Rom. 8:16
Spirit's leading. . . . . .Rom. 8:14
"Abba, Father". . . . . .Rom. 8:15
Changed life. . . . . 1 John 3:9–17
Father's chastening . . . . Prov. 3:11, 12;
Heb. 12:5–11
G. The blessings of:
A new nature . . . . 2 Cor. 5:17
A new name . . . . Is. 62:2, 12; Rev. 3:12
Access to God . . . . Eph. 2:18
Fatherly love . . . . .1 John 3:1
Help in prayer . . . . Matt. 6:5–15
Spiritual unity. . . . . . . .John 17:11, 21; Eph. 2:18–22
A glorious inheritance. . . . . John 14:1–3;
Rom. 8:17, 18

Adoraim—*double honor*
A city fortified by Rehoboam . . . . . . .2 Chr. 11:5, 9

Adoram (see Adoniram)

Adoration—*reverential praise*
A. Rendered falsely to:
Idols. . . . . .Is. 44:15, 17, 19
An image . . . . .Dan. 3:5–7
Heavenly hosts . . . . 2 Kin. 17:16
Satan . . . . Luke 4:6–8
People . . . . .Acts 10:25, 26
Angels . . . . Col. 2:18, 23
B. Rendered properly to God:
Illustrated. . . . . Is. 6:1–5
Taught. . . . . .Ps. 95–100
Proclaimed. . . . . Rev. 4:8–11
C. Rendered properly to Christ as God by:
Wise men . . . . Matt. 2:1, 11
Leper . . . . .Matt. 8:2
Ruler . . . . .Matt. 9:18
Disciples . . . . Matt. 14:22, 33
Woman . . . . Matt. 15:25
Mother . . . . Matt. 20:20
Blind man. . . . . .John 9:1, 38
Every creature . . . . Phil. 2:10, 11
See Worship

Adornment
A. Used literally of:
A harlot. . . . . .Rev. 17:3, 4
A woman. . . . . .Is. 3:16–24; 1 Tim. 2:9
A building . . . . .Luke 21:5
A bride. . . . . .Rev. 21:2
B. Used spiritually of:
Believer as justified . . . . .Is. 61:10
Believer as sanctified. . . . . .Titus 2:10
Israel restored . . . . .Jer. 31:4

Saintly woman. . . . . 1 Tim. 2:9
C. Guidelines for:
In modesty. . . . . 1 Tim. 2:9
Not external. . . . . 1 Pet. 3:3–5

Adrammelech—*Adar is king*
1. A god worshiped by the Samaritans . . . 2 Kin. 17:31
2. Killed Sennacherib . . . . . . 2 Kin. 19:36, 37; Is. 37:38

Adramyttium—*a seaport of Mysia in Asia Minor*
Travels of Paul. .Acts 27:2–6

Adriatic Sea
A part or the whole of the Adriatic Sea named
after Adria, a city of Italy . . . . Acts 27:27

Adriel—*my help is God*
Marries Saul's eldest daughter . . . . . . .1 Sam. 18:19
Sons of, slain to atone Saul's
crime. . . . . 2 Sam. 21:8, 9

Adullam—*refuge*
A town of Canaan. . . . . Gen. 38:1, 12, 20
Conquered by Joshua. . . . . .Josh. 12:7, 15
Assigned to Judah. . . . . .Josh. 15:20, 35
Fortified by Rehoboam. . . . . .2 Chr. 11:5–7
Symbol of Israel's glory. . . . . .Mic. 1:15
Reoccupied. . . . . .Neh. 11:25, 30
David seeks refuge in caves of. . . . . . 1 Sam. 22:1, 2
Exploits of mighty men while
there . . . . .2 Sam. 23:13–17

Adullamite—*a citizen of Adullam*
Judah's friend . . . . Gen. 38:1, 12, 20

Adulterer—*a man who commits adultery*
Punishment of. . . . . .Lev. 20:10
Waits for the twilight . . . . Job 24:15
Offspring of. . . . . .Is. 57:3
Land is full of . . . . Jer. 23:10
Shall not inherit the kingdom
of God. . . . . 1 Cor. 6:9
God will judge. . . . . Heb. 13:4
Examples of:
Judah . . . . .Gen. 38:15–18
David. . . . . 2 Sam. 11:2–5
Herod . . . . Matt. 14:3, 4

Adulteress—*a woman guilty of adultery; seductress*
A. Sin of:
Punished by death . . . . .Lev. 20:10
Ensnares the simple . . . . Prov. 7:6–23
Brings a man to poverty . . . . .Prov. 6:26
Leads to death. . . . . Prov. 2:16–19
Increases transgressors. . . . . Prov. 23:27, 28
Defined by Christ. . . . . Matt. 5:32
Forgiven by Christ . . . . .John 8:1–11
Mentioned by Paul. . . . . .Rom. 7:3
B. Examples of:
Tamar . . . . Gen. 38:13–24
Potiphar's wife (attempted) . . . . .Gen. 39:7–20
Midianite women. . . . . .Num. 25:6–8
Rahab . . . . Josh. 2:1
Bathsheba. . . . . 2 Sam. 11:4, 5

Herodias...........................Matt. 14:3, 4
Unnamed woman..................John 8:1–11
See Harlot

WORD
STUDY

ADULTERY, *moicheia* (moy-*kheye*-ah). A noun meaning "illicit sexual relations between a married person and someone other than that person's spouse." In the OT "adultery" applied specifically to a married (or betrothed) woman who had sexual relations with any man other than her husband; it was strictly forbidden (Ex. 20:14; Lev. 18:20; Deut. 5:18) and punishable by death (Deut. 22:22–24; cf. John 7:53–8:11). Although "adultery" is prohibited by NT writers (Rom. 13:9; Gal. 5:19; James 2:11), the definition seems to have been expanded in the teaching of Jesus to mean that a husband could be held accountable for committing "adultery" against his wife (Mark 10:11; Luke 16:18). The term is also used figuratively to refer to the spiritual infidelity of God's people (James 4:4). (Strong's #3430)

Adultery—*sexual intercourse outside marriage*
A. Defined:
    In God's Law...........................Ex. 20:14
    By Christ........................ Matt. 5:28, 32
    In mental attitude .... Matt. 5:28
    As a work of the flesh ....Gal. 5:19
B. Sin of:
    Breaks God's Law....................Deut. 5:18
    Punishable by death.............. Lev. 20:10–12
    Brings death.......................Prov. 2:18, 19
    Makes one poor.......................Prov. 29:3
    Produces moral insensibility........Prov. 30:20;
        2 Cor. 12:21
    Corrupts a land...................... Hos. 4:1–3
    Justifies divorce .... Matt. 19:7–9
    Excludes from Christian
        fellowship ....1 Cor. 5:1–13
    Excludes from God's kingdom ......1 Cor. 6:9, 10
    Merits God's judgments.............. Heb. 13:4
    Ends in hell (Sheol) .... Prov. 7:27; Rev. 21:8
C. Forgiveness of, by:
    Man .... Judg. 19:1–4
    Christ...........................John 8:10, 11
    Repentance .... 2 Sam. 12:7–14
    Regeneration ....1 Cor. 6:9–11
D. Examples of:
    Lot ....Gen. 19:31–38
    Shechem .... Gen. 34:2
    Judah..........................Gen. 38:1–24
    Eli's sons .... 1 Sam. 2:22
    David .... 2 Sam. 11:1–5
    Amnon .... 2 Sam. 13:1–20
    The Samaritan woman .... John 4:17, 18

Adultery, spiritual
Seen in Israel's idolatry............Judg. 2:11, 17
Described graphically .... Ezek. 16
Symbolized in Hosea's marriage....... Hos. 1:1–3

Figurative of friendship with
    the world .... James 4:4
Figurative of false teaching... Rev. 2:14, 15, 20–22

Adummim—*red spots*
A hill between Jerusalem and
    Jericho ....Josh. 15:5, 7, 8
The probable site of Good Samaritan
    parable in................... Luke 10:30–37

Advancement—*progression*
A. Promotion to a higher office:
    Moses and Aaron, by the Lord .... 1 Sam. 12:6
    Promised to Balaam..............Num. 22:16, 17
    Joseph, by true interpretation..... Gen. 41:38–46
    Levites, for loyalty ....Ex. 32:26–28
    Phinehas, by decisive action .... Num. 25:7–13
    Haman, by intrigue ....Esth. 3:1, 2
    Mordecai, by ability...................Esth. 10:2
    Daniel, by fidelity.....................Dan. 2:48
    Deacons, by faithfulness .... 1 Tim. 3:10, 13
B. Conditions of, seen in:
    Humility........................... Matt. 18:4
    Faithfulness....................Matt. 25:14–30
    Skilled in work ....Prov. 22:29
    Service to others .... Luke 22:24–30
C. Hindrances to, occasioned by:
    Self-glory .... Is. 14:12–15; 1 Cor. 4:6–9
    Pride .... Ezek. 28:11–19; 1 Pet. 5:5, 6

Advantage—*superior circumstance or ability*
A. In God's kingdom, none by:
    Birth............................. Matt. 3:8, 9
    Race............................ Gal. 2:14–16
    Position...........................John 3:1–6
    Works .... Matt. 5:20
    Wealth..............................Luke 9:25
B. In God's kingdom, some by:
    Industry .... 1 Cor. 15:10
    Faithfulness....................Matt. 25:14–30
    Kindred spirit ....Phil. 2:19–23
    Works ....1 Cor. 3:11–15
    Dedication .... Rev. 14:1–5

Advent of Christ, the First
A. Announced in the Old Testament by:
    Moses........................... Deut. 18:18, 19
    Samuel............................. Acts 3:24
    David................. Ps. 40:6–8; Heb. 10:5–8
    Prophets .... Luke 24:26, 27
B. Prophecies fulfilled by His:
    Birth........................Is. 7:14; Matt. 1:23
    Forerunner.............. Mal. 3:1, 2; Matt. 3:1–3
    Incarnation .... Is. 9:6
    Time of arrival .... Dan. 9:24, 25; Mark 1:15
    Rejection..............Is. 53:1–4; Rom. 10:16–21
    Crucifixion .... Ps. 2:1, 2; Acts 4:24–28
    Atonement............Is. 53:1–12; 1 Pet. 1:18–21
    Resurrection .... Ps. 16:8–11; Acts 2:25–31
    Priesthood .... Ps. 110:4, 5; Heb. 5:5, 6
C. His first coming:
    Introduces gospel age .... Acts 3:24

Establishes new covenant.......... Jer. 31:31–34; Heb. 8:6–13

Fulfills prophecy................ Luke 24:44, 45

Nullifies the ceremonial system.......... Heb. 9

Brings Gentiles in................ Acts 15:13–18

Advent of Christ, the Second (see Second Coming of Christ)

Advents of Christ, compared

A. First Advent:

Prophesied ....Deut. 18:18, 19; Is. 7:14

Came as man ....Phil. 2:5–8

Announced......................Luke 2:10–14

Time predicted .... Dan. 9:25

To save the lost .... Matt. 18:11

Subject to government...........Matt. 17:24–27

B. Second Advent:

Prophesied ....John 14:1–3; 1 Thess. 4:16

Come as God..................... 1 Thess. 4:16

As a thief......................... 1 Thess. 5:2

At a time unknown .... Matt. 24:36

To judge people.......... Matt. 25:31–33, 41–46

Source of government .... Rev. 20:4–6; 22:3–5

Adversaries—*those who actively oppose*

A. Descriptive of:

Satan ....1 Pet. 5:8

Gospel's enemies .... 1 Cor. 16:9

Israel's enemies.......................Josh. 5:13

An enemy .... Esth. 7:6

A rival ....1 Sam. 1:6

God's agent ....1 Kin. 11:14, 23

God's angel .... Num. 22:22

B. Believer's attitude toward:

Pray for ....Matt. 5:43, 44

Use God's weapons against .... Luke 21:15

Not to be terrified by................. Phil. 1:28

Not to give opportunity to............1 Tim. 5:14

Remember God's judgment on .... Heb. 10:27

Adversity—*adverse circumstances*

A. Caused by:

Sin...........................Gen. 3:16–19

Disobedience to God's Law........ Lev. 26:14–20

B. Purposes of, to:

Punish for sin ....2 Sam. 12:9–12

Humble us ....2 Chr. 33:12

Lead us to God's Word .... Deut. 8:2, 3

Chasten and correct.................Heb. 12:5–11

Test our faith.................... 1 Pet. 1:5–8

Give us final rest.................... Ps. 94:12, 13

C. Reactions to:

Rebellious.................. Ex. 14:4–8; Job 2:9

Distrustful.........................Ex. 6:8, 9

Complaining ....Ruth 1:20, 21

Questioning...................... Jer. 20:7–10

Fainting ....Prov. 24:10

Arrogant...........................Ps. 10:6

Hopeful........................ Lam. 3:31–40

Submissive .... Job 5:17–22

Joyful..............................James 1:2–4

D. God's relation to, He:

Troubles nations with ....2 Chr. 15:5, 6

Knows the soul in...................... Ps. 31:7

Saves out of .... 1 Sam. 10:19

Redeems out of ....2 Sam. 4:9

E. Helps under:

By prayer...........................Jon. 2:1–7

By understanding God's purpose...Lam. 3:31–39; Rom. 5:3

Advertise—*to make known publicly*

Messiah's advent.................Num. 24:14–19

A piece of property..................... Ruth 4:4

Advice—*one's judgment or counsel*

A. Sought by:

A king .... Esth. 1:13–15

Another ruler.....................Acts 25:13–27

A usurper ....2 Sam. 16:20–23

Five men .... 2 Kin. 22:12–20

B. Sought from:

The ephod ....1 Sam. 23:9–12

A prophet .... Jer. 42:1–6

A dead prophet .... 1 Sam. 28:7–20

A council...................... Acts 15:1–22

A grieving husband .... Judg. 20:4–7

C. Kinds of:

Helpful .... Ex. 18:12–25

Rejected .... 1 Kin. 12:6–8

Timely.....................1 Sam. 25:32–34

Good ....2 Kin. 5:13, 14

God-inspired .... 2 Sam. 17:6–14

Foolish...............................Job 2:9

Humiliating....................... Esth. 6:6–11

Fatal...................Esth. 5:14; 7:9, 10

Ominous........................ Matt. 27:19

Accepted......................Acts 5:34–41

D. Sought from:

Congregation of Israel.................Judg. 20:7

Advocate, Christ our

A. His interest in believers, by right of:

Election............................ John 15:16

Redemption ....Eph. 1:7

Regeneration ....Col. 1:27

Imputed righteousness ...... 2 Cor. 5:21; Phil. 3:9

B. His defense of believers by:

Prayer .... Luke 22:31–34

Protection............................ Heb. 13:6

Provision.................Ps. 23:1; John 10:28

Perseverance .... 2 Tim. 4:17, 18

C. His blessings upon believers:

Another Helper..................John 14:16, 17

New commandment ....John 13:34, 35

New nature......................... 2 Cor. 5:17

New name.........................Rev. 2:17

New life........................ John 4:14

New relationship .... John 15:15

D. Our duties prescribed by Him:

Our mission—world evangelization ....Matt. 28:16–20

Our means—the Holy Spirit . . . . Acts 1:8
Our might—the gospel . . . . Rom. 1:16
Our motivation—the love
    of Christ. 2 Cor. 5:14, 15

Aeneas—*praise*
A paralytic healed by Peter . . . . Acts 9:32–35

Aenon—*springs*
A place near Salim where John the
    Baptist baptized. . . . . John 3:22, 23

Afar off—*at a far distance*
A. Applied physically to:
    Distance . . . . Gen. 22:4
    A journey . . . . Num. 9:10
    Sound of joy. .Ezra 3:13
    Ostracism . . . . Luke 17:12
B. Applied spiritually to:
    God's knowledge . . . . .Ps. 139:2
    Unworthiness . . . . Luke 18:13
    Eternal separation . . . . Luke 16:23
    Gentiles. . . . . Acts 2:39
    God's promises . . . . Heb. 11:13

Affability—*a personality overflowing with benign
    sociability*
A. Manifested in:
    Cordiality. . . . . .Gen. 18:1–8
    Compassion . . . . Luke 10:33–37
    Generosity . . . . .Phil. 4:10, 14–18
    Unantagonizing speech . . . . 1 Sam. 25:23–31
B. Examples of:
    Jonathan. 1 Sam. 18:1–4
    The Shunammite woman. . . . . 2 Kin. 4:8–10
    Lydia . . . . Acts 16:14, 15
    Titus . . . . .2 Cor. 8:16–18
    Timothy .Phil. 2:17–20
    Gaius. . . . . 3 John 1–6
    Demetrius. . . . . 3 John 12

Affectation—*a studied pretense*
    Parade of egotism. . . . . Esth. 6:6–9
    Boast of the power . . . . Dan. 4:28–30
    Sign of hypocrisy . . . . Matt. 6:1, 2, 16
    Outbreak of false teachers . . . . 2 Pet. 2:18, 19
    Sign of antichrist . . . . .2 Thess. 2:4, 9
    Proof of spiritual decay. . . . . 1 Cor. 4:6–8

Affection—*an inner feeling or emotion*
A. Kinds of:
    Natural . . . . .Rom. 1:31
    Paternal. . . . . .Luke 15:20
    Maternal. 1 Kin. 3:16–27
    Fraternal. Gen. 43:30–34
    Filial. . . . . .Gen. 49:29, 30
    National . . . . .Ps. 137:1–6
    Racial. . . . . Rom. 9:1–3
    For wife. . . . . .Eph. 5:25–33
    For husband. . . . . .Titus 2:4
    Christian. . . . . .Rom. 12:10
    Heavenly. . . . . .Col. 3:1, 2

B. Good, characteristics of:
    Loyal, intense . . . . .Ruth 1:14–18
    Memorable. 2 Sam. 1:17–27
    Natural, normal . . . . .2 Sam. 13:37–39
    Tested, tried. . . . . .Gen. 22:1–19
    Emotional. .John 11:33–36
    Grateful . . . . Luke 7:36–50
    Joyous . . . . Ps. 126:1–6
    Christ-centered. . . . . .Matt. 10:37–42
C. Evil, characteristics of:
    Unnatural. Rom. 1:18–32
    Pretended .Matt. 26:47–49
    Abnormal. . . . . .2 Tim. 3:3
    Fleshly. . . . . Rom. 13:13, 14
    Worldly. . . . . 2 Tim. 4:10
    Defiling, degrading. . . . . .2 Pet. 2:10–12
    Agonizing, in Hades . . . . Luke 16:23–28

Afflictions—*hardships; trials; tribulations*
A. Visited upon:
    Israel in Egypt. . . . . Gen. 15:13
    Samson by Philistines . . . . .Judg. 16:5, 6, 19–21
    David by God .Ps. 88:7
    Judah by God. . . . . .Lam. 3:33
    Israel by the world . . . . .Ps. 129:1, 2
    The just by the wicked . . . . Amos 5:12; Heb. 11:37
    Christians by the world. . . . . 2 Cor. 1:6
B. Design of, to:
    Show God's mercy . . . . Is. 63:9
    Make us seek God . . . . Hos. 5:15
    Bring us back to God. . . . . .Ps. 119:67
    Humble us .2 Chr. 33:12
    Test us . . . . Is. 48:10
C. In the Christian's life:
    A means of testing . . . . .Mark 4:17
    A part of life. . . . . Matt. 24:9
    To be endured . . . . 2 Tim. 4:5
    Part of gospel. . . . . 1 Thess. 1:6
    Must not be shaken by. . . . . 1 Thess. 3:3
    Commendable examples of . . . . .2 Tim. 3:11
    Momentary . . . . 2 Cor. 4:17
    Cannot separate from God . . . . Rom. 8:35–39
    Deliverance from, promised . . . . .Ps. 34:19
    Terminated at Christ's return . . . . . .2 Thess. 1:4–7
See Trials

Afraid—*overcome with fear*
A. Caused by:
    Nakedness . . . . Gen. 3:10
    Unusual dream . . . . .Gen. 28:16, 17
    God's presence . . . . .Ex. 3:6
    Moses' approach. . . . . Ex. 34:30
    A burning mountain . . . . .Deut. 5:5
    Giant's raging . . . . 1 Sam. 17:11, 24
    A prophet's words. . . . . 1 Sam. 28:20
    Angel's sword . . . . .1 Chr. 21:30
    God's deeds . . . . Ps. 65:8
    Gabriel's presence . . . . Dan. 8:17
    A terrifying storm . . . . .Jon. 1:5, 10
    Peter's sinking. . . . . Matt. 14:30
    Changed person . . . . .Mark 5:15

Heavenly hosts . . . . Luke 2:9

B. Overcome by:

The Lord's presence. . . . . Ps. 3:5, 6

Trusting God. . . . . Ps. 27:1–3

God's protection. . . . . Ps. 91:4, 5

Stability of heart. Ps. 112:7, 8

God's coming judgment . . . . Is. 10:24–26

The Messiah's advent . . . . Is. 40:9–11

God's sovereign power . . . . Is. 51:12, 13

Christ's comforting words . . . . Matt. 14:27

Afternoon—*part of the day following noon*

Called cool of the day . . . . Gen. 3:8

Afterthought—*a later reflection*

Of Esau . . . . Heb. 12:16, 17

Of the Israelites . . . . Num. 14:40–45

Of one of two sons . . . . Matt. 21:28–30

Of the lost son . . . . Luke 15:17

Of the unjust steward . . . . Luke 16:1–8

Of the rich man in hell . . . . Luke 16:23–31

Of Judas . . . . Matt. 27:3–5

Afterward(s)

Your hands shall be . . . . Judg. 7:11

Those who are invited. . . . . 1 Sam. 9:13

David's conscience bothered him. . . . . 1 Sam. 24:5

His mouth will . . . . Prov. 20:17

Jesus finds him . . . . John 5:14

Agabus—*he loved*

A Christian prophet who foretells a famine and warns Paul. . . . . Acts 11:27, 28; 21:10, 11

Agag—*flaming or violent*

1. A king of Amalek in Balaam's prophecy . . . Num. 24:7

2. Amalekite king spared by Saul, but slain by Samuel. . . . . 1 Sam. 15:8, 9, 20–24, 32, 33

Agagite—*descendant of Agag*

A title applied to the father of Haman, enemy of the Jews . . . . Esth. 3:1, 10

Agape—*Greek word rendered "love"*

Descriptive of God. . . . . 1 John 4:8

Demanded toward God . . . . Matt. 22:37

Demanded toward neighbors . . . . Matt. 22:39

Fulfills Law . . . . Matt. 22:40

Activity of described . . . . 1 Cor. 13:1–13

Agate—*a stone of translucent quartz*

Worn by the high priest . . . . Ex. 28:19; 39:12

Sold by Syrians . . . . Ezek. 27:16

Age—*time counted by years*

A. Handicaps of, seen in:

Physical infirmities . . . . Gen. 48:10

Unwillingness to adventure. . . . . . 2 Sam. 19:31–39

Declining strength. . . . . Ps. 71:9

Deterioration of body . . . . Eccl. 12:1–7

B. Glories of, manifested in:

Wisdom . . . . Job 12:12

Maturity. . . . . Job 5:26

Spiritual beauty. Prov. 16:31

Fruitfulness . . . . Ps. 92:12–15

Judgment . . . . 1 Kin. 12:6–8

Strong faith . . . . Josh. 24:15, 29

C. Attitude of others toward:

Respect . . . . Lev. 19:32

Disrespect. . . . . 2 Chr. 36:17

Insolence. . . . . Is. 3:5

D. Unusual things connected with:

Retaining physical vigor. . . . . Deut. 34:7

Becoming a father . . . Gen. 18:9–15; Luke 1:18, 36

Living to see Christ . . . . Luke 2:25–32

Knowing kind of death in . . . . John 21:18, 19

E. Attaining unto, by:

Honoring parents. . . . . Ex. 20:12; Eph. 6:2, 3

Keeping God's law . . . . Prov. 3:1, 2

Following wisdom . . . . Prov. 3:13, 16

The fear of the Lord. . . . . Ps. 128:1, 6

Keeping from evil. . . . . Ps. 34:11–14

God's promise . . . . Gen. 15:15

F. Those of Bible times who lived beyond age of 100:

Methuselah . . . . Gen. 5:27

Jared. . . . . Gen. 5:20

Noah . . . . Gen. 9:29

Adam. . . . . Gen. 5:5

Seth . . . . Gen. 5:8

Cainan. . . . . Gen. 5:14

Enosh. . . . . Gen. 5:11

Mahalalel . . . . Gen. 5:17

Lamech . . . . Gen. 5:31

Enoch. . . . . Gen. 5:23

Terah . . . . Gen. 11:32

Isaac. . . . . Gen. 35:28

Abraham. . . . . Gen. 25:7

Jacob . . . . Gen. 47:28

Ishmael . . . . Gen. 25:17

Jehoiada . . . . 2 Chr. 24:15

Sarah . . . . Gen. 23:1

Aaron. . . . . Num. 33:39

Moses. . . . . Deut. 34:7

Joseph . . . . Gen. 50:26

Joshua . . . . Josh. 24:29

Agee—*fugitive*

Shammah's father . . . . 2 Sam. 23:11

Ages—*extended periods of time*

Descriptive of the times before Christ . . . Eph. 3:5

Descriptive of eternity . . . . Eph. 2:7

Agitation—*a disturbance*

A. Physically of:

Mountain . . . . Ex. 19:16–18

The earth . . . . Matt. 27:51–53

The world. . . . . Ps. 46:2–6

End-time events . . . . Luke 21:25–27

World's end . . . . 2 Pet. 3:7–12

B. Emotionally of:

Extreme grief. 2 Sam. 19:1–4

Remorse . . . . Matt. 27:3, 4

Fear . . . . Matt. 28:1–4

C. Figuratively of:

Messiah's advent. . . . . Hag. 2:6, 7

Enraged people .Acts 4:25–28
The wicked. . . . . Is. 57:20
The drunkard . . . . Prov. 23:29–35

Agony—*extreme suffering*
Descriptive of:
Christ in Gethsemane. . . . . .Luke 22:44
Christ on the cross . . . . .Mark 15:34–37
Paul's sufferings . . . . 2 Cor. 1:8, 9
The Christians' race . . . . .1 Cor. 9:24, 25

Agree, agreement
A. Forbidden between:
Israel and pagans . . . . Ex. 34:12–16
God and Baal. . . . . 1 Kin. 18:21–40
Believers, demons. . . . . .1 Cor. 10:21
Truth, error . . . . 1 John 4:1–6
B. Necessary between:
Prophecy, fulfillment . . . . .Acts 15:15
Doctrine, life. .James 2:14–21
Words, performance . . . . 2 Cor. 10:9–11
Believers in prayer . . . . Matt. 18:19
Adversaries. . . . . Matt. 5:24, 25
Christian workers. . . . . Gal. 2:7–9
C. Examples of:
Laban and Jacob . . . . Gen. 31:43–53
God and Israel. . . . . Ex. 19:3–8
David and Jonathan. . . . . 1 Sam. 18:1–4
The wicked and Sheol . . . . Is. 28:15, 18
Employer and employees . . . . .Matt. 20:10–13
Judas and the Sanhedrin. . . . . .Matt. 26:14–16
Witnesses . . . . Mark 14:56, 59
Husband and wife . . . . .Acts 5:9
The Jews and Gamaliel. . . . . .Acts 5:34–40
Conspiring Jews . . . . Acts 23:20
The people of the Antichrist . . . . .Rev. 17:17

Agriculture—*the cultivation of the soil*
A. Terms and implements involved:
Binding. . . . . Gen. 37:7
Cultivating. . . . . Luke 13:6–9
Gleaning. . . . . Ruth 2:3
Grafting . . . . Rom. 11:17–19
Harrowing . . . . Is. 28:24
Harvesting. . . . . Matt. 13:30
Mowing. . . . . Amos 7:1
Planting. . . . . Prov. 31:16
Plowing. . . . . .Job 1:14
Pruning. . . . . .Is. 5:6
Reaping. . . . . .Is. 17:5
Removing stones. .Is. 5:2
Sowing. . . . . Matt. 13:3
Stacking . . . . .Ex. 22:6
Threshing. . . . . .Judg. 6:11
Treading. . . . . Neh. 13:15
Watering. . . . . 1 Cor. 3:6–8
Weeding . . . . .Matt. 13:28, 29
Winnowing . . . . Ruth 3:2
B. Virtues required in:
Wisdom . . . . Is. 28:24–29
Diligence. Prov. 27:23–27

Labor . . . . 2 Tim. 2:6
Patience. . . . . James 5:7
Industry . . . . .Prov. 28:19
Faith. . . . . .Hab. 3:17–19
Bountifulness .2 Cor. 9:6, 7
Hopefulness. . . . . 1 Cor. 9:10
C. Enemies of:
War . . . . Jer. 50:16
Pestilence . . . . .Joel 1:9–12
Fire. . . . . Joel 1:19
Animals. . . . . Song 2:15
Dry seasons . . . . .Jer. 14:1, 4
D. Restrictions involving:
Coveting another's field . . . . Deut. 5:21
Removing boundaries. . . . . Deut. 19:14
Roaming cattle . . . . .Ex. 22:5
Spreading fire . . . . .Ex. 22:6
Military service. . . . . Deut. 20:5, 6
Working on the Sabbath. . . . . Ex. 34:21
Complete harvest . . . . .Lev. 19:9, 10
E. God's part in:
Began in Eden . . . . Gen. 2:15
Sin's penalty. . . . . Gen. 3:17
Providence of, impartial. . . . . Matt. 5:45
Goodness of, recognized . . . . Acts 14:16, 17
Judgments against, cited . . . . .Hag. 1:10, 11
F. Figurative of:
Gospel seed . . . . Matt. 13:1–9
Gospel dispensation . . . . . Matt. 13:24–30, 36–43
God's workers . . . . John 4:36–38
God's Word . . . . Is. 55:10, 11
Spiritual barrenness. . . . . Heb. 6:7, 8
Spiritual bountifulness. . . . . .2 Cor. 9:9, 10
Final harvest . . . . Mark 4:28, 29

Aground—*stranded in shallow water*
Ship carrying Paul . . . . Acts 27:41

Agur—*collector*
Writer of proverbs . . . . Prov. 30:1–33

Ahab—*father's brother*
1. A wicked king of Israel . . . . 1 Kin. 16:29
Marries Jezebel . . . . .1 Kin. 16:31
Introduces Baal worship. . . . . 1 Kin. 16:31–33
Denounced by Elijah . . . . 1 Kin. 17:1
Gathers prophets of Baal . . . . 1 Kin. 18:17–46
Wars against Ben-Hadad . . . . 1 Kin. 20:1–43
Covets Naboth's vineyard . . . . .1 Kin. 21:1–16
Death of, predicted . . . . 1 Kin. 21:17–26
Repentance of, delays judgment . . . 1 Kin. 21:27–29
Joins Jehoshaphat against Syrians . . . 1 Kin. 22:1–4
Rejects Micaiah's warning. . . . . 1 Kin. 22:5–33
Slain in battle. . . . . 1 Kin. 22:34–37
Seventy sons of, slain . . . . .2 Kin. 10:1–11
Prophecies concerning, fulfilled . . . . .1 Kin. 22:38
2. Lying prophet . . . . Jer. 29:21–23

Aharah—*after his brother*
1. Son of Benjamin . . . . .1 Chr. 8:1
2. Called Ahiram . . . . Num. 26:38
3. Called Ehi . . . . Gen. 46:21

Aharhel—*brother of Rachel*
  A descendant of Judah .... 1 Chr. 4:8

Ahasbai—*blooming; shining*
  The father of Eliphelet .... 2 Sam. 23:34

Ahasuerus—*king*
1. The father of Darius the Mede........... Dan. 9:1
2. Persian king............................. Esth. 1:1
  Makes Esther queen................ Esth. 2:16, 17
  Follows Haman's intrigue .... Esth. 3:1, 8–12
  Orders Jews annihilated........... Esth. 3:13–15
  Responds to Esther's plea............. Esth. 7:1–8
  Orders Haman hanged .... Esth. 7:9, 10
  Promotes Mordecai .... Esth. 8:1, 2
  Reverses Haman's plot .... Esth. 8:3–17
  Exalts Mordecai .... Esth. 10:1–3
3. A king of Persia; probably Xerxes,
    486–465 B.C. .... Ezra 4:6

Ahava—*a town and a river in Babylonia*
  Jewish exiles gather here........... Ezra 8:15–31

Ahaz—*he has grasped*
1. A king of Judah; son of Jotham ...... 2 Kin. 16:1, 2
  Pursues evil ways .... 2 Kin. 16:3, 4
  Defends Jerusalem against Rezin and
    Pekah .... 2 Kin. 16:5, 6
  Refuses a divine sign .... Is. 7:1–16
  Defeated with great loss .... 2 Chr. 28:5–15
  Becomes subject to Assyria .... 2 Kin. 16:7–9
  Makes Jerusalem a pagan city.... 2 Kin. 16:10–18
  Erects sundial .... 2 Kin. 20:11
  Death of .... 2 Kin. 16:19, 20
2. A descendant of
    Jonathan.............. 1 Chr. 8:35, 36; 9:40–42
3. Ancestor of Jesus .... Matt. 1:9

Ahaziah—*Yahweh has grasped*
1. A king of Israel; son of Ahab and
    Jezebel........................ 1 Kin. 22:40, 51
  Worships Baal .... 1 Kin. 22:52, 53
  Seeks alliance with Jehoshaphat.. 1 Kin. 22:48, 49
  Falls through lattice; sends to Baal-Zebub, the god
    of Ekron for help .... 2 Kin. 1:2–16
  Dies according to Elijah's word..... 2 Kin. 1:17, 18
2. A king of Judah; son of Jehoram and
    Athaliah...................... 2 Kin. 8:25, 26
  Made king by Jerusalem
    inhabitants .... 2 Chr. 22:1, 2
  Taught evil by his mother .... 2 Chr. 22:2, 3
  Follows Ahab's wickedness .... 2 Chr. 22:4
  Joins Joram against the Syrians .... 2 Kin. 8:28
  Visits wounded Joram............... 2 Kin. 9:16
  Slain by Jehu .... 2 Kin. 9:27, 28
  Called Jehoahaz .... 2 Chr. 21:17
  Called Azariah .... 2 Chr. 22:6

Ahban—*brother of intelligence*
  A son of Abishur.................... 1 Chr. 2:29

Aher—*another*
  A Benjamite....................... 1 Chr. 7:12

Ahi—*brother*
1. Gadite chief......................... 1 Chr. 5:15
2. Asherite chief .... 1 Chr. 7:34

Ahiam—*mother's brother*
  One of David's mighty men........ 2 Sam. 23:33

Ahian—*fraternal*
  A Manassite....................... 1 Chr. 7:19

Ahiezer—*brother is help*
1. Head of the tribe of Dan .... Num. 1:12
2. Benjamite chief, joined David
    at Ziklag......................... 1 Chr. 12:3

Ahihud—*brother is majesty*
1. Asherite leader, helped Moses divide
    Canaan........................ Num. 34:27
2. A Benjamite....................... 1 Chr. 8:6, 7

Ahijah—*brother of Yahweh*
1. A great-grandson of Judah............. 1 Chr. 2:25
2. One of David's warriors.............. 1 Chr. 11:36
3. A Levite treasurer in David's reign .... 1 Chr. 26:20
4. A prophet of Shiloh who foretells
    division of Solomon's kingdom . 1 Kin. 11:29–39
  Foretells elimination of Jeroboam's
    line........................... 1 Kin. 14:1–18
  A writer of prophecy .... 2 Chr. 9:29
5. The father of Baasha.............. 1 Kin. 15:27, 33
6. A Jew who seals Nehemiah's covenant... Neh. 10:26
7. A secretary of Solomon................. 1 Kin. 4:3
8. A Benjamite.......................... 1 Chr. 8:7
9. A priest during Saul's reign .... 1 Sam. 14:3, 18

Ahikam—*my brother has arisen*
  A son of Shaphan the scribe.......... 2 Kin. 22:12
  Sent in Josiah's mission
    to Huldah .... 2 Kin. 22:12–14
  Protects Jeremiah...................... Jer. 26:24
  The father of Gedaliah, governor under
    Nebuchadnezzar ...... 2 Kin. 25:22; Jer. 39:14

Ahilud—*a child's brother*
1. The father of Jehoshaphat, the recorder under
    David and Solomon............... 2 Sam. 8:16
2. The father of Baana, a district
    governor....................... 1 Kin. 4:7, 12

Ahimaaz—*brother of anger*
1. The father of Ahinoam, wife of
    King Saul .... 1 Sam. 14:50
2. A son of Zadok the high priest........ 1 Chr. 6:8, 9
  Warns David of Absalom's
    plans .... 2 Sam. 15:27, 36
  Good man........................ 2 Sam. 18:27
  First to tell David of Absalom's
    defeat .... 2 Sam. 18:19–30
3. Solomon's son-in-law and commissioner in
    Naphtali....................... 1 Kin. 4:15
  May be the same as 2.

Ahiman—*my brother is a gift*
1. A giant son of Anak seen by
    Israelite spies.................. Num. 13:22, 33

Driven out of Hebron by Caleb . . . . . Josh. 15:13, 14

Slain by tribe of Judah . . . . Judg. 1:10

2. A Levite gatekeeper . . . . 1 Chr. 9:17

Ahimelech—*my brother is king*

1. The high priest at Nob during

Saul's reign . . . . 1 Sam. 21:1

Feeds David the showbread . . . . 1 Sam. 21:2–6

Gives Goliath's sword to David . . . . 1 Sam. 21:8, 9

Betrayed by Doeg . . . . 1 Sam. 22:9–16

Slain by Doeg at

Saul's command . . . . 1 Sam. 22:17–19

Abiathar, son of, escapes . . . . 1 Sam. 22:20

David wrote concerning . . . . Ps. 52 (title)

2. Abiathar's son . . . . 2 Sam. 8:17

Copriest with Zadok . . . . 1 Chr. 24:3, 6, 31

3. David's Hittite warrior . . . . 1 Sam. 26:6

Ahimoth—*my brother is death*

A Kohathite Levite . . . . 1 Chr. 6:25

Ahinadab—*my brother is noble*

One of Solomon's officers . . . . 1 Kin. 4:14

Ahinoam—*my brother is delight*

1. Wife of Saul . . . . 1 Sam. 14:50

2. David's wife . . . . 1 Sam. 25:43

Lived with David at Gath . . . . 1 Sam. 27:3

Captured by Amalekites at Ziklag . . . . 1 Sam. 30:5

Rescued by David . . . . 1 Sam. 30:18

Lives with David in Hebron . . . . 2 Sam. 2:1, 2

Mother of Amnon . . . . 2 Sam. 3:2

Ahio—*brotherly*

1. Abinadab's son . . . . 2 Sam. 6:3

2. A Benjamite . . . . 1 Chr. 8:14

3. A son of Jeiel . . . . 1 Chr. 8:31; 9:35, 37

Ahira—*my brother is evil*

A tribal leader . . . . Num. 1:15

Ahisamach—*my brother supports*

A Danite . . . . Ex. 31:6

Ahishahar—*brother of dawn*

A Benjamite . . . . 1 Chr. 7:10

Ahishar—*my brother has sung*

A manager of Solomon's household . . . . . 1 Kin. 4:6

Ahithophel—*brother of folly*

David's counselor . . . . 2 Sam. 15:12

Joins Absalom's insurrection . . . . 2 Sam. 15:31

Plans of, prepared against by David . . . . 2 Sam.
15:31–34

Counsels Absalom . . . . 2 Sam. 16:20–22

Reputed wise . . . . 2 Sam. 16:23

Counsel of, rejected by Absalom . . . 2 Sam. 17:1–22

Commits suicide . . . . 2 Sam. 17:23

Ahitub—*my brother is goodness*

1. Phinehas's son . . . . 1 Sam. 14:3

2. The father of Zadok the priest . . . . 2 Sam. 8:17

3. The father of another Zadok . . . . 1 Chr. 6:11, 12

Ahlab—*fruitful*

A city of Asher . . . . Judg. 1:31

Ahlai—*O would that!*

1. Father of a warrior of David . . . . 1 Chr. 11:41

2. Woman who married an Egyptian

servant . . . . 1 Chr. 2:31–35

Ahoah—*brotherly*

A son of Bela . . . . 1 Chr. 8:4

Ahohite—*a descendant of Ahoah*

Applied to Dodo, Zalmon, and Ilai . . . 2 Sam. 23:9,
28; 1 Chr. 11:29

Aholiab—*a father's tent*

Son of Ahisamach . . . . Ex. 31:6

Ahumai—*meaning unknown*

A descendant of Judah . . . . 1 Chr. 4:2

Ahuzzam—*possessor*

A man of Judah . . . . 1 Chr. 4:6

Ahuzzath—*possession*

A friend of Abimelech . . . . Gen. 26:26

Ahzai—*Yahweh has grasped*

A postexilic priest . . . . Neh. 11:13

Also called Jahzerah . . . . 1 Chr. 9:12

Ai—*ruin*

1. A city east of Bethel in central Palestine . . . Josh. 7:2

Abraham camps near . . . . Gen. 12:8

A royal city of Canaan . . . . Josh. 10:1

Israel defeated at . . . . Josh. 7:2–5

Israel destroys completely . . . . Josh. 8:1–28

Occupied after exile . . . . Ezra 2:28

2. An Ammonite city near Heshbon . . . . Jer. 49:3

Aiah—*falcon*

The father of Rizpah, Saul's concubine . . . 2 Sam. 3:7

Aijalon—*place of gazelles*

1. A town assigned to Dan . . . . Josh. 19:42

Amorites not driven from . . . . Judg. 1:35

Miracle there . . . . Josh. 10:12, 13

Assigned to Kohathite Levites . . . . Josh. 21:24

City of refuge . . . . 1 Chr. 6:66–69

Included in Benjamin's territory . . . . . . 1 Chr. 8:13

Fortified by Rehoboam . . . . 2 Chr. 11:5, 10

Captured by Philistines . . . . 2 Chr. 28:18

2. The burial place of Elon, a judge . . . . Judg. 12:12

Ain—*spring*

1. A town near Riblah . . . . Num. 34:11

2. Town of Judah . . . . Josh. 15:32

Transferred to Simeon . . . . Josh. 19:7

Later assigned to the priests . . . . Josh. 21:16

Called Ashan . . . . 1 Chr. 6:59

Air—*the atmosphere around the earth*

Adam given dominion over . . . . Gen. 1:26–30

Adam names birds of . . . . Gen. 2:19, 20

God destroys birds of . . . . Gen. 6:7

Mystery of eagle in . . . . Prov. 30:19

Satan, prince of . . . . Eph. 2:2

Believers meet Jesus in . . . . 1 Thess. 4:17

God's wrath poured out in . . . . Rev. 9:2

Figurative of emptiness . . . . 1 Cor. 9:26

Ajah—*falcon*
    A Horite .... Gen. 36:24

Akel Dama
    Field called "Field of Blood" .... Acts 1:19

Akkub—*cunning*
1. Elioenai's son........................ 1 Chr. 3:24
2. A Levite head of a family of porters .... 1 Chr. 9:17
3. A family of Nethinim .... Ezra 2:45
4. A Levite interpreter..................... Neh. 8:7

Akrabbim—*scorpions*
    An "ascent" on the south of the
        Dead Sea .... Num. 34:4
    One border of Judah .... Josh. 15:3

Alabaster—*container made of fine textured, usually*
    white and translucent, material
    Used by woman anointing Jesus....... Matt. 26:7

Alammelech—*oak of a king*
    Village of Asher .... Josh. 19:26

Alamoth—*virgins*
    A musical term probably indicating a
        women's choir................... 1 Chr. 15:20

Alarm—*sudden and fearful surprise*
A. Caused physically by:
    Sudden attack .... Judg. 7:20–23
    Death plague .... Ex. 12:29–33
    A mysterious manifestation...... 1 Sam. 28:11–14
    Prodigies of nature.............. Matt. 27:50–54
B. Caused spiritually by:
    Sin.......................... 1 Sam. 12:17–19
    Remorse .... Gen. 27:34–40
    Conscience...................... Acts 24:24, 25
    Hopelessness in hell............. Luke 16:22–31
C. Shout of jubilee or warning:
    Instruction to Israel................. Num. 10:9
    Causes anguish......................... Jer. 4:19
    Prophecy of judgment.................. Jer. 49:2
    See Agitation

Alas—*an intense emotional outcry*
A. Emotional outcry caused by:
    Israel's defeat........................ Josh. 7:7–9
    An angel's appearance................. Judg. 6:22
    A vow's realization.............. Judg. 11:34, 35
    Army without water................ 2 Kin. 3:9, 10
    Loss of an ax head .... 2 Kin. 6:5
    Servant's fear.................... 2 Kin. 6:14, 15
B. Prophetic outcry caused by:
    Israel's future.................... Num. 24:23, 24
    Israel's punishment .... Amos 5:16–20
    Jacob's trouble...................... Jer. 30:7–9
    Babylon's fall .... Rev. 18:10–19

Alemeth—*hidden*
1. A Benjamite......................... 1 Chr. 7:8
2. A descendant of Saul............... 1 Chr. 8:36
3. A Levitical city .... 1 Chr. 6:60

Aleph
    The first letter in the Hebrew
        alphabet...................... Ps. 119:1–8

Alert—*watchful*
    In battle......................... Judg. 7:15–22
    In personal safety............... 1 Sam. 19:9, 10
    In readiness for attack............... Neh. 4:9–23
    In prayer......................... Matt. 26:41
    In spiritual combat................... Eph. 6:18
    In waiting for Christ's return ..... Matt. 24:42–51
    Daily living .... 1 Cor. 16:13
    Times of testing .... Luke 21:34–36
    Against false teachers .... Acts 20:29–31

Alexander—*man-defending*
1. A son of Simon of Cyrene............. Mark 15:21
2. A member of the high-priestly family ..... Acts 4:6
3. A Jew in Ephesus .... Acts 19:33, 34
4. An apostate condemned by Paul .... 1 Tim. 1:19, 20

Alexander the Great—*Alexander III of Macedonia*
    (356–323 B.C.)
A. Not named in the Bible, but referred to as:
    The four-headed leopard .... Dan. 7:6
    The goat with a great horn........ Dan. 8:5–9, 21
    A mighty king....................... Dan. 11:3
B. Rule of, described:
    His invasion of Palestine .... Zech. 9:1–8
    His kingdom being divided............ Dan. 7:6

Alexandria—*a city of Egypt founded by Alexander the*
    Great (332 B.C.)
    Men of, persecute Stephen............... Acts 6:9
    Apollos, native of .... Acts 18:24
    Paul sails in ship .... Acts 27:6

Algum, almug—*a tree (probably the red sandalwood)*
    Imported from Ophir by Hiram's
        navy........................ 1 Kin. 10:11, 12
    Used in constructing the temple.... 2 Chr. 9:10, 11
    Also imported from Lebanon .... 2 Chr. 2:8

Alienation—*a withdrawing or separation*
    Descriptive of Israel's
        apostasy.............. Ezek. 23:17, 18, 22, 28
    Spiritual deadness .... Eph. 4:18

Aliens—*citizens of a foreign country; strangers*
A. Descriptive, naturally, of:
    Israel in the Egyptian bondage........ Gen. 15:13
    Abraham in Canaan .... Gen. 23:4
    Moses in Egypt .... Ex. 18:2, 3
    Israel in Babylon...................... Ps. 137:4
B. Descriptive, spiritually, of:
    Estrangement from friends .... Job 19:15
    The condition of the Gentiles......... Eph. 2:12

Alive—*the opposite of being dead*
A. Descriptive of:
    Natural life..................... Gen. 43:7, 27, 28
    Spiritual life..................... Luke 15:24, 32
    Restored physical life.................. Acts 9:41
    Christ's resurrected life................. Acts 1:3
    The believer's glorified life .... 1 Cor. 15:22

Korah, Dathan, and Abiram's descent
into Sheol . . . . Num. 16:27, 33
B. The power of keeping:
Belongs to God . . . . Deut. 32:39
Not in human power . . . . Ps. 22:29
Promised to the godly . . . . Ps. 33:18, 19
Gratefully acknowledged . . . . Josh. 14:10
Transformed by Christ's
return . . . . 1 Thess. 4:15, 16

Allegory—*an extended figure of speech using symbols*
A. Of natural things:
A king's doom . . . . Judg. 9:8–20
Old age . . . . Eccl. 12:1–7
Israel as a transplanted vine . . . . Ps. 80:8–19
B. Of spiritual things:
Christian as sheep . . . . John 10:1–16
Two covenants . . . . Gal. 4:21–31
Israel and the Gentiles . . . . Rom. 11:15–24
Christ and His church . . . . Eph. 5:22–33
The Christian's armor . . . . Eph. 6:11–17

Alleluia—*praise the Lord*
The Greek form of the Hebrew
Hallelujah . . . . Rev. 19:1–6

Alliances—*treaties between nations or individuals*
A. In the time of the patriarchs:
Abraham with Canaanite chiefs . . . . Gen. 14:13
Abraham with Abimelech . . . . Gen. 21:22–34
Isaac with Abimelech . . . . Gen. 26:26–33
Jacob with Laban . . . . Gen. 31:44–54
B. In the time of the wilderness:
Israel with Moab . . . . Num. 25:1–3
C. In the time of the conquest:
Israel with Gibeonites . . . . Josh. 9:3–27
D. In the time of David:
David with Achish . . . . 1 Sam. 27:2–12
E. In the time of Solomon:
Solomon with Hiram . . . . 1 Kin. 5:12–18
Solomon with Egypt . . . . 1 Kin. 3:1
F. In the time of the divided kingdom:
Asa with Ben-Hadad . . . . 1 Kin. 15:18–20
Ahab with Ben-Hadad . . . . 1 Kin. 20:31–34
Israel with Assyria . . . . 2 Kin. 16:5–9
Hoshea with Egypt . . . . 2 Kin. 17:1–6
G. In the time of Judah's sole kingdom:
Hezekiah with Egypt . . . . 2 Kin. 18:19–24
Jehoiakim with Egypt . . . . 2 Kin. 23:31–35

Alliance with evil
A. Forbidden to:
Israel . . . . Ex. 34:11–16
Christians . . . . Rom. 13:12
Christ . . . . Matt. 4:1–11
B. Forbidden because:
Leads to idolatry . . . . Ex. 23:32, 33
Deceives . . . . Num. 25:1–3, 18
Enslaves . . . . 2 Pet. 2:18, 19
Defiles . . . . Ezra 9:1, 2
Brings God's anger . . . . Ezra 9:13–15
Corrupts . . . . 1 Cor. 15:33

Incompatible with Christ . . . . 2 Cor. 6:14–16
Defiles . . . . Jude 23
C. The believer should:
Avoid . . . . Prov. 1:10–15
Hate . . . . Ps. 26:4, 5
Confess . . . . Ezra 10:9–11
Separate from . . . . 2 Cor. 6:17
D. Examples of:
Delilah . . . . Judg. 16:5, 6, 18
Solomon . . . . 1 Kin. 11:1–11
Jeroboam . . . . 1 Kin. 12:25–33
Jehoshaphat . . . . 2 Chr. 20:35–37
Judas Iscariot . . . . Matt. 26:14–16
Heretics . . . . Rev. 2:14, 15, 20
See Association

All in all—*complete*
Descriptive of:
God . . . . 1 Cor. 15:28
Christ . . . . Eph. 1:23

Allon—*oak*
A Simeonite prince . . . . 1 Chr. 4:37

Allon Bachuth—*oak of weeping*
A tree marking Deborah's grave . . . . Gen. 35:8

Allowance—*a stipulated amount*
Daily to Jehoiachin . . . 2 Kin.25:27–30, Jer. 52:34

WORD STUDY   **ALMIGHTY,** *shadday* (shad-*dah*-ee). *Shadday* is a noun meaning "almighty," used as a name of God. The original meaning of the name may have been "God of the Mountains," offsetting Canaanite religion, which had a separate god who lived in the high places in the mountains. In the Pentateuch and Ezek. 10:5, the word is used in the compound form of God's name, *'Ēl Shaddai,* usually translated "God *Almighty.*" Elsewhere, most frequently in Job where it occurs thirty-one times, the name is used independently, "the *Almighty.*" The emphasis of this name is the power and majesty of deity. (Strong's #7706)

Almighty—*a title of God*
Applied to God . . . . Gen. 17:1, 2; 2 Cor. 6:18
Applied to Christ . . . . Rev. 1:8

Almodad—*the beloved*
Eldest son of Joktan . . . . Gen. 10:26

Almond—*a small tree bearing fruit*
Sent as a present to Pharaoh . . . . Gen. 43:11
Used in the tabernacle . . . . Ex. 25:33, 34
Aaron's rod produces . . . . Num. 17:2, 3, 8
Used figuratively of old age . . . . Eccl. 12:5
Used by Jacob . . . . Gen. 30:37

Almon Diblathaim—*Almon of the double cake of figs*
An Israelite encampment . . . . Num. 33:46, 47

Alms—*gifts prompted by love to help the needy*
A. Design of, to:
Help the poor . . . . Lev. 25:35
Receive a blessing . . . . Deut. 15:10, 11

B. Manner of bestowing with:

A willing spirit . . . . Deut. 15:7–11

Simplicity . . . . Matt. 6:1–4

Cheerfulness . . . . 2 Cor. 9:7

True love . . . . 1 Cor. 13:3

Fairness to all . . . . Acts 4:32–35

Regularity . . . . Acts 11:29, 30

Law of reciprocity . . . . Rom. 15:25–27

C. Cautions concerning:

Not for human honor . . . . Matt. 6:1–4

Not for lazy . . . . 2 Thess. 3:10

Needful for the rich . . . . 1 Tim. 6:17, 18

D. Rewarded:

Now . . . . Deut. 14:28, 29; 2 Cor. 9:9, 10

In heaven . . . . Matt. 19:21

E. Examples of:

Zacchaeus . . . . Luke 19:8

Dorcas . . . . Acts 9:36

Cornelius . . . . Acts 10:2

The early Christians . . . . Acts 4:34–37

Aloes—*a perfume-bearing tree*

A. Used on:

Beds . . . . Prov. 7:17

The dead . . . . John 19:39

B. Figurative of:

Israel . . . . Num. 24:5, 6

Aloth—*ascents, steeps*

A town in Asher . . . . 1 Kin. 4:16

Alpha and Omega—*first and last letters of the Greek alphabet ("A to Z")*

Expressive of God and Christ as initiator and fulfillment of all that happens . . . . Rev. 1:8; 21:6, 7

Alphabet—*the letters of a language*

The Hebrew, seen in . . . . Ps. 119

Alphaeus—*leader, chief*

1. The father of Levi (Matthew) . . . . Mark 2:14

2. The father of James . . . . Matt. 10:3

WORD STUDY

ALTAR, *mizbeach* (miz-*bay*-akh). *Mizbeach* is a noun meaning "altar." The OT records altars built by many people including Noah, Abraham, Isaac, Jacob, and Moses. The same word is used to refer to altars built for the Hebrew God and altars built for foreign deities. The altar, a place for sacrifice, could also be a place of refuge (see Ex. 21:14; 1 Kin. 1:50, 51) when the horns of the altar were grasped. Altars were made of various materials from the early versions of heaped up earth or stone (for example, see Ex. 20:24–26) to the two elaborate altars of Solomon's temple, one of which was made of cedar and plated with gold. (Strong's #4196)

Altar—*an elevated structure*

A. Uses of:

Sacrifice . . . . Gen. 8:20

Incense . . . . Ex. 30:1, 7, 8; Luke 1:10, 11

National unity . . . . Deut. 12:5, 6

A memorial . . . . Ex. 17:15, 16

Protection . . . . Ex. 21:13, 14

B. Made of:

Earth . . . . Ex. 20:24

Unhewn stone . . . . Ex. 20:25

Stones . . . . Deut. 27:5, 6

Natural rock . . . . Judg. 6:19–21

Bronze . . . . Ex. 27:1–6

C. Built worthily by:

Noah . . . . Gen. 8:20

Abraham . . . . Gen. 12:7, 8

Isaac . . . . Gen. 26:25

Jacob . . . . Gen. 33:18, 20

Moses . . . . Ex. 17:15

Joshua . . . . Deut. 27:4–7

Eastern tribes . . . . Josh. 22:10, 34

Gideon . . . . Judg. 6:26, 27

Manoah . . . . Judg. 13:19, 20

Israelites . . . . Judg. 21:4

Samuel . . . . 1 Sam. 7:17

Saul . . . . 1 Sam. 14:35

David . . . . 2 Sam. 24:18–25

Elijah . . . . 1 Kin. 18:31, 32

D. Built unworthily (for idolatry) by:

Gideon's father . . . . Judg. 6:25–32

King Jeroboam . . . . 1 Kin. 12:32, 33

King Ahab . . . . 1 Kin. 16:30–32

King Ahaz . . . . 2 Chr. 28:1, 3, 5

Israelite people . . . . Is. 65:3

Athenians . . . . Acts 17:23

E. Pagan altars destroyed by:

Gideon . . . . Judg. 6:25–29

King Asa . . . . 2 Chr. 14:2, 3

Jehoiada . . . . 2 Kin. 11:17, 18

King Hezekiah . . . . 2 Kin. 18:22

King Josiah . . . . 2 Kin. 23:12, 16, 17

F. Burnt offering:

1. *Of the tabernacle, features concerning:*

Specifications . . . . Ex. 27:1–8

Bezalel, builder of . . . . Ex. 31:1–6, 9

Place of, outside tabernacle . . . . Ex. 40:6, 29

Only priests allowed at . . . . Num. 18:3, 7

The defective not acceptable on . . . . Lev. 22:22

The putting on of blood . . . . Ex. 29:12

2. *Of Solomon's temple:*

Described . . . . 1 Kin. 8:63, 64

Renewed by King Asa . . . . 2 Chr. 15:8

Cleansed by King Hezekiah . . . . . 2 Chr. 29:18–24

Repaired by King Manasseh . . . . . 2 Chr. 33:16–18

Vessels of, carried to Babylon . . . . 2 Kin. 25:14

3. *Of the postexilic (Zerubbabel's) temple:*

Described . . . . Ezra 3:1–6

Polluted . . . . Mal. 1:7, 8

4. *Of Ezekiel's vision:*

Described . . . . Ezek. 43:13–27

G. Incense:

In the tabernacle, described . . . . Ex. 30:1–10

Location of . . . . Ex. 30:6

Anointed with oil . . . . Ex. 30:26, 27

Annual atonement made at . . . . .Ex. 30:10
In Solomon's temple. . . . . .1 Kin. 7:48
In John's vision . . . . .Rev. 8:3
H. New covenant:
    A place of spiritual sacrifices. . . . . . . .Rom. 12:1, 2
    Christ, our pattern. . . . . .Heb. 13:10–16

Altruism—*living for the good of others*
A. Manifested in:
    Service. . . . . Matt. 20:26–28
    Doing good . . . . Acts 10:38
    Seeking the welfare of others . . . . . . Gal. 6:1, 2, 10
    Helping the weak . . . . Acts 20:35
B. Examples of:
    Moses. . . . . .Ex. 32:30–32
    Samuel. . . . . 1 Sam. 12:1–5
    Jonathan . . . . 1 Sam. 18:1–4
    Christ. . . . . .John 13:4–17
    Paul . . . . 1 Cor. 9:19–22

Alush—*wild place*
    An Israelite encampment. . . . . .Num. 33:13, 14

Alvah—*high; tall*
    An Edomite chief. . . . . .Gen. 36:40
    Also called Aliah . . . . 1 Chr. 1:51

Alvan—*tall*
    A son of Shobal the Horite. . . . . .Gen. 36:23
    Also called Alian . . . . .1 Chr. 1:40

Always—*continually, forever*
A. Of God's:
    Care . . . . Deut. 11:12
    Covenant . . . . 1 Chr. 16:15
    Striving. . . . . .Ps. 103:9
B. Of Christ's:
    Determination . . . . Ps. 16:8–11; Acts 2:25–28
    Rejoicing. . . . . Prov. 8:30–31
    Presence . . . . Matt. 28:20
    Obedience . . . . .John 8:29
    Prayer . . . . .John 11:42
C. Of the believer's:
    Prayer . . . . .Luke 21:36
    Peace . . . . 2 Thess. 3:16
    Obedience . . . . Phil. 2:12
    Work . . . . .1 Cor. 15:58
    Defense. . . . . .1 Pet. 3:15
    Rejoicing. . . . . Phil. 4:4
    Thanksgiving . . . . 1 Thess. 1:2
    Victory . . . . 2 Cor. 2:14
    Conscience. . . . . .Acts 24:16
    Confidence. . . . . .2 Cor. 5:6
    Sufficiency. . . . . .2 Cor. 9:8
D. Of the unbeliever's:
    Probation . . . . Gen. 6:3
    Turmoil. . . . . .Mark 5:5
    Rebellion . . . . .Acts 7:51
    Lying . . . . .Titus 1:12

Amad—*people of duration*
    A city of Asher. . . . . .Josh. 19:26

Amal—*toil*
    Asher's descendant. . . . . .1 Chr. 7:35

Amalek—*warlike*
    A son of Eliphaz .1 Chr. 1:36
    Grandson of Esau. . . . . .Gen. 36:11, 12
    A chief of Edom . . . . .Gen. 36:16
    First among nations. . . . . .Num. 24:20

Amalekites—*a nation hostile to Israel*
A. Defeated by:
    Chedorlaomer .Gen. 14:5–7
    Joshua . . . . Ex. 17:8, 13
    Gideon. . . . . Judg. 7:12–25
    Saul. . . . . .1 Sam. 14:47, 48
    David. . . . . 1 Sam. 27:8, 9
    Simeonites . . . . 1 Chr. 4:42, 43
B. Overcame Israel during:
    Wilderness. Num. 14:39–45
    Judges . . . . .Judg. 3:13
C. Destruction of:
    Predicted . . . . .Ex. 17:14
    Reaffirmed. . . . . Deut. 25:17–19
    Fulfilled in part by David. . . . . .1 Sam. 27:8, 9;
        2 Sam. 1:1–16
    Fulfilled by the Simeonites . . . . 1 Chr. 4:42, 43

Amam—*gathering place*
    A city of Judah. .Josh. 15:26

Amana—*permanent*
    A summit in the Anti-Lebanon mountain
        range. . . . . Song 4:8

Amaranthine—*like the amaranth flower: unfading,*
    perennial
    From a Greek word used to describe our
        inheritance and our glory . . . . . . .1 Pet. 1:4; 5:4

Amariah—*Yahweh said*
1. The grandfather of Zadok
    the priest . . . . 1 Chr. 6:7, 8, 52
2. A priest. . . . . 1 Chr. 6:11
3. Levite in David's time. . . . . 1 Chr. 23:19
4. A high priest . . . . 2 Chr. 19:11
5. A Levite in Hezekiah's reign. . . . . 2 Chr. 31:14, 15
6. Son of King Hezekiah. . . . . .Zeph. 1:1
7. One who divorced his foreign wife . . . Ezra 10:42, 44
8. A signer of Nehemiah's document . . . . . . .Neh. 10:3
9. A postexilic chief priest . . . . Neh. 12:1, 2, 7

Amasa—*burden-bearer*
1. The son of Jithra; David's nephew. . . . .2 Sam. 17:25
    Commands Absalom's rebels. . . . . 2 Sam. 17:25
    Made David's commander. . . . . 2 Sam. 19:13
    Treacherously killed by Joab . . . . . .2 Sam. 20:9–12
    Death avenged. . . . . 1 Kin. 2:28–34
2. An Ephraimite leader . . . . .2 Chr. 28:9–12

Amasai—*Yahweh has borne*
1. A Kohathite Levite . . . . 1 Chr. 6:25, 35
2. David's officer . . . . 1 Chr. 12:18
3. A priestly trumpeter in David's time . . . 1 Chr. 15:24
4. A Kohathite Levite . . . . 2 Chr. 29:12

Amashai—*carrying spoil*
  A priest .... Neh. 11:13

Amasiah—*Yahweh bears*
  One of Jehoshaphat's commanders ... 2 Chr. 17:16

Amazement—*an intense emotional shock*
A. Caused by:
  Christ's miracles .... Matt. 12:22, 23;
    Luke 5:25, 26
  Christ's teaching .... Matt. 19:25
  God's power .... Luke 9:42, 43
  Apostolic miracle .... Acts 3:7–10
B. Manifested by:
  Christ's parents .... Luke 2:48
  Christ's disciples .... Matt. 19:25
  The Jews .... Mark 9:15
  The early Christians .... Acts 9:19–21

Amaziah—*Yahweh is strong*
1. King of Judah .... 2 Kin. 14:1–4
  Kills his father's assassinators ...... 2 Kin. 14:5, 6
  Raises a large army .... 2 Chr. 25:5
  Employs troops from Israel .... 2 Chr. 25:6
  Rebuked by a man of God .... 2 Chr. 25:7–10
  Defeats Edomites .... 2 Kin. 14:7
  Worships Edomite gods .... 2 Chr. 25:14
  Rebuked by a prophet .... 2 Chr. 25:15, 16
  Defeated by Israel .... 2 Kin. 14:8–14
  Killed by conspirators .... 2 Chr. 25:25–28
2. A priest of Bethel .... Amos 7:10–17
3. A Simeonite .... 1 Chr. 4:34, 42, 43
4. A Merarite Levite .... 1 Chr. 6:45

| WORD STUDY | **AMBASSADOR, BE AN,** *presbeuō* (pres-byoo-oh). The literal meaning of *presbeuō* |

is "to be an ambassador" or "envoy." Paul characterizes his apostolic work as being an "ambassador" (Eph. 6:20) on behalf of Christ (2 Cor. 5:20). This figurative use of *presbeuō* draws upon the role of the emperor's legates, who were dispatched by the emperor as his official representatives to make his presence felt and his intentions known. (Strong's #4243)

Ambassador—*an official sent to deal with a foreign government or sovereign*
A. Some purposes of, to:
  Grant safe passage .... Num. 20:14–21
  Settle disputes .... Judg. 11:12–28
  Arrange business .... 1 Kin. 5:1–12
  Stir up trouble .... 1 Kin. 20:1–12
  Issue an ultimatum .... 2 Kin. 19:9–14
  Spy .... 2 Kin. 20:12–19
  Learn God's will .... Jer. 37:3–10
B. Some examples of:
  Judah to Egypt .... Is. 30:1–4
  Babylonians to Judah .... 2 Chr. 32:31
  Necho to Josiah .... 2 Chr. 35:20, 21
C. Used figuratively of:
  Christ's ministers .... 2 Cor. 5:20
  Paul in particular .... Eph. 6:19, 20

Amber—*a yellow, fossilized resin*
  Descriptive of the divine glory ...... Ezek. 1:4, 27

Ambidextrous—*equally skilled with either hand*
  True of some of David's warriors .... 1 Chr. 12:1, 2

Ambition, Christian
A. Good, if for:
  The best gifts .... 1 Cor. 12:31
  Spiritual goals .... Phil. 3:12–14
  The gospel's extension .... Rom. 15:17–20
  Acceptance before God .... 2 Cor. 5:9, 10
  Quietness .... 1 Thess. 4:11
B. Evil, if it leads to:
  Strife .... Matt. 20:20–28
  Sinful superiority .... Matt. 18:1–6
  A pharisaical spirit .... Mark 12:38–40
  Contention about gifts .... 1 Cor. 3:3–8
  Selfish ambition .... Phil. 1:14–17

Ambition, worldly
A. Inspired by:
  Satan .... Gen. 3:1–6; Luke 4:5–8
  Pride .... Is. 14:12–15; 1 Tim. 3:1, 6
  Jealousy .... Num. 12:2
B. Leads to:
  Sin .... Acts 8:18–24
  Strife .... James 4:1, 2
  Suicide .... 2 Sam. 17:23
  Self-glory .... Hab. 2:4, 5
C. Examples of:
  Builders of Babel .... Gen. 11:4
  Korah's company .... Num. 16:3–35
  Abimelech .... Judg. 9:1–6
  Absalom .... 2 Sam. 15:1–13
  Adonijah .... 1 Kin. 1:5–7
  Haman .... Esth. 5:9–14
  Nebuchadnezzar .... Dan. 3:1–7
  James and John .... Mark 10:35–37
  The Antichrist .... 2 Thess. 2:3, 4
  Diotrephes .... 3 John 9, 10

Ambush—*strategic concealment for surprise attack*
  Joshua at Ai .... Josh. 8:1–24
  Abimelech against Shechem .... Judg. 9:31–40
  Israel at Gibeah .... Judg. 20:29–48
  David against the Philistines ...... 2 Sam. 5:23–25
  Jehoshaphat against his
    enemies .... 2 Chr. 20:22–25

Amen—*a strong assent to a prayer (also translated "assuredly")*
A. Used in the Old Testament to:
  Confirm a statement .... Num. 5:22
  Close a doxology .... 1 Chr. 16:36
  Confirm an oath .... Neh. 5:13
  Give assent to laws .... Deut. 27:15–26
B. Used in the New Testament to:
  Close a doxology .... Rom. 9:5
  Close epistle .... Rom. 16:27
  Describe God's promises .... 2 Cor. 1:20
  Close prayer .... 1 Cor. 14:16

Give assent..........................Rev. 1:7
Emphasize a truth (translated "most
    assuredly")...................John 3:3, 5, 11

Amethyst—*a form of quartz purple to blue-violet*
Worn by the high priest.........Ex. 28:19; 39:12
In the New Jerusalem.................Rev. 21:20

Ami
Head of a family of Solomon's
    servants........................Ezra 2:57
Called Amon........................Neh. 7:59

Amittai—*true*
The father of Jonah the prophet.........Jon. 1:1

Ammah—*mother or beginning*
A hill near Giah....................2 Sam. 2:24

Ammiel—*my kinsman is God*
1. A spy representing the tribe of Dan.....Num. 13:12
2. The father of Machir................2 Sam. 9:4, 5
3. The father of Bathshua (Bathsheba), one of David's
    wives.............................1 Chr. 3:5
    Called Eliam......................2 Sam. 11:3
4. A son of Obed-Edom................1 Chr. 26:4, 5

Ammihud—*my kinsman is glorious*
1. An Ephraimite.......................Num. 1:10
2. A Simeonite, father of Shemuel.......Num. 34:20
3. A Naphtalite.......................Num. 34:28
4. The father of king of Geshur.........2 Sam. 13:37
5. A Judahite...........................1 Chr. 9:4

Amminadab—*my kinsman is noble*
1. Man of Judah........................1 Chr. 2:10
    The father of Nahshon...............Num. 1:7
    Aaron's father-in-law...................Ex. 6:23
    An ancestor of David...............Ruth 4:19, 20
    An ancestor of Christ...................Matt. 1:4
2. Chief of a Levitical house.........1 Chr. 15:10, 11
3. Son of Kohath......................1 Chr. 6:22

Ammishaddai—*my kinsman is the Almighty*
A captain representing the Danites....Num. 1:12

Ammizabad—*my kinsman has endowed*
A son of Benaiah.....................1 Chr. 27:6

Ammon—*a people*
A nation fathered by Lot..........Gen. 19:36, 38

Ammonites—*descendants of Ben-Ammi*
A. Characterized by:
    Cruelty...........................Amos 1:13
    Pride............................Zeph. 2:9, 10
    Callousness.......................Ezek. 25:3, 6
    Idolatry..........................1 Kin. 11:7, 33
B. Hostility toward Israel, seen in:
    Not aiding Israel..................Deut. 23:3, 4
    Helping the Amalekites..............Judg. 3:13
    Proposing a cruel treaty...........1 Sam. 11:1–3
    Abusing David's ambassadors.....2 Sam. 10:1–4
    Hiring Syrians against David........2 Sam. 10:6
    Assisting the Chaldeans..............2 Kin. 24:2
    Harassing postexilic Jews..........Neh. 4:3, 7, 8

C. Defeated by:
    Jephthah.......................Judg. 11:4–33
    Saul..............................1 Sam. 11:11
    David...........................2 Sam. 10:7–14
    Jehoshaphat.....................2 Chr. 20:1–25
    Jotham..........................2 Chr. 27:5, 6
D. Prohibitions concerning:
    Exclusion from worship............Deut. 23:3–6
    No intermarriage with...............Ezra 9:1–3
E. Prophecies concerning their:
    Captivity........................Amos 1:13–15
    Subjection.......................Jer. 25:9–21
    Destruction.......................Ps. 83:1–18

Ammonitess—*a female Ammonite*
Naamah.........................1 Kin. 14:21, 31
Shimeath.........................2 Chr. 24:26

Amnesty—*a pardon granted to political offenders*
To Shimei......................2 Sam. 19:16–23
To Amasa...................2 Sam. 17:25; 19:13

Amnon—*faithful*
1. A son of David.........................2 Sam. 3:2
    Rapes his half sister..............2 Sam. 13:1–18
    Killed by Absalom..............2 Sam. 13:19–29
2. Son of Shimon.....................1 Chr. 4:19–33

Amok—*deep, inscrutable*
A chief priest......................Neh. 12:7, 20

Amon—*master workman*
1. King of Judah....................2 Kin. 21:18, 19
    Follows evil......................2 Chr. 33:22, 23
    Killed by conspiracy............2 Kin. 21:23, 24
2. A governor of Samaria............1 Kin. 22:10, 26

Amorites—*mountain dwellers*
A. Described as:
    Descendants of Canaan...........Gen. 10:15, 16
    Original inhabitants of Palestine.......Ezek. 16:3
    One of seven nations..............Gen. 15:19–21
    A confederation....................Josh. 10:1–5
    Ruled by great kings..............Ps. 136:17–19
    Of great size.........................Amos 2:9
    Very wicked......................Gen. 15:16
    Worshipers of idols..................Judg. 6:10
B. Contacts of, with Israel:
    Their defeat by Joshua............Josh. 10:1–43
    Their not being destroyed.........Judg. 1:34–36
    Peace with.........................1 Sam. 7:14
    Solomon uses for forced labor.....1 Kin. 9:20, 21
    Intermarriage with..................Judg. 3:5, 6

Amos—*burden-bearer*
1. A prophet of Israel......................Amos 1:1
    Pronounces judgment against
        nations......................Amos 1:1–3, 15
    Denounces Israel's sins...........Amos 4:1–7:9
    Condemns Amaziah, the priest of
        Bethel......................Amos 7:10–17
    Predicts Israel's downfall...........Amos 9:1–10
    Foretells great blessings...........Amos 9:11–15
2. An ancestor of Christ.................Luke 3:25

Amos, Book of—*a book of the Old Testament*

Amoz—*strong*
    The father of Isaiah the prophet ....Is. 1:1

Amphipolis—*a city in Macedonia*
    Visited by Paul ....Acts 17:1

Amplias
    Christian at Rome ....Rom. 16:8

Amram—*a people exalted*
1. Son of Kohath.....................Num. 3:17–19
    The father of Aaron, Moses
       and Miriam...........Ex. 6:18–20; 1 Chr. 6:3
2. One who divorced his foreign wife ......Ezra 10:34

Amramites—*descendants of Amram*
    A subdivision of the Levites.......... Num. 3:27

Amraphel—*powerful people*
    A king of Shinar who invaded Canaan during
      Abraham's time; identified by some as the
      Hammurabi of the monuments... Gen. 14:1, 9

Amulet—*charm worn to protect against evil*
    Condemned.......................Is. 3:18–23

Amusements—*entertainment*
A. Found in:
    Dancing .... Ex. 32:18, 19, 25
    Music........................... 1 Sam. 18:6, 7
    Earthly pleasures .... Eccl. 2:1–8
    Drunkenness............. Amos 6:1–6; 1 Pet. 4:3
    Feasting....................... Mark 6:21, 22
    Games.............................Luke 7:32
    Gossip ....Acts 17:21
B. Productive of:
    Sorrow.........................Prov. 14:13
    Poverty ....Prov. 21:17
    Vanity ....Eccl. 2:1–11
    Immorality...................... 1 Cor. 10:6–8
    Spiritual deadness .... 1 Tim. 5:6
C. Prevalence of:
    In the last days .... 2 Tim. 3:1, 4
    In Babylon .... Rev. 18:21–24
    At Christ's return.............. Matt. 24:36–39

Amzi—*strong one*
1. A Merarite Levite.................... 1 Chr. 6:46
2. A priest...........................Neh. 11:12

Anab—*grapes*
    A town of Judah ....Josh. 11:21

Anah—*answer*
1. Father of Esau's wife .... Gen. 36:2, 14, 18
2. A Horite chief..................... Gen. 36:20, 29
3. Son of Zibeon .... Gen. 36:24

Anaharath—*narrow way*
    A city in the valley of Jezreel.........Josh. 19:19

Anaiah—*Yahweh has answered*
1. A Levite assistant.....................Neh. 8:4
2. One who sealed the new covenant...... Neh. 10:22

Anak—*long-necked*
    Descendant of Arba................Josh. 15:13

    Father of three sons................ Num. 13:22

Anakim—*descendants of Anak; a race of giants*
A. Described as:
    Giants .... Num. 13:28–33
    Very strong................... Deut. 2:10, 11, 21
B. Defeated by:
    Joshua .... Josh. 10:36–39, 11:21
    Caleb ....Josh. 14:6–15
C. A remnant left:
    Among the Philistines................Josh. 11:22
    Possibly in Gath .... 1 Sam. 17:4–7

Anamim—*rockmen*
    A tribe or people listed among Mizraim's
      (Egypt's) descendants............. Gen. 10:13

Anammelech—*Anu is king*
    A god worshiped at Samaria ......2 Kin. 17:24, 31

Anan—*cloud*
    A signer of Nehemiah's document..... Neh. 10:26

Anani—*my cloud*
    Son of Elioenai ....1 Chr. 3:24

Ananiah—*Yahweh has covered*
1. The father of Maaseiah ....Neh. 3:23
2. A town inhabited by Benjamite
      returnees ....Neh. 11:32

Ananias—*Yahweh has been gracious*
1. Disciple at Jerusalem slain for lying to
    God ....Acts 5:1–11
2. A Christian disciple at Damascus .... Acts 9:10–19;
    22:12–16
3. A Jewish high priest...................Acts 23:1–5

Anarchy—*a reign of lawlessness in society*
A. Manifested in:
    Moral looseness................... Ex. 32:1–8, 25
    Idolatry........................Judg. 17:1–13
    Religious syncretism .... 2 Kin. 17:27–41
    A reign of terror .... Jer. 40:13–16
    Perversion of justice................Hab. 1:1–4
B. Instances of:
    At Kadesh....................... Num. 14:1–10
    During the judges................Judg. 18:1–31
    In the northern kingdom........ 1 Kin. 12:26–33
    At the Crucifixion .... Matt. 27:15–31
    At Stephen's death .... Acts 7:54, 57, 58
    At Ephesus ....Acts 19:28–34
    In the time of the Antichrist..... 2 Thess. 2:3–12

Anath—*answer*
    Father of Shamgar ....Judg. 3:31

Anathoth—*answers*
1. A Benjamite, son of Becher ....1 Chr. 7:8
2. A leader who signed the document......Neh. 10:19
3. A Levitical city in Benjamin ....Josh. 21:18
    Birthplace of Jeremiah ....Jer. 1:1
    Citizens of, hate Jeremiah .... Jer. 11:21, 23
    Jeremiah bought property there......Jer. 32:6–15
    Home of famous mighty man....... 2 Sam. 23:27
    Home of Abiathar, the high priest.....1 Kin. 2:26

Reoccupied after exile............... Ezra 2:1, 23
To be invaded by Assyria .... Is. 10:30
Reproved Jeremiah of .... Jer. 29:27

Anathothite—*a native of Anathoth*
Abiezer thus called................ 2 Sam. 23:27

Anchor—*a weight used to hold a ship in place*
Literally, of Paul's ship ....Acts 27:29, 30, 40
Figuratively of the believer's hope ...... Heb. 6:19

Ancient—*that which is old*
Applied to the beginning (eternity)...... Is. 45:21
Applied to something very old .... Prov. 22:28
Applied to old men (elders) ....1 Sam. 24:13;
Ps. 119:100

Ancient of Days
Title applied to God ....Dan. 7:9, 13, 22

Andrew—*manly*
A fisherman..........................Matt. 4:18
A disciple of John the Baptist .... John 1:40
Brought Peter to Christ............ John 1:40–42
Called to Christ's discipleship...... Matt. 4:18, 19
Enrolled among the Twelve.......... Matt. 10:2
Told Jesus about a lad's lunch .... John 6:8, 9
Carried a request to Jesus........ John 12:20–22
Sought further light on
Jesus' words................... Mark 13:3, 4
Met in the Upper Room ....Acts 1:13

Andronicus—*conqueror of men*
A notable Christian at Rome..........Rom. 16:7

Anem—*double fountain*
Levitical city ....1 Chr. 6:73

Aner—*waterfall*
1. Amorite chief .... Gen. 14:13, 24
2. A Levitical city .... 1 Chr. 6:70

WORD
STUDY
ANGEL, *mal'ak* (mal-*awk*). *Mal'ak* is a noun used throughout the OT meaning "messenger" or "angel." Messengers specifically from God could include prophets (Is. 42:19) and priests (Mal. 2:7), but were generally heavenly beings. Angels performed various duties including caring for the faithful (Ps. 91:11), destroying enemies (Ps. 35:5), and praising God. Theophanic angels, representing God, brought messages and acted as guides (see Ex. 14:19; Judg. 6:20, 21). They frequently appeared in human form and were only recognized as angels after the event in which they were involved. For example, read about the time Abraham entertained the three strangers (Gen. 18:2–22; 19:1). (Strong's #4397)

Angels—*heavenly beings created by God*
A. Described as:
Spiritual beings................... Heb. 1:13, 14
Created .... Ps. 148:2, 5; Col. 1:16
Immortal ....Luke 20:36
Holy............................. Matt. 25:31
Innumerable ....Heb. 12:22
Wise........................... 2 Sam. 14:17, 20
Powerful ....Ps. 103:20

Elect............................. 1 Tim. 5:21
Respectful of authority................... Jude 9
Sexless .... Matt. 22:30
Invisible ....Num. 22:22–31
Obedient..........................Ps. 103:20
Possessing emotions .... Luke 15:10
Judged in future by Christians .... 1 Cor. 6:3
Concerned in human things ....1 Pet. 1:12
Incarnate in human form at times....Gen. 18:2–8
Not perfect............................Job 4:18
Organized in ranks or orders ....Is. 6:1–3;
1 Thess. 4:16
B. Ministry of, toward believers:
Guide....................Gen. 24:7, 40
Provide for .... 1 Kin. 19:5–8
Protect......................... Ps. 34:7; 91:11
Deliver.................Dan. 6:22; Acts 12:7–11
Gather........................... Matt. 24:31
Direct activities....................... Acts 8:26
Comfort ....Acts 27:23, 24
Minister to.......................... Heb. 1:14
C. Ministry of, toward unbelievers:
A destruction.................. Gen. 19:1, 13
A curse............................Judg. 5:23
A pestilence .... 2 Sam. 24:15–17
Sudden death......................... Acts 12:23
Persecution.........................Ps. 35:5, 6
D. Ministry of, in Christ's life, to:
Announce His conception .... Matt. 1:20, 21
Herald His birth............. Luke 2:10–12
Sustain Him......................Matt. 4:11
Witness His resurrection ....1 Tim. 3:16
Proclaim His resurrection .... Matt. 28:5–7
Accompany Him to heaven .... Acts 1:9–11
E. Ministry of, on special occasions, at:
The world's creation .... Job 38:7
Sinai............................. Acts 7:38, 53
Satan's binding .... Rev. 20:1–3
Christ's return......Matt. 13:41, 49; 1 Thess. 4:16
F. Appearance of, during the Old Testament, to:
Abraham.........................Gen. 18:2–15
Hagar............................Gen. 16:7–14
Lot ....Gen. 19:1–22
Jacob .... Gen. 28:10–12
Moses...........................Ex. 3:1, 2
Balaam ....Num. 22:31–35
Joshua ....Josh. 5:13–15
All Israel .... Judg. 2:1–4
Gideon........................... Judg. 6:11–24
Manoah........................Judg. 13:6–21
David.................... 2 Sam. 24:16, 17
Elijah .... 1 Kin. 19:2–8
Daniel ....Dan. 6:21, 22
Zechariah...........................Zech. 2:3
G. Appearances of, during the New Testament, to:
Zacharias ....Luke 1:11–20
The virgin Mary.................. Luke 1:26–38
Joseph ....Matt. 1:20–25
Shepherds........................Luke 2:8–15

Certain women . . . . Matt. 28:1–7

Mary Magdalene . . . . John 20:11–13

The apostles. . . . . Acts 1:10, 11

Peter. . . . . Acts 5:19, 20

Philip . . . . Acts 8:26

Cornelius . . . . Acts 10:3–32

Paul . . . . Acts 27:23, 24

John . . . . Rev. 1:1

Seven churches . . . . Rev. 1:20

Angels, fallen

Fall of, by pride . . . . Is. 14:12–15; Jude 6

Seen by Christ . . . . Luke 10:18

Make war on saints . . . . Rev. 12:7–17

Imprisoned. . . . . 2 Pet. 2:4

Everlasting fire prepared for . . . . Matt. 25:41

Angel of God, the—*distinct manifestation of God*

A. Names of:

Angel of God . . . . Gen. 21:17

Angel of the Lord . . . . Gen. 22:11

Captain of the army of the Lord . . . . Josh. 5:14

B. Appearances of, to:

Hagar. . . . . Gen. 16:7, 8; 21:17

Abraham. . . . . Gen. 18:1–33; 22:11, 15

Jacob . . . . Gen. 31:11–13; 32:24–30

Moses. . . . . Ex. 3:1, 2

Children of Israel . . . . Ex. 13:21, 22; 14:19

Balaam . . . . Num. 22:22–35

Joshua . . . . Judg. 2:1

Donkey and Manoah and wife . . . . . Judg. 13:1–21

David. . . . . 1 Chr. 21:16–18

Zechariah, in vision, concerning

Joshua. . . . . Zech. 3:1–10

C. Divine characteristics:

Deliver Israel . . . . 2 Kin. 19:14–20, 35, 36

Extend blessings . . . . Gen. 16:7–12

Pardon sin . . . . Ex. 23:20–22

Angels’ food

Eaten by humans . . . . Ps. 78:25

Eaten by Elijah . . . . 1 Kin. 19:5–8

> **WORD STUDY**
>
> **ANGER,** '*aph* (*awf*). The noun '*aph* means “nostril,” “nose,” “face,” or “anger.” Sometimes the anger is human as it is in Gen. 27:45, where Jacob is sent away by Rebekah to escape Esau’s anger. Most often, however, the anger is divine anger and occurs 177 times in the OT. God was so angry after the Israelites had made the gold calf that He planned to destroy them (Ex. 32:12) and only Moses’ intervention saved them. The word '*aph* implies wrath, probably from the visual image of flaring nostrils. Frequently the word is used in the phrase his or her “anger was kindled.” (Strong’s #639)

> **WORD STUDY**
>
> **ANGER,** *cha'as* (kaw-*as*). *Cha'as* is a noun meaning “vexation,” “anger,” or “grief.” Such anger was provoked by repeated offenses. Humans could be provoked by unwarranted treatment from others (Prov. 12:16). This anger also

has the aspect of grief. God was most often provoked by the worship of other gods. This can be seen in 1 Kin. 15:30. The phrase “do evil in the sight of the LORD to provoke [Him] to anger” appears in several places, including Deut. 4:25. (Strong’s #3708)

Anger of God

A. Caused by humankind’s:

Sin. . . . . Num. 32:10–15

Unbelief . . . . Ps. 78:21, 22

Error . . . . 2 Sam. 6:7

Disobedience. . . . . Josh. 7:1, 11, 12

Idolatry . . . . Judg. 2:11–14

B. Described as:

Sometimes delayed. . . . . 2 Kin. 23:25–27

Slow . . . . Neh. 9:17

Brief. . . . . Ps. 30:5

Restrained . . . . Ps. 78:38

Fierceness . . . . Ps. 78:49, 50

Consuming . . . . Ps. 90:7

Powerful . . . . Ps. 90:11

Not forever . . . . Mic. 7:18

To be feared . . . . Ps. 76:7

C. Visitation of, upon:

Miriam and Aaron . . . . Num. 12:9–15

Israelites . . . . Num. 11:4–10

Balaam . . . . Num. 22:21, 22

Moses. . . . . Deut. 4:21, 22

Israel . . . . Deut. 9:8

Aaron. . . . . Deut. 9:20

Wicked cities . . . . Deut. 29:23

A land . . . . Deut. 29:24–28

A king . . . . 2 Chr. 25:15, 16

D. Deliverance from, by:

Intercessory prayer. . . . . Num. 11:1, 2;

Deut. 9:19, 20

Decisive action . . . . Num. 25:3–12

Obedience . . . . Deut. 13:16–18

Executing the guilty. . . . . Josh. 7:1, 10–26

See Wrath of God

Anger of Jesus

Provoked by unbelievers . . . . Mark 3:1–6

In the temple . . . . Matt. 21:12; Mark 11:15

Anger, human

A. Caused by:

A brother’s deception . . . . Gen. 27:42–45

A wife’s complaint . . . . Gen. 30:1, 2

Rape. . . . . Gen. 34:1–7

Inhuman crimes . . . . Gen. 49:6, 7

A leader’s indignation . . . . Ex. 11:8

A people’s idolatry . . . . Ex. 32:19, 22

Disobedience. . . . . Num. 31:14–18

The Spirit’s arousal . . . . 1 Sam. 11:6

A brother’s jealousy . . . . 1 Sam. 17:28;

Luke 15:25–28

A king’s jealousy . . . . 1 Sam. 20:30

Righteous indignation . . . . 1 Sam. 20:34

Priestly rebuke . . . . 2 Chr. 26:18, 19

Unrighteous dealings . . . . Neh. 5:6, 7

Wife's disobedience....................Esth. 1:12
Lack of respect ....Esth. 3:5
Failure of astrologers........... Dan. 2:2, 10, 12
Flesh.............................Gal. 5:19, 20
Harsh treatment.................... Eph. 6:4
B. Justifiable, seen in:
Jacob .... Gen. 31:36
Moses...........................Ex. 32:19
Samson ....Judg. 14:1, 19
Saul...........................1 Sam. 11:6
Samuel.................... 1 Sam. 15:16–31
Jonathan...................... 1 Sam. 20:34
Christ........................Mark 3:5
C. Unjustifiable, seen in:
Cain......................... Gen. 4:5, 6
Simeon and Levi....................Gen. 49:5–7
Potiphar .... Gen. 39:1, 19
Moses........................Num. 20:10–12
Balaam ....Num. 22:27, 28
Saul......................... 1 Sam. 20:30
Naaman ....2 Kin. 5:11, 12
Asa..................................2 Chr. 16:10
Uzziah...........................2 Chr. 26:19
Ahasuerus........................Esth. 1:9, 12
Haman .... Esth. 3:5
Nebuchadnezzar....................Dan. 3:12, 13
Jonah ....Jon. 4:1–11
Herod ....Matt. 2:16
The Jews ....Luke 4:28
Jewish officialdom....................Acts 5:17
D. The Christian attitude toward:
To be slow in ....Prov. 14:17
Not to sin in..........................Eph. 4:26
To put away ....Eph. 4:31
E. Effects of, seen in:
Attempted assassination ....Esth. 2:21
Punishment........................Prov. 19:19
Mob action......................Acts 19:28, 29
F. Pacified by:
Kindly suggestion .... 2 Kin. 5:10–14
Righteous execution ....Esth. 7:10
Gentle answer ....Prov. 15:1

Anguish—*extreme pain*
A. Caused by:
Physical hardships ....Ex. 6:9
Physical pain ....2 Sam. 1:9
Impending destruction.............. Deut. 2:25
Conflict of soul......................Job 7:11
National distress.................... Is. 8:21, 22
Childbirth ....John 16:21
A spiritual problem ....2 Cor. 2:4
B. Reserved for:
People who refuse wisdom........ Prov. 1:20–27
The wicked.......................Job 15:20, 24
Those in Hades................. Luke 16:23, 24

Aniam—*lament of the people*
A Manassite........................ 1 Chr. 7:19

Anim—*springs*
A city in south Judah.................Josh. 15:50
Animals
A. Described as:
Domesticated and wild.............. 2 Sam. 12:3
Clean and unclean ... Lev. 11:1–31; Deut. 14:1–20
For sacrifices .... Lev. 16:3, 5; Ex. 12:3–14
B. List of, in the Bible:
Antelope........................... Deut. 14:5
Ape...............................1 Kin. 10:22
Badger................................Ex. 25:5
Bat .... Deut. 14:18
Bear .... 1 Sam. 17:34
Boar ....Ps. 80:13
Bull............................... Jer. 52:20
Calf .... Gen. 18:7
Camel .... Gen. 12:16
Cattle........................... Gen. 1:25
Chameleon......................Lev. 11:30
Cobra...............................Is. 11:8
Colt ....Zech. 9:9
Cow .... Gen. 32:15
Deer........................... Deut. 14:5
Dog................................Ex. 22:31
Donkey .... Gen. 22:3
Elephant ("ivory") ....1 Kin. 10:22
Ewe lamb .... Gen. 21:30
Fox ....Judg. 15:4
Frog .... Ex. 8:2–14
Gazelle .... Deut. 14:5
Gecko ....Lev. 11:30
Goat........................... Gen. 27:9
Greyhound.......................Prov. 30:31
Hare .... Deut. 14:7
Heifer .... Gen. 15:9
Hind........................... Hab. 3:19
Horse........................... Gen. 47:17
Hyena .... Is. 13:22
Hyrax........................... Lev. 11:5
Jackal........................... Is. 13:22
Lamb .... Ex. 29:39
Leopard........................Rev. 13:2
Lion .... 1 Sam. 17:34
Lizard .... Lev. 11:29, 30
Mole........................... Is. 2:20
Monkey........................1 Kin. 10:22
Mouse ....Lev. 11:29
Mule........................... 2 Sam. 13:29
Ox................................Ex. 21:28
Porcupine........................ Is. 14:23
Ram .... Gen. 15:9
Roe deer .... Deut. 14:5
Scorpion ....Deut. 8:15
Serpent .... Matt. 10:16
Sheep .... Gen. 4:2
Spider........................Prov. 30:28
Swine...........................Is. 65:2–4
Whale (great sea creatures) .... Gen. 1:21
Wolf................................Is. 11:6

C. Used figuratively of:

Human traits . . . . Gen. 49:9–14, 21

Universal peace . . . . Is. 11:6–9

Man's innate nature . . . . Jer. 13:23

World empires . . . . Dan. 7:2–8

Satanic powers . . . . Rev. 12:4, 9

Christ's sacrifice . . . . 1 Pet. 1:18–20

Anise—*a plant for seasoning; the dill*

Tithed by the Jews . . . . Matt. 23:23

Ankle—*joint connecting foot and leg*

Lame man's healed . . . . Acts 3:7

Anklet—*an ornament worn by women on the ankles*

Included in Isaiah's denunciation . . . . . Is. 3:16, 18

Anna—*grace*

Aged prophetess . . . . Luke 2:36–38

Annas—*gracious*

A Jewish high priest . . . . Luke 3:2

Christ appeared before . . . . John 18:12–24

Peter and John appeared before . . . . Acts 4:6

| WORD STUDY | **ANOINT,** *mashach* (maw-*shawkh*). *Mashach* is a verb meaning "smear" or "anoint." It can simply mean to coat, as in |

painting a house, Jer. 22:14. Usually, however, it means anointing with oil on the head and carries the significance of consecrating or setting apart for special office. Kings could be anointed (Judg. 9:8) as could prophets (for example, Elijah anointed Elisha, 1 Kin. 19:16). Priests were anointed for religious office as in Ex. 28:41 when Aaron and his sons were first set apart as priests. Objects can also be anointed to set them apart, especially the tabernacle and sacred vessels (Ex. 29:36). (Strong's #4886)

Anointing—*pouring oil upon*

A. Performed upon:

The patriarchs . . . . 1 Chr. 16:15–17, 21, 22

Priest . . . . Ex. 29:1, 7

Prophets . . . . 1 Kin. 19:16

Israel's kings . . . . 1 Sam. 10:1

Foreign kings . . . . 1 Kin. 19:15

The messianic King . . . . Ps. 2:2

Sacred objects . . . . Ex. 30:26–28

B. Ordinary, purposes of, for:

Adornment . . . . Ruth 3:3

Invigoration . . . . 2 Sam. 12:20

Hospitality . . . . Luke 7:38, 46

Battle . . . . Is. 21:5

Burial . . . . Matt. 26:12

Sanctifying . . . . Ex. 30:29

C. Medicinal, purposes of, for:

Wound . . . . Luke 10:34

Healing . . . . Mark 6:13; James 5:14

D. Sacred, purposes of, to:

Memorialize an event . . . . Gen. 28:18

Confirm a covenant . . . . Gen. 35:14

Set apart . . . . Ex. 30:22–29

Institute into office . . . . 1 Sam. 16:12, 13

E. Absence of:

Sign of judgment . . . . Deut. 28:40

Fasting . . . . 2 Sam. 12:16, 20

Mourning . . . . 2 Sam. 14:2

F. Of Christ the Messiah "the Anointed One," as:

Predicted . . . . Ps. 45:7; Is. 61:1

Fulfilled . . . . Luke 4:18; Heb. 1:9

Interpreted . . . . Acts 4:27

Symbolized in His name
("the Christ") . . . . . . Matt. 16:16, 20; Acts 9:22

Typical of the believer's anointing . . . . . 1 John 2:27

G. Significance of, as indicating:

Divine appointment . . . . 2 Chr. 22:7

Special honor . . . . 1 Sam. 24:6, 10

Special privilege . . . . Ps. 105:15

God's blessing . . . . Ps. 23:5

Anointing of the Holy Spirit

A. Of Christ:

Predicted . . . . Is. 61:1

Fulfilled . . . . John 1:32–34

Explained . . . . Luke 4:18

B. Of Christians:

Predicted . . . . Ezek. 47:1–12

Foretold by Christ . . . . John 7:38, 39

Fulfilled at Pentecost . . . . Acts 2:1–41

Fulfilled at conversion . . . . 2 Cor. 1:21, 22;
1 John 2:20, 27

Answer—*a reply*

A. Good:

Soft . . . . Prov. 15:1

Confident . . . . Dan. 3:16–18

Convicting . . . . Dan. 5:17–28

Astonished . . . . Luke 2:47

Unanswerable . . . . Luke 20:3–8

Spontaneous . . . . Luke 21:14, 15

Spirit-directed . . . . Luke 12:11, 12

Ready . . . . 1 Pet. 3:15

B. Evil:

Unwise . . . . 1 Kin. 12:12–15

Incriminating . . . . 2 Sam. 1:5–16

Insolent . . . . 2 Kin. 18:27–36

Humiliating . . . . Esth. 6:6–11

Satanic . . . . Job 1:8–11

Ant—*a small insect*

An example of industry . . . . Prov. 6:6–8; 30:24

Antagonism—*unceasing opposition*

A. Of men, against:

God's people . . . . Ex. 5:1–19; Deut. 2:26–33

The prophets . . . . Amos 7:10–17; Zech. 1:2–6

The light . . . . John 3:19, 20

The truth . . . . John 8:12–47; Acts 7:54–60

Christians . . . . Acts 16:16–24

B. Of Satan, against:

Job . . . . Job 1:9–12

Christ . . . . Luke 4:1–13

Peter . . . . Luke 22:31–34

Paul . . . . 1 Thess. 2:18

Christians . . . . Eph. 6:11–18

Antediluvians—*those who lived before the Flood*

A. Described as:

Long-lived ....Gen. 5:3–32

Very wicked .... Gen. 6:5

A mixed race ....Gen. 6:1–4; Jude 6, 7

Of great size......................... Gen. 6:4

B. Warnings against, made by:

Enoch............................Jude 14, 15

Noah ....2 Pet. 2:5

Christ.......................... 1 Pet. 3:19, 20

C. Destruction of:

Only Noah's family escaped ....Gen. 7:21–23

Predicted ....Gen. 6:5–7

Comparable to Christ's return ... Matt. 24:37–39; Luke 17:26, 27

Comparable to the world's end.......2 Pet. 3:3–7

Antelope

Listed as clean....................... Deut. 14:5

Anthropomorphisms—*applying human attributes to God*

A. Physical likenesses, such as:

Feet.................................Ex. 24:10

Hands ....Ex. 24:11

Face .... Num. 12:7, 8

Eyes .... Hab. 1:13

Arms ....Ex. 6:6

B. Nonphysical characteristics, such as:

Memory .... Gen. 9:16

Anger............................ Ex. 22:24

Jealousy............................Ps. 78:58

Repentance ....Jon. 3:10

Antichrist—*Satan's final opponent of Christ and Christians*

A. Called:

Man of sin..........................2 Thess. 2:3

Son of perdition ....2 Thess. 2:3

Lawless one ....2 Thess. 2:8

Antichrist..................... 1 John 2:18, 22

Beast ....Rev. 11:7

B. Described as:

Lawless .... 2 Thess. 2:3–12

Opposing God......................2 Thess. 2:4

Working wonders...................2 Thess. 2:9

Deceiving the world.........2 John 7; Rev. 19:20

Persecuting Christians ....Rev. 13:7

Satan-inspired.....................2 Thess. 2:9

Denying Christ's incarnation .... 1 John 4:3; 2 John 7

A person and a system.............2 Thess. 2:3, 7

Seeking man's worship ....2 Thess. 2:4

One and many................... 1 John 2:18–22

C. Coming of:

Foretold..........................2 Thess. 2:5

In the last time ....1 John 2:18

Now restrained ....2 Thess. 2:6

Follows removal of hindrance......2 Thess. 2:7, 8

Before Christ's return ....2 Thess. 2:3, 8

By Satan's deception ....2 Thess. 2:9, 10

D. Destruction of:

At Christ's return .... 2 Thess. 2:8; Rev. 19:20

Eternal in lake of fire................ Rev. 20:10

Antidote—*a remedy given to counteract poison*

A. Literal:

A tree............................. Ex. 15:23–25

Meal........................... 2 Kin. 4:38–41

B. Figurative and spiritual, for:

Sin, Christ ....Num. 21:8, 9; John 3:14, 15

Christ's absence, the Holy Spirit....John 14:16–18

Sorrow, joy .... John 16:20–22

Satan's lies, God's truth .... 1 John 4:1–6

Earth's trials, faith................. 1 Pet. 1:6–8

Testings, God's grace .... 1 Cor. 10:13; 2 Cor. 12:7–9

Suffering, heaven's glory.............. Rom. 8:18; 2 Cor. 5:1–10

Antinomianism—*the idea that Christian liberty exempts one from the moral law*

A. Prevalence of, among:

Christians........................ Rom. 6:1–23

False teachers.................2 Pet. 2:19; Jude 4

B. Based on error, that:

Grace allows sin ....Rom. 6:1, 2

Moral law is abolished..............Rom. 7:1–14

Liberty has no bounds.......... 1 Cor. 10:23–33

C. Corrected by remembering, that liberty is:

Not a license to sin................. Rom. 6:1–23

Limited by moral law............... Rom. 8:1–4

Controlled by Holy Spirit........... Rom. 8:5–14

Not to be a stumbling block.......Rom. 14:1–23; 1 Cor. 8:1–13

Motivated by love.................. Gal. 5:13–15

Antioch—*a city of Syria*

Home of Nicolas......................Acts 6:5

Haven of persecuted Christians........Acts 11:19

Home of first Gentile church ...... Acts 11:20, 21

Name "Christian" originated in....... Acts 11:26

Barnabas ministered here.........Acts 11:22–24

Barnabas and Paul minister in church of ....Acts 11:25–30

Paul commissioned by church of .... Acts 13:1–4; 15:35–41

Paul reports to...................Acts 14:26–28

Church of, troubled by Judaizers .... Acts 15:1–4; Gal. 2:11–21

Antioch—*a city of Pisidia*

Jewish synagogue .... Acts 13:14

Paul visits ....Acts 13:14, 42

Jews of, reject the gospel..........Acts 13:45–51

Paul revisits .... Acts 14:21

Paul recalls persecution at ....2 Tim. 3:11

Antipas

A Christian martyr of Pergamos ....Rev. 2:13

Antipatris—*belonging to Antipater*

A city between Jerusalem and Caesarea... Acts 23:31

Antitype—*the fulfillment of a type*
The ark, baptism .... 1 Pet. 3:21
The Greek word translated
   "copies" in .... Heb. 9:24
Generally, a fulfillment of an Old Testament
   type.............. Matt. 12:39, 40; John 1:29

Antonia, Tower of—*fortress built by Herod the Great; not mentioned by name in Scripture*
Called "the barracks" .... Acts 21:30–40
Possible site of Jesus' trial, called
   "The Pavement"................... John 19:13

Antothijah—*answers of Yahweh*
A Benjamite .... 1 Chr. 8:24

Anub—*strong*
A man of Judah..................... 1 Chr. 4:8

Anvil—*a block for forging hot metals*
Used figuratively in .... Is. 41:7

Anxiety—*a disturbed state of mind produced by real or imaginary fears*
A. Caused by:
   Brother's hatred .... Gen. 32:6–12
   Son's rebellion .... 2 Sam. 18:24–33
   King's decree .... Esth. 4:1–17
   Child's absence .... Luke 2:48
   Son's sickness.................... John 4:46–49
   Friend's delay.................... 2 Cor. 2:12, 13
B. Overcome by:
   Trust .... Ps. 37:1–5
   Reliance upon the Holy Spirit........ Mark 13:11
   God's provision................. Luke 12:22–30
   Upward look .... Luke 21:25–28
   Assurance of God's sovereignty .... Rom. 8:28
   Angel's word .... Acts 27:21–25
   Prayer .... Phil. 4:6
   God's care........................ 1 Pet. 5:6, 7
See Cares, worldly

Ape—*a monkey*
Article of trade .... 1 Kin. 10:22

Apelles
A Christian in Rome .... Rom. 16:10

Apharsathchites
Assyrian colonists in Samaria opposing
   Zerubbabel's work.................. Ezra 4:9

Aphek—*strength, fortress*
1. A town in Plain of Sharon .... Josh. 12:18
   Site of Philistine camp .... 1 Sam. 4:1; 29:1
2. A city assigned to Asher.............. Josh. 19:30
3. Border city......................... Josh. 13:4
4. A city in Jezreel................. 1 Kin. 20:26–30
   Syria's defeat prophesied here .... 2 Kin. 13:14–19

Aphekah—*fortress*
A city of Judah...................... Josh. 15:53

Aphiah—*striving*
An ancestor of King Saul .... 1 Sam. 9:1

Aphik—*strength, fortress*
Spared by Asher .... Judg. 1:31
See Aphek 2

Apocalypse—*an unveiling of something unknown*
The Greek word usually translated
   "revelation" .... Rom. 16:25; Gal. 1:12

Apocrypha—*hidden things*
Writings in Greek written during the period
   between the Testaments; rejected by
   Protestants as uninspired

Apollonia—*pertaining to Apollo*
A town between Amphipolis and
   Thessalonica...................... Acts 17:1

Apollos—*a short or pet name for Apollonios*
An Alexandrian Jew mighty in the
   Scriptures..................... Acts 18:24, 25
Receives further instruction .... Acts 18:26
Sent to preach in Achaia........... Acts 18:27, 28
A minister in Corinth .... 1 Cor. 1:12; 3:4, 22
Cited by Paul .... 1 Cor. 4:6
Urged to revisit Corinth............. 1 Cor. 16:12
Journey of, noted by Paul .... Titus 3:13

Apollyon—*the destroyer*
Angel of the bottomless pit .... Rev. 9:11

Apostasy—*a falling away from God's truth*
A. Kinds of:
   National .... 1 Kin. 12:26–33
   Individual.............. 2 Kin. 21:1–9; Heb. 3:12
   Satanic........................... Rev. 12:7–9
   Angelic .... 2 Pet. 2:4
   General .... 2 Tim. 3:1–5
   Imputed .... Acts 21:21
   Final......................... 2 Thess. 2:3
   Irremedial....................... Heb. 6:1–8
B. Caused by:
   Satan .... Luke 22:31
   False teachers.................... Acts 20:29, 30
   Perversion of Scripture............. 2 Tim. 4:3, 4
   Persecution....................... Matt. 13:21
   Unbelief .... Heb. 4:9–11
   Love of world..................... 2 Tim. 4:10
   Hardened heart................... Acts 7:54, 57
   Spiritual blindness .... Acts 28:25–27
C. Manifested in:
   Resisting truth .... 2 Tim. 3:7, 8
   Resorting to deception .... 2 Cor. 11:13–15
   Reverting to immorality........ 2 Pet. 2:14, 19–22
D. Safeguards against, found in:
   God's Word .... Ps. 119:11; 2 Tim. 3:13–17
   Spiritual growth .... 2 Pet. 1:5–11
   Indoctrination.................... Acts 20:29–31
   Faithfulness..................... Matt. 24:42–51
   Spiritual perception................ 1 John 4:1–6
   Being grounded in the truth .... Eph. 4:13–16
   Using God's armor................. Eph. 6:10–20
   Preaching the Word................ 2 Tim. 4:2, 5

E. Examples of, seen in:

Israelites .... Ex. 32:1–35

Saul................................1 Sam. 15:11

Solomon ....1 Kin. 11:1–10

Amaziah .... 2 Chr. 25:14–16

Judas ....Matt. 26:14–16

Hymenaeus and Philetus .... 2 Tim. 2:17, 18

Demas........................... 2 Tim. 4:10

Certain men........................... Jude 4

Apostles—*men divinely commissioned to represent Christ*

A. Descriptive of:

Christ................................ Heb. 3:1

The twelve .... Matt. 10:2

Others (Barnabas, James, etc.) ....Acts 14:14; Gal. 1:19

Simon Peter .... Matt. 10:2

Andrew.............................. Matt. 10:2

James, son of Zebedee............... Matt. 10:2

John .... Matt. 10:2

Philip.............................. Matt. 10:3

Bartholomew (Nathanael)... Matt. 10:3; John 1:45

Thomas............................. Matt. 10:3

Matthew (Levi)............ Matt. 10:3; Luke 5:27

James, son of Alphaeus.............. Matt. 10:3

Thaddaeus (Judas)........ Matt. 10:3; John 14:22

Simon the Zealot .... Luke 6:15

Judas Iscariot........................ Matt. 10:4

Matthias............................ Acts 1:26

Paul .... 2 Cor. 1:1

Barnabas............................Acts 14:14

James, the Lord's brother ....Gal. 1:19

Silvanus and Timothy........... 1 Thess. 1:1; 2:9

Andronicus and Junia.................Rom. 16:7

B. Mission of, to:

Perform miracles .... Matt. 10:1, 8

Preach gospel.................... Matt. 28:19, 20

Witness Christ's resurrection ....Acts 1:22; 10:40–42

Write Scripture .... Eph. 3:5

Establish the church .... Eph. 2:20

C. Limitations of, before Pentecost:

Lowly in position ....Matt. 4:18

Unlearned........................... Acts 4:13

Subject to disputes .... Matt. 20:20–28

Faith often obscure ....Matt. 16:21–23

Need of instruction ....Matt. 17:4, 9–13

D. Position of, after Pentecost:

Interpreted prophecy............... Acts 2:14–36

Defended truth .... Phil. 1:7, 17

Exposed heretics..................... Gal. 1:6–9

Upheld discipline ....2 Cor. 13:1–6

Established churches............. Rom. 15:17–20

Appaim—*nostrils*

A man of Judah...................1 Chr. 2:30, 31

Apparel—*clothing*

A. Kinds of:

Harlot's ....Gen. 38:14, 15

Virgin's .... 2 Sam. 13:18

Mourner's...................... 2 Sam. 12:19, 20

Gorgeous .... Luke 7:25

Rich .... Ezek. 27:24

Worldly............................1 Pet. 3:3

Showy .... Luke 16:19

Official .... 1 Kin. 10:5

Royal .... Esth. 6:8

Priestly ....Ezra 3:10

Angelic .... Acts 1:10

Heavenly............................Rev. 19:8

B. Attitude toward:

Not to covet .... Acts 20:33

Without show .... 1 Pet. 3:3, 4

Be modest in .... 1 Tim. 2:9, 10

C. Figurative of:

Christ's blood .... Is. 63:1–3

Christ's righteousness .... Zech. 3:1–5

The church's purity ....Ps. 45:13, 14

Apparition—*appearance of ghost or disembodied spirit*

Samuel.........................1 Sam. 28:12–14

Christ mistaken for... Matt. 14:26; Luke 24:37, 39

Appeal—*petition for higher judgment*

To Christ ....Luke 12:13, 14

Of Paul, to Caesar ...... Acts 25:11, 25–27; 26:32

Appearance, outward

A. Can conceal:

Deception.......... Josh. 9:3–16; James 1:10, 11

Hypocrisy.......................Matt. 23:25–28

Rottenness ....Acts 12:21–23

Rebellion .... 2 Sam. 15:7–13

False apostles....................2 Cor. 11:13–15

Inner glory .... Is. 53:1–3; Matt. 17:1, 2

B. Can be:

Misunderstood .... Josh. 22:10–31

Mistaken....................... 1 Sam. 1:12–18

Misleading ....2 Cor. 10:7–11

Misjudged........................... John 7:24

Misinterpreted .... Matt. 11:16–19

Appearances, divine

A. Of the Lord in the Old Testament:

To Abraham........................ Gen. 12:7

To Isaac.........................Gen. 26:1, 2, 24

To Jacob .... Gen. 35:1, 9

To Moses........................ Ex. 3:1, 2, 16

To Israel ....Ex. 16:10

In mercy seat ....Lev. 16:2

In tabernacle .... Num. 14:10

To Gideon ....Judg. 6:11, 12

To Manoah and wife ....Judg. 13:2, 3, 10, 21

To Samuel........................ 1 Sam. 3:21

To David......................... 2 Chr. 3:1

To Solomon ....1 Kin. 3:5

B. Of Christ's first advent, in:

Nativity.............................2 Tim. 1:10

Transfiguration .... Luke 9:29–31
Resurrected form ....Luke 24:34
Priestly intercession.................... Heb. 9:24
Return ....Col. 3:4
C. Of Christ resurrected, to, at:
Mary Magdalene ....John 20:11–18
Other women.................... Matt. 28:9, 10
Disciples on road to Emmaus ..... Luke 24:13–35
Ten disciples ....John 20:19–25
Thomas....................... John 20:26–31
Sea of Galilee.....................John 21:1–25
Give Great Commission.........Matt. 28:16–20
Five hundred brethren .... 1 Cor. 15:6
His ascension...................... Acts 1:4–11
Paul ....Acts 9:3–6
John .... Rev. 1:10–18
D. Of Christ's second advent, a time of:
Salvation........................... Heb. 9:28
Confidence........................ 1 John 2:28
Judgment ....2 Tim. 4:1
Reward .... 2 Tim. 4:8
Blessedness..........................Titus 2:13
Joy............................i Pet. 1:7, 8
Rulership .... 1 Tim. 6:14, 15
See Theophany

Appeasement—*means used to reconcile two parties*
A. Kinds of, between:
Brothers ....Gen. 32:20
Nations .... 1 Kin. 20:31–34
Tribes......................... Josh. 22:10–34
Jews and Gentiles.................. Eph. 2:11–17
B. Means of, by:
Gifts.......................Gen. 43:11–16
Special pleading .... 1 Sam. 25:17–35
Correcting an abuse................... Acts 6:1–6
Slowness to anger ....Prov. 15:18
Wisdom ....Prov. 16:14
C. None allowed between:
Righteousness, evil ....2 Cor. 6:14–17
Truth, error ....Gal. 1:7–9
Faith, works......................... Gal. 5:1–10
Flesh, Spirit .... Gal. 5:16–26
Christ, Satan .... Matt. 4:1–11
Heaven, Sheol .... Is. 28:18
D. Of God's wrath, by:
Righteous action............... Num. 16:44–50
Repentance ....2 Sam. 12:10–14
Atoning for an evil.............. 2 Sam. 21:1–14
Christ's death .... Is. 53:1–7
Christ's righteousness..............Zech. 3:1–5;
    2 Cor. 5:18–21

Appetite—*desire to fulfill some basic need*
A. Kinds of:
Physical........................1 Sam. 14:31–33
Sexual ....1 Cor. 7:1–9
Lustful........................... Matt. 5:28
Insatiable ....Prov. 27:20
Spiritual .... Ps. 119:20, 131

B. Perversion of, by:
Gluttony ....Prov. 23:1, 2
Adultery ....Prov. 6:24–29; Ezek. 23:1–49
Impurity .... Rom. 1:24–32
C. Loss of, by:
Age............................. 2 Sam. 19:35
Trouble ....1 Sam. 28:21–23
Visions..........................Dan. 10:3–16
Deep concern......................John 4:31–34
D. Spiritual, characteristics of:
Satisfying .... Is. 55:1, 2
Sufficient ....Matt. 5:6
Spontaneous ....John 7:37–39
Sanctifying.........................1 Pet. 2:2
Sublime.........................Col. 3:1–3
See Gluttony; Hunger; Temperance

Apphia
Christian lady of Colosse............. Philem. 2

Appii Forum—*a town about 40 miles south of Rome*
Paul meets Christians here .... Acts 28:15

Applause—*a visible expression of public approval*
Men seek after..................... Matt. 6:1–5

"Apple of the eye"—*a figurative expression for
            something very valuable*
A. Translated as:
"The apple of His eye" .... Zech. 2:8
B. Figurative of:
God's care......................... Deut. 32:10
God's Law........................... Prov. 7:2
The saint's security .... Ps. 17:8

Apples of gold—*something of great value*
A word fitly spoken ....Prov. 25:11

Appoint—*to set in an official position or relationship*
A. Descriptive of ordination, to:
Priesthood .... Num. 3:10
Prophetic office .... Heb. 3:2
Ruler .... 2 Sam. 6:21
Apostleship ....Luke 10:1
Deacon's office ....Acts 6:3
Christ as High Priest................. Heb. 5:1, 5
Paul as a preacher.....................1 Tim. 2:7
Elders...............................Titus 1:5
Royal officer ....Dan. 2:24
B. Descriptive of God's rule, over:
Earth .... Ps. 104:19, 20
World history .... Acts 17:26
Israel's history.......................2 Chr. 33:8
Nations ....Jer. 47:7
Human life............................Job 14:5
Death............................. Heb. 9:27
Final judgment ....Acts 17:31
Human destiny..................... Matt. 24:51
C. Descriptive of the believer's life:
Trials.............................1 Thess. 3:3
Service............................ Acts 22:10
Government........................Rom. 13:1
Salvation...............Acts 13:48; 1 Thess. 5:9

> **WORD STUDY**

APPOINTED TIME, *mo'ed* (moh-*ayd*). *Mo'ed* is a noun meaning "appointed time," "appointed place," or "meeting." The simplest use of the word refers to a fixed time for an event (Gen. 18:14) or even the seasons, which change at fixed intervals. By connection, the word refers to sacred festivals or feasts held at appointed times (Deut. 31:10). Often these festivals were related to the season because they were agricultural festivals. Also by connection, the word means sacred assemblies or meetings held at appointed places. The assemblies were usually specially called and held at an appointed time. (Strong's #4150)

Appreciation—*favorable recognition of blessings*
Sought for among people . . . . Ps. 107:8–21
Of favors, rebuffed. . . . . 2 Sam. 10:1–5
Of blessings, unnoticed. . . . . Acts 14:15–18

Apprehension—*the ability to understand*
God . . . . .Job 11:7
God's Word . . . . .Acts 17:11
Prophecy. . . . . 1 Pet. 1:10–12
Parables. . . . . Matt. 13:10–17
Spiritual truths .1 Cor. 2:7–16
Christ. . . . . Phil. 3:12–14

Appropriation—*possessing for one's use*
God's promises .Heb. 11:8–16
God's Word . . . . Ps. 119:11
Salvation. . . . . .Acts 16:30–34

Approval—*favorable acceptance*
A. Means of, by:
God . . . . Acts 2:22
The Lord. . . . . .2 Cor. 10:18
The Jews . . . . .Rom. 2:17, 18
A church . . . . 1 Cor. 16:3
Humankind. . . . . .Rom. 14:18
B. Obtained by:
Endurance . . . . .2 Cor. 6:4–10
Innocence. . . . . 2 Cor. 7:11
Spiritual examination . . . . 2 Cor. 13:5–8
Spiritual judgment. . . . . Phil. 1:9, 10
Diligence. . . . . .2 Tim. 2:15

Aprons—*articles of clothing*
Item of miraculous healing . . . . Acts 19:12

Aquila—*eagle*
Jewish tentmaker; husband
   of Priscilla . . . . Acts 18:2, 3
Paul stays with. . . . . Acts 18:1–3
Visits Syria . . . . .Acts 18:18
Resides in Ephesus . . . . .Acts 18:19
Instructs Apollos . . . . .Acts 18:24–26
Esteemed by Paul . . . . Rom. 16:3, 4
Church in their house . . . . Rom. 16:3, 5

Ar—*city*
A chief Moabite city. . . . . Num. 21:15
On Israel's route . . . . .Deut. 2:18
Destroyed by Sihon . . . . Num. 21:28

Destroyed by God . . . . .Is. 15:1

Ara—*strong*
A descendant of Asher . . . . 1 Chr. 7:38

Arab—*a court*
A mountain city of Judah. . . . . .Josh. 15:52

Arabia—*steppe*
A. Place of:
Mt. Sinai . . . . .Gal. 4:25
Gold mines. . . . . 2 Chr. 9:14
Paul visited. . . . . .Gal. 1:17
B. People of:
Nomadic. . . . . Is. 13:20
Paid tribute to Solomon . . . . .1 Kin. 10:14, 15
Plundered Jerusalem . . . . .2 Chr. 21:16, 17
Defeated by Uzziah . . . . .2 Chr. 26:1, 7
Sold sheep and goats to Tyre . . . . . Ezek. 27:1, 2, 21
Opposed Nehemiah. . . . . Neh. 2:19
Denounced by prophets . . . . .Is. 21:13–17
Visited Jerusalem at Pentecost . . . . .Acts 2:11

Arad—*fugitive*
1. A Benjamite. . . . . 1 Chr. 8:15
2. A city south of Hebron . . . . .Num. 21:1–3
Defeated by Joshua. . . . . .Josh. 12:14
Kenites settled near . . . . .Judg. 1:16

Arah—*wayfarer*
1. A descendant of Asher . . . . 1 Chr. 7:39
2. A family of returnees . . . . Ezra 2:5

Aram—*high; exalted*
1. A son of Shem . . . . Gen. 10:22, 23
2. A grandson of Nahor . . . . Gen. 22:21
3. A descendant of Asher . . . . 1 Chr. 7:34

Aramaic—*a Semitic language*
Used by the Syrians . . . . .2 Kin. 18:26
The language of the postexilic period. . . . Ezra 4:7;
   Dan. 2:4
Portions of the Bible written in, include. . . . . . Ezra
   4:8–6:18; 7:12–26; Dan. 2:4–7:28
The same as "Hebrew" in . . . . .John 19:20
Words and phrases of, found in . . . . . .Matt. 27:46;
   Mark 5:41; 7:34

Aran—*wild goat*
Esau's descendant. . . . . .Gen. 36:28

Ararat—*a high mountain range in eastern Armenia*
Site of ark's landing . . . . Gen. 8:4
Assassins flee to . . . . .2 Kin. 19:37; Is. 37:38

Aratus—*a Greek poet living about 270 B.C.; not mentioned by name in the Bible*
Paul quotes from his *Phaenomena* . . . . . . Acts 17:28

Araunah—*Yahweh is firm*
A Jebusite . . . . .2 Sam. 24:15–25
His threshing floor bought by
   David . . . . .2 Sam. 24:18–25
Became site of temple . . . . 2 Chr. 3:1
Also called Ornan . . . . 1 Chr. 21:18–28

Arba—*four*
The father of the Anakim . . . . Josh. 14:15

Arbathite—*a native of Beth Arabah*
Two of David's mighty men......... 2 Sam. 23:31

Arbite—*a native of Arab*
In Judah .... 2 Sam. 23:35

Arbitrator—*one authorized to settle disputes*
A. Exercised by:
Judges .... Ex. 18:18–27
Priests .... Deut. 17:8–13
Kings............................. 1 Kin. 3:9, 16–28
Christ............................ Matt. 22:17–33
Apostles .... Acts 6:1–6
Church .... Acts 15:1–29
B. Purposes of:
Determine the Lord's will ..... Lev. 24:11–16, 23;
Num. 15:32–36
Settle disputes................... Josh. 22:9–34
Settle labor disputes..... Matt. 18:23–35; 20:1–16

Archaeology—*the science of digging up ancient
civilizations*
Truth springs out of the earth.......... Ps. 85:11
The stones cry out .... Luke 19:40

Archangel—*a chief angel*
Contends with Satan.................... Jude 9
Will herald the Lord's return .... 1 Thess. 4:16

Archelaus—*leader of the people*
Son of Herod the Great.............. Matt. 2:22

Archers—*experts with the bow and arrow*
A. Descriptive of:
Ishmael........................... Gen. 21:20
Jonathan.................... 1 Sam. 20:34–39
Sons of Ulam.......................1 Chr. 8:40
B. Instrumental in the death of:
Saul................................1 Sam. 31:3
Uriah the Hittite................... 2 Sam. 11:24
Josiah........................ 2 Chr. 35:23, 24
C. Figurative of:
Invincibility.....................Gen. 49:23, 24
The Lord's chastisements.............Job 16:13
Loss of glory...........................Is. 21:17
Divine judgment..................... Jer. 50:29

Archippus—*master of the horse*
A church worker.......................Col. 4:17

Archite—*the long*
Canaanite tribe.......................Josh. 16:2
David's friend .... 2 Sam. 15:32

Architect—*one who draws plans for a building*
Plan of, given to Noah...............Gen. 6:14–16
Plan of, shown to Moses.......... Ex. 25:8, 9, 40
Bezalel, an inspired .... Ex. 35:30–35
Plan of, given to Solomon........ 1 Chr. 28:11–21
Seen in Ezekiel's vision .... Ezek. 40–42

Archives—*storage place for public and historical
documents*
The Book of the Law found in ....2 Kin. 22:8
Jeremiah's roll placed in ....Jer. 36:20, 21
Record book kept in....................Ezra 4:15

Genealogies kept in .... Neh. 7:5, 64

Ard—*humpbacked*
A son of Benjamin .... Gen. 46:21
Progenitor of the Ardites .... Num. 26:40
Also called Addar..................... 1 Chr. 8:3

Ardon—*descendant*
A son of Caleb........................ 1 Chr. 2:18

Areli—*valiant, heroic*
A son of Gad .... Gen. 46:16

Areopagite—*a member of the court*
A convert .... Acts 17:34

Areopagus—*a rocky hill at Athens; also the name of a
court*
Paul preached .... Acts 17:18–34

Aretas—*pleasing*
The title borne by four Nabatean rulers, the last of
whom Paul mentions (Aretas IV, Philopatris,
9 B.C.–A.D. 40) ....2 Cor. 11:32, 33

Argob—*mound or region of clods*
1. District of Bashan with 60
fortified cities ....Deut. 3:4; 1 Kin. 4:13
2. Guard killed by Pekah .... 2 Kin. 15:25

Aridai
A son of Haman .... Esth. 9:9

Aridatha
A son of Haman .... Esth. 9:8

Arieh—*lion*
Guard killed by Pekah...............2 Kin. 15:25

Ariel—*lion of God*
1. Ezra's friend........................Ezra 8:15–17
2. Name applied to Jerusalem ....Is. 29:1, 2, 7

Arimathea—*a height*
Joseph's native city................... John 19:38

Arioch—*lionlike*
1. King of Ellasar ....Gen. 14:1, 9
2. Captain of Nebuchadnezzar......... Dan. 2:14, 15

Arisai
A son of Haman .... Esth. 9:9

Arise—*to stand up*
A. Descriptive of:
Natural events........................ Eccl. 1:5
Standing up .... 1 Sam. 28:23
Regeneration ....Luke 15:18, 20
Resurrection .... Matt. 9:24, 25
A miracle ....Luke 4:38, 39
B. Descriptive of prophetic events:
World kingdoms..................... Dan. 2:39
The Messiah's advent .... Is. 60:1–3
Persecution....................... Mark 4:16, 17
False christs....................... Matt. 24:24

Aristarchus—*the best ruler*
A Macedonian Christian .... Acts 19:29
Accompanied Paul.................... Acts 20:1, 4
Imprisoned with Paul ....Col. 4:10

Aristobulus—*the best counselor*
  A Christian at Rome . . . . .Rom. 16:10

Ark of bulrushes—*a basket made of reeds (papyrus)*
  Moses placed in. Ex. 2:1–6
  Made by faith . . . . Heb. 11:23

Ark of Noah
  Construction. . . . . .Gen. 6:14–16
  Cargo. . . . . .Gen. 6:19–21
  Ready for the flood . . . . .Matt. 24:38, 39
  Rested on Mt. Ararat. . . . . Gen. 8:1–16
  A type of baptism. . . . . 1 Pet. 3:20, 21

Ark of the Covenant—*a small box containing the
    tablets of the Law*
A. Called:
  Ark of the covenant. . . . . Num. 10:33
  Ark of the Testimony . . . . .Ex. 30:6
  Ark of the Lord. . . . . Josh. 4:11
  Ark of God. . . . . .1 Sam. 3:3
  Ark of God's strength . . . . .2 Chr. 6:41
B. Construction of:
  Described. . . . . Ex. 25:10–22
  Executed. . . . . Ex. 37:1–5
C. Contained:
  The Ten Commandments . . . . Deut. 10:4, 5
  Aaron's rod. . . . . Num. 17:10; Heb. 9:4
  Pot of manna. Ex. 16:33, 34
D. Conveyed:
  By Levites. . . . . .Num. 3:30, 31
  Before Israel. . . . . .Josh. 3:3–17
  Into battle. . . . . 1 Sam. 4:4, 5
  On a cart. . . . . 1 Sam. 6:7–15
E. Purposes of:
  Symbol of God's Law. . . . . Ex. 25:16, 21
  Memorial of God's provision. . . . . Ex. 16:33, 34
  Place to know God's will . . . . . .Ex. 25:22; 30:6, 36
  Place of entreaty. . . . . .Josh. 7:6–15
  Symbol of God's holiness. . . . . 1 Sam. 6:19;
    2 Sam. 6:6, 7
  Place of atonement. . . . . .Lev. 16:2, 14–17
  Symbol of heaven . . . . .Rev. 11:19
F. History of:
  Placed in Most Holy Place . . . . Ex. 26:34
  Carried across Jordan . . . . .Josh. 3:14–17
  Caused Jordan's stoppage. . . . . . . .Josh. 4:5–11, 18
  Carried around Jericho. . . . . Josh. 6:6–20
  At Mt. Ebal ceremony . . . . Josh. 8:30–33
  Set up at Shiloh. Josh. 18:1
  Moved to house of God. . . . . Judg. 20:26, 27
  Returned to Shiloh. . . . . .1 Sam. 1:3
  Carried into battle . . . . 1 Sam. 4:3–22
  Captured. . . . . 1 Sam. 4:10–22
  Caused Dagon's fall . . . . 1 Sam. 5:1–4
  Brought a plague. . . . . 1 Sam. 5:6–12
  Returned to Israel. . . . . 1 Sam. 6:1–21
  Set in Abinadab's house . . . . .1 Sam. 7:1, 2
  Moved illegally on cart . . . . 2 Sam. 6:1–9
  In Obed-Edom's house . . . . 2 Sam. 6:10–12
  Established in Jerusalem. . . . . 2 Sam. 6:12–17

During Absalom's rebellion. . . . . .2 Sam. 15:24–29
  Placed in temple . . . . .1 Kin. 8:1–11
  Restored by Josiah . . . . .2 Chr. 35:3
  Prophetic fulfillment . . . . .Jer. 3:16, 17;
    Acts 15:13–18

Arkite—*belonging to Arka*
  Canaan's descendants . . . . . Gen. 10:17; 1 Chr. 1:15

Arm of God
A. Described as:
  Stretched out. . . . . Deut. 4:34
  Everlasting. . . . . Deut. 33:27
  Strong, mighty . . . . .Ps. 89:10, 13
  Holy. . . . . Ps. 98:1
  Glorious . . . . Is. 63:12
B. Descriptive of, God's:
  Redeeming. . . . . .Ex. 6:6
  Saving . . . . .Ps. 44:3
  Victorious. . . . . Ps. 98:1
  Ruling . . . . Is. 40:10
  Strengthening . . . . Ps. 89:21
  Protecting. . . . . .Deut. 7:19
  Destroying. . . . . Is. 30:30

Arm of the wicked—*expression for molestation*
  Shall be broken . . . . Ps. 10:15

Armageddon—*Mount Megiddo*
Site of:
  Historic wars. . . . . .Judg. 5:19
  Final battle. . . . . .Rev. 16:16

Armholes
  Armpits, protected with rags. . . . . Jer. 38:12

Armoni—*belonging to the palace*
  A son of Saul . . . . 2 Sam. 21:8–11

Armor—*a protective article of warfare*
A. As a protective weapon:
  Shield. . . . . .1 Sam. 17:7, 41
  Helmet . . . . 1 Sam. 17:38
  Scale armor . . . . 1 Sam. 17:5, 38; 1 Kin. 22:34
  Greaves . . . . .1 Sam. 17:6
  Body armor . . . . .2 Chr. 26:14; Jer. 46:4
B. As an aggressive weapon:
  Rod. . . . . Ps. 2:9
  Sling. . . . . 1 Sam. 17:40
  Bow and arrow . . . . .2 Sam. 1:18
  Spear . . . . Is. 2:4
  Sword. . . . . .1 Sam. 17:51
  See Armor, spiritual

Armorbearer—*one who bears the arms of another*
  Assists kings in battle . . . . .Judg. 9:54
  David serves Saul as. . . . . 1 Sam. 16:21
  Jonathan's, a man of courage. . . . . . 1 Sam. 14:7, 12
  Saul's, dies with him . . . . 1 Sam. 31:4–6
  Goliath's, precedes him . . . . .1 Sam. 17:7, 41

Armor, spiritual
  The Christian's, complete . . . . .Eph. 6:11–17;
    1 Thess. 5:8
  Of light . . . . .Rom. 13:12

Of righteousness...................... 2 Cor. 6:7
The Bible, the sword .... Eph. 6:17
Not of flesh ....2 Cor. 10:4, 5

Armory—*an arsenal*
Armor stored in .... Neh. 3:19
God's, opened for war................. Jer. 50:25
David's, well stocked.................. Song 4:4

Army—*group organized and disciplined for battle*
A. Consisted of:
Men over 20........................ Num. 1:3
Infantrymen ....2 Chr. 25:5
Archers .... 1 Chr. 5:18
Slingstones ....2 Chr. 26:14
Chariots ....1 Kin. 4:26
Foreigners........................2 Sam. 15:18
Choice men .... 2 Sam. 10:7–9
B. Led by:
God ....Josh. 5:13–15
Judges .... Judg. 11:1, 5, 6, 32
Commander........................2 Sam. 2:8
Kings......................2 Sam. 12:28, 29
C. Commands regarding:
Use of chariots.....................Deut. 17:16
Deferred certain classes ....Num. 2:33;
   Deut. 20:1–9
Division of spoil ....1 Sam. 30:21–25
Fearfulness.......................... Deut. 20:1
D. Units of:
Fifties .... 2 Kin. 1:9
Hundreds .... Num. 31:14, 48
Legions .... Matt. 26:53
Garrison ....Acts 21:31
Guards........................... Acts 28:16
Squads .... Acts 12:4
Thousands .... Num. 31:14, 48
E. Of Israel, conquered:
Egyptians .... Ex. 14:19–31
Jericho............................Josh. 6:1–25
Midianites .... Judg. 7:1–23
Philistines......................1 Sam. 14:14–23
Syrians...........................2 Kin. 7:1–15
Assyrians .... 2 Kin. 19:35, 36

Army, Christian
A. Warfare against:
The world............. James 4:4; 1 John 2:15–17
The flesh..........................Gal. 5:17–21
Satan .... 1 Pet. 5:8, 9
Evil men .... 2 Tim. 3:8
False teachers........................Jude 3, 4
Spiritual wickedness .... Eph. 6:12
Worldly "idle babblings" .... 1 Tim. 6:20
B. Equipment for:
Sufficient for total war .... Eph. 6:12–17;
   1 Thess. 5:8
Spiritual in nature ....2 Cor. 10:3, 4
Sharper than any sword .... Heb. 4:12
C. The soldier in, must:
Enlist.......................Matt. 28:18–20

Obey ....2 Cor. 10:5, 6
Please one who enlisted him .... 2 Tim. 2:4
Use self-control................. 1 Cor. 9:25–27
Stand firm ....Eph. 6:13–17
Endure hardship.................... 2 Tim. 2:3
Show courage..................... 2 Tim. 4:7–18
Fight hard.......................... 1 Tim. 6:12
Be pure .... 1 Pet. 2:11, 12
Be alert ....1 Pet. 5:8
Be faithful ....1 Tim. 1:18–20
D. Jesus Christ, the Captain of, is:
Perfect............................ Heb. 2:10
Undefiled .... Heb. 7:26
Powerful..........................2 Thess. 2:8

Arnan—*strong*
A descendant of David ....1 Chr. 3:1, 21

Arnon—*a river*
Boundary between Moab and
   Ammon ....Num. 21:13, 26
Border of Reuben .... Deut. 3:12, 16
Ammonites reminded of.......... Judg. 11:18–26

Arod—*hunchbacked*
A son of Gad .... Num. 26:17
Called Arodi .... Gen. 46:16

Aroer—*naked*
1. A town in east Jordan ....Deut. 2:36
An Amorite boundary city......Josh. 13:9, 10, 16
Sihon ruled......................... Josh. 12:2
Assigned to Reuben .... Deut. 3:12
Rebuilt by Gadites .... Num. 32:34
Beginning of David's census .... 2 Sam. 24:1, 5
Taken by Hazael............... 2 Kin. 10:32, 33
Possessed by Moab.............. Jer. 48:19
2. A city of Judah ....1 Sam. 30:28
3. A city of Gad .... Josh. 13:25

Aroma—*a pleasant smell*
Of sacrifices.......................Lev. 26:31
Figurative of gifts.................... Phil. 4:18

Arpad—*a couch, resting place*
A town in Samaria ....2 Kin. 18:34
End of, predicted .... Jer. 49:23

Arphaxad
A son of Shem .... Gen. 10:22, 24
Born two years after the flood .....Gen. 11:10–13
An ancestor of Christ ....Luke 3:36

Arrogance—*overbearing pride*
Mentioned with other evils .... Prov. 8:13
To be punished by God................. Is. 13:11
Seen in haughtiness .... Jer. 48:29

 WORD STUDY   **ARROGANT, PROUD,** *huperēphanos* (hoop-er-*ay*-fan-oss). This adjective is formed from *huper,* "over," and *phainomai,* "to appear" or "to make one's appearance." In the NT *huperēphanos* evokes the unsavory attitude of superiority and means "arrogant," "haughty," "proud." It is cataloged among other vices (Rom. 1:30; 2 Tim. 3:2), and Jesus uses the cognate noun *huperēphania,* "arrogance" or "pride," in a list of evil things that "come from within and defile" (Mark 7:22). The "arrogant" are often contrasted to those who are "lowly" or "humble" (*tapeinos*), as in Luke 1:51, 52; James 4:6; and 1 Pet. 5:5. (Strong's #5244)

Arrows—*sharp instruments hurled by a bow*
A. Uses of:
    Hunting .... Gen. 27:3
    Send message................. 1 Sam. 20:20–22
    Divination ....Ezek. 21:21
    Prophecy...................... 2 Kin. 13:14–19
    War ....2 Kin. 19:32
B. Described as:
    Deadly.............................Prov. 26:18
    Sharp ....Ps. 120:4
    Bright..............................Jer. 51:11
    Like lightning ....Zech. 9:14
C. Figurative of:
    God's judgments.................Deut. 32:23, 42
    Intense affliction ....Job 6:4
    Wicked intentions .... Ps. 11:2
    Messiah's mission.......................Ps. 45:5
    Bitter words ....Ps. 64:3
    God's power.........................Ps. 76:3
    Daily hazards......................... Ps. 91:5
    Children ....Ps. 127:4
    A false witness......................Prov. 25:18
    A deceitful tongue ....Jer. 9:8

Arson—*setting fire to property maliciously*
A. Features concerning:
    A law forbidding.......................Ex. 22:6
    A means of revenge ....Judg. 12:1
B. Instances of, by:
    Samson ....Judg. 15:4, 5
    Danites .... Judg. 18:26, 27
    Absalom .... 2 Sam. 14:30
    Enemies............................. Ps. 74:7, 8

Art
    Ointment after the.................... Ex. 30:25
    Stones graven by .... Acts 17:29

Artaxerxes—*great king*
    Artaxerxes I, king of Persia (465–425 B.C.),
      authorizes Ezra's mission to
      Jerusalem...................... Ezra 7:1–28
    Temporarily halts rebuilding program
      at Jerusalem .... Ezra 4:7–23
    Commissions Nehemiah's mission ...Neh. 2:1–10
    Permits Nehemiah to return .... Neh. 13:6

Artemas—*gift of Artemis*
    Paul's companion at Nicopolis ....Titus 3:12

Artisans—*skilled workers; craftspersons*
    Tubal-Cain, the earliest .... Gen. 4:22
    Women, work of in tabernacle ....Ex. 35:25
    Employed in temple construction .....1 Chr. 29:5
    Removed in judgment.................. Is. 3:1–3

Arts and crafts in the Bible
    Armorer .... 1 Sam. 8:12
    Baker ....Gen. 40:1
    Barber ....Ezek. 5:1
    Blacksmith...................... 1 Sam. 13:19
    Brickmaker ....Ex. 5:7
    Carpenter...........................Mark 6:3
    Carver ....Ex. 31:5
    Caulker............................Ezek. 27:9
    Cook ....1 Sam. 8:13
    Coppersmith .... 2 Tim. 4:14
    Draftsman ....Ezek. 4:1
    Dyer.......................... Ex. 25:1–5
    Embalmer.......................Gen. 50:2, 3
    Engraver ....Ex. 28:11
    Farmer............................. Gen. 4:2
    Fisherman.........................Matt. 4:18
    Gardener........................ John 20:15
    Goldsmith .... Is. 40:19
    Jeweler....................... Ex. 28:17–21
    Lapidary ....Ex. 35:33
    Launderer.........................Mark 9:3
    Mason ....2 Sam. 5:11
    Molder............................Ex. 32:4
    Musician.........................2 Sam. 6:5
    Oarsmen...................... Ezek. 27:8, 9
    Painting ....Jer. 22:14
    Perfumer....................... Ex. 30:25, 35
    Potter............................Jer. 18:3
    Refiner .... Mal. 3:2, 3
    Ropemaker.......................Judg. 16:11
    Sewing...........................Ezek. 13:18
    Shipbuilding ....1 Kin. 9:26
    Silversmith......................... Acts 19:24
    Smelter .... Job 28:1, 2
    Spinner .... Prov. 31:19
    Stonecutter.........................Ex. 31:5
    Tailor............................ Ex. 28:3, 4
    Tanner............................. Acts 10:6
    Tapestry maker.....................Ex. 35:35
    Tentmaking........................Acts 18:3
    Weaver ....Ex. 35:35
    Winemaker .... Neh. 13:15
    Worker in metal .... Gen. 4:22; Ex. 31:3, 4
    Writer ....Judg. 5:14

Arubboth—*the lattices*
    A town in one of Solomon's districts... 1 Kin. 4:10

Arumah—*height*
    A village near Shechem; Abimelech's
      refuge ....Judg. 9:41

Arvad—*wandering*
    A Phoenician city built on an island
      north of Tyre.................. Ezek. 27:8, 11

Arvadites—*inhabitants of Arvad*
    Of Canaanite ancestry ....Gen. 10:18; 1 Chr. 1:16

Arza—*earth*
    King Elah's steward in Tirzah ....1 Kin. 16:9

Asa—*physician*

1. Third king of Judah. . . . . 1 Kin. 15:8–10
   Reigns 10 years in peace . . . . 2 Chr. 14:1
   Overthrows idolatry . . . . 2 Chr. 14:2–5
   Removes his grandmother . . . . 1 Kin. 15:13
   Fortifies Judah . . . . 2 Chr. 14:6–8
   Defeats the Ethiopians . . . . 2 Chr. 14:9–15
   Leads in national revival. . . . . .2 Chr. 15:1–15
   Hires Ben-Hadad against Baasha . . 2 Chr. 16:1–6
   Reproved by a prophet . . . . .2 Chr. 16:7–10
   Diseased, seeks physicians rather than
      the Lord . . . . .2 Chr. 16:12
   Buried in Jerusalem . . . . .2 Chr. 16:13, 14
   An ancestor of Christ . . . . .Matt. 1:7
2. A Levite among returnees . . . . 1 Chr. 9:16

Asahel—*God has made*

1. A son of Zeruiah, David's sister . . . . 1 Chr. 2:16
   Noted for valor . . . . 2 Sam. 2:18; 23:24
   Pursues Abner. . . . . .2 Sam. 2:19
   Killed by Abner. . . . . 2 Sam. 2:23
   Avenged by Joab . . . . 2 Sam. 3:27, 30
   Made a captain in David's army . . . . 1 Chr. 27:7
2. A Levite teacher . . . . 2 Chr. 17:8
3. A collector of tithes . . . . 2 Chr. 31:12, 13
4. A priest who opposes Ezra's reforms. . . . . Ezra 10:15

Asaiah—*Yahweh has made*

1. A Simeonite chief. . . . . 1 Chr. 4:36
2. A Levite during David's reign. . . . . 1 Chr. 6:30
   Helps restore ark to Jerusalem . . . . .1 Chr. 15:6, 11
3. An officer sent to Huldah . . . . .2 Chr. 34:20–22;
   2 Kin. 22:12–14
4. The firstborn of the Shilonites. . . . . 1 Chr. 9:5
   Probably called Maaseiah. . . . . Neh. 11:5

Asaph—*collector*

1. A Gershonite Levite choir leader in the time of
      David and Solomon. . . . 1 Chr. 15:16–19; 16:1–7;
   2 Chr. 5:6, 12
   Called a seer. . . . . .2 Chr. 29:30
   Sons of, made musicians. . . . . .1 Chr. 25:1–9
   Twelve psalms assigned to . . . . 2 Chr. 29:30;
   Ps. 50; 73–83
   Descendants of, among returnees . . . . . . Ezra 2:41;
   Neh. 7:44
   In dedication ceremony . . . . .Ezra 3:10
2. The father of Hezekiah's recorder . . . 2 Kin. 18:18, 37
3. A chief forester whom Artaxerxes commands
      to supply timber to Nehemiah . . . . .Neh. 2:8
4. A Korahite Levite . . . . 1 Chr. 26:1
   Also called Ebiasaph . . . . 1 Chr. 9:19

Asarel—*God has bound*

   A son of Jehallelel. . . . . 1 Chr. 4:16

Ascension—*rising to a higher place*

A. Descriptive of:
   Physical rising of smoke . . Ex. 19:18; Josh. 8:20, 21
   Going up hill . . . . Luke 19:28
   Rising to heaven . . . . Ps. 139:8
   Christ's ascension. John 6:62
   Sinful ambition. . . . . Is. 14:13, 14

B. Of saints:
   Enoch, translation of. . . . . Gen. 5:24; Heb. 11:5
   Elijah, translation of . . . . 2 Kin. 2:11; Matt. 17:1–9
   Christians, at Christ's return. . . . . 1 Cor. 15:51, 52;
   1 Thess. 4:13–18

C. Of Christ:
   Foretold in the Old Testament . . . . Ps. 68:18;
   Eph. 4:8–10
   Announced by Christ . . . . John 20:17
   Forty days after His resurrection. . .Luke 24:48–51;
   Acts 1:1–12
   Enters heaven by redemption . . . . . . Heb. 6:19, 20;
   9:12, 24
   Crowned with glory and honor. . . . . Heb. 2:9
   Rules from David's throne. . . . . .Acts 2:29–36
   Sits at the Father's side . . . . Eph. 1:20; Heb. 1:3
   Intercedes for the saints . . . . Rom. 8:34
   Preparing place for His people . . . . John 14:2
   Highly exalted. . . . . .Acts 5:31; Phil. 2:9
   Reigns triumphantly . . . . 1 Cor. 15:24–28;
   Heb. 10:12, 13
   Exercises priestly ministry. . . .Heb. 4:14–16; 8:1, 2

Ascent of Akrabbim—*steep*

   Ascent south of the Dead Sea . . . . Josh. 15:3

Asceticism—*stern restraint upon bodily appetites*

A. Forms of, seen in:
   Nazirite vow . . . . Num. 6:1–21
   Manoah's wife. . . . . Judg. 13:3–14
   Samson . . . . .Judg. 16:16, 17
   Elijah's life . . . . .1 Kin. 19:1–9
   The Rechabites . . . . Jer. 35:1–19
   John the Baptist . . . . Matt. 3:4; 11:18
   Jesus Christ . . . . Matt. 4:2
   Paul . . . . .1 Cor. 9:27

B. Teaching concerning:
   Extreme, repudiated . . . . Luke 7:33–36
   False, rejected . . . . Col. 2:20–23; 1 Tim. 4:3, 4
   Some, necessary . . . . .1 Cor. 9:26, 27; 2 Tim. 2:3, 4
   Temporary, helpful . . . Ezra 8:21–23; 1 Cor. 7:3–9
   Figurative of complete consecration. . .Matt. 19:12;
   Rev. 14:1–5

Asenath—*belonging to the goddess Neith*

   Daughter of Poti-Pherah and wife
      of Joseph . . . . Gen. 41:45
   Mother of Manasseh and
      Ephraim. . . . . Gen. 41:50–52; 46:20

Ashamed—*shame instilled by evildoing*

A. Caused by:
   Mistreatment. . . . . 2 Sam. 10:4, 5
   Sad tidings . . . . .2 Kin. 8:7–13
   Transgression . . . . Ps. 25:3
   Inconsistent action. . . . . Ezra 8:22
   Idolatry. . . . . .Is. 44:9–17
   Rebellion against God . . . . Is. 45:24
   Lewdness . . . . Ezek. 16:27
   False prophecy. . . . . Zech. 13:3, 4
   Rejecting God's mercy . . . . Is. 65:13

Unbelief . . . . Mark 8:38
Unpreparedness . . . . .2 Cor. 9:4
B. Avoidance of, by:
Waiting for the Lord . . . . .Ps. 34:5; Is. 49:23
Regarding God's commands . . . . .Ps. 119:6
Sound in statutes . . . . .Ps. 119:80
Trusting God. . . . . .Ps. 25:20
Believing in Christ. . . . . Rom. 9:33; 10:11
Christian diligence . . . . .2 Tim. 2:15
Assurance of faith . . . . .2 Tim. 1:12
Abiding in Christ . . . . 1 John 2:28
C. Possible objects of, in the Christian's life:
Life's plans . . . . Phil. 1:20
God's message. . . . . .2 Tim. 1:8
The gospel . . . . .Rom. 1:16
The old life. . . . . Rom. 6:20, 21
One's faith . . . . .1 Pet. 4:16

Ashan—*smoke*
A city of Judah. .Josh. 15:42
Later allotted to Judah . . . . Josh. 19:7
Assigned to the Levites. . . . . .1 Chr. 6:59

Asharelah—*Yahweh is joined*
A son of Asaph in David's time. . . . . . . .1 Chr. 25:2
Called Jesharelah . . . . .1 Chr. 25:14

Ashbea—*let me call as witness*
A descendant of Shelah. . . . . .1 Chr. 4:21

Ashbel—*having a long upper lip*
A son of Benjamin . . . . .Gen. 46:21; 1 Chr. 8:1
Progenitor of the Ashbelites . . . . Num. 26:38

Ashdod—*stronghold; fortress*
One of five Philistine cities . . . . .Josh. 13:3
Anakim refuge . . . . .Josh. 11:22
Assigned to Judah. . . . . .Josh. 15:46, 47
Seat of Dagon worship . . . . 1 Sam. 5:1–8
Captured by Tartan. . . . . Is. 20:1
Opposed Nehemiah. . . . . Neh. 4:7
Women of, marry Jews . . . . .Neh. 13:23, 24
Called Azotus . . . . Acts 8:40

Asher—*happy*
1. Jacob's second son by Zilpah. . . . . Gen. 30:12, 13
Goes to Egypt with Jacob. . . . . .Gen. 46:8, 17
Father of five children. . . . . Gen. 46:17
Blessed by Jacob . . . . Gen. 49:20
2. The tribe fathered by Asher,
Jacob's son . . . . .Deut. 33:24
Census of . . . . Num. 1:41; 26:47
Tolerant of Canaanites . . . . .Judg. 1:31, 32
Failure of, in national crisis . . . . .Judg. 5:17
Among Gideon's army. . . . . .Judg. 6:35; 7:23
A godly remnant among. . . . . .2 Chr. 30:11
Anna, descendant of . . . . Luke 2:36–38
12,000 of sealed . . . . .Rev. 7:6
3. A town in Manasseh . . . . .Josh. 17:7

Asherah—*a goddess of the Phoenicians and Arameans*
1. The female counterpart of Baal . . . . .Judg. 3:7;
1 Kin. 18:19
Asa's mother worships. . . . . .1 Kin. 15:13

Image of, erected by Manasseh in the
temple. . . . . .2 Kin. 21:7
Vessels of, destroyed by Josiah . . . . .2 Kin. 23:4
2. Translated "wooden images, " idols used in the
worship of Asherah . . . . . . Ex. 34:13; Deut. 12:3;
16:21; 1 Kin. 16:32, 33; 2 Kin. 23:6, 7

Ashes—*the powdery residue of burned material*
A. Used for:
A miracle . . . . Ex. 9:8–10
Purification . . . . .Num. 19:1–10; Heb. 9:13
B. Symbolic of:
Mourning. . . . . 2 Sam. 13:19; Esth. 4:1, 3
Dejection . . . . .Job 2:8
Repentance . . . . .Job 42:6; Dan. 9:3;
Matt. 11:21
C. Figurative of:
Frailty . . . . Gen. 18:27
Destruction . . . . Ezek. 28:18
Victory . . . . Mal. 4:3
Worthlessness . . . . Job 13:12
Transformation. . . . . .Is. 61:3
Deceit . . . . Is. 44:20
Afflictions . . . . .Ps. 102:9
Destruction . . . . Jer. 6:26

Ashhur—*blackness*
A descendant of Judah . . . . 1 Chr. 2:24; 4:5–7

Ashima—*heaven*
A god or idol worshiped by Assyrian
colonists at Samaria . . . . .2 Kin. 17:30

Ashkelon—*holm oak*
One of five Philistine cities . . . . Josh. 13:3;
Jer. 47:5, 7
Captured by Judah. . . . . .Judg. 1:18
Men of, killed by Samson . . . . .Judg. 14:19, 20
Repossessed by Philistines. . . . . .1 Sam. 6:17;
2 Sam. 1:20
Doom of, pronounced by
the prophets . . . . .Jer. 47:5, 7; Amos 1:8;
Zeph. 2:4, 7; Zech. 9:5

Ashkenaz
1. A descendant of Noah through Japheth . . . Gen. 10:3;
1 Chr. 1:6
2. A nation associated with Ararat, Minni . . Jer. 51:27

Ashnah—*hard, firm*
1. A village of Judah near Zorah. . . . . .Josh. 15:33
2. Another village of Judah . . . . Josh. 15:43

Ashpenaz
The chief of Nebuchadnezzar's
eunuchs . . . . Dan. 1:3

Ashtaroth, Astaroth—*plural of Ashtoreth*
1. A city in Bashan; residence of
King Og . . . . .Deut. 1:4; Josh. 12:4
Captured by Israel . . . . Josh. 9:10
Assigned to Manasseh. . . . . .Josh. 13:31
Made a Levitical city ("Be Eshterah") . . .Josh. 21:27
Uzzia, a native of . . . . .1 Chr. 11:44

2. A general designation of the
Canaanite female deities .... 1 Sam. 7:3, 4; 31:10

Ashteroth Karnaim—*twin peaks near Ashtaroth*
A fortified city in Gilead occupied by the
Rephaims......................... Gen. 14:5

Ashtoreth—*the name given by Hebrews to the goddess Ashtart (Astarte)*
A. A mother goddess of love, fertility, and war
worshiped by:
Philistines......................... 1 Sam. 31:10
Sidonians .... 1 Kin. 11:5, 33
Hebrews (see below)
B. Israel's relation to:
Ensnared by .... Judg. 2:13; 10:6
Worship of, by Solomon .... 1 Kin. 11:5, 33
Destroyed by Josiah .... 2 Kin. 23:13
See Ashtaroth 2

Ashurites
A people belonging to Ishbosheth's
kingdom...................... 2 Sam. 2:8, 9

Ashvath—*made*
An Asherite .... 1 Chr. 7:33

Asia—*in New Testament times, the Roman province of proconsular Asia*
People from, at Pentecost........... Acts 2:9, 10
Paul forbidden to preach in .... Acts 16:6
Paul's later ministry in .... Acts 19:1–26
Paul plans to pass by .... Acts 20:16, 17
Paul's great conflict in............... 2 Cor. 1:8
Peter writes to saints of............... 1 Pet. 1:1
Seven churches of................... Rev. 1:4, 11

Asiel—*God has made*
A Simeonite .... 1 Chr. 4:35

Asking in prayer
A. Based upon:
God's foreknowledge................. Matt. 6:8
God's willingness................ Luke 11:11–13
God's love....................... John 16:23–27
Abiding in Christ.................... John 15:7
B. Receiving of answer, based upon:
Having faith....................... James 1:5, 6
Keeping God's commands........... 1 John 3:22
Regarding God's will............. 1 John 5:14, 15
Believing trust..................... Matt. 21:22
Unselfishness...................... James 4:2, 3
In Christ's name .... John 14:13, 14; 15:16

Asnah—*thornbush*
The head of a family of Nethinims ..... Ezra 2:50

Asp—*a deadly snake*
Figurative of man's evil nature .... Ps. 140:3;
Rom. 3:13

Aspatha—*horse-given*
A son of Haman .... Esth. 9:7

Asphalt
In Babel's tower...................... Gen. 11:3
In Moses' ark........................ Ex. 2:3

Kings fall in .... Gen. 14:10

Aspiration—*exalted desire combined with holy zeal*
A. Centered in:
God Himself .... Ps. 42:1, 2
God's kingdom .... Matt. 6:33
The high calling .... Phil. 3:8–14
Heaven .... Col. 3:1, 2
Acceptableness with Christ.......... 2 Tim. 2:4
B. Inspired by:
Christ's love .... 2 Cor. 5:14–16
Work yet to be done............ Rom. 15:18–20;
2 Cor. 10:13–18
Christ's grace.................... 2 Cor. 12:9–15
The reward........................ 2 Tim. 4:7, 8
The Lord's return............... Matt. 24:42–47;
1 John 3:1–3
World's end .... 2 Pet. 3:11–14

Asriel—*God has filled with joy*
A descendant of Manasseh and progenitor
of the Asrielites ...... Num. 26:31; Josh. 17:2;
1 Chr. 7:14

Assassination—*killing by secret and sudden assault*
A. Actual cases of:
Eglon by Ehud................. Judg. 3:17, 20, 21
Sisera by Jael .... Judg. 4:17–21
Abner by Joab .... 2 Sam. 3:27
Ishbosheth by sons of Rimmon ..... 2 Sam. 4:5–8
Amnon by Absalom............. 2 Sam. 13:28, 29
Absalom by Joab................... 2 Sam. 18:14
Amasa by Joab..................... 2 Sam. 20:10
Elah by Zimri...................... 1 Kin. 16:8–10
Ben-Hadad by Hazael........... 2 Kin. 8:7, 8, 15
Jehoram by Jehu .... 2 Kin. 9:24
Ahaziah by Jehu .... 2 Kin. 9:27
Jezebel by Jehu.................. 2 Kin. 9:30–37
Joash by servants .... 2 Kin. 12:20, 21
Zechariah by Shallum............ 2 Kin. 15:8–10
Shallum by Menahem .... 2 Kin. 15:14
Pekahiah by Pekah................. 2 Kin. 15:25
Pekah by Hoshea .... 2 Kin. 15:30
Amon by servants................... 2 Kin. 21:23
Gedaliah by Ishmael .... 2 Kin. 25:25
Sennacherib by his sons .... 2 Kin. 19:36, 37
B. Attempted cases of:
Jacob by Esau.................... Gen. 27:41–45
Joseph by his brothers............ Gen. 37:18–22
David by Saul.................... 1 Sam. 19:10–18
David by Absalom .... 2 Sam. 15:10–14
Joash by Athaliah.................. 2 Kin. 11:1–3
Ahasuerus by servants .... Esth. 2:21–23
Jesus by the Jews...... Luke 4:14, 28–30; John 7:1
Paul by the Jews .... Acts 9:23–25; 23:12–31
C. Crime of:
Against God's image in man............ Gen. 9:6
Punishable by death.... Ex. 21:12–15; Num. 35:33
Not to be condoned .... Deut. 19:11–13
Puts the guilty under a curse......... Deut. 27:24
Abhorred by the righteous........ 2 Sam. 4:4–12

WORD STUDY

ASSEMBLY, *qahal* (kaw-*hawl*). *Qahal* is a noun meaning "assembly," "company," or "congregation." Assemblies were convened for special purposes, such as war or civil affairs, but could also be religious in nature, as when the people gathered to wait for Moses to come down from the mountain. The *congregation* was an organized body and thus could mean all of Israel (Num. 16:3; Mic. 2:5). In Ezra the *congregation* is the restored community (Ezra 10:12), and in Ps. the *assembly* is a company of angels (Ps. 89:5). (Strong's #6951)

Assembly—*a large gathering for official business*
A. Descriptive of:
Israel as a people....................Num. 10:2–8
Israel as a nation.......Judg. 20:1, 2; 2 Chr. 30:23
God's elect people .... Ps. 111:1
A civil court.....................Acts 19:32–41
A church gathering ....James 2:2–4
B. Purposes of:
Proclaim war.......Judg. 10:17, 18; 1 Sam. 14:20
Establish the ark in Zion ....1 Kin. 8:1–6
Institute reforms........Ezra 9:4–15; Neh. 9:1, 2
Celebrate victory ....Esth. 9:17, 18
Condemn Christ...............Matt. 26:3, 4, 57
Worship God.............. Acts 4:31; Heb. 10:25
C. Significant ones, at:
Sinai........................... Ex. 19:1–19
Joshua's farewell..........Josh. 23:1–16; 24:1–28
David's coronation................. 2 Sam. 5:1–3
The temple's dedication ....2 Chr. 5:1–14
Josiah's reformation........2 Kin. 23:1–3, 21–23
Ezra's reading the Law...............Neh. 8:1–18
Jesus' trial......................Matt. 27:11–26
Pentecost ....Acts 2:1–21
The Jerusalem Council............. Acts 15:5–21

Assent—*agreeing to the truth of a statement or fact*
A. Concerning good things:
Accepting God's covenant.............Ex. 19:7, 8
Agreeing to reforms1 Sam. 7:3, 4; Ezra 10:1–12, 19
Accepting a scriptural decision.....Acts 15:13–22
Receiving Christ as Savior........ Rom. 10:9, 10
B. Concerning evil things:
Tolerating idolatry.................Jer. 44:15–19
Condemning Christ to death ..... Matt. 27:17–25
Putting Stephen to death ....Acts 7:51–60
Refusing to hear the gospel ....Acts 13:44–51

Asshur—*level plain*
1. One of the sons of Shem; progenitor
of the Assyrians .... Gen. 10:22; 1 Chr. 1:17
2. The chief god of the Assyrians; seen in names
like Ashurbanipal (Osnapper) ....Ezra 4:10
3. A city in Assyria or the nation of
Assyria ....Num. 24:22, 24

Asshurim—*mighty ones*
Descendants of Abraham by Keturah... Gen. 25:3

Assir—*prisoner*
1. A son of Korah .... Ex. 6:24; 1 Chr. 6:22

2. A son of Ebiasaph.................1 Chr. 6:23, 37
3. A son of King Jeconiah................ 1 Chr. 3:17

Assistance, divine
A. Offered, in:
Battle........................... 2 Chr. 20:5–17
Trouble ....Ps. 50:15
Crises............................Luke 21:14, 15
Prayer ....Rom. 8:16–27
Testimony.......................... 2 Tim. 4:17
Wisdom ....James 1:5–8
B. Given:
Internally .... Phil. 2:13; Heb. 13:21
By God .... 2 Cor. 8:9; 1 John 4:9, 10
By Christ........................... Phil. 4:13
By the Spirit...................... Zech. 4:6
By God's Word ....1 Thess. 2:13
By grace........................... 1 Cor. 15:10
By prayer........................James 5:15–18
By trusting God ....Ps. 37:3–7
By God's providence ....Rom. 8:28

Association—*joining together for mutually beneficial purposes*
A. Among believers, hindered by:
Sin................................. Acts 5:1–11
Friction............................ Acts 6:1–6
Inconsistency...................... Gal. 2:11–14
Disagreement .... Acts 15:36–40
Selfishness .... 3 John 9–11
Ambition .... Matt. 20:20–24
Error .... 2 John 7–11
Partiality.............................James 2:1–5
B. Among believers, helped by:
Common faith....................Acts 2:42–47
Mutual helpfulness .... Gal. 6:1–5
United prayer.................... Matt. 18:19, 20
Impending dangers ....Neh. 4:1–23
Grateful praise ....Acts 4:23–33
See Alliance with evil; Fellowship

Assos—*a seaport of Mysia in Asia Minor*
Paul walks to, from Troas......... Acts 20:13, 14

Assurance—*the security of knowing that one's name is written in heaven*
A. Objects of, one's:
Election............................. 1 Thess. 1:4
Adoption...................... Eph. 1:4, 5
Union with Christ .... 1 Cor. 6:15
Possession of eternal life.............. John 5:24;
1 John 5:13
Peace ....Rom. 5:1
B. Steps in:
Believing God's Word.............. 1 Thess. 2:13
Accepting Christ as Savior........ Rom. 10:9, 10
Standing upon the promises ...... John 10:28–30
Desiring spiritual things ....1 Pet. 2:2
Growing in grace .... 2 Pet. 1:5–11
Knowing life is changed.............2 Cor. 5:17;
1 John 3:14–22

Having inner peace and joy . . . . Rom. 15:12, 13; Phil. 4:7

Victorious living. . . . . 1 John 5:4, 5

The Spirit's testimony. . . . . Rom. 8:15, 16

Absolute assurance . . . Rom. 8:33–39; 2 Tim. 1:12

C. Compatible with:

A nature still subject to sin. . . . . 1 John 1:8–10; 2:1

Imperfection of life . . . . Gal. 6:1

Limited knowledge . . . . 1 Cor. 13:9–12

Fatherly chastisement . . . . Heb. 12:5–11

> **WORD STUDY**
>
> **ASSUREDLY,** *amēn* (ahm-*ayn*). This is the transliteration of a Hebrew word (*'āmēn*) into Greek. It echoes the liturgical formula spoken by the congregation in worship and functions as an exclamation of affirmation in response to prayer (Matt. 6:13), to doxologies (Rom. 1:25; Gal. 1:5; 1 Pet. 4:11; Rev. 7:12), and to blessings (Gal. 6:18; Rev. 22:21); in these cases it is best translated as "so be it" or "let it be so." Jesus often prefaces a solemn teaching with "Amen, I say to you," thereby stressing the importance and truthfulness of His words (Mark 3:28). In these instances "amen" can be translated as "truly" or "assuredly." (Strong's #281)

Assyria—*the nation ruled from Asshur (first) and Nineveh (later)*

A. Significant facts regarding:

Of remote antiquity. . . . . Gen. 2:14

Of Shem's ancestry. . . . . Gen. 10:22

Founded by Nimrod . . . . . . Gen. 10:8–12; Mic. 5:6

Nineveh, principal city of. . . . . Gen. 10:11

Hiddekel (Tigris) River flows through . . . Gen. 2:14

Proud nation . . . . Is. 10:5–15

A cruel military power . . . . Nah. 3:1–19

Agent of God's purposes . . . . . . Is. 7:17–20; 10:5, 6

B. Contacts of, with Israel:

Pul (Tiglath-Pileser III, 745–727 B.C.)

captures Damascus. . . . . Is. 8:4

Puts Menahem under tribute . . . . . 2 Kin. 15:19, 20

Occasions Isaiah's prophecy . . . . Is. 7; 8

Puts Pekah under tribute . . . . 2 Kin. 15:29

Shalmaneser (727–722 B.C.) besieges

Samaria . . . . 2 Kin. 17:3–5

Sargon II (722–705 B.C.) captures

Israel. . . . . 2 Kin. 17:6–41

C. Contacts of, with Judah:

Sargon's general takes Ashdod

(in Philistia) . . . . Is. 20:1–6

Sennacherib (704–681 B.C.) invades

Judah . . . . 2 Kin. 18:13

Puts Hezekiah under tribute. . . . . 2 Kin. 18:14–16

Threatens Hezekiah through

Rabshakeh. . . . . 2 Kin. 18:17–37

Army of, miraculously slain. . . . . 2 Kin. 19:35

D. Prophecies concerning:

Destruction of, anciently

foretold. . . . . Num. 24:22–24

Israel captive in land of. . . . . Hos. 10:6; 11:5

Doom of, mentioned . . . . . . Is. 10:12, 19; 14:24, 25

End eulogized . . . . Nah. 3:1–19

Shares, figuratively,

in gospel blessings . . . . Is. 19:23–25

Astonishment—*an emotion of perplexed amazement*

A. Caused by:

God's judgments. . . . . 1 Kin. 9:8, 9; Jer. 18:16

Racial intermarriage . . . . Ezra 9:2–4

Urgent message. . . . . Ezek. 3:14, 15

A miracle . . . . Dan. 3:24

An unexplained vision . . . . Dan. 8:27

Christ's knowledge. . . . . Luke 2:47

Christ's teaching. . . . . Luke 4:32

Christ's miracles. . . . . Mark 5:42; Luke 5:9

Gentile conversions . . . . Acts 10:45

Miracles . . . . Acts 12:5–7, 13–16; 13:6–12

B. Applied figuratively to:

God . . . . Jer. 14:9

Babylon. . . . . Jer. 51:37, 41

Jerusalem . . . . Ezek. 5:5, 15

Priests . . . . Jer. 4:9

Astrologers—*those who search the heavens for supposed revelations*

Cannot save Babylon . . . . Is. 47:1, 12–15

Cannot interpret dreams . . . . Dan. 2:2, 10–13; 4:7

Cannot decipher handwriting. . . . . Dan. 5:7, 8

Daniel surpasses. Dan. 1:20

Daniel made master of . . . . Dan. 5:11

God does not speak through . . . . Dan. 2:27, 28

Asylum—*protection, refuge*

Afforded by altar . . . . 1 Kin. 1:50–53; 2:28

Cities of refuge . . . . . . Ex. 21:12–14; Deut. 19:1–13

Asyncritus—*incomparable*

A Christian at Rome . . . . Rom. 16:14

Atad—*thorn*

A mourning site east of Jordan . . . . . Gen. 50:9–13

Atarah—*crown*

A wife of Jerahmeel . . . . 1 Chr. 2:26

Ataroth—*crowns*

1. Town of Gad . . . . Num. 32:3, 34

2. A town of Ephraim . . . . Josh. 16:7

3. A town between Ephraim

and Benjamin . . . . Josh. 16:2

Probably the same as Ataroth

Addar . . . . Josh. 16:5; 18:13

4. A village near Bethlehem. . . . . 1 Chr. 2:54

Ataroth Addar—*crowns of Addar*

A frontier town of Ephraim. . . . . Josh. 16:5

See Ataroth 3

Ater—*crippled one*

1. The ancestor of a family of returnees. . . . Ezra 2:16; Neh. 7:21

2. The ancestor of a family of gatekeepers. . Ezra 2:42; Neh. 7:45

3. A signer of Nehemiah's document. . . . . . Neh. 10:17

Athach—*lodging, inn*

A town in south Judah. . . . . 1 Sam. 30:30

Athaiah—*Yahweh is helper*

    A Judahite in Nehemiah's time......... Neh. 11:4

Athaliah—*Yahweh is exalted*

1. The daughter of Ahab
    and Jezebel....... 2 Kin. 8:18, 26; 2 Chr. 22:2, 3
    Wife of King Jehoram................2 Kin. 8:18
    Mother of King Ahaziah ....2 Kin. 8:26
    Destroys all the royal seed
        except Joash ... 2 Kin. 11:1, 2; 2 Chr. 22:10, 11
    Usurps throne for six years ....2 Kin. 11:3
    Killed by priestly uprising ....2 Kin. 11:4–16;
       2 Chr. 23:1–21
    Called wicked ....2 Chr. 24:7
2. A Benjamite.......................1 Chr. 8:26, 27
3. The father of Jeshaiah .... Ezra 8:7

Atharim—*spies*

    Israel attacked there .... Num. 21:1

Atheism—*the denial of God's existence*

A. Defined as:
    The fool's philosophy .... Ps. 14:1; 53:1
    Living without God..... Rom. 1:20–32; Eph. 2:12
B. Manifestations of, seen in:
    Defiance of God........Ex. 5:2; 2 Kin. 18:19–35
    Irreligion............................Titus 1:16
    Corrupt morals........ Rom. 13:12, 13; 1 Pet. 4:3
C. Evidences against, seen in:
    Human inner conscience .... Rom. 2:14, 15
    Design in nature........... Job 38:1–41; 39:1–30
    God's works...........................Ps. 19:1–6
    God's providence ....Ps. 104:1–35; Acts 14:17
    Clear evidence.................... Rom. 1:19, 20
    The testimony of pagans .... Dan. 4:24–37
    Fulfillment of prophecy ....Is. 41:20–23;
       46:8–11

Athens—*a Greek city named after the goddess Athena*

    Paul preaches in .... Acts 17:15–34
    Paul resides in .... 1 Thess. 3:1

Athlai—*Yahweh is strong*

    One who divorced his foreign wife .... Ezra 10:28

Athletes

    Discipline...................... 1 Cor. 9:24–27
    Removal of weights .... Heb. 12:1
    Prize................................. Phil. 3:14

WORD STUDY

ATONE, *kaphar* (kaw-*fawr*). *Kaphar* is a verb used in the OT to mean "cover" or "atone." Usually the act that covers uncleanness, including sin, is an offering. The word appears frequently in the legal codes describing rites to bring atonement. In Lev. there is a ceremony by which the sins of the people were transferred to a scapegoat. The goat was then released to take the sins away (Lev. 16:9, 10). There is also atonement or covering of sin without the sacrifice, as in Deut. 32:43. At these times, God provides what humans cannot do for themselves (Ps. 65:3; 78:38). (Strong's #3722)

Atonement—*reconciliation of the guilty by divine sacrifice*

A. Elements involved in, seen in:
    Human sin .... Ex. 32:30; Ps. 51:3, 4
    The blood sacrificed ..... Lev. 16:11, 14–20; Heb.
       9:13–22
    Guilt transferred......... Lev. 1:3, 4; 2 Cor. 5:21
    Guilt removed.............Lev. 16:21; 1 Cor. 6:11
    Forgiveness granted.....Lev. 5:10, 11; Rom. 4:6, 7
    Righteousness given ...... Rom. 10:3, 4; Phil. 3:9
B. Fulfilled by Christ:
    Predicted ....Is. 53:10–12; Dan. 9:24–26
    Symbolized...............Is. 63:1–9; Zech. 3:3–9
    Realized ....Rom. 3:23–26; 1 Pet. 1:18–21

Atonement, Day of

A. Features regarding:
    Time specified.................... Lev. 23:26, 27
    The ritual involved in .... Lev. 16:3, 5–15
    A time of humiliation .... Lev. 16:29, 31
    Exclusive ministry of the high
       priest in .... Lev. 16:2, 3; Heb. 9:7
B. Benefits of, for:
    The Holy Place ....Lev. 16:15, 16
    The people ....Lev. 16:17, 24
    The high priest ....Lev. 16:11; Heb. 9:7
C. Result of, seen in:
    Atonement for sin.................Rom. 3:24–26
    Removal of sin........... Heb. 9:7–28; 13:10–13

Atonement of Christ

A. Typified by:
    The paschal lamb ..... Ex. 12:5, 11, 14; John 1:29;
       1 Cor. 5:7
    The Day of Atonement............Lev. 16:30, 34;
       Heb. 9:7–28
B. What human is:
    A sinner...........................Rom. 5:8
    Alienated in mind ....Col. 1:21
    Strangers............................ Eph. 2:12
C. What God does:
    Loves us............................. John 3:16
    Demonstrates His love toward us........Rom. 5:8
    Sends Christ to save us ....Gal. 4:4, 5
    Spared not His own Son ....Rom. 8:32
D. What Christ does:
    Becomes a man .... Heb. 2:14
    Becomes our ransom .... Matt. 20:28
    Dies in our place....................1 Pet. 3:18
    Dies for our sins .... 1 Pet. 2:24
    Dies as a sacrifice .... Eph. 5:2
    Dies willingly...................... John 10:18
    Reconciles us to God................Rom. 5:10
    Brings us to God......................1 Pet. 3:18
    Restores our fellowship............. 1 Thess. 5:10
    See Blood of Christ
E. What the believer receives:
    Forgiveness...........................Eph. 1:7
    Peace ....Rom. 5:1
    Reconciliation...................... 2 Cor. 5:19
    Righteousness .... 2 Cor. 5:21

Justification . . . . Rom. 3:24–26
Access to God . . . . Eph. 2:18
Cleansing . . . . 1 John 1:7
Liberty. . . . . Gal. 5:1
Freedom from the devil's power . . . . Heb. 2:14
Christ's intercession. . . . . Heb. 2:17, 18

Atroth Beth Joab
A village near Bethlehem . . . . 1 Chr. 2:54

Atroth Shophan
A city built by the Gadites . . . . Num. 32:34, 35

Attai—*timely*
1. A half-Egyptian Judahite . . . . 1 Chr. 2:35, 36
2. A Gadite in David's army . . . . 1 Chr. 12:11
3. Rehoboam's son . . . . 2 Chr. 11:18–20

Attalia—*a seaport town of Pamphylia named after*
Attalus II
Paul sails from, to Antioch . . . . Acts 14:25, 26

Attend
To care for . . . . Esth. 4:5

Attendance, church
Taught by example . . . . Acts 11:25, 26;
14:19, 20, 26, 27
Not to be neglected . . . . Heb. 10:25

Attitude—*the state of mind toward something*
A. Of Christians toward Christ, must:
Confess . . . . Rom. 10:9, 10
Obey . . . . John 14:15, 23
Follow . . . . Matt. 16:24
Imitate. . . . . 1 Pet. 2:21
B. Of Christians toward the world, not to:
Conform to . . . . Rom. 12:2
Abuse. . . . . 1 Cor. 7:29–31
Love . . . . 1 John 2:15
Be friend of. . . . . James 4:4
Be entangled with. . . . . 2 Tim. 2:4
Be defiled with . . . . Jude 23
C. Of Christians toward sinners:
Seek their salvation . . . . 1 Cor. 9:22
Pray for . . . . Rom. 9:1–3
Plead with. . . . . Acts 17:22–31
Rebuke . . . . Titus 1:10–13
Persuade . . . . 2 Cor. 5:11

Audience—*an assembly of hearers*
Disturbed . . . . Neh. 13:1–3
Attentive. . . . . Luke 7:1
Hostile. . . . . Luke 4:28–30
Receptive . . . . Acts 2:1–41
Menacing . . . . Acts 7:54–60
Rejecting. . . . . Acts 13:44–51
Critical . . . . Acts 17:22–34
Sympathetic. . . . . Acts 20:17–38
Vast . . . . Rev. 5:9; 7:9, 10
See Assembly

Auditorium—*a room for assembly*
Hearing. . . . . Acts 25:23

Augustus's regiment—*a battalion of Roman soldiers*
Paul placed in custody of . . . . Acts 27:1

Author—*creator; originator; writer*
God of peace . . . . 1 Cor. 14:33
Christ of salvation . . . . Heb. 5:9
Christ of faith . . . . Heb. 12:2
Solomon of many proverbs and songs. . . 1 Kin. 4:32

Authority—*the lawful right to enforce obedience, power*
A. As rulers:
Governor . . . . Matt. 10:18; Acts 23:24, 26
B. Delegated to, man as:
Created . . . . Gen. 1:26–31
A legal state . . . . Esth. 9:29; Luke 22:25
Agent of the state . . . . Matt. 8:9; Rom. 13:1–6
Husband. . . . . 1 Cor. 14:35
Agent of religious leaders . . . . Acts 26:10, 12
C. Christ's, seen in His power:
Over demons . . . . Mark 1:27
In teaching. . . . . Matt. 7:29
To forgive . . . . Luke 5:24
To judge . . . . John 5:22, 27
To rule . . . . Matt. 2:6; 1 Cor. 15:24; 1 Pet. 3:22
To commission . . . . Matt. 28:18–20
D. Purpose:
Protection. . . . . Heb. 13:17
Instruction. . . . . 1 Pet. 5:2, 3
Example of Christ's power . . . . Matt. 8:5–13
Testimony to unbelievers . . . . 1 Tim. 6:1;
1 Pet. 3:13–15
E. Of Christians, given to:
Apostles . . . . 2 Cor. 10:8
Ministers . . . . Titus 2:15
The righteous . . . . Prov. 29:2

Ava—*a region or city in Assyria*
Colonists from, brought to Samaria by
Sargon. . . . . 2 Kin. 17:24
Worshipers of Nibhaz and Tartak . . . . 2 Kin. 17:31

Avarice—*covetousness; greed*
A. Productive of:
Defeat . . . . Josh. 7:11, 21
Death. . . . . 1 Kin. 21:5–16
Discontent . . . . James 4:1–4
B. Examples of:
Balaam . . . . 2 Pet. 2:15
Achan . . . . Josh. 7:20, 21
Ahab . . . . 1 Kin. 21:1–4
Judas Iscariot. Matt. 26:14–16
Ananias and Sapphira . . . . Acts 5:1–10
Rich men. . . . . Luke 12:16–21; James 5:1–6

Aven—*wickedness*
1. The city of On in Egypt near Cairo;
known as Heliopolis . . . . Gen. 41:45; Ezek. 30:17
2. A name contemptuously applied to
Bethel . . . . Hos. 10:5, 8
3. Valley in Syria . . . . Amos 1:5

Avenge—*to retaliate for an evil done*
A. Examples of:
    Commanded by God.............. Num. 31:1, 2
    Given strength for ....Judg. 16:28–30
    Sought maliciously............... 1 Sam. 18:25
    Possible but not done.............. 1 Sam. 24:12
    Attempted but hindered........1 Sam. 25:26–33
    Obtained in self-defense...........Esth. 8:12, 13
B. Sought because of:
    A murdered neighbor .....Num. 35:12; Josh. 20:5
    A wife's mistreatment............. Judg. 15:6–8
    Judah's sins............................Jer. 5:9
    Mistreatment................... Acts 7:24, 25
    Impurity......................1 Thess. 4:5–7
C. Performed by:
    God Himself .... Lev. 26:25; Luke 18:7, 8
    Wicked people.................2 Sam. 4:8–12
    Impetuous general.......... 2 Sam. 18:18, 19, 31
    An anointed king ....2 Kin. 9:6, 7
    A judge ....Luke 18:3, 5
    God ....Rev. 19:2
D. Restrictions on:
    Personal, prohibited................Lev. 19:17, 18
    Christians prohibited ....Rom. 12:19

Avenger of blood (literally, "redeemer of blood")
    An ancient practice .... Gen. 4:14
    Seen also in kinsman as "avenger" of
        a murdered relative..........Num. 35:11–34
    Avenger alone must kill
        murderer ....Deut. 19:6, 11–13
    Practice of, set aside by David.....2 Sam. 14:4–11
    Figurative of a violent person .... Ps. 8:2

Avim, Avims, Avites—*villagers*
1. A tribe of early Canaanites living near Gaza;
    absorbed by the Caphtorim
    (Philistines)........................Deut. 2:23
2. A city of Benjamin near Bethel........ Josh. 18:23
3. Colonists brought from Ava in
    Assyria ....2 Kin. 17:24, 31

Avith—*ruin*
    An Edomite city ....Gen. 36:35

Awakening, spiritual
A. Produced by:
    Returning to Bethel.................Gen. 35:1–7
    Discovering God's Word .... 2 Kin. 22:8–13
    Reading God's Word...............Neh. 8:2–18
    Confessing sin.....................Ezra 10:1–17
    Receiving the Spirit .... John 7:38, 39;
        Acts 2:1–47
B. Old Testament examples of, under:
    Joshua ....Josh. 24:1–31
    Samuel...........................1 Sam. 7:3–6
    Elijah .... 1 Kin. 18:21–40
    Hezekiah .... 2 Chr. 30:1–27; 31:1
    Josiah........................ 2 Kin. 23:1–25
    Ezra .... Ezra 10:1–17
C. New Testament examples of:
    John the Baptist ....Luke 3:2–14

Jesus in Samaria .... John 4:28–42
Philip in Samaria .... Acts 8:5–12
Peter at Lydda .... Acts 9:32–35
Peter with Cornelius .... Acts 10:34–48
Paul at Antioch in Pisidia.........Acts 13:14–52
Paul at Thessalonica ....Acts 17:11, 12;
    1 Thess. 1:1–10
Paul at Corinth .... 2 Cor. 7:1–16

Awe—*fear mingled with reverence*
    Proper attitude toward God .... Ps. 33:8
    Also toward God's Word ....Ps. 119:161

Awl—*a sharp tool for piercing*
    Used on the ear as a symbol of
        perpetual obedience .....Ex. 21:6; Deut. 15:17

Ax—*a sharp instrument for cutting wood*
A. Used in:
    Cutting timber ....Judg. 9:48
    War ....1 Chr. 20:3
    Malicious destruction.................Ps. 74:5–7
    A miracle; floated in water...........2 Kin. 6:5, 6
B. As a figure of:
    Judgment ....Matt. 3:10
    God's sovereignty..................... Is. 10:15

Ayin
    Sixteenth letter of the Hebrew
        alphabet.................... Ps. 119:121–128

Ayyah
    Ephraimite town.....................1 Chr. 7:28

Azal, Azel
1. A descendant of Jonathan .... 1 Chr. 8:37, 38
2. A place near Jerusalem ....Zech. 14:5

Azaliah—*Yahweh has set aside*
    Father of Shaphan ....2 Kin. 22:3

Azaniah—*Yahweh has heard*
    A Levite who signs the document ...... Neh. 10:9

Azarel, Azareel—*God has helped*
1. A Levite in David's army at Ziklag ..... 1 Chr. 12:6
2. A musician in David's time .... 1 Chr. 25:18
3. A prince of Dan under David .... 1 Chr. 27:22
4. A Jew who divorced his foreign wife.....Ezra 10:41
5. A postexilic priest ....Neh. 11:13
6. A musician in dedication service....... Neh. 12:36

Azariah—*Yahweh has helped*
1. Man of Judah........................ 1 Chr. 2:8
2. A Kohathite Levite .... 1 Chr. 6:36
3. A son of Zadok the high priest .... 1 Kin. 4:2
4. A son of Ahimaaz.................... 1 Chr. 6:9
5. A great-grandson of Ahimaaz........ 1 Chr. 6:9, 10
6. Son of Nathan....................... 1 Kin. 4:5
7. A son of Jehu, with Egyptian
    ancestry ....1 Chr. 2:34–38
8. A prophet who encourages King Asa... 2 Chr. 15:1–8
9. Son of King Jehoshaphat .... 2 Chr. 21:2
10. A captain under Jehoiada .... 2 Chr. 23:1
11. Another under Jehoiada.............. 2 Chr. 23:1
12. A head of Ephraim .... 2 Chr. 28:12

13. King of Judah . . . . .2 Kin. 15:1
14. A high priest who rebukes
    King Uzziah . . . . .2 Chr. 26:16–20
15. Kohathite, father of Joel. . . . . 2 Chr. 29:12
16. A reforming Levite . . . . 2 Chr. 29:12
17. Chief priest in time of Hezekiah . . . 2 Chr. 31:9, 10
18. A high priest, son of Hilkiah . . . . . . 1 Chr. 6:13, 14
19. Ancestor of Ezra. Ezra 7:1–3
20. An opponent of Jeremiah . . . . .Jer. 43:2
21. The Hebrew name of Abed-Nego . . . . .Dan. 1:7
22. Postexilic Jew . . . . .Neh. 7:6, 7
23. A workman under Nehemiah. . . . . . . Neh. 3:23, 24
24. A prince of Judah. . . . . Neh. 12:32, 33
25. An expounder of the Law . . . . .Neh. 8:7
26. A signer of the covenant . . . . .Neh. 10:1, 2
27. A descendant of Hilkiah . . . . 1 Chr. 9:11

Azaz—*strong*
    A Reubenite. . . . . 1 Chr. 5:8

Azaziah—*Yahweh is strong*
1. A musician. . . . . 1 Chr. 15:21
2. Father of Hoshea . . . . 1 Chr. 27:20
3. A temple overseer. . . . . 2 Chr. 31:13

Azbuk—*pardon*
    Father of a certain Nehemiah; but not the
        celebrated one. Neh. 3:16

Azekah—*tilled*
    Great stones cast upon . . . . .Josh. 10:11
    Camp of Goliath. . . . . 1 Sam. 17:1, 4, 17
    Fortified by Rehoboam. . . . . .2 Chr. 11:5, 9
    Reoccupied after exile. . . . . Neh. 11:30
    Besieged by Nebuchadnezzar . . . . Jer. 34:7

Azgad—*fate is hard*
    Head of exile family. . . . . Ezra 2:12; 8:12
    Among document signers. . . . . Neh. 10:15

Aziel—*God strengthens*
    A Levite musician. . . . . .1 Chr. 15:20
    Called Jaaziel. . . . . 1 Chr. 15:18

Aziza—*strong*
    Divorced foreign wife . . . . Ezra 10:27

Azmaveth—*death is strong*
1. One of David's mighty men. . . . . .2 Sam. 23:31
2. A Benjamite. . . . . 1 Chr. 12:3
3. David's treasurer . . . . 1 Chr. 27:25
4. A son of Jehoaddah . . . . 1 Chr. 8:36
5. A village near Jerusalem. . . . . Neh. 12:29
    Also called Beth Azmaveth . . . . Neh. 7:28

Azmon—*strong*
    A place in south Canaan. . . . . .Num. 34:4, 5

Aznoth Tabor—*peaks of Tabor*
    Place in Naphtali . . . . .Josh. 19:34

Azor—*helper*
    Ancestor of Christ . . . . Matt. 1:13, 14

Azotus—*fortress*
    Philip went there . . . . Acts 8:40
    Same as Ashdod . . . . .1 Sam. 6:17

Azriel—*God is a help*
1. A chief of Manasseh . . . . 1 Chr. 5:24
2. Father of Jerimoth. . . . . 1 Chr. 27:19
3. Father of Seraiah . . . . .Jer. 36:26

Azrikam—*my help has arisen*
1. Son of Neariah . . . . 1 Chr. 3:23
2. A son of Azel. . . . . 1 Chr. 8:38
3. A Merarite Levite. . . . . 1 Chr. 9:14
4. Official under King Ahaz . . . . 2 Chr. 28:7

Azubah—*forsaken*
1. Wife of Caleb . . . . 1 Chr. 2:18, 19
2. Mother of Jehoshaphat. . . . . 1 Kin. 22:42

Azur, Azzur—*helpful*
1. Father of Hananiah. . . . . .Jer. 28:1
2. Father of Jaazaniah . . . . Ezek. 11:1
3. A covenant signer. . . . . .Neh. 10:17

Azzan—*strong*
    Father of Paltiel . . . . Num. 34:26

B

WORD STUDY   **BAAL,** *ba'al* (baw-*awl*). *Ba'al* means "master," "husband," "owner," or "lord." The word at its most basic means "the owner of something," such as the ox's owner, who is responsible for damages by the ox (Ex. 21:28). The word can also mean "husband" as it does in Gen. 20:3 and Ex. 21:22, as well as in many other places. Specifically, the word is used as the name of one the deities of Israel's neighbors. The name is often used in compound form as in *Baal-Peor,* a Moabite deity; *Baal-Berith,* a Shechemite deity; and *Baal-Zebub,* the god of Ekron. In Hosea the word is used with the dual meaning of "master" and "foreign god," when God says that Israel chased after her Baals. (Strong's #1168)

Baal—*lord, possessor, husband*
A. The nature of:
    The male god of the Phoenicians and Canaanites;
        the counterpart of the female
        Ashtaroth . . . . .2 Kin. 23:5
    Connected with immorality . . . . . Num. 25:1, 3, 5;
        Hos. 9:10
    Incense burned to. .Jer. 7:9
    Kissing the image of . . . . 1 Kin. 19:18;
        Hos. 13:1, 2
    Dervish rites by priests of. . . . . 1 Kin. 18:26, 28
    Children burned in fire of . . . . .Jer. 19:5
    Eating sacrifices .Ps. 106:28
B. History of:
    Among Moabites in Moses' time . . . . . Num. 22:41
    Altars built to, during time of
        judges . . . . .Judg. 2:11–14; 6:28–32
    Overthrown by Gideon. . . . . Judg. 6:25, 27
    Jezebel introduces into Israel . . . . .1 Kin. 16:31, 32
    Elijah's overthrow of,
        on Mt. Carmel . . . . 1 Kin. 18:17–40

Athaliah encourages it
    into Judah .... 2 Kin. 11:14–20; 2 Chr. 22:2–4
Revived again in Israel and Judah ...... Hos. 2:8;
    Amos 5:26
Manasseh worships .... 2 Kin. 21:3
Altars everywhere .... Jer. 11:13
Overthrown by Josiah............. 2 Kin. 23:4, 5
Denounced by prophets .... Jer. 19:4–6;
    Ezek. 16:1, 2, 20, 21
Historic retrospect................... Rom. 11:4

Baal—*master; possessor*
1. A Benjamite, from Gibeon............. 1 Chr. 8:30
2. A descendant of Reuben .... 1 Chr. 5:5, 6
3. A village of Simeon .... 1 Chr. 4:33
    Also called Baalath Beer.............. Josh. 19:8

Baalah—*mistress*
1. A town also known as
    Kirjath Jearim................... Josh. 15:9, 10
2. A hill in Judah......................... Josh. 15:11
3. A town in south Judah .... Josh. 15:29
    Probably the same as Bilhah .... 1 Chr. 4:29
    May be the same as Balah............. Josh. 19:3

Baalath—*mistress*
    A village of Dan .... Josh. 19:44
    Fortified by Solomon................. 1 Kin. 9:18

Baalath Beer—*mistress of the well*
    A border town of Simeon .... Josh. 19:8
    Called Ramah of the South .... Josh. 19:8
    Also called Baal..................... 1 Chr. 4:33

Baal-Berith—*lord of covenant*
    A god (Baal) of Shechem.......... Judg. 8:33; 9:4
    Also called Berith.................... Judg. 9:46

Baale Judah
    A town of Judah .... 2 Sam. 6:2
    Also called Baalah and
    Kirjath Jearim .... Josh. 15:9, 10

Baal Gad—*lord of good fortune*
    A place in the valley of Lebanon....... Josh. 11:17

Baal Hamon—*lord of a multitude*
    Site of Solomon's vineyard........... Song 8:11

Baal-Hanan—*lord of grace*
1. Edomite king........................ Gen. 36:38
2. David's gardener .... 1 Chr. 27:28

Baal Hazor—*lord of a village*
    A place near Ephraim .... 2 Sam. 13:23

Baal Hermon—*lord of Hermon*
    A mountain east of Jordan............. Judg. 3:3

Baals—*lords (plural of Baal)*
    Deities of Canaanite polytheism... Judg. 10:10–14
    Ensnared Israelites............. Judg. 2:11–14; 3:7
    Rejected in Samuel's time.............. 1 Sam. 7:4
    Historic reminder.................. 1 Sam. 12:10
    Ahaz makes images to............. 2 Chr. 28:1–4

Baalis
    An Ammonite king .... Jer. 40:14

Baal Meon—*lord of Meon (habitation)*
    An Amorite city on the Moabite
    boundary......................... Ezek. 25:9
    Rebuilt by Reubenites............. Num. 32:38;
    Josh. 13:15, 17

Baal Peor, Baal of Peor—*lord of Peor*
    A Moabite god..................... Num. 25:1–5
    Infected Israel; 24,000 died........ Num. 25:1–9
    Vengeance taken on.............. Num. 31:1–18
    Sin long remembered................ Deut. 4:3, 4;
    Josh. 22:17; Ps. 106:28, 29
    Historic reminder................... 1 Cor. 10:1–8

Baal Perazim—*lord of breaking through*
    Where David defeated the
    Philistines .... 2 Sam. 5:18–20
    Same as Perazim....................... Is. 28:21

Baal Shalisha—*lord of Shalisha*
    A place from which Elisha received
    food......................... 2 Kin. 4:42–44

Baal Tamar—*lord of the palm*
    A place in Benjamin.................. Judg. 20:33

Baal-Zebub—*lord of flies*
    A Philistine god at Ekron.............. 2 Kin. 1:2
    Ahaziah inquired of.............. 2 Kin. 1:2, 6, 16
    Also called Beelzebub .... Matt. 10:25; 12:24

Baal Zephon—*lord of darkness*
    Israelite campsite .... Ex. 14:2, 9; Num. 33:7

Baana—*affliction*
1. Supply officer .... 1 Kin. 4:12
2. Zadok's father........................ Neh. 3:4

Baanah—*affliction*
1. A murderer of Ishbosheth .... 2 Sam. 4:1–12
2. Heled's father .... 1 Chr. 11:30
3. A returning exile .... Ezra 2:2; Neh. 7:7
    Signs document...................... Neh. 10:27
4. Supply officer .... 1 Kin. 4:16

Baara—*foolish*
    Shaharaim's wife...................... 1 Chr. 8:8

Baaseiah—*work of Yahweh*
    A Levite ancestor of Asaph .... 1 Chr. 6:40

Baasha—*boldness*
    Gains throne by murder.......... 1 Kin. 15:27, 28
    Kills Jeroboam's household ...... 1 Kin. 15:29, 30
    Wars against Asa .... 1 Kin. 15:16, 32
    Restricts access to Judah .... 1 Kin. 15:17
    Contravened by Asa's league with
    Ben-Hadad .... 1 Kin. 15:18–22
    Evil reign...................... 1 Kin. 15:33, 34
    Jehu's prophecy concerning........ 1 Kin. 16:1–7

WORD STUDY **BABBLER,** *spermologos* (sper-mol-*og*-oss). This adjective literally means "picking up seeds" and is commonly used as a substantive to refer to a type of bird (for example, a crow). As a figurative description of a person, *spermologos* refers to "one who picks up scraps" of information, hence a "babbler," "chatterer," "gossip." The philosophers in Athens, who subscribe to a unified system of thought (Epicureanism or Stoicism), disdain Paul as a pseudointellectual—"one who picks up scraps" from various philosophical systems; thus, they insult him with the term "babbler" (Acts 17:18). (Strong's #4691)

Babbler—*an inane talker*

The mumblings of drunkards..... Prov. 23:29–35
Like a serpent .... Eccl. 10:11
Paul called such...................... Acts 17:18
Paul's warnings against ....1 Tim. 6:20;
   2 Tim. 2:16

Babe, Baby—*an infant child*
A. Natural:
Moses................................Ex. 2:6
John Baptist......................Luke 1:41, 44
Christ.............................Luke 2:12, 16
B. Figurative of:
Unenlightened .... Rom. 2:20
True believers .... Matt. 11:25; 21:16
New Christians......................1 Pet. 2:2
Carnal Christians.......... 1 Cor. 3:1; Heb. 5:13

Babel—*confusion*
A city built by Nimrod in the plain of
   Shinar........................Gen. 10:8–10

Babel, Tower of
A huge brick structure intended to magnify
   humankind and preserve the unity of
   the race.........................Gen. 11:1–4
Objectives thwarted by God ....Gen. 11:5–9

Babel; Babylon, city of
A. History of:
Built by Nimrod ....Gen. 10:8–10
Tower built in Babel................. Gen. 11:1–9
Occupied by Assyrians in Manasseh's
   time...........................2 Chr. 33:11
Greatest power under
   Nebuchadnezzar .... Dan. 4:30
A magnificent city .... Is. 13:19; 14:4
Wide walls of......................... Jer. 51:44
Gates of........................... Is. 45:1, 2
Bel, god of............................. Is. 46:1
Jews carried captive to........... 2 Kin. 25:1–21;
   2 Chr. 36:5–21
B. Inhabitants, described as:
Enslaved by magic ....Is. 47:1, 9–13
Idolatrous..............Jer. 50:35, 38; Dan. 3:18
Sacrilegious ....Dan. 5:1–3
C. Prophecies concerning:
Babylon, God's agent...........Jer. 25:9; 27:5–8
God fights with...................... Jer. 21:1–7
Jews, 70 years in .... Jer. 25:12; 29:10
First of great empires........ Dan. 2:31–38; 7:2–4
Cyrus, God's agent................... Is. 45:1–4

Perpetual desolation of............. Is. 13:19–22;
   Jer. 50:13, 39
Downfall of .... Is. 13:1–22; Jer. 50:1–46

Babylon in the New Testament
A. The city on the Euphrates
Listed as a point of reference.... Matt. 1:11, 12, 17
As the place of Israel's exile............ Acts 7:43
As the place of Peter's residence ....1 Pet. 5:13
B. The prophetic city
Fall predicted.........................Rev. 14:8
Wrath taken on......................Rev. 16:19
Called "the Mother of Harlots" ..... Rev. 17:1–18
Fall described .... Rev. 18:1–24

Babylonians—*sons of Babel*
Inhabitants of Babylonia ....Ezek. 23:15–23

Babylonian garment—*a valuable robe worn in Babylon*
Coveted by Achan .... Josh. 7:21

Baca—*weeping*
Figurative of sorrow.....................Ps. 84:6

Bachelor—*unmarried man*
Described literally .... 1 Cor. 7:26–33
Described figuratively.... Is. 56:3–5; Matt. 19:12;
   Rev. 14:1–5
Not for elders........................Titus 1:5, 6

Bachrites
Family of Becher.................... Num. 26:35

Backbiting—*reviling another in secret; slander*
A fruit of sin...................... Rom. 1:28–30
Expressed by the mouth ....Ps. 50:20
An offspring of anger ....Prov. 25:23
Merits punishment..................... Ps. 101:5
Keeps from God .... Ps. 15:1, 3
To be laid aside ....1 Pet. 2:1
Unworthy of Christians ....2 Cor. 12:20

Backsliding—*to turn away from God after conversion*
A. Described as:
Turning from God................... 1 Kin. 11:9
Turning to evil ....Ps. 125:5
Turning to Satan.....................1 Tim. 5:15
Turning back to the world .... 2 Tim. 4:10
Tempting Christ.....................1 Cor. 10:9
Turning from first love..................Rev. 2:4
Turning from the gospel........ Gal. 1:6, 7; 3:1–5
B. Prompted by:
Haughty spirit......................Prov. 16:18
Spiritual blindness.......... 2 Pet. 1:9; Rev. 3:17
Murmuring ....Ex. 17:3
Lusting after evil ....Ps. 106:14
Material things .... Mark 4:18, 19; 1 Tim. 6:10
Prosperity........................ Deut. 8:11–14
Tribulation......................Matt. 13:20, 21
C. Results:
Displeases God .... Ps. 78:56–59
Punishment .... Num. 14:43–45; Jer. 8:5–13
Blessings withheld .... Is. 59:2
Unworthiness ....Luke 9:62

D. Examples of Israel's:
  At Meribah . . . . .Ex. 17:1–7
  At Sinai . . . . Ex. 32:1–35
  In wilderness . . . . Ps. 106:14–33
  After Joshua's death. . .Judg. 2:8–23; Ps. 106:34–43
  In Solomon's life . . . . . .1 Kin. 11:4–40; Neh. 13:26
  During Asa's reign . . . . .2 Chr. 15:1–4
  During Manasseh's reign . . . . .2 Chr. 33:1–10
E. Examples of, among believers:
  Lot . . . . .Gen. 19:1–22
  David . . . . .2 Sam. 11:1–5; Ps. 51:1–19
  Peter . . . . .Matt. 26:69–75; Luke 22:31, 32
  Galatians . . . . Gal. 1:6; 4:9–11
  Corinthians .1 Cor. 5:1–13
  Churches of Asia . . . . .2 Tim. 1:15; Rev. 2; 3
  See Apostasy

WORD STUDY

BACKSLIDINGS, *meshubah* (mesh-oo-*baw*). *Meshubah* is a noun derived from the verb meaning "to turn," and therefore means a "turning back" or "apostasy." The word has the negative connotation of turning away from the correct way, not turning back to God. There are quite a few references to the apostasy of Israel (Hos. 14:4) and the apostasy of Judah (Jer. 2:19; 3:22). Jeremiah also refers to the peoples' enduring apostasy (Jer. 8:5). (Strong's #4878)

Badger
1. *Probably a specie of dolphin or porpoise*
  Skins of, used in tabernacle
    coverings . . . . Ex. 26:14; 35:7
  Used for sandals .Ezek. 16:10
2. *The Syrian rock hyrax*
  Called "rock hyrax" . . . . Lev. 11:5; Deut. 14:7
  Lives among rocks .Ps. 104:18
  Likened to people .Prov. 30:26

Bag—*a purse or pouch*
A. Used for:
  Money . . . . .2 Kin. 12:10
  Stones . . . . 1 Sam. 17:40, 49
  Food ("vessels") . . . . .1 Sam. 9:7
  Weights . . . . .Deut. 25:13; Prov. 16:11
B. Figurative of:
  Forgiveness . . . . .Job 14:17
  True righteousness . . . . .Prov. 16:11
  True riches . . . . .Luke 12:33
  Insecure riches . . . . Hag. 1:6

Bahurim—*young men*
  A village near Jerusalem . . . . .2 Sam. 3:16
  Where Shimei cursed David . . . . 2 Sam. 16:5
  Where two men hid in a well . . . . . .2 Sam. 17:17, 18

Bakbakkar—*investigator*
  A Levite . . . . 1 Chr. 9:15

Bakbuk—*a flask*
  Head of postexilic family . . . . .Ezra 2:51; Neh. 7:53

Bakbukiah—*Yahweh has poured out*
1. A Levite of high position . . . . .Neh. 11:17

2. Levite porter . . . . Neh. 12:25
Baker—*one who cooks food (bread)*
A. Kinds of:
  Household . . . . Gen. 18:6
  Public . . . . .Jer. 37:21
  Royal . . . . .Gen. 40:1, 2
B. Features of:
  Usually a woman's job . . . . Lev. 26:26
  Considered menial . . . . .1 Sam. 8:13

Balaam—*destroyer of the people*
A. Information concerning:
  A son of Beor . . . . Num. 22:5
  From Mesopotamia . . . . Deut. 23:4
  A soothsayer . . . . .Josh. 13:22
  A prophet . . . . .2 Pet. 2:15
  Killed because of his sin . . . . Num. 31:1–8
B. Mission of:
  Balak sent to curse Israel . . . . Num. 22:5–7;
    Josh. 24:9
  Hindered by speaking donkey . . .Num. 22:22–35;
    2 Pet. 2:16
  Curse becomes a blessing . . . . Deut. 23:4, 5;
    Josh. 24:10
C. Prophecies of:
  Under divine control . . . . Num. 22:18, 38;
    23:16, 20, 26
  By the Spirit's prompting . . . . Num. 24:2
  Blessed Israel three times . . . . Num. 24:10
  Spoke of the Messiah in final
    message . . . . .Num. 24:14–19
D. Nature of:
  "Unrighteousness"—greed . . . . 2 Pet. 2:14, 15
  "Error"—rebellion . . . . Jude 11

Baladan—*(Marduk) has given a son*
  Father of Merodach-Baladan (*also spelled*
    Berodach-Baladan) . . . . .2 Kin. 20:12

Balak, Balac—*empty*
  A Moabite king . . . . Num. 22:4
  Hired Balaam to curse Israel . . . . Num. 22–24

Balances—*an instrument for weighing; scales*
A. Used for weighing:
  Things . . . . .Lev. 19:36
  Money . . . . .Jer. 32:10
B. Laws concerning:
  Must be just . . . . .Lev. 19:36
  False, an abomination . . . . Prov. 11:1
  Deceit, condemned . . . . Amos 8:5
C. Figurative of:
  God's justice . . . . .Job 31:6
  Human smallness . . . . .Ps. 62:9; Is. 40:12, 15
  God's judgment . . . . .Dan. 5:27
  Human tribulation .Rev. 6:5

Baldness—*a head without hair*
A. Natural:
  Not a sign of leprosy . . . . Lev. 13:40, 41
  Elisha mocked for . . . . 2 Kin. 2:23, 24

B. Artificial:

A sign of mourning .... Is. 22:12

An idolatrous practice....... Lev. 21:5; Deut. 14:1

Inflicted upon captives............. Deut. 21:12

Forbidden to priests................ Ezek. 44:20

A part of Nazirite vow........... Num. 6:2, 9, 18

C. Figurative of judgment, upon:

Israel .... Is. 3:24; Amos 8:10

Moab............................... Is. 15:2

Philistia.............................Jer. 47:5

Tyre .... Ezek. 27:2, 31

Ball—*spherical object*

Prophetic .... Is. 22:18

Ballad singers

Rendered "those who speak in
     proverbs" .... Num. 21:27

Balm—*an aromatic resin or gum*

A product of Gilead.................... Jer. 8:22

Sent to Joseph .... Gen. 43:11

Exported to Tyre.....................Ezek. 27:17

Healing qualities of ....Jer. 46:11; 51:8

Bamah—*high place*

A place of idolatry .... Ezek. 20:29

Bamoth—*high places*

Encampment site .... Num. 21:19, 20

Also called Bamoth Baal............. Josh. 13:17

Bamoth Baal—*high places of Baal*

Assigned to Reuben.................. Josh. 13:17

Ban (see Excommunication)

Bandage

Used as disguise .... 1 Kin. 20:37–41

In prophecy against Egypt........Ezek. 30:20–22

Bani—*built*

1. Gadite warrior ....2 Sam. 23:36

2. A Judahite .... 1 Chr. 9:4

3. A postexilic family..........Ezra 2:10; Neh. 10:14

4. A Merarite Levite..................... 1 Chr. 6:46

5. A Levite; father of Rehum...............Neh. 3:17

6. Signed document ....Neh. 10:13

7. Head of Levitical family...............Ezra 10:34

8. A postexilic Levite...................Ezra 10:38

9. A descendant of Asaph.................Neh. 11:22

Banishment—*forceful expulsion from one's place*

A. Political, of:

Absalom by David .... 2 Sam. 14:13, 14

The Jews into exile.............. 2 Chr. 36:20, 21

The Jews from Rome.................. Acts 18:2

B. Moral and spiritual, of:

Adam and Eve from Eden .... Gen. 3:22–24

Cain from others ....Gen. 4:12, 14

Lawbreaker .... Ezra 7:26

John to Patmos .... Rev. 1:9

Satan from heaven .... Rev. 12:7–9

The wicked to lake of fire........ Rev. 20:15; 21:8

Bank—*A place for money*

Exchange charges.................... John 2:15

Interest paid on deposits ....Matt. 25:27;
     Luke 19:23

Bankruptcy—*inability to pay one's debts*

A. Literal:

Condition of David's men .... 1 Sam. 22:1, 2

Unjust steward ....Matt. 18:23–27

B. Moral and spiritual:

Israel's condition .... Hos. 4:1–5

Humankind's condition... Rom. 1:20–32; 3:9–19

Individual's condition.... Phil. 3:4–8; 1 Tim. 1:13

Banner—*a flag or standard*

A. Literal:

Used by armies .... Num. 2:2, 3

Signal for assembling.................. Is. 18:3

Hosts............................. Num. 1:52

Enemy ....Ps. 74:4, 5

B. Figurative of:

God's salvation ....Ps. 20:5; 60:4

God's protection..................... Song 2:4

God's power.......................Song 6:4, 10

Enemy force........................... Is. 5:26

God's uplifted hand.....................Is. 31:9

Christ............................ Is. 11:10, 12

Banquet—*a sumptuous feast*

A. Reasons for:

Birthday ....Gen. 40:20

Marriage...........................Gen. 29:22

Reunion .... Luke 15:22–25

State affairs ....Esth. 1:3, 5; Dan. 5:1

B. Features of:

Invitations sent....... Esth. 5:8, 9; Luke 14:16, 17

Nonacceptance merits censure.... Luke 14:18–24

Courtesies to guests............... Luke 7:34–46

Special garment..........Matt. 22:11; Rev. 3:4, 5

A presiding governor................... John 2:8

Protocol of seating...... Gen. 43:33; Prov. 25:6, 7

Anointing oil........................ Ps. 45:7

Honor guest noted ....1 Sam. 9:22–24

Baptism, Christian

A. Commanded by:

Christ........... Matt. 28:19, 20; Mark 16:15, 16

Peter.......................... Acts 10:46–48

Christian ministers ....Acts 22:12–16

B. Administered by:

The apostles...................... Acts 2:1, 41

Ananias...........................Acts 9:17, 18

Philip...................... Acts 8:12, 36–38

Peter.......................... Acts 10:44–48

Paul ....Acts 18:8; 1 Cor. 1:14–17

C. Places:

Jordan ....Matt. 3:13–16; Mark 1:5–10

Jerusalem .... Acts 2:5, 41

Samaria.......................... Acts 8:5, 12

A house .... Acts 10:44–48

A jail.........................Acts 16:25–33

D. Subjects of:

Believing Jews.................... Acts 2:14, 41

Believing Gentiles . . . . Acts 10:44–48; 18:8
Households . . . . . Acts 16:14, 15, 27, 33; 1 Cor. 1:16
E. Characteristics of:
By water . . . . Acts 10:47
Only one . . . . Eph. 4:5
Necessary . . . . Acts 2:38, 41
Source of power . . . . Acts 1:5
Follows faith . . . . Acts 2:41; 18:8
F. Symbolism of:
Forecast in prophecy . . . . Joel 2:28, 29;
Acts 2:16–21
Prefigured in types . . . . . 1 Cor. 10:2; 1 Pet. 3:20, 21
Visualized by the Spirit's descent . . . John 1:32, 33;
Acts 2:3, 4, 41
Expressive of spiritual unity . . . . 1 Cor. 12:13;
Gal. 3:27, 28
Figurative of regeneration . . . . John 3:3, 5, 6;
Rom. 6:3, 4, 11
Illustrative of cleansing . . . . . Acts 22:16; Titus 3:5

Baptism, John's
Administrator—John . . . . Matt. 3:4–7
Place—at Jordan; in Aenon . . . . . Matt. 3:6, 13, 16;
John 3:23
Persons—people and Jesus . . . . Mark 1:5, 9;
Acts 13:24
Character—repentance . . . . Luke 3:3
Reception—rejected by some . . . . Luke 7:29, 30
Nature—of God . . . . Matt. 21:25, 27
Insufficiency—rebaptism . . . . Acts 19:1–7
Intent—to prepare . . . . Matt. 3:11, 12;
Acts 11:16; 19:4
Jesus' submission to—fulfilling all
righteousness . . . . Matt. 3:13–17

| WORD STUDY | **BAPTIZE,** *baptizō* (bap-*tid*-zoh). The English word "baptize" is derived from the Greek verb *baptizō,* which means "to |

dip," "immerse." In the NT *baptizō* is used with respect to religious rituals involving water: for example, Jewish ritual washings (Mark 7:4); the ritual performed by John (Matt. 3:6ff.), and later by the disciples of Jesus and John (see John 3:22–4:2). It also designates a ritual of Christian initiation after Jesus' death (Acts 2:41; 1 Cor. 1:14–17). The initiate is baptized in the "name of the Lord" or "Christ" (Acts 10:48; Rom. 6:3; Gal. 3:27)—or, according to Matthew, in the name of the Father, Son, and Holy Spirit (28:19). The word can be used figuratively (Luke 12:50; 1 Cor. 10:2). (Strong's #907)

Barabbas—*son of Abba (father)*
A murderer released in
place of Jesus . . . . Matt. 27:16–26; Acts 3:14, 15

Barachel—*God has blessed*
Father of Elihu . . . . Job 32:2, 6

Barak—*lightning*
Defeats Jabin . . . . Judg. 4:1–24
A man of faith . . . . Heb. 11:32

Barbarian—*rude*
Primitive people . . . . Rom. 1:14
Those included in the gospel . . . . Col. 3:11

Barber—*one who cuts hair*
Expressive of divine judgment . . . . Is. 7:20;
Ezek. 5:1

Bare—*uncovered; naked*
Figurative of:
Destitution . . . . Ezek. 16:22, 39
Uncleanness . . . . Lev. 13:45
Undeveloped state, immaturity . . . . Ezek. 16:7
Power revealed . . . . Is. 52:10
Destruction . . . . Joel 1:7
Mourning . . . . Is. 32:9–11

Barefoot—*bare feet*
Expression of great distress . . . . 2 Sam. 15:30
Forewarning of judgment . . . . Is. 20:2–4
Indicative of reverence . . . . Ex. 3:5

Bargain—*an agreement between persons*
A disastrous . . . . Gen. 25:29–34
A blessed . . . . Gen. 28:20–22
Involving a wife . . . . Gen. 29:15–20
Deception of . . . . Prov. 20:14
Resulting in death . . . . Matt. 14:7–10
History's most notorious . . . . Matt. 26:14–16

Barhumite (another form of Baharumite)
One of David's mighty men . . . . 2 Sam. 23:31

Bariah—*fugitive*
A descendant of David . . . . 1 Chr. 3:22

Bar-Jesus (Elymas)
A Jewish impostor . . . . Acts 13:6–12

Bar-Jonah—*son of Jonah*
Surname of Peter . . . . Matt. 16:17

Barkos—*parti-colored*
Postexilic family . . . . Ezra 2:53

Barley—*a bearded cereal grass*
Food for animals . . . . 1 Kin. 4:28
Used by the poor . . . . Ruth 2:17
A product of Palestine . . . . Deut. 8:8; Ruth 1:22
Used in trade . . . . 2 Chr. 2:10
In a miracle . . . . John 6:9, 13

Barn—*a storehouse*
A. Literal:
A place of storage . . . . Deut. 28:8; Joel 1:17
Full, prayed for . . . . Ps. 144:13
B. Spiritual, of:
God's blessings . . . . Prov. 3:10; Mal. 3:10
Human vanity . . . . Luke 12:16–21
Heaven itself . . . . Matt. 13:30, 43

Barnabas—*son of exhortation*
Called Joses . . . . Acts 4:36
Gives money . . . . Acts 4:37
Supports Paul . . . . Acts 9:27
Assists in Antioch . . . . Acts 11:22–24
Brings Paul from Tarsus . . . . Acts 11:25, 26
Carries relief to Jerusalem . . . . Acts 11:27–30

Travels with Paul . . . . Acts 13:2
Called Zeus by the multitudes . . . . Acts 14:12
Named as apostle .Acts 14:14
Speaks before Jerusalem Council . . . Acts 15:1, 2, 12
With Paul, takes letter of instruction
    to churches . . . . .Acts 15:22–31
Breaks with Paul over John Mark. . .Acts 15:36–39
Highly regarded by Paul. . . . 1 Cor. 9:6; Gal. 2:1, 9
Not always steady. .Gal. 2:13

Barren—*unable to reproduce*
A. Physically, of:
    Unproductive soil. . . . . Ps. 107:34; Joel 2:20
    Trees . . . . Luke 13:6–9
    Females. . . . . .Prov. 30:16
B. Significance of:
    A reproach . . . . Gen. 16:2
    A judgment. . . . . 2 Sam. 6:23
    Absence of God's blessing . . .Ex. 23:26; Deut. 7:14
    God's protection. Ps. 113:9
C. Spiritually:
    Removal of, in new Israel . . . . . . .Is. 54:1; Gal. 4:27
    Remedy against. 2 Pet. 1:5–8
D. Examples of:
    Sarah . . . . Gen. 21:2
    Rebekah . . . . Gen. 25:21
    Rachel . . . . .Gen. 30:22
    Manoah's wife. . . . . .Judg. 13:2, 3, 24
    Hannah. . . . . .1 Sam. 1:18–20
    The Shunammite woman. . . . . 2 Kin. 4:12–17
    Elizabeth. . . . . .Luke 1:7, 13, 57

Barsabas—*son of Saba*
1. Nominated to replace Judas . . . . Acts 1:23
2. Sent to Antioch. . . . . .Acts 15:22

Barter—*to exchange for something*
    Between Joseph and
        the Egyptians . . . . .Gen. 47:15–17
    Between Solomon and Hiram. . . . . .1 Kin. 5:10, 11

Bartholomew—*son of Talmai*
    Called Nathanael . . . . .John 1:45, 46
    One of Christ's apostles . . . . .Matt. 10:3; Acts 1:13

Bartimaeus—*son of Timaeus*
    Blind beggar healed by Jesus . . . . .Mark 10:46–52

Baruch—*blessed*
1. Son of Neriah . . . . .Jer. 32:12, 13
    Jeremiah's faithful friend and scribe. . .Jer. 36:4–32
    The Jewish remnant takes him
        to Egypt . . . . Jer. 43:1–7
2. Son of Zabbai . . . . .Neh. 3:20
    Signs document. Neh. 10:6
3. A Shilonite of Judah . . . . .Neh. 11:5

Barzillai—*of iron*
1. Helps David with food . . . . 2 Sam. 17:27–29
    Age restrains him from following
        David . . . . .2 Sam. 19:31–39
2. Father of Adriel . . . . 2 Sam. 21:8
3. A postexilic priest . . . . Ezra 2:61

Basemath—*fragrance*
1. Wife of Esau . . . . Gen. 26:34
    Called Adah. .Gen. 36:2, 3
2. Wife of Esau . . . . Gen. 36:3, 4, 13
    Called Mahalath. . . . . Gen. 28:9
3. A daughter of Solomon. . . . . 1 Kin. 4:15

Bashan—*smooth soil*
    A vast highland east of the Sea of Chinnereth
        (Galilee). .Num. 21:33–35
    Ruled by Og. . . . . Deut. 29:7
    Conquered by Israel. . . . . Neh. 9:22
    Assigned to Manasseh. . . . . Deut. 3:13
    Smitten by Hazael . . . . 2 Kin. 10:32, 33
    Fine cattle. . . . . .Ezek. 39:18
    Typical of cruelty . . . . .Ps. 22:12; Amos 4:1
    Called Havoth Jair. . . . . .Deut. 3:14

Basin—*cup or bowl for containing liquids*
    Moses used. . . . . .Ex. 24:6
    Made for the altar. . . . . .Ex. 27:3; 38:3
    Brought for David . . . . 2 Sam. 17:28, 29
    Hiram made. . . . . 1 Kin. 7:40

Baskets—*something made to hold objects*
A. Used for carrying:
    Produce. . . . . Deut. 26:2
    Food. . . . . Matt. 14:20
    Ceremonial offerings. . . . . Ex. 29:3, 23
    Paul . . . . Acts 9:24, 25
    Other objects (heads) . . . . .2 Kin. 10:7
B. Symbolic of:
    Approaching death . . . . Gen. 40:16–19
    Israel's judgment. . . . . Amos 8:1–3
    Judah's judgment . . . . Jer. 24:1–10
    Hiding good works . . . . .Matt. 5:15

Bat—*a flying mammal*
    Listed among unclean birds. . . . . Lev. 11:19;
      Deut. 14:18
    Lives in dark places . . . . Is. 2:19–21

Bath—*a liquid measure (about 6 gallons)*
    A tenth of a homer . . . . Ezek. 45:10, 11
    For measuring oil and wine . . . 2 Chr. 2:10; Is. 5:10

Bathing
A. For pleasure:
    Pharaoh's daughter . . . . .Ex. 2:5
    Bathsheba. . . . . 2 Sam. 11:2, 3
B. For purification:
    Cleansing the feet. . . . . .Gen. 24:32; John 13:10
    Ceremonial cleansing . . . Lev. 14:8; 2 Kin. 5:10–14
    Jewish rituals. . . . . .Mark 7:2
    Before performing priestly duties . . . Ex. 30:19–21;
      Lev. 16:4, 24

Bath Rabbim—*daughter of multitudes*
    Gate of Heshbon. Song 7:4

Bathsheba—*daughter of an oath*
    Wife of Uriah . . . . 2 Sam. 11:2, 3
    Commits adultery with David . . . . . 2 Sam. 11:4, 5
    Husband's death contrived
        by David. . . . . .2 Sam. 11:6–25

Mourns husband's death .... 2 Sam. 11:26
Becomes David's wife .... 2 Sam. 11:27
Her first child dies .... 2 Sam. 12:14–19
Solomon's mother.................. 2 Sam. 12:24
Secures throne for Solomon........ 1 Kin. 1:15–31
Deceived by Adonijah .... 1 Kin. 2:13–25

Bathshua—*daughter of prosperity*
Same as Bathsheba.................... 1 Chr. 3:5

Batten—*a wooden or metal peg*
Used in a weaver's loom .... Judg. 16:13, 14
See Nail

Battering ram (see Armor)
Used in destroying walls........ Ezek. 4:2; 21:22

Battle (see War)

Battle-ax—*an instrument of war*
Applied to Israel .... Jer. 51:19, 20

Bavai—*wisher*
Postexilic worker .... Neh. 3:18

Bay—*inlet*
Dead Sea's cove at Jordan's mouth ...... Josh. 15:5

Bazluth—*stripping*
Head of a family .... Ezra 2:52
Called Bazlith in..................... Neh. 7:54

Bdellium—*an oily gum, or a white pearl*
A valuable mineral of Havilah .... Gen. 2:12
Manna colored like .... Num. 11:7

Beach—*coast; shore*
Place of:
Jesus' preaching .... Matt. 13:2
Fisherman's task..................... Matt. 13:48
Jesus' meal with disciples .... John 21:8, 9
A prayer meeting ....Acts 21:5
A notable shipwreck ....Acts 27:39–44
A miracle .... Acts 28:1–6

Bealiah—*Yahweh is Lord*
A warrior .... 1 Chr. 12:5

Bealoth—*mistresses*
Village of Judah .... Josh. 15:24

Beam
A. Physical:
Wood undergirding floors............. 1 Kin. 7:2
Part of weaver's frame............... 1 Sam. 17:7
B. Figurative of:
The cry for vengeance................ Hab. 2:11
God's power.........................Ps. 104:3

Bean—*a food*
Brought to David by friends ..... 2 Sam. 17:27, 28
Mixed with grain for bread ....Ezek. 4:9

Bear—*a wild animal*
A. Natural:
Killed by David................. 1 Sam. 17:34, 35
Two tore up forty-two lads........ 2 Kin. 2:23, 24
B. Figurative of:
Fierce revenge .... 2 Sam. 17:8
Fool's folly .... Prov. 17:12

Wicked rulers ....Prov. 28:15
World empire....................... Dan. 7:5
Final antichrist ....Rev. 13:2
Messianic times ....Is. 11:7
A constellation ....Job 9:9

Bear—*to carry, yield*
A. Used literally of:
Giving birth......................... Gen. 17:19
Carrying a load............. Josh. 3:13; Jer. 17:21
Cross .... Matt. 27:32
B. Used figuratively of:
Excessive punishment................. Gen. 4:13
Divine deliverance ....Ex. 19:4
Responsibility for sin............Lev. 5:17; 24:15
Burden of leadership .... Deut. 1:9, 12
Personal shame .... Ezek. 16:54
Evangelism..........................Acts 9:15
Spiritual help.........................Gal. 6:1, 2
Spiritual productivity ....John 15:2, 4, 8

Beard—*hair grown on the face*
A. Long, worn by:
Aaron...............................Ps. 133:2
David.................... 1 Sam. 21:12, 13
B. In mourning:
Plucked ....Ezra 9:3
Clipped .... Jer. 48:37, 38
C. Features regarding:
Leper's must be shaven .... Lev. 13:29–33
Half-shaven, an indignity .... 2 Sam. 10:4, 5
Marring of, forbidden ....Lev. 19:27
Shaven, by Egyptians................. Gen. 41:14
Spittle on, sign of lunacy......... 1 Sam. 21:12, 13
Holding to, a token of respect....... 2 Sam. 20:9

Beasts—*four-footed animals; mammals*
A. Characteristics of:
God-created......................... Gen. 1:21
Of their own order................. 1 Cor. 15:39
Named by Adam..................... Gen. 2:20
Suffer because of human sin .... Rom. 8:20–22
Perish at death..................... Ps. 49:12–15
Follow instincts................... Is. 1:3; Jude 10
Under God's control .... 1 Sam. 6:7–14
Wild...............................Mark 1:13
For human food .... Gen. 9:3; Acts 10:12, 13
Used in sacrifices .... Lev. 27:26–29
Spiritual lessons from ... 1 Kin. 4:30–33; Job 12:7
Eat people............. 1 Sam. 17:46; 1 Cor. 15:32
B. Treatment of:
No sexual relation with........... Lev. 20:15, 16
Proper care of, sign of a
righteous person .. Gen. 33:13, 14; Prov. 12:10
Abuse of, rebuked............... Num. 22:28–32
Extra food for, while working........Deut. 25:4;
1 Tim. 5:18
C. Typical of:
Human folly........................Ps. 73:22
Unregenerate individuals.............Titus 1:12

False prophets . . . . 2 Pet. 2:12
Antichrist . . . . Rev. 13:1–4
See Animals

Beaten silver—*silver shaped by hammering*
Overlaid idols . . . . Is. 30:22; Hab. 2:19
In trade . . . . .Jer. 10:9

Beatings—*striking the body with blows; floggings*
A. Inflicted on:
   The wicked . . . . Deut. 25:3
   The guilty . . . . .Lev. 19:20
   Children . . . . .Prov. 22:15
   The disobedient . . . . Prov. 26:3; Luke 12:47, 48
B. Victims of unjust beatings:
   A servant . . . . .Luke 20:10, 11
   Christ . . . . .Is. 50:6; Mark 15:19
   The apostles . . . . Acts 5:40
   Paul . . . . .Acts 16:18–24

Beatitudes—*pronouncements of blessings*
Jesus begins His sermon with . . . . . . Matt. 5:3–12;
   Luke 6:20–22

Beautiful Gate—*gate at east of temple area*
Lame man healed there . . . . Acts 3:1–10

Beauty, physical
A. Temporal:
   Seen in nature . . . . Hos. 14:6; Matt. 6:28, 29
   Consumed in dissipation . . . . Is. 28:1
   Contest, Abishag winner of . . . . .1 Kin. 1:1–4
   Esther, winner of . . . . .Esth. 2:1–17
   Destroyed by sin . . . . Ps. 39:11
   Ends in grave . . . . Ps. 49:14
B. In Women:
   Vain . . . . .Prov. 31:30
   Without discretion . . . . .Prov. 11:22
   Enticements of . . . . .Prov. 6:25
   Source of temptation . . . . . Gen. 6:2; 2 Sam. 11:2–5
   Leads to marriage . . . . .Deut. 21:10–13
   A bride's . . . . Ps. 45:11
   Sarah's . . . . Gen. 12:11
   Rebekah's . . . . .Gen. 24:15, 16
   Rachel's . . . . Gen. 29:17
   Daughters of Job . . . . Job 42:15
   Abigail's . . . . 1 Sam. 25:3
   Bathsheba's . . . . 2 Sam. 11:2, 3
   Tamar's . . . . .2 Sam. 13:1
   Abishag's . . . . .1 Kin. 1:3, 4
   Vashti's . . . . Esth. 1:11
   Esther's . . . . Esth. 2:7
C. In Men:
   Of man . . . . Is. 44:13
   Of the aged . . . . .Prov. 20:29
   Joseph's . . . . Gen. 39:6
   David's . . . . 1 Sam. 16:12, 13
   Absalom's . . . . 2 Sam. 14:25

Beauty, spiritual
The Messiah . . . . Ps. 110:3; Is. 52:7
The true Israel . . . . Ps. 45:8–11; Song 1:8
The meek . . . . .Ps. 149:4

Spiritual worship . . . . .2 Chr. 20:21
Christian ministers . . . . .Rom. 10:15
Holy garments . . . . Is. 52:1
Christ's rejection by Israel . . . . Zech. 11:7–14

Bebai—*fatherly*
1. Family head . . . . Ezra 2:11
2. One who signs document . . . . .Neh. 10:15

Becher—*young camel*
1. Benjamin's son . . . . Gen. 46:21
2. Son of Ephraim . . . . .Num. 26:35
   Called Bered . . . . .1 Chr. 7:20

Bechorath—*the first birth*
Ancestor of Saul .1 Sam. 9:1

Bed
A. Made of:
   The ground . . . . Gen. 28:11
   Iron, 13 1/2 feet long . . . . .Deut. 3:11
   Ivory . . . . Amos 6:4
   Gold and silver . . . . Esth. 1:6
B. Used for:
   Sleep . . . . Luke 11:7
   Rest . . . . 2 Sam. 4:5–7
   Sickness . . . . Gen. 49:33
   Meals . . . . Amos 6:4
   Prostitution .Prov. 7:16, 17
   Evil . . . . Ps. 36:4
   Marriage . . . . Song 3:1; Heb. 13:4
   Singing . . . . Ps. 149:5
C. Figurative of:
   The grave . . . . Job 17:13–16
   Divine support . . . . Ps. 41:3
   Worldly security . . . . .Is. 57:7

Bed—*a garden plot*
Used literally . . . . Song 6:2
Used figuratively . . . . Song 5:13

Bedad—*separation*
Father of Hadad . . . . Gen. 36:35

Bedan—*son of judgment*
1. Judge of Israel . . . . 1 Sam. 12:11
2. Descendant of Manasseh . . . . .1 Chr. 7:17

Bedeiah—*servant of Yahweh*
Son of Bani . . . . Ezra 10:34, 35

Bedfellows
Provide mutual warmth . . . . Eccl. 4:11

Bedroom
A place of sleep . . . . .2 Sam. 4:7
Elisha's special . . . . .2 Kin. 4:8, 10
Secrets of . . . . 2 Kin. 6:12
Joash hidden in . . . . 2 Kin. 11:2

Bee—*insect*
Abundant in Canaan . . . . .Judg. 14:8
Amorites compared to . . . . Deut. 1:44
David's enemies compared to . . . . Ps. 118:12
Assyria compared to . . . . .Is. 7:18
See Honey

Beef, boiled
    Elisha gives people . . . . 1 Kin. 19:21

Beeliada—*the Lord knows*
    Son of David . . . . 1 Chr. 14:7
    Called Eliada. 2 Sam. 5:14–16

Beelzebub
    Prince of demons . . . . Matt. 12:24
    Identified as Satan . . . . Matt. 12:26, 27
    Jesus thus called . . . . Matt. 10:25

Beer—*a well*
1. Moab station . . . . Num. 21:16–18
2. Jotham's place of refuge . . . . Judg. 9:21

Beera—*a well*
    An Asherite . . . . 1 Chr. 7:37

Beerah—*a well*
    Reubenite prince . . . . 1 Chr. 5:6

Beer Elim
    Well dug by leaders of Israel . . . . Is. 15:8

Beeri—*expounder*
1. Esau's father-in-law . . . . Gen. 26:34
2. Hosea's father . . . . Hos. 1:1

Beer Lahai Roi—*Well of the One who lives and sees me*
    Angel met Hagar there . . . . Gen. 16:7–14
    Isaac dwelt in. . . . . Gen. 24:62

Beeroth—*wells*
    Gibeonite city . . . . Josh. 9:17

Beerothite, Berothite
    An inhabitant of Beeroth . . . . 2 Sam. 4:2;
    1 Chr. 11:39

Beersheba—*well of the oath*
A. God appeared to:
    Hagar. . . . . .Gen. 21:14, 17–19
    Isaac. . . . . Gen. 26:19–24
    Jacob . . . . .Gen. 46:1–5
    Elijah . . . . 1 Kin. 19:3–7
B. Other features of:
    Named after an oath . . . .Gen. 21:31–33; 26:26–33
    Isaac's residence at . . . . Gen. 26:23–25
    Jacob's departure from . . . . Gen. 28:10
    Assigned to Judah. . . . . .Josh. 15:20, 28
    Later assigned to Simeon . . . . .Josh. 19:1, 2, 9
    Judgeship of Samuel's sons. . . . . .1 Sam. 8:2
    Became seat of idolatry. . . . . Amos 5:5; 8:14
    "From Dan to Beersheba". . . . . .2 Sam. 17:11

Be Eshterah—*temple of Ashterah*
    A Levitical city .Josh. 21:27
    Same as Ashtaroth . . . . 1 Chr. 6:71

Beggar—*needy*
A. Statements concerning:
    Shame of. . . . . .Luke 16:3
    Seed of righteous, kept from . . . . .Ps. 37:25
    Punishment of. .Ps. 109:10
    Object of prayer . . . . 1 Sam. 2:1, 8
B. Examples of:
    Bartimaeus. . . . . Mark 10:46

    Lazarus . . . . Luke 16:20–22
    Blind man. . . . . Luke 18:35
    Lame man. . . . . Acts 3:2–6

Beginning—*the starting point; origin of*
    Creation . . . . .Gen. 1:1 ; John 1:1–3
    Sin. . . . . .Gen. 3:1–6; Rom. 5:12–21
    Death. . . . . Gen. 3:3, 22–24
    Salvation. . . . . .2 Thess. 2:13, 14
    Satan . . . . John 8:44
    The gospel . . . . .Gen. 3:15; Gal. 3:8
    The old covenant . . . . Ex. 19:1–5; Heb. 8:7–9
    The new covenant . . . . Jer. 31:31–34; Matt. 26:28;
    Heb. 9:14–28

Begotten—*from "beget" meaning to bring into being*
A. Applied to Christ:
    Predicted . . . . Ps. 2:7; Acts 13:33
    Prefigured . . . . Heb. 11:17
    Proclaimed. . . . . John 1:14
    Proffered. . . . . John 3:16
    Professed. . . . . Heb. 1:5, 6
B. Applied to Christians:
    By the gospel . . . . 1 Cor. 4:15
    In bonds . . . . Philem. 10
    Unto hope. . . . . .1 Pet. 1:3
    For safekeeping. . . . . .1 John 5:18

Behavior—*one's conduct*
A. Strange:
    Feigned insanity . . . . 1 Sam. 21:12, 13
    Supposed drunkenness . . . . 1 Sam. 1:12–16
    Pretended grief . . . . 2 Sam. 14:1–8
    Professed loyalty. . . . . Matt. 26:48–50
    Insipid hypocrisy . . . . Esth. 6:5–11
    Counterfeit religion. . . . . .2 Cor. 11:13–15
B. True:
    Reverent . . . . .Titus 2:7
    Orderly . . . . 2 Thess. 3:7
    Good . . . . 1 Tim. 3:2
    Without blame . . . . 1 Thess. 2:10

Beheading—*a form of capital punishment*
    Ishbosheth . . . . 2 Sam. 4:5–7
    John the Baptist . . . . Matt. 14:10
    James. . . . . Acts 12:2
    Martyrs. . . . . Rev. 20:4

Behemoth—*a colossal beast*
    Described . . . . .Job 40:15–24

Bekah (see Weights and measures)
    Half a shekel . . . . Ex. 38:26

Bel—*lord*
    Patron god of Babylon. . . . . .Is. 46:1; Jer. 51:44
    Merodach title. . . . . Jer. 50:2

Bela, Belah—*destruction*
1. King of Edom . . . . Gen. 36:32
2. Reubenite chief. . . . . 1 Chr. 5:8
3. Benjamin's son . . . . Gen. 46:21
4. A city. . . . . Gen. 14:2, 8

Belial
A. Hebrew word translated:
    Corrupt............................ Deut. 13:13
    Perverted ....Judg. 19:22
    Worthless...................... 1 Sam. 30:22
    Scoundrels ....1 Kin. 21:10, 13
B. Applied to:
    Satan .... 2 Cor. 6:15

WORD STUDY   **BELIEVE,** *'aman,* (aw-*man*). The verb *'aman* means "to believe" or "trust," "to be firm" or "to be faithful." Therefore, "to believe" is to have assurance. Trust can be placed in a person as when God gave signs to the Israelites so that they would believe in Moses (Ex. 19:9). More usually, one believes in God as the Israelites did after seeing the miracles God performed in releasing them from Egypt (see Ex. 14:31; Deut. 1:32; Ps. 78:22). (Strong's #539)

WORD STUDY   **BELIEVE, TRUST (HAVE FAITH IN),** *pisteuō* (pist-yoo-oh). *Pisteuō* is a verb occurring frequently in the NT, meaning "believe," "have faith," "trust," "put confidence in." It most often refers to faith in God or Christ, or, frequently in John, to belief in things Christ taught. It can also mean to believe any kind of claim, as in Acts 9:26 when some did not *believe* that Paul was a disciple. Occasionally (as in Luke 16:11) it can mean to entrust someone with something. (Strong's #4100)

Believers—*those who have received Christ; Christians*
    Applied to converts ....Acts 5:14; 1 Tim. 4:12

Bellows—*an instrument used in forcing air at fire*
    A figure of affliction .... Jer. 6:29
    Descriptive of God's judgment.......Jer. 6:27–30

Bells
    On Aaron's garment...... Ex. 28:33, 34; 39:25, 26
    Attention-getters .... Is. 3:16, 18
    Symbols of consecration............. Zech. 14:20

Beloved—*a title of endearment*
A. Applied naturally to:
    A husband ....Song 6:1–3
B. Applied spiritually to:
    Christ..............................Matt. 3:17
    Spiritual Israel.......................Rom. 9:25
    Believers ....Col. 3:12
    Christian friends .... Rom. 16:8, 9
    Saints' abode ....Rev. 20:9

Belshazzar—*Bel protect the king*
    Son of Nebuchadnezzar .... Dan. 5:2
    Gives feast .... Dan. 5:1, 4
    Disturbed by handwriting..........Dan. 5:5–12
    Seeks Daniel's aid.................Dan. 5:13–16
    Daniel interprets for him..........Dan. 5:17–29
    Last Chaldean king ....Dan. 5:30, 31

Belteshazzar—*Bel protect his life*
    Daniel's Babylonian name .... Dan. 1:7

Ben—*son*
    Levite porter .... 1 Chr. 15:18

Benaiah—*Yahweh has built*
1. Jehoiada's son ....2 Sam. 23:20
    A mighty man ....2 Sam. 23:20, 21
    David's bodyguard..................2 Sam. 8:18
    Faithful to David .... 2 Sam. 15:18; 20:23
    Escorts Solomon to the throne .... 1 Kin. 1:38–40
    Executes Adonijah, Joab,
        and Shimei...........1 Kin. 2:25, 29–34; 2:46
    Commander-in-chief............. 1 Kin. 2:28–35
2. One of David's mighty men ....2 Sam. 23:30
    Divisional commander .... 1 Chr. 27:14
3. Levite musician ....1 Chr. 15:18–20
4. Priestly trumpeter .... 1 Chr. 15:24; 16:6
5. Levite of Asaph's family.............. 2 Chr. 20:14
6. Simeonite............................ 1 Chr. 4:36
7. Levite overseer .... 2 Chr. 31:13
8. Father of leader Pelatiah .... Ezek. 11:1, 13
9–12. Four postexilic Jews who divorced
      their foreign wives............. Ezra 10:25–43

Ben-Ammi—*son of my kinsman*
    Son of Lot; father of the Ammonites... Gen. 19:38

Ben-Deker—*piercing; mattock*
    One of Solomon's officers.............. 1 Kin. 4:9

Bene Berak—*sons of berak (lightning)*
    A town of Dan.......................Josh. 19:45

Benediction—*an act of blessing*
A. Characteristics of:
    Instituted by God...................Gen. 1:22, 28
    Divinely approved .... Deut. 10:8
    Aaronic form......................Num. 6:23–26
    Apostolic form .... 2 Cor. 13:14
    Jesus' last words .... Luke 24:50, 51
B. Pronounced upon:
    Creation ....Gen. 1:22, 28
    New world .... Gen. 9:1, 2
    Abraham.........................Gen. 14:19, 20
    Marriage...........................Gen. 24:60
    Son (Jacob).......................Gen. 27:27–29
    Monarch (Pharaoh) .... Gen. 47:7, 10
    Sons (Joseph's) .... Gen. 48:15, 16, 20
    Tribes (Israel's) ....Deut. 33:1–29
    Foreigner .... Ruth 1:8, 9
    People ....2 Sam. 6:18
    Jesus.............................Luke 2:34
    Song of Zacharias................. Luke 1:68–79
    Children's blessing.................. Mark 10:16

Benefactor—*one who bestows benefits*
A. Materially, God as:
    Israel's...........................Deut. 7:6–26
    Unbeliever's......................Acts 14:15–18
    Christian's .... Phil. 4:19
B. Spiritually:
    By God ....Eph. 1:3–6
    Through Christ....................Eph. 2:13–22
    For enrichment...................Eph. 1:16–19

C. Attitudes toward:

Murmuring .... Num. 11:1–10
Forgetfulness...................... Ps. 106:7–14
Rejection........................ Acts 13:44–47
Remembrance .... Luke 7:1–5
Gratefulness .... Acts 13:48

Benefice—*an enriching act or gift*

Manifested by a church............ Phil. 4:15–17
Encouraged in a friend ....Philem. 17–22
Justified in works ....James 2:14–17
Remembered in heaven.......... 1 Tim. 6:17–19

Bene Jaakan—*sons of Jaakan*

A wilderness station................ Num. 33:31

Benevolence—*generosity toward others*

A. Exercised toward:

The poor...............................Gal. 2:10
The needy........................... Eph. 4:28
Enemies...........................Prov. 25:21
God's servant......................Phil. 4:14–17

B. Measured by:

Ability............................. Acts 11:29
Love............................... 1 Cor. 13:3
Sacrifice ....Mark 12:41–44
Bountifulness ....2 Cor. 9:6–15

C. Blessings of:

Fulfills a grace.................... Rom. 12:6, 13
Performs a spiritual sacrifice......... Heb. 13:16
Makes us "more blessed" .... Acts 20:35
Enriches the giver.......Prov. 11:25; Is. 58:10, 11
Reward .... 1 Tim. 6:17–19

Ben-Hadad—*son of the god Hadad*

1. Ben-Hadad I, king of Damascus.
Hired by Asa, king of Judah, to attack
   Baasha, king of Israel .... 1 Kin. 15:18–21
2. Ben-Hadad II, king of Damascus.
Makes war on Ahab,
   king of Israel................. 1 Kin. 20:1–21
Defeated by Israel............... 1 Kin. 20:26–34
Fails in siege against
   Samaria .... 2 Kin. 6:24–33; 7:6–20
Killed by Hazael...................2 Kin. 8:7–15
3. Ben-Hadad III, king of Damascus.
Loses all Israelite conquests made by
   Hazael, his father .... 2 Kin. 13:3–25

Ben-Hail—*son of strength*

A teacher........................... 2 Chr. 17:7

Ben-Hanan—*son of the gracious one*

A son of Shimon ....1 Chr. 4:20

Ben Hesed—*son of mercy*

Father of one of Solomon's officers... 1 Kin. 4:7, 10

Beninu—*our son*

A Levite document signer .... Neh. 10:13

Benjamin—*son of the right hand*

Jacob's youngest son .... Gen. 35:16–20
Jacob's favorite son........... Gen. 42:4; 43:1–14
Loved by Joseph .... Gen. 43:29–34

Judah intercedes for.............. Gen. 44:18–34
Joseph's gifts to.....................Gen. 45:22
Father of five sons .... 1 Chr. 8:1, 2
Head of a tribe................. Num. 26:38–41
Jacob's prophecy concerning.........Gen. 49:27

Benjamin (others bearing this name)

1. A son of Bilhan ....1 Chr. 7:10
2. Son of Harim............. Ezra 10:18, 31, 32
Same as in........................... Neh. 3:23

Benjamin, tribe of

A. Background features of:

Descendants of Jacob's youngest
   son........................Gen. 35:17, 18, 24
Family divisions of............. Num. 26:38–41
Strength of.......................Num. 1:36, 37
Bounds of........................Josh. 18:11–28
Prophecies respecting .... Gen. 49:27; Deut. 33:12

B. Memorable events of:

Almost destroyed for protecting men
   of Gibeah....................Judg. 20:12–48
Wives provided for, to preserve the
   tribe..................... Judg. 21:1–23
Furnished Israel her first king ..... 1 Sam. 9:1–17
Hailed David's return .... 2 Sam. 19:16, 17
12,000 sealed.......................Rev. 7:8

C. Celebrities belonging to:

Ehud, a judge.......................Judg. 3:15
Saul, Israel's first king................1 Sam. 9:1
Abner, David's general ....1 Sam. 17:55
Mordecai............................ Esth. 2:5
The apostle Paul...................... Phil. 3:5

Beno—*his son*

A Merarite Levite.............. 1 Chr. 24:26, 27

Ben-Oni—*son of my sorrow*

Rachel's name for Benjamin ....Gen. 35:16–18

Ben-Zoheth—*son of Zoheth*

A man of Judah....................1 Chr. 4:20

Beon—*house of On*

A locality east of Jordan .... Num. 32:3
Same as Baal Meon...............Num. 32:37, 38

Beor—*a burning*

1. Father of Bela .... Gen. 36:32
2. Father of Balaam .... Num. 22:5; 2 Pet. 2:15

Bera—*excellent*

A king of Sodom..................... Gen. 14:2

Berachah—*blessing*

1. David's warrior..................... 1 Chr. 12:3
2. A valley in Judah near Tekoa .... 2 Chr. 20:26

Berachiah, Berechiah—*blessed by Yahweh*

1. Asaph's father .... 1 Chr. 6:39
2. Levite door-keepers............... 1 Chr. 15:23, 24
3. Head man of Ephraim .... 2 Chr. 28:12
4. Son of Zerubbabel .... 1 Chr. 3:20
5. Levite .... 1 Chr. 9:16
6. Postexilic workman.................. Neh. 3:4, 30
7. Father of Zechariah .... Zech. 1:1, 7; Matt. 23:35

Beraiah—*Yahweh has created*
A Benjamite chief....................1 Chr. 8:21

Berea—*watered*
A city of Macedonia visited
by Paul ....Acts 17:10–15

Bereavement—*the emotional state after a loved one's death*
A. General attitudes in:
Horror...........................Ex. 12:29, 30
Great emotion....................2 Sam. 18:33
Complaint ....Ruth 1:20, 21
Genuine sorrow ....Gen. 37:33–35
Submission........................Job 1:18–21
B. Christian attitudes in:
Unlike world's.................. 1 Thess. 4:13–18
Yet sorrow allowed......John 11:32–35; Acts 9:39
With hope of reunion .... John 11:20–27
C. Unusual circumstances of, mourning:
Forbidden............................Lev. 10:6
Of great length ....Gen. 50:1–11
Turned to joy........ Matt. 28:8; John 11:41–44

Bered—*hail*
1. A place in the wilderness of Shur......Gen. 16:7, 14
2. An Ephraimite .... 1 Chr. 7:20

Beri—*belonging to a well*
An Asherite ....1 Chr. 7:36

Beriah—*evil*
1. Son of Asher .... Gen. 46:17
2. Ephraim's son ....1 Chr. 7:22, 23
3. Chief of Benjamin .... 1 Chr. 8:13, 16
4. Levite ....1 Chr. 23:10, 11

Beriites
Descendants of Beriah ....Num. 26:44

Berites
A people in north Palestine ...... 2 Sam. 20:14, 15

Berith—*covenant*
Shechem idol ....Judg. 9:46
Same as Baal-Berith.............Judg. 8:33; 9:4

Bernice—*victorious*
Sister of Herod Agrippa II .... Acts 25:13, 23
Hears Paul's defense ....Acts 26:1–30

Berodach-Baladan
A king of Babylon............... 2 Kin. 20:12–19
Also called Merodach-Baladan.......... Is. 39:1

Berothah, Berothai—*wells*
City of Syria taken by David ....2 Sam. 8:8
Boundary in the ideal kingdom ....Ezek. 47:16

Beryl—*a precious stone*
In breastplate of high priest........ Ex. 28:15–21;
39:8–14
Ornament of a king ....Ezek. 28:12, 13
Describes a lover.....................Song 5:14
Applied to an angel ....Dan. 10:5, 6
Wheels like color of..................Ezek. 1:16
In New Jerusalem.....................Rev. 21:20

Besai
A family head .... Ezra 2:49

Besodeiah—*in the counsel of Yahweh*
Father of Meshullam...................Neh. 3:6

Besor—*cold*
A brook south of Ziklag ....1 Sam. 30:9, 10, 21

Bestial—*beastlike*
Condemned..........................Ex. 22:19
Punishment of.......................Lev. 20:13

Best seats—*seats or places of honor*
Sought by scribes and Pharisees.....Matt. 23:1, 6;
Mark 12:38, 39
Not to be sought...................Luke 14:7–11

Betah—*trust, confidence*
Cities of Hadadezer...................2 Sam. 8:8
Called Tibhath ....1 Chr. 18:8

Beten—*valley*
City of Asher ....Josh. 19:25

Beth—*house*
Second letter of the
Hebrew alphabet ....Ps. 119:9–16

Bethabara—*house of passage*
A place beyond Jordan where John
baptized ....John 1:28

Beth Acacia
A town of Judah ....Judg. 7:22

Beth Anath—*house of Anath (the goddess)*
A town of Naphtali ....Josh. 19:38, 39
Canaanites remain in ....Judg. 1:33

Beth Anoth—*house of Anoth (the goddess)*
A town of Judah ....Josh. 15:59

Bethany—*house of poverty*
A town on Mt. of Olives ....Luke 19:29
Home of Lazarus .... John 11:1
Home of Simon, the leper............. Matt. 26:6
Jesus visits there .... Mark 11:1, 11, 12
Scene, Ascension................. Luke 24:50, 51

Beth Aphrah—*house of dust*
A Philistine city; symbolic of doom .....Mic. 1:10

Beth Arabah—*house of desert*
A village of Judah..................Josh. 15:6, 61
Assigned to Benjamin ....Josh. 18:21, 22

Beth Arbel—*house of God's ambush*
A town destroyed by Shalman......... Hos. 10:14

Beth Aven—*house of nothingness (vanity)*
A town of Benjamin....................Josh. 7:2
Israel defeated Philistines there ...... 1 Sam. 13:5

Beth Baal Meon
City of Reuben ....Josh. 13:17

Beth Barah—*house of the ford*
A passage over Jordan.................Judg. 7:24

Beth Biri—*house of my creation*
A town of Simeon....................1 Chr. 4:31
Probably same as Beth Lebaoth........Josh. 19:6

Beth Car—*house of a lamb*
Site of Philistines' retreat.............1 Sam. 7:11

Beth Dagon—*house of Dagon*
1. Village of Judah ....Josh. 15:41
2. Town of Asher .... Josh. 19:27

Beth Diblathaim—*house of fig cakes*
A Moabite town ....Jer. 48:21, 22

Bethel—*house of God*
1. A town of Benjamin.................. Judg. 21:19
Abraham settles near................ Gen. 12:7, 8
Site of Abraham's altar .... Gen. 13:3, 4
Scene of Jacob's ladder ....Gen. 28:10–19
Luz becomes Bethel.................. Gen. 28:19
Jacob returns to.....................Gen. 35:1–15
On Ephraim's border................Josh. 16:1–4
Samuel judged there............ 1 Sam. 7:15, 16
Site of worship and sacrifice .... 1 Sam. 10:3
Center of idolatry.............. 1 Kin. 12:28–33
School of prophets ....2 Kin. 2:1, 3
Youths from, mock Elisha .... 2 Kin. 2:23, 24
Josiah destroys altars of ....2 Kin. 23:4, 15–20
Denounced by a man of God.......1 Kin. 13:1–10
Denounced by Amos.............Amos 7:10–13
Denounced by Jeremiah............... Jer. 48:13
Denounced by Hosea................. Hos. 10:15
2. Simeonite town......................1 Sam. 30:27
Called Bethul and Bethuel........... Josh. 19:4;
1 Chr. 4:30

Beth Emek—*house of the valley*
A town of Asher ....Josh. 19:27

Bether—*separation*
Designates mountains................ Song 2:17

Bethesda—*house of mercy*
Jerusalem pool......................John 5:2–4

Beth Ezel—*a place near*
A town of Judah ....Mic. 1:11

Beth Gader—*house of the wall*
A town of Judah ....1 Chr. 2:51
Probably same as Geder ....Josh. 12:13

Beth Gamul—*house of recompense*
A Moabite town .... Jer. 48:23

Beth Haccerem—*house of the vineyard*
Town of Judah.........................Jer. 6:1

Beth Haram—*mountain house*
A town of Gad......................Josh. 13:27
Same as Beth Haran................. Num. 32:36

Beth Hoglah—*house of the partridge*
A village of Benjamin ....Josh. 15:6; 18:19, 21

Beth Horon—*house of the hollow*
Twin towns of Ephraim ....Josh. 16:3, 5
Built by Sheerah ....1 Chr. 7:24
Assigned to Kohathite Levites .....Josh. 21:20, 22

Fortified by Solomon............... 2 Chr. 8:3–5
Prominent in battles ....Josh. 10:10–14;
1 Sam. 13:18

Beth Jeshimoth, Beth Jesimoth—*house of the wastes*
A town near Pisgah ....Josh. 12:3
Israel camps near .... Num. 33:49
Assigned to Reubenites...............Josh. 13:20
Later a town of Moab ....Ezek. 25:9

Beth Lebaoth—*house of lionesses*
A town in south Judah; assigned to
Simeonites.......................Josh. 19:6
Called Lebaoth....................Josh. 15:32

Bethlehem (of Judah)—*house of bread*
A. Significant features of:
Built by Salma ....1 Chr. 2:51
Originally called Ephrath............. Gen. 35:16
Burial of Rachel .... Gen. 35:19
Two wandering
Levites of ....Judg. 17:1–13; 19:1–30
Naomi's home .... Ruth 1:1, 19
Home of Boaz ....Ruth 4:9–11
Home of David .... 1 Sam. 16:1–18
Stronghold of Philistines .... 2 Sam. 23:14, 15
Fortified by Rehoboam..............2 Chr. 11:5, 6
Refuge of Gedaliah's murderers..... Jer. 41:16, 17
B. Messianic features of:
Sought for the tabernacle........... Ps. 132:5–7
Predicted place of the Messiah's birth ... Mic. 5:2
Fulfillment cited.............. Matt. 2:1, 5, 6
Infants of, slain by Herod..............Jer. 31:15;
Matt. 2:16–18

Bethlehem (of Zebulun)
Town assigned to Zebulun........Josh. 19:15, 16
Home of judge Ibzan.............. Judg. 12:8–11

Beth Maachah—*house of Maachah*
Tribe of Israel .... 2 Sam. 20:14, 15

Beth Marcaboth—*house of the chariots*
Town of Simeon .... Josh. 19:5

Beth Meon—*house of habitation*
Moabite town .... Jer. 48:23

Beth Millo—*house of a terrace*
Stronghold at Shechem............. Judg. 9:6, 20

Beth Nimrah—*house of the leopard*
Town of Gad ....Num. 32:3, 36

Beth Pazzez—*house of dispersion*
Town of Issachar ....Josh. 19:21

Beth Pelet—*house of escape*
Town of Judah.......................Josh. 15:27

Beth Peor—*house of Peor*
Town near Pisgah.................... Deut. 3:29
Valley of Moses' burial place.......... Deut. 34:6
Assigned to Reubenites............Josh. 13:15, 20

Bethphage—*house of unripe figs*
Village near Bethany..................Mark 11:1
Near Mt. of Olives ....Matt. 21:1

Beth-Rapha—*house of a giant*
A town or family of Judah . . . . 1 Chr. 4:12

Beth Rehob—*house of a street*
A town in north Palestine . . . . .Judg. 18:28
Inhabited by Syrians . . . . 2 Sam. 10:6

Bethsaida—*place of fishing*
A city of Galilee . . . . Mark 6:45
Home of Andrew, Peter and
    Philip .John 1:44; 12:21
Blind man healed . . . . Mark 8:22, 23
Near feeding of 5,000 . . . . .Luke 9:10–17
Unbelief of, denounced. . . Matt. 11:21; Luke 10:13

Beth Shan, Beth Shean—*house of security*
A town in Issachar . . . . Josh. 17:11
Assigned to Manasseh. . . . . 1 Chr. 7:29
Tribute paid by . . . . .Josh. 17:12–16
Users of iron chariots . . . . Josh. 17:16
Saul's corpse hung up at . . . . 1 Sam. 31:10–13;
    2 Sam. 21:12–14

Beth Shemesh—*house of the sun*
1. A border town between Judah and Dan. . .Josh. 15:10
Also called Ir Shemesh . . . . Josh. 19:41
Assigned to priests . . . . .Josh. 21:16
Ark brought to . . . . 1 Sam. 6:12–19
Joash defeats Amaziah at . . . . .2 Kin. 14:11
Taken by Philistines . . . . .2 Chr. 28:18
2. A town of Naphtali . . . . Josh. 19:38
3. A town of Issachar. . . . . Josh. 19:22
4. Egyptian city. . . . . .Jer. 43:13

Beth Tappuah—*house of apples*
A town of Judah . . . . .Josh. 15:53

Bethuel—*abode of God*
1. Father of Laban and
    Rebekah . . . . Gen. 22:20–23; 24:29
2. Simeonite town. . . . . 1 Chr. 4:30
Called Bethul. . . . . .Josh. 19:4

Beth Zur—*house of a rock*
A town of Judah .Josh. 15:58
Fortified by Rehoboam. . . . . 2 Chr. 11:7
Help to rebuild . . . . Neh. 3:16

Betonim—*pistachio nuts*
A town of Gad. . . . . .Josh. 13:26

Betrayal—*a breach of trust*
A. Of Christ:
    Predicted . . . . Ps. 41:9
    Frequently mentioned. . . . Matt. 17:22; John 13:21
    Betrayer identified. . . . . .John 13:26
    Sign of, a kiss . . . . .Matt. 26:48, 49
    Guilt of . . . . Matt. 27:3, 4
    Supper before. . . . . 1 Cor. 11:23
B. Examples of:
    Israelites by Gibeonites. . . . . .Josh. 9:22
    Samson by Delilah . . . . Judg. 16:18–20
    The woman of En Dor by Saul . . . .1 Sam. 28:9–12
    Jesus by Judas . . . . .Matt. 26:14–16
    Christians. . . . . Matt. 10:21

Betrothed—*given in marriage*
Treatment of . . . . .Ex. 21:8, 9

Beulah—*married*
A symbol of true Israel . . . . Is. 62:4, 5

Beverage—*a drink*
A. Literal:
    Milk. . . . . .Judg. 4:19; 5:25
    Strong drink. . . . . Prov. 31:6
    Water. . . . . Matt. 10:42
    Wine . . . . 1 Tim. 5:23
B. Figurative:
    Christ's blood . . . . John 6:53
    Cup of suffering . . . . John 18:11
    Living water. . . . . John 4:10
    Water of life. .Rev. 22:17

Beware—*be wary of; guard against*
A. Of evil things:
    False prophets . . . . .Matt. 7:15
    Evil men . . . . Matt. 10:17
    Covetousness. . . . . .Luke 12:15
    Dogs (figurative) . . . . Phil. 3:2
B. Of possibilities:
    Disobeying God . . . . Ex. 23:20, 21
    Forgetting God. . . . . Deut. 6:12
    Being led away. . . . . .2 Pet. 3:17

Bewitch—*to charm, captivate, or astound*
Activity of Simon . . . . Acts 8:9–11
Descriptive of legalism . . . . .Gal. 3:1

Bezai—*shining; high*
Postexilic family head . . . . .Ezra 2:17; Neh. 7:23
Signs document. Neh. 10:18

Bezalel—*in the shadow (protection) of God*
1. Hur's grandson . . . . 1 Chr. 2:20
Tabernacle builder . . . . .Ex. 31:1–11; 35:30–35
2. Divorced foreign wife . . . . .Ezra 10:18, 30

Bezek—*scattering*
1. Town near Jerusalem. . . . . Judg. 1:4, 5
2. Saul's army gathered there. . . . . 1 Sam. 11:8

Bezer—*fortress*
1. An Asherite . . . . 1 Chr. 7:37
2. City of Reuben . . . . .Deut. 4:43
Place of refuge. . . . . .Josh. 20:8

Bible history, outlined
A. Prepatriarchal period, the:
    Creation . . . . Gen. 1:1–2:25
    Fall of man . . . . .Gen. 3:1–24
    Development of wickedness . . . . .Gen. 4:1–6:8
    Flood. . . . . .Gen. 6:9–8:22
    Establishment of nations . . . . .Gen. 9:1–10:32
    Confusion of tongues . . . . .Gen. 11:1–32
B. Patriarchal period:
    Abraham. .Gen. 12:1–25:11
    Isaac. . . . . Gen. 21:1–28:9; 35:27–29
    Jacob . . . . Gen. 25:19–37:36; 45:21–46:7; 49:1–33
    Joseph . . . . .Gen. 7:1–50:26

Peter confesses Jesus is Christ..... Matt. 16:5–16; Mark 8:27–29

Foretells death..... Matt. 16:21–26; Luke 9:22–25

Transfiguration .... Matt. 17:1–13; Luke 9:28–36

Forgiving of adulteress .... John 7:53–8:11

Resurrection of Lazarus .... John 11:1–44

Blesses the children .... Matt. 19:13–15; Mark 10:13–16

Bartimaeus healed .... Matt. 20:29–34; Mark 10:46–52

Meets Zacchaeus .... Luke 19:1–10

Triumphant entry... Matt. 21:1–9; Luke 19:29–44

Anointed.......... Matt. 26:6–13; Mark 14:3–9

The Passover ..... Matt. 26:17–19; Luke 22:7–13

The Lord's Supper .... Matt. 26:26–29; Mark 14:22–25

Gethsemane..................... Luke 22:39–46

Betrayal and arrest.............. Matt. 26:47–56; John 18:3–12

Before the Sanhedrin........... Matt. 26:57–68; Luke 22:54–65

Denied by Peter................... John 18:15–27

Before Pilate .... Matt. 27:2–14; Luke 23:1–7

Before Herod................... Luke 23:6–12

Returns to Pilate................ Matt. 27:15–26; Luke 23:13–25

Crucifixion ..... Matt. 27:35–56; Luke 23:33–49

Burial.......... Matt. 27:57–66; Luke 23:50–56

Resurrection .... Matt. 28:1–15; John 20:1–18

Appearance to disciples .... Luke 24:36–43; John 20:19–25

Appearance to Thomas.......... John 20:26–31

Great commission ....Matt. 28:16–20

Ascension .... Luke 24:50–53

N. The early church:

Pentecost .... Acts 2:1–42

In Jerusalem...................... Acts 2:3–6:7

Martyrdom of Stephen .... Acts 6:8–7:60

In Judea and Samaria .... Acts 8:1–12:25

Conversion of Saul.................. Acts 9:1–18

First missionary journey......... Acts 13:1–14:28

Jerusalem conference.............. Acts 15:1–35

Second missionary journey ..... Acts 15:36–18:22

Third missionary journey ...... Acts 18:23–21:16

Captivity of Paul.............. Acts 21:27–28:31

Bichri—*firstborn*

Father of Sheba .... 2 Sam. 20:1

Bidkar—*servant of Kar*

Captain under Jehu .... 2 Kin. 9:25

Bigamist—*having more than one wife*

First, Lamech........................ Gen. 4:19

Bigamy (see Marriage)

Bigotry—*excessive prejudice; blind fanaticism*

A. Characteristics of:

Name-calling.......................John 8:48, 49

Spiritual blindness................ John 9:39–41

Hatred.......................... Acts 7:54–58

Self-righteousness .... Phil. 3:4–6

Ignorance .... 1 Tim. 1:13

B. Examples of:

Haman .... Esth. 3:8–10

The Pharisees .... John 8:33–48

Saul (Paul) .... Acts 9:1, 2

Peter............................. Acts 10:14, 28

See Intolerance; Persecution

Bigtha—*gift of God*

An officer of Ahasuerus .... Esth. 1:10

Bigthan, Bigthana—*gift of God*

Conspired against Ahasuerus ...... Esth. 2:21; 6:2

Bigvai—*happy*

1. Zerubbabel's companion ..... Ezra 2:2; Neh. 7:7, 19

2. One who signs covenant................ Neh. 10:16

Bildad—*Bel has loved*

One of Job's friends .... Job 2:11

Makes three speeches .... Job 8:1–22; 18:1–21; 25:1–6

Bileam—*greed*

A town of Manasseh .... 1 Chr. 6:70

Bilgah—*brightness; cheerfulness*

1. A descendant of Aaron........... 1 Chr. 24:1, 6, 14

2. A chief of the priests .... Neh. 12:5, 7, 18

Same as Bilgai; signs document .... Neh. 10:8

Bilhah—*foolish; simple*

1. Rachel's maid .... Gen. 29:29

The mother of Dan and Naphtali ....Gen. 30:1–8

Commits incest with Reuben .... Gen. 35:22

2. Simeonite town....................... 1 Chr. 4:29

Same as Baalah .... Josh. 15:29

Bilhan—*foolish; simple*

1. A Horite chief; son of Ezer ....Gen. 36:27; 1 Chr. 1:42

2. A Benjamite family head .... 1 Chr. 7:10

Bilshan—*searcher*

A postexilic leader .... Ezra 2:2; Neh. 7:7

Bimhal—*with pruning*

An Asherite .... 1 Chr. 7:33

Bin

For food storage .... 1 Kin. 17:12–16

Binding—*a restraint; a tying together*

A. Used literally of:

Tying a man......................... Gen. 22:9

Imprisonment.............. 2 Kin. 17:4; Acts 22:4

B. Used figuratively of:

A fixed agreement .... Num. 30:2

God's Word .... Prov. 3:3

The broken-hearted................... Is. 61:1

Satan .... Luke 13:16

The wicked...................... Matt. 13:30

Ceremonialism .... Matt. 23:4

The keys .... Matt. 16:19

A determined plan .... Acts 20:22

Marriage........................... Rom. 7:2

Binea
　　A son of Moza . . . . .1 Chr. 8:37

Binnui—*built*
1. Head of postexilic family. . . . . .Neh. 7:15
　　Called Bani . . . . .Ezra 2:10
2. Son of Pahath-Moab . . . . .Ezra 10:30
3. Son of Bani. . . . . .Ezra 10:38
4. Postexilic Levite. . . . . .Neh. 12:8
　　Henadad's son. . . . . Neh. 10:9
　　Family of, builds wall . . . . Neh. 3:24

Bird cage
　　Used figuratively . . . . .Jer. 5:27

Birds—*vertebrates with feathers and wings*
A. List of:
　　Buzzard. . . . . .Lev. 11:13
　　Dove. . . . . Gen. 8:8
　　Eagle . . . . Job 39:27
　　Falcon . . . . Deut. 14:13
　　Hawk . . . . Job 39:26
　　Hen . . . . Matt. 23:37
　　Heron . . . . .Lev. 11:19
　　Hoopoe . . . . .Lev. 11:19
　　Jackal. . . . . Job 30:29
　　Kite . . . . Deut. 14:13
　　Ostrich . . . . Job 30:29
　　Owls. . . . . .Lev. 11:16
　　Desert . . . . .Ps. 102:6
　　Fisher. . . . . .Lev. 11:17
　　Screech . . . . .Lev. 11:17
　　Little . . . . .Lev. 11:17
　　Partridge. . . . . 1 Sam. 26:20
　　Pelican. . . . . .Ps. 102:6
　　Pigeon . . . . .Lev. 12:6
　　Quail . . . . Num. 11:31, 32
　　Raven. . . . . Job 38:41
　　Rooster . . . . Matt. 26:34, 74; Mark 14:30;
　　　　Luke 22:61; John 18:27
　　Sparrow. . . . . .Matt. 10:29–31
　　Stork . . . . .Ps. 104:17
　　Swallow. . . . . .Ps. 84:3
　　Swift. . . . . .Jer. 8:7
　　Turtledove . . . . .Song 2:12
　　Vulture . . . . .Lev. 11:13
B. Features regarding:
　　Created by God. . . . . .Gen. 1:20, 21
　　Named by Adam. . . . . .Gen. 2:19, 20
　　Clean, unclean. Gen. 8:20
　　Differ from animals. . . . . .1 Cor. 15:39
　　Under man's dominion . . . . Ps. 8:6–8
　　For food . . . . .Gen. 9:2, 3
　　Belong to God . . . . .Ps. 50:11
　　God provides for. . . Ps. 104:10–12; Luke 12:23, 24
　　Can be tamed. . . . . James 3:7
　　Differ in singing . . . . .Song 2:12
　　Some migratory . . . . .Jer. 8:7
　　Solomon writes of. . . . . .1 Kin. 4:33
　　Clean, used in sacrifices . . . . Lev. 1:14;
　　　　Luke 2:23, 24

　　Worshiped . . . . .Rom. 1:23
C. Figurative of:
　　Escape from evil . . . . .Ps. 124:7
　　A wanderer. . . . . .Prov. 27:8
　　Snares of death . . . . .Eccl. 9:12
　　Cruel kings. . . . . Is. 46:11
　　Hostile nations . . . . .Jer. 12:9
　　Wicked rich . . . . .Jer. 17:11
　　Kingdom of heaven . . . . Matt. 13:32
　　Maternal love. . . . . Matt. 23:37

Birsha—*with wickedness*
　　A king of Gomorrah . . . . .Gen. 14:2, 8, 10

Birth—*the act of coming into life*
A. Kinds of:
　　Natural . . . . Eccl. 7:1
　　Figurative. . . . . Is. 37:3
　　Supernatural . . . . Matt. 1:18–25
　　The new . . . . John 3:5
　　See New birth
B. Natural, features regarding:
　　Pain of, results from sin . . . . Gen. 3:16
　　Produces a sinful being. . . . . Ps. 51:5
　　Makes ceremonially unclean. . . . . .Lev. 12:2, 5;
　　　　Luke 2:22
　　Affliction from . . . . John 9:1
　　Twins of, differ . . . . .Gen. 25:21–23
　　Sometimes brings death . . . . Gen. 35:16–20
　　Pain of, forgotten . . . . John 16:21

Birthday—*date of one's birth*
　　Job and Jeremiah curse theirs . . . . .Job 3:1–11;
　　　　Jer. 20:14, 15
Celebration:
　　Pharaoh's . . . . .Gen. 40:20
　　Herod's . . . . Mark 6:21

Birthright—*legal rights inherited by birth*
A. Blessings of:
　　Seniority. . . . . .Gen. 43:33
　　Double portion . . . . Deut. 21:15–17
　　Royal succession .2 Chr. 21:3
B. Loss of:
　　Esau's—by sale . . . . Gen. 25:29–34; Heb. 12:16
　　Reuben's—as a punishment. . . . . Gen. 49:3, 4;
　　　　1 Chr. 5:1, 2
　　Manasseh's—by Jacob's will . . . . . .Gen. 48:15–20;
　　　　1 Chr. 5:1, 2
　　David's brother—by divine will . . .1 Sam. 16:2–22
　　Adonijah's—by the Lord . . . . .1 Kin. 2:13, 15
　　Hosah's son's—by his father's will. . . .1 Chr. 26:10
C. Transferred to:
　　Jacob . . . . Gen. 27:6–46
　　Judah. . . . . .Gen. 49:8–10
　　Solomon . . . . 1 Chr. 28:5–7
　　See Firstborn

Birth pangs—*the labor pains of childbirth*
A. Descriptive of:
　　Anguish. . . . . Is. 53:11
B. Of a woman's, described as:
　　Fearful. . . . . .Ps. 48:6

Painful............................... Is. 13:8
Hazardous.....................Gen. 35:16–19
Joyful afterward.................... John 16:21

C. Figurative of:
New Israel.......................... Is. 66:7, 8
Messiah's birth.................... Mic. 4:9, 10
Redemption..........................Mic. 5:3
New birth...........................Gal. 4:19
Creation's rebirth...................Rom. 8:22

Births, foretold

A. Over a short period:
Ishmael's.......................... Gen. 16:11
Isaac's............................ Gen. 18:10
Samson's......................... Judg. 13:3, 24
Samuel's......................... 1 Sam. 1:11, 20
Shunammite's son's...............2 Kin. 4:16, 17
John the Baptist's.................... Luke 1:13

B. Over a longer period:
Josiah's...........................1 Kin. 13:2
Cyrus's........................... Is. 45:1–4
Christ's.................. Gen. 3:15; Mic. 5:1–3

Birthstool
Used during childbirth.................Ex. 1:16

Birzaith—*olive well*
An Asherite........................ 1 Chr. 7:31

Bishlam—*in peace*
A Persian officer.......................Ezra 4:7

Bishop—*an overseer; elder*

A. Qualifications of, given by:
Paul.............................. 1 Tim. 3:1–7
Peter, called "elder"................. 1 Pet. 5:1–4

B. Office of:
Same as overseer or elder.......... Acts 20:17, 28
Several in a church...............Acts 20:17, 28;
    Phil. 1:1
Follows ordination...................Titus 1:5, 7
Held by Christ....................... 1 Pet. 2:25

C. Duties of:
Oversee the church............Acts 20:17, 28–31
Feed God's flock.......................1 Pet. 5:2
Watch over believers' souls........... Heb. 13:17
Teach.............................1 Tim. 5:17

Bit—*a part of a horse's bridle*
Figurative, of humankind's
    stubborn nature...........Ps. 32:9; James 3:3

Bithiah—*daughter of Yahweh*
Pharaoh's daughter; wife of Mered.... 1 Chr. 4:18

Bithron—*ravine; gorge*
A district east of Jordan.............. 2 Sam. 2:29

Bithynia—*a province of Asia Minor*
The Spirit keeps Paul from.............Acts 16:7
Peter writes to Christians of............1 Pet. 1:1

Bitter

A. Used of:
The soul............................ Job 3:20
Words.............................Ps. 64:3

Water........................... Num. 5:24
Demanding woman.................. Eccl. 7:26
Sin............................. Prov. 5:4
Death.............................Jer. 31:15

B. Avoidance of:
Toward a wife.......................Col. 3:19
As contrary to the truth.............. James 3:14

Bitter herbs
Part of Passover meal........Ex. 12:8; Num. 9:11

"Bitter is sweet"
Descriptive of human hunger.......... Prov. 27:7

Bittern—*a nocturnal member of heron family*
Sings in desolate windows........... Zeph. 2:14

Bitterness—*extreme enmity; sour temper*

A. Kinds of:
The heart..........................Prov. 14:10
Death.......................... 1 Sam. 15:32

B. Causes of:
Childlessness.................... 1 Sam. 1:5, 10
A foolish son......................Prov. 17:25
Sickness............................. Is. 38:17

C. Avoidance of:
Toward others....................... Eph. 4:31
As a source of defilement............. Heb. 12:15

Bitter waters
Made sweet by a tree............... Ex. 15:23–25
Swallowed by suspected wife....... Num. 5:11–31

Bizjothjah—*contempt of Yahweh*
A town in south Judah................Josh. 15:28

Biztha—*eunuch*
An officer under Ahasuerus........... Esth. 1:10

Blackness—*destitute of light*

A. Literally of:
Hair............................... Song 5:11
Horse............................. Zech. 6:2
Sky...............................1 Kin. 18:45
Mountain......................... Heb. 12:18
Night............................. Prov. 7:9

B. Figuratively of:
Hell................................. Jude 13

C. Specifically:
Let blackness of the day.................Job 3:5
Clothe heaven with.................... Is. 50:3

Blamelessness—*freedom from fault; innocency*

A. Used ritualistically of:
Priests............................ Matt. 12:5
Proper observance..................... Luke 1:6
Works, righteousness.................. Phil. 3:6

B. Desirable in:
Bishops (elders)...........1 Tim. 3:2; Titus 1:6, 7
Deacons........................... 1 Tim. 3:10
Widows............................1 Tim. 5:7

C. Attainment of:
Desirable now...................... Phil. 2:15
At Christ's return.......1 Cor. 1:8; 1 Thess. 5:23;
    2 Pet. 3:14

WORD STUDY

BLASPHEME, *blasphēmeō* (blas-fay-meh-oh). In its wider sense this verb means "to injure the reputation of," "to defame," "to slander," "to revile," and it is used in relation to humans (as in Rom. 3:8). Most NT usages of *blasphēmeō* pertain to the defamation of the sacred, and it is properly translated as "blaspheme," especially in instances where people "blaspheme" God (Rev. 16:11), God's name (Rom. 2:24), and Jesus (Luke 23:39). Jesus Himself is accused of blaspheming (Matt. 9:3), as were the early Christians (cf. the cognate noun in Acts 6:11). Jesus gravely warns against blaspheming the Holy Spirit (Mark 3:29). (Strong's #987)

Blasphemy—*cursing God*
A. Arises out of:
     Pride .... Ps. 73:9, 11; Ezek. 35:12, 13
     Hatred .... Ps. 74:18
     Affliction .... Is. 8:21
     Injustice .... Is. 52:5
     Defiance .... Is. 36:15–20
     Skepticism .... Ezek. 9:8; Mal. 3:13, 14
     Self-deification ...... Dan. 11:36, 37; 2 Thess. 2:4
     Unworthy conduct .... 2 Sam. 12:13, 14;
        Rom. 2:24
B. Instances of:
     Job's wife .... Job 2:9
     Shelomith's son .... Lev. 24:11–16, 23
     Sennacherib .... 2 Kin. 19:4, 10, 22
     The Beast .... Dan. 7:25; Rev. 13:1, 5, 6
     The Jews .... Luke 22:65
     Saul of Tarsus .... 1 Tim. 1:13
     Gentiles .... Rom. 1:28–32
     Hymenaeus .... 1 Tim. 1:20
C. Those falsely accused of:
     Naboth .... 1 Kin. 21:12, 13
     Jesus .... Matt. 9:3; 26:65
     Stephen .... Acts 6:11, 13
D. Guilt of:
     Punishable by death .... Lev. 24:11, 16
     Christ accused of .... John 10:33, 36
See Revile

Blasphemy against the Holy Spirit
     Attributing Christ's miracles to
        Satan .... Matt. 12:22–32
     Never forgivable .... Mark 3:28–30

Blasting—*injure severely*
     Shows God's power .... Ex. 15:8
     Sent as judgment .... Amos 4:9
     Figurative of death .... Job 4:9

Blastus—*sprout*
     Herod's chamberlain .... Acts 12:20

WORD STUDY

BLEMISH, WITHOUT, *tamim* (taw-meem). *Tamim* is an adjective used in the OT to indicate that which is "complete" or "sound." Therefore, it is that which is "without blemish." The word can refer to humans (Prov. 1:12) or plants (Ezek. 15:5), but most often the term is used in describing sacrificial animals that had no imperfections and were thus acceptable to God. Sometimes the word is used to refer to God's way, meaning a way that is perfect (Ps. 18:30). (Strong's #8549)

Blemish—*any deformity or injury*
A. Those without physical:
     Priests .... Lev. 21:17–24
     Absalom .... 2 Sam. 14:25
     Animals used in sacrifices .... Lev. 22:19–25;
        Mal. 1:8
B. Those without moral:
     Christ .... Heb. 9:14
     The church .... Eph. 5:27
C. Those with:
     Apostates .... 2 Pet. 2:13

WORD STUDY

BLESS, *barak* (baw-rak). *Barak* is a verb meaning "kneel" or "bless." It is used frequently referring to God in the phrase "Blessed be the LORD" (Ex. 18:10; Ruth 4:14), indicating an act of adoration sometimes on bended knee. Frequently God blesses humans, meaning that they are given benefits (Ps. 115:12 and many others). Occasionally God blesses things, such as a sabbath (Gen. 2:3), fields (Gen. 27:27), work (Deut. 28:12), or bread (Ex. 23:25). Humans could also bless humans, as when fathers on their deathbed blessed their children (Gen. 27). The term can have the opposite meaning of "curse," as in Job where Job's wife and friends tell him to "curse God and die" (Job 2:9). (Strong's #1288)

Bless—*to bestow blessings upon*
     To give divine blessings .... Gen. 1:22; 9:1–7
     To adore God for His blessings .... Gen. 24:48;
        Ps. 103:1
     To invoke blessings upon another .... Gen. 24:60;
        27:4, 27

WORD STUDY

BLESSED, *makarios* (mak-ar-ee-oss). This adjective is usually translated "blessed," "fortunate," or "happy," and in the NT it carries with it the obvious religious sense of "privileged recipient of divine favor." This is certainly the case with the Beatitudes spoken by Jesus (Matt. 5), as well as with blessings spoken by others (Luke 1:45; Rev. 22:7). Even in situations where the translation "fortunate" or "happy" seems warranted (Acts 26:2; 1 Cor. 7:40), the religious connotation cannot be excluded. Parts of the body are deemed objects of a special grace, and thus "blessed" (for example, the eyes in Matt. 13:16 and Luke 10:23). (Strong's #3107)

Blessed—*the objects of God's favors*
A. Reasons for, they:
     Are chosen .... Eph. 1:3, 4
     Believe .... Gal. 3:9
     Are forgiven .... Ps. 32:1, 2
     Are justified .... Rom. 4:6–9

Are instructed.........................Ps. 94:12
Keep God's Word......................Rev. 1:3
B. Time of:
Eternal past .... Eph. 1:3, 4
Present............................Luke 6:22
Eternal future .... Matt. 25:34

Blessings—*the gift of God's grace*
A. Physical and temporal:
Prosperity......................Mal. 3:10–12
Food, clothing............... Matt. 6:26, 30–33
Sowing, harvest.....................Acts 14:17
Longevity............................Ex. 20:12
Children .... Ps. 127:3–5
B. National and Israelitish:
General............................Gen. 12:1–3
Specific .... Rom. 9:4, 5
Fulfilled .... Rom. 11:1–36
Perverted .... Rom. 2:17–29
Rejected ....Acts 13:46–52
C. Spiritual and eternal:
Salvation........................... John 3:16
Election............................ Eph. 1:3–5
Regeneration....................... 2 Cor. 5:17
Forgiveness...........................Col. 1:14
Adoption...................... Rom. 8:15–17
No condemnation...................Rom. 8:1
Holy Spirit ....Acts 1:8
Justification...................Acts 13:38, 39
New covenant ....Heb. 8:6–13
Fatherly chastisement.............Heb. 12:5–11
Christ's intercession.................. Rom. 8:34
Sanctification .... Rom. 8:3–14
Perseverance ....John 10:27–29
Glorification ....Rom. 8:30

Blindfold—*a covering over the eyes*
A prelude to execution .... Esth. 7:8
Put on Jesus .... Luke 22:63, 64

Blindness—*destitute of vision*
A. Causes of:
Old age .... Gen. 27:1
Disobedience...................Deut. 28:28, 29
Miracle .... 2 Kin. 6:18–20
Judgment ....Gen. 19:1–11
Captivity........................ Judg. 16:20, 21
Condition of servitude ....1 Sam. 11:2
Defeat in war.......................2 Kin. 25:7
Unbelief .... Acts 9:8, 9
God's glory........................John 9:1–3
B. Disabilities of:
Keep from priesthood..............Lev. 21:17, 18
Offerings unacceptable.......Lev. 22:22; Mal. 1:8
Make protection.....................Lev. 19:14
Helplessness.......................Judg. 16:26
Occasional derision ....2 Sam. 5:6–8
C. Remedies for:
Promised in Christ.................. Is. 42:7, 16
Proclaimed in the gospel ....Luke 4:18–21;
Acts 26:18

Portrayed in a miracle...John 9:1–41; Acts 9:1–18
Perfected in faith .... John 11:37; Eph. 1:15–19
Perverted by disobedience...........1 John 2:11

Blood
A. Used to designate:
Unity of humankind .... Acts 17:26
Human nature....................... John 1:13
Human depravity .... Ezek. 16:6, 22
The individual soul ....Ezek. 33:8
The essence of life ....Gen. 9:4; Lev. 17:11, 14
The sacredness of life .... Gen. 9:5, 6
Means of atonement .... Lev. 17:10–14
Regeneration ....Is. 4:4; Ezek. 16:9
New covenant .... Matt. 26:28
The new life.....................John 6:53–56
Christ's atonement.................... Heb. 9:14
Redemption.......................Zech. 9:11
B. Miracles connected with:
Water turns to..................... Ex. 7:20, 21
Water appears like .... 2 Kin. 3:22, 23
The moon turns to..........Acts 2:20; Rev. 6:12
Flow of, stops..................... Mark 5:25, 29
Sea becomes ....Rev. 11:6
Believers become white in .... Rev. 7:14
C. Figurative of:
Sin.................................... Is. 59:3
Cruelty .... Hab. 2:12
Abominations .... Is. 66:3
Inherited guilt..................... Matt. 23:35
Guilt...................2 Sam. 1:16; Matt. 27:25
Vengeance ....Ezek. 35:6
Retribution ....Is. 49:25, 26
Slaughter.........................Is. 34:6–8
Judgment ....Rev. 16:6
Victory .... Ps. 58:10

Blood of Christ
A. Described as:
Innocent.......................... Matt. 27:4
Precious..........................1 Pet. 1:19
Necessary ....Heb. 9:22, 23
Sufficient ....Heb. 9:13, 14
Final............................. Heb. 9:24–28
Cleansing ....1 John 1:7
Conquering ....Rev. 12:11
B. Basis of:
Reconciliation...................Eph. 2:13–16
Redemption..................... Rom. 3:24, 25
Justification.........................Rom. 5:9
Sanctification .... Heb. 10:29
Communion .... Matt. 26:26–29
Victory ....Rev. 12:11
Eternal life ....John 6:53–56

Bloodguiltiness—*guilt incurred by murder*
Incurred by willful murderer ....Ex. 21:14
Not saved by altar....................1 Kin. 2:29
Provision for innocent...Ex. 21:13; 1 Kin. 1:50–53
David's prayer concerning .... Ps. 51:14
Judas's guilt in.................... Matt. 27:3, 4

The Jews' admission of . . . . .Matt. 27:23–25
Of Christ-rejectors . . . . Acts 18:5, 6

Blood money
Payment made to Judas . . . . .Matt. 26:14–16

Bloodthirsty
Descriptive of:
Saul's house . . . . .2 Sam. 21:1
David . . . . 2 Sam. 16:6, 7

Bloody
Descriptive of:
Cities . . . . .Ezek. 22:2; 24:6, 9

Bloody sweat—*(believed to be caused by agony or stress)*
Agony in Gethsemane . . . . .Luke 22:44

Blossom—*to open into blossoms; to flower*
Aaron's rod . . . . Num. 17:5, 8
A fig tree . . . . Hab. 3:17
A desert . . . . Is. 35:1, 2
Israel . . . . Is. 27:6

Blot—*to rub or wipe off*
One's name in God's Book . . . . Ex. 32:32, 33
Legal ordinances .Col. 2:14
One's sins . . . . Ps. 51:1, 9; Acts 3:19
Amalek . . . . Deut. 25:19
Israel as a nation . . . . .2 Kin. 14:27

Blue
Often used in tabernacle . . . . Ex. 25:4; 28:15
Used by royalty . . . . .Esth. 8:15
Imported . . . . .Ezek. 27:7

Blush—*to redden in the cheeks*
Sin makes impossible . . . . .Jer. 6:15; 8:12

Boanerges—*sons of thunder*
Surname of James and John . . . . .Mark 3:17

Boar—*male wild hog*
Descriptive of Israel's enemies . . . . .Ps. 80:13

Boasting—*to speak of with pride; to brag*
A. Excluded because of:
Man's limited knowledge . . . . .Prov. 27:1, 2
Uncertain issues . . . . .1 Kin. 20:11
Evil incurred thereby . . . Luke 12:19–21; James 3:5
Salvation by grace . . . . Eph. 2:9
God's sovereignty . . . . Rom. 11:17–21
B. Examples of:
Goliath . . . . 1 Sam. 17:44
Ben-Hadad . . . . .1 Kin. 20:10
Rabshakeh .2 Kin. 18:27, 34
Satan . . . . .Is. 14:12–15; Ezek. 28:12–19
See Haughtiness; Pride

Boasting in God
Continual duty . . . . .Ps. 34:2
Always in the Lord . . . . 2 Cor. 10:13–18
Necessary to refute the wayward . . .2 Cor. 11:5–33
Of spiritual rather than natural . . . . . . Phil. 3:3–14

Boats
In Christ's time . . . . . Matt. 8:23–27; John 6:22, 23
Lifeboats . . . . Acts 27:30

Ferryboats . . . . .2 Sam. 19:18
Used for fishing . . . . .John 21:3–8

Boaz—*strength*
1. A wealthy Bethlehemite . . . . Ruth 2:1, 4–18
Husband of Ruth . . . . Ruth 4:10–13
Ancestor of David . . . . Ruth 4:17
Ancestor of Christ . . . . .Matt. 1:5
2. Pillar of temple . . . . 1 Kin. 7:21

Bocheru—*firstborn*
A son of Azel . . . . .1 Chr. 8:38

Bochim—*weepers*
A place near Gilgal . . . . .Judg. 2:1–5

| WORD STUDY | **BODY,** *sōma* (soh-mah). In the NT this noun is used in reference to the physical "body" of persons (Luke 11:34), animals |

(James 3:3), and even plants (1 Cor. 15:37, 38). Most frequently, *sōma* denotes the material or physical aspect of a person, the "body"—as opposed to the nonmaterial "spirit" (James 2:26) or "soul" (Matt. 10:28). Hence, *sōma* can also refer to dead bodies or "corpses" (Matt. 14:12; Acts 9:40). The physical "body" is contrasted to the resurrection body (1 Cor. 15:44; Phil. 3:21). Figuratively, *sōma* is used to refer to the Christian community as a unified "body" (Rom. 12:5) or the "body of Christ" (Col. 1:18). (Strong's #4983)

Body of Christ
A. Descriptive of His own body:
Prepared by God . . . . Heb. 10:5
Conceived by the Holy Spirit . . . . . . .Luke 1:34, 35
Subject to growth . . . . .Luke 2:40, 52;
Heb. 5:8, 9
Part of our nature . . . . Heb. 2:14
Without sin . . . . 2 Cor. 5:21
Subject to human emotions . . . . Heb. 5:7
Raised without corruption . . . . .Acts 2:31
Glorified by resurrection . . . . Phil. 3:21
Communion with . . . . .1 Cor. 11:27
B. Descriptive of the church:
Identified . . . . .Col. 1:24
Described . . . . Eph. 2:16
Christ, the head of . . . . Eph. 1:22
Christ dwells in . . . . .Eph. 1:23

Body of human
A. By creation:
Made by God .Gen. 2:7, 21, 22
Various organs of . . . . 1 Cor. 12:12–25
Bears God's image . . . . .Gen. 9:6; Col. 3:10
Wonderfully made . . . . .Ps. 139:14
B. By sin:
Subject to death .Rom. 5:12
Destroyed . . . . Job 19:26
Instrument of evil . . . . Rom. 1:24–32
C. By salvation:
A temple of the Holy Spirit . . . . 1 Cor. 6:19
A living sacrifice .Rom. 12:1
Dead to the law . . . . .Rom. 7:4

Dead to sin........................ Rom. 8:1–4
Control over..................... Rom. 6:12–23
Christ, the center of... Rom. 6:8–11; Phil. 1:20, 21
Sins against, forbidden ....1 Cor. 6:13, 18
Needful requirements of .... 1 Cor. 7:4; Col. 2:23

D. By resurrection, to be:
Redeemed...........................Rom. 8:23
Raised ....John 5:28, 29
Changed .... Phil. 3:21
Glorified...................... Rom. 8:29, 30
Judged ....2 Cor. 5:10–14
Perfected......................1 Thess. 5:23

E. Figurative descriptions of:
House .... 2 Cor. 5:1
House of clay.........................Job 4:19
Earthen vessel ....2 Cor. 4:7
Tent ....2 Pet. 1:13
Temple of God ....1 Cor. 3:16, 17
Members of Christ................. 1 Cor. 6:15

Bohan—*thumb*
1. Reuben's son ....Josh. 15:6
2. Border mark ....Josh. 18:17

Boil—*an inflamed ulcer*
Sixth Egyptian plague................ Ex. 9:8–11
A symptom of leprosy .... Lev. 13:18–20
Satan afflicts Job with...................Job 2:7
Hezekiah's life endangered by ......2 Kin. 20:7, 8

Boiling—*the state of bubbling*
A part of cooking ....1 Kin. 19:21
Of a child, in famine ....2 Kin. 6:29

WORD STUDY | **BOLDNESS, OPENNESS,** *parrhēsia* (par-rhay-*see*-ah). This noun originally applied to a manner of speaking that neither conceals nor omits anything, and thus means "frankness," "plainness," "openness." In John this type of speech is contrasted to a manner of speech in which the meaning is concealed in enigmatic maxims (16:29). The sense of "openness" sometimes develops into "openness to the public" or "publicly," as in John 7:26 and Acts 28:31. An additional nuance of *parrhēsia* moves in the direction of "courage," "confidence," or "boldness" (Acts 4:13; Eph. 6:19; 1 John 3:21). (Strong's #3954)

Boldness—*courage; bravery; confidence*
A. Comes from:
Righteousness.......................Prov. 28:1
Prayer .... Eph. 6:18, 19
Fearless preaching ....Acts 9:26–29
Christ................. Eph. 3:11, 12; Phil. 1:20
Testimony........................... Phil. 1:14
Communion with God .... Heb. 4:16
Perfect love..........................1 John 4:17

B. Examples of:
Tribe of Levi ....Ex. 32:26–28
David.......................1 Sam. 17:45–49
Three Hebrew men ....Dan. 3:8–18
Daniel .... Dan. 6:10–23

The apostles....................... Acts 4:13–31
Paul ....Acts 9:26–29
Paul, Barnabas...................... Acts 13:46
See Courage; Fearlessness

Bondage, literal
Israel in Egypt...................... Ex. 1:7–22
Gibeonites to Israel ....Josh. 9:17–23
Judah in Babylon ....2 Kin. 25:1–21
Israel in Assyria .... 2 Kin. 17:6, 20, 23
Denied by Jews ....John 8:33

Bondage, spiritual
A. Subjection to:
The devil........................... 2 Tim. 2:26
Sin.................................John 8:34
Fear of death .... Heb. 2:14, 15
Death...............................Rom. 7:24
Corruption..........................2 Pet. 2:19

B. Deliverance from:
Promised........................... Is. 42:6, 7
Proclaimed....................Luke 4:18, 21
Through Christ...................... John 8:36
By obedience .... Rom. 6:17–19
By the truth .... John 8:32

Bones—*structural parts of the body*
A. Descriptive of:
Unity of male and female.............. Gen. 2:23
Physical being ....Luke 24:39
Family unity .... Gen. 29:14
Tribal unity .... 1 Chr. 11:1

B. Prophecies concerning:
The paschal lamb's......... Ex. 12:46; John 19:36
Jacob's ....Gen. 50:25; Heb. 11:22
Valley of dry..................... Ezek. 37:1–14

C. Figurative of health, affected by:
Shameful wife ....Prov. 12:4
Good report..........................Prov. 15:30
Broken spirit ....Prov. 17:22

Books—*written compositions*
A. Features of:
Old...............................Job 19:23, 24
Made of papyrus reeds .... Is. 19:7
Made of parchment .... 2 Tim. 4:13
Made in a roll...................... Jer. 36:2
Written with ink..................... 3 John 13
Dedicated......................... Luke 1:3
Sealed ....Rev. 5:1
Many .... Eccl. 12:12
Quotations in .... Matt. 21:4, 5
Written by secretary .... Jer. 36:4, 18

B. Contents of:
Genealogies .... Gen. 5:1
Law of Moses.................Deut. 31:9, 24, 26
Geography ....Josh. 18:9
Wars............................ Num. 21:14
Records...........................Ezra 4:15
Miracles ....Josh. 10:13
Legislation .... 1 Sam. 10:25
Lamentations......................2 Chr. 35:25

Proverbs . . . . Prov. 25:1

Prophecies . . . . .Jer. 51:60–64

Symbols. . . . . Rev. 1:1

The Messiah . . . . Luke 24:27, 44; Heb. 10:7

C. Mentioned but not preserved:

Book of wars . . . . Num. 21:14

Book of Jasher . . . . .Josh. 10:13

Chronicles of David. . . . . .1 Chr. 27:24

Book of Gad. . . . . .1 Chr. 29:29

Story of prophet Iddo . . . . .2 Chr. 13:22

Book of Nathan. . . . . .1 Chr. 29:29

Book of Jehu. . . . . .2 Chr. 20:34

Book of God's judgment

In visions of Daniel and John . . . . .Dan. 7:10; Rev. 20:12

Book of the Law

Called "the Law of Moses". . . . . .Josh. 8:31, 32

Copied. . . . . .Deut. 17:18

Placed in the ark . . . . Deut. 31:26

Foundation of Israel's religion . . . . Deut. 28:58

Lost and found . . . . .2 Kin. 22:8

Produces reformation . . . . 2 Kin. 23:2–14

Produces revival . . . . Neh. 8:2, 8–18

Quoted . . . . .2 Kin. 14:6

To be remembered . . . . Josh. 1:7, 8; Mal. 4:4

Prophetic of Christ . . . . Luke 24:27, 44

Book of Life

A. Contains:

The names of the saved. . . . . Phil. 4:3

The deeds of the righteous. . . . . Mal. 3:16–18

B. Excludes:

Renegades. . . . . Ex. 32:33; Ps. 69:28

Apostates . . . . .Rev. 13:8; 17:8

C. Affords, basis of:

Joy. . . . . .Luke 10:20

Hope . . . . .Heb. 12:23

Judgment . . . . .Dan. 7:10; Rev. 20:12–15

Booths—*stalls made of branches*

Used for cattle. . . . . Gen. 33:17

Required in Feast of Tabernacles. . . Lev. 23:40–43; Neh. 8:14–17

Booty—*spoils taken in war*

A. Stipulations concerning:

No Canaanites. . . . . .Deut. 20:14–17

No accursed thing . . . . .Josh. 6:17–19

Destruction of Amalek . . . . 1 Sam. 15:2, 3

Destruction of Arad. . . . . Num. 21:1–3

The Lord's judgment. . . . . .Jer. 49:30–32

B. Division of:

On percentage basis. . . . . Num. 31:26–47

Rear troops share in. . . . . .1 Sam. 30:22–25

Border—*boundary*

A. Marked by:

Natural landmarks. . . . . .Josh. 18:16

Rivers. . . . . .Josh. 18:19

Neighbor's landmark. . . . . Deut. 19:14

B. Enlargement of:

By God's power. . . . . Ex. 34:24

A blessing . . . . 1 Chr. 4:10

Born again—*new birth, regeneration*

A. Necessity of, because of:

Inability . . . . .John 3:3, 5

The flesh. . . . . John 3:6

Deadness . . . . .Eph. 2:1

B. Produced by:

The Holy Spirit. . . . . .John 3:5, 8; Titus 3:5

The Word of God. . . . . James 1:18; 1 Pet. 1:23

Faith. . . . . .1 John 5:1

C. Results of:

New creature . . . . 2 Cor. 5:17

Changed life. . . . . Rom. 6:4–11

Holy life . . . . .1 John 3:9

Righteousness .1 John 2:29

Love. . . . . .1 John 3:10

Victory . . . . .1 John 5:4

Borrow—*to get by loan*

A. Regulations regarding:

From other nations, forbidden. . . . . Deut. 15:6; 28:12

Obligation to repay . . . . Ex. 22:14, 15

Nonpayment, wicked. . . . . Ps. 37:21

Involves servitude . . . . .Prov. 22:7

Evils of, corrected. . . . . .Neh. 5:1–13

Christ's words on . . . . Matt. 5:42

B. Examples of:

Jewels. . . . . .Ex. 11:2

A widow's vessels . . . . 2 Kin. 4:3

A woodsman's ax . . . . .2 Kin. 6:5

Christ's transportation . . . . Matt. 21:2, 3

Bosom—*the breast as center of affections*

A. Expressive of:

Prostitution . . . . Prov. 6:26, 27

Anger. . . . . Eccl. 7:9

Protection. . . . . Is. 40:11

Iniquity. . . . . .Job 31:33

B. Symbolic of:

Human impatience . . . . Ps. 74:11

Christ's deity . . . . John 1:18

Eternal peace. . . . . Luke 16:22, 23

Bottle—*a hollow thing (vessel)*

A. Used for:

Milk. . . . . .Judg. 4:19

Water. . . . . Gen. 21:14

Wine . . . . Hab. 2:15

B. Made of:

Clay . . . . Jer. 19:1, 10, 11

Skins .Matt. 9:17; Mark 2:22

C. Figurative of:

God's remembrance. . . . . .Ps. 56:8

God's judgments. . . . . .Jer. 13:12–14

Sorrow. . . . . .Ps. 119:83

Impatience. . . . . .Job 32:19

Clouds of rain . . . . Job 38:37

Old and new covenants. . . . . .Matt. 9:17

Bottomless pit

Apollyon, king of ....Rev. 9:11
Beast comes from ....Rev. 11:7; 17:8
Devil, cast into .... Rev. 20:1–3
A prison............................Rev. 20:7

Bough—*branch of a tree*

A. Used:
To make ceremonial booths ....Lev. 23:39–43
In siege of Shechem ....Judg. 9:45–49
B. Figurative of:
Joseph's offspring....................Gen. 49:22
Judgment .... Is. 17:1–11
Israel .... Ps. 80:8–11

Bow—*an instrument for shooting arrows*

A. Uses of:
For hunting .... Gen. 27:3
For war .... Is. 7:24
As a token of friendship .... 1 Sam. 18:4
As a commemorative song...........2 Sam. 1:18
B. Illustrative of:
Strength .... Job 29:20
The tongue............................ Ps. 11:2
Defeat .... Hos. 1:5
Peace .... Hos. 2:18, 19

Bowed down—*bent*

As an act of:
Respect ....Ex. 18:7
Reverence..........................Matt. 2:11
Flaunting fidelity................. 2 Sam. 1:2–16
Fawning favor ....2 Sam. 14:2–4
Feigned flattery .... 2 Sam. 15:5, 6

Bowing, Bowing the knee

A. Wrong:
Before idols ....Ex. 20:5
In mockery........................ Matt. 27:29
Before an angel .... Rev. 22:8, 9
B. True, in:
Prayer ....1 Kin. 8:54
Homage............................2 Kin. 1:13
Repentance .... Ezra 9:5, 6
Worship ....Ps. 95:6
Submission................. Eph. 3:14; Phil. 2:10

Bowl—*a vessel*

Full of incense..........................Rev. 5:8
Filled with God's wrath .... Rev. 16:1–17

Box tree—*an evergreen tree*

Descriptive of messianic times .... Is. 41:19, 20

Boy—*male child*

Esau and Jacob .... Gen. 25:27
Payment for a harlot .... Joel 3:3
Play in streets........................Zech. 8:5
See Children; Young men

Bozez—*shining*

Rock of Michmash............... 1 Sam. 14:4, 5

Bozkath—*height*

A town in south Judah...............Josh. 15:39
Home of Jedidah.....................2 Kin. 22:1

Bozrah—*fortress; sheepfold*

1. City of Edom....................... Gen. 36:33
Destruction of, foretold .... Amos 1:12
Figurative, of Messiah's victory .... Is. 63:1
2. City of Moab..........................Jer. 48:24

Bracelet—*ornament*

Worn by both sexes ....Ezek. 16:11
Given to Rebekah....................Gen. 24:22
Worn by King Saul..................2 Sam. 1:10
A sign of worldliness ....Is. 3:19

Braided hair

Contrasted to spiritual adornment... 1 Tim. 2:9, 10

Bramble—*a thorny bush*

Emblem of a tyrant .... Judg. 9:8–15
Symbol of destruction................. Is. 34:13

Branch—*a limb*

A. Used naturally of:
Limbs of tree .... Num. 13:23
B. Used figuratively of:
Israel .... Rom. 11:16, 21
The Messiah ....Is. 11:1
Christians..........................John 15:5, 6
Adversity .... Job 15:32
Nebuchadnezzar's kingdom ....Dan. 4:10–12

Brass—*an alloy of copper and zinc (tin)*

Used of:
Christ's glory..........................Rev. 1:15

Bravery, moral

Condemning sin................. 2 Sam. 12:1–14
Denouncing hypocrisy .... Matt. 23:1–39
Opposing enemies .... Phil. 1:28
Exposing inconsistency............. Gal. 2:11–15
Uncovering false teachers .... 2 Pet. 2:1–22
Rebuking Christians............... 1 Cor. 6:1–8;
James 4:1–11

Breach—*a break*

Used figuratively of:
Sin.................................. Is. 30:13

Bread—*food*

A. God's provision for:
Earned by sweat .... Gen. 3:19
Object of prayer ....Matt. 6:11
Without work, condemned ....2 Thess. 3:8, 12
A gift ....Ruth 1:6; 2 Cor. 9:10
B. Uses of unleavened, for:
Heavenly visitors .... Gen. 19:3
The Passover ....Ex. 12:8
Priests ....2 Kin. 23:9
Nazirites........................ Num. 6:13, 15
Lord's Supper.....................Luke 22:7–19
C. Special uses of:
Provided by ravens.................. 1 Kin. 17:6
Strength .... 1 Kin. 19:6–8

Satan's ....Matt. 4:3

Miracle .... Matt. 14:19–21

Insight............................Luke 24:35

D. Figurative of:

Adversity .... Is. 30:20

Christ...........................John 6:33–35

Christ's death .... 1 Cor. 11:23–28

Communion with Christ.............Acts 2:46;
     1 Cor. 10:17

Extreme poverty.......................Ps. 37:25

Heavenly food........................Ps. 78:24

Prodigality....................... Ezek. 16:49

Wickedness .... Prov. 4:17

Idleness............................Prov. 31:27

E. Bread of life:

Christ is........................John 6:32–35

Same as manna .... Ex. 16:4, 5

Fulfilled in Lord's Supper........1 Cor. 11:23, 24

Breaking of bread—*a meal*

Prayer before .... Matt. 14:19

Insight through....................Luke 24:35

Fellowship thereby.................. Acts 2:42

Strength gained by.................. Acts 20:11

See Lord's Supper

Breastplate—*protection*

A. Worn by:

High priest.....................Ex. 28:4, 15–20

"Locusts" ....Rev. 9:7, 9

B. Figurative of:

Christ's righteousness................. Is. 59:17

Faith's righteousness................. Eph. 6:14

Breasts—*the female teats*

A. Literally of:

Married love...............Prov. 5:19; Song 1:13

An infant's life................. Job 3:12; Ps. 22:9

Posterity .... Gen. 49:25

B. Figuratively, of:

Mother Jerusalem................... Is. 66:10, 11

WORD
STUDY   **BREATH,** *neshamah* (nesh-aw-*maw*).
Neshamah is a noun meaning "breath."
The *breath* of God is frequently seen as
wind: a hot wind (Is. 30:33) or a wind giving breath to
humans (Gen. 2:7). The "breath" of humans is the
equivalent of life. In Is. 42:5 we read that God gives
breath to the people. In Job 27:3 Job says that as long as
he has breath (or as long as he lives), he will not speak
wickedness. Often this life is seen as God's breath in
humans (Gen. 2:7; 7:22). This meaning is seen frequently in Job. The term can also mean the spirit of a
person as it does in Prov. 20:27. (Strong's #5397)

Breath

Comes from God .... Gen. 2:7

Necessary for all...................... Eccl. 3:19

Held by God.......................... Dan. 5:23

Taken by God .... Ps. 104:29

Figurative, of new life .... Ezek. 37:5–10

Breath of God

Cause of:

Life.................................Job 33:4

Destruction ....2 Sam. 22:16; Is. 11:4

Death................................Job 4:9

Brevity of human life

A. Compared to:

Pilgrimage .... Gen. 47:9

A sigh..............................Ps. 90:9

Sleep................................Ps. 90:5

Flower ....Job 14:2

Grass .... 1 Pet. 1:24

Vapor......................... James 4:14

Shadow .... Eccl. 6:12

Moment .... 2 Cor. 4:17

A weaver's shuttle.......................Job 7:6

B. Truths arising from:

Prayer can prolong....................Is. 38:2–5

Incentive to improvement ....Ps. 90:12

Some kept from old age.......... 1 Sam. 2:32, 33

Some know their end............. 2 Pet. 1:13, 14

Hope regarding.................. Phil. 1:21–25

Life's completion .... 2 Tim. 4:6–8

Bribery—*gifts to pervert*

A. The effects of:

Makes sinners .... Ps. 26:10

Corrupts conscience ....Ex. 23:8

Perverts justice .... Is. 1:23

Brings chaos....................... Amos 5:12

Merits punishment.................... Amos 2:6

B. Examples of:

Balak ....Num. 22:17, 18, 37

Delilah............................Judg. 16:4, 5

Samuel's sons..........................1 Sam. 8:3

Ben-Hadad.....................1 Kin. 15:18, 19

Shemaiah ....Neh. 6:10–13

Haman ....Esth. 3:8, 9

Judas and priests............... Matt. 27:3–9

Soldiers ....Matt. 28:12–15

Simon..............................Acts 8:18

Felix.........................Acts 24:25, 26

Brick—*baked clay*

Babel built of........................ Gen. 11:3

Israel forced to make....................Ex. 1:14

Altars made of........................ Is. 65:3

Forts made of..........................Is. 9:10

Bridal

A. Gift:

A burned city...................... 1 Kin. 9:16

B. Veil:

Rebekah wears .... Gen. 24:64–67

Bride—*newly wed woman*

Wears adornments.....................Is. 61:10

Receives presents .... Gen. 24:53

Has damsels.................Gen. 24:59, 61

Adorned for husband...............Rev. 19:7, 8

Husband rejoices .... Is. 62:5

Stands near husband .... Ps. 45:9

Receives benediction..............Ruth 4:11, 12
Must forget father's house ....Ruth 1:8–17
Must be chaste......................2 Cor. 11:2
Figurative of Israel..............Ezek. 16:8–14
Figurative of church .... Rev. 21:2, 9

Bridegroom—*newly wed man*
Wears special garments.................Is. 61:10
Attended by friends................John 3:29
Rejoices over bride.................... Is. 62:5
Returns with bride................Matt. 25:1–6
Exempted from military service....... Deut. 24:5
Figurative of God.................Ezek. 16:8–14
Figurative of Christ..................John 3:29

Bridle—*a harness*
A. Used literally of:
Â donkey............................Prov. 26:3
B. Used figuratively of:
God's control......................... Is. 30:28
Self-control........................James 1:26
Imposed control.......................Ps. 32:9

Briers—*thorny shrubs*
A. Used literally of:
Thorns...........................Judg. 8:7, 16
B. Used figuratively of:
Sinful nature ....Mic. 7:4
Change of nature .... Is. 55:13
Rejection................................Is. 5:6

Brimstone—*sulphur*
Falls upon Sodom...................Gen. 19:24
Sent as judgment................. Deut. 29:23
State of wicked ....Ps. 11:6
Condition of hell ....Rev. 14:10

Broiled fish
Eaten by Jesus .... Luke 24:42, 43

Broken-handed
Disqualifies for priesthood ....Lev. 21:19

Brokenhearted—*grieving*
Christ's mission to .... Is. 61:1; Luke 4:18

Bronze—*an alloy of copper and tin*
A. Used for:
Tabernacle vessels .... Ex. 38:2–31
Temple vessels................... 1 Kin. 7:41–46
Armor ....2 Chr. 12:10
Mirrors ....Ex. 38:8; Is. 45:2
B. Workers in:
Tubal-Cain......................... Gen. 4:22
Huram.........................1 Kin. 7:13, 14
C. Figurative of:
Grecian Empire..................... Dan. 2:39
Obstinate sinners .... Is. 48:4
Endurance .... Jer. 15:20
God's decrees........................Zech. 6:1
Christ's glory .... Dan. 10:6

Bronze serpent
Made by Moses .... Num. 21:8, 9
Occasion of ruin..................2 Kin. 18:4

Brooks—*streams*
A. Characteristics of:
Numerous...........................Deut. 8:7
Produce grass.......................1 Kin. 18:5
Abound in fish .... Is. 19:8
Afford protection..................... Is. 19:6
B. Names of:
Arnon .... Num. 21:14, 15
Besor .... 1 Sam. 30:9
Gaash......................2 Sam. 23:30
Cherith....................1 Kin. 17:3, 5
Kidron.....................2 Sam. 15:23
Kishon........................Ps. 83:9
C. Figurative of:
Wisdom .... Prov. 18:4
Prosperity.......................... Job 20:17
Deception...........................Job 6:15
Refreshment ....Ps. 110:7
Desire .... Ps. 42:1

Broth—*thin, watery soup*
Served by Gideon ....Judg. 6:19, 20
Figurative of evil...................... Is. 65:4

WORD STUDY   **BROTHER,** *'ach* (*awkh*). The noun *'ach* means "brother." Literally, it indicates persons who share the same mother, meaning that they may be half brothers. The word is used with a wider meaning for other relatives, as when Abraham's nephew Lot is referred to as his brother (Gen. 14:16). Further extension of the term includes belonging to the same tribe or people (Ex. 2:11; Num. 16:10). In Job 30:29 the word is used for a figurative resemblance, so that Job is "a brother of jackals." (Strong's #251)

Brother, brethren
A. Used naturally of:
Sons of same parents .... Gen. 42:4
Common ancestry ....Gen. 14:12–16
Same race .... Deut. 23:7
Same humanity....................... Gen. 9:5
B. Used figuratively of:
An ally............................. Amos 1:9
Christian disciples .... Matt. 23:8
A spiritual companion................. 1 Cor. 1:1
C. Characteristics of Christian brothers:
One Father........................ Matt. 23:8, 9
Believe...............................Luke 8:21
Some weak ....1 Cor. 8:11–13
In need............................. James 2:15
Of low degree........................ James 1:9
Disorderly.........................2 Thess. 3:6
Evil............................... James 4:11
Falsely judge .... Rom. 14:10–21
Need admonishment.............. 2 Thess. 3:15

Brotherhood of man
A. Based on common:
Creation ....Gen. 1:27, 28
Blood.......................... Acts 17:26

Needs.....................Prov. 22:2; Mal. 2:10
B. Disrupted by:
Sin..................................1 John 3:12
Satan ....John 8:44

Brotherly kindness (love)
A. Toward Christians:
Taught by God ....1 Thess. 4:9
Commanded ....Rom. 12:10
Explained......................1 John 4:7–21
Fulfills the law....................Rom. 13:8–10
Badge of new birth...................John 13:34
A Christian grace...................2 Pet. 1:5–7
Must continue.......................Heb. 13:1
B. Toward others:
Neighbors.........................Matt. 22:39
Enemies............................Matt. 5:44

Brothers (brethren) of Christ
Four: James, Joses, Simon,
    Judas (Jude)...........Matt. 13:55; Mark 6:3
Born after Christ ....Matt. 1:25; Luke 2:7
Travel with Mary ....Matt. 12:47–50
Disbelieve Christ ....John 7:4, 5
Become believers ....Acts 1:14
Work for Christ ....1 Cor. 9:5
One (James) becomes prominent......Acts 12:17
Wrote an epistle ....James 1:1
Another (Jude) wrote an epistle............Jude

Brothers, Twin
Figurehead on Paul's ship to Rome,
    called Castor and Pollux ....Acts 28:11

Brought up—*reared*
Ephraim's children—by Joseph ....Gen. 50:23
Esther—by Mordecai ....Esth. 2:5–7, 20
Jesus—at Nazareth ....Luke 4:16
Paul—at Gamaliel's feet..............Acts 22:3

Brow
The forehead.........................Is. 48:4
Top of hill...........................Luke 4:29

Bruised—*injured*
A. Used literally of:
Physical injuries ....Luke 9:39
B. Used figuratively of:
Evils................................Is. 1:6
The Messiah's pains....................Is. 53:5
Satan's defeat............Gen. 3:15; Rom. 16:20

Bucket—*container for water*
Figurative of blessing ....Num. 24:7
Pictures God's magnitude ....Is. 40:15

Buffet—*to strike*
Descriptive of Paul..................2 Cor. 12:7

Build—*construct or erect*
A. Used literally, of:
City ....Gen. 4:17
Altar................................Gen. 8:20
Tower................................Gen. 11:4
House ....Gen. 33:17

Sheepfolds .... Num. 32:16
Fortifications............. Deut. 20:20; Ezek. 4:2
Temple.................. 1 Kin. 6:1, 14; Ezra 4:1
High place .... 1 Kin. 11:7
Walls .... Neh. 4:6
Tombs ....Matt. 23:29; Luke 11:47
Synagogue ....Luke 7:2–5
B. Used figuratively, of:
Obeying Christ..................Matt. 7:24–27
Church .... Matt. 16:18
Christ's resurrection ...Matt. 26:61; John 2:19–21
Return to legalism .... Gal. 2:16–20
Christian unity ....Eph. 2:19–22
Spiritual growth ... Acts 20:32; Col. 2:7; 1 Pet. 2:5
See Edification

Bukki
1. Danite chief....................... Num. 34:22
2. A descendant of Aaron............. 1 Chr. 6:5, 51

Bukkiah—*proved of Yahweh*
A Levite musician.................1 Chr. 25:4, 13

Bul—*growth*
Eighth Hebrew month ....1 Kin. 6:38

Bull—*male of any bovine animal*
Used in sacrifices .... Heb. 9:13
Blood of, insufficient.................. Heb. 10:4
Symbol of evil men....................Ps. 22:12
Symbol of mighty men ....Ps. 68:30
Restrictions on .... Deut. 15:19, 20
Sacrifices of, inadequate........... Ps. 69:30, 31
Blood of, unacceptable ....Is. 1:11
Figurative of the Lord's sacrifice .... Is. 34:6, 7
Figurative of strength .... Deut. 33:17

Bullock—*young bull*
Used in sacrifices .... Ex. 29:1, 10–14
Figurative of the Lord's sacrifice .... Is. 34:6, 7

Bulrush—*a reed*
Used in Moses' ark....................Ex. 2:3
Found in river banks ....Job 8:11
Figurative of judgment..................Is. 9:14
See Papyrus; Rush

Bulwark—*defensive wall*
Around Jerusalem ....Ps. 48:13
Used in wars.........................Eccl. 9:14

Bunah—*intelligence*
A descendant of Judah ....1 Chr. 2:25

Bunni—*erected*
1. A preexilic Levite....................Neh. 11:15
2. A postexilic Levite...................Neh. 9:4
3. Signer of document...................Neh. 10:15

Burden—*load*
A. Used physically of:
Load, cargo .... Neh. 4:17
B. Used figuratively of:
Care ....Ps. 55:22
Prophet's message.....................Hab. 1:1
Rules, rites ....Luke 11:46

Sin. . . . . Ps. 38:4
Responsibility . . . . Gal. 6:2, 5
Christ's law. . . . . Matt. 11:30

Burden-bearer
Christ is the believer's . . . . Ps. 55:22

Burial
A. Features regarding:
Body washed . . . . Acts 9:37
Ointment used . . . . Matt. 26:12
Embalm sometimes . . . . Gen. 50:26
Body wrapped . . . . John 11:44
Placed in coffin . . . . Gen. 50:26
Carried on a bier. . . . . Luke 7:14
Mourners attend. . . . . John 11:19
Graves provided . . . . Gen. 23:5–20
Tombs erected. . . . . Matt. 23:27–29
B. Places of:
Abraham and Sarah. . . . . Gen. 25:7–10
Deborah . . . . Gen. 35:8
Rachel . . . . Gen. 35:19, 20
Isaac and Rebekah . . . . Gen. 49:31
Leah. . . . . Gen. 49:31
Jacob . . . . Gen. 50:13
Miriam . . . . Num. 20:1
Moses. . . . . Deut. 34:5, 6
Aaron. . . . . Josh. 10:6
Joshua . . . . Josh. 24:29, 30
Joseph . . . . Josh. 24:32
Eleazar. . . . . Josh. 24:33
Gideon. . . . . Judg. 8:32
Samson and Manoah. . . . . Judg. 16:30, 31
Saul and his sons. . . . . 1 Sam. 31:12, 13
David. . . . . 1 Kin. 2:10
Joab . . . . 1 Kin. 2:33, 34
Solomon . . . . 1 Kin. 11:43
Rehoboam . . . . 1 Kin. 14:31
Asa . . . . 1 Kin. 15:24
Manasseh . . . . 2 Kin. 21:18
Amon. . . . . 2 Kin. 21:23–26
Josiah. . . . . 2 Chr. 35:23, 24
Jesus. . . . . Luke 23:50–53
Lazarus . . . . John 11:14, 38

Buried alive
Two rebellious families. . . . . Num. 16:27–34
Desire of some. . . . . Rev. 6:15, 16

Burning bush
God speaks from. . . . . Ex. 3:2

Business—*one's work*
A. Attitudes toward:
See God's hand . . . . James 4:13
Be diligent . . . . Prov. 22:29
Be industrious . . . . Rom. 12:8, 11
Be honest . . . . 2 Cor. 8:20–22
Put God's first. . . . . Matt. 6:33, 34
Keep heaven in mind. . . . . Matt. 6:19–21
Give portion. Mal. 3:8–12
Avoid anxiety . . . . Luke 12:22–30
Remember the fool. . . . . Luke 12:15–21

B. Those diligent in:
Joseph . . . . Gen. 39:11
Moses. . . . . Heb. 3:5
Workers in Israel . . . . 2 Chr. 34:11, 12
Daniel . . . . Dan. 6:4
Mordecai. . . . . Esth. 10:2, 3
Paul . . . . Acts 20:17–35

Busybodies—*meddlers*
Young widows may become. . . . . 1 Tim. 5:13
Some Christians . . . . 2 Thess. 3:11, 12
Admonitions against. . . . . 1 Pet. 4:15
See Slander; Whisperer

Butler—*an officer*
Imprisonment of Pharaoh's . . . . Gen. 40:1–13
Same as "cupbearer" . . . . 1 Kin. 10:5

Butter—*curdled milk*
Set before visitors . . . . Gen. 18:8
Got by churning . . . . Prov. 30:33
Figurative of smooth words. . . . . Ps. 55:21
See Curds

Buz—*contempt*
1. A Gadite . . . . 1 Chr. 5:14
2. An Aramean tribe descending from
Nahor . . . . Gen. 22:20, 21

Buzi—*descendant of Buz*
Father of Ezekiel. . . . . Ezek. 1:3

Buzite—*belonging to Buz*
Of the tribe of Buz . . . . Job 32:2

Buzzard
Unclean bird . . . . Lev. 11:13

Byway—*winding or secluded path*
Used by travelers. . . . . Judg. 5:6

Byword—*saying; remark*
Predicted as a taunt . . . . Deut. 28:37
Job describes himself. . . . . Job 17:6

C

Cabbon—*surround*
Village of Judah . . . . Josh. 15:40

Cabul—*unproductive*
1. Town of Asher. . . . . Josh. 19:27
2. A district of Galilee offered
to Hiram. . . . . 1 Kin. 9:12, 13
Solomon placed people in. . . . . 2 Chr. 8:2

Caesar—*a title of Roman emperors*
A. Used in reference to:
1. Augustus Caesar (31 B.C.–A.D. 14) Decree of brings
Joseph and Mary to Bethlehem . . . . Luke 2:1
2. Tiberius Caesar (A.D. 14–37) Christ's
ministry dated by. . . . . Luke 3:1–23
Tribute paid to . . . . Matt. 22:17–21
Jews side with . . . . John 19:12

3. Claudius Caesar (A.D. 41–54) Famine in
    time of.............................Acts 11:28
    Banished Jews from Rome............ Acts 18:2
4. Nero Caesar (A.D. 54–68) Paul
    appealed to...................... Acts 25:8–12
    Converts in household of............. Phil. 4:22
    Paul before.......................2 Tim. 4:16–18
    Called Augustus..................... Acts 25:21
B. Represented Roman authority:
    Image on coins .... Matt. 22:19–21;
    Mark 12:15, 16; Luke 20:24
    Received tax......Matt. 22:19, 21; Mark 12:14, 17;
    Luke 20:25
    Jesus called threat to ....Luke 23:2; John 19:12
    Pilate's loyalty to questioned......... John 19:12
    Chosen over Jesus.................... John 19:12

Caesarea—*pertaining to Caesar*
    Home of Philip .... Acts 8:40; 21:8
    Roman capital of Palestine ..... Acts 12:19; 23:33
    Home of Cornelius............Acts 10:1, 24, 25
    Peter preached at .... Acts 10:34–43
    Paul escorted to...................Acts 23:23, 33
    Paul imprisoned at.................... Acts 25:4
    Paul appealed to Caesar at.........Acts 25:8–13
    Paul preached here three times..... Acts 9:26–30;
    18:22; 21:8

Caesarea Philippi
    A city in north Palestine; scene of
    Peter's great confession ....Matt. 16:13–20
    Probable place of the
    Transfiguration.............. Matt. 17:1–13

Caesar's household—*the imperial staff*
    Greeted the Philippians .... Phil. 4:22

Cage—*an enclosure*
    Judah compared to.....................Jer. 5:27
    Figurative of captivity................Ezek. 19:9
    Babylon called........................Rev. 18:2

Caiaphas—*depression*
    Son-in-law of Annas; high priest ...... John 18:13
    Makes prophecy ....John 11:49–52
    Jesus before ....John 18:23, 24
    Apostles before .... Acts 4:1–22

Cain—*smith; spear*
    Adam's son............................ Gen. 4:1
    Offering rejected ....Gen. 4:2–7; Heb. 11:4
    Was of the Wicked One ....1 John 3:12
    Murders Abel....................... Gen. 4:8
    Becomes a vagabond ....Gen. 4:9–15
    Builds city........................Gen. 4:16, 17
    A type of evil .... Jude 11

Cainan—*fixed*
1. A son of Arphaxad.................... Luke 3:36
2. A son of Enosh .... Gen. 5:9–14; 1 Chr. 1:1, 2;
    Luke 3:37, 38

Cake—*a bread*
A. Kinds of:
    Unleavened .... Num. 6:19

    Fig............................. 1 Sam. 30:12
    Raisin ....1 Chr. 16:3
    Barley..........................Ezek. 4:12
    Of fine flour .... Lev. 2:4
    Baked with oil.............Ex. 29:23; Num. 11:8
B. Used literally of:
    Food........................... 2 Sam. 13:6
    Idolatry........................... Jer. 44:19
    Food prepared for Elijah............. 1 Kin. 17:13
C. Used figuratively of:
    Defeat ....Judg. 7:13
    Weak religion .... Hos. 7:8

Calah
    A great city of Assyria built by Nimrod Gen. 10:11,
    12

Calamities—*disasters*
A. Kinds of:
    Personal ....Job 6:2
    Tribal........................Judg. 20:34–48
    National ....Lam. 1:1–22
    Punitive.......................Num. 16:12–35
    Judicial .... Deut. 32:35
    Worldwide .... Luke 21:25–28
    Sudden.................Prov. 6:15; 1 Thess. 5:3
B. Attitudes toward:
    Unrepentance .... Prov. 1:24–26
    Repentance ....Jer. 18:8
    Hardness of heart.............. Ex. 14:8, 17
    Bitterness ....Ruth 1:20, 21
    Defeat .... 1 Sam. 4:15–18
    Submission........................ Job 2:9, 10
    Prayerfulness........................Ps. 141:5
    Hopefulness........................Ps. 27:1–3

Calamus—*the sweet cane*
    Figurative of love .... Song 4:14
    Rendered "sweet cane" .... Jer. 6:20

Calcol, Chalcol
    A son of Zerah.......................1 Chr. 2:6
    Famous for wisdom .... 1 Kin. 4:31

Caldron—*a large kettle*
A. Used literally of:
    Temple vessels....................2 Chr. 35:13
B. Used figuratively of:
    Safety......................... Ezek. 11:3, 7, 11
    Oppression........................... Mic. 3:3

Caleb—*dog; also bold*
1. Son of Jephunneh.....................Josh. 15:13
    Sent as spy .... Num. 13:2, 6
    Gave good report .... Num. 13:27, 30
    His life saved ....Num. 14:5–12
    Told to divide Canaan............ Num. 34:17, 19
    Entered Canaan .... Num. 14:24–38
    Eighty-five at end of conquest...... Josh. 14:6–13
    Given Hebron .... Josh. 14:14, 15; 15:13–16
    Gave daughter to Othniel .... Judg. 1:12–15
    Descendants of ....1 Chr. 4:15
2. Son of Hezron.................... 1 Chr. 2:18, 42

Caleb Ephrathah

    Hezron died at.........................1 Chr. 2:24

Calendar—*a system of dating*

    Year divided......................1 Chr. 27:1–15

    Determined by moon ....Ps. 104:19

  See Jewish calendar

Calf—*the young of a cow*

A. Characteristics of:

    Playfulness of ....Ps. 29:6

    Used for food........................Amos 6:4

    A delicacy..................... Luke 15:23, 27

    In sacrifice..........................Lev. 9:2, 3

    Redeemed, if firstborn .... Num. 18:17

B. Figurative of:

    Saints sanctified...................... Mal. 4:2

    Nimbleness...........................Ezek. 1:7

Calf, Calves of Gold

A. Making of:

    Inspired by Moses' delay.............. Ex. 32:1–4

    Repeated by Jeroboam .... 1 Kin. 12:25–28

    To represent God .... Ex. 32:4, 5

    To replace temple worship .... 1 Kin. 12:26, 27

    Priests appointed for .... Ex. 32:6; 1 Kin. 12:31

    Sacrifices offered to............. 1 Kin. 12:32, 33

B. Sin of:

    Immorality...................... 1 Cor. 10:6–8

    Great .... Ex. 32:21, 30, 31

    An apostasy ....Ex. 32:8

    Wrathful.......................Deut. 9:14–20

    Brings punishment.............Ex. 32:26–29, 35

    Repeated by Jeroboam .... Hos. 1:1; 8:5, 6

Call

To:

    Name................................ Gen. 1:5

    Pray .... Gen. 4:26

    Be in reality .... Ex. 31:2; Luke 1:35

    Set in office .... Is. 22:20

    Give privileges....................Luke 14:16, 17

    Offer salvation .... Matt. 9:13

    Engage in work .... 1 Cor. 7:20

Calling—*one's vocation*

    Faith and one's .... 1 Cor. 7:20–22

Calling, the Christian

A. Manifested through:

    Christ............................. Matt. 9:13

    Holy Spirit ....Rev. 22:17

    Gospel........................ 2 Thess. 2:14

B. Described as:

    Heavenly............................ Heb. 3:1

    Holy................................2 Tim. 1:9

    High................................ Phil. 3:14

    Irrevocable..........................Rom. 11:29

    By grace.................... Gal. 1:15; 2 Tim. 1:9

    According to God's purpose ....2 Tim. 1:9

C. Goals of:

    Fellowship with Christ .... 1 Cor. 1:9

    Holiness .... 1 Thess. 4:7

    Liberty.............................Gal. 5:13

    Peace .... 1 Cor. 7:15

    Glory and virtue......................2 Pet. 1:3

    Eternal glory .... 2 Thess. 2:14

    Eternal life .... 1 Tim. 6:12

D. Attitudes toward:

    Walk worthy of.......................Eph. 4:1

    Make it sure.......................2 Pet. 1:10

    Of Gentiles..................... Eph. 4:17–19

Calneh—*fort of Ana*

1. Nimrod's city .... Gen. 10:9, 10

2. A city linked with Hamath and Gath.....Amos 6:2

    Same as Calno......................... Is. 10:9

Calvary—*from the Latin "calvaria" (skull)*

    Christ was crucified there ....Luke 23:33

    Same as "Golgotha" in Hebrew........ John 19:17

Camel—*humpbacked animal*

A. Used for:

    Riding ....Gen. 24:61, 64

    Trade............................... Gen. 37:25

    War ....Judg. 7:12

    Hair of, used for garment worn by

        John the Baptist...................Matt. 3:4

    Wealth........................... Job 42:12

B. Features of:

    Docile .... Gen. 24:11

    Unclean..........................Lev. 11:4

    Adorned .... Judg. 8:21, 26

    Prize for booty ....Job 1:17

    Treated well ....Gen. 24:31, 32

    Illustrative of the impossible........ Matt. 19:24

Camon—*elevation*

    Jair was buried there ....Judg. 10:5

Camp—*to pitch a tent; take residence*

A. The Lord's guidance of, by:

    An angel .... Ex. 14:19; 32:34

    His presence..........................Ex. 33:14

    A cloud ....Ps. 105:39

B. Israel's:

    On leaving Egypt .... Ex. 13:20

    At Sinai..............................Ex. 18:5

    Orderly ....Num. 2:2–34

    Tabernacle in center of .... Num. 2:17

    Exclusion of:

        Unclean ....Deut. 23:10–12

        Lepers......................Lev. 13:46

        Dead ....Lev. 10:4, 5

    Executions outside...................Lev. 24:23

    Log kept of......................Num. 33:1–49

    In battle........................ Josh. 10:5, 31, 34

C. Spiritual significance of:

    Christ's crucifixion outside........Heb. 13:12, 13

    God's people ....Rev. 20:9

Cana of Galilee

    A village of upper Galilee; home of

        Nathanael .... John 21:2

Christ's first miracle at . . . . John 2:1–11
Healing at. . . . . John 4:46–54

Canaan—*low*
1. A son of Ham . . . . .Gen. 10:6
Cursed by Noah . . . . Gen. 9:20–25
2. Promised Land . . . . .Gen. 12:5

Canaan, land of
A. Specifications regarding:
Boundaries. . . . . Gen. 10:19
Fertility. . . . . .Ex. 3:8, 17
Seven nations. . . . . .Deut. 7:1
Language . . . . Is. 19:18
B. God's promises concerning, given to:
Abraham. . . . . .Gen. 12:1–3
Isaac. . . . . .Gen. 26:2, 3
Jacob . . . . Gen. 28:10–13
Israel . . . . .Ex. 3:8
C. Conquest of:
Announced. . . . . .Gen. 15:7–21
Preceded by spies . . . . .Num. 13:1–33
Delayed by unbelief . . . . .Num. 14:1–35
Accomplished by the Lord . . . . .Josh. 23:1–16
Done only in part . . . . Judg. 1:21, 27–36

Canaan, names of
Canaan . . . . Gen. 11:31
Land of Hebrews . . . . Gen. 40:15
Philistia. . . . . .Ex. 15:14
Land of Israel. . . . . 1 Sam. 13:19
Immanuel's land. . . . . .Is. 8:8
Beulah . . . . Is. 62:4
Glorious . . . . Dan. 8:9
The Lord's land. Hos. 9:3
Holy land . . . . Zech. 2:12
Land of the Jews . . . . Acts 10:39
Land of promise . . . . Heb. 11:9

Canaanites—*original inhabitants of Palestine*
A. Described as:
Descendants of Ham. . . . . .Gen. 10:5, 6
Under a curse. . . . . .Gen. 9:25, 26
Amorites. . . . . Gen. 15:16
Seven nations. . . . . .Deut. 7:1
Fortified . . . . Num. 13:28
Idolatrous. . . . . Deut. 29:17
Defiled . . . . Lev. 18:24–27
B. Destruction of:
Commanded by God. . . . . Ex. 23:23, 28–33
Caused by wickedness. . . . . .Deut. 9:4
In God's time. . . . . .Gen. 15:13–16
Done in degrees . . . . Ex. 23:29, 30
C. Commands prohibiting:
Common league with . . . . .Deut. 7:1, 2
Intermarriage with. . . . . .Deut. 7:1, 3
Idolatry of . . . . Ex. 23:24
Customs of . . . . Lev. 18:24–27

Canaanites—*of Tyre and Sidon*
Woman from that region . . . . Matt. 15:22

Candace—*dynastic title of Ethiopian queens*
Conversion of eunuch of. . . . . .Acts 8:27–39

Cane—*a tall sedgy grass*
Used in sacrifices . . . . Is. 43:24; Jer. 6:20
Used in holy oil . . . . Ex. 30:23

Canneh
Trading city . . . . Ezek. 27:23

Cannibalism—*using human flesh as food*
Predicted as a judgment . . . . .Deut. 28:53–57
Fulfilled in a siege . . . . 2 Kin. 6:28, 29

Capacity—*ability to perform*
Hindered by sin . . . . .Gal. 5:17
Fulfilled in Christ . . . . Phil. 4:13

Capernaum—*village of Nahum*
A. Scene of Christ's healing of:
Centurion's servant . . . . Matt. 8:5–13
Nobleman's son. . . . . John 4:46–54
Peter's mother-in-law. . . . . Matt. 8:14–17
The demoniac . . . . Mark 1:21–28
The paralytic. . . . . Matt. 9:1–8
Various diseases . . . . Matt. 8:16, 17
B. Other events connected with:
Jesus' headquarters . . . . .Matt. 4:13–17
Simon Peter's home . . . . Mark 1:21, 29
Jesus' sermon on the Bread of Life . . John 6:24–71
Other important messages. . . . . .Mark 9:33–50
Judgment pronounced upon . . . . . . Matt. 11:23, 24

Caphtor—*cup*
The place (probably Crete) from which
the Philistines came to Palestine. . . . .Jer. 47:4

Caphtorim
Those of Caphtor . . . . Deut. 2:23
Descendants of Mizraim . . . . .Gen. 10:13, 14
Conquerors of the Avim . . . . Deut. 2:23

Capital punishment—*the death penalty*
A. Institution of:
By God . . . . Gen. 9:5, 6; Ex. 21:12–17
B. Crimes punished by:
Murder . . . . Gen. 9:5, 6
Adultery . . . . .Lev. 20:10
Incest. . . . . Lev. 20:11–14
Sodomy . . . . .Lev. 20:13
Rape. . . . . Deut. 22:25
Witchcraft . . . . .Ex. 22:18
Disobedience to parents . . . . .Ex. 21:17
Blasphemy . . . . Lev. 24:11–16, 23
False doctrines . . . . Deut. 13:1–10

Capitals—*tops of posts or columns*
Variegated decorations of. . . . . Ex. 36:38
Part of temple . . . . .1 Kin. 7:16, 19, 20

Cappadocia—*a province of Asia Minor*
Natives of, at Pentecost. . . . . .Acts 2:1, 9
Christians of, addressed by Peter. . . . . . . .1 Pet. 1:1
Adnah . . . . 2 Chr. 17:14

Capstone
Placed with shouts of "Grace". . . . . .Zech. 4:7

Captain—*a civil or military officer*
Arioch .... Dan. 2:15
Potiphar .... Gen. 37:36
David as leader .... 1 Sam. 22:2
Jehohanan .... 2 Chr. 17:15
Temple police head .... Luke 22:4

Captain, chief of the temple—*priest who kept order*
Conspired with Judas .... Luke 22:3, 4
Arrested Jesus .... Luke 22:52–54
Arrested apostles .... Acts 5:24–26

Captive—*an enslaved person*
A. Good treatment of:
Compassion........................ Ex. 6:4–8
Kindness........................... 2 Chr. 28:15
Mercy............................. 2 Kin. 6:21–23
B. Bad treatment of:
Forced labor...................... 2 Sam. 12:31
Blinded ....Judg. 16:21
Maimed............................Judg. 1:6, 7
Ravished.......................... Lam. 5:11–13
Enslaved .... 2 Kin. 5:2
Killed.......................... 1 Sam. 15:32, 33
C. Applied figuratively to those:
Under Satan....................... 2 Tim. 2:26
Under sin .... 2 Tim. 3:6
Liberated by Christ .... Luke 4:18

Captivity—*a state of bondage; enslavement*
A. Foretold regarding:
Hebrews in Egypt................. Gen. 15:13, 14
Israelites .... Deut. 28:36–41
Ten Tribes (Israel) .... Amos 7:11
Judah................................. Is. 39:6
B. Fulfilled:
In Egypt ....Ex. 1:11–14
In many captivities............... Judg. 2:14–23
In Assyria...................... 2 Kin. 17:6–24
In Babylon .... 2 Kin. 24:11–16
Under Rome....................... John 19:15
C. Causes of:
Disobedience.................. Deut. 28:36–68
Idolatry.........................Amos 5:26, 27

Caravan—*a group traveling together*
Ishmaelite traders .... Gen. 37:25
Jacob's family ....Gen. 46:5, 6
Jacob's funeral.....................Gen. 50:7–14
Queen of Sheba.................. 1 Kin. 10:1, 2
Returnees from exile .... Ezra 8:31

Carcas—*severe*
Eunuch under Ahasuerus............. Esth. 1:10

Carcass—*a dead body; corpse*
A. Used literally of:
Sacrificial animals .... Gen. 15:9, 11
Unclean beasts ....Lev. 5:2
Lion ....Judg. 14:8
Men ....Deut. 28:25, 26
Idols ....Jer. 16:18

B. Used figuratively of:
Those in hell .... Is. 66:24
Idolatrous kings .... Ezek. 43:7, 9
Attraction......................... Matt. 24:28
C. Laws regarding:
Dwelling made unclean by........Num. 19:11–22
Contact with, makes unclean ....Lev. 11:39
Food made unclean ....Lev. 11:40

Carchemish
Eastern capital of Hittites on the
Euphrates...................... 2 Chr. 35:20
Conquered by Sargon II .... Is. 10:9
Josiah wounded here .... 2 Chr. 35:20–24

WORD STUDY **CARE, ANXIETY,** *merimna* (mer-im-nah). This noun means "anxiety," "worry," "care," "concern." Both *merimna* and the cognate verb *merimnaō* clearly refer to a state of concern that carries with it the sense of anxiety or worry. So it is that in 1 Pet. 5:7 we find the exhortation to cast all "worry" on the Lord (cf. the verb in Phil. 4:6). Jesus refers to the same kind of anxious concerns in Matt. 6:25–34. Such extreme "concern" is not entirely negative, for Paul "cares" greatly about the spiritual well-being of others (2 Cor. 11:28; cf. Phil. 2:20). (Strong's #3308)

Care, carefulness—*wise and provident concern*
A. Natural concern for:
Children .... Luke 2:44–49
Duties ....Luke 10:40
Mate........................... 1 Cor. 7:32–34
Health............................. Is. 38:1–22
Life............................... Mark 4:38
Possessions.......................Gen. 33:12–17
B. Spiritual concern for:
Duties .... Phil. 2:20
Office .... 1 Tim. 3:1–8
A minister's needs ....Phil. 4:10–12
The flock of God .... John 10:11; 1 Pet. 5:2, 3
Christians......................... 1 Cor. 12:25
Spiritual things................... Acts 18:12–17

Care, divine—*God's concern for His creatures*
For the world..................... Ps. 104:1–10
For animals .... Ps. 104:11–30
For pagans ....Jon. 4:11
For Christians.................... Matt. 6:25–34
Nineveh.......................... Zeph. 2:10–15

Careah—*made bold*
Father of Johanan.................. 2 Kin. 25:23
Same as Kareah...................... Jer. 40:8

Carelessness—*lack of proper concern*
Babylon........................... Is. 47:1, 8–11
Ethiopians .... Ezek. 30:9
Inhabitants of coastlands............. Ezek. 39:6
Nineveh........................... Zeph. 2:15
Women of Jerusalem .... Is. 32:9–11
Gallio............................. Acts 18:12–17

Cares, worldly—*overmuch concern for earthly things; anxiety*
A. Evils of:
    Chokes the Word .... Matt. 13:7, 22
    Gluts the soul. .... Luke 21:34
    Obstructs the gospel .... Luke 14:18–20
    Hinders Christ's work .... 2 Tim. 2:4
    Manifests unbelief .... Matt. 6:25–32
    Limits time with the Lord .... Luke 10:38–42
B. Antidotes for, God's:
    Protection .... Ps. 37:5–11
    Provision .... Matt. 6:25–34
    Promises .... Phil. 4:6, 7

Carmel—*field, park, garden*
1. Rendered as: "Fruitful field" .... Is. 10:18
    "Plentiful field" .... Is. 16:10
    "Bountiful country" .... Jer. 2:7
2. City of Judah .... Josh. 15:55
    Site of Saul's victory .... 1 Sam. 15:12
    Home of David's wife .... 1 Sam. 27:3
3. A mountain of Palestine .... Josh. 19:26
    Joshua defeated king there .... Josh. 12:22
    Scene of Elijah's triumph .... 1 Kin. 18:19–45
    Elisha visits .... 2 Kin. 2:25
    Place of beauty .... Song 7:5
    Figurative of strength .... Jer. 46:18
    Barrenness foretold .... Amos 1:2

Carmelite, Carmelitess
    Nabal .... 1 Sam. 30:5; 2 Sam. 2:2
    Hezrai .... 2 Sam. 23:35
    Abigail .... 1 Sam. 27:3

Carmi—*vinedresser*
1. Son of Reuben .... Gen. 46:9
2. Father of Achan .... Josh. 7:1

Carnal—*fleshly, worldly*
Used literally of:
    Sexual relations .... Lev. 19:20
    Paul calls himself .... Rom. 7:14
    Paul calls brethren at Corinth .... 1 Cor. 3:1, 3

Carob pod—*seedcase of the carob, or locust tree*
    Rendered "pod"; fed to swine .... Luke 15:16

Carpenter—*a skilled woodworker*
    David's house built by .... 2 Sam. 5:11
    Temple restored by .... 2 Chr. 24:12; Ezra 3:7
    Joseph works as .... Matt. 13:55

Carpentry tools—*implements for the carpentry trade*
    Ax .... Deut. 19:5
    Hammer .... Jer. 23:29
    Line .... Zech. 2:1
    Nail .... Jer. 10:4
    Saw .... 1 Kin. 7:9

Carpus—*fruit*
    Paul's friend at Troas .... 2 Tim. 4:13

Carriage
    A vehicle .... Is. 46:1

Carrion vulture
    Unclean bird .... Lev. 11:18

Carshena—*plowman*
    Prince of Persia .... Esth. 1:14

Cart—*a wagon*
    Used in moving .... Gen. 45:19, 21
    Made of wood .... 1 Sam. 6:14
    Sometimes covered .... Num. 7:3
    Drawn by cows .... 1 Sam. 6:7
    Used in threshing .... Is. 28:28
    Used for hauling .... Amos 2:13
    Ark carried by .... 2 Sam. 6:3
    Figurative of sin .... Is. 5:18

Carving—*cutting figures in wood or stone; grave*
    Used in worship .... Ex. 31:1–7
    Found in homes .... 1 Kin. 6:18
    Employed by idolaters .... Judg. 18:18
    Used in the temple .... 1 Kin. 6:35

Casiphia—*silvery*
    Home of exiled Levites .... Ezra 8:17

Casluhim
    A tribe descended from Mizraim ...... Gen. 10:14
    Descendant of Ham .... 1 Chr. 1:8, 12

Cassia—*amber*
    An ingredient of holy oil .... Ex. 30:24, 25
    An article of commerce .... Ezek. 27:19
    Noted for fragrance .... Ps. 45:8

Castaway—*worthless; reprobated*
    The rejected .... Matt. 25:30; 2 Pet. 2:4

Caste—*divisions of society*
    Some leaders of low .... Judg. 11:1–11
    David aware of .... 1 Sam. 18:18, 23
    Jews and Samaritans observe .... John 4:9
    Abolished .... Acts 10:28–35

Castle—*fortress*
Used figuratively of:
    Offended brother .... Prov. 18:19

Castor and Pollux—*sons of Jupiter*
    Gods in Greek and Roman mythology; figurehead on Paul's ship to Rome .... Acts 28:11

Castration—*removal of testicles*
    Disqualified for congregation .... Deut. 23:1
    Rights restored in new covenant .... Is. 56:3–5
    Figurative of absolute devotion ...... Matt. 19:12

Caterpillar—*an insect living on vegetation*
    Works with locust .... Is. 33:4

Cattle—*animals (collectively)*
    Created by God .... Gen. 1:24
    Adam named .... Gen. 2:20
    Entered the ark .... Gen. 7:13, 14
    Taken as plunder .... Josh. 8:2, 27
    Belong to God .... Ps. 50:10
    Nebuchadnezzar eats like .... Dan. 4:33
    Pastureless .... Joel 1:18

Caulkers—*sealers*

    Used on Tyrian vessels .... Ezek. 27:9, 27

Caution—*provident care; alertness*

    For safety .... Acts 23:10, 16–24

    For defense....................... Neh. 4:12–23

    For attack.................... 1 Sam. 20:1–17

    A principle .... Prov. 14:15, 16

    Neglect of.................... 1 Sam. 26:4–16

Cave—*a cavern*

A. Used for:

    Habitation .... Gen. 19:30

    Refuge............................. 1 Kin. 18:4

    Burial............................. John 11:38

    Concealment..................... 1 Sam. 22:1

    Protection.................. Is. 2:19; Rev. 6:15

B. Mentioned in Scripture:

    Machpelah .... Gen. 23:9

    Makkedah .... Josh. 10:16, 17

    Adullam .... 1 Sam. 22:1

    En Gedi........................ 1 Sam. 24:1, 3

Cedar—*an evergreen tree*

A. Used in:

    Ceremonial cleansing .... Lev. 14:4–7

    Building temple .... 1 Kin. 5:5, 6

    Building palaces .... 2 Sam. 5:11

    Gifts............................. 1 Chr. 22:4

    Making idols .... Is. 44:14, 17

B. Figurative of:

    Israel's glory...................... Num. 24:6

    Christ's glory................... Ezek. 17:22, 23

    Growth of saints..................... Ps. 92:12

    Mighty nations .... Amos 2:9

    Arrogant rulers...................... Is. 2:13

Ceiling—*upper surface of a room*

    Temple's .... 1 Kin. 6:15

Celebrate—*to commemorate; observe; keep*

    Feast of Weeks .... Ex. 34:22

    Feast of Ingathering .... Ex. 34:22

    The Sabbath.................... Lev. 23:32, 41

    Passover .... 2 Kin. 23:21

    Feast of Unleavened Bread.......... 2 Chr. 30:13

    Feast of Tabernacles .... Zech. 14:16

Celestial—*heavenly*

    Bodies called .... 1 Cor. 15:40

Celibacy—*the unmarried state*

    Useful sometimes............... Matt. 19:10, 12

    Not for bishops .... 1 Tim. 3:2

    Requiring, a sign of apostasy........ 1 Tim. 4:1–3

    Figurative of absolute devotion .... Rev. 14:4

Cemetery—*a burial place*

    Bought by Abraham............... Gen. 23:15, 16

    Pharisees compared to .... Matt. 23:27

    Man dwelt in .... Mark 5:2, 3

    A resurrection from................ Matt. 27:52

Cenchrea—*millet*

    A harbor of Corinth.................. Acts 18:18

    A church in........................... Rom. 16:1

Censer—*firepan*

    Used for incense .... Num. 16:6, 7, 39

    Made of bronze.................... Num. 16:39

    Used in idol worship .... Ezek. 8:11

    Typical of Christ's intercession........ Rev. 8:3, 5

Censoriousness—*a critical spirit*

    Rebuked by Jesus .... Matt. 7:1–5

    Diotrephes .... 3 John 9, 10

    Apostates .... Jude 10–16

Census—*counting the population*

    At Sinai .... Ex. 38:25, 26

    Military....................... Num. 1:2, 18, 20

    In Moab .... Num. 26:1–64

    By David .... 2 Sam. 24:1–9

    Provoked by Satan .... 1 Chr. 21:1

    Completed by Solomon.............. 2 Chr. 2:17

    Of exiles .... Ezra 2:1–70

    By Rome .... Luke 2:1, 2

Centurion—*a Roman officer*

    Servant of, healed................. Matt. 8:5–13

    Watches crucifixion................. Matt. 27:54

    Is converted .... Acts 10:1–48

    Protects Paul .... Acts 22:25–28

    Takes Paul to Rome................... Acts 27:1

Cephas—*stone*

    Name of Peter .... John 1:42

Ceremonialism—*adherence to forms and rites*

    Jews guilty of....................... Is. 1:11–15

    Christ condemns .... Matt. 15:1–9

    Apostles reject................... Acts 15:12–28

    Sign of apostasy .... 1 Tim. 4:1–3

    Exhortations against.............. Col. 2:14–23

Certainties—*absolute truths*

    Sin's exposure .... Num. 32:23

    The gospel .... Luke 1:4

    Jesus' claims....................... Acts 1:3

    Apostolic testimony.............. 2 Pet. 1:16–21

    Death's approach .... Heb. 9:27

    Ultimate judgment................. Acts 17:31

Chaff—*the husk of threshed grain*

    Describes the ungodly................... Ps. 1:4

    Emptiness........................... Is. 33:11

    False doctrine .... Jer. 23:28

    God's judgment..................... Is. 17:13

    Punishment .... Matt. 3:12

Chain—*a series of connected links*

A. A badge of office:

    On Joseph's neck.................... Gen. 41:42

    Promised to Daniel .... Dan. 5:7

B. An ornament:

    Worn by women .... Is. 3:20

C. A means of confinement of:

    Paul .... Eph. 6:20

D. Used figuratively of:
  Oppression...........................Lam. 3:7
  Sin's bondage.......................Jer. 40:3, 4
  Punishment .... Jude 6
  Satan's defeat........................Rev. 20:1

Chalcedony—*from Chalcedon*
  Variegated stone.....................Rev. 21:19

Chaldea
  Originally, the south portion
    of Babylonia .... Gen. 11:31
  Applied later to all Babylonia .... Dan. 3:8
  Abraham came from ....Gen. 11:28, 31
  Ezekiel prophesies in ....Ezek. 1:3

Chaldeans
  Abraham, a native .... Gen. 11:31
  Ur, a city of........................... Neh. 9:7
  Babylon, "the glory of" .... Is. 13:19
  Attack Job ....Job 1:17
  Nebuchadnezzar, king of.............2 Kin. 24:1
  God's agent .... Hab. 1:6
  Predicted captivity of Jews among....Jer. 25:1–26
  Jerusalem defeated by.............2 Kin. 25:1–21
  Noted for astrologers.............Dan. 2:2, 5, 10

Chalkstone—*limestone*
  Used figuratively .... Is. 27:9

Chamber—*inner room; enclosed place*
A. Used literally of:
  Place of idolatry ....2 Kin. 23:12
B. Used figuratively of:
  Heavens........................... Ps. 104:3, 13
  Death................................Prov. 7:27

Chamberlain—*a high official; a eunuch*
  Blastus, serving Herod .... Acts 12:20
  See Eunuch

Chameleon—*a lizardlike reptile*
  Unclean............................Lev. 11:30

Champion—*a mighty one; a winner*
  Goliath .... 1 Sam. 17:23, 51
  David........................1 Sam. 17:45–54

Chance, second
Not given to:
  Angels ....2 Pet. 2:4
  Noah's world ....2 Pet. 2:5
  Esau..............................Heb. 12:16, 17
  Israelites...................... Num. 14:26–45
  Saul............................ 1 Sam. 16:1, 14
  Judas .... John 13:26–30
  Apostates .... Heb. 10:26–31
  Those in hell .... Luke 16:19–31

Change of garments—*gala, festal clothes*
  A gift ....Gen. 45:22
  A wager ....Judg. 14:12–19
  From a king .... 2 Kin. 5:5

Character—*one's total personality*
A. Traits of:
  Described prophetically ....Gen. 49:1–28

Indicated before birth........... Gen. 25:21–34
Seen in childhood....................Prov. 20:11
Fixed in hell .... Rev. 22:11, 15
B. Manifested by:
  Decisions (Esau) .... Gen. 25:29–34
  Destiny (Judas)..................John 6:70, 71
  Desires (Demas) .... 2 Tim. 4:10
  Deeds (Saul)................... 1 Sam. 15:1–35

Character of God's people
A. Their dedication:
  Hear Christ ....John 10:3, 4
  Follow Christ....................John 10:4, 5, 27
  Receive Christ...................... John 1:12
B. Their standing before God:
  Blameless .... Phil. 2:15
  Faithful...........................Rev. 17:14
  Godly..............................2 Pet. 2:9
  Holy................................Col. 3:12
C. Their graces:
  Humble............................1 Pet. 5:5
  Loving............................ 1 Thess. 4:9
  Humility......................... Phil. 2:3, 4
  Gentle ....Matt. 5:5
  Merciful ....Matt. 5:7
  Obedient..........................Rom. 16:19
  Pure ....Matt. 5:8
  Sincere......................... 2 Cor. 1:12
  Zealous ....Titus 2:14
  Courteous..........................1 Pet. 3:8
  Unity of mind .... Rom. 15:5–7
  Hospitable ....1 Pet. 4:9
  Generous ....2 Cor. 8:1–7
  Peaceable .... Heb. 12:14
  Patient........................... James 5:7, 8
  Content........................... Heb. 13:5
  Steadfast.........................1 Cor. 15:58

Character of the wicked
A. Their attitude toward God:
  Hostile............................Rom. 8:7
  Denial .... Ps. 14:1
  Disobedience.......................Titus 1:16
B. Their spiritual state:
  Blindness .... 2 Cor. 4:4
  Slavery to sin .... 2 Pet. 2:14, 19
  Deadness ....Eph. 2:1
  Inability ....Rom. 8:8
C. Their works:
  Boastful.......................... Ps. 10:3–6
  Full of evil .... Rom. 1:29–32
  Haters of the gospel...............John 3:19, 20
  Sensual ....2 Pet. 2:12–22

Chariot—*a vehicle*
A. Used for:
  Travel.............................Gen. 46:29
  War ....1 Kin. 20:25
B. Employed by:
  Kings..............................1 Kin. 22:35
  Persons of distinction .... Gen. 41:43

God ....2 Kin. 2:11, 12
C. Illustrative of:
Clouds.......................Ps. 104:3
God's judgments.....................Is. 66:15
Angels.........................2 Kin. 6:16, 17

Chariot, war machine
A. Used by:
Egyptians...........................Ex. 14:7
Canaanites....................... Josh. 17:16
Philistines.................... 1 Sam. 13:5
Syrians......................... 2 Sam. 10:18
Assyrians .... 2 Kin. 19:20, 23
Jews ....2 Kin. 8:21
B. Numbers employed by:
Pharaoh—600.........................Ex. 14:7
Jabin—900..........................Judg. 4:3
Philistines—30,000................. 1 Sam. 13:5

Chariot cities
Many in Solomon's time .... 1 Kin. 9:19

Chariot horses
Hamstrung........................1 Chr. 18:4

Chariot of fire
Used in Elijah's exit from earth .... 2 Kin. 2:11

Chariots of the sun—*used in sun worship*
Destroyed.........................2 Kin. 23:11

Charitableness—*a generous spirit toward others*
Bearing burdens .... Gal. 6:2–4
Showing forgiveness ....2 Cor. 2:1–10
Seeking concord .... Phil. 4:1–3
Helping the tempted ....Gal. 6:1
Encouraging the weak............. Rom. 14:1–15
Not finding fault .... Matt. 7:1–3
Descriptive of Dorcas .... Acts 9:36

Charmers—*users of magic*
Falsified by God ....Ps. 58:4, 5

Chastisement—*fatherly correction*
A. Sign of:
Sonship ....Prov. 3:11, 12
God's love............................Deut. 8:5
B. Design of, to:
Correct .... Jer. 24:5, 6
Prevent sin ....2 Cor. 12:7–9
Bless.............................. Ps. 94:12, 13
C. Response to:
Penitence .... 2 Chr. 6:24–31
Submission......................2 Cor. 12:7–10

Chastity—*sexual purity*
A. Manifested in:
Dress .... 1 Pet. 3:1–6
Looks...........................Matt. 5:28, 29
Speech .... Eph. 5:4
Intentions......................Gen. 39:7–12
B. Aids to:
Shun the unchaste .... 1 Cor. 5:11
Consider your sainthood .... Eph. 5:3, 4
Dangers of unchastity............. Prov. 6:24–35

Let marriage suffice................ 1 Cor. 7:1–7
"Keep yourself pure" .... 1 Tim. 5:22
C. Examples of:
Job ....Job 31:1, 9–12
Joseph ....Gen. 39:7–20
Ruth..........................Ruth 3:10, 11
Boaz..........................Ruth 3:13, 14
Saints..............................Rev. 14:4

Cheating—*defrauding by deceitful means; depriving*
The Lord............................ Mal. 3:8, 9
One's soul.......................... Matt. 16:26
The needy............................ Amos 8:4, 5
Others .... 1 Cor. 7:5
See Dishonesty

Chebar—*joining*
River in Babylonia by which Jewish captives were
situated......................... Ezek. 1:1–3
Site of Ezekiel's visions .... Ezek. 10:15, 20

Chedorlaomer—*servant of the god Lagamar*
A king of Elam; invaded Canaan .... Gen. 14:1–16

Cheek—*side of face*
Micaiah struck on ....1 Kin. 22:24
Struck on ....Job 16:10
Messiah's plucked........................ Is. 50:6
Description of:
Beauty............................. Song 5:13
Patience........................... Matt. 5:39
Victory .... Ps. 3:7
Attack ....Mic. 5:1

Cheerfulness—*serene joyfulness*
A. Caused by:
A merry heart ....Prov. 15:13
The Lord's goodness .... Zech. 9:16, 17
The Lord's presence............... Mark 6:54, 55
Victory ....John 16:33
Confidence........................ Acts 24:10
B. Manifested in:
Giving .... 2 Cor. 9:7
Christian graces ....Rom. 12:8
Times of danger ....Acts 27:22–36

Cheese—*a dairy product*
Used for food.......................1 Sam. 17:18
Received by David .... 2 Sam. 17:29
Figurative of trials .... Job 10:10

Chelal—*completeness; perfection*
A son of Pahath-Moab .... Ezra 10:30

Chelub—*basket; bird's cage*
1. A brother of Shuhah .... 1 Chr. 4:11
2. Father of Ezri .... 1 Chr. 27:26

Chelubai
A son of Hezron ....1 Chr. 2:9

Cheluh—*robust*
A son of Bani.......................... Ezra 10:35

Chemosh—*fire, hearth*
The god of the Moabites............. Num. 21:29
Children sacrificed to .... 2 Kin. 3:26, 27

Solomon builds altars to . . . . 1 Kin. 11:7
Josiah destroys altars of . . . . 2 Kin. 23:13

Chenaanah—*feminine form of Canaan*
1. A Benjamite .1 Chr. 7:10
2. Father of Zedekiah . . . . 2 Chr. 18:10

Chenani—*contraction of Chenaniah*
A reforming Levite. . . . . Neh. 9:4

Chenaniah—*Yahweh has established*
A chief Levite in David's reign . . . 1 Chr. 15:22, 27

Chephar Haammoni—*village of the Ammonite*
A village of Benjamin . . . . .Josh. 18:24

Chephirah—*village*
A city of the Gibeonites . . . . Josh. 9:17
Assigned to Benjamin . . . . .Josh. 18:26
Residence of exiles . . . . Ezra 2:25

Cheran—*lyre*
A Horite, son of Dishon . . . . 1 Chr. 1:41

Cherethites—*Cretans in southwest Palestine*
Tribes in southwest Canaan . . . . 1 Sam. 30:14
Identified with Philistines. . . . . .Ezek. 25:16
In David's bodyguard . . . . .2 Sam. 8:18
Serve Solomon. 1 Kin. 1:37, 38

Cherith—*cut; brook*
Elijah hid and was sustained there. . . 1 Kin. 17:3–6

Cherub
A district in Babylonia . . . . . . Ezra 2:59; Neh. 7:61

WORD STUDY   **CHERUBIM,** *kerubim* (*cher*-uh-bim or *ker*-oo-beem). *Kerubim* is the plural of the singular noun *kerub*. Cherubim are winged celestial beings, a type of angel. It was cherubim who guarded the Garden of Eden after Adam and Eve were driven out (Gen. 3:24). Images of cherubim were placed above the ark of the covenant, on the throne of God in Ex. In Solomon's temple they were used to decorate the inner sanctuary (1 Kin. 6:23–35). In Ezek. 10 there is a description of a vision featuring cherubim with wheels. These beings are associated with the dwelling and throne of God (see Ps. 80:1; 99:1). (Strong's #3742)

Cherubim (plural of cherub)
A. Appearances of:
 Fully described . . . . Ezek. 1:5–14
B. Functions of:
 Guard . . . . Gen. 3:22–24
 Fulfill God's purposes. . . . . Ezek. 10:9–16
 Show God's majesty. . . . . 2 Sam. 22:11
C. Images of:
 On the mercy seat. . . . . Ex. 25:18–22
 On the veil . . . . .Ex. 26:31
 On curtains . . . . .Ex. 36:8
 In the temple . . . . .1 Kin. 8:6, 7

Chesalon—*trust*
A town of Judah . . . . Josh. 15:10

Chesed
Fourth son of Nahor . . . . Gen. 22:22

Chesil—*a fool*
A village of Judah. . . . . .Josh. 15:30
Probably same as Bethul and Bethuel . . Josh. 19:4;
 1 Chr. 4:30

Chest—*case or box*
For offering . . . . .2 Kin. 12:9, 10
For levy fixed by Moses. . . . . .2 Chr. 24:8, 9
Used to safeguard valuables. . . . . 1 Sam. 6:8–15

Chestnut tree—*plane tree*
Used by Jacob . . . . Gen. 30:37
In Eden, God's garden. . . . . Ezek. 31:8, 9

Chesulloth—*loins or slopes*
A border town of Issachar . . . . Josh. 19:18

Chezib—*deceitful*
Birthplace of Shelah. . . . . Gen. 38:5
Same as Azib . . . . .Josh. 15:44

Chicken—*domestic fowl*
Hen and brood . . . . .Luke 13:34
Rooster . . . . .Luke 22:34

Chicks—*the young of a hen*
Figurative of Israel. . . . . Matt. 23:37

Chiding—*to reprove or rebuke*
A. Between men:
 Jacob with Laban . . . . Gen. 31:36
 Israelites with Moses. . . . . .Ex. 17:2
 Ephraimites with Gideon. . . . . . . Judg. 7:24, 25; 8:1
 Paul with Peter . . . . .Gal. 2:11, 14
B. By Christ, because of:
 Unbelief . . . . .Matt. 11:20–24
 Spiritual dullness . . . . Matt. 16:8–12
 Censoriousness . . . . Mark 10:13–16
 Sluggishness. . . . . Matt. 26:40

Chidon—*a javelin*
Where Uzza was struck dead. . . . . . .1 Chr. 13:9, 10
Called Nachon . . . . 2 Sam. 6:6

WORD STUDY   **CHILD,** *teknon* (*tek*-non). "Child" is a very common word in the NT, and it is used without designating gender (Mark 13:12), although the context can give indication that the child in question is a "son" (Matt. 21:28; Luke 2:48). The plural "children" more generally refers to descendants or posterity (Acts 2:39). Used figuratively, *teknon* describes a spiritual relationship, for example, of a follower to an apostle or teacher (1 Cor. 4:14; 2 Tim. 1:2), or of believers to God (John 1:12: "children of God"). Used with an abstract noun, *teknon* suggests the moral nature of people (Matt. 11:19; Eph. 5:8). (Strong's #5043)

Childbearing
Agreeable to God's command. . . . . Gen. 1:28
Result of marriage . . . . .1 Tim. 5:14
Attended with pain . . . . Gen. 3:16
Productive of joy. John 16:21

Productive of the Messiah . . . . Luke 2:7
Means of salvation . . . . .1 Tim. 2:15
Expressed in symbols. . . . . Rev. 12:2, 5

Childhood, characteristics of
Dependence. . . . . 1 Thess. 2:7
Immaturity . . . . 1 Cor. 13:11
Foolishness. . . . . .Prov. 22:15
Unstableness . . . . Eph. 4:14
Humility. . . . . Matt. 18:1–5
Need for instruction . . . . .Prov. 22:6
Influence on adults . . . . Is. 49:15

Childishness—*an immature spirit*
Manifested by Saul. . . . . 1 Sam. 18:8, 9
Seen in Haman . . . . Esth. 6:6–9

Childlikeness
Requirement of God's kingdom. . . . . . Mark 10:15
An element in spiritual growth. . . . . .1 Pet. 2:2
A model to be followed. . . . . 1 Cor. 14:20

Children, figurative
Disciples of a teacher. . . . . Mark 10:24
God's own. . . . . Rom. 8:16, 17
Christians. . . . . Eph. 5:8
Devil's own. . . . . .1 John 3:10
Those who show such trait. . . . . Matt. 11:16–19
See Sonship of believers

Children, illegitimate
A. Characteristics of:
  No inheritance . . . . .Gal. 4:30
  Not in congregation. . . . . Deut. 23:2
  Despised . . . . .Judg. 11:2
B. Examples of:
  Moab and Ammon. . . . . Gen. 19:36–38
  Sons of Tamar by Judah . . . . Gen. 38:12–30
  Jephthah. . . . . .Judg. 11:1
C. Figurative of:
  A mixed race . . . . Zech. 9:6
  The unregenerate state. . . . . Heb. 12:8

Children, natural
A. Right estimate of:
  God's gifts . . . . Gen. 33:5
  God's heritage. Ps. 127:3–5
  Crown of old men. . . . . Prov. 17:6
B. Characteristics of:
  Imitate parents . . . . .1 Kin. 15:11, 26
  Diverse in nature . . . . .Gen. 25:27
  Playful. . . . . Matt. 11:16–19
C. Capacities of:
  Glorify God. . . . . Matt. 21:15, 16
  Come to Christ . . . . Mark 10:13–16
  Understand Scripture . . . . .2 Tim. 3:15
  Receive the promises. . . . . Acts 2:39
  Believe. . . . . Matt. 18:6
  Receive training . . . . Eph. 6:4
  Worship in God's house . . . . 1 Sam. 1:24, 28
D. Parental obligations toward:
  Nourishment. 1 Sam. 1:22
  Discipline . . . . Eph. 6:4

Instruction. . . . . .Gal. 4:1, 2
Employment. . . . . .1 Sam. 17:15
Inheritance. . . . . Luke 12:13, 14
E. Duties of:
  Obedience . . . . Eph. 6:1–3
  Honor to parents . . . . Heb. 12:9
  Respect for age .1 Pet. 5:5
  Care for parents . . . . .1 Tim. 5:4
  Obedience to God . . . . Deut. 30:2
  Remembering God. . . . . Eccl. 12:1
F. Description of ungrateful:
  Stubborn. . . . . Deut. 21:18–21
  Scorners . . . . .Prov. 30:17
  Robbers. . . . . .Prov. 28:24
  Strikers . . . . .Ex. 21:15
  Cursers . . . . .Lev. 20:9
G. Examples of good:
  Isaac. . . . . Gen. 22:6–10
  Joseph . . . . Gen. 45:9, 10
  Jephthah's daughter. . . . . Judg. 11:34–36
  Samuel. . . . . 1 Sam. 2:26
  David. . . . . 1 Sam. 17:20
  Josiah. . . . . 2 Chr. 34:1–3
  Esther . . . . .Esth. 2:20
  Daniel . . . . .Dan. 1:1–6
  John the Baptist . . . . .Luke 1:80
  Jesus. . . . . Luke 2:51
  In the temple . . . . Matt. 21:15, 16
  Timothy . . . . .2 Tim. 3:15
H. Examples of bad:
  Esau . . . . Gen. 26:34, 35
  Job's haters. . . . . .Job 19:18
  Sons of Eli. 1 Sam. 2:12, 17
  Sons of Samuel . . . . 1 Sam. 8:1–3
  Absalom . . . . 2 Sam. 15:10
  Adonijah . . . . .1 Kin. 1:5, 6
  Elisha's mockers . . . . 2 Kin. 2:22, 23
  Adrammelech .2 Kin. 19:37
I. Acts performed upon:
  Naming. . . . . Ruth 4:17
  Blessing. . . . . Luke 1:67, 76–79
  Circumcision. Luke 2:21
J. Murder of:
  By Pharaoh. . . . . .Ex. 1:15, 16
  By Herod the Great . . . . Matt. 2:16–18
  In war . . . . Num. 31:12–17
K. Jesus' relationship with:
  Blessed them . . . . Matt. 19:13–15
  Healed them . . . . .Matt. 15:22–28
  Raised girl from
    dead. . . . . Matt. 9:18, 19, 23–25; Luke 8:49–56

Chileab—*restraint of father*
  A son of David. .2 Sam. 3:3
  Also called Daniel . . . . 1 Chr. 3:1

Chilion—*wasting away*
  Elimelech's son . . . . Ruth 1:2
  Orpah's deceased husband. . . . . .Ruth 1:4, 5
  Boaz redeems his estate . . . . Ruth 4:9

Chilmad

A town or country trading with Tyre... Ezek. 27:23

Chimham—*pining*

A son of Barzillai ....2 Sam. 19:37–40

Inn bearing his name...................Jer. 41:17

Chinnereth, Chinneroth—*lyre*

1. A city of Naphtali..................... Deut. 3:17

2. The region of Chinneroth .... 1 Kin. 15:20

Same as plain of Gennesaret .... Matt. 14:34

3. The Old Testament name for

Sea of Galilee ....Num. 34:11

Also called Lake of Gennesaret

and Sea of Galilee .... Matt. 4:18; Luke 5:1

Chios—*snow*

An island of the Aegean Sea; on Paul's

voyage.......................... Acts 20:15

Chislev

Ninth month of Hebrew year .... Neh. 1:1

Chislon—*trust, hope*

Father of Elidad .... Num. 34:21

Chisloth Tabor—*the flanks of Tabor*

A locality near Mt. Tabor............. Josh. 19:12

Probably same as Chesulloth......... Josh. 19:18

Chiun—*detestable thing*

Pagan deity worshiped by Israel....... Amos 5:26

Chloe—*verdure*

Woman of Corinth.................. 1 Cor. 1:11

Choice, choose

A. Of human things:

Wives............................ Gen. 6:2

Land............................. Gen. 13:11

Soldiers ....Ex. 17:9

King..............................1 Sam. 8:18

Apostles .... Luke 6:13

Church officers.......................Acts 6:5

Missionaries....................... Acts 15:40

Delegates .... Acts 15:22, 25

B. Of God's choice:

Moses as leader .... Num. 16:28

Levites to priesthood............... 1 Sam. 2:28

Kings............................ 1 Sam. 10:24

Jerusalem .... Deut. 12:5

Israel as His people .... Deut. 7:6–8

Cyrus as deliverer.................... Is. 45:1–4

The Servant (the Messiah)............ Is. 42:1–7

The new Israel (the church)............1 Pet. 2:9

The weak as God's own .... 1 Cor. 1:27, 28

The elect.......................... Matt. 20:16

C. Kind of:

God and the devil................... Gen. 3:1–11

Life and death .... Deut. 30:19, 20

God and idols .... Josh. 24:15–28

Obedience and disobedience...... 1 Sam. 15:1–35

God and Baal.................... 1 Kin. 18:21–40

Wisdom and folly................... Prov. 8:1–21

Obedience and sin ....2 Pet. 2:4

Christ and the Antichrist........ 1 John 2:18, 19

D. Factors determining choice, human:

First choice..........................Rom. 5:12

Depraved nature...................John 3:19–21

Spiritual deadness .... Eph. 4:17–19

Blindness .... John 9:39–41

Inability ....Rom. 8:7, 8

E. Bad choice made by:

Disobeying God ....Num. 14:1–45

Putting the flesh first .... Gen. 25:29–34

Following a false prophet........ Matt. 24:11, 24

Letting the world overcome.......Matt. 19:16–22

Rejecting God's promises......... Acts 13:44–48

F. Good choice made by:

Using God's Word ....Ps. 119:9–11

Believing God .... Heb. 11:24–27

Obedience ....Acts 26:19–23

Prayer .... Eph. 1:16–19

Faith............................Heb. 11:8–10

Choir—*musicians trained to sing together*

Appointed by Nehemiah .... Neh. 12:31

In house of God ....Neh. 12:40

Under instructor................ 1 Chr. 15:22, 27

> **WORD STUDY** **CHOOSE,** *bachar* (baw-*khar*). *Bachar* is a verb meaning "choose," "select," or "appoint." The word can refer to divine choice, which makes the chosen person or thing special. Among God's choices were Abraham (Neh. 9:7), Israel (Deut. 7:7), David (1 Sam. 10:24), and Jerusalem (2 Chr. 6:6). Human choices could be religious or secular in nature and include ways (Prov. 3:31), life or death (Deut. 30:19), gods (Judg. 10:14), and wives (Gen. 6:2). (Strong's #977)

Chorazin

A city denounced for its unbelief..... Matt. 11:21

Chozeba

Town of Judah.......................1 Chr. 4:22

> **WORD STUDY** **CHRIST,** *Christos* (khris-*toss*). Derived from the verb *chriō*, "to anoint," *christos* is technically an adjective. However, in the NT it is used as a noun, and most frequently as a name meaning "the Anointed One," "the Messiah," "the Christ." Although not all references are to a particular person (Matt. 2:4), it is clear that in most instances *Christos* does not apply to the Messiah in general, but to a specific Person as Messiah—Jesus (Acts 5:42). *Christos* came to be understood as a personal name used in tandem with "Jesus" (Mark 1:1), especially in the epistles, either as Jesus *Christos* or *Christos* Jesus. (Strong's #5547)

Christ—*the Anointed One*

A. Preexistence of:

Affirmed in Old Testament.............. Ps. 2:7

Confirmed by Christ.................. John 8:58

Proclaimed by apostles .... Col. 1:15–19

B. Birth of:

Predicted ....Is. 7:14

Firstborn of creation . . . . Col. 1:15
Firstborn among many brethren . . . . . . .Rom. 8:29
Firstfruits . . . . .1 Cor. 15:23
First and last . . . . Rev. 22:13
Forerunner . . . . Heb. 6:20
Foundation laid in Zion . . . . Is. 28:16
Friend of tax collectors and sinners . . . . . Luke 7:34
God . . . . .John 20:28
God blessed forever . . . . .Rom. 9:5
God of Israel . . . . Is. 45:15
God, our Savior . . . . 1 Tim. 2:3
God with us . . . . Matt. 1:23
Good Master . . . . Mark 10:17
Great God . . . . .Titus 2:13
Great High Priest . . . . Heb. 4:14
Great Shepherd . . . . Heb. 13:20
Head, even Christ . . . . Eph. 4:15
Head of all . . . . .Col. 2:10
Head of every man . . . . 1 Cor. 11:3
Head of the body, the church . . . . .Col. 1:18
Head over all things . . . . Eph. 1:22
Heir of all things . . . . Heb. 1:2
High Priest . . . . Heb. 4:14
His beloved Son . . . . Col. 1:13
Holy One . . . . 1 John 2:20
Holy and Just One .Acts 3:14
Holy One of God .Luke 4:34
Holy One of Israel . . . . Is. 37:23
Holy Servant . . . . Acts 4:27
Hope of glory . . . . .Col. 1:27
Horn of salvation .Luke 1:69
Husband . . . . 2 Cor. 11:2
I Am . . . . John 8:58
Image of God . . . . 2 Cor. 4:4
Image of the Invisible God . . . . .Col. 1:15
Immanuel . . . . .Is. 7:14
Jesus . . . . Luke 1:31
Jesus Christ . . . . .Rom. 1:3
Jesus Christ our Lord . . . . .Rom. 6:23
Jesus Christ our Savior . . . . .Titus 3:6
Jesus of Nazareth .Luke 24:19
Jesus, the Son of God . . . . Heb. 4:14
Jesus, the (supposed) son of Joseph . . . . . Luke 3:23
Judge of Israel . . . . .Mic. 5:1
Judge of the living and the dead . . . . Acts 10:42
Just man . . . . Matt. 27:19
King . . . . John 12:13
King eternal . . . . .1 Tim. 1:17
King of glory . . . . Ps. 24:7
King of Israel . . . . John 12:13
King of kings . . . . .1 Tim. 6:15
King of the Jews . . . . Matt. 27:37
King of Zion . . . . .Zech. 9:9
Lamb . . . . .Rev. 13:8
Lamb of God . . . . John 1:36
Leader . . . . Is. 55:4
Life . . . . John 14:6
Light . . . . John 1:9
Light of the Gentiles . . . . Acts 13:47

Light of the World . . . . John 9:5
Lily of the valleys . . . . Song 2:1
Lion of the tribe of Judah . . . . .Rev. 5:5
Living bread . . . . John 6:51
Living stone . . . . .1 Pet. 2:4
Lord . . . . John 21:7
Lord Christ . . . . .Col. 3:24
Lord God Almighty . . . . .Rev. 4:8
Lord Jesus . . . . .Acts 19:17
Lord Jesus Christ . . . . 2 Thess. 2:1
Lord and Savior Jesus Christ . . . . 2 Pet. 2:20
Lord both of dead and living . . . . .Rom. 14:9
Lord of all . . . . Acts 10:36; Rom. 10:12
Lord of glory . . . . 1 Cor. 2:8
Lord of hosts . . . . Is. 54:5
Lord of lords . . . . .1 Tim. 6:15
Lord of Sabbath . . . . Luke 6:5
Lord our righteousness . . . . Jer. 23:6
Lord, your redeemer . . . . Is. 43:14
Majestic Lord . . . . Is. 33:21
Man of Sorrows . . . . Is. 53:3
Mediator . . . . .Heb. 12:24
Messenger of the covenant . . . . .Mal. 3:1
Messiah . . . . .John 4:25, 26
Mighty God . . . . Is. 9:6
Mighty One . . . . Ps. 45:3
Mighty One of Jacob . . . . Is. 60:16
Minister of the circumcision . . . . .Rom. 15:8
Minister of the sanctuary . . . . Heb. 8:1, 2
Morning star . . . . .Rev. 22:16
Nazarene . . . . Matt. 2:23
Only begotten of the Father . . . . John 1:14
Only begotten Son . . . . John 1:18
Only wise God . . . . .1 Tim. 1:17
Our Passover . . . . 1 Cor. 5:7
Our peace . . . . Eph. 2:14
Physician . . . . .Luke 4:23
Power of God . . . . 1 Cor. 1:24
Precious cornerstone . . . . Is. 28:16; 1 Pet. 2:6
Priest . . . . Heb. 5:6
Prince . . . . .Acts 5:31
Prince of life . . . . .Acts 3:15
Prince of Peace . . . . Is. 9:6
Prophet . . . . Deut. 18:15, 18
Propitiation . . . . .Rom. 3:25
Purifier and refiner . . . . Mal. 3:3
Rabbi . . . . .John 6:25
Rabboni . . . . John 20:16
Ransom . . . . 1 Tim. 2:6
Redeemer . . . . Is. 59:20
Resurrection and the life . . . . John 11:25
Righteous Judge . . . . 2 Tim. 4:8
Righteous Servant . . . . Is. 53:11
Rock . . . . .1 Cor. 10:4
Rock of offense . . . . .Rom. 9:33
Rod from the stem of Jesse . . . . .Is. 11:1
Root of David . . . . .Rev. 22:16
Root of Jesse . . . . .Is. 11:10
Rose of Sharon . . . . Song 2:1

Ruler in Israel . . . . .Mic. 5:2; Matt. 2:6
Ruler over the kings of the earth . . . . .Rev. 1:5
Salvation. . . . . .Luke 2:30
Savior. . . . . 1 Tim. 4:10
Savior Jesus Christ. . . . . 2 Pet. 2:20
Savior, God our. . . . . .Titus 1:3
Savior of the world. . . . . .1 John 4:14
Scepter out of Israel . . . . Num. 24:17
Second Man. . . . . 1 Cor. 15:47
Seed of David. . . . . John 7:42
Seed of the woman. . . . . Gen. 3:15
Shepherd. . . . . .John 10:11
Shepherd and Overseer of souls . . . . 1 Pet. 2:25
Son of the Blessed. . . . . Mark 14:61
Son of David . . . . Matt. 9:27
Son of God. . . . . .Rom. 1:4
Son of Man. . . . . .Acts 7:56
Son of Mary . . . . .Mark 6:3
Son of the Father . . . . .2 John 3
Son of the Highest . . . . .Luke 1:32
Sower . . . . Matt. 13:3, 37
Star out of Jacob . . . . Num. 24:17
Stone . . . . Dan. 2:45
Stone rejected .Luke 20:17
Stone of stumbling. . . . . Rom. 9:32, 33
Sun of Righteousness . . . . Mal. 4:2
Teacher from God . . . . John 3:2
Tried stone. . . . . Is. 28:16
True vine . . . . John 15:1
Truth. . . . . John 14:6
Unspeakable gift. . . . . 2 Cor. 9:15
Way . . . . John 14:6
Wonderful . . . . Is. 9:6
Word . . . . .1 John 1:1
Word of God . . . . .Rev. 19:13
Word of Life. . . . . .1 John 1:1

Christian attributes
A. Manifested toward God:
Belief. . . . . Heb. 11:6
Holiness . . . . .Heb. 12:10, 14
Godliness. . . . . .Titus 2:12
Love. . . . . .Matt. 22:36, 37
Faith. . . . . Mark 11:22
Joy. . . . . Phil. 4:4
B. Manifested toward Christ:
Faith. . . . . .2 Tim. 1:12
Worship . . . . .Phil. 2:4–11
Obedience . . . . 2 Thess. 1:8
Imitation . . . . 1 Cor. 11:1
Fellowship . . . . .1 John 1:3
C. Manifested toward the Holy Spirit:
Walking in . . . . .Gal. 5:16
Filled with . . . . .Eph. 5:18
Guided by. . . . . John 16:13
Praying in. . . . . Jude 20
Quench not . . . . 1 Thess. 5:19
Taught by . . . . .John 14:26
Living in . . . . .Gal. 5:25
Grieve not. . . . . Eph. 4:30

D. Manifested in the world:
Chastity . . . . 1 Tim. 5:22
Contentment. . . . . Heb. 13:5
Diligence. . . . . 1 Thess. 3:7, 8
Forbearance. . . . . Eph. 4:2
Honesty. . . . . Eph. 4:25
Industry . . . . .1 Thess. 4:11, 12
Love toward enemies. . . . . Matt. 5:44
Peacefulness. Rom. 14:17–19
Temperance . . . . .1 Cor. 9:25
Tolerance . . . . Rom. 14:1–23
Zealous for good deeds. . . . . .Titus 2:14
E. Manifested toward other Christians:
Bearing burdens . . . . .Gal. 6:2
Helping the needy . . . . Acts 11:29, 30
Fellowship . . . . Acts 2:42
Brotherly kindness. . . . . 1 Pet. 4:7–11
Mutual edification. . . . . 1 Thess. 5:11
F. Manifested as signs of faith:
Spiritual growth . . . . .2 Pet. 3:18
Fruitfulness . . . . .John 15:1–6
Perseverance . . . . 1 Cor. 15:58
Persecution. . . . . 2 Tim. 3:9–12
Obedience . . . . Phil. 2:12
Good works .James 2:14–26
G. Manifested as internal graces:
Kindness. . . . . Col. 3:12, 13
Humility. . . . . 1 Pet. 5:5, 6
Gentleness . . . . James 3:17, 18
Love . . . . .1 Cor. 13:1–13
Self-control. . . . . .Gal. 5:23
Peace . . . . Phil. 4:7

Christianity, a way of life
Founded on Christ. . . . . .1 Cor. 3:10, 12
Based on doctrines. . . . . .1 Cor. 15:1–4
Designed for all. . . . . .Matt. 28:18–20
Centers in salvation . . . . Acts 4:12
Produces change. . . . . 1 Cor. 6:11

Christians—*believers in Jesus Christ*
A. Bible occurrences of term:
First applied at Antioch . . . . Acts 11:26
Agrippa almost becomes . . . . Acts 26:28
Proof of, by suffering. . . . . .1 Pet. 4:16
B. Sometimes referred to as:
Believers . . . . .Acts 5:14
Brethren. . . . . .Rom. 7:1
Brethren, beloved. . . . . 1 Thess. 1:4
Brethren, holy . . . . Heb. 3:1
Children . . . . 2 Cor. 6:13
Children of God . . . . .Rom. 8:16
Children of light. . . . . Eph. 5:8
Dear children .Eph. 5:1
Disciples . . . . Acts 9:25
Elect, the. . . . . .Rom. 8:33
Friends . . . . John 15:14
Heirs of God and joint heirs with. . . . . . .Rom. 8:17
Light in the Lord. . . . . Eph. 5:8
Light of the world. . . . . .Matt. 5:14
Little children .1 John 2:1

Christlikeness

Chronicles—*two books of the Old Testament from Heb. meaning "the words of the days"*

Chrysolite—*gold stone*

Chrysoprase—*golden-green stone*

Chub

Chun—*founding*

WORD STUDY   **CHURCH,** *ekklēsia* (ek-klay-*see*-ah). This noun means "assembly," and it typically refers to a regularly convened political body (Acts 19:39). *Ekklēsia* is also used to designate the congregation of Israel (Acts 7:38). The predominate usage in the NT is in reference to a Christian "assembly," "congregation," "church," whether that be a house-church (Rom. 16:5), the totality of Christians living in one location (Acts 8:1; Phil. 4:15), or the "church" universal—to which all believers belong (Matt. 16:18; Eph. 1:22) and which Paul calls the *ekklēsia* of God (2 Cor. 1:1) or the *ekklēsia* of Christ (Rom. 16:16). (Strong's #1577)

Church—*the called-out ones*
A. Descriptive of:
B. Title applied to:

C. Relation to Christ:
D. Members of:
E. Organization of:
F. Mission of:
G. Local, examples of:

Galatia. . . . . .Gal. 1:2
Jerusalem . . . . .Acts 8:1
Judea . . . . .Gal. 1:22
Laodicea . . . . .Col. 4:15
Macedonia . . . . 2 Cor. 8:1
Pergamos . . . . .Rev. 2:12
Philadelphia. . . . . .Rev. 3:7
Philippi . . . . .Phil. 1:1
Rome . . . . .Rom. 1:7
Sardis. . . . . .Rev. 3:1
Smyrna . . . . .Rev. 2:8
Thyatira . . . . .Rev. 2:18
Thessalonica . . . . 1 Thess. 1:1

Church sleeper
Falls from window during Paul's
    sermon . . . . Acts 20:7–12

Chuza
Herod's steward . . . . Luke 8:3

Cilicia—*a province of Asia Minor*
Paul's country . . . . Acts 21:39
Students from, argued with Stephen. . . . . .Acts 6:9
Paul labors in. . . . . .Gal. 1:21

Cinnamon—*a laurel-like spicy plant*
Used in holy oil. . . . . Ex. 30:23
A perfume . . . . Prov. 7:17
In Babylon's trade. . . . . .Rev. 18:13
Figurative of a lover. . . . . .Song 4:12, 14

Circle—*a curved line equally distant from a common center*
Used of the earth . . . . Is. 40:22

Circuit—*circle, regular course*
Judge's itinerary .1 Sam. 7:16
Sun's orbit. . . . . .Ps. 19:6

Circumcision—*a cutting*
A. The physical rite:
    Instituted by God. . . . . .Gen. 17:9–14
    A seal of righteousness . . . . Rom. 2:25–29
    Performed on the eighth day. . . . . Luke 1:59
    Child named when performed . . . . . .Luke 1:59, 60
    Allowed right to Passover. . . . . Ex. 12:48
    Neglect of, punished . . . . Ex. 4:24, 25
    Neglected during wilderness journey . . . . Josh. 5:7
    A sign of covenant relation . . . . .Rom. 4:11
B. Necessity of:
    Asserted in old dispensation . . . . .Gen. 17:9–14
    Abolished by the gospel . . . . .Gal. 5:1–4;
        Eph. 2:11, 15
    Avails nothing. . . . . Gal. 5:6; Col. 3:10, 11
    Avowed by false teachers . . . . .Acts 15:1
    Acclaimed a yoke . . . . .Acts 15:10
    Abrogated by apostles. . . . . Acts 15:5–29;
        1 Cor. 7:18, 19
C. Spiritual significance of:
    Regeneration . . . . Deut. 10:16; 30:6; Jer. 4:4
    The true Jew (Christian) . . . . .Rom. 2:29
    The Christian . . . . Phil. 3:3; Col. 2:11

Circumstances
A. Relationship to Christian:
    Work for good. . . . . .Rom. 8:28
    Produce perseverance . . . . .Rom. 5:3
    Not cause for anxiety . . . . Phil. 4:6
    Test and purify . . . . 1 Pet. 1:5–7
    To be met with thanksgiving. . . Eph. 5:20; Phil. 4:6
    Can be overcome . . . . Phil. 4:11–13
B. Examples, victory over:
    Moses. . . . . Ex. 14:10–31
    Joshua . . . . .Josh. 6:8–21
    Shamgar . . . . .Judg. 3:31
    Gideon. . . . . Judg. 7:19–23
    Hannah. . . . . 1 Sam. 1:9–20
    David. . . . . .1 Sam. 17:40–51
    Widow of Zarephath. . . . . .1 Kin. 17:8–16
    Hezekiah . . . . 2 Kin. 20:1–11
    Peter. . . . . .Acts 12:5–17
    Paul . . . . Acts 14:19, 20; 16:19–26

Cistern—*an underground reservoir for water*
A. Literal uses of:
    Water. . . . . .2 Kin. 18:31
    Imprisonment (when empty). . . . . Jer. 38:6
B. Figurative uses of:
    Wife. . . . . Prov. 5:15
    False religion . . . . .Jer. 2:13
C. Kinds of:
    Family cisterns . . . . Is. 36:16

Cities—*organized population centers*
A. Features regarding:
    Walled. . . . . Lev. 25:29–31; Deut. 3:5
    Earliest . . . . Gen. 4:17
    Often built on hills. . . . . .Matt. 5:14
    Gates guarded. . . . . Acts 9:24
    Guard posted. . . . . .2 Kin. 7:10; Neh. 13:19
    Difficult to attack . . . . .Prov. 16:32
    Business at gate. . . . . . . Gen. 23:10, 11; Ruth 4:1–11
B. Descriptions of:
    Sodom—wicked . . . . Gen. 13:13
    Jerusalem—like Sodom . . . . Is. 1:1, 10
    Nineveh—repentant . . . . .Jon. 3:5–10
    Capernaum—arrogant . . . . Matt. 11:23
    Athens—idolatrous . . . . .Acts 17:16

Cities, Levitical
Forty-eight. . . . . Num. 35:7
Six designed for refuge . . . . Deut. 19:1–13

Cities of refuge
Given to Levites . . . . Num. 35:6
For the manslayer. . . . . Num. 35:11

Cities of the mountains
Avoided by Israel . . . . Deut. 2:37

Cities of the plain
Admah . . . . Gen. 14:8
Bela . . . . Gen. 14:2
Gomorrah. . . . . Gen. 19:28; Jude 7
Sodom . . . . .Gen. 19:28, 29

Zeboiim .... Gen. 14:8
Dibon, Bamoth Baal,
   Beth Baal Meon .... Josh. 13:17

Cities of the lowland
Restored .... Jer. 32:44

Citizen, citizenship
A. Kinds of:
   Hebrew .... Eph. 2:12
   Roman........................Acts 22:25–28
   Spiritual .... Eph. 2:19, 20; Phil. 3:20
   Christian (see below)
B. Duties of Christian citizens:
   Be subject to rulers................ Rom. 13:1–7
   Pray for rulers .... 1 Tim. 2:1, 2
   Honor rulers ....1 Pet. 2:17
   Seek peace ....Jer. 29:7
   Pay taxes......................... Matt. 22:21
   Obey God first .... Acts 5:27–29
   Love one's nation .... Neh. 2:3
   Live righteously .... 1 Pet. 3:8–17

Citron—*a fragrant wood from the sandarac tree*
Wood of, used for furniture...........Rev. 18:12

City builder
Cain builds first .... Gen. 4:17
Woe to, who uses bloodshed .... Hab. 2:12

City clerk—*a keeper of court records*
Appeases the people................. Acts 19:35

City, Holy
Applied to Jerusalem........ Dan. 9:24; Rev. 11:2
Prophecy concerning.................. Joel 3:17
Clothed with beautiful garments........ Is. 52:1
New Jerusalem .... Rev. 21:2

City of David
Applied to the stronghold of Zion ..... 1 Chr. 11:5
Taken by David from Jebusites..... 1 Chr. 11:4–8
Ark brought to ....1 Chr. 15:1–29
Bethlehem called .... Luke 2:4

City of destruction
Prophecy concerning an Egyptian city... Is. 19:18

City of God
Prophetic description of Zion ....Ps. 48:1–14
Dwelling place of God ....Ps. 46:4, 5
Sought by the saints............ Heb. 11:9, 10, 16
Descriptive of the heavenly Jerusalem ...Rev. 21:2

City of Moab
Where Balak met Balaam........... Num. 22:36

City of palm trees—*Jericho*
Seen by Moses..................... Deut. 34:1–3
Occupied by Kenites .... Judg. 1:16
Captured by Eglon .... Judg. 3:12–14

City of Salt
Near the Dead Sea .... Josh. 15:62

Civil
1. Righteousness:
   Principle of........................Prov. 14:34

   Precepts of .... Zech. 8:16, 17
   Practice of.......................... Mic. 4:2
   Perversion of .... Mic. 7:1–4
2. Service:
A. Characteristics of:
   Loyalty .... Neh. 2:3
   Industry ....Gen. 41:37–57
   Esteem............................Esth. 10:3
B. Examples of:
   Joseph ....Gen. 39:1–6
   Daniel .... Dan. 1:17–21
   Mordecai.......................Esth. 8:1, 2, 9
   Nehemiah........................Neh. 2:1–8
3. Authority:
   Obedience to commanded.......... Eccl. 8:2–7;
     Rom. 13:1–7
   Submit for Christ's sake .... 1 Pet. 2:13–15

Civility—*good breeding; courtesy*
Shown by Joseph...................Gen. 47:1–10
Taught by Christ.................. Luke 14:8–10
Shown by Timothy.................Phil. 2:19–23
Shown by Gaius .... 3 John 1–6

| WORD STUDY | **CLAP,** *taqa'* (taw-kah). *Taqa'* is a verb meaning "thrust," "clap," or "give a blow." Most often it can mean to thrust a weapon |

or drive a peg. It can also mean to blow a horn or other instrument. When the word is used to mean a hand clap, the meaning is a gesture of triumph (Ps. 47:1; Nah. 3:19) or the sign of the sealing of a pledge given (Job 17:3; Prov. 22:26). (Strong's #8628)

Class distinction
Egyptians—against Hebrews ....Gen. 43:32
Haman—against Hebrews ....Esth. 3:8, 9
Jews—against Samaritans .... John 4:9
Jews—against Gentiles........... Acts 22:21, 22
Forbidden........................ Ex. 12:48, 49

Clauda—*lamentable*
Small island southeast of Crete.........Acts 27:16

Claudia
Disciple at Rome.................... 2 Tim. 4:21

Claudius Lysias
Roman commander who
   protected Paul .. Acts 23:24–30; 24:22–24, 26

Clay—*firm, plastic earth*
A. Uses of:
   Making bricks...................... 2 Sam. 12:31
   Making pottery........................ Is. 41:25
   Sealing.............................. Job 38:14
   Miracle .... John 9:6, 15
B. Figurative of:
   Man's weakness........................ Is. 64:8
   Unstable kingdom .... Dan. 2:33–35, 42
   Trouble ....Ps. 40:2

Clean—*pure, innocent*
A. Used physically:
   Outward purity.................... Matt. 23:26

B. Used ceremonially of:

Clean animals	Gen. 7:2
Freedom from defilement	Luke 5:14, 15

C. Used spiritually of:

Human nature	Job 9:30, 31
Repentance	Gen. 35:2; James 4:8
Regeneration	Ezek. 36:25
Sanctification	Ps. 24:4
Glorification	Rev. 19:8, 14

Cleanliness

Required of priests	Is. 52:11
Acceptability of worship	Heb. 10:22
Inner, better than outward	Matt. 23:25–28

WORD STUDY **CLEANSE**, *taher* (taw-*hayr*). The verb *taher* can mean both a state in which someone or something is "clean" or "pure" or the action of "cleansing" or "purifying." A person might become clean miraculously as in 2 Kin. 5, which relates that Naaman was cured of his leprosy. Ceremonial cleanliness is addressed in the legal codes of the Pentateuch where cleanness is accomplished by washing or by passing through fire. Jeremiah, speaking for God, asks the people how long it will be before they are morally clean (Jer. 13:27). The action of cleansing, another form of the verb, can be accomplished in the physical realm where metal is cleansed from dross, the heavens from clouds, the land and cities from Asherim. Ceremonial cleansing is addressed (Lev. 16:9; Num. 8:6, 7; Ezek. 43:26), and moral cleansing is also treated in a number of places (see Lev. 16:30; Ps. 51:4; Ezek. 36:33; 37:23; and others). A person might also purify himself for sacred duties. (Strong's #2891)

Cleansing, spiritual

Promise of	Jer. 33:8
Need of	Ps. 51:2
Extent of	Ps. 19:12
Command regarding	2 Cor. 7:1
Means of	1 John 1:7, 9
Perfection of	Eph. 5:25, 26

Cleanthes—*Stoic teacher not mentioned by name in the Bible*

Quoted by Paul	Acts 17:28

WORD STUDY **CLEARS OF GUILT**, *naqah* (naw-*kaw*). To be "empty" or "clean" is indicated by the verb *naqah*. Sometimes the word means something which is cleaned out or purged as in Zech. 5:3 where thieves and liars are cut off or purged from the land. More often the word means "clean" in the sense that someone is free from guilt or made innocent. In a variation of this meaning, someone may be free or exempt from punishment though not necessarily free of guilt. In another form, the verb can mean "hold innocent" or "acquit." In this form the verb is used most often to mean that someone is left unpunished, sometimes by humans, but most often by God (see Ex. 34:7). (Strong's #5352)

Clement—*mild, merciful*

Paul's companions	Phil. 4:3

Cleopas—*of a renowned father*

Christ appeared to	Luke 24:18

Climate—*temperature and weather conditions*

A. Elements of:

Cold	Job 37:9; Acts 28:2
Clouds	Job 35:5
Thirsty ground	Deut. 8:15
Heat	Is. 49:10
Rain	Ezra 10:13
Snow	1 Chr. 11:22
Sunshine	Ex. 16:21
Wind	Matt. 14:24

B. Order of:

Promised	Gen. 8:22
Controlled by God	Job 37:5–13
Used in judgment	Jer. 50:38; Hag. 1:9–11
Tool of correction	Jon. 1:3, 4
Shows deity of Christ	Mark 4:37–39

Cloak—*outer garment*

A. Used literally of:

Outer garment	Matt. 5:40

B. Used figuratively of:

Covering for sin	1 Thess. 2:5
Covering for vice	1 Pet. 2:16

Clopas—*of a renowned father*

Husband of Mary	John 19:25
Called Alphaeus	Matt. 10:3

Closet

A place of prayer	Matt. 6:6

Clothing—*garments*

A. Need of:

Cover nakedness	Gen. 3:10, 11
Maintain modesty	1 Pet. 3:1–5
Keep warm	2 Tim. 4:13
Remove anguish	Esth. 4:3, 4

B. Unusual features regarding:

Lasted forty years	Deut. 8:4
Torn into twelve pieces	1 Kin. 11:29, 30
Obtained from enemies	Ex. 12:35
Some stripped of	Luke 10:30

C. Regulations concerning:

Wearing opposite sex's, forbidden	Deut. 22:5
Gaudy, denounced	Is. 3:16–24
Ostentatious, prohibited	1 Tim. 2:9
Warnings concerning	Matt. 7:15
Judgments by, deceptive	Luke 16:19–23
Proper sign of sanity	Mark 5:15

Clothing, tearing of—*symbolic expression of grief*

By Reuben	Gen. 37:29, 34
By Joshua	Josh. 7:6
By Tamar	2 Sam. 13:19
By Job	Job 1:20
By Ezra	Ezra 9:3
By high priest	Mark 14:63

By Paul and Barnabas . . . . .Acts 14:14
Forbidden to Aaron . . . . Lev. 10:6

Cloud—*a visible mass of vapor*
A. Miraculous uses of:
Israel's guidance . . . . Ex. 13:21, 22
Manifesting the divine glory . . . . .Ex. 16:10
Manifesting the divine presence . . . . . . 2 Chr. 5:13
Jesus' transfiguration . . . . .Luke 9:34, 35
Jesus' ascension . . . . Acts 1:9–11
Jesus' return . . . . Matt. 24:30
B. Figurative of:
God's unsearchableness . . . . Ps. 97:2
Sins . . . . Is. 44:22
Witnesses . . . . Heb. 12:1
False teachers . . . . .2 Pet. 2:17
Baptism . . . . 1 Cor. 10:1, 2
Boasting . . . . Prov. 25:14

Cloudburst—*a sudden downpour of rain*
Sent as a punishment . . . . Ezra 10:9–14

Cloud, pillar of
A. Designed to:
Regulate Israel's movements . . . . Ex. 40:36, 37
Guide Israel . . . . .Ex. 13:21
Defend Israel . . . . Ex. 14:19, 20
Cover the tabernacle . . . . Ex. 40:34
B. Special manifestations of, at:
Time of murmuring . . . . Ex. 16:9, 10
Giving of Law . . . . .Ex. 19:9, 16
Rebellion of Aaron and Miriam . . . . . Num. 12:1–9
Korah's rebellion . . . . Num. 16:19–21, 42

Clusters—*bunches*
Kinds of:
Grapes . . . . Num. 13:23
Henna blossoms . . . . Song 1:14
Raisins . . . . 1 Sam. 25:18

Cnidus—*age*
City of Asia Minor on Paul's voyage . . . . .Acts 27:7

Coal—*charcoal*
A. Uses of:
Heating . . . . John 18:18
Cooking . . . . John 21:9
By smiths . . . . Is. 44:11, 12
B. Figurative of:
Lust . . . . Prov. 6:25–28
Purification . . . . Is. 6:6, 7
Good deeds . . . . Rom. 12:20
Posterity . . . . 2 Sam. 14:7

Coat of mail
Worn by priests . . . . Ex. 28:32; 39:23

Cobra—*venomous snake*
Figurative of evil deeds . . . . .Is. 11:8
Figurative of man's evil nature . . . . Deut. 32:33

Coffin—*a boxlike container for a corpse*
In Joseph's burial . . . . .Gen. 50:26
Jesus touched . . . . Luke 7:14

Coins—*metal mediums of exchange*
Bekah (1/2 shekel) . . . . Ex. 38:26
Copper . . . . Matt. 10:9, 29
Daric . . . . 1 Chr. 29:7
Denarius . . . . Matt. 20:2
Drachma . . . . Ezra 2:69
Gerah . . . . .Ex. 30:13
Mina . . . . Ezek. 45:12
Mite . . . . Mark 12:42
Penny . . . . Matt. 5:26
Shekels of gold . . . . 2 Kin. 5:5
Piece of money . . . . Matt. 17:27
Piece of silver . . . . Matt. 26:15

Cold—*absence of heat*
A. Used literally of:
Winter . . . . Gen. 8:22
Cold weather . . . . John 18:18
B. Used figuratively of:
God's power . . . . Ps. 147:17
Indolence . . . . .Prov. 20:4
Good news . . . . .Prov. 25:25
Apostasy . . . . .Jer. 18:14
Spiritual decay . . . . Matt. 24:12

Col-Hozeh—*all-seeing*
A man of Judah . . . . Neh. 3:15; 11:5

Collaborators
Delilah . . . . Judg. 16:4–21
Doeg . . . . 1 Sam. 21:7; 22:7–23
Judas . . . . .Matt. 26:14–16

Collection box
For temple offerings . . . . .2 Kin. 12:9

Collection of money
The temple tax . . . . 2 Chr. 24:6, 9
For saints . . . . Rom. 15:25, 26

Colony—*citizens transported to another land*
A. Illustrated by:
Israel in Egypt . . . . Gen. 46:26–28
Israel in Assyria . . . . .2 Kin. 17:6, 24
Judah in Babylon . . . . 2 Kin. 25:8–12
B. Applied to:
Philippi as a Roman colony . . . . Acts 16:12
Philippian Christians . . . . Phil. 3:20

Colors
A. White, descriptive of:
Glory and majesty . . . . Dan. 7:9; Rev. 20:11
Purity, glory . . . . .Rev. 1:14
Victory . . . . .Rev. 6:2
Completion . . . . John 4:35
B. Black, descriptive of:
Sorrow, calamity .Rev. 6–12
Hell . . . . Jude 13
C. Green, descriptive of:
Spiritual privileges .Jer. 11:16
Spiritual life . . . . Ps. 52:8; 92:12–15
D. Red (crimson), descriptive of:
Atonement . . . . Is. 63:2
Military might . . . . Nah. 2:3

Persecution............................Rev. 12:3
Drunkenness.......................Prov. 23:29
Sinfulness...............................Is. 1:18
E. Purple, descriptive of:
Royalty ....Judg. 8:26
Wealth............................Luke 16:19
Luxury................................Rev. 17:4
F. Blue, descriptive of:
Heavenly character ....Ex. 28:31

Colosse—*punishment*
A city in Asia Minor ....Col. 1:2
Evangelized by Epaphras ....Col. 1:7
Not visited by Paul......................Col. 2:1
Paul writes against errors of .... Col. 2:16–23

Colossians, the epistle to the
Written by Paul......................Col. 1:1

Colt—*young beast of burden*
Descriptive of Messiah ....Gen. 49:10, 11
Christ rides on.................. Matt. 21:2, 5, 7
Of camel, as gift ....Gen. 32:13, 15

Come—*to approach; arrive*
Of invitation ....Is. 1:18
Of salvation .... Matt. 18:11
Of rest .... Matt. 11:28
Of promise.......................... John 14:3
Of prayer........................... Heb. 4:16
The final....................... Rev. 22:17, 20

WORD STUDY **COME, LORD!** *marana tha* (mar-*an*-ah *thah*). This phrase is the Greek transliteration of an Aramaic saying that early tradition associates with the liturgy of the Lord's Supper, and its only occurrence in the NT is in 1 Cor. 16:22. Depending upon which way the Aramaic words are divided, the expression could mean either "(our) Lord has come" (*maran atha*) or "(our) Lord, come!" (*marana tha*). Although the early church fathers favored the former understanding of the expression, the rendering given here represents *tha* as an imperative, a plea that the Lord should "come" (cf. the echo of this in Rev. 22:20). (Strong's #3134)

WORD STUDY **COMFORT,** *nacham* (naw-*kham*). To "be sorry" or "console" are indicated by the same verb, *nacham.* In one sense, the word describes those who have compassion for others as in Ps. 90:13 where the psalmist pleads for God to have compassion on His people. In other cases the word describes those who repent from their own actions. Most frequently, though, the term refers to those who comfort others. In some cases, the comforter is human as in Job where Job describes himself as one who has comforted mourners in the past or in ch. 42, where Job's friends come to comfort him. At other times, the Comforter is God as in Is. 49:13. In Ps. sometimes *nacham* comes in a cry for comfort from God and at others in the assertion that God has comforted. (Strong's #5162)

Comfort—*to relieve distress; to console*
A. Sources of:
God ....2 Cor. 1:3, 4
Christ............................. Matt. 9:22
Holy Spirit ....Acts 9:29–31
The Scriptures.....................Rom. 15:4
Christian friends .... 2 Cor. 7:6
B. Those in need of:
Afflicted............................ Is. 40:1, 2
Sorrowful ....2 Cor. 2:6, 7
Weak .... 1 Thess. 5:14
Discouraged.......................2 Cor. 2:6, 7
Troubled.........................2 Cor. 7:5–7
One another...................... 1 Thess. 4:18

Coming of Christ (see Second Coming of Christ)

Commander—*a leading official*
A. Names of:
Phichol .... Gen. 21:32
Sisera ....Judg. 4:7
Saul............................. 1 Sam. 9:15, 16
Abner...........................1 Sam. 17:55
Shobach........................ 2 Sam. 10:16
Joab .... 2 Sam. 24:2
Amasa ....1 Kin. 2:32
Zimri ....1 Kin. 16:9
Omri ....1 Kin. 16:16
Shophach ....1 Chr. 19:16
Rehum ....Ezra 4:8
Lysias............................. Acts 24:7
B. Applied spiritually to:
Angel of the Lord .... Josh. 5:14

WORD STUDY **COMMANDMENT,** *mitzvah* (mits-*vaw*). The noun *mitzvah*, "commandment," comes from the verb meaning "charge" or "command." Generally, the word is considered to be a late word. Occasionally the commandments are those of the king. Most often the commandments are those coming from God, usually the entire code of the law. When the singular is used, it can indicate the code of law as opposed to a single commandment (see 2 Chr. 8:13). In Prov. a commandment is a wise way of living instructed by a teacher (Prov. 6:23). The word *mitzvah* is most recognizable today in the phrase *Bar Mitzvah* or *Bas Mitzvah,* the ceremonies marking Jewish boys' and girls' coming of age and being ready to assume responsibility for keeping the commandments. (Strong's #4687)

Commandment—*a rule imposed by authority*
A. God's, described as:
Faithful............................Ps. 119:86
Broad..............................Ps. 119:96
A lamp.............................Prov. 6:23
Holy.................................Rom. 7:12
Not burdensome....................1 John 5:3
B. Christ's, described as:
New .... John 13:34
Obligatory .... Matt. 5:19, 20

WORD STUDY | **COMMON,** *koinos* (koy-*noss*). This adjective literally means "common." Used in a positive sense, it refers to something shared in common, such as a "common faith" (Titus 1:4) or "common salvation" (Jude 3). According to Acts, the early Christian community "had all things in common" (2:44; 4:32), which probably means that the individual members of the community made their possessions common property. Used in a negative sense, *koinos* means "common," "profane," "unclean" (cf. the cognate verb in Matt. 15:11–20; Acts 21:28)—that is, anything that has been made ritually "unclean" or impure (e.g., food, as in Acts 10:14 and 11:8). (Strong's #2839)

WORD STUDY | **COMPANION,** *chaber* (khaw-*bayr*). "Associates" or "companions" are indicated by the noun *chaber* coming from the verb meaning "unite" or "touch." The word indicates that there is some similarity between the individuals. In Ps. 45:7 the similarity is one of rank, while in Song 1:7 the resemblance comes from their calling as shepherds. At other times the word denotes similarity in character as in Is. 1:23 and Prov. 28:24, where the comparison is negative, suggesting that a person is a thief because the companions are thieves. (Strong's #2270)

Violence, death . . . . Acts 23:12–22
Persecution. . . . . Acts 17:5–9
B. Warnings against:
Do not consent with them . . . . Prov. 1:10–19
Avoid them. . . . . 1 Cor. 5:9–11
Remember their end . . . . Rev. 22:11, 14, 15

Comparison—*likeness; similarity*
A. Worthy comparisons, between:
God's holiness and human
sinfulness. . . . . Is. 46:12, 13; 55:6–9
Christ's glory and humiliation . . . . Phil. 2:5–11
Israel's call and responsibility . . . . . . Rom. 2:17–29
Faith and unbelief . . . . Matt. 12:41, 42
Former and present unbelief . . . . . . Matt. 11:20–24
Old and new covenants. . . . . 2 Cor. 3:6–18
The believer's status now
and hereafter . . . . 1 John 3:1–3
B. Unworthy comparisons, based on:
Position. . . . . Num. 16:3
Privileges . . . . 1 Cor. 3:1–9
Wealth. . . . . James 2:1–9

Compassion—*suffering with another, mercy*
A. God's, described as:
Overabundant. Ps. 86:13, 15
New every morning . . . . Lam. 3:22, 23
Great . . . . Is. 54:7
Kindled. . . . . Hos. 11:8
B. God's, expressed:
Fully. . . . . Ps. 78:38
Sovereignly. . . . . Rom. 9:15
Unfailingly. . . . . Lam. 3:22
Willingly. . . . . Luke 15:18–20
C. Christ's, expressed toward the:
Weary . . . . Matt. 11:28–30
Tempted . . . . Heb. 2:17, 18
Helpless. . . . . Mark 9:20–22
Sorrowful . . . . Luke 7:13, 14
Multitude. . . . . Matt. 15:32
Sick. . . . . Matt. 20:34; Mark 1:41
D. Examples of:
David in sorrow. . . . . Ps. 51:1–12
God to Israel . . . . Hos. 11:8
Christ to sinners . . . . Matt. 9:12, 13
E. Christian's:
Commanded . . . . Zech. 7:9; Col. 3:12;
Jude 22
Expressed . . . . 1 Pet. 3:8; Heb. 10:34
Illustrated. Luke 10:30, 33
Unified . . . . Phil. 2:1, 2

WORD STUDY **COMPLETE**, *teleioō* (tel-eye-*ah*-oh). This verb, encountered often in the NT, is used to denote the final intended stage in a process of development. The meaning of *teleioō* is usually captured by translating it as "to complete," "to bring to an end," "to finish," "to bring to its goal," "to bring to its accomplishment," or even "to make perfect." Jesus uses this word to indicate that He must "finish" ("complete") the work of God (John 4:34; cf.

17:4). In instances where *teleioō* implies that an imperfect state has been overcome, as in Heb. 5:9 and 7:28, it is perhaps best to translate it "to make perfect" (1 John 4:12, 17, 18) (Strong's #5048)

Complete—*to finish*
Used of:
Purification rites . . . . Esth. 2:12
Priestly ministry. . . . . Luke 1:23
Time of pregnancy. . . . . Luke 2:6

Complicity—*partnership in wrongdoing*
In Adam's sin. . . . . Rom. 5:12
In the sins of others . . . . Ps. 50:18
In national guilt . . . . Matt. 27:24–26

Composure—*calmness; tranquility; self-possession*
Before enemies . . . . Neh. 4:1–23
Under great strain . . . . Acts 27:21–26
Facing death . . . . Acts 7:59, 60
Lack of. . . . . Dan. 6:18–20

WORD STUDY **COMPREHEND, OVERTAKE,** *katalambanō* (kat-al-am-*bahn*-oh). This verb can be translated in several ways, but the meaning revolves around the notion of "to take into one's possession." Thus, *katalambanō* can mean "to seize," "to win," "to attain" (as in Rom. 9:30; 1 Cor. 9:24; Phil. 3:12, 13); or it can mean "to seize," "to overtake," "to come upon," usually with sinister intent (Mark 9:18). With respect to the coming of day and especially the coming of night, *katalambanō* can be translated as "come upon" or "overtake" (John 1:5; 12:35; 1 Thess. 5:4); with reference to cognition, it can be translated "to comprehend" (Eph. 3:18) or "to perceive" (Acts 10:34). (Strong's #2638)

Compromise—*agreement by concession*
A. Forbidden with:
Ungodly . . . . Ps. 1:1
Evil. . . . . Rom. 12:9
Unbelievers . . . . 2 Cor. 6:14–18
False teachers. . . . . Gal. 1:8–10; 2 John 7–11
Spiritual darkness . . . . Eph. 5:11
B. Examples:
Lot . . . . Gen. 13:12, 13; 19:1–29
Samson . . . . Judg. 16:1–21
Solomon . . . . 1 Kin. 11:1–14
Asa . . . . 2 Chr. 16:1–9
Jehoshaphat . . . . 2 Chr. 18:1–3; 19:1, 2;
2 Chr. 20:35–37

Concealment—*keeping something secret*
Of sin, impossible. . . . . Is. 29:15
Of intrigue, exposed . . . . Esth. 2:21–23
Of intentions, revealed . . . . Acts 23:12–22

Conceit—*self-flattery*
A. Of persons:
Goliath . . . . 1 Sam. 17:42–44
Haman . . . . Esth. 6:6–9
The wicked. . . . . Prov. 6:12–17
Christians, deplored . . . . Rom. 12:16

B. Characteristic of:

    False teachers. 1 Tim. 6:3, 4

    New convert. . . . . 1 Tim. 3:6

Conceited—*a self-righteous spirit; haughty*

    Christians warned against. . . . . .Rom. 11:20

    Rich tempted to . . . . .1 Tim. 6:17

    To prevail in last days . . . . 2 Tim. 3:1–5

Conception of children

    In marriage . . . . Gen. 21:1–3

    In adultery . . . . 2 Sam. 11:2–5

    In virginity. . . . . Matt. 1:18–21

Conclude—*to finish*

    The main issue . . . . Eccl. 12:13

Concubine—*a "wife" who is not legally a wife*

A. Features regarding:

    Could be divorced . . . . .Gen. 21:10–14

    Has certain rights. . . . . Deut. 21:10–14

    Children of, legitimate . . . . Gen. 22:24

    Unfaithfulness of . . . . .Judg. 19:1, 2

    Source of trouble. . . . . .Gen. 21:9–14

    Incompatible with Christianity . . . . Matt. 19:5

B. Men who had:

    Abraham. . . . . Gen. 25:6

    Nahor . . . . Gen. 22:23, 24

    Jacob . . . . Gen. 30:1, 4

    Eliphaz . . . . Gen. 36:12

    Gideon. . . . . Judg. 8:30, 31

    The Levite . . . . .Judg. 19:1

    Saul. . . . . .2 Sam. 3:7

    David. . . . . .2 Sam. 5:13

    Solomon . . . . .1 Kin. 11:1–3

    Caleb . . . . .1 Chr. 2:46

    Manasseh . . . . 1 Chr. 7:14

    Rehoboam . . . . .2 Chr. 11:21

    Belshazzar . . . . Dan. 5:2

Condemnation—*the judicial act of declaring one guilty*

A. Causes of:

    Adam's sin . . . . Rom. 5:12, 15–19

    Actual sin . . . . Matt. 27:3

    Our words . . . . Matt. 12:37

    Self-judgment . . . . Rom. 2:1; Titus 3:10, 11

    Legal requirements . . . . 2 Cor. 3:9

    Rejection of Christ. . . . . John 3:18, 19

B. Escape from:

    In Christ. . . . . .Rom. 8:1, 3

    By faith . . . . John 3:18, 19

C. Described as:

    Having degrees . . . . Matt. 23:14

    Just. . . . . .Rom. 3:8

    Self-inflicted . . . . 1 Cor. 11:29

    Merited . . . . 1 Tim. 5:11, 12

D. Inflicted:

    Now . . . . Rom. 14:23

    In eternity . . . . Matt. 23:33

Condescend—*to humble oneself to the level of others*

    Christ's example. . . . . .John 13:3–5

    The believer's practice. . . . . .Rom. 12:16

    The divine model . . . . Phil. 2:3–11

Condolence—*an expression of sympathy*

A. Received by:

    Job from friends . . . . .Job 2:11

    Hanun from David. . . . . 2 Sam. 10:2

    Hezekiah from a king . . . . .2 Kin. 20:12

    Mary from Jesus . . . . .John 11:23–35

B. Helps in expressing, assurance of:

    Trust . . . . .Ps. 23:1–6

    Hope . . . . .John 14:1–4

    Resurrection . . . . 1 Thess. 4:13–18

    Help. . . . . Is. 40:10, 11

Confessing Christ

A. Necessity of:

    For salvation . . . . Rom. 10:9, 10

    A test of faith. . . . . .1 John 2:23

    An evidence of spiritual union . . . . .1 John 4:15

    His confessing us . . . . Matt. 10:32

B. Content of:

    Christ's incarnation. . . . . 1 John 4:2, 3

    Christ's lordship . . . . Phil. 2:11

C. Prompted by:

    Holy Spirit . . . . 1 Cor. 12:3

    Faith. . . . . .Rom. 10:9

D. Hindrances to:

    Fear . . . . John 7:13

    Persecution. . . . . Mark 8:34, 35

    False teachers. .2 John 7

Confession of sin

A. Manifested by:

    Repentance . . . . .Ps. 51:1–19

    Self-abasement . . . . .Jer. 3:25

    Godly sorrow. . . . . Ps. 38:18

    Turning from sin . . . . .Prov. 28:13

    Restitution . . . . Num. 5:6, 7

B. Results in:

    Forgiveness. . . . . .1 John 1:9, 10

    Pardon. . . . . .Ps. 32:1–5

    Renewed fellowship. . . . . .Ps. 51:12–19

    Healing. . . . . James 5:16

C. Instances of:

    Aaron. . . . . Num. 12:11

    Israelites . . . . 1 Sam. 12:19

    David. . . . . 2 Sam. 24:10

    Ezra . . . . .Ezra 9:6

    Nehemiah . . . . Neh. 1:6, 7

    Daniel . . . . Dan. 9:4

    Peter. . . . . Luke 5:8

    Thief . . . . Luke 23:39–43

Confidence—*assurance*

A. True, based upon:

    God's Word . . . . .Acts 27:22–25

    Assurance. . . . . .2 Tim. 1:12

    Trust . . . . .Hab. 3:17–19

    Christ's promise . . . . Phil. 1:6

    Belief in God's power . . . . .1 Sam. 17:45–50

B. False, based upon:

    Unwarranted use of sacred things. . . 1 Sam. 4:5–11

Presumption .... Num. 14:40–45
Pride .... 1 Sam. 17:43, 44
C. The believer's:
Source of........................ 1 John 3:21, 22
In prayer .... 1 John 5:14, 15
In testimony........................ Acts 28:31
In others .... 2 Cor. 2:3; 7:16
Of God's will.................... Phil. 1:25, 26
Of faith's finality .... Phil. 1:6
Of future things .... 2 Cor. 5:6, 8
Must be held .... Heb. 10:35

| WORD STUDY | **CONFIRM, ESTABLISH,** *bebaioō* (beb-ah-*yah*-oh). The literal meaning of this verb is "to make firm," "to establish," |

especially in the sense of "to strengthen" (2 Cor. 1:21; Col. 2:7) or "to make reliable." In a legal context *bebaioō* and its cognates function as technical terms that designate a reliable and dependable security that serves as a confirmation. This usage informs several NT passages, particularly those places that speak of the activities of God in and through Jesus that establish the reliability of the apostles' proclamation (Mark 16:20); God's promises (Rom. 15:8); or the "testimony of Christ" (1 Cor. 1:6; cf. 1:8). (Strong's #950)

Confirmation—*making something steadfast and sure; establishing*
Human things.......... Ruth 4:7; Esth. 9:31, 32
A kingdom .... 2 Kin. 14:5
An oath............................. Heb. 6:17
A covenant........................... Gal. 3:17
Prophecy........................Dan. 9:12, 27
Promises.........................Rom. 15:8
Defense of faith....................... Phil. 1:7
Establishing faith..........Acts 14:22; 15:32, 41
To the world, forbidden ....Rom. 12:2

Conform—*to make one thing like another*
Used of:
The world, forbidden ....Rom. 12:2
World's lust .... 1 Pet. 1:14
Believer, to Christ..................... Phil. 3:21

Confused—*disorderly; perplexed*
Concerning:
God's will...................... 1 Sam. 23:1–12
The Messiah .... Matt. 11:2, 3
A great event .... Acts 2:1–13

Confusion—*bewilderment, perplexity*
A. Aspects of:
God not author of................... 1 Cor. 14:33
Typical of evil .... James 3:16
Prayer concerning .... Ps. 70:2
Illustrations of...................... Acts 19:29
B. Examples of:
Babel .... Gen. 11:9
Philistines.........................1 Sam. 7:10
Egyptians .... Ex. 14:24
City of Shushan..................... Esth. 3:15
Jerusalem ....Acts 21:31

Congratulate—*to express happiness to another*
Tou to David .... 1 Chr. 18:9, 10

| WORD STUDY | **CONGREGATION,** *edah* (ay-*daw*). A "congregation," the noun coming from the verb which means "to appoint," is a |

company of those assembled by appointment or acting concertedly. Most often the term refers to the gathered body of Israel, especially the company of Israel of the Exodus. In Ps. the word indicates a company of angels (82:1), a company of people (7:7), and a company of righteous people (1:5), all of whom are gathered round God, some of them for judgment. In the negative sense, the word can mean a company of evildoers (Job 15:34). A rare usage of the term appears in Judg. 14:8 in reference to a swarm of bees. (Strong's #5712)

Congregation—*an assembly of people*
A. Used of:
The political Israel.............. Ex. 12:3, 19, 47
A religious assembly ....Acts 13:42, 43
B. Regulations concerning:
Ruled by representatives.............. Num. 16:6
Summoned by trumpets......... Num. 10:3, 4, 7
Bound by decisions of
representatives.................Josh. 9:15–21
Atonement of sin of .... Lev. 4:13–21
Exclusion of certain ones from ...... Deut. 23:1–8

Coniah—*Yahweh is creating*
King of Judah ....Jer. 22:24, 28
Same as Jehoiachin.................2 Kin. 24:8

Connivance at wrong—*tacit approval of evil*
Involves guilt..................... Ps. 50:18–22
Aaron's, at Sinai .... Ex. 32:1, 2, 22
Pilate's, at Jesus' trial............. Matt. 27:17–26
Saul's (Paul's) at Stephen's
death......................Acts 7:57–60; 8:1

Cononiah, Conaniah—*Yahweh has established*
1. A Levite .... 2 Chr. 31:11–13
2. A Levite official .... 2 Chr. 35:9

Conscience—*the inner judge of moral issues*
A. Described as:
Good .... Acts 23:1
Pure .... 1 Tim. 3:9
Evil..............................Heb. 10:22
Defiled .... 1 Cor. 8:7
Seared .... 1 Tim. 4:2
B. Functions of:
A witness......................... Rom. 2:14, 15
An accuser .... John 8:9
An upholder.......................1 Tim. 1:19
Server of good..................... Rom. 13:4, 5
Source of joy....................... 2 Cor. 1:12
Dead..........................Prov. 30:20
C. Limitations of:
Needs cleansing .... Heb. 9:14
Subject to others' .... 1 Cor. 10:28, 29

Differs...........................1 Cor. 8:7–13
Fallible............................Prov. 16:25

Conscience, clear—*freedom from guilt feelings*
A. Necessary for:
    Freedom from dead works.........Heb. 9:13, 14
    Access to God....................Heb. 10:21, 22
    Liberty in witnessing.............. 1 Pet. 3:15, 16
    Christian love ....1 Tim. 1:5
    Confidence in prayer............. 1 John 3:21, 22
    Proud confidence .... 2 Cor. 1:12
B. Requirements for:
    Doctrinal purity......1 Tim. 1:3–5, 18–2:1; 4:1, 2
    Proper conduct....Acts 24:10–13, 16; Rom. 13:4–6
    Faith in Christ's blood....... Heb. 10:19–22; 9:14
    Knowledge...........................1 Cor. 8:7
    Belief.............................Titus 1:15
    Submissive spirit.................. 1 Pet. 2:18, 19
    Faith in God's greatness.............1 John 3:20
    Consideration of others .... 1 Cor. 10:28, 29
    Seeking forgiveness ... Prov. 28:13; Matt. 5:23, 24

Conscription—*to enroll for compulsory service*
    Employed by Solomon.... 1 Kin. 7:13, 14; 9:20, 21
    To build temple................. 1 Kin. 5:2, 3, 13
    To restore cities...................1 Kin. 9:15–17
    Led to revolt..................... 1 Kin. 12:3–16
    See Levy

Consecration—*dedication to God's service*
A. Applied to:
    Israel ....Ex. 19:6
    Priests ....Lev. 8:1–13
    Levites..........................Num. 8:5, 6, 14
    Individuals...........................1 Sam. 1:11
    Firstborn.......................... Ex. 13:2, 12
    Possessions....................... Lev. 27:28, 29
    Christ............................. Heb. 2:10
B. The Christian's:
    By Christ.......................... John 17:23
    Complete and entire ....Rom. 12:1, 2
    Separation from world ....2 Cor. 6:14–18
    Devotion to Christ.................. Rev. 14:1–7
    Sacred anointing................. 1 John 2:20, 27
    New priesthood .... 1 Pet. 2:5, 9

Conservation—*preserving worthwhile things*
    Material things.....................John 6:12, 13
    Spiritual things...................... Rev. 3:2, 3
    Good ....Acts 26:22, 23
    Unwise...........................Luke 5:36, 37

Consolation—*comfort fortified with encouragement*
    God, source of.......................Rom. 15:5
    Simeon waits for......................Luke 2:25
    Source of joy..................... Acts 15:30, 31
    To be shared......................2 Cor. 1:4–11

Conspiracy—*a plot to overthrow lawful authority*
Against:
    Joseph ....Gen. 37:18–20
    Moses...........................Num. 16:1–35
    Samson .... Judg. 16:4–21

Daniel ....Dan. 6:4–17
Jesus............................. Matt. 12:14
Paul ....Acts 23:12–15

Constancy—*firmness of purpose*
    Ruth's, to Naomi .... Ruth 1:16
    Jonathan's, to David............1 Sam. 20:12–17
    Virgins, to Christ .... Rev. 14:4, 5

Constellation—*a group of stars*
    The Great Bear.................. Job 9:9; 38:32
    The Serpent........................ Job 26:13
    Orion.................... Job 38:31; Amos 5:8
    Pleiades (seven stars)............. Job 9:9; 38:31
    Castor and Pollux................... Acts 28:11
    Judgment on .... Is. 13:10, 11
    Incense burned to.................2 Kin. 23:5

Consultation—*seeking advice from others*
    Demonical .... 1 Sam. 28:7–25
    Divided...........................1 Kin. 12:6, 8
    Determined .... Dan. 6:7
    Devilish............Matt. 26:3, 4; John 12:10, 11

Contempt—*scorn compounded with disrespect*
A. Forbidden toward:
    Parents ....Prov. 23:22
    Weak Christians..........Matt. 18:10; Rom. 14:3
    Believing masters .... 1 Tim. 6:2
    The poor.........................James 2:1–3
B. Objects of:
    The righteous ....Ps. 80:6
    Spiritual things....................Matt. 22:2–6
    Christ.........................John 9:28, 29
C. Examples of:
    Nabal......................... 1 Sam. 25:10, 11
    Michal...........................2 Sam. 6:16
    Sanballat............................ Neh. 2:19
    Jews .... Matt. 26:67, 68
    False teachers.......................2 Cor. 10:10
    The wicked..........................Prov. 18:3

Contention—*a quarrelsome spirit*
A. Caused by:
    Pride ....Prov. 13:10
    Disagreement ....Acts 15:36–41
    Divisions........................1 Cor. 1:11–13
    A quarrelsome spirit ....Gal. 5:15
B. Antidotes:
    Avoid the contentious ....Prov. 21:19
    Avoid controversies ....Titus 3:9
    Abandon the quarrel................ Prov. 17:14
    Follow peace .... Rom. 12:18–21

Contentious woman
    Gets Samson's secret ....Judg. 16:13–17;
        Prov. 21:9, 19
    Undesirable ....Prov. 25:24; 27:15

Contentment—*an uncomplaining acceptance of one's*
        share
A. Opposed to:
    Worry .... Matt. 6:25, 34
    Murmuring ....1 Cor. 10:10

Greed............................. Heb. 13:5
Envy............................. James 3:16

B. Shown by our recognition of:

Our unworthiness .... Gen. 32:9, 10
Our trust....................... Hab. 3:17–19
God's care...................... Ps. 145:7–21
God's provisions................. 1 Tim. 6:6–8
God's promises .... Heb. 13:5

WORD STUDY | **CONTINUALLY,** *tamid* (taw-*meed*). The adverb *tamid,* meaning "continuously" or "without interruption" is used frequently in the OT in a variety of settings. It can refer to the regular repetition of meals or rituals, including sacrifices. In Jer. 6:7, God's people are accused of sinning continuously. The word appears frequently in Ps., where there is a feeling of hyperbole as the psalmist says of human actions that his "eyes *are* continually on the LORD" (25:15) or indicates that praise is a continual action, as are sorrow and repentance. The psalmist asks for continuous aid and continually places offerings before God. There is also a continual seeking of revenge on enemies. (Strong's #8548)

Contracts—*covenants legally binding*

A. Ratified by:

Giving presents................. Gen. 21:25–30
Public witness .... Ruth 4:1–11
Oaths........................... Josh. 9:15, 20
Joining hands .... Prov. 17:18
Pierced ear .... Ex. 21:2–6

B. Examples of:

Abraham and Abimelech .... Gen. 21:25–32
Solomon and Hiram .... 1 Kin. 5:8–12

Contrition—*a profound sense of one's sinfulness*

Of the heart .... Ps. 51:17
The tax collector.................... Luke 18:13
Peter's example .... Matt. 26:75

Controversy—*dispute between people*

Between men .... Deut. 25:1
A public.......................... Acts 15:1–35
A private......................... Gal. 2:11–15

Conversion—*turning to God from sin*

A. Produced by:

God .... Acts 21:19
Christ............................. Acts 3:26
Holy Spirit .... 1 Cor. 2:13
The Scriptures..................... Ps. 19:7
Preaching .... Rom. 10:14

B. Of Gentiles:

Foretold........................... Is. 60:1–5
Explained .... Acts 15:3; Rom. 15:8–18
Illustrated............... Acts 10:1–48; 16:25–34
Confirmed .... Acts 15:1–31
Defended .... Gal. 3:1–29

C. Results in:

Repentance .... Acts 26:20
New creation .... 2 Cor. 5:17
Transformation................... 1 Thess. 1:9, 10

D. Fruits of:

Faithfulness................... Matt. 24:45–47
Gentleness .... 1 Thess. 2:7
Patience....................... Col. 1:10–12
Love .... 1 John 3:14
Obedience .... Rom. 15:18
Peacefulness................... James 3:17, 18
Self-control....................... 2 Pet. 1:6
Self-denial .... John 12:25

Conviction—*making one conscious of one's guilt*

A. Produced by:

Holy Spirit .... John 16:7–11
The gospel .... Acts 2:37
Conscience................. John 8:9; Rom. 2:15
The Law .... James 2:9

B. Instances of:

Adam........................... Gen. 3:8–10
Joseph's brothers................. Gen. 42:21, 22
Israel .... Ex. 33:2–4
David............................ Ps. 51:1–17
Isaiah............................ Is. 6:1–5
Men of Nineveh .... Matt. 12:41
Peter............................. Luke 5:8
Saul of Tarsus .... Acts 9:4–18
Philippian jailer .... Acts 16:27–30

Convocation—*a gathering for worship*

A. Applied to:

Sabbaths .... Lev. 23:2, 3
Passover .... Ex. 12:16
Pentecost .... Lev. 23:16–21
Feast of Trumpets .... Num. 29:1
Feast of Weeks .... Num. 28:26
Feast of Tabernacles .... Lev. 23:34–36
Day of Atonement .... Lev. 23:27

B. Designed to:

Gather the people................. Josh. 23:1–16
Worship God................... 2 Kin. 23:21, 22

Cooking—*making food palatable*

Done by women .... Gen. 18:2–6
Carefully performed .... Gen. 27:3–10
Savory dish...................... Gen. 27:4
Vegetables....................... Gen. 25:29
Forbidden on the Sabbath .... Ex. 35:3
Small cake .... 1 Kin. 17:13
Fish.............................. Luke 24:42

Cooperation—*working together*

A. Kinds of:

Person with person................. Ex. 17:12
God with person................. Phil. 2:12, 13

B. Needed to:

Complete job .... Neh. 4:16, 17
Secure results.................... Matt. 18:19
Win converts..................... John 1:40–51
Maintain peace .... Mark 9:50

C. Basis:

Obedience to God .... Ps. 119:63
Faith............................ Rom. 14:1–4

Copper
A. Used for:
Money . . . . Matt. 10:9
B. Workers in:
Alexander . . . . 2 Tim. 4:14

Coral—*a rocklike substance formed from skeletons of sea creatures*
Wisdom more valuable than . . . . Job 28:18
Bought by traders . . . . Ezek. 27:16

Corban—*an offering*
Money dedicated . . . . Mark 7:11

Cordiality—*sincere affection and kindness*
Abraham's . . . . Gen. 18:1–8
Seen in Jonathan . . . . 1 Sam. 20:11–23
Lacking in Nabal . . . . 1 Sam. 25:9–13

Coriander
A plant whose seed is compared to manna . . . . . Ex. 16:31

Corinth—*a city of Greece*
Paul labors at . . . . Acts 18:1–18
Site of church . . . . 1 Cor. 1:2
Visited by Apollos . . . . Acts 19:1
Abode of Erastus . . . . 2 Tim. 4:20

Corinthians, the Epistles to the—*two books of the New Testament*
Written by Paul . . . . 1 Cor. 1:1; 2 Cor. 1:1

Cornelius—*a horn*
A religious Gentile . . . . Acts 10:1–48

Cornerstone—*a stone placed to bind two walls together*
Laid in Zion . . . . Is. 28:16
Rejected . . . . Ps. 118:22
Christ is . . . . 1 Pet. 2:6, 8
Christ fulfills . . . . Acts 4:11; 1 Pet. 2:7

Correction—*punishment designed to restore*
A. Means of:
God's judgments . . . . Jer. 46:28
The rod . . . . Prov. 22:15
Wickedness . . . . Jer. 2:19
Prayer . . . . Jer. 10:24
Scriptures . . . . 2 Tim. 3:16
B. Benefits of:
Needed for children . . . . Prov. 23:13
Sign of sonship . . . . Prov. 3:12
Brings rest . . . . Prov. 29:17
Makes happy . . . . Job 5:17

Corrosion (see Rust)

Corruption—*rottenness; depravity*
A. Descriptive of:
Physical blemishes . . . . Mal. 1:14
Physical decay . . . . Matt. 6:19, 20
Moral decay . . . . Gen. 6:12
Eternal ruin . . . . Gal. 6:8
B. Characteristics of:
The unregenerate . . . . Luke 6:43–45
Apostates . . . . 2 Cor. 2:6, 7; 2 Pet. 2:12, 19

C. Deliverance from:
By Christ . . . . Acts 2:27, 31
Promised . . . . Rom. 8:21
Through conversion . . . . 1 Pet. 1:18, 23
Perfected in heaven . . . . 1 Cor. 15:42, 50

Corruption, mount of
Site of pagan altars . . . . 1 Kin. 11:7
Altars of, destroyed . . . . 2 Kin. 23:13

Corruption of body
Results from Adam's sin . . . . Rom. 8:21
Begins in this life . . . . 2 Cor. 5:4
Consummated by death . . . . John 11:39
Freedom from, promised . . . . Rom. 8:21
Freedom from, accomplished . . . . 1 Cor. 15:42

Cos
An island between Rhodes and Miletus . . Acts 21:1

Cosam—*a diviner*
Father of Addi . . . . Luke 3:28

Cosmetics
Used by Jezebel . . . . 2 Kin. 9:30
Futility of . . . . Jer. 4:30

Cosmic conflagration—*to destroy by fire*
Day of judgment . . . . 2 Pet. 3:7–10

Council—*Jewish Sanhedrin, Jewish governing body*
A judicial court . . . . Matt. 5:22
Christ's trial . . . . Matt. 26:57–59
Powers of, limited . . . . John 18:31
Apostles before . . . . Acts 4:5–30
Stephen before . . . . Acts 6:12–15
Paul before . . . . Acts 23:1–5

Counsel, God's
A. Called:
Immutable . . . . Heb. 6:17
Faithful . . . . Is. 25:1
Wonderful . . . . Is. 28:29
Great . . . . Jer. 32:19
Sovereign . . . . Dan. 4:35
Eternal . . . . Eph. 3:11
B. Events determined by:
History . . . . Is. 46:10, 11
Christ's death . . . . Acts 2:23
Salvation . . . . Rom. 8:28–30
Union in Christ . . . . Eph. 1:9, 10
C. Attitudes toward:
Christians declare . . . . Acts 20:27
Proper reserve . . . . Acts 1:7
Wicked despise . . . . Is. 5:19
They reject . . . . Luke 7:30

Counsel, human
Jethro's, accepted . . . . Ex. 18:13–27
Hushai's followed . . . . 2 Sam. 17:14
Of a woman, brings peace . . . . 2 Sam. 20:16–20
David's dying . . . . 1 Kin. 2:1–10
Of old men, rejected . . . . 1 Kin. 12:8, 13
Of friends, avenged . . . . Esth. 5:14; 7:10

Counselor—*an adviser*

    Christ is.................................... Is. 9:6

    Your testimonies are ....Ps. 119:24

    Safety in many........................ Prov. 11:14

    Brings security ....Prov. 15:22

    Jonathan, a..........................1 Chr. 27:32

    Gamaliel...........................Acts 5:33–40

Count—*to number*

Things counted:

    Stars.................................. Gen. 15:5

    Days...................................Lev. 15:13

    Years ....Lev. 25:8

    Plunder .... Num. 31:26

    Weeks .... Deut. 16:9

    Money ....2 Kin. 22:4

    People ....1 Chr. 21:17

    Bones..................................Ps. 22:17

    Towers................................Ps. 48:12

    Houses................................ Is. 22:10

Countenance—*facial expression, visage*

A. Kinds of:

    Unfriendly .... Gen. 31:1, 2

    Fierce.............................. Deut. 28:50

    Awesome............................Judg. 13:6

    Sad .... 1 Sam. 16:12

    Handsome .... 1 Sam. 16:12

    Cheerful .... Prov. 15:13

    Angry................................Prov. 25:23

B. Transfigured:

    Moses'............................. 2 Cor. 3:7

    Christ's ....Matt. 17:1, 2

    The believer's....................... 2 Cor. 3:18

Counterfeit—*a spurious imitation of the real thing*

A. Applied to persons:

    Christ.........................Matt. 24:4, 5, 24

    Apostles .... 2 Cor. 11:13

    Ministers ....2 Cor. 11:14, 15

    Christians...........................Gal. 2:3, 4

    Teachers ....2 Pet. 2:1

    Prophets ....1 John 4:1

    The Antichrist .... Rev. 19:20

B. Applied to things:

    Worship .... Matt. 15:8, 9

    Gospel............................ Gal. 1:6–12

    Miracles ....2 Thess. 2:7–12

    Knowledge......................... 1 Tim. 6:20

    Commandments.................. Titus 1:13, 14

    Doctrines .... Heb. 13:9

    Religion.............................James 1:26

    Prayers............................ James 4:3

Country—*the land of a nation*

    Commanded to leave.................Gen. 12:1–4

    Love of native ....Gen. 30:25

    Exiled from ....Ps. 137:1–6

    A prophet in his own ....Luke 4:24

    A heavenly .... Heb. 11:16

Courage—*fearlessness in the face of danger*

A. Manifested:

    Among enemies .... Ezra 5:1–17

    In battle.......................... 1 Sam. 17:46

    Against great foes.................Judg. 7:7–23

    Against great odds .... 1 Sam. 17:32, 50

    When threatened .... .Dan. 3:16–18

    When intimidated ....Dan. 6:7–13

    When facing death..............Judg. 16:28–30

    In youth ....1 Sam. 14:6–45

    In old age .... Josh. 14:10–12

    Before a king ....Esth. 4:8, 16

    In moral crises....................Neh. 13:1–31

    In preaching Christ ....Acts 3:12–26

    In rebuking .... Gal. 2:11–15

B. Men encouraged to:

    Leaders ....Deut. 31:7

    Joshua ....Josh. 1:5–7

    Gideon.......................... .Judg. 7:7–11

    Philistines.........................1 Sam. 4:9

    Zerubbabel.......................... Hag. 2:4

    Solomon ....1 Chr. 28:20

Course—*onward movement; advance*

    A ship's direction ....Acts 16:11

    A prescribed path ....Judg. 5:20

    The age .... Eph. 2:2

    The cycle of life.................... James 3:6

Courtesy—*visible signs of respect*

A. Shown in:

    Manner of address .... Gen. 18:3

    Gestures of bowing .... Gen. 19:1

    Rising before superiors...............Lev. 19:32

    Well-wishing remarks...............Gen. 43:29

    Expressions of blessing .... Ruth 2:4

B. Among Christians:

    Taught......................... Rom. 12:9–21

    Illustrated.......................3 John 1–6, 12

Courts—*institution designed for justice*

A. Kinds of:

    Circuit......................... 1 Sam. 7:15–17

    Superior and inferior.............. Ex. 18:21–26

    Ecclesiastical .... Matt. 18:15–18

B. Places held:

    At the tabernacle .... Num. 27:1–5

    Outside the camp................. Lev. 24:13, 14

    At the city's gates .... Ruth 4:1, 2

    Under a tree.......................Judg. 4:4, 5

C. Features of:

    Witness examined ....Deut. 19:15–21

    Accused speaks.................... Mark 15:1–5

    Sentence of, final ....Deut. 17:8–13

    Contempt of, forbidden .... Acts 23:1–5

    Corruption of, deplored .... Matt. 26:59–62

Courtship—*the period leading to marriage*

    Isaac and Rebekah............... Gen. 24:1–67

    Jacob and Rachel .... Gen. 29:9–30

    Samson ....Judg. 14:1–7

Boaz and Ruth......................Ruth 3:4–14
Ahasuerus and Esther................Esth. 2:17

Courtyard, Court—*an enclosed area*
Tabernacle...........................Ex. 27:9
Temple.............................1 Kin. 6:36
Prison..............................Jer. 32:2
House.............................2 Sam. 17:18
Garden place.......................Esth. 1:5

WORD STUDY

COVENANT, *berith* (ber-*eeth*). The "covenant," *berith,* in the OT is a noun that can describe a treaty or alliance between equals or heads of state. For example, Abraham made a covenant with the Amorites, and Judah had a covenant with Assyria. The contract can be between a monarch and his subject, such as the one between David and Abner in 2 Sam. 3, or between friends, such as between David and Jonathan. The covenants between God and humans is a divine construct with signs and pledges. The first divine covenant is the one given to Noah in which God promises that He will never again flood the whole earth. God also made covenants with Abraham, Isaac, and Jacob, promising many descendants and the land of Canaan. The most frequently mentioned covenant is the one made at Sinai between God and the people of Israel. David was promised an ever-lasting kingdom in the covenant God made with him. The prophets discuss a new construct with new precepts as Jeremiah states that there will be a new covenant (Jer. 31:31). The idea also appears in Is. 42:6; 49:8; 55:3; Ezek. 16:60–62; and Hos. 2:18. (Strong's #1285)

WORD STUDY

COVENANT, *diathēkē* (dee-ath-*ay*-kay). In the language of the day this noun referred exclusively to a "last will and testament" (as in Heb. 9:16, 17; perhaps Gal. 3:15, 17). The impact of the Septuagint, where *diathēkē* translates the Heb. word for "covenant" (*berith*), is evident in the NT. Doubtlessly, *diathēkē* was employed in the Septuagint because a *diathēkē* is the declaration of a person's will and not a contractual agreement; in the OT it is clear that God alone sets the conditions of the "covenant" with His people (Israel). NT writers emphasize that God's *diathēkē* directed toward Christians is "new" (Luke 22:20; 1 Cor. 11:25; Heb. 8:8, 9), and that (like OT covenants) the shedding of blood puts this "covenant" into effect (Heb. 9:20; 10:29; cf. Matt. 26:28 and Mark 14:24). (Strong's #1242)

Covenant—*agreement between two or more parties*
A. Designed for:
    Mutual protection...............Gen. 31:50–52
    Securing peace...................Josh. 9:15, 21
    Friendship......................1 Sam. 18:3
    Promoting commerce............1 Kin. 5:6–11
B. Requirements of:
    Witnessed......................Gen. 23:16–18
    Confirmed by an oath...........Gen. 21:23, 31

Specified.........................1 Sam. 11:1, 2
Written and sealed..................Neh. 9:38
C. Examples of:
    Abraham and Abimelech.........Gen. 21:27–32
    Laban and Jacob..............Gen. 31:43–55
    David and elders..............2 Sam. 5:1–3
    Ahab and Ben-Hadad.............1 Kin. 20:34
    New covenant.....................Matt. 26:28
    New Testament dispensation..........2 Cor. 3:6
D. Characteristics of:
    Superiority of the new..............Heb. 8:6–13
    Descriptive of a person's will.......Heb. 9:15–17

Covenant—*spiritual agreement*
A. Between a leader and people:
    Joshua's........................Josh. 24:1–28
    Jehoiada's.....................2 Kin. 11:17
    Hezekiah's....................2 Chr. 29:1, 10
    Josiah's........................2 Kin. 23:3
    Ezra's..........................Ezra 10:3
B. Between God and man:
    Adam........................Gen. 2:16, 17
    Noah..........................Gen. 9:1–17
    Abraham......................Gen. 15:18
    Isaac..........................Gen. 26:1–5
    Jacob........................Gen. 28:13–22
    Israel..........................Ex. 19:5
    Levi..........................Mal. 2:4–10
    Phinehas......................Num. 25:11–13
    David.........................Ps. 89:3, 28, 34
C. The old (Sinaitic):
    Instituted at Sinai....................Ex. 19:5
    Ratified by sacrifice........Ex. 24:6–8; Heb. 9:16
    Does not annul the Abrahamic......Gal. 3:16–18
    Designed to lead to Christ..........Gal. 3:17–25
    Consists of outward rites...........Heb. 9:1–13
    Sealed by circumcision...........Gen. 17:9–14
    Prefigures the gospel..............Heb. 9:8–28
D. The new (evangelical):
    Promised in Eden.....................Gen. 3:15
    Proclaimed to Abraham..............Gen. 12:3
    Dated in prophecy...............Dan. 9:24–27
    Fulfilled in Christ................Luke 1:68–79
    Ratified by His blood.............Heb. 9:11–23
    Remembered in the Lord's Supper....1 Cor. 11:25
    Called everlasting....................Heb. 13:20

Covenant-breakers
    Under God's judgment..................Is. 24:5
    By abominations....................Ezek. 44:7

Covenant-keepers
    God's blessing upon....................Ex. 19:5

Covenant of salt—*of perpetual purity*
    Descriptive of priests...............Num. 18:19
    Descriptive of David................2 Chr. 13:5
    Used figuratively...................Mark 9:50

Covered carts
    Used as offerings....................Num. 7:3

Coverings
Symbolic of:
Immorality. . . . . Prov. 7:16

Covert—*hiding place*
Used by Abigail. . . . . 1 Sam. 25:20
Figurative of protection . . . . Is. 32:2

Covetousness—*an insatiable desire for worldly gain; greed*
A. Described as:
Idolatry. . . . . Col. 3:5
Root of evil. . . . . 1 Tim. 6:9–11
Never satisfied . . . . Hab. 2:9
Vanity . . . . Ps. 39:6
B. Productive of:
Theft . . . . Josh. 7:20, 21
Lying . . . . 2 Kin. 5:20–27
Murder . . . . Prov. 1:18, 19
Falsehood. . . . . Acts 5:1–10
Harmful lusts . . . . 1 Tim. 6:9
Apostasy. . . . . 1 Tim. 6:10
C. Excludes from:
God's kingdom . . . . 1 Cor. 6:10; Eph. 5:5
Sacred offices. .1 Tim. 3:3
Heaven . . . . .Eph. 5:5
D. Examples of:
Achan . . . . Josh. 7:21
Saul. . . . . 1 Sam. 15:9, 19
Judas . . . . Matt. 26:14, 15
Ananias and Sapphira. . . . . Acts 5:1–11
See Avarice

Cowardice, spiritual
A. Causes of:
Fear of life . . . . .Gen. 12:11–13
Fear of others. . . . . .Ex. 32:22–24
Unbelief . . . . Num. 13:28–33
Fear of rulers . . . . John 9:22
B. Results in:
Defeat . . . . Num. 14:40–45
Escape . . . . 2 Sam. 15:13–17
Compromise .John 19:12–16
Denial . . . . .Matt. 26:69–74
C. Guilty conscience makes:
Joseph's brothers. . . . . Gen. 42:21–28
David. . . . . 2 Sam. 12:1–14
Pharisees. . . . . John 8:1–11

Cows
Jacob's possessions. . . . . Gen. 32:15
Found in Egypt. . . . . Gen. 41:2
Use of milk. . . . . 2 Sam. 17:29
Used in rituals. . . . . Lev. 3:1

Cozbi—*false*
Slain by Phinehas . . . . .Num. 25:6–18

Craft
A trade. . . . . Rev. 18:22
See Arts and crafts in the Bible

Craftiness—*cunning deception*
Applied to David . . . . .1 Sam. 23:19–22

Human's, thwarted by God . . . . .Job 5:13
A harlot's heart . . . . Prov. 7:10
Human's, known by God . . . . 1 Cor. 3:19
Enemies', perceived by Christ . . . . .Luke 20:23
Use of, rejected . . . . 2 Cor. 4:2
Warning against. Eph. 4:14

Craftsmen—*men who work at a trade*
Makers of idols . . . . Deut. 27:15
Destroyed in Babylon . . . . Rev. 18:21, 22

Crane—*a migratory bird*
Chatters . . . . Is. 38:14

> **WORD STUDY**   **CREATE,** *bara'* (baw-*raw*). The verb translated "shape" or "create," *bara',* is always used to indicate divine activity, never human. God created objects, such as heaven and earth, humans, and the host of heavens. Malachi indicates that individuals are created by God. A third category of creative activity is that of new conditions, such as righteousness and salvation, cloud and flame (Is. 4:5), and a new thing (Jer. 31:22). Just as God originates creations, He can transform other creations, making a clean heart, a new heaven and earth, and in Is. 65:18 a new Jerusalem, which is a delight and cause for rejoicing. (Strong's #1254)

Creation—*causing what did not exist to exist*
A. Author of:
God . . . . Heb. 11:3
Jesus Christ . . . . .Col. 1:16, 17
Holy Spirit . . . . .Ps. 104:30
B. Objects of:
Heaven, earth . . . . Gen. 1:1–10
Vegetation . . . . Gen. 1:11, 12
Animals. . . . . .Gen. 1:21–25
Man and woman. . . . . Gen. 1:26–28
Stars . . . . Is. 40:26
C. Expressive of God's:
Deity . . . . .Rom. 1:20
Power. . . . . .Is. 40:26, 28
Glory . . . . Ps. 19:1
Goodness . . . . Ps. 33:5, 6
Wisdom . . . . .Ps. 104:24
Sovereignty . . . . .Rev. 4:11
D. Illustrative of:
The new birth . . . . 2 Cor. 5:17
Renewal of believers . . . . Ps. 51:10
The eternal world. . . . . .Is. 65:17; 2 Pet. 3:11, 13
E. The first:
Subject to vanity. . . . . Rom. 8:19, 20
Will be delivered. . . . . .Rom. 8:21

Creator—*the Supreme Being*
A title of God. . . . . Is. 40:28
People's disrespect of. . . . . .Rom. 1:25
To be remembered . . . . Eccl. 12:1

Creditor—*one to whom a debt is payable*
Interest, forbidden. . . . . Ex. 22:25
Debts remitted . . . . .Neh. 5:10–12

Some very cruel . . . . .Matt. 18:28–30
Christian principle . . . . .Rom. 13:8

Cremation—*burning a body*
Two hundred fifty were consumed . . . Num. 16:35
Zimri's demise . . . . 1 Kin. 16:15–19

Crescens—*growing*
Paul's assistant . . . . 2 Tim. 4:10

Crete—*an island in the Mediterranean Sea*
Some from, at Pentecost . . . . .Acts 2:11
Paul visits . . . . Acts 27:7–21
Titus dispatched to . . . . .Titus 1:5
Inhabitants of, evil and lazy . . . . .Titus 1:12

Crib
Animals feed from . . . . .Is. 1:3

Criminal—*a lawbreaker*
Paul considered a . . . . Acts 25:16, 27
Christ accused of . . . . John 18:28–30
Christ crucified between . . . . Luke 23:32, 33
One unrepentant; one repentant . . . Luke 23:39–43

Cripple—*one physically impaired*
Mephibosheth, by a fall . . . . .2 Sam. 4:4
Paul's healing of . . . . Acts 14:8–10
Jesus heals . . . . Matt. 15:30, 31

Crisis—*the crest of human endurance*
Bad advice in . . . . Job 2:9, 10
God's advice in . . . . Luke 21:25–28

Crispus—*curled*
Chief ruler of synagogue at Corinth . . . . Acts 18:8
Baptized by Paul . . . . 1 Cor. 1:14

Crop—*the craw of a bird*
Removed by priest . . . . Lev. 1:16

Cross—*a method of execution*
A. Used literally of:
Christ's death . . . . Matt. 27:32
B. Used figuratively of:
Duty . . . . Matt. 10:38
Christ's sufferings . . . . 1 Cor. 1:17
The Christian faith . . . . 1 Cor. 1:18
Reconciliation . . . . Eph. 2:16

Crown—*an emblem of glory*
A. Worn by:
High priest . . . . .Lev. 8:9
Kings . . . . 2 Sam. 12:30
Queens . . . . Esth. 2:17
Ministers of state . . . . Esth. 8:15
B. Applied figuratively to:
A good wife . . . . .Prov. 12:4
Old age . . . . .Prov. 16:31
Grandchildren . . . . Prov. 17:6
Honor . . . . .Prov. 27:24
Material blessings . . . . .Ps. 65:11
C. Applied spiritually to:
Christ . . . . .Ps. 132:18
Christ at His return . . . . .Rev. 19:12
Christ glorified . . . . .Heb. 2:7–9
The church . . . . Is. 62:3

The Christian's reward . . . . 2 Tim. 2:5
The minister's reward . . . . Phil. 4:1
Soul winners . . . . 1 Thess. 2:19
The Christian's incorruptible prize . . . . 1 Cor. 9:25

Crown—*the top of the head*
Figurative of retribution . . . . Ps. 7:16

Crown of thorns
Placed on Christ . . . . Matt. 27:29; John 19:2

Crowns of Christians
Joy . . . . 1 Thess. 2:19
Righteousness . . . . 2 Tim. 4:8
Life . . . . James 1:12
Glory . . . . .1 Pet. 5:4
Imperishable . . . . 1 Cor. 9:25

Crucifixion—*death on a cross*
A. Jesus' death by:
Predicted . . . . Matt. 20:19
Demanded . . . . Mark 15:13, 14
Gentiles . . . . Matt. 20:19
Jews . . . . .Acts 2:22, 23, 36
Between thieves . . . . Matt. 27:38
Nature of, unrecognized . . . . 1 Cor. 2:7, 8
B. Figurative of:
Utter rejection . . . . Heb. 6:6
Apostasy . . . . .Rev. 11:8
Union with Christ . . . . .Gal. 2:20
Separation . . . . Gal. 6:14
Sanctification . . . . .Rom. 6:6
Dedication . . . . 1 Cor. 2:2

Cruelty—*violence*
Descriptive of the wicked . . . . .Ps. 74:20
To animals, forbidden . . . . .Num. 22:27–35

Crumbs—*fragments of bread*
Dogs eat of . . . . Matt. 15:27
Lazarus begs for . . . . Luke 16:20, 21

Crying—*an emotional upheaval*
Accusation . . . . Gen. 4:10
Remorse . . . . Heb. 12:17
Pretense . . . . Judg. 14:15–18
Sorrow . . . . 2 Sam. 18:33
Others' sins . . . . .Ps. 119:136
Pain . . . . Heb. 5:7, 8
None in heaven . . . . .Rev. 21:4

Crystal—*rock crystal*
Wisdom surpasses . . . . .Job 28:17–20
Gates of Zion . . . . Is. 54:12
Descriptive of heaven . . . . .Rev. 4:6

Cubs—*offspring of beasts*
Figurative of:
Babylonians . . . . .Jer. 51:38
Assyrians . . . . .Nah. 2:11, 12
Princes of Israel . . . . Ezek. 19:2–9

Cucumber—*an edible fruit grown on a vine*
Lusted after . . . . Num. 11:5
Grown in gardens .Is. 1:8

Cud—*partly digested food*

Animals chew again. . . . . Lev. 11:3–8

Cummin—*an annual of the parsley family*

Seeds threshed by a rod. . . . . Is. 28:25, 27

A trifle of tithing . . . . Matt. 23:23

Cup

A. Literal use of:

For drinking . . . . 2 Sam. 12:3

B. Figurative uses of:

One's portion. . . . . Ps. 11:6

Blessings . . . . Ps. 23:5

Suffering. . . . . Matt. 20:23

New covenant . . . . 1 Cor. 10:16

Hypocrisy. . . . . Matt. 23:25, 26; Luke 11:39

Cupbearer—*a high court official*

Many under Solomon . . . . 1 Kin. 10:5

Nehemiah, a faithful. . . . . Neh. 1:11

Curds

Article of diet . . . . 2 Sam. 17:29

Fed to infants. . . . . Is. 7:15, 22

Illustrative of prosperity. . . . . Deut. 32:14

Cure—*to restore to health*

Of the body . . . . Matt. 17:16

Of the mind . . . . Mark 5:15

Of the demonized. . . . . Matt. 12:22

With means . . . . Is. 38:21

By faith . . . . Num. 21:8, 9

By prayer. . . . . James 5:14, 15

By God's mercy. . . . . Phil. 2:27

Hindered . . . . 2 Kin. 8:7–15

Curiosity—*desire to know*

Into God's secrets, forbidden . . . . . . John 21:21, 22

Moses', concerning burning bush. . . . . Ex. 3:3

Leads 50,070 to death . . . . 1 Sam. 6:19

Examples of curiosity seekers:

Eve . . . . Gen. 3:6

Israelites . . . . Ex. 19:21, 24

Babylonians . . . . 2 Kin. 20:12, 13

Herod . . . . Matt. 2:3–8

Zacchaeus. . . . . Luke 19:1–6

Certain Greeks . . . . John 12:20, 21

Lazarus's visitors . . . . John 12:9

Peter. . . . . Matt. 26:58

At the Crucifixion . . . . Matt. 27:46–49

Athenians. . . . . Acts 17:21

Curse, cursing—*a violent expression of evil upon others*

A. Pronounced upon:

Serpent . . . . Gen. 3:14, 15

The earth . . . . Gen. 3:17, 18

Cain. . . . . Gen. 4:9–11

Canaan . . . . Gen. 9:25

Two sons. . . . . Gen. 49:5–7

Lawbreakers. . . . . Deut. 28:15–45

Jericho's rebuilder. . . . . Josh. 6:26

Meroz. . . . . Judg. 5:23

Abimelech . . . . Judg. 9:26, 27

B. Forbidden upon:

Parents . . . . Ex. 21:17

Ruler . . . . Ex. 22:28

Deaf. . . . . Lev. 19:14

Enemies. . . . . Luke 6:28

God . . . . Job 2:9

God's people . . . . Gen. 12:3

C. Instances of:

Goliath's. . . . . 1 Sam. 17:43

Balaam's attempted . . . . Num. 22:1–12

Shimei on David. . . . . 2 Sam. 16:5–7

The fig tree. . . . . Mark 11:21

Peter's . . . . Matt. 26:69–74

The crucified Christ . . . . Deut. 21:23; Gal. 3:13

D. Manifested by:

Rebellious. . . . . 2 Sam. 16:5–8

Curtains—*an awninglike screen*

Ten, in tabernacle. . . . . Ex. 26:1–13

Figurative of the heavens . . . . Ps. 104:2

Cush—*black*

1. Ham's oldest son. . . . . 1 Chr. 1:8–10

2. Means Ethiopia . . . . Is. 18:1

3. A Benjamite. . . . . Ps. 7 (Title)

Cushan—*blackness*

Probably same as Cush . . . . Hab. 3:7

Cushan-Rishathaim—*extra wicked*

A Mesopotamian king; oppressed Israel . . . Judg. 3:8

Othniel delivers Israel from. . . . . Judg. 3:9, 10

Cushi—*an Ethiopian*

1. Ancestor of Jehudi. . . . . Jer. 36:14

2. Father of Zephaniah . . . . Zeph. 1:1

Cushite—*an Ethiopian*

David's servant . . . . 2 Sam. 18:21–32

Custom—*tax; usage*

A. As a tax:

Levites excluded from . . . . Ezra 7:24

Imposed by Jews. . . . . Ezra 4:20

Imposed upon Jews . . . . Ezra 4:13

Kings require. Matt. 17:25

B. As a common practice:

Abominable . . . . Lev. 18:30

Vain . . . . Jer. 10:3

Worthy . . . . Luke 4:16

Traditional. . . . . Acts 21:21

Cuth, Cuthah—*burning*

People from, brought to

Samaria . . . . 2 Kin. 17:24, 30

Cymbal—*hollow of a vessel*

A musical instrument . . . . 1 Chr. 13:8; 15:28

Figurative of lacking love. . . . . 1 Cor. 13:1

Cypress—*a hardwood tree*

Used by idol-makers . . . . Is. 44:14–17

Cyprus—*fairness*

Ships of, in Balaam's prophecy . . . . Num. 24:24

A haven for Tyre's ships . . . . Is. 23:1–12

Mentioned in the prophets. . . . . Jer. 2:10

A large Mediterranean island; home of
Barnabas .... Acts 4:36
Christians reach .... Acts 11:19, 20
Paul visits .... Acts 13:4–13
Barnabas visits .... Acts 15:39
Paul twice sails past ....Acts 21:3

Cyrene—*wall*
A Greek colonial city in north Africa;
home of Simon .... Matt. 27:32
People from, at Pentecost.............Acts 2:10
Synagogue of ....Acts 6:9
Some from, become missionaries ...... Acts 11:20

Cyrus—*sun; throne*
Prophecies concerning, God's:
"Anointed"........................... Is. 45:1
Liberator............................. Is. 45:1
Rebuilder .... Is. 44:28

D

Dabbasheth—*hump*
Town of Zebulun ....Josh. 19:10, 11

Daberath—*pasture*
Correct rendering of Dabareh........Josh. 21:28
Assigned to Gershomites ....1 Chr. 6:71, 72

Dagon—*fish*
The national god of the Philistines ....Judg. 16:23
Falls before ark .... 1 Sam. 5:1–5

Daleth
The fourth letter in the Hebrew
alphabet..................... Ps. 119:25–32

Dalmanutha
A place near the Sea of Galilee ....Mark 8:10

Dalmatia—*deceitful*
A region east of the Adriatic Sea; Titus
departs to...................... 2 Tim. 4:10

Dalphon—*crafty*
A son of Haman ....Esth. 9:7–10

Damages and remuneration
A. In law for:
Personal injury ....Ex. 21:18, 19
Causing miscarriage ....Ex. 21:22
Injuries by animals................. Ex. 21:28–32
Injuries to animals .... Ex. 21:33–35
Losses .... Ex. 22:1–15
Stealing.........................Lev. 6:1–7
Defaming a wife ....Deut. 22:13–19
Rape............................Deut. 22:28, 29
B. In practice:
Jacob's .... Gen. 31:38–42
Samson's ....Judg. 16:28–30
Tamar's ....2 Sam. 13:22–32
Zacchaeus's .... Luke 19:8
Paul's...........................Acts 16:35–39
Philemon's ....Philem. 10–18

Damaris—*gentle*
An Athenian woman converted by
Paul.......................... Acts 17:33, 34

Damascus—*chief city of Aram*
A. In the Old Testament:
Abram passed through ....Gen. 14:14, 15
Abram heir from................. Gen. 15:2
Captured by David................. 2 Sam. 8:5, 6
Rezon, king of................. 1 Kin. 11:23, 24
Ben-Hadad, king of ....1 Kin. 15:18
Rivers of, mentioned .... 2 Kin. 5:12
Elisha's prophecy in ....2 Kin. 8:7–15
Taken by Assyrians ....2 Kin. 16:9
Prophecies concerning .... Is. 8:3, 4
B. In the New Testament, Paul:
Journeys to .... Acts 9:1–9
Is converted near .... Acts 9:3–19
First preaches at ....Acts 9:20–22
Escapes from ....2 Cor. 11:32, 33
Revisits ....Gal. 1:17

Dan—*judge*
1. Jacob's son by Bilhah................. Gen. 30:5, 6
Prophecy concerning.............Gen. 49:16, 17
2. *Tribe of:*
Census of .... Num. 1:38, 39
Position of .... Num. 2:25, 31
Blessing of .... Deut. 33:22
Inheritance of .... Josh. 19:40–47
Conquest by......................Josh. 19:47
Failure of .... Judg. 1:34, 35
Idolatry of ....Judg. 18:1–31
3. *Town of:*
Called Leshem.......................Josh. 19:47
Captured by Danites ....Josh. 19:47
Northern boundary of Israel..........Judg. 20:1
Center of idolatry............... 1 Kin. 12:28–30
Destroyed by Ben-Hadad............1 Kin. 15:20
Later references to .... Jer. 4:15–17

Dance—*an emotional movement of the body*
A. Kinds of:
Joyful................................Ps. 30:11
Evil................................Ex. 32:19
B. Designed to:
Express joy in victory .... 1 Sam. 18:6, 7
Greet a returning son .... Luke 15:21–25
Rejoice in the Lord.............. 2 Sam. 6:14–16
Inflame lust .... Matt. 14:6
C. Performed by:
Children .... Matt. 11:16, 17
Women ....Judg. 11:34
David.......................... 2 Sam. 6:14, 16
Worshipers........................Ps. 149:3

Dancing
Israelites before the gold calf...........Ex. 32:18
David only .... 2 Sam. 6:14–16
Greeting a prodigal ....Luke 15:20, 23–25
Lustful exhibition .... Mark 6:22
Religious exercise............... 1 Chr. 15:25–29

Time of rejoicing .... 1 Sam. 18:6, 7
Time to dance .... Eccl. 3:4
Young women alone............. Judg. 21:20, 21

Danger—*risk; peril*
Physical...........................Acts 27:9–44
Spiritual ....Heb. 2:1–3
Comfort in......................Acts 27:22–25
Jesus sought in.................... Luke 8:22–24
Of judgment....................... Matt. 5:22
Of many kinds................. 2 Cor. 11:23–33
Paul's escape from ....Acts 9:22–25

Daniel—*God is my judge*
1. Son of David ....1 Chr. 3:1
Called Chileab .... 2 Sam. 3:2, 3
2. Postexilic priest .... Ezra 8:1, 2
Signs covenant....................... Neh. 10:6
3. Taken to Babylon.................... Dan. 1:1–7
Refuses king's choice foods............. Dan. 1:8
Interprets Nebuchadnezzar's
    dreams ....Dan. 2:1–45; 4:4–27
Honored by Nebuchadnezzar ...... Dan. 2:46–49
Interprets handwriting............Dan. 5:10–29
Made a high official.................Dan. 6:1–3
Conspired against ....Dan. 6:4–15
Cast into lions' den .... Dan. 6:16–22
Honored by Belshazzar................ Dan. 5:29
Vision of beasts....................Dan. 7:1–28
Vision of ram and goat ....Dan. 8:1–27
Great confession of ....Dan. 9:1–19
Vision of the seventy weeks....... Dan. 9:20–27
Vision by the great river ....Dan. 10:1–21
Vision of the kings.................Dan. 11:1–45
Vision of the two men.............Dan. 12:1–13
Jesus mentions his prophecy .... Matt. 24:15

Daniel, Book of—*a book of the Old Testament*
History in Babylon.................... Dan. 1–6
Prophecy of nations................ Dan. 2:4–45
Visions...............................Dan. 7; 8
Kingdom............................ Dan. 9–12

Danites
Descendants of Dan..................Judg. 13:2

Dan Jaan
Town near Sidon.................... 2 Sam. 24:6

Dannah—*low ground*
A city of Judah......................Josh. 15:49

Darda—*pearl of wisdom*
Famed for wisdom ....1 Kin. 4:31
Also called Dara .... 1 Chr. 2:6

Darius—*possessing the good*
1. *Darius the Mede:*
Son of Ahasuerus .... Dan. 9:1
Conquers Babylon ....Dan. 5:30, 31
Coruler with Cyrus ....Dan. 6:28
Made king of the Chaldeans .... Dan. 9:1
2. *Darius Hystaspis* (521–486 B.C.)
King of all Persia ....Ezra 4:5
Confirms Cyrus's royal edict......... Ezra 6:1–14

Temple work dated by his reign .... Ezra 4:24
Prophets during his reign.............. Hag. 1:1
3. *Darius the Persian* (424–404 B.C.)
Priestly records made during
    his reign ....Neh. 12:22

Dark sayings
Speaks openly .... Num. 12:8
Utter of old........................... Ps. 78:2

Darkness—*absence of light*
A. Kinds of:
Precreational ....Gen. 1:2–4
Natural .... Gen. 15:17
Miraculous....................... Ex. 10:21, 22
Supernatural .... Matt. 27:45
Spiritual .... Luke 11:34–36
Eternal............................. Matt. 8:12
B. Illustrative of:
God's unsearchableness .... Ps. 97:2
The way of sin ....Eph. 5:11
Afflictions ....Ps. 112:4
Moral depravity ....Rom. 13:12
Ignorance .... 1 John 2:8–11
Death............................ Job 10:21, 22
Hell .... Matt. 22:13

Darkon—*scatterer*
Founder of a family .... Neh. 7:58

Dart—*a pointed weapon*
Figurative of Satan's weapons.......... Eph. 6:16

Dathan—*fount*
A Reubenite.....................Num. 26:7–11
Joins Korah's rebellion .... Num. 16:1–35
Swallowed up by the earth.............Ps. 106:17

Daughter—*a female descendant*
A. Applied to:
Female child......................... Gen. 20:12
Female inhabitants of a city............Judg. 21:1
Female worshipers of God .... Is. 43:6
Citizens of a town...................... Ps. 9:14
B. Described as:
Licentious...................... Gen. 19:30–38
Dutiful .... Judg. 11:36–39
Ideal..............................Prov. 31:29
Beautiful.......................... Ps. 45:9–13
Complacent .... Is. 32:9–11
Prophesying........................Joel 2:28
C. Daughter-in-law:
Ruth, a loyal......................Ruth 1:11–18
Strife against .... Matt. 10:35

Daughter of Zion—*a name referring to Jerusalem and
    the inhabitants therein*
Show praise to .... Ps. 9:14
Gaze on Solomon .... Song 3:11
Left desolate ....Is. 1:8
The King comes to...................Matt. 21:5

David—*well beloved*
A. Early life of:
Born at Bethlehem..................1 Sam. 17:12

David, Root of—*a title of Christ*

David, Tower of—*fortress built by David, location now*
    unknown

Dawn, Dawning

WORD
STUDY
DAY, *yom* (*yohm*). The noun used throughout the OT meaning "day," *yom,* alludes to a variety of different meanings, many of which are also found in the English word "day." First, day is the opposite of night as in Gen. 7:4. One of the most common usages is as a division of time. The unit might be a working day, a day's journey, or some other duration. Sometimes the unit specifically states

that evening and morning are combined to form a day as in Gen. 1. In union with other nouns, specific times are mentioned: a day of judgment or a holy day (Sabbath). A third general use is found in the term "the day of Yahweh," a time when the Lord will come in judgment. This is a time when the righteous will be blessed and the wicked destroyed (Is. 2:12; Jer. 46:10; Amos 5:18). (Strong's #3117)

Day—*a division of time*
A. Natural uses of:
  The daylight .... Gen. 1:5, 16
  Twelve hours .... John 11:9
  Opposite of night ....Mark 5:5
  The civil day (24 hours) .... Luke 13:14
  Divisions of .... Neh. 9:3
  Security of .... Gen. 8:22
B. Extended uses of:
  Noah's time .... Matt. 24:37
  Gospel age .... John 9:4
  Long period ....2 Pet. 3:8
C. Descriptive of:
  Believers ....1 Thess. 5:5, 8
  Christ's return..................... 1 Thess. 5:2
  Prophetic period.......... Dan. 12:11; Rev. 2:10
  Eternity............................. Dan. 7:9, 13
  Present age .... Heb. 1:2

Day of the Lord
A. In Old Testament:
  Punishment of faithless .... Is. 13:6–13;
    Joel 1:15; Amos 5:18–20
  Day of wrath ....Is. 2:6–22
  Restoration of remnant...... Is. 4:2–6; 10:20–22;
    Hos. 2:16–20
B. In New Testament:
  The last times .... Matt. 24:29; 2 Pet. 3:10
  The great day........................Rev. 16:14

Day, Joshua's long
  Described .... Josh. 10:12–14

Day's journey
Described as:
  A distance....................Gen. 30:36; 31:23
  Traveled to make a sacrifice ....Ex. 3:18; 5:3; 8:27

Deaconess—*a female attendant in church ministry*
  Phoebe thus called ("a servant").......Rom. 16:1

Deacons—*church officers*
  Ordained by the apostles .... Acts 6:1–6
  Stephen, the first martyr of .... Acts 6:5–15
  Named with bishops ....Phil. 1:1
  Qualifications of .... 1 Tim. 3:8–13

Dead—*lacking life*
A. Used literally of:
  Lost physical functions................Rom. 4:19
  Those in the other world .... Rev. 20:12
B. Used figuratively of:
  Unregenerate..........................Eph. 2:1
  Unreal faith .... James 2:17, 19
  Decadent church.......................Rev. 3:1

  Legal requirements .... Heb. 9:14
  Freedom from sin's power .... Rom. 6:2, 8, 11
  Freedom from the Law .... Rom. 7:4

Dead Sea
Called the:
  Salt Sea .... Gen. 14:3
  Sea of the Arabah ....Deut. 3:17

Deaf—*unable to hear*
  Protection afforded ....Lev. 19:14
  Healing of. ....Matt. 11:5
  Figurative of spiritual inability....... Is. 42:18, 19
  Figurative of patience .... Ps. 38:13

Death, eternal
A. Described as:
  Everlasting punishment .... Matt. 25:46
  Resurrection of condemnation........ John 5:29
  God's wrath....................... 1 Thess. 1:10
  Destruction .... 2 Thess. 1:9; 2 Pet. 2:12
  Second death ....Rev. 20:14
B. Truths regarding:
  A consequence of one's sin .... Gen. 3:17–19
  The punishment of the wicked.... Matt. 25:41, 46
  Separates from God .... 2 Thess. 1:9
  Christ saves from .... John 3:16
  Saints shall escape from ....1 Cor. 15:54–58;
    Rev. 2:11
  Vividly described .... Luke 16:22–26
C. As sentence upon:
  Those not believing the Son .... John 3:36
  Angels who sinned....................2 Pet. 2:4
  The Beast and the False Prophet ...... Rev. 19:20
  The devil. .... Rev. 20:10
  Death and Hades ....Rev. 20:14

Death, natural
A. Features regarding:
  Consequence of sin ....Rom. 5:12
  Lot of all .... Heb. 9:27
  Ends earthly life .... Eccl. 9:10
  Christ delivers from fear of .... Heb. 2:14, 15
  Some escaped from .... Gen. 5:24
  Some will escape................1 Cor. 15:51, 52
  All to be raised from .... Acts 24:15
  Illustrates regeneration.................Rom. 6:2
B. Described as:
  Return to dust....................... Gen. 3:19
  Removal of breath .... Gen. 25:8; Acts 5:10
  Removal from tent .... 2 Cor. 5:1
  Naked ....2 Cor. 5:3, 4
  Sleep............................. John 11:11–14
  Departure........................... Phil. 1:23
C. Recognition after:
  Departed saints recognized by the
    living................Matt. 17:1–8; 27:52, 53
  Greater knowledge in future world ... 1 Cor. 13:12
  The truth illustrated .... Luke 16:19–24

Death of saints
A. Described as:
  Sleep in Jesus .... 1 Thess. 4:14

Blessed..............................Rev. 14:13
A gain ....Phil. 1:21
Peace ....Is. 57:1, 2
Crown of righteousness .... 2 Tim. 4:8
B. Exemplified in:
Abraham.......................... Gen. 25:8
Isaac............................Gen. 35:28, 29
Jacob .... Gen. 49:33
Elisha............................ 2 Kin. 13:14, 20
The criminal ....Luke 23:39–43

Death of wicked
Result of sin ....Rom. 5:12
Often punishment .....Ex. 23:25–29; Is. 65:11, 12
Unpleasant for God ....Ezek. 33:11
Without hope ....1 Thess. 4:13; Rev. 20:10, 14, 15

Death penalty—*legal execution*
By stoning..................Deut. 13:6–10; 17:5

Debate—*discussion, contention*
With a neighbor ....Prov. 25:9
Wicked, full of ....Rom. 1:29
Saints must avoid ....2 Cor. 12:20

WORD STUDY   **DEBAUCHERY (LEWDNESS)**, *aselgeia* (ahs-*elg*-eye-ah). The noun *aselgeia* refers to "debauchery" or "licentiousness," and it is used especially of sexual excesses (Rom. 13:13; 2 Cor. 12:21; Gal. 5:19). *Aselgeia* appears twice in catalogs of vices (Mark 7:22; 1 Pet. 4:3). In addition to the meaning associated with sexual immorality ("lewdness"), the use of *aselgeia* in Jude 4 may point to the "insolence" of one who scoffs. (Strong's #766)

Debir—*oracle*
1. King of Eglon ....Josh. 10:3–26
2. City of Judah ....Josh. 15:15
Also called Kirjath Sepher............Josh. 15:15
Captured by Joshua ....Josh. 10:38, 39
Recaptured by Othniel ....Josh. 15:15–17; Judg. 1:11–13
Assigned to priests ....Josh. 21:13, 15
3. A place east of the Jordan............. Josh. 13:26
4. Town of Judah ....Josh. 15:7

Deborah—*a bee*
1. Rebekah's nurse ....Gen. 35:8
2. A prophetess and judge...............Judg. 4:4–14
Composed song of triumph ....Judg. 5:1–31

WORD STUDY   **DEBT**, *opheilēma* (ahf-*eye*-lay-mah). The literal meaning of this noun is "debt," that is, "what is owed," "one's due." Paul writes (Rom. 4:4) that wages for work is not a gracious gift, but "debt," or "one's due." In Matt. 6:12 Jesus uses *opheilēma* in a figurative way to refer to sins (cf. Luke 11:4). (Strong's #3783)

Debt, debtor
A. Safeguards regarding:
No oppression allowed ....Deut. 23:19, 20
Collateral protected...............Ex. 22:25–27

Time limitation of .... Deut. 15:1–18
Nonpayment forbidden ....Neh. 5:4, 5
Debts to be honored...................Rom. 13:6
Interest (usury) forbidden .... Ezek. 18:8–17
Love, the unpayable...................Rom. 13:8
Parable concerning ....Matt. 18:23–35
B. Evils of:
Causes complaint ....2 Kin. 4:1–7
Produces strife ....Jer. 15:10
Makes outlaws..................... 1 Sam. 22:2
Endangers property.................Prov. 6:1–5
Brings slavery .... Lev. 25:39, 47, 48
C. Figurative of:
Sins................................. Matt. 6:12
Works ....Rom. 4:4
Moral obligation.....................Rom. 1:14
God's mercy..........................Ps. 37:26

Decalogue (see Ten Commandments)

Decapolis—*league of ten cities*
Multitudes from, follow Jesus........ Matt. 4:25
Jesus healed demon-possessed,
preaches in...................... Mark 5:20

Deceit, deceivers, deception
A. The wicked:
Devise ....Ps. 35:20
Speak................................Jer. 9:8
Are full of...........................Rom. 1:29
Increase in .... 2 Tim. 3:13
B. Agents of:
Satan ....2 Cor. 11:13, 14
Sin................................Rom. 7:11
Self.....................1 Cor. 3:18; James 1:22
Others .... 2 Thess. 2:3; 2 Tim. 3:13
C. Warnings against:
Among religious workers ....2 Cor. 11:3–15
As a sign of apostasy ....2 Thess. 2:9, 10
Sign of latter days.....................1 Tim. 4:1
As a sign of the Antichrist .... 1 John 4:1–6
D. Examples of:
Eve ....1 Tim. 2:14
Abram ....Gen. 12:11–13
Isaac............................Gen. 26:6, 7
Jacob ....Gen. 27:18–27
Joseph's brothers.................. Gen. 37:28–32
Pharaoh..............................Ex. 8:29
David........................... 1 Sam. 21:12, 13
Amnon ....2 Sam. 13:6–14
Gehazi .... 2 Kin. 5:20–27
Elisha............................ 2 Kin. 6:18–23
Herod ....Matt. 2:7, 8
Pharisees...................... Matt. 22:15, 16
Peter............................ Mark 14:70, 71
Ananias and Sapphira............... Acts 5:1–11
The earth .... Rev. 13:11–14

Deceive—*to delude or mislead*
A. In Old Testament:
Eve, by Satan .... Gen. 3:13
Israel, by the Midianites......... Num. 25:17, 18

Joshua, by the Gibeonites. . . . . .Josh. 9:22
B. Of Christians:
　By flattering words . . . . .Rom. 16:18
　By false report. . . . . 2 Thess. 2:3
　By false reasoning. . . . . .Col. 2:4
　By evil spirits. . . . . .1 Tim. 4:1
　By false prophets. . . . . . . Mark 13:22; 2 Tim. 3:13

Decision—*determination to follow a course of action*
A. Sources of:
　Loyalty . . . . Ruth 1:16
　Prayer . . . . 1 Sam. 23:1–13
　The Lord. . . . . .1 Kin. 12:15
　Satan . . . . 1 Chr. 21:1
　The world. . . . . Luke 14:16–24
　Human need . . . . Acts 11:27–30
　Disagreement .Acts 15:36–41
　Faith. . . . . Heb. 11:24–28
B. Wrong, leading to:
　Spiritual decline . . . . .Gen. 13:7–11
　Repentance . . . . .Heb. 12:16, 17
　Defeat . . . . Num. 14:40–45
　Rejection. . . . . .1 Sam. 15:6–26
　Apostasy. . . . . .1 Kin. 11:1–13
　Division. . . . . 1 Kin. 12:12–20
　Death. . . . . Acts 1:16–20
C. Good, manifested in:
　Siding with the Lord . . . . Ex. 32:26
　Following God . . . . .Num. 14:24; Josh. 14:8
　Loving God . . . . .Deut. 6:5
　Seeking God . . . . 2 Chr. 15:12
　Obeying God. . . . . Neh. 10:28–30

Decision, valley of—*location unknown*
　Called "Valley of Jehoshaphat". . . . . . . .Joel 3:2, 12
　Refers to final judgment. . . . . .Joel 3:1–21

Decisiveness—*showing firmness of decision*
　In serving God . . . . Josh. 24:15, 16; Heb. 11:24, 25
　Toward family. .Ruth 1:15–18
　Toward a leader. . . . . .2 Kin. 2:1–6
　To complete a task . . . . .Neh. 4:14–23
　In morality. . . . . Gen. 39:10–12; Dan. 1:8
　In prayer . . . . Dan. 6:1–16

Decree—*a course of action authoritatively determined*
A. As a human edict:
　Issued by kings .Dan. 6:7–14
　Considered inflexible . . . . .Dan. 6:15–17
　Published widely. . . . . Esth. 3:13–15; Luke 2:1
　Providentially nullified. . . . . Esth. 8:3–17
　Sometimes beneficial . . . . Dan. 4:25–28
B. As a divine edict, to:
　Govern nature. . . . . .Jer. 5:22

Dedan—*low*
1. Raamah's son . . . . .Gen. 10:7
2. Jokshan's son. . . . . .Gen. 25:3
3. Descendants of Raamah;
　a commercial people . . . . . Ezek. 27:15, 20; 38:13

Dedication—*setting apart for a sacred use*
A. Of things:
　Tabernacle . . . . .Ex. 40:34–38
　Solomon's temple . . . . 1 Kin. 8:12–66
　Second temple . . . . Ezra 6:1–22
B. Offerings in, must be:
　Voluntary . . . . Lev. 22:18–25
　Without blemish. . . . . Lev. 1:3
　Unredeemable. Lev. 27:28, 29
C. Examples of:
　Samuel. . . . . 1 Sam. 1:11, 22
　The believer. . . . . .Rom. 12:1, 2

Dedication, Feast of
　Jesus attended .John 10:22, 23

Deeds—*things done*
A. Descriptive of one's:
　Past record . . . . .Luke 11:48
　Present achievements . . . . Acts 7:22
　Future action. . . . . 2 Cor. 10:11
B. Expressive of one's:
　Evil nature . . . . .2 Pet. 2:7, 8
　Parentage . . . . John 8:41
　Record. . . . . .Luke 24:19
　Profession. . . . . 3 John 10
　Love . . . . 1 John 3:18
　Judgment . . . . .Rom. 2:5, 6
C. Toward God:
　Weighed . . . . .1 Sam. 2:3
　Wrong punished. . . . . .Luke 23:41
D. Lord's are:
　Righteous . . . . Judg. 5:11; 1 Sam. 12:7
　Mighty. . . . . .Ps. 106:2
　Beyond description . . . . .Ps. 106:2
E. Considered positively:
　Example of . . . . .Titus 2:7
　Zealous for . . . . .Titus 2:14
　Careful to engage in. . . . . Titus 3:8, 14
　Stimulate to . . . . Heb. 10:24
　In heaven . . . . .Rev. 14:13

Deeds, the unbeliever's
A. Described as:
　Evil. . . . . .Col. 1:21
　Done in dark place . . . . Is. 29:15
　Abominable. . . . . Ps. 14:1
　Unfruitful. . . . . .Eph. 5:11
B. God's attitude toward, will:
　Never forget. . . . . Amos 8:7
　Render according to . . . . .Prov. 24:12
　Bring to judgment . . . . Rev. 20:12, 13
C. Believer's relation to:
　Lay aside. . . . . .Rom. 13:12
　Not participate in. . . . . .Eph. 5:11
　Be delivered from . . . . 2 Tim. 4:18

Deer
A. Literally:
　Listed as clean . . . . Deut. 14:5
　Hurt by drought . . . . .Jer. 14:5

B. Figurative of:

Spiritual vivacity .... 2 Sam. 22:34
Buoyancy of faith .... Hab. 3:19
Good wife........................... Prov. 5:19

WORD
STUDY

DEFENSE, REPLY, *apologia* (ap-ol-og-ee-ah). In a legal setting this noun refers to the accused's response or "reply" to formal charges, hence the meaning "defense." The use of this word in Acts often reflects a legal background (22:1; 25:16; cf. the cognate verb in 24:10; 26:24); the same is perhaps the case in Paul's reference to his "defense of the gospel" (Phil. 1:7, 17; cf. 2 Tim. 4:16). Other occurrences of this word may mean a more general "reply" to accusations or a response to critical questions (1 Cor. 9:3; 2 Cor. 7:11; 1 Pet. 3:15). (Strong's #627)

Defense—*protection during attack*

Of a city............................2 Kin. 19:34
Of Israel ....Judg. 10:1
Of a plot .... 2 Sam. 23:11, 12
Of the upright .... Ps. 7:10
Of one accused .... Acts 22:1
Of the gospel .... Phil. 1:7, 16

Deference—*respectful yielding to another*

To a woman's entreaty..............Ruth 1:15–18
To an old man's wish ....2 Sam. 19:31–40
Results in exaltation .... Matt. 23:12
Commanded .... Heb. 13:17

Defilement—*making the pure impure*
A. Ceremonial causes of:

Childbirth .... Lev. 12:2–8
Leprosy .... Lev. 13:3, 44–46
Bodily discharge....................Lev. 15:1–15
Copulation............................Lev. 15:17
Menstruation..................... Lev. 15:19–33
Touching the dead .... Lev. 21:1–4, 11
B. Spiritual manifestations of:

Abominations .... Jer. 32:34
C. Objects of:

Conscience............................1 Cor. 8:7
Fellowship .... Heb. 12:15
Flesh.................................... Jude 8
Hands ....Mark 7:2

Defrauding—*depriving others through deceit*

Forbidden........................ Mark 10:19
To be accepted.....................1 Cor. 6:5–8
Paul, not guilty of.................... 2 Cor. 7:2
Product of sexual immorality ..... 1 Thess. 4:3–6

Degrees—*ascents; steps*

The sundial .... 2 Kin. 20:9–11
Rank in society.......................Luke 1:52
Advancement in service .... 1 Tim. 3:13

Dehavites—*people who settled in Samaria during the Exile*

Opposed rebuilding of Jerusalem..... Ezra 4:9–16

Deity of Christ (see Christ)

Delaiah—*Yahweh has delivered*

1. Descendant of Aaron .... 1 Chr. 24:18
2. Son of Shemaiah; urges Jehoiakim not
to burn Jeremiah's scroll..........Jer. 36:12, 25
3. Founder of a family....................Ezra 2:60
4. A son of Elioenai .... 1 Chr. 3:24

Delegation—*an official commission*

Coming to seek peace ....Luke 14:32

Deliberation—*careful consideration of elements involved in a decision*

Necessary in life .... Luke 14:28–32
Illustrated in Jacob.................Gen. 32:1–23

Delicacies—*savory food*

Used as a warning.................. Prov. 23:3–6
Unrighteous fellowship................. Ps. 141:4

Delight—*great pleasure in something*
A. Wrong kind of:

Showy display .... Esth. 6:6–11
Physical strength .... Ps. 147:10
Abominations .... Is. 66:3
Sacrifices..................... Ps. 51:16; Is. 1:11
B. Right kind of:

God's will............................. Ps. 40:8
God's commandments .... Ps. 112:1
God's goodness....................... Neh. 9:25
Lord Himself.................. Ps. 37:4; Is. 58:14

WORD
STUDY

DELIGHT IN, *chafets* (khaw-*fets*). The verb *chafets,* usually translated "delight in," indicates desire or favor. When the word refers to human actions, it can mean "to take pleasure in a person" as in Esth. 2:14 or it can indicate something a person would like to do (1 Kin. 9:1). God also "delights in" a person (Num. 14:8). There are also characteristics that delight God, while their absence angers Him; among these are mercy, justice, and righteousness (Is. 56:4; 65:12; Jer. 9:24). (Strong's #2654)

Delilah—*lustful*

Deceives Samson .... Judg. 16:4–22

Deliver—*to rescue or save from evil*
A. By Christ, from:

Trials ....2 Tim. 3:11
Evil.......................2 Tim. 4:18; 2 Pet. 2:9
Death............................... 2 Cor. 1:10
Power of darkness ....Col. 1:13
God's wrath .... 1 Thess. 1:10
B. Examples of, by God:

Noah ....Gen. 8:1–22
Lot ....Gen. 19:29, 30
Jacob .... Gen. 33:1–16
Israel .... Ex. 12:29–51
David............................ 1 Sam. 23:1–29
Jews ....Esth. 9:1–19
Daniel .... Dan. 6:13–27
Jesus......................... Matt. 2:13–23
Apostles .... Acts 5:17–26
Paul .... 2 Cor. 1:9, 10

Deluge, the—*the Flood*

A. Warnings of:

    Believed by Noah .... Heb. 11:7

    Disbelieved by the world ....2 Pet. 2:5

B. Coming of:

    Announced........................Gen. 6:5–7

    Dated............................. Gen. 7:11

    Sudden.......................Matt. 24:38, 39

C. Purpose of:

    Punish sin..........................Gen. 6:1–7

    Destroy the world................... 2 Pet. 3:5, 6

D. Its nonrepetition based on God's:

    Promise..........................Gen. 8:21, 22

    Covenant ....Gen. 9:9–11

    Token (the rainbow) ....Gen. 9:12–17

    Pledge .... Is. 54:9, 10

E. Type of:

    Baptism........................ 1 Pet. 3:20, 21

    Christ's coming................ Matt. 24:36–39

    Destruction .... Is. 28:2, 18

    The end.......................... 2 Pet. 3:5–15

Delusions, common—*self-deception*

    Rejecting God's existence .... Ps. 14:1

    Supposing God does not see ....Ps. 10:1–11

    Trusting in one's heritage..............Matt. 3:9

    Living for time alone.............Luke 12:17–19

    Presuming on time.............. Luke 13:23–30

    Believing the Antichrist..........2 Thess. 2:1–12

    Denying facts .... 2 Pet. 3:5, 16, 17

Demagogue—*one who becomes a leader by mass prejudice*

    Absalom .... 2 Sam. 15:2–12

    Haman ....Esth. 3:1–11

    Judas of Galilee...................... Acts 5:37

Demas—*popular*

    Follows Paul.........................Col. 4:14

    Forsakes Paul....................... 2 Tim. 4:10

Demetrius

1. A silversmith at Ephesus ....Acts 19:24–40

2. A good Christian .... 3 John 12

Demon—*an evil spirit*

A. Nature of:

    Evil............................Luke 10:17, 18

    Powerful..........................Luke 8:29

    Numerous........................ Mark 5:8, 9

    Unclean........................... Matt. 10:1

    Under Satan.................... Matt. 12:24–30

B. Ability of:

    Recognize Christ ...Matt. 8:28, 29; Mark 1:23, 24

    Recognize Paul .... Acts 19:13–16

    Possess human beings .... Matt. 8:28, 29

    Overcome men .... Acts 19:13–16

    Know their destiny .... Matt. 8:29–33

    Receive sacrifice.................... 1 Cor. 10:20

    Instigate deceit ....1 Tim. 4:1

Demon possession

A. Recognized as:

    Not insanity....................... Matt. 4:24

    Not disease.........................Mark 1:32

    Productive harm................... Mark 5:1–5

B. Instances of deliverance from:

    Man in the synagogue............Mark 1:23–26

    Blind and mute man ....Matt. 12:22, 23

    Two men of the Gergesenes.......Matt. 8:28–34

    Mute man....................... Matt. 9:32, 33

    Canaanite woman's daughter .....Matt. 15:22–28

    Epileptic child................... Matt. 17:14–21

    Mary Magdalene ....Mark 16:9

Denarius, Denarii

    Debt of 100........................ Matt. 18:28

    Day laborer's pay.................Matt. 20:2–13

    Roman coin ....Matt. 22:19–21

    Two, the cost of lodging ....Luke 10:35

    Ointment, worth 300 .... John 12:5

    Famine prices ....Rev. 6:6

Den of lions

    Daniel placed in .... Dan. 6:16–24

Denial of Christ

A. The realm of:

    Doctrine ....Mark 8:38; 2 Tim. 1:8

    Practice............................Titus 1:16

B. The agents of:

    Individuals.....................Matt. 26:69–75

    Jews ....John 18:39, 40

    False teachers......................2 Pet. 2:1

    Antichrist...................... 1 John 2:22, 23

C. The consequences of:

    Christ denies them.................. Matt. 10:33

    They merit destruction................2 Pet. 2:1

Deportation—*exile from a nation*

    Captives carried into................2 Kin. 15:29

    To Babylon..................... 2 Kin. 24:8–17

Deposit—*a pledge of full payment*

    The Holy Spirit in the heart ....2 Cor. 1:22

    Given by God........................ 2 Cor. 5:5

    Guarantee of future redemption .... Eph. 1:13, 14

Depravity of humankind

A. Extent of:

    Universal........................... Gen. 6:5

    In the heart ....Jer. 17:9

    The whole being................... Rom. 3:9–19

    From birth .... Ps. 51:5

B. Effects of:

    Impenitence........................Rom. 2:5

    Inability to listen ....Jer. 17:23; 2 Pet. 2:14, 19

    Lovers of evil...................... John 3:19

    Defilement of conscience..........Titus 1:15, 16

Deputy—*a person empowered to act for another*

    King............................1 Kin. 22:47

Derbe—*a city of Lycaonia*

    Paul visits .... Acts 14:6, 20

    Paul meets Timothy here ....Acts 16:1

    Gaius, native of..................... Acts 20:4

Derision—*contempt manifested by laughter*
Heaped on God's people............. Jer. 20:7, 8

Descend
As a dove.................. Matt. 3:16; John 1:32
The angels of God .... John 1:51
Lord to lower parts of earth........... Eph. 4:9
Lord from Heaven .... 1 Thess. 4:17

Desert—*a wilderness place*
Israel journeys through................ Is. 48:21
Place of great temptation .... Ps. 106:14
Rejoicing of, predicted .... Is. 35:1
A highway in .... Is. 40:3
John's home in...................... Luke 1:80
Israel received manna in.............. John 6:31

Desertion—*forsaking a person or thing*
Jesus, by His disciples .... Matt. 26:56
Jesus, by God...................... Matt. 27:46
Paul, by others.................... 2 Tim. 4:16
Christ, by professed followers.........2 Pet. 2:15

Desire, sinful
A. Causes of:
Learning evil........................Rom. 16:19
Making provision for flesh ....Rom. 13:14
Not fearing God ....Prov. 8:13; 9:10
Not seeing consequences of sin.......Ex. 34:6, 7;
Rom. 6:23; Heb. 11:25
B. Fruits of:
Evil inclinations .... Rom. 7:7, 8
Unchastity .... 1 Thess. 4:5
Reprobation...................... Rom. 1:21–32
C. Remedy for:
Repentance ....2 Cor. 7:9, 10; James 4:9, 10
Submitting to God....... Rom. 12:1, 2; James 4:7
Resisting the devil .... James 4:7
Drawing near to God................. James 4:8
Walking in the Spirit............... Rom. 8:1–8

Desire, spiritual
Renewed fellowship................ 1 Thess. 2:17
Church office........................1 Tim. 3:1
Spiritual knowledge.................1 Pet. 2:2
Spiritual gifts...................... 1 Cor. 14:1

Desire of All Nations
A title descriptive of the Messiah...... Hag. 2:6, 7

Despair—*a hopeless state*
A. Results from:
Heavy burdens ....Num. 11:10–15
Disobedience..................1 Sam. 28:16–25
Disappointment .... 2 Sam. 17:23
Impending death ....Esth. 7:1–10
Futility of human things ....Eccl. 6:1–12
Rejection.........................Matt. 27:3–5
Rebellion against God .... Rev. 9:4–6
Hopelessness .... Luke 16:23–31
B. Remedies against:
Hope in God ....Ps. 42:5, 11
God's faithfulness .... 1 Cor. 10:13

Accept God's chastening ....Heb. 12:5–11
Cast your care upon the Lord ....1 Pet. 5:7

Despondency—*depression of spirits*
A. Causes of:
Mourning......................Gen. 37:34, 35
Sickness...........................Is. 38:9–12
Sorrow.............2 Sam. 18:32, 33; 2 Cor. 2:7
Adversity ....Job 9:16–35
Fears............................. 2 Cor. 7:5, 6
B. Examples of:
Moses..........................Ex. 14:15
Joshua ....Josh. 7:7–9
Elijah ....1 Kin. 19:2, 4
David.........................Ps. 42:6
Jonah ....Jon. 4:3, 8
Two disciples................... Luke 24:13–17

Destitute—*a state of extreme need*
The soul ....Ps. 102:17
The body........................James 2:14–17
Spiritual realities ....Prov. 15:21

> WORD STUDY
>
> **DESTROY, LOSE,** *apollumi* (ap-*ol*-loo-mee). This verb has to do with the destruction or ruination of things or persons. With respect to the destruction of persons, it is often translated as "destroy," in the sense of "to kill," "to put to death" (Mark 11:18), or "to perish" (Matt. 8:25; Luke 15:17; John 3:16); and it can refer to eternal "destruction" (Matt. 10:28; John 10:28). *Apollumi* can express "loss," for example, the loss of life (Mark 8:35); relatedly, it applies to sheep gone astray (Luke 15:4, 6) and in a religious sense to people gone astray—"the lost" (Luke 19:10). *Apollumi* is also used to describe the fate of transitory things (James 1:11; 1 Pet. 1:7; Rev. 18:14). (Strong's #622)

Destruction—*a state of ruin*
A. Past:
Cities .... Gen. 19:29
People ....1 Cor. 10:9, 10
Nations .... Jer. 48:42
B. Present:
Satan's power of .... 1 Cor. 5:5
Power of lusts....................... 1 Tim. 6:9
Wicked on way to....................Rom. 3:16
C. Future:
Those appointed to .... Prov. 31:8; 2 Pet. 2:12
Those fitted for......................Rom. 9:22
End of the enemies of Christ........ Phil. 3:18, 19
Sudden............................ 1 Thess. 5:3
Swift................................2 Pet. 2:1
Everlasting....................... 2 Thess. 1:9

Determinate counsel
God's fixed purpose................Acts 2:22, 23

Determination—*resolute persistence*
Against popular opposition...... Num. 13:26–31;
14:1–9
Against great numbers .... 1 Sam. 14:1–5
Beyond human advice..............2 Kin. 2:1–6

In perilous situation .... Esth. 4:10–16
In spite of persecution............. Acts 6:8–7:60

Deuel—*invocation of God*
Father of Eliasaph .... Num. 1:14

Deuteronomy, Book of—*a book of the Old Testament*
Written and spoken by Moses...Deut. 31:9, 22, 24

WORD STUDY

DEVIL, *diabolos* (dee-*ab*-ol-oss). This adjective, which literally means "slanderous," is derived from the verb *diaballō*, "to bring charges with hostile intent" (justly or slanderously, usually the latter). Although *diabolos* retains its adjectival meaning occasionally in the NT (1 Tim. 3:11; Titus 2:3), in most instances it is used substantively as a proper name for a specific "slanderer"—the "devil" (Matt. 4; Luke 4; Eph. 6:11). This use of the word is already established in the Septuagint, where it occurs frequently as a translation of the Heb. *sātān* ("adversary"). The association of the "devil" with Satan continues in the NT (e.g., John 13:2, 27; Rev. 20:2). (Strong's #1228)

Devil—*the chief opponent of God*
A. Titles of:
Abaddon.............................Rev. 9:11
Accuser ....Rev. 12:10
Adversary...........................1 Pet. 5:8
Angel of the bottomless pit ....Rev. 9:11
Apollyon............................Rev. 9:11
Beelzebub......................... Matt. 12:24
Belial .... 2 Cor. 6:15
God of this age .... 2 Cor. 4:4
Murderer...........................John 8:44
Prince of demons .... Matt. 12:24
Prince of the power of the air .... Eph. 2:2
Ruler of darkness .... Eph. 6:12
Ruler of this world .... John 14:30
Satan .... Luke 10:18
Serpent .... Gen. 3:4
Serpent of old .... Rev. 20:2
Wicked one .... Matt. 13:19
B. Origin of:
Heart lifted up in pride.............Is. 14:12–20
Perfect until sin came ....Ezek. 28:14–19
Greatest of fallen angels............ Rev. 12:7–9
Tempts man to sin ....Gen. 3:1–7
Father of lies ....John 8:44
C. Character of:
Cunning .... Gen. 3:1; 2 Cor. 11:3
Slanderous ....Job 1:9
Fierce.............................Luke 8:29
Deceitful.......................... 2 Cor. 11:14
Powerful .... Eph. 2:2
Proud............................. 1 Tim. 3:6
Cowardly .... James 4:7
Wicked ....1 John 2:13
D. Power of, over the wicked:
They are his children......Acts 13:10; 1 John 3:10
They do his will ....John 8:44
He possesses ....Luke 22:3

He blinds .... 2 Cor. 4:4
He deceives ....Rev. 20:7, 8
He ensnares ....1 Tim. 3:7
They are punished with him .... Matt. 25:41
E. Power of, over God's people:
Tempt .... 1 Chr. 21:1
Afflict ....Job 2:7
Oppose ....Zech. 3:1
Sift ....Luke 22:31
Deceive .... 2 Cor. 11:3
Disguise ....2 Cor. 11:14, 15
F. The believer's power over:
Watch against ....2 Cor. 2:10, 11
Fight against .... Eph. 6:11–16
Resist ....James 4:7; 1 Pet. 5:9
Overcome............1 John 2:13; Rev. 12:10, 11
G. Christ's triumph over:
Predicted .... Gen. 3:15
Portrayed .... Matt. 4:1–11
Proclaimed..........................Luke 10:18
Perfected........................Mark 3:22–28

Devotion to God
A. How?
With our whole selves ....Prov. 3:9; Rom. 12:1;
1 Cor. 6:20
B. Why? Because of:
God's goodness.......1 Sam. 12:24; 1 Thess. 2:12
Christ's death .... 2 Cor. 5:15
Our redemption ....1 Cor. 6:19, 20

Devotion to the ministry of saints
Household of Stephanas........ .... 1 Cor. 16:15

Devotions, morning
Jacob's ....Gen. 28:16–18
Samuel's parents' .... 1 Sam. 1:17–19
Hezekiah's .... 2 Chr. 29:20–31
Job's ....Job 1:5
The psalmist's (David's)................. Ps. 5:3
Jesus' ....Mark 1:35

Devout—*pious, religious, sincere*
Simeon.............................Luke 2:25
Cornelius .... Acts 10:1, 2, 7
Ananias .... Acts 22:12
Those who buried Stephen..............Acts 8:2
Converts .... Acts 13:43
Women of Antioch.............. Acts 13:50
Greeks in Thessalonica................Acts 17:4
Gentiles..........................Acts 17:17
Men ....Is. 57:1

Dew—*moisture condensed on the earth*
A. Used literally of:
Natural dew...................... Ex. 16:13, 14
Brought manna...................... Num. 11:9
A miraculous test ....Judg. 6:37–40
A curse................... 1 Kin. 17:1; Hag. 1:10
B. Used figuratively of:
God's blessings .... Gen. 27:28
God's truth......................... Deut. 32:2
The Messiah .... Is. 26:19

Human fickleness. . . . . Hos. 6:4
Peace and harmony . . . . Ps. 133:3

Dexterity—*skill in using one's hands or body*
Of 700 men . . . . Judg. 20:16
David's . . . . 1 Sam. 17:40–50

Diadem—*a crown*
Reserved for God's people . . . . Is. 28:5
Restored by grace . . . . Is. 62:3

Dial—*an instrument for telling time*
Miraculous movement of . . . . Is. 38:8

Diamond—*crystallized carbon*
Sacred . . . . Ex. 28:18
Precious. . . . . Ezek. 28:13

Diana, Artemis—*the mother-goddess of Asia Minor (known as Cybele)*
Worship of, at Ephesus, creates
uproar. . . . . Acts 19:23–41

Diblah—*rounded cake*
An unidentified place . . . . Ezek. 6:14

Diblaim—*twin fig cakes*
Hosea's father-in-law. . . . . Hos. 1:3

Dibon—*a wasting away*
1. Amorite town . . . . Num. 21:30
Taken by Israel . . . . Num. 32:2–5
Rebuilt by Gadites . . . . Num. 32:34
Called Dibon Gad . . . . Num. 33:45, 46
Later given to Reubenites. . . . . . . Josh. 13:9, 15, 17
Destruction of, foretold . . . . Jer. 48:18, 22
2. A village of Judah. . . . . Neh. 11:25

Dibri—*loquacious; wordy*
A Danite . . . . Lev. 24:11–14

Dictator—*ruler with absolute authority*
A. Powers of, to:
Take life . . . . 1 Kin. 2:45, 46
Judge . . . . 1 Kin. 10:9
Tax. . . . . 2 Kin. 15:19, 20
Levy labor. . . . . 1 Kin. 5:13–15
Make war . . . . 1 Kin. 20:1
Form alliances. . . . . 1 Kin. 15:18, 19
B. Examples, evil:
Pharaoh. . . . . Ex. 1:8–22
Ahab . . . . 1 Kin. 16:28–33
Herod . . . . Matt. 2:16
C. Examples, benevolent:
Solomon . . . . 1 Kin. 8:12–21; 10:23, 24
Cyrus. . . . . Ezra 1:1–4

Diet
Of the Hebrews. . . . . Lev. 11:1–47

Differing weights
Prohibited. Deut. 25:13, 14

Difficulties—*problems hard to solve*
A. Kinds of:
Mental. . . . . Ps. 139:6, 14
Moral. . . . . Ps. 38:1–22
Theological . . . . John 6:48–60

B. Examples of:
Birth of a child in old age . . . . Gen. 18:9–15
Testing of Abraham. . . . . Gen. 22:1–14
Slaughter of Canaanites . . . . Ex. 23:27–33
God's providence . . . . Ps. 44:1–26
Prosperity of wicked . . . . Ps. 73:1–28
Israel's unbelief. . . . . John 12:39–41
C. Negative attitudes toward:
Rebellion against . . . . Num. 21:4, 5
Unbelief under . . . . Heb. 3:12–19
D. Positive attitudes toward:
Submission under. . . . . Num. 14:7–9
Prayer concerning . . . . Mark 11:23, 24
Admission of . . . . 2 Pet. 3:15, 16

Diklah—*palm tree*
Son of Joktan. Gen. 10:27

Dilean—*cucumber*
Town of Judah. . . . . Josh. 15:38

Dilemma—*unpleasant alternatives*
Given to David . . . . 1 Chr. 21:9–17
Presented to Jews . . . . Matt. 21:23–27

Diligence—*faithful applications to one's work*
A. Manifested in:
A child's education. . . . . Deut. 6:6, 7
Dedicated service. . . . . Rom. 12:11
A minister's task. . . . . 2 Tim. 4:1–5
B. Special objects of:
The soul . . . . Deut. 4:9
God's commandments . . . . Deut. 6:17
The heart . . . . Prov. 4:23
Christian qualities . . . . 2 Pet. 1:5–9
One's calling . . . . 2 Pet. 1:10
C. Rewards of:
Prosperity. . . . . Prov. 10:4
Ruling hand. . . . . Prov. 12:24
Perseverance . . . . 2 Pet. 1:10

Dimnah—*dung heap*
City of Zebulun. . . . . Josh. 21:35
Same as Rimmon . . . . 1 Chr. 6:77

Dimon—*riverbed*
Place in Moab . . . . Is. 15:9

Dimonah
Town in Judah. . . . . Josh. 15:22
Same as Dibon. . . . . Neh. 11:25

Dinah—*judgment*
Daughter of Leah . . . . Gen. 30:20, 21
Defiled by Shechem. . . . . Gen. 34:1–24
Avenged by brothers . . . . Gen. 34:25–31
Guilt concerning . . . . Gen. 49:5–7

Dinaites
Foreigners who settled in Samaria. . . . . . . Ezra 4:9

Dinhabah—*give judgment*
City of Edom . . . . Gen. 36:32

Dionysius—*of the (god) Dionysos*
Prominent Athenian; converted
by Paul . . . . Acts 17:34

Spirit of truth.....................John 14:16, 17
Word is truth............Ps. 119:160; John 17:17
Satan, father of lies...................John 8:44
C. Between God's Word and man's:
  Paul preached ....1 Thess. 2:13
  God's Word inspired...............2 Tim. 3:16
  By Spirit ....1 Cor. 2:10–16

Diseases—*physical impairments of health*
A. Kinds of:
  Atrophy...............................Job 16:8
  Blindness .... Matt. 9:27
  Boil.............................2 Kin. 20:7
  Boils..............................Ex. 9:10
  Bowed back ....Luke 13:13
  Consumption.....................Deut. 28:22
  Deafness...........................Mark 7:32
  Dropsy............................Luke 14:2
  Dumbness........................ Matt. 9:32
  Dysentery....................2 Chr. 21:12–19
  Epilepsy......................... Matt. 4:24
  Fever .... Matt. 8:14, 15
  Flow of blood.................... Matt. 9:20
  Inflammation .... Deut. 28:22
  Insanity............................Dan. 4:33
  Itch............................ Deut. 28:27
  Leprosy .... 2 Kin. 5:1
  Paralysis .... Matt. 4:24
  Plague ....2 Sam. 24:15–25
  Scab .... Deut. 28:27
  Sores...........................Luke 16:20
  Tumors .... 1 Sam. 5:6, 12
  Weakness ....Ps. 102:23
B. Causes of:
  Man's original sin.................Gen. 3:16–19
  Man's actual sin ....2 Kin. 5:25–27;
    2 Chr. 21:12–19
  Satan's afflictions........... Job 2:7; Luke 13:16
  God's sovereign will... John 9:1–3; 2 Cor. 12:7–10
C. Cures of:
  From God............. 2 Chr. 16:12; Ps. 103:2, 3
  By Jesus..........................Matt. 4:23, 24
  By prayer........................James 5:14, 15
  By the use of means ....Is. 38:21; Luke 10:34
  By laying on of hands .... Acts 28:8, 9
  See Sick

Disfigured face
  Disqualifies for service...............Lev. 21:18

Disgrace—*shame produced by evil conduct*
  Treachery...................... 2 Sam. 10:1–5
  Private.......................2 Sam. 13:6–20
  Public.......................... Esth. 6:6–13
  Posthumous......................... Jer. 8:1–3
  Permanent......................Matt. 27:21–25
  Paramount .... Matt. 27:26–44

Disgraceful—*contemptuous reproach or shame*
  Immorality..........................Gen. 34:7
  Transgression ....Josh. 7:15
  Rape.......................... 2 Sam. 13:12

Dish
  Tabernacle implement.................Ex. 25:29
  Figurative of annihilating Jerusalem ... 2 Kin. 21:13

Dishan—*antelope*
  Son of Seir ....Gen. 36:21, 28

Dishes—*platters used for food*
  In the tabernacle.....................Ex. 25:29
  A common .... Matt. 26:23
  Devastating judgment compared to
    washing of.....................2 Kin. 21:13

Dishon—*antelope*
1. Son of Seir .... Gen. 36:21–30
2. Grandson of Seir .... Gen. 36:25

Dishonesty—*untruthfulness*
A. Manifested in:
  Half-truths.....................Gen. 12:11–20
  Trickery .... Gen. 27:6–29
  Falsifying one's word...............Gen. 34:1–31
  Wicked devices...................Prov. 1:10–19
  Theft ....John 12:4–6
  Unpaid wages .... James 5:4
B. Consequences of:
  Uncovered by God .... 1 Kin. 21:17–26
  Uncovered by men ....Josh. 9:3–22
  Condemned by conscience......... Matt. 27:3–5

Disobedience—*rebellion against recognized authority*
A. Sources of:
  Satan's temptations ....Gen. 3:1–13
  Lust ....James 1:13–15
  Rebellion ......Num. 20:10–24; 1 Sam. 15:16–23
B. Consequences of:
  Death......................... Rom. 5:12–19
  The Flood.......................1 Pet. 3:18–20
  Exclusion from the
    Promised Land.............. Num. 14:26–39
  Defeat .... Judg. 2:2, 11–15
  Doom.........................1 Pet. 2:7, 8

Disorderly—*unruly and irregular*
  Paul not guilty.................... 1 Thess. 5:14
  Some guilty .... 2 Thess. 3:6–11

Dispensation—*a stewardship or administration*
  Of divine working ....Eph. 1:10
  Paul's special privilege in .... Eph. 3:2

WORD STUDY | **DISPERSION**, *diaspora* (dee-as-por-*ah*). Derived from the verb meaning "to scatter," the noun *diaspora* is used in the Septuagint to refer to the "dispersion" of the Jewish people among the Gentiles, and it retains that meaning in John 7:35. Elsewhere in the NT the "dispersion" is figuratively meant to designate Christians scattered throughout regions perceived as hostile (James 1:1; 1 Pet. 1:1). Compare the cognate verb in Acts 8:1; 11:19. (Strong's #1290)

Dispersion—*a scattering abroad*
  Of Noah's generation .... Gen. 11:8
  Of Israelites ....2 Kin. 17:5, 6

Because of disobedience............Hos. 9:1–12
Of the early Christians.................1 Pet. 1:1

Display—*an unusual exhibition*
A. Of God's:
Power...........................Ex. 14:23–31
Glory.............................Ex. 33:18–23
Wrath.........................Num. 16:23–35
Universe...........................Job 38:1–41
Holiness...........................Is. 6:1–10
Love...............................John 3:16
B. Of human:
Kingdom........................Esth. 1:2–7
Pride.............................Esth. 5:10, 11
Wealth............................Is. 39:1, 2
Hypocrisy......................Luke 20:46, 47

Displeasure—*disapproval; anger*
God's, at people.....................1 Chr. 21:7
Person's, at God.......................Jon. 4:1
People's, at people..................Mark 10:41

Disposition—*natural temperament*
Ambitious Absalom...............2 Sam. 15:1–6
Boastful Nebuchadnezzar.............Dan. 4:30
Cowardly Peter.................Matt. 26:57, 58
Devilish Judas.................John 13:20–30
Envious Saul.....................1 Sam. 18:6–12
Foolish Nabal.................1 Sam. 25:10–25
Gullible Haman....................Esth. 6:6–11
Humble Job.........................Job 1:20–22

Distress, distressed
Used of:
Lust...............................2 Sam. 13:2
God's punishment.......................Ps. 2:5

Ditch—*a trench*
Miraculously filled...............2 Kin. 3:16–20
Wicked fall into.......................Ps. 7:15
Blind leaders fall into.................Luke 6:39

Diversity—*variety*
Among hearers....................Mark 13:3–8
Of God's gifts.................1 Cor. 12:4–11
Of God's times.......................Heb. 1:1

Divination—*attempt to foretell the unknown by occult
means*
A. Considered as:
System of fraud....................Ezek. 13:6, 7
Lucrative employment..............Acts 16:16
Abomination....................Deut. 18:11, 12
Punishable by death.................Lev. 20:6, 27
B. Practiced by:
Astrologers...........................Is. 47:13
Diviners...........................Deut. 18:14
False prophets.......................Jer. 14:14
Magicians.........................Gen. 41:8
Medium.................Deut. 18:11; 1 Sam. 28:7
Necromancer.......................Deut. 18:11
Soothsayers...........................Is. 2:6
Sorcerers.........................Acts 13:6, 8

Sorceress...........................Ex. 22:18
Spiritist...........................Deut. 18:11

Diviner's Terebinth Tree
Tree or place where soothsayers
performed.......................Judg. 9:37

Division—*diversity; discord*
A. Causes of:
Real faith.......................Luke 12:51–53
Carnal spirit.........................1 Cor. 3:3
B. Opposed to:
Prayer of Christ...................John 17:21–23
Unity of Christ.....................1 Cor. 1:13
Unity of the church...John 10:16; 1 Cor. 12:13–25

Division of priests—*assignments for service*
Outlined by David...............1 Chr. 24:1–19
Determined by casting lots.........1 Chr. 24:5, 7
Of Zacharias.........................Luke 1:5

Divorce—*breaking of the marriage tie*
A. The Old Testament teaching:
Permitted.........................Deut. 24:1–3
Divorced may not return to first
husband.........................Deut. 24:4
Denied to those making
false claims.................Deut. 22:13–19
Denied to those seducing
a virgin......................Deut. 22:28, 29
Unjust, reproved...................Mal. 2:14–16
Required, foreign wives put away....Ezra 10:1–16
Disobedience, a cause
among heathen................Esth. 1:10–22
A prophet's concern with...........Hos. 2:1–22
B. In the New Testament:
Marriage binding as long as life....Mark 10:2–9;
Rom. 7:2, 3
Divorce allowed because
of adultery....................Matt. 5:27–32
Marriage of the divorced constitutes
adultery.........................Luke 16:18
Reconciliation encouraged........1 Cor. 7:10–17

Dizahab—*abounding in gold*
Location of Moses' farewell addresses...Deut. 1:1

Doctrine—*teaching*
A. Statements of:
Foundational........................Heb. 6:1, 2
Traditional........................1 Cor. 15:1–4
Creedal...........................2 Tim. 3:16
B. Essentials of:
The Bible's inspiration..............2 Tim. 3:16
Christ's deity.......................1 Cor. 12:3
Christ's incarnation...............1 John 4:1–6
Christ's resurrection............1 Cor. 15:12–20
Christ's return....................2 Pet. 3:3–13
Salvation by faith...................Acts 2:38
C. Attitudes toward:
Obey...........................Rom. 6:17
Receive.........................1 Cor. 15:1–4

Hold fast...........................2 Tim. 1:13
Adorn ....Titus 2:10

Doctrine, false
A. What constitutes:
Perverting the gospel.....Gal. 1:6, 7; 1 John 4:1–6
Satanic deception................2 Cor. 11:13–15
B. Teachers of:
Deceive many ....Matt. 24:5, 24
Attract many........................2 Pet. 2:2
Speak perverse things .... Acts 20:30
Are savage .... Acts 20:29
Deceitful......................... 2 Cor. 11:13
Ungodly .... Jude 4, 8
Proud........................... 1 Tim. 6:3, 4
Corrupt.......................... 2 Tim. 3:8
Love error...................... 2 Tim. 4:3, 4
C. Christian attitude toward:
Avoid ....Rom. 16:17, 18
Test................................1 John 4:1
Detest .... Jude 23

Dodai
An Ahohite ....1 Chr. 27:4

Dodanim
Fourth son of Javan .... Gen. 10:4

Dodavah—*beloved of Yahweh*
Eliezer's father......................2 Chr. 20:37

Dodo—*loving*
1. A descendant of Issachar .... Judg. 10:1
2. A mighty man of David's.............2 Sam. 23:9
Called Dodai........................1 Chr. 27:4
3. Father of Elhanan ....2 Sam. 23:24

Doe—*female deer*
Figurative of peaceful quietude .... Song 2:7

Doeg—*fearful*
An Edomite; chief of Saul's herdsmen .1 Sam. 21:7
Betrays David .... 1 Sam. 22:9, 10
Kills 85 priests................. 1 Sam. 22:18, 19

Dogs—*a domesticated animal*
A. Described as:
Carnivorous....................... 1 Kin. 14:11
Blood-eating .... 1 Kin. 21:19
Dangerous ....Ps. 22:16
Domesticated ....Matt. 15:26, 27
Unclean................................ Is. 66:3
B. Figurative of:
Promiscuity...................... Deut. 23:18
Contempt....................... 1 Sam. 17:43
Worthlessness.......................2 Sam. 9:8
Satan ....Ps. 22:20
Hypocrite...........................Matt. 7:6
Gentiles......................... Matt. 15:26
False teachers.................... 2 Pet. 2:22
The unsaved.......................Rev. 22:15

Dominion—*supreme authority to govern*
A. Humankind's:
Delegated by God................. Gen. 1:26–28

Under God's control .... Jer. 25:12–33
Misused.........................Dan. 5:18–23
B. Satan's:
Secured by rebellion................. Is. 14:12–16
Offered to Christ .... Luke 4:6
Destroyed by Christ...................1 John 3:8
Abolished at Christ's return ....2 Thess. 2:8, 9
C. Christ's:
Predicted .... Is. 11:1–10
Announced.......................Luke 1:32, 33
Secured by His resurrection........ Acts 2:24–36;
Rev. 1:18
Perfected at His return .... 1 Cor. 15:24–28

Donkey
A. Used for:
Riding................................ Gen. 22:3
Carrying burdens.....................Gen. 42:26
Food...............................2 Kin. 6:25
Royalty ....Judg. 5:10
B. Regulations concerning:
Not to be yoked with an ox .... Deut. 22:10
To be rested on Sabbath .... Ex. 23:12; Luke 13:15
To be redeemed with a lamb .... Ex. 34:20
C. Special features regarding:
Spoke to Balaam................ Num. 22:28–31
Knowing his owner ....Is. 1:3
Jawbone kills many .... Judg. 15:15–17
Jesus rides upon one...... Zech. 9:9; Matt. 21:2, 5
All cared for by God .... Ps. 104:1, 10, 11
D. Figurative of:
Wildness (in Hebrew, "wild donkey') ... Gen. 16:12
Stubbornness........................ Hos. 8:9
Promiscuity .... Jer. 2:24

Door—*an entrance*
A. Used literally of:
City gates ....Neh. 3:1–6
Prison gates ....Acts 5:19
B. Used figuratively of:
Christ............................ John 10:7, 9
Christ's return.................... Matt. 24:33
Day of salvation .... Matt. 25:10
Inclusion of Gentiles................ Acts 14:27
Opportunity .... 2 Cor. 2:12

Doorkeeper
Descriptive of:
Maaseiah ....Jer. 35:4
Watchman .... Mark 13:34
Good Shepherd...................... John 10:3
One who was spoken to by a disciple... John 18:16

Doorpost
Private homes ....Ex. 12:7
Servant's ears pierced at ....Ex. 21:6
Tabernacle ....1 Sam. 1:9
Command to strike .... Amos 9:1

Dophkah—*cattle driving*
A desert encampment ....Num. 33:12, 13

Dor—*habitation*
Jabin's ally..........................Josh. 11:1, 2
Taken by Joshua ....Josh. 12:23
Assigned to Manasseh................. Josh. 17:11
Inhabitants not driven out............Judg. 1:27

Dorcas—*gazelle*
Good woman........................ Acts 9:36
Raised to life ....Acts 9:37–42
Called Tabitha.....................Acts 9:36, 40

Dothan—*wells*
Ancient town.....................Gen. 37:14–25
Joseph sold there..................Gen. 37:17–28
Elisha strikes Syrians at .... 2 Kin. 6:8–23

Double-mindedness—*inability to hold a fixed belief*
Makes one unstable .... James 1:8

Double-tongued—*two-faced, hypocritical*
Condemned in deacons.............. 1 Tim. 3:8

Doubt—*uncertainty of mind*
A. Objects of, Christ's:
Miracles .... Matt. 12:24–30
Resurrection .... John 20:24–29
Messiahship......................Luke 7:19–23
Return.............................2 Pet. 3:4
B. Causes of:
Satan .... Gen. 3:4
Unbelief .... Luke 1:18–20
Worldly wisdom..................1 Cor. 1:18–25
Spiritual instability ....James 1:6, 7
C. Removal of, by:
Putting God to the test.......... Judg. 6:36–40;
    John 7:16–18
Searching the Scriptures.......... Acts 17:11, 12
Believing God's Word........... Luke 16:27–31

Dove—*pigeon*
A. Features regarding:
Sent from ark....................Gen. 8:8, 10, 12
Sold in temple .... Matt. 21:12
B. Figurative of:
Loveliness........................... Song 2:14
Desperate mourning .... Is. 38:14
Foolish insecurity.................... Hos. 7:11
Israel's restoration .... Hos. 11:11
Holy Spirit ....Matt. 3:16
Harmlessness...................... Matt. 10:16

Dove's dropping
Sold in Samaria.....................2 Kin. 6:25

Dowry—*gifts given to bride's father for the bride*
A. Regulations regarding:
Sanctioned in the Law.............. Ex. 22:16, 17
Amount of, specified.............Deut. 22:28, 29
Sometimes given by bride's father . . .Josh. 15:16–19
B. Instances of:
Abraham (Isaac) for Rebekah..... Gen. 24:22–53
Jacob for Rachel .... Gen. 29:15–20
Shechem for Dinah ....Gen. 34:11–14
David for Michal ....1 Sam. 18:20–25

Dragon
Applied to:
Satan ....Rev. 12:9
Antichrist...........................Rev. 12:3

Drawers of water—*a lowly servant classification*
Women .... Gen. 24:13; 1 Sam. 9:11
Defeated enemies....................Josh. 9:21
Young men .... Ruth 2:9
Included in covenant............Deut. 29:10–13

DREAM, *chalom* (khal-*ohm*). The noun *chalom*, translated "dream," has two basic meanings. The first are those ordinary dreams associated with sleep. The second type of dreams are prophetic dreams—the lowest grade of prophecy and most familiar to us from the story of Joseph. Others who dreamed prophetic dreams were Abimelech (Gen. 20:3), Jacob (Gen. 31:10), and Laban (Gen. 31:24). Saul desired prophetic dreams as a word from God and sought aid from the witch or medium of Endor as a substitute. There is also mention of prophetic dreams in relation to false prophets (Deut. 13:1, 3, 5; Jer. 23:27, 28, 32). (Strong's #2472)

Dreams—*thoughts visualized in sleep*
A. Purposes of:
Restrain from evil .... Gen. 20:3
Reveal God's will ....Gen. 28:11–22
Encourage........................ Judg. 7:13–15
Reveal future......................Gen. 37:5–10
Instruct........................... Matt. 1:20
B. The interpretation of:
Sought anxiously ....Dan. 2:1–3
Belong to God......................Gen. 40:8
Revealed by God......................Gen. 40:8
Sought for God's will................. Num. 12:6
Sometimes delusive .... Is. 29:7, 8
False, by false prophets............Deut. 13:1–5
C. Notable examples of:
Abimelech .... Gen. 20:3
Jacob ....Gen. 28:10, 12
Laban............................. Gen. 31:24
Joseph .... Gen. 37:5
Pharaoh.........................Gen. 41:1–13
Unnamed person ....Judg. 7:13, 14
Solomon .... 1 Kin. 3:5–10
Job ....Job 7:14
Nebuchadnezzar....................Dan. 2:1–13
Joseph .... Matt. 1:19, 20
Pilate's wife .... Matt. 27:13, 19

Dregs—*the sediments of liquids; grounds*
Wicked shall drink down................ Ps. 75:8
Contains God's fury .... Is. 51:17, 22
Figurative of negligence and ease....... Jer. 48:11

Drink—*to swallow liquids*
A. Used literally of:
Water............................... Gen. 24:14
Wine .... Gen. 9:21

B. Used figuratively of:

Famine	2 Kin. 18:27
Misery	Is. 51:22, 23
Married pleasure	Prov. 5:15–19
Unholy alliances	Jer. 2:18
God's blessings	Zech. 9:15–17
Spiritual communion	John 6:53, 54
Holy Spirit	John 7:37–39

Drink offerings

Of wine	Hos. 9:4
Of water	1 Sam. 7:6

Dromedary—*a specie of camel*

Noted for speed	Jer. 2:23
Figurative of gospel blessings	Is. 60:6

Dropsy—*an unnatural accumulation of fluid in parts of the body*

Healing of	Luke 14:2–4

Dross—*impurities separated from metals*

Result of refinement	Prov. 25:4
Figurative of Israel	Is. 1:22, 25

Drought—*an extended dry season*

Unbearable in the day	Gen. 31:40
Seen in the wilderness	Deut. 8:15
Comes in summer	Ps. 32:4
Sent as a judgment	Hag. 1:11
Only God can stop	Jer. 14:22
Descriptive of spiritual barrenness	Jer. 14:1–7
The wicked dwell in	Jer. 17:5, 6
The righteous endure	Jer. 17:8
Longest	1 Kin. 18:1; Luke 4:25

Drown

Of the Egyptians	Ex. 14:27–30
Jonah saved from	Jon. 1:15–17
Of severe judgment	Matt. 18:6
The woman saved from	Rev. 12:15, 16
Figurative of lusts	1 Tim. 6:9

Drowsiness—*the mental state preceding sleep*

Prelude to poverty	Prov. 23:21
Disciples guilty of	Matt. 26:36–43

Drunkenness—*state of intoxication*

A. Evils of:

Debases	Gen. 9:21, 22
Provokes brawling	Prov. 20:1
Poverty	Prov. 23:21
Perverts justice	Is. 5:22, 23
Confuses the mind	Is. 28:7
Licentiousness	Rom. 13:13
Disorderliness	Matt. 24:48–51
Hinders watchfulness	1 Thess. 5:6, 7

B. Actual instances of the evil of:

Defeat in battle	1 Kin. 20:16–21
Degradation	Esth. 1:10, 11
Debauchery	Dan. 5:1–4
Weakness	Amos 4:1
Disorder	1 Cor. 11:21, 22

C. Penalties of:

Death	Deut. 21:20, 21

Exclusion from fellowship	1 Cor. 5:11
Exclusion from heaven	1 Cor. 6:9, 10

D. Figurative of:

Destruction	Is. 49:26
Roaring waves	Ps. 107:25–27
Giddiness	Is. 19:14
Error	Is. 28:7
Spiritual blindness	Is. 29:9–11
International chaos	Jer. 25:15–29
Persecution	Rev. 17:6

Drusilla—*feminine of "Drusus"*

Wife of Felix; hears Paul	Acts 24:24, 25

Dumah—*silence*

1. Descendants (a tribe) of Ishmael ... Gen. 25:14
2. Town in Judah ... Josh. 15:52

Dumb—*inability to speak*

A. Used literally of dumbness:

Imposed	Ezek. 3:26, 27
Demonized	Mark 9:17, 25

B. Used figuratively of:

Inefficient leaders	Is. 56:10
Helplessness	1 Cor. 12:2

See Mute

Dung—*excrement; refuse*

A. Used for:

Fuel	Ezek. 4:12, 15
Food in famine	2 Kin. 6:25

B. Figurative of:

Something worthless	2 Kin. 9:37

Dungeon—*an underground prison*

Joseph in	Gen. 40:8, 15
Jeremiah in	Jer. 37:16

Dunghills—*heaps of manure*

Pile of manure	Luke 14:34, 35

Dura—*circuit, wall*

Site of Nebuchadnezzar's golden image	Dan. 3:1

Dust—*powdery earth*

A. Used literally of:

The human body	Gen. 2:7
Dust of Egypt	Ex. 8:16, 17
Particles of soil	Num. 5:17

B. Used figuratively of:

Humankind's mortality	Gen. 3:19
Descendants	Gen. 13:16
Judgment	Deut. 28:24
Act of cursing	2 Sam. 16:13
Dejection	Job 2:12
Subjection	Is. 49:23
The grave	Is. 26:19
Rejection	Matt. 10:14

Duty—*an obligation*

A. Toward others:

Husband to wife	Eph. 5:25–33
Wife to husband	Eph. 5:22–24
Parents to children	Eph. 6:4
Children to parents	Eph. 6:1–3

Subjects to rulers . . . . 1 Pet. 2:12–20
Rulers to subjects . . . . Rom. 13:1–7
One toward another. . . . . 1 Pet. 3:8–16
The weak . . . . .1 Cor. 8:1–13
B. Toward God:
Love . . . . .Deut. 11:1
Obey . . . . Matt. 12:50
Serve . . . . 1 Thess. 1:9
Worship . . . . John 4:23

Dwarf—*a diminutive person*
Excluded from priesthood . . . . .Lev. 21:20

Dwell, to
A. Descriptive of:
Abram in Egypt. . . . . Gen. 12:10
Jacob with Laban . . . . Gen. 32:4
Israel in Egypt. . . . . Gen. 47:4
Stranger . . . . Ex. 12:48, 49
Wandering Levite. . . . . Deut. 18:6
Naomi in Moab. . . . . Ruth 1:1
Remnant in Egypt . . . . .Jer. 42:15–22
Jews in captivity . . . . .Ezra 1:4
B. Characterized by:
Simplicity of living. . . . . Heb. 11:9
Being among enemies . . . . 2 Kin. 8:1, 2
Lord's blessing. . . . . .Gen. 26:2, 3
C. Figurative of:
Christian in the world. . . . . .1 Pet. 1:17
See Foreigners; Strangers

Dwelling, God
In the tabernacle. . . . . .Ex. 29:43–46
In the temple . . . . 1 Kin. 6:11–13; 2 Chr. 7:1–3
In Zion . . . . .Is. 8:18
In Christ. . . . . Col. 2:9
Among people. . . . . John 1:14
In our hearts . . . . 1 John 4:12–16
In the Holy Spirit . . . . 1 Cor. 3:16
In the New Jerusalem . . . . Rev. 7:15

Dyeing—*coloring*
Leather . . . . .Ex. 25:5

Dysentery
Cured by Paul . . . . Acts 28:8

E

Eagle—*a bird of prey of the falcon species*
A. Described as:
Unclean. . . . . .Lev. 11:13
A bird of prey. . . . . Job 9:26
Large . . . . .Ezek. 17:3, 7
Swift. . . . . 2 Sam. 1:23
Keen in vision .Job 39:27–29
Nesting high . . . . .Jer. 49:16
B. Figurative of:
God's care. . . . . .Ex. 19:4
Swift armies. . . . . .Jer. 4:13
Spiritual renewal. . . . . Is. 40:31

Flight of riches . . . . .Prov. 23:5
False security. . . . . .Jer. 49:16

Ear—*the organ of hearing*
A. Ceremonies respecting:
Priest's, anointed . . . . Ex. 29:20
Leper's, anointed . . . . Lev. 14:2, 14, 25
Servant's bored . . . . .Ex. 21:5, 6
B. The hearing of the unregenerate:
Deafened . . . . Deut. 29:4
Stopped. . . . . .Ps. 58:4
Dulled . . . . Matt. 13:15
Disobedient . . . . .Jer. 7:23, 24
Uncircumcised . . . . .Acts 7:51
Itching. . . . . 2 Tim. 4:3, 4
C. Promises concerning, in:
Prophecy. . . . . Is. 64:4
Fulfillment. . . . . Matt. 13:16, 17
A miracle . . . . .Mark 7:35
A foretaste . . . . .2 Cor. 12:4
Final realization . . . . 1 Cor. 2:9

Early, arose
A. For spiritual purposes:
Abraham—looked on Sodom and
Gomorrah .Gen. 19:27, 28
Abraham—to offer a burnt offering. . .Gen. 22:2, 3
Jacob—to worship the Lord. . . . . . . Gen. 28:18–22
Moses—to meet God on Sinai. . . . . Ex. 34:4, 5
Elkanah and Hannah—to worship
God. . . . . 1 Sam. 1:19–28
Hezekiah—to worship God. . . . . .2 Chr. 29:20–24
Job—to offer sacrifices. . . . . .Job 1:5
Jesus—to pray . . . . .Mark 1:35
Jesus—to prepare to teach . . . . John 8:2
The people—to hear Jesus . . . . .Luke 21:38
B. For military reasons:
Joshua—to lead Israel over Jordan. . . .Josh. 3:1–17
Joshua—to capture Jericho . . . . Josh. 6:12–27
Joshua—to capture Ai. . . . . .Josh. 8:10
People of Jerusalem—to see
dead men . . . . .2 Kin. 19:35
C. For personal reasons:
Gideon—to examine the fleece . . . . Judg. 6:36–38
Samuel—to meet Saul . . . . 1 Sam. 15:12
David—to obey his father . . . . 1 Sam. 17:20
The ideal woman—to do her work . . . . Prov. 31:15
Drunkards—to pursue strong drink. . . . . . .Is. 5:11
Certain women—to visit
Christ's grave . . . . Mark 16:1, 2

Early rising
Hezekiah to worship God . . . . 2 Chr. 29:20–24

Earnest—*a pledge of full payment*
The Holy Spirit in the heart . . . . 2 Cor. 1:22
Given by God. . . . . 2 Cor. 5:5
Guarantee of future redemption . . . . Eph. 1:13, 14

Earnestness—*a serious and intense spirit*
Warning men. . . . . . . .Gen. 19:15–17; Ezek. 18:1–32
Accepting promises . . . . Gen. 28:12–22
Admonishing a son . . . . .1 Chr. 28:9, 10

Public prayer . . . . 2 Chr. 6:12–42
Asking forgiveness . . . . Ps. 51:1–19
Calling to repentance . . . . .Acts 2:38–40
Seeking salvation . . . . .Acts 16:30–34
Preaching the gospel . . . . .Acts 20:18–38
Contend for the faith . . . . .Jude 3–5

Earrings—*ornaments worn on the ear*
Sign of worldliness . . . . .Gen. 35:2–4
Made into a gold calf . . . . Ex. 32:2–4
Spoils of war .Judg. 8:24–26
Used figuratively . . . . .Ezek. 16:12

Earth—*our planet*
A. Described as:
Inhabitable . . . . Is. 45:18
God's footstool . . . . Is. 66:1
A circle . . . . Is. 40:22
Full of minerals .Deut. 8:9
B. Glory of God's:
Goodness . . . . Ps. 33:5
Glory . . . . .Is. 6:3
Riches . . . . .Ps. 104:24
Mercy . . . . .Ps. 119:64
C. History of:
Created by God . . . . Gen. 1:1
Given to humankind . . . . .Gen. 1:27–31
Affected by sin . . . . .Rom. 8:20–23
Destroyed . . . . .Gen. 7:6–24
Final destruction . . . . 2 Pet. 3:7–12
To be renewed . . . . Is. 65:17
D. Unusual events of:
Swallows several families . . . . .Num. 16:23–35
Reversed in motion . . . . 2 Kin. 20:8–11
Shaking . . . . .Heb. 12:26
Striking . . . . Mal. 4:6
Earthquake . . . . Matt. 27:51–54
E. Our relation to:
Made of . . . . .1 Cor. 15:47, 48
Given dominion over . . . . Gen. 1:26
Brings curse on . . . . Gen. 3:17
Returns to dust . . . . Gen. 3:19
F. Promises respecting:
Continuance of seasons . . . . Gen. 8:21, 22
No more flood . . . . Gen. 9:11–17
God's knowledge to fill . . . . .Is. 11:9
The meek shall inherit . . . . .Matt. 5:5
Long life upon . . . . Eph. 6:2, 3
To be renewed . . . . Is. 65:17

Earthquake—*a trembling of the earth*
A. Expressive of God's:
Power . . . . Heb. 12:25–29
Presence . . . . Ps. 68:7, 8
Anger . . . . Ps. 18:7
Judgments . . . . .Is. 24:18–21
Overthrowing of kingdoms . . . . Hag. 2:6, 7;
    Rev. 16:18–21
B. Reported occurrences:
Mt. Sinai . . . . .Ex. 19:18
The wilderness . . . . Num. 16:31, 32

Saul's time . . . . 1 Sam. 14:15, 16
Ahab's reign . . . . .1 Kin. 19:11, 12
Uzziah's reign . . . . .Amos 1:1; Zech. 14:5
Christ's death . . . . Matt. 27:50, 51
Christ's resurrection . . . . Matt. 28:2
Philippi . . . . Acts 16:26
C. Prophesied:
End of this age . . . . Matt. 24:7; Mark 13:8;
    Luke 21:11
Opening of sixth seal . . . . .Rev. 6:12
Following ascension of the two
    witnesses . . . . Rev. 11:3, 7, 11–13
Temple open in heaven . . . . .Rev. 11:19
At Armageddon . . . . .Rev. 16:18

Ease—*contentment of body and mind*
Israel's . . . . Amos 6:1
Pagan nations' . . . . .Zech. 1:15

East country—*southeastern Palestine; Arabia*
Abraham sent family there . . . . Gen. 25:6

East gate—*a gate of Jerusalem*
In temple area . . . . .Ezek. 10:19; 11:1

East wind—*a violent and often scorching wind*
Destroys vegetation . . . . Gen. 41:6; Ezek. 17:10
Destroys ships . . . . .Ps. 48:7; Ezek. 27:25, 26
Brings judgment . . . . Is. 27:8
Dries springs and fountains . . . . Hos. 13:15
Afflicts Jonah . . . . .Jon. 4:8
Called Euroclydon . . . . .Acts 27:14

Eat, eating
A. Restrictions on:
Forbidden tree . . . . Gen. 2:16, 17
Blood . . . . Acts 15:19, 20
Unclean things . . . . . . Lev. 11:1–47; Deut. 14:1–29
Excess, condemned . . . . . Eccl. 10:16, 17; Phil. 3:19
Anxiety concerning, prohibited . . . .Matt. 6:24–34
B. Spiritual significance of:
Covenant . . . . .Ex. 24:11
Adoption . . . . .Jer. 52:33, 34
Fellowship . . . . Luke 22:15–20
C. Christian attitude toward:
Tradition rejected . . . . Mark 7:1–23
Disorderliness condemned . . . . 1 Cor. 11:20–22
Regard for weaker brother . . . . Rom. 14:1–23
No work, no eating . . . . .2 Thess. 3:7–10

Ebal—*to be bare, stony*
1. Son of Shobal . . . . Gen. 36:23
Same as Obal . . . . .Gen. 10:28
2. Mountain in Samaria . . . . .Deut. 27:12, 13
Law to be written upon . . . . Deut. 27:1–8
Fulfilled by Joshua . . . . Josh. 8:30–35

Ebed—*slave*
1. Gaal's father . . . . .Judg. 9:28, 30
2. Son of Jonathan . . . . Ezra 8:6

Ebed-Melech—*slave of the king*
Ethiopian eunuch; rescues Jeremiah . . . Jer. 38:7–13
Promised divine protection . . . . Jer. 39:15–18

Ebenezer—*stone of help*
     Site of Israel's defeat .... 1 Sam. 4:1–10
     Ark transferred from................... 1 Sam. 5:1
     Site of memorial stone........... 1 Sam. 7:10, 12

Eber—*the region beyond*
1. Great-grandson of Shem .... Gen. 10:21–24;
     1 Chr. 1:25
     Progenitor of the: Hebrews ....Gen. 11:16–26
     Arabians and Arameans.......... Gen. 10:25–30
     Ancestor of Christ .... Luke 3:35
2. Son of Elpaal........................ 1 Chr. 8:12
3. Son of Shashak .... 1 Chr. 8:22, 25
4. Postexilic priest .... Neh. 12:20

Ebiasaph—*gatherer*
     Forefather of Samuel................. 1 Chr. 6:23
     Same as Abiasaph.............. Ex. 6:16, 18, 24

Ebony
     Dark, heavy hardwood; article
         of trade.........................Ezek. 27:15

Ebron—*alliance*
     Town of Asher.......................Josh. 19:28
     See Hebron

Ecclesiastes, Book of—*a book of the Old Testament; from Gr. word for "assembly" and Heb. word for "one who assembles"*
     Vanity of earthly things .... Eccl. 1:2
     Material goods ....Eccl. 5:10–12

Eclipse of the sun
     Foretold............................. Amos 8:9

Economy—*living thriftily*
     The law of..........................Prov. 11:24
     The wrong kind ....Hag. 1:6, 9–11
     Exemplified by Jesus .... John 6:11, 12

Eczema
     Makes an animal unacceptable........Lev. 22:22

Eden—*delight; pleasantness*
1. First home .... Gen. 2:8–15
     Zion becomes like........................Is. 51:3
     Called the "garden of God".......... Ezek. 28:13
     Terrible contrast...................... Joel 2:3
2. Region in Mesopotamia...................Is. 37:12
3. Gershonite Levite .... 2 Chr. 29:12

Eder—*a flock*
1. Tower ....Gen. 35:21
2. Town in Judah ....Josh. 15:21
3. Benjamite............................ 1 Chr. 8:15
4. Levite .... 1 Chr. 23:23

WORD STUDY

EDIFY, BUILD, *oikodomeō* (oy-kod-om-*eh*-oh). This verb appears forty times in the NT. Literally, it means "to build" or "to erect" an edifice (Matt. 7:24, 26; Mark 12:1); as a participle it can refer to "the builders" (Luke 20:17). Figuratively, *oikodomeō* refers to the "building up" of the Christian church (Matt. 16:18; 1 Pet. 2:5). It is also used in a religious sense to mean "edify," "strengthen,"

"establish." This particular usage normally occurs in contexts where the reference is to the strengthening and development of Christian communities (Acts 9:31) or the character of believers (1 Cor. 8:1; 1 Thess. 5:11). (Strong's #3618)

Edification—*building up one's faith*
A. Objects of:
     The church...................... 1 Cor. 14:4–12
     The body of Christ.................... Eph. 4:12
     One another........................Rom. 14:19
B. Accomplished by:
     The ministry .... 2 Cor. 12:19
     Christian gifts.................... 1 Cor. 14:3–12
     Word of God .... Acts 20:32
     Love .... 1 Cor. 8:1
     Spiritual things ....Rom. 14:19
     Seeking another's goods............... Rom. 15:2
     God's authority..................... 2 Cor. 10:8
C. Hindrances of:
     Carnal spirit........................ 1 Cor. 3:1–4
     Disputes .... 1 Tim. 1:3, 4
     Spiritual lukewarmness .... Rev. 3:14–22
     Worldly spirit ....James 4:1–6

Edom—*red*
1. Name given to Esau................... Gen. 25:30
2. Edomites .... Num. 20:18–21
3. Land of Esau; called Seir ....Gen. 32:3
     Called Idumea.......................Mark 3:8
     Mountainous land .... Jer. 49:16, 17
     People of, cursed..................... Is. 34:5, 6

Edomites—*descendants of Esau*
A. Character of:
     Warlike............................ Gen. 27:40
     Idolatrous.................... 2 Chr. 25:14, 20
     Superstitious .... Jer. 27:3, 9
     Proud................................Jer. 49:16
     Strong...............................Jer. 49:19
     Vindictive..........................Ezek. 25:12
B. Relations with Israel:
     Descendants of Esau .... Gen. 36:9
     Refused passage to.............. Num. 20:18–20
     Enemies of .... Ezek. 35:5–7
     Wars against .... 1 Sam. 14:47
     Joined enemies of ....2 Chr. 20:10
     Aided Babylon against .... Ps. 137:7
C. Well-known:
     Doeg........................1 Sam. 22:9, 18–22
     Hadad .... 1 Kin. 11:14
D. Prophecies concerning:
     Subjection to Israel.................. Gen. 27:37
     Punishment for persecuting Israel......Is. 34:5–8
     Utter desolation of....................Is. 34:9–17
     Babylonian conquest of.............. Jer. 49:7–12
     God's vengeance on.............. Ezek. 25:12–14
     Figurative of Gentiles .... Amos 9:11, 12
     Judgment of God against........... Obad. 1–21

Edrei—*mighty*
1. Capital of Bashan......................Deut. 3:10
   Site of Og's defeat................Num. 21:33–35
2. City of Naphtali......................Josh. 19:37

Education—*instruction in knowledge*
A. Performed by:
   Parents........................... Eph. 6:4
   Guardians........................... Gal. 4:1–3
   Teachers ....2 Chr. 17:7–9
   Learned men .... Acts 22:3
B. Method of:
   Sharing ....Gal. 6:6
   Recalling God's works ....Ps. 78:1–8
   Learning from nature .... Prov. 6:6–11
   Step-by-step........................ Is. 28:10
   Asking questions ....Luke 2:46
C. Examples of:
   Moses........................... Acts 7:22
   Daniel .... Dan. 1:17
   Paul .... Acts 22:3
   Timothy .... 2 Tim. 3:15, 16

Effeminate—*a man with female traits*
   Curse on Egypt .... Is. 19:16
   The weakness of Nineveh .... Nah. 3:13
   Rebuked by Paul................... 1 Cor. 16:13
   Shall not inherit the kingdom of God... 1 Cor. 6:9

Effort—*using energy to get something done*
   Organized........................Neh. 4:15–23
   Diligence in ....Neh. 6:1–4
   Inspired to ....Hag. 1:12–14
   Ill-considered .... Luke 14:28–30
   The highest .... Phil. 3:11–14

Egg
   Prohibition concerning that of birds... Deut. 22:6
   Article of food......................Luke 11:12
   White of, without taste.................Job 6:6

Eglah—*heifer*
   Wife of David .... 2 Sam. 3:2, 5

Eglaim—*two ponds*
   Moabite town .... Is. 15:8

Eglon—*heiferlike*
1. Moabite king......................Judg. 3:12–15
2. City of Judah....................... Josh. 15:39

Egotism—*a sinful exultation of one's self*
   Satan .... Is. 14:13–15; Luke 4:5, 6
   Goliath .... 1 Sam. 17:4–11
   Haman .... Esth. 6:6–12
   Simon............................. Acts 8:9–11
   Herod ....Acts 12:20–23
   Diotrephes .... 3 John 9, 10
   Sign of the Antichrist .... 2 Thess. 2:3, 4
   Sign of the last days .... 2 Tim. 3:1–5

Egypt—*black*
A. Israel's contact with, up to the Exodus:
   Abram visits......................Gen. 12:10
   Joseph sold into..................Gen. 37:28, 36

Joseph becomes leader in ....Gen. 39:1–4
Hebrews move to ....Gen. 46:5–7
Persecution by...................... Ex. 1:15–22
Israel leaves .... Ex. 12:31–33
Army of, perishes ....Ex. 14:26–28
B. Israel's contact with, after the Exodus:
   Solomon marries Pharaoh's daughter... 1 Kin. 3:1
   Hadad flees to...................... 1 Kin. 11:17
   Jeroboam flees to ....1 Kin. 11:40
   King Josiah killed by king of........ 2 Kin. 23:29;
     2 Chr. 35:20
   After death of Gedaliah, people
     flee to ....2 Kin. 25:26
   Jeremiah captured and taken there .... Jer. 43:1–7
   Joseph takes Mary and
     the Child there...................Matt. 2:14
   Joseph, Mary, and the Child return
     home from..................... Matt. 2:20
C. Characteristics of:
   Superstitious .... Is. 19:3
   Unprofitable .... Is. 30:1–7
   Treacherous....................... Is. 36:6
   Ambitious.......................... Jer. 46:8, 9
D. Prophecies concerning:
   Israel's sojourn in .... Gen. 15:13
   Destruction of.................Ezek. 30:24, 25
   Ever a lowly kingdom .... Ezek. 29:14, 15
   Conversion of ....Is. 19:18–25
   Christ, called out of ....Matt. 2:15

Egyptian, the—*an unknown insurrectionist*
   Paul mistaken for .... Acts 21:37, 38

Ehi—*brotherly*
   Benjamin's son ....Gen. 46:21
   Same as Ahiram .... Num. 26:38

Ehud—*union*
1. Great-grandson of Benjamin............1 Chr. 7:10
2. Judge, son of Gera .... Judg. 3:15
   Slays Eglon...................... Judg. 3:16–26

Eker—*offshoot*
   Descendant of Judah................. 1 Chr. 2:27

Ekron—*extermination*
   Philistine city ....Josh. 13:3
   Captured by Judah...................Judg. 1:18
   Assigned to Dan .... Josh. 19:40, 43
   Ark sent to ....1 Sam. 5:10
   Baal-Zebub, god of.................2 Kin. 1:2, 3
   Denounced by the prophets......... Jer. 25:9, 20

El—*ancient word for God, often used as prefix to*
    Hebrew names
   El Bethel ....Gen. 35:6, 7

Eladah—*God has adorned*
   A descendant of Ephraim............. 1 Chr. 7:20

Elah—*an oak*
1. Duke of Edom.................... Gen. 36:41
2. Son of Caleb .... 1 Chr. 4:15
3. King of Israel.................1 Kin. 16:6, 8–10
4. Benjamite.............................. 1 Chr. 9:8

5. Father of Hoshea . . . . 2 Kin. 15:30
6. Valley of . . . . 1 Sam. 17:2, 19
7. Father of Shimei . . . . 1 Kin. 4:18

Elam—*hidden*
1. Son of Shem . . . . Gen. 10:22
2. Benjamite . . . . 1 Chr. 8:24
3. Korahite Levite . . . . 1 Chr. 26:1, 3
4. Head of postexilic families . . . . Ezra 2:7
5. Another family head . . . . Ezra 2:31
6. One who signs covenant . . . . Neh. 10:1, 14
7. Priest . . . . Neh. 12:42

Elamites—*descendants of Elam*
A Semite (Shem) people . . . . Gen. 10:22
An ancient nation . . . . Gen. 14:1
Connected with Media . . . . Is. 21:2
Destruction of . . . . .Jer. 49:34–39
In Persian Empire . . . . .Ezra 4:9
Jews from, at Pentecost . . . . .Acts 2:9

Elasah—*God has made*
1. Shaphan's son . . . . .Jer. 29:3
2. Son of Pashhur . . . . .Ezra 10:22

Elath—*a grove*
Seaport on Red Sea . . . . .1 Kin. 9:26
Built by Azariah . . . . 2 Kin. 14:21, 22
Captured by Syrians . . . . 2 Kin. 16:6
Same as Ezion Geber . . . . 2 Chr. 8:17

El Bethel—*God of Bethel*
Site of Jacob's altar . . . . Gen. 35:6, 7

Eldaah—*God has called*
Son of Midian . . . . Gen. 25:4

Eldad—*God has loved*
Elder of Moses . . . . .Num. 11:26–29

WORD STUDY   **ELDER, PRESBYTER**, *presbuteros* (pres-*byoo*-ter-oss). This comparative adjective is used to denote age in relation to another person ("older" as in Luke 15:25). Outside the NT it is used as a noun, "elder," to designate officials of local councils in individual cities or of Jewish congregations (or synagogues). In the NT it can refer to members of a group within the Sanhedrin (Matt. 16:21) or to "elders" of the people of Israel (Acts 4:23). In Christian groups the use of *presbuteros* as a title is influenced by Jewish tradition. Thus, we read of "elders" within the Jerusalem church (Acts 15; 16). Rev. speaks of a council of twenty-four "elders" (5:5–14). The rank of the "elder" in relation to other officials, such as "bishop" (*episkopos*), is debated. (Strong's #4245)

Elderly
A. Contributions of:
Counsel . . . . 1 Kin. 12:6–16; Job 12:12
Spiritual service . . . . Luke 2:36–38
Fruitfulness . . . . .Ps. 92:13, 14
Leadership . . . . .Josh 24:2, 14, 15, 29;
    Titus 2:2–5
B. Attitude toward:
Minister to needs . . . . 1 Kin. 1:15
Respect . . . . .Ps. 71:18, 19

As cared for by God . . . . Is. 46:4
Honor . . . . Lev. 19:32; Prov. 16:31

WORD STUDY   **ELDERS**, *zaqen* (zaw-*kayn*). *Zaqen* is an adjective meaning "old aged" or used substantively meaning "old man" or "elders." Among the texts where the term is used to mean "old aged" is Gen. 18:11. Generally the word refers to an old man or old woman (1 Sam. 2:31, 32), but in some cases the old men are "elders," a technical term, indicating that these men within the community had more authority and power over the affairs of the community. This technical use of the term occurs over 100 times and is used especially to refer to the elders of Israel. During the times of the judges, a council of seventy elders made decisions for all of Israel (Num. 11:16). (Strong's #2205)

Elders of Israel
A. Functions of, in Mosaic period:
Rule the people . . . . .Judg. 2:7
Represent the nation . . . . .Ex. 3:16, 18
Share in national guilt . . . . Josh. 7:6
Assist in government . . . . .Num. 11:16–25
Perform religious acts . . . . Ex. 12:21, 22
B. Functions of, in later periods:
Choose a king . . . . 2 Sam. 3:17–21
Ratify a covenant .2 Sam. 5:3
Assist at a dedication . . . . 1 Kin. 8:1–3
Counsel kings . . . . 1 Kin. 12:6–8, 13
Legislate reforms . . . . Ezra 10:7–14
Try civil cases . . . . Matt. 26:3–68

Elders in the church
A. Qualifications of, stated by:
Paul . . . . Titus 1:5–14
Peter . . . . 1 Pet. 5:1–4
B. Duties of:
Administer relief . . . . Acts 11:29, 30
Correct error . . . . Acts 15:4, 6, 23
Hold fast the faithful word . . . . .Titus 1:5, 9
Rule well . . . . .1 Tim. 5:17
Minister to the sick . . . . James 5:14, 15
C. Honors bestowed on:
Ordination . . . . Acts 14:21, 23
Obedience . . . . Heb. 13:7, 17
Due respect . . . . 1 Tim. 5:1, 19
See Bishop

Elders in heaven
Twenty-four, seated on thrones and wearing
    crowns and white robes . . . . .Rev. 4:4
Having harps and incense . . . . .Rev. 5:8
Ask and answer questions . . . . Rev. 7:13–17
Worship God . . . . Rev. 4:10, 11; 5:9–14;
    7:11, 12; 19:4

Elead—*God has testified*
Ephraimite . . . . 1 Chr. 7:21

Elealeh—*God has ascended*
Moabite town . . . . Is. 15:1, 4
Rebuilt by Reubenites . . . . Num. 32:37

Eleasah—*God has made*
1. Descendant of Judah................1 Chr. 2:2–39
2. Descendant of Saul ....1 Chr. 8:33–37

Eleazar—*God has helped*
1. Son of Aaron .... Ex. 6:23
   Father of Phinehas......................Ex. 6:25
   Consecrated a priest ....Ex. 28:1
   Ministers in priest's position..........Lev. 10:6, 7
   Made chief over Levites .... Num. 3:32
   Succeeds Aaron................. Num. 20:25–28
   Takes second wilderness census.....Num. 26:1–4
   Aids Joshua ....Josh. 14:1
   Buried at Ephraim ....Josh. 24:33
2. Merarite Levite...................1 Chr. 23:21, 22
3. Son of Abinadab; custodian of the ark... 1 Sam. 7:1
4. One of David's mighty men ....2 Sam. 23:9
5. Priest..................................Ezra 8:33
6. Son of Parosh ....Ezra 10:25
7. Musician priest ....Neh. 12:27–42
8. Ancestor of Jesus ....Matt. 1:15

Elect, Election—*chosen*
A. Descriptive of:
   The Messiah .... Is. 42:1
   Israel .... Is. 45:4
   Good angels........................ 1 Tim. 5:21
   Christians......................Matt. 24:22, 31
   Christian ministers ....Acts 9:15
   Lady or church .... 2 John 1, 13
B. Characteristics of:
   Eternal................................Eph. 1:4
   Personal ....Acts 9:15
   Sovereign .... Rom. 9:11–16
   Unmerited ....Rom. 9:11
   God's foreknowledge................. 2 Pet. 1:3, 4
   Grace.............................Rom. 11:5, 6
   Through faith ....2 Thess. 2:13
   Recorded in heaven ....Luke 10:20
   Knowable .... 1 Thess. 1:4
   Of high esteem .... 2 Tim. 2:4
C. Results in:
   Adoption...........................Eph. 1:5
   Salvation.........................2 Thess. 2:13
   Conformity to Christ ....Rom. 8:29
   Good works .... Eph. 2:10
   Eternal glory ....Rom. 9:23
   Inheritance...................... 1 Pet. 1:2, 4, 5
D. Proof of:
   Faith................................2 Pet. 1:10
   Holiness .... Eph. 1:4, 5
   Divine protection.................. Mark 13:20
   Manifest it in life ....Col. 3:12

El Elohe Israel—*God, the God of Israel*
   Name of Jacob's altar.................Gen. 33:20

Elements—*basic parts of anything*
A. Used literally of:
   Basic forces of nature.............. 2 Pet. 3:10, 12
B. Used figuratively of:
   Basic principles of religion............Gal. 4:3, 9

Rudiments of tradition.............. Col. 2:8, 20
First principles of religion .... Heb. 5:12

Eleph—*ox*
   Town of Benjamin ....Josh. 18:28

Eleven, the—*the disciples without Judas*
   Were told of resurrection .... Luke 24:9, 33, 34
   Met Jesus .... Matt. 28:16, 17
   At Pentecost...................... Acts 2:1, 14
   Jesus appeared to ....Mark 16:14
   Cast lots for Judas's replacement .... Acts 1:21–26

Elhanan—*God has been gracious*
1. Son of Dodo........................2 Sam. 23:24
   Brave man..........................1 Chr. 11:26
2. Son of Jair .... 1 Chr. 20:5
   Slays a giant ....2 Sam. 21:19

Eli—*my God*
   Jesus' cry on the cross .... Matt. 27:46
   Same as "Eloi"..................... Mark 15:34

Eli—*high (that is, God is high)*
   High priest, officiates in Shiloh ....1 Sam. 1:3
   Blesses Hannah.................. 1 Sam. 1:12–19
   Becomes Samuel's guardian.......1 Sam. 1:20–28
   Samuel ministers before ....1 Sam. 2:11
   Sons of............................ 1 Sam. 2:12–17
   Rebukes sons .... 1 Sam. 2:22–25
   Rebuked by a man of God .... 1 Sam. 2:27–36
   Instructs Samuel.................. 1 Sam. 3:1–18
   Death of .... 1 Sam. 4:15–18

Eliab—*God is father*
1. Son of Helon ....Num. 1:9
   Leader of Zebulun ....Num. 7:24, 29
2. Father of Dathan and Abiram ....Num. 16:1, 12
3. Ancestor of Samuel .... 1 Chr. 6:27, 28
4. Brother of David .... 1 Sam. 16:5–13
   Fights in Saul's army ....1 Sam. 17:13
   Discounts David's worth .... 1 Sam. 17:28, 29
5. Gadite warrior .... 1 Chr. 12:1–9
6. Levite musician ....1 Chr. 15:12–20

Eliada, Eliadah—*God has known*
1. Son of David .... 2 Sam. 5:16
   Also called Beeliada..................1 Chr. 14:7
2. Father of Rezon .... 1 Kin. 11:23
3. Benjamite warrior ....2 Chr. 17:17

Eliah—*my God is Yahweh*
   Divorced foreign wife .... Ezra 10:18, 26

Eliahba—*God conceals*
   One of David's mighty men......... 2 Sam. 23:32

Eliakim—*God will establish*
1. Son of Hilkiah .... 2 Kin. 18:18
   Confers with Rabshakeh ....Is. 36:3, 11–22
   Sent to Isaiah.......................Is. 37:2–5
   Becomes type of the Messiah ....Is. 22:20–25
2. Son of King Josiah................... 2 Kin. 23:34
   Name changed to Jehoiakim..........2 Chr. 36:4
3. Postexilic priest .... Neh. 12:41
4. Ancestor of Christ.........Matt. 1:13; Luke 3:30

Eliam—*God of the people*
1. Father of Bathsheba . . . . 2 Sam. 11:3
   Called Ammiel . . . . 1 Chr. 3:5
2. Son of Ahithophel . . . . .2 Sam. 23:34

Eliasaph—*God has added*
1. Gadite prince . . . . .Num. 1:4, 14
   Presents offering. . . . . Num. 7:41, 42
2. Levite . . . . .Num. 3:24

Eliashib—*God will restore*
1. Davidic priest . . . . 1 Chr. 24:1, 12
2. Divorced foreign wife . . . . Ezra 10:24, 27
3. High priest. . . . . .Neh. 12:10
   Rebuilds Sheep Gate . . . . .Neh. 3:1, 20, 21
   Allies with foreigners . . . . .Neh. 13:4, 5, 28
4. Descendant of Zerubbabel . . . . .1 Chr. 3:19–24

Eliathah—*God has come*
   Son of Heman . . . . 1 Chr. 25:4, 27

Elidad—*God has loved*
   Benjamite leader. . . . . Num. 34:17, 21

Eliehoenai—*toward God are my eyes*
1. Son of Zerahiah . . . . Ezra 8:4
2. Korahite gatekeeper . . . . 1 Chr. 26:1–3

Eliel—*God is God*
1. Ancestor of Samuel . . . . 1 Chr. 6:33, 34
2. One of David's mighty men . . . . 1 Chr. 11:26, 46
3. Another of David's mighty men. . . . . . . 1 Chr. 11:47
4. Gadite warrior . . . . 1 Chr. 12:1–11
5. Levite . . . . 1 Chr. 15:9, 11
6. Benjamite . . . . 1 Chr. 8:1–21
7. Benjamite, son of Shashak . . . . 1 Chr. 8:22, 25
8. Manassite chief. 1 Chr. 5:23, 24
9. Overseer of tithes. . . . . 2 Chr. 31:12, 13

Elienai—*toward God are my eyes*
   Benjamite chief. . . . . .1 Chr. 8:1, 20

Eliezer—*God of help*
1. Abraham's servant. . . . . .Gen. 15:2
2. Son of Moses. . . . . .Ex. 18:2–4
3. Son of Zichri . . . . 1 Chr. 27:16
4. Son of Becher . . . . .1 Chr. 7:8
5. Priest of David . . . . 1 Chr. 15:24
6. Prophet. . . . . 2 Chr. 20:37
7. Ezra's delegate . . . . Ezra 8:16
8, 9, 10. Three men who divorced their
       foreign wives . . . . Ezra 10:18–31
11. An ancestor of Christ . . . . Luke 3:29

Elihoreph—*God of autumn*
   One of Solomon's scribes . . . . 1 Kin. 4:3

Elihu—*He is my God*
1. Ancestor of Samuel . . . . 1 Sam. 1:1
   Also called Eliab and Eliel . . . . .1 Chr. 6:27, 34
2. David's brother. 1 Chr. 27:18
   Called Eliab . . . . 1 Sam. 16:6
3. Manassite captain . . . . 1 Chr. 12:20
4. Temple servant. 1 Chr. 26:1, 7
5. One who reproved Job and
   his friends . . . . Job 32:2, 4–6

Elijah—*Yahweh is God*
A. Life of the prophet:
   Proclaims drought . . . . 1 Kin. 17:1
   Hides by the Brook Cherith. . . . . 1 Kin. 17:3
   Fed by ravens. .1 Kin. 17:4–7
   Fed by widow. .1 Kin. 17:8–16
   Restores life to widow's son . . . . . . .1 Kin. 17:17–24
   Sends message to Ahab. . . . . .1 Kin. 18:1–16
   Overthrows Baal prophets . . . . 1 Kin. 18:17–46
   Flees from Jezebel. . . . . .1 Kin. 19:1–3
   Fed by angels . . . . 1 Kin. 19:4–8
   Hears God . . . . 1 Kin. 19:9–14
   Sent on a mission . . . . 1 Kin. 19:15–18
   Throws mantle on Elisha . . . . 1 Kin. 19:19–21
   Condemns Ahab. . . . . 1 Kin. 21:15–29
   Condemns Ahaziah. . . . . .2 Kin. 1:1–16
   Taken up to heaven . . . . .2 Kin. 2:1–15
B. Miracles of:
   Widow's oil .1 Kin. 17:14–16
   Dead child raised . . . . .1 Kin. 17:17–24
   Causes rain. 1 Kin. 18:41–45
   Causes fire to consume sacrifices . . . 1 Kin. 18:24–38
   Causes fire to consume soldiers . . . . 2 Kin. 1:10–12
   Divides the Jordan . . . . 2 Kin. 2:8
C. Prophecies of:
   Drought . . . . 1 Kin. 17:1
   Ahab's destruction. . . . . .1 Kin. 21:17–29
   Ahaziah's death . . . . .2 Kin. 1:2–17
   Plague . . . . 2 Chr. 21:12–15
D. Significance of:
   Prophecy of his coming. . . . . Mal. 4:5, 6
   Appears with Christ . . . . Matt. 17:1–4
   Type of John the Baptist. . . . . Luke 1:17
   Prayers of the righteous, effective . . . James 5:17, 18

Elijah—*Yahweh is God*
1. Priest who divorced his foreign wife . . . . . Ezra 10:21
2. Son of Jeroham . . . . 1 Chr. 8:27

Elika—*God has spewed out*
   David's warrior . . . . 2 Sam. 23:25

Elim—*large trees*
   Israel's encampment . . . . .Ex. 15:27
   Place of palm trees . . . . Num. 33:9, 10

Elimelech—*God is king*
   Man of Judah. . . . . Ruth 1:1, 2
   Dies in Moab . . . . Ruth 1:3
   Kinsman of Boaz . . . . Ruth 2:1, 3
   Boaz buys his land . . . . Ruth 4:3–9

Elioenai—*toward God are my eyes*
1. Descendant of Benjamin . . . . .1 Chr. 7:8
2. Simeonite head. 1 Chr. 4:36
3. Son of Neariah . . . . 1 Chr. 3:23, 24
4. Postexilic priest . . . . Neh. 12:41
   Divorced his foreign wife . . . . Ezra 10:19, 22
5. Son of Zattu; divorced his foreign wife . . .Ezra 10:27

Eliphal—*God has judged*
   David's warrior . . . . 1 Chr. 11:26, 35
   Called Eliphelet . . . . 2 Sam. 23:34

Eliphaz—*God is fine gold*
1. Son of Esau......................... Gen. 36:2, 4
2. One of Job's friends..................... Job 2:11
    Rebukes Job........................... Job 4:1, 5
    Is forgiven........................... Job 42:7–9

Elipheleh—*whom God makes distinguished*
    Levite singer ....1 Chr. 15:18, 21

Eliphelet—*God is deliverance*
1. Son of David .... 1 Chr. 3:5, 6
2. Another son of David .... 2 Sam. 5:16
3. Descendant of Jonathan............. 1 Chr. 8:33, 39
4. David's warrior.....................2 Sam. 23:34
5. Returnee from Babylon .... Ezra 8:13
6. Son of Hashum; divorced his
      foreign wife ....Ezra 10:33

Elisha—*God is salvation*
A. Life of:
    Called to succeed Elijah .... 1 Kin. 19:16
    Follows Elijah .... 1 Kin. 19:19–21
    Sees Elijah translated...............2 Kin. 2:1–12
    Requests double portion of Elijah's
      spirit .... 2 Kin. 2:9–14
    Is recognized as a prophet .... 2 Kin. 2:13–22
    Mocked..................... 2 Kin. 2:23–25
    Deals with kings................. 2 Kin. 3:11–20
    Helps two women..................2 Kin. 4:1–17
    Rebukes King Joash............... 2 Kin. 13:19
    Death of Elisha ....2 Kin. 13:20
B. Miracles of:
    Divides Jordan .... 2 Kin. 2:14
    Purifies water .... 2 Kin. 2:19–22
    Increases widow's oil...............2 Kin. 4:1–7
    Raises Shunammite's son .... 2 Kin. 4:18–37
    Neutralizes poison............... 2 Kin. 4:38–41
    Multiplies bread .... 2 Kin. 4:42–44
    Heals Naaman the leper...........2 Kin. 5:1–19
    Inflicts Gehazi with leprosy ...... 2 Kin. 5:26, 27
    Causes iron to float .... 2 Kin. 6:6
    Reveals secret counsels........... 2 Kin. 6:8–12
    Opens servant's eyes .... 2 Kin. 6:13–17
    Strikes Syrian army
      with blindness .... 2 Kin. 6:18–23
    Dead man raised by touching of his
      bones........................2 Kin. 13:21
C. Prophecies of:
    Birth of a child .... 2 Kin. 4:16
    Abundance........................... 2 Kin. 7:1
    Official's death .... 2 Kin. 7:2
    Great famine ....2 Kin. 8:1–3
    Hazael's cruelty...................2 Kin. 8:7–15
    Joash's victories................. 2 Kin. 13:14–19

Elishah—*God is salvation*
    Son of Javan........................ Gen. 10:4

Elishama—*God has heard*
1. Son of Ammihud ....Num. 1:10
    Ancestor of Joshua................... 1 Chr. 7:26
2. Man of Judah .... 1 Chr. 2:41
3. Son of David .... 1 Chr. 3:1, 5, 6

    Also called Elishua...................2 Sam. 5:15
4. Another son of David .... 2 Sam. 5:16
5. Teaching priest....................2 Chr. 17:7, 8
6. Scribe .... Jer. 36:12, 20, 21

Elishaphat—*God has judged*
    Captain............................. 2 Chr. 23:1

Elisheba—*God is an oath*
    Wife of Aaron ....Ex. 6:23

Elishua—*God is salvation*
    Son of David ....2 Sam. 5:15
    Called Elishama .... 1 Chr. 3:6

Eliud—*God is mighty*
    Father of Eleazar.................. Matt. 1:14, 15

Elizabeth—*God is an oath*
    Wife of Zacharias..................... Luke 1:5
    Barren .... Luke 1:7, 13
    Conceives a son....................Luke 1:24, 25
    Relative of Mary.................... Luke 1:36
    Filled with the Holy Spirit .... Luke 1:41
    Salutation to Mary............... Luke 1:42–45
    Mother of John the Baptist .... Luke 1:57–60

Elizaphan—*God has concealed*
1. Chief of Kohathites....................Num. 3:30
    Heads family ....1 Chr. 15:5, 8
    Family consecrated .... 2 Chr. 29:12–16
2. Son of Parnach ....Num. 34:25

Elizur—*God is a rock*
    Reubenite warrior .... Num. 1:5

Elkanah—*God has possessed*
1. Father of Samuel.....................1 Sam. 1:1–23
2. Son of Korah........................... Ex. 6:24
    Escapes judgment.............. Num. 26:11
3. Levite ....1 Chr. 6:23–36
4. Descendant of Korah .... 1 Chr. 6:22, 23
5. Levite .... 1 Chr. 9:16
6. Korahite warrior .... 1 Chr. 12:1, 6
7. Officer under Ahaz .... 2 Chr. 28:7
8. Doorkeeper of the ark................ 1 Chr. 15:23

Elkoshite—*an inhabitant of Elkosh*
    Descriptive of Nahum.................. Nah. 1:1

Ellasar
    Place in Babylon .... Gen. 14:1, 9

Elmodam
    Ancestor of Christ .... Luke 3:28

Elnaam—*God is pleasantness*
    Father of two warriors.............. 1 Chr. 11:46

Elnathan—*God has given*
1. Father of Nehushta .... 2 Kin. 24:8
    Goes to Egypt .... Jer. 26:22
    Entreats with king .... Jer. 36:25
2, 3, 4. Three Levites .... Ezra 8:16

Eloi (same as Eli)
    Jesus' cry........................... Mark 15:34

Elon—*oak*
1. Hittite............................. Gen. 26:34

2. Son of Zebulun . . . . Gen. 46:14
3. Judge in Israel . . . . Judg. 12:11, 12
4. Town of Dan . . . . Josh. 19:43

Elon Beth Hanan—*oak of house of grace*
Town of Dan . . . . 1 Kin. 4:9

Elonites—*belonging to Elon*
Descendants of Elon . . . . Num. 26:26

Eloquent—*fluent and persuasive in speech*
Moses is not . . . . Ex. 4:10
Paul rejects . . . . 1 Cor. 2:1, 4, 5
Apollos is . . . . Acts 18:24
False prophets boast of . . . . 2 Pet. 2:18

Elpaal—*God has wrought*
Benjamite . . . . 1 Chr. 8:11–18

El Paran—*oak of Paran*
Place in Canaan . . . . Gen. 14:6

Elpelet—*God of deliverance*
Son of David . . . . 1 Chr. 14:3, 5
Same as Eliphelet . . . . 1 Chr. 3:6

Eltekeh—*God is dread*
City of Dan . . . . Josh. 19:44
Assigned to Levites . . . . Josh. 21:23

Eltekon—*founded by God*
Village in Judah . . . . Josh. 15:59

Eltolad—*kindred of God*
Town in Judah . . . . Josh. 15:21, 30
Assigned to Simeonites . . . . Josh. 19:4
Called Tolad . . . . 1 Chr. 4:29

Elul—*vine*
Sixth month of Hebrew year . . . . Neh. 6:15

Eluzai—*God is my defense*
Ambidextrous warrior of David . . . . . 1 Chr. 12:1, 5

Elymas—*a wise man*
Arabic name of Bar-Jesus, a false
prophet . . . . Acts 13:6–12

Elzabad—*God has bestowed*
1. Gadite warrior . . . . 1 Chr. 12:8, 12
2. Korahite Levite . . . . 1 Chr. 26:7, 8

Elzaphan (contraction of Elizaphan)
Son of Uzziel . . . . Ex. 6:22
Given instructions by Moses . . . . Lev. 10:4

Emancipation—*a setting free from slavery*
Of Hebrew nation . . . . Ex. 12:29–42
Of Hebrew slaves . . . . Ex. 21:2
In the Year of Jubilee . . . . Lev. 25:8–41
Proclaimed by Zedekiah . . . . Jer. 34:8–11
By Cyrus . . . . 2 Chr. 36:23; Ezra 1:1–4

Emasculation—*castration*
Penalty of . . . . Deut. 23:1

Embalming—*preserving a corpse from decay*
Unknown to Abraham . . . . Gen. 23:1–4
Practiced in Egypt . . . . Gen. 50:2, 3, 26
Manner of, among Jews . . . . 2 Chr. 16:14
Limitation of . . . . John 11:39, 44

Embroider—*to decorate by needlework*
In tabernacle curtains . . . . Ex. 26:1, 36
Bezalel and Aholiab inspired
concerning . . . . Ex. 35:30–35
On Sisera's garments . . . . Judg. 5:30

Emek Keziz—*cut off*
City of Benjamin . . . . Josh. 18:21

Emerald—*a precious stone of the beryl variety*
In high priests' garments . . . . Ex. 28:17
In Tyre's trade . . . . Ezek. 27:16
Used for ornamentation . . . . Ezek. 28:13
Foundation stone . . . . Rev. 21:19

Emim—*terrors*
Giant race of Anakim east of the
Dead Sea . . . . Gen. 14:5

Emmaus—*hot spring*
Town near Jerusalem . . . . Luke 24:13–18

Emotion—*a person's response to living situations*
A. Objects of:
Self . . . . Job 3:1–26
Nation . . . . Ps. 137:1–6
Family . . . . Gen. 49:1–28
Mate . . . . 1 Sam. 25:24, 25
Foreigners . . . . Ruth 1:16–18
B. Kinds of:
Conviction . . . . Acts 2:37
Contempt . . . . 1 Sam. 17:42–44
Despondency . . . . 1 Kin. 19:4–10
Disappointment . . . . Luke 18:23
Disgust . . . . Neh. 4:1–3
Envy . . . . 1 Sam. 17:28
Fear . . . . 1 Kin. 19:1–3
Flattery . . . . 1 Sam. 25:23–31
Hate . . . . Acts 7:54, 57
Joy . . . . Luke 15:22–24
Love . . . . Ex. 32:26–29
Loyalty . . . . 2 Sam. 18:32, 33
Regret . . . . Luke 16:27–31
Revenge . . . . Gen. 27:41–45
Sorrow . . . . 2 Sam. 12:13–19
C. Control of:
Unsuppressed . . . . 1 Sam. 20:30–33
Suppressed . . . . Is. 36:21
Uncontrollable . . . . Mark 5:4, 5
Controlled . . . . Mark 5:18, 19

Employees—*those who work for others*
A. Types of:
Diligent . . . . Gen. 30:27–31
Discontented . . . . Matt. 20:1–15
Unworthy . . . . Matt. 21:33–41
B. Duties of:
Contentment . . . . Luke 3:14
Fulfilling terms . . . . Matt. 20:1–15
Respect . . . . 1 Tim. 6:1
Diligence . . . . Prov. 22:29
Honesty . . . . Ex. 20:18

C. Rights of:
    Equal wage . . . . Matt. 10:10
    Prompt payment . . . . .Lev. 19:13
    Good treatment . . . . Ruth 2:4
D. Oppression of, by:
    Arbitrary changes . . . . Gen. 31:38–42
    Unscrupulous landowners . . . . .James 5:4–6

Employers—*those who hire others to work for them*
    Must not oppress . . . . Deut. 24:14
    Must be considerate . . . . .Job 31:31
    Must be just and fair . . . . .Col. 4:1

Employment—*the state of one who has regular work*
A. Usefulness of:
    Manifest graces . . . . Prov. 31:10–31
    Provided food . . . . .2 Thess. 3:7–12
B. Examples of:
    Adam . . . . Gen. 2:15
    Workmen after the Exile . . . . .Neh. 4:15–23
    Paul . . . . .1 Thess. 2:9–11

Enam—*two springs*
    Village of Judah . . . . .Josh. 15:20, 34

Enan—*having fountains*
    Father of Ahira . . . . Num. 1:15

Encampment—*a resting place on a march or journey*
    Israel's, on leaving Egypt . . . . Ex. 13:20
    At Sinai . . . . .Ex. 18:5
    List of . . . . Num. 33:10–49
    In battle . . . . Josh. 10:5, 31, 34

Enchantment—*the practice of magical arts*
A. Practiced in:
    Egypt . . . . .Ex. 7:11
    Judah . . . . .2 Kin. 17:16, 17
    Babylon . . . . .Ezek. 21:21
    Chaldea . . . . Dan. 5:11
    Greece . . . . Acts 16:16
    Asia Minor . . . . Acts 19:13, 19
B. Futility of:
    Vanity of . . . . Is. 47:9–15
    Inability of . . . . .Ex. 7:11, 12
    Abomination of . . . . Deut. 18:9–12
C. Examples of:
    Simon . . . . .Acts 8:9
    Bar-Jesus . . . . .Acts 13:6–12
    Slave girl . . . . Acts 16:16
    Itinerant Jews . . . . Acts 19:13
    Jannes and Jambres . . . . 2 Tim. 3:8

Encouragement—*inspiration to hope and service*
A. Needed by:
    Prophets . . . . .1 Kin. 19:1–19
    People . . . . .Neh. 4:17–23
    Servants . . . . .2 Kin. 6:15–17
    Kings . . . . 2 Kin. 11:10–21
    Heathen . . . . .Dan. 6:18–23
B. Paul, for churches at:
    Rome . . . . .Rom. 1:7, 8
    Corinth . . . . .1 Cor. 1:1–9; 2 Cor. 1:1, 2
    Galatia . . . . .Gal. 1:1–5

    Ephesus . . . . .Eph. 1:1, 2
    Philippi . . . . Phil. 1:1–6
    Colosse . . . . .Col. 1:1–4
    Thessalonica . . . . . . 1 Thess. 1:1–4; 2 Thess. 1:1–4
C. Agents of:
    Angels . . . . Gen. 32:1, 2
    A dream . . . . .Gen. 28:11–22
    God's promises .Josh. 1:1–9
    A friend . . . . 1 Sam. 23:16–18
    A relative . . . . Esth. 4:13–16
    Paul . . . . Acts 27:21–26
D. Reasons for, Christ is:
    Risen . . . . .1 Cor. 15:11–58
    Present . . . . Matt. 28:19, 20
    Coming . . . . Luke 21:25–28

Encumbrance—*that which hinders freedom of action*
    Universal . . . . .Gen. 3:16–19
    Imposed . . . . .Gen. 32:31, 32
    Perpetual . . . . Matt. 27:25
    Moral . . . . Titus 1:12, 13
    Spiritual . . . . Heb. 12:1

End of the world
A. Events connected with:
    Day of salvation ended . . . . Matt. 24:3, 14
    Harvest of souls . . . . Matt. 13:36–43
    Defeat of Man of Sin . . . . .2 Thess. 2:1–12
    Judgment . . . . .Matt. 25:31–46
    Destruction of world . . . . .2 Thess. 1:6–10
B. Coming of:
    Denied by scoffers . . . . 2 Pet. 3:3–5
    Preceded by lawlessness . . . . Matt. 24:12
    Preceded by apostasy . . . . Luke 18:8
    Without warning . . . . Matt. 24:37–42
    With fire . . . . .2 Thess. 1:7–10
C. Attitude toward:
    Watchfulness . . . . Matt. 25:1–13
    Industry . . . . .Matt. 25:14–30
    Hopefulness . . . . Luke 21:25–28
    Holy living . . . . Rom. 13:12–14; 2 Pet. 3:11, 14
    Seeking the lost . . . . 2 Pet. 3:9, 15
    Waiting for eternity . . . . 2 Pet. 3:13; Rev. 21:1

En Dor—*fountain of habitation*
    Town of Manasseh . . . . Josh. 17:11
    Site of memorable defeat . . . . .Ps. 83:9, 10
    Home of notorious witch . . . . 1 Sam. 28:1–10

Endurance, blessedness of
    Commanded . . . . Matt. 10:22; 2 Tim. 2:3
    Exemplified . . . . .2 Tim. 2:10; Heb. 10:32, 33
    Rewarded . . . . .2 Tim. 3:11; James 1:12

Enduring things
    God's faithfulness . . . . .Ps. 89:33
    God's mercies . . . . .Ps. 103:17
    God's Word . . . . Matt. 24:35
    Spiritual nourishment . . . . John 6:27
    Spiritual rewards . . . . 1 Cor. 3:14
    Graces . . . . 1 Cor. 13:13
    The real things . . . . 2 Cor. 4:18
    God's kingdom . . . . .Heb. 12:27, 28

En Eglaim—*fountain of calf*
Place near the Dead Sea ....Ezek. 47:10

Enemies—*foes; adversaries; opponents*
A. Applied to:
   Foreign nations......................Gen. 14:20
   Israel .... Mic. 2:8
   Gentiles.............................Col. 1:21
   The unregenerate....................Rom. 5:10
   The world........................ Matt. 22:44
   Satan .... Matt. 13:39
   Death............................1 Cor. 15:26
B. Characteristics of, hate for:
   God ....Rom. 1:30
   The gospel ....1 Thess. 2:14–18
   The light.........................John 3:19–21
C. Examples of:
   Amalek against Israel .... Ex. 17:8–16
   Saul against David .... 1 Sam. 18:29
   Jezebel against Elijah............... 1 Kin. 19:1, 2
   Ahab against Elijah ....1 Kin. 21:20
   Haman against the Jews.............. Esth. 3:10
   Jews against Christians........... Acts 7:54–60;
      22:13, 21, 22
D. Christian attitude toward:
   Overcome by kindness ....1 Sam. 26:18–21
   Do not curse...................... Job 31:29, 30
   Feed .... Rom. 12:20
   Love.............................Luke 6:27, 35
   Forgive .... Matt. 6:12–15
   Pray for ....Luke 23:34

Energy—*effective force to perform work*
A. God's, in nature:
   Creative...........................Job 38:4–11
   Beyond natural law .... Job 26:12
   Maintains matter .... Heb. 1:3
B. God's, in people:
   To be witnesses........................Acts 1:8
   For abundant living..................Rom. 15:13
   For edification ....Rom. 15:14
   To raise dead ....1 Cor. 6:14; 2 Cor. 13:4

En Gannim—*fountains of gardens*
1. Village of Judah .... Josh. 15:34
2. Border town of Issachar...............Josh. 19:21
   Assigned to Levites ....Josh. 21:29

En Gedi—*fountain of a kid*
May have been originally called
    Hazazon Tamar..................2 Chr. 20:2
Occupied by the Amorites .... Gen. 14:7
Assigned to Judah.................Josh. 15:62, 63
David's hiding place .... 1 Sam. 23:29
Noted for vineyards.................. Song 1:14

Engraving—*cutting or carving on some hard substance*
Stone set in priest's breastplate....Ex. 28:9–11, 21
Bezalel, inspired in.................Ex. 35:30–33
Of a signet .... Ex. 28:21; 39:6
Of cherubim ....1 Kin. 6:29

En Haddah—*swift fountain*
Frontier village of Issachar ....Josh. 19:17, 21

En Hakkore—*fountain of him who called*
Miraculous spring .... Judg. 15:14–19

En Hazor—*fountain of a village*
City of Naphtali ....Josh. 19:32, 37

Enjoyment—*satisfaction in something*
A. Of material things:
   Depends upon obedience.......... Deut. 7:9–15
   Withheld for disobedience ....Hag. 1:3–11
   Must not trust in................. Luke 12:16–21
   Cannot fully satisfy................. Eccl. 2:1–11
B. Of spiritual things:
   Abundant..........................1 Tim. 6:17
   Never-ending....................... Is. 58:11
   Satisfying .... Is. 55:1, 2
   Internal.........................John 7:37–39
   For God's people only ....Is. 65:22–24
   Complete in heaven .... Ps. 16:11

Enlargement—*extension in quantity or quality*
Japheth's territory .... Gen. 9:27
Israel's prosperity .... Ex. 34:24
Solomon's kingdom .... 1 Kin. 4:20–25
Solomon's wisdom .... 1 Kin. 4:29–34
Pharisaical hypocrisy .... Matt. 23:5
Spiritual: Relationship ....2 Cor. 6:11, 13
Knowledge....................... Eph. 1:15–19
Opportunity .... Is. 54:1–3

Enlightenment, spiritual
A. Source of:
   From God...........................Ps. 18:28
   Through God's Word .... Ps. 19:8
   By prayer.........................Eph. 1:18
   By God's ministers............... Acts 26:17, 18
B. Degrees of:
   Partial now...................... 1 Cor. 13:9–12
   Hindered by sin .... 1 Cor. 2:14
   Complete in heaven .... Is. 60:19

Enoch—*dedicated*
1. Son of Cain ....Gen. 4:17
2. City built by Cain ....Gen. 4:17
3. Father of Methuselah ....Gen. 5:21
   Walks with God .... Gen. 5:22
   Taken up to heaven .... Gen. 5:24
   His faith an example .... Heb. 11:5
   Prophecy of, cited.................... Jude 14, 15

Enosh—*mortal*
Grandson of Adam ....Gen. 4:25, 26
Son of Seth ....Gen. 5:6–11
Ancestor of Christ ....Luke 3:38
Genealogy of .... 1 Chr. 1:1

En Rimmon—*fount of pomegranates*
Reinhabited after the Exile .... Neh. 11:29
Same as Rimmon .... Zech. 14:10

En Rogel—*the fuller's fountain*
Fountain outside Jerusalem.........2 Sam. 17:17

On Benjamin's boundary . . . . .Josh. 18:11, 16
Seat of Adonijah's plot . . . . .1 Kin. 1:5–9

En Shemesh—*fountain of the sun*
Spring and town near Jericho . . . . Josh. 15:7

En Tappuah—*fountain of the apple tree*
Town of Ephraim . . . . Josh. 17:7, 8

Entertainment—*affording an enjoyable occasion*
A. Occasions of:
Child's weaning . . . . Gen. 21:8
Ratifying covenants. . . . . Gen. 31:54
King's coronation. . . . . .1 Kin. 1:9, 18, 19
National deliverance . . . . .Esth. 9:17–19
Marriage. . . . . Matt. 22:2
Return of loved ones . . . . Luke 15:23–25
B. Features of:
Invitations sent. . . . . .Luke 14:16
Preparations made. . . . . Matt. 22:4
Helped by servants. . . . . John 2:5
Under a leader. . . . . John 2:8, 9
Often with music . . . . .Luke 15:25
Sometimes out of control . . . . 1 Sam. 25:36
Unusual. . . . . Heb. 13:2

Enthusiasm—*a spirit of intense zeal*
Caleb's. . . . . Num. 13:30–33
Phinehas's. . . . . .Num. 25:7–13
David's . . . . .2 Sam. 6:12–22
Saul's (Paul's). .Acts 9:1, 2
Paul's . . . . Phil. 3:7–14

Enticers—*those who allure to evil*
A. Means of:
Man . . . . .Ex. 22:16
Spirit . . . . .2 Chr. 18:20
Sinners. . . . . Prov. 1:10
Lusts. . . . . James 1:14
Human wisdom . . . . 1 Cor. 2:4
Satan . . . . .Gen. 3:4, 5; Matt. 4:3, 6, 9
B. Reasons proposed:
Turn from God . . . . .Deut. 13:6–8
Obtain secrets .Judg. 16:4, 5
Defeat a king. 2 Chr. 18:4–34
Commit a sin. . . . . James 1:14

Entrails—*bowels, intestines*
Used literally:
Amasa's poured out . . . . 2 Sam. 20:10
Jehoram's came out . . . . 2 Chr. 21:14–19
Judas's gushed out . . . . Acts 1:16–18

Envy—*resentment against another's success, jealousy*
A. Characterized as:
Powerful. . . . . Prov. 27:4
Dominant in unregenerate nature. . . . . .Rom. 1:29
Of the flesh . . . . Gal. 5:19–21
Source of evil. . . . . 1 Tim. 6:4
B. The evil of, among Christians:
Hinders growth. . . . . .1 Pet. 2:1, 2
C. Examples of:
Philistines. . . . . Gen. 26:14
Joseph's brothers. . . . . Gen. 37:5, 11

Aaron and Miriam . . . . Num. 12:1, 2
Korah. . . . . Num. 16:1–3
Asaph. . . . . .Ps. 73:3, 17–20
Haman . . . . .Esth. 5:13
Chief priests. . . . . .Mark 15:10
The Jews . . . . Acts 13:45

Epaenetus
Addressed by Paul . . . . .Rom. 16:5

Epaphras
Leader of the Colossian church . . . . Col. 1:7, 8
Suffers as a prisoner in Rome . . . . Philem. 23

Epaphroditus—*lovely, charming*
Messenger from Philippi . . . . .Phil. 2:25–27
Brings a gift to Paul . . . . Phil. 4:18

Ephah—*dark one*
1. Son of Midian . . . . .Gen. 25:4
2. Concubine of Caleb. . . . . 1 Chr. 2:46
3. Son of Jahdai . . . . 1 Chr. 2:47

Ephah—*a measure*
Dry measure . . . . .Ex. 16:36
Used for measuring barley. . . . . Ruth 2:17

Ephai—*birdlike*
Netophathite. . . . . Jer. 40:8

Epher—*young deer*
1. Son of Midian . . . . .Gen. 25:4
2. Man of Judah . . . . 1 Chr. 4:17
3. Chief in Manasseh. . . . . 1 Chr. 5:23, 24

Ephes Dammim—*end of bloods*
Philistine encampment. . . . . .1 Sam. 17:1
Called Pasdammim . . . . 1 Chr. 11:13

Ephesians, the Epistle to the—*a book of the
New Testament*
Written by Paul. . . . . .Eph. 1:1
Election. . . . . .Eph. 1:4–6
Salvation by grace. . . . . Eph. 1:7, 8; 2:8
Headship of Christ. . . . . Eph. 4:15, 16

Ephesus—*a city of Asia Minor*
Site of Jewish synagogue. . . . . .Acts 18:19
Paul visits . . . . .Acts 18:18–21
Apollos taught here . . . . .Acts 18:24–26
Miracles done here. . . . . Acts 19:11–21
Demetrius stirs up riot in . . . . .Acts 19:24–29
Temple of Diana at. . . . . Acts 19:35
Elders of, addressed by Paul at
Miletus. .Acts 20:17–38
Letter sent to . . . . .Eph. 1:1
Paul sends Tychicus. . . . . Eph. 6:21
Paul leaves Timothy. . . . . .1 Tim. 1:3
One of seven churches. . . . . .Rev. 1:11

Ephlal—*judgment*
A descendant of Judah . . . . 1 Chr. 2:37

Ephod—*a vest*
1. *Worn by:*
The high priest . . . . Ex. 28:4–35
Samuel. . . . . .1 Sam. 2:18
David. . . . . .2 Sam. 6:14

WORD STUDY **EQUIP, RESTORE,** *katartizō* (kat-ar-*tid*-zoh). This verb is translated in a variety of ways in the NT. The central meanings of *katartizō* are "to put something in its former condition," "to put something in its proper condition," or "to prepare." The context determines how these meanings are best rendered into English. Thus, *katartizō* can be translated "mend" (Mark 1:19), "restore" (Gal. 6:1), "to make complete" (Heb. 13:21), or even "to prepare"—in the sense of "make" or "create" (Heb. 10:5; 11:3), or "to train fully" (Luke 6:40). (Strong's #2675)

WORD STUDY **EQUIPPING,** *katartismos* (kat-ar-tis-*moss*). This noun occurs only in Eph. 4:12 in the NT. In other literature of the period, *katartismos* is a medical technical term for the "setting of a bone," and it is sometimes used more generally to refer to "preparation." In Eph. 4:12 it is translated as "equipping," even though an equally acceptable translation would be "preparation" or "training." Compare the cognate verb *katartizō*. (Strong's #2677)

Hairy . . . . Gen. 25:25
Hunter . . . . Gen. 25:27
Isaac's favorite son . . . . Gen. 25:28
Also named Edom . . . . Gen. 25:30
Sells his birthright . . . . Gen. 25:29–34
Unable to repent . . . . Heb. 12:16, 17
Marries two women . . . . Gen. 26:34
Deprived of blessing . . . . Gen. 27:1–40
Hates his brother Jacob . . . . Gen. 27:41–45
Marries Ishmael's daughter . . . . Gen. 28:8, 9
Reconciled to Jacob . . . . Gen. 33:1–17
With Jacob, buries his father . . . . Gen. 35:29
Descendants of . . . . Gen. 36:1–43
Ancestor of Edomites . . . . Jer. 49:7, 8
Prophecy concerning . . . . Obad. 18
Not elect . . . . Rom. 9:11–13

Escape—*to flee from*
A. Physical things:
Flood . . . . Gen. 7:7, 8
City of destruction . . . . Gen. 19:15–30
Egyptian army . . . . Ex. 14:26–30
Mob . . . . Luke 4:28–30
Insane king . . . . 1 Sam. 19:9–18
Wicked queen . . . . 2 Kin. 11:1–3
Assassination . . . . Esth. 2:21–23
Hanging . . . . Esth. 5:14; 7:9
Prison . . . . Acts 5:18–20
Sinking ship . . . . Acts 27:30–44
B. Spiritual things:
Sin . . . . Gen. 39:10–12
Destruction . . . . Luke 21:36
Corruption . . . . 2 Pet. 1:4
God's wrath . . . . 1 Thess. 1:9, 10
The Great Tribulation . . . . Rev. 7:13–17

Eschatology—*teaching dealing with final destiny*
A. In Old Testament:
Judgment . . . . Is. 2:12–22
Messianic kingdom . . . . Jer. 23:4–18; 33:14–17
B. In New Testament:
Coming of Christ . . . . Matt. 24; Luke 21:5–36
Resurrection of dead . . . . 1 Cor. 15:51–58;
    1 Thess. 4:13–18
Destruction of earth . . . . 2 Pet. 3:10–13
Reign of Christ . . . . Rev. 20:4, 6

Esek—*strife*
A well in Gerar . . . . Gen. 26:20

Esh-Baal—*man of Baal*
Son of Saul . . . . 1 Chr. 8:33

Eshban—*wise man*
Son of Dishon . . . . Gen. 36:26

Eshcol—*cluster of grapes*
1. Brother of Aner and Mamre . . . . Gen. 14:13, 24
2. Valley near Hebron . . . . Num. 13:22–27; Deut. 1:24

Eshean—*support*
City of Judah . . . . Josh. 15:52

Eshek—*oppression*
Descendant of Saul . . . . 1 Chr. 8:39

Eshtaol—*a way*
Town of Judah . . . . Josh. 15:20, 33
Assigned to Danites . . . . Josh. 19:40, 41
Near Samson's home and burial site . . . Judg. 16:31

Eshtaolites
Inhabitants of Eshtaol . . . . 1 Chr. 2:53

Eshtemoa, Eshtemoh—*obedience*
Town of Judah . . . . Josh. 15:20, 50
Assigned to Levites . . . . Josh. 21:14
David sends spoils to . . . . 1 Sam. 30:26, 28

Eshton—*restful*
Man of Judah . . . . 1 Chr. 4:1–12

Esli—*reserved*
Ancestor of Christ . . . . Luke 3:25

Establish—*a permanent condition*
A. Of earthly things:
Kingdom . . . . 2 Chr. 17:5
Festival . . . . Esth. 9:21
B. Of spiritual things:
Messiah's kingdom . . . . 2 Sam. 7:13
God's Word . . . . Ps. 119:38
Our:
Hearts . . . . 1 Thess. 3:13
Faith . . . . Col. 2:7
Works . . . . 2 Thess. 2:17
Lives . . . . 1 Pet. 5:10
C. Accomplished by:
God . . . . 2 Cor. 1:21, 22

Esther—*star*
Daughter of Abihail . . . . Esth. 2:15
Mordecai's cousin . . . . Esth. 2:7, 15
Selected for harem . . . . Esth. 2:7–16
Chosen queen . . . . Esth. 2:17, 18
Seeks to help Mordecai . . . . Esth. 4:4–6
Told of Haman's plot . . . . Esth. 4:7–9
Sends message to Mordecai . . . . Esth. 4:10–12
Told to act . . . . Esth. 4:13, 14
Seeks Mordecai's aid . . . . Esth. 4:15–17
Appears before Ahasuerus . . . . Esth. 5:1–5
Invites Ahasuerus to banquet . . . . Esth. 5:4–8
Reveals Haman's plot . . . . Esth. 7:1–7
Given Haman's house . . . . Esth. 8:1, 2
New decree allows Jews to fight . . . . . Esth. 8:3–11
Makes further request . . . . Esth. 9:12, 13
With Mordecai, institutes Purim . . . Esth. 9:29–32

Esther, Book of—*a book of the Old Testament*

Estrangement from God
Caused by:
Adam's sin . . . . Gen. 3:8–11, 24
Personal sin . . . . Ps. 51:9–12
National sin . . . . Jer. 2:14–17

Etam—*Wild beasts' lair*
1. Village of Simeon . . . . 1 Chr. 4:32
2. Rock where Samson took refuge . . . . . Judg. 15:8–19
3. Town of Judah . . . . 2 Chr. 11:6

Eternal, everlasting—*without end*
A. Applied to Trinity:
  God .... Ps. 90:2
  Christ .... Prov. 8:23
  Holy Spirit .... Heb. 9:14
B. Applied to God's attributes:
  Home .... Eccl. 12:5
  Power .... Rom. 1:20
  Covenant .... Is. 55:3
  Gospel .... Rev. 14:6
  Counsels .... Eph. 3:10, 11
  Righteousness .... Ps. 119:142, 144
  Kingdom .... Ps. 145:13
  Truth .... Ps. 100:5
  Love .... Jer. 31:3
  Father .... Is. 9:6
C. Applied to the believer:
  Comfort .... 2 Thess. 2:16
  Life .... John 3:15
  Redemption .... Heb. 9:12
  Salvation .... Heb. 5:9
  Inheritance .... Heb. 9:15
  Glory .... 1 Pet. 5:10
  Kingdom .... 2 Pet. 1:11
  Reward .... John 4:36
  Name .... Is. 56:5
  Glory .... 2 Tim. 2:10
  Light .... Is. 60:19, 20
  Joy .... Is. 51:11
  Dwellings .... Luke 16:9
  Purpose .... Eph. 3:11
D. Applied to the wicked:
  Condemnation .... Mark 3:29
  Judgment .... Heb. 6:2
  Punishment .... Matt. 25:46
  Destruction .... 2 Thess. 1:9
  Contempt .... Dan. 12:2
  Chains .... Jude 6
  Fire .... Matt. 25:41
  Sin .... Mark 3:29

Eternity—*time without end mentioned once*
  God's habitation .... Is. 57:15

Etham—*sea bound*
  Israel's encampment .... Ex. 13:20

Ethan—*perpetuity*
1. One noted for wisdom .... 1 Kin. 4:31
2. Levite, son of Kishi .... 1 Chr. 6:44
3. Ancestor of Asaph .... 1 Chr. 6:42, 43

Ethanim—*incessant rains*
  Seventh month in the Hebrew year ..... 1 Kin. 8:2

Ethbaal—*with Baal*
  Father of Jezebel .... 1 Kin. 16:31

Ether—*plenty*
  Town of Judah .... Josh. 15:42

Ethics—*a system setting forth standards of right conduct*
  Perversion of .... Rom. 1:19–32
  Law of .... Rom. 2:14–16
  Summary of Christian .... Rom. 12:1–21

Ethiopia (Cush)—*burnt face*
  Country south of Egypt .... Ezek. 29:10
  Home of the sons of Ham .... Gen. 10:6
  Famous for minerals .... Job 28:19
  Merchandise of .... Is. 45:14
  Wealth of .... Is. 43:3
  Militarily strong .... 2 Chr. 12:2, 3
  Anguished people .... Ezek. 30:4–9
  Defeated by Asa .... 2 Chr. 14:9–15
  Subdued .... Dan. 11:43
  Prophecies against .... Is. 20:1–6
  Hopeful promise .... Ps. 68:31

Ethiopians—*descendants of Cush*
  Skin of, unchangeable .... Jer. 13:23
  Moses' marriage to .... Num. 12:1
  Ebed-Melech saves Jeremiah .... Jer. 38:7
  Eunuch converted .... Acts 8:26–40

Eth Kazin—*time of a judge*
  On border of Zebulun .... Josh. 19:13, 16

Ethnan—*hire*
  Judahite .... 1 Chr. 4:5–7

Ethni—*liberal*
  Levite .... 1 Chr. 6:41

Eubulus—*prudent*
  Christian at Rome .... 2 Tim. 4:21

Eucharist (see Lord's Supper)

Eunice—*blessed with victory*
  Mother of Timothy .... 2 Tim. 1:5

Eunuch—*an officer or official, emasculated*
A. Rules concerning:
  Excluded from congregation .... Deut. 23:1
  Given promise .... Is. 56:3–5
B. Duties of:
  Keeper of harem .... Esth. 2:3, 14
  Attendant .... Dan. 1:3, 7, 10, 11
  Treasurer .... Acts 8:27
  Seven, serving Ahasuerus .... Esth. 1:10, 15
C. The Ethiopian:
  Philip preaches to .... Acts 8:27–35
  Is baptized .... Acts 8:36–38

Euodia—*good journey*
  Christian woman at Philippi .... Phil. 4:2

Euphrates—*that which makes fruitful*
  River of Eden .... Gen. 2:14
  Assyria bounded by .... 2 Kin. 23:29
  Babylon on .... Jer. 51:13, 36
  Boundary of Promised Land .... Gen. 15:18;
     1 Kin. 4:21, 24
  Scene of battle .... Jer. 46:2, 6, 10
  Exiled Jews weep there .... Ps. 137:1
  Angels bound there .... Rev. 9:14
  Waters of will dry up .... Rev. 16:12

Euroclydon—*east wind*
  Violent wind .... Acts 27:14

Eutychus—*fortunate*
Sleeps during Paul's sermon .... Acts 20:9
Restored to life .... Acts 20:12

Evangelism—*declaring gospel to the unregenerate*
A. Scope:
  To all nations................. Matt. 28:19, 20;
    Mark 16:15
  House to house .... Acts 5:42
  Always................................1 Pet. 3:15
  As ambassadors................. 2 Cor. 5:18–20
B. Source:
  Jesus Christ .... Gal. 1:6–12
  The Father ....John 6:44, 65
  The Spirit ....Acts 1:8

Evangelist—*one who proclaims the Good News*
Distinct ministry .... Eph. 4:11
Applied to Philip ....Acts 21:8
Timothy works as.................... 2 Tim. 4:5

Eve—*life*
Created in God's image............... Gen. 1:27
Made from Adam's rib ....Gen. 2:18–22
Named by Adam...................... Gen. 3:20
Mother of all living .... Gen. 3:20
Deceived by Satan ....Gen. 3:1–24
Fell into sin...................... 1 Tim. 2:13, 14
Cursed............................. Gen. 3:16
Evicted from Garden.................. Gen. 3:24
Names first son Cain.................. Gen. 4:1
Second son is Abel .... Gen. 4:2
Bears Seth........................... Gen. 4:25

Evening—*last hours of sunlight*
Labor ceases..............Judg. 19:16; Ruth 2:17
Workers paid....................... Deut. 24:15
Ritual impurity ends .. Lev. 11:24–28; Num. 19:19
Meditation...........................Gen. 24:63
Prayer .... Matt. 14:15, 23
Eating .... Luke 24:29, 30
Sacrifice ....Ex. 29:38–42; Num. 28:3–8

Evening sacrifice—*part of Israelite worship*
Ritual described ....Ex. 29:38–42
Part of continual offering..........Num. 28:3–8

Events, Biblical, classified
A. Originating, originating other events:
  Creation .... Gen. 1
  Fall of man..........................Rom. 5:12
B. Epochal, introducing new period:
  Flood............................... Gen. 6–8
  Giving of Law at Sinai............... Ex. 20:1–17
  The death of Christ.............Matt. 27:50, 51;
    Heb. 9
C. Typical, foreshadowing some New Testament event:
  The Passover—Christ as Lamb ....Ex. 12;
    John 1:35–37; 1 Cor. 5:7, 8
  Serpent on pole—Christ on the cross...Num. 8:10;
    John 3:14, 15
  Jonah and great fish—Christ's death and
    resurrection.........Jon. 1; 2; Matt. 12:38–41

D. Prophetic, prophesying future events:
  Return from exile..... 2 Chr. 36:22, 23; Jer. 29:10
  Destruction of Jerusalem........ Luke 19:41–44;
    21:20–24
E. Redemptive, connected with humankind's salvation:
  Advent of Christ.......... Luke 2:11; Gal. 4:4, 5
  Death of Christ...... Luke 24:44–47; 1 Tim. 1:15
F. Unique, those without parallel:
  Creation ....Gen. 1
  Virgin birth .... Matt. 1:18–25; Luke 1:30–37
G. Miraculous, those produced by supernatural
    means:
  Plagues on Egypt .... Ex. 7–12
  Crossing Red Sea .... Ex. 14; 15
  Fall of Jericho ....Josh. 6
  Sun's standing still................Josh. 10:12–14
H. Judgmental, those judging people for sins:
  Flood ....2 Pet. 2:5
  Sodom and Gomorrah .... Gen. 19; 2 Pet. 2:6
  Killing of Israelites................ Ex. 32:25–35;
    Num. 25:1–9
I. Transforming, those producing a change:
  Christ's transfiguration .... Matt. 17:1–8
  Conversion of Paul........ Acts 9; 1 Tim. 1:12–14
  Believer's regeneration ....John 3:1–8; 2 Cor. 5:17
J. Providential, those manifesting God's providence:
  Baby's cry .... Ex. 2:5–10
  Joseph's being sold into Egypt.....Gen. 37:26–28;
    45:1–9
  King's sleepless night...............Esth. 6:1–10
K. Confirmatory, those confirming some promise:
  Rainbow ....Gen. 9:11–17
  Worship at Sinai........................Ex. 3:12
  Aaron's rod...................... Num. 17:1–11
  Thunder and rain............... 1 Sam. 12:16–18
  Sun's shadow moved backward....2 Kin. 20:8–11;
    Is. 38:1–8
L. Promissory, those fulfilling some promise:
  Pentecost .... Joel 2:28–32; Acts 2
  Spirit's coming........Luke 24:49; Acts 1:4, 5, 8;
    2:1–4
  Possession of land................ Gen. 15:18–21;
    Josh. 24:3, 11–19
M. Eschatological, those connected with Christ's return:
  Doom of the Antichrist ....2 Thess. 2:1–12
  Resurrection and translation..... 1 Cor. 15:35–38,
    42; 1 Thess. 4:13–18
  Resurrection and judgment...... Matt. 25:31–46;
    Acts 17:31; Rev. 20:11–15
  Destruction of the world .... 2 Pet. 3:7–15

WORD STUDY   **EVER,** *'ad (awd).* Translated "perpetuity" or "forever," the noun *'ad* has a variety of nuances. It can refer to past time and take on the meaning of ancient, as in the ancient mountains of Hab. 3:6. The word can also mean the opposite, a future time or forever as in Job 19:24 and Ps. 21:6. A slight variation of "forever" is a meaning of continuous existence. Under this translation come the continued existence of nations and of anger. Both God and divine promises are also said to exist forever (1 Chr. 28:9; Ps. 111:3; Is. 57:15). (Strong's #5703)

Evi—*desirous*
   King of Midian .... Num. 31:8
   Land of, assigned to Reuben ...... Josh. 13:15, 21

Evidence—*ground for belief*
A. Based upon:
   Testimony of witnesses .... Matt. 18:16
   Personal testimony .... Acts 26:1–27
   Fulfilled prophecy .... Matt. 1:22, 23
   Supernatural testimony .... Matt. 3:17
   New life .... 1 John 3:14
B. Kinds of:
   Circumstantial .... Gen. 39:7–19
   False .... Matt. 26:59–61
   Fabricated .... Gen. 37:29–33
   Confirmed .... Heb. 2:3, 4
   Satanic .... 2 Thess. 2:9, 10
   Indisputable .... 1 Cor. 15:1–19
C. Need of:
   Confirm weak faith .... Luke 7:19, 22
   Remove doubt .... John 20:24–29
   Refute mockers .... 2 Pet. 3:3–7
   Attest a messenger of God .... Ex. 8:18, 19
   Produce faith .... John 20:30, 31

> **WORD STUDY**   **EVIL,** *ra'* (*raw*). The adjective *ra'* is usually translated as "bad" or "evil." It can mean "bad" as in stating that something is malignant, including poisonous herbs, boils, disease, arrows, and wild beasts. It can also mean "that which is unpleasant, giving pain or unhappiness." In this sense are mentioned evil days or evil reports (Ex. 33:4). Similarly, it may describe some individual thing that is bad, while not all of its kind are bad, such as bad water or figs. The word is also used for a thing that has little value. *Ra'* most commonly describes someone or something that is ethically bad or wicked, such as an evil man or evil deeds. The same spelling in Hebrew can also be translated as the noun form of the word meaning "evil," "distress," or "injury." (Strong's #7451)

Evil—*that which is morally injurious*
A. Origin of:
   Begins with Satan .... Is. 14:12–14
   Enters world .... Rom. 5:12
   Comes from the heart .... Matt. 15:18, 19
   Inflamed by lust .... James 1:14
B. Applied to:
   People .... Matt. 12:35
   Heart .... Jer. 17:9
   Imaginations .... Gen. 6:5
   Generation .... Matt. 12:39
   Age .... Gal. 1:4
   Our days .... Eph. 5:16
   Conscience .... Heb. 10:22
   Spirits .... Matt. 12:45

C. Satan as "the evil one":
   Lord safeguards against .... John 17:15
D. The Christian should guard against, evil:
   Heart of unbelief .... Heb. 3:12
   Thoughts .... James 2:4
   Boastings .... James 4:16
   Things .... Rom. 12:9
   Deeds .... 2 John 9–11
   Appearance .... 1 Thess. 5:22

Evil—*that which is physically harmful: floods,*
     earthquakes, etc.
   Part of man's curse .... Gen. 3:17–19
   Men cry out against .... Rev. 9:18–21
   Can be misinterpreted .... Luke 13:1–3
   Foreseen by prudent .... Prov. 22:3
   Will continue to the end .... Matt. 24:6–8, 14
   Believers share in .... 2 Cor. 12:7–10
   To be borne patiently ..... Job 2:7–10; James 5:11
   Prospects of relief from .... Rom. 8:18–39
   Relieved now by faith .... Heb. 3:17–19
   None in heaven .... Rev. 7:14–17

Evil companions (see Association)

Evildoers—*workers of evil*
   Christians wrongly called .... 1 Pet. 2:12
   Christians should not be .... 1 Pet. 4:15
   Christians cry against .... Ps. 119:115
   Punished by magistrates .... Rom. 13:1–4
   End of, certain .... Ps. 34:16

Evil eye
   Descriptive of one's inner being .... Mark 7:21, 22
   Shown in attitudes .... Matt. 20:15

Evil-Merodach—*man of Marduk*
   Babylonian king (562–560 B.C.); succeed
     Nebuchadnezzar .... 2 Kin. 25:27–30

Evil-mindedness
   Full of envy .... Rom. 1:29

Evil speaking
A. The evil of:
   Sign of unregeneracy .... Ps. 10:7
   Aimed at righteous .... Ps. 64:2–5
   Defiles the whole body .... James 3:5–10
   Disrupts fellowship .... 3 John 9–11
   Severely condemned .... James 4:11
   Punished .... 1 Cor. 6:9, 10
B. Not to be confused with:
   Denunciation of vice .... Titus 1:12, 13
   Description of sinners .... Acts 13:9, 10
   Defense of the faith .... Jude 4, 8–16

Evil spirits—*demons*
   Sent upon King Saul .... 1 Sam. 16:14
   Ahab prompted to evil by .... 1 Kin. 22:1–23
   To be cast out by believers in Jesus'
     name .... Mark 16:17
   Cast out by Jesus .... Luke 7:21
   Cast out by Paul .... Acts 19:11, 12

Evolution—*development of life from lower to higher forms*
A. Conflicts with:
    God's description . . . . Gen. 1:26, 27; 2:21–25
    Moses' record. . . . . .Ex. 20:11; Deut. 4:32
B. Not accepted by:
    Jesus . . . . .Matt. 19:4–6; Rom. 5:12–19
    Paul . . . . 1 Cor. 15:22, 45; 1 Tim. 2:13, 14

Exaltation—*the state of being raised up*
A. Of evil people:
    Originates in Satan . . . . .Luke 4:5, 6
    Defies God. 2 Kin. 18:28–35
    Perverts religion . . . . .Dan. 11:36, 37
    Brings downfall. . . . . Esth. 6:6–14; 7:9
    Merits punishment. . . . . 1 Kin. 16:1–4
    Displayed by Herod . . . . .Acts 12:21–23
    Seen in the Antichrist . . . . 2 Thess. 2:4, 9
B. Of good men:
    Principle of. . . . . Matt. 23:12
    Follows humility. .1 Pet. 5:6
    Restrictions upon . . . . 2 Cor. 10:5
    Brings glory . . . . James 1:9
    False, brings sorrow . . . . .1 Cor. 4:6–14
    Final, in heaven. .Rev. 22:5
C. Of Christ:
    Promised. . . . . .Ps. 2:8, 9
    Predicted by Christ . . . . Matt. 26:64
    The Ascension. . . . . Acts 2:33, 34
    Seen by Stephen . . . . Acts 7:55, 56
    Taught by the apostles . . . . .Eph. 1:20–22
    Set forth as a reward . . . . Phil. 2:9–11
    Introduces priestly intercession . . . . Heb. 1:3

WORD STUDY   **EXALTED, TO BE,** *rum* (*room*). The verb *rum* can be translated as "be high," "be exalted," or "rise." To be high refers to a location. A throne, a hill, trees, or human stature can all be in a high position or be set on high (Job 22:12; Ps. 61:2). The same word can also mean something is raised or lifted up, such as a highway or voice. This usage especially describes a hand raised as a symbol of might (Deut. 32:27). A person, such as a king, can be exalted (Num. 24:7); but often the one being exalted is God. In this case humans are showing His exaltation rather than raising Him up (Ps. 18:46; Is. 30:18). A final and only negative use of the term is a sign of haughtiness in humans as in Prov. 6:17, which speaks of "a proud look." (Strong's #7311)

Examination of others
    Of Jesus . . . . .Luke 23:13, 14
    Of Peter. . . . . Acts 4:8, 9
    Of Paul . . . . .Acts 22:24, 25

Examination of self
    Sought by David . . . . .Ps. 26:2
    Must precede Lord's Supper . . . . 1 Cor. 11:28
    Necessary for real faith. . . . . 2 Cor. 13:5

Example—*a pattern*
A. Purposes of:
    Set forth sin's punishment . . . . .2 Pet. 2:6

    Show unbelief's consequences. . . . . Heb. 4:11
    Restrain from evil . . . . 1 Cor. 10:6–11
    Illustrate humility . . . . . . John 13:14, 15; 1 Pet. 3:5
    Exemplify patience . . . . James 5:10, 11;
        1 Pet. 2:20–22
    Portray Christian conduct . . . . Phil. 3:17
B. Of evil people:
    Covetousness—Achan . . . . .Josh. 7:20, 21
    Immorality—Eli's sons . . . . .1 Sam. 2:22–25
    Rebellion—Saul . . . . 1 Sam. 15:17–23
    Folly—Nabal . . . . .1 Sam. 25:25–37
    Idolatry—Jeroboam. . . . . 1 Kin. 12:26–33
    Vindictiveness—Herodias. . . . . . .Matt. 14:3, 6–11
C. Of good men:
    Humility—Moses. . . . . Num. 12:3
    Holy zeal—Phinehas. . . . . .Num. 25:7–13
    Faith—Caleb. . . . . .Josh. 14:6–15
    Fidelity—Joshua. . . . . .Josh. 24:15–25
    Loyalty—Ruth . . . . .Ruth 1:14–17
    Courage—David. . . . . 1 Sam. 17:32–37
    Holy life—Daniel. . . . . Ezek. 14:14, 20
    Servanthood—Mary . . . . .John 12:3, 7, 8
    Perseverance—Job . . . . .James 5:10, 11
    Christian living—Paul . . . . Phil. 3:17

Example of Christ, the
A. Virtues illustrated by:
    Compassion . . . . Matt. 9:36
    Gentleness . . . . Matt. 11:29
    Self-denial . . . . Matt. 16:24
    Love . . . . .John 13:34
    Obedience . . . . John 15:10
    Benevolence . . . . 2 Cor. 8:7, 9
    Humility. . . . . .Phil. 2:5–8
    Forgiveness. . . . . .Col. 3:13
    Suffering wrongfully . . . . 1 Pet. 2:21–23
    Purity. . . . . .1 John 3:3
B. The Christian approach to:
    Progressive . . . . 2 Cor. 3:18
    Instructive .Eph. 4:20–24
    Imitative . . . . 1 Pet. 2:21–23
    Perfective . . . . .Rom. 8:29

WORD STUDY   **EXCESS, EXCELLENCE,** *huperbolē* (hoop-er-bol-*ay*). This noun denotes something that exceeds or surpasses the ordinary, hence its meaning "excess" or "extraordinary." It usually occurs in phrases to indicate the "extraordinary" quality or character of something (e.g., the "abundance" of revelation in 2 Cor. 12:7, or the "extraordinary" quality of power in 4:7). *Huperbolē* and the preposition *kata* form an idiomatic expression, which means "to an extraordinary degree," usually translated as "beyond measure" or "exceedingly" (Rom. 7:13; 2 Cor. 1:8; Gal. 1:13). (Strong's #5236)

Excitement—*something that stirs us emotionally*
A. Causes of:
    Great sin . . . . Ex. 32:17–20

Great victory . . . . 1 Sam. 17:52
God's power . . . . 1 Kin. 18:22–41
King's coronation . . . . 2 Kin. 11:12–16
Human destruction . . . . Esth. 9:1–19
Handwriting on the wall . . . . Dan. 5:5–9
Miracle . . . . Acts 19:13–20

B. Time of:

The giving of the Law . . . . Heb. 12:18–21
Christ's death . . . . Matt. 27:51–54
Pentecost . . . . Acts 2:1–47
Christ's return . . . . Luke 21:25–28

Exclusiveness—*setting boundaries against others*

A. Christianity's, only one:

Door . . . . John 10:1, 7, 9
Way . . . . John 14:6
Salvation . . . . Acts 4:12

B. The Bible's, only book:

Inspired . . . . 1 Tim. 3:16
Revealing God . . . . Heb. 1:1
Written to save humankind . . . . John 20:30, 31
Containing true prophecies . . . . John 5:45–47

Excommunication—*expulsion from membership in a body*

A. Separation from:

Kingship . . . . 1 Sam. 16:1
Foreigners . . . . Neh. 13:1–3
Priesthood . . . . Neh. 13:27, 28

B. Practice of:

To intimidate people . . . . John 9:19–23
Against true Christians . . . . John 16:1, 2
Against false teachers . . . . 2 John 10, 11

C. Method of:

Described . . . . Matt. 18:15–17
Illustrated . . . . 1 Cor. 5:1–13
Perverted . . . . 3 John 9, 10

Excuse—*an invalid reason for neglect of duty*

A. Nature of, blaming:

Wife . . . . Gen. 3:12
The people . . . . 1 Sam. 15:20, 21
God's mercy . . . . Jon. 4:1–4
God's providence . . . . Num. 14:1–23

B. Invalidity of:

Shown to Moses . . . . Ex. 3:10–12
Proved to Gideon . . . . Judg. 6:36–40
Made plain to Esther . . . . Esth. 4:13–17
Illustrated by Christ . . . . Luke 14:16–24
Relayed to the inhabitants
    of Hades . . . . Luke 16:27–31
Made evident to Thomas . . . . John 20:24–28

Exhortation—*encouraging others to commendable conduct*

A. Objects of:

Call to repentance . . . . Luke 3:17, 18
Continue in the faith . . . . Acts 14:22
Convict contradictors . . . . Titus 1:9
Warn the unruly . . . . 1 Thess. 5:14
Encourage soberness . . . . Titus 3:1
Strengthen godliness . . . . 1 Thess. 4:1–6
Stir up liberality . . . . 2 Cor. 9:5–7

B. Office of:

Commended . . . . Rom. 12:8
Part of the ministry . . . . Titus 2:15
Needed before times of hardening . . . 2 Tim. 4:2–5

C. Nature of:

Daily duty . . . . Heb. 3:13
For holiness . . . . 1 Thess. 2:3, 4
Worthy of reception . . . . Heb. 13:22
Belongs to all . . . . Heb. 10:25
Special need of . . . . Jude 3, 4

Exile—*banished from one's native land; captive*

Chemosh . . . . Jer. 48:7
Christ . . . . Matt. 2:13–15
David . . . . 1 Sam. 21:10–15
Israel—Ten Tribes . . . . Amos 7:11
Jeconiah . . . . Jer. 27:20
Jehoiachin . . . . 2 Kin. 24:15
Jeremiah . . . . Jer. 43:4–7
Jeroboam . . . . 1 Kin. 11:40
John . . . . Rev. 1:9
Judah . . . . 2 Kin. 25:21
Nebuchadnezzar . . . . Jer. 29:1
Syrians . . . . Amos 1:5

  See Captivity

Exodus, the—*a departure*

Leave Egypt . . . . Ex. 12:31–42
Cross Red Sea . . . . Ex. 14:1–31
Bitter water sweetened . . . . Ex. 15:22–26
Manna in wilderness . . . . Ex. 16:1–36
Water from a rock . . . . Ex. 17:1–7
Defeat of Amalek . . . . Ex. 17:8–16
At Sinai . . . . Ex. 19:1–25
Depart Sinai . . . . Num. 10:33, 34
Lord sends quail . . . . Num. 11:1–35
Twelve spies . . . . Num. 13:1–33
Rebellion at Kadesh . . . . Num. 14:1–45
Korah's rebellion . . . . Num. 16:1–34
Aaron's rod . . . . Num. 17:1–13
Moses' sin . . . . Num. 20:2–13
Fiery serpents . . . . Num. 21:4–9
Balak and Balaam . . . . Num. 22:1–24:25
Midianites conquered . . . . Num. 31:1–24
Death of Moses . . . . Deut. 34:1–8
Accession of Joshua . . . . Deut. 34:9

Exodus, Book of—*a book of the Old Testament*

Escape from Egypt . . . . Ex. 12:31–42
The Law . . . . Ex. 20:1–17
The tabernacle and priesthood . . . Ex. 24:12–31:18

Exorcists—*those who use oaths to dispel evil spirits*

Paul encounters . . . . Acts 19:13, 19

Expanse—*firmament; vault*

Created by God . . . . Gen. 1:8
Stars placed in . . . . Gen. 1:14, 17
Compared to a tent curtain . . . . Ps. 104:2
Expressive of God's glory . . . . Ps. 19:1
Saints compared to . . . . Dan. 12:3

Expectation—*looking forward*
Conquest.........................Num. 14:1–24
Victory ....Josh. 7:4–13
Relief............................1 Kin. 12:4–15
Impending doom ....2 Kin. 23:25–27
Elevation........................ Esth. 6:6–14
The wicked.......................Prov. 10:28
Righteous...........................Ps. 62:5
Death...........................Acts 28:3–6

Expediency—*a method of justifying an act*
To fulfill God's plan .... John 11:50
To avoid offense ....1 Cor. 8:8–13
To save others .... 1 Cor. 9:19–23
To accomplish a task .... 2 Cor. 8:10–12
Illustrations .... Acts 16:3

Expense—*the cost involved*
Royalty, foretold................. 1 Sam. 8:11–18
Royalty, realized................. 1 Kin. 4:22, 23
Of soul's salvation ....Mark 8:34–38

Experiment—*a test designed to prove something*
Jacob .... Gen. 30:37–43
Aaron's sons.......................Lev. 10:1–3
Philistines....................... 1 Sam. 6:1–18
Daniel ....Dan. 1:11–16
God's goodness....................Mal. 3:10–12

Expiation—*atonement*
Under Law ....Lev. 14:11–20; 16:11–28
Prophecy of Isaiah .... Is. 53:1–12
Fulfilled in Christ....Acts 8:27–39; 1 Pet. 2:21–25

Explanation—*making simple and plain*
Of a condition................... Luke 16:25–31
Of a phenomenon.................. Acts 2:1–21
Of a decision .... Acts 15:15–31

Expulsion—*driving out by force*
From:
Eden........................... Gen. 3:22–24
The priesthood .... Neh. 13:27–29
A city .... Luke 4:16–29
By persecution.................... Acts 13:50, 51

Extortion—*money obtained by force or threat*
Innocency from, pretended .... Matt. 23:25
Fellowship with, forbidden ....1 Cor. 5:10, 11
Sin of, proscribed ....Luke 3:13, 14
Examples of .... Gen. 47:13–26

Extremity—*the greatest degree of something*
Human faith ....Gen. 22:1–3
Grief............................ 2 Sam. 18:33
Pride .... Is. 14:13, 14
Pain ....Matt. 27:46–50
Degradation..................... Luke 15:13–16
Torments .... Luke 16:23, 24
Human endurance.................2 Cor. 1:8–10

Eye—*the organ of sight*
A. Affected by:
Age............................. Gen. 27:1
Wine .... Gen. 49:12

Sorrow..............................Job 17:7
Disease ....Lev. 26:16
Grief............................... Ps. 6:7
Light .... Acts 22:11
B. Of God, figurative of:
Omniscience ....2 Chr. 16:9
Holiness .... Hab. 1:13
Guidance .... Ps. 32:8
Protection......................... Ps. 33:18
C. Of human, figurative of:
Revealed knowledge .... Num. 24:3
Lawlessness ....Judg. 17:6
Jealousy......................... 1 Sam. 18:9
Understanding .... Ps. 19:8
Agreement .... Is. 52:8
Great sorrow ....Jer. 9:1
Retaliation .... Matt. 5:38
The essential nature .... Matt. 6:22, 23
Moral state .... Matt. 7:3–5
Spiritual inability................... Matt. 13:15
Spiritual dullness ....Mark 8:17, 18
Future glory...................... 1 Cor. 2:9
Enlightenment ....Eph. 1:18
Unworthy service .... Eph. 6:6
Worldliness ....1 John 2:16
Evil desires.........................2 Pet. 2:14
D. Prophecies concerning:
Shall see the Redeemer ....Job 19:25–27
Gentiles shall see .... Is. 42:6, 7
Blind shall see .... Is. 29:18
Will see the King .... Is. 33:17
Will see Jesus.....................Rev. 1:7
Tears of, shall be wiped away...........Rev. 7:17

Eyebrows—*the arch of hair over the eyes*
Of lepers, shaved off ....Lev. 14:2, 9

Eye salve—*an ointment*
Christ mentions ....Rev. 3:18

Eyeservice—*service performed only when watched by*
another
Highly obnoxious...................... Eph. 6:6

Eyewitness—*a firsthand observer*
Consulted by Luke................... Luke 1:1, 2
Of Christ's majesty ....2 Pet. 1:16

Ezbai—*shining*
Naarai's father.......................1 Chr. 11:37

Ezbon—*bright*
1. Son of Gad......................... Gen. 46:16
2. Benjamite..........................1 Chr. 7:7

Ezekiel—*God strengthens*
A. Life of:
Priest; son of Buzi.....................Ezek. 1:3
Carried captive to Babylon .... Ezek. 1:1–3
Lived among exiles................ Ezek. 3:15–17
His wife died .... Ezek. 24:18
Persecuted ....Ezek. 3:25
Often consulted ....Ezek. 8:1
Prophetic minister .... Ezek. 3:17–21

B. Visions of:

Ezra, Book of—*a book of the Old Testament*

God's glory........................ Ezek. 1:4–28

Return from exile............ Ezra 1:1–2:70

Abominations .... Ezek. 8:5–18

Rebuilding the temple............ Ezra 3:1–6:22

Valley of dry bones............... Ezek. 37:1–14

Celebrated Passover............ Ezra 7:19–22

Messianic times .... Ezek. 40–48

Reformation.................... Ezra 9:1–10:44

River of life .... Ezek. 47:1–5

Ezrahite—*belonging to Ezrach*

C. Methods employed by:

Family name of Ethan and Heman .... 1 Kin. 4:31

Muteness.......................... Ezek. 3:26

Ezri—*my help*

Illustrates siege of Jerusalem........ Ezek. 4:1–3

David's farm overseer .... 1 Chr. 27:26

Lay on left side 390 days............ Ezek. 4:4, 5

Lay on right side 40 days ....Ezek. 4:6

Shaves himself..................... Ezek. 5:1–4

Removes belongings .... Ezek. 12:3–16

F

Uses boiling pot .... Ezek. 24:1–14

Does not mourn for wife ....Ezek. 24:16–27

Fable—*a fictitious story*

Uses parables..................... Ezek. 17:2–10

A. Form of allegory:

The trees.........................Judg. 9:7–15

Ezekiel, Book of—*a Book of the Old Testament*

The thistle .... 2 Kin. 14:9

Prophecies against Israel .... Ezek. 1:1–24:27

B. Form of fiction, contrary to:

Prophecies against the nations... Ezek. 25:1–32:32

Edification...........................1 Tim. 1:4

Prophecies of restoration .... Ezek. 33:1–39:29

Godliness .... 1 Tim. 4:6, 7

The messianic kingdom .... Ezek. 40:1–48:35

Truth................................ 2 Tim. 4:4

Ezel—*departure*

Facts................................2 Pet. 1:16

David's hiding place .... 1 Sam. 20:19

Face—*front part of head*

Ezem—*bone*

A. Acts performed on:

Village of Judah ....Josh. 15:29

Spitting on .... Deut. 25:9

Assigned to Simeon .... Josh. 19:3

Disfiguring of ....Matt. 6:16

Painting of ....2 Kin. 9:30

Ezer—*help*

Hitting .... 2 Cor. 11:20

1. Horite tribe .... 1 Chr. 1:38

B. Acts indicated by:

Son of Seir .... Gen. 36:21

Falling on—worship .... Gen. 17:3

2. Ephraimite........................ 1 Chr. 7:21

Covering of—mourning .... 2 Sam. 19:4

3. Judahite .... 1 Chr. 4:1, 4

Hiding of—disapproval .... Deut. 31:17, 18

4. Gadite warrior .... 1 Chr. 12:9

Turning away of—rejection ....2 Chr. 30:9

5. Son of Jeshua.......................Neh. 3:19

Setting of—determination.......... 2 Kin. 12:17

6. Postexilic priest .... Neh. 12:42

Face of the Lord

Ezion Geber—*backbone of a giant*

A. Toward the righteous:

Town on the Red Sea.................1 Kin. 9:26

Shine on .... Num. 6:25

Israelite encampment .... Num. 33:35

Do not hide ....Ps. 102:2

Seaport of Israel's navy..............1 Kin. 22:48

Hide from our sins..................... Ps. 51:9

See Elath

Shall see.............................Rev. 22:4

B. Toward the wicked:

Eznite—*spear; to be sharp*

Is against............................Ps. 34:16

Adino, the warrior of David .... 2 Sam. 23:8

Set against ....Jer. 21:10

Called Tachmonite .... 2 Sam. 23:8

They hide from ....Rev. 6:16

Called Hachmonite .... 1 Chr. 11:11

Failure

Ezra—*help*

A. Causes of:

1. Postexilic priest ....Neh. 12:1, 7

Actions contrary to God's will ....Gen. 11:3–8

Called Azariah .... Neh. 10:2

Disobedience.................. Num. 14:40–45

2. Scribe, priest and reformer of postexilic

Sin.................................Josh. 7:3–12

times ....Ezra 7:1–6

Lack of prayer .... Matt. 17:15–20; Mark 9:24–29

Commissioned by Artaxerxes........Ezra 7:6–28

Not counting the cost .... Luke 14:28–32

Takes exiles with him .... Ezra 8:1–20

Unbelief .... Heb. 4:6

Proclaims a fast..................... Ezra 8:21–23

B. Examples of:

Commits treasures to the priests ....Ezra 8:24–30

Esau .... Gen. 25:29–34

Comes to Jerusalem.................. Ezra 8:31, 32

Eli's sons .... 1 Sam. 2:12–17

Institutes reforms................... Ezra 9:1–15

King Saul ....1 Sam. 16:1

Reads the Law to the people .... Neh. 8:1–18

Absalom .... 2 Sam. 18:6–17

Helps in dedication .... Neh. 12:27–43

Hananiah . . . . Jer. 28:1–17
Haman . . . . Esth. 7:1–10

Fainting, faintheartedness—*a loss of vital powers; weary; lacking courage*
A. Causes of:
    Physical fatigue . . . . Gen. 25:29, 30
    Famine . . . . Gen. 47:13
    Unbelief . . . . Gen. 45:26
    Fear . . . . Josh. 2:24
    Sin . . . . Lev. 26:31
    Sickness . . . . Job 4:5
    Human weakness . . . . Is. 40:29–31
    Ecstasy of visions . . . . Dan. 8:27
    Disappointment . . . . Jon. 4:8
B. Antidotes against:
    Removal of the fearful . . . . Deut. 20:8

Fair—*English rendering of numerous Hebrew and Greek words*
    Beautiful . . . . Song 1:15, 16
    Good . . . . Matt. 16:2

Fair Havens
    Harbor of Crete . . . . Acts 27:8

WORD STUDY

FAITH, TRUST, *pistis* (*pis*-tis). This noun occurs over two hundred times in the NT. By far the most common usage of *pistis* is to refer to the active sense of believing—"faith" in God (Mark 11:22), Jesus Christ (Rom. 3:22; Col. 1:4), as well as Their revelations and promises (e.g., Gal. 3:2–29). "Faith" is regarded as a fundamental Christian virtue, often mentioned with love and hope (1 Cor. 13:13; Gal. 5:22; 1 Thess. 3:6; Heb. 11:1; 1 Pet. 1:21). *Pistis* can also refer to that which is believed—that is, to "doctrine" (Jude 3). A less common use of the word is with respect to that which effects "trust" or "faith," hence "faithfulness" (Rom. 3:3; cf. Titus 2:10). (Strong's #4102)

Faith—*confidence in the testimony of another*
A. Nature of:
    Work of God . . . . John 6:29
    God's gift . . . . Eph. 2:8
    Comes from the heart . . . . Rom. 10:9, 10
    Substance of unseen things . . . . Heb. 11:1
B. Obtained from:
    Scriptures . . . . John 20:30, 31
    Preaching . . . . John 17:20
    Gospel . . . . Acts 15:7
    Hearing the word . . . . Rom. 10:17
C. Objects of:
    God . . . . John 14:1
    Christ . . . . John 20:31
    Moses' writings . . . . John 5:46
    Writings of the prophets . . . . Acts 26:27
    Gospel . . . . Mark 1:15
    God's promises . . . . Rom. 4:21
D. Kinds of:
    Saving . . . . Rom. 10:9, 10
    Temporary . . . . Luke 8:13

    Intellectual . . . . James 2:19
    Dead . . . . James 2:17, 20
E. Described as:
    Boundless . . . . John 11:21–27
    Common . . . . Titus 1:4
    Great . . . . Matt. 8:10
    Holy . . . . Jude 20
    Humble . . . . Luke 7:6, 7
    Little . . . . Matt. 8:26
    Mutual . . . . Rom. 1:12
    Perfect . . . . James 2:22
    Precious . . . . 2 Pet. 1:1
    Rootless . . . . Luke 8:13
    Small . . . . Matt. 17:20
    Unfeigned . . . . 1 Tim. 1:5
    United . . . . Mark 2:5
    Venturing . . . . Matt. 14:28, 29
F. The fruits of:
    Remission of sins . . . . Acts 10:43
    Justification . . . . Acts 13:39
    Freedom from condemnation . . . . John 3:18
    Salvation . . . . Mark 16:16
    Sanctification . . . . Acts 15:9
    Freedom from spiritual death . . . . . . John 11:25, 26
    Spiritual light . . . . John 12:36, 46
    Spiritual life . . . . John 20:31
    Eternal life . . . . John 3:15, 16
    Adoption . . . . John 1:12
    Access to God . . . . Eph. 3:12
    Edification . . . . 1 Tim. 1:4
    Preservation . . . . John 10:26–29
    Inheritance . . . . Acts 26:18
    Peace and rest . . . . Rom. 5:1
G. Place of, in Christian life:
    Live by . . . . Rom. 1:17
    Walk by . . . . Rom. 4:12
    Pray by . . . . Matt. 21:22
    Resist evil by . . . . Eph. 6:16
    Overcome world by . . . . 1 John 2:13–17
    Fight the good fight of . . . . 1 Tim. 6:12
    Die in . . . . Heb. 11:13
H. Growth of, in Christian life:
    Stand fast in . . . . 1 Cor. 16:13
    Continue in . . . . Acts 14:22
    Be strong in . . . . Rom. 4:20–24
    Abound in . . . . 2 Cor. 8:7
    Be grounded in . . . . Col. 1:23
    Hold fast . . . . 1 Tim. 1:19
    Pray for increase of . . . . Luke 17:5
    Have assurance of . . . . 2 Tim. 1:12
I. Examples of, in Old Testament:
    Abel . . . . Heb. 11:4
    Enoch . . . . Heb. 11:5
    Noah . . . . Heb. 11:7
    Abraham . . . . Rom. 4:16–20
    Sarah . . . . Heb. 11:11
    Jacob . . . . Heb. 11:21
    Joseph . . . . Heb. 11:22
    Moses . . . . Heb. 11:23–29

Faith as a body of belief

Faithfulness—*living out one's faith in daily life*
A. Manifested in:
B. Illustrated in lives of:

Faithfulness of God
A. Described as:
B. Manifested in:

Falcon

Fall of humankind
A. Occasion of:
B. Temporal consequences of:
C. Spiritual consequences of:

Change from, not in man............. Jer. 2:22
Only God can change .... John 3:16

Fallow ground—*a field plowed and left unplanted*
Used figuratively .... Jer. 4:3; Hos. 10:12

False accusations
A. Against men:
Joseph ....Gen. 39:7–20
Moses.........................Num. 16:1–3, 13
Ahimelech ....1 Sam. 22:10–16
David............................Ps. 41:5–9
Elijah.......................1 Kin. 18:17, 18
Naboth ....1 Kin. 21:1–14
Jeremiah ....Jer. 26:8–11
Amos ....Amos 7:10, 11
Stephen .... Acts 6:11, 13
Paul ....Acts 21:27–29
Those first to receive Holy Spirit.... Acts 2:14, 15
B. Against Christ:
Gluttony ....Matt. 11:19
Blasphemy ....Matt. 26:64, 65
Insanity........................... Mark 3:21
Demon possession .... John 7:20
Sabbath desecration................. John 9:16
Treason....................... John 19:12

False apostles
Opposed Paul .... 2 Cor. 11:1–15

False christs
Christ foretells their coming........ Matt. 24:24
Christ warns against .... Mark 13:21–23
See Antichrist

False confidence
A. Characteristics of:
Self-righteous ....Rom. 2:3
Spiritually blind .... Is. 28:15, 19
Sensualist...........................Gal. 6:7, 8
Worldly secure .... 1 Thess. 5:3
B. Causes of trusting in:
Riches ....1 Tim. 6:17
Worldly success.................Luke 12:19, 20
Men ....Is. 30:1–5
Oneself ....Matt. 26:33–35
Ignoring God's providence ....James 4:13–15
C. Warnings against:
Curse on ....Jer. 17:5
Do not glory in human beings........ 1 Cor. 3:21
Human limitation .... 2 Cor. 1:9
Mighty will fail.....................Ps. 33:16, 17
Boasting ....1 Kin. 20:11
D. Instances of:
Babel's men .... Gen. 11:4
Sennacherib .... 2 Kin. 19:20–37
Asa ....2 Chr. 16:7–12
Peter .... Luke 22:33, 34

Falsehood—*turning truth into a lie*
A. Manifested by false:
Witnesses ....Ps. 27:12
Balances .... Prov. 11:1

Tongue ....Ps. 120:3
Report ....Ex. 23:1
Prophets ....Jer. 5:2, 31
Knowledge.........................1 Tim. 6:20
B. God's people:
Must avoid ....Ex. 23:7
Must hate .... Ps. 119:104, 128
Must endure.........................Acts 6:13
Are falsely charged with.....Jer. 37:14; Matt. 5:11

False professions
A. Pretending to be:
Harmless..........................Josh. 9:3–16
Innocent...................... Matt. 27:24
Divine ....Acts 12:21–23
Sincere.....................Matt. 26:47–49
True prophets .... 1 Kin. 22:6–12
B. Exposed by:
Prophets .... Jer. 28:1–17
Christ.......................John 13:21–30
Apostles .... Acts 5:1–11

False prophets
A. Tests of:
Doctrine............................. Is. 8:20
Prophecies .... 1 Kin. 13:1–32
Lives.......................... Matt. 7:15, 16
Spirit behind .... 1 John 4:1–3
B. Characteristics of:
Prophesy peace ....Jer. 23:17
Speak a lie.........................Jer. 28:15
Pretend to be true........... Matt. 7:22, 23
Teach corruption .... 2 Pet. 2:10–22
Seduce to immorality ....Rev. 2:20
C. Examples of:
Zedekiah.....................1 Kin. 22:11, 12
Hananiah .... Jer. 28:1–17
In the last days .... Matt. 24:3, 11

False teachers
A. Characteristics of:
Grace-perverters.................... Gal. 1:6–8
Money-lovers..................... Luke 16:14
Christ-deniers.....................2 Pet. 2:1
Truth-resisters.................... 2 Tim. 3:8
Fable-lovers .... 2 Tim. 4:3, 4
Destitute of the truth .... 1 Tim. 6:3–5
Bound by traditions................. Matt. 15:9
Unstable ....1 Tim. 1:6, 7
Deceitful........................... Eph. 4:14
Lustful.......................... 2 Pet. 2:12–19
B. Prevalence of:
In Paul's time.................. 2 Tim. 1:14, 15
During this age .... 1 Tim. 4:1–3
At Christ's return .... 2 Tim. 4:3, 4
C. Examples of:
Balaam ....Rev. 2:14
Bar-Jesus......................... Acts 13:6
Ephesian elders .... Acts 20:30; Rev. 2:2
Epicureans ....Acts 17:18
False apostles..............2 Cor. 11:5, 13; 12:11

Freedmen . . . . Acts 6:9
Herodians. . . . . Mark 3:6; 12:13
Hymenaeus . . . . .2 Tim. 2:17
Nicolaitans. . . . . Rev. 2:15
Pharisees. . . . . Matt. 23:26
Philetus. . . . . .2 Tim. 2:17
Sadducees. . . . . Matt. 16:12
Scribes. . . . . Matt. 12:38, 39
Serpent (Satan) . . . . Gen. 3:4
Stoic philosophers .Acts 17:18
Those of the circumcision . . . . Titus 1:10–14

False weights
Prohibited. . . . . Deut. 25:13, 14
An abomination . . . . Prov. 11:1

False witnesses
A. Defined as:
   Deceptive . . . . Prov. 12:17
   Cruel . . . . Prov. 25:18
   Speaks lies . . . . Prov. 6:19
   Shall perish. . . . . Prov. 21:28
   Hated by God . . . . .Zech. 8:17
   Forbidden. . . . . .Ex. 20:16
B. Sin of:
   Comes from corrupt heart . . . . .Matt. 15:19
   Causes suffering. . . . . Ps. 27:12
   Merits punishment. . . . . .Prov. 19:5, 9
C. Punishment of:
   Specified. . . . . .Lev. 6:1–5
   Described . . . . .Deut. 19:16–20
   Visualized. . . . . Zech. 5:3, 4
D. Examples of, against:
   Ahimelech . . . . .1 Sam. 22:8–18
   Naboth . . . . .1 Kin. 21:13
   Jeremiah . . . . .Jer. 37:12–14
   Jesus. . . . . .Matt. 26:59–61
   Stephen . . . . Acts 6:8–13
   Paul . . . . Acts 16:19–21

Fame—*report; renown; news*
A. As report or news of:
   Joseph's brothers. . . . . Gen. 45:16
   Israel's departure . . . . Num. 14:15
   Jesus' ministry. Matt. 4:24
B. As reputation or renown of:
   Nation. . . . . Ezek. 16:14, 15
   Joshua's exploits . . . . .Josh. 6:27
   God's works. . . . . .Josh. 9:9
   Solomon's wisdom . . . . .1 Kin. 4:30, 31
   David's power . . . . .1 Chr. 14:17
   The temple's greatness . . . . .1 Chr. 22:5
   God's glory. . . . . Is. 66:19
   Mordecai's fame . . . . Esth. 9:4
   Jesus' works . . . . Matt. 4:24; 9:31

Familiar spirits
A. Described as:
   Source of defilement . . . . Lev. 19:31
   Abominable. .Deut. 18:10–12
   Vain . . . . .Is. 8:19

B. The practicers of, to be:
   Cut off. . . . . .Lev. 20:6
   Put to death . . . . Lev. 20:27
C. Consulted by:
   Saul. . . . . .1 Sam. 28:3–25
   Manasseh . . . . .2 Kin. 21:6

WORD STUDY   **FAMILY,** *mishpachah* (mish-paw-*khaw*). A "clan" or "family" is indicated by the noun *mishpachah*. The family in question might be an extended family as in Gen. 24:38 or in a rather loose and popular usage of the term, a tribe as in Judg. 13:2. The more technical use of the term (Ex. 6:14, 15; Num. 11:10; Jer. 2:4) indicates a division of the people of Israel. In its widest sense, the word means people or nations as in Amos 3:2. There are several rare uses of *mishpachah* in the OT: something similar to a guild (1 Chr. 2:55); aristocrats (Job 31:34); a species of animal (Gen. 8:19); and a kind of judgment (Jer. 15:3). (Strong's #4940)

Family
A. Founded on:
   Divine creation . . . . Gen. 1:27, 28
   Marriage. . . . . Matt. 19:6
   Monogamy. . . . . .Ex. 20:14
   Unity of parents .Ex. 20:12
   Headship of husband. . . . . .1 Cor. 11:3–7
   Obedience of children. . . . . Eph. 6:1–3
   Common concern. . . . . .Luke 16:27, 28
B. Disturbed by:
   Polygamy . . . . .Gen. 4:19–24
   Jealousy. . . . . Gen. 37:3, 4, 18–27
   Hatred. . . . . Gen. 4:5, 8
   Disrespect. . . . . .Gen. 9:21, 22
   Deceit . . . . .Gen. 37:31–35
   Ambition . . . . 2 Sam. 15:1–16
   Waywardness . . . . .Luke 15:11–18
   Insubordination . . . . Gen. 34:6–31
   Unbelief . . . . .John 7:3–10
   Lust . . . . .Gen. 34:1–31
C. Unity of:
   Husband and wife . . . . 1 Cor. 7:3
   Parents and children . . . . Jer. 35:1–19
   Worship . . . . 1 Cor. 16:19
   Faith. . . . . .2 Tim. 1:5
   Baptism. . . . . Acts 16:14, 15
D. Worship in:
   Led by the father. . . . . Gen. 18:19
   Instructed in the Scriptures. . . . . Eph. 6:4
   Observing religious rites . . . . .Acts 10:2, 47, 48
   Common consecration . . . . .Josh. 24:15

Famine—*deficiency; a great shortage of food*
A. Kinds of:
   Physical. . . . . Gen. 12:10
   Prophetic . . . . Matt. 24:7; Rev. 6:5–8
   Spiritual . . . . .2 Chr. 15:3; Amos 8:11
B. Causes of:
   Divine judgment. . . . . Is. 65:13, 14

Hailstorms ....Ex. 9:23
Insects .... Joel 1:4
Enemies.......................Deut. 28:49–51
Siege........................ 2 Kin. 6:24, 25
Sin........................ Ezek. 14:12, 13
Punishment ....2 Kin. 8:1

C. Characteristics of:

Often long .... Gen. 41:27
Often severe.....................Deut. 28:49–53
Suffering intense .... Jer. 14:1, 5, 6
Destructive .... Jer. 14:12, 15

D. Instances of, in:

Abram's time......................Gen. 12:10
Isaac's time.......................Gen. 26:1
Joseph's time .... Gen. 41:53–56; Acts 7:11–13
Time of judges......................... Ruth 1:1
David's reign ....2 Sam. 21:1
Elijah's time........................ 2 Kin. 17:1
Elisha's time.................2 Kin. 4:38; 8:1
Samaria's siege.............. 2 Kin. 6:24, 25
Reign of Claudius Caesar............ Acts 11:28
Jeremiah's time.................. Jer. 14:1–6
Ahab's reign...................... 1 Kin. 17:1
Nehemiah's day...................... Neh. 5:3
Joel's time.................Joel 1:9–12, 16–18

Fan—*to toss about*

A. Used literally of:

Fork for winnowing grain .... Is. 30:24

B. Used figuratively of judgments:

God's............................... Is. 30:24
Christ's .... Matt. 3:12

Fanaticism—*unbridled obsession*

A. Kinds of:

Personal ....Acts 9:1, 2
Group .... 1 Kin. 18:22–29
Civic...........................Acts 19:24–41
National .... John 19:15

B. Characteristics of:

Intolerance.........................Acts 7:57
Persecution.................1 Thess. 2:14–16
Inhumanity .... Rev. 11:7–10
Insanity....................... 1 Sam. 18:9–12

Fangs

Used figuratively of:

Power over the wicked...... Job 29:17; Prov. 30:14

Farewell message

Moses' .... Deut. 29:1–31:13
Joshua's .... Josh. 24:1–28
David's ....1 Kin. 2:1–9
Christ's ....Matt. 28:18–20
Paul's .... 2 Tim. 4:1–8

Farewells—*expressions at departing*

Naomi's, to Orpah ....Ruth 1:11–14
Paul's, to Ephesians ....Acts 18:18–21
Paul's, to elders ....Acts 20:17–38
Paul's, to Tyrians ....Acts 21:3–6
Paul's, to Jews ....Acts 28:23–29

Farm—*a cultivated field*

Preferred more than a wedding ..... Matt. 22:1–5

Farmer—*one who farms*

Cain, the first .... Gen. 4:2
Noah .... Gen. 9:20
Elisha ....1 Kin. 19:19, 20
Remain in land .... 2 Kin. 25:12
Uzziah......................2 Chr. 26:9, 10
Diligence required in........... Prov. 24:30–34
Reward of......................2 Cor. 9:6–11
Unwise.......................... Luke 12:16–21
Takes share of crops................ 2 Tim. 2:6

Farming—*the art of agriculture*

Rechabites forbidden to engage in.... Jer. 35:5–10

Fasting—*abstaining from physical nourishment*

A. Occasions of:

Before receiving Law ....Ex. 34:28; Deut. 9:9
Day of Atonement .... Lev. 16:29, 31
Death of a friend.............. 1 Sam. 31:11–13
Private emotions.....................1 Sam. 1:7
Grief............................. 2 Sam. 12:16
Anxiety.......................... Dan. 6:18–20
Intercession .... Dan. 9:3, 4
Approaching danger .... Esth. 4:16
National repentance .... 1 Sam. 7:5, 6
Sad news .... Neh. 1:4
Sacred ordination.................... Acts 13:3

B. Accompaniments of:

Prayer ....Luke 2:37
Confession .... Neh. 9:1, 2
Mourning.........................Joel 2:12
Humiliation .... Neh. 9:1

C. Correct method:

Avoid display.................... Matt. 6:16–18
Remember God.................... Zech. 7:5–7
Chasten the soul....................Ps. 69:10
Humble the soul....................Ps. 35:13
Consider the true meaning of........ Is. 58:1–14

D. Results of:

Divine guidance ....Judg. 20:26–28
Victory over temptation........... Matt. 4:1–11

E. Instances of:

Moses....................... Ex. 34:27, 28
Israelites .... Judg. 20:26
Samuel...................... 1 Sam. 7:5, 6
David........................ 2 Sam. 12:16
Elijah ....1 Kin. 19:2, 8
Esther .... Esth. 4:16
Ninevites .... Jon. 3:5–8
Nehemiah...................... Neh. 1:4
Darius ....Dan. 6:9, 18
Daniel .... Dan. 9:3
Anna ....Luke 2:36, 37
Jesus......................... Matt. 4:1, 2
John's disciples and the Pharisees ......Mark 2:18
Early Christians .... Acts 13:2
Apostles ....2 Cor. 6:4, 5
Paul ....2 Cor. 11:27

Fat

Figurative of best	Gen. 45:18
Of sacrifices, burned	Ex. 29:13; Lev. 4:26
Figurative of pride	Ps. 119:69, 70
Sacrificed by Abel	Gen. 4:4
Offered to God	Ex. 23:18; Lev. 3:14–16

WORD STUDY

FATHER, *'ab* (*awb*). The noun *'ab* has various translations all loosely based on the word "father," many of which have counterparts in English. Most often, the term means "father" in the literal sense. This father-figure is seen in a variety of roles—commanding, instructing, begetting, loving, pitying, blessing, and rebuking. The term is also used to portray God as the Father who controls, guides, and lovingly watches His people, as He is described as doing in Hos. 11:1. God is especially featured as the Father of the Davidic line. A father can also be the head of the household or clan. Ancestors are referred to as fathers or forefathers. A less literal meaning of the word is seen in Job 29:16 and Is. 22:21 where the term describes a figure of benevolence and protection. A final use is as a term of respect and honor and is applied, for example, to a master, priest, or prophet. (Strong's #1)

WORD STUDY

FATHER, *Abba* (ab-*bah*). *Abba* is the Greek transliteration of an Aramaic word used to address fathers. Although the Greek translation "father" is supplied each time *Abba* is used in the NT, it is likely that the word is a term of endearment more similar to the English "Dada" or "Papa." Evidence indicates that early on Greek-speaking Christians took up this Aramaic form of addressing God in prayer. See Jesus' poignant and prayerful plea to His "Father" in Gethsemane (Mark 14:36). Paul claims that believers, adopted by the Spirit into the family of God, may rightfully address God as *Abba* (Rom. 8:15; cf. Gal. 4:6). (Strong's #5)

Father—*male parent*

A. Kinds of:

Natural	Gen. 28:13
Ancestors	Jer. 35:6
Natural leaders	Rom. 9:5
Head of households	Ex. 6:14

B. Figurative of:

Source	Job 38:28
Original inventor	Gen. 4:20
Creator	James 1:17
Spiritual likeness	John 8:44
Counselor	Gen. 45:8
Superior	2 Kin. 2:12
Praise seeking	Matt. 23:9

C. Powers of, in Old Testament times:

Arrange son's marriage	Gen. 24:1–9
Sell children	Ex. 21:7

D. Duties of, toward his children:

Bless	Gen. 27:27–29, 39, 40; 49:1–28
Love	Gen. 37:4
Command	Gen. 50:16
Instruct	Prov. 1:8
Guide and warn	1 Thess. 2:11
Train	Hos. 11:1–3
Rebuke	Gen. 34:30
Restrain	1 Sam. 3:12, 13
Punish	Deut. 21:18–21
Chasten	Heb. 12:7
Nourish	Is. 1:2
Supply needs	Matt. 7:8–11
Do not provoke	Eph. 6:4

E. Examples of devout:

Abraham	Gen. 18:18, 19
Isaac	Gen. 26:12, 13
Joshua	Josh. 24:15
Job	Job 1:5

F. Christ's command about:

"Do not call anyone on earth your father"	Matt. 23:9

Fatherhood of God

Of all men	Mal. 2:10
Of Israel	Jer. 31:9
Of Gentiles	Rom. 3:29
Of Christians	John 1:12, 13

Fatherless—*orphans*

A. Proper attitude toward:

Share blessings with	Deut. 14:28, 29
Leave gleanings for	Deut. 24:19–22
Do not defraud	Prov. 23:10
Defend	Ps. 82:3
Visit	James 1:27
Oppress not	Zech. 7:10
Do no violence to	Jer. 22:3

B. God's help toward:

Father of	Ps. 68:5
Helper of	Ps. 10:14
Hears cry of	Ex. 22:22, 23
Executes judgment of	Deut. 10:18

Father's house

The family home	Gen. 12:1; 1 Sam. 18:2
A household	Ex. 12:3
Tribal divisions	Num. 3:15, 20; 17:2, 3
Temple	John 2:14–16
Heaven	John 14:2

Fathom—*a sea measure; about six feet*

Mentioned in Paul's shipwreck	Acts 27:28

Fatigue—*physical or mental exhaustion*

From:

Marching	1 Sam. 30:9, 10
Fighting	2 Sam. 23:10, 15
Much study	Eccl. 12:12
Fasting	Acts 27:21

In:

Sleeping	Matt. 26:45

Fault—*an imperfection*
A. Examples of:
    A promise forgotten................... Gen. 41:9
    Unworthy conduct................. 1 Sam. 29:3
    Guilt................................John 18:38
    Deficient behavior................. Matt. 18:15
B. Absence of:
    Flawless devotion.....................Rev. 14:5
    Ultimate sinlessness...................Jude 24

Faultfinders—*those who notice and stress faults*
A. Motives behind:
    Supposed injustice ....Matt. 20:9–12
    Supposed defilement.............Luke 5:29, 30
    Greed and avarice................... John 12:3–6
B. Against God's:
    Choice........................... Num. 12:1, 2
    Leading...........................Num. 14:1–4
    Mercy............................Jon. 4:1–11
    Government..................... Rom. 9:19–23
C. Guilt of:
    Punishable .... Num. 12:2, 8–13
    Productive of evil..................... 3 John 10

Faultless—*without blame*
    David......................... 1 Sam. 29:3, 6
    Daniel .... Dan. 6:4
    Christ........................Luke 23:4, 14

Favoritism—*being unfairly partial*
A. Forbidden to:
    Parents .... Deut. 21:15–17
    Judges .... Deut. 25:1–3
    Ministers .... 1 Tim. 5:21
B. Results in:
    Family friction .... Gen. 27:6–46
    Jealousy...........................Gen. 37:3–35

WORD STUDY   **FEAR,** *yare'* (yaw-*ray*). The verb translated "fear" is used throughout the OT. It can mean literal fear and is seen frequently in the imperative phrase "fear not." The verb can also mean "to stand in awe of." This translation can apply to humans as in Ex. 34:30 where the people stood in awe of Moses' radiance after he came down from Mount Sinai. More often, the term is used with reference to deity (see Ps. 33:8). Although *yare'* means more than "fear" in this usage, often there is an element of trepidation in connection with the awe. This word can also mean simply to have "reverence" or "honor"; and people are instructed to show reverence for parents, oaths, and commandments. (Strong's #3372)

Fear—*anxiety caused by approaching danger*
A. Causes of:
    Disobedience........................ Gen. 3:10
    Impending judgment................. Heb. 11:7
    Persecution.........................John 20:19
    Events of nature .... Acts 27:17, 29
    Suspicion........................... Acts 9:26
    Uncertainty .... 2 Cor. 11:3
    Final events ....Luke 21:26

    Death............................. Heb. 2:15
B. Effects of:
    Demoralization................... 1 Sam. 13:5–8
    Paralysis .... Matt. 28:4
    Silent testimony .... John 9:22
C. Instances of:
    Abraham......................... Gen. 20:11
    Jacob ....Gen. 32:9–11
    Soldiers .... Matt. 27:54
    Mariners.........................Jon. 1:5, 10

Fear, godly
A. Defined as:
    Hating evil.......................... Prov. 8:13
    Life-giving ....Prov. 14:27
    Sanctifying......................... Ps. 19:9
    Beginning of wisdom .... Prov. 9:10
B. Motives to, God's:
    Majesty ....Jer. 10:7
    Holiness ....Rev. 15:4
    Forgiveness.......................Ps. 130:4
    Power.........................Josh. 4:23, 24
    Goodness .... 1 Sam. 12:24
    Judgment ....Rev. 14:7
C. Examples of:
    Noah .... Heb. 11:7
    Abraham......................... Gen. 22:12
    Jacob ....Gen. 28:16, 17
    Joseph .... Gen. 42:18
    David............................. Ps. 5:7
    Obadiah .... 1 Kin. 18:7, 12
    Job ....Job 1:8
    Nehemiah........................ Neh. 5:15
    Early Christians ....Acts 9:31

Fearlessness—*without fear*
A. Source of:
    Believing God's promises........... Num. 13:30
    Challenge of duty..................Ex. 32:26–29
    Regard for God's holiness .... Num. 25:1–9
    Believing God ....Acts 27:22–26
B. Exemplified by:
    Abram ....Gen. 14:14–16
    Jonathan .... 1 Sam. 14:6–14
    David........................ 1 Sam. 17:34–37
    Nehemiah........................Neh. 4:1–23
    Hebrew men..................... Dan. 3:16–30
    Peter and John........................Acts 4:13
    Paul .... Acts 21:10–14

Feasts, Hebrew
A. Annual:
    Passover .... Ex. 12:1–14; Lev. 23:5–8
    Unleavened Bread .... Ex. 12:15–20
    Harvest (Weeks or Pentecost)..........Ex. 23:16
    Firstfruits....................... Lev. 23:9–14
    Tabernacles ....Lev. 23:34–44
B. Other, celebrated:
    Sabbath................ Ex. 20:8–11; Lev. 23:2, 3
    Sabbath year ....Lev. 25:1–7
    Year of Jubilee .... Lev. 25:8–17

The New Moon.........Num. 28:11–15; Ps. 81:3
Dedication..........................John 10:22
Purim.........................Esth. 9:18–32
C. Purposes of:
Unify the nation.................Deut. 12:5–14
Worship God.........................Ex. 5:1
Illustrate spiritual truths..........John 7:37–39
Foretell the Messiah...........1 Cor. 11:23–26
D. Brief history of:
Pre-Sinaitic observance.............Ex. 12:1–27
Three instituted at Sinai...........Ex. 23:14–17
Celebrated in the wilderness........Num. 9:3–5
Again at beginning of conquest.....Josh. 5:10, 11
At dedication of temple...........1 Kin. 8:2, 65
"Dedication" introduced by Solomon......2 Chr. 7:9–11
Idolatrous counterfeits introduced by Jeroboam................1 Kin. 12:27–33
Observed in Hezekiah's reign.........2 Chr. 30:1
Perversion of, by Jews...............Is. 1:13, 14
Restored in Josiah's reformation . 2 Kin. 23:22, 23
Failure in, cause of exile.........2 Chr. 36:20, 21
Restored after the Exile.................Ezra 3:4
Purim instituted by Mordecai.......Esth. 9:17–32
Christ attends....................John 2:23; 13:1
Christ fulfills the Passover..........1 Cor. 5:7, 8
Christianity begins with Pentecost...Acts 2:1–41
All fulfilled in Christ..............2 Cor. 3:3–18

Feasts, social
A. Worldly, occasions of:
Idolatry.............................Ex. 32:6
Drunkenness.....................1 Sam. 25:36
Proud display.......................Esth. 1:1–8
Profane carousals...................Dan. 5:1–16
Licentiousness...................Mark 6:21, 22
B. Proper, occasions of:
Refreshment......................Gen. 19:1–3
Reconciliation...................Gen. 31:54, 55
Reunion.........................Gen. 43:16–34
Restoration.....................Luke 15:22–24
See Entertainment

Feeble—*powerless*
Moab................................Is. 16:14

Feed—*to supply food to*
A. Used naturally of:
Food for men.....................2 Sam. 19:33
Food for animals.....................Gen. 30:36
God's provision.....................Matt. 6:26
B. Used figuratively of:
Messiah...........................Ezek. 34:23
Good deeds......................Matt. 25:37
Supernatural supply.................Rev. 12:6
Elemental teaching...............1 Cor. 3:2
Change of nature.......................Is. 11:7
Corruption.........................Ps. 49:14
Vanity..............................Hos. 12:1

C. Miracles:
Feeding children of Israel:
Manna..............................Ex. 16:4
Quail..............................Ex. 16:13
Feeding Elijah:
By ravens........................1 Kin. 17:4–6
Widow's oil and meal.............1 Kin. 17:8–16
By Elisha feeds:
100 prophets with 20 loaves.......2 Kin. 4:42–44
Sons of the prophets.............2 Kin. 4:38–41
By Jesus feeds:
4,000..........................Matt. 15:32–38
5,000............................John 6:1–13

Feet—*the lower parts of the body*
A. Acts performed by or on, indicating:
Subjection.........................Josh. 10:24
Conquest........................2 Sam. 22:39
Humiliation.........................Judg. 5:27
Submission and entreaty........1 Sam. 25:24, 41
Great love.....................Luke 7:38, 44–46
Worship............................Rev. 19:10
Learner's position...................Luke 10:39
Humility.........................John 13:5–14
Changed nature.....................Luke 8:35
Rejection..........................Matt. 10:14
B. Figurative of:
God's holiness.........................Ex. 3:5
God's nature.......................Ex. 24:10
Clouds..............................Nah. 1:3
God's messengers...........Is. 52:7; Rom. 10:15
Final conquest.....................Rom. 16:20
C. Unusual features concerning:
No swelling........................Neh. 9:21
Lameness.......................2 Sam. 9:3, 13
Neglected.......................2 Sam. 19:24
Impotent........................Acts 14:8–10
Binding...........................Acts 21:11
See Foot

Feet washing
Performed on guests.................Gen. 18:4
Proffered by Abigail.............1 Sam. 25:40, 41
On Jesus, with tears..................Luke 7:44
Performed by Jesus....................John 13:5
Duty of saints.......................1 Tim. 5:10

Felix—*happy*
Governor of Judea................Acts 23:24, 26
Letter addressed to..............Acts 23:25–30
Paul's defense before..............Acts 24:1–21
Convicted, but unchanged.........Acts 24:22–25
Subject to bribery.................Acts 24:26, 27

Fellow citizens
With the saints......................Eph. 2:19

Fellow countryman
Shall not hate.......................Lev. 19:17
Becomes poor......................Lev. 25:25
Judge righteously....................Deut. 1:16
Lord gives rest.....................Deut. 3:20
Save some.........................Rom. 11:14

Fellow servant

Who owed a hundred denarii	Matt. 18:28–33
Evil slave beats	Matt. 24:48, 49
Were to be killed.	Rev. 6:11
Who hold fast the testimony of Jesus	Rev. 19:10
Who heed the words	Rev. 22:9

FELLOWSHIP, COMMUNION, *koinōnia* (koy-nohn-ee-ah). This noun is used in the NT as an expression for the "close relationship" or "fellowship" that exists between believers and God (1 John 1:3); Jesus Christ (1 Cor. 1:9); the Spirit (Phil. 2:1; cf. 2 Cor. 13:13); and other believers (1 John 1:7). *Koinōnia* can also be used in the sense of "participation" or "sharing" in something, such as Christ's sufferings (Phil. 3:10). Paul speaks of the Christian ritual of blessing the cup and breaking bread as "communion" in the blood and body of Christ (1 Cor. 10:16). Figuratively, *koinōnia* can refer to altruistic acts of unity, for example, to gifts or contributions (Rom. 15:26). (Strong's #2842)

Fellowship—*sharing together*

A. Based upon common:

Purpose	Ps. 133:1–3
Belief	Acts 2:42
Conviction	1 Pet. 3:8
Work	Neh. 4:1–23
Hope	Heb. 11:39, 40
Faith	1 Sam. 20:30–42
Suffering	Dan. 3:16–30
Need	2 Cor. 8:1–15

B. Persons sharing together:

Father, the Son, and Christians	1 John 1:3
Christ and Christians	1 Cor. 1:9
Holy Spirit and Christians	Phil. 2:1
Apostles	Acts 2:42
Believers	1 John 1:7

C. Things shared together:

Material things	2 Cor. 8:4
Suffering	Phil. 3:10
The gospel ministry	Gal. 2:9
Gospel privileges	Phil. 1:5
Gospel mystery	Eph. 3:9
Lord's Supper	Mark 14:22–25; 1 Cor. 10:16, 17

Fellow workers

In the truth	3 John 8
In the kingdom	Col. 4:11
Priscilla and Aquila described as	Rom. 16:3
Urbanus	Rom. 16:9
Timothy	Rom. 16:21
Paul	1 Cor. 3:1–9
Titus	2 Cor. 8:23
Epaphroditus	Phil. 2:25
Philemon	Philem. 1
Mark, Aristarchus, Demas, Luke	Philem. 24

Ferryboats

David's use of	2 Sam. 19:16–18

FERVENT, BE, *zeō* (*dzeh*-oh). The literal meaning of this verb is "to boil" or "to seethe." It is often used figuratively with respect to emotions (e.g., anger or love) or to indicate an eagerness to do good or evil. In the NT *zeo* is used figuratively twice, and both times the reference is to a spiritual "fervor" or "zeal" (cf. the cognate noun in Rom. 10:2; Phil. 3:6). Apollos is described as "fervent in spirit" (Acts 18:25); compare Paul's exhortation in Rom. 12:11. (Strong's #2204)

Festus—*feastful, joyful*

Governor of Judea	Acts 24:27
Paul's defense made to	Acts 25:1–22

Fetters—*shackle for binding the feet*

A. Used literally of:

Imprisonment	Ps. 105:18

B. Used figuratively of:

Trouble	Job 36:8
Subjection	Ps. 149:8

Fetus—*unborn child*

Protected by law	Ex. 21:22, 23
Possesses sin nature	Ps. 51:5
Fashioned by God	Ps. 139:13–16
Called by God	Is. 49:1; Jer. 1:5
Active	Luke 1:41

Fever—*abnormal body temperature*

Sent as a judgment	Deut. 28:22
Rebuked by Christ	Luke 4:38, 39
Healed by Paul	Acts 28:8

Few—*the opposite of many*

Days	Gen. 47:9
Do not determine God's power	1 Sam. 14:6
Words in prayer	Eccl. 5:2
The saved	Matt. 7:14
Gospel messengers	Matt. 9:37
The chosen	Matt. 22:14

Fidelity—*faithfulness in the performance of duty*

In finances	2 Kin. 12:15
In industry	2 Chr. 34:11, 12
Seen in Joseph	Gen. 39:6
Seen in Daniel	Dan. 6:1–3, 28

Field—*open or cleared land*

A. Used literally of:

Cultivated land	Gen. 47:20
A city	Ps. 78:12, 43

B. Laws regarding:

Fires	Ex. 22:6
Coveting others'	Deut. 5:21
Destruction of trees	Deut. 20:19, 20
Total harvest of	Deut. 24:19–22
Sabbath rest	Lev. 25:3–12
Redemption of	Lev. 27:16–24
Title of	Ruth 4:5–11

C. Figurative of:

World	Matt. 13:38
Harvest of souls	John 4:35

Field of Blood

A field, predicted in the Old Testament, bought as a cemetery for Judas's burial . . . . Zech. 11:12, 13; Matt. 27:1–10

Fiery serpents

Attack Israelites . . . . Num. 21:6, 8

Fig—*pear-shaped fruit of fig tree*

Destruction foretold . . . . Hos. 2:12

Prescribed for boils . . . . 2 Kin. 20:7; Is. 38:21

Fig tree

A. The leaves of, used for:

Covering nakedness. . . . . Gen. 3:7

Shade . . . . John 1:48, 50

B. Fruit of:

Used for food. . . . . 1 Sam. 30:12

Sent as present. . . . . 1 Sam. 25:18

Sold in markets . . . . Neh. 13:15

Used for healing . . . . Is. 38:21

Sometimes fails. Hab. 3:17

C. Figurative of:

Prosperity and peace . . . . 1 Kin. 4:25

Righteous and the wicked . . . . Jer. 24:1–10

Fathers of Israel . . . . Hos. 9:10

Barren religion . . . . Matt. 21:18–22

Jewish nation. Luke 13:6–9

Christ's return. . . . . Matt. 24:32, 33

Final judgment . . . . Rev. 6:13

Fight—*a conflict*

A. Used literally of:

War . . . . Ex. 17:8, 10

Individual combat . . . . 1 Sam. 17:10, 32

B. Used figuratively of:

Determined resolve . . . . 1 Cor. 9:26

Opposition of evil men . . . . 1 Cor. 15:32

Christian life . . . . 1 Tim. 6:12

Dissension . . . . James 4:1, 2

Spiritual conflict . . . . Rev. 12:7

Fighting against God

A. Manifested by:

Pharaoh. . . . . Ex. 5:1, 2

Rabshakeh . . . . 2 Kin. 18:28–36

Jeroboam . . . . 2 Chr. 13:8–19

B. Futility of:

Seen by Gamaliel . . . . Acts 5:34, 39

Admitted by Pharisees . . . . Acts 23:9

Experienced by Satan . . . . Rev. 12:7–17

Blasphemy of unregenerate . . . . Rev. 16:9–21

Figurehead—*symbol on ship's prow*

Twin Brothers . . . . Acts 28:11

Figures of speech

Allegory . . . . Gal. 4:24

Fable. . . . . Judg. 9:8–15; 1 Tim. 4:7

Hyperbole. . . . . 1 Sam. 13:5; John 21:25

Interrogation. . . . . 1 Cor. 12:29, 30

Irony . . . . Luke 15:7–10

Metaphor . . . . Luke 13:32

Parable. . . . . Matt. 13:10

Parallelism . . . . Gen. 4:23, 24

Personification . . . . Is. 55:12

Proverb . . . . 1 Kin. 4:32

Sarcasm. . . . . Matt. 27:29

Simile. . . . . Is. 1:8, 9

Similitude. . . . . Ps. 90:4–6

Filial devotion

A. Duty of:

Commanded . . . . Ex. 20:12

Corrupted. Matt. 15:4–6

Confirmed . . . . Eph. 6:1–3

B. Examples of:

Joseph . . . . Gen. 47:12

David. . . . . 1 Sam. 22:3

Solomon . . . . 1 Kin. 2:19

Elisha. . . . . 1 Kin. 19:19, 20

Young man. . . . . Matt. 19:16–20

C. Obedience:

Continual . . . . Prov. 6:20–22

Total. . . . . Col. 3:20

Lack of, severely punished . . . . Deut. 21:18–21

Lack of, cursed . . . . Prov. 20:20

Filth—*uncleanness, defilement, corruption*

Men . . . . Job 15:16; Ps. 14:2, 3

Garments and furniture . . . . Is. 4:1–4; 28:8; James 2:2

Ceremonial uncleanness. . . . . Ezek. 22:15

Unrighteousness. . . . . Is. 64:6; Ezek. 16:6

Fine—*penalty payment*

Paid by guilty. . . . . Ex. 21:23–30; Deut. 22:19

Restitution . . . . Ex. 22:5–15; Num. 5:6, 7

Finger

A. Used literally of:

Human fingers . . . . John 20:25, 27

Deformity. . . . . 2 Sam. 21:20

Measurement. Jer. 52:21

Mysterious hand. . . . . Dan. 5:5

B. Used figuratively of:

God's power. . . . . Ex. 8:19

Inspiration . . . . Ex. 31:18

Suggestiveness. . . . . Prov. 6:13

Contrast of burdens. . . . . 1 Kin. 12:10

Lord's authority . . . . Luke 11:20

Finish

Used of:

The Messiah's advent . . . . Dan. 9:24–27

Final events . . . . Dan. 12:7

Jesus' mission. . . . . John 19:28–30

Fins

Signs of a clean fish . . . . Lev. 11:9

Fir—*a tree of the pine family*

Used in ships . . . . Ezek. 27:5

Used for musical instruments . . . . 2 Sam. 6:5

Fire

A. Physical uses of:

Productive:

Warmth. . . . . John 18:18

Cooking . . . . .Ex. 16:23
Signal. . . . . .Judg. 20:38, 40
Sacrifice . . . . .Gen. 8:20, 21
Refining . . . . .Ps. 12:6
Evil:
Torture . . . . Dan. 3:6
Sacrificing children . . . . .2 Kin. 16:3
Burning fields . . . . .Judg. 15:4, 5
War . . . . 1 Sam. 30:1
B. Supernatural uses of:
Express God's nature. . . . . .Deut. 4:24; Heb. 12:29
Seal a covenant . . . . Gen. 15:17
Burning bush. . . . . .Ex. 3:2
Pillar of fire . . . . Ex. 13:21, 22
Mt. Sinai on fire . . . . .Ex. 19:18
Holy fire on altar .Lev. 9:24
Chariot, horses of .2 Kin. 2:11
Tongues as of fire . . . . .Acts 2:1–4
Eyes like . . . . .Rev. 1:14
Destroy the world. . . . . 2 Pet. 3:10, 11
Punish the wicked . . . . Matt. 25:41
C. Figurative uses of:
Affliction . . . . Is. 43:2
Angels . . . . Heb. 1:7
Christ. . . . . Mal. 3:2
God's protection. . . . . .Zech. 2:5
God's vengeance. . . . . Heb. 12:29
God's Word . . . . .Jer. 5:14
Love . . . . Song 8:6
Lust . . . . .Prov. 6:27, 28
Persecution. . . . . Luke 12:49–53
Purification . . . . Is. 6:5–7
The tongue. . . . . James 3:6

Fire, lake of—*place of eternal punishment*
The Beast . . . . Rev. 19:20
The False Prophet . . . . Rev. 19:20
The devil. . . . . Rev. 20:10
Death and Hades . . . . .Rev. 20:14
Sinners. . . . . .Rev. 21:8

Firebrand—*torch*
Figurative of enemies . . . . .Is. 7:4
Thrown by a madman. . . . . .Prov. 26:18
Have no fear of . . . . .Is. 7:4
All who encircle . . . . Is. 50:11
Snatched from a blaze . . . . Amos 4:11

Firepan—*a shovel used for carrying fire*
Part of the altar. . . . . .Ex. 27:3

Firmament—*expanse*
Created by God. Gen. 1:8
Stars placed in . . . . Gen. 1:14, 17
Compared to a tent . . . . .Ps. 104:2
Expressive of God's glory. . . . . Ps. 19:1
Saints compared to. . . . . .Dan. 12:3

First
Came out red . . . . Gen. 25:25
This came out . . . . Gen. 38:28
These should set forth. . . . . Num. 2:9
Amalek, of nations. . . . . Num. 24:20

Hands of witness shall be. . . . . .Deut. 17:7
Altar Saul built . . . . 1 Sam. 14:35
Case pleaded . . . . .Prov. 18:17
Seek . . . . Matt. 6:33
Cast out plank. . . . . Matt. 7:5; Luke 6:42
Last state worse than. . . . . .Luke 11:26
The blade, then the head . . . . Mark 4:28
Let the children. . . . . .Mark 7:27
Desire to be . . . . Mark 9:35
Commandment. . . . . Mark 12:28
Gospel must, be preached. . . . . Mark 13:10
Appeared to Mary Magdalene . . . . .Mark 16:9
Not sit down . . . . .Luke 14:28
Stepped in, made whole . . . . John 5:4
Gave themselves. . . . . 2 Cor. 8:5
Trusted in Christ . . . . Eph. 1:12
A falling away . . . . 2 Thess. 2:3
Let these also. . . . . 1 Tim. 3:10
Dwelt. . . . . .2 Tim. 1:5
He takes away . . . . Heb. 10:9

First (things mentioned)
Altar. . . . . Gen. 8:20
Archer . . . . Gen. 21:20
Bigamist . . . . Gen. 4:19
Birthday celebration . . . . .Gen. 40:20
Book. . . . . Gen. 5:1
Bridal veil. Gen. 24:64–67
Cave dwellers. Gen. 19:30
Christian martyr . . . . Acts 22:19, 20
City builder . . . . Gen. 4:17
Coffin . . . . .Gen. 50:26
Command . . . . Gen. 1:3
Commanded by Christ . . . . Matt. 6:33
Craftsman . . . . Gen. 4:22
Cremation . . . . .1 Sam. 31:12
Curse . . . . Gen. 3:14
Death. . . . . Gen. 4:8
Doubt . . . . Gen. 3:1
Dream . . . . Gen. 20:3
Drunkenness .Gen. 9:20, 21
Emancipator . . . . Ex. 3:7–22
Embalming . . . . .Gen. 50:2, 3
European convert. . . . . Acts 16:14, 15
Execution . . . . Gen. 40:20–22
Family . . . . Gen. 4:1, 2
Famine . . . . Gen. 12:10
Farewell address . . . . .Josh. 23:1–16
Farmer. . . . . Gen. 4:2
Female government . . . . .Judg. 4:4, 5
Ferryboat . . . . .2 Sam. 19:18
Food control . . . . Gen. 41:25–36
Frying pan . . . . .Lev. 2:7
Gardener. . . . . Gen. 2:15
Gold. . . . . Gen. 2:11
Harp . . . . Gen. 4:21
Hebrew (Jew). Gen. 14:13
High priest. . . . . .Ex. 28:1
Hunter. . . . . .Gen. 10:8, 9
Idolatry . . . . .Josh. 24:2

Firstfruits

A. Regulations concerning:

Law specified.......................Lev. 23:9–14

Brought to God's house ....Ex. 34:26

Firstfruits offering.................Lev. 23:9–14

Considered holy ....Ezek. 20:40

God honored by ....Prov. 3:9

B. Figurative of:

Israel's position.....................Rom. 11:16

Christ's place in resurrection...... 1 Cor. 15:20, 23

Christians...........................James 1:18

First converts.......................Rom. 16:5

Fish

A. Features regarding:

Created by God.....................Gen. 1:20, 21

Worship of forbidden ....Deut. 4:15–18

Caught by net ....Matt. 4:18

Some disciples called while
fishermen.....................Matt. 4:18–21

B. Miracles involving:

Jonah's life in.........................Jon. 1:17

Multiplied by Christ .... Matt. 14:17–21

Containing a coin................... Matt. 17:27

Miraculous catch ...... Luke 5:4–7; John 21:6–10

C. Figurative of:

Ministers as fishermen ....Matt. 4:19

Ignorant men........................ Eccl. 9:12

Fish Gate—*a gate of Jerusalem*

Manasseh built wall there ....2 Chr. 33:13, 14

Built by sons of Hassenaah .... Neh. 3:3

Two choirs took their stand....... Neh. 12:38–40

A cry there prophesied .... Zeph. 1:10

Fishhook—*hook for catching fish*

Cannot catch Leviathan.................Job 41:1

Sorrow of those using .... Is. 19:8

Fist fighting

Punishment of.....................Ex. 21:18, 19

Flask—*a small vessel*

Used for anointing.................. 1 Sam. 10:1

Used in prophecy .... Jer. 19:1–15

Of alabaster .... Matt. 26:7; Luke 7:37

Flattery—*unjustified praise*

A. Used by:

False prophets.......................Rom. 16:18

Hypocrites ....Ps. 78:36

Wicked .... Ps. 36:1–4

Seductresses........................ Prov. 2:16

B. Attitude of saints toward:

Should avoid users of................Prov. 20:19

Pray against.........................Ps. 5:8, 9

Should not use...................... 1 Thess. 2:5

C. Dangers of:

Leads to ruin ....Prov. 26:28

Brings deception.....................Prov. 29:5

Corrupts.....................Dan. 11:21, 25, 27

Brings death.......................Acts 12:21–23

Flax—*the flax plant*

Grown in Egypt and Palestine ....Ex. 9:31

Used for:

Cords..............................Judg. 15:14

Weaving .... Is. 19:9

Garments ("linen") .... Deut. 22:11

Figurative use of:

Messiah will not extinguish.............Is. 42:3;
Matt. 12:20

Flea—*a parasitic, blood-sucking insect*

Figurative of insignificance......... 1 Sam. 24:14

Fleece—*freshly sheared wool*

Given to priests.................... Deut. 18:3, 4

Sign to Gideon.....................Judg. 6:36–40

Warm................................ Job 31:20

WORD STUDY **FLESH,** *basar* (baw-*sawr*). The flesh of the body of an animal is the most common use of the noun *basar* (Deut. 14:8), usually translated "flesh." The same word can also be used to refer to the flesh of a human body as in Gen. 40:19. Alternatively, the word can refer to the entire body, and not just to the flesh as it does in Lev. 16:4. As an extension of this, *basar* is the opposite of the soul or breath (Job 14:22; Is. 10:18), so that humans are seen to be made up of two parts—the body, which is tangible, and the intangible life force that originates with God. It can refer to blood relations who are of the same flesh. The word is also used to compare the frail and erring with God. (Strong's #1320)

WORD STUDY **FLESH,** *sarx* (*sarks*). This noun literally refers to the material covering of the body (1 Cor. 15:39), but it can refer to the "body" itself (Eph. 5:29), sometimes as the opposite of the "spirit" (1 Cor. 5:5). *Sarx* describes human beings of "flesh and blood" (1 Cor. 15:50) in contrast to God (Matt. 16:17), the resurrected Christ (Gal. 1:16), or other supernatural entities (Eph. 6:12). *Sarx* is used with reference to the "physical nature" of Christ (John 1:14; Col. 1:22; Heb. 5:7) or to emphasize the corporeality of His earthly body (1 John 4:2; 2 John 7): Christ became "flesh." Paul uses "flesh" as a metaphor for the baser nature of human beings, which is subject to sin (Rom. 8). (Strong's #4561)

Flesh

A. Used to designate:

All created life...................Gen. 6:13, 17, 19

Kinsmen (of same nature) .... Rom. 9:3, 5, 8

The body............................ Job 33:25

Marriage........................... Matt. 19:5

Human nature....................... John 1:14

Christ's mystical nature .... John 6:51, 53–63

Human weakness................... Matt. 16:17

Outward appearance................. 2 Cor. 5:16

The evil principle in man ....Rom. 7:18

B. In a bad sense, described as:

Having passions ....Gal. 5:24

Producing evil works................ Gal. 5:19–21
Dominating the mind.................. Eph. 2:3
Absorbing the affections ....Rom. 13:14
Seeking outward display........... Gal. 6:12, 13
Antagonizing the Spirit ....Gal. 5:17
Fighting against God's Law......... Rom. 8:5–9
Reaping corruption ....Gal. 6:8
Producing death ....Rom. 7:5

C. Christian's attitude toward:
Still confronts .... Rom. 7:18–23
Source of opposition ....Gal. 5:17
Make no provision for...............Rom. 13:14
Do not love.................... 1 John 2:15–17
Do not walk in.....................Rom. 8:1, 4
Do not live in.................... Rom. 8:12, 13
Crucified ....Gal. 5:24
Spirit to be poured out on all.......... Joel 2:28;
     Acts 2:16, 17

Fleshhook—*fork*
In tabernacle ....Ex. 27:3; Num. 4:14
By priests .... 1 Sam. 2:12–14
In temple........... 1 Chr. 28:11, 17; 2 Chr. 4:16

Flies—*small winged insects*
Cause of evil odor.................... Eccl. 10:1
Figurative of Egypt ....Is. 7:18
Plague upon the Egyptians ....Ex. 8:21–31;
     Ps. 78:45

Flint—*a very hard stone*
Water from.........................Deut. 8:15
Oil from .... Deut. 32:13
Turning into fountain of water......... Ps. 114:8
Hoofs shall seem like.................... Is. 5:28
Figurative of a fixed course .....Is. 50:7; Ezek. 3:9

Flock—*a group of domesticated animals; a group under
the guidance of a leader*
Sheep and goats....................... Gen. 27:9
Nations................................Jer. 51:23
National leaders ....Jer. 25:34, 35
Jewish people...................... Jer. 13:17, 20
The church................ Is. 40:11; Acts 20:28

Flood—*overflowing of water*
A. Used literally of:
Earth's flood .... Gen. 6:17
B. Used figuratively of:
Great trouble...........................Ps. 32:6
Hostile world powers.....................Ps. 93:3
An invading army.................... Jer. 46:7, 8
Great destruction................... Dan. 9:26
Testing .... Matt. 7:25, 27
Persecution..................... Rev. 12:15, 16

Floor
For threshing wheat...... Judg. 6:37; 1 Kin. 22:10
Of a building .... 1 Kin. 6:15

Flour—*finely ground wheat*
Offered in sacrifices................Lev. 5:11, 13
Used of, in bread................. 1 Sam. 28:24

Increased ....1 Kin. 17:12–16
Antidote .... 2 Kin. 4:38–41

Flowers
A. Described as:
Wild..........................Ps. 103:15, 16
Beautiful.................... Matt. 6:28, 29
Sweet .... Song 5:13
Fading .... Is. 40:7, 8
B. Figurative of:
Shortness of life ....Job 14:2
Israel .... Is. 28:1
Human glory ....James 1:10, 11
C. Specific kinds:
Aloes .... John 19:39
Anise .... Matt. 23:23
Cummin ....Is. 28:25, 27
Flax ....Ex. 9:31
Hemlock........................ Hos. 10:4
Lentil....................... Gen. 25:34
Lily.................... Song 2:1, 16; 4:5
Mandrake....................... Gen. 30:14
Mint.......................Luke 11:42
Rose .... Song 2:1; Is. 35:1
Rue ....Luke 11:42
Saffron............................. Song 4:4

Flute—*a hollow musical instrument*
A. Used in:
Babylon............................. Dan. 3:5
Prophecy...................... 1 Sam. 10:5
Worship ....Ps. 150:4
B. Figurative of:
Joyful deliverance................ Is. 30:29
Mournful lamentation .... Jer. 48:36
Inconsistent reactions...............Matt. 11:17
Spiritual discernment .... 1 Cor. 14:7

Foal—*a colt, young donkey*
Given to Esau....................Gen. 32:13–15
Ridden by Christ ....Zech. 9:9; Matt. 21:5

Fodder—*food for domestic animals*
Given to oxen and wild donkey ....Job 6:5;
     Is. 30:24

Following
A. In Old Testament:
Commanded .... Deut. 8:6
Brought reward..................... Deut. 19:9
Covenant ....2 Kin. 23:3
B. In New Testament:
Multitudes .... Matt. 4:25; 12:15
Disciples ....Matt. 8:19; Luke 5:11, 27, 28
Left all...........................Matt. 4:18–22
In light............................. John 8:12
After Christ's example .....John 13:15; 1 John 2:6
Examples of godly people....Phil. 3:17; Heb. 6:12;
     James 5:10

Folly—*contemptuous disregard of holy things*
A. Associated with:
Deception...........................Prov. 14:8

Hasty spirit ....Prov. 14:29
Gullibility...........................Prov. 13:16
Ferociousness ....Prov. 17:12
Disgust ....Prov. 26:11
Lack of wisdom.....................Eccl. 7:25

B. Warnings against:

Saints not to return to..................Ps. 85:8
Samaritan prophets guilty of.......... Jer. 23:13
Apostles subject to .... 2 Cor. 11:1

Food

A. Features regarding:

Given by God.................... Ps. 104:21, 27
Necessary for life ....Gen. 1:29, 30
Gives physical strength...............Acts 9:19
Revives the spirit .... 1 Sam. 30:12
Object of daily prayer ....Matt. 6:11
Object of thanksgiving..............1 Sam. 9:13
Sanctified by prayer............... 1 Tim. 4:4, 5
Scruples recognized .... Rom. 14:2–23

B. Lack of:

Testing of faith .... Hab. 3:17

C. Provided by:

God ....Ps. 145:15
Christ.............................John 21:5, 6

D. Prohibitions concerning:

Dead animals........................Ex. 22:31
Eating blood .... Deut. 12:16
Clean and unclean ....Deut. 14:4–20
Wine .... Prov. 23:29–35
Strangled animals.................... Acts 21:25
Not in itself commendable............ 1 Cor. 8:8
Not to be a stumbling block.......... 1 Cor. 8:13
Life more important than .... Matt. 6:25

E. Miracles connected with:

Destruction of.................... Ps. 105:29–35
Provision for .... Ps. 105:40, 41
Supply of........................ 1 Kin. 17:4–6
Multiplication of.... Matt. 15:32–38; John 6:5–13
Refused........................... Matt. 4:1–4

F. Figurative of:

God's will.........................John 4:32, 34
Christ............................John 6:27, 55
Strong doctrines .... 1 Cor. 3:2

Food control

Physical..................... Gen. 41:25–36
Spiritual .... Rev. 13:11–17

Food, spiritual

A. Elements of:

The Word..........................Ps. 19:9, 10
Christ...........................John 6:48–51

B. Need of, by:

The naive ....Prov. 9:1–5
The immature..................... 1 Cor. 3:1, 2
The mature .... Heb. 5:14
All............................... Matt. 22:4

C. Characteristics of:

Abundant .... Is. 55:1–3
Satisfying ....Ps. 22:26

Enduring.........................John 6:48–51
Life-giving ....John 6:53–63

Foods of Bible times

A. Obtaining; storing; use:

Shall be for .... Gen. 6:21
Let them gather...................... Gen. 41:35
Come to buy......................... Gen. 42:10
Go again, buy .... Gen. 43:2
Buy................................ Gen. 43:4
Much ....Prov. 13:23
Of the offering .... Lev. 3:11
Of holy things ....Lev. 22:7
In giving him....................... Deut. 10:18
Seeking in wilderness .... Job 24:5
People did eat that of angels ....Ps. 78:25
Bring forth ....Ps. 104:14

B. Specific kinds:

Almonds........................... Gen. 43:11
Barley.............................Judg. 7:13
Beans ....Ezek. 4:9
Beef .... 1 Kin. 4:22, 23
Beef stew........................1 Kin. 19:21
Bread ....1 Sam. 17:17
Broth ....Judg. 6:19
Cakes............................ 2 Sam. 13:8
Cheese .... Job 10:10
Cucumbers.......................... Num. 11:5
Curds of cows .... Deut. 32:14
Eggs .... Deut. 22:6
Figs............................. Num. 13:23
Fish.............................Matt. 7:10
Fowl ....1 Kin. 4:23
Fruit............................. 2 Sam. 16:2
Garlic............................ Num. 11:5
Goat's milk........................Prov. 27:27
Grain .... Ruth 2:14
Grapes........................... Deut. 23:24
Grasshoppers.....................Lev. 11:22
Herbs............................Ex. 12:8
Honey ....Is. 7:15
Leeks .... Num. 11:5
Lentils ....Gen. 25:34
Locusts ....Matt. 3:4
Meal............................. Matt. 13:33
Melons........................... Num. 11:5
Milk .... Gen. 18:7, 8
Nuts .... Gen. 43:11
Oil ....Prov. 21:17
Olives...........................Deut. 28:40
Onions........................... Num. 11:5
Pomegranates .... Num. 13:23
Quail ....Num. 11:32, 33
Raisins..........................2 Sam. 16:1
Salt ....Job 6:6
Sheep .... Deut. 14:4
Spices............................ Gen. 43:11
Stew .... Gen. 25:30
Vinegar .... Num. 6:3
Venison .... Gen. 25:28

Wild honey............................Matt. 3:4
Wine ....John 2:3, 10

Foolish—*those who misuse wisdom*
A. Those described as:
Clamorous woman....................Prov. 9:13
Builder on sand..................... Matt. 7:26
Five virgins...................... Matt. 25:1–13
Galatians ....Gal. 3:1, 3
Gentiles.............................Titus 3:3
Pharisees.......................Luke 11:39, 40
B. Things described as:
The heart ....Rom. 1:21
Things............................ 1 Cor. 1:27
Lusts............................. 1 Tim. 6:9
Disputes .... 2 Tim. 2:23
C. Characteristics of:
Destructive ....Prov. 10:14
Despicable ....Prov. 15:20
Disappointing ....Prov. 19:13

Foolishness—*a disregard of final issues*
A. Characteristics of:
Form of sin.........................Prov. 24:9
Originates in the heart .... Mark 7:21–23
Sign of wickedness................. Eccl. 7:25
Known by God ....Ps. 69:5
B. Consequences of:
Brings sorrow .... Ps. 38:4–10
Perverts man's way................. Prov. 19:3
Spiritual blindness.................. 1 Cor. 1:18

Fools—*those who lack true wisdom*
A. Described as:
Atheistic............................. Ps. 14:1
Blasphemous .... Ps. 74:18
Contentious........................Prov. 18:6
Corrupt............................. Ps. 14:1
Hypocritical......................Luke 11:39, 40
Idle.............................. Eccl. 4:5
Vexation ....Prov. 12:16
Materialistic .... Luke 12:16–21
Quarrelsome ....Prov. 20:3
Mischievous.......................Prov. 10:23
Mocking ....Prov. 14:9
Raging............................Prov. 14:16
Self-confident ....Prov. 28:26
Self-righteous ....Prov. 12:15
Self-sufficient ....Rom. 1:22
Slandering ....Prov. 10:18
Wasteful..........................Prov. 21:20
Wordy ....Eccl. 10:12–14
B. Further characteristics of:
Deny God......................... Ps. 14:1
Hate knowledge ....Prov. 1:22
Come to shame ....Prov. 3:35
Mock at sin........................Prov. 14:9
Cannot attain to wisdom.............Prov. 24:7
Trust in their hearts...............Prov. 28:26
Walk in darkness .... Eccl. 2:14

C. Examples of:
Nabal.......................... 1 Sam. 25:3, 25
Rehoboam .... 1 Kin. 12:6–13
Pharisees....................... Matt. 23:17, 19
The rich man.................... Luke 12:16–21
Apostles ....1 Cor. 14:9, 10

Foot
A. To sit at, figurative of:
Teachableness ....Luke 10:39
B. To be under, figurative of:
Humankind's sovereignty .... Ps. 8:6
Christ's victory ....Ps. 110:1
Conquest.......................Josh. 10:24
C. Examples, figurative of:
Prosperity......................... Deut. 33:24
Possession......................... Josh. 1:3
Stability........................ Prov. 4:26, 27
Reverence....................... Josh. 5:15
Whole person .... Prov. 1:15
See Feet

Footstool
A. Used literally of:
In the temple .... 2 Chr. 9:18
Prominent seat .... James 2:3
B. Used figuratively of:
Earth .... Matt. 5:35
Ark................................1 Chr. 28:2
Temple worship.......................Ps. 99:5
Subjection....................... Acts 2:35

Forbearance of God
A. God's withholding of judgment upon:
The Amorites .... Gen. 15:16
Sodom .... Gen. 18:23–32
Israel ....Neh. 9:30, 31
Nineveh........................Jon. 4:10, 11
The world......................Rom. 3:25
B. Attitudes toward:
Not to be despised ....Rom. 2:4
To be remembered .... 2 Pet. 3:8–10
Means of preparation .... Mal. 3:1–6

Forbearance toward others
Expression of love.................... 1 Cor. 13:7
Christian grace .... Eph. 4:2

Forced labor—*conscripted workers or slaves*
In brickmaking.................... Ex. 5:11–14
Prisoners of war .... Deut. 20:10, 11
As slaves ....Ex. 13:3
By Solomon .... 1 Kin. 9:20, 21

Forces—*military power*
Assembling great ....Dan. 11:10, 38
Weakness of........................ Zech. 4:6
Destruction of great............. Rev. 20:7–10

Forceful—*powerful*
Power of right words .... Job 6:25

Ford—*a shallow part of a body of water used for crossing*
Of the Jabbok ....Gen. 32:22
Of the Jordan.......................Judg. 3:28

Forehead—*the upper part of the face*
A. Used literally of:
    Aaron's .... Ex. 28:38
    Philistine's .... 1 Sam. 17:49
    Uzziah's........................ 2 Chr. 26:19, 20
B. Used figuratively of:
    Shamelessness ....Rev. 17:5
    Stronger power .... Ezek. 3:8, 9
    Devotion to God....................Ezek. 9:4
    Christ's true servants................... Rev. 7:3

Foreign affairs—*dealings with other countries*
    War .... Gen. 14:1–16; Josh. 8:1–29
    Treaties ....Josh. 9:1–27
    Trade agreement...................1 Kin. 5:1–18
    Alliances...............1 Kin. 15:16–22; 22:1–6
    Conquest........................2 Kin. 25:1–11

Foreigners—*sojourners in Israel*
    Kept from feast....................Ex. 12:43–45
    Taxable .... Deut. 15:2, 3
    Figurative of Gentiles .... Eph. 2:19
  See Strangers

Foreign missionaries
    Jonah as.............................Jon. 1:1, 2
    Came from Antioch church......... Acts 13:1–3
    Report of........................ Acts 15:7–12

Foreknowledge of Christ
Concerning:
    Human nature.....................John 1:47, 48
    Human acts ....John 6:64
    His death and resurrection ...... Matt. 20:18, 19;
        John 13:1
    Jerusalem's destruction.......... Luke 19:41–44
    Prophetic events .... Matt. 24:1–51

Foreknowledge of God
A. Manifested in:
    Naming a person ....1 Kin. 13:2, 3
    Naming a place..................... Matt. 2:5, 6
    Setting a time ....Mark 1:15
    Determining the boundaries
      of nations...................... Acts 17:26
    Indicating successive nations ...... Dan. 2:26–47
    Announcing Israel's captivity....... Jer. 25:11, 12
    Foretelling Christ's death.............. Acts 2:23
B. Based upon God's:
    Infinite knowledge..................Is. 41:22, 23
    Eternal being ....Is. 43:9–13
    Foredetermination of events..........Rom. 8:29
C. Plan of Salvation:
    Planned in eternity..................Eph. 1:3–12
    Announces from beginning........... Gen. 3:15
    Expanded to include Gentiles...........Gal. 3:8
    Elaborated in details .... Is. 53:1–12
    Visualized in prophecy .... Zech. 3:1–10
    Consummated in Christ's death....... John 19:30

Foresee—*to see something before it takes place*
    Approaching evil ....Prov. 22:3
    Resurrection of Christ ....Acts 2:31

    Salvation of Gentiles ....Gal. 3:8

Foreskin (see Circumcision)
A. Used literally of:
    Circumcision.....................Gen. 17:9–17
    Death......................... 1 Sam. 18:25
B. Figuratively of:
    Regeneration ....Jer. 4:4

Forest
A. Descriptive of wooded areas in:
    Hereth...................... 1 Sam. 22:5
    Lebanon .... 1 Kin. 7:2
    Bethel .... 2 Kin. 2:23, 24
    Arabia .... Is. 21:13
B. Used figuratively of:
    Army .... Is. 10:18, 19
    Kingdom...........................Jer. 21:14
    Unfruitfulness.............. Jer. 26:18; Hos. 2:12

Forethought—*thinking ahead*
    In meeting a danger.............. Gen. 32:3–23
    In anticipating evil.....................Prov. 22:3
    Concerning physical needs ....Phil. 4:10–19
    Neglect of, dangerous .... Matt. 25:8–13
    Examples of ant, in................. Prov. 6:6–8
    For eternal riches .... Luke 12:23–34

Foretold—*made known beforehand*
    Destruction of Jerusalem .... Mark 13:1, 2
    Christ's suffering ....Acts 3:18
    Outpouring of the Holy Spirit .....Joel 2:28–32;
      Acts 2:14–21
    Gospel blessings .... Acts 3:24
    Paul's trip to Corinth.................2 Cor. 13:2

Forewarn—*to warn beforehand*
    God's judgment.......................Luke 12:5
    God's vengeance.................... 1 Thess. 4:6

Forfeit—*loss incurred by one's failure*
    Leadership .... 1 Sam. 15:16–28
    Possessions....................... Ezra 10:8
    Salvation........................... Matt. 16:26

Forfeiting spiritual rights
    Birthright.........................Gen. 25:34
    Headship ....Gen. 49:3, 4
    Discipleship ....Matt. 19:16–22
    Apostleship ....Matt. 26:14–16
    Spiritual heritage ....Acts 13:45–48

Forger—*a counterfeiter*
    Applied to David's enemies ....Ps. 119:69

Forget—*be unable to remember*
    God does not .... Is. 49:15
    Our sinful past .... Phil. 3:13

Forgetful—*unable to remember*
    Concerning our hearing............. James 1:25

Forgetting of God
A. Seen in forgetting God's:
    Covenant .... Deut. 4:23
    Works .... Ps. 78:7, 11
    Blessings .... Ps. 103:2

Law............................Ps. 119:153, 176
Word ....James 1:25
B. Characteristics of:
   Wicked .... Is. 65:11
   Form of backsliding................. Jer. 3:21, 22
   Instigated by false teachers ....Jer. 23:26, 27

| WORD STUDY | **FORGIVE,** *salach* (saw-*lakh*). The verb *salach,* which means "forgive" or "pardon," is always used in reference to God |

as the One who forgives. Sometimes God is said to forgive a particular sin as in Num. 14:19 where Moses pleads for God to forgive the people of Israel and in Jer. 31:34 where God says that in the future people will not have to ask for forgiveness, for He will forgive their sin. At other times, God is said to forgive sinners (1 Kin. 8:50). *Salach* is used in the technical phrase "it shall be forgiven" seen frequently in Lev. (4:26, 31; 5:10, 13, 16) and Num. (15:28). (Strong's #5545)

Forgiveness—*an act of pardon*
A. Synonyms of:
   "Blots out" .... Is. 43:25
   "Remission"....................... Matt. 26:28
   "Pardon"................................. Is. 55:7
   "Remember no more" .... Jer. 31:34
   "Healed"..................... 2 Chr. 30:18–20
B. Basis of:
   God's nature .... Ps. 86:5
   God's grace......................... Luke 7:42
   Shedding of blood .... Heb. 9:22
   Christ's death .... Col. 1:14
   Son's power...................... Luke 5:21–24
   Repentance .... Acts 2:38
   Our forgiveness.................. Matt. 6:12–14
   Faith in Christ...................... Acts 10:43
C. Significance of:
   Shows God's righteousness .... Rom. 3:25, 26
   Makes salvation real .... Luke 1:77
   Must be preached...................Luke 24:47

Forgiving one another
A. The measure of:
   Seventy times seven............. Matt. 18:21, 22
   Unlimited......................... Luke 17:3, 4
   As God in Christ forgave us........... Eph. 4:32
B. Benefits of:
   Means of our forgiveness .... Mark 11:25, 26
   Restored Christian fellowship ......2 Cor. 2:7–10
   Spiritual cleansing ....James 5:15, 16
C. Examples of:
   Esau and Jacob ....Gen. 33:4–15
   Joseph ....Gen. 45:8–15
   Moses..........................Num. 12:1–13
   David..........................2 Sam. 19:18–23
   Solomon ....1 Kin. 1:52, 53
   Jesus...........................Luke 23:34
   Stephen .... Acts 7:59, 60
   Paul .... 2 Tim. 4:16

Fork
   In tabernacle .... Ex. 27:3; Num. 2:12–14
   In temple........... 1 Chr. 28:11, 17; 2 Chr. 4:16

Form—*the outward appearance*
A. Of physical things:
   Earth without .... Gen. 1:2
   Baby in the womb.....................Is. 44:24
   Sexes .... 1 Tim. 2:13
   Idols.................................Is. 44:10
B. Of spiritual realities:
   Incarnate Christ.............Is. 53:2; Rom. 9:20
   Molder............................. Rom. 9:20
   Christian truth ....Rom. 6:17
   New birth ....Gal. 4:19
   World passing away.................. 1 Cor. 7:31

Formalism—*forms performed mechanically*
A. Characterized by:
   Outward forms of religion........... Is. 1:10–15
   Lifelessness........................ Is. 58:1–14
   Lukewarmness .... Rev. 3:14–18
B. Sign of:
   Hypocrisy...................... Luke 18:10–14
   Deadness ....Phil. 3:4–8
   Last days.......................... 2 Tim. 3:1, 5

Formula—*a prescribed method*
   Success............................Prov. 22:29
   Prosperity...................... Matt. 6:32, 33
   Peace .... Is. 26:3
   Making friends ....Prov. 18:24

Fornication—*sexual relations among the unmarried*
Evil of:
   Comes from evil heart...............Matt. 15:19
   Sins against the body................. 1 Cor. 6:18
   Excludes from God's kingdom .... 1 Cor. 6:9
   Disrupts Christian fellowship.......1 Cor. 5:9–11
   Spiritual fornication symbolized in
      final apostasy .... Rev. 17:1–5

Forsaken—*left deserted*
   God's house .... Neh. 13:11
   God's children........................Ps. 37:25
   Messiah............................... Is. 53:3
   God's Son .... Matt. 27:46

Forsaking Christ
   Disciples left .... Matt. 26:56
   Cause of separation .... John 6:66–70
   By His Father....................... Matt. 27:46

Forsaking God
A. Manifested in:
   Going after idols..................... 1 Kin. 11:33
   Going backward.....................Jer. 15:6
   Following human forms.................Jer. 2:13
B. Evil of:
   Manifests ingratitude .... Jer. 2:5–12
   Brings confusion....................Jer. 17:13
   Merits God's wrath .... Ezra 8:22

Fraud—*something designed to deceive*
A. Examples of:
    Rebekah's, on Isaac . . . . .Gen. 27:5–36
    Laban's, on Jacob . . . . .Gen. 29:21–25
    Gibeonites', on Israelites . . . . .Josh. 9:3–9
    Jonathan's, on Saul. . . . . 1 Sam. 20:11–17
B. Discovery of, by:
    A miracle . . . . Ex. 7:9–12
    Events . . . . Matt. 28:11–15
    Character . . . . .Matt. 26:47–50

Free moral agency of humankind—*ability to choose*
    Resulted in sin. Gen. 2:16, 17
    Recognized by God . . . . . . .Gen. 4:6–10; John 7:17
    Appealed to . . . . Is. 1:18–20; Jer. 36:3, 7

Freedmen
    Jews opposing Stephen . . . . .Acts 6:9

Freedom—*unrestricted action*
A. Of the unregenerate, limited by:
    Sin. . . . . John 8:34
    Inability . . . . John 8:43
    Satan . . . . .John 8:41, 44
    Bondage . . . . Rom. 6:20
    Deadness . . . . .Eph. 2:1
B. Of the regenerate:
    Made free by Christ. . . . . John 8:36
    Freed from sin's bondage . . . . Rom. 6:18, 22
    Not of license. .1 Pet. 2:16
    Not of bondage again . . . . Gal. 5:1
    Not of the flesh . . . . Gal. 5:13

Freewill offerings
    Obligatory . . . . Deut. 12:6
    Must be perfect. . . . . Lev. 22:17–25
    Eaten in tabernacle by the priests. . . . .Lev. 7:16, 17
    Firstfruits . . . . Prov. 3:9
    According to one's ability. . . . . Deut. 16:17
    Willing mind. . . . . 2 Cor. 8:10–12
    Cheerful heart. . . . . .2 Cor. 9:6, 7

Fretting—*a peevish state of mind*
    Of the saints, forbidden . . . . Ps. 37:1, 7, 8

WORD
STUDY

FRIEND, *philos* (*fee*-loss). Derived from the verb *phileo* ("to love," "to have affection for"), this adjective means "beloved" or "dear" in the passive sense and "loving" or "devoted" (as perhaps in Acts 19:31) in the active sense. In the NT *philos* is used mostly as a substantive meaning "friend" (Luke 7:6). It can also be used as a form of address (Luke 11:5). Usually, *philos* implies a close association, which helps explain the scandal of Jesus' being called the "friend of tax collectors and sinners" (Matt. 11:19). Other uses of the term suggest a special relationship (John 15:13–15; James 2:23). (Strong's #5384)

Friend
A. Nature of, mutual:
    Interest . . . . .1 Sam. 18:1
    Love . . . . 1 Sam. 20:17
    Sympathy . . . . .Job 2:11

    Sacrifice . . . . John 15:13
    Loyalty . . . . Ps. 41:9
    Encouragement. .3 John 5
B. Value of:
    Constructive criticism. . . . . Prov. 27:6
    Helpful advice. . . . . Prov. 27:7
    Valuable in time of need . . . . Prov. 27:10
    Always faithful . . . . Prov. 17:17
C. Dangers of:
    May entice to sin. . . . . .Deut. 13:6–8
    Some attracted to riches . . . . .Prov. 14:20
    Some are untrustworthy. . . . . Ps. 41:9
    Poor counsel . . . . 1 Kin. 12:8–14
D. Examples of:
    God and Abraham . . . . 2 Chr. 20:7; Is. 41:8
    David and Jonathan. . . . . .1 Sam. 18:1
    David and Hushai . . . . 2 Sam. 15:37
    Elijah and Elisha. . . . . .2 Kin. 2:1–14
    Job and his three. . . . . .Job 2:11
    Jesus and Lazarus. . . . . John 11:11
    Christ and His disciples . . . . .John 15:13–15
    Paul and Timothy . . . . .2 Tim. 1:2
    Paul and Philemon. . . . . Philem. 1

Friendless—*lacking friends*
    David's plight . . . . .Ps. 142:4
    Prodigal son. . . . . .Luke 15:15, 16

Friendship
A. Kinds of:
    True . . . . 1 Sam. 18:1–3
    Close . . . . .Prov. 18:24
    Ardent. . . . . .2 Cor. 2:12, 13
    Treacherous. . . . . Matt. 26:48–50
    Dangerous . . . . .Deut. 13:6–9
    Unfaithful . . . . Job 19:14–19
    False. . . . . .2 Sam. 16:16–23
    Worldly. . . . . James 4:4
B. Tests of:
    Continued loyalty. . . . . 2 Sam. 1:23
    Willingness to sacrifice . . . . John 15:13
    Obedient spirit . . . . .John 15:14, 15
    Likemindedness . . . . .Phil. 2:19–23

Frog—*a small, leaping creature*
    Plague on Egypt .Ps. 78:45
    Unclean spirits like . . . . .Rev. 16:13

Frontlets—*ornaments worn on the forehead*
    Of God's Word .Deut. 6:6–9

Frost
    Figurative of God's creative ability . . . . . Job 38:29
    Manna's texture compared to . . . . .Ex. 16:14

Frugality—*thrift*
    Manifested by Jesus. . . . . .John 6:11–13
    Wrong kind . . . . Prov. 11:24, 25

Fruit—*product of life*
A. Used literally of:
    Produce of trees . . . . Gen. 1:29
    Produce of the earth . . . . Gen. 4:3

B. Factors destructive of:

Blight	Joel 1:12
Locusts	Joel 1:4
Enemies	Ezek. 25:4
Drought	Hag. 1:10, 11
God's anger	Jer. 7:20

C. Used figuratively of:

Repentance	Matt. 3:8
Industry	Prov. 31:16, 31
Christian graces	Gal. 5:22, 23
Holy life	Prov. 11:30
Christ	Ps. 132:11
Sinful life	Matt. 7:15, 16
Reward of righteousness	Phil. 1:11

Fruit-bearing—*productiveness of*

Old age	Ps. 92:14
Good hearers	Matt. 13:23
Christian converts	Col. 1:6, 10
Abiding	John 15:2–8

Fruitfulness

A. Literally, dependent upon:

Right soil	Matt. 13:8
Rain	James 5:18
Sunshine	Deut. 33:14
Seasons	Matt. 21:34
Cultivation	Luke 13:8
God's blessing	Acts 14:17

B. Spiritually, dependent upon:

Death	John 12:24
New life	Rom. 7:4
Abiding in Christ	John 15:2–8
Yielding to God	Rom. 6:13–23
Christian effort	2 Pet. 1:5–11
Absence of, reprobated	Matt. 21:19

Fruitless discussion—*self-conceited talk against God*

Characteristic of false teachers	1 Tim. 1:6, 7

Fruit of the Spirit

Defined	Gal. 5:22, 23
Christian life characterized by	Rom. 14:17
Unity to be pursued	Eph. 3:15, 16; 4:2, 3
In relations with others	Col. 3:12–15
Virtues	2 Pet. 1:5–7

Fruit trees

Protected by Law	Lev. 19:23–25

Fulfill—*to bring to its designed end*

A. Spoken of God's:

Word	Ps. 148:8
Prophecy	1 Kin. 2:27
Threat	2 Chr. 36:20, 21
Promise	Acts 13:32, 33
Righteousness	Matt. 3:15
Good pleasure	2 Thess. 1:11

B. Spoken of the believer's:

Love	Rom. 13:8
Righteousness	Rom. 8:4
Burden-bearing	Gal. 6:2

Mission	Col. 1:25
Ministry	Col. 4:17

Full—*complete*

A. Of natural things:

Years	Gen. 25:8
Pails	Job 21:24
Children	Ps. 127:5
Cart	Amos 2:13
Leprosy	Luke 5:12
Darkness	Lev. 16:10

B. Of miraculous things:

Guidance	Judg. 6:38
Supply	2 Kin. 4:4, 6
Protection	2 Kin. 6:17

C. Of evil emotions:

Evil	Eccl. 9:3
Fury	Dan. 3:19
Wrath	Acts 19:28
Envy	Rom. 1:29
Cursing	Rom. 3:14
Deadly poison	James 3:8
Adultery	2 Pet. 2:14

D. Of good things:

Power	Mic. 3:8
Grace, truth	John 1:14
Joy	John 15:11
Faith	Acts 6:5, 8
Good works	Acts 9:36
Holy Spirit	Acts 11:24

Fuller—*one who treats or dyes cloth*

Outside city	2 Kin. 18:17; Is. 7:3
God is like	Mal. 3:2

Fullness—*completion*

A. Of time:

Christ's advent	Gal. 4:4
Gentile age	Rom. 11:25
Age of grace	Eph. 1:10

B. Of Christ:

Eternal Christ	Col. 2:9
Incarnate Christ	John 1:16
Glorified Christ	Eph. 1:22, 23

Funeral—*burial rites*

Sad	1 Kin. 13:29, 30
Joyful	Luke 7:11–17

Furnace—*fire made very hot*

A. Used literally of:

Smoke from Sodom and Gomorrah	Gen. 19:28
Baker's oven	Hos. 7:4
Fiery, of Nebuchadnezzar	Dan. 3:20–27

B. Used figuratively of:

Egyptian bondage	Deut. 4:20
Spiritual refinement	Ps. 12:6
Lust	Hos. 7:4
Hell	Matt. 13:42, 50
Punishment	Ezek. 22:18–22

Furniture

Tabernacle	Ex. 31:7

G

Freedom from the Law . . . . Gal. 2:15–4:31
Fruit of the Holy Spirit . . . . Gal. 5:22, 23

Galbanum—*a yellowish-brown aromatic resin*
Used in the holy oil . . . . Ex. 30:34

Galeed—*heap of witness*
Memorial site. . . . . Gen. 31:48

Galilean—*an inhabitant of Galilee*
Speech of. . . . . Mark 14:70
Slaughter of . . . . Luke 13:1
Faith of . . . . John 4:45
Pilate's cruelty toward. . . . . Luke 13:1, 2

Galilee—*circle, circuit*
A. History of:
Moses' prophecy concerning . . . . . . Deut. 33:18–23
Allotted to tribe of Naphtali . . . . Josh. 20:7
Twenty cities of, given to Hiram . . . . . . 1 Kin. 9:11
Conquered by Syrians . . . . 1 Kin. 15:18, 20
Conquered by Assyrians. . . . . 2 Kin. 15:29
Called Galilee of the Gentiles. . . . . Is. 9:1
Dialect of, distinctive . . . . Matt. 26:73
Herod's jurisdiction over . . . . Luke 3:1; 23:5–7
Christian churches in . . . . Acts 9:31
B. Christ's contacts with:
Reared there. . . . . Matt. 2:22
Called Jesus of Galilee . . . . Matt. 26:69
Chooses disciples from . . . . Matt. 4:18, 21
Fulfills prophecy concerning . . . . . . Matt. 4:14, 15
Performs many miracles in . . . . Matt. 4:23
People of, receive Him . . . . Matt. 4:25
Seeks refuge in . . . . John 4:1, 3
Women of, minister to Him . . . . Matt. 27:55
Seen in, after His resurrection . . . . Matt. 26:32
Great Commission issued there . . . Matt. 28:16–20

Galilee, Sea of
Scene of many events in Christ's life such as:
Calls four fishermen on,
    as disciples. . . . . Matt. 4:18–22
Teaches multitude from boat on. . . . . . Luke 5:1–3
Walks on waters of. . . . . John 6:19
Feeds 5,000 on shore of. . . . . John 6:1–11
Heals deaf and mute man at . . . . Mark 7:31–35
Called Chinnereth . . . . Num. 34:11
Later called Gennesaret . . . . Luke 5:1

Gall—*bile*
Used literally of:
Liver secretion. . . . . Job 16:13
Poisonous herb . . . . Amos 6:12; Matt. 27:34

Gallantry—*a chivalrous act of bravery*
Example of . . . . Ex. 2:16–21

Gallim—*heaps*
Village north of Jerusalem. . . . . Is. 10:29, 30
Home of Palti . . . . 1 Sam. 25:44

Gallio—*who lives on milk*
Roman proconsul of Achaia; dismisses
    charges against Paul . . . . Acts 18:12–17

Gallows—*a structure used for hanging*
Haman had made. . . . . Esth. 5:14
Haman hanged on . . . . Esth. 7:9, 10
Haman's sons hanged on . . . . Esth. 9:13, 25

Gamaliel—*God has rewarded*
1. Leader of Manasseh. . . . . Num. 2:20
2. Famous Jewish teacher. . . . . Acts 22:3
Respected by people. . . . . Acts 5:34–39

Game—*the flesh of wild animals*
Isaac's favorite dish . . . . Gen. 27:1–33

Games—*various kinds of contests*
Figurative examples of (as of a race):
Requiring discipline . . . . 1 Cor. 9:25–27
Requiring obedience to rules . . . . 2 Tim. 2:5
Testing the course . . . . Gal. 2:2
Press on to the goal . . . . Phil. 3:13, 14

Gammad—*warrior*
Manned Tyre's towers . . . . Ezek. 27:11

Gamul—*rewarded*
Descendant of Aaron. . . . . 1 Chr. 24:17

Garden—*a protected and cultivated place*
A. Notable examples of:
In Eden . . . . Gen. 2:15
In Egypt . . . . Deut. 11:10
In Shushan . . . . Esth. 1:5
In Gethsemane . . . . Mark 14:32
A royal. . . . . 2 Kin. 25:4
B. Used for:
Festivities. . . . . Esth. 1:5
Idolatry. . . . . Is. 65:3
Meditations . . . . Matt. 26:36
Burial. . . . . John 19:41
C. Figurative of:
Desolation . . . . Amos 4:9
Fruitfulness . . . . Is. 51:3
Prosperity. . . . . Is. 58:11
Righteousness . . . . Is. 61:11

Gardener—*one whose work is gardening*
Adam, the first . . . . Gen. 2:15
Christ, mistaken for . . . . John 20:15, 16

Gareb—*scab*
1. One of David's warriors . . . . 2 Sam. 23:38
2. Hill near Jerusalem . . . . Jer. 31:39

Garland—*ceremonial headdress or wreath*
Brought by priests of Zeus . . . . Acts 14:13

Garlic—*an onionlike plant*
Egyptian food . . . . Num. 11:5

Garments (see Clothing)

Garmite—*bony*
Gentile name applied to Keilah . . . . . . 1 Chr. 4:19

Garrison—*a military post*
Smitten by Jonathan . . . . 1 Sam. 13:3, 4
Attacked by Jonathan . . . . 1 Sam. 14:1–15

Gatam—*puny*

Esau's grandson; chief of Edomite
clan . . . . .Gen. 36:11–16

Gate—*an entrance*

A. Made of:

Wood. . . . . Neh. 2:3, 17

Iron . . . . Acts 12:10

Bronze. . . . . .Ps. 107:16

Stones . . . . .Rev. 21:12

B. Opening for:

Cities. . . . . .Judg. 16:3

Citadel. . . . . Neh. 2:8

Sanctuary. . . . . Ezek. 44:1, 2

Tombs . . . . Matt. 27:60

Prisons. Acts 12:5, 10

C. Used for:

Business transactions . . . . .1 Kin. 22:10

Legal business . . . . .Ruth 4:1–11

Criminal cases. . . . . .Deut. 25:7–9

Proclamations. . . . . .Jer. 17:19, 20

Festivities . . . . Ps. 24:7

Protection. . . . . .2 Sam. 18:24, 33

D. Figurative of:

Satanic power . . . . Matt. 16:18

Death. . . . . Is. 38:10

Righteousness. . . . . .Ps. 118:19, 20

Salvation. . . . . .Matt. 7:13

Holy Jerusalem . . . . .Rev. 21:25

Gatekeeper

Duty of:

Zechariah .1 Chr. 9:21

Shallum. . . . . .1 Chr. 9:17

Akkub . . . . .1 Chr. 9:17

Talmon . . . . 1 Chr. 9:17

Ahiman. . . . . .1 Chr. 9:17

Heman. . . . . 1 Chr. 15:17

Asaph. . . . . .1 Chr. 15:17

Ethan. . . . . .1 Chr. 15:17

Ben. . . . . .1 Chr. 15:18

Jaaziel . . . . .1 Chr. 15:18

Shemiramoth. . . . . .1 Chr. 15:18

Jehiel . . . . .1 Chr. 15:18

Unni. . . . . .1 Chr. 15:18

Eliab. . . . . .1 Chr. 15:18

Benaiah. . . . . .1 Chr. 15:18

Maaseiah . . . . .1 Chr. 15:18

Mattithiah .1 Chr. 15:18

Elipheleh. . . . . .1 Chr. 15:18

Mikneiah . . . . .1 Chr. 15:18

Obed-Edom . . . . .1 Chr. 15:18

Jeiel. . . . . .1 Chr. 15:18

Berechiah . . . . .1 Chr. 15:23

Elkanah. . . . . .1 Chr. 15:23

Jehiah . . . . .1 Chr. 15:24

Jeduthun . . . . .1 Chr. 16:38

Hosah . . . . .1 Chr. 16:38

Gates of Jerusalem

1. Corner Gate. . . . . 2 Chr. 26:9

2. Refuse Gate. . . . . .Neh. 12:31

3. Of Ephraim . . . . .Neh. 8:16

4. Fish Gate . . . . .Zeph. 1:10

5. Fountain Gate. Neh. 12:37

6. Horse Gate. . . . . .Jer. 31:40

7. Benjamin's Gate . . . . .Zech. 14:10

8. "Gate of the Prison" . . . . Neh. 12:39

9. Sheep Gate. . . . . .Neh. 3:1

10. Upper Benjamin Gate. . . . . .Jer. 20:2

11. Valley Gate . . . . .Neh. 2:13

12. Water Gate . . . . .Neh. 8:16

Gath—*winepress*

1. Philistine city . . . . 1 Sam. 6:17

Last of Anakim here . . . . .Josh. 11:22

Ark carried to . . . . .1 Sam. 5:8

Home of Goliath. . . . . .1 Sam. 17:4

David takes refuge in. . . . . 1 Sam. 21:10–15

David's second flight to . . . . 1 Sam. 27:3–12

Captured by David. . . . . .1 Chr. 18:1

Captured by Hazael. . . . . .2 Kin. 12:17

Rebuilt by Rehoboam . . . . .2 Chr. 11:5, 8

Uzziah broke down walls of. . . . . .2 Chr. 26:6

Destruction of, prophetic. . . . . .Amos 6:1–3

Name becomes proverbial . . . . .Mic. 1:10

2. Musical instrument or tune. . . . . Ps. 8; 81; 84 (titles)

Gath Hepher—*winepress of the pit*

Birthplace of Jonah . . . . .2 Kin. 14:25

Boundary of Zebulun . . . . .Josh. 19:13

Gath Rimmon—*pomegranate press*

1. City of Dan . . . . .Josh. 19:40–45

Assigned to Levites . . . . .Josh. 21:24

2. Town in Manasseh. . . . . .Josh. 21:25

Gaza—*strong place*

Philistine city . . . . .Josh. 13:3

Conquered by Joshua. . . . . .Josh. 10:41

Refuge of Anakim . . . . .Josh. 11:22

Assigned to Judah. . . . . .Josh. 15:47

Gates of, removed by Samson . . . . . . .Judg. 16:1–3

Samson deceived by Delilah here. . . Judg. 16:1–20

Samson blinded here . . . . .Judg. 16:21

Temple of Dagon here; pulled

down . . . . .Judg. 16:21–25, 29, 30

Ruled by Solomon . . . . 1 Kin. 4:22, 24

Sin of, condemned . . . . Amos 1:6, 7

Judgment pronounced upon . . . . Jer. 25:20

Philip preaches on road to . . . . Acts 8:26

Gazelle—*medium-sized antelope; translated "roe"; "roebuck"*

A. Described as:

Fit for food. . . . . Deut. 12:15, 22

Swift. . . . . .1 Chr. 12:8

Wild. . . . . .2 Sam. 2:18

Hunted by men . . . . Prov. 6:5

In Solomon's provisions . . . . .1 Kin. 4:23

B. Figurative of:

Timidity. . . . . Is. 13:14

Swiftness. . . . . .2 Sam. 2:18

Church . . . . Song 4:5

Christ. . . . . Song 2:9, 17

Gazez—*shearer*
1. Son of Caleb. . . . . 1 Chr. 2:46
2. Grandson of Caleb . . . . 1 Chr. 2:46

Gazites
     Inhabitants of Gaza. . . . . .Judg. 16:2

Gazzam—*consuming*
     Head of family of temple servants. . . . . . Ezra 2:48

Geba, Gaba—*a hill*
     City of Benjamin . . . . .Josh. 18:24
     Assigned to Levites . . . . Josh. 21:17
     Rebuilt by Asa. .1 Kin. 15:22
     Idolatrous. . . . . .2 Kin. 23:8
     Repossessed after the Exile . . . . Neh. 11:31

Gebal—*mountain*
1. Phoenician maritime town . . . . Ezek. 27:9
     Inhabitants called Gebalites . . . . Josh. 13:5;
         1 Kin. 5:18
2. Mountainous region in Edom. . . . . Ps. 83:7

Geber—*strong one; hero*
     Solomon's purveyors . . . . 1 Kin. 4:19

Gebim—*ditches*
     Place north of Jerusalem. . . . . Is. 10:31

Gedaliah—*Yahweh has made great*
1. Jeduthun's son. . . . . 1 Chr. 25:3, 9
2. Pashhur's son . . . . Jer. 38:1
3. Grandfather of Zephaniah . . . . Zeph. 1:1
4. Ahikam's son. . . . . Jer. 39:14
     Made governor of Judah. . . . . 2 Kin. 25:22–26
     Befriends Jeremiah. . . . . Jer. 40:5, 6
     Murdered by Ishmael. . . .2 Kin. 25:25; Jer. 41:2, 18
5. Postexilic priest . . . . Ezra 10:18

Geder—*wall*
     Town of Judah. .Josh. 12:13

Gederah—*sheepfold*
     Town in Judah. .Josh. 15:36

Gederathite
     Native of Gederah . . . . 1 Chr. 12:4

Gederite
     Native of Geder. . . . . .1 Chr. 27:28

Gederoth—*sheepfolds*
     Town of Judah. .Josh. 15:41
     Captured by Philistines . . . . .2 Chr. 28:18

Gederothaim—*two sheepfolds*
     Town of Judah. .Josh. 15:36

Gedor—*wall*
1. Town of Judah. Josh. 15:58
2. Simeonite town. 1 Chr. 4:39
3. Town of Benjamin . . . . 1 Chr. 12:7
4. Family in Judah . . . . 1 Chr. 4:4
5. A son of Jeiel and brother of Ner . . . 1 Chr. 8:30, 31;
     9:35–37
6. The son of Jered . . . . 1 Chr. 4:18

Ge Harashim
1. A craftsman . . . . 1 Chr. 4:14
2. Called the "Valley of Craftsmen" . . . . . . .Neh. 11:35

Gehazi—*valley of vision*
     Elisha's servant .2 Kin. 5:25
     Seeks reward from Naaman. . . . . . . 2 Kin. 5:20–24
     Afflicted with leprosy. . . . . 2 Kin. 5:25–27
     Relates Elisha's deeds to Jehoram. . . . 2 Kin. 8:4–6

WORD STUDY   **GEHENNA, HELL,** *geenna* (*gheh*-en-nah). This noun is the Greek representation of the Hebrew words for "Valley of the Sons of Hinnom" (see 2 Chr. 28:3), the name for a ravine south of Jerusalem—the site, according to popular belief, of the Last Judgment. In the first three Gospels, *geenna* is apparently thought of as the site of eternal punishment or condemnation in the afterlife (Matt. 5:29; Luke 12:5), sometimes depicted as a place of fire (Matt. 18:9; Mark 9:43, 45), called "hell." The word is also used figuratively to describe the unruly and evil tongue (James 3:6). (Strong's #1067)

Gehenna (see Hell)

Geliloth—*circles*
     Probably Gilgal, in the land
         of Benjamin. . . . . .Josh. 18:17

Gemalli—*camel driver*
     Father of Ammiel. . . . . Num. 13:12

Gemariah—*Yahweh has perfected*
1. Hilkiah's son. . . . . .Jer. 29:3
2. Shaphan's son . . . . Jer. 36:10–25

Gems—*precious stones*
     On breastplate. Ex. 28:15–21
     Figurative of value . . . . Prov. 3:15; 31:10
     In commerce . . . . .Ezek. 27:16
     In New Jerusalem. . . . . Rev. 21:19–21

Genealogies—*ancestral lineage*
A. Importance:
     Tribal inheritance . . . . .Num. 36:1–13
     Royal line . . . . .Matt. 1:1, 6
     Chronology . . . . .Matt. 1:17
     Priesthood claims. . . . .Ezra 2:61, 62; Neh. 7:63, 64
     Messiahship. . . . . Matt. 1:1–17
B. Lists of:
     Patriarchs' . . . . .Gen. 5:1–32
     Noah's . . . . .Gen. 10:1–32
     Shem's . . . . .Gen. 10:21–32
     Abraham's . . . . 1 Chr. 1:28–34
     Jacob's . . . . Gen. 46:8–27
     Esau's. . . . . Gen. 36:1–43
     Israel's . . . . 1 Chr. 9:1
     David's . . . . .1 Chr. 3:1–16
     Levites' . . . . .1 Chr. 6:1–81
     Saul's . . . . 1 Chr. 9:35–44

Genealogy of Jesus
     Seed of Abraham . . . . .Gal. 3:16
     Through Joseph . . . . Matt. 1:2–17
     Through Mary . . . . Luke 3:23–38

General—*chief military authority*
     Commander. . . . . 1 Chr. 27:34; Rev. 6:15
     Also rendered "princes" . . . . Gen. 12:15

WORD STUDY **GENERATION,** *dor* (*dohr*). The noun *dor,* which is usually translated "generation," can also mean "period" or "dwelling." Usually the term is used in poetic literature to refer to a period or age or generation and can indicate former ages. More commonly the term points to future ages. *Dor* can also refer to a generation from a particular time in either the present or past. It is especially seen in references to the future as in Gen. 15:16 and Ps. 48:14. Sometimes a generation is characterized by a particular quality such as a "wicked generation" or a "righteous generation." (Strong's #1755)

Generation
Descriptive of:
Period of time .... Gen. 9:12
Living people or race .... Matt. 24:34

Genesis, Book of—*a book of the Old Testament*
Creation .... Gen. 1:1–2:25
The Fall............................. Gen. 3:1–24
The Flood............................ Gen. 6:8–7:24
Abraham........................ Gen. 12:1–25:18
Isaac......................... Gen. 25:19–26:35
Jacob .... Gen. 27:1–36:43
Joseph .... Gen. 37:1–50:26

Genius—*unusual mental ability*
Applicable to Solomon .... 1 Kin. 4:29–34

WORD STUDY **GENTILE, NATION,** *ethnos* (*eth*-noss). As a singular noun it means "nation" or "people" (Acts 8:9; 10:22). Although the plural form can be a general reference to "nations," it functions also as an idiomatic expression to refer to non-Jewish people (Heb. *goyim*), or "Gentiles" (Matt. 6:32; Luke 2:32). While Paul certainly speaks of "Gentile" Christians (Rom. 16:4), the word can be used to differentiate "Christians" from non-Christians (1 Pet. 2:12; 4:3). These usages are not inconsistent with the Greek and later Roman practice of calling foreign (i.e., non-Greek or non-Roman) people "heathens" or "pagans," which are also possible translations. (Strong's #1484)

WORD STUDY **GENTILES,** *goyim* (*goh*-yeem). The plural noun *goyim* can be translated "nation" or "people." The singular noun *goy* is used to describe Abraham, Sarah, Ishmael, Jacob, and others. Occasionally the plural is used of Israel (Ex. 19:6). Usually the word refers to non-Hebrew people, such as those from Egypt or Tyre. Frequently the word has a negative connotation, referring especially to those people who are heathen or idolatrous. However, the legal codes do emphasize the care to be given to the "foreigner in the midst" of the people, reasoning that Israel was also once a foreigner. (Strong's #1471)

Gentiles—*non-Jews*
A. Described as:
Superstitious .... Deut. 18:14

Knowing God .... Rom. 1:21
Without the Law..................... Rom. 2:14
Wicked .... Rom. 1:23–32
Idolatrous.......................... 1 Cor. 12:2
Uncircumcised .... Eph. 2:11
Without Christ .... Eph. 2:12
Dead in sins .... Eph. 2:1
B. Blessings promised to:
Given to Christ .... Ps. 2:8
Included in God's covenant....Gen. 12:3; Gal. 3:8
Conversion predicted .... Is. 11:10; Rom. 15:9–16
Christ their light.................... Is. 49:6
Included in "all flesh" .... Joel 2:28–32
Called "other sheep" .... John 10:16
C. Conversion of:
Predicted .... Is. 60:1–14
Proclaimed...................... Matt. 4:12–17
Anticipated .... John 10:16
Questioned...................... Acts 10:9–29
Realized .... Acts 10:34–48
Explained .... Acts 11:1–18
Hindered .... Acts 13:45–51
Debated........................ Acts 15:1–22
Confirmed .... Acts 15:23–31
Vindicated .... Acts 28:25–29
D. Present position:
Barrier removed .... Eph. 2:11–22
Brought near .... Eph. 2:13
Fellow citizens.................... Eph. 2:19
Fellow heirs .... Eph. 3:6
In body .... Eph. 3:6

WORD STUDY **GENTLE,** *epieikēs* (ep-ee-eye-*kayce*). Adjective meaning "gentle," "kind." In James 3:17 *epieikēs* is an attribute of "wisdom from above." Paul exhorts the Philippians to let their "gentleness" be known to all (4:5; cf. Titus 3:2). It is also listed among the qualifications of a bishop (1 Tim. 3:3). Generally speaking, *epieikēs* describes an amiable and agreeable disposition. (Strong's #1933)

WORD STUDY **GENTLENESS, MEEKNESS,** *praotēs* (prah-*ot*-ayce). This noun means "gentleness," "humility," "courtesy," "considerateness," "meekness." It is listed with other virtues at Gal. 5:23; Eph. 4:2; Col. 3:12. Paul specifies "gentleness and meekness" as attributes of Christ, and he appeals to the Corinthians in the same spirit (2 Cor. 10:1). Believers are to show *praotēs* to everyone (Titus 3:2). (Strong's #4236)

Gentleness—*mildness combined with tenderness*
A. Examples of:
God's........................... 2 Sam. 22:36
Christ's .... Matt. 11:29; 2 Cor. 10:1
Paul's........................... 1 Thess. 2:7
Fruit of the Spirit .... Gal. 5:22, 23
B. A Christian essential in:
Living in the world.................. Titus 3:1, 2

Instruction......................2 Tim. 2:24, 25
Restoring a brother ....Gal. 6:1
Calling..............................Eph. 4:1, 2
Marriage..........................1 Pet. 3:1–4
C. Commandments concerning:
Follow after ....1 Tim. 6:11

Genubath—*theft*
Edomite ....1 Kin. 11:20

Geology—*study of the earth*
Allusions to ....Gen. 1:9, 10

Gera—*grain*
1. Son of Bela...........................Gen. 46:21
2. A descendant of Bela.................1 Chr. 8:3–8
3. Father of Ehud ....Judg. 3:15
4. Father of Shimei.....................2 Sam. 16:5

Gerah—*smallest coin and weight among the Jews*
Twentieth part of a shekel ...Ex. 30:13; Lev. 27:25

Gerar—*region*
Town of Philistia ....Gen. 10:19
Visited by Abraham.................Gen. 20:1–18
Visited by Isaac.....................Gen. 26:1–17
Abimelech, king of.................Gen. 26:1, 26

Gerizim—*cutters*
Mountain of blessing in Ephraim.....Deut. 11:29
Jotham's parable.......................Judg. 9:7
Samaritans' sacred mountain ....John 4:20, 21

Gershom, Gershon—*exile*
1. Son of Levi............... Ex. 6:16; 1 Chr. 6:16–20
Father of Libni and Shimei ....Ex. 6:17
Founder of Gershonites ....Num. 3:17–26
2. Son of Moses.........................Ex. 2:21, 22
Circumcised..........................Ex. 4:25
Founder of Levite family ....1 Chr. 23:14–16
3. Descendant of Phinehas.................Ezra 8:2
4. Father of Jonathan....................Judg. 18:30

Gershonites
Descendants of Gershon...........Num. 3:21, 22
Tabernacle servants...............Num. 3:25, 26
Achievements of..................1 Chr. 15:7–19

Geshan—*firm*
Descendant of Caleb ....1 Chr. 2:47

Geshem—*shower*
Opposes Nehemiah ....Neh. 6:6

Geshur—*bridge*
Not expelled........................Josh. 13:13
Talmai, king of ....2 Sam. 3:3
Absalom flees to ....2 Sam. 13:37, 38

Geshurites
1. People of Geshur ....Deut. 3:14
2. People living south of Philistia.........1 Sam. 27:8

Gether—*fear*
Son of Aram........................Gen. 10:23

Gethsemane—*oil press*
Garden near Jerusalem..........Matt. 26:30, 36

Scene of Christ's agony and
  betrayal .... Matt. 26:36–56; John 18:1–12
Often visited by Christ..............Luke 22:39

Geuel—*majesty of God*
Gadite spy ....Num. 13:15, 16

Gezer—*portion*
Canaanite city......................Josh. 10:33
Not expelled........................Josh. 16:10
Assigned to Kohathites............Josh. 21:21
Scene of warfare ....1 Chr. 14:16
Burned by Egyptian king ....1 Kin. 9:16
Rebuilt by Solomon ....1 Kin. 9:17

Ghost
Christ thought to be ..... Matt. 14:26; Mark 6:49

Giah—*waterfall*
Place near Ammah..................2 Sam. 2:24

Giants—*men of unusual size*
A. Names of:
Rephaim............................Gen. 14:5
Anakim............ Num. 13:28–33; Josh. 11:21
Emim...............................Gen. 14:5
Zamzummim......................Deut. 2:20
Goliath ....1 Sam. 17:4–7
Og................................Deut. 3:11, 13
Others.........................2 Sam. 21:16–22
B. Destroyed by:
Moses...........................Deut. 3:3–11
Joshua ....Josh. 11:21
David.........................1 Sam. 17:48–51
David and his men ....2 Sam. 21:16–22

Gibbar—*huge*
Family head........................ Ezra 2:20

Gibbethon—*mound*
Town of Dan ....Josh. 19:44
Assigned to Levites .... Josh. 21:20–23
Nadab's assassination at.........1 Kin. 15:27, 28
Besieged by Omri ....1 Kin. 16:17

Gibea—*hill*
Caleb's grandson ....1 Chr. 2:49

Gibeah—*hill*
1. Village of Judah ....Josh. 15:57
2. Town of Benjamin.................Judg. 19:14–16
Known for wickedness ....Judg. 19:12–30
Destruction ....Judg. 20:1–48
Saul's birthplace .... 1 Sam. 10:26
Saul's political capital .... 1 Sam. 15:34
Saul's sons executed..............2 Sam. 21:6–10
Wickedness of, long remembered .... Hos. 9:9

Gibeathites
Inhabitants of Gibeah................1 Chr. 12:3

Gibeon—*hill town*
Hivite town ....Josh. 9:3, 7
Mighty, royal city .... Josh. 10:2
Sun stands still at ....Josh. 10:12
Assigned to Benjamin ....Josh. 18:25
Given to Levites ....Josh. 21:17

Location of tabernacle ....1 Chr. 16:39
Joab struck Amasa here ....2 Sam. 20:8–10
Joab killed here .... 1 Kin. 2:28–34
Site of Solomon's sacrifice
    and dream ....1 Kin. 3:5–15
Natives of, return from exile .... Neh. 3:7

Gibeonites—*inhabitants of Gibeon*
Deceive Joshua ....Josh. 9:3–15
Deception discovered .... Josh. 9:16–20
Made woodcutters ....Josh. 9:21–27
Rescued by Joshua .... Josh. 10:1–43
Massacred by Saul ....2 Sam. 21:1
Avenged by David................ 2 Sam. 21:2–9

Giddalti—*I have made great*
Son of Heman ....1 Chr. 25:4

Giddel—*very great*
1. Head of family of temple servants.......Ezra 2:47
2. Children of Solomon's servants .... Ezra 2:56;
    Neh. 7:58

Gideon—*cutter of trees*
Son of Joash ....Judg. 6:11
Called by an angel .... Judg. 6:11–24
Destroys Baal's altar .... Judg. 6:25–32
Fleece confirms call from God .....Judg. 6:36–40
His army reduced................... Judg. 7:2–8
Encouraged by a dream............Judg. 7:9–15
Unusual strategy successful........ Judg. 7:16–25
Soothes angry Ephraimites ....Judg. 8:1–3
Takes revenge on Succoth
    and Penuel.....................Judg. 8:4–22
Refuses kingship.................. Judg. 8:22, 23
Unwisely makes an ephod ....Judg. 8:24–27
Judgeship of forty years .... Judg. 8:28, 29
Father of 71 sons................... Judg. 8:30, 31
His death brings apostasy .... Judg. 8:32–35
Called Jerubbaal......................Judg. 8:35
Man of faith........................ Heb. 11:32

Gideoni—*a cutting down*
Benjamite.......................... Num. 1:11
Father of Abidan..................... Num. 1:11
Brought offering for the tribe of
    Benjamin.................... Num. 7:60–65
Over tribal army of Benjamin........ Num. 10:24

Gidom—*a cutting off*
Village of Benjamin.................Judg. 20:45

> **WORD STUDY**   **GIFT OF GRACE**, *charisma* (*khar*-is-mah). The literal meaning of this noun is "gift (freely and graciously given)," "favor bestowed," and in the NT it is used only of divinely bestowed gifts. Paul identifies perhaps the crowning "gift of God"—"eternal life in Christ Jesus our Lord" (Rom. 6:23; cf. 11:29). The Pastoral Epistles speak of the "gift" of office (1 Tim. 4:14; 2 Tim. 1:6). *Charisma* is also used in a particular sense to refer to special "gifts" of ministry, called "spiritual gifts" (probably following Rom. 1:11); on the variety of

spiritual gifts, see Rom. 12; 1 Cor. 12; compare 1 Pet. 4:10. (Strong's #5486)

Gifts
A. Of God:
1. *Material:*
Food............................ Matt. 6:25, 26
Rain .... Matt. 5:45
Health........................Phil. 2:25–30
Sleep........................ Prov. 3:23–25
Rest .... Deut. 12:10
All things ....1 Tim. 6:17
All needs .... Phil. 4:19
2. *Spiritual:*
Christ........................... John 3:16
Holy Spirit ....Luke 11:13
Grace..........................James 4:6
Wisdom .... James 1:5
Repentance ....Acts 11:18
Faith.......................... Eph. 2:8
New spirit.....................Ezek. 11:19
Peace .... Phil. 4:7
Rest .... Heb. 4:1, 9
Glory ....1 Pet. 5:10
Eternal life ....John 10:28
B. Of humankind:
1. *Purposes of:*
Confirm covenants ....Gen. 21:27–32
Appease anger................. 1 Sam. 25:27–35
Show respect .... Judg. 6:18–21
Manifest friendship............1 Sam. 30:26–31
Reward .... 2 Sam. 18:11, 12
Memorialize an event .... Esth. 9:20–22
Render worship.....................Matt. 2:11
Give help........................Phil. 4:10–18
Seal friendship .... 1 Sam. 18:3, 4
2. *Times given:*
Betrothals..................... Gen. 24:50–53
Weddings..................... Ps. 45:12
Departures.................... Gen. 45:21–24
Returns home .... Luke 15:22, 23
Times of recovery............. Job 42:10, 11
Trials, forbidden.......................Ex. 23:8
C. Spiritual:
Listed and explained .... Rom. 12:6–8;
    1 Cor. 12:4–30; Eph. 4:11–16
Come from God .... James 1:17
Assigned sovereignty.............1 Cor. 12:11, 28
Cannot be bought.................. Acts 8:18–20
Always for edification................Rom. 1:11
Counterfeited by Satan..........2 Cor. 11:13–15
Spiritually discerned..............1 Cor. 12:2, 3
Love, the supreme................1 Cor. 13:1–13

Gihon—*bursting forth*
1. River of Eden............................Gen. 2:13
2. Spring outside Jerusalem...........1 Kin. 1:33–45
3. Source of water supply .... 2 Chr. 32:30

Gilalai—*weighty*
Levite musician.....................Neh. 12:36

Gilboa—*bubbling fountain*
    Range of limestone hills in Issachar . . . 1 Sam. 28:4
    Scene of Saul's death . . . . 1 Sam. 31:1–7
    Philistines desecrate Saul's
        body here . . . . 1 Sam. 31:8, 9
    Under David's curse . . . . .2 Sam. 1:17, 21

Gilead—*rocky or strong*
1. Grandson of Manasseh . . . . Num. 26:29, 30
2. Father of Jephthah . . . . Judg. 11:1
3. Gadite . . . . 1 Chr. 5:14
4. Condemned city . . . . .Hos. 6:8
5. Mountain . . . . Judg. 7:3
6. Tableland east of the Jordan between the
        Arnon and Jabbok rivers . . . . Judg. 20:1
    Possessed by Israel . . . . Num. 21:21–31
    Assigned to Reuben, Gad, and
        Manasseh . . . . Deut. 3:12–17
    Rebuked by Deborah . . . . Judg. 5:17
    Hebrews flee to . . . . 1 Sam. 13:7
    Ishbosheth's rule over . . . . 2 Sam. 2:8, 9
    David takes refuge in . . . . . . 2 Sam. 17:26, 27; 19:31
    In David's census . . . . 2 Sam. 24:1, 6
    Elijah's birthplace . . . . 1 Kin. 17:1
    Smitten by Hazael . . . . 2 Kin. 10:32, 33
    Mentioned by Amos . . . . Amos 1:3, 13

Gilead, balm of—*an aromatic gum for medicinal*
        purposes
Figurative of:
    National healing . . . . Jer. 8:22; 51:8

Gilgal—*a circle, a wheel*
1. Memorial site between Jordan and
        Jericho . . . . .Josh. 4:19–24
    Israel circumcised . . . . .Josh. 5:2–9
    Passover observed . . . . Josh. 5:10
    Site of Gibeonite covenant . . . . .Josh. 9:3–15
    On Samuel's circuit . . . . 1 Sam. 7:15, 16
    Saul made king . . . . .1 Sam. 11:15
    Saul rejected . . . . 1 Sam. 13:4–15
    Denounced for idolatry . . . . Hos. 9:15
2. Town near Bethel . . . . .2 Kin. 2:1
    Home of Elisha .2 Kin. 4:38

Giloh—*exile*
    Town of Judah . . . . Josh. 15:51

Gilonite—*Giloh native*
    Ahithophel called . . . . 2 Sam. 15:12

Gimel
    Third letter in Hebrew alphabet . . . Ps. 119:17–24

Gimzo—*producing sycamores*
    Village of Judah . . . . .2 Chr. 28:18

Ginath—*protection*
    Father of Tibni . . . . 1 Kin. 16:21, 22

Ginnethoi—*gardener*
    Postexilic priest . . . . Neh. 12:4

Ginnethon—*gardener*
    Family head and signer of document . . . Neh. 10:6
    Probably same as Ginnethoi

Gird—*to put on, as a belt*
A. Purposes of:
    Strengthening . . . . Prov. 31:17
B. Figurative of:
    Gladness . . . . .Ps. 30:11
    Truth . . . . Eph. 6:14
    Readiness . . . . .1 Pet. 1:13
C. Those girding:
    Priests . . . . Ex. 28:4, 39
    Warriors . . . . 1 Sam. 18:4
    Jesus . . . . John 13:3, 4

Girgashites—*an original tribe of Canaan*
    Descendants of Canaan . . . . Gen. 10:15, 16
    Land of, given to Abraham's
        descendants . . . . Gen. 15:18, 21
    Delivered to Israel . . . . .Josh. 24:11

Girl—*a female child; young woman*
    Sold for wine . . . . Joel 3:3
    Prophecy concerning . . . . Zech. 8:4, 5
    Raised by Jesus . . . . .Mark 5:39–42
    Demands John's head . . . . Matt. 14:10, 11
    Questions Peter . . . . John 18:17
    Is disbelieved . . . . Acts 12:13–17
    Healed by Paul . . . . Acts 16:16–18

Girzites—*inhabitants of Gezer*
    Raided by David . . . . 1 Sam. 27:8

Gishpa—*attentive*
    Overseer . . . . Neh. 11:21

Gittaim—*two winepresses*
    Village of Benjamin . . . . Neh. 11:31, 33
    Refuge of the Beerothites . . . . 2 Sam. 4:2, 3

Gittites—*natives of Gath*
    600 follow David . . . . 2 Sam. 15:18–23

Giving to God
A. Manner of:
    Without show . . . . Matt. 6:1–4
    According to ability . . . . 1 Cor. 16:1, 2
    Willingly . . . . 1 Chr. 29:3–9
    Liberally . . . . .2 Cor. 9:6–15
    Cheerfully . . . . 2 Cor. 9:7
    Proportionately . . . . Mal. 3:10
B. Examples of:
    Israelites . . . . Ex. 35:21–29
    Leaders of Israel . . . . .Num. 7:2–28
    Poor widow . . . . .Luke 21:1–4
    Macedonian churches . . . . .2 Cor. 8:1–5

Gizonite
    Hashem thus described . . . . 1 Chr. 11:34

Gladness—*cheerfulness*
A. Reasons for:
    Salvation . . . . Is. 51:3, 11; John 8:56
    Forgiveness . . . . Ps. 51:8
    Recovery of a son . . . . .Luke 15:32
    Restoration of hope . . . . John 20:20
    Temporal blessings . . . . .Acts 14:17
    Christ's coming . . . . 1 Pet. 4:13

B. Wrong kinds of:

At an enemy's downfall	Prov. 24:17
At wickedness	Hos. 7:3

Glass

A. Used literally of:

Crystal	Job 28:17, 18

B. Used figuratively of:

God's nature	Rev. 4:6
New Jerusalem	Rev. 21:18, 21

Gleaning—*gathering grain left by reapers*

Laws providing for	Lev. 19:9, 10
Illustrated by Ruth	Ruth 2:2–23
Gideon's reference to	Judg. 8:2

Glorification of Christ

A. Nature of:

Predicted	Is. 55:5
Prayed for	John 12:28
Not of Himself	Heb. 5:5
Predetermined	John 17:1

B. Accomplished by:

Father	John 13:31, 32
Holy Spirit	John 16:13, 14
Miracles	John 11:4
His resurrection	Acts 3:13
Believers	Acts 21:20

Glorifying God

A. By means of:

Praise	Ps. 50:23
Fruitfulness	John 15:8
Service	1 Pet. 4:11
Suffering	1 Pet. 4:14, 16

B. Reason for:

Deliverance	Ps. 50:15
Mercy shown	Rom. 15:9
Subjection	2 Cor. 9:13

C. Extent of:

Universal	Ps. 86:9
In body and soul	1 Cor. 6:20

WORD STUDY **GLORY,** *kabod* (kaw-*vohd*). The noun form of the verb meaning "heavy" or "weighty" is translated "abundance," "glory," or "honor." Occasionally the word is seen in a context where it obviously means abundance or riches as in Is. 10:3. Most commonly it refers to honor or glory that is an external condition or circumstance. A human can have honor as Joseph did in Egypt (Gen. 45:13). Material things, such as a throne or kingdom or even priestly robes, can have glory (1 Sam. 2:8). The glory of God is seen in the historic theophanies where it is almost a separate entity. In 1 Sam. 4:21 the glory of God went from Israel when the ark was captured and taken away. Glory is seen to be a feature of God so that God's name is a name of glory and God's eyes are eyes of glory. God's glory is great, and the whole earth is filled with it (Ps. 72:19). The honor that is not an external condition is a position, though this use is less frequent. (Strong's #3519)

WORD STUDY **GLORY,** *doxa* (*doks*-ah). This noun is usually translated "glory," but because it carries with it other meanings and nuances, it can also be translated as "brightness," "splendor," "radiance" (especially with reference to God or beings who appear before God; see Acts 7:2; Luke 2:9; 2 Cor. 3:7), or "magnificence," "splendor" (e.g., the eyecatching "splendor" of kings, as in Matt. 6:29), or "fame," "renown," "honor" (i.e., esteem, a good reputation, as in John 8:54). The last sense is perhaps behind the expression "Glory be to God" (Luke 2:14; Rom. 11:36). "Glory" is also used for the state of being present with God in the hereafter (Luke 24:26; 1 Pet. 1:11). (Strong's #1391)

Glory—*honor; renown*

A. Of temporal things:

Granted by God	Dan. 2:37
Used to entrap	Matt. 4:8
Not to be sought	1 Thess. 2:6
Quickly passes	1 Pet. 1:24

B. Of believers:

Given by God	John 17:22
Transformed by the Spirit	2 Cor. 3:18
Through Christ's death	Heb. 2:9, 10
Follows salvation	2 Tim. 2:10
In suffering	Rom. 5:3
In the cross	Gal. 6:14
Greater than present suffering	Rom. 8:18
Hope of	Col. 1:27
At Christ's advent	Col. 3:4

Glory of Christ

A. Aspects of:

Manifested	John 2:11
Not selfish	John 8:50
Given by God	John 17:22
Crowned with	Heb. 2:9
Ascribed to forever	Heb. 13:21

B. Stages of:

Before creation	John 17:5
Revealed in Old Testament	John 12:41
In His incarnation	John 1:14
In His transfiguration	Luke 9:28–36
In His resurrection	Luke 24:26
In His exaltation	1 Tim. 3:16
At His return	Matt. 25:31
In heaven	Rev. 5:12

Glory of God

A. Manifested to:

Moses	Ex. 24:9–17
Stephen	Acts 7:55

B. Reflected in:

Christ	John 1:14
Man	1 Cor. 11:7

C. Appearances of:

The tabernacle	Ex. 40:34
The temple	1 Kin. 8:11
At Jesus' birth	Luke 2:8–11

D. The believer's relation to:
Does all for.........................1 Cor. 10:31
Illuminated by.......................2 Cor. 4:6
Will stand in presence of ....Jude 24
E. Humankind's relation to:
Corrupts...........................Rom. 1:23
Falls short of ....Rom. 3:23
Refuse to give to God ....Acts 12:23

Glory of humankind
Prefigured in creation...............Heb. 2:6–8
Lost by sin ....Rom. 3:23
Soon passes away ....1 Pet. 1:24
Removed by death ....Ps. 49:17
Restored by Christ..................2 Cor. 5:17

Gluttony—*excessive appetite*
Sternly forbidden ....Prov. 23:1–3
Characteristic of the wicked ....Phil. 3:19
Leads to poverty....................Prov. 23:21
Christ accused of ....Matt. 11:19

Gnat—*small insect*
Used as illustration ....Matt. 23:24

Gnosticism—*early heresy based on knowledge instead of faith*
Warned against.....................Col. 2:8, 18
Arrogant............................1 Cor. 8:1
False..............................1 Tim. 6:20
Surpassed by Christ..................Eph. 3:19

Goad—*a pointed rod*
Used as a weapon ....Judg. 3:31
Figurative of pointed morals.........Eccl. 12:11
Figurative of conscience.............Acts 26:14
Sharpened by files ....1 Sam. 13:21

Goals, spiritual
Provide motivation ....Phil. 3:12–14
Promise reward...................1 Cor. 9:24, 25

Goat—*a domesticated animal*
A. Literal uses of:
Clothing ....Num. 31:20; Heb. 11:37
Milk of, food ....Prov. 27:27
Curtains ....Ex. 26:7
Wineskins ....Josh. 9:4
Sacrifices..........................Ex. 12:5
B. Figurative uses of:
Kingdom of Greece ....Dan. 8:5, 21
Wicked ....Matt. 25:32, 33

Goath—*constance*
Place near Jerusalem ....Jer. 31:39

Gob—*a pit*
Plain where Hebrews and Philistines
fought.....................2 Sam. 21:18, 19
Also called Gezer ....1 Chr. 20:4

Goblet—*a bowl or basin*
Used as a comparison .... Song 7:2
Same word translated "basins"
and "cups" ....Ex. 24:6; Is. 22:24

WORD STUDY **GOD,** *Elohim* (el-oh-*heem*). *Elohim* is a plural noun meaning "gods." It is also a name for deity, sometimes clearly meaning other gods. Occasionally *elohim* is used for rulers, judges, or angels. Most often, however, the word refers to the one true God, and the plural is called the plural of majesty. It is used in phrases to identify people or things belonging to God, such as "a man of God" (1 Kin. 13) or "the ark of God" (1 Sam. 3:3). Many times the word is used in conjunction with an attribute as in such phrases as "righteous God" (Ps. 7:9) or "God who is a rock" (Ps. 18:31). When *Elohim* is used in combination with *Yahweh,* as it is several hundred times, the two names together are translated "Lord God." (Strong's #430)

God—*the Supreme Being*
A. Names of:
God .... Gen. 1:1
Lord God .... Gen. 2:4
God Most High................Gen. 14:18–22
Lord God.........................Gen. 15:2, 8
Almighty God...................... Gen. 17:1, 2
Everlasting God .... Gen. 21:33
Almighty God...................... Gen. 28:3
I AM..............................Ex. 3:14
Jealous..........................Ex. 34:14
Eternal God .... Deut. 33:27
Living God....................... Josh. 3:10
God of hosts...................... Ps. 80:7
Lord of hosts .... Is. 1:24
Holy One of Israel ....Is. 43:3, 14, 15
Mighty God......................Jer. 32:18
God of heaven .... Jon. 1:9
Heavenly Father .... Matt. 6:26
King eternal......................1 Tim. 1:17
Only Potentate ....1 Tim. 6:15
Father of lights .... James 1:17
B. Manifestations of:
Face of...........................Gen. 32:30
Voice of.......................Deut. 5:22–26
Glory of.........................Ex. 40:34, 35
Angel of........................Gen. 16:7–13
Name of .... Ex. 34:5–7
Form of ....Num. 12:6–8
Comes from Teman .... Hab. 3:3
C. Nature of:
Spirit .... John 4:24
One.............................. Deut. 6:4
Personal .... John 17:1–3
Trinitarian ....2 Cor. 13:14
Omnipotent......................Rev. 19:6
D. Attributes of:
Incomparable .... 2 Sam. 7:22
Invisible .... John 1:18
Inscrutable....................... Is. 40:28
Unchangeable .... Num. 23:19
Unequaled ....Is. 40:13–25
Unsearchable................... Rom. 11:33, 34

Infinite . . . . 1 Kin. 8:27
Eternal. . . . . .Is. 57:15
Omnipotence (All-powerful) . . . . Jer. 32:17, 27
Omnipresence (Ever-present) . . . . Ps. 139:7–12
Omniscience (All-knowing) . . . . 1 John 3:20
Foreknowledge . . . . Is. 48:3, 5
Wise. . . . . .Acts 15:18

E. Moral attributes of:
Goodness (see Goodness of God)
Hatred. . . . . Ps. 5:5, 6
Holiness . . . . Rev. 4:8
Impartiality. . . . . 1 Pet. 1:17
Justice . . . . Ps. 89:14
Long-suffering . . . . Ex. 34:6, 7
Love. . . . . 1 John 4:8, 16
Mercy. . . . . Lam. 3:22, 23
Peace . . . . .Gal. 3:15
Truth . . . . Ps. 117:2
Vengeance . . . . Deut. 32:34–41
Wrath . . . . Deut. 32:22

F. Human expressions applied to:
Fear . . . . .Deut. 32:26, 27
Grief. . . . . Gen. 6:6
Repentance . . . . Gen. 6:7
Jealousy. . . . . .Ex. 34:14
Swearing. . . . . Jer. 44:26
Laughing . . . . Ps. 2:4
Sleeping. . . . . .Ps. 78:65

Human parts:
Face . . . . .Num. 6:25, 26
Eyes . . . . 2 Chr. 16:9
Ears . . . . Neh. 1:6
Nose. . . . . .Ex. 15:8
Mouth . . . . .Deut. 8:3
Voice . . . . Gen. 3:9, 10; Ex. 15:26
Hand . . . . .Ezra 7:9
Fingers. . . . . Ps. 8:3
Arms . . . . Deut. 33:27
Back. . . . . Ex. 33:21–23
Feet. . . . . Ps. 18:9

G. Titles given to:
Creator . . . . Is. 40:12, 22, 26
Judge . . . . .Ps. 96:10, 13
King. . . . . Ps. 47:2, 7, 8
Defender. . . . . Ps. 59:1
Preserver. . . . . Ps. 121:3–8
Shepherd. . . . . .Gen. 49:24
Healer. . . . . .Ex. 15:26

H. Works of, described as:
Awesome. . . . . .Ps. 66:3
Incomparable . . . . Ps. 86:8
Great . . . . Ps. 92:5
Manifold. . . . . .Ps. 104:24
Marvelous. . . . . .Ps. 139:14
Wondrous. . . . . 1 Chr. 16:9

I. Ways of, described as:
Perfect. . . . . .Ps. 18:30
Knowledgeable . . . . Ps. 86:11
Made known . . . . Ps. 103:7

Righteous. . . . . Ps. 145:17
Not like human. . . . . Is. 55:8, 9
Everlasting . . . . Hab. 3:6
Inscrutable. . . . . .Rom. 11:33
Just and true. . . . . Rev. 15:3
See Goodness of God; Love of God; Power of God

Godhead—*the Deity*
Revealed to humankind . . . . .Rom. 1:20
Corrupted by humankind . . . . Acts 17:29
Incarnated in Jesus Christ . . . . .Col. 2:9

Godliness—*holy living*
Profitable . . . . 1 Tim. 4:7, 8
Perverted . . . . 1 Tim. 6:5
Pursue . . . . .1 Tim. 6:11
Duty. . . . . .Titus 2:12
See Holiness of Christians

Gods, false

A. Names of:
Adrammelech (Syria) . . . . 2 Kin. 17:31
Anammelech (Babylon) . . . . 2 Kin. 17:31
Ashtoreth (Canaan). . . . . .1 Kin. 11:5, 33
Baal (Canaan) . . . . 1 Kin. 18:19
Baal of Peor (Moab). . . . . Num. 25:1–9
Beelzebub (Philistine). . . . . Luke 11:19–23
Bel (Babylon). . . . . Jer. 51:44
Calf worship (Egypt). . . . . Ex. 32:1–6
Chemosh (Moab) . . . . 1 Kin. 11:7
Dagon (Philistine) . . . . 1 Sam. 5:1–7
Diana (Ephesian) . . . . Acts 19:34
Hermes (Greek) . . . . Acts 14:12, 13
Milcom (Ammon) . . . . 1 Kin. 11:5
Molech (Ammon) . . . . 1 Kin. 11:7
Nebo (Babylon). Is. 46:1
Nisroch (Assyria) . . . . 2 Kin. 19:37
Rimmon (Syria) . . . . 2 Kin. 5:18
Tammuz (Babylon) . . . . .Ezek. 8:14
Zeus (Greek) . . . . Acts 14:12, 13

B. Evils connected with:
Immorality. . . . . Num. 25:1–9
Prostitution . . . . 2 Kin. 23:7
Divination . . . . Lev. 20:1–6
Sacrilege . . . . Dan. 5:4
Pride . . . . 2 Kin. 18:28–35
Persecution. . . . . .1 Kin. 19:1–3
Child sacrifice. .Jer. 7:29–34

Gog—*mountain*
1. Reubenite. . . . . 1 Chr. 5:4
2. Prince of Rosh, Meshech, and Tubal . . . .Ezek. 38:2, 3
3. Leader of the final battle . . . . .Rev. 20:8–15

Golan—*circuit*
City of Bashan. . . . . Deut. 4:43
Assigned to Levites . . . . .Josh. 21:27
City of refuge. . . . . .Josh. 20:8

Gold

A. Found in:
Havilah. . . . . Gen. 2:11, 12
Ophir. . . . . 1 Kin. 9:28

Sheba . . . . 1 Kin. 10:2, 10
Arabia . . . . 2 Chr. 9:14
B. Used for:
Money . . . . Matt. 10:9
Offerings . . . . Ex. 35:22; 1 Sam. 6:4
Gift . . . . Matt. 2:11
Tabernacle:
Frame . . . . Ex. 26:29, 32
Furnishings . . . . Ex. 25:10–40; 30:3–5
Priest's garment . . . . Ex. 39:2–30
Temple:
Building . . . . 1 Kin. 6:20–35
Furnishings . . . . 1 Kin. 7:48–51
Shields . . . . 1 Kin. 10:16, 17
Holy adornment . . . . Ex. 28:4–6
Jewelry . . . . Gen. 24:22
Physical adornment . . . . Ex. 36:34, 38
Idols . . . . Ex. 32:31
C. Figurative of:
Saints refined . . . . Job 23:10
Babylonian Empire . . . . Dan. 2:38
Redeemed . . . . 2 Tim. 2:20
Faith purified . . . . 1 Pet. 1:7
Christ's doctrine . . . . Rev. 3:18

Golden apples
Appropriate word . . . . Prov. 25:11

Golden city
Babylon called . . . . Is. 14:4

Golden rule
For Christian conduct . . . . Matt. 7:12;
Luke 6:31

Golden wedge
Figurative term . . . . Is. 13:12

Goldsmiths
In building the tabernacle . . . . Ex. 31:1–4
Refiners . . . . Mal. 3:3
Shapers of objects . . . . Ex. 25:11, 18
Makers of idols . . . . Num. 33:52
Guilds . . . . Neh. 3:8, 32

Golgotha—*place of a skull*
Where Jesus died . . . . Matt. 27:33–35

Goliath—*exile*
1. Giant of Gath . . . . 1 Sam. 17:4
Challenged Israel . . . . 1 Sam. 17:8–11
Killed by David . . . . 1 Sam. 17:50
2. Brother of above; killed by Elhanan . . . 2 Sam. 21:19
See Giants

Gomer—*completion*
1. Son of Japheth . . . . Gen. 10:2, 3; 1 Chr. 1:5, 6
Northern nation . . . . Ezek. 38:6
2. Wife of Hosea . . . . Hos. 1:2, 3

Gomorrah—*submersion*
In a fruitful valley . . . . Gen. 13:10
Defeated by Chedorlaomer . . . . Gen. 14:8–11
Destroyed by God . . . . Gen. 19:23–29
Symbol of evil . . . . Is. 1:10

Symbol of destruction . . . . Amos 4:11
Punishment of . . . . Matt. 10:15

WORD STUDY   **GOOD,** *agathos* (ag-ath-*oss*). This adjective means "good," and it appears numerous times in the NT. This word describes a thing or person as "good" in the sense of "fit," "capable," "useful" (e.g., "good" tree in Matt. 7:17; "good" servant in 25:21), but it is used especially of moral "goodness." Jesus reserves the term in an absolute sense ("perfect goodness") for God alone (Matt. 19:17). *Agathos* can be used in the singular as a substantive to denote that which is intrinsically valuable or morally good (cf. Rom. 2:10); as a plural substantive it refers to "goods" or "possessions," "treasures" (Luke 12:18). (Strong's #18)

Good for evil
Illustrated by Joseph . . . . Gen. 45:5–15
Christian duty . . . . . . Luke 6:27, 35; Rom. 12:14, 20

WORD STUDY   **GOODNESS, KINDNESS,** *chesed* (*kheh*-sehd). The noun *chesed* is translated as "goodness" or "kindness." When used in reference to humans, it indicates kindness to other humans, especially to the lowly and needy (1 Sam. 20:8). A rare use means the affection of Israel to God, which is piety. This use carries over today in the name of the ultra-conservative Jewish group, the Hasidim. *Chesed,* describing God's kindness, is also lovingkindness to the needs of His creatures, which is seen as mercy. The kindness of God can come in the form of redemption from either sin or enemies, or it can be seen when God keeps the covenant. The kindness of God is abundant (Num. 14:18), great in extent (Ps. 145:8), and everlasting (Jer. 33:11). (Strong's #2617)

Goodness of God
A. Described as:
Abundant . . . . Ex. 34:6
Great . . . . Ps. 31:19
Enduring . . . . Ps. 52:1
Satisfying . . . . Ps. 65:4
Universal . . . . Ps. 145:9
B. Manifested in:
Material blessings . . . . Matt. 5:45; Acts 14:17
Spiritual blessings . . . . Ps. 31:19
Forgiving sin . . . . Ps. 86:5
C. Saints' attitude toward:
Rejoice in . . . . Ex. 18:9
Remember . . . . Ps. 145:7
Be satisfied with . . . . Jer. 31:14

Gopherwood
Used in Noah's ark . . . . Gen. 6:14

Gore—*to push or thrust*
By an ox . . . . Ex. 21:28–32
Rendered "push" . . . . Deut. 33:17; Ezek. 34:21

Goshen

1. District of Egypt where Israel lived......Gen. 45:10
    Land of pastures......................Gen. 47:1–6
    Called the land of Rameses ....Gen. 47:6–11
2. Region in south Judah ....Josh. 10:41
3. City of Judah.........................Josh. 15:51

Gospel—*good news*

A. Described as, of:
    God ....Rom. 1:1
    Christ............................2 Cor. 2:12
    The kingdom.................... Matt. 24:14
    Grace of God.................... Acts 20:24
    Peace .... Eph. 6:15
    Salvation........................Eph. 1:13
    Glory of Christ ....2 Cor. 4:4

B. Defined as:
    Of supernatural origin .... Gal. 1:10–12
    God's power.......................Rom. 1:16
    Mystery.......................... Eph. 6:19
    Revelation .... Eph. 3:1–6
    Deposit of truth ....1 Cor. 15:1–4

C. Source of:
    Hope ....Col. 1:23
    Salvation.......................2 Thess. 2:13, 14
    Faith.............................Acts 15:7
    Life............................. 1 Cor. 4:15
    Immortality.......................2 Tim. 1:10
    Afflictions .... Phil. 1:16
    Peace .... Eph. 6:15

D. Proclaimed by or in:
    Scriptures........................Gal. 3:8
    Prophets ....Rom. 1:1, 2
    Angels to shepherds................Luke 2:8–14
    John .... Mark 1:1–4
    Jesus Christ .... Mark 1:14, 15
    The Twelve.......................Luke 9:1, 2, 6
    Dispersion ....Acts 8:4
    Philip........................... Acts 8:5, 6
    Peter and John.................... Acts 8:14, 25
    Paul .... Acts 20:25
    Angel............................Rev. 14:6

E. Should be proclaimed:
    To all people..................... Mark 16:15, 16
    Everywhere .... Rom. 15:19, 20
    At all times......................Rev. 14:6
    With great urgency .... 1 Cor. 9:16
    With boldness..................... Eph. 6:19
    As a testimony.................... Matt. 24:14

F. Proclaimers of, are:
    Separated ....Rom. 1:1
    Called .... Acts 16:10
    Entrusted with it.................. 1 Thess. 3:2
    Set apart for its defense.......... Phil. 1:7, 16, 27
    Under divine orders................ 1 Cor. 9:16

G. Negative reactions to, some:
    Disobey.......................... 2 Thess. 1:8
    Are blinded to ....2 Cor. 4:3, 4
    Hinder...........................1 Cor. 9:12
    Pervert...........................Gal. 1:7

H. Believer's reaction to:
    Believing...........................Eph. 1:13
    Submitting to .... 2 Cor. 9:13
    Being established by .... Rom. 16:25
    Living by.......................... Phil. 1:27
    Defending .... Phil. 1:7, 16, 27

Gossip—*idle talk or rumors about others; talebearer*

    Forbidden.........................Lev. 19:16
    Cause of friction...................Prov. 16:28
    Destructive .... 1 Tim. 5:13
    Warns against associating with ......Prov. 20:19
    Called "talebearer"............Prov. 11:13; 20:19
    Called "talkers"..................... Ezek. 36:3
    Called "whisperers" ....Rom. 1:29
    Called "whisperings".................2 Cor. 12:20

Gourd—*a running plant with large leaves*

    Poison variety .... 2 Kin. 4:39–41

Government—*recognized rulership*

A. Types of:
    Patriarchal, in families .... Gen. 27:29–39
    Theocratic, under God............. Ex. 18:13–26
    Monarchial, under kings .... 1 Sam. 8:5–22
    Antichristian, under the
        Antichrist .... 2 Thess. 2:3–12
    Absolute and final, under Christ .... Is. 9:6, 7

B. Characteristics of:
    Ruled by God..................... Is. 45:1–13
    Successions of, determined
        by God .... Dan. 2:28–45
    Ignorant of spiritual things........... 1 Cor. 2:8
    Providentially used .... Acts 26:32

C. Christian attitude toward:
    Occupy positions in................. Gen. 42:6
    Pay taxes to ....Matt. 22:18–21
    Pray for .... 1 Tim. 2:1–3
    Obey rules of..................... Rom. 13:1–7
    Obey God first .... Acts 5:29

Governor—*a ruler*

    Title used of Zerubbabel .... Ezra 2:63
    Applied to Nehemiah .... Neh. 8:9
    Prime minister .... Gen. 42:6
    Provincial ruler...................Acts 23:24, 26

Gozan—*quarry*

    Town and district in Mesopotamia....2 Kin. 17:6
    Israelites deported to................2 Kin. 18:11

 WORD STUDY   **GRACE, FAVOR,** *charis* (*khar*-iss). This noun, which means "favor," "grace," is used with reference to a voluntary act of "goodwill," or that which one grants freely even though there is no obligation to do so. In the NT *charis* is used mostly with respect to God's gracious intentions and deeds toward humans, especially to His act of redemption through Christ (Gal. 1:6), and thus the meaning of the word is extended to refer to the state of "grace" (= being in God's favor) experienced by believers (Rom. 5:2). It can also be used to express "thanks" or "gratitude" to God (2 Cor. 9:15). At the beginning and end of letters *charis* is used—with the sense of divine "grace" or "favor"—in formulaic expressions (Rom. 1:7; Col. 4:18). (Strong's #5485)

Grace—*unmerited favor*

A. Descriptive of:
God's favor............................. Gen. 6:8
God's forgiving mercy................Rom. 11:6
Gospel.............................. John 1:17
Gifts (miracles, etc.) ....1 Pet. 4:10
Eternal life ....1 Pet. 1:13

B. Is the source of:
Salvation...........................Acts 15:11
Call of God...........................Gal. 1:15
Faith............................... Acts 18:27
Justification........................ Rom. 3:24
Forgiveness...........................Eph. 1:7
Consolation .... 2 Thess. 2:16
Eternal life ....Rom. 5:21

C. Described as:
All-abundant..................... Rom. 5:15–20
All-sufficient..................... 2 Cor. 12:9
Glorious ....Eph. 1:6
Great .... Acts 4:33
Manifold..........................1 Pet. 4:10
Rich .... Eph. 2:4, 5
Undeserved .... 1 Tim. 1:12–16
Gift of God in Christ................. Rom. 5:15;
  Eph. 2:8

D. Believers:
Are under ....Rom. 6:14
Receive .... John 1:16
Stand in............................Rom. 5:2
Abound in .... 2 Cor. 9:8
Be strong in ....2 Tim. 2:1
Grow in.............................2 Pet. 3:18
Speak with .... Eph. 4:29
Inherit...............................1 Pet. 3:7
Serve God by ....Heb. 12:28

E. Dangers of, can:
Be abused .... Jude 4
Be frustrated ....Gal. 2:21
Be turned from ....Gal. 5:3, 4

Graces, Christian
Growth in, commanded .... 2 Pet. 1:5–8

Grafting—*uniting a portion of one plant to another*
Gentiles, on Israel's stock..........Rom. 11:17, 24

Grain—*the generic term for cereal grasses*

A. Features regarding:
Grown in Palestine...................2 Kin. 18:32
Article of food....................Gen. 42:1, 2, 19
Offered mixed with oil ....Lev. 2:14, 15
Roasted........................... Ruth 2:14

B. Figurative of:
Blessings.......................... Ezek. 36:29
Christ..............................John 12:24
Life's maturity....................... Job 5:26

Grandchildren
Lot becomes father of, through
  incest....................... Gen. 19:30–38
Abdon's........................ Judg. 12:13, 14
Widow's ....1 Tim. 5:4
Iniquity visited on ....Ex. 34:7
Served idols ....2 Kin. 17:41
Crown of old men................... Prov. 17:6
Practice piety toward family ....1 Tim. 5:4
Leave inheritance to ....Prov. 13:22

Grandmother
Lois thus called....................2 Tim. 1:5

Grapes
Grown in Palestine................. Num. 13:23
Used for wine........................ Num. 6:3
"Sour grapes"........................Ezek. 18:2
Figurative of judgment...............Rev. 14:18
See Vine, vineyard

Grass

A. Features:
Created by God.................. Gen. 1:11, 12
Produced by rain................. Deut. 32:2
Adorns earth .... Matt. 6:30
Shall not make.......................Ex. 20:4
Failure of, a calamity................. Jer. 14:5, 6
Nebuchadnezzar eats ....Dan. 4:1, 33
Disappears ....Prov. 27:25
Withered away .... Is. 15:6

B. Figurative of:
Life's shortness ....Ps. 90:5, 6
Prosperous wicked.....................Ps. 92:7
God's grace......................... Ps. 72:6

Grasshopper—*locust*
Used as food.........................Lev. 11:22
Inferiority........................... Num. 13:33
Insignificance .... Is. 40:22
Burden............................. Eccl. 12:5
See Locust

Gratitude (see Thankfulness)

Gratitude to man

A. Reasons for:
Deliverance from an enemy........ Judg. 8:22, 23
Deliverance from death ....1 Sam. 26:21–25
Interpretation of a dream......... Dan. 2:46–48
Rescue from murderers..............Esth. 6:1–6

B. Examples of:
Ruth to Boaz ....Ruth 2:8–17
Israelites to Jonathan.............. 1 Sam. 14:45
Abigail to David .... 1 Sam. 25:40–42
David to Jonathan ....2 Sam. 9:1
David to Hanun .... 2 Sam. 10:1, 2
Pagans to Paul.....................Acts 28:1–10

Grave—*a place of burial*

A. Features regarding:
Dug in ground........................ Gen. 50:5
Some in caves......................... Gen. 23:9

Marker set on. . . . . Gen. 35:20

Touching of, makes unclean . . . . . . Num. 19:16, 18

B. Resurrection from:

Symbolized. . . . . Ezek. 37:1–14

Evidenced. . . . . Matt. 28:5, 6; Luke 24:2–8

Lazarus's. John 11:38, 43, 44

Graveclothes—*clothes for the dead*

Lazarus attired in. . . . . .John 11:43, 44

Jesus lays His aside. . . . . .Luke 24:12

Gravel—*small pebbles*

Figurative of:

Distress. . . . . .Prov. 20:17

Numerous offspring; rendered "grains". . . Is. 48:19

Suffering. . . . . Lam. 3:16

Graven image—*an idol*

Shall not make. . . . . .Ex. 20:4

Of Canaanites, to be destroyed. . . Deut. 7:1–5, 25;
12:2, 3

Cause of God's anger. . . . . Ps. 78:58; Jer. 8:19

See Idols, idolatry

WORD STUDY   **GREAT,** *rab* (*rahb*). This adjective can be translated as "much," "many," or "great." When translated "much," it means a great amount of something, such as gold or silver. When it is translated as "many," it means a great number of people, days, or times, for example. When used in combination with another word, *rab* generally means "abounding in," as in Prov. 28:20, where one is abounding in blessings. Less often, the word actually means "great." One example of this usage is found in Amos 7:4 with its reference to "the great deep." (Strong's #7227)

Great

A. Descriptive of:

Sun and moon . . . . Gen. 1:16

Euphrates . . . . Gen. 15:18

Mediterranean . . . . Josh. 1:4

Nineveh. . . . . .Jon. 3:2, 3

Babylon. . . . . .Rev. 14:8

B. Applied to God's:

Nature. . . . . Deut. 10:17

Works . . . . .Judg. 2:7

Victory . . . . 2 Sam. 23:10, 12

Mercy. . . . . 2 Chr. 1:8

Wrath . . . . .2 Chr. 34:21

Glory . . . . .Ps. 21:5

Love . . . . Eph. 2:4, 5

C. Descriptive of Christ as:

God . . . . .Titus 2:13

Prophet. . . . . Luke 7:16

Priest . . . . Heb. 4:14

King. . . . . Luke 1:32, 33; Rev. 11:17

Shepherd. . . . . .Heb. 13:20

D. Applied to the believer's:

Reward . . . . Matt. 5:12

Faith. . . . . Matt. 15:28

Joy. . . . . .Acts 8:8

Zeal . . . . .Col. 4:13

Affliction . . . . 2 Cor. 8:2

Boldness . . . . 1 Tim. 3:13

Promises. . . . . .2 Pet. 1:4

E. Applied to final things:

Gulf fixed. . . . . .Luke 16:26

Wrath . . . . .Rev. 6:17

Tribulation. . . . . Rev. 7:14

White throne judgment . . . . .Rev. 20:11

Great fish

Swallows Jonah. . . . . Jon. 1:17; Matt. 12:40

Greatness, true

Hinges on:

God's gentleness. . . . . .Ps. 18:35

Great work . . . . Neh. 6:3

Unselfishness. . . . . .Jer. 45:5

Servanthood . . . . Matt. 23:11

God's estimate .Matt. 5:19

Great Tribulation

A specific period of time. . . . . Rev. 7:14

Time of distress . . . . Dan. 12:1

Jesus predicted . . . . .Matt. 24:15–28

Time will be shortened. . . . . Matt. 24:22

Greece—*the southern extremity of the Balkan peninsula*

Prophecy concerning. . . . . Dan. 8:21

Paul preaches in . . . . Acts 17:16–31

Called Javan. . . . . Is. 66:19

Vision of, in Daniel's visions . . . . Dan. 8:21

Conflict with. . . . . Zech. 9:13

Greed—*excessive desire for things*

A. Productive of:

Defeat . . . . .Josh. 7:11–26

Murder . . . . .1 Kin. 21:1–16

Betrayal. . . . . Luke 22:1–6

B. Examples of:

Samuel's sons. . . . . .1 Sam. 8:1, 3

False prophets . . . . Is. 56:10, 11

False teachers. . . . . 2 Pet. 2:14, 15

See Avarice; Covetousness

Greek

1. Native of Greece. . . . . .Joel 3:6; Acts 16:1

Spiritual state of . . . . .Rom. 10:12

Some believe . . . . .Acts 14:1

2. Foreigners speaking Greek . . . . John 12:20

3. Language of Greece. . . . . .Acts 21:37

Greeting

A. Normal between:

Brothers . . . . 1 Sam. 17:22

Social ranks . . . . Gen. 47:7

Strangers. . . . . 1 Sam. 10:3, 4

Christians. . . . . .1 Pet. 5:14

On visits . . . . Rom. 16:21–23

B. Examples of forms used in:

"God be gracious". . . . . Gen. 43:29

"Peace be with you" . . . . .Judg. 19:20

"The Lord be with you" . . . . Ruth 2:4

"The Lord bless you". . . . . Ruth 2:4

"Blessed are you" . . . . Ruth 3:10

"Rejoice"..................Matt. 28:9; Luke 1:28
"Hail" .... John 19:3
See Benediction

Greyhound—*a tall, slender hound*
   Poetically described............. Prov. 30:29, 31

Grief
A. Human causes of:
   Son's marriage.................. Gen. 26:34, 35
   Barrenness .... 1 Sam. 1:11, 16
   Death........................... 2 Sam. 19:1, 2
   Disease .... Job 2:11–13
   Sinners........................... Ps. 119:158
   Foolish son......................Prov. 17:25
B. Divine:
   Messiah..........................Is. 53:3, 4, 10
   God .... Ps. 95:10
   Holy Spirit .... Is. 63:10; Eph. 4:30
See Sorrow

> **WORD STUDY**   **GRIEVE, MOURN,** *pentheō* (pen-*theh*-oh). This verb means "to grieve," "to mourn (over)," and it can apply either to an inner and private feeling of sorrow or to an outward expression of grief (especially in conjunction with weeping; see, e.g., Luke 6:25; Rev. 18:11, 15, 19). In the NT *pentheō* is used in the obvious context of mourning the dead (Mark 16:10), but more often it is used with reference to grieving over sin, either one's own wrongdoing (James 4:9) or the wrongdoing of others (2 Cor. 12:21). The mourning mentioned in Matt. 5:4 is more likely to be a sad response to the oppression of the righteous by the wicked. (Strong's #3996)

Grow—*to increase*
A. Of natural things:
   Plants..............................Ps. 90:5, 6
Humans:
   Samuel........................... 1 Sam. 2:21
   John ....Luke 1:80
   Jesus...............................Luke 2:52
B. Of material things:
   Power............................2 Sam. 3:1
C. Of immaterial things:
   Spirituality...........................Luke 2:40
   Old covenant...................... Heb. 8:13
   God's kingdom ....Luke 13:18, 19
D. Parables of growth:
   Sower........................... Mark 4:2–20
   Tares ....Matt. 13:24–30
   Mustard seed...................Luke 13:18, 19
   Yeast............................. Matt. 13:33
   Seed ....Mark 4:26–29

Growth, spiritual
A. Expressed by words indicating:
   Fruitfulness ....John 15:2, 5
   Increase......................... 2 Cor. 9:10
   Addition .... 2 Pet. 1:5–10
   Growth ....1 Pet. 2:2

   Building up .... Jude 20
B. Hindrances to:
   Lack of knowledge.................Acts 18:24–28
   Carnality ....1 Cor. 3:1–3
   Instability.........................Eph. 4:14, 15
   Dullness ....Heb. 5:11–14
C. Means of:
   Milk of the Word .... 1 Pet. 2:1–3
   By knowledge of God ....Col. 1:10

Grudge—*to harbor resentment*
   Forbidden............................Lev. 19:18

> **WORD STUDY**   **GUARANTEE, PLEDGE,** *arrhabōn* (ar-rhab-*ohn*). This noun is a technical term, meaning "first installment," "deposit," or "pledge" in legal and commercial contexts. Specifically, it refers to a partial payment made in advance in order to secure a valid legal claim to the item purchased. Paul uses *arrhabōn* figuratively with respect to the Holy Spirit as God's "pledge" given to believers as a "guarantee" of His promises (2 Cor. 1:22; 5:5; Eph. 1:14). (Strong's #728)

Guard
A. Aspects of:
   Called mighty ....2 Sam. 23:8–23
   Often foreigners .... 2 Sam. 20:7
   Respected ....Jer. 40:1–5
B. Duties of:
   Run before chariots ....2 Sam. 15:1
   Form a military guard............. 1 Sam. 22:17
   Keep watch.......................2 Kin. 11:5, 6
   Carry out commandments......... Jer. 39:11–14
   Execute criminals.................... Dan. 2:14

Guardian angels
   Helpers ....Gen. 24:7; Heb. 1:1–14
   Protectors............................ Ps. 91:11
   Aided apostles.......Acts 5:17–19; 8:26; 12:7–11

Guardians, stewards—*custodians*
   Christ, of our souls..................2 Tim. 1:12
   Referred to by Paul.....................Gal. 4:2

Gudgodah—*cutting; cleft*
   Israelite encampment .... Deut. 10:7
   Also called Hor Hagidgad .... Num. 33:32

Guest
Kinds of:
   Terrified ....1 Kin. 1:41, 49
   Dead............................. Prov. 9:18
   Unwelcomed ....Prov. 25:17
   Unprepared .... Matt. 22:11
   Criticized .... Luke 7:39–50
   Congenial......................... Acts 18:1–3
   Courteous........................1 Cor. 10:27
   Angelic .... Heb. 13:2

Guidance, divine
   To meek .... Ps. 25:9
   To wise .... Prov. 23:19
   To good person .... Ps. 112:5

In God's strength . . . . Ex. 15:13
On every side . . . . .2 Chr. 32:22
With God's eye . . . . Ps. 32:8
With counsel . . . . .Ps. 73:24
Like a flock . . . . Ps. 78:52
By skillfulness . . . . .Ps. 78:72
Continually . . . . Is. 58:11

Guide—*a leader*
A. Kinds of:
Human . . . . .Num. 10:29–32
Supernatural . . . . .Ex. 13:20–22
Blind . . . . Matt. 23:16, 24
B. Goals of:
Peace . . . . Luke 1:79
Truth . . . . John 16:13
God's word . . . . Acts 8:30, 31

Guilt, universality of
All as filthy rags . . . . Is. 64:6
All fall short . . . . .Rom. 3:23
All declared . . . . Rom. 5:12–14; Gal. 3:22

Guni—*colored*
1. One of Naphtali's sons . . . . . Gen. 46:24; 1 Chr. 7:13
Descendants called Gunites . . . . .Num. 26:48
2. Gadite . . . . 1 Chr. 5:15

Gur—*lion's cub*
Site of Ahaziah's death . . . . .2 Kin. 9:27

Gur Baal—*sojourn of Baal*
Place in Arabia . . . . .2 Chr. 26:7

H

Haahashtari—*runner*
Son of Ashhur . . . . .1 Chr. 4:5, 6

Habaiah—*Yahweh has hidden*
Father of excommunicated Jewish
priests . . . . .Ezra 2:61, 62; Neh. 7:63, 64

Habakkuk—*embrace*
A. Complaints of:
God's silence . . . . .Hab. 1:2–4
God's response . . . . .Hab. 1:5–11
Chaldean cruelty . . . . .Hab. 1:12–17
God's response . . . . .Hab. 2:1–20
B. Prayer of:
Praise of God . . . . .Hab. 3:1–19

Habakkuk, Book of—*a book of the Old Testament*
Author . . . . Hab. 1:1
Setting . . . . .Hab. 1:2–4
Historical reference . . . . Hab. 1:6
The life of the just . . . . Hab. 2:4

Habazziniah
Grandfather of Jaazaniah . . . . .Jer. 35:3

Habit—*a custom*
A. Kinds of:
Doing evil . . . . Jer. 13:23
Doing good . . . . Acts 10:38

Of animals, instinctive . . . . 2 Pet. 2:22
B. Examples of:
Jesus'—worship at synagogue . . . . Luke 4:16
Daniel's—daily prayer . . . . Dan. 6:10

Habitation—*a place of residence*
A. Used literally of:
Canaan . . . . Num. 15:2
A tree . . . . .Dan. 4:20, 21
Nation . . . . Acts 17:26
B. Used figuratively of:
Eternity . . . . .Is. 57:15
God's throne . . . . Is. 63:15
Sky . . . . Hab. 3:11
Heaven . . . . .Luke 16:9
New Jerusalem . . . . Is. 33:20

Habor—*joined together*
The River of Gozan . . . . .2 Kin. 17:6

Hachaliah—*darkness of Yahweh*
Father of Nehemiah . . . . Neh. 1:1

Hachilah—*dark; gloomy*
Hill in the wilderness of Ziph where
David hid . . . . .1 Sam. 23:19–26

Hachmoni
Father of a tutor to David's sons . . . . . .1 Chr. 27:32

Hadad—*fierceness*
1. Ishmael's son . . . . 1 Chr. 1:30
2. King of Edom . . . . Gen. 36:35, 36
3. Another king of Edom . . . . 1 Chr. 1:50
Called Hadar . . . . Gen. 36:39
4. Edomite leader . . . . 1 Kin. 11:14–25

Hadadezer—*Hadad is a help*
King of Zobah . . . . 2 Sam. 8:3–13
Defeated by David . . . . .2 Sam. 10:6–19

Hadad and Rimmon
Name of the two Aramean deities; a place
in Jezreel . . . . Zech. 12:11

Hadashah—*new*
Village of Judah .Josh. 15:37

Hadassah—*myrtle*
Esther's Jewish name . . . . Esth. 2:7

Hadattah—*new*
Town in south Judah; possibly should be read as
Hazor Hadattah . . . . Josh. 15:25

 WORD STUDY

HADES, *hadēs* (ha-dayce). Outside the NT this noun, originally the proper name for the mythological god of the underworld, functions as the name for the place of the dead—the "underworld." This is paralleled in the NT where Hades is personified alongside "Death" (Rev. 6:8; 20:13, 14; cf. 1 Cor. 15:55). In Acts 2:27 it serves as the translation for the Hebrew *sheol*. The depths of Hades, guarded by gates (according to Matt. 16:18), are contrasted to heaven (Matt. 11:23; Luke 10:15; 16:23ff.). (Strong's #86)

Hadid—*sharp*
Town of Benjamin .... Neh. 11:31, 34

Hadlai—*restful*
Ephraimite .... 2 Chr. 28:12

Hadoram—*Hadar is exalted*
1. Son of Joktan .... Gen. 10:26, 27
2. Son of Tou .... 1 Chr. 18:9, 10
3. Rehoboam's tribute officer .... 2 Chr. 10:18
   Called Adoram .... 1 Kin. 12:18
   Probably same as Adoniram .... 1 Kin. 4:6

Hadrach—*periodical return*
Place in Syria .... Zech. 9:1

Hagab—*locust*
Head of a family of temple servants .... Ezra 2:46

Hagaba, Hagabah—*locust*
Head of a family of temple
   servants .... Neh. 7:46, 48; Ezra 2:43, 45

Hagar—*flight*
Sarai's Egyptian maidservant .... Gen. 16:1
Conceives by Abram .... Gen. 16:4
Flees from Sarai .... Gen. 16:5, 6
Angel of the Lord meets her .... Gen. 16:7, 8
Returns; becomes mother
   of Ishmael .... Gen. 16:9–16
Abraham sends her away .... Gen. 21:14
Paul's allegory of .... Gal. 4:22–26

Haggai—*festive*
Postexilic prophet .... Ezra 5:1, 2
Contemporary of Zechariah .... Ezra 6:14
Prophecies of, dated in reign of Darius
   Hystaspes (520 B.C.) ... Hag. 1:1, 15; 2:1, 10, 20

Haggai, Book of—*a book of the Old Testament*
Purpose .... Hag. 1:1–15
The coming glory .... Hag. 2:4–9
On Levitical cleanliness .... Hag. 2:10–14

Hagri—*a Hagerite*
Father of one of David's warriors ..... 1 Chr. 11:38
Called "Bani the Gadite" in .... 2 Sam. 23:36

Haggi—*festal*
Son of Gad .... Gen. 46:16
Head of tribal family .... Num. 26:15

Haggiah—*festival of Yahweh*
Merarite Levite .... 1 Chr. 6:30

Haggith—*festal*
One of David's wives .... 2 Sam. 3:4
Mother of Adonijah .... 1 Kin. 1:5

Hagri—*a Hagrite*
Father of one of David's warriors ..... 1 Chr. 11:38

Hagrites—*descendants of Hagar*
Nomad people east of Gilead ..... 1 Chr. 5:10–22;
   Ps. 83:6
Jaziz, keeper of David's flocks .... 1 Chr. 27:31

Hail—*frozen rain*
Illustrative of God's:
Wonders .... Job 38:22

Glory .... Ps. 18:12
Chastening .... Is. 28:2, 17
Wrath .... Rev. 8:7
Power .... Ps. 147:17

Hair
A. Of women:
Covering .... 1 Cor. 11:15
Uses of .... Luke 7:38
Prohibitions concerning ..... 1 Tim. 2:9; 1 Pet. 3:3
B. Of men:
Not to be worn long .... 1 Cor. 11:14
Rules for cutting .... Lev. 19:27
Long, during Nazirite vow .... Num. 6:5
Gray, sign of age .... 1 Sam. 12:2
Absalom's beautiful .... 2 Sam. 14:25, 26
Numbered .... Matt. 10:30
C. Figurative of:
Minuteness .... Judg. 20:16
Complete safety .... 1 Sam. 14:45
Fear .... Job 4:14, 15
Great numbers .... Ps. 40:12
Grief .... Ezra 9:3
Respect .... Prov. 16:31
Attractiveness .... Song 5:2, 11
Affliction .... Is. 3:17, 24
Entire destruction .... Is. 7:20
Decline and fall .... Hos. 7:9

Hakkatan—*the smallest*
Johanan's father .... Ezra 8:12

Hakkoz—*the thorn*
Descendant of Aaron .... 1 Chr. 24:1, 10
Called Koz .... Ezra 2:61, 62
Descendants of, kept from
   priesthood .... Neh. 7:63, 64

Hakupha—*crooked*
Ancestor of certain Temple
   servants .... Ezra 2:42, 43, 51

Halah—*a district of Assyria*
Israelite captives carried to .... 2 Kin. 17:6

Halak—*smooth*
Mountain near Seir .... Josh. 11:17

Half-shekel tax—*a temple tax*
Commanded .... Ex. 30:13, 14
Christ paid .... Matt. 17:24–27

Half-tribe of Manasseh—*the part of Manasseh east of the Jordan*
Clans of:
Machir .... Josh. 17:1

Halhul—*contorted*
A city in Judah .... Josh. 15:20, 21, 58

Hali—*necklace*
Town of Asher .... Josh. 19:25

Hallohesh—*enchanter*
Repairs walls and signs covenant ...... Neh. 3:12;
   10:24

Ham—*hot*
1. Noah's youngest son .Gen. 5:32
   Enters ark . . . . Gen. 7:7
   His immoral behavior merits Noah's
      curse . . . . Gen. 9:22–25
   Father of descendants of repopulated
      earth . . . . Gen. 10:6–20
2. Poetical name of Egypt. . . . . .Ps. 105:23, 27
3. Hamites at Gedor . . . . .1 Chr. 4:39, 40
4. Place where Chedorlaomer defeated the
      Zuzim . . . . .Gen. 14:5

Haman
   Agagite . . . . .Esth. 3:1, 2
   Plots to destroy Jews . . . . Esth. 3:3–15
   Invited to Esther's banquet . . . . .Esth. 5:1–14
   Forced to honor Mordecai . . . . Esth. 6:5–14
   Hanged on his own gallows . . . . .Esth. 7:1–10

Hamath—*fortification*
   Hittite city north of Damascus. . . . . . . .Josh. 13:5
   Spies visit . . . . Num. 13:21
   Israel's northern limit . . . . Num. 34:8
   Solomon's boundary . . . . .1 Kin. 8:65
   Storage cities built . . . . .2 Chr. 8:3, 4
   Captured by the Assyrians. . . . . 2 Kin. 18:30, 34
   People of, deported to Samaria. . . 2 Kin. 17:24, 30
   Israelites exiled. . . . . .Is. 11:11
   Mentioned by Jeremiah. . . . . Jer. 49:23
   Boundary in Ezekiel's prophecy . . . Ezek. 47:16–20

Hamathites
   People of Hamath. . . . . Gen. 10:18

Hamath Zobah—*fortress of Zobah*
   Captured by Solomon . . . . .2 Chr. 8:3

Hammath—*hot springs*
1. City of
   Naphtali . . . . .Josh. 19:35
   Probably the same as Hammon and
      Hammoth Dor . . . . . . .Josh. 21:32; 1 Chr. 6:76
2. Founder of the Rechabites. . . . . 1 Chr. 2:55

Hammedatha—*given by Ham*
   Father of Haman . . . . Esth. 3:1

Hammer—*a worker's tool*
A. Literal uses of:
   Drive tent pegs . . . . .Judg. 4:21
   Not used in temple . . . . 1 Kin. 6:7
   Straighten metal. . . . . .Is. 41:7
B. Figurative uses of:
   God's Word . . . . Jer. 23:29
   Babylon. . . . . Jer. 50:23

Hammered gold—*gold shaped by forceful blows*
   Ornamental shields . . . . 1 Kin. 10:16, 17;
      2 Chr. 9:15, 16

Hammoleketh—*the queen*
   Sister of Gilead . . . . 1 Chr. 7:17, 18

Hammon—*glowing*
1. Village of Asher .Josh. 19:28

2. Town of Naphtali. . . . . 1 Chr. 6:76
   See Hammath 1

Hammoth Dor—*hot springs of Dor*
   City of refuge. . . . . .Josh. 21:32
   See Hammath 1

Hamonah—*multitude*
   Site of Gog's defeat. . . . . Ezek. 39:11–16

Hamon Gog—*multitude of Gog*
   Memorial name of Gog's burial . . . . . . .Ezek. 39:11

Hamor—*ass*
   Sells land to Jacob. . . . . . .Gen. 33:18–20; Acts 7:16
   Killed by Jacob's sons . . . . .Gen. 34:1–31

Hamran
   Descendant of Seir. . . . . 1 Chr. 1:41
   See Hemdan

Hamstring—*to cut the tendons of the leg*
   To render captured animals useless . . . Josh. 11:6, 9;
      2 Sam. 8:4

Hamuel—*anger of God*
   Son of Mishma . . . . .1 Chr. 4:26

Hamul—*spared*
   Son of Perez . . . . .Gen. 46:12
   Founder of tribal family . . . . Num. 26:21

Hamutal—*kinsman of dew*
   Wife of King Josiah . . . . 2 Kin. 23:30, 31
   Mother of Jehoahaz and Zedekiah . . .2 Kin. 24:18
   Daughter of Jeremiah of Libnah. . . . . . . .Jer. 52:1

Hanamel—*God has pitied*
   Cousin of Jeremiah the prophet . . . . .Jer. 32:7

Hanan—*merciful*
1. One of David's mighty men. . . . . . . 1 Chr. 11:26, 43
2. Benjamite. . . . . .1 Chr. 8:23, 25
3. Descendant of Jonathan. . . . . 1 Chr. 8:38
4. Prophet. . . . . .Jer. 35:4
5. Head of temple servants. . . . . .Ezra 2:46
6. Explained Law . . . . .Neh. 8:7
7. Nehemiah's assistant treasurer. . . . . .Neh. 13:13
8, 9. Signers of the covenant. . . . . Neh. 10:22, 26

Hananel—*God has been gracious*
   Tower at Jerusalem . . . . .Jer. 31:38

Hanani—*gracious*
1. Father of Jehu the prophet. . . . . 1 Kin. 16:1, 7
   Rebukes Asa; confined to prison . . .2 Chr. 16:7–10
2. Son of Heman; head of Levitical
      course . . . . 1 Chr. 25:4, 25
3. Priest who divorced his foreign wife. . . . .Ezra 10:20
4. Nehemiah's brother; brings news
      concerning the Jews. . . . . .Neh. 1:2
   Becomes a governor of Jerusalem. . . . . . . Neh. 7:2
5. Levite musician . . . . Neh. 12:35, 36

Hananiah—*Yahweh has been gracious*
1. Benjamite chief. . . . . .1 Chr. 8:24, 25
2. Son of Heman; head of Levitical
      division. . . . . .1 Chr. 25:4, 23
3. One of King Uzziah's captains. . . . . . . 2 Chr. 26:11

4. Father of Zedekiah . . . . .Jer. 36:12
5. False prophet who contradicts
    Jeremiah . . . . .Jer. 28:1–17
6. Ancestor of Irijah . . . . .Jer. 37:13–15
7. Hebrew name of Shadrach . . . . Dan. 1:6, 7, 11
8. Son of Zerubbabel . . . . 1 Chr. 3:19–21
    Perhaps the same as Joannas . . . . .Luke 3:27
9. Son of Bebai; divorced his foreign wife . . .Ezra 10:28
10. Postexilic workman . . . . Neh. 3:8, 30
11. Postexilic priest . . . . Neh. 12:41
12. Postexilic chief; signs document . . . . . . Neh. 10:23
13. Postexilic ruler . . . . .Neh. 7:2
14. Priest of Joiakim's time . . . . .Neh. 12:12

> **WORD STUDY**
>
> **HAND,** *yad (yawd).* The noun *yad,* used many times in the OT, is translated "hand" and means an open hand as opposed to the word for "hand" that means "the palm of the hand." Literally, *yad* refers to hands, but by extension it also specifies the means by which something is done, so that it appears in phrases, such as "stretch out the hand to" (Ex. 7:19) or "a weapon in the hand" (Judg. 4:21). Frequently the word appears with a preposition so that it is translated "in hand" or "by the hand of." Figuratively, the word means "strength" or "power" as in Job 27:11. Another figurative use is the meaning "side," as Eli sat by the side of the way in 1 Sam. 4:13. (Strong's #3027)

Hand, Hands
    Mysterious . . . . .Dan. 5:1–6
    Healing withered . . . . Mark 3:1–3
    Offending, to be cut off . . . . Matt. 18:8
    Clapping—in joy .2 Kin. 11:12
    Washing—in innocency . . . . Matt. 27:24
    Joining—in agreement . . . . .2 Kin. 10:15
    Shaking—in pledge . . . . .Prov. 17:16–18
    Striking—in anger . . . . Num. 24:10
    Under thigh—in oaths . . . . .Gen. 47:29, 31

Right hand, expressive of:
    Honor . . . . Ps. 45:9
    Power . . . . Ps. 110:1
    Love . . . . Song 2:6
    Oath . . . . Is. 62:8
    Opposition . . . . .Zech. 3:1
    Self-denial . . . . Matt. 5:30
    Fellowship . . . . .Gal. 2:9

Handbreadth—*a linear measurement*
    Border of . . . . .Ex. 37:12
    Figurative of human life . . . . .Ps. 39:5

Handful
    Of fine flour . . . . .Lev. 2:2–5:12
    Of grain offering . . . . Num. 5:26
    Of barley . . . . .Ezek. 13:19

Handkerchief
    Touch of, brings healing . . . . Acts 19:12
    Placed on the dead .John 20:7

Handle—*to manage with the hands*
    Hold . . . . .2 Chr. 25:5
    Touch . . . . .Luke 24:39
    Feel . . . . .Ps. 115:7

Handmaid—*female servant*
Examples of:
    Hagar . . . . Gen. 16:1
    Zilpah . . . . .Gen. 29:24
    Bilhah . . . . .Gen. 30:4

Hand of God
Expressive of:
    Judgment . . . . .Ex. 9:3
    Chastening . . . . Job 19:21
    Security . . . . .John 10:29
    Miracles . . . . .Ex. 3:20
    Providence . . . . Ps. 31:15
    Provision . . . . .Ps. 145:16
    Protection . . . . .Ps. 139:10
    Punishment . . . . Ps. 75:8
    Pleading . . . . Is. 65:2

Hands, laying on of
A. In the Old Testament:
    Blessing a person . . . . .Gen. 48:14, 20
    Transferring one's guilt . . . . .Lev. 4:14, 15
    Setting apart for service . . . . Num. 8:10, 11
    Inaugurating a successor . . . . .Num. 27:18–23
B. In the New Testament:
    Blessing . . . . Matt. 19:13–15
    Healing . . . . .Matt. 9:18
    Ordaining deacons . . . . .Acts 6:6
    Sending out missionaries . . . . Acts 13:2, 3
    Ordaining officers . . . . 1 Tim. 4:14
    In bestowing the Holy Spirit . . . . .Acts 8:17, 18

Handwriting
    Of a king, changeable . . . . Dan. 6:8–27
    Of God, unchangeable . . . . .Dan. 5:5–31

Hanes—*mercury*
    Probably an Egyptian city . . . . Is. 30:4

Hanging—*a form of punishment*
    Absalom . . . . 2 Sam. 18:9–17
    Ahithophel . . . . 2 Sam. 17:23
    Judas . . . . Matt. 27:5
    Chief baker . . . . .Gen. 40:19, 22
    King of Ai . . . . .Josh. 8:29
    Five Canaanite kings . . . . Josh. 10:26, 27
    Ishbosheth's murderers . . . . 2 Sam. 4:12
    Bodies of Saul and Jonathan . . . . . . 2 Sam. 21:5–12
    Law of . . . . .Ezra 6:11
    Haman . . . . Esth. 7:10
    Haman's sons . . . . .Esth. 9:14
    Curse of . . . . .Gal. 3:13
    Saul's descendants . . . . 2 Sam. 21:8, 9
    Jesus Christ . . . . .John 19:17, 18, 31

Haniel—*God has been gracious*
    Descendant of Asher . . . . .1 Chr. 7:30, 39

Hannah—*graciousness*
    Favored wife of Elkanah . . . . .1 Sam. 1:5

Childless..........................1 Sam. 1:5, 6
Provoked by Peninnah...........1 Sam. 1:2, 6, 7
Prayerful............................1 Sam. 1:10
Wrongly accused by Eli..............1 Sam. 1:14
Bears child, Samuel..............1 Sam. 1:19, 20
Attentive to her child...............1 Sam. 1:22
Fulfills her vows.................1 Sam. 1:11–28
Magnifies God....................1 Sam. 2:1–10
Recognizes the Messiah
   ("His anointed")..................1 Sam. 2:10
Has other children..................1 Sam. 2:21
Model of Mary's song.............Luke 1:46–54

Hannathon—*regarded with favor*
Town of Zebulun.....................Josh. 19:14

Hanniel—*God has been gracious*
Manassite prince....................Num. 34:23

Hanoch—*dedicated*
1. Descendant of Abraham....Gen. 25:4; 1 Chr. 1:33
2. Son of Reuben.........................Gen. 46:9
3. Head of tribal family...................Num. 26:5

Hanun—*favored*
1. King of Ammon......................2 Sam. 10:1
   Disgraces David's ambassadors....2 Sam. 10:2–5
   Is defeated by David.............2 Sam. 10:6–14
2, 3. Postexilic workmen..............Neh. 3:13, 30

Haphraim—*double pit*
Town of Issachar.....................Josh. 19:19

Happiness of the saints
A. Is derived from:
   Fear of God..........................Ps. 128:1, 2
   Trust in God.........................Prov. 16:20
   Obedience to God................John 13:15, 17
   Wisdom's ways...................Prov. 3:13–18
B. Examples of:
   Israel.............................Deut. 33:29
   Mary............................Luke 1:46–55
   Paul...............................Acts 26:2
C. In spite of:
   Discipline...........................Job 5:17
   Suffering.......................1 Pet. 4:12–14
   Persecution.....................Matt. 5:10–12
   Lack.............................Phil. 4:6, 7
   Trouble.........................2 Cor. 4:7–18
D. Described as:
   Blessed.........................Matt. 5:3–12
   Filled..............................Ps. 36:8
   In God alone.....................Ps. 73:25, 26
See Gladness; Joy

Happiness of the wicked
A. Described as:
   Short..............................Job 20:5
   Uncertain.........................Luke 12:20
   Vain..............................Eccl. 2:1, 2
   Limited to this life.............Luke 16:24, 25
   Under God's judgment............Job 15:20, 21;
      Ps. 73:12, 18–20

B. Derived from:
   Prominence.................Job 21:7; Ps. 37:35
   Prosperity.......................Ps. 17:14; 37:7
   Sensuality..........................Is. 22:13
C. Saints:
   Sometimes stumble at.................Ps. 73:2, 3
   Should not envy.....................Ps. 37:1, 7
   Will see end......................Ps. 73:17–20

Happizzez
Chief of a priestly group............1 Chr. 24:15

Hara—*hill*
Place in Assyria where captive Israelites
   settled...........................1 Chr. 5:26

Haradah—*fear*
Israelite encampment...............Num. 33:24

Haran—*mountainous*
1. Abram's younger brother and Lot's
   father..........................Gen. 11:26–31
2. Gershonite Levite...................1 Chr. 23:9
3. Son of Caleb.......................1 Chr. 2:46
4. City of Mesopotamia.................Gen. 11:31
   Abraham lives in.....................Acts 7:2, 4
   Abram leaves.......................Gen. 12:4, 5
   Jacob flees to........................Gen. 27:43
   Jacob dwells at.....................Gen. 29:4–35
   Center of idolatry........Gen. 35:2; 2 Kin. 19:12

Hararite—*mountaineer*
Applied to David's mighty men...2 Sam. 23:11, 33;
   1 Chr. 11:34, 35

Harass, harassed
Used of:
   Temptations.......................Num. 25:18
   King................................Acts 12:1
   Enemies............................Judg. 10:8

Harbona—*bald man*
Eunuch under Ahasuerus..............Esth. 1:10
Same as Harbonah....................Esth. 7:9

Harbor—*a sheltered bay*
Unacceptable.......................Acts 27:12

Hard labor
A. Spiritual:
   Subduing flesh..................1 Cor. 9:24–27
   Striving against sin................Heb. 12:4
   Reaching goal....................Phil. 3:11–14
B. Physical:
   Jacob...........................Gen. 31:40–42
   Israelites.........................Ex. 1:11–14
   Gibeonites........................Josh. 9:3–27
   Samson.........................Judg. 16:20, 21

Hardness of heart
A. Causes of:
   God.................................Rom. 9:18
   Human...............................Job 9:4
   Unbelief............................John 12:40
   Sin................................Heb. 3:13

B. Examples of:
 Pharaoh.............................Ex. 4:21
 Zedekiah................ 2 Chr. 36:11–13
 Israel...........................Ezek. 3:7
 Nebuchadnezzar......................Dan. 5:20
 Jews...........................Mark 3:5
 Believers .... Mark 6:52
 The eleven ....Mark 16:14
C. Warnings against:
 Recognized by Egyptians............. 1 Sam. 6:6
 Unheeded by Israel......................Jer. 5:3
 Lamented by the prophets............. Is. 63:17
 Addressed to Christians........Heb. 3:8–15; 4:7

Harem—*group of females associated with one man*
 Esther a member of
 King Ahasuerus's.............. Esth. 2:8–14

Hareph—*plucking*
 Son of Caleb.....................1 Chr. 2:50, 51

Harhaiah—*Yahweh is protecting*
 Father of Uzziel....................... Neh. 3:8

Harhas—*splendor*
 Grandfather of Shallum.............2 Kin. 22:14

Harhur—*fever*
 Ancestor of returning
 temple servants .... Ezra 2:43, 51

Harim—*consecrated to God*
1. Descendant of Aaron .... 1 Chr. 24:1, 6, 8
2. Postexilic leader...................Ezra 2:32, 39
3. Father of Malchijah...................Neh. 3:11
4. Signer of the covenant ....Neh. 10:1, 5
5. Signer of the covenant .... Neh. 10:1, 27
6. Family house of priests............ Neh. 12:12, 15
7. Descendants of, divorced foreign
 wives ....Ezra 10:19, 21

Hariph—*autumn rain*
 Family of returnees .... Neh. 7:24
 Signers of covenant .... Neh. 10:19
 Same as Jorah ....Ezra 2:18

Harlot—*a prostitute*
A. Characteristics of:
 Shameless............................Jer. 3:3
 Painted ....Ezek. 23:30, 40
 Enticing......................... Prov. 9:14–18
 Roaming streets .... Prov. 7:12
 Expensive .... Prov. 29:3
B. Evils of:
 Profanes God's name.................. Amos 2:7
 Connected with idolatry............ Ex. 34:15, 16
 Brings spiritual error...............Hos. 4:10–19
 Cause of divorce .... Jer. 3:8, 14
C. Prohibitions concerning:
 Forbidden in Israel...................Lev. 19:29
 Priests not to marry..............Lev. 21:1, 7, 14
 To be shamed..................... Prov. 5:3–20
 Punishment .... Lev. 21:9
D. Examples of:
 Tamar .... Gen. 38:13–20

 Rahab ....Josh. 2:1–21
 Jephthah's mother ....Judg. 11:1
 Samson's ....Judg. 16:1
 Hosea's wife...................... Hos. 1:2
 The great .... Rev. 17:1–18
E. Figurative of:
 Tyre .... Is. 23:15, 17
 Israel .... Is. 1:21
 Spiritual adultery .... Is. 57:7–9; Rev. 17:1–18
 See Adultery

Harmony—*agreement, cooperation*
 Husband and wife ....1 Cor. 7:3–6;
 Eph. 5:22, 23; Col. 3:18, 19
 Christians..........John 13:34, 35; Rom. 15:5–7
 Christians and unbelievers ...... Rom. 12:16–18;
 Heb. 12:14

Harnepher
 Asherite.........................1 Chr. 7:36

Harness—*to equip*
 Horses .... Jer. 46:4

Harod—*fountain of trembling*
 Well near Gideon's camp .... Judg. 7:1

Harodite
 Inhabitant of Harod .... 2 Sam. 23:25
 Same as Harorite ....1 Chr. 11:27

Haroeh—*the seer*
 Judahite........................ 1 Chr. 2:50, 52
 Called Reaiah ....1 Chr. 4:2

Harosheth Hagoyim—*carving of the nations*
 Residence of Sisera............. Judg. 4:2, 13, 16

Harp—*a stringed musical instrument*
Used by:
 The wicked........................ Is. 5:11, 12
 David........................ 1 Sam. 16:16, 23
 Prophets .... 1 Sam. 10:5
 Temple orchestra .... 1 Chr. 16:5
 Temple worshipers.....................Ps. 33:2
 Celebrators..................... 2 Chr. 20:27, 28
 Jewish captives ....Ps. 137:2
 Worshipers in heaven ....Rev. 5:8

Harpoon—*a barbed spear for hunting large fish*
 Used against Leviathan ....Job 41:7

Harsha—*enchanter*
 Head of temple servants.......... Ezra 2:43, 52;
 Neh. 7:46, 54

Harum—*exalted*
 Judahite.............................1 Chr. 4:8

Harumaph—*flat-nosed*
 Father of Jedaiah .... Neh. 3:10

Haruphite
 Designation of Shephatiah............1 Chr. 12:5
 Member of Hariph's family............ Neh. 7:24

Haruz—*active*
 Father-in-law of King Manasseh ..... 2 Kin. 21:19

Harvest—*the time when the crops are ripe*
A. Occasion of:
Great joy..................................Is. 9:3
Bringing the first-fruits ....Lev. 23:10
Remembering the poor.............Lev. 19:9, 10
B. Figuratively of:
Seasons of grace ....Jer. 8:20
Judgment ....Jer. 51:33
God's wrath..........................Rev. 14:15
Gospel opportunities............. Matt. 9:37, 38
World's end ....Matt. 13:30, 39
Measure of fruitfulness...............2 Cor. 9:6
C. Promises concerning:
To continue ....Gen. 8:22
Rain.................................. Jer. 5:24
Patience............................James 5:7
D. Failure caused by:
Drought .... Amos 4:7
Locusts ....Joel 1:4
Sin...................................Is. 17:4–12

Hasadiah—*Yahweh has been gracious*
Son of Zerubbabel ....1 Chr. 3:20

Hashabiah—*Yahweh has imputed*
1. Merarite Levite....................1 Chr. 6:44, 45
Perhaps the same as in...............1 Chr. 9:14
2. Levite musician .... 1 Chr. 25:3, 19
3. Kohathite Levite ....1 Chr. 26:30
4. Levite ruler .... 1 Chr. 27:17
5. Chief Levite during Josiah's reign ...... 2 Chr. 35:9
6. Postexilic Levite.....................Ezra 8:19, 24
Probably the same in .... Neh. 10:11
7. Postexilic ruler ....Neh. 3:17
8. Descendant of Asaph ....Neh. 11:22
9. Priest in the time of Joiakim........... Neh. 12:21

Hashabnah—*covenant sealer*
Signed covenant ....Neh. 10:25

Hashabniah—*Yahweh has regarded me*
1. Father of Hattush ....Neh. 3:10
2. Postexilic Levite.........................Neh. 9:5
Probably the same as Hashabiah 6

Hashbadana—*thoughtful judge*
Assistant to Ezra...................... Neh. 8:4

Hashem—*shining*
Father of David's warriors ....1 Chr. 11:34
Also called Jashen.................. 2 Sam. 23:32

Hashmonah—*fertility*
Israelite encampment .... Num. 33:29

Hashub, Hasshub—*thoughtful*
1. Postexilic workman....................Neh. 3:11
2. Signer of the covenant .... Neh. 10:23
3. Levite chief ....Neh. 11:15

Hashubah—*esteemed*
Son of Zerubbabel ....1 Chr. 3:19, 20

Hashum—*opulent*
Founder of postexilic family ....Ezra 2:19
Assists Ezra and signs document .. Neh. 8:4; 10:18

Hasrah—*want*
Grandfather of Shallum.............2 Chr. 34:22
Called Harhas......................2 Kin. 22:14

Hassenaah—*thorny*
Father of postexilic workmen .... Neh. 3:3
Same as Senaah............. Ezra 2:35; Neh. 7:38

Hassenuah—*thorny*
Benjamite family .... 1 Chr. 9:7
Called Senuah ....Neh. 11:7–9

Haste—*to do something quickly*
Prompted by good ..... 2 Chr. 35:21; Luke 19:5, 6
Prompted by evil............. Prov. 14:29; 28:20

Hasupha—*naked*
Head of temple servants..... Ezra 2:43; Neh. 7:46

Hate—*to dislike something with strong feeling*
A. Meanings of:
React as God does ....Rev. 2:6
Twist moral judgments................Prov. 8:36
Esteem of less value ....John 12:25
Make a vital distinction ....Luke 14:26
Despise ....Is. 1:14
B. Causes of:
Parental favoritism............... Gen. 37:4, 5
Rape.....................2 Sam. 13:14, 15, 22
Failure to please .... 1 Kin. 22:8
God's purpose.......................Ps. 105:25
Six things God hates .... Prov. 6:16–19
Belonging to Christ .... Matt. 24:9, 10
Evil nature ....John 3:20
C. Objects of:
God's people ....Gen. 26:27
God ....Ex. 20:5
Christ...............................John 15:25
Light ....John 3:20
Evil men ....Ps. 26:5
Wickedness ....Ps. 45:7
D. Toward Christians, sign of their:
Discipleship........................ Matt. 24:9
Election.............................John 15:19
Regeneration .... 1 John 3:13–15

Hathach—*chamberlain*
Esther's attendant .... Esth. 4:5–10

Hathath—*terror*
Son of Othniel.......................1 Chr. 4:13

Hatipha—*captive*
Head of temple servants........... Ezra 2:43, 54

Hatita—*dug up*
Father of porters........... Ezra 2:42; Neh. 7:45

Hattil—*vacillating*
Ancestor of Solomon's servants .....Ezra 2:55, 57;
Neh. 7:57–59

Hattush—*assembled*
1. Descendant of David.................... Ezra 8:2
2. Man of Judah .... 1 Chr. 3:22
Probably the same as 1
3. Priest returning with Zerubbabel ......Neh. 12:1, 2

4. Postexilic workman . . . . Neh. 3:10
5. Priest who signs covenant . . . . Neh. 10:1, 4

Haughtiness—*an arrogant spirit*
  Precedes a fall . . . . Prov. 16:18
  To be brought low . . . . Is. 2:11, 17
  Guilt of Jerusalem for . . . . Ezek. 16:50; Zeph. 3:11

Hauran—*hollow land*
  District southeast of Mt. Hermon . . . . . Ezek. 47:16

Haven—*a sheltered area*
  Zebulun's assets . . . . Gen. 49:13
  Desired . . . . Ps. 107:30
  Near Lasea . . . . Acts 27:8

Havilah—*circle*
1. Son of Cush . . . . Gen. 10:7
2. Son of Joktan . . . . Gen. 10:29
3. District of Arabia . . . . Gen. 2:11
  Limit of Ishmaelite territory . . . . Gen. 25:18
  Saul defeated Amalekites . . . . 1 Sam. 15:7

Havoth Jair—*tent villages of Jair*
  Villages of Jordan in Gilead . . . . . . Num. 32:40, 41
  Formerly called Bashan . . . . Deut. 3:13, 14
  Taken by Jair . . . . Num. 32:41

Hawk—*a plundering bird*
  Ceremonially unclean . . . . Lev. 11:16
  Migratory . . . . Job 39:26

Hay—*food for cattle*
  Build with . . . . 1 Cor. 3:12
  Rendered "leeks" . . . . Num. 11:5

Hazael—*God has seen*
  Anointed by Elijah . . . . 1 Kin. 19:15
  Kills Ben-Hadad . . . . 2 Kin. 8:14, 15
  Becomes king of Syria . . . . 2 Kin. 8:15
  Defeats Joram of Israel . . . . 2 Kin. 8:25–29
  Defeats Jehu . . . . 2 Kin. 10:31, 32
  Oppresses Israel . . . . 2 Kin. 13:3–7, 22
  His son defeated . . . . 2 Kin. 13:24, 25

Hazaiah—*Yahweh has seen*
  Man of Judah . . . . Neh. 11:5

Hazar Addar—*village of Addar*
  Place in Canaan . . . . Num. 34:4

Hazar Enan—*village of springs*
  Village of north Palestine . . . . Num. 34:9, 10

Hazar Gaddah—*village of good fortune*
  Town on the border of Judah . . . . . . Josh. 15:21, 27

Hazar Hatticon—*the middle village*
  Town on the border of Hauran . . . . Ezek. 47:16

Hazarmaveth—*village of death*
  Descendants of Joktan . . . . Gen. 10:26

Hazar Shual—*fox village*
  Town in south Judah . . . . Josh. 15:21, 28
  Assigned to Simeon . . . . Josh. 19:1, 3
  Reoccupied after the Exile . . . . Neh. 11:27

Hazar Susah—*village of a mare*
  Simeonite village . . . . Josh. 19:5

Hazazon Tamar, Hazezon Tamar—*pruning of the palm*
  Dwelling of Amorites . . . . Gen. 14:7
  Also called En Gedi . . . . 2 Chr. 20:2

Hazeleponi—*give shade, you who turn toward me*
  Female descendant of Judah . . . . 1 Chr. 4:3

Hazeroth—*courts*
  Israelite camp . . . . Num. 33:17
  Scene of sedition of Miriam
    and Aaron . . . . Num. 12:1–16

Haziel—*God sees*
  Gershonite Levite . . . . 1 Chr. 23:9

Hazo—*seer*
  Son of Nahor . . . . Gen. 22:22, 23

Hazor—*enclosure*
1. Royal Canaanite city destroyed by
    Joshua . . . . Josh. 11:1–13
  Rebuilt and assigned
    to Naphtali . . . . Josh. 19:32, 36
  Army of, defeated by Deborah and
    Barak . . . . Judg. 4:1–24
  Fortified by Solomon . . . . 1 Kin. 9:15
  Captured by Tiglath-Pileser . . . . 2 Kin. 15:29
2. Town in south Judah . . . . Josh. 15:21, 25
3. Town of south Judah . . . . Josh. 15:21, 23
4. Town of Benjamin . . . . Neh. 11:31, 33
5. Region in the Arabian desert . . . . Jer. 49:28–33

He
  Fifth letter of Hebrew alphabet . . . . Ps. 119:33–40

WORD STUDY **HEAD,** *rosh* (rohsh). The noun *rosh*, occurring about 230 times in the OT, most commonly refers to the "head" of a human or animal, although it can indicate the top of something, such as a mountain, hill, ladder, or throne (Gen. 8:5). It can also be used of a chief or leader as in Judg. 10:18. By extension, *rosh* describes one that is first in a series, such as a chief priest or the head of a family (2 Chr. 24:11). *Rosh* (head) can also mean "front," which is a leader's place (Mic. 2:13) or the head of time, which is "the beginning of time" (Ezek. 40:1). (Strong's #7218)

Head
A. Attitudes expressed by:
  Covered, in grief . . . . 2 Sam. 15:30
  Covered, in subjection . . . . 1 Cor. 11:5
  Hand upon, in sorrow . . . . 2 Sam. 13:19
  Dust upon, in dismay . . . . Josh. 7:6
  Uncovered, in leprosy . . . . Lev. 13:45
  Wagging, in derision . . . . Matt. 27:39
  Anointed, in dedication . . . . Matt. 6:17
  Not to be shaved, in consecration . . . . . . Judg. 13:5
  Bowed, in worship . . . . 2 Chr. 29:30
  See Hands, laying on of
B. Figurative of:
  God . . . . 1 Cor. 11:3
  Christ . . . . Eph. 1:22
  Husband . . . . 1 Cor. 11:3, 7

Protection............................Ps. 140:7
Judgment .... Is. 15:2
Confidence..........................Luke 21:28
Pride ....Ps. 83:2
Exaltation ....Ps. 27:6
Joy and prosperity ....Ps. 23:5

Headdresses
Part of feminine attire .... Is. 3:20

Head of the church—*position of preeminence in the church*
Christ.................Eph. 1:22; 5:23; Col. 1:18
Prophesied ....Dan. 7:13, 14

Headship—*office of authority, responsibility*
A. Of Christ:
Over all things....................... Eph. 4:15
Over people .... 1 Cor. 11:3
Over the church ....Eph. 5:23; Col. 1:18
The chief cornerstone ......Acts 4:11; 1 Pet. 2:7, 8
B. Of the Father:
Over Christ .... 1 Cor. 11:3
Gives authority...................John 5:26, 27;
1 Cor. 15:25–28
C. Of man:
Of human race................ Rom. 5:12, 18, 21
Over woman .... 1 Cor. 11:3; Eph. 5:23

Heads of grain
Seen in Pharaoh's dream............Gen. 41:5–7
Regulations concerning ....Lev. 2:14
Ruth gleans .... Ruth 2:2
Christ's disciples pluck .... Matt. 12:1

| WORD STUDY | **HEAL**, *rapha'* (raw-*faw*). *Rapha'* is a verb, which means quite literally "to heal of hurts." Sometimes God is the Healer as |

He is in Gen. 20:17 and Ps. 107:20. At other times humans are the healers or physicians (2 Chr. 16:12; Eccl. 3:3). In the figurative sense, God heals the hurts of the nation, which indicates restored favor and forgiveness. There are many uses of the word in this context. The other figurative use of the word comes in the context of individual distress, which can be healed as in Job 5:18 and Ps. 41:5. (Strong's #7495)

| WORD STUDY | **HEALING**, *marpe'* (mawr-*pay*). *Marpe'* is a noun, usually translated "healing" or "cure." It is used in the context of healing |

of national woes (2 Chr. 36:16; Jer. 8:15; 33:6). Figuratively, the word means "health" or "profit" as it does in Prov. 4:22. It can mean spiritual healing as it does in Mal. 4:2 where the "Sun of Righteousness shall arise with healing in His wings." The adjectival form of the word can be used to mean a healthy mind (Prov. 14:30). (Strong's #4832)

Healing—*restoration of health*
A. Resulting from:
Intercession ....Num. 12:10–15
Repentance .... 1 Kin. 13:1–6

Prayer ....James 5:14, 15
Faith..........................Matt. 9:20–22;
John 4:46–53
God's Word ....Ps. 107:20
Laying on of hands...................Acts 28:8
B. Power of:
Belongs to God ....Gen. 20:17, 18
Possessed by Jesus .... Matt. 4:24; 8:16
Given to apostles .... Matt. 10:1–8
Given as a gift ....1 Cor. 12:9
Eternal in heaven ....Rev. 22:2
See Diseases; Sickness

Healing, spiritual
A. Source of:
Only in God.........................Jer. 17:14
Through Christ........................ Is. 53:5
Through the gospel .... Ezek. 47:8–11
B. Provided for:
Heartbroken ....Ps. 147:3
Repentant........................ 2 Chr. 7:14
Egyptians ....Is. 19:22–25
Faithful........................... Mal. 4:2
Oppression......................... Acts 10:38
C. Necessary because of human:
Sin............................... Ps. 41:4
Backsliding .... Jer. 3:22
Spiritual sickness .... Is. 6:10

Health—*the body freed from disease*
A. Factors conducive to:
Exercise........................... 1 Tim. 4:8
Food............................. Acts 27:34
Temperance......................Jer. 35:5–8
Obedience ....Prov. 4:20–22
Cheerfulness ....Prov. 17:22
God's will..........................John 9:1–3
B. Factors destructive of:
Moral looseness.................. Prov. 7:22–27
Wickedness ....Ps. 55:23
Disease .... 1 Sam. 5:6–12
Injury............................Luke 10:30
Debauchery ....Titus 1:12

| WORD STUDY | **HEALTHY, BE; BE SOUND**, *hugiainō* (hoog-ee-*eye*-no). This noun literally means "to be in good health," "to be in |

sound health." Luke uses the term three times with reference to physical health (5:31; 7:10; 15:27). In the Pastoral Epistles, however, *hugiainō* is used figuratively to refer to "sound" faith (Titus 1:13; 2:2), "sound" teaching (1 Tim. 1:10; 2 Tim. 4:3; Titus 1:9; 2:1), or "sound" words (1 Tim. 6:3; 2 Tim. 1:13). That is, it refers to correct Christian teaching, which engenders a robust faith and gives rise to wholesome values. (Strong's #5198)

Heap of stones—*a monument of stones*
Symbolic of:
Shameful acts ....Josh. 7:20–26
Covenant .... Gen. 31:46–52

Hearers—*those who hear*

A. Element necessary in:

Action	James 1:22–25
Attentiveness	Neh. 8:1–3
Belief	Rom. 10:14
Conviction	Acts 2:37
Discrimination	Luke 8:18

B. Reactions of:

Responsiveness	2 Sam. 7:17–29
Repentance	2 Sam. 12:12, 13
Rebellion	Ezek. 33:30–33
Retreat	John 6:60–66
Resistance	Acts 7:51–54
Rejoicing	Acts 13:48
Rejection	Acts 28:23–29
Research	Acts 17:11

> **WORD STUDY**
>
> **HEART,** *leb* (*layb*). The noun *leb*, which is translated "heart," can refer to the inner person as opposed to the outer form, "my heart and my flesh" (Ps. 84:2). The figurative use of the word indicates feelings either of sorrow and pain or of gladness. It can also mean the "will" or "inclination" (Ps. 10:17; Eccl. 1:13). Differing from English usage, the term can also mean "the mind" as in Num. 16:28 and Jer. 3:16. The heart is the center of anything so that the heart of the sea is the midst of the sea in Ex. 15:8. The word is often used in phrases describing moral character, such as "broken heart," "clean heart," "new heart," or "evil heart." (Strong's #3820).

Heart

A. Seat of:

Adultery	Matt. 5:28
Belief	Rom. 10:10
Concern	Jer. 31:20
Condemnation	1 John 3:20
Desire	Rom. 10:1
Doubt	Mark 11:23
Evil	Ps. 28:3
Fear	Is. 35:4
Hatred	Lev. 19:17
Joy	Eccl. 5:20
Love	Mark 12:30, 33
Lust	Rom. 1:24
Meditation	Ps. 19:14
Obedience	Rom. 6:17
Pride	Prov. 16:5
Purity	Matt. 5:8
Purpose	2 Cor. 9:7
Reason	Mark 2:8
Rebellion	Jer. 5:23
Rejoicing	Acts 2:26
Sorrow	John 14:1
Suffering	Ps. 22:14
Thought	Matt. 9:4
Wisdom	Prov. 14:33

B. Of the wicked, described as:

Blind	Eph. 4:18
Darkened	Rom. 1:21
Covetous	2 Pet. 2:14
Full of evil	Gen. 6:5
Unrepentant	Rom. 2:5
Lustful	Prov. 6:25
Proud	Jer. 49:16
Rebellious	Jer. 5:23
Uncircumcised	Acts 7:51

C. God:

Knows	Ps. 44:21
Searches	1 Chr. 28:9
Enlightens	2 Cor. 4:6
Opens	Acts 16:14
Recreates	Ezek. 11:19
Tests	Jer. 12:3
Strengthens	Ps. 27:14
Establishes	1 Thess. 3:13

D. Regenerate's, described as:

Circumcised	Rom. 2:29
Contrite	Ps. 51:17
Enlarged	Ps. 119:32
Enlightened	2 Cor. 4:6
Joyful in God	1 Sam. 2:1
Meditative	Ps. 4:4
Perfect	Ps. 101:2
Pure	Ps. 73:1; Matt. 5:8
Prayerful	1 Sam. 1:12, 13
Glad and sincere	Acts 2:46
Steadfast	Ps. 57:7
Tender	2 Kin. 22:19
Treasury of good	Matt. 12:35
Wise	Prov. 10:8

E. Regenerate's, responses of:

Believe with	Rom. 10:10
Keep with diligence	Prov. 4:23
Love God with all	Matt. 22:37
Sanctify God in	1 Pet. 3:15
Serve God with all	Deut. 26:16
Walk before God with all	1 Kin. 2:4
Trust the Lord with all	Prov. 3:5
Regard not iniquity in	Ps. 66:18
Do God's will from	Eph. 6:6

Hearth—*a place for fire*

Bed of live coals	Is. 30:14; Ps. 102:3

Heartlessness—*without moral feeling; cruelty*

A. Among unbelievers:

Pharaoh, toward Israel's baby boys	Ex. 1:15–22
Philistines, toward Samson	Judg. 16:21
Saul, toward David	1 Sam. 18:25
Nabal, toward David	1 Sam. 25:4–12
Haman, toward Jews	Esth. 8–10
Herod, toward male babies	Matt. 2–16
Levite, toward a certain man	Luke 10:30–32
Multitude, toward Jesus	Luke 23:13–25

B. Among professing believers:

Laban, toward Jacob	Gen. 31:7, 36–42
Jacob's sons, toward Joseph	Gen. 37:18–35
David, toward Uriah	2 Sam. 11:9–27

Heat, hot

Figurative of:

God's wrath	Deut. 9:19
Human anger	Deut. 19:6
Determination	Gen. 31:36
Zeal	Ps. 39:3
Persecution	Matt. 13:6, 21
Heavy toil	Matt. 20:12
Real faith	Rev. 3:15

Heathen (see Gentiles)

Heave offering

A. Consisted of:

Firstfruits	Num. 15:18–21
Tenth of all tithes	Num. 18:21–28

B. Part of:

All gifts	Num. 18:29
Spoils	Num. 31:26–47
Offerings	Ex. 29:27; Lev. 7:14, 32

C. Requirements concerning:

To be the best	Num. 18:29
Brought to God's house	Deut. 12:5, 6
Given to priests	Ex. 29:27, 28
Sanctified the whole offering	Num. 18:27–32
Eaten in a clean place	Lev. 10:12–15

WORD STUDY   **HEAVEN (EXPANSE ABOVE EARTH),** *shamayim* (shaw-*mah*-yim). The noun *shamayim* is a plural noun that is usually used in the singular context. It means the visible heavens where the stars are. Birds fly beneath heaven, and rain comes from this heaven. The other meaning is the abode of God where He sits enthroned. From heaven God rains down brimstone, hailstones, and bread. God is said to look down from heaven and talk to Israel from the same place. Certain of God's aspects are in heaven also, such as His mercy, righteousness, and faithfulness. Occasionally, heaven is personified as it is in Is. 1:2 and Jer. 2:12. (Strong's #8064)

Heaven—*the place of everlasting bliss*

A. Inhabitants of:

God	1 Kin. 8:30
Christ	Heb. 9:12, 24
Holy Spirit	Ps. 139:7, 8
Angels	Matt. 18:10
The just	Heb. 12:22, 23

B. Things lacking in:

Marriage	Matt. 22:30
Death	Luke 20:36
Flesh and blood	1 Cor. 15:50
Perishable	1 Cor. 15:42, 50
Sorrow	Rev. 7:17
Pain	Rev. 21:4
Curse	Rev. 22:3
Night	Rev. 22:5
Weeping	Is. 65:19
Wicked people	Rev. 22:15
End	Matt. 25:46; Rev. 22:5

C. Positive characteristics of:

Joy	Luke 15:7, 10
Rest	Rev. 14:13
Peace	Luke 16:19–25
Righteousness	2 Pet. 3:13
Service	Rev. 7:15
Reward	Matt. 5:11, 12
Inheritance	1 Pet. 1:4
Glory	Rom. 8:17, 18
Authority of God's word	Ps. 119:89

D. Entrance into, for:

Righteous	Matt. 5:20
Changed	1 Cor. 15:51
Saved	John 3:5, 18, 21
Called	2 Pet. 1:10, 11
Overcomers	Rev. 2:7, 10, 11
Those recorded	Luke 10:20
Obedient	Rev. 22:14
Holy	Rev. 19:8

E. Believer's present attitude toward:

Given foretaste of	Acts 7:55, 56
Earnestly desires	2 Cor. 5:2, 8
Looks for	2 Pet. 3:12
Considers "far better" than now	Phil. 1:23
Puts treasure there	Luke 12:33

F. Described as:

House	John 14:2
Kingdom	Matt. 25:34
Abraham's bosom	Luke 16:22, 23
Paradise	2 Cor. 12:2, 4
Better country	Heb. 11:10, 16
Holy city	Rev. 21:2, 10–27; 22:1–5

Heavens, natural

A. Facts regarding:

Created by God	Gen. 1:1
Stretched out	Is. 42:5; Jer. 10:12
Will be destroyed	Heb. 1:10–12; 2 Pet. 3:10
New heavens to follow	Is. 65:17; 2 Pet. 3:13

B. Purposes of:

To declare God's glory	Ps. 19:1
To declare God's righteousness	Ps. 50:6
To manifest God's wisdom	Prov. 8:27

Heaviness—*a spirit of grief or anxiety*

Unrelieved by mirth	Prov. 14:13
God's children experience	Phil. 2:26
Needed exchange	James 4:9
Experienced by Christ	Ps. 69:20, 21
Remedy for	Prov. 12:25

Heavy—*oppressive*

A. Used literally of:

Eli's weight	1 Sam. 4:18
Absalom's hair	2 Sam. 14:26
Stone	Prov. 27:3

B. Used figuratively of:

Fatigue	Matt. 26:43
Burdens	2 Chr. 10:11, 14
Sins	Is. 24:20
God's judgments	1 Sam. 5:6, 11

Heber, Eber—*associate*
1. Son of Beriah........................ Gen. 46:17
   Descendants called Heberites........ Num. 26:45
2. Husband of Jael, the slayer of Sisera...Judg. 4:11–24
3. Descendant of Ezra .... 1 Chr. 4:17, 18
4. Gadite chief....................... 1 Chr. 5:11, 13
5. Benjamite.......................... 1 Chr. 8:17

Hebrew—*one from the other side*
Applied to:
   Abram............................. Gen. 14:13
   Israelites .... 1 Sam. 4:6, 9
   Jews ....Acts 6:1
   Paul, a sincere .... Phil. 3:5

Hebrew language
   Spoken by Rabshakeh........... 2 Kin. 18:26, 28
   Alphabet of, in divisions..................Ps. 119
   Language of Christ's time .... John 19:13, 20;
      Acts 21:40
   See Aramaic

Hebrews, the Epistle to the—*a book of the
      New Testament*
   Christ greater than the angels........ Heb. 1:3, 4
   Christ of the order of
      Melchizedek ....Heb. 4:14–5:10
   The new covenant .... Heb. 8:1–10:18
   The life of faith...............Heb. 10:19–13:17

Hebron—*alliance*
1. Ancient town in Judah ....Num. 13:22
   Originally called Kirjath Arba .... Gen. 23:2
   Called Mamre .... Gen. 23:19
   Abram dwells here .... Gen. 13:18
   Abraham buys cave here.......... Gen. 23:2–20
   Isaac and Jacob sojourn here .... Gen. 35:27
   Visited by spies ....Num. 13:21, 22
   Defeated by Joshua..................Josh. 10:1–37
   Caleb expels Anakim from ....Josh. 14:12–15
   Assigned to Levites ....Josh. 21:10–13
   City of refuge....................Josh. 20:5–7
   David's original capital......... 2 Sam. 2:1–3, 11
   Birthplace of David's sons ....2 Sam. 3:2
   Abner's death here ....2 Sam. 4:1
   Absalom's rebellion here.......... 2 Sam. 15:7–10
   Fortified by Rehoboam.............. 2 Chr. 11:10
2. Son of Kohath.......................... Ex. 6:18
   Descendants called Hebronites .... Num. 3:19, 27
3. Descendant of Caleb..............1 Chr. 2:42, 43

Hebronites (see Hebron 3)

Hedge—*a fence or barrier*
Illustrative of:
   God's protection......................Job 1:10
   Afflictions ....Job 19:8
   Laziness ....Prov. 15:19
   Removal of protection.................Ps. 80:12

Heedfulness—*giving proper attention to something
      important*
A. Objects of:
   God's commandments ....Josh. 22:5

Our ways............................. Ps. 39:1
False teachers..................... Matt. 16:6
God's Word ....2 Pet. 1:19
B. Admonitions to Christians, concerning:
   Deception .... Matt. 24:4
   Outward display...................Matt. 6:1
   Worldliness ....Luke 21:34
   Duty..........................Acts 20:28–31
   Foundation...................... 1 Cor. 3:10
   Liberty.......................... 1 Cor. 8:9
   Security.........................1 Cor. 10:12
   Effectiveness ....Gal. 5:15
   Ministry ....Col. 4:17
   Fables...........................1 Tim. 1:4
   Unbelief .... Heb. 3:12
See Caution

Heel—*the back part of the human foot*
A. Used literally of:
   Esau's............................. Gen. 25:26
B. Used figuratively of;
   Seed of the woman................... Gen. 3:15
   Enemy of Dan .... Gen. 49:17
   The wicked.......................... Job 18:5, 9
   Friend of David...................... Ps. 41:9

Hegai—*the sprinkler*
   Eunuch under King Ahasuerus ... Esth. 2:3, 8, 15

Heifer—*a young cow*
A. Ceremonial uses of:
   In a covenant...................... Gen. 15:9
   In purification.................... Num. 19:1–22
B. Red heifer, ceremony concerning:
   Without spot .... Num. 19:2
   Never yoked........................ Num. 19:2
   Slaughtered and burned outside the
      camp ....Num. 19:3–8
   Ashes kept .... Num. 19:9, 10
   Ashes, with water, used to purify... Num. 19:11–22
   Significance of...................... Heb. 9:13, 14
C. Figurative of:
   Improper advantage ....Judg. 14:18
   Contentment......................Jer. 50:11

Heirs, natural
A. Persons and property involved:
   Firstborn...................... Deut. 21:15–17
   Sons of concubines.................. Gen. 21:10
   Daughters...................... Num. 27:1–11
   Widows..........................Ruth 3:12, 13
   Order of succession .... Num. 27:8–11
B. Exceptions:
   Father could make concubines'
      sons heirs.................. Gen. 49:1, 12–27
   Daughters receive marriage
      portion...................... Gen. 29:24, 29
   Daughters sometimes share with sons ... Job 42:15
   Daughters receive, if no sons......... Num. 27:8
C. Examples of heirship changes by divine election:
   Ishmael to Isaac ....Gen. 21:10, 11
   Esau to Jacob ....Gen. 27:35–37; Rom. 9:13

Reuben to Joseph .... Gen. 49:22–26
Adonijah to Solomon. .... 1 Kin. 1:11–14
See Birthright; Inheritance, earthly

Heirs, spiritual
A. Of Christ:
    Recognized. .... Matt. 21:38
    Appointed .... Heb. 1:2
B. Of Christians, means of:
    By promise .... Gal. 3:29
    Through Christ. .... Gal. 4:7
    Through faith .... Rom. 4:13, 14
    By grace. .... Gal. 4:21–31
C. Of Christians, receiving:
    Grace .... 1 Pet. 3:7
    Promise. .... Heb. 11:9
    Kingdom. .... James 2:5
    Salvation. .... Heb. 1:14
    Righteousness .... Heb. 11:7
    Eternal life .... Titus 3:7
See Inheritance, spiritual

Helah—*ornament*
One of Ashhur's wives. .... 1 Chr. 4:5, 7

Helam—*fortress*
Place between Damascus and Hamath where
    David defeated Syrians ...... 2 Sam. 10:16–19

Helbah—*fertility*
City of Asher .... Judg. 1:31

Helbon—*fertile*
City north of Damascus .... Ezek. 27:18

Heldai—*worldly*
1. One of David's captains .... 1 Chr. 27:15
    Probably same as Heled
    and Heleb .... 2 Sam. 23:29; 1 Chr. 11:30
2. Exile from Babylon bearing gifts ..... Zech. 6:10, 11
    Called Helem. .... Zech. 6:14

Helek—*portion*
Son of Gilead. .... Num. 26:30
Founder of a family .... Josh. 17:2

Helem—*strength*
1. Asherite .... 1 Chr. 7:34, 35
2. Same as Heldai .... Zech. 6:10, 11
    Called Hotham .... 1 Chr. 7:32

Heleph—*strong*
Frontier town of Naphtali .... Josh. 19:32, 33

Helez—*strong*
1. One of David's captains .... 2 Sam. 23:26
2. Judahite .... 1 Chr. 2:39

Heli—*climbing*
Father of Joseph, husband of Mary ..... Luke 3:23

Helkai—*portion*
Postexilic priest. .... Neh. 12:15

Helkath—*portion, field*
Frontier town of Asher .... Josh. 19:24, 25
Assigned to Levites .... Josh. 21:31
Same as Hukok .... 1 Chr. 6:75

Hell—*the place of eternal torment*
A. Described as:
    Everlasting fire .... Matt. 25:41
    Everlasting punishment .... Matt. 25:46
    Outer darkness .... Matt. 8:12
    Everlasting destruction .... 2 Thess. 1:9
    Lake of fire. .... Rev. 19:20
B. Prepared for:
    Devil and his angels. .... Matt. 25:41
    Wicked .... Rev. 21:8
    Disobedient .... Rom. 2:8, 9
    Fallen angels .... 2 Pet. 2:4
    Beast and the False Prophet. .... Rev. 19:20
    Worshipers of the Beast .... Rev. 14:11
    Rejectors of the gospel .... Matt. 10:15
C. Punishment of, described as:
    Bodily .... Matt. 5:29, 30
    In the soul. .... Matt. 10:28
    With degrees .... Matt. 23:14

Hellenists
Greek-speaking Jews .... Acts 6:1
Hostile to Paul .... Acts 9:29
Gospel preached to. .... Acts 11:20

Helmet—*armor for the head*
Used figuratively of salvation:
    Prepared .... Is. 59:17
    Provided .... Eph. 6:17
    Promised. .... 1 Thess. 5:8

Helon—*strong*
Father of Eliab. .... Num. 1:9

WORD STUDY   **HELPER,** *paraklētos* (par-*ak*-lay-toss). This noun is derived from the verb *parakaleo,* which means "to call to one's side," "to summon (to one's aid)," "to appeal to," "to exhort," "to request," "to implore," "to comfort." Originally, *paraklētos* was used in the passive sense for "one who is called to someone's aid." In the NT, however, *paraklētos* carries an active meaning of "one who appears on another's behalf," thus "medi-ator," "intercessor," "helper." In 1 John 2:1 *paraklētos* is described as one who intercedes with God on behalf of sinners. In the Gospel of John the Spirit is designated as the "Helper" (14:16, 26; 15:26; 16:7). (Strong's #3875)

Helper—*one who assists another*
A. Used of:
    God .... Heb. 13:6
    Christ. .... Heb. 4:15, 16
    Holy Spirit .... Rom. 8:26
    Angels .... Dan. 10:13
    Woman .... Gen. 2:18, 20
    Christians. .... Acts 16:9
B. The Holy Spirit as:
    Abides with believers. .... John 14:16
    Teaches .... John 14:26
    Testifies of Christ. .... John 15:26
    Convicts .... John 16:7–11

Guides into truth . . . . John 16:13
Glorifies Christ. . . . . John 16:14, 15

Helps—*the acts of bearing another's burden*
A gift to the church . . . . 1 Cor. 12:28
Christians admonished to . . . . 1 Thess. 5:14
Elders admonished to . . . . Acts 20:28, 35

Hemam—*raging*
Son of Lotan . . . . Gen. 36:22
Same as Homam. . . . . 1 Chr. 1:39

Heman—*faithful*
1. Famous wise man. . . . . 1 Kin. 4:31
Judahite. . . . . 1 Chr. 2:6
Composer of a psalm. . . . . Ps. 88 (Title)
2. Musician under David; grandson
of Samuel . . . . 1 Chr. 6:33
Appointed as chief singer. . . . . 1 Chr. 15:16, 17
Man of spiritual insight . . . . 1 Chr. 25:5

Hemdan—*pleasant*
Descendant of Seir. . . . . Gen. 36:26
Same as Hamran. . . . . 1 Chr. 1:41

Hemorrhage—*a flow of blood*
Healing of woman who suffered for 12 years
from . . . . Matt. 9:20–22; Mark 5:25–29;
Luke 8:43, 44

Hen—*favor*
Son of Zephaniah .Zech. 6:14

Hen—*domestic fowl*
God's nurturing care compared to. . . . Matt. 23:37

Hena—*lowland*
City captured by the Assyrians. . . . . . .2 Kin. 18:34

Henadad—*favor of Hadad*
Postexilic Levite . . . . .Ezra 3:9
Sons of, help Nehemiah . . . . Neh. 3:18, 24

Henna—*a fragrant shrub*
Illustrative of beauty . . . . Song 1:14

Hepher—*pit, well*
1. Town west of the Jordan. . . . . .Josh. 12:17
Name applied to a district . . . . 1 Kin. 4:10
2. Founder of Hepherites . . . . Num. 26:30, 32
3. Son of Ashhur. 1 Chr. 4:5, 6
4. One of David's guards . . . . 1 Chr. 11:26, 36

Hephzibah—*my delight is in her*
Mother of King Manasseh. . . . . 2 Kin. 21:1

Herald
Of Nebuchadnezzar. . . . . .Dan. 3:3–6
Of Pharaoh. . . . . .Gen. 41:42, 43
Zion . . . . Is. 40:9

Herbs—*grass or leafy vegetables*
Bitter, used at Passover. . . . . .Ex. 12:8
Poisonous, not fit . . . . 2 Kin. 4:39, 40

Herdsman—*one who tends cattle*
Conflict among. . . . . Gen. 13:7, 8

Heredity—*transmission of physical and mental traits*
A. Factors involved:
Likeness of nature . . . . Gen. 5:3
Common transgression. . . . . .Rom. 5:12
Sinful nature . . . . John 3:6, 7
Family and national traits . . . . .Titus 1:12
God's purpose of plan. . . . . Gen. 9:22–27
B. Consistent with:
Individual responsibility . . . . Jer. 31:29, 30
God's sovereign plan . . . . Rom. 9:6–16
Need of a new nature. . . . . . Matt. 3:9; John 3:1–12
Family differences . . . . 1 John 3:11, 12
Child different from his parents. . . . . 1 Sam. 8:1–5

Heres—*sun*
1. Mountain in Dan . . . . .Judg. 1:35, 36
Probably connected with Beth Shemesh
or Ir Shemesh . . . . . . Josh. 19:40, 41; 1 Kin. 4:9
2. Egyptian city; probably is the "City of
Destruction" referred to. . . . . Is. 19:18

Heresh—*silent*
Levite. . . . . 1 Chr. 9:15

> **WORD STUDY**
>
> **HERESY, FACTION,** *hairesis* (heye-res-iss). This noun is translated in a variety of ways in the NT, but it apparently meant "choice" originally (cf. the cognate verb in Matt. 12:18). It is used to designate a "sect," "faction," or "party," whose members subscribe to distinctive views or opinions (e.g., Sadducees in Acts 5:17 and Pharisees in 15:5). Since the word is also used with reference to groups that hold divisive or dissenting opinions, *hairesis* is translated as "heresy" or "faction" (1 Cor. 11:19; Gal. 5:20; 2 Pet. 2:1). (Strong's #139)

Heresy—*a teaching contrary to the truth*
A. Characteristics of:
Damnable. . . . . .2 Pet. 2:1
Contagious. . . . . .2 Pet. 2:2
Subversive. . . . . Gal. 1:7
B. Attitude toward:
Recognize purpose. . . . . 1 John 2:18, 19
Withdraw. 1 Tim. 6:4, 5, 11
Do not receive . . . . 2 John 9–11

Hereth
Forest in Judah . . . . 1 Sam. 22:5

Heritage, earthly
A. Of believers:
Children . . . . Ps. 127:3
Long life . . . . Ps. 91:16
B. Of Israel:
Promised Land . . . . .Ex. 6:8
Forsaken of God. . . . . Jer. 12:7–9
Discontinue . . . . .Jer. 17:4
Return to . . . . .Jer. 12:15

Heritage, spiritual
A. Described as:
Laid up . . . . .Ps. 31:19; Col. 1:5
Reserved. . . . . .1 Pet. 1:4

Healed; his life prolonged

    15 years........................ 2 Kin. 20:1–11

    His thanks .... Is. 38:9–22

    Rebuked for his pride .... 2 Kin. 20:12–19

    Death of .... 2 Kin. 20:20, 21

    Ancestor of Christ ....Matt. 1:9

2. Ancestor of returning exiles .... Ezra 2:1, 16

3. Ancestor of Zephaniah.................. Zeph. 1:1

4. Postexilic workman who returned with

    Zerubbabel .... Ezra 2:16

5. Son of Neariah .... 1 Chr. 3:23

6. Ancestor of returning exiles ....Neh. 10:17

Hezion—*vision*

    Grandfather of Ben-Hadad......... 1 Kin. 15:18

Hezir—*swine*

1. Descendant of Aaron .... 1 Chr. 24:1, 15

2. One who signs document........... Neh. 10:1, 20

Hezro—*having a fixed habitation*

    One of David's mighty men......... 1 Chr. 11:37

Hezron—*enclosure*

1. Place in south Judah ....Josh. 15:1, 3

2. Son of Reuben....................... Gen. 46:9

    Founder of the Hezronites........... Num. 26:6

3. Son of Perez......................... Gen. 46:12

    Head of tribal family............... Num. 26:21

    Ancestor of David .... Ruth 4:18–22

    Ancestor of Christ ....Matt. 1:3

Hiddai—*joyful*

    One of David's warriors .... 2 Sam. 23:30

    Same as Hurai......................1 Chr. 11:32

Hiddekel—*rapid*

    Hebrew name of the river Tigris ....Gen. 2:14;

    Dan. 10:4

Hide—*to conceal*

A. Used literally of:

    Man in Eden .... Gen. 3:10

    Baby Moses ....Ex. 2:2, 3

    Spies.............................Josh. 6:17, 25

B. Used figuratively of:

    God's face...................... Deut. 31:17, 18

    Protection............................ Is. 49:2

    Darkness.........................Ps. 139:12

    Believer's life ....Col. 3:3

Hiel—*God lives*

    Native of Bethel; rebuilds Jericho ....1 Kin. 16:34

    Fulfills Joshua's curse ....Josh. 6:26

Hierapolis—*sacred city*

    City of Asia Minor; center of Christian

    activity............................Col. 4:13

High—*exalted, lofty*

Descriptive of:

    Rich ....Ps. 49:2

    Eminent people.................... 1 Chr. 17:17

    God's mercy........................Ps. 103:11

High places—*places of idolatrous worship*

A. Evils of:

    Contrary to one sanctuary......... Deut. 12:1–14

    Source of idolatry...................2 Kin. 12:3

    Place of child sacrifices...............Jer. 7:31

    Cause of God's wrath ....1 Kin. 14:22, 23;

    Ps. 78:58

    Denounced by the prophets.........Ezek. 6:1–6;

    Hos. 4:11–14

    Cause of exile..................... Lev. 26:29–34

B. Built by:

    Solomon ....1 Kin. 11:7–11

    Jeroboam .... 1 Kin. 12:26–31

    Jehoram.........................2 Chr. 21:9, 11

    Ahaz........................... 2 Chr. 28:24, 25

    Manasseh ....2 Kin. 21:1, 3

    People of Judah............... 1 Kin. 14:22, 23

    People of Israel .... 2 Kin. 17:9

    Sepharvites.......................2 Kin. 17:32

C. Destroyed by:

    Asa.............................2 Chr. 14:3, 5

    Jehoshaphat .... 2 Chr. 17:6

    Hezekiah ....2 Kin. 18:4, 22

    Josiah........................ 2 Kin. 23:5, 8, 13

High priest

A. Duties of:

    Offer gifts and sacrifices .... Heb. 5:1

    Make atonement.................. Lev. 16:1–34

    Inquire of God ....1 Sam. 23:9–12

    Consecrate Levites................ Num. 8:11–21

    Anoint kings .... 1 Kin. 1:34

    Bless the people...................Num. 6:22–27

    Preside over courts........... Matt. 26:3, 57–62

B. Typical of Christ's priesthood:

    Called of God .... Heb. 5:4, 5

    Making atonement............... Lev. 16:32, 33

    Subject to temptation .... Heb. 2:18

    Exercise of compassion .... Heb. 4:15, 16

    Holiness of position...............Lev. 21:14, 15

    Marrying a virgin.................... 2 Cor. 11:2

    Alone entering Most Holy Place ....Heb. 9:7, 12, 24

    Ministry of intercession ....Num. 16:43–48;

    Heb. 7:25

    Blessing people .... Acts 3:26

Highway—*a thoroughfare, road*

A. Characteristics of:

    Roads for public use................. Num. 20:19

    Straight and broad .... Is. 40:3

    Robbers use .... Luke 10:30–33

    Animals infest..................... Is. 35:8, 9

    Beggars sit by.................... Matt. 20:30

    Byways sometimes better..............Judg. 5:6

B. Figurative of:

    Holy way..........................Prov. 16:17

    Israel's restoration ....Is. 11:16

    Gospel's call...................... Is. 40:3

    Way of salvation .... Is. 35:8–10

    Two destinies.................... Matt. 7:13, 14

    Christ......................... John 14:6

Hilen—*strong place*

Town of Judah.....................1 Chr. 6:57, 58

Also called Holon....................Josh. 15:51

Hilkiah—*Yahweh is my portion*

1. Levite, son of Amzi ....1 Chr. 6:45, 46

2. Levite, son of Hosah .... 1 Chr. 26:11

3. Father of Eliakim......................Is. 22:20

4. Priest, father of Jeremiah.................. Jer. 1:1

5. Father of Gemariah....................Jer. 29:3

6. Shallum's son........................ 1 Chr. 6:13

High priest in Josiah's reign....... 2 Chr. 34:9–22

Oversees temple work.............. 2 Kin. 22:4–7

Finds the Book of the Law........ 2 Kin. 22:8–14

Aids in reformation...................2 Kin. 23:4

7. Chief of postexilic priest ....Neh. 12:1, 7

Later descendants of ....Neh. 12:12, 21

8. One of Ezra's assistants ....Neh. 8:4

Hill, hill country—*an elevation of the earth's surface*

Rendered "Gibeah" ....1 Sam. 11:4

Sinners plead for their covering ....Luke 23:30

Hillel—*he has praised*

Father of Abdon the judge........ Judg. 12:13, 15

Hindrances—*things which obstruct one's way*

A. Physical:

Heavy armor .... 1 Sam. 17:38, 39

Ship's cargo ....Acts 27:18–38

B. Spiritual:

Satanic temptations................ Matt. 4:8–10

Riches .... Matt. 19:24

Unbelief ....Matt. 11:21–24

Ceremonialism ....Matt. 15:1–9

Love of world..................... 2 Tim. 4:10

Sin................................. Heb. 12:1

C. Removal of, by:

Faith......................... Matt. 17:20, 21

God's armor...................... Eph. 6:11–18

Walking in the Spirit...............Gal. 5:16, 17

Self-control..................... 1 Cor. 9:25–27

Love .... 1 Cor. 13:4–8

Hinge—*a pivot of a door*

Of gold ....1 Kin. 7:50

Hinnom, Valley of (Ben-Hinnom)

A. Location of:

Near Jerusalem.......................Jer. 19:2

Boundary line ....Josh. 15:8

Tophet......................Jer. 19:6, 11–14

B. Uses of:

For idol worship ....1 Kin. 11:7

For sacrificing children ....2 Chr. 28:3

Defiled by Josiah .... 2 Kin. 23:10–14

Jeremiah addresses people here .... Jer. 19:1–5

Will become "Valley of Slaughter".... Jer. 7:31, 32

Make holy........................ Jer. 31:40

Hirah—*nobility*

Adullamite, a friend of Judah ....Gen. 38:1, 12

Hiram, Huram—*highborn*

1. King of Tyre .... 2 Sam. 5:11

Provides men and material for David's

palace ....1 Chr. 14:1

David's friend .... 1 Kin. 5:1

Provides men and material for

Solomon's temple...............1 Kin. 5:1–12

Refuses gifts of cities

from Solomon................ 1 Kin. 9:10–13

Helps Solomon with money

and seamen ....1 Kin. 9:14, 26–28; 10:11

2. Craftsman; a son of a Tyrian and a

widow of Naphtali.............. 1 Kin. 7:13, 14

Sent by King Solomon to work

on temple................. 1 Kin. 7:14–40, 45

Writes to Solomon .... 2 Chr. 2:11

Hire—*wages*

A. Used literally of payments to:

Prostitute .... Deut. 23:18

Priests ....Judg. 18:4

Mercenary soldiers.................. 2 Sam. 10:6

Mercenary prophets................. Deut. 23:4

B. Used figuratively of:

Spiritual adultery .... Ezek. 16:33

Sexual relations..................... Gen. 30:16

See Wages, hire

Hireling—*a common laborer*

Anxious for the day to close ....Job 7:1, 2

Figurative of human life................Job 14:6

Guilty of neglect.................John 10:12, 13

History, biblical

A. Characteristics of:

Dated with human events ....Hag. 1:1, 15;

Luke 3:1

Inspired...........................2 Tim. 3:16

Free of fables ....2 Pet. 1:16

B. Valuable for:

Outline of ancient history .... Acts 7:1–53

Spiritual lessons ....1 Cor. 10:1–11

Prophecy and fulfillment..........Acts 4:24–28

Hittites—*an ancient nation*

A. Facts concerning:

Descendants of Canaan .... Gen. 10:15

One of seven Canaanite nations........Deut. 7:1

Original inhabitants of Palestine... Ezek. 16:3, 45

Ruled by kings.....................1 Kin. 10:29

Great nation........................ 2 Kin. 7:6

Their land promised to Israel ......Gen. 15:18, 20

Destruction of, commanded ...... Deut. 7:1, 2, 24

Destruction of, incomplete ....Judg. 3:5

B. Intermarriage with:

By Esau .... Gen. 36:2

By Israelites after the conquest........Judg. 3:5, 6

By Solomon .... 1 Kin. 11:1

By Israelites after the Exile ....Ezra 9:1, 2

C. Notable persons of:

Ephron............................. Gen. 49:30

Ahimelech . . . . 1 Sam. 26:6
Uriah . . . . 2 Sam. 11:6, 21

Hivites
Descendants of Canaan . . . . Gen. 10:15, 17
One of seven Canaanite nations . . . . .Deut. 7:1
Esau intermarries with . . . . Gen. 36:2
Gibeonites belong to . . . . .Josh. 9:3, 7
Land of, promised to Israel . . . . Ex. 3:8; 23:23
Destruction of:
Commanded . . . . Deut. 7:1, 2, 24
Incomplete . . . . .Judg. 3:3

Hizki—*my strength*
Benjamite . . . . 1 Chr. 8:17

Hobah—*hiding place*
Town north of Damascus . . . . Gen. 14:15

Hod—*majesty*
Asherite . . . . .1 Chr. 7:30, 37

Hodaviah—*praise Yahweh*
1. Son of Elioenai . . . . 1 Chr. 3:24
2. Chief of Manasseh . . . . 1 Chr. 5:23, 24
3. Benjamite . . . . 1 Chr. 9:7
4. Levite, founder of a family . . . . .Ezra 2:40
Called Judah . . . . .Ezra 3:9

Hodesh—*new moon*
Wife of Shaharaim . . . . .1 Chr. 8:8, 9

Hodiah, Hodijah—*splendor of Yahweh*
1. Judahite . . . . 1 Chr. 4:1, 19
2. Levite interpreter .Neh. 8:7
Leads in prayer . . . . Neh. 9:5
Probably the same as one of the signers
of the covenant . . . . .Neh. 10:10, 13
3. Signer of the covenant . . . . .Neh. 10:18

Hoglah—*partridge*
Daughter of Zelophehad . . . . Num. 26:33

Hoham—*Yahweh protests*
Amorite king defeated by Joshua . . . Josh. 10:3–27

Hold fast
Good thing . . . . 1 Thess. 5:21
Faithful word . . . . .Titus 1:9
Our confidence . . . . Heb. 3:6
Our confession . . . . Heb. 4:14
What we have .Rev. 2:25; 3:11

Holiness of Christ
A. Announced in:
Psalms . . . . Ps. 16:10
Prophets . . . . Is. 11:4, 5
B. Proclaimed by:
Gabriel . . . . Luke 1:35
Demons . . . . Mark 1:24
Centurion . . . . .Luke 23:47
Peter . . . . Acts 4:27, 30
Paul . . . . 2 Cor. 5:21
John . . . . .1 John 2:1, 29
C. Manifested negatively in freedom from:
Sin . . . . .1 John 3:5
Guilt . . . . .John 8:46

Defilement . . . . .Heb. 7:26, 27
D. Manifested as "the Holy One" applied by:
Demons . . . . Mark 1:24
Peter . . . . Acts 2:27
Paul . . . . Acts 13:35
John . . . . 1 John 2:20
Christ Himself .Rev. 3:7

Holiness of Christians
A. In their calling:
Elected to . . . . .Rom. 8:29
Called to . . . . 1 Thess. 4:7
Created in . . . . Eph. 4:24
Possessed by .1 Cor. 3:16, 17
B. In their lives:
Bodies . . . . Rom. 6:13, 19
Manner of life . . . . .1 Pet. 1:15
Fruitfulness . . . . John 15:8
C. Reasons for:
God's holiness . . . . 1 Pet. 1:15, 16
God's mercies .Rom. 12:1, 2
Christ's love . . . . 2 Cor. 5:14, 15
World's end . . . . .2 Pet. 3:11
Inheritance in kingdom . . . . .Eph. 5:5
D. God's means of:
Word . . . . John 17:17
Chastisement . . . . Heb. 12:10
Grace . . . . Titus 2:3, 11, 12
See Godliness; Sanctification

Holiness to the Lord
Breastplate insignia . . . . Ex. 28:36
Israel . . . . .Jer. 2:3
On bells of horses . . . . Zech. 14:20

Holon—*strong place*
1. City of Judah . . . . .Josh. 15:51
2. City of Moab . . . . .Jer. 48:21

WORD STUDY
HOLY (SET ASIDE FOR HOLY PURPOSE), qadosh (kaw-*dohsh*). The adjective *qadosh*, meaning "sacred" or "holy," comes from the verb for "to set something apart" or "to consecrate" it. When applied to God, the term means "set apart" and therefore "sacred" or "holy." There are a number of aspects to God's holiness. First, He is exalted and thus different from others. Next, He is separate from human impurity and sin. *Qadosh* is used as part of a name of God, "the Holy One of Israel," frequently in Is. and occasionally in Ps. and Jer. On the human plane, there are holy places, such as the chambers of priests and the camp of Israel. People can be holy as is said of priests, Aaron, and prophets. In Ps. 89:6 angels are called holy. Time can also be holy when it is set apart for a special purpose as the Sabbath is in Neh. 8:9 and Is. 58:13. (Strong's #6918)

WORD STUDY
HOLY, hagios (hag-ee-oss). Adjective meaning "holy" or "sacred" in the sense of dedicated or set apart for God. It is used to describe places (Jerusalem, Matt. 4:5; the temple,

Acts 6:13) and persons (prophets, Luke 1:70; apostles, Eph. 3:5) consecrated to God—even angels (Col. 1:12) and Jesus (Acts 4:27, 30). As a substantive the word can designate "that which is holy" (the "sanctuary" in Heb. 8:2) and can be used as a name for God ("The Holy One," as in John 2:20) or Christ (Luke 4:34) or God's Spirit ("Holy" Spirit, as in Matt. 28:19). As a plural substantive (literally, "holy ones") the word is used to refer to believers as "saints" (1 Cor. 6:1, 2). (Strong's #40)

Holy day—*any of the Jewish religious holidays*

Sabbath ....Ex. 35:2
"Festival" ....Col. 2:16
Rendered "Feast" ....Luke 2:41

Holy Land (see Canaan, Land of)

Holy Spirit

A. Titles applied to:

Spirit of:

God .... Gen. 1:2
The Lord God ....Is. 61:1
Your Father .... Matt. 10:20
Grace...............................Zech. 12:10
Truth .... John 14:17
Holiness ....Rom. 1:4
Life................................Rom. 8:2
Christ................................Rom. 8:9
Adoption..............................Rom. 8:15
His Son ....Gal. 4:6
Glory ....1 Pet. 4:14
Prophecy...............................Rev. 19:10
My Spirit................................ Gen. 6:3
Holy Spirit .... Ps. 51:11
The Helper.......................John 14:16, 26
Eternal Spirit........................ Heb. 9:14

B. Deity of:

Called God........................ Acts 5:3, 4
Joined with the Father and Son ......Matt. 28:19;
   2 Cor. 13:14
Eternal............................. Heb. 9:14
Omnipotent........................Luke 1:35
Omniscient ....1 Cor. 2:10, 11
Omnipresent ....Ps. 139:7–13
Creator .... Gen. 1:2
Sovereign ....1 Cor. 12:6, 11
New creation ....John 3:3, 8
Sin against, eternal............... Matt. 12:31, 32

C. Personality of:

Speaks .... Acts 28:25
Teaches.............................John 14:26
Strives with sinners .... Gen. 6:3
Comforts ....Acts 9:31
Helps our weaknesses .... Rom. 8:26
Is grieved .... Eph. 4:30
Is resisted ....Acts 7:51

D. Work in the world:

Creates ....Job 33:4
Renews .... Is. 32:15
Convicts ....John 16:8–11

E. Work of, in Christ's ministry:

Christ conceived by .... Luke 1:35
Cast out demons by .... Matt. 12:28
Anointed by.........................Matt. 3:16
Supported by ....Luke 4:1, 17, 18
Filled by .... Luke 4:1
Offered to God by .... Heb. 9:14
Raised by ....Rom. 1:4
Justified by..........................1 Tim. 3:16
Glorified by .... John 16:14

Witnesses to Christ:

In heaven ....1 John 5:7
On earth...........................1 John 5:8

F. Work of, in the Scriptures:

Speaks in:

Prophets .... Acts 28:25
Psalms .... Acts 1:16, 17
All Scripture ....2 Tim. 3:16
His sword .... Eph. 6:17

G. Ministry of, among believers:

Regenerates .... John 3:3, 5
Indwells.............................Rom. 8:11
Anoints .... 1 John 2:20, 27
Baptizes.........................Acts 2:17–41
Guides............................. John 16:13
Empowers......................... Mic. 3:8
Sanctifies .... Rom. 15:16; 2 Thess. 2:13
Bears witness............ Rom. 8:16; Heb. 10:15
Helps ....John 14:16–26
Gives joy ....Rom. 14:17
Gives discernment ....1 Cor. 2:10–16;
   1 John 4:1–6
Bears fruit......................... Gal. 5:22, 23
Gives gifts...................... 1 Cor. 12:3–11
Invites ....Rev. 22:17

H. Ministry of, in the church:

Fills ....Acts 2:4
Baptizes............................1 Cor. 12:13
Appoints officers .... Acts 20:17, 28
Sends out missionaries .... Acts 13:2, 4
Directs missionaries .... Acts 8:29
Comforts the church ....Acts 9:31
Sanctifies the church.................Rom. 15:16

I. Reception of:

Promised........................Joel 2:28–32
Awaits Christ's glorification ....John 7:38, 39
Realized at Pentecost................ Acts 2:1–21
Realized by Gentiles .... Acts 10:45
Contingent...................... Acts 2:38; 5:32

J. Filling of:

Bezalel...............................Ex. 31:2
Samson ....Judg. 14:19
Saul.............................. 1 Sam. 10:10
David.............................. 1 Sam. 16:13
Jesus................................ Luke 4:1
John the Baptist ....Luke 1:15, 60
Elizabeth............................Luke 1:41
Zacharias ....Luke 1:67
Pentecost Christians .... Acts 2:1–4

Peter . . . . .Acts 4:8
Prayer meeting . . . . Acts 4:31
Seven men . . . . .Acts 6:3–5
Stephen . . . . .Acts 7:55
Barnabas . . . . Acts 11:22, 24
Paul . . . . Acts 13:9
Certain disciples . . . . Acts 13:52
K. As teacher:
    Illuminates the mind . . . . 1 Cor. 2:12, 13;
      Eph. 1:16, 17
    Reveals things of God . . . . Is. 40:13, 14;
      1 Cor. 2:10, 13

Home—*center of family life*
Things associated with:
    Eating . . . . 1 Cor. 11:34
    Homemaking . . . . .Titus 2:5
    Religious training . . . . .1 Tim. 5:4
    Entertainment . . . . .Luke 15:6
Domestic:
    Counsel . . . . 1 Cor. 14:35
    Discord . . . . Ruth 4:3; 2 Sam. 14:13–24
    Land . . . . Ruth 4:3
    Friends . . . . .Mark 5:19
    Present life . . . . 2 Cor. 5:6
See House

Homeless
    Christ's condition .Luke 9:58
    True of apostles also . . . . 1 Cor. 4:11

Homer—*a heap*
    Measure; equal to about
      11 bushels . . . . Ezek. 45:11, 14

Homesickness
    Jacob . . . . Gen. 30:25
    Edomite Hadad . . . . .1 Kin. 11:21, 22
    Exiles . . . . .Ps. 137:1–6
    Prodigal son . . . . .Luke 15:11–19
    Epaphroditus .Phil. 2:25, 26

Homestead—*the family dwelling*
    Redeemable . . . . Lev. 25:25–30

Homicide
Provisions provided:
    Distinction between guilty
      and innocent . . . .Ex. 21:12–14; Num. 35:16–23
    Determination of guilt . . . . .Num. 35:24, 30
    Detention in cities
      of refuge . . . . Num. 35:11, 15, 25–29
    Defilement of land by
      slack justice . . . . .Num. 35:31–34
    See Murder

Homosexuality
    Forbidden . . . . .Lev. 18:22
    Considered an abomination . . . . .1 Kin. 14:24
    Punishment . . . . .Lev. 20:13
    Unclean .Rom. 1:24, 26, 27

Honest, honesty—*uprightness*
A. Necessity of:
    Means of testimony . . . . 1 Pet. 2:12

Obligatory upon Christians . . . . 2 Cor. 13:7
Signs of a righteous person . . .Ps. 1:1–3; Luke 8:15
B. Blessings of:
    Brings advancement . . . . Is. 33:15–17
    Makes acceptable with God . . . . .Ps. 15:1, 2
C. Examples of:
    Samuel . . . . 1 Sam. 12:1–5
    David . . . . 1 Sam. 25:7, 15
    Workmen . . . . 2 Kin. 12:15
    Zacchaeus . . . . .Luke 19:8
    Paul . . . . .2 Cor. 8:20, 21

Honey—*a sweet substance*
A. Characteristics of:
    Product of bees .Judg. 14:8, 9
    Not acceptable in offerings . . . . .Lev. 2:11
    Offered as part of firstfruits . . . . 2 Chr. 31:5
B. Figurative of:
    God's Word . . . . Ps. 19:10
    God's blessings .Ex. 3:8, 17
    Wisdom . . . . Prov. 24:13, 14
    Prostitute's enticements . . . . Prov. 5:3
    Immanuel's diet . . . . Is. 7:14, 15

WORD STUDY

HONOR, *hadar* (haw-*dar*). When *hadar* is a verb, it means "honor" or "adorn." The positive sense of the word, "to show honor for a person," can be seen in Lev. 19:32 where one honors the face of an old man. The negative side of the word appears in Lev. 19:15 and means "to show favoritism." As a noun, *hadar* can be translated "splendor," "ornament," or "honor." The term implies dignity when it appears in Job 40:10, Ps. 96:6, and other places; but it is not used to refer to a quality by which God is recognized in the same way *kabod*, meaning "glory" and "honor," is used. (Strong's #1921, #1926)

Honor—*to esteem or regard highly*
A. Those worthy of:
    God . . . . .1 Tim. 1:17
    Christ . . . . John 5:23
    Parents . . . . Eph. 6:2
    Aged . . . . 1 Tim. 5:1, 3
    Church officers .Phil. 2:25, 29
B. Obtainable by:
    Wisdom . . . . Prov. 3:16
    Graciousness . . . . Prov. 11:16
    Discipline . . . . .Prov. 13:18
    Humility . . . . .Prov. 15:33
    Peaceableness .Prov. 20:3
    Righteousness and mercy . . . . .Prov. 21:21
    Honoring God . . . . 1 Sam. 2:30
    Serving Christ . . . . .John 12:26
C. Those advanced to:
    Joseph . . . . Gen. 41:41–43
    Phinehas . . . . .Num. 25:7–13
    Joshua . . . . .Num. 27:18–20
    Solomon . . . . 1 Kin. 3:13
    Hezekiah . . . . .2 Chr. 32:33
    Abishai . . . . .1 Chr. 11:20, 21

Daniel . . . . Dan. 2:48
Mordecai. . . . . Esth. 8:15
Apostles . . . . Matt. 19:27–29

Hoof—*the covering of horn protecting the extremities of certain animals*
Test of clean animals. . . . . Lev. 11:3–8
All must leave with Israel. . . . . Ex. 10:26
Like flint. . . . . Is. 5:28
Cause noise . . . . .Jer. 47:3

Hook
Used:
  For curtains . . . . Ex. 26:32, 37
  In fishing . . . . .Job 41:1, 2
  For pruning . . . . Is. 2:4
  Expressive of God's sovereignty . . . . . .2 Kin. 19:28

Hoopoe—*a bird of the plover family*
Unclean bird . . . . .Lev. 11:19

Hope—*the expectation of future good*
A. Kinds of:
  Continual. . . . . Ps. 71:14
  Natural expectation. . . . . Acts 27:20
  Sinful expectation . . . . Acts 24:26
  Impossible . . . . .Rom. 4:18
  Spiritual assurance. . . . . 2 Cor. 1:7
  One. . . . . Eph. 4:4
B. Described as:
  Living . . . . .1 Pet. 1:3
  Blessed. . . . . .Titus 2:13
  Good . . . . 2 Thess. 2:16
  Better. . . . . Heb. 7:19
  Sure and steadfast . . . . Heb. 6:19
  One of the great virtues . . . . .1 Cor. 13:13
C. Productive of:
  Purity. . . . . .1 John 3:3
  Patience. . . . . .Rom. 8:25
  Courage. . . . . Rom. 5:4, 5
  Joy. . . . . .Rom. 12:12
  Salvation. . . . . .Rom. 8:23
  Assurance. . . . . Heb. 6:18, 19
  Stability. . . . . .Col. 1:23
D. Grounds of:
  God's Word . . . . .Ps. 119:42–81; Rom. 15:4
  God's promises . . . . .Acts 26:6, 7; Titus 1:2
  Christ. . . . . .Col. 1:27
E. Objects of:
  God . . . . Ps. 39:7
  Christ. . . . . 1 Cor. 15:19
  Salvation. . . . . Rom. 5:1–5
  Resurrection . . . . Acts 23:6
  Eternal life . . . . .Titus 1:2
  Glory . . . . .Rom. 5:2
  Christ's return. . . . . Rom. 8:22–25

Hopelessness—*without hope*
Condition of the wicked. . . . . Eph. 2:12
Their unchangeable condition . . . . Luke 16:23–31

Hophni—*fighter*
Son of Eli; brother of Phinehas. . . . . .1 Sam. 1:3

Called "reprobates" . . . . 1 Sam. 2:12
Guilty of unlawful practices . . . . . . 1 Sam. 2:13–17
Immoral . . . . 1 Sam. 2:22
Eli's warning rejected by. . . . . .1 Sam. 2:23–25
Cursed by a man of God. . . . . .1 Sam. 2:27–36
Warned by Samuel. . . . . 1 Sam. 3:11–18
Ark taken to battle by . . . . 1 Sam. 4:1–8
Slain in battle. .1 Sam. 4:11
News of, causes Eli's death. . . . . 1 Sam. 4:12–18

Hor—*mountain*
1. Mountain of Edom . . . . Num. 20:23
  Scene of Aaron's death . . . . .Num. 20:22–29;
  33:37–39
2. Prominent peak of the Lebanon range. Num. 34:7, 8

Horam—*elevated*
King of Gezer . . . . .Josh. 10:33

Horeb—*desert*
God appears to Moses. . . . . Ex. 3:1–22
Water flows from . . . . .Ex. 17:6
Law given here. . . . . Mal. 4:4
Site of Israel's great sin . . . .Deut. 9:8, 9; Ps. 106:19
Covenant made. Deut. 29:1
Elijah lodged here 40 days . . . . .1 Kin. 19:8, 9
See Sinai

Horem—*consecrated*
City of Naphtali . . . . .Josh. 19:32, 38

Hor Hagidgad—*cavern of Gidgad*
Israelite encampment . . . . Num. 33:32
See Gudgodah

Hori—*cave dweller*
1. Son of Lotan . . . . Gen. 36:22; 1 Chr. 1:39
2. Horites . . . . Gen. 36:21–30
3. Father of Shaphat the spy. . . . . .Num. 13:5

Horites—*cave dwellers*
Inhabitants of Mt. Seir . . . . Gen. 36:20
Defeated by Chedorlaomer . . . . Gen. 14:5, 6
Ruled by chieftains . . . . .Gen. 36:29, 30
Driven out by Esau's descendants . . .Gen. 36:20–29;
  Deut. 2:12, 22

Hormah—*devoted to destruction*
Originally called Zephath . . . . .Judg. 1:17
Scene of Israel's defeat . . . . Num. 14:45
Destroyed by Israel . . . . Num. 21:1–3
Assigned to Judah. . . . . .Josh. 15:30
Transferred to Simeon . . . . Josh. 19:4
David sends spoils to. . . . . .1 Sam. 30:26, 30

WORD STUDY   **HORN,** *qeren (keh*-rehn). The "horn" of a ram is the most literal translation of the noun *qeren*. In this sense, the word refers to a horn used as an oil flask or a wind instrument. In the figurative use of the term, horn is a symbol of strength and refers to a person (Deut. 33:17). Strength is especially indicated when the horn is lifted up as in Lam. 2:17, where it indicates increasing dignity and might. A lifted horn can also indicate haughtiness or arrogance (Ps. 75:5, 6). When used in the phrase "to cut off the horns," the implication is humiliation or reduction in status (Jer. 48:25). Another context in which the word appears is "the horn of an altar," where it describes hornlike projections on the corners of an altar. These horns can be grasped for sanctuary or refuge (1 Kin. 1:50; 2:28). (Strong's #7161)

Horn—*bonelike protrusion from an animal's head*
A. Descriptive of:
    Ram's...............................Gen. 22:13
    Ox's ....Ex. 21:29
    Wild ox ....Ps. 92:10
    Goat's.............................Dan. 8:5
    Altar's ....1 Kin. 1:50
B. Uses of:
    For trumpets ....Josh. 6:4, 13
    For vessels........................1 Sam. 16:1–13
C. Figurative of:
    Christ's power.....................Rev. 5:6
    Power of the wicked................Ps. 22:21
    Power of earthly kingdoms ....Dan. 7:7, 8, 24
    Power of the Antichrist...........Rev. 13:1
    Arrogance..........................1 Kin. 22:11
    Conquests..........................Deut. 33:17
    Exaltation.........................1 Sam. 2:1, 10
    Destruction ....Jer. 48:25
    Salvation..........................Luke 1:69
D. As musical instrument:
    Used on occasions ....1 Chr. 15:28
    A part of worship ....2 Chr. 15:14
    Used in Babylon ....Dan. 3:7, 10

Hornets—*a large, strong wasp*
    God's agents ....Ex. 23:28; Deut. 7:20
    Kings driven out by ....Josh. 24:12

Horns of the altar—*the protruding points at the four corners of an altar*
    Description ....Ex. 27:2
    Provides sanctuary.................1 Kin. 1:50

Horonaim—*two caverns*
    Moabite city.......................Is. 15:5

Horonite
    Native of Horonaim.................Neh. 2:10, 19

Horoscope—*fortune-telling by astrology*
    Forbidden..........................Jer. 10:2
    Unprofitable ....Deut. 17:2–5
    Punishment ....Is. 47:13, 14

Horse
A. Used for:
    Travel.............................Deut. 17:16
    War ....Ex. 14:9
    Bearing burdens ....Neh. 7:68
    Showing honor ....Esth. 6:11
    Sending messages...................Esth. 8:10
    Idolatry...........................2 Kin. 23:11
B. Figurative of:
    Human trust ....Hos. 14:3
    Obstinacy..............Ps. 20:7; 32:9; James 3:3
    Impetuosity in sin ....Jer. 8:6

C. Spiritual:
    Of fire ....2 Kin. 2:11
    Angelic host.......................2 Kin. 6:17
    Visions of ....Zech. 1:7, 8; Rev. 6:1–8; 19:11

Horse Gate—*a gate of Jerusalem*
    Restored by Nehemiah ....Neh. 3:28

Horse traders
    Tyre famous for....................Ezek. 27:2, 14

Hosah—*seeking refuge*
1. Village of Asher ....Josh. 19:29
2. Temple porter.......................1 Chr. 16:38

Hosanna—*save, now, we beseech you*
    Triumphal acclaim......Matt. 21:9, 15; Mark 11:9

Hosea—*salvation*
    Son of Beeri, prophet to the northern
        kingdom............................Hos. 1:1
    Unfaithful wife pictures backsliding
        Israel............................Hos. 1:2–11
    Children's names prophetic..........Hos. 1:6, 9
    Reproved idolatry.....................Hos. 1; 2
    Threatens God's judgment; calls to
        repentance........................Hos. 3–6
    Foretells impending judgment ....Hos. 7–10
    Calls an ungrateful people to repentance;
        promises God's blessings..........Hos. 11–14

Hosea, Book of—*a book of the Old Testament*

Hoshaiah—*Yahweh has saved*
1. Father of Jezaniah and Azariah ......Jer. 42:1; 43:2
2. Participant in a dedication .... Neh. 12:31, 32

Hoshama—*Yahweh has heard*
    Son of King Jeconiah..............1 Chr. 3:17, 18

Hoshea—*save*
1. Original name of Joshua,
    the son of Nun ..... Deut. 32:44; Num. 13:8, 16
  See Joshua, Jeshua
2. Ephraimite chieftain.................1 Chr. 27:20
3. One who signs covenant............. Neh. 10:1, 23
4. Israel's last king; usurps throne .... 2 Kin. 15:30
5. Reigns wickedly; Israel taken to
    Assyria during reign .... 2 Kin. 17:1–23

Hospitality—*reception and entertainment of strangers*
A. Kinds of:
    Treacherous.......................Judg. 4:17–21
    Rewarded..........................Josh. 6:17–25
    Unwise............................2 Kin. 20:12–19
    Critical ....Luke 7:36–50
    Unwelcomed ....Luke 9:51–53
    Joyful.............................Luke 19:5, 6
    Turbulent ....Acts 17:5–9
    Forbidden.........................3 John 1, 9, 10
B. Act of:
    Commanded ....Rom. 12:13
    Required of church leaders ....1 Tim. 3:2
    Discipleship.......................Matt. 25:35
C. Courtesies of:
    Protection provided................Gen. 19:6–8

Food............................Luke 11:5–8
Washing of feet......................Luke 7:44
Kissing ....Luke 7:45
Denied with indignities ....Judg. 19:15–28;
    Luke 10:10–16
D. Examples of:
    Abraham to angels..................Gen. 18:1–8
    Lot to angels ....Gen. 19:1–11
    Laban to Abraham's servant ....Gen. 24:31–33
    Joseph to his brothers .... Gen. 43:31–34
    Pharaoh to Jacob................. Gen. 45:16–20
    Rahab to the spies ....Josh. 2:1–16
    David to Mephibosheth ....2 Sam. 9:6–13
    Martha to Jesus.................Luke 10:38–42
    Lydia to Paul and Silas .... Acts 16:14, 15
    Barbarians to Paul .... Acts 28:2, 7

Host—*one who entertains*
    Gaius hospitable.................... Rom. 16:23

Hostage—*a person held as security*
    Captive for pledge ..... 2 Kin. 14:14; 2 Chr. 25:24

Host of heaven
A. Used of stars as objects of worship:
    Objects of idolatry ....Deut. 4:19
    Practiced in Israel.................... 2 Kin. 17:16
    Introduced by Manasseh ....2 Kin. 21:5
    Abolished by Josiah .... 2 Kin. 23:4–12
    Worship of, on roofs ....Jer. 19:13
B. Used of stars as created things:
    Created by God....................... Is. 45:12
    Cannot be numbered.................. Jer. 33:22
    Named by God .... Is. 40:26
    To be dissolved .... Is. 34:4
C. Used of angels:
    Created by God...................... Neh. 9:6
    Around the throne..................1 Kin. 22:19

Hosts, Lord of—*a title of God*
Commander of:
    Israel's armies ....1 Sam. 17:45; Is. 31:4
    Armies (angels) of heaven .... Gen. 28:12, 13;
        Ps. 89:6–8; Hos. 12:4, 5
    Same as Sabaoth ....Rom. 9:29

Hotham—*determination*
1. Asherite .... 1 Chr. 7:30, 32
2. Father of two of David's
    mighty men ....1 Chr. 11:26, 44

Hothir—*abundance*
    Son of Heman; a musician .... 1 Chr. 25:4, 28

WORD STUDY **HOUR, TIME,** *hōra* (*hoh*-rah). This noun is used as a measurement of time and is usually translated literally as "hour." It can be used as a general reference to a short period of time (Rev. 18:10, 17, 19) or a portion of the day (Mark 11:11), and it can specify the time of day (e.g., "the sixth hour" [= noon], as in Luke 23:44). The word is also used to designate an opportune or propitious moment when a particular event has occurred

(Luke 22:53) or will take place (Rev. 14:7). In the Gospel of John *hōra* is used figuratively to speak of the "hour" or time of Jesus' death and glorification (7:30; 12:23, 27, 28; 13:1; 17:1). (Strong's #5610)

Hour—*a division of time*
A. Used literally of:
    One-twelfth of daylight ....Matt. 20:1–12
    One-twelfth of night ....Luke 12:39
B. Jewish reckoning (from 6 P.M. and from 6 A.M.):
    Third (9 A.M.) .... Matt. 20:3
    Sixth and ninth (12 noon; 3 P.M.)...... Matt. 20:5
    Ninth (3 P.M.) ....Acts 3:1
    Eleventh (5 P.M.)...............Matt. 20:6, 9, 12
    Third (9 P.M.) .... Acts 23:23
C. Used literally and descriptively of Christ's:
    Death.................... Mark 14:35; John 13:1
    Betrayal........................... Matt. 26:45
    Set time............................ John 7:30
    Predestined time..................... John 12:27
D. Used prophetically of:
    Gospel age .... John 4:21
    Great Tribulation....................Rev. 3:10
    God's judgment.....................Rev. 14:7, 15
    Christ's return.............. Matt. 24:42, 44, 50

Hour of prayer
A. Characteristics of:
    Jewish custom .... Luke 1:10
    Directed toward Jerusalem ....1 Kin. 8:48
B. Times of:
    Three times daily .... Dan. 6:10
    First, at third hour (9 A.M.) ....Acts 2:15
    Second, at sixth hour (12 noon) .... Acts 10:9
    Third, at ninth hour (3 P.M.).............Acts 3:1

WORD STUDY **HOUSE,** *bayith* (*bah*-yith). The noun *bayith,* which occurs over 2,000 times in the OT, can refer quite literally to a house that is a dwelling. Occasionally it is used to mean a tent that is a dwelling, but usually it refers to a solid building. The word is used in combination to form phrases, such as "the house of the king," which is a palace, or "a house of women," which is a harem. While *bayith* can mean a structure that shelters family, by extension it can refer to the household or family itself. In this vein, the term can refer to a family of descendants, such as the house of Saul or the house of David (Is. 7:2). It can also mean the Hebrew people and some of the subdivisions within that group as in the phrases "house of Jacob" or "house of Israel." (Strong's #1004)

House
A. Descriptive of:
    Family dwelling ....Gen. 14:14; Judg. 11:34;
        Acts 16:34
    Descendants ....Luke 2:4
    Racial or religious group........Is. 7:13; Jer. 31:31
    Tabernacle or temple........Ex. 34:26; 1 Kin. 6:1
B. Figurative of:
    Grave................................. Job 30:23

Body................................. 2 Cor. 5:1
True church .... Heb. 10:21
Earthly life........................... Ps. 119:54
Heaven .... John 14:2
Security and insecurity........... Matt. 7:24–27
Division............................. Mark 3:25
See Home

Household idols
Laban's stolen by Rachel.......... Gen. 31:19–35

Housekeeper
Sarah .... Gen. 18:6
Rebekah ....Gen. 27:6–9
Abigail.......................... 1 Sam. 25:41, 42
Happy .... Ps. 113:9
Virtuous wife................... Prov. 31:10–31
Martha .... Luke 10:40, 41

House of God
Tabernacle called .... Luke 6:4
Temple described .... Ezra 5:2, 8
Church named..................... 1 Tim. 3:15
Center of God's worship................. Ps. 42:4

House of prayer
Corrupted into a den of
    thieves .... Matt. 21:13; Mark 11:17

Houses—*dwellings made for habitations*
Rechabites refuse to dwell in........ Jer. 35:5–10

Hukkok—*decreed*
Border town of Naphtali.......... Josh. 19:32, 34

Hukok
Land given as place of refuge......... 1 Chr. 6:75

Hul—*circle*
Aram's second son .... Gen. 10:23

Huldah—*weasel, mole*
Wife of Shallum .... 2 Kin. 22:14
Foretells Jerusalem's ruin........ 2 Kin. 22:15–17;
    2 Chr. 34:22–25
Exempts Josiah from trouble..... 2 Kin. 22:18–20

Human dignity
Based on:
God's image........................ Gen. 1:26
God's elevation of..................... Ps. 8:3–8
Love .... John 3:16
Being chosen .... John 15:16

Humaneness—*a kind spirit*
Toward animals .... Ex. 23:5
Not shown by Balaam .... Num. 22:27–30

Humanitarianism—*promoting the welfare of humanity*
Illustrated by Jesus.............. Luke 10:30–37
Enjoined on Christians............. 1 Thess. 5:15

Human nature of Christ
A. Predicted as Seed of:
Woman .... Gen. 3:15
Abraham......................... Gal. 3:8, 16
David........................... Luke 1:31, 32

B. Proved by:
Virgin's conception .... Matt. 1:18
Birth............................ Matt. 1:16, 25
Incarnation .... John 1:14
Circumcision....................... Luke 2:21
Growth............................ Luke 2:52
Genealogy .... Matt. 1:1–17; Luke 3:23–38

C. Manifested in:
Hunger .... Matt. 4:2
Thirst .... John 19:28
Weariness .... John 4:6
Sleep............................. Matt. 8:24
Suffering......................... Luke 22:44
Death............................ John 19:30
Burial......................... Matt. 27:59, 60
Resurrection .... Luke 24:39
Touch........................... 1 John 1:1, 2

D. Importance of, necessary for:
Sinlessness .... John 8:46
His death .... Heb. 2:14, 17
His resurrection .... 2 Tim. 2:8
His exaltation .... Phil. 2:9–11
His priestly intercession .... Heb. 7:26, 28
His return....................... Heb. 9:24–28
Faith............................ 2 John 7–11
See Incarnation of Christ

Human sacrifice
A. Practiced by:
Canaanites........................ Deut. 12:31
Ammonites .... Lev. 20:2, 3
Moabites....................... 2 Kin. 3:26, 27
Phoenicians .... Jer. 19:5
Israel .... 2 Kin. 16:3, 4
Judah............................ 2 Chr. 28:3

B. Sin of:
Condemned....................... Lev. 18:21
Source of defilement .... Ezek. 20:31
Source of demonism .... Ps. 106:37, 38
Cause of captivity............... 2 Kin. 17:17, 18

 WORD STUDY

HUMBLE, *shaphel* (shaw-*fayl*). Translated as "humble," the verb *shaphel* means "to be abased" or "to become low." It can mean "to be low" in the sense of sinking down (Is. 10:33). It can also mean to be humble (Is. 2:9). In another form the verb means "bringing down" or "laying low," an action done to another person. This form can be seen in Ezek. 17:24 where God brings down the high tree. It can also mean "to put someone at a lower place" as in Ps. 75:7. The natural extension of this meaning is seen in 1 Sam. 2:7 and Jer. 13:18 where someone is humiliated or abased. (Strong's #8213)

Humiliation—*state of deflated pride*
A. Causes of:
Pride .... Esth. 6:6–13
Arrogance...................... Dan. 4:29–33
Boastfulness................... 1 Sam. 17:42–50
National sins .... Dan. 9:1–21

Self-will. . . . . .Luke 15:11–19

B. Remedies against:

Be humble. . . . . Luke 14:8–11

Avoid improper associations . . . . . . Judg. 16:16–21

Obey God. . . . . .Josh. 7:11–16

Avoid self-sufficiency . . . . Luke 22:31–34

Rely upon God's grace. . . . . 2 Cor. 12:6–10

Humiliation of Christ—*the state that He took while on earth*

A. Exhibited in His:

Taking our nature . . . . Phil. 2:7

Birth. . . . . Matt. 1:18–25

Obedience . . . . Luke 2:51

Submission to ordinances. . . . . Matt. 3:13–15

Becoming a servant . . . . Matt. 20:28

Menial acts. . . . . John 13:4–15

Suffering. . . . . Matt. 26:67, 68

Death. . . . . John 10:15–18

B. Rewards of:

Exalted by God .Acts 2:22–36

Crowned king . . . . Heb. 1:1, 2

Perfected forever . . . . Heb. 2:10

Acceptable high priest. . . . . Heb. 2:17

WORD STUDY

HUMILITY, *tapeinophrosunē* (tap-eye-nof-ros-*oo*-nay). Noun meaning "humility" or "modesty." Although to some ancient Greeks "humility" was perceived in a negative light—as an abasement or humiliation, and thus a source of shame—it is valued positively in the NT. "Humility" describes an attitude that leads one to consider oneself "lower" than others (cf. the related verb *tapeinoō* in Phil. 2:8, especially Luke 14:11) or, as Paul states, "others as better" than oneself (Phil. 2:3). "Humility" is listed among other virtues (Col. 3:12); it is said to contribute to Christian unity (Eph. 4:2) if it is not wrongly directed (Col. 2:18, 23). (Strong's #5012)

Humility

A. Factors involved in sense of:

One's sinfulness . . . . .Luke 18:13, 14

One's unworthiness . . . . .Luke 15:17–21

One's limitations . . . . 1 Kin. 3:6–14

God's holiness. . . . . Is. 6:1–8

God's righteousness. . . . . .Phil. 3:4–9

B. Factors producing:

Affliction . . . . .Deut. 8:3

Impending doom . . . . 2 Chr. 12:5–12

Submissiveness . . . . .Luke 10:39

Christ's example . . . . Matt. 11:29

C. Rewards of:

Road to honor .1 Kin. 3:11–14

Leads to riches. . . . . .Prov. 22:4

Brings blessings. . . . . .2 Chr. 7:14, 15

Guarantees exaltation. . . . . .Matt. 23:12; James 4:10

Insures God's presence . . . . .Is. 57:15

Makes truly great . . . . Matt. 18:4

Unlocks more grace . . . . .Prov. 3:34; James 4:6

Healing for a nation. . . . . 2 Chr. 7:14

D. Christians exhorted to:

Put on . . . . .Col. 3:12

Be clothed with . . . . .1 Pet. 5:5

Walk with . . . . Eph. 4:1, 2

Avoid false . . . . Col. 2:18–23

E. Examples of:

Abraham. . . . . .Gen. 18:27, 32

Jacob . . . . Gen. 32:10

Moses. . . . . .Ex. 3:11

Joshua . . . . Josh. 7:6

David. . . . . .1 Sam. 18:18–23

Job . . . . .Job 42:2–6

Jeremiah . . . . .Jer. 1:6

Daniel . . . . Dan. 2:30

Elizabeth. . . . . Luke 1:43

John the Baptist . . . . .John 3:29, 30

Jesus. . . . . Matt. 11:29

Paul . . . . Acts 20:19

Humtah—*a place of lizards*

Town of Judah. . . . . .Josh. 15:54

Hunchback

Barred from priesthood . . . . Lev. 21:20, 21

Hundred, Tower of the

Restored by Eliashib . . . . Neh. 3:1

Hunger, physical

A. Causes of:

Fasting. . . . . Matt. 4:1–3

Fatigue . . . . .Gen. 25:29, 30

Famine . . . . .Luke 15:14–17

God's judgment. . . . . Is. 9:19–21

B. Some results of:

Selling birthright . . . . Gen. 25:30–34

Murmuring . . . . Ex. 16:2, 3

Breaking God's Law. . . . . .1 Sam. 14:31–34

Cannibalism . . . . 2 Kin. 6:28, 29

Cursing God . . . . Is. 8:21

C. Satisfaction of:

Supplied:

By friends .2 Sam. 17:27–29

Supernaturally. . . . . Ex. 16:4–21

Sent as a judgment . . . . .Ps. 106:14, 15

Provided by God. . . . . .Matt. 6:11

Christian duty. . . . . 1 Sam. 30:11, 12

Complete in heaven . . . . Rev. 7:14–17

D. Examples of:

David. . . . . 1 Sam. 21:3–6

Elijah . . . . .1 Kin. 17:11–13

Jeremiah . . . . .Jer. 38:9

Peter. . . . . Acts 10:10

Paul . . . . 1 Cor. 4:11

E. Strike:

By forty men . . . . Acts 23:11–16

Hunger, spiritual

More important than physical . . . . .Deut. 8:3; Matt. 4:4

Sent as a judgment . . . . .Amos 4:11–13

Will be satisfied . . . . .Is. 55:1, 2

Blessing of . . . . .Matt. 5:6
Satisfied by Christ . . . . .John 6:33–35

Hunter, hunting
A. Purposes of:
Secure food . . . . Gen. 27:3
Kill harmful beasts . . . . .1 Sam. 17:34–36
B. Methods of:
Noose. . . . . .Job 18:10
Snare . . . . Amos 3:5
Pits . . . . 2 Sam. 23:20
Bows and quiver . . . . Gen. 27:3
Sword, etc. . . . . .Job 41:26–30
C. Examples of:
Nimrod . . . . Gen. 10:8, 9
Ishmael . . . . Gen. 21:20
Esau . . . . .Gen. 27:3, 5, 30

Hupham—*protected*
Son of Benjamin; founder of
Huphamites . . . . Num. 26:39
Called Huppim . . . . Gen. 46:21

Huppah—*covering*
Descendant of Aaron. . . . . .1 Chr. 24:1, 13

Huppim—*protection*
1. Son of Benjamin . . . . Gen. 46:21
2. Son of Ir . . . . .1 Chr. 7:12
See Hupham

Hur—*splendor*
1. Man of Judah; of Caleb's house . . . . .1 Chr. 2:18–20
Grandfather of Bezalel . . . . .Ex. 31:1, 2
Supports Moses' hands . . . . Ex. 17:10–12
Aids Aaron. . . . . .Ex. 24:14
2. Prince of Midian . . . . Josh. 13:21
3. Father of Rephaiah . . . . .Neh. 3:9

Hurai—*free, noble*
One of David's mighty men. . . . . .1 Chr. 11:32

Huram—*noble, free*
Son of Bela . . . . 1 Chr. 8:5

Huri—*linen worker*
Gadite . . . . 1 Chr. 5:14

Husband—*married man*
A. Regulations concerning:
One flesh . . . . Matt. 19:5, 6
Until death. . . . . .Rom. 7:2, 3
Rights of. . . . . .1 Cor. 7:1–5
Sanctified by wife. . . . . .1 Cor. 7:14–16
B. Duties of, toward wife:
Love . . . . .Eph. 5:25–33
Live with for life . . . . Matt. 19:3–9
Be faithful to . . . . Mal. 2:14, 15
Be satisfied with . . . . .Prov. 5:18, 19
Instruct. . . . . 1 Cor. 14:34, 35
Honor . . . . .1 Pet. 3:7
Confer with . . . . .Gen. 31:4–16
Provide for . . . . .1 Tim. 5:8
Serve as leader . . . . Gen. 3:16

C. Kinds of:
Adam, blaming . . . . .Gen. 3:9–12
Isaac, loving. . . . . .Gen. 24:67
Elkanah, sympathetic . . . . 1 Sam. 1:8–23
Nabal, evil. . . . . 1 Sam. 25:3
Ahab, weak. . . . . 1 Kin. 21:5–16
David, ridiculed . . . . 2 Sam. 6:20
Job, strong . . . . Job 2:7–10
Joseph, just. . . . . .Matt. 1:19

Hushah—*haste*
Judahite. . . . . .1 Chr. 4:4

Hushai—*hasty*
Archite; David's friend . . . . .2 Sam. 15:32–37
Feigns sympathy with
Absalom. 2 Sam. 16:16–19
Defeats Ahithophel's advice . . . . . . 2 Sam. 17:5–23

Husham—*hastily*
Temanite king of Edom . . . . Gen. 36:34, 35

Hushathite
Inhabitant of Hushah . . . . .2 Sam. 21:18

Hushim—*hasters*
1. Head of a Danite family. . . . . Gen. 46:23
Called Shuham . . . . Num. 26:42
2. Son of Aher . . . . .1 Chr. 7:12
3. Wife of Shaharaim . . . . 1 Chr. 8:8, 11

Huz
Son of Nahor . . . . .Gen. 22:20, 21

Huzzab—*uncertain meaning*
May refer to Assyrian queen or to Nineveh;
or may be rendered "it is decreed". . . . Nah. 2:7

Hymenaeus—*belonging to Hymen*
False teacher excommunicated by
Paul . . . . 1 Tim. 1:19, 20
Teaches error. 2 Tim. 2:17, 18

Hymn—*a spiritual song*
A. Occasions producing:
Great deliverance . . . . Ex. 15:1–19
Great victory . . . . .Judg. 5:1–31
Prayer answered . . . . 1 Sam. 2:1–10
Mary's "Magnificat" . . . . Luke 1:46–55
Father's ecstasy . . . . Luke 1:68–79
Angel's delight . . . . Luke 2:14
Elderly man's faith . . . . Luke 2:29–32
Heaven's eternal praise . . . . Rev. 5:9–14
B. Purposes of:
Worship God. . . . . .2 Chr. 23:18
Express joy . . . . Matt. 26:30
Edify . . . . 1 Cor. 14:15
Testify to others . . . . Acts 16:25

WORD STUDY **HYPOCRISY,** *hupokrisis* (hoop-*ok*-ris-iss). This noun is derived from a verb meaning "to play a part on stage," thus "to pretend," "to playact" (see Luke 20:20). In vernacular Greek *hupokrisis* was a word applied to the playing of a role in a theatrical production—literally, "playing a part"—and used negatively to mean "playacting"

(="acting insincerely"), "pretense," or "outward show," "hypocrisy." In the NT it is used of an outward appearance (Matt. 23:28) projected by someone whose intent is to dissemble (e.g., Mark 12:15). This kind of "pretense," when accompanied by haughty criticism of others, is condemned by Paul (Gal. 2:13) and characterized as malicious and deceitful (1 Pet. 2:1). (Strong's #5272)

WORD STUDY

HYPOCRITE, *hupokritēs* (hoop-ok-ri-*tayce*). This is the name given to actors in Greek theaters. A "playactor" is someone who plays a role on stage and pretends to be someone else. Thus, this noun could carry with it the negative connotation of "pretender." In the NT it is usually translated as "hypocrisy." Jesus is the only One who uses the word against another (see Matt. 6:2, 5, 16; 23:13–29; Mark 7:6; Luke 6:42), and in most instances He castigates others for acting insincerely. See the word study "hypocrisy" for the cognate noun *hupokrisis*. (Strong's #5273)

Hypocrisy, hypocrite—*showy, empty display of religion*
A. Kinds of:
    Worldly .... Matt. 23:5–7
    Legalistic ....Rom. 10:3
    Evangelical......................2 Pet. 2:10–22
    Satanic..........................2 Cor. 11:13–15
B. Described as:
    Self-righteous ....Luke 18:11, 12
    "Holier than you".......................Is. 65:5
    Blind ....Matt. 23:17–26
    Covetous............................2 Pet. 2:3
    Showy .... Matt. 6:2, 5, 16
    Highly critical..................... Matt. 7:3–5
    Indignant .... Luke 13:14–16
    Destructive .... Prov. 11:9
    Bound by traditions............... Matt. 15:1–9
    Neglectful of major duties .... Matt. 23:23, 24
    Pretended but unpracticed........ Ezek. 33:31, 32
    Interested in the externals .... Luke 20:46, 47
    Fond of titles .... Matt. 23:6, 7
    Inwardly unregenerate ....Luke 11:39
C. Examples of:
    Jacob ....Gen. 27:6–35
    Jacob's sons .... Gen. 37:29–35
    Delilah.........................Judg. 16:4–20
    Ishmael .... Jer. 41:6, 7
    Herod ....Matt. 2:7, 8
    Pharisees.........................John 8:4–9
    Judas .... Matt. 26:25–49
    Ananias.......................... Acts 5:1–10
    Peter.............................. Gal. 2:11–14

Hyssop—*a small plant*
    Grows from walls.....................1 Kin. 4:33
    Used in sprinkling blood .... Ex. 12:22
    Used to offer Jesus vinegar ....John 19:28, 29
    Typical of spiritual cleansing .... Ps. 51:7

I

I AM—*a title indicating self-existence*
    Revealed to Moses ....Ex. 3:14
    Said by Christ ....John 8:57, 58
Christ expressing, refers to:
    Bread of life .... John 6:35, 41, 48, 51
    Light of the world................ John 8:12; 9:5
    Door of the sheep .... John 10:7, 9
    Good shepherd ....John 10:11, 14
    Resurrection and the life .... John 11:25
    Way, truth, and life .... John 14:6
    True vine .... John 15:1, 5

Ibleam—*he destroys the people*
    City assigned to Manasseh.........Josh. 17:11, 12
    Canaanites remain in ....Judg. 1:27
    Called Bileam ....1 Chr. 6:70
    Ahaziah slain near ....2 Kin. 9:27

Ibneiah—*Yahweh builds up*
    Head of a Benjamite family............ 1 Chr. 9:8

Ibnijah—*Yahweh builds up*
    Father of Reuel .... 1 Chr. 9:8

Ibri—*a Hebrew*
    Son of Jaaziah ....1 Chr. 24:27

Ibzan—*active*
    Judge of Israel ....Judg. 12:8
    Father of 60 children...............Judg. 12:8, 9

Ice
Figurative of:
    By reason of ....Job 6:16

Ichabod—*inglorious*
    Son of Phinehas ....1 Sam. 4:19–22

Iconium—*imagelike*
    City of Asia Minor; visited by Paul .... Acts 13:51
    Many converts in .... Acts 14:1–6
    Paul visits again .... Acts 14:21
    Timothy's ministry .... Acts 16:1, 2
    Paul persecuted.....................2 Tim. 3:11

Iconoclast—*a breaker of images*
    Moses, an angry .... Ex. 32:19, 20
    Gideon, an inspired .... Judg. 6:25–32
    Jehu, a subtle .... 2 Kin. 10:18–31
    Josiah, are forming.............. 2 Kin. 23:12–25

Idalah—*memorial of God*
    Border town of Zebulun .... Josh. 19:15

Idbash—*honey-sweet*
    Man of Judah....................... 1 Chr. 4:3

Iddo—*festal*
1. Chief officer under David .... 1 Chr. 27:21
2. Father of Ahinadab.................. 1 Kin. 4:14
3. Leader of Jews at Casiphia...........Ezra 8:17–20
4. Gershonite Levite .... 1 Chr. 6:20, 21
    Called Adaiah ....1 Chr. 6:41
5. Seer whose writings are cited .... 2 Chr. 9:29

6. Grandfather of Zechariah the prophet . . . Zech. 1:1, 7
7. Postexilic priest. Neh. 12:4, 16

Identification—*proving something or somebody to be what it or he really is*
A. Among men:
    At birth . . . . Gen. 25:22–26
    By the life . . . . Luke 6:43–45
    By speech . . . . .Judg. 12:6
    By a search . . . . .2 Kin. 10:23
    By a kiss. . . . . .Matt. 26:48, 49
B. Of Christ the Messiah, by:
    A divine sign . . . . .John 1:31–34
    A divine voice .Matt. 17:5
    Divine works . . . . Matt. 11:2–6
    Human testimony . . . . John 3:26–36
    Scriptures . . . . John 5:39–47
C. Of spiritual things:
    New birth . . . . 2 Cor. 5:17
    Apostates . . . . Matt. 7:22, 23
    Antichrist. . . . . .2 Thess. 2:1–12
    Believers and unbelievers. . . . . .Matt. 25:31–46

Identifying with Christ
A. Proper time, when tempted:
    To harm . . . . .Prov. 1:10–19
    To violate convictions. . . . . Dan. 1:8
    To conform to world . . . . .Rom. 12:2
    To rebellion . . . . Rom. 13:1–5
    With improper associations. . . . . . . .2 Cor. 6:14–17
    To learn evil. . . . . Prov. 19:27; Rom. 16:19
B. Results:
    Hatred. . . . . John 17:14
    Separation . . . . Luke 6:22, 23
    Suffering. . . . . 1 Pet. 2:20, 21
    Witness. . . . . .1 Pet. 3:15
    Good conscience. . . . . .1 Pet. 3:16
C. Basis:
    Future glory. . . . . .Rom. 8:18
    Life of Christ. . . . . .Gal. 2:20
    Reward . . . . 2 Tim. 2:12

Idleness—*inactivity; slothfulness*
A. Consequences of:
    Poverty . . . . .Prov. 20:13
    Begging. . . . . .Prov. 20:4
    Hunger . . . . Prov. 19:15
    Bondage . . . . .Prov. 12:24
    Ruin. . . . . .Prov. 24:30–34
B. Admonitions against, consider:
    Ant. . . . . Prov. 6:6–11
    Ideal woman . . . . Prov. 31:10–31
    Lord . . . . John 9:4
    Apostles . . . . .2 Thess. 3:7–9
    Judgment . . . . .1 Cor. 3:8–15
    See Laziness; Slothfulness

Idol makers
    Maachah. . . . . .1 Kin. 15:13
    Foreign peoples. . . . . Is. 45:16
    Men of Judah. . . . . Is. 2:1, 20
    People of Jerusalem . . . . Ezek. 22:3

Idol making
    Described by Isaiah . . . . .Is. 44:9–18

Idols, idolatry—*worship of idols*
A. Described as:
    Irrational . . . . Acts 17:29
    Degrading . . . . Rom. 1:22, 23
    Demonical . . . . 1 Cor. 10:20, 21
    Defiling. . . . . .2 Cor. 6:15–18
    Enslaving . . . . .Gal. 4:8, 9
    Abominable. . . . . .1 Pet. 4:3
B. Brief history of:
    Begins in humankind's apostasy . . . Rom. 1:21–25
    Prevails in Ur. .Josh. 24:2, 14
    In Laban's household. . . . . .Gen. 31:19–35
    Judgments on Egyptian . . . . Num. 33:4
    Brought from Egypt by Israel . . . . .Josh. 24:14
    Forbidden in Law at Sinai . . . . Ex. 20:1–5
    Warnings against, at Sinai. . . . . Ex. 34:13–16
    Israel yields to, at Sinai . . . . Ex. 32:1–8
    Moabites entice Israel to. . . . . Num. 25:1–18
    Early zeal against . . . . Josh. 22:10–34
    Gideon destroys . . . . Judg. 6:25–32
    Gideon becomes an occasion of . . . . Judg. 8:24–27
    Enticements to Baalism . . . . Judg. 10:6–16
    Levite corrupted by . . . . .Judg. 17:1–13
    Danites establish, at Shiloh . . . . Judg. 18:30, 31
    Overthrow of Philistines'. . . . . 1 Sam. 5:1–12
    Revival against, under Samuel . . . . . . 1 Sam. 7:3–6
    Solomon yields to . . . . .1 Kin. 11:1–8
    Jeroboam establishes in
        Jerusalem. . . 1 Kin. 12:26–33; 2 Chr. 11:14, 15
    Rehoboam tolerates in Judah . . . . 1 Kin. 14:22–24
    Conflict—Elijah and Ahab . . . . 1 Kin. 18:1–46
    Wicked kings of Israel. . . . . .1 Kin. 21:25, 26;
        2 Kin. 16:2, 3
    Prophet denounces in Israel. . . . . . . .Hos. 4:12–19
    Cause of Israel's exile . . . . 2 Kin. 17:5–23
    Judah follows Israel's example . . . . . 2 Chr. 28:1–4
    Manasseh climaxes Judah's
        apostasy in. . . . . 2 Kin. 21:1–18; 2 Chr. 33:1–11
    Reformation against, under Asa. . . . 2 Chr. 14:3–5
    Under Hezekiah . . . . 2 Chr. 29:15–19
    Under Josiah . . . . 2 Kin. 23:1–20
    Prophets denounce in Judah . . . . Jer. 16:11–21
    Cause of Judah's exile . . . . 2 Kin. 23:26, 27
C. Christians warned against:
    No company with. . . . . 1 Cor. 5:11
    Flee from. . . . . 1 Cor. 10:14
    No fellowship with. . . . . .1 Cor. 10:19, 20
    Keep from. . . . . .1 John 5:21
    Testify against. . . . . .Acts 14:15
    Turn from. . . . . 1 Thess. 1:9
D. Enticements to, due to:
    Heathen background. . .Josh. 24:2; Ezek. 16:44, 45
    Contact with idolaters. . . . . .Num. 25:1–6
    Intermarriage . . . . .1 Kin. 11:1–13
    Imagined good . . . . .Jer. 44:15–19
    Corrupt heart . . . . Rom. 1:21–23

E. Removed through:
    Punishment . . . . Deut. 17:2–5
    Display of powerlessness. . . . . .1 Sam. 5:1–5;
        1 Kin. 18:25–29
    Logic . . . . .Is. 44:6–20
    Display of God's power. . . . . 2 Kin. 19:10–37
    Denunciation. . . . . Mic. 1:5–7
    Exile . . . . Hos. 8:5–14; Zeph. 1:4–6
    New birth . . . . Hos. 14:1–9; Amos 5:26, 27

Idumea—*pertaining to Edom*
    Name used by Greeks and Romans to
        designate Edom .Mark 3:8
    See Edom

Igal—*He (God) redeems*
1. Issachar's spy. . . . . Num. 13:2, 7
2. One of David's mighty men . . . . .2 Sam. 23:36
3. Shemaiah's son . . . . 1 Chr. 3:22

Igdaliah—*great is Yahweh*
    Father of Hanan the prophet. . . . . .Jer. 35:4

Ignorance—*lack of knowledge*
A. Kinds of:
    Pardonable . . . . .Luke 23:34
    Pretended . . . . Luke 22:57–60
    Innocent . . . . Acts 19:2–5
    Excusable . . . . Acts 17:30
    Judicial . . . . .Rom. 1:28
    Guilty . . . . Rom. 1:19–25
    Partial . . . . .1 Cor. 13:12
    Confident. . . . . Heb. 11:8
B. Causes of:
    Unregeneracy . . . . Eph. 4:18
    Unbelief . . . . .1 Tim. 1:13
Spiritual:
    Darkness. . . . . .1 John 2:11
    Immaturity . . . . .1 Cor. 8:7–13
C. Productive of:
    Unbelief . . . . .John 8:19–43
    Error . . . . Matt. 22:29
D. Objects of:
    God . . . . John 8:55
    Scriptures . . . . Matt. 22:29
    Christ's return. . . . . .1 Thess. 4:13, 14
    Spiritual gifts. . . . . 1 Cor. 12:1

Ijim—*ruins*
    Town of Judah. .Josh. 15:29

Ije Abarim—*ruins of the Abarim (regions beyond)*
    Wilderness camp . . . . Num. 21:11
    Same as Ijim. .Num. 33:44, 45

Ijon—*heap*
    Town of Naphtali; captured by
        Ben-Hadad . . . . .1 Kin. 15:20
    Captured by Tiglath-Pileser . . . . .2 Kin. 15:29

Ikkesh—*crooked*
    Father of Ira. . . . . 2 Sam. 23:26
    Commander of 24,000 . . . . .1 Chr. 27:9

Ilai—*supreme*
    One of David's mighty men. . . . . . . 1 Chr. 11:26, 29
    Called Zalmon . . . . 2 Sam. 23:28

Illumination—*enlightenment, understanding*
    Of Daniel . . . . Dan. 5:11, 14

Illumination, spiritual
    By Christ. . . . . John 1:9
    At conversion. . . . . Heb. 6:4
    In Christian truth . . . . .Eph. 1:18
    By Holy Spirit . . . . .John 16:13–16
    By God . . . . 1 Cor. 4:5

Illustration—*something used to explain something else*
From:
    Ancient history . . . . .1 Cor. 10:1–14
    Current history . . . . Mark 12:1–11
    Nature. . . . . Prov. 6:6–11

Illyricum—*a province of Europe*
    Paul preaches. . . . . .Rom. 15:19

Image (see Idols, idolatry)

Image of God
A. In human beings:
    Created in. . . . . .Gen. 1:26, 27
    Reason for sanctity of life. . . . . Gen. 9:6
    Reason for husband's headship. . . . . 1 Cor. 11:7
    Restored by grace .Col. 3:10
    Transformed into. . . . . 2 Cor. 3:18
B. In Christ:
    In essential nature .Col. 1:15
    Manifested on earth . . . . John 1:14, 18
    Believers conformed . . . . . ,. . . . . . . .Rom. 8:29

Imagination—*creating mental picture of*
A. Described as:
    Evil. . . . . Gen. 8:21
    Willful. . . . . .Jer. 18:12
    Deceitful. . . . . .Prov. 12:20
B. Cleansing of:
    Promised. . . . . .Jer. 3:17
    See Thought

Imitation—*attempting to duplicate*
Of the good:
    God . . . . .Eph. 5:1
    Paul's conduct. 2 Thess. 3:7, 9
    Apostles . . . . 1 Thess. 1:6
    Heroes of the faith . . . . Heb. 6:12
    Good . . . . 3 John 11
    Other churches . . . . 1 Thess. 2:14
    See Example of Christ, the

Imla, Imlah—*fullness*
    Father of Micaiah the prophet . . . . . 1 Kin. 22:8, 9;
        2 Chr. 18:7, 8

Immanuel—*God (is) with us*
    Name given to the Child born of
        the virgin . . . . .Is. 7:14; Matt. 1:23

Immer—*eloquent*
1. Descendant of Aaron . . . . 1 Chr. 24:1–14
2. Father of Pashhur .Jer. 20:1

3. Founder of a postexilic family . . . . Ezra 2:37
The same as the father
of Meshillemith . . . . 1 Chr. 9:12
Also the ancestor of priests marrying
foreigners. . . . . Ezra 10:19, 20
4. Person or place in Babylonia. . . . . .Neh. 7:61
5. Zadok's father. . . . . .Neh. 3:29

Immorality—*state of a wrongful act or relationship; fornication*
Consider sanctity of the body . . . . . 1 Cor. 6:13–20
Flee from it. . . . . 1 Cor. 6:18
Get married . . . . 1 Cor. 7:2
Abstain from it . . . . 1 Thess. 4:3
Mention it not . . . . Eph. 5:3
Corrupts the earth . . . . .Rev. 19:2

Immortality—*eternal existence*
A. Proof of, based upon:
God's image in humankind . . . . .Gen. 1:26, 27
Translation of Enoch and Elijah. . . . . . Gen. 5:24;
2 Kin. 2:11, 12
Promises of Christ . . . . John 11:25, 26; 14:2, 3
Appearance of Moses and Elijah . . . . Matt. 17:2–9
Eternal rewards and punishments . . . Matt. 25:31–46; Luke 16:19–31
Resurrection of Christ . . . . Rom. 8:11;
1 Cor. 15:12–58
Resurrection of humankind . . . . Dan. 12:2, 3;
John 5:28, 29
B. Expression indicative of:
"I am" . . . . Matt. 22:32
"Today". . . . . .Luke 23:43
"Shall never die" . . . . .John 11:25, 26
"The redemption of our body" . . . . . Rom. 8:22, 23
"Neither death" . . . . Rom. 8:38, 39
"We know". . . . . .2 Cor. 5:1–10
"A living hope" . . . . 1 Pet. 1:3–8
"We shall be like Him" . . . . .1 John 3:2
See Eternal, everlasting; Life, eternal

Immunity—*exemption from something*
From:
Egyptian plagues . . . . Ex. 8:22, 23
Disease . . . . .Deut. 7:15
Corruption. .Ps. 16:10, 11
Harm. . . . . Luke 10:19
Second death . . . . Rev. 20:6

Immutability—*unchangeableness*
A. Of God, expressed by:
"I AM". . . . . .Ex. 3:14
"You are the same". . . . . Ps. 102:25–27
"I do not change" . . . . Mal. 3:6
"Are irrevocable" . . . . .Rom. 11:29
"Who cannot lie" . . . . .Titus 1:2
"The immutability". . . . . Heb. 6:17, 18
"No variation". James 1:17
B. Of Christ, expressed by:
"I AM". . . . . .John 8:58
"You are the same". . . . . Heb. 1:12
"Unchangeable" . . . . Heb. 7:22–24

"The same" . . . . Heb. 13:8
"I am the Alpha and the Omega". . . . . Rev. 1:8–18
C. Of God, characteristics of:
Unique. . . . . Is. 43:10
Purposive . . . . .Ps. 138:8
Active . . . . Phil. 1:6

Imna—*he keeps back*
Asherite chief . . . . 1 Chr. 7:35

Imnah—*prosperity*
1. Eldest son of Asher . . . . 1 Chr. 7:30
Called Jimna and Jimnah. . . . . Gen. 46:17;
Num. 26:44
2. Levite in Hezekiah's reign. . . . . .2 Chr. 31:14

Impartiality—*that which is equitable, just, and fair*
In God's:
Material blessings. . . . . Matt. 5:45
Spiritual blessings. . . . . Acts 10:34, 35
Judgments . . . . Rom. 2:3–12

Impatience—*inability to control one's desire for action*
A. Causes of:
Lust . . . . .Gen. 19:4–9
Revenge. . . . . Gen. 34:25–27
Irritability . . . . Num. 20:10
B. Consequences of:
Kept from Promised Land . . . . . . .Num. 20:10–12
Great sin . . . . Ex. 32:1, 21, 30
Loss of kingdom . . . . 1 Sam. 13:8–14
Foolish statements . . . . Job 2:7–9
Loss of birthright . . . . Gen. 25:29–34
Shipwreck. . . . . .Acts 27:29–34

Impeccability (see Holiness of Christ)

Impediment—*something that hinders one's activity*
In speech, cured . . . . Mark 7:32–35
Avoided by obedience . . . . .Prov. 4:10, 12

Impenitence—*without a change of mind*
A. Expressed by:
Willful disobedience. . . . . .Jer. 44:15–19
Hardness of heart. . . . . John 12:37–40
Refusing to hear . . . . .Luke 16:31
Rebellion against the truth . . . . . .1 Thess. 2:15, 16
B. Consequences of:
Spiritual bondage. . . . . John 8:33–44
Judicial blindness . . . . John 9:39–41
Eternal destruction . . . . .2 Thess. 1:8, 9

Imperfection of humankind
A. Manifested in:
Falling short of God's glory. . . . . .Rom. 3:23
Total corruption . . . . Is. 1:5, 6
B. Remedy for:
New creature . . . . 2 Cor. 5:17
Conformity to Christ . . . . 1 John 3:2, 3

Impertinence—*an action or remark inappropriate for the occasion*
Christ rebukes Peter's . . . . Mark 8:31–33

Impetuousness—*acting suddenly with little thought*
Characterized by:
    Ill-considered judgment . . . . Esth. 1:10–22
    Enraged disposition . . . . Gen. 34:25–31
    Hasty action . . . . Josh. 22:10–34

Import—*to receive from other countries*
Things imported:
    Horses . . . . .1 Kin. 10:28
    Chariots . . . . 2 Chr. 1:17
    Fish. . . . . Neh. 13:16

Impossibilities—*powerless, weak*
A. Natural:
    Change one's color . . . . Jer. 13:23
    Hide from God . . . . Ps. 139:7–12
    Change one's size . . . . Matt. 6:27
    Control the tongue. . . . . James 3:7, 8
B. Spiritual:
    God to sin . . . . Hab. 1:13
    Save one's self . . . . Mark 10:26, 27
    God to fail His promises. . . . . Titus 1:2
    Believers to perish . . . . John 10:27–29

Impostor—*a pretender*
A. Characteristics of:
    Not believed as . . . . Jer. 40:14–16
    Speaks falsely. . . . . Josh. 9:3–14
    Poses as real . . . . .2 Cor. 11:13–15
    Much like the real. . . . . Matt. 7:21–23
    Deception of, revealed to prophets . . . Acts 13:8–12
B. Examples of:
    Jannes and Jambres . . . . 2 Tim. 3:8
    Judas . . . . John 13:18–30
    Antichrist. . . . . .2 Thess. 2:1–4
    False apostles. . . . . 2 Cor. 11:13
    Satan . . . . 2 Cor. 11:14

Imprecation—*pronouncing a curse*
    God's enemies . . . . .Ps. 55:5–15
    One's enemies . . . . Ps. 35:4–8, 26
    Heretics. . . . . .Gal. 1:9
    Persecutors. . . . . .Jer. 11:18–20
    On the disobedient . . . . .Deut. 28:15–68
    Forbidden. . . . . Luke 9:54–56
  See Curse, cursing

Imprisonment—*physical confinement in jail*
A. Of Old Testament persons:
    Joseph . . . . .Gen. 39:20
    Simeon. . . . . .Gen. 42:19, 24
    Samson . . . . Judg. 16:21, 25
    Jehoiachin . . . . 2 Kin. 25:27–29
    Micaiah. . . . . 2 Chr. 18:25, 26
    Jeremiah . . . . .Jer. 32:2, 8, 12
B. Of New Testament persons:
    John the Baptist . . . . Mark 6:17–27
    Apostles . . . . .Acts 5:18
    Peter. . . . . Acts 12:4
    Paul and Silas. Acts 16:24
    Paul . . . . Acts 23:10, 18
    John . . . . .Rev. 1:9
  See Prisoners

Improvement—*a betterment*
Expressed by:
    Growth . . . . .1 Pet. 2:2
    Addition . . . . 2 Pet. 1:5–11
    Press on . . . . .Phil. 3:13–15

Improvidence—*wasting present possession*
    Material things . . . . .Luke 15:11–13
    Spiritual things . . . . Luke 12:16–23
    Eternal things . . . . Luke 16:19–31

Impurity (see Unclean)

Imputation—*counting or crediting something to another*
A. Described as charging:
    Evil to an innocent person . . . . Philem. 18
    Evil to an evil person . . . . .Lev. 17:4
    Good to a good person . . . . Ps. 106:30, 31
B. Of Adam's sin to the race:
    Based on the Fall. . . . . Gen. 3:1–19
    Explained fully . . . . Rom. 5:12–21
    The wider implications of . . . . Rom. 8:20–23
C. Of the believer's sin to Christ:
    Our iniquity laid on Him. . . . . Is. 53:5, 6
    Made to be sin for us . . . . 2 Cor. 5:21
    Became a curse for us . . . . .Gal. 3:13
    Takes away our sins . . . . .John 1:29; Heb. 9:28
D. Of Christ's righteousness to the believer:
    Negatively stated . . . . Rom. 4:6–8
    Positively affirmed. . . . . Rom. 10:4–10
    Explained graphically . . . . Luke 15:22–24
    God justifies the ungodly. . . . . Rom. 5:18, 19
    Christ becomes our righteousness . . . . . 1 Cor. 1:30
    We become the righteousness of God
        in Him . . . . 2 Cor. 5:21
    Illustrated by Abraham's faith . . . . .Rom. 4:3
  See Justification

Imrah—*He (God) resists*
    Son of Zophah. . . . . .1 Chr. 7:36

Imri—*eloquent*
1. Son of Bani. . . . . 1 Chr. 9:4
2. Father of Zaccur. .Neh. 3:2

Inability (see Impossibilities)

Incarnation of Christ
A. Foreshadowed by:
    Angel. . . . . .Josh. 5:13–15
    Prophecies . . . . .Is. 7:14
B. Described as:
    Becoming flesh . . . . John 1:14
    Born of woman . . . . .Gal. 4:4
    Coming in flesh . . . . .1 John 4:2
    Appearing in flesh . . . . .1 Tim. 3:16
    Our likeness. . . . . .Rom. 8:3; Heb. 2:14
    Body. . . . . Heb. 10:5, 10; 1 John 1:1–3
    Dying in flesh . . . . .1 Pet. 3:18; 4:1
C. Purposes of:
    Reveal the Father . . . . .John 14:8–11
    Do God's will. .Heb. 10:5–9
    Fulfill prophecy . . . . .Luke 4:17–21
    Die for our sins . . . . .1 Pet. 3:18

Fulfill all righteousness ....Matt. 3:15
Reconcile the world ....2 Cor. 5:18–21
Become our High Priest .... Heb. 7:24–28
Become our example .... 1 Pet. 2:21–23
Destroy works of the devil.............1 John 3:8
D. Importance of:
Evidence Christ's deity .... Rom. 9:3–5
Confirm Christ's resurrection.......Acts 2:24–32
Mark of believers .... 1 John 4:1–6
See Human nature of Christ

Incense—*sweet perfume; frankincense*
A. Offered:
By priests .... Lev. 16:12, 13
On the altar .... Ex. 30:1–8
On Day of Atonement.............Lev. 16:12, 13;
   1 Chr. 6:49
According to strict formula........ Ex. 30:34–36;
   Lev. 10:1, 2; Num. 16:35–38
Twenty-four elders..................Rev. 5:8; 8:4
B. Illegal offering of:
Forbidden...................... Ex. 30:37, 38
Excluded from certain offerings........ Lev. 5:11
Punished severely....Lev. 10:1, 2; 2 Chr. 26:16–21
Among idolaters .... Is. 65:3
C. Typical of:
Worship ....Ps. 141:2
Prayer .... Rev. 5:8; 8:3, 4
Praise.............................Mal. 1:11
Approved service .... Eph. 5:2
D. Purposes of:
Used in grain offerings ....Lev. 2:1, 2, 15
Excluded from certain offerings.........Lev. 5:11
Used in the showbread ....Lev. 24:7
Product of Arabia...................... Is. 60:6
Presented to Jesus.....................Matt. 2:11
Figurative of worship .... Ps. 141:2

Incentives to good works
Reap kindness...................... Hos. 10:12
Eternal impact...................... John 15:16
Reap what we sow.................. Gal. 6:7–10

Incest—*sexual relations between persons related*
A. Relations prohibited:
Same family....................... Lev. 18:6–12
Grandchildren ....Lev. 18:10
Aunts and uncles .... Lev. 18:12–14
In-laws...........................Lev. 18:15, 16
Near kin ....Lev. 18:17, 18
B. Punishment for:
Death........................... Lev. 20:11–17
Childlessness..................... Lev. 20:19–21
A curse.........................Deut. 27:20–23
C. Examples of:
Lot—with his daughters.......... Gen. 19:30–38
Reuben—with his father's concubine... Gen. 35:22
Amnon—rape of sister Tamar ....2 Sam. 13:1–20

Inconsistency—*the nonagreement of two things*
Between:
Criticism of ourselves and others........Matt. 7:3

Legalism and human mercy........... John 7:23
Profession and reality .... Luke 22:31–62
Preaching and practice .... Rom. 2:21–23
Private and public convictions ...... Gal. 2:11–14
Faith and works ....James 2:14–26
Profession and works..................Titus 1:16

Inconstancy—*inability to stand firm in crisis*
A. Causes of:
Little faith ....Matt. 13:19–22
Satan .... Luke 22:31–34
False teachers...................... Gal. 1:6–10
Doubt ....James 1:6–8
Immaturity .... 2 Pet. 1:5–10
Strife ....Mark 3:24–26
B. Remedies against:
Firm foundation..................Matt. 7:24–27
Strong faith ....Hab. 3:16–19
Full armor ....Eph. 6:10–20

Incorruptible—*enduring; lasting forever*
Resurrected body .... 1 Cor. 15:42, 52, 53
Christian's inheritance ....1 Pet. 1:4
Seed of Christian life................. 1 Pet. 1:23

Increase—*to become more abundant*
A. Used literally of:
Knowledge...........................Dan. 12:4
Wealth..................... Gen. 24:35; Rev. 3:17
B. Used spiritually of:
Messiah's kingdom ....Is. 9:7
Wisdom ....Luke 2:52
Faith.............................Luke 17:5
Esteem ....John 3:30
Fruits of righteousness .... 2 Cor. 9:10
Knowledge of God.....................Col. 1:10
Love ....1 Thess. 4:9, 10
Ungodliness........................ 2 Tim. 2:16

Incredulity—*an unwillingness to believe*
Characterized by:
Exaggerated demand for
   evidence.....................John 20:24, 25
Desire for more signs............. Judg. 6:37–40
Attempts to nullify plain
   evidence.....................John 9:13–41
Blindness of mind ....Acts 28:22–29

Indecency
Noah guilty of.....................Gen. 9:21–23
Forbidden, to priests .... Ex. 20:26
Michal rebukes David for.........2 Sam. 6:20–23
Men committing.....................Rom. 1:27

Indecision—*inability to decide between vital issues*
A. Manifested in, mixing:
Truth and idolatry..................1 Kin. 18:21
Duty and compromise.............John 19:12–16
Holiness and sin ....Gal. 5:1–7
Faith and works .... Gal. 3:1–5
B. Results in:
Spiritual unfitness .... Luke 9:59–62
Instability..........................James 1:6–8

Sinful compromise . . . . 2 Cor. 6:14–18
Spiritual defeat . . . . Rom. 6:16–22
Spiritual deadness . . . . Rev. 3:15–17
C. Examples of:
   Israel at Kadesh . . . . Num. 13:26–33
   Joshua at Ai . . . . Josh. 7:6–10
   David at Keilah . . . . 1 Sam. 23:1–5
   Pilate . . . . Matt. 27:11–24
   Felix . . . . Acts 24:25, 26
   See Inconstancy

Independence—*control of one's affairs apart from outside influences*
A. Virtues of:
   Freedom of action . . . . Gen. 14:22–24
   Responsibility . . . . John 9:21, 23
B. Evils of:
   Arbitrary use of authority . . . . . . 1 Sam. 14:24–45
   Selfishness . . . . 1 Sam. 25:1–11
   Mismanagement . . . . Luke 15:12–16
   Arrogance . . . . 3 John 9, 10

Indescribable
God's gift . . . . 2 Cor. 9:15

India
Eastern limit of Persian Empire . . . . Esth. 1:1

Indictment—*formal accusation for a crime*
A. For real crimes:
   Korah's company . . . . Num. 16:1–50
   Achan . . . . Josh. 7:1–26
   Baal worshipers . . . . 1 Kin. 18:19–42
   David . . . . 2 Sam. 12:1–14
   Ananias . . . . Acts 5:1–10
B. For supposed crimes:
   Certain tribes . . . . Josh. 22:10–34
   Naboth . . . . 1 Kin. 21:1–16
   Three Hebrew men . . . . Dan. 3:1–28
   Jews . . . . Ezra 5:3–17; Esth. 3:8, 9
   Christ . . . . Matt. 26:61–65
   Stephen . . . . Acts 6:11, 13
   Paul . . . . Acts 16:20, 21; 17:7

Indifference—*not concerned for or against something*
A. Characteristic of:
   Unbelievers . . . . Luke 17:26–30
   Backsliders . . . . Rev. 3:15, 16
B. As a good feature concerning, worldly:
   Comforts . . . . Phil. 4:11–13
   Applause . . . . Gal. 1:10
   Traditions . . . . Col. 2:16–23
C. As a bad feature:
   Inhumanitarianism . . . . Luke 10:30–32
   In the use of one's talents . . . . Luke 19:20–26
   Moral callousness . . . . Matt. 27:3, 4
   Religious unconcern . . . . Acts 18:12–16

Indignation—*boiling wrath against something sinful*
A. God's:
   Irresistible . . . . Nah. 1:6
   Victorious . . . . Hab. 3:12
   Poured out . . . . Zeph. 3:8

Toward His enemies . . . . Is. 66:14
On Israel . . . . Deut. 29:28
Against Edom forever . . . . Mal. 1:4
Angels, instruments of . . . . Ps. 78:49
On believers . . . . Job 10:17
Will hide His own from . . . . Is. 26:20
Entreated, on the wicked . . . . Ps. 69:24
As punishment . . . . Rom. 2:8
B. Human against:
   Others . . . . Esth. 5:9
   Jews . . . . Neh. 4:1
   Christ . . . . Luke 13:14
   Christians . . . . Acts 5:17

Indignities suffered by Christ
A. Against His body:
   Spit on . . . . Matt. 26:67
   Struck . . . . John 18:22, 23
   Crowned with thorns . . . . Matt. 27:29
   Crucified . . . . Matt. 27:31–35
B. Against His Person:
   Called guilty without a trial . . . . John 18:30, 31
   Mocked and derided . . . . . . Matt. 27:29, 31, 39–44
   Rejected in favor of a murderer . . . Matt. 27:16–21
   Crucified between two men . . . . John 19:18

Indiscrimination—*showing lack of distinction in*
   Devastation . . . . Is. 24:1–4
   Judgment . . . . Ezek. 18:1–32
   God's providences . . . . Matt. 5:45

Indulge—*to yield to desires*
   Fleshly desires . . . . Eph. 2:3
   Corrupt desires . . . . 2 Pet. 2:10
   Gross immorality . . . . Jude 7

Indulgence—*a kindness often misused*
   Parental . . . . 1 Sam. 3:11–14
   Kingly . . . . 2 Sam. 13:21–39
   Priestly . . . . Judg. 17:1–13

Industry—*diligence in one's work*
A. Characteristics of:
   Established . . . . Gen. 2:15
   Commanded . . . . 1 Thess. 4:11
   Commendable . . . . Prov. 27:23–27
   Done willingly . . . . Prov. 31:13
   Mark of wisdom . . . . Prov. 10:5
   Suspended on Sabbath . . . . Ex. 20:10
   Neglect of, rebuked . . . . 2 Thess. 3:10–12
B. Necessity of:
   Our needs . . . . 1 Thess. 2:9
   Needs of others . . . . Acts 20:35
   Faithful witness . . . . 1 Tim. 5:8
C. Blessings of:
   Wealth . . . . Prov. 10:4, 5
   Praise . . . . Prov. 31:28, 31
   Food sufficient . . . . Prov. 12:11
   Will rule . . . . Prov. 12:24

Indwelling, of believers

A. By Christ:

Through faith . . . . Eph. 3:14–19

Mystery . . . . Col. 1:27

B. By Holy Spirit:

Every believer . . . . Rom. 8:9–11

Body, the temple of . . . . 1 Cor. 6:19

Infant salvation

Suggested by Scripture . . . . Matt. 18:3–5, 10; 19:14

Infants

A. Acts performed upon:

Naming . . . . Ruth 4:17

Blessing . . . . Luke 1:67, 76–79

Circumcision . . . . Luke 2:21

B. Capacity to:

Believe . . . . Matt. 18:6

Know the Scriptures . . . . 2 Tim. 3:15

Receive training . . . . Eph. 6:4

Worship in God's house . . . . 1 Sam. 1:24, 28

C. Murder of:

By Pharaoh . . . . Ex. 1:16

By Herod the Great . . . . Matt. 2:16–18

In war . . . . Num. 31:17

Infidelity—*lack of belief in God's revelation*

A. Causes of:

Unregenerate heart . . . . Rom. 2:5

Hatred of the light . . . . John 3:19–21

Spiritual blindness . . . . 1 Cor. 2:8, 14

Self-trust . . . . Is. 47:10, 11

Unbelief . . . . Acts 6:10–15

Inveterate prejudice . . . . Acts 7:54, 57

Worldly wisdom . . . . 1 Cor. 1:18–22

B. Manifested in:

Rejecting God's Word . . . . 2 Pet. 3:3–5

Scoffing at God's servants . . . . 2 Chr. 30:6, 10

Hiding under lies . . . . Is. 28:15

Living without God . . . . Job 22:13–17

Using derisive words . . . . Matt. 12:24

Doubting God's righteousness . . . . Ps. 10:11, 13

Calling religion worthless . . . . Mal. 3:14

C. Punishment of:

Eternal separation from God . . . . 2 Thess. 1:8, 9

God's wrath . . . . 1 Thess. 2:14–16

Hell . . . . Luke 16:23–31

Severe punishment . . . . Heb. 10:28, 29

D. Remedies against:

Remember the end . . . . Ps. 73:16–28

Trust when you can't explain . . . . Job 2:9, 10

Stand upon the Word . . . . Matt. 4:3–11

Use God's armor . . . . Eph. 6:10–19

Grow spiritually . . . . 2 Pet. 1:4–11

Infinite—*extending immeasurably*

God's understanding . . . . Ps. 147:5

Infirmities—*weaknesses of our human nature*

A. Kinds of:

Sickness or disease . . . . Matt. 8:17

Imperfections of the body . . . . 2 Cor. 11:30

B. Our duties with reference to:

Rejoice in . . . . 2 Cor. 12:10

Help those afflicted with . . . . Gal. 6:1

Not to despise in others . . . . Gal. 4:13, 14

Influence—*the power of one's personality that causes others to act*

Christians, should be:

As salt . . . . Matt. 5:13

As light . . . . Matt. 5:14–16; Phil. 2:15

As examples . . . . 1 Thess. 1:7, 8

Beneficial to spouse . . . . 1 Cor. 7:14, 16;
1 Pet. 3:1, 2

Above criticism . . . . 1 Cor. 8:10–13

Honorable . . . . 1 Tim. 6:1

Permanent . . . . Heb. 11:4

Beneficial to others . . . . 1 Pet. 2:11, 12

Without reproach . . . . Phil. 2:15, 16

Ingenuity—*skill shown in unusual contrivances*

Of God . . . . Gen. 27:7–29; Job 38:4–41;
Ps. 139:13–16

Of humankind . . . . Ex. 2:1–9; 35:30–33

Ingratitude—*unthankfulness for blessings received*

A. Characteristics of:

Inconsiderate . . . . Deut. 32:6, 7

Unreasonable . . . . Jer. 2:5–7

Unnatural . . . . Is. 1:2, 3

Ungrateful . . . . Jer. 5:7–9, 24

B. Causes of:

Prosperity . . . . Deut. 6:10–12

Self-sufficiency . . . . Deut. 8:12–18

Fear . . . . 1 Sam. 23:5, 12

Greed . . . . 1 Sam. 25:4–11

Pride . . . . Dan. 5:18–20

C. Responses to:

Acknowledged . . . . 1 Sam. 24:17–19

Abused . . . . 2 Chr. 24:22

Revealed . . . . 1 Sam. 23:5–12

Forgiven by kindness . . . . 1 Sam. 25:14–35

Long remembered . . . . Deut. 25:17–19

Overcome by faithfulness . . . . Gen. 31:38–44

D. Examples of:

Moses by Israel . . . . Ex. 17:1–3

Gideon by Israel . . . . Judg. 8:33–35

God by Saul . . . . 1 Sam. 15:16–23

God by David . . . . 2 Sam. 12:7–14

Jeremiah by Judah . . . . Jer. 18:19, 20

Christ by lepers . . . . Luke 17:12–17

God by the world . . . . Luke 6:35; Rom. 1:21

WORD STUDY   **INHERITANCE,** *cheleq* (*khay*-lek). The noun *cheleq* is usually translated "inheritance," although it can also mean "portion," "tract," or "territory," and is used infrequently in the OT. As a "portion," it usually refers to a portion of land. The references to property also usually indicate someone's share of the land. Opposite to this, the word can also mean an obligation, rather than something that is gained. (Strong's #2506)

INHERITANCE, *nachalah* (nakh-al-aw). *Nachalah* is also a Hebrew word usually translated "inheritance." This word has a more religious overtone than *cheleq,* referring to Canaan as Israel's "inheritance" from God or saying that God is the "inheritance" of the Levites who had no land. It is also used to identify Israel as the "property" of God. (Strong's #5159)

Inheritance, earthly

A. Among Israelites:

God the owner	Lev. 25:23, 28
Possessed by families	Num. 27:4, 7
Law of transmission	Num. 27:8–11
If sold, restored in Year of Jubilee	Lev. 25:25–34
Must remain in tribe	Num. 36:6–10
Repossessed by relative	Ruth 4:3–5, 10

B. General characteristics of:

From fathers	Prov. 19:14
Uncertain use	Eccl. 2:18, 19
Object of seizure	1 Kin. 21:3, 4; Matt. 21:38
Squandered	Luke 15:11–13
Foolish not blessed	Prov. 11:29
Descendants blessed	Ps. 25:12, 13

See Heirs, natural

Inheritance of Israel

A. Basic features of:

Lord, Israel's	Deut. 9:26, 29
Land promised to Abraham's seed	Gen. 15:7–18
Limits defined	Gen. 15:18–21
Limits fulfilled	1 Kin. 4:21, 24
Possession of, based on obedience	2 Kin. 21:12–15
Blessed by the Lord	Deut. 15:4
Tribes destroyed from	Deut. 20:16–18
Apportioned	Josh. 13:7–33
Tribes encouraged to possess	Josh. 18:1–10
Levites excluded from	Num. 18:20–24
Lost by sin	Ps. 79:1
Restored after the captivity	Neh. 11:20

B. Figurative of:

Messianic blessings	Ps. 2:8
Call of the Gentiles	Is. 54:3
Elect remnant	Is. 65:8, 9
Eternal possessions	Is. 60:21

Inheritance, spiritual

A. Objects of:

Kingdom	Matt. 25:34
Eternal life	Matt. 19:29
Promises	Heb. 6:12
Blessing	1 Pet. 3:9
All things	Rev. 21:7
Glory	Prov. 3:35

B. Nature of:

Sealed by the Spirit	Eph. 1:13, 14
Received from the Lord	Col. 3:24
Results from Christ's death	Heb. 9:15
Depends on belief	Gal. 3:18, 22

Incorruptible	1 Pet. 1:4
Final, in heaven	1 Pet. 1:4

C. Restrictions upon, only:

For the righteous	1 Cor. 6:9, 10
For the sanctified	Acts 20:32
In Christ	Eph. 1:11, 12
For the transformed	1 Cor. 15:50–53

See Heirs, spiritual

Inhospitality—*unwillingness to entertain strangers*

Edomites	Num. 20:17–21
Sihon	Num. 21:22, 23
Gibeah	Judg. 19:15
Nabal	1 Sam. 25:10–17
Samaritans	Luke 9:53
Diotrephes	3 John 10
Penalty for	Deut. 23:3, 4; Luke 10:10–16

INIQUITY, (CROOKED DIRECTION, WARPED DEED), *'avon* (aw-vohn). The noun *'avon* indicates "iniquity," "guilt," or the "punishment of iniquity." When the word is translated "iniquity," it usually refers to those actions that are confessed and cause shame. In this context the word appears frequently in phrases of punishment or forgiveness, including covering over or cleansing from the wrongdoing. The term can also indicate the guilt due to iniquity as seen in Jer. 2:22. Sometimes the guilt is a condition in a person's life as can be noted in Ps. 51:7. Used to describe the punishment resulting from wrong (2 Kin. 7:9), *'avon* can also refer to someone bearing the guilt of others as in Ex. 28:38 or Lev. 10:17. (Strong's #5771)

Iniquity—*the depth of sin; lawlessness*

A. Sources of:

Heart	Ps. 41:6; Matt. 23:28

B. Effects upon humankind:

Insatiable appetite for	Ezek. 7:16, 19
Perversion	Ezek. 9:9

C. God's attitude toward:

Cannot look on	Hab. 1:13
Remembers and punishes	Jer. 14:10
Visits on children	Ex. 34:7
Pardons and subdues	Mic. 7:18, 19
Takes away from us	Zech. 3:4
Lays upon the Messiah	Is. 53:5, 6, 11
Remembers no more	Heb. 8:12

D. Christ's relation to:

Bears our	Is. 53:5, 6, 11
Makes reconciliation for	Dan. 9:24
Redeems us	Titus 2:14

E. Believer's relation to:

Will declare it	Ps. 38:18
Confesses	Neh. 9:2
Prays for pardon of	Ps. 25:11
Forgiven of	Ps. 32:5
Must depart from	2 Tim. 2:19
Protection from	Ps. 125:3
Separation from God	Is. 59:2

Prays for freedom from.............Ps. 119:133
Hindrance to prayer ....Ps. 66:18

F. Punishment for:
Wanderings ....Num. 14:34
Loss of strength ....Ps. 31:10
Destruction ....Gen. 19:15
Captivity...........................Ezra 9:7
Death......................Ezek. 18:24, 26
Less than deserved....................Ezra 9:13
Remembered forever ....1 Sam. 3:13, 14
In hell ....Ezek. 32:27

Injustice—*violation of another's rights*
A. Examples of, among men:
Laban's treatment of Jacob........Gen. 31:36–42
Saul's treatment of:
Priests ....1 Sam. 22:15–23
David............1 Sam. 24:8–22; 26:14–25
David's treatment of Uriah ....2 Sam. 12:1–12
Irijah's treatment of Jeremiah.......Jer. 37:11–21

B. Charges made against God for His:
Choice...........................Num. 16:1–14
Inequality.......................Ezek. 18:25
Partiality..........................Rom. 9:14
Delay ....Rev. 6:10

C. Punishment on, executed:
Severely......................1 Sam. 15:32, 33
Swiftly.........................Esth. 7:9, 10
According to prophecy ....1 Kin. 22:34–38
See Just, justice

Ink—*a writing fluid*
Used for writing a book ....Jer. 36:18
Used in letter writing ....2 John 12; 3 John 13

Inkhorn—*a case for pens and ink*
Writer's tool.......................Ezek. 9:2, 3

Inn—*a shelter providing lodging for travelers*
Lodging place ....Jer. 9:2
Place for rest ....Luke 2:7

Inner group
At girl's bedside..................Mark 5:35–40
At Christ's transfiguration ....Mark 9:2
In Gethsemane ....Matt. 26:36, 37

Inner natures, conflict of
A. Sin nature:
Called flesh ....Rom. 8:5
Called old self ....Col. 3:9
Corrupt and deceitful.................Eph. 4:22
Works of........................Gal. 5:19–21
Cannot please God.....................Rom. 8:8
To be mortified........................Col. 3:5

B. New nature:
By Spirit's indwelling.................1 Cor. 3:16
Strengthened by Spirit ....Eph. 3:16
Called "inward man".................2 Cor. 4:16
Called "new *man*"......................Col. 3:10
Fruit of ....Gal. 5:22, 23

C. Conflict:
Called warfare..........Rom. 7:19–23; Gal. 5:17

D. Victory:
Recognize source ....James 1:14–16
Realize former condition ....Eph. 2:1–7
Put off former conduct ....Eph. 4:22
Make no provision ....Rom. 13:14
Complete surrender to God.........Rom. 12:1, 2
Spiritual food........................1 Pet. 2:1, 2

Inner person—*one's genuine identity*
Often hidden..................... Matt. 23:27, 28
Seen by God..................... 1 Sam. 16:7
Strengthened..................... Eph. 3:16

Innocence—*freedom from guilt or sin*
A. Loss of, by:
Disobedience........................Rom. 5:12
Idolatry.......................Ps. 106:34–39

B. Kinds of:
Absolute ....2 Cor. 5:21
Legal ....Luke 23:4
Moral........................Josh. 22:10–34
Spiritual ....2 Pet. 3:14

C. Of Christ:
In prophecy ....Is. 53:7–9
In type.............................1 Pet. 1:19
In reality.........................1 Pet. 3:18
By examination................. Luke 23:13–22
By testimony ....Acts 13:28

Innocents, massacre of
Mourning foretold....................Jer. 31:15
After Jesus' birth ....Matt. 2:16–18

Inns, Three
Place about 30 miles south of Rome ...Acts 28:15

Innumerable—*uncounted multitude*
Evils................................Ps. 40:12
Animal life.........................Ps. 104:25
Descendants ....Heb. 11:12
People ....Luke 12:1
Angels ....Heb. 12:22

Inquiry—*a consulting or seeking for counsel*
By Israel ....Ex. 18:15
With ephod .... 1 Sam. 23:9, 11
Unlawful method................ 1 Sam. 28:6, 7
Through prayer.........2 Cor. 12:7–9; James 1:5

Insanity—*mental derangement*
A. Characteristics of:
Abnormal behavior ....Dan. 4:32–34
Self-destruction ....Matt. 17:14–18
Distinct from demon possession ......Matt. 4:24

B. Figurative of:
The result of moral
instability ....Jer. 25:15–17; 51:7
God's judgment......................Zech. 12:4

Inscription—*a statement written or engraved*
On Christ's cross......Luke 23:38; John 19:19–22
On an altar.........................Acts 17:23
Roman coin ....Mark 12:16

Insects of the Bible

A. Characteristics of:

B. List of:

C. Illustrative of:

Insecurity—*a state of anxiety about earthly needs*

A. Descriptive of:

B. Cure of:

Insensibility—*deadness of spiritual life*

A. Kinds of:

B. Causes of:

Insincerity—*hypocritical deceitfulness*

A. Manifested in:

B. Those guilty of:

See Hypocrisy

Insomnia—*inability to sleep*

A. Causes of:

B. Cure of:

Inspiration of the Scriptures

A. Expressed by:

B. Described as:

C. Modes of:

D. Proofs of:

E. Design of:

F. Results of:

See Word of God

Instability—*lack of firmness of convictions*

A. Causes of:

Lack of depth . . . . Heb. 5:11–14
Unsettled mind . . . . Eph. 4:14; James 1:6–8
B. Examples of:
Pharaoh . . . . Ex. 10:8–20
Israel . . . . Judg. 2:17
Solomon . . . . 1 Kin. 11:1–8
Disciples . . . . John 6:66
John Mark . . . . Acts 15:37, 38
Galatians . . . . Gal. 1:6

Instinct—*inbred characteristic*
Of animals . . . . Is. 1:3
Of birds . . . . Jer. 8:7

Instruction—*imparting knowledge to others*
A. Given by:
Parents . . . . Deut. 6:6–25
Priests . . . . Deut. 24:8
God . . . . Jer. 32:33
Pastors . . . . Eph. 4:11
Teachers . . . . Neh. 8:7, 8
Paraclete (the Holy Spirit) . . . . John 14:26
B. Means of:
Nature . . . . Prov. 6:6–11
Human nature . . . . Prov. 24:30–34
Law . . . . Rom. 2:18
Proverbs . . . . Prov. 1:1–30
Songs . . . . Deut. 32:1–44
History . . . . 1 Cor. 10:1–11
God's Word . . . . 2 Tim. 3:15, 16
See Education; Teaching, teachers

Instrument—*a tool or implement*
For threshing . . . . 2 Sam. 24:22
For sacrifices . . . . Ezek. 40:42
Of iron . . . . 2 Sam. 12:31
Body members, used as . . . . Rom. 6:13
See Music

Insult—*to treat insolently*
Ignored by King Saul . . . . 1 Sam. 10:26, 27
Job treated with . . . . Job 30:1, 9, 10
Children punished because of . . . . . 2 Kin. 2:23, 24
Pharisees treat Jesus with . . . . Matt. 12:24, 25
Paul's reaction to . . . . Acts 23:1–5
Forbidden . . . . 1 Pet. 3:8, 9

Insurrection—*rebellion against constituted authority*
In Jerusalem . . . . Ezra 4:19
Absalom's miserable . . . . 2 Sam. 18:32, 33
Attempted by Jews . . . . Mark 15:7

Integrity—*moral uprightness*
A. Manifested in:
Moral uprightness . . . . Gen. 20:3–10
Unselfish service . . . . Num. 16:15
Performing vows . . . . Jer. 35:12–19
Rejecting bribes . . . . Acts 8:18–23
Honest behavior . . . . 2 Cor. 7:2
B. Illustrated in:
Job's life . . . . Job 2:3, 9, 10
David's kingship . . . . Ps. 7:8
Nehemiah's service . . . . Neh. 5:14–19

Daniel's rule . . . . Dan. 6:1–4
Paul's ministry . . . . 2 Cor. 4:2

Intemperance—*not restraining the appetites*
A. Manifested in:
Drunkenness . . . . Prov. 23:19–35
Gluttony . . . . Titus 1:12
Immorality . . . . Rom. 1:26, 27
B. Evils of:
Puts the flesh first . . . . Phil. 3:19
Brings about death . . . . 1 Sam. 25:36–38
See Drunkenness

Intention—*a fixed determination to do a specified thing*
A. Good:
Commended but not allowed . . . . . . 1 Kin. 8:17–19
Planned but delayed . . . . Rom. 15:24–28
B. Evil:
Restrained by God . . . . Gen. 31:22–31
Turned to good by God . . . . Gen. 45:4–8
Overruled by God's providence . . . . Esth. 9:23–25
C. Of Christ:
Predicted . . . . Ps. 40:6–8
Announced . . . . Matt. 20:18–28
Misunderstood . . . . Matt. 16:21–23
Fulfilled . . . . John 19:28–30
Explained . . . . Luke 24:25–47

Interbreeding—*crossbreed*
Forbidden:
In animals, vegetables, cloth . . . . Lev. 19:19

WORD STUDY

INTERCESSION, MAKE, *paga'* (paw-gah'). *Paga'* is a verb, which can be translated as "meet," "encounter," or "reach." Usually one "meets with" kindness and "encounters" hostility so that the choice of word is context specific. The attitudes and relationships of the people involved are the determining factor. One can encounter or meet with a request, that is, one can "entreat." When one makes entreaty for another, one makes intercession (see, for example, Is. 53:12; Jer. 7:16; 27:18; 36:25). (Strong's #6293)

Intercession—*prayer offered in behalf of others*
A. Purposes of:
Secure healing . . . . James 5:14–16
Avert judgment . . . . Num. 14:11–21
Insure deliverance . . . . 1 Sam. 7:5–9
Give blessings . . . . Num. 6:23–27
Obtain restoration . . . . Job 42:8–10
For infilling of the Holy Spirit . . . . . . Acts 8:15–17;
Eph. 3:14–19
Encourage repentance . . . . Rom. 10:1–4
B. Characteristics of:
Pleading . . . . Gen. 18:23–33
Specific . . . . Gen. 24:12–15
Victorious . . . . Ex. 17:9–12
Very intense . . . . Ex. 32:31, 32
Quickly answered . . . . Num. 27:15–23
Confessing . . . . 2 Sam. 24:17
Personal . . . . 1 Chr. 29:19

Covenant pleading.................Neh. 1:4–11
Unselfish...........................Acts 7:60
C. Examples of:
　Abraham...................... Gen. 18:23–32
　David...........................1 Chr. 29:19
　Moses..........................Ex. 32:11–13
　Joshua ....Josh. 7:6–9
　Jehoshaphat.................... 2 Chr. 20:5–13
　Isaiah...........................2 Chr. 32:20
　Daniel ....Dan. 9:3–19
　Christ.................John 17:1–26; Rom. 8:34
　Stephen .... Acts 7:60
　Christians...................... Acts 12:12
　Holy Spirit .... Rom. 8:26
　Paul .... Col. 1:9–12

Intercourse—*copulation*
Kinds of, forbidden:
　With neighbor's wife.................Lev. 18:20
　With animal.......................Lev. 18:23

Interest—*money charged on borrowed money; usury*
　From poor man, forbidden............ Ex. 22:25
　From a stranger, permitted .... Deut. 23:19, 20
　Exaction of, unprofitable ....Prov. 28:8
　Condemned as a sin.............. Ezek. 18:8–17
　Exaction of, rebuked ....Neh. 5:1–13
　Reward for nonexaction of.............. Ps. 15:5
　Used to illustrate ....Luke 19:23

Intermediate state—*the state of the believer between death and the resurrection*
A. Described as:
　Like sleep ....John 11:11–14
　"Far better" ....Phil. 1:21, 23
　"Present with the Lord" ....2 Cor. 5:6, 8
B. Characteristics of:
　Persons identifiable ....Matt. 17:3
　Conscious and enjoyable ....Ps. 17:15; Luke 16:25
　Unchangeable ....Luke 16:26
　Without the body..........2 Cor. 5:1–4; Rev. 6:9
　Awaiting the
　　resurrection... Phil. 3:20, 21; 1 Thess. 4:13–18
　See Immortality

Interpretation—*making the unknown known*
A. Things in need of:
　Dreams ....Gen. 41:15–36
　Languages ....Gen. 42:23
　Writings ....Dan. 5:7–31
　Scripture..........................Acts 8:30–35
　Tongues..........................1 Cor. 12:10
B. Agents of:
　Jesus Christ ....Luke 24:25–47
　Holy Spirit ....1 Cor. 2:11–16
　Angels ....Luke 1:26–37
　Prophets and apostles ....Eph. 3:2–11

Intestines (see Entrails)

Intimidation—*suggesting possible harm if one acts contrary to another's wishes*
Attitudes toward:
　Discovers its deceit.................Neh. 6:5–13
　Do not yield ....Jer. 26:8–16
　Go steadfastly on ....Dan. 6:6–10
　Answer boldly ....Amos 7:12–17

Intolerance—*active opposition to the views of others*
A. Of the state against:
　Jews ....Esth. 3:12, 13
　Rival religions ....Dan. 3:13–15
　Christian faith..................... Rev. 13:1–18
B. Of the Jews against:
　Their prophets .... Matt. 23:31–35
　Christ...................... Luke 4:28–30
　Christians...................... Acts 5:40, 41
　Christianity .... Acts 17:1–8
C. Of the church against:
　Evil.............................2 Cor. 6:14–18
　False teaching .... 2 John 10, 11
　False religions .... Gal. 1:6–9
D. Manifestations of:
　Prejudice........................Acts 21:27–32
　Persecution......................... Acts 13:50
　Passion .... Acts 9:1, 2, 21

Intrigue—*using hidden methods to cause another's downfall*
A. Characteristics of:
　Deceit .... Gen. 27:6–23
　Plausible arguments................. Judg. 9:1–6
　Subtle maneuvers .... 2 Sam. 15:1–13
　False front .... 2 Kin. 10:18–28
　Political trickery.................. Esth. 3:5–10
B. Against Christ by:
　Herod ....Matt. 2:8, 12–16
　Satan .... Matt. 4:3–11
　Jews ....Luke 11:53, 54

Investigation—*close examination*
A. Characteristics of:
　Involves research .... Ezra 6:1–13
　Causes sought out .... Eccl. 1:13, 17
　Claims checked...................Num. 13:1–25
　Suspicions followed through...... Josh. 22:10–30
　Historic parallels cited ....Jer. 26:17–24
B. Lack of:
　Cause of later trouble ....Josh. 9:3–23
　Productive of evil.................Dan. 5:22, 23

Investments, spiritual
　In heavenly riches................. Matt. 6:20
　Dividends later paid ....1 Tim. 6:19

Invisible—*the unseeable*
　Created by Christ...................Col. 1:15, 16
　God is ....1 Tim. 1:17
　Faith sees .... Heb. 11:27

Invitations of the Bible
Come:

And reason	Is. 1:18
My people	Is. 26:20
Buy wine and milk	Is. 55:1
"To Me"	Is. 55:3; Matt. 11:28
And see	John 1:46
And rest	Matt. 11:28
After Me	Mark 1:17
Take up the cross	Mark 10:21
To the marriage	Matt. 22:4
Everything is ready	Luke 14:17
The blessed	Matt. 25:34
Threefold	Rev. 22:17

Iphdeiah—*the Lord redeems*
A descendant of Benjamin .... 1 Chr. 8:1, 25

Ira—*watchful*
1. Priest to David .... 2 Sam. 20:26
2. One of David's mighty men .... 2 Sam. 23:26;
    1 Chr. 11:28
3. Ithrite .... 2 Sam. 23:38; 1 Chr. 11:40

Irad—*fugitive*
Son of Enoch; grandson of Cain .... Gen. 4:18

Iram—*aroused*
Edomite chief .... Gen. 36:43; 1 Chr. 1:54

Iri—*urbane*
Benjamite .... 1 Chr. 7:7

Irijah—*Yahweh sees*
Accuses Jeremiah of desertion ...... Jer. 37:13, 14

Ir-Nahash—*serpent city*
City of Judah .... 1 Chr. 4:1, 12

Iron—*a useful metal*
A. Features concerning:

Used very early	Gen. 4:22
Used in weapons	Job 20:24

B. Items made of:

Armor	2 Sam. 23:7
Ax	2 Kin. 6:5
Bedstead	Deut. 3:11
Chariot	Josh. 17:16, 18
Gate	Acts 12:10
Gods	Dan. 5:4, 23
Pen	Job 19:24
Tools	1 Kin. 6:7; 2 Sam. 12:31
Vessels	Josh. 6:24
Weapons	Job 20:24
Yokes	Deut. 28:48
Implements	Gen. 4:22

C. Figurative of:

Affliction	Deut. 4:20
Barrenness	Deut. 28:23
Authority	Ps. 2:9
Stubbornness	Is. 48:4
Slavery	Jer. 28:13, 14
Strength	Dan. 2:33–41
Insensibility	1 Tim. 4:2

Iron—*conspicuous*
City of Naphtali .... Josh. 19:38

Irony—*a pretense of ignorance*

Show contempt	2 Sam. 6:20
Mockery	1 Kin. 18:27
Rebuke distrust	1 Kin. 22:13–17
Multiply transgression	Amos 4:4
Mocked honor	Matt. 27:29
Deflate the wise	2 Cor. 11:19, 20

Irpeel—*God heals*
Town of Benjamin .... Josh. 18:21, 27

Irreconcilable—*violators of agreements; opposing compromise*
Characteristic of the last days .... 2 Tim. 3:1, 3

Irrigation—*supply with water*

Not usually needed	Deut. 11:11, 14
Source of	Eccl. 2:5, 6
Figurative of spiritual life	Is. 43:19, 20; 58:11

Irritability—*the quality of easily being provoked to anger*
A. Characteristics of:

Quick temper	1 Sam. 20:30–33
Morose disposition	1 Sam. 25:3, 36–39
Hotheaded	Gen. 49:6
Complaining	Ex. 14:10–14

B. Cure by God's:

Love	1 Cor. 13:4–7
Peace	Phil. 4:7, 8
Spirit	Gal. 5:22–26

Ir Shemesh—*city of the sun*

Danite city	Josh. 19:41
Same as Beth Shemesh	1 Kin. 4:9

Iru—*watchful*
Son of Caleb .... 1 Chr. 4:15

Isaac—*laughter*
A. Life of:

Son of Abraham and Sarah	Gen. 21:1–3
His birth promised	Gen. 17:16–18
Heir of the covenant	Gen. 17:19, 21
Born and circumcised	Gen. 21:1–8
Weaned	Gen. 21:8
Offered up as a sacrifice	Gen. 22:1–19; Heb. 11:17–19
Secures Rebekah as wife	Gen. 24:1–67
Buries his father	Gen. 25:8, 9
Father of Esau and Jacob	Gen. 25:19–26
Prefers Esau	Gen. 25:27, 28
Lives in Gerar	Gen. 26:1, 6
Covenant reaffirmed with	Gen. 26:2–5
Lies to Abimelech	Gen. 26:7–11
Becomes prosperous	Gen. 26:12–14
Trouble over wells	Gen. 26:14–22
Covenant with Abimelech	Gen. 26:23–33
Grieves over Esau	Gen. 26:34, 35
Deceived by Jacob	Gen. 27:1–25
Blesses his sons	Gen. 27:26–40
Dies in his old age	Gen. 35:28, 29

B. Character of:

    Obedient..............................Gen. 22:9

    Peaceable .... Gen. 26:14–22

    Thoughtful ....Gen. 24:63

    Prayerful......................Gen. 25:21; 26:25

C. Significance of:

    Child of promise..................Gal. 4:22, 23

    Man of faith......................Heb. 11:9, 20

    Type of believers..................Gal. 4:28–31

    Ancestor of Christ ....Luke 3:34

    Patriarch of Israel......................Ex. 32:13

Isaiah—*Yahweh is salvation*

A. Life of:

    Son of Amoz ....Is. 1:1

    Prophesies during reigns of Uzziah, Jotham,

        Ahaz and Hezekiah....................Is. 1:1

    Contemporary of Amos and

        Hosea ....Hos. 1:1; Amos 1:1

    Responds to prophetic call............. Is. 6:1–13

    Protests against policy of Ahaz........Is. 7:1–25;

        8:1–22

    Gives symbolic names to his sons.....Is. 8:1–4, 18

    Walks naked and barefoot.............Is. 20:2, 3

    Encourages Hezekiah .... 2 Kin. 19:1–34

    Warns Hezekiah of death.............2 Kin. 20:1

    Instructs Hezekiah concerning his

        recovery .... 2 Kin. 20:4–11

    Upbraids Hezekiah for his acts... 2 Kin. 20:12–19

    Writes Uzziah's biography...........2 Chr. 26:22

    Writes Hezekiah's biography ....2 Chr. 32:32

B. Messianic prophecies of:

    Christ's birth......Is. 7:14; 11:1–9; Matt. 1:22, 23

    John's coming .... Is. 40:3; Matt. 3:3

    Christ's mission ....Is. 61:1, 2; Luke 4:17–19

    Christ's death ......Is. 53:1–12; Matt. 8:17; 1 Pet.

        2:21–25

    Christ as Servant ......Is. 42:1–4; Matt. 12:17–21

    Gospel invitation ....Is. 55:1–13; Acts 13:34

    Conversion of Gentiles ... Is. 11:10; Rom. 15:8–12

C. Other prophecies of:

    Assyrian invasion...................... Is. 8:1–4

    Babylon's fall ....Is. 13:1–22

    Devastation of Moab.................Is. 16:1–14

    Tyre and Sidon condemned...........Is. 23:1–18

    Destruction of Sennacherib.........Is. 37:14–38

    Babylonian captivity ....Is. 39:3–7

D. Other features concerning:

    Calls Christ Immanuel...................Is. 7:14

    Names Cyrus.........................Is. 45:1–3

    Eunuch reads from.............Acts 8:27, 28, 30

    Quoted in New Testament........Rom. 9:27, 29;

        10:16, 20, 21; 11:26, 27

Isaiah, Book of—*a book of the Old Testament*

    Call of Isaiah.............................. Is. 6

    Promise of Immanuel ....Is. 7:10–25

    Prophecies against nations..............Is. 13–23

    Historical section......................Is. 36–39

    Songs of the Servant ....Is. 42; 49–53

    Future hope of Zion......................Is. 66

Iscah—*watchful*

    Daughter of Haran...................Gen. 11:29

Iscariot, Judas—*man of Kerioth*

A. Life of:

    Listed among the Twelve .... Mark 3:14, 19

    Called Iscariot and a traitor ....Luke 6:16

    Criticizes Mary.....................John 12:3–5

    Treasurer ....John 13:29

    Entered by Satan....................Luke 22:3

    Identified as betrayer ....John 13:21–26

    Sells out Christ ....Matt. 26:14–16

    Betrays Christ with a kiss... Mark 14:10, 11, 43–45

    Returns betrayal money ....Matt. 27:3–10

    Commits suicide.................... Matt. 27:5

    Goes to his own place ....Acts 1:16–20, 25

    Better not to have been born .... Matt. 26:24

B. Described as:

    Thief ....John 12:6

    Callous ....John 12:4–6

    Deceitful.......................Matt. 26:14–16

    Possessed by Satan ....John 13:27

    Son of perdition ....John 17:12

    Devil............................John 6:70, 71

Ishbah—*he praises*

    Man of Judah......................1 Chr. 4:17

Ishbak—*leaving*

    Son of Abraham and Keturah.......... Gen. 25:2

Ishbi-Benob—*my dwelling is at Nob*

    Philistine giant .... 2 Sam. 21:16, 17

Ishbosheth—*man of shame*

    One of Saul's sons....................2 Sam. 2:8

    Made king .... 2 Sam. 2:8–10

    Offends Abner .... 2 Sam. 3:7–11

    Slain; but assassins executed .... 2 Sam. 4:1–12

Ishhod—*man of majesty*

    Manassite............................ 1 Chr. 7:18

Ishi—*salutary*

1. Son of Appaim .... 1 Chr. 2:31

2. Descendant of Judah................. 1 Chr. 4:20

3. Simeonite whose sons destroyed

    Amalekites....................... 1 Chr. 4:42

4. Manassite leader................... 1 Chr. 5:23, 24

Ishiah—*Yahweh will lend*

    Son of Izrahiah .... 1 Chr. 7:3

See Isshiah

Ishijah—*Yahweh will lend*

    Son of Harim...................... Ezra 10:31

Ishma—*desolate*

    Man of Judah......................1 Chr. 4:1, 3

Ishmael—*God hears*

1. Abram's son by Hagar............. Gen. 16:3, 4, 15

    Angel foretells his name and character.......Gen.

        16:11–16

    Circumcised at 13.................... Gen. 17:25

    Mocks at Isaac's feast .... Gen. 21:8, 9

    Evidence of fleshly origin.......... Gal. 4:22–31

Becomes an archer . . . . Gen. 21:20
Dwells in wilderness . . . . Gen. 21:21
Marries an Egyptian . . . . Gen. 21:21
Buries his father . . . . Gen. 25:9
Dies at age 137. Gen. 25:17
His genealogy . . . . .Gen. 25:12–19; 1 Chr. 1:29–31
2. Descendant of Jonathan. . . . . 1 Chr. 8:38
3. Father of Zebadiah . . . . 2 Chr. 19:11
4. Military officer under Joash. . . . . . 2 Chr. 23:1–3, 11
5. Son of Nethaniah; instigates murder
    of Gedaliah . . . . .2 Kin. 25:22–25
6. Priest who divorced his foreign wife . . . . .Ezra 10:22

Ishmaelites—*descendants of Ishmael*
Settle at Havilah. . . . . Gen. 25:17, 18
Joseph sold to. . . . . Gen. 37:25–28
Sell Joseph to Potiphar . . . . Gen. 39:1
Wear golden earrings . . . . Judg. 8:22, 24
Become known as Arabians. . . . . 2 Chr. 17:11

Ishmaiah—*Yahweh hears*
1. Gibeonite . . . . 1 Chr. 12:4
2. Tribal chief in Zebulun . . . . 1 Chr. 27:19

Ishmerai—*Yahweh keeps*
Benjamite. . . . . 1 Chr. 8:18

Ishpan—*he will hide*
Son of Shashak . . . . 1 Chr. 8:22, 25

Ish-Tob—*man of Tob*
Small kingdom of Aram. . . . . 2 Sam. 10:6, 8
Jephthah seeks asylum in . . . . .Judg. 11:3, 5

Ishuah—*he is equal*
Son of Asher. . . . . Gen. 46:17
Called Ishvah. . . . . 1 Chr. 7:30

Ishvi—*man of Yahweh*
Son of Asher and chief . . . . 1 Chr. 7:30
Called Isui . . . . Gen. 46:17

Island—*surrounded by water*
List of:
Caphtor (Crete?). .Jer. 47:4
Clauda. . . . . .Acts 27:16
Chios . . . . Acts 20:15
Cos . . . . .Acts 21:1
Crete . . . . Acts 27:12
Cyprus. . . . . .Acts 11:19
Elishah . . . . .Ezek. 27:7
Malta . . . . Acts 28:1, 7, 9
Patmos. . . . . Rev. 1:9
Rhodes . . . . .Acts 21:1
Samos . . . . Acts 20:15
Samothrace . . . . .Acts 16:11
Syracuse . . . . Acts 28:12
Tyre . . . . Is. 23:1, 2

Ismachiah—*Yahweh will sustain*
Temple overseer . . . . 2 Chr. 31:13

Ispah—*to lay bare*
Benjamite. . . . . 1 Chr. 8:16

Israel—*God strives*
A. Used literally of:
Jacob . . . . .Gen. 32:28
Descendants of Jacob . . . . .Gen. 49:16, 28
Ten northern tribes (in contrast to
    Judah). . . . . .1 Sam. 11:8
Restored nation after exile. . . . . .Ezra 9:1
B. Used spiritually of:
Messiah. . . . . Is. 49:3
God's redeemed ones. . . . . Rom. 9:6–13
The church. . . . . .Gal. 6:16

Israelites—*descendants of Israel (Jacob)*
A. Brief history of:
Begin as a nation in Egypt . . . . Ex. 1:12, 20
Afflicted in Egypt . . . . Ex. 1:12–22
Moses becomes their leader. . . . . Ex. 3:1–22
Saved from plagues . . . . Ex. 9:4, 6, 26
Expelled from Egypt . . . . .Ex. 12:29–36
Pass through Red Sea . . . . Ex. 14:1–31
Receive Law at Sinai . . . . Ex. 19:1–25
Sin at Sinai . . . . Ex. 32:1–35
Rebel at Kadesh . . . . .Num. 13:1–33
Wander 40 years. . . . . Num. 14:26–39
Cross Jordan .Josh. 4:1–24
Conquer Canaan . . . . .Josh. 12:1–24
God's promise fulfilled. . . . . Josh. 21:43–45
Ruled by judges. . . . . Judg. 2:1–23
Samuel becomes leader . . . . 1 Sam. 7:1–17
Seek to have a king. . . . . 1 Sam. 8:1–22
Saul chosen king. . . . . .1 Sam. 10:18–27
David becomes king. . . . . 2 Sam. 2:1–4
Solomon becomes king . . . . 1 Kin. 1:28–40
Kingdom divided . . . . 1 Kin. 12:1–33
Israel (northern kingdom) carried
    captive . . . . 2 Kin. 17:5–23
Judah (southern kingdom) carried
    captive . . . . 2 Kin. 24:1–20
70 years in exile. . . . . 2 Chr. 36:20, 21
Return after exile. . . . . Ezra 1:1–5
Nation rejects Christ. . . . . .Matt. 27:20–27
Nation destroyed . . . . Luke 21:20–24;
    1 Thess. 2:14–16
B. Blessed with:
Great leaders . . . . Heb. 11:8–40
Inspired prophets. . . . . 1 Pet. 1:10–12
God's oracles .Rom. 3:2
Priesthood . . . . Rom. 9:3–5
The Law . . . . Gal. 3:16–25
Messianic promises . . . . Acts 3:18–26
Tabernacle . . . . .Heb. 9:1–10
Messiah. . . . . Dan. 9:24–27
God's covenant . . . . Jer. 31:31–33
Regathering. . . . . Is. 27:12; Jer. 16:15, 16
C. Sins of:
Idolatry. . . . . .Hos. 13:1–4
Hypocrisy. . . . . Is. 1:11–14
Disobedience. . . . . .Jer. 7:22–28
Externalism . . . . Matt. 23:1–33
Unbelief . . . . Rom. 11:1–31

Works—righteousness .... Phil. 3:4–9
D. Punishments upon:
Defeat .... Lev. 26:36–38
Curses upon .... Deut. 28:15–46
Captivity .... Judg. 2:13–23
Destruction .... Luke 19:42–44
Dispersion .... Deut. 4:26–28
Blindness .... Rom. 11:25
Forfeiture of blessings .... Acts 13:42–49
Replaced by Gentiles .... Rom. 11:11–20
See Jews

Israel, the religion of
A. History of:
Call of Abram .... Gen. 12:1–3
Canaan promised .... Gen. 15:18–21
Covenant at Sinai .... Ex. 20
Covenant at Shechem .... Josh. 24:1–28
Ark brought to Jerusalem .... 2 Sam. 6
Dedication of the temple .... 1 Kin. 8:1–66
Reform movements .... 2 Kin. 23:4–14;
2 Chr. 29:3–36
Destruction of Jerusalem .... Jer. 6
Restoration of the Law .... Neh. 8; 9
B. Beliefs about God:
Creator .... Gen. 1:1; Ps. 104:24
Sustainer of creation .... Ps. 104:27–30
Active in human affairs .... Deut. 26:5–15
Omniscient .... Ps. 139:1–6
Omnipresent .... Jer. 23:23, 24
Everlasting .... Ps. 90:2
Moral .... Ex. 34:6, 7

Issachar—*man of hire*
1. Jacob's fifth son .... Gen. 30:17, 18
2. Tribe of, descendants of Jacob's
fifth son .... Num. 26:23, 24
Prophecy concerning .... Gen. 49:14, 15
Census at Sinai .... Num. 1:28, 29
Second census .... Num. 26:25
On Gerizim .... Deut. 27:12
Inheritance of .... Josh. 19:17–23
Assists Deborah .... Judg. 5:15
At David's coronation .... 1 Chr. 12:32
Census in David's time .... 1 Chr. 7:1–5
Attended Hezekiah's Passover .... 2 Chr. 30:18
Prominent person of .... Judg. 10:1
12,000 of, sealed .... Rev. 7:7
3. Gatekeeper .... 1 Chr. 26:1, 5

Isshiah, Jisshiah, Jesshiah—*Yahweh exists*
1. Mighty man of David .... 1 Chr. 12:1, 6
2. Kohathite Levite .... 1 Chr. 23:20; 24:25
3. Levite and family head .... 1 Chr. 24:21

Isui (see Ishvi)

Italy—*a peninsula of southern Europe*
Soldiers of, in Caesarea .... Acts 10:1
Jews expelled from .... Acts 18:2
Paul sails for .... Acts 27:1, 6
Christians in .... Acts 28:14

Itching ears—*descriptive of desire for something exciting*
Characteristic of the last days .... 2 Tim. 4:2, 3

Ithai—*with me (is Yahweh)*
Son of Ribai .... 1 Chr. 11:31
Also called Ittai .... 2 Sam. 23:29

Ithamar—*island of palms*
Youngest son of Aaron .... Ex. 6:23
Consecrated as priest .... Ex. 28:1
Duty entrusted to .... Ex. 38:21
Jurisdiction over Gershonites and
Merarites .... Num. 4:21–33
Founder of Levitical family .... 1 Chr. 24:4–6

Ithiel—*God is with me*
1. Man addressed by Agur .... Prov. 30:1
2. Benjamite .... Neh. 11:7

Ithmah—*bereavement*
Moabite of David's mighty men ...... 1 Chr. 11:46

Ithnan—*perennial*
Town in south Judah .... Josh. 15:23

Ithran, Jithran—*excellent*
1. Son of Dishon .... Gen. 36:26
2. Son of Zophah .... 1 Chr. 7:37
Same as Jether .... 1 Chr. 7:38

Ithream—*residue of the people*
Son of David .... 2 Sam. 3:2–5

Ithrite—*preeminence*
Family dwelling at Kirjath Jearim ..... 1 Chr. 2:53
One of David's guard .... 2 Sam. 23:38

Ittai—*with me (is Yahweh)*
1. One of David's guard .... 2 Sam. 23:23–29
2. Native of Gath; one of David's
commanders .... 2 Sam. 15:18–22

Iturea—*pertaining to Jetur*
Ruled by Philip .... Luke 3:1

Ivah—*sky*
City conquered by the Assyrians .... Is. 37:13

Ivory—*the tusks of certain mammals*
Imported from Tarshish .... 1 Kin. 10:22
Imported from Cyprus .... Ezek. 27:6, 15
Ahab's palace made of .... 1 Kin. 22:39
Thrones made of .... 1 Kin. 10:18
Beds made of .... Amos 6:4
Sign of luxury .... Amos 3:15
Figuratively used .... Song 5:14
Descriptive of wealth .... Ps. 45:8
Among Babylon's trade .... Rev. 18:12

Izhar, Izehar—*shining*
Son of Kohath .... Ex. 6:18, 21; Num. 3:19
Ancestor of the Izharites .... Num. 3:27;
1 Chr. 6:38

Izrahiah—*Yahweh will shine*
Chief of Issachar .... 1 Chr. 7:1, 3

Izrahite—*descendant of Izrah*
Applied to Shamhuth .... 1 Chr. 27:8

J

Jaakan, Akan
Son of Ezer . . . . 1 Chr. 1:42
Also called Akan. . . . . Gen. 36:27
Of Horite origin . . . . Gen. 36:20–27
Tribe of, at Beeroth . . . . Deut. 10:6
Dispossessed by Edomites . . . . Deut. 2:12
Same as Bene Jaakan . . . . Num. 33:31, 32

Jaakobah—*heel catcher*
Simeonite . . . . .1 Chr. 4:36

Jaala—*wild she-goat*
Family head of exile returnees . . . . Ezra 2:56
Descendants of Solomon's servants. . . Neh. 7:57, 58

Jaalam
Son of Esau. . . . . .Gen. 36:5, 18

Jaanai—*answerer*
Gadite chief. . . . . .1 Chr. 5:12

Jaare-Oregim—*forests of weavers*
Father of Elhanan. . . . . .2 Sam. 21:19
Also called Jair .1 Chr. 20:5

Jaareshiah—*Yahweh nourishes*
Benjamite head . . . . .1 Chr. 8:27

Jaasai—*Yahweh makes*
Son of Bani; divorced foreign wife. . . . . Ezra 10:37

Jaasiel—*God makes*
1. One of David's mighty men. . . . . 1 Chr. 11:47
2. Son of Abner . . . . 1 Chr. 27:21

Jaazaniah—*Yahweh hearkens*
1. Military commander supporting
　　Gedaliah. . . . . 2 Kin. 25:23
2. Rechabite leader. . . . . .Jer. 35:3
3. Idolatrous Israelite elder . . . . Ezek. 8:11
4. Son of Azzur; seen in Ezekiel's vision. . . . Ezek. 11:1

Jaaziah—*Yahweh strengthens*
Merarite Levite . . . . 1 Chr. 24:26, 27

Jaaziel—*God strengthens*
Levite musician. . . . . .1 Chr. 15:18, 20

Jabal—*moving*
Son of Lamech; father of herdsmen. . . . . Gen. 4:20

Jabbok—*luxuriant river*
River entering the Jordan about 20 miles north of
　　the Dead Sea. Num. 21:24
Scene of Jacob's conflict. . . . . Gen. 32:22–32
Boundary marker. . . . . .Deut. 3:16

Jabesh—*dry*
1. Father of Shallum. . . . . .2 Kin. 15:10, 13, 14
2. Abbreviated name of
　　Jabesh Gilead . . . . .1 Sam. 11:1–10

Jabesh Gilead—*Jabesh of Gilead*
Consigned to destruction. . . . . Judg. 21:8–15
Saul struck the Ammonites here. . . 1 Sam. 11:1–11

Citizens of, rescue Saul's body . . . 1 Sam. 31:11–13
David thanks citizens of. . . . . 2 Sam. 2:4–7

Jabez—*he makes sorrowful*
1. City of Judah. . . . . 1 Chr. 2:55
2. Man of Judah noted for his prayer. . . . 1 Chr. 4:9, 10

Jabin—*He (God) perceives*
1. Canaanite king of Hazor; leads confederacy
　　against Joshua. . . . . Josh. 11:1–14
2. Another king of Hazor; oppresses
　　Israelites . . . . Judg. 4:2
Defeated by Deborah and Barak . . . . Judg. 4:3–24
Immortalized in poetry . . . . .Judg. 5:1–31

Jabneel—*built of God*
1. Town in north Judah. . . . . .Josh. 15:11
Probably same as Jabneh. . . . . .2 Chr. 26:6
2. Town of Naphtali. . . . . Josh. 19:33

Jachan—*troubled*
Gadite chief. . . . . 1 Chr. 5:13

Jachin—*He (God) establishes*
1. Son of Simeon . . . . Gen. 46:10
Family head . . . . Num. 26:12
Called Jarib . . . . .1 Chr. 4:24
2. Descendant of Aaron . . . . 1 Chr. 24:1, 17
Representatives of . . . . Neh. 11:10
3. One of two pillars in front of
　　Solomon's temple . . . . 1 Kin. 7:21, 22

Jacinth—*a sapphire stone*
In high priest's breastplate. . . . . .Ex. 28:19
Foundation stone . . . . .Rev. 21:20

Jacob—*supplanter*
Son of Isaac and Rebekah. . . . . .Gen. 25:20–26;
　　Hos. 12:2, 3
Younger of twins . . . . Gen. 25:24–26
Born in answer to prayer. . . . . Gen. 25:21
Rebekah's favorite . . . . .Gen. 25:27, 28
Obtains Esau's birthright. . . . . .Gen. 25:29–34;
　　Heb. 12:16
Obtains Isaac's blessing . . . . .Gen. 27:1–40
Hated by Esau . . . . Gen. 27:41–46
Departs for Haran . . . . .Gen. 28:1–5
Sees heavenly ladder . . . . Gen. 28:12
Makes a vow. Gen. 28:20–22
Covenant renewed with . . . . Gen. 28:13–15
Meets Rachel and Laban . . . . .Gen. 29:1–14
Serves for Laban's daughters . . . . . . Gen. 29:15–30
His children. . . . . .Gen. 29:31–35
Requests departure from Laban. . . Gen. 30:25–43
Flees from Laban . . . . .Gen. 31:1–21
Overtaken by Laban . . . . Gen. 31:22–43
Covenant with Laban . . . . Gen. 31:44–55
Meets angels . . . . Gen. 32:1, 2
Sends message to Esau . . . . .Gen. 32:3–8
Prays earnestly . . . . .Gen. 32:9–12
Sends gifts to Esau . . . . Gen. 32:13–21
Wrestles with an angel . . . . .Gen. 32:22–32;
　　Hos. 12:3, 4
Name changed to Israel . . . . .Gen. 32:28

Reconciled to Esau . . . . Gen. 33:1–16
Erects altar at Shechem . . . . Gen. 33:17–20
Trouble over Dinah . . . . Gen. 34:1–31
Renewal at Bethel . . . . Gen. 35:1–15
Buries Rachel . . . . Gen. 35:16–20
List of 12 sons . . . . Gen. 35:22–26
Buries Isaac . . . . Gen. 35:27–29
His favoritism toward Joseph . . . . Gen. 37:1–31
Mourns over Joseph . . . . Gen. 37:32–35
Sends sons to Egypt for food . . . . Gen. 42:1–5
Allows Benjamin to go . . . . Gen. 43:1–15
Revived by good news . . . . Gen. 45:25–28
Goes with family to Egypt . . . . Gen. 46:1–27
Meets Joseph . . . . Gen. 46:28–34
Meets Pharaoh . . . . Gen. 47:7–12
Makes Joseph swear . . . . Gen. 47:28–31
Blesses Joseph's sons . . . . Gen. 48:1–22
Blesses his own sons . . . . Gen. 49:1–28
Dies in Egypt . . . . Gen. 49:29–33
Burial in Canaan . . . . Gen. 50:1–14

Jacob
Father of Joseph, Mary's husband . . Matt. 1:15, 16

Jacob's oracles—*blessings and curses on Twelve Tribes*
Recorded . . . . Gen. 49:1–27

Jacob's well
Christ teaches a Samaritan
    woman at . . . . John 4:5–26

Jada—*knowing*
Grandson of Jerahmeel . . . . 1 Chr. 2:26, 28, 32

Jaddai—*praised*
Son of Nebo . . . . Ezra 10:43

Jaddua—*known*
1. Chief layman who signs
    the document . . . . Neh. 10:21
2. Levite who returns
    with Zerubbabel . . . . Neh. 12:8, 11

Jadon—*he judges*
Meronothite worker . . . . Neh. 3:7

Jael—*mountain goat*
Wife of Heber the Kenite . . . . Judg. 4:17
Slays Sisera . . . . Judg. 4:17–22
Praised by Deborah . . . . Judg. 5:24–27

Jagur—*lodging place*
Town in south Judah . . . . Josh. 15:21

Jahath—*comfort, revival*
1. Grandson of Judah . . . . 1 Chr. 4:2
2. Great-grandson of Levi . . . . 1 Chr. 6:20, 43
3. Son of Shimei . . . . 1 Chr. 23:10
4. Son of Shelomoth . . . . 1 Chr. 24:22
5. Merarite Levite . . . . 2 Chr. 34:12

Jahaz, Jahaza—*a place trodden underfoot*
Town in Moab at which Sihon was
    defeated . . . . Num. 21:23
Assigned to Reubenites . . . . Josh. 13:18
Levitical city . . . . Josh. 21:36

Regained by Moabites . . . . Is. 15:4
Same as Jahzah . . . . 1 Chr. 6:78

Jahaziah—*Yahweh sees*
Postexilic returnee . . . . Ezra 10:15

Jahaziel—*God sees*
1. Kohathite Levite . . . . 1 Chr. 23:19
2. Benjamite warrior . . . . 1 Chr. 12:4
3. Priest . . . . 1 Chr. 16:6
4. Inspired Levite . . . . 2 Chr. 20:14

Jahdai—*Yahweh leads*
Judahite . . . . 1 Chr. 2:47

Jahdiel—*God makes glad*
Manassite chief . . . . 1 Chr. 5:24

Jahdo—*union*
Gadite . . . . 1 Chr. 5:14

Jahleel—*wait for God*
Son of Zebulun . . . . Gen. 46:14
Family head . . . . Num. 26:26

Jahleelites
Descendants of Jahleel . . . . Num. 26:26

Jahmai—*may God protect*
Descendant of Issachar . . . . 1 Chr. 7:1, 2

Jahzeel—*God divides*
Son of Naphtali . . . . Gen. 46:24
Same as Jahziel . . . . 1 Chr. 7:13

Jahzeelites
Descendants of Jahzeel . . . . Num. 26:48

Jahzerah—*prudent*
Priest . . . . 1 Chr. 9:12
Called Ahzai . . . . Neh. 11:13

Jahziel (see Jahzeel)

Jailer—*one who guards a prison*
At Philippi, converted by Paul . . . . . Acts 16:19–34

Jair—*he enlightens*
1. Manassite warrior . . . . Num. 32:41; Deut. 3:14
    Conquers towns in Gilead . . . . Num. 32:41
2. Eighth judge of Israel . . . . Judg. 10:3–5
3. Father of Mordecai, Esther's uncle . . . . Esth. 2:5
4. Father of Elhanan . . . . 1 Chr. 20:5
    Called Jaare-Oregim . . . . 2 Sam. 21:19

Jairite
Descendant of Jair, the Manassite . . . 2 Sam. 20:26

Jairus—*Greek form of "Jair"*
Ruler of the synagogue; Jesus raises
    his daughter . . . . Mark 5:22–24, 35–43

Jakeh—*pious*
Father of Agur . . . . Prov. 30:1

Jakim—*He (God) raises up*
1. Descendant of Aaron . . . . 1 Chr. 24:1, 12
2. Benjamite . . . . 1 Chr. 8:19

Jalon—*passing the night*
Calebite, son of Ezrah . . . . 1 Chr. 4:17

Jambres (see Jannes and Jambres)

James—*a form of Jacob*
1. Son of Zebedee . . . . .Matt. 4:21
 Fisherman. . . . . Matt. 4:21
 One of the Twelve. . . . . Matt. 10:2
 In business with Peter . . . . .Luke 5:10
 Called Boanerges . . . . .Mark 3:17
 Of fiery disposition . . . . Luke 9:52–55
 Causes contention . . . . .Mark 10:35–45
 One of inner circle . . . . .Matt. 17:1
 Present at transfiguration . . . . Matt. 17:1–13
 Sees the risen Lord . . . . John 21:1, 2
 Awaits the Holy Spirit. . . . . .Acts 1:13
 Slain by Herod Agrippa I . . . . Acts 12:2
2. Son of Alphaeus; one of the Twelve. . . .Matt. 10:3, 4
 Identified usually as "the Less". . . . . . Mark 15:40
 Brother of Joses. Matt. 27:56
3. Son of Joseph and Mary . . . . Matt. 13:55, 56
 Lord's brother . . . . .Gal. 1:19
 Rejects Christ's claim . . . . Mark 3:21
 Becomes a believer . . . . Acts 1:13, 14
 Sees the risen Lord . . . . 1 Cor. 15:7
 Becomes moderator of Jerusalem
  Council. . . . . .Acts 15:13–23
 Paul confers with him . . . . .Gal. 2:9, 12
 Wrote an epistle . . . . James 1:1
 Brother of Jude . . . . Jude 1

James, the Epistle of—*a book of the New Testament*
 Trials . . . . .James 1:2–8
 Temptation .James 1:12–18
 Doing the word . . . . .James 1:19–25
 Faith and works . . . . .James 2:14–26
 Patience. . . . . .James 5:7–11
 Converting the sinner . . . . .James 5:19, 20

Jamin—*the right hand*
1. Son of Simeon . . . . Gen. 46:10
 Family head . . . . .Ex. 6:14, 15
2. Man of Judah . . . . 1 Chr. 2:27
3. Postexilic Levite; interprets the Law . . . .Neh. 8:7, 8

Jaminites
 Descendants of Jamin . . . . Num. 26:12

Jamlech—*whom He (God) makes king*
 Simeonite chief . . . . .1 Chr. 4:34

Janna—*a form of John*
 Ancestor of Christ . . . . Luke 3:23, 24

Jannes and Jambres
 Two Egyptian magicians;
  oppose Moses . . . . 2 Tim. 3:8
 Compare account . . . . Ex. 7:11–22

Janoah—*rest; quiet*
 Town of Naphtali . . . . .2 Kin. 15:29

Janohah
 Border town of Ephraim. . . . . .Josh. 16:6, 7

Janum—*sleep*
 Town near Hebron . . . . Josh. 15:53

Japheth—*wide-spreading*
 One of Noah's three sons . . . . Gen. 5:32
 Saved in the ark. 1 Pet. 3:20
 Covers father's nakedness . . . . Gen. 9:23
 Receives messianic blessing. . . . . Gen. 9:20–27
 His descendants occupy Asia Minor
  and Europe .Gen. 10:2–5

Japhia—*may He (God) cause to shine forth*
1. King of Lachish; slain by Joshua . . . . .Josh. 10:3–27
2. One of David's sons. . . . . .2 Sam. 5:13–15
3. Border town of Zebulun. . . . . .Josh. 19:10, 12

Japhlet—*He (God) will deliver*
 Asherite family . . . . .1 Chr. 7:32, 33

Japhletites
 Unidentified tribe on Joseph's
  boundary . . . . .Josh. 16:1, 3

Jarah—*honeycomb*
 Descendant of King Saul . . . . .1 Chr. 9:42
 Called Jehoaddah . . . . .1 Chr. 8:36

Jareb—*he will contend*
 Figurative description of Assyrian king. Hos. 5:13

Jared—*descent*
 Father of Enoch. . . . . .Gen. 5:15–20
 Ancestor of Noah . . . . 1 Chr. 1:2
 Ancestor of Christ . . . . Luke 3:37

Jarha
 Egyptian slave; marries master's
  daughter. . . . . .1 Chr. 2:34–41

Jarib—*he contends*
1. Head of a Simeonite family . . . . 1 Chr. 4:24
 Called Jachin . . . . Gen. 46:10
2. Man sent to search for Levites . . . . . . .Ezra 8:16, 17
3. Priest who divorced his foreign wife . . . . . Ezra 10:18

Jarmuth—*height*
1. Royal city of Canaan . . . . .Josh. 10:3
 King of, slain by Joshua . . . . Josh. 10:3–27
 Assigned to Judah. . . . . .Josh. 15:20, 35
 Inhabited after Exile . . . . Neh. 11:29
2. Town in Issachar assigned to the
  Levites. . . . . .Josh. 21:28, 29
 Called Ramoth . . . . .1 Chr. 6:73
 Called Remeth . . . . .Josh. 19:21

Jaroah—*new moon*
 Gadite chief . . . . 1 Chr. 5:14

Jashen—*sleeping*
 Sons of, in David's bodyguard. . . . . . . 2 Sam. 23:32
 Called Hashem .1 Chr. 11:34

Jasher—*upright*
 Book of, quoted. . . . . .Josh. 10:13

Jashobeam—*let the people return*
1. Chief of David's mighty men . . . . .1 Chr. 11:11
 Becomes military captain. . . . . .1 Chr. 27:2, 3
2. Benjamite warrior . . . . 1 Chr. 12:1, 2, 6

Jashub—*he returns*
1. Issachar's son. . . . . .1 Chr. 7:1

Head of family .... Num. 26:24
Called Job........................... Gen. 46:13
2. Son of Bani; divorced his foreign wife ... Ezra 10:29

Jashubi-Lehem—*bread returns*
A man of Judah...................... 1 Chr. 4:22

Jashubites
Descendants of Jashub .... Num. 26:24

Jason—*Greek equivalent for "Joshua" or "Jesus"*
Welcomes Paul at Thessalonica ...... Acts 17:5–9
Described as Paul's kinsman .... Rom. 16:21

Jasper—*a precious stone (quartz)*
Set in high priest's breastplate......... Ex. 28:20
Descriptive of:
Tyre's adornments .... Ezek. 28:12, 13
Heavenly vision....................... Rev. 4:3

Jathniel—*God bestows*
Korahite gatekeepers.............. 1 Chr. 26:1, 2

Jattir—*preeminence*
Town of Judah...................... Josh. 15:48
Assigned to Aaron's children....... Josh. 21:13, 14
David sends spoil to............. 1 Sam. 30:26, 27

Javan—*Greece (Ionia)*
Son of Japheth..................... Gen. 10:2, 4
Descendants of, to receive
Good News .... Is. 66:19, 20
Trade with Tyre .... Ezek. 27:13, 19
King of, in Daniel's visions .... Dan. 8:21
Conflict with...................... Zech. 9:13

Javelin—*a light, short spear*
Used by Saul...................... 1 Sam. 18:10

Jaw—*jawbone*
Used figuratively of:
God's sovereignty...................... Is. 30:28

Jawbone—*cheekbone*
Weapon used by Samson .... Judg. 15:15–19

Jazer—*helpful*
Town east of Jordan near Gilead ..... 2 Sam. 24:5
Amorites driven from .... Num. 21:32
Assigned to Gad .... Josh. 13:24, 25
Becomes Levitical city............ Josh. 21:34, 39
Taken by Moabites................... Is. 16:8, 9
Desired by sons of Reuben
and Gad .... Num. 32:1–5

Jaziz—*shining*
Shepherd over David's flocks .... 1 Chr. 27:31

Jealous, jealousy
A. Kinds of:
Divine .... Ex. 20:5
Marital .... Num. 5:12–31
Motherly........................... Gen. 30:1
Brotherly...................... Gen. 37:4–28
Sectional................... 2 Sam. 19:41–43
National .... Judg. 8:1–3
B. Good causes of:
Zeal for the Lord.................. Num. 25:11

Concern over Christians............. 2 Cor. 11:2
C. Evil causes of:
Favoritism .... Gen. 37:3–11
Regard for names .... 1 Cor. 3:3–5
Carnality .... Amos 3:12–15; 2 Cor. 12:20
D. Described as:
Implacable .... Prov. 6:34, 35
Cruel .... Song 8:6
Burning........................... Deut. 29:20
Godly.............................. 2 Cor. 11:2
E. Of God:
His name.......................... Ex. 34:14
For His preeminence....Ex. 20:5; 1 Cor. 10:21, 22
Over idolatry........................ Ps. 78:58

Jearim—*forests*
Mountain 10 miles west of Jerusalem .. Josh. 15:10

Jeatherai—*steadfast*
Descendant of Levi .... 1 Chr. 6:21
Also called Ethni .... 1 Chr. 6:41

Jeberechiah—*Yahweh blesses*
Father of Zechariah (not the prophet) ...... Is. 8:2

Jebus—*trodden underfoot*
Same as Jerusalem .... 1 Chr. 11:4
Entry denied to David............... 1 Chr. 11:5
Levite came near.................. Judg. 19:1, 11
See Zion; Sion

Jebusites
Descendants of Canaan .... Gen. 10:15, 16
Mountain tribe .... Num. 13:29
Land of, promised to Israel .... Gen. 15:18–21
Adoni-Zedek, their king, raises
confederacy.................... Josh. 10:1–5
Their king killed by Joshua .... Josh. 10:23–26
Join fight against Joshua .... Josh. 11:1–5
Assigned to Benjamin .... Josh. 18:28
Royal city not taken................. Judg. 1:21
Taken by David.................... 2 Sam. 5:6–8
Old inhabitants remain.......... 2 Sam. 24:16–25
Become slaves .... 1 Kin. 9:20, 21

Jecamiah (see Jekamiah)

Jecholiah—*Yahweh is able*
Mother of King Azariah... 2 Kin. 15:2; 2 Chr. 26:3

Jeconiah—*Yahweh establishes*
Variant form of Jehoiachin .... 1 Chr. 3:16, 17
Abbreviated to Coniah .... Jer. 22:24, 28
Son of Josiah .... Matt. 1:11
See Jehoiachin

Jedaiah—*Yahweh has been kind*
1. Priestly family...................... 1 Chr. 24:7
2. Head of the priests.................... Neh. 12:6
3. Another head priest................. Neh. 12:7, 21
4. Simeonite......................... 1 Chr. 4:37
5. Postexilic worker .... Neh. 3:10
6. One who brings gifts for the temple ... Zech. 6:10, 14

Jediael—*known of God*
1. Son of Benjamin and
     family head .... 1 Chr. 7:6, 10, 11
2. Manassite; joins David............... 1 Chr. 12:20
3. One of David's mighty men .... 1 Chr. 11:45
4. Korahite gatekeeper .... 1 Chr. 26:1, 2

Jedidah—*beloved*
     Mother of King Josiah................. 2 Kin. 22:1

Jedidiah—*beloved of Yahweh*
     Name given to Solomon
         by Nathan .... 2 Sam. 12:24, 25

Jeduthun—*praising*
1. Levite musician appointed
     by David...................... 1 Chr. 16:41, 42
     Heads a family of musicians .... 2 Chr. 5:12
     Name appears in Psalm titles .... Ps. 39; 62; 77
     Family officiates after Exile .... Neh. 11:17
     Possibly same as Ethan .... 1 Chr. 15:17, 19
2. Father of Obed-Edom............... 1 Chr. 16:38

Jegar Sahadutha—*heap of testimony*
     Name given by Laban to memorial
         stones .... Gen. 31:46, 47

Jehallelel—*God will flash light*
1. Man of Judah and family head .... 1 Chr. 4:16
2. Merarite Levite...................... 2 Chr. 29:12

Jehdeiah—*Yahweh will make glad*
1. Kohathite Levite .... 1 Chr. 24:20
2. Meronothite in charge of David's
     donkeys......................... 1 Chr. 27:30

Jehezekel—*God will strengthen*
     Descendant of Aaron.............. 1 Chr. 24:1, 16

Jehiah—*Yahweh lives*
     Doorkeeper .... 1 Chr. 15:24

Jehiel—*God lives*
1. Levite musician................... 1 Chr. 15:18, 20
2. Gershonite and family head .... 1 Chr. 23:8
3. Son of Hachmoni................... 1 Chr. 27:32
4. Son of King Jehoshaphat .... 2 Chr. 21:2, 4
5. Hemanite Levite.................... 2 Chr. 29:14
6. Overseer in Hezekiah's reign .... 2 Chr. 31:13
7. Official of the temple .... 2 Chr. 35:8
8. Father of Obadiah, a returned exile .... Ezra 8:9
9. Father of Shechaniah .... Ezra 10:2
10. Postexilic priest .... Ezra 10:21
11. Postexilic priest .... Ezra 10:26

Jehieli
     A Levite family .... 1 Chr. 26:21, 22

Jehizkiah—*Yahweh strengthens*
     Ephraimite chief.................... 2 Chr. 28:12

Jehoaddah—*whom Yahweh adorns*
     Descendant of Saul .... 1 Chr. 8:36
     Also called Jarah................... 1 Chr. 9:42

Jehoaddan—*Yahweh delights*
     Mother of Amaziah .... 2 Kin. 14:2

Jehoahaz—*Yahweh has taken hold of*
1. Son and successor of Jehu, king of
     Israel .... 2 Kin. 10:35
     Seeks the Lord in defeat .... 2 Kin. 13:2–9
2. Son and successor of Josiah, king
     of Judah .... 2 Kin. 23:30–34
     Called Shallum .... 1 Chr. 3:15
3. Another form of Ahaziah, youngest son
     of King Joram .... 2 Chr. 21:17

Jehoash (see Joash)

Jehohanan—*Yahweh is gracious*
1. Korahite Levite....................... 1 Chr. 26:3
2. Captain under Jehoshaphat........ 2 Chr. 17:10, 15
3. Father of Ishmael,
     Jehoiada's supporter .... 2 Chr. 23:1
4. Priestly family head................... Neh. 12:13
5. Priest who divorced his foreign wife..... Ezra 10:28
6. Son of Tobiah the Ammonite .... Neh. 6:17, 18
7. Postexilic singer .... Neh. 12:42
     See Johanan

Jehoiachin—*Yahweh establishes*
     Son of Jehoiakim; next to the last king
         of Judah .... 2 Kin. 24:8
     Deported to Babylon .... 2 Kin. 24:8–16
     Liberated by Evil-Merodach .... Jer. 52:31–34
     See Jeconiah

Jehoiada—*Yahweh knows*
1. Aaronite supporter of David.......... 1 Chr. 12:27
2. Father of Benaiah, one of David's
     officers .... 2 Sam. 8:18
3. Son of Benaiah; one of David's
     counselors .... 1 Chr. 27:34
4. High priest.......................... 2 Kin. 11:9
     Proclaims Joash king............. 2 Kin. 11:4–16
     Institutes a covenant............. 2 Kin. 11:17–21
     Instructs Joash .... 2 Kin. 12:2
     Commanded to repair
         the temple .... 2 Kin. 12:3–16
     Receives honorable burial .... 2 Chr. 24:15, 16
5. Deposed priest .... Jer. 29:26
6. Postexilic returnee...................... Neh. 3:6
     See Joiada

Jehoiakim—*Yahweh raises up*
     Son of King Josiah .... 2 Kin. 23:34, 35
     Made Pharaoh's official .... 2 Kin. 23:34, 36
     Wicked king .... 2 Chr. 36:5, 8
     Burns Jeremiah's scroll .... Jer. 36:1–32
     Becomes Nebuchadnezzar's servant ... 2 Kin. 24:1
     Punished by the Lord .... 2 Kin. 24:2–4
     Taken by Nebuchadnezzar .... 2 Chr. 36:5, 6
     Returns to idolatry................. 2 Chr. 36:5, 8
     Treats Jeremiah with contempt ..... Jer. 36:21–28
     Kills a true prophet .... Jer. 26:20–23
     Bound in fetters .... 2 Chr. 36:6
     Buried as a donkey................. Jer. 22:18, 19
     Curse on .... Jer. 36:30, 31

Jehoiarib—*Yahweh contends*
  Descendant of Aaron............ 1 Chr. 24:1, 6, 7
  Founder of an order of priests......1 Chr. 9:10, 13

Jehonadab—*Yahweh is liberal*
  A Rechabite.........................2 Kin. 10:15
  See Jonadab

Jehonathan—*Yahweh has given*
  1. Levite teacher........................ 2 Chr. 17:8
  2. Postexilic priest.................... Neh. 12:1, 18
  3. Uncle of King David................ 1 Chr. 27:32
  See Jonathan

Jehoram—*Yahweh is high*
  1. King of Judah; son and successor of
      Jehoshaphat...................... 1 Kin. 22:50
      Called Joram.................. 2 Kin. 8:21, 23, 24
      Marries Athaliah, who leads him
          astray..........................2 Kin. 8:18, 19
      Reigns eight years.................2 Kin. 8:16, 17
      Killed his brothers............. 2 Chr. 21:2, 4, 13
      Edom revolts from............. 2 Kin. 8:20–22
      Elijah predicts his terrible end... 2 Chr. 21:12–15
      Nations fight against............2 Chr. 21:16, 17
      Smitten by the Lord; dies in
          disgrace.................... 2 Chr. 21:18–20
  2. King of Israel; son of Ahab.............2 Kin. 1:17
      Reigns 12 years....................... 2 Kin. 3:1
      Puts away Baal........................2 Kin. 3:2
      Called Joram................. 2 Kin. 8:16, 25, 28
      Joins Jehoshaphat against
          Moabites......................2 Kin. 3:1–27
      Naaman sent to, for cure..........2 Kin. 5:1–27
      Informed by Elisha of
          Syria's plans................... 2 Kin. 6:8–23
      Wounded in war with Syria....... 2 Kin. 8:28, 29
  3. Levite teacher........................ 2 Chr. 17:8
  See Joram

Jehoshabeath—*Yahweh is an oath*
  Safeguards Joash from Athaliah......2 Chr. 22:11

Jehoshaphat—*Yahweh has judged*
  1. King of Judah; son and successor
      of Asa........................... 1 Kin. 15:24
      Godly king........................1 Kin. 22:43
      Reigns 25 years.................... 1 Kin. 22:42
      Fortifies his kingdom............... 2 Chr. 17:2
      Institutes reforms.................... 2 Chr. 17:3
      Inaugurates public instruction......2 Chr. 17:7–9
      Honored and respected.........2 Chr. 17:10–19
      Joins Ahab against
          Ramoth Gilead............... 1 Kin. 22:1–36
      Rebuked by a prophet..............2 Chr. 19:2, 3
      Develops legal system........... 2 Chr. 19:4–11
      By faith defeats invading forces... 2 Chr. 20:1–30
      Navy of, destroyed.............. 2 Chr. 20:35–37
      Provision for his children..........2 Chr. 21:2, 3
      Death of........................... 2 Chr. 21:1
      Ancestor of Christ...................Matt. 1:8
  2. Son of Ahilud....................... 2 Sam. 8:16

  Recorder under David
      and Solomon................... 2 Sam. 20:24
  3. Father of King Jehu.................... 2 Kin. 9:2

Jehoshaphat, Valley of
  Described as a place of judgment......Joel 3:2, 12

Jehosheba—*Yahweh is an oath*
  King Joram's daughter............... 2 Kin. 11:2

Jehozabad—*Yahweh has bestowed*
  1. Son of Obed-Edom................... 1 Chr. 26:4
  2. Son of a Moabitess; assassinates
      Joash.........................2 Kin. 12:20, 21
      Put to death.........................2 Chr. 25:3
  3. Military captain under King
      Jehoshaphat.......................2 Chr. 17:18

Jehozadak—*Yahweh has justified*
  Son of Seraiah, the high priest........ 1 Chr. 6:14
  His father killed................ 2 Kin. 25:18–21
  Carried captive to Babylon........... 1 Chr. 6:15
  Father of Joshua the high priest...Hag. 1:1, 12, 14

Jehu—*Yahweh is He*
  1. Benjamite warrior.................... 1 Chr. 12:3
  2. Prophet and son of Hanani........... 1 Kin. 16:1
      Denounces Baasha.............. 1 Kin. 16:2–4, 7
      Rebukes Jehoshaphat..............2 Chr. 19:2, 3
      Writes Jehoshaphat's biography......2 Chr. 20:34
  3. Descendant of Judah................. 1 Chr. 2:38
  4. Simeonite........................... 1 Chr. 4:35
  5. Grandson of Nimshi................... 2 Kin. 9:2
      Commander under Ahab.............2 Kin. 9:25
      Elijah anoints him to be king........ 1 Kin. 19:16
      Divinely commissioned to destroy
          Ahab's house.................1 Kin. 19:16, 17
      Anointed by Elisha's servant.......2 Kin. 9:1–10
      Carries out orders with zeal.......2 Kin. 9:11–37
      Killed Ahab's sons.............2 Kin. 10:1–17
      Destroys worshipers of Baal..... 2 Kin. 10:18–28
      Serves the Lord outwardly....... 2 Kin. 10:29–31
      His death..................... 2 Kin. 10:35, 36

Jehubbah—*he hides*
  Asherite............................1 Chr. 7:34

Jehucal—*Yahweh is able*
  Son of Shelemiah; sent by Zedekiah to
      Jeremiah..........................Jer. 37:3
      Also called Jucal......................Jer. 38:1

Jehud—*praise*
  Town of Dan....................Josh. 19:40, 45

Jehudi—*a man of Judah; a Jew*
  Reads Jeremiah's roll...........Jer. 36:14, 21, 23

Jehudijah—*a Jewess*
  One of Mered's two wives; should be
      rendered "the Jewess"............. 1 Chr. 4:18

Jeiel—*God snatches away*
  1. Ancestor of Saul...................1 Chr. 9:35–39
  2. One of David's mighty men.......... 1 Chr. 11:44
      Reubenite prince..................1 Chr. 5:6, 7
  3. Levite musician..................... 1 Chr. 16:5

4. Gatekeeper . . . . 1 Chr. 15:18, 21
    May be the same as 3 . . . . 1 Chr. 16:5
    Called Jehiah . . . . 1 Chr. 15:24
5. Inspired Levite . . . . 2 Chr. 20:14
6. Levite chief . . . . 2 Chr. 35:9
7. Scribe . . . . 2 Chr. 26:11
8. Temple Levite . . . . 2 Chr. 29:13
9. One who divorced his foreign wife . . . Ezra 10:19, 43

Jekabzeel—*God will gather*
    Town in Judah . . . . Neh. 11:25
    Called Kabzeel . . . . Josh. 15:21
    Home of Benaiah, David's friend . . . . 2 Sam. 23:20

Jekameam—*people will rise*
    Kohathite Levite . . . . 1 Chr. 23:19

Jekamiah, Jecamiah—*Yahweh will rise*
1. Son of Shallum . . . . 1 Chr. 2:41
2. Son of Jeconiah . . . . 1 Chr. 3:17, 18

Jekuthiel—*God will support*
    Man of Judah . . . . 1 Chr. 4:18

Jemimah—*dove*
    Job's daughter . . . . Job 42:14

Jemuel—*day of God*
    Son of Simeon . . . . Gen. 46:10
    Called Nemuel . . . . Num. 26:12

Jephthah—*he will open*
    Gilead's son by a harlot . . . . Judg. 11:1
    Flees to Tob; becomes a leader . . . . . Judg. 11:2–11
    Cites historical precedents against
       invading Ammonites . . . . Judg. 11:12–27
    Makes a vow before battle . . . . Judg. 11:28–31
    Defeats Ammonites . . . . Judg. 11:32, 33
    Fulfills vow . . . . Judg. 11:34–40
    Defeats quarrelsome Ephraimites . . . Judg. 12:1–7
    Cited by Samuel . . . . 1 Sam. 12:11
    In faith's chapter . . . . Heb. 11:32

Jephunneh—*it will be prepared*
1. Caleb's father . . . . Num. 13:6
2. Asherite . . . . 1 Chr. 7:38

Jerah—*moon*
    Son of Joktan; probably an
       Arabian tribe . . . . Gen. 10:26; 1 Chr. 1:20

Jerahmeel—*may God have compassion*
1. Great-grandson of Judah . . . . 1 Chr. 2:9, 25–41
2. Son of Kish, not Saul's father . . . . 1 Chr. 24:29
3. King Jehoiakim's officer . . . . Jer. 36:26

Jerahmeelites
    Raided by David . . . . 1 Sam. 27:10

Jered—*descent*
    A descendant of Judah . . . . 1 Chr. 4:18
    See Jared

Jeremai—*high*
    One who divorced his foreign wife . Ezra 10:19, 33

Jeremiah—*Yahweh establishes*
A. Life of:
    Son of Hilkiah; a Benjamite . . . . Jer. 1:1

    Native of Anathoth . . . . Jer. 1:1
    Called before birth . . . . Jer. 1:4–10
    Prophet under kings Josiah, Jehoiakim,
       and Zedekiah . . . . Jer. 1:2, 3
    Forbidden to marry . . . . Jer. 16:1–13
    Imprisoned by Pashhur . . . . Jer. 20:1–6
    Commanded by God to purchase
       a field . . . . Jer. 32:1–15
    Writes his prophecy; Jehoiakim
       burns it . . . . Jer. 36:1–26
    Prophecy rewritten . . . . Jer. 36:27–32
    Accused of defection . . . . Jer. 37:1–16
    Released by Zedekiah . . . . Jer. 37:17–21
    Cast into a dungeon . . . . Jer. 38:1–6
    Saved by an Ethiopian . . . . Jer. 38:7–28
    Set free by Nebuchadnezzar . . . . Jer. 39:11–14
    Given liberty of choice by
       Nebuzaradan . . . . Jer. 40:1–6
    Forced to flee to Egypt . . . . Jer. 43:5–7
    Last prophecies at Tahpanhes,
       Egypt . . . . Jer. 43:8–13
B. Characteristics of:
    Has internal conflicts . . . . Jer. 20:7–18
    Has incurable pain . . . . Jer. 15:18
    Motives misunderstood . . . . Jer. 37:12–14
    Tells captives to build in Babylon . . . . . Jer. 29:4–9
    Denounces false prophets
       in Babylon . . . . Jer. 29:20–32
    Rebukes idolatry . . . . Jer. 7:9–21
C. Prophecies of, foretell:
    Egypt's fall . . . . Jer. 43:8–13
    70 years of captivity . . . . 2 Chr. 36:21
    Restoration to land . . . . Jer. 16:14–18
    New covenant . . . . Jer. 31:31–34
    Herod's massacre . . . . Jer. 31:15
D. Teachings of:
    God's sovereignty . . . . Jer. 18:5–10
    God's knowledge . . . . Jer. 17:5–10
    Shame of idolatry . . . . Jer. 10:14, 15
    Spirituality of worship, etc. . . . . Jer. 3:16, 17
    Need of regeneration . . . . Jer. 9:26
    Man's sinful nature . . . . Jer. 2:22
    Gospel salvation . . . . Jer. 23:5, 6
    Call of the Gentiles . . . . Jer. 3:17–19

Jeremiah
1. Benjamite warrior . . . . 1 Chr. 12:4
2. Gadite warrior . . . . 1 Chr. 12:10
3. Another Gadite warrior . . . . 1 Chr. 12:13
4. Manassite head . . . . 1 Chr. 5:23, 24
5. Father of Hamutal, a wife of Josiah . . . . 2 Kin. 23:31
6. Father of Jaazaniah . . . . Jer. 35:3
7. Postexilic priest . . . . Neh. 12:1, 7
    Head of a priestly line . . . . Neh. 12:12
8. Priest who signs the covenant . . . . Neh. 10:2

Jeremiah, Book of—*a book of the Old Testament*
    Jeremiah's call . . . . Jer. 1:1–19
    Jeremiah's life . . . . Jer. 26:1–45:5
    Israel's sin against God . . . . Jer. 2:1–10:25
    Against false prophets . . . . Jer. 23:9–40

Against foreign nations .... Jer. 46:1–51:64
The messianic King................. Jer. 23:1–8

Jeremoth—*elevation*
1. Benjamite........................... 1 Chr. 8:14
2. Merarite Levite..................... 1 Chr. 23:23
3. Musician of David .... 1 Chr. 25:22
4. One who divorced his foreign wife ....Ezra 10:26
5. Another who divorced his foreign wife ...Ezra 10:27
6. Spelled Jerimoth.................... 1 Chr. 24:30
See Jerimoth

Jeriah, Jerijah—*Yahweh sees*
Kohathite Levite................. 1 Chr. 23:19, 23
Hebronite chief.................... 1 Chr. 26:31

Jeribai—*Yahweh contends*
One of David's warriors .... 1 Chr. 11:46

Jericho—*place of fragrance*
City near the Jordan .... Num. 22:1
Viewed by Moses .... Deut. 34:1–3
Called the city of palm trees .... Deut. 34:3
Viewed by spies........................ Josh. 2:1
Home of Rahab the harlot .... Heb. 11:31
Scene of Joshua's vision............ Josh. 5:13–15
Destroyed by Joshua .... Heb. 11:30, 31
Curse of rebuilding of .... Josh. 6:26
Assigned to Benjamin .... Josh. 16:1, 7
Moabites retake .... Judg. 3:12, 13
David's envoys stay here........... 2 Sam. 10:4, 5
Rebuilt by Hiel .... 1 Kin. 16:34
Visited by Elijah and Elisha........ 2 Kin. 2:4–22
Zedekiah captured here .... 2 Kin. 25:5
Reinhabited after Exile........... Ezra 2:34
People of, help rebuild Jerusalem........ Neh. 3:2
Blind men of, healed by Jesus .... Matt. 20:29–34
Home of Zacchaeus................. Luke 19:1–10

Jeriel—*God sees*
Son of Tola....................... 1 Chr. 7:2

Jerimoth
1. Son of Bela...................... 1 Chr. 7:7
2. Warrior of David .... 1 Chr. 12:5
3. Musician of David .... 1 Chr. 25:4
4. Son of David .... 2 Chr. 11:18
5. Levite overseer .... 2 Chr. 31:13
6. Son of Becher .... 1 Chr. 7:8
7. Ruler of Naphtali .... 1 Chr. 27:19
8. Spelled Jeremoth .... 1 Chr. 23:23
See Jeremoth

Jerioth—*tent curtains*
One of Caleb's wives .... 1 Chr. 2:18

Jeroboam—*may the people increase*
1. Son of Nebat .... 1 Kin. 11:26
Rebels against Solomon .... 1 Kin. 11:26–28
Ahijah's prophecy concerning.... 1 Kin. 11:29–39
Flees to Egypt .... 1 Kin. 11:40
Recalled, made king .... 1 Kin. 12:1–3, 12, 20
Perverts the true religion .... 1 Kin. 12:25–33
Casts Levites out.................... 2 Chr. 11:14
Rebuked by a man of God .... 1 Kin. 13:1–10

Leads people astray .... 1 Kin. 13:33, 34
His wife consults Ahijah .... 1 Kin. 14:1–18
War with Abijam .... 1 Kin. 15:7
Reigns 22 years .... 1 Kin. 14:20
Struck by the Lord .... 2 Chr. 13:20
2. Jeroboam II; king of Israel .... 2 Kin. 13:13
Successor of Joash (Jehoash)...... 2 Kin. 14:16, 23
Conquers Hamath
and Damascus .... 2 Kin. 14:25–28
Reigns wickedly 41 years .... 2 Kin. 14:23, 24
Denounced by Amos .... Amos 7:7–13
Death of .... 2 Kin. 14:29

Jeroham—*he is pitied*
1. Grandfather of Samuel................ 1 Sam. 1:1
2. Benjamite........................... 1 Chr. 9:8
3. Father of Benjamite chief men .... 1 Chr. 8:27
4. Benjamite of Gedor.................... 1 Chr. 12:7
5. Father of Adaiah .... 1 Chr. 9:12
6. Danite chief's father .... 1 Chr. 27:22
7. Military captain .... 2 Chr. 23:1

Jerubbaal—*Baal contends*
Name given to Gideon for destroying
Baal's altar...................... Judg. 6:32

Jerubbesheth—*let shame contend*
Father of Abimelech .... 2 Sam. 11:21

Jeruel—*founded by God*
Wilderness west of the Dead Sea ..... 2 Chr. 20:16

Jerusalem—*possession of peace*
A. Names applied to:
City of God .... Ps. 46:4
City of David...................... 2 Sam. 5:6, 7
City of Judah .... 2 Chr. 25:28
Zion................................. Ps. 48:12
Jebus .... Josh. 18:28
Holy city........................... Matt. 4:5
Faithful city .... Is. 1:21, 26
City of righteousness.................. Is. 1:26
City of Truth .... Zech. 8:3
City of the great King .... Ps. 48:2
Salem............................... Gen. 14:18
THE LORD IS THERE............... Ezek. 48:35
Ariel................................. Is. 29:1
B. History of:
Originally Salem.................... Gen. 14:18
Occupied by Jebusites .... Josh. 15:8
King of, defeated by Joshua........ Josh. 10:5–23
Assigned to Benjamin .... Josh. 18:28
Attacked by Judah .... Judg. 1:8
Jebusites remain in............... Judg. 1:21
David brings Goliath's head to...... 1 Sam. 17:54
Conquered by David .... 2 Sam. 5:6–8
Name changed .... 2 Sam. 5:7–9
Ark brought to .... 2 Sam. 6:12–17
Saved from destruction............ 2 Sam. 24:16
Solomon builds temple here........ 1 Kin. 5:5–8
Suffers in war..................... 1 Kin. 14:25–27
Plundered by Israel................ 2 Kin. 14:13, 14
Besieged by Syrians .... Is. 7:1

Earthquake damages..................Amos 1:1
Miraculously saved ....2 Kin. 19:31–36
Ruled by Egypt ....2 Kin. 23:33–35
Besieged by Babylon ....2 Kin. 24:10, 11
Captured by Babylon.................Jer. 39:1–8
Desolate 70 years ....Jer. 25:11, 12
Temple rebuilt in ....Ezra 1:1–4
Exiles return to....................Ezra 2:1–70
Work on, hindered..................Ezra 5:1–17
Walls of, rebuilt ....Neh. 3:1–33
Walls of, dedicated..............Neh. 12:27–47
Christ:
  Enters as King.............Matt. 21:9, 10
  Laments for ....Matt. 23:37
  Crucified at ....Luke 9:31
  Weeps over.....................Luke 19:41, 42
  Predicts destruction ....Luke 19:43, 44
  Crucified in ....Luke 24:18–20
  Gospel preached at.................Luke 24:47
  Many miracles performed in..........John 4:45
  Church begins here ....Acts 2:1–47
  Christians of, persecuted ....Acts 4:1–30
  Stephen martyred at ....Acts 7:1–60
  First Christian council held here ....Acts 15:1–29
Paul:
  Visits ....Acts 20:16
  Arrested in ....Acts 21:30–36
  Taken from ....Acts 23:12–33
C. Prophecies concerning:
  Destruction by Babylon ....Jer. 20:5
  Utter ruin............................Jer. 26:18
  Rebuilding by Cyrus ....Is. 44:26–28
  Christ's entry into ....Zech. 9:9
  Gospel proclaimed from.................Is. 2:3
  Perilous times ....Matt. 24:1–22
  Being under Gentiles.................Luke 21:24
D. Described:
  Physically—strong..........Ps. 48:12, 13; 125:2;
  Morally—corrupt...........Is. 1:1–16; Jer. 5:1–5
  Spiritually—the redeemed..........Gal. 4:26–30
  Prophetically—New Jerusalem......Rev. 21:1–27
  See Zion; Sion

Jerusha—*possessed (married)*
  Wife of King Uzziah ....2 Kin. 15:33
  Called Jerushah......................2 Chr. 27:1

Jeshaiah—*Yahweh saves*
1. Musician of David ....1 Chr. 25:3
2. Grandson of Zerubbabel ....1 Chr. 3:21
3. Levite in David's reign ....1 Chr. 26:25
4. Son of Athaliah; returns from Babylon ....Ezra 8:7
5. Levite who returns with Ezra ....Ezra 8:19
6. Benjamite.........................Neh. 11:7

Jeshanah—*old*
  City of Ephraim taken by Abijah .....2 Chr. 13:19

Jesharelah—*upright toward God*
  Levite musician....................1 Chr. 25:14
  Called Asharelah ....1 Chr. 25:2

Jeshebeab—*may the father tarry (live)*
  Descendant of Aaron................1 Chr. 24:13

Jesher—*uprightness*
  Caleb's son ....1 Chr. 2:18

Jeshimon—*waste*
  Wilderness west of the
    Dead Sea ....1 Sam. 23:19, 24

Jeshishai—*aged*
  Gadite.............................1 Chr. 5:14

Jeshohaiah—*humbled by Yahweh*
  Leader in Simeon ....1 Chr. 4:36

Jeshua—*Yahweh is salvation*
1. Descendant of Aaron ....Ezra 2:36
2. Levite treasurer ....2 Chr. 31:14, 15
3. Postexilic high priest....................Zech. 3:8
  Returns with Zerubbabel................Ezra 2:2
  Aids in temple rebuilding.............Ezra 3:2–8
  Withstands opponents ....Ezra 4:1–3
  Figurative act performed on ....Zech. 3:1–10
4. Called Joshua ....Hag. 1:1
  See Joshua 3
5. Levite assistant........................Ezra 2:40
  Explains the Law ....Neh. 8:7
  Leads in worship....................Neh. 9:4, 5
  Seals the covenant ....Neh. 10:1, 9
6. Repairer of the wall....................Neh. 3:19
7. Man of the house of Pahath-Moab ....Ezra 2:6
8. Village in south Judah ....Neh. 11:26

Jeshurun—*upright one*
  Poetic name of endearment
    for Israel.......................Deut. 32:15

Jesimiel—*God sets up*
  Simeonite leader....................1 Chr. 4:36

Jesse—*Yahweh exists*
  Grandson of Ruth and Boaz ....Ruth 4:17–22
  Father of:
    David........................1 Sam. 16:18, 19
    Eight sons.....................1 Sam. 16:10, 11
    Two daughters...................1 Chr. 2:15, 16
    Citizen of Bethlehem.............1 Sam. 16:1, 18
    Protected by David...............1 Sam. 22:1–4
    Of humble origin ....1 Sam. 18:18, 23
    Mentioned in prophecy..............Is. 11:1, 10
    Ancestor of Christ ....Matt. 1:5, 6; Luke 3:32

Jesshiah (see Isshiah)

Jesting—*mocking; joking*
  Condemned..........................Eph. 5:4
  Lot appeared to be ....Gen. 19:14
  Of godless men ....Ps. 35:16

> **WORD STUDY**   **JESUS,** *Iesous* (eeyay-*soos*). This proper noun was a very popular name chosen by Jewish parents for their sons. Transliterated into Greek as *Iesous,* the Hebrew name *Yēshuaʿ* (a later form of "Joshua") means "God Is Salvation." An angel reveals to Joseph that this is the appropriate name for his

son (Matt. 1:21), and in the NT the name almost always identifies Jesus of Nazareth. However, the name is not exclusive to the one "called Christ" (Matt. 27:17): Paul refers to one of his coworkers as "Jesus who is called Justus" (Col. 4:11), and a magician in Acts (13:6) is called "Bar-Jesus." (Strong's #2424)

Jesus (see Christ)

Jether—*abundance*
1. Gideon's oldest son ....Judg. 8:20, 21
2. Descendant of Judah..................1 Chr. 2:32
3. Son of Ezra.........................1 Chr. 4:17
4. Asherite; probably same as Jithran...1 Chr. 7:30–38
5. Amasa's father ....1 Kin. 2:5, 32

Jetheth—*subjection*
Chief of Edom........................Gen. 36:40

Jethlah—*an overhanging place*
Danite town..........................Josh. 19:42

Jethro—*excellent*
Priest of Midian; Moses'
   father-in-law....................Num. 10:29
Also called Reuel ....Num. 10:29
Moses marries his
   daughter Zipporah ....Ex. 2:16–22
Moses departs from..................Ex. 4:18–26
Visits and counsels Moses ....Ex. 18:1–27

Jetur
Son of Ishmael......................Gen. 25:15
Conflict with Israel ....1 Chr. 5:18, 19
Tribal descendants of; the Itureans......Luke 3:1

Jeuel—*snatching away*
Son of Zerah ....1 Chr. 9:6

Jeush—*may he aid*
1. Son of Esau and Edomite chief.......Gen. 36:5, 18
2. Benjamite head.......................1 Chr. 7:10
3. Gershonite Levite ....1 Chr. 23:10, 11
4. Descendant of Jonathan..............1 Chr. 8:39
5. Rehoboam's son ....2 Chr. 11:19

Jeuz—*counseling*
Benjamite.........................1 Chr. 8:8, 10

Jewels—*ornaments used on the body*
A. Used for:
Ornaments...........................Is. 3:18–24
Evil offering.......................Ex. 32:1–5
Good offering ....Ex. 35:22
Spoils of war.......................2 Chr. 20:25
Farewell gifts......................Ex. 11:2
B. Significance of:
Betrothal present ....Gen. 24:22, 53
Sign of wealth ....James 2:2
Standard of value ....Prov. 3:15
Tokens of repentance ....Gen. 35:4
Tokens of love ....Ezek. 16:11–13
Indications of worldliness ....1 Tim. 2:9
Figurative of God's own ....Matt. 13:45, 46

Jewish alphabet
Given topically ....Ps. 119

Jewish calendar
A. List of months of:
Abib or Nisan (March—April)..........Ex. 13:4
Ziv or Iyar (April—May) ....1 Kin. 6:1, 37
Sivan (May—June)....................Esth. 8:9
Tammuz (June—July)..................Jer. 39:2
Ab (July—August)...................Num. 33:38
Elul (August—September)............Neh. 6:15
Ethanim or Tishri
   (September—October) ....1 Kin. 8:2
Bul or Heshvan
   (October—November)............1 Kin. 6:38
Chislev (November—December)........Neh. 1:1
Tebeth (December—January)..........Esth. 2:16
Shebat or Sebat (January—February)....Zech. 1:7
Adar (February—March)..............Esth. 3:7
B. Feasts of:
Abib (14)—Passover ....Ex. 12:18
Abib (15–21)—Unleavened Bread ....Lev. 23:5, 6
Abib (16)—Firstfruits.............Lev. 23:10, 11
Ziv (14)—Later Passover ....Num. 9:10, 11
Sivan (6)—Pentecost, Feast of Weeks,
   Harvest ....Lev. 23:15–21
Ethanim (1)—Trumpets...............Lev. 23:24
Ethanim (10)—Day of Atonement...Lev. 16:29–34
Ethanim (15–21)—Tabernacles ....Lev. 23:34, 35
Ethanim (22)—Holy Convocation .....Lev. 23:36
Chislev (25)—Dedication ....John 10:22

Jewish measures (Metrology)
A. Long measures:
Finger (¾ inch) ....Jer. 52:21
Handbreadth (3 to 4 inches) ....Ex. 25:25
Span (about 9 inches)................Ex. 28:16
Cubit of man (about 18 inches)........Gen. 6:15
Pace (about 3 feet) ....2 Sam. 6:13
Fathom (about 6 feet) ....Acts 27:28
Rod (about 11 feet).................Ezek. 40:5
Line ....Ezek. 40:3
B. Land measures:
Cubit of God (1¾ feet)...............Josh. 3:4
Mile (1,760 yards)..................Matt. 5:41
Sabbath day's journey (⅗ mile)........Acts 1:12
Day's journey (24 miles) ....Gen. 30:36
C. Weights and dry measures:
Kab (about 2 quarts) ....2 Kin. 6:25
Omer (about 7 pints).............Ex. 16:16–18, 36
Ephah (about 4½ pecks)..............Ex. 16:36
Homer (about 11 bushels) ... Num. 11:32; Hos. 3:2
Talent (about 93 pounds)............Ex. 25:39
D. Liquid measures:
Log (about 1 pint)................Lev. 14:10, 15
Hin (about 1½ gallons) ....Num. 15:4–10
Bath (about 9 gallons) ....Is. 5:10
Homer or kor (c. 85 gallons) ......Ezek. 45:11, 14

Jews—*the Hebrew people*
A. Descriptive of:
Hebrew race........... Esth. 3:6, 13; Acts 24:24
Postexilic Hebrew nation.............Ezra 5:1, 5
Believers ....Rom. 2:28, 29

B. Their sins:

Self-righteousness .... Rom. 10:1–3
Hypocrisy....................... Rom. 2:17–25
Persecution.................... 1 Thess. 2:14, 15
Rejection of Christ.............. Matt. 27:21–25
Rejection of the gospel .... Acts 13:42–46
Embitter Gentiles.................Acts 14:2–6
Spiritual blindness.................. John 3:1–4
Ignorance ....Luke 19:41, 42

C. Their punishment:

Blinded ....Rom. 11:25
Cast out......................... Matt. 8:11, 12
Desolation as a nation........... Luke 21:20–24
Scattered....................... Deut. 28:48–64

Jezaniah—*Yahweh answers*
Judahite military officer.............. Jer. 40:7, 8
Seeks advice from Jeremiah.......... Jer. 42:1–3
Called Jaazaniah................... 2 Kin. 25:23

Jezebel—*unmarried, chaste*
1. Daughter of Ethbaal; Ahab's wife ..... 1 Kin. 16:31
Destroyed Yahweh's prophets..... 1 Kin. 18:4–13
Plans Elijah's death .... 1 Kin. 19:1, 2
Secures Naboth's death........... 1 Kin. 21:1–15
Sentence:
Pronounced upon................... 1 Kin. 21:23
Fulfilled by Jehu .... 2 Kin. 9:7, 30–37
2. Type of paganism in the church......... Rev. 2:20

Jezer—*form, purpose*
Son of Naphtali.....................Gen. 46:24
Family head of the Jezerites......... Num. 26:49

Jeziah—*Yahweh sprinkles*
One who divorced his foreign wife .... Ezra 10:25

Jeziel—*God sprinkles*
Benjamite warrior .... 1 Chr. 12:2, 3

Jezrahiah—*Yahweh shines*
Leads singing at dedication service.... Neh. 12:42

Jezreel—*God sows*
1. Fortified city of Issachar .... Josh. 19:17, 18
Gideon fights Midianites in valley of ... Judg. 6:33
Israelites camp here .... 1 Sam. 29:1, 11
Center of Ishbosheth's rule .... 2 Sam. 2:8, 9
Capital city..........................1 Kin. 18:45
Home of Naboth................... 1 Kin. 21:1, 13
Site of Jezebel's tragic end .... 1 Kin. 21:23
Heads of Ahab's sons piled here....2 Kin. 10:1–10
City of bloodshed...................... Hos. 1:4
Judgment in valley of.................. Hos. 1:5
2. Town of Judah .... Josh. 15:56
David's wife from................... 1 Sam. 25:43
3. Judahite .... 1 Chr. 4:3
4. Symbolic name of Hosea's son .... Hos. 1:4
5. Symbolic name of the new Israel ..... Hos. 2:22, 23

Jezreelite, Jezreelitess—*a person from Jezreel*
Ahinoam........................... 1 Sam. 30:5
Naboth .... 1 Kin. 21:1

Jibsam—*fragrant*
Descendant of Issachar................ 1 Chr. 7:2

Jidlaph—*he weeps*
Son of Nahor .... Gen. 22:22

Jimnah—*prosperity*
Son of Asher........................ Gen. 46:17

Jiphtah—*he will open*
City of Judah .... Josh. 15:43

Jiphthah El—*God will open*
Valley between Asher and Naphtali Josh. 19:10–27

Jishui
Son of Saul .... 1 Sam. 14:49

Jithra—*excellence*
Israelite (or Ishmaelite); father of
Amasa......................... 2 Sam. 17:25
Called Jether .... 1 Kin. 2:5, 32

Jizliah—*Yahweh delivers*
Son of Elpaal .... 1 Chr. 8:18

Jizri—*fashioner*
Leader of Levitical choir............. 1 Chr. 25:11
Also called Zeri..................... 1 Chr. 25:3

Joab—*Yahweh is father*
1. Son of Zeruiah, David's half sister...... 2 Sam. 8:16
Leads David's army to victory over
Ishbosheth.................... 2 Sam. 2:10–32
Assassinates Abner deceptively ... 2 Sam. 3:26, 27
David rebukes him.............. 2 Sam. 3:28–39
Commands David's army against
Edomites .... 1 Kin. 11:14–17
Defeats Syrians and Ammonites ... 2 Sam. 10:1–14
Obeys David's orders concerning
Uriah...................... 2 Sam. 11:6–27
Allows David to besiege Rabbah ......2 Sam. 11:1
Makes David favorable toward
Absalom..................... 2 Sam. 14:1–33
Remains loyal to David........... 2 Sam. 18:1–5
Killed Absalom.................. 2 Sam. 18:9–17
Rebukes David's grief .... 2 Sam. 19:1–8
Demoted by David................. 2 Sam. 19:13
Puts down Sheba's revolt .... 2 Sam. 20:1–22
Killed Amasa.................... 2 Sam. 20:8–10
Regains command .... 2 Sam. 20:23
Opposes David's numbering
of the people .... 2 Sam. 24:1–9; 1 Chr. 21:1–6
Supports Adonijah................... 1 Kin. 1:7
David's dying words against .... 1 Kin. 2:1–6
His crimes punished by Solomon.. 1 Kin. 2:28–34
2. Son of Seraiah.................... 1 Chr. 4:13, 14
3. Family head of exiles.................... Ezra 2:6

Joah—*Yahweh is brother*
1. Son of Obed-Edom .... 1 Chr. 26:4
2. Gershonite Levite .... 1 Chr. 6:21
Hezekiah's assistant .... 2 Chr. 29:12
3. Son of Asaph; a recorder under
Hezekiah .... Is. 36:3, 11, 22
4. Son of Joahaz...................... 2 Chr. 34:8

Joahaz—*Yahweh has laid hold of*
Father of Joah, a recorder.............2 Chr. 34:8

Joanna—*Yahweh has been gracious*
Wife of Chuza, Herod's steward ......Luke 8:1–3
With others, heralds Christ's
resurrection.....................Luke 24:10

Joannas—*Yahweh has been gracious*
Ancestor of Christ ....Luke 3:27

Joash, Jehoash—*Yahweh has given*
1. Father of Gideon ....Judg. 6:11–32
2. Judahite .... 1 Chr. 4:21, 22
3. Benjamite warrior .... 1 Chr. 12:3
4. Son of Ahab........................ 1 Kin. 22:26
5. Son and successor of Ahaziah, king
of Judah ....2 Kin. 11:1–21
Rescued and hid by Jehosheba ......2 Kin. 11:1–3
At age 7 proclaimed king by Jehoiada...... 2 Kin.
11:4–12
Instructed by Jehoiada ....2 Kin. 12:1, 2
Repairs the temple .... 2 Kin. 12:4–16
Turns to idols after
Jehoiada's death............. 2 Chr. 24:17–19
Murdered Zechariah, Berechiah's
son.............2 Chr. 24:20–22; Matt. 23:35
Killed, not buried with kings ....2 Chr. 25:23–28
6. Son and successor of Jehoahaz, king
of Israel.......................2 Kin. 13:10–13
Follows idolatry ....2 Kin. 13:11
Laments Elisha's sickness........ 2 Kin. 13:14–19
Defeats:
Syria........................ 2 Kin. 13:24, 25
Amaziah ....2 Kin. 13:12

Joash—*Yahweh has come to help*
1. Benjamite..........................1 Chr. 7:8
2. Officer of David.................... 1 Chr. 27:28

Job—*returning*
A. Life of:
Lives in Uz ....Job 1:1
Afflicted by Satan ....Job 1:6–19
Deplores his birth....................Job 3:3–19
Debate between Job and his
three friends ....Job 3–33
Elihu intervenes ....Job 34–37
Lord answers Job ....Job 38–41
His final reply ....Job 42:1–6
The Lord rebukes Job's three friends ...Job 42:7–9
Restored to prosperity...............Job 42:10–15
Dies "old and full of days" ....Job 42:16, 17
B. Strength of his:
Faith........................Job 19:23–27
Perseverance ....James 5:11
Integrity ....Job 31:1–40
C. Sufferings of:
Lost property...................... Job 1:13–17
Lost children .... Job 1:18, 19
Lost health ....Job 2:4–8
Misunderstood by friends ...... Job 4:1–8; 8:1–6;
11:1–20

D. Restoration of:
After repentance.....................Job 42:1–6
After prayer ....Job 42:8–10
To greater prosperity...............Job 42:11–17

Job, Book of—*a book of the Old Testament*
Wisdom described .... Job 1:1–5
Wisdom tested .... Job 1:6–2:10
Wisdom sought.....................Job 3–37
God challenges Job ....Job 38–41
Wisdom in humility ....Job 42:1–6

Jobab—*to call shrilly*
1. Son of Joktan........................ Gen. 10:29
Tribal head......................1 Chr. 1:23
2. King of Edom .... Gen. 36:31, 33
3. Canaanite king defeated
by Joshua .... Josh. 11:1, 7–12
4. Benjamite........................... 1 Chr. 8:9
5. Another Benjamite .... 1 Chr. 8:18

Jochebed—*Yahweh is glory*
Daughter of Levi; mother of Miriam, Aaron,
and Moses ....Ex. 6:20
Faith of .... Heb. 11:23

Joed—*Yahweh is witness*
Benjamite .... Neh. 11:7

Joel—*Yahweh is God*
1. Son of Samuel .... 1 Sam. 8:1, 2; 1 Chr. 6:28, 33
Father of Heman the singer.......... 1 Chr. 15:17
2. Kohathite Levite .... 1 Chr. 6:36
3. Leader of Simeon .... 1 Chr. 4:35
4. Reubenite chief.................. 1 Chr. 5:4, 8, 9
5. Gadite chief......................... 1 Chr. 5:12
6. Chief man of Issachar................1 Chr. 7:3
7. One of David's mighty men........... 1 Chr. 11:38
8. Gershonite Levite .... 1 Chr. 15:7, 11, 17
Probably the same as in.............1 Chr. 23:8
9. Manassite chief officer............... 1 Chr. 27:20
10. Kohathite Levite during Hezekiah's
reign........................... 2 Chr. 29:12
11. Son of Nebo; divorced his
foreign wife ....Ezra 10:43
12. Benjamite overseer under Nehemiah....Neh. 11:9
13. Prophet.............................Joel 1:1

Joel, Book of—*a book of the Old Testament*
Prophecies of:
Predict Pentecost .... Joel 2:28–32
Proclaim salvation in Christ ....Joel 2:32
Portray the universal judgment ......Joel 3:1–16
Picture the eternal age ....Joel 3:17–21

Joelah—*let him help*
David's recruit at Ziklag.............. 1 Chr. 12:7

Joezer—*Yahweh is help*
One of David's supporters at Ziklag ... 1 Chr. 12:6

Jogbehah—*lofty*
Town in Gilead ....Judg. 8:11

Jogli—*exiled*
Father of Bukki, a Danite prince ..... Num. 34:22

Joha—*Yahweh is living*
1. Benjamite............................ 1 Chr. 8:16
2. One of David's mighty men .... 1 Chr. 11:45

Johanan—*Yahweh is gracious*
1. One of David's mighty men.......... 1 Chr. 12:2, 4
2. Gadite captain of David........... 1 Chr. 12:12, 14
3. Father of Azariah the priest .... 1 Chr. 6:10
4. Ephraimite leader .... 2 Chr. 28:12
5. Son of King Josiah.................... 1 Chr. 3:15
6. Son of Careah ....2 Kin. 25:22, 23
   Supports Gedaliah................... Jer. 40:8, 9
   Warns Gedaliah of
      assassination plot............... Jer. 40:13, 14
   Avenges Gedaliah's murder......... Jer. 41:11–15
   Removes Jewish remnant to Egypt against
      Jeremiah's warning............. Jer. 41:16–18
7. Elioenai's son......................... 1 Chr. 3:24
8. Returned exile .... Ezra 8:12
9. Postexilic high priest................. Neh. 12:22
   See Jehohanan

John—*Yahweh has been gracious*
1. Jewish official........................... Acts 4:6
2. Also called Mark .... Acts 12:12, 25
3. John the Baptist .... Matt. 3:1
4. John the apostle .... Matt. 4:21

John the apostle
A. Life of:
   Son of Zebedee; brother of James...... Matt. 4:21
   Fisherman.......................Luke 5:1–11
   Leaves his business for Christ...... Matt. 4:21, 22
   Called to be an apostle .... Matt. 10:2
   One of the inner circle.................Matt. 17:1
   Witnessed the Transfiguration.....Matt. 17:1–13;
      Mark 9:1–13
   Rebuked by Christ......Mark 13:3; Luke 9:54, 55
   Sent to prepare Passover........... Luke 22:8–13
   Close to Jesus at Last Supper...... John 13:23–25
   Went to Gethsemane............ Matt. 26:36–56
   Christ commits His mother to .....John 19:26, 27
   Ran to the tomb .... John 20:2–8
   Met Jesus at Sea of Tiberias........ John 21:1–14
   Witnesses Christ's ascension........ Acts 1:9–13
   With Peter, heals a man .... Acts 3:1–11
   Imprisoned with Peter .... Acts 4:1–21
   With Peter, becomes a missionary... Acts 8:14–25
   Encourages Paul.......................Gal. 2:9
   Exiled on Patmos ....Rev. 1:9
   Wrote a Gospel ....John 21:23–25
   Wrote three epistles........1 John; 2 John; 3 John
   Wrote the Revelation.........Rev. 1:1, 4, 9
B. Described as:
   Uneducated ....Acts 4:13
   Bold ....Acts 4:13
   Intolerant .... Mark 9:38
   Ambitious.......................Mark 10:35–37
   Trustworthy.....................John 19:26, 27
   Humble..............................Rev. 19:10
   Beloved by Jesus .... John 21:20

John the Baptist
A. Life of:
Prophecies:
   Concerning ....Is. 40:3–5
   Fulfilled by...........................Matt. 3:3
   Angel announces birth of........... Luke 1:5–20
   Set apart as Nazirite...... Num. 6:2, 3; Luke 1:15
   Leaps in Elizabeth's womb............ Luke 1:41
   Filled with the Holy Spirit from the
      womb .... Luke 1:15
   Named John...................... Luke 1:60–63
   Prophecy by Zacharias concerning
      his call. .... Luke 1:76–79
   Lives in deserts ....Luke 1:63, 80
   Ministry of, dated ....Luke 3:1–3
   Public confusion.................... Luke 3:15
   Identifies Jesus as the Messiah .....John 1:29–36
   Bears witness to Christ................ John 5:33
   Exalts Christ ....John 3:25–36
   Baptizes Christ .... Matt. 3:13–16
   Doubts............................. Matt. 11:2–6
   Identified with Elijah .... Matt. 11:13, 14
   Public reaction to .... Matt. 11:16–18
   Christ's testimony concerning ..... Matt. 11:9–13
   Considered a prophet .... Matt. 21:26
   Reproves Herod for adultery.......Mark 6:17, 18
   Imprisoned by Herod .... Matt. 4:12
   Beheaded by Herod ....Matt. 14:3–12
B. Described as:
   Fearless .... Matt. 14:3, 4
   Holy.............................. Mark 6:20
   Humble ....John 3:25–31
   Faithful.......................Acts 13:24, 25
   Resourceful ....Matt. 3:4
   Baptism of, insufficient ... Acts 18:24–26; 19:1–5
   Preaching a baptism of repentance ...Luke 3:2–18

John, the Epistles of—*three books of the New
      Testament*
A. 1 John:
   God is light........................ 1 John 1:5–7
   True knowledge ....1 John 2:3, 4
   Love one another .... 1 John 3:11–24
   God is love .... 1 John 4:7–21
   Eternal life .... 1 John 5:13–21
B. 2 John:
   Commandment to love...............2 John 4–6
   Warning against deceit.............. 2 John 7–11
C. 3 John:
   Walking in truth................... 3 John 3, 4
   Service to the brethren .... 3 John 5–8
   Rebuke to Diotrephes .... 3 John 9, 10
   Do good .... 3 John 11, 12

John, the Gospel of—*a book of the New Testament*
   Deity of Christ .... John 1:1–18
   Testimony of the Baptist ....John 1:19–34
   Wedding at Cana .... John 2:1–11
   Samaritan mission .... John 4:1–42
   Feast of Tabernacles .... John 7:1–53
   The Good Shepherd................John 10:1–42

Lazarus raised . . . . John 11:1–57
Priestly prayer . . . . John 17:1–26
Sufferings and glory . . . . John 18:1–20:31
Purpose of . . . . John 20:30, 31

Joiada—*Yahweh knows*
Postexilic high priest . . . . Neh. 12:10, 11, 22
Son banished from priesthood . . . . Neh. 13:28
See Jehoiada

Joiakim—*Yahweh establishes*
Postexilic high priest; son of Jeshua Neh. 12:10–26

Joiarib—*Yahweh contends*
1. Teacher sent by Ezra . . . . Ezra 8:16, 17
2. Postexilic Judahite chief . . . . Neh. 11:5
3. Founder of an order of priests . . . . Neh. 11:10
4. Postexilic priest . . . . Neh. 12:6

> **WORD STUDY**   **JOIN,** *proskollaō* (pros-kol-*lah*-oh). The verb literally means "to stick to" and carries with it the figurative sense "to adhere closely to," "to join someone" (as in Acts 5:36). Besides its use in Acts, the verb describes the feeling of attachment between husband and wife in a marriage relationship (Matt. 19:5; Mark 10:7; Eph. 5:31). (Strong's #4347)

Jokdeam—*anger of the people*
City of Judah . . . . Josh. 15:56

Jokim—*Yahweh raises up*
Judahite . . . . 1 Chr. 4:22

Jokmeam—*let the people arise*
Town of Ephraim . . . . 1 Chr. 6:68
Home of Kohathite Levites . . . . 1 Chr. 6:66, 68
Same as Kibzaim in . . . . Josh. 21:22
Called Jokneam . . . . 1 Kin. 4:12

Jokneam—*let the people inquire*
1. Town near Mt. Carmel . . . . Josh. 12:22
In tribe of Zebulun . . . . Josh. 19:11
Assigned to Levites . . . . Josh. 21:34
2. Town of Ephraim . . . . 1 Kin. 4:12
See Jokmeam

Jokshan—*fowler*
Son of Abraham and Keturah . . . . Gen. 25:1, 2

Joktan—*he will be made small*
A descendant of Shem . . . . Gen. 10:21, 25

Joktheel—*God's reward of victory*
1. Village of Judah . . . . Josh. 15:20, 38
2. Name given by King Amaziah to Sela . . 2 Kin. 14:7

Jonadab—*Yahweh is bounteous*
1. Son of Shimeah; David's nephew . . . . . . 2 Sam. 13:3
Very subtle man . . . . 2 Sam. 13:3–6, 32–36
2. Son of Rechab . . . . Jer. 35:6
Makes Rechabites primitive and
temperate . . . . Jer. 35:5–17
Blessing upon . . . . Jer. 35:18, 19
Opposes idolatry . . . . 2 Kin. 10:15, 16, 23
Called Jehonadab . . . . 2 Kin. 10:15, 23

Jonah—*dove*
1. Son of Amittai . . . . Jon. 1:1
Ordered to go to Nineveh . . . . Jon. 1:2
Flees to Tarshish . . . . Jon. 1:3
Cause of storm; cast into sea . . . . Jon. 1:4–16
Swallowed by a great fish . . . . Jon. 1:17
Prays in fish's belly . . . . Jon. 2:1–9
Vomited onto land . . . . Jon. 2:10
Obeys second order to go to Nineveh . . . Jon. 3:1–10
Grieved at Nineveh's repentance . . . . Jon. 4:1–3
Taught God's mercy . . . . Jon. 4:4–11
Type of Christ's resurrection . . . . . . Matt. 12:39, 40
2. Father of Simon Peter . . . . John 1:42
Peter called Bar-Jonah . . . . Matt. 16:17

Jonah, Book of—*a book of the Old Testament*
1. Jonah's disobedience . . . . Jon. 1:1–3
2. Results of disobedience . . . . Jon. 1:4–17
3. Jonah's prayer and deliverance . . . . Jon. 2:1–10
4. Jonah's message and Nineveh's
repentance . . . . Jon. 3:1–10
5. Jonah's negative reaction . . . . Jon. 4:1–11

Jonan—*Yahweh has been gracious*
Ancestor of Christ . . . . Luke 3:30

Jonathan—*Yahweh has given*
1. Levite; becomes Micah's priest . . . . . . Judg. 17:1–13
Follows Danites to
idolatrous Dan . . . . Judg. 18:3–31
Grandson of Moses (Manasseh) . . . . . . Judg. 18:30
2. King Saul's eldest son . . . . 1 Sam. 14:49
Smites Philistine garrison . . . . 1 Sam. 13:2, 3
Attacks Michmash . . . . 1 Sam. 14:1–14
Saved from his father's vow . . . . . 1 Sam. 14:24–45
Loved David as his own soul . . . . 1 Sam. 18:1
Makes covenant with David . . . . 1 Sam. 18:2–4
Pleads for David's life . . . . 1 Sam. 19:1–7
Warns David of Saul's wrath . . . . . . 1 Sam. 20:1–42
Makes second covenant
with David . . . . 1 Sam. 23:15–18
Killed by Philistines . . . . 1 Sam. 31:2, 8
Mourned by David . . . . 2 Sam. 1:17–27
David provides for his son . . . . 2 Sam. 9:1–8
3. Son of the high priest Abiathar . . . . 2 Sam. 15:27
Remains faithful to David . . . . 2 Sam. 15:26–36
Brings David Absalom's plans . . . . 2 Sam. 17:15–22
Informs Adonijah of
David's choice . . . . 1 Kin. 1:41–49
4. Son of Shimea . . . . 2 Sam. 21:21, 22
5. One of David's mighty men . . . . 2 Sam. 23:32
6. Judahite . . . . 1 Chr. 2:32, 33
7. Son of Kareah . . . . Jer. 40:8, 9
8. Scribe . . . . Jer. 37:15, 20
9. Opponents of Ezra's reforms . . . . Ezra 10:15
10. Descendant of Adin . . . . Ezra 8:6
11. Levite of Asaph's line . . . . Neh. 12:35
12. Head of a priestly house . . . . Neh. 12:14
13. Postexilic high priest . . . . Neh. 12:11

Joppa—*beauty*
Allotted to Dan . . . . Josh. 19:40, 46

Seaport city . . . . 2 Chr. 2:16
Center of commerce. . . . . .Ezra 3:7
Scene of Peter's vision . . . . Acts 10:5–23, 32

Jorah—*rain*
Family of returnees . . . . .Ezra 2:18
Called Hariph . . . . Neh. 7:24

Jorai—*rainy*
Gadite chief. . . . . 1 Chr. 5:13

Joram, Jehoram—*Yahweh is exalted*
1. Son of Toi, king of Hamath. . . . . 2 Sam. 8:10
   Called Hadoram. 1 Chr. 18:10
2. Levite . . . . 1 Chr. 26:25
3. Son of Ahab, king of Israel . . . . .2 Kin. 3:1
   Institutes some reforms . . . . 2 Kin. 3:2, 3
   Joins Judah against Moab . . . . .2 Kin. 3:1–27
   Slain by Jehu . . . . 2 Kin. 9:14–26
   Called Jehoram. . . . . 2 Kin. 1:17
4. Priest sent to teach the people . . . . 2 Chr. 17:8
5. Son and successor of Jehoshaphat, king
     of Judah . . . . 2 Kin. 8:16
   Murders his brothers. . . . . .2 Chr. 21:1–4
   His wife, Ahab's daughter, leads him
     astray . . . . 2 Kin. 8:17, 18
   Edomites revolt against . . . . 2 Chr. 21:8–10
   Unable to withstand invaders . . . . .2 Chr. 21:16, 17
   Elijah's prophecy against . . . . 2 Chr. 21:12–15
   Dies horribly without mourners. . 2 Chr. 21:18–20
   Called Jehoram. . . . . .2 Chr. 21:1, 5
   See Jehoram

Jordan—*the descender; a river in Palestine*
Canaan's eastern boundary . . . . Num. 34:12
Lot dwells near .Gen. 13:8–13
Jacob crosses . . . . Gen. 32:10
Moses forbidden to cross . . . . Deut. 3:27
Israel crosses miraculously. . . . . .Josh. 3:1–17
Stones commemorate crossing of. . . . .Josh. 4:1–24
David crosses in flight. . . . . 2 Sam. 17:22, 24
Divided by Elijah . . . . 2 Kin. 2:5–8
Divided by Elisha . . . . .2 Kin. 2:13, 14
Despised by foreigners . . . . .2 Kin. 5:10, 12
Naaman healed in . . . . .2 Kin. 5:10, 14
John's baptism in . . . . Matt. 3:6
Christ baptized in. . . . . Matt. 3:13–17

Jorim—*Yahweh is exalted*
Ancestor of Christ . . . . .Luke 3:29

Jorkoam
Judahite family name . . . . .1 Chr. 2:44
May be same as Jokdeam in . . . . .Josh. 15:56

Jose
Ancestor of Christ . . . . .Luke 3:29

Joseph—*may He (Yahweh) add*
1. Son of Jacob by Rachel . . . . .Gen. 30:22–24
   Tribe of, 12,000 sealed . . . . .Rev. 7:8
2. Father of one of the spies . . . . .Num. 13:7
3. Son of Asaph . . . . 1 Chr. 25:2, 9
4. One who divorced his foreign wife . . . Ezra 10:32, 42
5. Preexilic ancestor of Christ. . . . . Luke 3:30

6. Priest in the days of Joiakim . . . . .Neh. 12:14
7. Postexilic ancestor of Christ . . . . Luke 3:26
8. Son of Mattathiah, in Christ's
     ancestry . . . . .Luke 3:24, 25
9. Husband of Mary, Jesus' mother . . . . Matt. 1:16
   Of Davidic lineage . . . . Matt. 1:20
   Angel explains Mary's
     condition to. . . . . Matt. 1:19–25
   With Mary at Jesus' birth. . . . . Luke 2:16
   Names child Jesus. . . . . Matt. 1:25
   Obeys Old Testament ordinances . . Luke 2:21–24
   Takes Jesus and Mary to Egypt. . . . . Matt. 2:13–15
   Returns to Nazareth with family . . . Matt. 2:19–23
   Attends Passover in Jerusalem . . . . . .Luke 2:41, 42
   Jesus subject to . . . . .Luke 2:51
   Referred to as a carpenter . . . . Matt. 13:55
10. Man of Arimathea. . . . . .John 19:38
    Devout man .Luke 23:50, 51
    Secret disciple . . . . John 19:38
    Obtains Christ's body;
      prepares it . . . . Mark 15:43, 46
    Receives Nicodemus's help. . . . . . . .John 19:39, 40
    Puts Christ's body in his new tomb . . . .Luke 23:53
11. Called Barsabas; one of two chosen to
      occupy Judas's place . . . . Acts 1:22–26

Joseph—*increaser*
A. Life of:
   Jacob's son by Rachel. . . . . Gen. 30:22–25
   Jacob's favorite . . . . Gen. 37:3
   Aroused his brothers' hatred. . . . . Gen. 37:4
   His prophetic dreams . . . . .Gen. 37:5–11
   Sold into Egypt . . . . Gen. 37:25–30
   His death faked. . . . . .Gen. 37:31–33
   In Potiphar's house . . . . .Gen. 39:1–19
   In prison . . . . Gen. 39:20–40:23
   Interprets Pharaoh's dream. . . . . .Gen. 41:1–37
   Made Pharaoh's prime minister . . . Gen. 41:38–46
   Marries Pharaoh's daughter Asenath . . . Gen. 41:45
   Two sons born—Manasseh and
     Ephraim. . . . . Gen. 41:50–52
   Joseph's plan for plentiful years . . . Gen. 41:47–49
   Joseph's plan for lean years . . . . Gen. 41:54–57
   Recognizes his brothers . . . . .Gen. 42:1–8
   Reveals his identity . . . . .Gen. 45:1–16
   Invites Jacob to Egypt. . . . . .Gen. 45:17–28
   Acquires Egypt's wealth
     for Pharaoh . . . . Gen. 47:13–26
   Put under oath by Jacob . . . . Gen. 47:28–31
   His sons blessed by Jacob . . . . .Gen. 48:1–22
   Blessed by Jacob . . . . Gen. 49:22–26
   Mourns his father's death. . . . . .Gen. 50:1–14
   Deals kindly with his brothers . . . . Gen. 50:15–21
   His death at 110 . . . . Gen. 50:22–26
   His body carried to Canaan for burial . . . Ex. 13:19;
     Josh. 24:32
   Descendants of . . . . Num. 26:28–37
B. Character of:
   Spiritually sensitive . . . . Gen. 37:2
   Honorable . . . . Gen. 39:2–20

Wise and prudent................ Gen. 41:38–49
Of strong emotions .... Gen. 43:29–31
Sees God's hand in human events .... Gen. 45:7, 8
Forgiving .... Gen. 50:19–21
Man of faith...................... Heb. 11:22

Joses—*increaser*
1. One of Christ's brothers.............. Matt. 13:55
2. The name of Barnabas .... Acts 4:36

Joshah—*Yahweh's gift*
Simeonite leader................. 1 Chr. 4:34, 38

Joshaphat—*Yahweh has judged*
1. Mighty man of David .... 1 Chr. 11:43
2. Priestly trumpeter .... 1 Chr. 15:24

Joshaviah—*Yahweh is equality*
One of David's mighty men.......... 1 Chr. 11:46

Joshbekashah—*he returns a hard fate*
Head of musical order........... 1 Chr. 25:4, 24

Josheb-Basshebeth—*one who sat on the seat*
Chief of David's mighty men .... 2 Sam. 23:8
Called Jashobeam................... 1 Chr. 11:11

Joshibiah—*Yahweh causes to dwell (in peace)*
Simeonite .... 1 Chr. 4:35

Joshua, Jeshua—*Yahweh is salvation*
1. Native of Beth Shemesh .... 1 Sam. 6:14, 18
2. Governor of Jerusalem during
   Josiah's reign .... 2 Kin. 23:8
3. High priest during Zerubbabel's
   time .... Hag. 1:1, 12, 14
   Called Jeshua in Ezra and Nehemiah .... Ezra 2:2;
   Neh. 7:7
   Type of Christ.................... Zech. 6:11–13
   Zechariah's vision concerning .... Zech. 3:1–9
4. Son of Nun....................... Num. 13:8, 16
   See Jeshua 4

Joshua—*Yahweh saves*
A. Life of:
   Defeats Amalek .... Ex. 17:8–16
   Minister under Moses.................. Ex. 24:13
   One of the spies.............. Num. 13:1–3, 8, 16
   Reports favorably................. Num. 14:6–10
   Moses' successor................ Num. 27:18–23
   Inspired by God .... Num. 27:18
   Unifies the people .... Josh. 1:10–18
   Sends spies out .... Josh. 2:1–24
   Crosses Jordan.................... Josh. 3:1–17
   Circumcision of males at Gilgal........ Josh. 5:1–9
   Meets Commander of the Lord's
   army .... Josh. 5:14, 15
   Destroys Jericho.................. Josh. 6:1–27
   Sun stands still;
   Amorites defeated............ Josh. 10:12–14
   Conquers Canaan.................... Josh. 10–12
   Divides the land .... Josh. 13–19
   Establishes cities of refuge.......... Josh. 20:1–9
   Orders Israel's leaders.............. Josh. 23:1–16
   Farewell address to the nation ..... Josh. 24:1–28

Dies at 110 .... Josh. 24:29, 30
Called Hoshea.................... Num. 13:8, 16
B. Character of:
   Courageous .... Num. 14:6–10
   Emotional........................ Josh. 7:6–10
   Wise military man................ Josh. 8:3–29
   Easily beguiled .... Josh. 9:3–27
   Prophetic .... Josh. 6:26, 27
   Strong religious leader .... Judg. 2:7

Joshua, Book of—*a book of the Old Testament*
   Entering Promised Land.......... Josh. 1:1–5:12
   The divine Commander.......... Josh. 5:13–6:5
   Capture of Jericho .... Josh. 6:6–27
   Capture of Ai..................... Josh. 8:1–29
   Apportionment of the land ..... Josh. 13:1–22:34
   Covenant at Shechem .... Josh. 24:1–28
   Death of Joshua................. Josh. 24:29–33

Josiah—*Yahweh heals*
1. Son and successor of Amon,
   king of Judah.................. 2 Kin. 21:25, 26
   Crowned at 8; reigns righteously
   31 years........................ 2 Kin. 22:1
   Named before birth .... 1 Kin. 13:1, 2
   Repairs the temple .... 2 Kin. 22:3–9
   Receives the Book of the Law .... 2 Kin. 22:10–17
   Saved from predicted doom...... 2 Kin. 22:18–20
   Reads the Law.................... 2 Kin. 23:1, 2
   Makes a covenant.................. 2 Kin. 23:3
   Destroys idolatry .... 2 Kin. 23:4, 20, 24
   Observes the Passover........... 2 Kin. 23:21–23
   Exceptional king................. 2 Kin. 23:25
   Slain in battle.................. 2 Chr. 35:20–24
   Lamented by Jeremiah .... 2 Chr. 35:25–27
   Commended by Jeremiah.......... Jer. 22:15–18
   Ancestor of Christ .... Matt. 1:10, 11
2. Son of Zephaniah..................... Zech. 6:10

Josiphiah, Ben- Yahweh will increase
   Father of a postexilic Jew .... Ezra 8:10

Jot—*Greek iota (i); Hebrew yod (y)*
   Figurative of the smallest detail....... Matt. 5:18

Jotbah—*pleasantness*
   City of Haruz, the father of
   Meshullemeth................. 2 Kin. 21:19

Jotbathah—*pleasantness*
   Israelite encampment .... Num. 33:33; Deut. 10:7

Jotham—*Yahweh is perfect*
1. Gideon's (Jerubbaal's) youngest son ...... Judg. 9:5
   Escapes Abimelech's massacre .... Judg. 9:5, 21
   Utters a prophetic parable .... Judg. 9:7–21
   Sees his prophecy fulfilled........ Judg. 9:22–57
2. Son and successor of Azariah (Uzziah),
   king of Judah.................... 2 Kin. 15:5, 7
   Reign of, partly good........... 2 Kin. 15:32–38
   Conquers Ammonites............. 2 Chr. 27:5–9
   Contemporary of Isaiah and Hosea........ Is. 1:1
   Ancestor of Christ .... Matt. 1:9
3. Son of Jahdai....................... 1 Chr. 2:47

Journey—*an extended trip*

Preparation for, by:

    Prayer . . . . .Rom. 1:10

    God's providence acknowledged . . . .James 4:13–17

> **WORD STUDY**   **JOY (LAUD, CHEERING IN TRI-UMPH)**, *rinnah* (rin-*naw*). *Rinnah* is a noun that indicates a ringing cry and is translated "joy." Occasionally the word appears in an entreaty or supplication to God as it does in Jer. 7:16 where God tells Jeremiah that he is not to "lift up a cry" for the people. Also, rarely, the term shows up in a proclamation form as in 1 Kin. 22:36. Most often the cry is one of joy, especially those cries in praise of God, such as found in 2 Chr. 20:22; Is. 35:10; 51:11. In Zeph. 3:17 it is God who is rejoicing over Israel. (Strong's #7440)

Joy—*gladness of heart*

A. Kinds of:

    Foolish. . . . . .Prov. 15:21

    Temporary . . . . Matt. 13:20

    Motherly. . . . . .Ps. 113:9

    Figurative. . . . . Is. 52:9

    Future . . . . Matt. 25:21, 23

B. Described as:

    Everlasting. . . . . .Is. 51:11

    Great . . . . .Acts 8:8

    Full. . . . . .1 John 1:4

    Abundant. . . . . 2 Cor. 8:2

    Unspeakable . . . . .1 Pet. 1:8

C. Causes of:

    Victory . . . . 1 Sam. 18:6

    Christ's birth . . . . .Luke 2:10, 11

    Christ's resurrection . . . . Matt. 28:7, 8

    Sinner's repentance . . . . .Luke 15:5, 10

    Miracles among the Gentiles. . . . . .Acts 8:7, 8

    Forgiveness. . . . . .Ps. 51:8, 12

    God's Word . . . . .Jer. 15:16

    Spiritual discovery. . . . . Matt. 13:44

    Names written in heaven . . . . .Luke 10:17, 20

    True faith . . . . .1 Pet. 1:8

    Right answer . . . . .Prov. 15:23

D. Place of, in:

    Prayer . . . . Is. 56:7

Christian:

    Fellowship . . . . Phil. 1:25

    Tribulation. . . . . .2 Cor. 7:4–7

    Giving . . . . 2 Cor. 8:2

E. Contrasted with:

    Weeping . . . . .Ezra 3:12, 13; Ps. 30:5

    Tears . . . . .Ps. 126:5

    Sorrow. . . . . Is. 35:10

    Mourning. . . . . .Jer. 31:13

    Pain . . . . .John 16:20, 21

    Loss . . . . .Heb. 10:34; 13:17

    Adversity . . . . Eccl. 7:14

    Discipline . . . . .Ps. 51:8; Heb. 12:11

    Persecution. . . . . Luke 6:22, 23

F. Of angels:

    At creation . . . . Job 38:4, 7

    At Christ's birth . . . . Luke 2:10, 13, 14

    At sinner's conversion . . . . .Luke 15:10

G. Expressed by:

    Songs . . . . Gen. 31:27

    Musical instruments . . . . 1 Sam. 18:6

    Sounds. . . . . .1 Chr. 15:16

    Praises. . . . . .2 Chr. 29:30

    Shouting . . . . Ezra 3:12, 13

    Heart. . . . . 1 Kin. 21:7

See Gladness; Happiness of the saints

> **WORD STUDY**   **JOYFUL**, *sameach* (saw-*may*-akh). The adjective *sameach* describes someone who is "joyful," "blithe," or "gleeful," and is one of several words translated this way. After anointing Solomon king (1 Kin. 1:45), Zadok the priest and Nathan the prophet were rejoicing so loudly that the whole city came to be in an uproar. In Deut. 16:15, at the Feast of Tabernacles, *sameach* is used for the people showing thankfulness to the Lord. Sometimes the adjective is used as a noun to indicate the ones who rejoice (Prov. 2:14; Amos 6:13). In at least one case, the term is used for one taking malicious joy in the calamity of others (Prov. 17:5). (Strong's #8056)

Jozabad—*Yahweh has bestowed*

1, 2, 3. Three of David's mighty men . . . 1 Chr. 12:4, 20

4. Levite overseer in Hezekiah's reign . . . 2 Chr. 31:13

5. Chief Levite in Josiah's reign . . . . 2 Chr. 35:9

6. Levite, son of Jeshua . . . . Ezra 8:33

    Probably the same as in. . . . . Ezra 10:23

7. Expounder of the Law. . . . . .Neh. 8:7

8. Levitical chief . . . . .Neh. 11:16

    Some consider 6, 7, 8 the same person

9. Priest who divorced his foreign wife. . . . .Ezra 10:22

Jozachar—*Yahweh has remembered*

    Assassin of Joash . . . . 2 Kin. 12:19–21

    Called Zabad. . . . . .2 Chr. 24:26

Jozadak—*Yahweh is righteous*

    Postexilic priest. . . . . .Ezra 3:2

Jubal—*playing*

    Son of Lamech. . . . . Gen. 4:21

Jubilee, Year of

A. Regulations concerning:

    Introduced by trumpet . . . . .Lev. 25:9

    After 49 years . . . . .Lev. 25:8

    Rules for fixing prices. . . . . . .Lev. 25:15, 16, 25–28

B. Purposes of:

    Restore liberty (to the enslaved). . . .Lev. 25:38–43

    Restore property (to the original

        owner). . . . . Lev. 25:23–28

    Remit debt (to the indebted) . . . . Lev. 25:47–55

    Restore rest (to the land) . . . .Lev. 25:11, 12, 18–22

C. Figurative of:

    Christ's mission . . . . Is. 61:1–3

    Earth's jubilee . . . . Rom. 8:19–24

Judah—*let Him (God) be praised*

1. Son of Jacob and Leah. . . . . Gen. 29:15–35

WORD STUDY **JUDGE**, *shaphat* (shaw-*fat*). To "judge" or "pronounce sentence" is indicated by the use of the verb *shaphat*. Both humans and God can fulfill the actions of lawgiving and deciding controversies. In Gen. 18:25 God is judging Sodom. Moses is a particularly well-known example of a human who executed law and decided controversies. "To judge" can also mean to execute judgment. The judgment might include vindicating a person as God does in Ps. 10:18 or delivering one as in 1 Sam. 24:16. Humans can vindicate or seek justice for others (Is. 1:17, 23). Alternatively, condemning and punishing might be the way in which the judgment is carried out. (Strong's #8199)

WORD STUDY **JUDGE**, *krinō* (*kree*-no). In legal contexts this verb is a technical term, which means literally "to judge." The NT reflects the various uses of the word common in the first century; for example, it can refer to being put on trial (Acts 25:10), going to court (1 Cor. 6:6; cf. Matt. 5:40), rendering a decision or judgment (John 18:31), especially with emphasis on an unfavorable verdict that leads to punishment or condemnation (Acts 13:27). Frequently, *krinō* is used in association with God's "judging" of humanity (Heb. 10:30; 1 Pet. 4:5; Rev. 18:8). The word is used figuratively to apply to judgments a person passes on others (Matt. 7:1, 2), especially in con-demnation (Rom. 2:1–3), or to cognitive acts involving an evaluative decision, deliberation, or consideration (Luke 7:43; Acts 4:19; 13:46; 1 Cor. 10:15). (Strong's #2919)

King acts as ....2 Sam. 15:2;
  1 Kin. 3:9, 28
Jehoshaphat established court .... 2 Chr. 19:5–11
Levites assigned .... 1 Chr. 23:1–4
Restored after exile ....Ezra 7:25
B. Procedure before:
  Public trial ....Ex. 18:13
  Case presented .... Deut. 1:16; 25:1
  Position of parties ....Zech. 3:1
  Accused heard........................ John 7:51
  Witness........................ Deut. 19:15–19
  Priests .... Deut. 17:8–13
  Oath.....................Ex. 22:11; Heb. 6:16
  Casting of lots sometimes used........ Prov. 18:18
  Divine will sought .... Lev. 24:12–14
C. Office of:
  Divinely instituted...................2 Sam. 7:11
  Limits to human affairs .... 1 Sam. 2:25
  Restricted by righteousness.......Deut. 16:18–20
  Needful of great wisdom .... 1 Kin. 3:9
  Easily corrupted ....Mic. 7:3
  Unjustly used.................Acts 23:3; 25:9–11
  Fulfilled perfectly in the Messiah ....Is. 2:4;
    11:3, 4; Acts 17:31

Judge, God as
Manner of:
  According to righteousness........... 1 Pet. 2:23
  According to one's works ....1 Pet. 1:17
  Openly..............................Rom. 2:16
  By Christ.........................John 5:22, 30
  In a final way.....................Joel 3:12–14

Judges of Israel
A. Characteristics of era:
  No central authority ....Judg. 17:6; 21:25
  Spiritual decline ....Judg. 2:16–18; 18:1–31
B. List of:
  Othniel .... Judg. 3:9–11
  Ehud............................Judg. 3:15–30
  Shamgar ....Judg. 3:31
  Deborah .... Judg. 4:4–9
  Gideon........................Judg. 6:11–40
  Abimelech .... Judg. 9:1–54
  Tola ....Judg. 10:1, 2
  Jair .... Judg. 10:3–5
  Jephthah ....Judg. 12:1–7
  Ibzan .... Judg. 12:8–10
  Elon ....Judg. 12:11, 12
  Abdon .... Judg. 12:13–15
  Samson ....Judg. 15:20
  Eli......................... 1 Sam. 4:15, 18
  Samuel.........................1 Sam. 7:15
  Samuel's sons..................... 1 Sam. 8:1–3

Judges, Book of—*a book of the Old Testament*
  The death of Joshua.............. Judg. 2:6–10
  Deborah and Barak ....Judg. 4:1–5:31
  Gideon........................Judg. 6:1–8:32
  Jephthah .... Judg. 10:6–11:40
  Samson ....Judg. 13:1–16:31

Micah and the Danites ....Judg. 18
The war against Benjamin.......Judg. 19:1–21:25

WORD STUDY **JUDGMENT, JUSTICE,** *mishpat* (mish-pawt). The noun *mishpat,* meaning "judgment" or "justice," is a derivative of the verb that is translated "judge." Judgment is sometimes the verdict of a case that has been decided. Frequently "justice" is an attribute of the judges. In some cases the judge is God, and justice is an inherent part of God's character (Is. 30:18). At other times justice is something God loves (Ps. 33:5) and demands of His people (Mic. 6:8). For humans, justice is an attribute of the righteous (Ps. 37:30). The term used for "justice" can also indicate a judge's ordinance, such as the Levitical ordinances or divine law. It can also indicate a legal right or privilege (Deut. 18:3; Jer. 32:7). An unusual use of the word is in describing the custom or manner in which something is done (Gen. 40:13; 1 Sam. 2:13). (Strong's #4941)

WORD STUDY **JUDGMENT,** *krisis* (kree-sis). This noun is a legal technical term meaning "judgment" (see the cognate verb *krinō* in the topical word study: "judge"). *Krisis* can refer to a local "court" (Matt. 5:21, 22), but the most common use of the word in the NT is with reference to God's or Christ's acting as judge, particularly on the Last Day or the Day of Judgment (Matt. 10:15; 11:22, 24; 2 Pet. 2:9; 1 John 4:17). *Krisis* can emphasize negative verdicts (John 3:19) or the punishment (Matt. 23:33). It can also mean "right" in the sense of "justice" or "righteousness" (Matt. 12:18; 23:23). (Strong's #2920)

Judgment, divine
A. Design of:
  Punish evil ....Ex. 20:5
  Chasten........................ 2 Sam. 7:14, 15
  Manifest God's righteousness........ Ex. 9:14–16
  Correct .... Hab. 1:12
  Warn others......................Luke 13:3, 5
B. Causes of:
  Disobedience.................... 2 Chr. 7:19–22
  Rejecting God's warnings ....2 Chr. 36:16, 17
  Idolatry...........................Jer. 7:30–34
  Sins of rulers ....2 Chr. 21:1–17
  Loving evil .... Rom. 1:18–32
C. Kinds of:
  Physical destruction ....Deut. 28:15–68
  Material loss...................... Mal. 3:11
  Spiritual blindness.................... Is. 6:9, 10
  Eternal destruction .....Luke 12:16–21; 16:19–31
D. Avoidance of, by:
  Turning to God.................... Deut. 30:1–3
  Turning from sin .... Jer. 7:3–7
  Humiliation........................Jon. 1:1–17
  Prayer .... 2 Kin. 19:14–36; 2 Chr. 20:5–30
  Refraining from judging others ...... Matt. 7:1, 2;
    Rom. 2:1–3

Judgment, Hall of
   Of Solomon . . . . 1 Kin. 7:1, 7

Judgment, human
A. Weaknesses of:
   Often circumstantial. . . . . Josh. 22:10–34
   Sometimes wrong. . . . . Gen. 39:10–20
   Hasty and revengeful . . . . .1 Sam. 25:20–35
   Full of conceit .Esth. 5:11–14
   Prejudicial . . . . Luke 7:38–50
B. Rules regarding:
   Begin with self-judgment . . . . Matt. 7:1–5
   Become spiritually minded . . . . . . .1 Cor. 2:12–15
   Abound in love . . . . Phil. 1:9, 10
   Await the final judgment . . . . .Rom. 14:10
C. Basis of:
   Circumstance . . . . Gen. 39:10–20
   Opinion. . . . . Acts 28:22
   Moral law . . . . Rom. 2:14–16
   Conscience. . . . . 1 Cor. 10:27–29
   Nature. . . . . .1 Cor. 11:13, 14
   Apostolic authority . . . . 1 Cor. 5:3, 4
   Law of Christ. . . . . Gal. 6:2–4
   Divine illumination. . . . . .Josh. 7:10–15

Judgment, the Last
A. Described as:
   Day of wrath . . . . .Rom. 2:5
   Day of judgment. . . . . .2 Pet. 3:7
B. Time of:
   After death. . . . . Heb. 9:27
   At Christ's return . . . . Matt. 25:31
   Appointed day. .Acts 17:31
C. Grounds of:
   One's works . . . . .1 Cor. 3:11–15
   One's faith . . . . Matt. 7:22, 23
   Conscience. . . . . .Rom. 2:12, 14–16
   Law. . . . . .Rom. 2:12
   Gospel . . . . James 2:12
   Christ's Word . . . . John 12:48
   Book of Life . . . . Rev. 20:12, 15
D. Results of:
   Separation of righteous from the
      wicked . . . . Matt. 13:36–43
   Retribution for disobedience . . . . .2 Thess. 1:6–10
   Crown of righteousness . . . . 2 Tim. 4:8
E. Attitudes toward:
   Be prepared for . . . . .1 Thess. 5:1–9
   Beware of deception . . . . Matt. 7:21–27
   Warn the wicked concerning. . . . . . .2 Cor. 5:10, 11

Judith—*Jewess*
   Hittite wife of Esau . . . . .Gen. 26:34
   Called Aholibamah . . . . Gen. 36:2

Julia—*feminine form of Julius*
   Christian woman at Rome. . . . . .Rom. 16:15

Julius—*the family name of the Caesars*
   Roman centurion assigned to guard
      Paul. . . . . Acts 27:1, 3
   Disregards Paul's warning . . . . .Acts 27:11
   Accepts Paul's warning. . . . . Acts 27:31

   Saves Paul's life . . . . Acts 27:42–44

Junia—*a kinsman of Paul*
   Jewish Christian at Rome. . . . . .Rom. 16:7

Juniper—*a shrub of the broom family*
   Symbolic of devastation . . . . Jer. 48:6

Jushab-Hesed—*kindness returned*
   Son of Zerubbabel . . . . .1 Chr. 3:20

Just, justice—*integrity of character*
A. Descriptive of:
   Righteous man . . . . Gen. 6:9
   Upright Gentile. . . . . Acts 10:22
   God's nature . . . . Deut. 32:4
   Promised Messiah . . . . .Zech. 9:9
   Christ. . . . . .Acts 3:14
   Saved . . . . Heb. 12:23
B. Produced by:
   True wisdom . . . . Prov. 8:15
   Parental instruction. . . . . Gen. 18:19
   True faith . . . . Heb. 10:38
See Injustice

Justification—*accounting the guilty just before God*
A. Negatively considered, not by:
   The Law . . . . Rom. 3:20, 28
   Human righteousness. . . . . Rom. 10:1–5
   Human works . . . . Rom. 4:1–5
   Faith mixed with works. . . .Acts 15:1–29; Gal. 2:16
   A dead faith .James 2:14–26
B. Positively considered, by:
   Grace. . . . . Rom. 5:17–21
Christ:
   Blood. . . . . .Rom. 5:9
   Resurrection .Rom. 4:25
   Righteousness. . . . . .Rom. 10:4
   Faith. . . . . Rom. 3:26, 27
C. Produces:
   Forgiveness of sins . . . . Acts 13:38, 39
   Peace . . . . .Rom. 5:1
   Holiness . . . . Rom. 6:22
   Imputed righteousness . . . . 2 Cor. 5:21
   Outward righteousness. . . . . .Rom. 8:4
   Eternal life . . . . .Titus 3:7
   Glorification . . . . .Rom. 8:30
D. Evidence of:
   Works (by faith) . . . . James 2:18
   Wisdom . . . . James 3:17
   Patience. . . . . James 5:7, 8
   Suffering. . . . . .James 5:10, 11
See Imputation

WORD STUDY **JUSTIFY,** *dikaioō* (dik-ah-*yah*-oh). The central meaning of this verb is "to justify" in the sense of "to treat as just" or "vindicate" (Matt. 11:19). It can be used with respect to self-justification (Luke 10:29; 16:15). In the NT *dikaioō* is used almost exclusively of God's judgment of a person as "just" or "righteous" (*dikaios*), thus, when *dikaioō* functions as a term to describe God's activity it means "to be pronounced and treated as righteous" and is usually translated as "to justify" (Rom. 8:33). Similarly, God may be "pronounced righteous" (Luke 7:29; 1 Tim. 3:16). A person's "being justified" is closely associated with God's forgiveness of sins (Acts 13:38, 39; Rom. 3:23, 24), His grace (Rom. 3:24), and a person's faith (according to Paul, Rom. 3:28; Gal. 2:16; 3:11) or works (James 2:24). (Strong's #1344)

Justus—*righteous*
1. Surname of Joseph......................Acts 1:23
2. Man of Corinth; befriends Paul.........Acts 18:7
3. Converted Jew..........................Col. 4:11

Juttah—*extended*
Town of Judah.......................Josh. 15:55
Assigned to the priests...........Josh. 21:13, 16

Juvenile delinquents
A. Examples of:
     Eli's sons.......................1 Sam. 2:12–17
     Samuel's sons....................1 Sam. 8:1–5
     Elisha's mockers.................2 Kin. 2:22–24
B. Safeguards against:
     Praying mother...................1 Sam. 1:9–28
     Strict discipline....................Prov. 13:24
     Early training ....Prov. 22:6

K

Kab—*a hollow vessel*
Jewish measure; about 2 quarts.......2 Kin. 6:25

Kabzeel—*God's gathering*
Town in south Judah.................Josh. 15:21
Benaiah's hometown..............2 Sam. 23:20
Called Jekabzeel....................Neh. 11:25

Kadesh—*holy*
Location of.........................Num. 27:14
Captured by Chedorlaomer.........Gen. 14:5–7
Hagar flees near...................Gen. 16:7, 14
Abraham dwells here.................Gen. 20:1
Spies sent from...................Num. 13:3, 26
Israel rebels here.................Num. 14:1–45
Miriam buried here..................Num. 20:1
Moses strikes rock here...........Num. 20:1–13
Messengers from, request passage
     through Edom..............Num. 20:14–22
Figurative of God's power..............Ps. 29:8
Boundary in the new Israel..........Ezek. 47:19

Kadesh Barnea—*another name for Kadesh*
Boundary of Promised Land.......Num. 34:1–4
Extent of Joshua's military campaign...Josh. 10:41

Kadmiel—*God is the Ancient One*
1. Levite family head; returns
     from Babylon.......................Ezra 2:40
2. Takes part in rebuilding..................Ezra 3:9
Participates in national repentance....Neh. 9:4, 5

Kadmonites—*easterners*
Tribe whose land Abraham is to
     inherit......................Gen. 15:18, 19

Kallai—*smith*
Postexilic priest....................Neh. 12:1, 20

Kanah—*place of reeds*
1. Brook between Ephraim and Manasseh...Josh. 16:8
2. Border town of Asher.................Josh. 19:28

Kaph
Eleventh letter of Hebrew alphabet. Ps. 119:81–88

Karkaa—*floor, ground*
Place in south Judah..................Josh. 15:3

Karkor—*even ground*
Place in east Jordan..................Judg. 8:10

Karnaim—*two peaks*
Conquered..........................Amos 6:13

Kartah—*city*
Levitical town in Zebulun...........Josh. 21:34

Kartan—*town*
Town in Naphtali assigned to Levites...Josh. 21:32
Called Kirjathaim...................1 Chr. 6:76

Kattath—*little*
Town of Zebulun................Josh. 19:15, 16
Same as Kitron.......................Judg. 1:30

Kedar—*dark*
Son of Ishmael..................Gen. 25:12, 13
Skilled archers........................Is. 21:17
Prophecy against.................Jer. 49:28, 29
Inhabit villages.......................Is. 42:11
Famous for flocks......................Is. 60:7
Tents of, called dark..................Song 1:5

Kedemah—*toward the east*
Ishmaelite tribe.....................Gen. 25:15

Kedemoth—*ancient places*
City east of the Jordan assigned to the
     tribe of Reuben...............Josh. 13:15, 18
Assigned to Merarite Levites......Josh. 21:34, 37
Messengers sent from................Deut. 2:26

Kedesh—*sacred place*
1. Town in south Judah...............Josh. 15:23
2. City of Issachar assigned to
     Gershonite Levites................1 Chr. 6:72
     Called Kishion...................Josh. 19:20
3. Canaanite town taken by Joshua and
     assigned to Naphtali..............Josh. 12:22
     Called Kedesh in Galilee...........Josh. 20:7
     Called Kedesh in Naphtali..........Judg. 4:6
     City of refuge..................Josh. 21:27, 32
     Home of Barak......................Judg. 4:6
     People of, carried captive.........2 Kin. 15:29

 WORD STUDY **KEEP A FEAST**, *chagag* (khaw-*gag*). The actions of "keeping a feast" or "making a pilgrim-feast" are indicated by the verb *chagag*. Some of the feasts, such as Passover and the Feast of Booths, were proposed by Moses. The term can also be used generally for any religious feasts as it is in Nah. 1:15. Many of the feasts indicated by this word were celebrated by a sacred procession and dances. This leads to the less common use of the word meaning "behave as at a feast." David found the Amalekites behaving in this manner because of the great spoil they "had taken from the land of the Philistines and from the land of Judah" (1 Sam. 30:16). This behavior can include reeling from festival excesses. (Strong's #2287)

KEEP UNDER GUARD, *phroureō* (froo-*reh*-oh). This verb literally means "to keep under guard" (see 2 Cor. 11:32). In the NT it is used figuratively to mean "to guard," "to protect," "to keep" with respect to God's protective care (Phil. 4:7; 1 Pet. 1:5). Paul may have this same meaning in mind when he speaks of believers as being "kept under guard by the law" before faith came, or he may use *phroureō* to mean "to hold in custody," "to confine" (Gal. 3:23). (Strong's #5432)

Keeper—*one who watches over, or guards*
Guardian of:
Sheep	Gen. 4:2
Brother	Gen. 4:9
Wardrobe	2 Kin. 22:14
Gate	Neh. 3:29
Door	1 Chr. 9:21
Women	Esth. 2:3, 8
Prison	Acts 16:27

Keeping—*holding or observing something firmly*
A. Christian objects of:
Christ's commandments	John 14:15–23
God's commandments	1 John 5:2
God's Word	Rev. 22:7, 9
Unity of the Spirit	Eph. 4:3
Faith	2 Tim. 4:7
Purity	1 Tim. 5:22
Oneself	1 John 5:18
In God's love	Jude 21

B. Manner of, by God's:
Power	John 10:28, 29
Name	John 17:11, 12

C. Promises respecting:
Provision	Ps. 121:3–8
Preservation	John 17:11, 12
Power	Rev. 2:26
Purity	Rev. 16:15

See Heart

Kehelathah—*assembly*
Israelite camp ....Num. 33:22, 23

Keilah—*enclosed*
Town of Judah ....Josh. 15:21, 44
Rescued from Philistines
   by David .... 1 Sam. 23:1–5
Betrays David ....1 Sam. 23:6–12
David escapes from .... 1 Sam. 23:13
Reoccupied after the Exile .... Neh. 3:17

Kelaiah—*Yahweh is light*
Levite who divorced
   foreign wife ....Ezra 10:18, 19, 23
See Kelita

Kelita—*dwarf*
Levite who divorced foreign wife ...... Ezra 10:23
Explains the Law .... Neh. 8:7
Called Kelaiah .... Ezra 10:23

Kemuel—*congregation of God*
1. Son of Nahor; father of six sons ..... Gen. 22:20, 21
2. Ephraimite prince .... Num. 34:24
3. Levite in David's time .... 1 Chr. 27:17

Kenath—*possession*
City of Gilead near Bozrah taken by
   Nobah ....Num. 32:40, 42
Reconquered by Geshur and Syria
   (Aram) .... 1 Chr. 2:23

Kenaz—*side, flank*
1. Descendant of Esau .... Gen. 36:10, 11
2. Edomite chief .... Gen. 36:42
3. Caleb's brother; father of Othniel ....Josh. 15:17
   Family called Kenizzites .... Num. 32:12
4. Grandson of Caleb .... 1 Chr. 4:15

Kenezzite
1. Canaanite tribe whose land is promised
   to Abraham's seed ....Gen. 15:19
2. Title applied to Caleb ....Num. 32:12
   Probably related to Kenaz, the
   Edomite .... Gen. 36:11–42

Kenites—*pertaining to coppersmiths*
Canaanite tribe whose land is promised
   to Abraham's seed .... Gen. 15:19
Subjects of Balaam's prophecy ... Num. 24:20–22
Mix with Midianites .... Num. 10:29
Member of, becomes
   Israel's guide ....Num. 10:29–32
Settle with Judahites .... Judg. 1:16
Heber separates from Kenites ....Judg. 4:11
Spared by Saul in war
   with Amalekites .... 1 Sam. 15:6
David shows friendship to .... 1 Sam. 30:29
Recorded among Judahites; ancestors
   of Rechabites .... 1 Chr. 2:55

Keren-Happuch—*horn of eye paint*
Daughter of Job .... Job 42:14

Kerioth—*cities*
1. Town in south Judah .... Josh. 15:25
2. City of Moab .... Amos 2:2

Keros—*bent*
Head of a Nethinim family returning
   from exile .... Ezra 2:44

Kettle—*pot*
Large cooking vessel .... 1 Sam. 2:14
Same word rendered "baskets" .... Ps. 81:6

Keturah—*incense*
Abraham's second wife .... Gen. 25:1

Sons of:
 Listed........................... Gen. 25:1, 2
 Given gifts and sent away............. Gen. 25:6

Key—*a small instrument for unlocking doors*
A. Used literally for:
 Doors...........................Judg. 3:25
B. Used figuratively of:
 Prophetic authority of Christ .... Is. 22:22
 Present authority of Christ ....Rev. 1:18
 Complete authority of
  Christ's apostles................ Matt. 16:19
 Knowledge........................Luke 11:52

Keziah—*cassia*
 Daughter of Job...................... Job 42:14

Kibroth Hattaavah—*graves of lust*
 Burial site of Israelites slain
  by God ....Num. 11:33–35

Kibzaim—*double heap*
 Ephraimite city assigned to Kohathite
  Levites ....Josh. 21:22
 Called Jokmeam.....................1 Chr. 6:68
 See Jokmeam

Kid—*a young goat*
A. Used for:
 Food............................... Gen. 27:9
 Payment ....Gen. 38:17–23
 Sacrifices.........................Lev. 4:23
 Offerings ....Judg. 13:15, 19
 Festive occasions ....Luke 15:29
B. Figurative of:
 Weakness ....Judg. 14:6
 Peacefulness.........................Is. 11:6
 See Goat

Kidnappers—*those who seize others by unlawful force*
 Condemned by law...................1 Tim. 1:10

Kidnapping
A. Punishment for:
 Death..............................Ex. 21:16
B. Examples of:
 Joseph .... Gen. 37:23–28
 Daughters of Shiloh.............Judg. 21:20–23
 Joash ....2 Kin. 11:1–12
 Jeremiah ....Jer. 43:1–8

Kidneys
 Select internal organs of an animal... Ex. 29:13, 22
 Translated "wheat" .... Deut. 32:14

Kidron—*dark, turbid*
 Brook (dry except for winter torrents)
  near Jerusalem ....John 18:1
 East boundary of Jerusalem........... Jer. 31:40
 Crossed by David and by Christ.....2 Sam. 15:23;
  John 18:1
 Site of dumping of idols ....2 Chr. 29:16

Killing—*causing life to cease*
A. Instances of, to:
 Take another's wife .... Gen. 12:12

Take another's property .... 1 Kin. 21:19
Life for life ....Ex. 21:23
Take revenge ....Gen. 27:42
Satisfy anger ....Num. 22:29
Satisfy hatred.........................John 5:18
Execute God's wrath ....Num. 31:2, 16–19
Destroy people ....Ex. 1:16
Seize a throne ....2 Kin. 15:25
Put down rebellion...................1 Kin. 12:27
Fulfill prophecy ....1 Kin. 16:1–11
For fear of punishment............... Acts 16:27
Get rid of an unwanted person .... Matt. 21:38
B. Reasons against:
 God's Law............................Ex. 20:13
Regard for:
 Life................................ Gen. 37:21
 One's position .... 1 Sam. 11; 24:10
C. Of Christians:
 In God's hand ....Luke 12:4, 5
 Result of persecution................. Matt. 24:9
 Time will come ....John 16:2
 Under the Antichrist.............Rev. 11:7; 13:15

Kinah—*lamentation*
 Village in south Judah................Josh. 15:22

WORD STUDY **KIND, GOOD,** *chrēstos* (khrace-*toss*). Adjective meaning literally "useful," "suitable," "worthy," "good." It can be used to describe morally "good" habits (1 Cor. 15:33), Jesus' yoke as "easy" (Matt. 11:30), or to make a comparative evaluation of old wine as "better" (Luke 5:39). *Chrēstos* can be used to exhort persons to be "good," "kind," or "benevolent" (Eph. 4:32), but in the NT this sense of the word applies mainly to God (Luke 6:35; 1 Pet. 2:3) or, as a substantive, to His "kindness" (Rom. 2:4). (Strong's #5543)

WORD STUDY **KINDNESS,** *philanthrōpia* (fil-an-throh-*pee*-ah). This noun means "love for humanity" or "(loving)kindness." Early on the word applied to the gods' benevolence to humans, and this is the sense in which it is used in Titus 3:4 to speak of the *philanthrōpia* of "God our Savior." Acts 28:2 tells of the "kindness" (or "hospitality") extended by the natives of Malta to Paul and the other victims of a shipwreck. (Strong's #5363)

Kindness—*a friendly attitude toward others*
A. Kinds of:
 Extraordinary .... Acts 28:2
 Acquired............................Col. 3:12
 Developed ....Prov. 31:26
 Commended .... 2 Cor. 6:6
 Divine .... Neh. 9:17
B. Of God:
 Great .... Neh. 9:17
 Everlasting........................... Is. 54:8
 Shall not depart....................... Is. 54:10
 Manifested........................ Ps. 31:21

Through Christ. . . . . Eph. 2:7
Results in salvation . . . . Titus 3:4–7
C. Manifestation of:
Rewarded . . . . 1 Sam. 15:6
Recalled . . . . 2 Sam. 2:5, 6
Rebuffed. . . . . .2 Sam. 3:8
Remembered . . . . 2 Sam. 9:1–7
Refused. . . . . 2 Sam. 10:1–6

Kindred—*one's family connections*
Manifestation of:
Felt with great emotion. . . . . Esth. 8:6
Through faith . . . . Josh. 6:23
By gospel. . . . . Acts 3:25; Rev. 14:6

King, Christ as
A. Old Testament prophecy:
Judah's tribe. . . . . Gen. 49:10
With a scepter . . . . Num. 24:15–17
David's lineage . . . . 2 Sam. 7:1–29
On David's throne . . . . Ps. 132:11, 12; Is. 9:6, 7;
Jer. 33:17
Divine origin . . . . Is. 9:6, 7
In righteousness . . . . Is. 11:1–5
At God's appointed time . . . . Ezek. 21:27
Will endure forever . . . . Dan. 2:44
To be born in Bethlehem . . . . Mic. 5:2, 3
As Priest-King. Zech. 6:9–15
Having salvation. .Zech. 9:9
He is coming . . . . Mal. 3:1–5
B. Christ's right to rule, determined by:
Divine decree. . . . . .Ps. 2:6, 7
Prophecy. . . . . .Ps. 45:6, 7
Birth. . . . . Is. 9:6, 7
Being seated at God's right hand . . . . . Ps. 16:8–11;
110:1, 2; Acts 2:34–36
Crowning . . . . Zech. 6:11–15
C. Described as:
Eternal. . . . . .Rev. 11:15
Spiritual . . . . .John 18:36, 37

Kingdom of God
A. Described as, of:
God . . . . .Mark 1:15
Heaven . . . . .Matt. 3:2
Christ and God. . . . . .Eph. 5:5
Not for immoral or impure person . . . . . . .Eph. 5:5
Their Father. . . . . Matt. 13:43
My Father's. . . . . Matt. 26:29
His dear Son . . . . .Col. 1:13
B. Special features of:
Gospel of. . . . . Matt. 24:14
Word of. . . . . Matt. 13:19
Mysteries of . . . . Mark 4:10–13
C. Entrance into, by:
New birth. . . . . .John 3:1–8
Granted. . . . . .Luke 22:29
Divine call . . . . 1 Thess. 2:12
Repentance . . . . .Matt. 3:2
D. Members of:
Seek it first . . . . Matt. 6:33

Suffer tribulation . . . . Acts 14:22
Preach it . . . . .Acts 8:12
Pray for it . . . . Matt. 6:10
Work in. . . . . .Col. 4:11
E. Nature of:
Spiritual . . . . .Rom. 14:17
Eternal. . . . . .2 Pet. 1:11

Kings, earthly
A. Some characteristics of:
Over a specific nation . . . . .Ex. 1:8
Desired by people. . . . . 1 Sam. 8:5, 6
Under God's control . . . . .Dan. 4:25, 37
Rule by God's permission. . . . . .Dan. 2:20, 21
Subject to temptations . . . 2 Sam. 11:1–5; Prov. 31:5
Good . . . . .2 Kin. 22:1, 2
Evil. . . . . .2 Kin. 21:1–9
B. Position of before God, by God:
Chosen . . . . 1 Chr. 28:4–6
Anointed. . . . . 1 Sam. 16:12
Removed and established. . . . . Dan. 2:21
Rejected . . . . .1 Sam. 15:10–26
C. Duties of:
Make covenants . . . . Gen. 21:22–32
Read Scriptures. .Deut. 17:19
Make war . . . . 1 Sam. 11:5–11
Pardon. . . . . .2 Sam. 14:1–11; 19:18–23
Judge . . . . .2 Sam. 15:2
Govern righteously . . . . 2 Sam. 23:3, 4
Keep the Law. . . . . 1 Kin. 2:3
Make decrees. . . . . Dan. 3:1–6, 29

King's Garden—*a garden of Jerusalem*
Near a gate . . . . 2 Kin. 25:4
By the Pool of Shelah. . . . . Neh. 3:15

King's Highway—*an important passageway connecting
Damascus and Egypt*
Use of, requested. . . . . Num. 20:17

Kings of ancient Israel
A. Over the United Kingdom:
Saul. . . . . 1 Sam. 11:15–31:13
David. . . . . 2 Sam. 2:4–1 Kin. 2:11
Solomon . . . . .1 Kin. 1:39–11:43
B. Over Israel (the northern kingdom):
Jeroboam (22 yrs.) . . . . 1 Kin. 12:20–14:20
Nadab (2 yrs.) . . . . 1 Kin. 15:25–27, 31
Baasha (24 yrs.). . . . . .1 Kin. 15:28–34; 16:1–7
Elah (2 yrs.) . . . . 1 Kin. 16:8–14
Zimri (7 days) .1 Kin. 16:15
Omri (12 yrs.) . . . . 1 Kin. 16:23–28
Ahab (22 yrs.) . . . . 1 Kin. 16:29–22:40
Ahaziah (2 yrs.). . . . . 1 Kin. 22:51–53
Jehoram (Joram)(12 yrs.) . . . . .2 Kin. 3:1–9:26
Jehu (28 yrs.) . . . . 2 Kin. 9:2–10:36
Jehoahaz (17 yrs.). . . . . .2 Kin. 13:1–9
Jehoash (Joash) (16 yrs.) . . . . 2 Kin. 13:10–25
Jeroboam II (41 yrs.) . . . . 2 Kin. 14:23–29
Zechariah (6 mos.) . . . . 2 Kin. 15:8–12
Shallum (1 mo.). . . . . 2 Kin. 15:13–15
Menahem (10 yrs.) . . . . 2 Kin. 15:16–22

Kings, Books of—*two books of the Old Testament*

Kingship of God—*the position of God as sovereign ruler of the universe*

Kinsman—*close relative, next of kin*

Kir—*wall*

Kirjath—*city*

Kirjathaim—*twin cities*

Kirjath Arba—*city of Arba, or fourfold city*

Kirjath Jearim—*city of forests*

Kirjath Sannah—*city of destruction*

Kirjath Sepher—*city of books*

Kish—*bow*

Kishi—*snarer*

Kishion—*hardness*

Kishon—*bending*

Kiss—*a physical sign of affection*

Separation .... Acts 20:37
Reunions........................... Luke 15:20
Great joy........................... Luke 7:38, 45
Blessing.................... Gen. 48:10–16
Anointings........................ 1 Sam. 10:1
Reconciliation....................... Gen. 33:4
Death............................... Gen. 50:1
B. Figurative of:
Complete:
Submission to evil .... Hos. 13:2
Submission to God.................... Ps. 2:12
Reconciliation....................... Ps. 85:10
Utmost affection .... Song 1:2
C. Kinds of:
Deceitful............ 2 Sam. 20:9, 10; Luke 22:48
Insincere............................2 Sam. 15:5
Fatherly............................ Gen. 27:26, 27
Friendship .... Ex. 18:7; 1 Sam. 20:41
Esteem..................... 2 Sam. 19:32, 39
Sexual love .... Gen. 29:11; Song 1:2
Illicit love .... Prov. 7:13
False religion .... 1 Kin. 19:18; Hos. 13:2
Holy love............... Rom. 16:16; 1 Cor. 16:20

Kite—*a bird of the falcon family*
Ceremonially unclean............. Lev. 11:12–14

Kithlish—*a man's wall*
Town of Judah..................... Josh. 15:1, 40

Kitron—*shortened, little*
Town in Zebulun .... Judg. 1:30

Kittim
The island of Cyprus; inhabited by descendants of
Japheth (through Javan) .... Gen. 10:4

Kneading—*mixing elements together*
Part of food process.................. Gen. 18:6
In making cakes to be used in idol
worship............................ Jer. 7:18

Kneading bowl—*used for kneading dough*
Covered with frogs...................... Ex. 8:3
Carried out of Egypt .... Ex. 12:33, 34

Knee
A. Place of weakness, due to:
Terror .... Dan. 5:6
Fasting........................... Ps. 109:24
Disease .... Deut. 28:35
Lack of faith...................... Is. 35:3
B. Lying upon:
Sign of true parentage or adoption ..... Gen. 30:3
Place of affectionate play .... Is. 66:12
Place of sleep .... Judg. 16:19
C. Bowing of:
Act of:
Respect .... 2 Kin. 1:13
False worship...................... 1 Kin. 19:18
True worship .... Rom. 14:11
D. Bowing of, in prayer:
Solomon .... 2 Chr. 6:13, 14
Ezra .... Ezra 9:5

Daniel .... Dan. 6:10
Christ........................... Luke 22:41
Stephen...................... Acts 7:59, 60
Peter............................ Acts 9:40
Paul .... Acts 20:36
Christians........................... Acts 21:5

Knife—*a sharp instrument for cutting*
A. Used for:
Slaying animals................... Gen. 22:6–10
Circumcision...................... Josh. 5:2, 3
Dismembering a body............... Judg. 19:29
B. Figurative of:
Inordinate appetite .... Prov. 23:2
Cruel oppressors..................... Prov. 30:14

Knob—*an ornament*
Round protrusions on lampstand.... Ex. 25:31–36

Knock—*to rap on a door*
Rewarded .... Luke 11:9, 10
Expectant........................... Luke 12:36
Disappointed................... Luke 13:25–27
Unexpected .... Acts 12:13, 16
Invitation .... Rev. 3:20

WORD
STUDY
KNOW, *yada'* (yaw-*dah*). In Gen. 3, when
Eve wanted to know good and evil, the
verb *yada'* is used. The term is applied to
both God and humans and can mean "to perceive,"
which means to observe and thereby gain knowledge
(Gen. 19:33). It can also mean "to distinguish" or "dis-
criminate," which is indicated in 2 Sam. 19:36. In Josh.
3:10 the word means "knowing by experience." In other
contexts the term means "to know" or "to be acquainted
with" a person. It is used in a negative form when God's
people are commanded to have no knowledge of other
gods or strange lands. The positive use is seen when
God knows a person, including his or her heart. The
word can also mean "to know sexually" (Gen. 4:1).
(Strong's #3145)

WORD
STUDY
KNOW, *ginōskō* (ghin-*ohs*-koh). This verb
occurs frequently in the NT. Its base
meaning is "to know," but translations
may range from "learn of," "understand," "comprehend," "perceive," to "recognize" in order to capture the
nuance of the context. John uses the word to speak of
the "knowledge" of God and Jesus Christ (17:3) and
other intensely close relationships (as in 10:27). *Ginōskō*
is also used as a euphemism for sexual relations (Matt.
1:25; Luke 1:34). (Strong's #1097)

WORD
STUDY
KNOW COMPLETELY, *epiginōskō* (ep-
ig-in-*ohs*-koh). The main meanings of
this verb are "to know" and "to recog-
nize" (as in Matt. 7:16, 20). In some instances *epiginosko*
is emphatic, meaning "to know exactly," "to know
completely" (as in Luke 1:4; Col. 1:6; 2 Cor. 6:9).
Epiginōskō can also mean "to acknowledge" (Matt.

17:12), "to learn of" (Mark 6:33), "to perceive" (Luke 5:22), or "to understand" (2 Cor. 1:13). (Strong's #1921)

Knowledge

A. Kinds of:

Natural	Matt. 24:32
Deceptive	Gen. 3:5
Sinful	Gen. 3:7
Personal	Josh. 24:31
Practical	Ex. 36:1
Intuitive	1 Sam. 22:22
Intellectual	John 7:15, 28
Saving	John 17:3
Spiritual	1 Cor. 2:14
Revealed	Luke 10:22

B. Sources of:

God	Ps. 94:10
Nature	Ps. 19:1, 2
Scriptures	2 Tim. 3:15
Doing God's will	John 7:17

C. Believer's attitude toward:

Not to be puffed up	1 Cor. 8:1
Should grow in	2 Pet. 3:18
Should add to	2 Pet. 1:5
Not to be forgetful of	2 Pet. 3:17
Not to be rejected	Hos. 4:6
Accept our limitations of	1 Cor. 13:8–12
Be filled with	Phil. 1:9

D. Christ's, of:

God	Luke 10:22
Human nature	John 2:24, 25
Human thoughts	Matt. 9:4
Believers	John 10:14, 27
Things future	2 Pet. 1:14
All things	Col. 2:3

E. Attitude of unrighteous toward:

Turn from	Rom. 1:21
Ignorant of	1 Cor. 1:21
Raised up against	2 Cor. 10:5
Did not acknowledge God	Rom. 1:28
Never able to come to	2 Tim. 3:7

F. Value of:

Superior to gold	Prov. 8:10
Increases strength	Prov. 24:5
Keeps from destruction	Is. 5:13
Insures stability	Is. 33:6

Koa

People described as enemies of Jerusalem	Ezek. 23:23

Kohath—*assembly*

Second son of Levi	Gen. 46:8, 11
Goes with Levi to Egypt	Gen. 46:11
Brother of Jochebed, mother of Aaron and Moses	Ex. 6:16–20
Dies at age 133	Ex. 6:18

Kohathites—*descendants of Kohath*

A. History of:

Originate in Levi's son (Kohath)	Gen. 46:11
Divided into 4 groups (Amram, Izehar, Hebron, Uzziel)	Num. 3:19, 27
Numbering of	Num. 3:27, 28
Duties assigned to	Num. 4:15–20
Cities assigned to	Josh. 21:4–11

B. Privileges of:

Aaron and Moses	Ex. 6:20
Special charge of sacred instruments	Num. 4:15–20
Temple music by Heman the Kohathite	1 Chr. 6:31–38
Under Jehoshaphat, lead in praise	2 Chr. 20:19
Under Hezekiah, help to cleanse temple	2 Chr. 29:12, 15

C. Sins of:

Korah (of Izhar) leads rebellion	Num. 16:1–35; Jude 11

Kolaiah—*voice of Yahweh*

1. Father of the false prophet Ahab	Jer. 29:21–23
2. Postexilic Benjamite family	Neh. 11:7

Korah—*baldness*

1. Son of Esau	Gen. 36:5, 14, 18
2. Son of Eliphaz and grandson of Esau	Gen. 36:16
3. Calebite	1 Chr. 2:42, 43
4. Son of Izhar the Kohathite	Ex. 6:21, 24
Leads a rebellion against Moses and Aaron	Num. 16:1–3
Warned by Moses	Num. 16:4–27
Supernaturally destroyed	Num. 16:28–35
Sons of, not destroyed	Num. 26:9–11
Sons of, gatekeepers	1 Chr. 26:19

Korahites

Descendants of Korah	Ex. 6:24

Some become:

David's warriors	1 Chr. 12:6
Servants	1 Chr. 9:19–31
Musicians	1 Chr. 6:22–32
A Contemplation of	Ps. 42 (Title)

Kore—*a partridge*

1. Korahite Levite	1 Chr. 9:19
2. Keeper of the eastern gate	2 Chr. 31:14

Koz—*thorn*

Father of Anub	1 Chr. 4:8

See Hakkoz

Kushaiah—*bow of Yahweh (that is, rainbow)*

Merarite Levite musician	1 Chr. 15:17
Called Kishi	1 Chr. 6:44

L

Laadah—*festival*

Judahite	1 Chr. 4:21

Laadan

1. Son of Gershon, the son of Levi	1 Chr. 23:7–9
Called Libni	1 Chr. 6:17
2. Ephraimite	1 Chr. 7:26

Laban—*white*
1. Son of Bethuel.....................Gen. 24:24, 29
    Brother of Rebekah ....Gen. 24:15, 29
    Father of Leah and Rachel........... Gen. 29:16
    Approves of Rebekah as bride for
        Isaac .... Gen. 24:29–60
    Entertains Jacob ....Gen. 29:1–14
    Deceives Jacob in marriage
        arrangement .... Gen. 29:15–30
    Agrees to Jacob's business
        arrangement .... Gen. 30:25–43
    Changes attitude toward Jacob....... Gen. 31:1–9
    Pursues fleeing Jacob ....Gen. 31:21–25
    Rebukes Jacob.................... Gen. 31:26–30
    Searches for stolen gods .... Gen. 31:30–35
    Rebuked by Jacob.................Gen. 31:31–42
    Makes covenant with Jacob....... Gen. 31:43–55
2. City in the wilderness.................. Deut. 1:1

Labor—*physical or mental effort*
A. Physical:
Nature of:
    As old as creation .... Gen. 2:5, 15
    Ordained by God ....Gen. 3:17–19
    One of the commandments.............Ex. 20:9
    From morning until night ....Ps. 104:23
    With the hands................... 1 Thess. 4:11
    To life's end .... Ps. 90:10
    Without God, vanity.................. Eccl. 2:11
    Shrinking from, denounced......... 2 Thess. 3:10
Benefits of:
    Profit...........................Prov. 14:23
    Happiness.........................Ps. 128:2
    Proclaim gospel..................... 1 Thess. 2:9
    Supply of other's needs ..... Acts 20:35; Eph. 4:28
    Restful sleep......................... Eccl. 5:12
    Double honor.......................1 Tim. 5:17
    Eternal life ....John 6:27
    Not in vain.............. 1 Cor. 15:58; Phil. 2:16
B. Spiritual:
Characteristics of:
    Commissioned by Christ .... John 4:38
    Accepted by few .... Matt. 9:37, 38
    Working with God.................... 1 Cor. 3:9
    By God's grace....................... 1 Cor. 15:10
    Result of faith .... 1 Tim. 4:10
    Characterized by love .... 1 Thess. 1:3
    Done in prayer.......................Col. 4:12
    Subject to discouragement......Is. 49:4; Gal. 4:11
    Interrupted by Satan .... 1 Thess. 3:5
    See Work, the Christian's
C. Problems:
    Inspired by opposition .... Ezra 4:1–6
    Complaint over wages............ Matt. 20:1–16
    Mistreatment of employees .... Matt. 21:33–35
    Characteristic of last days ....James 5:1–6

Labor (childbirth)
A. Of a woman's, described as:
    Fearful............................Ps. 48:6
    Painful.............................. Is. 13:8

    Hazardous ....Gen. 35:16–19
    Joyful afterwards .... John 16:21
B. Figurative of:
    New Israel............................ Is. 66:7, 8
    Messiah's birth .... Mic. 4:9, 10
    Redemption..........................Mic. 5:3
    New birth...........................Gal. 4:19
    Creation's rebirth ....Rom. 8:22

Lachish
    Town in south Judah ....Josh. 15:1, 39
    Joins coalition against Gibeonites....Josh. 10:3–5
    Defeated by Joshua............... Josh. 10:6–33
    Fortified by Rehoboam.............2 Chr. 11:5, 9
    City of sin.........................Mic. 1:13
    Amaziah murdered here............ 2 Kin. 14:19;
      2 Chr. 25:27
    Taken by Sennacherib........... 2 Kin. 18:13–17
    Military headquarters............ Is. 36:1, 2; 37:8
    Fights against Nebuchadnezzar .... Jer. 34:1, 7
    Reoccupied after exile................ Neh. 11:30

Lack—*something still needed*
A. How to avoid:
    Remember God's promises ....Deut. 2:7
    Work diligently................1 Thess. 4:11, 12
    Live chastely ....Prov. 6:32
    Seek the Lord....................... Ps. 34:10
    Share in common .... Acts 4:34
    Obey .... Amos 4:6
B. Things subject to:
    Food............................. 2 Sam. 3:29
    Physical needs ....2 Chr. 8:14; 2 Cor. 11:9
    Possessions..................... 1 Sam. 30:19
    Service to others .... Phil. 2:30
    Entire commitment ....Luke 18:22
    Wisdom .... James 1:5
    Graces ....2 Pet. 1:9
    Faith............................ 1 Thess. 3:10
    See Want

Lad—*a young boy*
    Heard by God ....Gen. 21:17–20
    Saved by God........................ Gen. 22:12
    Loved by his father.............. Gen. 44:22–34
    Slain with Samson ....Judg. 16:26–30
    Unsuspecting...................1 Sam. 20:21–41
    Tattling.........................2 Sam. 17:18
    Providing .... John 6:9

Ladder
    Jacob's .... Gen. 28:10–12

Lady
    Applied to females of high rank ....Judg. 5:29
    Among royalty .... Esth. 1:18
    Elect............................. 2 John 1, 5
    Figurative of Babylon .... Is. 47:5–7

Lael—*belonging to God*
    Gershonite Levite................... Num. 3:24

Lahad—*oppression*
    Judahite............................1 Chr. 4:2

Lahai Roi—*of the Living One who sees me*
Name of a well . . . . Gen. 16:7, 14
Same as Beer Lahai Roi . . . . Gen. 24:62

Lahmas—*place of light*
City of Judah . . . . Josh. 15:1, 40

Lahmi—*Bethlehemite*
Brother of Goliath slain by Elhanan . . . 1 Chr. 20:5

Laish—*lion*
1. Benjamite . . . . 1 Sam. 25:44
2. City in north Palestine at the head of
   the Jordan . . . . Judg. 18:7, 14
   Called Leshem . . . . Josh. 19:47
3. Village in Benjamin between Anathoth
   and Gallim . . . . Is. 10:30

Lake
Sea of Galilee is called . . . . Luke 5:1, 2; 8:22–33
Bottomless pit described as . . . . Rev. 19:20

Lake of fire—*the place of final punishment*
A. Those consigned to:
   The Beast and False Prophet . . . . Rev. 19:20
   The devil . . . . Rev. 20:10
   Death and hell . . . . Rev. 20:14
   Those whose names are not in Book
      of Life . . . . Rev. 20:15
B. Described as:
   Burning brimstone . . . . Rev. 19:20
   Second death . . . . Rev. 20:14

Lakkum—*obstruction*
Town of Naphtali . . . . Josh. 19:32, 33

Lama—*the Aramaic for "why"*
Spoken by Christ on the cross . . . . Matt. 27:46

Lamb—*a young sheep*
A. Used for:
   Food . . . . 2 Sam. 12:4
   Clothing . . . . Prov. 27:26
   Trade . . . . Ezra 7:17
   Tribute . . . . 2 Kin. 3:4
   Covenants . . . . Gen. 21:28–32
   Sacrifices . . . . Ex. 12:5
B. Figurative of:
   God's people . . . . Is. 5:17
   Weak believers . . . . Is. 40:11
   God's ministers . . . . Luke 10:3
   Messiah's reign . . . . Is. 11:6

Lamb of God, the (Christ)
A. Descriptive of Christ as:
   Prophesied . . . . Is. 53:7
   Presented to Israel . . . . John 1:29
   Our Passover sacrifice . . . . 1 Cor. 5:7
   Preached to world . . . . Acts 8:32–35
   Leader of 144,000 . . . . Rev. 14:1–5
   Praised throughout eternity . . . . Rev. 5:6, 13
B. Descriptive of Christ as:
   Sacrifice . . . . 1 Pet. 1:19; Rev. 7:13, 14
   Redeemer . . . . Rev. 5:9
   King . . . . Rev. 15:3

Lame, lameness—*inability to walk properly*
A. Healing of, by:
   Christ . . . . Matt. 11:5
   Peter . . . . Acts 3:2–7
   Philip . . . . Acts 8:5–7
B. Figurative of:
   Extreme weakness . . . . 2 Sam. 5:6, 8
   Inconsistency . . . . Prov. 26:7
   Weak believers . . . . Jer. 31:8
   The lowly . . . . Is. 35:6
C. Causes of:
   Birth defect . . . . Acts 3:2
   Accident . . . . 2 Sam. 4:4
D. Renders unfit for:
   Priesthood . . . . Lev. 21:17, 18
   Sacrifice . . . . Deut. 15:21
   Active life . . . . 2 Sam. 9:13; 19:24–26

Lamech—*wild man*
1. Son of Methushael, of Cain's race . . . . . Gen. 4:17, 18
   Had two wives . . . . Gen. 4:19
2. Son of Methuselah; father of Noah . . . Gen. 5:25–31
   Man of faith . . . . Gen. 5:29
   In Christ's ancestry . . . . Luke 3:36

Lamed
Twelfth letter of the
   Hebrew alphabet . . . . Ps. 119:89–96

Lamentation—*mournful speeches; elegies; dirges*
A. Historical of:
   Daughters of Israel over daughter of
      Jephthah . . . . Judg. 11:29–40
   Jeremiah over Josiah . . . . 2 Chr. 35:25
   David over Saul . . . . 2 Sam. 1:17–27
   David over Abner . . . . 2 Sam. 3:33, 34
   Jeremiah over Jerusalem . . . . Lam. 1:1
B. Prophetic of:
   Isaiah over Babylon . . . . Is. 14:1–32
   Jeremiah over Jerusalem . . . . Jer. 7:28–34
   Ezekiel over Tyre . . . . Ezek. 27:2–36
   Christ over Jerusalem . . . . Luke 19:41–44
   Kings over Babylon . . . . Rev. 18:1–24

Lamentations, Book of—*a book of the Old Testament*
The suffering of Zion . . . . Lam. 1:1–2:22
Individual prayer . . . . Lam. 3:1–66
Collective prayer . . . . Lam. 5:1–22

Lamp
A. Used in:
   Tabernacle . . . . Ex. 37:23
   Temple . . . . 1 Chr. 28:15
   Processions . . . . Matt. 25:1–8
B. Figurative of:
   God . . . . 2 Sam. 22:29
   God's Word . . . . Ps. 119:105; Prov. 6:23
   God's justice . . . . Zeph. 1:12
   Conscience . . . . Prov. 20:27
   Prosperity . . . . Job 29:2–6
   Industry . . . . Prov. 31:18
   Death . . . . Job 18:6

Churches..............................Rev. 1:20
Christ...............................Rev. 1:14

Lampstand, the golden
A. Specifications regarding:
    Made of gold ....Ex. 25:31
    After a divine model ....Ex. 25:31–40
    Set in holy place ....Heb. 9:2
    Continual burning of ....Ex. 27:20, 21
    Carried by Kohathites...............Num. 4:4, 15
    Temple's ten branches of.........1 Kin. 7:48–50
    Taken to Babylon ....Jer. 52:19
B. Used figuratively of:
    Christ...........................Zech. 4:2, 11
    The church......................Rev. 1:13, 20

Lance—*a spear*
    Used in war ....Jer. 50:42
    Used by Baal's priests ....1 Kin. 18:28

Landmark—*a boundary marker*
    Removal of, forbidden..............Deut. 19:14

WORD STUDY   **LAND,** *'eretz* (eh-*rets*). "Earth" or "land" is indicated by the use of the noun *'eretz.* At times it means the whole earth as it does in Jer. 25:26. Sometimes the word is used to indicate that which is opposite to heaven as in Gen. 1:1. Other uses include all the inhabitants of the earth. This use is familiar from the story of Noah (Gen. 6:11) where we read that the whole earth was corrupt. When *'eretz* means "land," it describes a country or territory, especially the land of Canaan, which the Israelites were to possess. *'Eretz* can also mean the surface of the land or soil, which is familiar from Gen. 1:26 with its reference to all things that creep on the land. (Strong's #776)

Land of Promise (Canaan)
A. Referred to as:
    The Land of Promise.................Heb. 11:9
    The land of Canaan...............Ezek. 16:3, 29
    The land of the Jews ....Acts 10:39
    The Holy Land ....Zech. 2:12
    "Beulah" ....Is. 62:4
B. Conquest of, by:
    Divine command ....Ex. 23:24
    God's angel ....Ex. 23:20, 23
    Hornets............................Ex. 23:28
    Degrees..........................Ex. 23:29, 30
C. Inheritance of:
    Promised to Abraham's seed ....Gen. 12:1–7
    Awaits God's time ....Gen. 15:7–16
    Boundaries of, specified..........Gen. 15:18–21
    Promise of possession fulfilled....Josh. 21:43–45
    Some kept from...................Deut. 1:34–40
    For the obedient ....Deut. 5:16
    Sin separates from ....Deut. 28:49–68
D. Laws concerning:
    Land allotted to 12 tribes........Num. 26:52–55
    None for priests ....Num. 18:20, 24
    Sale and redemption of...........Lev. 25:15–33
    Transfer of title....................Ruth 4:3–8

Witness of sale ....Ruth 4:9–11
Relieved of debt on ....Neh. 5:3–13
Leased to others ....Matt. 21:33–41
Widow's right in ....Ruth 4:3–9
Rights of unmarried women in..... Num. 27:1–11
Rest of, every seventh year.............Ex. 23:11
E. Original inhabitants of:
    Seven Gentile nations ...... Deut. 7:1; Josh. 24:11
    Mighty............................. Deut. 4:38
    Tall............................... Deut. 9:1, 2
    Mingled with Israel ....Ps. 106:34–38
    Idolatrous........ Ex. 23:23, 24; Deut. 12:29–31
    Corrupt.............. Lev. 18:1–30; Ezek. 16:47

Language—*human means of communication*
A. Kinds of:
    Hebrew ....2 Kin. 18:28
    Chaldean .... Dan. 1:4
    Aramaic ....2 Kin. 18:26
    Egyptian........................... Ps. 114:1
    Arabic ....Acts 2:11
    Greek............................. Acts 21:37
    Latin ....John 19:19, 20
    Lycaonian.........................Acts 14:11
    Medes and Persians ....Esth. 3:12
B. Varieties of:
    Result of confusion (Babel) ....Gen. 11:1–9
    Result of division of Noah's
        three sons................. Gen. 10:5, 20, 31
    Seen in one empire..... Esth. 1:22; Dan. 3:4, 7, 29
    Seen in Christ's inscription ....John 19:19, 20
    Witnessed at Pentecost.............Acts 2.6–12
    Evident in heaven ....Rev. 5:9
See Tongue

Lantern—*an enclosed lamp*
    Used by soldiers arresting Jesus .... John 18:3

Laodicea—*a chief city of Asia Minor*
    Church of, sharply rebuked............Rev. 1:11
    Epaphras labors here .... Col. 4:12, 13
    Paul writes letter to ....Col. 4:16
    Not visited by Paul.................Col. 2:1; 4:15

Lap
A. As a loose skirt of a garment:
    For carrying objects.................2 Kin. 4:39
    Lots cast into......................Prov. 16:33
B. Use of the tongue to drink:
    For selecting Gideon's army..........Judg. 7:5–7

Lapidoth—*torches*
    Husband of Deborah the prophetess.....Judg. 4:4

Lasea
    Seaport of Crete ....Acts 27:8

Lash—*a punishment imposed with a whip or scourge*
    Rendered "blows"................... Deut. 25:3
    Imposed on Paul
        (rendered "stripes")..............2 Cor. 11:24

Lasha—*bursting forth*
    Boundary town of southeast Palestine . Gen. 10:19

Lasharon—*to Sharon*
Town possessed by Joshua ....Josh. 12:1, 18

Last—*the terminal point*
A. Senses of:
Final consequence ....Prov. 23:32
God .... Is. 44:6
B. Of events, last:
Day (resurrection) ....John 6:39, 40
Day (judgment).......................John 12:48
Days (present age) ....Acts 2:17
Hour (present age) ....1 John 2:18
Times (present age) .... 1 Pet. 1:20
Days (time before Christ's return).....2 Tim. 3:1; 2 Pet. 3:3
Enemy (death)......................1 Cor. 15:26
Time (Christ's return)................1 Pet. 1:5
Trumpet (Christ's return) ....1 Cor. 15:52

Last Supper
At Feast of Unleavened
Bread...............Matt. 26:17; Mark 14:12
Fulfills Passover .... Luke 22:15–18

Latin—*the Roman language*
Used in writing Christ's
inscription...................John 19:19, 20

Lattice—*a framework of crossed wood or metal strips*
Window of Sisera's mother ....Judg. 5:28
Ahaziah fell through ....2 Kin. 1:2
Looked through ....Prov. 7:6

> **WORD STUDY** **LAUGH,** *tsachaq* (tsaw-*khak*). *Tsachaq* is a verb, which is usually translated "laugh." It can mean the act of laughing. Sarah laughs when God tells Abraham that they will have a son (Gen. 18:12–15); in this case laughter is a cynical reaction. In Gen. 21, after Isaac is born, Sarah indicates that laughter now will be done in happiness. *Tsachaq* can also be used to mean "joking" (Gen. 19:14). In some cases "play" is obviously the context as it is in Ex. 32:6. One use, which is perhaps an extension of "play," occurs in Gen. 26:8, which speaks of Isaac caressing Rebekah. (Strong's #6711)

Laughter—*an emotion expressive of joy, mirth, or ridicule*
A. Kinds of:
Divine .... Ps. 59:8
Natural ....Job 8:21
Derisive.............................. Neh. 2:19
Fake...............................Prov. 14:13
Scornful ....2 Chr. 30:10
Confident.......................... Job 5:22
Joyful..............................Ps. 126:2
B. Causes of:
Human folly........................... Ps. 2:4
Something unbelievable...........Gen. 18:12–15
Something untrue .... Matt. 9:24
Ridicule............................2 Chr. 30:10
Highly contradictory.................Ps. 22:7, 8

Laver—*a basin for washing*
Made for the tabernacle ....Ex. 30:18

> **WORD STUDY** **LAW,** *torah* (toh-*raw*). "Direction," "instruction," and "law" are all translations of the noun *torah*. This word is derived from the verb, meaning "to teach" or "to instruct." The meaning of instruction can refer to instruction from either humans or God. In Prov., where human instruction occurs most frequently, are many examples, as in 1:8 where a son is receiving instruction from father and mother. Godly instruction can also be received through His servants (Is. 30:9). Instruction can be an entire body of prophetic or priestly teaching. "Law" can refer to special laws, such as the Sabbath law (Ex. 16:4), or to entire law codes, such as the Ten Commandments or the code of law in Deut. Sometimes, *torah* is used to refer to the entire Pentateuch, the first five books of the OT. (Strong's #8451)

Law—*an authoritative rule of conduct*
Law of man.........................Luke 20:22
Natural law written upon
the heart..................... Rom. 2:14, 15
Law of Moses...................... Gal. 3:17–21
Entire Old Testament ....John 10:34
Expression of God's will........... Rom. 7:2–9
Operating principle ....Rom. 3:27

Law of Moses
A. History of:
Given by God at Sinai .... Ex. 20:1–26
Called a covenant................. Deut. 4:13, 23
Dedicated with blood ....Heb. 9:18–22
Called the Law of Moses........... Josh. 8:30–35
Restated in Deuteronomy .... Deut. 4:44–46
Written on stone.................... Deut. 4:13
Whitewashed stone ....Deut. 27:3–8
Placed in the ark .... Deut. 31:9, 26
Given to Joshua....................Josh. 1:1–9
Repeated by Joshua .... Josh. 23:6–16
Disobeyed by:
Israel ....Judg. 2:10–20
Israel's kings ....2 Kin. 10:31
The Jews..........................Is. 1:10–18
Finding of Book of.............. 2 Chr. 34:14–33
Disobedience to, cause of exile.... 2 Kin. 17:3–41
Read to postexilic assembly..........Neh. 8:1–18
Recalled at close of Old Testament ...... Mal. 4:4
Meaning of, fulfilled by Christ.....Matt. 5:17–48
Pharisees insist on observance of....Acts 15:1–29
B. Purposes of:
Knowledge of sin .... Rom. 3:20
Manifest God's righteousness..........Rom. 7:12
Lead to Christ .... Gal. 3:24, 25
C. Christ's relation to:
Born under..........................Gal. 4:4
Explains proper meaning of...... Matt. 5:17–48; 12:1–14
Redeems sinners from curse of.........Gal. 3:13

Shows fulfillment of, in Himself . . . Luke 24:27, 44; Rom. 10:4

D. Christian's relation to:

Freed from . . . . Acts 15:1–29
Spirit of, fulfilled in love. . . . . Rom. 13:8–10

E. Inadequacies of, cannot:

Make worshiper perfect . . . . Heb. 9:9–15
Justify . . . . Acts 13:38, 39

Lawgiver—*a lawmaker*

Only one . . . . James 4:12
The Lord is . . . . Is. 33:22

Lawlessness—*living outside or contrary to law*

A. Described as:

Wickedness . . . . Acts 2:23
Iniquity . . . . Matt. 13:41
Unrighteousness . . . . 2 Cor. 6:14

B. Features concerning:

Called sin . . . . 1 John 3:4
Incompatible with righteousness . . . . . . 2 Cor. 6:14
Torments the righteous. . . . . Matt. 24:12; 2 Pet. 2:8
Led to Jesus' crucifixion . . . . Acts 2:22, 23
Descriptive of the Antichrist. . . . . . . 2 Thess. 2:7, 8
Scribes and Pharisees full of . . . . . Matt. 23:27, 28
Basis for condemnation . . . . Matt. 7:23
Law made for . . . . 1 Tim. 1:9
Forgiven . . . . Rom. 4:7; Titus 2:14
Forgotten . . . . Heb. 8:12; 10:17

Lawsuits—*suing another for damages*

Between Christians, forbidden. . . . Matt. 5:25, 40;
1 Cor. 6:1–8

Lawyers—*interpreters of the law*

Test Jesus . . . . Matt. 22:34–40
Rejected the will of God . . . . Luke 7:30
Jesus answers one . . . . Luke 10:25–37
Condemned by Jesus . . . . Luke 11:45–52
Zenas, a Christian . . . . Titus 3:13

Lazarus—*God has helped*

1. Beggar described in a parable . . . . . . Luke 16:20–25
2. Brother of Mary and Martha; raised
   from the dead . . . . John 11:1–44
   Attends a supper . . . . John 12:1, 2
   Chief priests seek to kill . . . . John 12:9–11

Laziness

A. Leads to:

Poverty . . . . Prov. 6:9–11
Waste . . . . Prov. 18:9
Loss of all . . . . Matt. 25:26–30

B. Admonitions against:

Make the most of time . . . . Eph. 5:16
Work day and night . . . . 1 Thess. 2:9
Consider the ant . . . . Prov. 6:6–8
No work, no eat. . . . . 2 Thess. 3:10–12

Lead—*a heavy metal*

Purified by fire . . . . Num. 31:22, 23
Engraved with . . . . Job 19:23, 24
Very heavy . . . . Ex. 15:10
Object of trade . . . . Ezek. 27:12

Leader—*a guide*

A. Kinds of:

False . . . . Is. 3:12
Blind . . . . Luke 6:39
Young . . . . Is. 11:6
Safe . . . . Ps. 78:53
Gentle . . . . Is. 40:11
Faithful . . . . Deut. 8:2, 15

B. Used of:

The Lord . . . . Ex. 13:21; Ps. 23:3
Christ . . . . John 10:3
The Lamb . . . . Rev. 7:17
The Spirit . . . . Luke 4:1; Gal. 5:18
Hananiah . . . . Neh. 7:2
Tribal heads . . . . Num. 2:3, 5

C. Course of, in:

God's truth . . . . Ps. 25:5
Righteousness . . . . Ps. 5:8
Way you should go . . . . Is. 48:17
Unknown ways . . . . Is. 42:16
Smooth path . . . . Ps. 27:11
Everlasting way . . . . Ps. 139:24

Leaf, leaves

Status of floodwaters indicated by . . . . . . Gen. 8:11
Trees . . . . Matt. 21:19

League—*an agreement between two or more parties*

Fraudulent . . . . Josh. 9:3–6
Forbidden . . . . Judg. 2:2
Secret . . . . 1 Sam. 22:8
Conditional . . . . 2 Sam. 3:12, 13
Acceptable . . . . 2 Sam. 3:21
Unifying . . . . 2 Sam. 5:1–3
International . . . . 1 Kin. 5:12
Purchased . . . . 1 Kin. 15:18–21
Deceitful . . . . Dan. 11:23

Leah—*a wild cow*

Laban's eldest daughter . . . . Gen. 29:16, 17
By Laban's deceit, becomes Jacob's
   wife . . . . Gen. 29:19–27
Unloved by Jacob . . . . Gen. 29:30–33
Mother of seven children . . . . Gen. 30:19–21
Buried in Machpelah's cave . . . . Gen. 49:30, 31
Builder of house of Israel . . . . Ruth 4:11

Leaping—*to spring or bound forward suddenly*

A. Used physically of:

Insects . . . . Joel 2:5
Men . . . . 1 Kin. 18:26
Unborn child . . . . Luke 1:41, 44
Lame man . . . . Acts 3:8

B. Expressive of:

Great joy . . . . 2 Sam. 6:16
Renewed life . . . . Is. 35:6
Victory in persecution . . . . Luke 6:22, 23

Learning—*knowledge acquired through experience or*
instructions

A. Aspects of:

God's statutes . . . . Ps. 119:71, 73
Righteousness . . . . Is. 26:9, 10

Good works . . . . Titus 3:14
Obedience . . . . Heb. 5:8
B. Objects of:
Abominable things . . . . Deut. 18:9
Heathen ways . . . . Deut. 18:9; Ps. 106:35
Fear of the Lord . . . . Deut. 14:23; 17:19; 31:13
C. Sources of:
Experience . . . . Gen. 30:27
Worldly knowledge . . . . John 7:15
Christian experience . . . . Phil. 4:11
Scriptures . . . . Rom. 15:4

Leather—*an animal's dried skin*
Worn by John the Baptist . . . . Matt. 3:4

Leaven—*dough in a state of fermentation*
A. Forbidden in:
Passover . . . . Ex. 12:8–20
Grain offerings . . . . Lev. 2:11
B. Permitted in:
Peace offerings . . . . Lev. 7:13
First fruits of grain . . . . Lev. 23:17; Num. 15:20, 21
C. Figurative of:
Kingdom of heaven . . . . Matt. 13:33
Corrupt teaching . . . . Matt. 16:6, 12
Infectious sin . . . . 1 Cor. 5:5–7
False doctrine . . . . Gal. 5:1–9

Lebanah—*white*
Founder of a family of
returning exiles . . . . . . Ezra 2:43, 45; Neh. 7:48
Called Lebana . . . . Neh. 7:48

Lebanon—*mountain range (10,000 ft.) in north*
Canaan
A. Source of:
Wood for Solomon's temple . . . . 1 Kin. 5:5, 6
Stones for Solomon's temple . . . . 1 Kin. 5:14, 18
Wood for the second temple . . . . Ezra 3:7
B. Significant as:
A sight desired by Moses . . . . Deut. 3:25
Israel's northern boundary . . . . Deut. 1:7
Captured by Joshua . . . . Josh. 11:16, 17; 12:7
Assigned to Israelites . . . . Josh. 13:5–7
Not completely conquered . . . . Judg. 3:1–3
Possessed by Assyria . . . . Is. 37:24
C. Figurative of:
Great kingdoms . . . . Is. 10:24, 34
Spiritual transformation . . . . Is. 29:17
Jerusalem and the temple . . . . Ezek. 17:3
Spiritual growth . . . . Hos. 14:5–7
Messiah's glory . . . . Is. 35:2
D. Noted for:
Blossoms . . . . Nah. 1:4
Wine . . . . Hos. 14:6, 7
Wild beast . . . . 2 Kin. 14:9
Snow . . . . Jer. 18:14
Cedars . . . . Song 5:15; Is. 14:8

Lebaoth—*lionesses*
Town of south Judah . . . . Josh. 15:32
Also called Beth Lebaoth . . . . Josh. 19:6

Lebbaeus (see Judas 3)
Surname of Judas (Jude) . . . . Matt. 10:3

Lebonah—*incense*
Town north of Shiloh . . . . Judg. 21:19

Lecah—*journey*
Descendant of Judah . . . . 1 Chr. 4:21

Ledge—*a protrusion around an altar*
Part of altar rendered *rim* . . . . Ex. 27:5

Leech
Figurative of insatiable appetite . . . . Prov. 30:15, 16

Leek—*an onionlike plant*
Desired by Israelites . . . . Num. 11:5

Left—*opposite of right*
A. Of direction:
Making a choice . . . . Gen. 13:9
Position . . . . Matt. 20:21–23
B. Of the hand:
Unusual capacity of 700 men . . . . . Judg. 20:15, 16
Lesser importance of . . . . Gen. 48:13–20
C. Figurative of:
Weakness . . . . Eccl. 10:2
Shame . . . . Matt. 25:33, 41
Bride's choice . . . . Song 2:6
Singleness of purpose . . . . Matt. 6:3
Riches . . . . Prov. 3:16
Ministry of God . . . . 2 Cor. 6:7

Left—*that which remains over*
A. Descriptive of:
Aloneness . . . . Gen. 32:24
Entire destruction . . . . Josh. 11:11, 12
Entire separation . . . . Ex. 10:26
Survival . . . . Num. 26:65
Remnant . . . . Is. 11:11, 16
Heir . . . . 2 Sam. 14:7
B. Blessings upon:
Equal booty . . . . 1 Sam. 30:9–25
Greater heritage . . . . Is. 49:21–23
Holiness . . . . Is. 4:3
Lord's protection . . . . Rom. 11:3–5
Not wasted . . . . Matt. 15:37

Legacy—*that which is bequeathed to heirs*
Left by:
Abraham . . . . Gen. 25:5, 6
David . . . . 1 Kin. 2:1–7
Christ . . . . John 14:15–27

Legal—*lawful*
Kingship, determined by David . . . . 1 Kin. 1:5–48
Priests' rights,
divinely enforced . . . . 2 Chr. 26:16–21
Priesthood, rejected . . . . Neh. 7:63–65
Right to rebuild, confirmed . . . . Ezra 5:3–17
Mixed marriages, condemned . . . . . . Ezra 10:1–44
David's act, justified . . . . Matt. 12:3–8
Christ's trial, exposed . . . . Matt. 27:4–31
Paul's right of appeal, recognized . . . Acts 26:31, 32

Legion—*a great number or multitude*
Demons............................ Mark 5:9, 15
Christ's angels..................... Matt. 26:53

Legs—*lower parts of human or animal body*
A. Used literally of:
Animal's..............................Ex. 12:9
Human ....1 Sam. 17:6
Christ's ....John 19:31, 33
B. Used figuratively of:
Fool ....Prov. 26:7
Human weakness.....................Ps. 147:10
Children of Israel ....Amos 3:12
Strength ....Dan. 2:33, 40
Christ's appearance ....Song 5:15

Lehabim—*flaming*
Nation (probably the Libyans) related to
the Egyptians ....Gen. 10:13

Lehi—*cheek, jawbone*
Place in Judah; Samson kills
Philistines ....Judg. 15:9–19

Leisure—*spare time*
None found ....Mark 6:31

Lemuel—*devoted to God*
King taught by his mother..........Prov. 31:1–31

Lending—*to give to another for temporary use*
A. As a gift to:
Expecting no return.............. Luke 6:34, 35
To the Lord .... 1 Sam. 1:28; 2:20
B. As a blessing:
Recognized by God ....Deut. 28:12, 44
Remembered by God.................Ps. 112:5, 6
Rewarded by God..................Ps. 37:25, 26
See Borrow

Length of life
A. Factors prolonging:
Keeping commandments... 1 Kin. 3:14; Prov 3:1, 2
Wisdom ....Prov. 3:13, 16
Prayer .... 2 Kin. 20:1–11
Honor to parents .... Eph. 6:3
Fear of the Lord ....Prov. 10:27
B. Factors decreasing:
Killing............................ 2 Sam. 3:27
God's judgment....................Job 22:15, 16
Suicide............................ Matt. 27:5

Lentil—*plant of the legume family*
Prepared as Esau's pottage........ Gen. 25:29–34
Bread made of ....Ezek. 4:9

Leopard—*a wild, spotted animal*
A. Characteristics of:
Swift............................... Hab. 1:8
Watches.............................Jer. 5:6
Lies in wait.......................... Hos. 13:7
Lives in mountains.................... Song 4:8
B. Figurative of:
Humankind's inability to change ...... Jer. 13:23
Transformation........................Is. 11:6

Greek Empire .... Dan. 7:6
Antichrist.............................Rev. 13:2

Leprosy—*scourge; a cancerlike disease*
A. Characteristics of:
Many diseased with ....Luke 4:27
Unclean.......................... Lev. 13:44, 45
Outcast .... 2 Kin. 15:5
Considered incurable .... 2 Kin. 5:7
Often hereditary.................... 2 Sam. 3:29
Excluded from the priesthood........ Lev. 22:2–4
B. Kinds of, in:
Humans .... Luke 17:12
House .... Lev. 14:33–57
Clothing .... Lev. 13:47–59
C. Treatment of:
Symptoms described .... Lev. 13:1–46
Cleansing prescribed............... Lev. 14:1–32
Healing by a miracle ..... Ex. 4:6, 7; 2 Kin. 5:1–14
D. Used as a sign:
Miriam .... Num. 12:1–10
Gehazi.........................2 Kin. 5:25, 27
Uzziah...................... 2 Chr. 26:16–21
Moses...............................Ex. 4:6, 7

Letters—*written communications; epistles*
A. Kinds of:
Forged .... 1 Kin. 21:7, 8
Rebellious.......................Jer. 29:24–32
Authoritative........................ Acts 22:5
Instructive ....Acts 15:23–29
Weighty .... 2 Cor. 10:10
Causing sorrow..................... 2 Cor. 7:8
Malicious ....Acts 9:1, 2
Commendation..................... 1 Cor. 16:3
B. Descriptive of:
One's writing.......................Gal. 6:11
Learning........................... John 7:15
Legalism ....Rom. 7:6
Christians........................ 2 Cor. 3:1, 2

"Let us"
"Arise, go from here"................. John 14:31
"Cast off the works of darkness" ......Rom. 13:12
"Walk properly" ....Rom. 13:13
"Be sober"......................... 1 Thess. 5:8
"Fear" .... Heb. 4:1
"Be diligent to enter that rest" .... Heb. 4:11
"Come boldly"....................... Heb. 4:16
"Go on to perfection" .... Heb. 6:1
"Draw near"........................Heb. 10:22
"Hold fast"........................Heb. 10:23
"Consider one another" ....Heb. 10:24
"Run with endurance"................. Heb. 12:1
"Go forth" ....Heb. 13:13
"Offer sacrifice" ....Heb. 13:15

Letushim—*sharpened*
Tribe descending from Dedan .... Gen. 25:3

Leummim—*peoples*
Tribe descending from Dedan .... Gen. 25:3

Israel .... Hos. 7:3, 13
Judah .... Jer. 9:1–5
C. Attitude of the wicked toward:
    Are always ....Titus 1:12
    Forge against the righteous ....Ps. 119:69
    Change God's truth for...............Rom. 1:25
D. Attitude of the righteous toward:
    Keep far from ....Prov. 30:8
    Shall not speak .... Zeph. 3:13
    Pray for deliverance from..............Ps. 120:2
    "Putting away" .... Eph. 4:25
E. Attitude of God toward:
    Will not........................... Num. 23:19
    Is an abomination .... Prov. 6:16–19
    Will discover human................ Is. 28:15, 17
    Is against...........................Ezek. 13:8
F. Punishment of, shall:
    Not escape .... Prov. 19:5
    Be stopped .... Ps. 63:11
    Be silenced .... Ps. 31:18
    Be short lived.......................Prov. 12:19
    End in lake of fire.................. Rev. 21:8, 27
G. The evils of:
    Produces error........................ Amos 2:4
    Increases wickedness................Prov. 29:12
    Destruction ....Hos. 10:13–15
    Death.................... Prov. 21:6; Zech. 13:3

Liberality—*a generous spirit*
A. Object of:
    Poor ....Deut. 15:11
    Strangers............................Lev. 25:35
    Afflicted......................... Luke 10:30–35
    Fatherless and widows...........Deut. 24:19–21
    Servants (slaves) .... Deut. 15:12–18
    All people ....Gal. 6:10
    God's children.................2 Cor. 8:1–9, 12
B. Reasons for:
    Make our faith real ....James 2:14–16
    Secure true riches.....Luke 12:33; 1 Tim. 6:17–19
    Follow Christ's example .... 2 Cor. 8:9
    Help God's kingdom..............Phil. 4:14–18
    Relieve distress .... 2 Cor. 9:12
C. Blessings of:
    God remembers ....Prov. 3:9, 10
    Will return abundantly..... Prov. 11:24–27
    Brings deliverance in time of need.... Is. 58:10, 11
    Insures sufficiency.................Ps. 37:25, 26
    Brings reward ....Ps. 112:5–9;
      Matt. 25:40
    Provokes others to .... 2 Cor. 9:2
D. Measure of, on:
    God's part........................... Mal. 3:10
    Israel's part......................... Ex. 36:3–7
    Judah's part .... 1 Chr. 29:3–9
    Christian's part....................2 Cor. 8:1–5

Liberty, civil
Obtained by:
    Purchase .... Acts 22:28
    Birth............................. Acts 22:28

Release ....Deut. 15:12–15
Victory .... Ex. 14:30, 31

Liberty, spiritual
A. Described as:
    Predicted ....Is. 61:1
    Where the spirit is .... 2 Cor. 3:17
B. Relation of Christians toward, they:
    Are called to.........................Gal. 5:13
    Abide by .... James 1:25
    Should walk at.......................Ps. 119:45
    Have in Jesus Christ ....Gal. 2:4, 5
See Freedom

Libnah—*whiteness*
1. Israelite camp .... Num. 33:20, 21
2. Canaanite city near Lachish.......Josh. 10:29–32
    Captured by Joshua ....Josh. 10:30, 39
    In Judah's territory ....Josh. 15:42
    Given to Aaron's descendants........ Josh. 21:13
    Fought against by Assyria ....2 Kin. 19:8, 9
    Home of Hamutal ....2 Kin. 23:31

Libni—*white, pure*
1. Son of Gershon ....Num. 3:18, 21
    Family of, called Libnites............. Num. 3:21
    Called Laadan.......................1 Chr. 23:7
2. Descendant of Merari................ 1 Chr. 6:29

Libya, Libyans—*the land and people west of Egypt*
    Called Lubim.......................... Nah. 3:9
    Will fall by the sword .... Ezek. 30:5
    Will be controlled.................... Dan. 11:43
    Some from, at Pentecost............. Acts 2:1–10

Lice—*some small, harmful insects*
    Third plague upon Egypt, produced
      from dust...................... Ex. 8:16–18

WORD STUDY   **LIFE,** *zōē* (dzoh-*ay*). This noun refers literally to physical "life" (Luke 16:25; 1 Cor. 15:19). It is a word used often in the NT, but usually with reference to eternal "life" (as in Mark 10:30; John 5:24). John uses the term "life" to refer to the result of believing in Christ (3:15, 16; 6:40–54; cf. 1 John 5:11–13)—indeed, Jesus calls Himself the "life" (14:6). The use of "life" (with eschatological overtones) to speak of life after death or eternal life is not limited to John (cf. Luke 18:30); see, for example, the numerous references to "the book of life" in Rev. (3:5; 17:8; 20:12, 15; cf. Phil. 4:3). (Strong's #2222)

Life, eternal
A. Defined as:
    Knowing the true God .... John 17:3
    God's commandment .... John 12:50
    Jesus Christ ....1 John 1:2
    Security of, in Christ..............John 10:28, 29
    God's gift ....Rom. 6:23
B. Christ's relation to:
    It is in Him..........................2 Tim. 1:1
    Manifested through Him............2 Tim. 1:10
    He has the words of .... John 6:68

It comes through Him. . . . . .Rom. 5:21

C. Means of securing, by:

God's gift . . . . Rom. 6:22, 23

Having the Son . . . . .1 John 5:11, 12

Knowing the true God . . . . John 17:3

Knowing the Scriptures . . . . John 20:31

Believing the Son . . . . .John 3:15–36

Drinking the Water of Life . . . . John 4:14

Eating the Bread of Life . . . . John 6:50–58

Reaping. . . . . John 4:36

Fighting the good fight of faith . . . 1 Tim. 6:12, 19

D. Present aspect of, for Christians, they:

Believe in the Son. . . . . John 3:36

Have assurance of. . . . . John 5:24

Have promise of .Titus 1:2

Have hope of . . . . .Titus 3:7

Take hold of. . . . . 1 Tim. 6:12, 19

Hate life in this world . . . . John 12:25

E. Future aspect of, for Christians, they shall:

Inherit. . . . . Matt. 19:29

Have, in the world to come . . . . .Luke 18:30

Reap. . . . . .Gal. 6:8

Life, natural

A. Origin of, by:

God's creation. . . . . Acts 17:28, 29

Natural birth. . . . . Gen. 4:1, 2

Supernatural conception . . . . .Luke 1:31–35

B. Shortness of, described as:

Dream . . . . Job 20:8

Shadow . . . . .1 Chr. 29:15

Cloud. . . . . .Job 7:9

Flower . . . . .Job 14:1, 2

Vapor. . . . . James 4:14

Sleep. . . . . .Ps. 90:5

Sigh . . . . .Ps. 90:9

Pilgrimage . . . . Gen. 47:9

Grass . . . . 1 Pet. 1:24

C. God's concern for, its:

Preservation. . . . . Gen. 7:1–3

Protection. .Ps. 34:7, 17, 19

Perpetuity (continuance) . . . . Gen. 1:28

Provisions. . . . . Ps. 104:27, 28

Perfection in glory . . . . .Col. 3:4

D. Believer's attitude toward:

Seeks to preserve it. . . . . .Acts 27:10–31

Attends to needs of . . . . Acts 27:34

Accepts suffering of. . . . . .Job 2:4–10

Makes God's kingdom first in . . . . .Matt. 6:25–33

Gives it up for Christ. . . . . Matt. 10:39

Lays it down for others . . . . Acts 15:26

Prizes it not too highly . . . . Acts 20:24

Puts Jesus first in . . . . 2 Cor. 4:10–12

Regards God's will in . . . . .James 4:13–15

Puts away the evil of . . . . Col. 3:5–9

Do not participate in its dissipation . . 1 Pet. 4:1–4

Praises God all the days of. . . . . .Ps. 63:3, 4

Does not fear enemies of . . . . Luke 12:4

E. Cares of:

Stunt spiritual growth. . . . . Luke 8:14

Divide loyalty . . . . .Luke 16:13

Delay preparedness . . . . .Luke 17:26–30; 21:34

Hinder service. . . . . 2 Tim. 2:4

Life, spiritual

A. Source of:

God . . . . .Ps. 36:9

Christ. . . . . John 14:6

Holy Spirit . . . . .Ezek. 37:14

God's Word . . . . James 1:18

B. Described as:

New birth. . . . . .John 3:3–8

Resurrection . . . . John 5:24

Translation. . . . . Acts 26:18

New creation . . . . 2 Cor. 5:17

Seed . . . . .1 John 3:9

Crucified . . . . .Gal. 2:20

C. Evidences of:

Growth . . . . .1 Pet. 2:2

Love . . . . .1 John 3:14

Obedience . . . . Rom. 6:16–22

Victory . . . . Rom. 6:1–15

Spiritual-mindedness . . . . .Rom. 8:6

Possession of the Spirit . . . . Rom. 8:9–13

Spirit's testimony . . . . Rom. 8:15–17

Walking in the Spirit. . . . . Gal. 5:16, 25

Bearing the fruit of the Spirit . . . . .Gal. 5:22

Name in the Book of Life . . . . . .Phil. 4:3; Rev. 17:8

D. Growth of:

Begins in new birth . . . . .John 3:3–8

Feeds on milk in infancy . . . . .1 Pet. 2:2

Must not remain in infancy . . . . Heb. 5:11–14

Comes to adulthood . . . . 1 John 2:13, 14

Arrives at maturity . . . . Eph. 4:14–16

E. Characteristics of:

Imperishable . . . . .John 11:25, 26

Transforming . . . . .Rom. 12:1, 2

Invisible . . . . .Col. 3:3, 4

Abides forever. . . . . .1 John 2:17

F. Enemies of:

Devil . . . . Eph. 6:11–17

World. . . . . 1 John 2:15–17

Flesh. . . . . Gal. 5:16–21

Life, triumphant Christian

A. Over:

Sorrow. . . . . John 16:22–24; 1 Thess. 4:13–18

The world. . . . . John 16:33; 1 John 5:4, 5

Transgressions . . . . .Rom. 6:6, 7, 11–18; 8:1–4;
     Eph. 2:5, 6; 1 John 5:4, 5

Circumstances . . . . Rom. 8:37; Phil. 4:11–13

Death. . . . . Rom. 6:6–9; 1 Cor. 15:54–57

B. Through:

Prayer . . . . John 16:22–24

Christ's death . . . . Rom. 6:6, 7

Doctrine. . . . . .Rom. 6:17

Holy Spirit . . . . .Rom. 8:1, 2

Christ. . . . . Phil. 4:13

Grace. . . . . .Rom. 6:14; Eph. 2:7

Exaltation with Christ . . . . Eph. 2:5, 6

God's will. . . . . Phil. 2:13

WORD STUDY **LIFT UP, EXALT,** *hupsoō* (hoop-*sah*-oh). This verb literally means "to lift up," "to raise," "to exalt." John uses *hupsoō* literally once (3:14), but more often figuratively and with a double meaning at that: Jesus' being "lifted up" on the cross cannot be separated from His heavenly "exaltation" (3:14; 8:28; 12:32). *Hupsoō* is also used figuratively to refer to an elevation in position, honor, fame, power (Acts 2:33; 5:31), even self-aggrandizement (Matt. 23:12; Luke 14:11). God will "exalt" the humble or lowly (Luke 1:52; cf. James 4:10; 1 Pet. 5:6). (Strong's #5312)

WORD STUDY **LIGHT,** *phōs* (*fohce*). Noun meaning "light." References to light in the NT may be literal (Luke 8:16; John 11:9); but more often than not, the uses of "light" are metaphoric or symbolic. "Light" is closely associated with God (1 John 1:7); in fact, it is said that "God is light" (1:5). The Gospel of John uses light symbolism to cast Jesus in the divine light and to show His oneness with the One who sent Him (1:4–9; 8:12; 9:5; 12:46; cf. Luke 2:32). Those who are enlightened with the truth (believers) are called "children of light" (Eph. 5:8; cf. Luke 16:8; John 12:36; 1 Thess. 5:5). This symbolic use of light explains the emphasis on the eyes as the organs of perception (e.g., Luke 11:34–36), the close association of "seeing" with "believing," and the antipathy toward darkness throughout the NT. (Strong's #5457)

Sacred veil. . . . . Ex. 26:31, 36
Garments for royalty. . . . . Esth. 8:15
Levitical singers . . . . 2 Chr. 5:12
Gifts to a woman . . . . Ezek. 16:10, 13
Clothing of the rich . . . . Luke 16:19
Embalming . . . . Matt. 27:59
B. Figurative of:
Righteousness. . . . . .Rev. 19:8
Purity. . . . . .Rev. 19:14
Babylon's pride . . . . Rev. 18:2, 16

Lintel—*a beam of wood overhanging the door*
Sprinkled with blood. . . . . Ex. 12:22, 23

Linus
Christian at Rome . . . . 2 Tim. 4:21

Lions
A. Described as:
Strongest among beasts . . . . .Prov. 30:30
Destructive . . . . Amos 3:12
Fierce. . . . . .Job 10:16
Stealthy. . . . . Ps. 10:9
Majestic. . . . . Prov. 30:29, 30
Provoking fear. Amos 3:8
Roaring. . . . . .1 Pet. 5:8
B. God's use of:
Slay the disobedient. . . . . 1 Kin. 13:24, 26
Punish idolaters . . . . .2 Kin. 17:25, 26
Show His power over. . . . . Dan. 6:16–24
C. Figurative of:
Tribe of Judah . . . . Gen. 49:9
Christ. . . . . .Rev. 5:5
Devil . . . . .1 Pet. 5:8
Transformation. . . . . .Is. 11:6–8
Victory . . . . Ps. 91:13
Boldness . . . . .Prov. 28:1
Persecutors. . . . . .Ps. 22:13
World empire. . . . . .Dan. 7:1–4
Antichrist. . . . . .Rev. 13:2

Lips
A. Described as:
Uncircumcised . . . . Ex. 6:12, 30
Unclean. . . . . Is. 6:5, 7
Stammering. . . . . Is. 28:11
Flattering . . . . .Ps. 12:2, 3
Perverse. . . . . .Prov. 4:24
Righteous. . . . . .Prov. 16:13
False. . . . . Prov. 17:4
Burning. . . . . .Prov. 26:23
B. Of the righteous, used for:
Knowledge. . . . . .Job 33:3
Prayer . . . . Ps. 17:1
Silent prayer. . . . . .1 Sam. 1:13
Righteousness . . . . Ps. 40:9
Grace . . . . Ps. 45:2
Praise. . . . . Ps. 51:15
Vows. . . . . .Ps. 66:13, 14
Singing . . . . Ps. 71:23
God's judgments. . . . . Ps. 119:13
Feeding many . . . . .Prov. 10:21

Spiritual fruitfulness. . . . . Hos. 14:2; Heb. 13:15
C. Of the wicked, used for:
Flattery . . . . Prov. 7:21
Mocking. . . . . Ps. 22:7
Defiance . . . . Ps. 12:4
Lying . . . . Is. 59:3
Poison . . . . .Ps. 140:3, 9
Troublemaking. . . . . .Prov. 24:2
Evil. . . . . .Prov. 16:27, 30
Deception. .Prov. 24:28
D. Warnings:
Put away perverse. . . . . .Prov. 4:24
Refrain from using. . . . . Prov. 17:28;
1 Pet. 3:10
Of an adulteress, avoid . . . . Prov. 5:3–13
Hypocrites . . . . .Mark 7:6

WORD STUDY   **LISTEN,** *shama'* (shaw-*mah*). The verb translated "hear" or "listen" is used in a variety of ways in the OT. In human terms, the simplest meaning indicates hearing a sound or a voice. The negative, "cannot hear," is used in discussion of idols in Deut. 4:28 and Ps. 115:6 as well as in other places. "To hear" can also mean "to pay attention" or "to understand." In discussion of judicial cases, one may hear a case (Deut. 1:17). *Shama'* may indicate giving heed to someone, which leads to granting their request. In this case, obedience is often suggested by the word (Jer. 3:13). God can also hear humans. This use implies God's favor on the one being heard. *Shama'* is used in contexts meaning "hear and forgive" or "hear and answer." Occasionally God hears and is angry. (Strong's #8085)

Litigation—*a lawsuit*
Christ's warning concerning. . . . . . . Matt. 5:25, 40
Paul's warning concerning. . . . . 1 Cor. 6:1, 2

Litter—*a covered framework for carrying a single passenger*
Of nations. . . . . Is. 66:20

WORD STUDY   **LITTLE CHILD,** *teknion* (tek-*nee*-ahn). This noun is the diminutive form of *teknon* ("child"); it can be translated as "little child." Jesus uses it as a term of endearment for His disciples (John 13:33). Similarly, the writer of 1 John uses *teknion* to address his spiritual children (2:12, 28; 3:7, 18; 4:4; 5:21). (Strong's #5040)

Liver—*body organ that secretes bile*
A. Used literally of:
Animals:
In sacrifice . . . . Ex. 29:13, 22
For divination . . . . .Ezek. 21:21
B. Used figuratively of:
Extreme pain or death. . . . . Prov. 7:23

Livestock
Struck by God . . . . Ex. 12:29
Firstborn of, belong to God. . . . . .Ex. 34:19
Can be unclean . . . . Lev. 5:2

East of Jordan good for . . . . Num. 32:1, 4
Given as ransom . . . . Num. 3:45
See Cattle

Living, Christian
Source—Christ. . . . . John 14:19
Length—forever. . . . . .John 11:25, 26
Means—faith in Christ. . . . . Rom. 1:17
Kind—resurrected. . . . . 2 Cor. 5:15
End—to God. . . . . .Rom. 14:7, 8
Purpose—for Christ . . . . 1 Thess. 5:10
Motivation—Christ. . . . . .Gal. 2:20
Atmosphere—in the Spirit. . . . . .Gal. 5:25
Manner—righteously . . . . .Titus 2:12
Enemies—flesh and sin . . . . Rom. 8:12, 13
Price—persecution . . . . 2 Tim. 3:12

Living creatures—*a phrase referring to animals or living beings*
Aquatic animals . . . . Gen. 1:21
Land animals. . . . . Gen. 1:24
Angelic beings. . . . . .Ezek. 1:5

Lizard—*a small, swift reptile with legs*
Ceremonially unclean. . . . . Lev. 11:29, 30

Lo-Ammi—*not my people*
Symbolic name of Hosea's son . . . . Hos. 1:8, 9

Loan (see Borrow; Lending)

Lock
Doors. . . . . Judg. 3:23, 24
Of hair. . . . . .Judg. 16:13, 19
City gates . . . . .Neh. 3:6, 13, 14

Locust—*devastating, migratory insects*
A. Types, or stages, of:
    Eating . . . . Joel 1:4
    Devastating . . . . .Lev. 11:22
B. Used literally of insects:
    Miraculously brought forth. . . . . Ex. 10:12–19
    Sent as a judgment . . . . . . .Deut. 28:38; 1 Kin. 8:37
    Used for food. .Matt. 3:4
C. Used figuratively of:
    Weakness . . . . Ps. 109:23, 24
    Running men. . . . . Is. 33:4
    Nineveh's departing glory . . . . Nah. 3:15, 17
    Final plagues . . . . .Rev. 9:3, 7
    See Grasshopper

Lod
Benjamite town. . . . . .1 Chr. 8:1, 12
Mentioned in postexilic books . . . . Ezra 2:33
Aeneas healed here, called Lydda. . . .Acts 9:32–35

Lo Debar
City in Manasseh (in Gilead) . . . . 2 Sam. 9:4, 5
Machir a native of . . . . 2 Sam. 17:27

Lodge—*to pass the night; to occupy a place temporarily*
Angels—with Lot. . . . . Gen. 19:1–3
Travelers—in a house . . . . Judg. 19:4–20
Spies—in a house . . . . Josh. 2:1
Animals—in ruins . . . . Zeph. 2:14

Righteousness—in a city . . . . Is. 1:21
Thoughts—in Jerusalem . . . . .Jer. 4:14

Loft—*a room upstairs*
Dead child taken to . . . . 1 Kin. 17:19–24
Young man falls from . . . . Acts 20:9

Loins
Used figuratively of source of hope . . . . .1 Pet. 1:13

Lois
Timothy's grandmother . . . . .2 Tim. 1:5

Loneliness
Jacob—in prayer. . . . . Gen. 32:23–30
Joseph—in weeping. . . . . .Gen. 43:30, 31
Elijah—in discouragement . . . . 1 Kin. 19:3–14
Jeremiah—in witnessing . . . . .Jer. 15:17
Nehemiah—in a night vigil. . . . . . . .Neh. 2:12–16
Jonah—in repentance . . . . .Jon. 1:17–2:9
Christ—in agony . . . . Matt. 26:36–45
Paul—in prison. . . . . 2 Tim. 4:16

Longevity—*a great span of life*
Allotted years, 70 .Ps. 90:10
See Length of life

Longsuffering—*forbearance*
A. Manifested in God's:
    Description of His nature . . . . .Ex. 34:6
    Delay in executing wrath . . . . .Rom. 9:22
    Dealing with sinful people. . . . . .Rom. 2:4
    Desire for humankind's salvation . . . 2 Pet. 3:9, 15
B. As a Christian grace:
    Exemplified by the prophets
        ("patience"). James 5:10
    Manifested by Old Testament saints
        ("patience"). Heb. 6:12
    Produced by the Spirit. . . . . .Gal. 5:22
    Witnessed in Paul's life. . . . . 2 Cor. 6:6
    Taught as a virtue. . . . . .Eph. 4:1
    Given power for . . . . Col. 1:11
    Set for imitation . . . . 2 Tim. 3:10
    Needed by preachers . . . . 2 Tim. 4:2

Look—*focusing the eyes toward something*
Promise. . . . . Gen. 15:5
Warning against looking back . . . . . Gen. 19:17, 26
Astonishment . . . . Ex. 3:2–6
Disdain . . . . 1 Sam. 17:42
Encouragement. .Ps. 34:5
Salvation. . . . . Is. 45:22
Glory . . . . .Acts 7:55
Faith. . . . . .Jon. 2:4, 9
Anticipation. . . . . .Luke 21:28
Self-examination . . . . .2 John 8

 LORD, MASTER, *despotēs* (des-pot-ayce). This noun, which means "lord" or "master," was originally used with reference to a householder as "owner" of property and slaves (cf. 1 Tim. 6:1, 2); and this is the background for metaphorical references to God as *despotēs* in Luke 2:29, 2 Tim. 2:21, and 2 Pet. 2:1. Other uses of *despotēs*

for God in the NT (Acts 4:24; Jude 4; Rev. 6:10) are more in line with the Greek usage of the term to refer to the gods as "Lords" or "Masters" with absolute power and sovereignty. (Strong's #1203)

WORD STUDY **LORD, MASTER,** *kurios (koo-ree-oss).* This noun refers to an "owner" of property (Matt. 20:8; Mark 13:35) or slaves (Luke 12:36). *Kurios* is used as a term of respect for any person of position or power: for example, slaves would address their owner as "Master" (Matt. 13:27), or a son might call his father "Sir" (Matt. 21:30). *Kurios* can be used as a form of address for any respected person in general and would be equivalent to "Sir" (Acts 16:30). The religious usage of *kurios* is predominant in the NT. Influenced by the Septuagint, where *kurios* is both the translation of the Hebrew *'Ādōnai* ("Lord") and the word substituted for the personal name of God (*Yahweh*), *Kurios* is used as a form of address for God and Jesus that acknowledges and honors Their deity. However, sometimes Jesus is respectfully addressed as "Sir," as in John 4:11. (Strong's #2962)

Lord—*title of majesty and kingship; master*
A. Applied to:
    God . . . . .Gen. 3:1–23
    Christ. . . . . .Luke 6:46
    Masters . . . . .Gen. 24:14, 27
    Men ("sir") . . . . Matt. 21:30
    Husbands . . . . Gen. 18:12; 1 Pet. 3:6
B. As applied to Christ, "kyrios" indicates:
    Identity with Yahweh . . . . .Joel 2:32
    Confession of Christ's lordship
      ("Jesus as Lord") . . . . .Rom. 10:9
    Absolute lordship . . . . Phil. 2:11

Lord's Day (see First day of week)

Lord's Prayer
    Taught by Jesus to His disciples . . . . . Matt. 6:9–13

Lord's Supper
A. Described as:
    Sharing of communion . . . . 1 Cor. 10:16
    Breaking of bread. . . . . .Acts 2:42, 46
    Lord's Supper. . . . . .1 Cor. 11:20
    Eucharist "giving of thanks" . . . . . . .Luke 22:17, 19
B. Features concerning:
    Instituted by Christ . . . . Matt. 26:26–29
    Commemorative of Christ's
      death . . . . .Luke 22:19, 20
    Introductory to the new covenant . . . . Matt. 26:28
    Means of Christian fellowship . . . . . .Acts 2:42, 46
    Memorial feast . . . . 1 Cor. 11:23–26
    Inconsistent with
      demon fellowship . . . . 1 Cor. 10:19–22
    Preparation for, required . . . . 1 Cor. 11:27–34
    Spiritually explained . . . . John 6:26–58

Lordship—*supreme authority*
    Human kings. . . . . Mark 10:42

Divine King . . . . .Phil. 2:9–11

Lo-Ruhamah—*not pitied*
    Symbolic name of Hosea's daughter . . . . . Hos. 1:6

Loss, spiritual
A. Kinds of:
    One's self. . . . . .Luke 9:24, 25
    Reward . . . . .1 Cor. 3:13–15
    Heaven . . . . Luke 16:19–31
B. Causes of:
    Love of this life .Luke 17:33
    Sin. . . . . .Ps. 107:17, 34

Lost—*unable to find the way*
Descriptive of humankind as:
    Separated from God . . . . Luke 15:24, 32
    Unregenerated. . . . . Matt. 15:24
    Objects of Christ's mission . . . . Luke 15:4–6
    Blinded by Satan. . . . . .2 Cor. 4:3, 4
    Defiled . . . . .Titus 1:15, 16

Lot—*covering*
A. Life of:
    Abram's nephew . . . . .Gen. 11:27–31
    Goes with Abram to Canaan. . . . . Gen. 12:5
    Accompanies Abram to Egypt . . . . Gen. 13:1
    Settles in Sodom . . . . .Gen. 13:5–13
    Rescued by Abram . . . . .Gen. 14:12–16
    Befriends angels . . . . Gen. 19:1–14
    Saved from Sodom's destruction . . .Gen. 19:15, 22
    His wife, disobedient, becomes
      pillar of salt . . . . .Gen. 19:15, 17, 26
    His daughters commit
      incest with . . . . Gen. 19:30–38
    Unwilling father of Moabites and
      Ammonites . . . . .Gen. 19:37, 38
B. Character of:
    Makes selfish choice . . . . .Gen. 13:5–13
    Lacks moral stability . . . . .Gen. 19:6–10
    Loses moral influence . . . . .Gen. 19:14, 20

Lotan—*a covering*
    Tribe of Horites in Mt. Seir . . . . . . .Gen. 36:20, 29;
      1 Chr. 1:38, 39

Lot(s)—*a means of deciding doubtful matters*
A. Characteristic of:
    Preceded by prayer . . . . .Acts 1:23–26
    With divine sanction. . . . . Num. 26:55
    Considered final . . . . Num. 26:56
    Used also by the ungodly . . . . Matt. 27:35
B. Used for:
    Selection of scapegoat . . . . .Lev. 16:8
    Detection of a criminal. . . . . .Josh. 7:14–18
    Selection of warriors . . . . Judg. 20:9, 10
    Choice of a king . . . . 1 Sam. 10:19–21
    Deciding priestly rotation . . . . Luke 1:9

Lot's wife
    Disobedient, becomes pillar of salt . . . . Gen. 19:26
    Event to be remembered . . . . Luke 17:32

WORD STUDY

LOVE, *agapē* (ag-*ah*-pay). Noun meaning "love." It can be used to denote a person's love for God (John 5:42; 1 John 2:15), God's love for humanity (Rom. 5:8), and God's love for Jesus (John 15:10; 17:26). Jesus reveals His love for believers by laying down His life, and He commands that believers love each other (John 15:9–13). A cornerstone of the NT teachings about God is that "God is love" (1 John 4:8, 16; cf. 2 Cor. 13:11). (Strong's #26)

Love, Christian

A. Toward God:

First commandment	Matt. 22:37, 38
With all the heart	Matt. 22:37
More important than ritual	Mark 12:31–33
Gives boldness	1 John 4:17–19
Must love his brother	1 John 4:20, 21

B. Toward Christ:

Sign of true faith	John 8:42
Manifested in obedience	John 14:15, 21, 23
Leads to service	2 Cor. 5:14

C. Toward others:

Second command	Matt. 22:37–39
Commanded by Christ	John 13:34
Described in detail	1 Cor. 13:1–13

Love of Christ, the

A. Objects of:

Father	John 14:31
Believers	Gal. 2:20
Church	Eph. 5:2, 25

B. Described as:

Knowing	Eph. 3:19
Personal	Gal. 2:20
Conquering	Rom. 8:37
Unbreakable	Rom. 8:35
Intimate	John 14:21
Imitative	1 John 3:16
Like the Father's	John 15:9
Sacrificial	Gal. 2:20

C. Expressions of:

In taking our nature	Heb. 2:16–18
In dying for us	John 15:13

Love of God, the

A. Objects of:

Christ	John 3:35
Christians	2 Thess. 2:16
Humankind	Titus 3:4
Cheerful giver	2 Cor. 9:7

B. Described as:

Great	Eph. 2:4
Everlasting	Jer. 31:3
Sacrificial	Rom. 5:8

C. As seen in believers':

Hearts	Rom. 5:5
Regeneration	Eph. 2:4, 5
Love	1 John 4:7–12
Faith	1 John 4:16
Security	2 Thess. 3:5

Daily lives	1 John 2:15–17
Obedience	1 John 2:5
Without fear	1 John 4:17–19
Glorification	1 John 3:1, 2

Love, physical

Isaac and Rebekah	Gen. 24:67
Jacob and Rachel	Gen. 29:11–30
Samson and Delilah	Judg. 16:4, 15

Lovingkindness—*gentle and steadfast mercy*

Attitude of believers, to:

Expect	Ps. 17:7; 36:10
Rejoice in	Ps. 63:3; 69:16

Loyalty—*fidelity to a person or cause*

A. Kinds of, to:

People	Acts 25:7–11
Relatives	Esth. 2:21–23
King	1 Sam. 24:6–10
Friend	1 Sam. 20:1–4
Cause	2 Sam. 11:9–11
Oath	2 Sam. 21:7

B. Signs of:

General obedience	Rom. 13:1, 2
Prayer for rulers	Ezra 6:10
Hatred of disloyalty	Josh. 22:9–20

Lucifer—*light-bearer*

Name applied to Satan	Is. 14:12
Allusion to elsewhere	Luke 10:18

Lucius—*of light*

1. Prophet and teacher at Antioch … Acts 13:1
2. Paul's companion in Corinth … Rom. 16:21

Lud, Ludim (plural)

1. Lud, a people descending from Shem … 1 Chr. 1:17
2. Ludim, a people descending from Mizraim (Egypt) … Gen. 10:13

Luhith—*of tablets or planks*

Moabite town … Is. 15:5

Luke—*another name for Lucius*

"The beloved physician"	Col. 4:14
Paul's last companion	2 Tim. 4:11

Luke, the Gospel of—*a book of the New Testament*

The annunciation	Luke 1:26–56
John the Baptist	Luke 3:1–22
The temptation	Luke 4:1–13
Public ministry begins	Luke 4:15
The disciples chosen	Luke 6:12–19
The disciples' instructions	Luke 10:25–13:21
The Jerusalem ministry	Luke 19:28–21:38
The Last Supper	Luke 22:1–38
The Crucifixion	Luke 22:39–23:56
The Resurrection	Luke 24:1–53

Lukewarm—*neither hot nor cold*

Descriptive of Laodicea … Rev. 3:14–16

Lunatic—*an insane person*

David acts as	1 Sam. 21:13–15
Nebuchadnezzar inflicted as	Dan. 4:31–36

Christ declared . . . . John 10:20
Paul called . . . . Acts 26:24
See Madness

> **WORD STUDY**
>
> **LUST,** *epithumia* (ep-ee-thoo-*mee*-ah). Noun meaning "desire," "longing," "craving." Although it is usually translated as "lust" in the NT, it may be used as a neutral term for "desire" (Mark 4:19; Rev. 18:14) or a positive term for "longing" (Phil. 1:23; 1 Thess. 2:17). Most often, though, the term is used negatively with reference to a "desire" for something that is forbidden: for example, "desires" of the flesh, worldly "desires," which, of course, include sexual "desires" (Gal. 5:16; 1 Thess. 4:5; Titus 2:12; 1 John 2:16). *Epithumia* is included in a list of vices in 1 Pet. 4:3. (Strong's #1939)

Lust—*evil desire*

A. Origin of, in:
- Satan . . . . 1 John 3:8–12
- Heart . . . . .Matt. 15:19
- Flesh . . . . .James 1:14, 15
- World . . . . .2 Pet. 1:4

B. Described as:
- Deceitful . . . . Eph. 4:22
- Enticing . . . . .James 1:14, 15
- Harmful . . . . 1 Tim. 6:9
- Numerous . . . . 2 Tim. 3:6

C. Among the unregenerate, they:
- Live and walk in . . . . Eph. 2:3
- Are punished with . . . . Rom. 1:24–32

D. Among false teachers, they:
- Walk after . . . . .2 Pet. 2:10–22
- Will prevail in the last days . . . . .2 Pet. 3:3
- Are received because of . . . . 2 Tim. 4:3, 4

E. Among Christians:
- Once lived in . . . . Eph. 2:3
- Consider it dead . . . . .Col. 3:5
- Deny . . . . .Titus 2:12
- Flee from . . . . 2 Tim. 2:22
- Not carry out . . . . .Gal. 5:16

Lute—*musical instrument*
- Used in worship . . . . .Ps. 150:3

Luxuries

A. Characteristic of:
- Egypt . . . . Heb. 11:24–27
- Tyre . . . . Ezek. 27:1–27
- Ancient Babylon . . . . .Dan. 4:30
- Israel . . . . Amos 6:1–7
- Persia . . . . .Esth. 1:3–11
- Harlot Babylon . . . . Rev. 18:10–13

B. Productive of:
- Temptation . . . . .Josh. 7:20, 21
- Physical weakness . . . . Dan. 1:8, 10–16
- Moral decay . . . . Nah. 3:1–19
- Spiritual decay . . . . Rev. 3:14–17

Luz—*almond tree*
1. Ancient Canaanite town . . . . .Gen. 28:19
- Called Bethel . . . . Gen. 35:6

2. Hittite town . . . . .Judg. 1:23–26

Lycaonia—*a rugged, inland district of Asia Minor*
- Paul preaches in three of its cities . . . Acts 14:6, 11

Lycia—*a province of Asia Minor*
Paul:
- Visits Patara, a city of . . . . .Acts 21:1, 2
- Lands at Myra, a city of . . . . Acts 27:5, 6

Lydia—*from Lud*
1. Woman of Thyatira; Paul's first
   European convert . . . . Acts 16:14, 15, 40
2. District of Asia Minor containing Ephesus,
   Smyrna, Thyatira, and Sardis . . . . Rev. 1:11

Lye
- Used for cleansing . . . . Jer. 2:22

Lying (see Liars)

Lyre—*a musical instrument*
- Used in Babylon . . . . Dan. 3:7, 10

Lysanias—*ending sadness*
- Tetrarch of Abilene . . . . Luke 3:1

Lysias, Claudius
- Roman captain who rescues Paul . . . . . . Acts 23:10
- Listens to Paul's nephew . . . . .Acts 23:16–22
- Sends Paul to Felix . . . . .Acts 23:23–31
- Felix awaits arrival of . . . . Acts 24:22

Lystra—*a city of Lycaonia*
- Visited by Paul . . . . Acts 14:6, 21
- Lame man healed here . . . . .Acts 14:8–10
- People of, attempt to worship Paul and
  Barnabas . . . . Acts 14:11–18
- Paul stoned here . . . . .2 Tim. 3:11
- Home of Timothy . . . . Acts 16:1, 2

M

Maacah, Maachah—*oppression*
1. Daughter of Nahor . . . . Gen. 22:24
2. Small Syrian kingdom near
   Mt. Hermon . . . . Deut. 3:14
   - Not possessed by Israel . . . . .Josh. 13:13
   - Called Syrian Maacah . . . . .1 Chr. 19:6, 7
3. Machir's wife . . . . 1 Chr. 7:15, 16
4. One of Caleb's concubines . . . . 1 Chr. 2:48
5. Father of Shephatiah . . . . 1 Chr. 27:16
6. Ancestress of King Saul . . . . 1 Chr. 8:29; 9:35
7. One of David's warriors . . . . 1 Chr. 11:43
8. Father of Achish, king of Gath . . . . 1 Kin. 2:39
9. David's wife and mother of Absalom . . . . 2 Sam. 3:3
10. Wife of Rehoboam; mother of
    King Abijah . . . . .2 Chr. 11:18–21
    - Makes idol, is deposed as
      queen mother . . . . .1 Kin. 15:13

Maachathites—*inhabitants of Maachah*
- Not conquered by Israel . . . . .Josh. 13:13
- Among Israel's warriors . . . . 2 Sam. 23:34
See Maacah

Maadai—*ornament of Yahweh*
Postexilic Jew; divorced his
foreign wife . . . . Ezra 10:34

Maadiah
Priest who returns from Babylon with
Zerubbabel . . . . Neh. 12:5, 7
Same as Moadiah in . . . . Neh. 12:17

Maai—*compassionate*
Postexilic trumpeter . . . . Neh. 12:35, 36

Maarath—*barren place*
Town of Judah . . . . Josh. 15:1, 59

Maaseiah—*work of Yahweh*
1. Levite musician during
David's reign . . . . 1 Chr. 15:16, 18
2. Levite captain under Jehoiada . . . . 2 Chr. 23:1
3. Official during King Uzziah's reign . . . 2 Chr. 26:11
4. Son of Ahaz, slain by Zichri . . . . 2 Chr. 28:7
5. Governor of Jerusalem during
King Josiah's reign . . . . 2 Chr. 34:1, 8
6. Father of the false prophet Zedekiah . . . . . Jer. 29:21
7. Father of Zephaniah the priest . . . . Jer. 21:1
8. Temple doorkeeper . . . . Jer. 35:4
9. Judahite postexilic Jew . . . . Neh. 11:5
10. Benjamite ancestor of a postexilic Jew . . . Neh. 11:7
11, 12, 13. Three priests who divorced their
foreign wives . . . . Ezra 10:18, 21, 22
14. Layman who divorced his foreign wife . Ezra 10:30
15. Representative who signs the
covenant . . . . Neh. 10:1, 25
16. One who stood by Ezra . . . . Neh. 8:4
17. Levite who explains the Law . . . . Neh. 8:7
18. Priest who takes part in dedication
services . . . . Neh. 12:41
19. Another participating priest . . . . Neh. 12:42
20. Father or ancestor of Azariah . . . . Neh. 3:23

Maasai—*work of Yahweh*
Priest of Immer's family . . . . 1 Chr. 9:12

Maath—*to be small*
Ancestor of Christ . . . . Luke 3:26

Maaz—*anger*
Judahite . . . . 1 Chr. 2:27

Maaziah—*Yahweh is a refuge*
1. Descendant of Aaron; heads a course
of priests . . . . 1 Chr. 24:1–18
2. One who signs the covenant . . . . Neh. 10:1, 8

Macedonia—*Greece (northern)*
A. In Old Testament prophecy:
Called the kingdom of Greece . . . . Dan. 11:2
Bronze part of Nebuchadnezzar's
image . . . . Dan. 2:32, 39
Described as a leopard with
four heads . . . . Dan. 7:6, 17
Described as a male goat . . . . Dan. 8:5, 21; 11:4
B. In New Testament missions:
Man of, appeals to . . . . Acts 16:9, 10

Paul preaches in,
at Philippi, etc . . . . Acts 16:10–17:14
Paul's troubles in . . . . 2 Cor. 7:5
Churches of, very generous . . . . Rom. 15:26;
2 Cor. 8:1–5

Machbanai—*clad with a cloak*
One of David's mighty men . . . . 1 Chr. 12:13

Machbenah—*lump*
Son of Sheva . . . . 1 Chr. 2:49

Machi
Father of the Gadite spy . . . . Num. 13:15

Machir—*sold*
1. Manasseh's only son . . . . Gen. 50:23
Founder of the family of Machirites . . . Num. 26:29
Conqueror of Gilead . . . . Num. 32:39, 40
Name used of Manasseh tribe . . . . Judg. 5:14
2. Son of Ammiel . . . . 2 Sam. 9:4, 5
Provides food for David . . . . 2 Sam. 17:27–29

Machnadebai—*gift of the noble one*
Son of Bani; divorced foreign wife . . . Ezra 10:34, 40

Machpelah—*double*
Field containing a cave; bought by
Abraham . . . . Gen. 23:9–18
Sarah and Abraham buried here . . . . . . Gen. 23:19;
25:9, 10
Isaac, Rebekah, Leah, and Jacob
buried here . . . . Gen. 49:29–31; 50:12, 13

Madai—*middle*
Third son of Japheth; ancestor of the
Medes . . . . Gen. 10:2

Made—*something brought into being*
A. Why Christ was made for us:
Sin . . . . 2 Cor. 5:21
In our likeness . . . . Phil. 2:7
High priest . . . . Heb. 6:20
B. What Christians are made by Him:
Righteous . . . . 2 Cor. 5:21
Heirs . . . . Titus 3:7
Kings and priests . . . . Rev. 1:4–6

Madmannah—*dunghill*
Town in south Judah . . . . Josh. 15:20, 31
Son of Shaaph . . . . 1 Chr. 2:49

Madmen—*dunghill*
Moabite town . . . . Jer. 48:2

Madmenah—*dunghill, or dungheap*
Town near Jerusalem . . . . Is. 10:31

Madness—*emotional or mental derangement*
A. Kinds of:
Extreme jealousy . . . . 1 Sam. 18:8–11
Extreme rage . . . . Luke 6:11
B. Causes of:
Disobedience to God's laws . . . . Deut. 28:28
Judgment sent by God . . . . Dan. 4:31–34;
Zech. 12:4
C. Manifestations of:
Irrational behavior . . . . 1 Sam. 21:12–15

Uncontrollable emotions .... Mark 5:1–5
Moral decay .... Jer. 50:38
See Insanity; Lunatic

Madon—*contention*
Canaanite town...................Josh. 12:19
Joins confederacy against Joshua....Josh. 11:1–12

Magbish—*strong*
Town of Judah....................... Ezra 2:30

Magdala—*tower*
City of Galilee..................... Matt. 15:39

Magdalene—*of Magdala*
Descriptive of one of the Marys ...... Matt. 27:56
See Mary 3

Magdiel—*God is glory*
Edomite chief ....Gen. 36:43

Magi—*a priestly sect in Persia*
Bring gifts to the infant Jesus .... Matt. 2:1, 2

Magic, magician—*the art of doing superhuman things by "supernatural" means*
A. Special manifestations of:
At the Exodus ....Ex. 7:11
During apostolic Christianity.....Acts 8:9, 18–24
B. Modified power of:
Acknowledged in history.............Ex. 7:11, 22
Recognized in prophecy .... 2 Thess. 2:9–12
Fulfilled in second beast.......... Rev. 13:13–18
C. Failure of, to:
Perform miracles ....Ex. 8:18, 19
Overcome demons .... Acts 19:13–19
D. Condemnation of, by:
Explicit law......................... Lev. 20:27
Their inability.........................Ex. 8:18
Final judgment ....Rev. 21:8
See Divination

Magistrates—*civil rulers*
A. Descriptive of:
Ruler ....Judg. 18:7
Authorities.........................Luke 12:11
B. Office of:
Ordained by God ....Rom. 13:1, 2
Due proper respect.................. Acts 23:5
C. Duties of:
To judge:
Impartially..........................Deut. 1:17
Righteously .... Deut. 25:1
D. Christian's attitude toward:
Pray for .... 1 Tim. 2:1, 2
Honor .... Ex. 22:28
Submit to .... 1 Pet. 2:13, 14

Magnanimity—*loftiness*
A. Expressions of, toward people:
Abram's offer to Lot...............Gen. 13:7–12
Jacob's offer to Esau...............Gen. 33:8–11
B. Expression of, toward God:
Moses' plea for Israel............... Ex. 32:31–33
Paul's prayer for Israel............... Rom. 9:1–3

Magnificat—*he magnifies*
Poem of the Virgin Mary .... Luke 1:46–55

Magnify—*to make or declare great*
A. Concerning God's:
Name............................ 2 Sam. 7:26
Word ....Ps. 138:2
Law.................................. Is. 42:21
Christ's name.......................Acts 19:17
B. Duty of, toward God:
With others ....Ps. 34:3
With thanksgiving....................Ps. 69:30
In the body.......................... Phil. 1:20

Magog—*region of Gog*
People among Japheth's
descendants..................... Gen. 10:2
Associated with Gog .... Ezek. 38:2
Representatives of final enemies .... Rev. 20:8

Magor-Missabib—*terror on every side*
Name indicating Pashhur's demise ...... Jer. 20:3

Magpiash—*collector of a cluster of stars*
Signer of the covenant................Neh. 10:20

Mahalalel—*praise of God*
1. Descendant of Seth ....Gen. 5:12
Ancestor of Christ ....Luke 3:37
2. Postexilic Judahite....................Neh. 11:4

Mahalath—*sickness*
1. One of Esau's wives ....Gen. 28:9
Called Basemath............... Gen. 36:3, 4, 13
2. One of Rehoboam's wives .... 2 Chr. 11:18
3. Musical term.......................Ps. 53 (Title)

Mahanaim—*two camps*
Name given by Jacob to a sacred site.... Gen. 32:2
On boundary between Gad and
Manasseh.................... Josh. 13:26, 30
Assigned to Merarite Levites......... Josh. 21:38
Becomes Ishbosheth's capital ......2 Sam. 2:8–29
David flees to, during Absalom's
rebellion.................. 2 Sam. 17:24, 27
Solomon places Ahinadab over........ 1 Kin. 4:14

Mahaneh Dan—*camp of Dan*
Place between Zorah and Eshtaol .....Judg. 13:25

Maharai—*swift, hasty*
One of David's mighty men......... 2 Sam. 23:28
Becomes an army captain...........1 Chr. 27:13

Mahath—*grasping*
1. Kohathite Levite .... 1 Chr. 6:35
2. Levite in Hezekiah's reign............ 2 Chr. 29:12
Appointed an overseer of tithes ...... 2 Chr. 31:13

Mahavite
Applied to Eliel.....................1 Chr. 11:46

Mahazioth—*visions*
Levite musician.................. 1 Chr. 25:4, 30

Maher-Shalal-Hash-Baz—*spoil speeds, prey hastes*
Symbolic name of Isaiah's second son; prophetic of
the fall of Damascus and Samaria .... Is. 8:1–4

Mahlah—*disease*
1. Zelophehad's daughter . . . . Num. 26:33
2. Child of Hammoleketh . . . . 1 Chr. 7:18

Mahli—*weak, silly*
1. Eldest son of Merari . . . . Ex. 6:19; Num. 3:20
   Father of three sons . . . . 1 Chr. 6:29
   Father of tribal family . . . . Num. 3:33
2. Another Merarite Levite; nephew of 1. . . . 1 Chr. 6:47;
   23:23; 24:30

Mahlon—*sickly*
   Husband of Ruth; without child . . . . . . Ruth 1:2–5

Mahol—*dance*
   Father of certain wise men . . . . 1 Kin. 4:31

Mahseiah
   Ancestor of Baruch . . . . Jer. 32:12

Maid—*a young woman*
A. Characteristic of:
   Obedient . . . . Ps. 123:2
B. Provision for:
   Physical needs of . . . . Prov. 27:27
   Accepted as wives . . . . Gen. 30:3

Maidservant
Expressive of humility:
   Ruth . . . . Ruth 2:13
   Woman of En Dor . . . . 1 Sam. 28:7, 21, 22
   Mary . . . . Luke 1:38

Mail
   Letters were sent . . . . Esth. 3:13

Mainsail—*the lowest sail on the foremast, providing directional control*
   Hoisted . . . . Acts 27:40

Maintenance—*provision for support*
   Household supply . . . . Prov. 27:27
   King's service . . . . Ezra 4:14
   Solomon's supply . . . . 1 Kin. 4:22, 23
   House of the Lord . . . . 1 Chr. 26:27

WORD STUDY — **MAJESTY,** *hod* (*hohd*). The noun *hod* is used most often in poetic passages. "Majesty" and "splendor" are the characteristics of kings, so that there are connotations of royalty in this word. In references to divinity, God wears light and glory as a king. God's voice and actions can also have splendor. In Hos. 14:7 Israel receives majesty as part of the divine blessing to come. In Num. 27:20 the word is translated "authority" when referring to a characteristic of Moses that he is to share with Joshua. The word can also be used to refer to manly vigor, which is seen in a person's appearance (Prov. 5:9; Dan. 10:8). (Strong's #1935)

WORD STUDY — **MAJESTY, MAGNIFICENCE,** *megaleiotēs* (*meg-al-eye-ot-ayce*). This noun appears only three times in the NT, and it is used exclusively to denote the "grandeur," "sublimity," or "majesty" of a deity. In Acts 19:27 it is used with reference to the goddess Artemis (Diana). Luke 9:43 describes the amazement of the people at the "majesty" of God. The writer of 2 Peter claims that he was among those who were eyewitnesses of the "majesty" of Christ (1:16). (Strong's #3168)

Majesty—*the dignity and power of a ruler*
A. Of God:
   Splendor of . . . . Is. 2:2, 19, 21
   Voice of . . . . Ps. 29:4
   Clothed with . . . . Ps. 93:1
B. Of Christ:
   Promised to . . . . Mic. 5:2–4
   Laid upon . . . . Ps. 21:5
   Eyewitness of . . . . 2 Pet. 1:16
C. Of kings:
   Solomon . . . . 1 Chr. 29:25
   Nebuchadnezzar . . . . Dan. 4:28, 30, 36; 5:18–21

Makaz—*end, boundary*
   Town in Judah . . . . 1 Kin. 4:9

Makheloth—*assemblies*
   Israelite camp . . . . Num. 33:25, 26

Makkedah—*place of shepherds*
   Canaanite town assigned
      to Judah . . . . Josh. 15:20, 41

Maktesh—*mortar*
   Valley in Jerusalem . . . . Zeph. 1:11

Malachi—*my messenger*
   Prophet and writer . . . . Mal. 1:1

Malachi, Book of—*a book of the Old Testament*
   God's love for Jacob . . . . Mal. 1:1–5
   The priesthood rebuked . . . . Mal. 1:6–2:17
   The messenger of the Lord . . . . Mal. 3:1–5
   Blessings of the tithe . . . . Mal. 3:6–12
   The day of the Lord . . . . Mal. 4:1–6

Malcam—*their king*
   Benjamite leader . . . . 1 Chr. 8:9

Malchiah (see Malchijah)

Malchiel—*God is king*
   Grandson of Asher; founder of
      Malchielites . . . . Gen. 46:17

Malchijah, Malchiah—*Yahweh is king*
1. Gershonite Levite . . . . 1 Chr. 6:40
2. The father of Pashhur (Pashur) . . . . 1 Chr. 9:12;
   Jer. 21:1
   Called Melchiah . . . . Jer. 21:1
3. Head of a priestly division . . . . 1 Chr. 24:1, 6, 9
4. Royal prince . . . . Jer. 38:1, 6
5, 6. Two sons of Parosh; divorced their
      foreign wives . . . . Ezra 10:25
7. Son of Harim; divorced his
      foreign wife . . . . Ezra 10:31
   Helps rebuild walls . . . . Neh. 3:11
8. Son of Rechab; repairs gates . . . . Neh. 3:14
9. Postexilic goldsmith . . . . Neh. 3:31
10. Ezra's assistant . . . . Neh. 8:4

11. Signer of the covenant ....Neh. 10:1, 3

12. Choir member .... Neh. 12:42

Malchiram—*the king is exalted*
    Son of King Jeconiah..............1 Chr. 3:17, 18

Malchishua—*the king is salvation*
    Son of King Saul................... 1 Sam. 14:49
    Killed at Gilboa ....1 Sam. 31:2

Malchus—*king*
    Servant of the high priest............ John 18:10

Malformation—*irregular features*
    Of a giant .... 2 Sam. 21:20

Malice—*active intent to harm others*
A. Causes of:
    Unregenerate heart .... Prov. 6:14–16, 18, 19
    Satanic hatred.......................1 John 3:12
    Jealousy..........................1 Sam. 18:8–29
    Racial prejudice .... Esth. 3:5–15
B. Christian's attitude toward:
    Pray for those guilty of .... Matt. 5:44
    Clean out .... 1 Cor. 5:7, 8
    Put away .... Eph. 4:31
    Put off.................................Col. 3:8
    Laying aside............................1 Pet. 2:1
    Avoid manifestations ....1 Pet. 2:16
C. Characteristics:
    Unregenerate.............. Rom. 1:29; Titus 3:3
    God's wrath .... Rom. 1:18, 29
    Brings own punishment .... Ps. 7:15, 16

Mallothi—*I have talked*
    Son of Heman .... 1 Chr. 25:4, 26

Mallow—*saltiness*
    Perennial shrub that grows in salty
        marshes .... Job 30:4

Malluch—*reigning*
1. Merarite Levite....................... 1 Chr. 6:44
2. Chief of postexilic priests .... Neh. 12:2, 7
3. Son of Bani; divorced his foreign wife ...Ezra 10:29
4. Son of Harim; divorced his
     foreign wife ....Ezra 10:32
5, 6. Two who sign the covenant....... Neh. 10:4, 27

Malta—*an island in the Mediterranean*
    Site of Paul's shipwreck.............. Acts 28:1–8

Mammon—*wealth*
    Served as a master other than God .... Matt. 6:24

Mamre—*firmness*
1. Town or district near Hebron..........Gen. 23:19
    West of Machpelah .... Gen. 23:17, 19
    Abram dwelt by the oaks of .... Gen. 13:18
2. Amorite, brother of Eshcol ....Gen. 14:13

> **WORD STUDY**   **MAN,** *'adam* (aw-*dawm*). The noun *'adam* is usually translated "man." One usage of the word signifies man as a human being and distinct from animals or heavenly beings. This sense is used throughout the OT except for Gen. 2 and 3 and Eccl. 7:28 where man is distinct from woman,

also. Many times "man" is used in a collective manner meaning "humankind" (see Gen. 1:27). Some verses explicitly state that God differs from humans as in 1 Sam. 15:29 and Is. 31:3 where God's strength and power are contrasted with human ability. The first man is named "Adam" because he was created from earth (*'adamah*). (Strong's #120)

> **WORD STUDY**   **MAN,** *'ish* (*eesh*). The noun *'ish* is translated "man" or "husband." This word is used specifically of men as opposed to women and emphasizes man as a sexual being. Man is a procreator and husband. In Hos. 2:16 God is to be called "my husband" by Israel when they turn from chasing other gods. Occasionally the term is used in contrast to beasts or animals (Ex. 11:7) or in contrast with God (Gen. 37:29). The term can be used to refer to the occupants of a place, for example in the phrase "men of Israel." A final and rather unusual use of the term is "followers" or "soldiers" (Ezek. 39:20). (Strong's #376)

Man—*human being, male or female*
A. Original state of:
    Created by God....................Gen. 1:26, 27
    Created for God's pleasure and glory .....Is. 43:7;
        Rev. 4:11
    Made in God's image.................. Gen. 9:6
    Formed of dust .... Gen. 2:7
    Made upright........................ Eccl. 7:29
    Endowed with intelligence........ Gen. 2:19, 20;
        Col. 3:10
    Wonderfully made................. Ps. 139:14–16
    Given wide dominion .... Gen. 1:28
    From one.......................Acts 17:26–28
    Male and female .... Gen. 1:27
    Superior to animals .... Matt. 10:31
    Living being........................... Gen. 2:7
B. Sinful state of:
    Result of Adam's and Eve's
        disobedience.............Gen. 2:16, 17; 3:1–6
    Makes all sinners ....Rom. 5:12
    Brings physical death .... Gen. 2:16, 17, 19;
        Rom. 5:12–14
    Makes spiritually dead ....Eph. 2:1
C. Redeemed state of:
    Originates in God's love............... John 3:16
    Provides salvation for ....Titus 2:11
    Accomplished by Christ's death.... 1 Pet. 1:18–21
    Fulfills the new covenant............Heb. 8:8–13
    Entered by new birth................John 3:1–12
D. Final state of:
    Continues eternally .... Matt. 25:46
    Cannot be changed ....Luke 16:26
    Determined by faith or by unbelief.... John 3:36;
        2 Thess. 1:6–10
E. Christ's relation to:
    Gives light to .... John 1:9
    Knows nature of .... John 2:25

Took nature of. . . . . .Heb. 2:14–16
In the likeness . . . . .Rom. 8:3
Only Mediator for . . . . 1 Tim. 2:5
Died for. . . . . Heb. 9:26, 28; 1 Pet. 1:18–21
F. Certain aspects of:
　First—Adam . . . . .1 Cor. 15:45, 47
　Last—Christ . . . . 1 Cor. 15:45
　Natural—unregenerate. . . . . 1 Cor. 2:14
　Outward—physical . . . . 2 Cor. 4:16
　Inner—spiritual .Rom. 7:22
　New—regenerate . . . . Eph. 2:15

Man of Sin (see Antichrist)

Manaen—*comforter*
Prophet and teacher in church at
　Antioch . . . . .Acts 13:1

Manahath—*resting place*
1. Son of Shobal. Gen. 36:23
2. City of exile for sons of Ehud . . . . 1 Chr. 8:6
　Citizens of, called Manahethites . . . . . .1 Chr. 2:54

Manasseh—*making to forget*
1. Joseph's firstborn son . . . . Gen. 41:50, 51
　Adopted by Jacob . . . . .Gen. 48:5, 6
　Loses his birthright to Ephraim . . . Gen. 48:13–20
　Ancestor of a tribe . . . . .Num. 1:34, 35
2. Sons of . . . . .Num. 26:28–34
　Census of . . . . .Num. 1:34, 35
　Second census of. . . . . Num. 26:34
　One half of, desire region in east
　　Jordan. . . . . Num. 32:33–42
　Help Joshua against Canaanites. . . . .Josh. 1:12–18
　Division of, into eastern and western . . . Josh. 22:7
　Region assigned to eastern half . . . . Deut. 3:12–15
　Land assigned to western half. . . . . . .Josh. 17:1–13
　Zelophehad's daughters included in . . . Josh. 17:3, 4
　Question concerning altar . . . . Josh. 22:9–34
　Joshua's challenge to . . . . .Josh. 17:14–18
　Designation of city (Golan) of refuge . . . . Josh. 20:8
　Did not drive out Canaanites . . . . . .Judg. 1:27, 28
　Gideon, a member of. . . . . .Judg. 6:15
　Some of, help David. . . . . 1 Chr. 12:19–31
　Many support Asa . . . . .2 Chr. 15:9
　Attend Passover . . . . 2 Chr. 30:1–18
　Idols destroyed in. . . . . .2 Chr. 31:1
　12,000 of, sealed. . . . . .Rev. 7:6
3. Intentional change of Moses' name to . . . Judg. 18:30
4. Son and successor of Hezekiah, king
　of Judah . . . . .2 Kin. 21:1
　Reigns wickedly; restores
　　idolatry. . . . . .2 Kin. 21:1–16; 2 Chr. 33:1–9
　Captured and taken to Babylon,. . .2 Chr. 33:10, 11
　Repents and is restored. . . . . 2 Chr. 33:12, 13
　Removes idols and altars . . . . 2 Chr. 33:14–20
5, 6. Two men who divorce their foreign
　wives . . . . Ezra 10:30, 33

Mandrake—*a rhubarblike herb, having narcotic qualities*
Supposed to induce human
　fertility. . . . . Gen. 30:14–16; Song 7:13
Gives off a fragrance . . . . Song 7:13

Manger—*a feeding place for cattle*
Place of Jesus' birth . . . . Luke 2:7, 12
Called "crib" . . . . .Is. 1:3
Same as "stall". . . . . .Luke 13:15

> **WORD STUDY**
> **MANIFEST, REVEAL,** *emphanizō* (em-fan-*id*-zoh). This verb literally means "to make visible." With reference to Jesus Christ, it is used in the sense of "reveal" or "manifest" (John 14:21, 22) and "appear" (Matt. 27:53; Heb. 9:24). *Emphanizō* can also mean "to make known," "to explain," "to inform" (Acts 23:15), "to make a report" (Acts 23:22), or even "to make charges against" (Acts 24:1; 25:2). (Strong's #1718)

Manifest—*to make something clear or evident*
A. Applied to God's:
　Nature. . . . . .Rom. 1:19
　Revelation . . . . .Col. 1:26
　Knowledge. . . . . 2 Cor. 2:14
　Love. . . . . .1 John 4:9
　Judgments . . . . .Rev. 15:4
B. Applied to Christ's:
　Nature. . . . . .1 Tim. 3:16
　Presence . . . . John 1:31
　Life. . . . . .1 John 1:2
　Glory. . . . . .John 2:11
　Purpose. . . . . .1 John 3:8
C. Applied to evil:
　Works of the flesh . . . . .Gal. 5:19
Humankind's:
　Deeds. . . . . John 3:21
　Folly. . . . . 2 Tim. 3:9

Manliness—*masculine characteristics at their best*
A. Qualities of:
　Self-control. 1 Cor. 9:25–27
　Mature understanding . . . . .1 Cor. 14:20
　Courage in danger . . . . 2 Sam. 10:11, 12
　Endure hardship. . . . . 2 Tim. 2:3–5
B. Examples of:
　Caleb . . . . Num. 13:30
　Joshua . . . . .Josh. 1:1–11
　Jonathan. .1 Sam. 14:1, 6–14
　Daniel . . . . .Dan. 6:1–28
　Paul . . . . 1 Cor. 11:23–28

Manna—*what is it?*
A. Features regarding:
　Description of . . . . Num. 11:7–9
　Bread given by God . . . .Ex. 16:4, 15; John 6:30–32
　Previously unknown . . . . Deut. 8:3, 16
　Fell at evening. Num. 11:9
　Despised by people. . . . . .Num. 11:4–6
　Ceased at conquest. . . . . .Josh. 5:12
B. Illustrative of:
　God's glory. . . . . .Ex. 16:7
　Christ as the true bread . . . . .John 6:32–35

Manners—*a way of life*
A. Evil kinds:
　Sexual immorality . . . . .Gen. 19:31–36

Customs of other nations . . . . .Lev. 20:23
Lovers of self . . . . 2 Tim. 3:2–4
Careless living. . . . . .Judg. 18:7
B. Good kinds:
Prayer . . . . .Matt. 6:9
Faithfulness. . . . . Acts 20:18
Holy conduct. 2 Pet. 3:11, 12

Manoah—*rest, quiet*
Danite; father of Samson . . . . Judg. 13:1–25
Speaks of Angel of God. . . . . Judg. 13:11–22
Disapproves of Philistine wife for
Samson. . . . . .Judg. 14:3

Mantle—*a garment*
Female garment . . . . Is. 3:22
Outer garment (robe) . . . . 1 Kin. 19:13, 19;
2 Kin. 2:8, 13, 14

Maoch—*oppression*
Father of Achish, king of Gath . . . . 1 Sam. 27:2

Maon—*abode*
1. Village in Judah . . . . .Josh. 15:55
David stayed at . . . . 1 Sam. 23:24, 25
House of Nabal. . . . . 1 Sam. 25:2
2. Shammai's son . . . . 1 Chr. 2:45
3. People called Maonites among Israel's
oppressors . . . . Judg. 10:12
Called Meunites . . . . .2 Chr. 26:7
Listed among returnees . . . . . Ezra 2:50; Neh. 7:52

Mara—*bitter*
Name chosen by Naomi . . . . Ruth 1:20

Marah—*bitterness*
First Israelite camp after passing
through the Red Sea . . . . Num. 33:8, 9

Maralah—*downward slope*
Village in Zebulun . . . . Josh. 19:11

Marble—*crystalline limestone*
In columns . . . . Esth. 1:6
In Babylon's trade. . . . . .Rev. 18:12

Mareshah—*summit*
1. Father of Hebron . . . . 1 Chr. 2:42
2. Judahite . . . . 1 Chr. 4:21
3. Town of Judah . . . . Josh. 15:44
City built for defense
by Rehoboam . . . . 2 Chr. 11:5, 8
Great battle here between
Asa and Zerah . . . . 2 Chr. 14:9–12

Mariners—*sailors; seamen*
Skilled . . . . .1 Kin. 9:27
Fearful. . . . . .Jon. 1:5
Weeping . . . . Ezek. 27:8–36
Storm-tossed . . . . Acts 27:27–31

Mark
As object, thing:
Sign for preservation . . . . Ezek. 9:4–6
Sign of those following the Antichrist . . . Rev. 13:16,
17; 14:9, 11; 20:4

Mark (John)—*a large hammer*
Son of Mary, a believer . . . . Acts 12:12
Cousin of Barnabas . . . . .Col. 4:10
Returns with Barnabas to Antioch . . . . Acts 12:25
Leaves Paul and Barnabas at Perga . . . . Acts 13:13
Paul refuses to take him again . . . . . Acts 15:37–39
Paul's approval of . . . . .2 Tim. 4:11
Peter's companion . . . . .1 Pet. 5:13
The author of the
second Gospel. . . . . Mark 1:1 (Title)

Mark, the Gospel of—*a book of the New Testament*
John the Baptist . . . . Mark 1:1–11
Choosing of the disciples . . . . Mark 3:13–19
Parables. . . . . Mark 4:1–34
Galilean tours . . . . Mark 1:21–45; 6:1–44
Peter's confession . . . . Mark 8:27–30
The Transfiguration . . . . Mark 9:1–13
Foretelling of Jesus' death . . . . .Mark 10:32–34
Entry into Jerusalem . . . . Mark 11:1–11
Controversy with religious
authorities . . . . .Mark 11:27–12:40
Events of the Crucifixion . . . . . . Mark 14:43–15:47
The Resurrection . . . . Mark 16:1–20

Marketplace
Place of:
Greetings . . . . Matt. 23:7
Public trial . . . . Acts 16:19, 20
Evangelism. . . . . .Acts 17:17
Trade, Tyre to all nations . . . . Is. 23:1–4

Maroth—*bitter fountains*
Town of Judah. . . . . .Mic. 1:12

Marred face
Disqualifies for service . . . . Lev. 21:18

Marriage
A. Described as:
Instituted by God. . . . . .Gen. 2:18–24
Honorable among all. . . . . Heb. 13:4
Permanent bond . . . . Matt. 19:6
Intimate bond . . . . Matt. 19:5
Blessed of God for having children . . . Gen. 1:27, 28
Dissolved by death. . . . . .Rom. 7:2, 3
Means of sexual love . . . . .Prov. 5:15–19
Centered in love and obedience . . . . . Eph. 5:21–33
Worthy of Jesus' presence. . . . . John 2:1–11
B. Prohibitions concerning:
Near of kin. . . . . Lev. 18:6–18
Fornication excludes remarriage . . . . . . Matt. 5:32
Polygamy forbidden. . . . . .Lev. 18:18
Idol worshipers . . . . .Ex. 34:16
C. Arrangements for (among Hebrews):
Arranged by parents . . . . Gen. 21:21
Parties consenting . . . . Gen. 24:8
Parental concern in . . . . Gen. 26:34, 35
Romance involved in. . . . . .Gen. 29:10, 11
Commitment considered
binding. . . . . Gen. 24:58, 60
Unfaithfulness in, brings
God's judgment . . . . Heb. 13:4

D. Ceremonies of (among Hebrews):

Time of joy . . . . .Jer. 7:34

Bride richly attired. . . . . Ps. 45:13–15

Bride veiled . . . . .Gen. 24:65

Bridegroom decks himself. . . . . .Is. 61:10

Wedding feast in bridegroom's
house. . . . . Matt. 22:1–10

Distinctive clothing of guests . . . . . Matt. 22:11, 12

Christ attends . . . . John 2:1–11

Festivities following . . . . .John 2:8–10

Gifts bestowed at . . . . .Ps. 45:12

Parental blessing on. . . . . .Gen. 24:60

Change of name . . . . .Ps. 45:10, 16

Consummation of . . . . Gen. 29:23

Proof of virginity . . . . .Deut. 22:13–21

E. Purposes of:

Man's happiness . . . . Gen. 2:18

Continuance of the race . . . . Gen. 1:28

Godly offspring . . . . Mal. 2:14, 15

Prevention of fornication. . . . . 1 Cor. 7:2, 9

Complete satisfaction . . . . . Prov. 5:19; 1 Tim. 5:14

F. Denial of:

As a prophetic sign. . . . . .Jer. 16:2

For a specific purpose . . . . Matt. 19:10–12

As a sign of apostasy . . . . 1 Tim. 4:1–3

To those in heaven . . . . Matt. 22:30

G. Figurative of:

God's union with Israel. . . . . Is. 54:5

Christ's union with His church. . . . . .Eph. 5:23–32

Marrow—*the vascular tissue which occupies the cavities
of bones*

A. Used literally of:

Healthy person .Job 21:23, 24

Inner being. . . . . Heb. 4:12

B. Used figuratively of:

Spiritual sustenance. . . . . .Ps. 63:5

Marsena—*forgetful man*

Persian prince . . . . Esth. 1:14

Mars' Hill (see Areopagus)

Marsh

Area of grassy, soft, wet land. . . . . .Ezek. 47:11

Martha—*lady, mistress*

Sister of Mary and Lazarus . . . . John 11:1, 2

Welcomes Jesus into her home . . . . .Luke 10:38

Rebuked by Christ. . . . . Luke 10:38–42

Affirms her faith . . . . .John 11:21–32

Serves supper. . . . . .John 12:1–3

Martyrdom—*death for the sake of one's faith*

A. Causes of:

Evil deeds. . . . . .1 John 3:12

Persecution by the Antichrist . . . . .Rev. 13:15

Harlot Babylon's hatred . . . . .Rev. 17:5, 6

Our Christian faith . . . . .Rev. 6:9

B. Believer's attitude toward:

Remember Christ's warning . . . . . . Matt. 10:21, 22

Do not fear. . . . . Matt. 10:28

Be prepared . . . . Matt. 16:24, 25

Be ready for, if necessary . . . . .Acts 21:13

C. Examples of:

Prophets and apostles . . . . .Luke 11:50, 51

John the Baptist . . . . Mark 6:18–29

Stephen . . . . .Acts 7:58–60

Early disciples of the Lord . . . . .Acts 9:1, 2

Marvel—*to express astonishment*

A. Expressed by Christ because of:

Centurion's faith. .Matt. 8:10

Unbelief of many .Mark 6:6

B. Expressed by men because of Christ's:

Power. . . . . Matt. 8:27

Knowledge. . . . . John 7:15

Word . . . . Matt. 22:22

Mary—*same as Miriam*

1. Jesus' mother. . . . . Matt. 1:16

Prophecies concerning . . . . .Is. 7:14

Engaged to Joseph . . . . .Luke 1:26, 27

Told of virginal conception . . . . Luke 1:28–38

Visits Elizabeth. . . . . Luke 1:39–41

Offers praise . . . . Luke 1:46–55

Gives birth to Jesus . . . . Luke 2:6–20

Flees with Joseph to Egypt. . . . . Matt. 2:13–18

Mother of other children . . . . .Mark 6:3

Visits Jerusalem with Jesus . . . . Luke 2:41–52

Entrusted to John's care . . . . .John 19:25–27

Involved in Jesus' first miracle . . . . . .John 2:3–11

In Upper Room. . . . . Acts 1:13, 14

2. Wife of Clopas . . . . .John 19:25

Mother of James and Joses. . . . . Matt. 27:56

One of the women at the Cross. . . . Matt. 27:55, 56

Follows Jesus' body to the tomb . . . . . Matt. 27:61

Sees the risen Lord . . . . Matt. 28:1, 9, 10

Tells His disciples of resurrection . . . Matt. 28:7–9;
Luke 24:9–11

3. Mary Magdalene . . . . .Matt. 27:56, 61

Delivered from seven demons. . . . . Luke 8:2

Contributes to support of Christ . . . . . .Luke 8:2, 3

Looks on the crucified Savior . . . . . Matt. 27:55, 56

Follows Jesus' body to the tomb . . . . . . Matt. 27:61

Visits Jesus' tomb with Mary, mother
of James . . . . Mark 16:1–8

Tells the disciples . . . . John 20:2

First to see the risen Lord. . . . . .Mark 16:9;
John 20:11–18

4. Mary, the sister of Martha
and Lazarus. . . . . .John 11:1, 2

Commended by Jesus . . . . Luke 10:38–42

Grieves for Lazarus . . . . John 11:19, 20, 28–33

Anoints Jesus. . . . . .John 12:1–3, 7

Commended again by Jesus. . . . . Matt. 26:7–13

5. Mark's mother . . . . Acts 12:12–17

6. Christian disciple at Rome . . . . Rom. 16:6

Mash

Division of the Arameans. . . . . Gen. 10:23

Called Meshech. . . . . 1 Chr. 1:17

Mashal

Refuge city given to the Levites . . . . 1 Chr. 6:74

Called Mishal . . . . .Josh. 19:26; 21:30

Mason—*one who lays stones or bricks*

A. Sent by Hiram to help:

David . . . . .2 Sam. 5:11

Solomon . . . . 1 Kin. 5:18

B. Used in temple:

Repairs . . . . .2 Chr. 24:12

Rebuilding . . . . .Ezra 3:7

Masrekah—*vineyard*

City of Edom . . . . Gen. 36:36

Massa—*burden*

Son of Ishmael . . . . .Gen. 25:12, 14

Massah and Meribah—*testing and strife*

Named together . . . . .Ex. 17:7

Named separately . . . . Deut. 33:8

First locality, at Rephidim, Israel just out

of Egypt . . . . .Ex. 17:1–7

Levites proved . . . . Deut. 33:8

Second locality, at Kadesh, 40 years

later . . . . .Num. 20:1–13

Moses and Aaron rebel here . . . . Num. 20:24

Tragic events recalled by Moses . . . . . . .Deut. 6:16

Used as a boundary of the land . . . . .Ezek. 47:17, 19

Used for spiritual lesson . . . . .Heb. 3:7–12

Mast—*a vertical support for sails and rigging on a sailing ship*

A. Used literally of:

Cedars of Lebanon . . . . .Ezek. 27:5

B. Used figuratively of:

Strength of enemies . . . . Is. 33:23

Master

A. Descriptive of:

Owner of slaves . . . . Ex. 21:4–6

King . . . . 1 Chr. 12:19

Prophet . . . . 2 Kin. 2:3, 5

B. Kinds of:

Unmerciful . . . . 1 Sam. 30:13–15

Angry . . . . .Luke 14:21

Good . . . . Gen. 24:9–35

Believing . . . . 1 Tim. 6:2

Heavenly . . . . .Col. 4:1

Master builder

Paul describes himself as . . . . 1 Cor. 3:10

Master workmen—*craftsmen*

Bezalel . . . . .Ex. 31:1–5

Hiram (Huram) of Tyre . . . . 1 Kin. 7:13–50

Aquila and Priscilla . . . . Acts 18:2, 3

Demetrius . . . . Acts 19:24

Mate—*the male or female of a pair*

God provides for . . . . Is. 34:15, 16

Materialistic—*concerned for worldly goods only*

Christ condemns . . . . Luke 12:16–21

Sadducees described as . . . . Acts 23:8

Christians forbidden to live as . . . 1 Cor. 15:30–34

Mathematics, spiritual

A. General:

Addition:

God's Word . . . . Deut. 4:2

Knowledge will increase . . . . Dan. 12:4

Increased riches . . . . .Ps. 62:10

Subtraction:

God's commandments . . . . Deut. 12:32

Multiplication:

Human family . . . . Gen. 1:28

B. Unrighteous:

Addition:

Wealth . . . . .Ps. 73:12

Guilt . . . . .2 Chr. 28:13

Sin . . . . Is. 30:1

Subtraction:

Wealth obtained by fraud . . . . .Prov. 13:11

Life shortened . . . . Ps. 55:23; Prov. 10:27

Multiplication:

Sorrow by idolatry . . . . Ps. 16:4

Transgression .Prov. 29:16

C. Righteous:

Addition:

Years . . . . .Prov. 3:1, 2; 4:10

Blessing without sorrow . . . . .Prov. 10:22

By putting God first . . . . Matt. 6:33

Graces . . . . 2 Pet. 1:5–7

In latter years . . . . Job 42:12

Subtraction:

Disease . . . . .Ex. 15:26

Taken from evil .Is. 57:1

Multiplication:

Prosperity . . . . Deut. 8:1, 11–13

Length of days . . . . .Deut. 11:18–21; Prov. 9:11

Mercy, peace, love . . . . Jude 2

Church . . . . .Acts 9:31

Matred—*expulsion*

Mother-in-law of Hadar (Hadad), an

Edomite king .Gen. 36:39

Matri—*rainy*

Saul's Benjamite family . . . . 1 Sam. 10:21

Mattan—*gift*

1. Priest of Baal . . . . 2 Kin. 11:18

Killed by the people . . . . .2 Chr. 23:16, 17

2. Father of Shephatiah .Jer. 38:1

Mattanah—*gift*

Israelite camp . . . . Num. 21:18, 19

Mattaniah—*gift of Yahweh*

1. King Zedekiah's original name . . . . 2 Kin. 24:17

2. Son of Micah, a Levite and Asaphite . . . 1 Chr. 9:15

3. Musician, son of Heman . . . . 1 Chr. 25:4, 16

4. Spirit of the Lord came upon . . . . 2 Chr. 20:14

5. Levite under King Hezekiah . . . . 2 Chr. 29:13

6. Postexilic Levite and singer . . . . .Neh. 11:17

7. Levite gatekeeper . . . . Neh. 12:25

8. Postexilic Levite . . . . Neh. 12:35

9. Levite in charge of treasuries . . . . .Neh. 13:13

10, 11, 12, 13. Four postexilic Jews who
divorced foreign wives .... Ezra 10:26–37

Mattattah—*gift (of God)*
Son of Nathan; ancestor of Christ ..... Luke 3:31

Mattathiah—*Greek form of Mattithiah*
1. Postexilic ancestor of Christ .... Luke 3:25
2. Another postexilic ancestor of Christ ... Luke 3:26

Mattattah—*gift of Yahweh*
One who put away his foreign wife .... Ezra 10:33

Mattenai—*gift of Yahweh*
1. Priest in the time of Joiakim .... Neh. 12:19
2, 3. Two who put away their foreign
wives .... Ezra 10:33, 37

Matter—*something*
A. Descriptive of:
Lawsuit .... 1 Cor. 6:1
Sum of something .... Eccl. 12:13
Love affair .... Ruth 3:18
News .... Mark 1:45
B. Kinds of:
Evil................................ Ps. 64:5
Unknown .... Dan. 2:5, 10

Matthan—*gift*
Ancestor of Joseph .... Matt. 1:15, 16

Matthat—*gift*
1. Ancestor of Christ .... Luke 3:24
2. Another ancestor of Christ .... Luke 3:29

Matthew—*gift of Yahweh*
Tax collector .... Matt. 9:9
Becomes Christ's follower .... Matt. 9:9
Appointed an apostle.............. Matt. 10:2, 3
Called Levi, the son of Alphaeus ...... Mark 2:14
Entertains Jesus with a great feast... Mark 2:14, 15
In the Upper Room .... Acts 1:13
Author of the first Gospel .... Matt. 1:1 (Title)

Matthew, the Gospel of—*a book of the New Testament*
Events of Jesus' birth .... Matt. 1:18–2:23
John the Baptist .... Matt. 3:1–17
The temptation.................... Matt. 4:1–11
Jesus begins His ministry......... Matt. 4:12–17
The Sermon on the Mount....... Matt. 5:1–7:29
Christ, about John the Baptist ..... Matt. 11:1–19
Conflict with the Pharisees and
Sadducees .... Matt. 15:39–16:6
Peter's confession .... Matt. 16:13–20
Prophecy of death and
resurrection.................. Matt. 20:17–19
Jerusalem entry.................... Matt. 21:1–11
Authority of Jesus............. Matt. 21:23–22:14
Woes to the Pharisees .... Matt. 23:1–36
Discourse on signs of end of age........ Matt. 24
Garden of Gethsemane......... Matt. 26:36–56
Crucifixion and burial .... Matt. 27:27–66
Resurrection of Christ .... Matt. 28:1–20

Matthias—*gift of Yahweh*
Chosen by lot to replace Judas....... Acts 1:15–26

Mattithiah—*gift of Yahweh*
1. Korahite Levite...................... 1 Chr. 9:31
2. Levite, son of Jeduthun, and temple
musician .... 1 Chr. 15:18, 21
3. One who put away his foreign wife ..... Ezra 10:43
4. Levite attendant to Ezra................. Neh. 8:4

Mattock—*an agricultural instrument for digging and hoeing*
Sharpened for battle .... 1 Sam. 13:20–22

WORD STUDY   **MATURE, COMPLETE, PERFECT,** *teleios* (*tel*-eye-oss). This adjective expresses the idea of something or someone "having attained the end (or purpose or full measure)" thus "complete" or "perfect" (James 1:4; 1 John 4:18). When it is used to describe persons, it can mean "full-grown," "mature," or "adult" (1 Cor. 14:20; cf. 2:6; Eph. 4:13, 14) in contrast to children, or it can mean "perfect" or "fully developed" in a moral sense (Matt. 19:21; Col. 4:12; James 1:4; 3:2). God is said to be "perfect" (Matt. 5:48) and to give "perfect" gifts (James 1:17). (Strong's #5046)

Maturity, spiritual
Do away with childish things .... 1 Cor. 13:11
Be mature in your thinking......... 1 Cor. 14:20
Solid food is for.................... Heb. 5:11–14
Overcoming the Evil One............. 1 John 2:14

Mazzaroth—*the signs of the zodiac or a constellation*
Descriptive of God's power .... Job 38:32

Meal—*ground grain used for food*
One-tenth of an ephah of............ Num. 5:15
Used in offerings .... 1 Kin. 4:22
Millstones and grind.................. Is. 47:2
Three measures of .... Matt. 13:33

Meals—*times of eating*
A. Times of:
Early morning..................... John 21:4–12
At noon (for laborers) .... Ruth 2:14
In the evening .... Gen. 19:1–3
B. Extraordinary and festive:
Guests invited .... Matt. 22:3, 4
Received with a kiss................. Luke 7:45
Feet washed .... Luke 7:44
Anointed with ointment.............. Luke 7:38
Fellowship for early believers ...... Acts 2:44–46
Proper dress..................... Matt. 22:11, 12
Seated according to rank .... Matt. 23:6
Special guest honored .... 1 Sam. 9:22–24
Entertainment provided............. Luke 15:25
Temperate habits taught........... Prov. 23:1–3
Intemperance condemned.......... Amos 6:4–6
See Entertainment; Feasts

Means of grace
A. Agents of:
Holy Spirit .... Gal. 5:16–26
God's Word .... 1 Thess. 2:13
Prayer .... Rom. 8:15–27

Christian fellowship .... Mal. 3:16–18
Public worship...................... 1 Thess. 5:6
Christian witnessing ....Acts 8:4
God's gift .... Eph. 2:8

B. Words expressive of:
Stir up the gift........................2 Tim. 1:6
Neglect not the spiritual gift........ 1 Tim. 4:14
Take heed to the ministry ....Col. 4:17
Grow in.............................2 Pet. 3:18
Riches of God's grace ....Eph. 1:7

C. Use of, brings:
Assurance........................ 2 Pet. 1:5–12
Stability........................... Eph. 4:11–16

D. Enemies of:
Devil .... 1 Thess. 3:5
World............................ 1 John 2:15–17
Coldness........................... Rev. 3:14–18

Mearah—*cave*
Unconquered by Joshua .... Josh. 13:1, 4

Measure—*a standard of size, quantity or values*
A. Objectionable:
Differing (different) .... Deut. 25:14, 15
Short .... Mic. 6:10
Using themselves as a gauge .... 2 Cor. 10:12

B. As indicative of:
Earth's weight....................... Is. 40:12
Punishment inflicted ....Matt. 7:2
Giving and receiving.................Luke 6:38

C. Figurative of:
Great size .... Hos. 1:10
Sin's ripeness .... Matt. 23:32
The Spirit's infilling .... John 3:34
Humankind's ability................ 2 Cor. 10:13
Perfection of faith .... Eph. 4:13, 16

Measuring line—*a cord of specified length for measuring*
Signifies hope .... Jer. 31:38–40; Zech. 2:1

Mebunnai—*built*
One of David's mighty men........ 2 Sam. 23:27
Called Sibbechai.................... 1 Chr. 11:29

Mecherathite—*a dweller in Mecherah*
Descriptive of Hepher, one of David's
mighty men.................... 1 Chr. 11:36

Meconah—*foundation*
Town of Judah.................... Neh. 11:25, 28

Medad—*beloved*
One of the seventy elders receiving
the Spirit .... Num. 11:26–29

Medan—*judgment*
Son of Abraham by Keturah .... Gen. 25:1, 2

Meddling—*interfering with the affairs of others*
Brings a king's death .... 2 Chr. 35:21–24
Christians........................... 1 Pet. 4:15
Such called "busybodies" .... 2 Thess. 3:11

Medeba—*full waters*
Old Moabite town .... Num. 21:29, 30
Assigned to Reuben .... Josh. 13:9, 16

Syrians defeated here............... 1 Chr. 19:6, 7
Reverts to Moab .... Is. 15:2

Medes, Media—*the people and country of the Medes*
A. Characteristics of:
Part of Medo-Persian Empire .... Esth. 1:19
Inflexible laws of .... Dan. 6:8, 12, 15
Among those at Pentecost ....Acts 2:9

B. Kings of, mentioned in the Bible:
Cyrus...............................Ezra 1:1
Ahasuerus............................Ezra 4:6
Artaxerxes ....Ezra 4:7; 6:14
Darius ....Ezra 6:1
Xerxes .... Dan. 11:2

C. Place of, in Bible history:
Israel (northern kingdom)
deported to .... 2 Kin. 17:6
Babylon falls to ....Dan. 5:30, 31
"Darius the Mede," new ruler of
Babylon .... Dan. 5:31
Daniel rises high in the kingdom of ...Dan. 6:1–28
Cyrus, king of Persia, allows Jews to
return .... 2 Chr. 36:22, 23
Esther and Mordecai live under
Ahasuerus, king of ....Esth. 1:3, 19

D. Prophecies concerning:
Agents in Babylon's fall.......... Is. 13:17–19
Cyrus, king of, God's servant .... Is. 44:28
"Inferior" kingdom .... Dan. 2:39
Compared to a bear .... Dan. 7:5
Kings of............................ Dan. 11:2
War with Greece..................... Dan. 11:2

Mediation—*a friendly intervention designed to render assistance*
A. Purposes of:
Save a life ....Gen. 37:21, 22
Save a people .... Ex. 32:11–13
Obtain a wife.................... 1 Kin. 2:13–25
Obtain justice ....Job 9:33

B. Motives prompting:
People's fear.........................Deut. 5:5
Regard for human life............... Jer. 38:7–13
Sympathy for a sick man...........2 Kin. 5:6–8;
Matt. 17:15

C. Methods used:
Intense prayer ....Deut. 9:20–29
Flattery .... 1 Sam. 25:23–35
Appeal to self-preservation .... Esth. 4:12–17

Mediator, Christ our
A. His qualifications:
Bears God's image, man's likeness.... Phil. 2:6–8;
Heb. 2:14–17
Is both sinless and sin-bearer .... Is. 53:6–10;
Eph. 2:13–18
Endures God's wrath, brings God's
righteousness .... Rom. 5:6–19
Is sacrifice and the priest ..... Heb. 7:27; 10:5–22

B. How He performs the function, by:
Taking our nature .... 1 John 1:1–3

Dying as our substitute............ 1 Pet. 1:18, 19
Reconciling us to God................. Eph. 2:16

Medicine—*something prescribed to cure an illness*
A. General prescriptions:
Merry heart ....Prov. 15:13
Rest ....Ps. 37:7–11
Sleep...........................John 11:12, 13
Quarantine.........................Lev. 12:1–4
Sanitation......................Deut. 23:10–14
B. Specific prescriptions:
Figs.................................. Is. 38:21
Leaves ....Ezek. 47:12
Wine .... 1 Tim. 5:23
C. Used figuratively of:
Salvation........................... Jer. 8:22
Incurableness....................... Jer. 46:11
Spiritual stubbornness .... Jer. 51:8, 9
See Diseases

> **WORD STUDY**
> **MEDITATE,** *hagah* (haw-*gaw*). The verb *hagah* has several variations of meaning, one of which is to "meditate" or "muse." This occurs mostly in Ps., but also appears in Josh. 1:8 where the Lord instructs Joshua to meditate on the Book of the Law, which was given by Moses, in order to prosper. In Is. 33:18 the Lord says the people will "meditate on terror." Presumably these meditations will be accompanied by mutterings or murmurings, since most often the word is used to mean "moan" or "growl"—inarticulate sounds, which have neither a positive nor a negative connotation. (Strong's #1897)

Meditation—*quiet contemplation of spiritual truths*
A. Objects of, God's:
Word ....Ps. 119:148
Law................................ Josh. 1:8
Instruction....................... 1 Tim. 4:15
Works .... Ps. 77:12
B. Value of, for:
Understanding .... Ps. 49:3
Spiritual satisfaction ....Ps. 63:5, 6
Superior knowledge..................Ps. 119:99
Pleasing God .... Ps. 19:14
C. Extent of:
All the day ....Ps. 119:97
At evening ....Gen. 24:63
In night watches ....Ps. 119:148

Mediterranean Sea
Described as:
Sea .... Gen. 49:13
Great Sea.........................Josh. 1:4; 9:1
Sea, Philistia ....Ex. 23:31
Western Sea .... Deut. 11:24; Joel 2:20; Zech. 14:8

Mediums
A. Described as:
Source of defilement ....Lev. 19:31
Abomination....................Deut. 18:10–12
Whisperers........................Is. 8:19

B. The practicers, to be:
Cut off..............................Lev. 20:6
Put to death .... Lev. 20:27
C. Consulted by:
Saul............................1 Sam. 28:3–25
Manasseh ....2 Kin. 21:6
D. Condemned by:
Josiah.............................2 Kin. 23:24

Meek
Receiving the Word................. James 1:21
Stating our assurance .... James 3:13
Blessing for.........................Matt. 5:5

Megiddo—*place of troops*
City conquered by Joshua.............Josh. 12:21
Assigned to Manasseh................ Josh. 17:11
Inhabitants of, made slaves ....Judg. 1:27, 28
Deborah and Barak defeat
Canaanites here .... Judg. 5:1, 19–21
Site of Baana's headquarters .... 1 Kin. 4:12
Fortified by Solomon..............1 Kin. 9:15–19
King Ahaziah dies here............... 2 Kin. 9:27
King Josiah killed here .... 2 Kin. 23:29, 30
Mentioned in prophecy............. Zech. 12:11
Site of Armageddon...................Rev. 16:16

Mehetabel—*God benefits*
1. King Hadar's wife .... Gen. 36:39
2. Father of Delaiah.......................Neh. 6:10

Mehida—*renowned*
Ancestor of a family of returning
temple servants .... Ezra 2:52

Mehir—*price*
Judahite.......................... 1 Chr. 4:11

Meholathite—*a native of Meholah*
Descriptive of Adriel................1 Sam. 18:19

Mehujael—*smitten of God*
Cainite; father of Methushael.......... Gen. 4:18

Mehuman—*faithful*
Eunuch under King Ahasuerus .... Esth. 1:10

Me Jarkon—*waters of yellow color*
Territory of Dan near Joppa ...... Josh. 19:40, 46

Melatiah—*Yahweh has set free*
Postexilic workman.................... Neh. 3:7

Melchi—*my king*
Two ancestors of Jesus............. Luke 3:24, 28

Melchizedek—*king of righteousness*
A. Described as:
King of Salem .... Gen. 14:18
Priest of God .... Gen. 14:18
Receiver of a tenth of
Abram's goods .... Gen. 14:18–20
King of righteousness .... Heb. 7:2
Without parentage.................... Heb. 7:3
Great man.......................... Heb. 7:4
B. Typical of Christ's:
Eternity............................. Heb. 7:3

Priesthood . . . . Ps. 110:4
Kingship . . . . Heb. 8:1

Melea
Ancestor of Jesus . . . . Luke 3:31

Melech—*king*
Son of Micah, grandson of Jonathan . . . 1 Chr. 8:35

Melichu—*reigning*
Head of a household . . . . Neh. 12:14

Melon—*the watermelon*
Desired by Israelites in wilderness . . . . . Num. 11:5

Melting—*making a solid a liquid*
Used figuratively of:
Complete destruction . . . . Ex. 15:15
Discouragement . . . . Josh. 7:5
Defeatism . . . . Josh. 5:1
National discouragement . . . . Is. 19:1
Destruction of the wicked . . . . Ps. 68:2
God's presence . . . . Mic. 1:4
Testings . . . . Jer. 9:7
Troubled sea . . . . Ps. 107:26
Christ's pain on the cross . . . . Ps. 22:14

Mem
Thirteenth letter of the
Hebrew alphabet . . . . Ps. 119:97–104

Member—*a part of a larger whole*
A. Descriptive of:
Parts of the body . . . . Matt. 5:29, 30
Union with Christ . . . . 1 Cor. 6:15
The church . . . . 1 Cor. 12:27
B. Of the body:
Effect of sin in . . . . Rom. 7:5
Struggle in . . . . Rom. 7:23
C. Illustrative of:
Variety of Christian gifts . . . . Rom. 12:4, 5
God's design in . . . . 1 Cor. 12:18, 24

| WORD STUDY | **MEMORIAL**, *zikron* (zihk-*rohn*). The noun zikron, translated "memorial" or "re-minder," comes from the verb mean- |

ing "remember." A memorial might be in the form of a day that is set aside for feasting and other activities to commemorate an event, such as the Passover (Ex. 12:14). Objects, such as altar plates and stones, also are used as reminders. After the people of Israel crossed the Jordan, Joshua had stones set up as a memorial to the event (Josh. 4:7). A memorial might be recorded in a book so that others could read about and meditate on the events as is described in Mal. 3:16. (Strong's #2146)

Memorials—*things established to commemorate an event or a truth*
A. Established by humans:
Jacob's stone . . . . Gen. 28:18–22
Altar at Jordan . . . . Josh. 22:9–16
Feast of Purim . . . . Esth. 9:28
B. Established by God:
Passover . . . . Ex. 12:14

Pot of manna . . . . Ex. 16:32–34
Lord's Supper . . . . Luke 22:19

Memories—*the ability to revive past experiences*
A. Uses of, to recall:
Past blessings . . . . Ezra 9:5–15
Past sins . . . . Josh. 22:12–20
God's blessings . . . . Neh. 9:1–38
God's promises . . . . Neh. 1:8–11
Christian truths . . . . 2 Pet. 1:15–21
Prophecies . . . . John 2:19–22
Lost opportunities . . . . Ps. 137:1–3
B. Aids to:
Reminder . . . . 2 Sam. 12:1–13
Prick of conscience . . . . Gen. 41:9
Holy Spirit . . . . John 14:26

Memphis—*haven of good*
Ancient capital of Egypt . . . . Hos. 9:6
Called Noph:
Prophesied against by Isaiah . . . . Is. 19:13
Jews flee to . . . . Jer. 44:1
Denounced by the prophets . . . . Jer. 46:19

Memucan
Persian prince . . . . Esth. 1:14–21

Menahem—*comforter*
Cruel king of Israel . . . . 2 Kin. 15:14–18

Menan
Ancestor of Jesus . . . . Luke 3:31

Mending—*restoring something*
Of nets . . . . Matt. 4:21
Used figuratively . . . . Luke 5:36

Mene, Tekel, Upharsin
Sentence of doom . . . . Dan. 5:25
Written by God . . . . Dan. 5:5, 25
Interpreted by Daniel . . . . Dan. 5:24–29

Menstruation—*a woman's monthly flow*
Intercourse during, prohibited . . . . Lev. 18:19
End of, in old age . . . . Gen. 18:11
Called:
"Sickness" . . . . Lev. 20:18
"The manner of women" . . . . Gen. 31:35

Meonothai—*my habitations*
Judahite . . . . 1 Chr. 4:14

Mephaath—*splendor*
Reubenite town . . . . Josh. 13:18
Assigned to Merarite Levites . . . . Josh. 21:34, 37
Repossessed by Moabites . . . . Jer. 48:21

Mephibosheth—*one who destroys shame*
1. Son of King Saul . . . . 2 Sam. 21:8
2. Grandson of King Saul; crippled son of
Jonathan . . . . 2 Sam. 4:4–6
Reared by Machir . . . . 2 Sam. 9:4–6
Sought out and honored by David . . . 2 Sam. 9:1–13
Accused by Ziba . . . . 2 Sam. 16:1–4
Later explains his side to David . . . 2 Sam. 19:24–30
Spared by David . . . . 2 Sam. 21:7

Father of Micha .... 2 Sam. 9:12
Called Merib-Baal ....1 Chr. 8:34

Merab—*increase*
King Saul's eldest daughter .... 1 Sam. 14:49
Saul promises her to David, but gives
her to Adriel .... 1 Sam. 18:17–19

Meraiah—*rebellious*
Postexilic priest...................... Neh. 12:12

Meraioth—*rebellious*
1. Levite............................... 1 Chr. 6:6, 7
2. Son of Ahitub and father of Zadok..... 1 Chr. 9:11
3. Priestly household in Joiakim's time.....Neh. 12:15
Called Meremoth .... Neh. 12:3

Merari—*bitter*
1. Third son of Levi; brother of Gershon
and Kohath .... Gen. 46:11
Goes with Jacob to Egypt...........Gen. 46:8, 11
2. Descendants of Merari; called
Merarites ....Num. 26:57
Divided into two groups................Ex. 6:19
Duties assigned to ....Num. 3:35–37
Twelve cities assigned to........ Josh. 21:7, 34–40
Superintend temple music .... 1 Chr. 6:31–47
Help David bring up the ark ....1 Chr. 15:1–6
Divided into groups.............. 1 Chr. 23:6–23
Their duties described .... 1 Chr. 26:10–19
Participate in cleansing the house of
the Lord .... 2 Chr. 29:12–19
After the Exile, help Ezra .... Ezra 8:18, 19

Merarites (see Merari 2)

Merathaim—*double rebellion*
Name applied to Babylon.............. Jer. 50:21

Merchandise—*things for sale in trade*
A. Characteristics of:
Countries employed in .... Is. 45:14
Men occupied with.................. Matt. 22:5
Not mixed with spiritual things........ John 2:16
To be abolished.................. Rev. 18:11, 12
B. Figurative of:
Wisdom's profit ....Prov. 3:13, 14
Gospel's transformation............... Is. 23:18

Merchants—*traders*
Characteristics of:
Crossed the sea .... Is. 23:2
Lamentation over.................. Ezek. 27:2–36
Some do not observe
the Sabbath..................Neh. 13:19–21
Burden people with debts...........Neh. 5:1–13
Peddle goods .... Neh. 13:16
Trade with farmers ....Prov. 31:24
Form guilds ....Neh. 3:8–32
Destroyed with Babylon .... Rev. 18:3–19
Sailors, in Solomon's service ....1 Kin. 9:27, 28
Bring gold to Solomon.............. 2 Chr. 9:14
Bring horses to Solomon.............2 Chr. 9:28
Kingdom of heaven compared to... Matt. 13:45, 46

WORD STUDY **MERCY,** *eleos* (*el*-eh-oss). A noun meaning "mercy," *eleos* is not simply sympathy for someone; rather, it implies an active sense of "compassion" or "pity" for someone suffering or in distress. The cognate verb *eleeō* is used to implore Jesus for "mercy" or "pity"—a cry so basic that it is entrenched in Christian liturgy (Matt. 17:15)—and when Jesus was approached by someone in misery (as in Luke 18:38, 39), He characteristically responded with compassion (Matt. 20:30–34). Indeed, Jesus teaches that the law requires "mercy" (Matt. 23:23) and that God desires it (Matt. 9:13). Both God and Christ manifest "mercy" toward humanity (Rom. 9:23; Eph. 2:4–7; 1 Pet. 1:3). (Strong's #1656)

Mercy
A. Described as:
Great .... Is. 54:7
Sure .... Is. 55:3
Abundant............................1 Pet. 1:3
Tender............................... Ps. 25:6
New every morning.............. Lam. 3:22, 23
Enduring.......................... Ps. 136:1–26
B. Of God, seen in:
Regeneration ....1 Pet. 1:3
Salvation............................Titus 3:5
Christ's mission ....Luke 1:72, 78
Forgiveness............................ Ps. 51:1
C. In the Christian life:
Received in salvation................. 1 Cor. 7:25
Taught as a principle of life ....Matt. 5:7
Practiced as a gift ....Rom. 12:8
Obtained in prayer..................... Heb. 4:16
Reason of consecration................Rom. 12:1
Reason for hope .... Jude 21
D. Special injunctions concerning:
Put on ....Col. 3:12
E. Examples of:
David to Saul................... 1 Sam. 24:10–17
Christ to sinners..................... Matt. 9:13
F. Attitude of believers, to:
Cast themselves on................. 2 Sam. 24:14
Look for .... Jude 21
Show with cheerfulness ....Rom. 12:8

Mercy seat—*the covering of the ark*
Made of pure gold ....Ex. 25:17
Blood sprinkled upon ....Lev. 16:14, 15
God manifested over....................Lev. 16:2
Figurative of Christ................Heb. 9:5–12

Mered—*rebellion*
Judahite.......................... 1 Chr. 4:17
Had two wives...................... 1 Chr. 4:17, 18

Meremoth—*elevations*
1. Signer of the covenant...................Neh. 10:5
Called Meraioth .... Neh. 12:15
2. One who divorced his foreign wife ... Ezra 10:34, 36

3. Priest, son of Uriah; weighs silver
     and gold .... Ezra 8:33
     Repairs wall of Jerusalem........... Neh. 3:4, 21

Meres—*the forgetful one*
     Persian prince .... Esth. 1:13, 14

Merib-Baal—*Baal contends*
     Another name for Mephibosheth...... 1 Chr. 8:34

Merit—*reward given for something done additionally*
A. Of humankind, impossible because:
     None is good .... Rom. 3:12
     None is righteous .... Rom. 3:10
     We are all sinful .... Is. 6:5
     Our good comes from God .... 1 Cor. 15:9, 10
Our righteousness:
     Is unavailing .... Matt. 5:20
     Is Christ's .... 2 Cor. 5:21
     Cannot save .... Rom. 10:1–4
B. Of Christ:
     Secured by obedience .... Rom. 5:17–21
     Secured by His death............... Is. 53:10–12
     Obtained by faith................... Phil. 3:8, 9

Merodach—*bold*
     Supreme deity of the Babylonians .... Jer. 50:2
     Otherwise called Bel .... Is. 46:1

Merodach-Baladan—*Merodach has given a son*
     Sends ambassadors to Hezekiah .... Is. 39:1–8
     Also called Berodach-Baladan .... 2 Kin. 20:12

Merom—*high place*
     Lake on Jordan north of the Sea of
     Galilee .... Josh. 11:5, 7

Meronothite
     Citizen of Meronoth .... 1 Chr. 27:30

Meroz—*refuge*
     Town cursed for failing to help
     the Lord .... Judg. 5:23

Merry—*a spirit of gaiety; cheerful*
A. Good, comes from:
     Heart........................... Prov. 15:13, 15
     Restoration........................ Jer. 30:18, 19
     Christian joy .... James 5:13
B. Evil, results from:
     Careless unconcern .... Judg. 9:27
     Drunkenness...................... 1 Sam. 25:36
     False optimism .... 1 Kin. 21:7; Luke 12:19
     Sinful glee........................... Rev. 11:10

Mesha—*retreat*
1. Border of Joktan's descendants .... Gen. 10:30
2. Benjamite........................... 1 Chr. 8:8, 9
3. Son of Caleb .... 1 Chr. 2:42
4. King of Moab .... 2 Kin. 3:4

Meshach—*the shadow of the prince*
     Name given to Mishael................ Dan. 1:7
     Advanced to high position............ Dan. 2:49
     Refused to worship image .... Dan. 3:1–12
     Delivered from fiery furnace....... Dan. 3:13–30

Meshech—*tall*
1. Son of Japheth........................ Gen. 10:2
     Famous traders .... Ezek. 27:13
     Confederates with Gog............. Ezek. 38:2, 3
     Inhabitants of the netherworld.... Ezek. 32:18, 26
2. Son of Shem......................... 1 Chr. 1:17
     Same as Mash .... Gen. 10:23

Meshelemiah—*Yahweh repays*
     Father of Zechariah................ 1 Chr. 9:21
     Gatekeeper in the temple .... 1 Chr. 26:1
     Called Shelemiah .... 1 Chr. 26:14

Meshezabel—*God delivers*
1. Postexilic workman..................... Neh. 3:4
2. One who signs covenant.............. Neh. 10:21
3. Judahite .... Neh. 11:24

Meshillemith—*recompense*
     Postexilic priest................. 1 Chr. 9:10–12
     Called Meshillemoth................. Neh. 11:13

Meshillemoth—*acts of recompense*
     Ephraimite leader................... 2 Chr. 28:12

Meshobab—*restored*
     Descendant of Simeon .... 1 Chr. 4:34–38

Meshullam—*recompensed; rewarded*
1. Benjamite........................... 1 Chr. 8:17
2. Gadite leader..................... 1 Chr. 5:11, 13
3. Shaphan's grandfather .... 2 Kin. 22:3
4. Hilkiah's father .... 1 Chr. 9:11
5. Son of Zerubbabel .... 1 Chr. 3:19
6. A priest........................... 1 Chr. 9:10–12
7. Kohathite overseer.................... 2 Chr. 34:12
8. A second Benjamite.................... 1 Chr. 9:7
9. Another Benjamite .... 1 Chr. 9:8
10. Man commissioned to secure Levites.... Ezra 8:16
11. Levite who supports Ezra's reforms..... Ezra 10:15
12. One who divorced his foreign wife ..... Ezra 10:29
13. Postexilic workman.................. Neh. 3:4, 30
     His daughter married Tobiah's son..... Neh. 6:18
14. Postexilic workman..................... Neh. 3:4
15. One of Ezra's attendants .... Neh. 8:4
16, 17. Two priests who sign covenant.. Neh. 10:7, 20
18, 19. Two priests in Joiakim's time .. Neh. 12:13, 16
20. Gatekeeper .... Neh. 12:25
21. Participant in dedication services ..... Neh. 12:33

Meshullemeth—*feminine form of Meshullam*
     Wife of King Manasseh .... 2 Kin. 21:18, 19

Mesopotamia—*the country between two rivers*
     Abraham's native home .... Acts 7:2
     Place of Laban's household ..... Gen. 24:4, 10, 29
Called:
     Padan Aram....................... Gen. 25:20
     Syria........................... Gen. 31:20, 24
     Balaam came from................... Deut. 23:4
     Israel enslaved to .... Judg. 3:8, 10
     Chariots and horsemen hired from .... 1 Chr. 19:6
     Called Haran; conquered by
     Sennacherib .... 2 Kin. 19:12, 16
     People from, at Pentecost............... Acts 2:9

Messenger—*one who bears a message or does an errand*

A. Mission of, to:

Appease wrath...................... Gen. 32:3–6

Ask for favors ....Num. 20:14–17

Spy out...........................Josh. 6:17, 25

Assemble a nation ....Judg. 6:35

Secure provisions ....1 Sam. 25:4–14

Relay news ....1 Sam. 11:3–9

Stir up war ....Judg. 11:12–28

Sue for peace ....2 Sam. 3:12, 13

Offer sympathy......................1 Chr. 19:2

Call for help......................2 Kin. 17:4

Issue an ultimatum .... 1 Kin. 20:2–9

Deliver the Lord's message .... Hag. 1:13

B. Reception of:

Rejected ....Deut. 2:26–30

Humiliated........................ 1 Chr. 19:2–4

Rebuked .... 2 Kin. 1:2–5, 16

C. Significant examples of:

John the Baptist ....Mal. 3:1

Paul's thorn ....2 Cor. 12:7

Gospel workers ....2 Cor. 8:23; Phil. 2:25

> **WORD STUDY**
>
> **MESSIAH,** *mashiach* (maw-*shee*-akh). The noun *mashiach* is derived from the verb meaning "anoint," so that a messiah is one who is anointed for a particular purpose. The title is used for a king of Israel anointed by divine command. The high priest of Israel is also an anointed one (Lev. 4:3, 5) as is Cyrus, the king of Persia (Is. 45:1). From Dan. 9:25, 26 comes the prophecy of a coming messianic Prince. As can be seen, there is not a clear OT picture of what a messiah's role is to be. (Strong's #4899)

> **WORD STUDY**
>
> **MESSIAH,** *Messias* (mehs-*see*-ahs). This noun, which appears only two times in the NT, is the Greek transliteration of the Hebrew and Aramaic words for "Anointed One" (Heb. *mashiach*). Both instances of *Messias* are found in the Gospel of John (1:41; 4:25), and each time the Greek translation *Christos* is provided. See the topical word study: "Christ." (Strong's #3323)

Messiah, the

A. Described as:

Seed of woman .... Gen. 3:15

Promised Seed............ Gen. 12:1–3; Gal. 3:16

Star out of Jacob ....Num. 24:17; Luke 3:34

Of Judah's tribe............. Gen. 49:10; Heb. 7:14

Son of David ....Is. 11:1–10; Matt. 1:1

Prophet ....Deut. 18:15–19; Acts 3:22, 23

Priest after Melchizedek's order........ Ps. 110:4;

Heb. 6:20

King of David's line.......Jer. 23:5; Luke 1:32, 33

Son of God.................. Ps. 2:7, 8; Acts 13:33

Son of Man................ Dan. 7:13; Mark 8:38

Immanuel................. Is. 7:14; Matt. 1:22, 23

Branch.....................Jer. 23:5; Zech. 3:8

Chief cornerstone.........Ps. 118:22; 1 Pet. 2:4, 7

Servant ....Is. 42:1–4; Matt. 12:18, 21

B. Mission of, to:

Introduce the new covenant .... Jer. 31:31–34;

Matt. 26:26–30

Preach the gospel ....Is. 61:1–3; Luke 4:17–19

Bring peace...............Is. 9:6, 7; Heb. 2:14–16

Die for humankind's sin.............. Is. 53:4–6;

1 Pet. 1:18–20

Unite God's people.... Is. 19:23–25; Eph. 2:11–22

Call the Gentiles......... Is. 11:10; Rom. 15:9–12

Rule from David's throne............. Ps. 45:5–7;

Acts 2:30–36

Be a priest.......... Zech. 6:12, 13; Heb. 1:3; 8:1

Destroy Satan ....Rom. 16:20; 1 John 3:8

Bring in everlasting righteousness..... Dan. 9:24;

Matt. 3:15; 2 Cor. 5:21

C. Christ the true Messiah, proved by:

Birth at Bethlehem..........Mic. 5:2; Luke 2:4–7

Born of a virgin........... Is. 7:14; Matt. 1:18–25

Appearing in the second temple.......Hag. 2:7, 9;

John 18:20

Working miracles........ Is. 35:5, 6; Matt. 11:4, 5

Rejection by the Jews.................. John 1:11

Vicarious death........... Is. 53:1–12; 1 Pet. 3:18

Coming at the appointed time .....Dan. 9:24–27;

Mark 1:15

D. Other prophecies concerning:

Worship .... Ps. 72:10–15; Matt. 2:1–11

Flight to Egypt .... Hos. 11:1; Matt. 2:13–15

Forerunner.................Mal. 3:1; Mark 1:1–8

Zeal ....Ps. 69:9; John 2:17

Triumphal Entry..... Zech. 9:9, 10; Matt. 21:1–11

Betrayal.................... Ps. 41:9; Mark 14:10

Being sold.............. Zech. 11:12; Matt. 26:15

Silent defense........... Is. 53:7; Matt. 26:62, 63

Being spit on .... Is. 50:6; Mark 14:65

Being crucified with sinners Is. 53:12; Matt. 27:38

Piercing of hands and feet .... Ps. 22:16;

John 19:36, 37

Being mocked .... Ps. 22:6–8; Matt. 27:39–44

Dying drink................Ps. 69:21; John 19:29

Side pierced .... Zech. 12:10; John 19:34

Prayer for the enemies...... Ps. 109:4; Luke 23:34

Garments gambled for .....Ps. 22:18; Mark 15:24

Death without broken bones..........Ps. 34:20;

John 19:33

Separation from God........Ps. 22:1; Matt. 27:46

Burial with the rich ......Is. 53:9; Matt. 27:57–60

Preservation from decay....Ps. 16:8–10; Acts 2:31

Ascension................. Ps. 68:18; Eph. 4:8–10

Exaltation............... Ps. 2:6–12; Phil. 2:9, 10

See Christ

Metallurgy—*mining and processing of metal*

Mining and refining .... Job 28:1, 2

Heat needed.......................... Jer. 6:29

Metaphors—*graphic comparisons*

A. Concerning God, as:

Rock.............................. Deut. 32:4

Sun and shield........................Ps. 84:11

Consuming fire..................... Heb. 12:29
Husbandman........................ John 15:1
B. Concerning Christ, as:
Bread of life .... John 6:35
Light of the world.................... John 8:12
Door.................................. John 10:9
Good Shepherd..................... John 10:14
Resurrection and the life .... John 11:25
Way, Truth, Life .... John 14:6
True vine .... John 15:1
C. Concerning Christians, as:
Light .... Matt. 5:14
Salt................................ Matt. 5:13
Epistles .... 2 Cor. 3:3
Living stones .... 1 Pet. 2:5
D. Concerning the Bible, as:
Fire............................... Jer. 5:14
Light; lamp........................ Ps. 119:105
Sword.............................. Eph. 6:17

Metheg Ammah—*power of the metropolis*
Probably a figurative name for Gath....2 Sam. 8:1

Methuselah—*man of a javelin*
Son of Enoch .... Gen. 5:21
Oldest man on record .... Gen. 5:27
Ancestor of Christ .... Luke 3:37

Methushael—*man of God*
Cainite, father of Lamech .... Gen. 4:18
See Maon

Meunites
Arabian tribe near Mount Seir ....2 Chr. 26:7
Smitten by Simeonites............ 1 Chr. 4:39–42
Descendants of, serve as Nethinim ..... Ezra 2:50

Mezahab—*waters of gold*
Grandfather of Mehetabel, wife of
King Hadar........................ Gen. 36:39

Mezobaite—*found of Yahweh*
Title given Jaasiel.................... 1 Chr. 11:47

Mibhar—*choice*
One of David's mighty men.......... 1 Chr. 11:38

Mibsam—*sweet odor*
1. Son of Ishmael .... Gen. 25:13
2. Simeonite.......................... 1 Chr. 4:25

Mibzar—*stronghold*
Edomite duke .... Gen. 36:42

Micah, Micha, Michah—*who is like Yahweh?*
1. Ephraimite who hires a traveling
Levite .... Judg. 17:1–13
2. Reubenite......................... 1 Chr. 5:1, 5
3. Son of Mephibosheth .... 2 Sam. 9:12
4. Descendant of Asaph .... 1 Chr. 9:15
Called Michaiah.................... Neh. 12:35
5. Kohathite Levite .... 1 Chr. 23:20
6. Father of Abdon.................... 2 Chr. 34:20
7. Prophet, contemporary of Isaiah ....Is. 1:1; Mic. 1:1
8. One who signs the covenant ....Neh. 10:11

Micah, Book of—*a book of the Old Testament*
Judgment of Israel and Judah .... Mic. 1:2–16
Promise to the remnant .... Mic. 2:12, 13
Judgment on those in authority ...... Mic. 3:1–12
The coming peace .... Mic. 4:1–8
The Redeemer from Bethlehem........ Mic. 5:1–4
Hope in God .... Mic. 7:8–20

Micaiah, Michaiah—*who is like Yahweh?*
1. Wife of King Rehoboam .... 2 Chr. 13:2
2. Prophet who predicts
Ahab's death .... 1 Kin. 22:8–28
3. Teaching official .... 2 Chr. 17:7
4. Father of Achbor .... 2 Kin. 22:12
Called Micah...................... 2 Chr. 34:20
5. Contemporary of Jeremiah .... Jer. 36:11–13
6. Descendant of Asaph .... Neh. 12:35
7. Priest in dedication service .... Neh. 12:41

Michael—*who is like God?*
1. Father of an Asherite spy .... Num. 13:13
2, 3. Two Gadites .... 1 Chr. 5:13, 14
4. Levite ancestor of Asaph .... 1 Chr. 6:40
5. Issacharian chief .... 1 Chr. 7:3
6. Benjamite.......................... 1 Chr. 8:16
7. Manassite chief under David.......... 1 Chr. 12:20
8. Father of Omri .... 1 Chr. 27:18
9. Son of King Jehoshaphat .... 2 Chr. 21:2
10. Father of Zebadiah .... Ezra 8:8
11. Chief prince....................... Dan. 10:13, 21
Archangel............................. Jude 9
Stands against forces................. Dan. 10:21
Disputes with Satan..................... Jude 9
Fights the Dragon................... Rev. 12:7–9

Michal—*who is like God?*
Daughter of King Saul .... 1 Sam. 14:49
Loves and marries David .... 1 Sam. 18:20–28
Saves David from Saul............ 1 Sam. 19:9–17
Given to Palti...................... 1 Sam. 25:44
David demands her from Abner... 2 Sam. 3:13–16
Ridicules David; becomes barren... 2 Sam. 6:16–23

Michmash, Michmas—*hidden place*
Town occupied by Saul's army .... 1 Sam. 13:2
Site of battle with
Philistines .... 1 Sam. 13:5, 11, 16, 23
Scene of Jonathan's victory .... 1 Sam. 14:1–18
Mentioned in prophecy................ Is. 10:28
Exiles return .... Ezra 2:1, 27

Michmethath—*lurking place*
Place on the border of Ephraim and
Manasseh........................ Josh. 16:5, 6

Michri—*purchase price*
Benjamite.......................... 1 Chr. 9:8

Michtam
Word of unknown meaning used in
titles of...................... Ps. 16; 56 to 60

Middin—*extensions*
In the wilderness .... Josh. 15:61

Midian—*place of judgment*
1. Son of Abraham by Keturah . . . . Gen. 25:1–4
2. Region in the Arabian desert occupied
    by the Midianites . . . . Gen. 25:6; Ex. 2:15

Midianites—*descendants of Midian*
A. Characteristics of:
    Descendants of Abraham
        by Keturah . . . . Gen. 25:1, 2
    Moses fled to . . . . Ex. 2:15
    Retain worship of Yahweh . . . . Ex. 2:16
    Ruled by kings. Num. 31:8
    Immoral people. . . . . Num. 25:18
B. Contacts with Israel:
    Took Joseph to Egypt . . . . Gen. 37:36
    Joined Moab in cursing. . . . . .Num. 22:4–7
    Seduction of. . . . . Num. 25:1–18
    Defeat because of . . . . Num. 31:1–18
    Sent as punishment . . . . Judg. 6:1–10
    Defeated by Gideon . . . . Judg. 7:1–25; 8:12, 21
Listed, well-known:
    Jethro, priest of Midian . . . . Ex. 3:1
    Zipporah, Moses' wife. . . . . .Ex. 2:21
    Cozbi, killed by Phinehas. . . . . . . .Num. 25:5–9, 15
    Oreb and Zeeb, princes killed
        by Gideon . . . . Judg. 7:24, 25
    Zebah and Zalmunna, kings killed
        by Gideon . . . . .Judg. 8:12

Midnight
A. Significant happenings at:
    Death in Egypt . . . . .Ex. 11:4
    Prayer meeting . . . . Acts 16:25
B. Other happenings at:
    Quick departure. . . . . .Judg. 16:2, 3
    Friend's need . . . . Luke 11:5
    Great fear . . . . Job 34:20

Midwife—*one who assists at childbirth*
    Helps in the birth of a child. . . . . Gen. 35:17
    Hebrew, disobey king's command . . . . Ex. 1:15–21

Migdal El—*tower of God*
    City of Naphtali .Josh. 19:38

Migdal Gad—*a tower of Gad (fortune)*
    Town of Judah. .Josh. 15:37

Migdol—*tower*
1. Israelite encampment . . . . Ex. 14:2
2. Place in Egypt to which Jews flee. . . . . . . .Jer. 44:1

Might—*effective power*
A. God's:
    Irresistible . . . . .2 Chr. 20:6
    Hand is . . . . .1 Chr. 29:12
    Unutterable . . . . .Ps. 106:2
B. Human physical:
    Boasted in, brings destruction . . . . . Dan. 4:30–33
    Not to be gloried in . . . . .Deut. 8:17
    Will fail. . . . . .Jer. 51:30
    Exhortation concerning . . . . Eccl. 9:10
C. Human intellectual and moral:
    Invites self-glory. . . . . .Jer. 9:23

    Makes salvation difficult . . . . 1 Cor. 1:26
D. Human spiritual, comes from:
    God . . . . .Eph. 1:19
    Christ. . . . . Col. 1:28, 29
    The Spirit . . . . Mic. 3:8

Mighty
Literally of:
    Hunter. . . . . Gen. 10:9
    Nation . . . . Gen. 18:18
    Prince . . . . Gen. 23:6
    Waters . . . . .Ex. 15:10
    Hand . . . . .Ex. 32:11
    Acts . . . . Deut. 3:24
    Men of valor. . . . . .1 Chr. 7:9–11
    Warrior . . . . .2 Chr. 32:21
    Kings . . . . Ezra 4:20
    Strength . . . . .Job 9:4
    Fear . . . . Job 41:25

Mighty man—*a powerful man; a valiant warrior*
    Men of renown . . . . Gen. 6:4
    Gideon. . . . . .Judg. 6:11, 12
    Warriors of David . . . . 2 Sam. 10:7

Migron—*precipitous (very steep)*
1. Place where Saul stayed . . . . 1 Sam. 14:2
2. Village north of Michmash. . . . . .Is. 10:28

Mijamin—*from the right side*
1. Descendant of Aaron . . . . 1 Chr. 24:1, 6, 9
2. Chief priest; returns
        with Zerubbabel. . . . . Neh. 12:5, 7
    Probably same as 1
3. Divorced his foreign wife. . . . . .Ezra 10:25
4. Priest who signs the covenant. . . . . .Neh. 10:7
    Same as Minjamin in. . . . . Neh. 12:17, 41

Mikloth—*rods*
1. Ruler under David. . . . . 1 Chr. 27:4
2. Benjamite. . . . . 1 Chr. 8:32

Mikneiah—*possession of Yahweh*
    Gatekeeper and musician in David's
        time. . . . . .1 Chr. 15:18, 21

Milalai—*eloquent*
    Levite musician in dedication service. . . Neh. 12:36

Milcah—*counsel*
1. Wife of Nahor. .Gen. 11:29
    Mother of eight children . . . . Gen. 22:20–22
    Grandmother of Rebekah . . . . .Gen. 22:23
2. Daughter of Zelophehad . . . . .Num. 26:33

Milcom—*an Ammonite god*
    Solomon went after . . . . 1 Kin. 11:5
    Altar destroyed by Josiah . . . . 2 Kin. 23:12, 13

Mildew—*a disease of grain due to dampness*
    Threatened as a punishment. . . . . Deut. 28:22
    Sent upon Israel . . . . Amos 4:9
    Removed by repentance . . . . 1 Kin. 8:37–39

Mile—*a thousand paces (about 12/13 of an English mile)*
    Used illustratively . . . . Matt. 5:41
See Jewish measures

Miletus—*a city of Asia Minor*
    Paul meets Ephesian elders here....Acts 20:15–38
    Paul leaves Trophimus here.........2 Tim. 4:20

Milk—*a white liquid secreted by mammary glands*
A. Produced by:
    Goats...........................Prov. 27:27
    Sheep........................... Deut. 32:14
    Camels........................... Gen. 32:15
    Cows .... 1 Sam. 6:7, 10
    Humans .... Is. 28:9
B. Figurative of:
    Abundance........................ Deut. 32:14
    Egypt's supposed blessings.......... Num. 16:13
    Elementary teaching .... 1 Cor. 3:2
    Pure doctrine......................1 Pet. 2:2

Mill, millstone
A. Uses of:
    Grinding grain .... Num. 11:8
    Weapon...........................Judg. 9:53
    Pledge, forbidden .... Deut. 24:6
    Weight........................... Matt. 18:6
B. Operated by:
    Women .... Matt. 24:41
    Maidservant..........................Ex. 11:5
    Prisoners..........................Judg. 16:21
C. Figurative of:
    Courage........................... Job 41:24
    Old age .... Eccl. 12:4
    Desolation ....Jer. 25:10
    Total destruction ....Rev. 18:21

Millennium—*thousand years*
    Binding of Satan and reign
        with Christ .... Rev. 20:1–10

Millet—*a cereal*
    Ezekiel makes bread of ....Ezek. 4:9

Millo—*terrace, elevation*
    Fort at Jerusalem ....2 Sam. 5:9
    Prepared by Solomon................. 1 Kin. 9:15
    Strengthened by Hezekiah............2 Chr. 32:5
    Scene of Joash's death .... 2 Kin. 12:20, 21

Mina—*Greek money*
    Used in parable .... Luke 19:12–27

Mincing—*affected elegance in walking*
    Denounced...........................Is. 3:16

Mind—*the reasoning faculty*
A. Faculties of:
    Perception .... Luke 9:47
    Remembrance......................Titus 3:1
    Reasoning....................... Rom. 7:23, 25
    Feelings.........................2 Sam. 17:8
    Desire .... Neh. 4:6
    Intent............................. Gen. 6:5
    Purpose........................2 Cor. 1:15, 17
B. Of the unregenerate, described as:
    Alienated ....Ezek. 23:17–22; Col. 1:21
    Spiteful .... Ezek. 36:5
    Debased ....Rom. 1:28

    Hardened .... 2 Cor. 3:14
    Defiled ....Titus 1:15
C. Of the regenerate, described as:
    Willing ....1 Chr. 28:9
    In peace.......... Is. 26:3; Rom. 8:6; Phil. 4:6, 7
    Right ....Luke 8:35
    Renewed.........................Rom. 12:2
    Having Christ's...................... 1 Cor. 2:16
    Obedient........................... Heb. 8:10
D. Dangers of, to the Christian:
    Worry ....Luke 12:29
    Doubt ....Rom. 14:5
    Disunity ....Rom. 12:16; Phil. 4:2
    Grow weary .... Heb. 12:3
    Mental disturbance .... 2 Thess. 2:2
    Spiritual disturbance.............. Rom. 7:23, 25
E. Exhortations concerning, to Christians:
    Love God with all.................. Matt. 22:37

Minerals of the Bible
A. Features concerning:
    Mined .... Job 28:1–11
    Plentiful in Canaan ....Deut. 8:9
    Refined by fire .... Ezek. 22:18, 20
    Trade in...........................Ezek. 27:12
B. List of:
    Asphalt (bitumen) .... Gen. 11:3
    Brimstone (sulphur)................. Deut. 29:23
    Bronze........................... Num. 21:9
    Chalk............................ Is. 27:9
    Clay .... Is. 41:25
    Copper............................Deut. 8:9
    Coral .... Job 28:18
    Flint............................. Deut. 32:13
    Gold.......................... Gen. 2:11, 12
    Iron .... Gen. 4:22
    Lead .... Job 19:24
    Lime .... Amos 2:1
    Pitch (asphalt) .... Gen. 6:14
    Salt............................. Gen. 14:3
    Sand............................ Prov. 27:3
    Silver ....Gen. 44:2
    Tin .... Num. 31:22

Mingle, mix—*to put different elements together*
A. Instances of:
    Offerings ....Lev. 2:4, 5
    Garment ....Lev. 19:19
    Judgments ....Rev. 8:7
    Human sacrifice ....Luke 13:1
    Intermarriage ....Ezra 9:2
B. Figurative of:
    Sorrow............................Ps. 102:9
    Wisdom ....Prov. 9:2, 5
    Instability......................... Is. 19:14
    Severity .... Ps. 75:8
    Impurity .... Is. 1:22
    Intoxication .... Is. 5:22
    Worldliness .... Hos. 7:8

Miniamin, Minjamin—*fortunate*
1. Levite assistant.................... 2 Chr. 31:14, 15
2. Postexilic priest ....Neh. 12:17
3. Priestly participant in dedication ...... Neh. 12:41

> **WORD STUDY**   **MINISTER,** *sharat* (shaw-*rath*). To "minister" or "serve" is the action indicated by the verb *sharat*. The ministerial service mentioned is usually higher than domestic service. Biblical examples of those involved in such service include Joseph in Pharaoh's house; Joshua ministering to Moses; Elisha acting as Elijah's aide; royal officers and angels. Usually *sharat* indicates service preparing for worship or actions during worship. Levitical priests, Levites, Zadokite priests, and Aaronic priests are the groups in the OT usually seen involved in this form of service. (Strong's #8334)

Minister—*one who serves*
A. Descriptive of:
    Court attendants ....1 Kin. 10:5
    Angels ....Ps. 103:20
    Priests and Levites ....Joel 1:9, 13
    Servant .... Matt. 20:22–27
    Ruler .... Rom. 13:3–5
    Christ.............................Rom. 15:8
    Christ's messengers .... 1 Cor. 3:5
    False teachers...................... 2 Cor. 11:15
B. Christian, qualifications of:
    Able to teach .... 1 Tim. 3:2
    Diligent...........................1 Cor. 15:10
    Faithful........................ Rom. 15:17–19
    Impartial .... 1 Tim. 5:21
    Industrious...................... 2 Cor. 10:12–16
    Meek .... 2 Tim. 2:25
    Obedient....................... Acts 16:9, 10
    Persevering...................... 2 Cor. 11:23–33
    Prayerful...........................Acts 6:4
    Sincere.........................2 Cor. 4:1, 2
    Spirit-filled...........................Acts 1:8
    Studious .... 1 Tim. 4:13, 15
    Sympathetic....................... Heb. 5:2
    Temperate .... 1 Cor. 9:25–27
    Willing ....1 Pet. 5:2
    Worthy of imitation................. 1 Tim. 4:12
C. Sins to avoid:
    Arrogance...........................1 Pet. 5:3
    Contentiousness......................Titus 1:7
    Discouragement....................2 Cor. 4:8, 9
    Insincerity .... Phil. 1:15, 16
    Perverting the truth...............2 Cor. 11:3–15
    Unfaithfulness ....Matt. 24:48–51
D. Duties of:
Preach:
    Gospel............................ 1 Cor. 1:17
    Christ crucified..................... 1 Cor. 1:23
    Christ's riches ....Eph. 3:8–12
    Feed the church...................John 21:15–17
    Edify the church..................... Eph. 4:12
    Pray for people ....Col. 1:9

Teach............................ 2 Tim. 2:2
Exhort ....Titus 1:9
Rebuke ....Titus 2:15
Warn of apostasy .... 2 Tim. 4:2–5
Comfort ....2 Cor. 1:4–6
Win souls .... 1 Cor. 9:19–23
E. Attitude of believers toward:
    Pray for ....Eph. 6:18–20
    Follow the example of................ 1 Cor. 11:1
    Obey .... Heb. 13:17
    Esteem highly ....1 Thess. 5:12, 13
    Provide for ....1 Cor. 9:6–18

Minni—*a people of Armenia*
    Summoned to destroy Babylon..........Jer. 51:27

Minnith—*distribution*
    Wheat-growing Ammonite town......Ezek. 27:17

Minority—*the lesser number*
    On God's side .... Num. 14:1–10
    To be preferred ....Ex. 23:2
    Saved are....................... Matt. 7:13–23

Mint—*a fragrant herb*
    Tithed by Pharisees .... Matt. 23:23

Miphkad—*appointed place*
    Gate of Jerusalem rebuilt
        by Nehemiah...................... Neh. 3:31

Miracle
A. Described:
    Signs.............................. Acts 4:30
    Wonders ,,,,,,,,,,,,,,,,,,,,,,,,,,,,.Acts 6:8
    Works .... John 10:25–38
B. Kinds of, over:
    Nature......................Josh. 10:12–14
    Animals...........................Num. 22:28
    Human beings.......................Gen. 19:26
    Nations ....Ex. 10:1, 2
    Sickness and disease .... 2 Kin. 5:10–14
    Natural laws.......................2 Kin. 6:5–7
    Future events.................... 2 Kin. 6:8–13
    Death........................... John 11:41–44
C. Produced by:
    God's power........................ Acts 15:12
    Christ's power .... Matt. 10:1
    Spirit's power..................... Matt. 12:28
D. Design of:
Manifest:
    God's glory................... John 11:40–42
    Christ's glory..................... John 2:11
    God's presence .... Judg. 6:11–24
    Proof of God's messengers............. Ex. 4:2–9
    Proof of Jesus as the Messiah........ Matt. 11:2–5
    Signs of a true apostle .... 2 Cor. 12:12
    Produce obedience......................Ex. 16:4
    Vindicate God.................... Ex. 17:4–7
    Produce faith.....................John 20:30, 31
    Authenticate the gospel .... Rom. 15:18, 19
    Fulfill prophecy .... John 12:37–41

E. Effect of, upon people:

Forced acknowledgment..... John 11:47; Acts 4:16

Amazement .... Mark 6:49–51

Faith........................... John 2:23; 11:42

God glorified...................... Matt. 9:1–8

F. False:

Not to be followed .... Deut. 13:1–3

Sign of the Antichrist... 2 Thess. 2:3, 9; Rev. 13:13

Predicted by Christ .... Matt. 24:24

G. Evidence of:

Logic .... John 9:16

Sufficient to convince .... John 3:2; 6:14

Insufficient to convince ...Luke 16:31; John 12:37

Sought by Jews .... John 2:18

Demanded unreasonably .... Matt. 27:42, 43

Incurs guilt......... Matt. 11:20–24; John 15:24

Miracles of the Bible—*Old Testament*

Creation .... Gen. 1:1–31

Enoch's translation .... Gen. 5:24

The Flood........................... Gen. 7:17–24

Confusion of tongues at Babel .... Gen. 11:3–9

Sodom and Gomorrah destroyed...... Gen. 19:24

Lot's wife turned to a pillar of salt..... Gen. 19:26

Donkey speaking .... Num. 22:21–35

Those associated with Moses and Aaron:

Burning bush.............................Ex. 3:3

Moses' rod changed into a serpent... Ex. 4:3, 4, 30

Moses' hand made leprous.......... Ex. 4:6, 7, 30

Aaron's rod changed into a serpent .... Ex. 7:8–10

Ten plagues:

River turned to blood .... Ex. 7:20–25

Frogs .... Ex. 8:1–15

Lice .... Ex. 8:16–19

Flies .... Ex. 8:20–24

Pestilence......................... Ex. 9:1–7

Boils .... Ex. 9:8–12

Hail .... Ex. 9:18–24

Locusts .... Ex. 10:1–20

Darkness .... Ex. 10:21–23

Firstborn destroyed............. Ex. 12:29, 30

Pillar of cloud and fire ....Ex. 13:21, 22; 14:19, 20

Crossing the sea .... Ex. 14:21, 23

Bitter waters sweetened ....Ex. 15:25

Manna sent .... Ex. 16:13–36

Water from the rock at Rephidim ..... Ex. 17:5–8

Amalek defeated..................... Ex. 17:9–13

Fire on Aaron's sacrifice................Lev. 9:24

Nadab and Abihu devoured..........Lev. 10:1, 2

Israel's judgment by fire .... Num. 11:1–3

Miriam's leprosy.................Num. 12:10–15

Destruction of Korah ....Num. 16:31–35

Aaron's rod blossoms................. Num. 17:8

Water from the rock in Kadesh.....Num. 20:8–11

Bronze serpent .... Num. 21:9

Those associated with Joshua:

Jordan divided....................Josh. 3:14–17

Fall of Jericho .... Josh. 6:6–20

Sun and moon stand still .... Josh. 10:12–14

Those associated with Samson:

Lion killed ....Judg. 14:5, 6

Thirty Philistines killed.............Judg. 14:19

Water from the hollow place in Lehi... Judg. 15:19

Gates of the city carried away ....Judg. 16:3

Dagon's house pulled down .... Judg. 16:29, 30

Those associated with Elijah:

Drought .... 1 Kin. 17:1; James 5:17

Fed by ravens.................... 1 Kin. 17:4–6

Widow's oil and meal increased ...1 Kin. 17:12–16

Widow's son raised from dead ....1 Kin. 17:17–23

Sacrifice consumed by fire...........1 Kin. 18:38

Rain in answer to prayer............. 1 Kin. 18:41

Captains consumed by fire ....2 Kin. 1:9–12

Jordan divided....................... 2 Kin. 2:8

Translated to heaven in
a chariot of fire................... 2 Kin. 2:11

Those associated with Elisha:

Jordan divided...................... 2 Kin. 2:14

Waters of Jericho healed.......... 2 Kin. 2:20–22

Mocking young men destroyed
by bears ....2 Kin. 2:24

Water supplied for Jehoshaphat ... 2 Kin. 3:16–20

Widow's oil multiplied ....2 Kin. 4:1–7

Shunammite's child raised
from dead .... 2 Kin. 4:19–37

Poisoned pottage made harmless.. 2 Kin. 4:38–41

Hundred fed with twenty loaves ..2 Kin. 4:42–44

Naaman cured of leprosy .... 2 Kin. 5:10–14

Gehazi struck with leprosy ....2 Kin. 5:27

Ax head caused to float.............2 Kin. 6:5–7

Ben-Hadad's plans revealed....... 2 Kin. 6:8–13

Syrian army defeated............. 2 Kin. 6:18–20

Revival of a man who touched
Elisha's bones ....2 Kin. 13:21

Those associated with Isaiah:

Hezekiah healed.....................2 Kin. 20:7

Shadow turns backward on sun dial...2 Kin. 20:11

Other miracles of the Old Testament:

Dew on Gideon's fleece............ Judg. 6:37–40

Dagon's fall before the ark .... 1 Sam. 5:1–12

Men of Beth Shemesh destroyed ... 1 Sam. 6:19, 20

Thunder and rain in harvest........ 1 Sam. 12:18

Uzzah's death .... 2 Sam. 6:6, 7

Jeroboam's hand withered and
restored .... 1 Kin. 13:4–6

Rending of the altar .... 1 Kin. 13:5

Sennacherib's army destroyed........2 Kin. 19:35

Uzziah afflicted with leprosy .... 2 Chr. 26:16–21

Three men protected from the fiery
furnace.......................Dan. 3:19–27

Daniel delivered from
the lion's den................. Dan. 6:16–23

Preservation of Jonah in stomach of fish
three days ....Jon. 2:1–10

Miracles of the Bible—*New Testament*

Of Christ (listed chronologically):

Water made wine (Cana) ....John 2:1–11

Son of nobleman healed (Cana) .... John 4:46–54

Peter's . . . . Acts 10:1–48; 11:1–30
Cornelius's . . . . Acts 10:3, 4, 30–32
Paul's . . . . Acts 16:9; 2 Cor. 12:1–5
John's on Patmos . . . . Rev. 1–10; 4–22
Miracles by the seventy . . . . Luke 10:17
Stephen performed great miracles . . . . Acts 6:8
Philip cast out unclean spirits . . . . Acts 8:6–13

Miracles pretended, or false
Egyptian magicians . . . . Ex. 7:11–22; 8:18, 19
In support of false religions . . . . Deut. 13:1–3
Witch of En Dor . . . . 1 Sam. 28:9–12
False prophets . . . . Matt. 7:22, 23; 24:24
False christs . . . . Matt. 24:24
Deceive the ungodly . . . . Rev. 13:13; 19:20
Sign of apostasy . . . . 2 Thess. 2:3, 9; Rev. 13:13

Mire—*deep mud*
A. Places of:
Dungeon . . . . Jer. 38:22
Streets . . . . Is. 10:6
B. Figurative of:
Affliction . . . . Job 30:19
Insecurity . . . . Is. 57:20
Plentifulness . . . . Zech. 9:3

Miriam—*obstinacy (stubbornness)*
1. Sister of Aaron and Moses . . . . Num. 26:59
Watches over Moses in river . . . . Ex. 2:4–6
Calls Moses' mother as nurse to help with Moses
for Pharaoh's daughter . . . . Ex. 2:7, 8
Chosen by God; called a prophetess . . . . . Ex. 15:20
Leads in victory song . . . . Ex. 15:20, 21
Opposes Moses . . . . Num. 12:1, 2
Punished for rebellion . . . . Num. 12:3–16
Buried at Kadesh . . . . Num. 20:1
2. Judahite . . . . 1 Chr. 4:17

Mirmah—*deceit*
Benjamite . . . . 1 Chr. 8:10

Mirror
In the tabernacle . . . . Ex. 38:8
Of cast metal . . . . Job 37:18
Used figuratively . . . . 1 Cor. 13:12; 2 Cor. 3:18;
James 1:23, 25

Mirth—*a spirit of gaiety*
Occasions of . . . . Gen. 31:27; Neh. 8:10–12
Absence of . . . . Jer. 25:10, 11; Hos. 2:11
Inadequacy of . . . . Prov. 14:13; Eccl. 2:1, 2

Miscarriage—*premature ejection of a fetus from the mother's womb, resulting in the death of the fetus*
Against the wicked . . . . Ps. 58:8
Wished for . . . . Job 3:16; Eccl. 6:3

Miscegenation—*intermarriage of different races*
A. Restrictions in the Law of
Moses . . . . Ex. 34:12–16
B. Notable examples:
Moses . . . . Num. 12:1–10
Ruth . . . . Matt. 1:5
C. Unity of all races:
Descended from Adam . . . . . Gen. 3:20; Rom. 5:12

From one . . . . Acts 17:26
D. Christian marriage:
Spiritual basis . . . . Matt. 19:6
In the Lord . . . . 1 Cor. 7:39; 2 Cor. 6:14

Miser—*a covetous person*
A. Characteristics of:
Selfish . . . . Eccl. 4:8
Covetous . . . . Luke 12:15
Divided loyalty . . . . Matt. 6:24
B. Punishment of:
Dissatisfaction . . . . Eccl. 5:10
Loss . . . . Matt. 6:19
Sorrows . . . . 1 Tim. 6:10
Destruction . . . . Ps. 52:5, 7
C. Examples of:
Rich fool . . . . Luke 12:16–21
Rich ruler . . . . Luke 18:18–23
Ananias and Sapphira . . . . Acts 5:1–11

Miserable—*the wretched*
A. State of:
Wicked . . . . Rom. 3:12–16
Trapped . . . . Rom. 7:24
Lost . . . . Luke 13:25–28
B. Caused by:
Forgetfulness of God . . . . Is. 22:12–14
Ignorance . . . . Luke 19:42–44
Self-deception . . . . Rev. 3:17

Misfortune—*an unexpected adversity*
Explained by the nations . . . . Deut. 29:24–28
Misunderstood by Gideon . . . . Judg. 6:13
Understood by David . . . . 2 Sam. 16:5–13
Caused by sin . . . . Is. 59:1, 2

Mishael—*who is like God?*
1. Kohathite Levite . . . . Ex. 6:22
Removes dead bodies . . . . Lev. 10:4, 5
2. Hebrew name of Meshach . . . . Dan. 1:6–19
3. One of Ezra's assistants . . . . Neh. 8:4

Mishal
Town in Asher . . . . Josh. 19:24, 26
Assigned to Levites . . . . Josh. 21:30
Called Mashal . . . . 1 Chr. 6:74

Misham—*swift*
Son of Elpaal . . . . 1 Chr. 8:12

Mishma—*hearing*
1. Son of Ishmael . . . . Gen. 25:13, 14; 1 Chr. 1:30
2. Descendant of Simeon . . . . 1 Chr. 4:25

Mishmannah—*fatness*
One of David's Gadite warriors . . . . . . 1 Chr. 12:10

Mishraites
Family living in Kirjath Jearim . . . . . . 1 Chr. 2:53

Mispar—*writing*
Exile returnee . . . . Ezra 2:2
Called Mispereth . . . . Neh. 7:7

Misrephoth—*burning of waters*
Haven of fleeing Canaanites . . . . Josh. 11:8
Near the Sidonians . . . . Josh. 13:6

Missionaries—*those sent out to spread the gospel*
Jonah ....Jon. 3:2, 3
The early church........................Acts 8:4
Philip ....Acts 8:5
Some from Cyrene become ....Acts 11:20
Paul and Barnabas ....Acts 13:1–4
Peter................................Acts 15:7
Apollos ....Acts 18:24
Noah ....2 Pet. 2:5

Mission of Christ
Do God's will........................John 6:38
Save sinners ....Luke 19:10
Bring in everlasting righteousness......Dan. 9:24
Destroy Satan's works ....Heb. 2:14; 1 John 3:8
Fulfill the Old Testament.............Matt. 5:17
Give life...........................John 10:10, 28
Stop sacrifices ....Dan. 9:27
Complete revelation ....Heb. 1:1–3

Missions
A. Commands concerning:
"Will be"........................ Matt. 24:14
"Go"...........................Matt. 28:18–20
"Tarry" ....Luke 24:49
"Come" .... Acts 16:9
"Preach" ....Mark 16:15
B. Motives prompting:
God's love........................... John 3:16
Christ's love ....2 Cor. 5:14, 15
Humankind's need................. Rom. 3:9–31
C. Equipment for:
Word .... Rom. 10:14, 15
Spirit ....Acts 1:8
Prayer .... Acts 13:1–4

Mist—*a vapor (physical and spiritual)*
Physical (vapor)........................ Gen. 2:6
Spiritual (blindness) .... Acts 13:11

Mistake—*an error arising from human weakness*
Causes of:
Motives misunderstood .... Josh. 22:9–29
Appearance misjudged .... 1 Sam. 1:13–15
Trust misplaced ....Josh. 9:3–27

Mistress—*a married woman*
In charge of a maid................Gen. 16:4, 8, 9
Figurative of Nineveh .... Nah. 3:4

Misunderstandings—*disagreements among*
Israelites ....Josh. 22:9–29
Christ's disciples................. Matt. 20:20–27
Apostles .... Gal. 2:11–15
Christians...........................Acts 6:1

Misused—*putting to a wrong use*
Guilt of, brings wrath ....2 Chr. 36:16

Mite—*Jews' smallest coin*
Widow's .... Mark 12:42

Mithkah—*sweetness*
Israelite encampment ....Num. 33:28, 29

Mithnite
Descriptive of Joshaphat,
David's officer ....1 Chr. 11:43

Mithredath—*consecrated to Mithra*
1. Treasurer of Cyrus...................... Ezra 1:8
2. Persian official .... Ezra 4:7

Mitylene—*a city on the island of Lesbos*
Visited by Paul ....Acts 20:13–15

Mix (see Mingle; Miscegenation)

Mizar—*small*
Hill east of Jordan ....Ps. 42:6

Mizpah—*watchtower*
1. Site of covenant between Jacob
and Laban ....Gen. 31:44–53
2. Town in Gilead; probably same as 1 .... Judg. 10:17
Jephthah's home.............. Judg. 11:11, 29, 34
Probably same as Ramath Mizpah.....Josh. 13:26
3. Region near Mt. Hermon............. Josh. 11:3, 8
4. Town in Judah .... Josh. 15:1, 38
5. Place in Moab; David brings his
parents to.......................1 Sam. 22:3, 4
6. Town of Benjamin .... Josh. 18:21, 26
Outraged Israelites gather here ..... Judg. 20:1, 3
Samuel gathers Israel.....1 Sam. 7:5–16; 10:17–25
Built by Asa ....1 Kin. 15:22
Residence of Gedaliah .... 2 Kin. 25:23, 25
Home of exile returnees .... Neh. 3:7, 15, 19

Mizraim—*Egypt*
1. Son of Ham; ancestor of Ludim,
Anamim, etc....................... 1 Chr. 1:8, 11
2. Hebrew name for Egypt................Gen. 50:11
Called the land of Ham........... Ps. 105:23, 27

Mizzah—*fear*
Grandson of Esau; a duke
of Edom ....Gen. 36:13, 17

Mnason
Christian of Cyprus and Paul's host ....Acts 21:16

Moab—*seed*
1. Son of Lot........................Gen. 19:33–37
2. Country of the Moabites .... Deut. 1:5

Moabites—*inhabitants of Moab*
A. History of:
Descendants of Moab, Lot's son....Gen. 19:36, 37
Became a great nation ....Num. 21:28, 30
Governed by kings .... Num. 23:7; Josh. 24:9
Driven out of their territory by
Amorites .... Num. 21:26
Refused to let Israel pass ....Judg. 11:17, 18
Midian joined with Moab
to curse Israel .... Num. 22:4
Excluded from worship in Israel.....Deut. 23:3–6
Friendly relation with Israel ....Ruth 1:1, 4, 16
Defeated by Saul.................... 1 Sam. 14:47
Refuge for David's parents........ 1 Sam. 22:3, 4
Defeated by David .... 2 Sam. 8:2, 12
Solomon married women of........1 Kin. 11:1, 3

Paid tribute to Israel . . . . 2 Kin. 3:4
Fought Israel and Judah . . . . .2 Kin. 3:5–7
Conquered by Israel and Judah. . . . . 2 Kin. 3:8–27
Daughters of, intermarried with Jews. . .Ezra 9:1, 2;
    Neh. 13:23
B. Characteristics of:
Idolatrous. . . . . 1 Kin. 11:7
Wealthy. . . . . Jer. 48:1, 7
Superstitious . . . . Jer. 27:3, 9
Satisfied . . . . .Jer. 48:11
Proud. . . . . Jer. 48:29
C. Prophecies concerning their:
Desolation . . . . Is. 15:1–9
Ruin and destruction . . . . Jer. 27:3, 8
Punishment . . . . Amos 2:1–3
Subjection. . . . . .Is. 11:14

Mob—*a lawless crowd*
Caused Pilate to pervert justice . . .Matt. 27:20–25
Made unjust charges . . . . Acts 17:5–9
Paul saved from. . . . . .Acts 21:27–40

Mocking—*imitating in fun or derision*
A. Evil agents of:
Children . . . . .2 Kin. 2:23
Men of Israel . . . . .2 Chr. 30:10
Men of Judah. .2 Chr. 36:16
Fools . . . . Prov. 14:9
Wine . . . . Prov. 20:1
Jews . . . . Matt. 20:19
Roman soldiers .Luke 23:36
False teachers. . . . . Jude 18
B. Good agents of:
Donkey . . . . Num. 22:29
Samson . . . . Judg. 16:10–15
Elijah . . . . .1 Kin. 18:27
Wisdom (God) . . . . Prov. 1:20, 26
The Lord. . . . . Ps. 2:4
C. Reasons for, to:
Show unbelief . . . . .2 Chr. 36:16
Portray scorn. . . . . .2 Chr. 30:10
Ridicule. . . . . .Acts 2:13
Insult. . . . . .Gen. 39:14, 17
D. Objects of:
Christ. . . . . .Luke 23:11, 36
Believers . . . . Heb. 11:36

Modesty in dress
A. Of women:
Instructed. . . . . 1 Tim. 2:9
Illustrated in Israel. . . . . 1 Pet. 3:3–5
Lack of, an enticement . . . . 2 Sam. 11:2–5
B. Of men:
Lack of, condemned. . . . . .Gen. 9:21–27
Illustrated. . . . . John 21:7
Manifested in conversion. . . . . .Mark 5:15

Moladah—*birth, origin*
Town of Judah. . . . . .Josh. 15:1, 26
Inheritance of Simeon. . . . . Josh. 19:1, 2
Returning Levites inhabit . . . . Neh. 11:26

Molded—*made of melted metal*
A. Applied to:
Great basin in the temple . . . . 1 Kin. 7:16–33
Mirror . . . . .Job 37:18
Images. . . . . Ex. 32:4, 8
B. Of images:
Making of forbidden . . . . .Ex. 34:17
Made by Israel. 2 Kin. 17:16
Worshiped by Israel. . . . . .Ps. 106:19
Destroyed by Josiah . . . . .2 Chr. 34:3, 4
Folly of . . . . Is. 42:17
Vanity . . . . Is. 41:29
See Gods, false

Molding—*a decorative ledge of gold*
Around:
Ark. . . . . .Ex. 25:11
Incense altar . . . . Ex. 30:3, 4

Moldy—*musty or stale*
Applied to bread. . . . . .Josh. 9:5, 12

Mole—*a small, burrowing mammal*
Among unclean animals. . . . . .Lev. 11:29

Molech—*king*
A. Worship of:
By Ammonites. . . . . 1 Kin. 11:7
By human sacrifice. . . . . .2 Kin. 23:10
Strongly condemned . . . . .Lev. 18:21
Introduced by Solomon . . . . 1 Kin. 11:7
B. Prevalence of, among Jews:
Favored by Solomon. . . . . 1 Kin. 11:7
See Human sacrifice

Molid—*begetter*
Judahite. . . . . .1 Chr. 2:29

Moment—*a small unit of time*
A. Descriptive of:
Life. . . . . Job 34:20
Lying tongues .Prov. 12:19
Satan's temptation . . . . Luke 4:5
Affliction . . . . 2 Cor. 4:17
Loss of loved ones. . . . . .Is 47:8, 9
B. Descriptive of God's:
Anger. . . . . Num. 16:21, 45
Punishment . . . . Is. 47:9
Destruction . . . . Jer. 4:20
C. Descriptive of the believer's:
Problems. . . . . .Job 7:18
Protection. . . . . .Is. 26:20, 21
Perfection in glory . . . . 1 Cor. 15:52

Monarchy—*the rule of one person (king or queen)*
Described by Samuel . . . . 1 Sam. 8:11–18

Money—*an authorized medium of exchange*
A. Wrong uses of:
Misuse of children's. . . . . Gen. 31:15
Forced tribute . . . . .2 Kin. 15:20
Make interest on. Ps. 15:5
Bribe . . . . Ps. 15:5
Miserliness. . . . . Matt. 25:18
Buy spiritual gifts. . . . . Acts 8:18, 20

B. Good uses of:

Buy property . . . . .Gen. 23:9, 13

Buy food . . . . Deut. 2:6, 28

Give as an offering . . . . .Deut. 14:22–26

Repair God's house . . . . 2 Kin. 12:4–15

Pay taxes . . . . .Matt. 17:27; 22:19–21

Use for the Lord . . . . Matt. 25:27

As wages . . . . .2 Kin. 12:15

C. Evils connected with:

Greed . . . . 2 Kin. 5:20–27

Debts . . . . .Neh. 5:2–11

Money changers—*dealers in changing money*

Christ drives them out . . . . Matt. 21:12

Monkeys

Imported by Solomon from Tarshish .1 Kin. 10:22

Trade item . . . . .2 Chr. 9:21

Monogamy—*marriage to one spouse*

Commanded . . . . .Matt. 19:3–9; 1 Cor. 7:1–16

Example of Christ and the church . . .Eph. 5:25–33

Demanded of bishop . . . . 1 Tim. 3:2

Monotheism—*a belief in one god*

Statements of:

The Great Commandment . . . . Deut. 6:4, 5

Song of Moses . . . . .Deut. 32:36–39

About eternal life . . . . .John 17:3, 22

Moon—*earth's natural satellite shining by the sun's reflected light*

A. Miraculous use of:

Standing still . . . . Hab. 3:11

Darkened . . . . Is. 13:10

To be turned to blood . . . . Acts 2:20

B. Worship of:

Among Jews . . . . .Jer. 7:18

Forbidden . . . . .Deut. 4:19

Punishable . . . . Jer. 8:1–3

C. Illustrative of:

Eternity . . . . .Ps. 72:5, 7

Universal praise . . . . Is. 66:23

God's faithfulness . . . . .Jer. 31:35–37

Greater light of gospel age . . . . Is. 30:26

D. Purpose of:

Rule the night . . . . Gen. 1:16

Marking time . . . . Gen. 1:14

Designating seasons . . . . .Ps. 104:19

Signaling prophetic events . . . . Matt. 24:29; Luke 21:25

Morality—*principles of right conduct*

A. Of the unregenerate:

Based upon conscience . . . . Rom. 2:14, 15

Commanded by law . . . . .John 8:3–5

Limited to outward appearance . . . . Is. 1:14, 15

Object of boasting . . . . Mark 10:17–20

B. Of the regenerated:

Based upon the new birth . . . . 2 Cor. 5:17

Prompted by the Spirit . . . . Gal. 5:22, 23

Comes from the heart . . . . Heb. 8:10

No boasting except in Christ . . . . 1 Cor. 15:10; Phil. 3:7–10

Mordecai—*dedicated to Mars*

1. Jew exiled in Persia . . . . Esth. 2:5, 6

Brings up Esther . . . . Esth. 2:7

Directs Esther's movements . . . . Esth. 2:10–20

Reveals plot to kill the king . . . . Esth. 2:22, 23

Refuses homage to Haman . . . . .Esth. 3:1–6

Calls on Esther to save the Jews . . . . . .Esth. 4:1–17

Gallows made for . . . . Esth. 5:14

Honored by the king . . . . .Esth. 6:1–12

Writes a new decree . . . . Esth. 8:8–10

Is highly exalted . . . . Esth. 8:7, 15

Becomes famous . . . . Esth. 9:4

Writes to Jews about Feast of Purim . . . . Esth. 9:20–31

2. Postexilic returnee . . . . Ezra 2:2

More—*something in addition*

A. "More than" promises:

Repentance . . . . Matt. 18:13

Love . . . . John 21:15

B. "Much more" promises:

Grace . . . . Rom. 5:9–17

Witnessing . . . . Phil. 1:14

Obedience . . . . Phil. 2:12

C. "No more" promises:

Christ's death . . . . .Rom. 6:9

Remember sin . . . . Heb. 8:12

Moreh—*teacher, soothsayer*

1. Place (oak tree or grove) near Shechem . . .Gen. 12:6

Probably place of:

Idol-burying . . . . Gen. 35:4

Covenant stone . . . . .Josh. 24:26

2. Hill in the Valley of Jezreel . . . . .Judg. 7:1

Moresheth Gath—*possession of Gath*

Birthplace of Micah the prophet . . . . .Mic. 1:14

Moriah

God commands Abraham to sacrifice Isaac here .Gen. 22:1–13

Site of Solomon's temple . . . . 2 Chr. 3:1

Morning—*the first part of the day*

A. Early risers in:

Do the Lord's will . . . . Gen. 22:3

Worship . . . . .Ex. 24:4

Do the Lord's work . . . . Josh. 6:12

Fight the Lord's battles . . . . Josh. 8:10

Depart on a journey . . . . .Judg. 19:5, 8

Correct an evil . . . . Dan. 6:19

Pray . . . . .Mark 1:35

Visit the tomb . . . . .Mark 16:2

Preach . . . . Acts 5:21

B. For the righteous, a time for:

Joy . . . . .Ps. 30:5

God's lovingkindness . . . . .Ps. 92:2

God's mercies . . . . Lam. 3:22, 23

C. For the unrighteous, a time of:

Dread . . . . Deut. 28:67

Destruction . . . . Is. 17:14
D. Figurative of:
   Our unrighteousness. . . . . Hos. 6:4
   Judgment . . . . Zeph. 3:5
   God's light . . . . Amos 5:8
   Christ's return. . . . . .Rev. 2:28

Morning sacrifice—*part of Israelite worship*
   Ritual described . . . . .Ex. 29:38–42
   Part of continual offering. . . . . .Num. 28:3–8
   Under Ahaz . . . . 2 Kin. 16:15

Morning Star
Figurative of Christ:
   To church at Thyatira . . . . Rev. 2:24, 28
   Christ, of Himself .Rev. 22:16
   Applied to Christ .2 Pet. 1:19

Morsel—*a small piece of food*
   Offered to angels . . . . Gen. 18:5
   Rejected by a doomed man . . . . 1 Sam. 28:22
   Asked of a dying woman. . . . . 1 Kin. 17:11, 12
   Better than strife . . . . Prov. 17:1
   Exchanged for a birthright. . . . . Heb. 12:16

WORD STUDY | **MORTAL,** *'enosh* (ehn-*ohsh*). The noun *'enosh* usually appears in poetic passages and is translated "mortal" or "man." This word indicates ordinary men. Sometimes *'enosh* refers to an individual as it does in Job 5:17 where Eliphaz says, "Happy *is* the man whom God corrects." At other times the word refers to men in the collective sense as it does in Ps. 66:12 and Is. 24:6. Frequently in Job and Ps. the word is used referring to humans, especially as opposed to God. This is the sense seen in 2 Chr. 14:11 when Asa cries to God, "Do not let man prevail against You!" (Strong's #582)

Mortar—*a vessel*
   Vessel used for beating grains . . . . Num. 11:8
   Used figuratively .Prov. 27:22

Mortar—*a building material*
Made of:
   Clay . . . . Is. 41:25
   Asphalt . . . . Gen. 11:3
   Plaster . . . . Lev. 14:42, 45

Mortgage—*something given in security for debt*
   Postexilic Jews burdened with . . . . Neh. 5:3

Mortification—*a putting to death*
A. Objects of:
   Law. . . . . .Rom. 7:4
   Sin. . . . . Rom. 6:6, 11
   Flesh. . . . . .Rom. 13:14
   Members of earthly body . . . . .Col. 3:5
B. Agents of:
   Holy Spirit . . . . .Rom. 8:13
   Our obedience. Rom. 6:17–19

Moserah (sing.), Moseroth (pl.)—*bond*
   Place of Aaron's death and burial. . . . . . Deut. 10:6
   Israelite encampment . . . . Num. 33:30, 31

Moses—*drawn out*
A. Early life of (first 40 years):
   Descendant of Levi .Ex. 2:1
   Son of Amram and Jochebed. . . . . Ex. 6:16–20
   Brother of Aaron and Miriam. . . . . .Ex. 15:20
   Born under slavery. . . . . Ex. 2:1–10
   Hidden by mother . . . . .Ex. 2:2, 3
   Found among reeds, adopted by
      Pharaoh's daughter. . . . . Ex. 2:3–10
   Educated in Egyptian wisdom . . . . Acts 7:22
   Refused Egyptian sonship . . . . Heb. 11:23–27
   Defended his people . . . . Ex. 2:11–14
   Rejected, flees to Midian . . . . .Ex. 2:15
B. In Midian (second 40 years):
   Married Zipporah . . . . Ex. 2:16–21
   Father of two sons . . . . .Ex. 2:22; Acts 7:29
   Became Jethro's shepherd. . . . . .Ex. 3:1
C. Leader of Israel (last 40 years; to the end of his life):
   Saw burning bush. . . . . .Ex. 3:2, 3
   Heard God's voice .Ex. 3:4
   God's plan revealed to him . . . . Ex. 3:7–10
   Argued with God . . . . Ex. 4:1–17
   Met by Aaron. . . . . Ex. 4:14–28
   Assembled elders of Israelites . . . . Ex. 4:29–31
   Rejected by Pharaoh and Israel. . . . . . . Ex. 5:1–23
   Conflict with Pharaoh; ten plagues sent . Ex. 7–12
   Commanded to institute
      the Passover . . . . .Ex. 12:1–29; Heb. 11:28
D. From Egypt to Sinai:
   Led people from Egypt . . . . .Ex. 12:30–38
   Observed the Passover . . . . Ex. 12:39–51
   Healed bitter waters. . . . . Ex. 15:22–27
   People hunger; flesh and
      manna supplied . . . . Ex. 16:1–36; John 6:31, 32
   Defeated Amalek; hands held up by Hur
      and Aaron . . . . Ex. 17:8–13
   Came to Sinai . . . . .Ex. 19:1, 2
E. At Sinai:
   Called to God's presence . . . . .Acts 7:38
   Prepared Israel for the Law . . . . Ex. 19:7–25
   Received the Law . . . . .Ex. 20–23
   Confirmed the covenant with Israel . . Ex. 24:1–11
   Stayed 40 days on Sinai. . . . . Ex. 24:12–16
   Shown the pattern of the tabernacle . . . . Ex. 25–31
   Israel sinned; Moses interceded . . . . . . Ex. 32:1–35
   Recommissioned and encouraged . . . . Ex. 33:1–23
   Instructions received; tabernacle
      erected . . . . .Ex. 36–40
   Consecrated Aaron . . . . Lev. 8:1–36
   Numbered the men . . . . .Num. 1:1–54
   Observed the Passover . . . . Num. 9:1–5
F. From Sinai to Kadesh Barnea:
   Resumed journey to Canaan . . . . . .Num. 10:11–36
   Complained; 70 elders appointed . . . Num. 11:1–35
   Spoken against by Miriam
      and Aaron .Num. 12:1–6
G. At Kadesh Barnea:
   Sent spies to Canaan . . . . .Num. 13:1–33
   Pleaded with rebellious Israel . . . . . .Num. 14:1–19

Announced God's judgment . . . . . Num. 14:20–45

H. Wanderings:

Instructions received. . . . . .Num. 15:1–41

Sinned in anger. . . . . .Num. 20:1–13

Sent messengers to Edom. . . . . .Num. 20:14–21

Made a bronze serpent . . .Num. 21:4–9; John 3:14

Traveled toward Canaan . . . . .Num. 21:10–20

Ordered destruction . . . . Num. 25:1–18

Numbered the people . . . . .Num. 26:1–65

Gave instruction concerning

inheritance . . . . Num. 27:1–11

Commissioned Joshua as his

successor .Num. 27:12–23

Received further laws . . . . Num. 28–30

Conquered Midianites . . . . .Num. 31:1–54

Final instruction and records . . . . Num. 32–36

Reinterpreted the Law. . . . . Deut. 1–31

Gave farewell messages. . . . . .Deut. 32; 33

Committed written Law to

the priests . . . . Deut. 31:9, 26

Saw the Promised Land. . . . . .Deut. 34:1–4

Died, in full strength, at 120 . . . . . . .Deut. 34:5–7

Israel wept over. . . . . Deut. 34:8

I. In the New Testament:

Appears with Elijah at Christ's

transfiguration. . . . . Matt. 17:2–4

J. Character of:

Believer. . . . . Heb. 11:23–28

Faithful. . . . . .Num. 12:7; Heb. 3:2–5

Humble. . . . . Num. 12:3

Respected. . . . . Ex. 33:8–10

Logical. . . . . .Num. 14:12–20

Impatient . . . . Ex. 5:22, 23

Given to anger. . . . . .Ex. 32:19

Moses, oracles of—*blessings on tribes of Israel*

Pronounced . . . . .Deut. 33:6–25

Song introduces . . . . .Deut. 33:2–5

Song concludes . . . . .Deut. 33:26–29

Most assuredly—*a strong affirmation*

A. Concerning Christ's:

Glory . . . . John 1:51

Eternity. . . . . John 8:58

Uniqueness. . . . . .John 10:1, 7

Mission . . . . John 6:32

Betrayal. . . . . John 13:21

Death. . . . . John 12:24

B. Concerning humankind's:

Spiritual bondage. . . . . John 8:34

Spiritual darkness . . . . John 6:26

Need of regeneration. . . . . John 3:3, 5

Need of salvation . . . . .John 5:24, 25

Means of salvation . . . . .John 6:47, 53

Life eternal. . . . . John 8:51

C. Concerning the believer's:

Fickleness. . . . . John 13:38

Work . . . . John 14:12

Mission . . . . .John 13:16, 20

Prayer . . . . John 16:23

Most High—*a name of God*

Melchizedek, priest of. . . . . Heb. 7:1

Demons called Jesus Son of . . . . .Mark 5:7, 8

Paul and Silas called servants of. . . . . . .Acts 16:17

Most Holy Place

A. Described as:

Sanctuary. . . . . .Lev. 4:6

Holy Sanctuary. . . . . .Lev. 16:33

Holy place. . . . . Ex. 28:29

Most Holy. . . . . Ex. 26:33

Holiest of All. . . . . Heb. 9:3

Inner sanctuary . . . . 1 Kin. 6:5–20

B. Contents of:

Ark of the Testimony . . . . Ex. 26:33

Mercy seat . . . . Ex. 26:34

Cherubim. . . . . Ex. 25:18–22

Altar of incense. . . . . Heb. 9:4

Pot of manna . . . . .Ex. 16:33

Aaron's rod. . . . . Num. 17:10

Written copy of the Law . . .Deut. 31:26; 2 Kin. 22:8

C. Entrance to, by the high priest:

Not at all times . . . . .Lev. 16:2

Alone, once a year . . . . Heb. 9:7

With blood. . . . . .Lev. 16:14, 15

To make atonement. . . . . .Lev. 16:15–17, 33, 34

D. Significance of:

Abolished by Christ's death. . . . . Matt. 27:51

Typical of heaven . . . . .Ps. 102:19

Believers now enter boldly. . . . . Heb. 10:19

See Tabernacle

Moth—*a garment-destroying insect*

Used figuratively of:

Inner corruption. . . . . Is. 50:9

God's judgments. Hos. 5:12

Humankind's insecurity. . . . . .Job 4:19

Humankind's fading glory . . . . Job 13:28

Mother

A. Described as:

Loving. . . . . Ex. 2:1–25

Appreciative. . . . . 2 Kin. 4:19–37

Weeping . . . . .Luke 7:12–15

Remembering . . . . Luke 2:51

B. Kinds of:

Idolatrous. . . . . .Judg. 17:1–4

Troubled. . . . . .1 Kin. 17:17–24

Cruel . . . . 2 Kin. 11:1, 2

Joyful. . . . . Ps. 113:9

Good . . . . Prov. 31:1

Scheming . . . . Matt. 20:20–23

Prayerful. . . . . Acts 12:12

C. Duties toward:

Honor . . . . Eph. 6:2

Obedience . . . . Deut. 21:18, 19

Protection. . . . . Gen. 32:11

Provision. . . . . .John 19:25–27

D. Figurative of:

Israel . . . . Hos. 2:2, 5

Judah. . . . . Ezek. 19:2, 10

Heavenly Jerusalem....................Gal. 4:26
E. Duties performed by:
    Selecting son's wife .... Gen. 21:21
    Hospitality...........................Gen. 24:55
    Nourishment........................Ex. 2:8, 9
    Provision........................1 Kin. 1:11–21
    Comfort ....Is. 66:12, 13
    Teaching........................... Prov. 31:1
F. Dishonor of, punished by:
    Death.............................Lev. 20:9
    Shame ....Prov. 19:26
    Darkness.........................Prov. 20:20
    Destruction ....Prov. 28:24

Motherhood
A. Described as:
    Painful............................. Gen. 3:16
    Sometimes dangerous........... Gen. 35:16–20
    Yet joyful .... John 16:21
    Object of prayer .... Gen. 25:21
B. Blessings of:
    Fulfills divine Law.................. Gen. 1:28
    Makes joyful .... Ps. 113:9
    Woman will be saved in ....1 Tim. 2:15

Mother-in-law
    Judith's—grief.................. Gen. 26:34, 35
    Ruth's—loved ....Ruth 1:14–17
    Peter's—healed by Christ......... Matt. 8:14, 15

Motive—*inner impulse producing outward action*
A. Good:
    Questioned....................... 2 Kin. 5:5–8
    Misapplied .... Esth. 6:6–11
    Misrepresented .... Job 1:9–11
    Misunderstood ....Acts 21:26–31
B. Evil:
    Prompted by Satan.............. Matt. 16:22, 23
    Designed to deceive................ Acts 5:1–10

Mount Baalah—*mistress*
    Part of the territory of Judah......... Josh. 15:11

Mount Baal Hermon—*possessor of Hermon*
    Lived on by nations that tested Israel ...Judg. 3:3, 4

Mount Carmel—*fruitful*
    Prophets gathered together here...1 Kin. 18:19, 20
    Elisha journeyed to ....2 Kin. 2:25
    Shunammite woman comes to Elisha ..2 Kin. 4:25

Mount Ebal—*bald*
    Cursed by God .... Deut. 11:29
    Joshua built an altar here ....Josh. 8:30

Mount Gaash—*quaking*
    Place of Joshua's burial ....Josh. 24:30

Mount Gerizim—*rocky*
    Place the blessed stood .... Deut. 27:12
    Jotham spoke to people of
        Shechem here ....Judg. 9:7

Mount Gilboa—*bubbling spring*
    Men of Israel slain here...............1 Sam. 31:1
    Saul and his sons slain here ....1 Sam. 31:8

Mount Gilead—*heap of witness*
    Gideon divides the people for battle ..... Judg. 7:3

Mount Hor—*mountain*
    Lord spoke to Moses and
        Aaron here.....................Num. 20:23
    Aaron died here .... Num. 20:25–28

Mount Horeb—*desolate*
    Sons of Israel stripped themselves of
        ornaments here ....Ex. 33:6
    The same as Sinai.......................Ex. 3:1

Mount of Olives
    Prophecy concerning................. Zech. 14:4
    Jesus sent disciples for donkey ......Matt. 21:1, 2;
        Mark 11:1, 2
    Jesus speaks of the signs of
        His coming .... Matt. 24:3; Mark 13:3, 4
    After the Lord's supper went out to... Matt. 26:30;
        Mark 14:26
    Called Mount Olivet ....Luke 19:29; 21:37

Mount Seir—*rugged*
    Horites defeated by Chedorlaomer ... Gen. 14:5, 6

Mount Shepher—*beauty*
    Israelites camped at..............Num. 33:23, 24

Mount Sinai
    Lord descended upon, in fire............Ex. 19:18
    Lord called Moses to the top ....Ex. 19:20
    The glory of the Lord rested on, for
        six days........................Ex. 24:16

Mount Tabor—*broken*
    Deborah sent Barak there to defeat
        Canaanites .... Judg. 4:6–14

Mount Zion
    Survivors shall go out from ....2 Kin. 19:31

Mountain—*a high elevation of earth*
A. Mentioned in the Bible:
    Abarim ....Num. 33:47, 48
    Ararat .... Gen. 8:4
    Bashan............................Ps. 68:15
    Carmel............................1 Kin. 18:19
    Ebal .... Deut. 27:13
    Gaash.............................Judg. 2:9
    Gerizim......................... Deut. 11:29
    Gilboa .... 2 Sam. 1:6, 21
    Hachilah....................... 1 Sam. 23:19
    Hermon..........................Josh. 13:11
    Hor........................... Num. 34:7, 8
    Horeb (same as Sinai)................Ex. 3:1
    Lebanon .... Deut. 3:25
    Moreh ....Judg. 7:1
    Moriah .... Gen. 22:2
    Nebo .... Deut. 34:1
    Olives or Olivet..................... Matt. 24:3
    Pisgah .... Num. 21:20
    Sinai............................Ex. 19:2–20
    Sion or Zion ....2 Sam. 5:7
    Tabor........................... Judg. 4:6–14

B. In Christ's life, place of:

Temptation .... Matt. 4:8
Sermon ....Matt. 5:1
Prayer .... Matt. 14:23
Transfiguration ....Matt. 17:1, 2
Prophecy........................ Matt. 24:3
Agony ....Matt. 26:30, 31
Ascension ....Luke 24:50

C. Uses of:

Boundaries....................... Num. 34:7, 8
Distant vision .... Deut. 3:27
Hunting .... 1 Sam. 26:20
Warfare...........................1 Sam. 17:3
Protection........................ Amos 6:1
Refuge........................ Matt. 24:16
Idolatrous worship.................... Is. 65:7
Assembly sites .... Josh. 8:30–33

D. Significant Old Testament events on:

Ark rested upon (Ararat) .... Gen. 8:4
Abraham's testing (Moriah) ....Gen. 22:1–19
Giving of the Law (Sinai) .... Ex. 19:2–25
Moses' view of Canaan (Pisgah)....... Deut. 34:1
Combat with Baalism (Carmel)... 1 Kin. 18:19–42
David's city (Zion) ....2 Sam. 5:7

E. Figurative of:
God's:

Protection...........................Is. 31:4
Dwelling...........................Is. 8:18
Judgments ....Jer. 13:16
Gospel age .... Is. 27:13
Messiah's advent.................... Is. 40:9
Great joy......................... Is. 44:23
Great difficulties .... Matt. 21:21
Pride of humankind.................... Luke 3:5
Supposed faith...................... 1 Cor. 13:2

Mourning—*expression of sorrow*

A. Caused by:

Death............................ Gen. 50:10
Defection .... 1 Sam. 15:35
Disobedience...................... Ezra 9:4–7
Desolation .... Joel 1:9, 10
Defeat ....Rev. 18:11
Discouragement ....Ps. 42:9
Disease ....Job 2:5–8
Disbelief .... Num. 14:26–39

B. Transformed into:

Gladness..........................Is. 51:11
Hope ....John 11:23–28
Everlasting joy....................... Is. 35:10
Comfort ....Matt. 5:4

C. Signs of:

Tearing of clothing .... 2 Sam. 3:31, 32
Ashes on head .... 2 Sam. 13:19
Sackcloth .... Gen. 37:34
Neglect of appearance............. 2 Sam. 19:24
Presence of mourners .... John 11:19, 31
Apparel.......................... 2 Sam. 14:2
Shaved head........................ Jer. 16:6, 7

Mouse, mice—*a small rodent*

Accounted unclean ....Lev. 11:29
Eaten by idolatrous Israelites .... Is. 66:17

Mouth

A. Descriptive of:

Top of a well.....................Gen. 29:2, 3, 8
Opening of a sack.................Gen. 42:27, 28
Man's...............................Job 3:1

B. Exhortations concerning:

Make all acceptable .... Ps. 19:14
Keep with a muzzle .... Ps. 39:1
Set a guard before..................... Ps. 141:3
Keep the corrupt from .... Eph. 4:29
Keep filthy language from ....Col. 3:8

C. Of unregenerate, source of:

Lying .... 1 Kin. 22:13, 22, 23
Idolatry............................ 1 Kin. 19:18
Unfaithfulness .... Ps. 5:9
Cursing .... Ps. 10:7
Pride .... Ps. 17:10
Evil............................... Ps. 50:19
Lies............................... Ps. 63:11
Vanity .... Ps. 144:8, 11
Foolishness......................Prov. 15:2, 14
Flattery .... Jude 16

D. Of regenerate, used for:

Prayer ....1 Sam. 1:12
God's Law........................ Josh. 1:8
Praise............................ Ps. 34:1
Wisdom ....Ps. 37:30
Testimony......................... Eph. 6:9
Confession .... Rom. 10:8–10
Righteousness .... Ps. 71:15
Truth .... Mal. 2:6

Move—*to change the position*

A. Of God's Spirit in:

Creation .... Gen. 1:2
Humankind.......................Judg. 13:25
Prophets ....2 Pet. 1:21

B. Of things immovable:

City of God ....Ps. 46:4, 5
Eternal kingdom...................... Ps. 96:10

Mowing—*to cut grass*

First growth for taxes .... Amos 7:1
Left on the ground .... Ps. 72:6

Moza—*a going forth*

1. Descendant of Judah................. 1 Chr. 2:46
2. Descendant of Saul .... 1 Chr. 8:36, 37

Mozah—*drained*

A Benjamite town...................Josh. 18:21, 26

Mulberry tree

Referred to by Jesus .... Luke 17:6

Mule—*a hybrid between a horse and a donkey*

Breeding of, forbidden ....Lev. 19:19
Sign of kingship .... 1 Kin. 1:33
Used in trade ....Ezek. 27:14
Considered stubborn.................... Ps. 32:9

Multiply—*to increase in quantity or quality*
A. Of good things:
    Churches...........................Acts 9:31
    Word of God .... Acts 12:24
    God's wonders...........................Ex. 7:3
    Loaves and fish ..... Matt. 15:32–39; John 6:1–15
    Good seed............................Mark 4:8
B. Secret of:
God's:
    Promise........................... Gen. 16:10
    Oath.............................Gen. 26:3, 4
    Human obedience .... Deut. 7:12, 13

Multitude—*a large number of people*
A. Dangers of:
    Mixed, source of evil.................. Ex. 12:38
    Follow after in doing evil...............Ex. 23:2
    Sacrifices, vain ....Is. 1:11
B. Christ's compassion upon:
    Teaching...........................Matt. 5:1
    Healing...................... Matt. 12:15
    Teaching parables to ....Matt. 13:1–3, 34
    Feeding...................... Matt. 14:15–21
C. Their attitude toward Christ:
    Reaction to...................... Matt. 9:8, 33
    Recognition of................ Matt. 14:5; 21:46
    Reception of...................... Matt. 21:8–11
    Running after .... John 6:2
    Rejection of .... Matt. 27:20

Muppim—*obscurities*
    Son of Benjamin ....Gen. 46:21
    Called Shupham .... Num. 26:39
    Shuppim and Shephuphan.....1 Chr. 7:12, 15; 8:5

Murder
A. Defined as:
    Coming out of the heart.............Matt. 15:19
    Resulting from anger.............. Matt. 5:21, 22
    Work of the flesh .... Gal. 5:19–21
    Excluding from eternal life ....1 John 3:15
B. Guilt of:
    Determined by witnesses .... Num. 35:30
    Not redeemable.................... Num. 35:30
    Not forgiven by flight to the altar ....Ex. 21:14
C. Penalty of:
    Ordained by God .... Gen. 9:6
    Executed by avenger of blood .... Deut. 19:6
  See Homicide

Murmuring—*sullen dissatisfaction with things*
A. Caused by:
    Thirst ....Ex. 15:24
    Hunger .... Ex. 16:2, 3, 8
    Fear ....Num. 14:1–4
B. Against Christ, because of His:
    Practices ....Luke 15:1, 2
    Pronouncements...................John 6:41–61
C. Of Christians:
    Provoked...........................Acts 6:1
    Forbidden..........................John 6:43
    Excluded............................ Phil. 2:14

Mushi—*drawn out*
    Son of Merari.........................Ex. 6:19
    Descendants of,
        called Mushites ....Num. 3:33; 26:58

Music
A. Used in:
    Farewells........................ Gen. 31:27
    Entertainments....................... Is. 5:12
    Weddings ....Jer. 7:34
    Funerals .... Matt. 9:18, 23
    Sacred processions .... 1 Chr. 13:6–8
    Victory celebrations............. Ex. 15:20, 21
    Coronation services.............2 Chr. 23:11, 13
    Dedication services ....2 Chr. 5:11–13
B. Influence of, upon:
    Mental disorders............1 Sam. 16:14–17, 23
    Sorrowful ....Ps. 137:1–4
C. List of instruments of:
    Cymbal .... 1 Cor. 13:1
    Flute.......................Ps. 150:4; Is. 30:29
    Harp .... 1 Sam. 16:16, 23
    Psaltery............... 1 Sam. 10:5; Dan. 3:5, 10
    Tambourine...................... Is. 5:12
    Horn .... Dan. 3:5, 7
    Lyre .... Dan. 3:5, 7
    Sistrums ....2 Sam. 6:5
    Timbrel.................. Gen. 31:27; Ex. 15:20
    Trumpet ....Josh. 6:4
    Complete orchestra ....2 Sam. 6:5

Music in Christian worship
    From heart ....Eph. 5:19
    Means of teaching ....Col. 3:16

Must—*something that is imperative*
A. Concerning Christ's:
    Preaching ....Luke 4:43
    Suffering......................... Matt. 16:21
    Death.............................. John 3:14
    Fulfillment of Scripture .... Matt. 26:54
    Resurrection ....John 20:9
    Ascension .... Acts 3:21
    Reign............................1 Cor. 15:25
B. Concerning the believer's:
    Belief .... Heb. 11:6
    Regeneration .... John 3:7
    Salvation........................... Acts 4:12
    Worship .... John 4:24
    Duty...............................Acts 9:6
    Suffering...........................Acts 9:16
    Mission .... Acts 19:21
    Moral life ....Titus 1:7
    Inner life.......................... 2 Tim. 2:24
    Judgment .... 2 Cor. 5:10
C. Concerning prophecy:
    Gospel's proclamation .... Mark 13:10
    Gentiles' inclusion .... John 10:16
    Earth's tribulations .... Matt. 24:6
    Resurrection .... 1 Cor. 15:53

Mustard seed—*very small seed*
Kingdom compared to . . . . Matt. 13:31
Faith compared to . . . . Matt. 17:20

Mutability—*capable of change*
A. Asserted of:
Physical world . . . . .Matt. 5:18
Earthly world. . . . . 1 John 2:15–17
Old covenant . . . . .Heb. 8:8–13
Present order . . . . 2 Cor. 4:18
B. Denied of:
God . . . . Mal. 3:6
Christ. . . . . .Heb. 1:10, 11; 13:8
See Immutability; Move

Mute—*inability to speak*
A. Used literally of dumbness:
Natural . . . . .Ex. 4:11
Penalized . . . . .Luke 1:20
B. Used figuratively of:
External calamity. . . . . .Ps. 38:13
Submissiveness . . . . Is. 53:7
Lamb before shearer is . . . . Acts 8:32
With silence. . . . . .Ps. 39:2

Mutilation—*to maim, to damage, to disfigure*
A. Object of, forbidden:
On the body . . . . .Lev. 19:28
For:
Priesthood . . . . .Lev. 21:18
Sacrifice . . . . .Lev. 22:22
Mourning. . . . . Jer. 41:5–7
B. Practiced by:
Jews . . . . Judg. 19:29, 30
Philistines. . . . . .Judg. 16:21
Canaanites . . . . .Judg. 1:6, 7
Baal prophets. . . . . .1 Kin. 18:28
C. Used of:
Legalistic circumcision . . . . Phil. 3:2

Mutiny—*revolt against authority*
By Israelites . . . . .Num. 14:1–4

Mutual—*a common interest*
Spoken of faith . . . . .Rom. 1:12

Muzzling
Applied:
To oxen . . . . Deut. 25:4
Figuratively, to Christians . . . . .1 Cor. 9:9–11

Myra—*a city of Lycia*
Paul changes ships here. . . . . Acts 27:5, 6

Myrrh
A. Dried gum (Heb., mor) of a balsam tree, used:
In anointing oil. Ex. 30:23
As a perfume . . . . Ps. 45:8
For beauty treatment. . . . . Esth. 2:12
Brought as gifts. .Matt. 2:11
Given as a sedative. . . . . Mark 15:23
Used for embalming . . . . .John 19:38, 39
B. Fragrant resin (Heb. , lot) used:
In commerce . . . . Gen. 37:25
As presents. . . . . Gen. 43:11

Myrtle—*a shrub*
Found in mountains; booths made of . . . Neh. 8:15
Figurative of the gospel. . . . . Is. 41:19
Used symbolically . . . . Zech. 1:10, 11

Mysia—*a province of Asia Minor*
Paul and Silas pass through . . . . .Acts 16:7, 8

| WORD STUDY | **MYSTERY,** *mustērion* (moos-*tay*-ree-on). Noun meaning "secret" or "mystery." |

In vernacular Greek this term often pertained to "mystery" religions with their "secret" teachings and rites. In the NT it applies to God's plans, which cannot be comprehended by human intellect and therefore remain a "mystery" until they are revealed by God or one of His agents. The "mysteries of the kingdom of God" remain only "parables" until explained by Jesus (Luke 8:10). Paul uses the word to refer to God's plans for the salvation of humanity, understood by few until the "mystery" of Christ is proclaimed (Col. 4:3; cf. 1:27; 2:2; Eph. 1:9; 3:4; 6:19). Mysteries uttered "in the Spirit" (1 Cor. 14:2) can only be understood by God. The author of Rev. recounts the "mystery of God." (10:7; cf. 1:20) (Strong's #3466).

Mystery—*a religious truth unknown except by divine revelation*
A. Concerning God's:
Secrets . . . . Deut. 29:29
Providence . . . . Rom. 11:33–36
Sovereignty . . . . Rom. 9:11–23
Prophecies . . . . 1 Pet. 1:10–12
Predestination. Rom. 8:29, 30
B. Concerning Christianity:
Christ's incarnation. . . . . .1 Tim. 3:16
Christ's nature. . . . . .Col. 2:2
Kingdom of God. . . . . Luke 8:10
Christian faith. . . . . 1 Tim. 3:9
Indwelling Christ. . . . . Col. 1:26, 27
Union of all believers. . . . . Eph. 3:4–9
Israel's blindness. . . . . .Rom. 11:25
Lawlessness . . . . 2 Thess. 2:7
Harlot Babylon .Rev. 17:5, 7
Resurrection of saints . . . . 1 Cor. 15:51
God's completed purpose. . . . . .Rev. 10:7

Mythology, referred to
Zeus . . . . Acts 14:12, 13
Hermes . . . . Acts 14:12
Pantheon . . . . Acts 17:16–23
Diana. . . . . .Acts 19:24–41
Castor and Pollux (Twin Brothers) . . . . Acts 28:11

Myths—*speculative and philosophical fable or allegory*
Condemned. . . . . .1 Tim. 1:4
Fables. . . . . .1 Tim. 4:7
False. . . . . 2 Tim. 4:4

N

Naam—*pleasantness*
Son of Caleb.........................1 Chr. 4:15

Naamah—*sweet, pleasant*
1. Daughter of Lamech ....Gen. 4:19–22
2. Ammonite wife of Solomon; mother
　　of King Rehoboam ....1 Kin. 14:21, 31
3. Town of Judah ....Josh. 15:1, 41

Naaman—*pleasant*
1. Son of Benjamin.....................Gen. 46:21
2. Captain in the Syrian army.........2 Kin. 5:1–11
　　Healed of his leprosy.............2 Kin. 5:14–17
　　Referred to by Christ.................Luke 4:27

Naamathite—*an inhabitant of Naamah*
Applied to Zophar, Job's friend ....Job 2:11

Naamites
Descendants of Naaman ....Num. 26:40

Naarah—*girl*
1. Wife of Ashhur.....................1 Chr. 4:5, 6
2. Town of Ephraim.....................Josh. 16:7
　　Same as Naaran.....................1 Chr. 7:28

Naarai—*pleasantness of Yahweh*
One of David's mighty men.........1 Chr. 11:37

Nabal—*fool*
Wealthy sheep owner..............1 Sam. 25:2, 3
Refuses David's request for food...1 Sam. 25:4–12
Abigail, wife of, appeases David's
　　wrath against ....1 Sam. 25:13–35
Drunk, dies of a stroke ....1 Sam. 25:36–39
Widow of, becomes
　　David's wife ....1 Sam. 25:39–42

Naboth—*sprout*
Owner of vineyard coveted by
　　King Ahab.....................1 Kin. 21:1–4
Accused falsely of blasphemy and
　　disloyalty.................... 1 Kin. 21:5–16
Murder of, avenged ....1 Kin. 21:17–25

Nachon—*prepared*
Threshing floor, site of
　　Uzzah's death.................. 2 Sam. 6:6, 7
Called:
Perez Uzzah ("breach")................2 Sam. 6:8
Chidon ....1 Chr. 13:9

Nadab—*willing, liberal*
1. Eldest of Aaron's four sons ....Ex. 6:23
　　Takes part in affirming covenant ...Ex. 24:1, 9–12
　　Becomes priest ....Ex. 28:1
　　Consumed by fire....................Lev. 10:1–7
　　Dies childless........................ Num. 3:4
2. Judahite ....1 Chr. 2:28, 30
3. Benjamite.......................... 1 Chr. 8:30
4. King of Israel ....1 Kin. 14:20
　　Killed by Baasha................1 Kin. 15:25–31

Naggai
Ancestor of Christ ....Luke 3:25

Nahalal, Nahallal, Nahalol—*drinking place for flocks*
Village of Zebulun ....Josh. 19:10, 15
Assigned to Merarite Levites.........Josh. 21:35
Canaanites not driven from...........Judg. 1:30

Nahaliel—*valley of God*
Israelite camp .... Num. 21:19

Naham—*consolation*
Father of Keilah ....1 Chr. 4:19

Nahamani—*compassionate*
Returned after the Exile............... Neh. 7:7

Naharai—*snorting*
Armor-bearer of Joab...2 Sam. 23:37; 1 Chr. 11:39

Nahash—*serpent*
1. King of Ammon; makes impossible
　　demands......................1 Sam. 11:1–15
2. King of Ammon who treats David
　　kindly ....2 Sam. 10:2
　　Son of, helps David.............2 Sam. 17:27–29
3. Father of Abigail and Zeruiah, David's
　　half sisters ....2 Sam. 17:25

Nahath—*descent*
1. Edomite chief .... Gen. 36:13
2. Kohathite Levite .... 1 Chr. 6:26
　　Called Tohu.......................1 Sam. 1:1
3. Levite in Hezekiah's reign........... 2 Chr. 31:13

Nahbi—*concealed*
Spy of Naphtali.................... Num. 13:14

Nahor—*snorting*
1. Grandfather of Abraham...........Gen. 11:24–26
2. Son of Terah, brother of Abraham ......Gen. 11:27
　　Marries Milcah, fathers eight sons by her and four
　　　by concubine.................... Gen. 11:29
　　God of............................ Gen. 31:53
3. City of Haran .... Gen. 24:10

Nahshon
Judahite leader .... Num. 1:4, 7
Aaron's brother-in-law ....Ex. 6:23
Ancestor of David ....Ruth 4:20–22
Ancestor of Christ ....Matt. 1:4

Nahum—*full of comfort*
Inspired prophet to Judah concerning
　　Nineveh .... Nah. 1:1

Nahum, Book of—*a book of the Old Testament*
The awesomeness of God...........Nah. 1:1–15
The destruction of Nineveh ....Nah. 2; 3

Nail
A. Significant uses of:
Killing a man.......................Judg. 4:21
Fastening Christ to cross ....John 20:25
B. Figurative uses of:
Words fixed in the memory.......... Eccl. 12:11
Atonement for humankind's sin........Col. 2:14

Nain—*pleasant*

    Village south of Nazareth; Jesus raises

        widow's son here . . . . Luke 7:11–17

Naioth—*habitations*

    Prophets' school in Ramah 1 Sam. 19:18, 19, 22, 23

Naked, nakedness—*nude, nudity*

A. Used of humankind's:

    Original state . . . . Gen. 2:25

    Sinful state . . . . Gen. 3:7, 10, 11

    State of grace . . . . Rom. 8:35

    Disembodied state . . . . 2 Cor. 5:3

B. Evil of:

    Strictly forbidden . . . . Lev. 18:6–20

    Brings a curse . . . . Gen. 9:21–25

    Judged by God . . . . Ezek. 22:10

C. Instances of:

    Noah guilty of . . . . Gen. 9:21–23

    Forbidden, to priests . . . . Ex. 20:26

    Michal rebukes David for . . . . 2 Sam. 6:20–23

D. Putting clothing on:

    Indicates a changed life . . . . Mark 5:15

    Promises a reward . . . . Matt. 25:34–40

    Takes away shame . . . . Rev. 3:18

    Sign of true faith . . . . James 2:15–17

E. Figurative of:

    Separation from God . . . . Is. 20:3

    Israel's unworthiness . . . . Ezek. 16:7–22

    Judah's spiritual adultery . . . . Ezek. 16:36–38

    God's judgment . . . . Ezek. 16:39

    Spiritual need . . . . Hos. 2:9

    Wickedness . . . . Nah. 3:4, 5

    Needy . . . . Matt. 25:36, 38

    God's knowledge . . . . Heb. 4:13

    Unpreparedness . . . . Rev. 16:15

WORD STUDY   **NAME,** *shem* (*shaym*). *Shem* is a noun, generally translated "name," but it can also mean "a marking of fame," a "memorial," or "character." The word is used when rivers, beasts, and cities are named. Usually the word is used in connection with a person, signifying something about that person. God is seen to change a person's name. When this happens, there is not a verb, just the phrase "name Israel," which is usually seen in translation as "Israel shall be your name." *Shem* is used in indicating a person's reputation and thus his or her fame and glory. In Hebrew thought a man's name continued his life even after his physical life ended as long as his family, especially his sons, existed. So, to wipe out someone's name is to destroy his family. In reference to God, to call on His name is to worship. The names of God embody the revealed character of God, so that after an encounter with God, many times that person gave God a name indicating how he or she had just experienced God: as provider, healer, and so on. Is. 55:13, where the word "name" means "memorial," says, "It shall be to the LORD for a name." From this passage comes the name of the Holocaust museum in Israel, *Yad Vashem.* (Strong's #8034)

WORD STUDY   **NAME,** *onoma* (*on*-ahm-ah). This noun, "name," occurs often in the NT, usually with reference to a person's name (Mark 5:22). In ancient times a "name" represented the actual nature or essence or power of the person or god it designated. Thus, for example, exorcists invoke the name of a renowned exorcist (Acts 19:13). The "name of the LORD" (Acts 2:21) is revered as being almost a manifestation of the nature and character and power of God. Jesus' character and identity seem bound up in His name: therefore, one believesin His name (1 John 3:23), is baptized in His name (Acts 2:38), bears His name (Acts 9:15), proclaims His name (Acts 9:27). Since the utterance of Jesus' name is believed to bring about the desired effect, believers pray while calling on His name (John 16:23; Eph. 5:20). (Strong's #3686)

Name—*a word used to identify a person, animal, or thing*

A. Determined by:

    Events of the time . . . . Gen. 30:8

    Prophetic position . . . . Gen. 25:26

    Fondness of hope . . . . Gen. 29:32–35

    Change of character . . . . John 1:42

    Innate character . . . . 1 Sam. 25:25

    Coming events . . . . Is. 8:1–4

    Divine mission . . . . Matt. 1:21

B. Of God, described as:

    Great . . . . Josh. 7:9

    Glorious . . . . Is. 63:14

    Everlasting . . . . Ps. 135:13

    Exalted . . . . Ps. 148:13

    Holy . . . . Is. 57:15

C. Of God, evil acts against:

    Taken in vain . . . . Ex. 20:7

    Sworn falsely . . . . Lev. 19:12

    Lies spoken in . . . . Zech. 13:3

    Despised . . . . Mal. 1:6

D. Of God, proper attitude toward:

    Exalt . . . . Ps. 34:3

    Praise . . . . Ps. 54:6

    Love . . . . Ps. 69:36

    Bless . . . . Ps. 103:1

    Call on . . . . Ps. 116:17

E. Of Christ:

    Given before birth . . . . Matt. 1:21, 23

    Hated by the world . . . . Matt. 10:22

    Believers baptized in . . . . Acts 2:38

    Miracles performed by . . . . Acts 3:16

    Believers suffer for . . . . Acts 5:41

    Speaking in . . . . Acts 9:27, 29

    Gentiles called by . . . . Acts 15:14, 17

    Final subjection to . . . . Phil. 2:9, 10

F. Of believers:

    Called everlasting . . . . Is. 56:5

    Written in heaven . . . . Luke 10:20

    Called evil by world . . . . Luke 6:22

    Known by Christ . . . . John 10:3

    Confessed by Christ . . . . Rev. 3:5

    "Called by" . . . . Is. 62:2; Rev. 3:12

Names of Christ (see Christ, names of)

Naomi—*my delight*

Widow of Elimelech . . . . Ruth 1:1–3
Returns to Bethlehem with Ruth. . . . Ruth 1:14–19
Arranges Ruth's marriage to Boaz. . . . . . Ruth 3; 4
Considers Ruth's child (Obed) her
own . . . . Ruth 4:16, 17

Naphish—*numerous*

Ishmael's eleventh son. . . . . Gen. 25:15

Naphtali—*my wrestling*

1. Son of Jacob by Bilhah . . . . Gen. 30:1, 8
Has four sons. . . . . .Gen. 46:24
Receives Jacob's blessing . . . . .Gen. 49:21, 28
2. Tribe of. . . . . .Num. 1:42
Stationed last. . . . . .Num. 2:29–31
First census . . . . .Num. 1:42, 43
Second census . . . . Num. 26:48–50
Territory assigned to . . . . Josh. 19:32–39
Canaanites not driven out by . . . . .Judg. 1:33
Barak becomes famous. . . . . Judg. 4:6, 14–16
Bravery of, praised . . . . .Judg. 5:18
Warriors of, under Gideon. . . . . .Judg. 7:23
Warriors of, help David . . . . .1 Chr. 12:34
Conquered by wars. . . . . .1 Kin. 15:20
Taken captive . . . . .2 Kin. 15:29
Prophecy of a great light in . . . . Is. 9:1–7
Prophecy fulfilled in Christ's
ministry in. Matt. 4:12–16
12,000 of tribe of sealed . . . . Rev. 7:6

Naphtuhim

Fourth son of Mizraim; probably district
around . . . . Gen. 10:13

Narcissus

Christian in Rome . . . . .Rom. 16:11

Nathan—*gift*

1. Son of David . . . . 2 Sam. 5:14
Mentioned in the prophets. . . . . Zech. 12:12
Jesus' lineage traced through. . . . . . . Luke 3:23–28
2. Judahite . . . . 1 Chr. 2:36
3. Prophet under David and Solomon. . . . 1 Chr. 29:29
Reveals God's plan to David . . . . 2 Sam. 7:2–29
Rebukes David's sin. . . . . 2 Sam. 12:1–15
Renames Solomon as Jedidiah . . .2 Sam. 12:24, 25
Reveals Adonijah's plot. . . . . 1 Kin. 1:10–46
Sons of, in official positions. . . . . . . .1 Kin. 4:1, 2, 5
4. Father of Igal. . . . . .2 Sam. 23:36
5. A chief among returnees . . . . Ezra 8:16
6. One who divorced his foreign wife . . . Ezra 10:34, 39

Nathanael—*God has given*

One of Christ's disciples. . . . . .John 1:45–51

Nathan-Melech—*the king has given*

An official in Josiah's reign . . . . .2 Kin. 23:11

Nations—*people under a sovereign government*
A. Of the world:
Descendants of Noah's sons . . . . Gen. 10:32
Made from one blood . . . . Acts 17:26

Separated by God. Deut. 32:8
Inherit separate characteristics . . . . Gen. 25:23
Laden with iniquity. . . . . Is. 1:4
Destroyed by corruption. . . . . Lev. 18:26–28
Exalted by righteousness . . . . .Prov. 14:34
Father of many nations. . . . . Gen. 17:4
Lord will set you high above all . . . . . . Deut. 28:1
Subject to repentance . . . . Jer. 18:7–10
Judged by God. . . . . Gen. 15:14
Under God's control . . . . Jer. 25:8–14
Future of, revealed . . . . Dan. 2:27–45
Gospel to be preached to all. . . . . Matt. 24:14
Sarah shall be mother of many . . . . Gen. 17:16
B. Of Israel:
Descendants of Abraham. . . . . Gen. 12:2;
John 8:33, 37
Designated. . . . . .Ex. 19:6
Given blessings . . . . Deut. 4:7, 8; Rom. 9:4, 5
Punished by God. . . . . Jer. 25:1–11
Scattered among nations . . . .Neh. 1:8; Luke 21:24
Christ died for. . . . . John 11:51
C. Of the true people of God:
Described as righteous . . . . Is. 26:2
Born in a day . . . . Is. 66:8
Accounted fruitful. . . . . Matt. 21:43
Believers are. . . . . .1 Pet. 2:9

Nations, table of

Record. . . . . .Gen. 10:1–32

WORD STUDY **NATURAL, UNSPIRITUAL,** *psuchikos* (psoo-khee-*koss*). Adjective meaning "pertaining to the soul" or "life" (see the cognate noun *psuchē* in the topical word study: "soul"). In the NT *psuchikos* describes the life and things of the "natural" world in contrast to the life and things of the supernatural or spiritual world *(pneumatikos),* as in 1 Cor. 15:46 (where both adjectives are used as substantives). Thus, it is translated as "natural" or "unspiritual." The "natural person" cannot comprehend the "things of the Spirit of God" (1 Cor. 2:14; cf. 2:11–16). See also James 3:15; Jude 19. (Strong's #5591)

Natural—*that which is innate and real; not artificial or man-made*
A. Described as:
Physical origin. . . . . James 1:23
Normal . . . . .Rom. 1:26
Unregenerate. . . . . 1 Cor. 2:14
Unnatural. . . . . 2 Pet. 2:12
Temporal . . . . .1 Cor. 15:46
B. Contrasted with:
Acquired. . . . . Rom. 11:21, 24
Perverted . . . . Rom. 1:26, 27
Spiritual (life) . . . . 1 Cor. 2:14
Spiritual (body). . . . . 1 Cor. 15:44–46

Naturalization—*becoming a citizen of an adopted country*
Natural level, rights of . . . . .Acts 22:25–28
Spiritual level, blessings of. . . . . .Eph. 2:12–19

Natural person
Does not accept things of God . . . . 1 Cor. 2:14
Contrasted with spiritual. . . . . 1 Cor. 15:44–46

Natural religion
A. Contents of, God's:
Glory . . . . .Ps. 19:1–3
Nature. . . . . Rom. 1:19, 20
Sovereignty . . . . Acts 17:23–31
Goodness . . . . Acts 14:15–17
B. Characteristics of:
Original. . . . . Rom. 1:19, 20
Universal. . . . . .Rom. 10:18
Inadequate. . . . . Rom. 2:12–15
Corrupted. . . . . Rom. 1:21–32
Valuable . . . . .Dan. 5:18–23

Nature—*the essential elements resident in something*
A. Descriptive of:
Right order of things. . . . . .Rom. 1:26
Natural sense of right . . . . .Rom. 2:14
Nonexistence. . . . . .Gal. 4:8
Humankind's natural depravity. . . . . Eph. 2:3
Divine . . . . .2 Pet. 1:4
B. Of humankind's unregenerate, described as:
Under wrath. . . . . Eph. 2:3
Source of:
Iniquity. . . . . James 3:6
Corruption. . . . . 2 Pet. 2:12

Nature, beauties of
Reveal God's glory. . . . . .Ps. 19:1–6
Greater than outward appearance. . .Matt. 6:28–30
Descriptive of spiritual blessings . . . . . . Is. 35:1, 2

Navel—*the point at which the umbilical cord is attached*
A. Used literally of:
Lover's appeal . . . . Song 7:2
B. Used figuratively of:
Israel's wretched condition . . . . .Ezek. 16:4

Navy—*ships owned by a country*
Solomon's . . . . .1 Kin. 9:26
Jehoshaphat's. . . . . .1 Kin. 22:48

Nazarene—*a native of Nazareth*
Jesus to be called. Matt. 2:23
Descriptive of Jesus' followers. . . . . Acts 24:5

Nazareth
A. Town in Galilee:
Considered obscure . . . . .John 1:46
City of Jesus' parents. . . . . Matt. 2:23
Early home of Jesus . . . . Luke 2:39–51
Jesus departs from . . . . .Mark 1:9
Jesus rejected by . . . . Luke 4:16–30
B. As a title of honor descriptive of Jesus:
Anointed by the Spirit. . . . . Acts 10:38
Risen Lord . . . . Acts 22:8

Nazirite—*one especially consecrated to God*
A. Methods of becoming, by:
Birth. . . . . .Judg. 13:5, 7
Vow . . . . Num. 6:2

B. Requirements of:
Separation . . . . Num. 6:4
No:
Wine . . . . Num. 6:3, 4
Shaving. . . . . Num. 6:5
Defilement. . . . . Num. 6:6, 7
Corruption. . . . . Amos 2:11, 12
Holiness . . . . Num. 6:8
C. Examples of:
Samson . . . . Judg. 16:14–17
Samuel. . . . . 1 Sam. 1:11–28
John the Baptist . . . . .Luke 1:13, 15
Christians. . . . . 2 Cor. 6:17

Neah—*the settlement*
Town in Zebulun . . . . .Josh. 19:13

Neapolis—*new city*
Seaport of Philippi. . . . . .Acts 16:11

Near—*close at hand (in place or time)*
A. Of dangers, from:
Prostitute . . . . Prov. 7:8
Destruction . . . . .Prov. 10:14
God's judgment. . . . . .Joel 3:14
B. Of the messianic salvation, as:
Promised. . . . . Is. 50:8
Available. . . . . .Is. 51:5
C. Of Christ's return, described by:
Christ. . . . . Matt. 24:33
Paul . . . . .Rom. 13:11

Neariah—*Yahweh drives away*
1. Descendant of David. . . . . 1 Chr. 3:22, 23
2. Simeonite captain . . . . 1 Chr. 4:42

Nearness of God
A. Old Testament:
In sense of time. . . . . Is. 46:13; Zeph. 1:14
In prayer . . . . Is. 55:6
B. New Testament:
In sense of time. . . . . Rev. 1:1–3; 22:10
In prayer . . . . .Phil. 4:5–9; James 4:8

Nebai—*projecting*
Leader who signs the sealed covenant . . . Neh. 10:19

Nebaioth, Nebajoth
Descendants of, from Arabian tribe . . . . . . Is. 60:7
Eldest son of Ishmael. . . . . Gen. 25:13

Neballat—*hard, firm*
Postexilic town of Benjamin . . . . . . .Neh. 11:31, 34

Nebat—*look*
Father of Jeroboam . . . . .1 Kin. 11:26

Nebo—*height*
1. Babylonian god of literature and science. . . .Is. 46:1
2. Mountain peak near Jericho . . . . .Num. 33:47
Name of Pisgah's summit. . . . . Deut. 34:1
3. Moabite town near Mt. Nebo . . . . .Num. 32:3
Restored by Reubenites. . . . . Num. 32:37, 38
Mentioned in prophecy against Moab . . . . Is. 15:2
4. Town in Judah . . . . .Ezra 2:29

Nebuchadnezzar—*Nebo, defend the boundary*
A. Life of:
Monarch of the Neo-Babylonian Empire
(605–562 B.C.); defeats Pharaoh Necho at
Carchemish............2 Chr. 35:20; Jer. 46:2
Besieges Jerusalem; carries captives to
Babylon ....Dan. 1:1–3
Shows kindness to Jeremiah .... Jer. 39:11, 12
Crushes Jehoiachin's revolt
(597 B.C.) .... 2 Kin. 24:10–17
Carries sacred vessels
to Babylon .... 2 Kin. 24:11–13
Destroys Jerusalem; captures Zedekiah
(587 B.C.) .... Jer. 39:5, 6
Dreams interpreted by
Daniel.................Dan. 2:14–47; 4:9–27
Builds golden image.................Dan. 3:1–7
Puts three Hebrews in
fiery furnace................. Dan. 3:13–30
Leads attack on Tyre................ Ezek. 26:7
B. Features concerning:
Builder of Babylon ....Dan. 4:30
First of four great empires .... Dan. 2:26–48
Instrument of God's judgment..........Jer. 27:8
Afflicted with insanity........... Dan. 4:28–37
C. Prophecies concerning his:
Conquest of Judah and Jerusalem .....Jer. 21:7, 10
Destruction of Jerusalem..........Jer. 32:28–36
Conquest of other nations .... Jer. 27:7–9
Conquest of Egypt ....Jer. 43:10–13
Destruction of Tyre.............. Ezek. 26:7–12
Utter destruction ....Is. 14:4–27

Nebushasban—*Nebo delivers me*
Babylonian officer .... Jer. 39:13

Nebuzaradan—*Nebo has given seed*
Nebuchadnezzar's captain at siege of
Jerusalem.................... 2 Kin. 25:8–20
Carries out Nebuchadnezzar's
commands................... 2 Kin. 25:8–20
Protects Jeremiah................. Jer. 39:11–14

Necessary, necessity—*something imperative*
A. As applied to God's plan:
Preaching to the Jews first........... Acts 13:46
Change of the Law.................... Heb. 7:12
Of Christ's sacrifice................... Heb. 8:3
B. In the Christian's life:
Wise decisions...................... 2 Cor. 9:5
Personal needs..................... Acts 20:34
See Must

Neck
A. Uses of:
Ornaments........................Ezek. 16:11
Beauty............................. Song 4:4
Authority ....Gen. 41:42
B. Significant acts performed by:
Emotional salutation................. Gen. 45:14
Subjection of enemies ....Josh. 10:24

C. Figurative of:
Servitude .... Gen. 27:40
Stubbornness....................... Neh. 9:16
Severe punishment.....................Is. 8:8
Rescue .... Is. 52:2
See Yoke

Necklace—*an ornament worn about the neck*
Signifying rank...................Gen. 41:41, 42
Worn by animals ....Judg. 8:26

Nedabiah—*Yahweh has been gracious*
Son of King Jeconiah................ 1 Chr. 3:18

Need(s)—*an inner or outward lack; a compulsion to
something*
A. Physical necessity, arising from lack of:
Food............................... Deut. 15:8
Provisions......................... 2 Chr. 2:16
B. Moral necessity, arising from:
Spiritual immaturity................. Heb. 5:12
Order of things ....Matt. 3:14
Spiritual need ....Luke 10:42
C. Promises concerning supply of:
Promised...................... Matt. 6:8, 32
Provided........................... Acts 2:45
Fulfilled ....Rev. 21:23
D. Caused by:
Riotous living .... Luke 15:14
E. Provision against, by:
Help of others .... 2 Cor. 9:12
F. Reaction to, shown in:
Humble submission to God's will ... Phil. 4:11, 12
See Must; Necessary, necessity

Needle—*a sharp instrument used in sewing or
embroidering*
Figurative of something impossible ... Matt. 19:24

Needy—*the poor*
A. Evil treatment of:
Oppression.......................... Amos 4:1
Injustice toward .... Is. 10:2
B. Promise toward:
God's:
Remembrance of...................... Ps. 9:18
Deliverance .... Ps. 35:10
Salvation of .... Ps. 72:4–13
Exaltation of .... Ps. 113:7
Strength of........................... Is. 25:4
C. Right treatment of:
Recommended .... Deut. 24:14, 15
Remembered .... Jer. 22:16
Rewarded .... Matt. 25:34–40
See Poor, poverty

Neglect—*to fail to respond to duties*
A. Of material things:
One's appearance .... 2 Sam. 19:24
Needs of the body.....................Col. 2:23
B. Of spiritual things:
Gospel..........................Matt. 22:2–5
Salvation.........................Heb. 2:1–3

C. Consequences of:

    Kept out .... Matt. 25:1–13

    Sent to hell ....Matt. 25:24–30

    Reward lost ....1 Cor. 3:10–15

Nehelamite

    Term applied to Shemaiah, a false

        prophet.......................Jer. 29:24–32

Nehemiah—*Yahweh has comforted*

1. Leader in the postexilic community .... Ezra 2:2

2. Postexilic workman.....................Neh. 3:16

Nehemiah—*Yahweh has comforted*

A. Life of:

    Son of Hachaliah .... Neh. 1:1

    Cupbearer to the Persian King Artaxerxes I

        (465–424 b.c.) .... Neh. 1:11

    Grieves over Jerusalem's desolation...Neh. 1:4–11

    Appointed governor................... Neh. 5:14

    Sent to rebuild Jerusalem ....Neh. 2:1–8

    Unwelcome by non-Jews............. Neh. 2:9, 10

    Views walls at night...............Neh. 2:11–20

    Continues work in spite

        of opposition...................Neh. 4:1–23

    Makes reforms among Jews..........Neh. 5:1–19

    Opposition continues, but work

        completed .... Neh. 6:1–19

    Introduces law and order .... Neh. 7:1–73

    Participates with Ezra in restored

        worship........................Neh. 8–10

    Registers inhabitants..............Neh. 11:1–36

    Registers priests and Levites ....Neh. 12:1–26

    Returns to Artaxerxes; revisits

        Jerusalem.....................Neh. 13:6, 7

    Institutes reforms.................Neh. 13:1–31

B. Character of:

    Patriotic ....Neh. 1:1–4

    Prayerful.........................Neh. 1:5–11

    Perceptive........................Neh. 2:17–20

    Persistent ....Neh. 4:1–23

    Persuasive........................Neh. 5:1–13

    Pure in motives...................Neh. 5:14–19

    Persevering.......................Neh. 6:1–19

    See Nehemiah, Book of

Nehemiah, Book of—*a book of the Old Testament*

    Nehemiah's prayer ....Neh. 1:4–11

    Inspection of the wall ....Neh. 2:11–16

    List of those rebuilding the wall......Neh. 3:1–32

    The enemies' plot...................Neh. 6:1–14

    The reading of the Law.............Neh. 8:1–18

    Confession of the priests ....Neh. 9:4–38

    Nehemiah's reform ....Neh. 13:7–31

Nehum—*consolation*

    Postexilic returnee.................... Neh. 7:7

    Called Rehum ....Ezra 2:2

Nehushta—*of bronze*

    Wife of King Jehoiakim ....2 Kin. 24:8

Nehushtan—*piece of brass*

    Applied to bronze serpent ....2 Kin. 18:4

Neiel—*dwelling of God*

    Town in Asher...................Josh. 19:24, 27

Neigh—*to cry lustfully*

Used of:

    Horses ....Jer. 8:16

    Lustful desires.......................Jer. 5:8

    Rendered "bellow"...................Jer. 50:11

Neighbor

A. Sins against, forbidden:

    False witness ....Ex. 20:16

    Coveting...........................Ex. 20:17

    Lying .... Lev. 6:2–5

    Hating...........................Deut. 19:11–13

    Despising ....Prov. 14:21

    Enticing...........................Prov. 16:29

    Deception..........................Prov. 26:19

    Flattery ....Prov. 29:5

    Failure to pay..................... Jer. 22:13

    Adultery .... Jer. 29:23

B. Duties toward, encouraged:

    Love............................ Rom. 13:9, 10

    Speak truth to .... Eph. 4:25

    Show mercy to...................Luke 10:29, 37

Nekoda—*dotted*

    Founder of a family of

        temple servants .... Ezra 2:48

    Genealogy of, rejected............. Ezra 2:59, 60

Nemuel—*God is spreading*

1. Brother of Dathan and Abiram ....Num. 26:9

2. Eldest son of Simeon................. 1 Chr. 4:24

    Head of Nemuelites................. Num. 26:12

    Called Jemuel ....Gen. 46:10

Nepheg—*sprout*

1. Izhar's son; Korah's brother .... Ex. 6:21

2. David's son born in Jerusalem ......2 Sam. 5:13–15

Nephtoah—*opening*

    Border town between Judah and

        Benjamin ....Josh. 15:9

Nepotism—*putting relatives in public offices*

    Joseph's..........................Gen. 47:11, 12

    Saul's .... 1 Sam. 14:50

    David's .... 2 Sam. 8:16–18

    Nehemiah's .... Neh. 7:2

Ner—*lamp*

    Father of Abner; grandfather

        of Saul..................... 1 Sam. 14:50, 51

Nereus—*the name of a sea god*

    Christian at Rome ....Rom. 16:15

Nergal—*a Babylonian god of war*

    Worshiped by men of Cuth ....2 Kin. 17:30

Nergal-Sharezer—*Nergal preserve the king*

    Babylonian prince during capture of

        Jerusalem.......................Jer. 39:3, 13

Neri

    Ancestor of Christ ....Luke 3:27

Neriah—*Yahweh is a lamp*
    Father of Baruch....................Jer. 32:12

Nest
A. Kinds of:
    Eagle's .... Job 39:27
    Swallow's...........................Ps. 84:3
    Snake's.............................. Is. 34:15
    Dove's .... Jer. 48:28
B. Figurative of:
    False security...................Num. 24:21, 22
    Lord's resting place .... Matt. 8:20
    Full maturity .... Job 29:18
    Something out of place ....Prov. 27:8
    Helplessness.......................... Is. 10:14

Net
A. Used for:
    Trapping a bird or animal .... Prov. 1:17
    Catching fish.....................John 21:6–11
B. Figurative of:
    Plots of evil people .... Ps. 9:15
    Predatory people...................... Ps. 31:4
    God's chastisements ....Job 19:6
    Flattery ....Prov. 29:5
    God's sovereign plan .... Ezek. 12:13; 17:20

Nethanel—*God has given*
1. Leader of Issachar .... Num. 1:8
2. Jesse's fourth son .... 1 Chr. 2:13, 14
3. Levite trumpeter .... 1 Chr. 15:24
4. Levite scribe .... 1 Chr. 24:6
5. Obed-Edom's fifth son .... 1 Chr. 26:4
6. Prince sent to teach Judah.............2 Chr. 17:7
7. Levite chief....................... 2 Chr. 35:9
8. Priest who married a foreign wife ... Ezra 10:18–22
9. Priest in Joiakim's time................ Neh. 12:21
10. Levite musician in dedication
    service .... Neh. 12:36

Nethaniah—*Yahweh has given*
1. Son of Asaph ....1 Chr. 25:2, 12
2. Levite teacher in Jehoshaphat's reign ... 2 Chr. 17:8
3. Father of Jehudi ....Jer. 36:14
4. Father of Ishmael, struck down
    Gedaliah.....................2 Kin. 25:23, 25

Nethinim—*given*
A. Described as:
    Servants of the Levites .... Ezra 8:20
B. Probable origin of:
    Midianites ....Num. 31:2, 41
    Gibeonites ....Josh. 9:23, 27
    Solomon's slaves .... 1 Kin. 9:20, 21
C. Characteristics of:
    Governed by captains .... Neh. 11:21
    Assigned certain cities .... 1 Chr. 9:2
    Exempt from taxes .... Ezra 7:24
    Zealous for Israel's covenant.......Neh. 10:28, 29
    Assigned important jobs...............Ezra 8:17
    Returned from exile in
       large numbers.................Ezra 2:43–54

Netophathite—*an inhabitant of Netophah*
    Town of Judah near Jerusalem ....1 Chr. 2:54
    Occupied by returning Levites .... 1 Chr. 9:16
    Applied to two of David's
       mighty men.................2 Sam. 23:28, 29
    Loyalty of, demonstrated........ 2 Kin. 25:23, 24

Nettles—*thornbushes*
Sign of:
    Indolence ....Prov. 24:31
    Desolation .... Is. 34:13
    Retreat for cowards .... Job 30:7

Network—*artistic handwork in*
    Tabernacle ....Ex. 27:4
    Temple......................1 Kin. 7:17–41

Neutrality
    Impossibility of, taught ....Matt. 6:24; 12:30
    Invitation to, rejected ....Josh. 24:15, 16

Never—*not ever*
A. Concerning God's spiritual promises:
    Satisfaction .... John 4:14
    Stability.............................Ps. 55:22
    Security.............................John 10:28
B. Concerning God's threats:
    Chastisement..................... 2 Sam. 12:10
    Desolation .... Is. 13:20
    Forgiveness........................ Mark 3:29

WORD STUDY   **NEW,** *kainos* (keye-*noss*). This adjective, meaning "new," can be used with reference to something that has not been used before (Matt. 9:17). *Kainos* is also used with the connotation of "remarkable" as a designation of something that is "new" and not known previously (Mark 1:27; John 13:34). The same word qualifies something as "new" in the sense of a replacement for something that is old and obsolete—as in the "new covenant" (Heb. 8:8). Converts are "new persons" (2 Cor. 5:17; Eph. 4:24). *Kainos* is used in an eschatological sense to describe the "new" heaven and earth (2 Pet. 3:13; Rev. 21:1). (Strong's #2537)

New—*something recent or fresh*
    Commandment.....................John 13:34
    Covenant ....Jer. 31:31
    Creature .... 2 Cor. 5:17
    Fruit..............................Ezek. 47:12
    Earth .... Is. 65:17
    Heart............................ Ezek. 36:26
    Spirit.............................Ezek. 11:19
    Heaven .... Is. 66:22
    Jerusalem ....Rev. 21:2
    Name............................... Is. 62:2
    Person .... Eph. 2:15
    Song................................ Is. 42:10
    New thing (Christ's birth) ....Jer. 31:22
    All things new ....Rev. 21:5

New Birth—*regeneration*
A. Described as:
    One heart ....Ezek. 11:19

Resurrection .... Rom. 6:4–10
New creature .... 2 Cor. 5:17
Circumcision..................... Deut. 30:6
Holy seed ....1 John 3:9
Begotten ....1 Pet. 1:3
Name written in heaven ....Luke 10:20
Life everlasting .... John 3:16
B. Productive of:
    Growth ....1 Pet. 2:1, 2
    Knowledge......................1 Cor. 2:12–16
    Change .... 2 Cor. 3:18
    Fruitfulness.......................John 15:1–8
    Victory ....1 John 5:4
    Discipline ....Heb. 12:3–11
    Love ....1 John 4:7
  See Born again

New covenant
A. Described as:
    Everlasting .... Is. 55:3
    Of peace .... Ezek. 34:25
    Of life .... Mal. 2:5
B. Elements of:
    Author—God .... Eph. 2:4
    Cause—God's love.................... John 3:16
    Mediator—Christ .... 1 Tim. 2:5
    Time originated—in eternity ...... Rom. 8:29, 30
    Time instituted—at humankind's sin ... Gen. 3:15
    Time realized—at Christ's death....Eph. 2:13–22
    Time consummated—in eternity....... Eph. 2:7
    Duties—faith and repentance.........Mark 1:15
C. Ratification of, by:
    God's promise....................... Gen, 3;15
    God's oath .... Is. 54:9, 10
    Christ's blood ....Heb. 9:12–26
    Spirit's sealing..................... 2 Cor. 1:22
D. Superiority of, to the old:
    Hope .... Heb. 7:19
    Priesthood .... Heb. 7:20–28
    Covenant .... Heb. 8:6
    Sacrifice .... Heb. 9:23

New Gate—*a temple gate*
  Princes meet at .... Jer. 26:10

New Jerusalem
  Vision, seen by Abraham .... Heb. 11:10, 16
  Reality of, experienced by believers ... Gal. 4:26, 31
  Consummation of, awaits eternity .... Heb. 13:14
  Vision, seen by John........Rev. 3:12; 21:2, 9–27

New moon
  A festival day..................Ps. 81:3; Col. 2:16
  A point of reference .... Is. 66:23

New person (see New birth)

News
A. Kinds of:
    Distressing........................ Gen. 32:6–8
    Disturbing .... Josh. 22:11–20
    Alarming ....1 Sam. 4:13–22
    Agonizing........................ 2 Sam. 18:31–33

Sorrowful ....Neh. 1:2–11
Joyful..............................Luke 2:8–18
Fatal .... 1 Sam. 4:14–19
B. Of salvation:
    Bringer of peace .... Is. 52:7
    By Christ........................ Is. 61:1–3
  See Tidings

New year
  Erection of the tabernacle on .... Ex. 40:17, 18

Neziah—*preeminent*
  Head of a Nethinim family .... Ezra 2:43, 54

Nezib—*garrison*
  Town of Judah..................... Josh. 15:1, 43

Nibhaz
  Idol of Avites .... 2 Kin. 17:31

Nibshan—*the furnace*
  Town of Judah.................... Josh. 15:1, 62

Nicanor—*victorious*
  One of the seven men chosen
    as deacons .... Acts 6:1–5

Nicodemus—*conqueror of the people*
  Pharisee; converses with Jesus .... John 3:1–12
  Protests unfairness of
    Christ's trial .... John 7:50–52
  Brings gifts to anoint
    Christ's body................. John 19:39, 40

Nicolaitans—*early Christian sect*
  Group teaching moral looseness...... Rev. 2:6–15

Nicolas—*victor over the people*
  Non-Jewish proselyte deacon ....Acts 6:5

Nicopolis—*city of victory*
  Town in Epirus ....Titus 3:12

Niger—*dark*
  Latin surname of Simeon, a teacher in
    Antioch ....Acts 13:1

Night—*the time of darkness*
A. Important facts concerning:
    Made by God........................Ps. 104:20
    Named at creation .... Gen. 1:5
    Begins at sunset .... Gen. 28:11
    Established by God's covenant........ Gen. 8:22
    Displays God's glory .... Ps. 19:2
    Designed for rest.....................Ps. 104:23
    Wild beasts creep in...............Ps. 104:20–22
    None in heaven .... Zech. 14:7
    Divided into "watches" and hours .... Mark 13:35
B. Special events in:
    Jacob's wrestling................. Gen. 32:22–31
    Egypt's greatest plague .... Ex. 12:12–31
    Ordinance of the Passover............ Ex. 12:42
    King's sleeplessness .... Esth. 6:1
    Nehemiah's vigil...................Neh. 2:11–16
    Belshazzar slain .... Dan. 5:30
    Angelic revelation ....Luke 2:8–15
    Nicodemus' talk .... John 3:2
    Release from prison ....Acts 5:19

Paul's escape .... Acts 9:24, 25
Wonderful conversion............Acts 16:25–33
C. Good acts in:
Toil................................. Luke 5:5
Prayer .... 1 Sam. 15:11; Luke 6:12
Song........................Job 35:10; Ps. 42:8
Flight from evil.........1 Sam. 19:10; Matt. 2:14
Dreams ....Matt. 2:12, 13, 19
D. Evil acts in:
Drunkenness...........................Is. 5:11
Thievery.................Obad. 5; Matt. 27:64
Lewdness ....1 Thess. 5:2–7
Betrayal................Matt. 26:31, 34, 46–50
Death.......................Luke 12:20
E. Figurative of:
Present age.................... Rom. 13:11, 12
Death............................. John 9:4
Unregenerate state.............. 1 Thess. 5:5, 7
Judgment .... Mic. 3:6

Night creature—*a nocturnal creature*
Dwells in ruins .... Is. 34:14

Nile—*Egypt's main river*
A. Called:
Shihor .... Is. 23:3
B. Characteristics of:
Has seven streams ....Is. 11:15
Overflows annually.................. Jer. 46:8
Source of Egyptian wealth............Is. 19:5–8
C. Events connected with:
Drowning of male children ....Ex. 1:22
Moses placed in.......................Ex. 2:3
Water of, turned to blood............Ex. 7:15, 20
D. Figurative of:
Judgment .... Ezek. 30:12; Amos 9:5
Army ....Jer. 46:7–9

Nimrah—*an abbreviation of Beth Nimrah*
Town in Gilead ....Num. 32:3, 36

Nimrim—*wholesome waters*
Place in south Moab.................... Is. 15:6

Nimrod—*strong*
Ham's grandson .... Gen. 10:6–8
Becomes a mighty hunter...........Gen. 10:8, 9
Establishes cities.................Gen. 10:10–12
Land of Assyria, thus described .... Mic. 5:6

Nimshi—*Yahweh reveals*
Grandfather of King Jehu ....2 Kin. 9:2, 14
Called Jehu's father ....2 Kin. 9:20

Nineveh—*the capital of ancient Assyria*
A. History of:
Built by Nimrod ....Gen. 10:8–12
Capital of Assyria....................2 Kin. 19:36
Jonah sent to ....Jon. 1:1, 2
Citizens of:
Repent..........................Jon. 3:5–9
At the judgment seat .... Matt. 12:41
B. Prophecies concerning its:
Destruction by Babylon ....Nah. 2:1–4

Internal weakness..................Nah. 3:11–17
Utter desolation ....Nah. 3:18, 19
C. Described as:
Great city ....Jon. 3:2, 3
Wealthy............................. Nah. 2:9
Fortified ....Nah. 3:8, 12
Wicked ....Jon. 1:2
Idolatrous........................... Nah. 1:14
Careless........................... Zeph. 2:15
Full of lies.......................... Nah. 3:1

Ninth hour—*that is, 3 P.M.*
Time of Christ's death .... Matt. 27:46
Customary hour of prayer ....Acts 3:1
Time of Cornelius's vision .... Acts 10:1, 3

Nisan—*beginning*
Name of Abib (first month of Jewish year)
after the Exile..................... Neh. 2:1
See Jewish calendar

Nisroch—*eagle, hawk*
Sennacherib's god..................2 Kin. 19:37

No Amon—*the Egyptian city Thebes*
Nineveh compared to .... Nah. 3:8

Noadiah—*Yahweh has met by appointment*
1. Levite in Ezra's time .... Ezra 8:33
2. Prophetess who tries to frighten
Nehemiah ....Neh. 6:14

Noah—*rest*
A. Life of:
Son of Lamech....................Gen. 5:28, 29
Father of Shem, Ham, and Japheth ..... Gen. 5:32
Finds favor with God .... Gen. 6:8
Lives in the midst of corruption......Gen. 6:1–13
Instructed to build the ark.........Gen. 6:13–22
Preacher of righteousness..............2 Pet. 2:5
Enters ark with family and animals...Gen. 7:1–24
Preserved during the Flood..........Gen. 8:1–17
Builds an altar......................Gen. 8:18–22
Covenant established with...........Gen. 9:1–19
Plants a vineyard; becomes drunk...Gen. 9:20, 21
Pronounces curse and blessings .... Gen. 9:22–27
Dies at 950 ....Gen. 9:28, 29
B. Character of:
Righteous............................. Gen. 6:9
Obedient............................. Heb. 11:7
In fellowship with God................ Gen. 6:9
Notable in history .... Ezek. 14:14, 20

Noah—*trembling*
Daughter of Zelophehad .... Num. 26:33

Nob—*height*
City of priests; David flees to ...... 1 Sam. 21:1–9
Priests of, killed by Saul ....1 Sam. 22:9–23
Near Jerusalem .... Is. 10:32
Reinhabited after the Exile .... Neh. 11:32

Nobah—*barking*
1. Manassite leader..................... Num. 32:42
2. Town in Gad.......................... Judg. 8:11

Nobleman—*one who belongs to the upper class*
Jesus:
    Heals son of .... John 4:46–54
    Cites in parable .... Luke 19:12–27

Nod—*wandering exile*
    Place (east of Eden) of
        Cain's abode .... Gen. 4:16, 17

Nodab—*nobility*
    Arabian tribe .... 1 Chr. 5:19

Nogah—*brilliance*
    One of David's sons .... 1 Chr. 3:1, 7

Nohah—*rest*
    Benjamin's fourth son .... 1 Chr. 8:1, 2

Noise—*a sound of something*
A. Kinds of:
    Sea .... Ps. 65:7
    Sound of songs .... Ezek. 26:13; Amos 5:23
    Battle .... Is. 13:4; Jer. 47:3
    Mourners .... Matt. 9:23
    Outcry .... 1 Sam. 4:13, 14
    Revelry .... Ex. 32:17, 18
    Growl of dog .... Ps. 59:6
    God's glory .... Ezek. 43:2
B. Figurative of:
    Strong opposition .... Is. 31:4
    Worthlessness .... Jer. 46:17

Nomad—*wanderer*
    Lifestyle of patriarchs ...... Gen. 12:1–9; 13:1–18
    Israel's history .... Deut. 26:5

Noon—*midday*
A. Time of:
    Eating .... Gen. 43:16, 25
    Resting .... 2 Sam. 4:5
    Praying .... Ps. 55:17
    Crying aloud .... Ps. 55:17
    Drunkenness .... 1 Kin. 20:16
    Destruction .... Ps. 91:6
    Death .... 2 Kin. 4:20
B. Figurative of:
    Blindness .... Deut. 28:29
    Cleansing .... Job 11:17

Noph (see Memphis)

Nophah—*windy place*
    Moabite town .... Num. 21:29, 30

North
Refers to:
    A geographical direction .... Gen. 28:14; Ps. 107:3
    Invading forces .... Is. 14:31; Jer. 6:1

Nose, nostrils—*the organ of breathing*
A. Used literally for:
    Breathing .... Gen. 2:7
    Smelling .... Amos 4:10
    Ornamentation .... Is. 3:21
    Bondage .... Is. 37:29
    Idols .... Ps. 115:6
    Nosebleed produced by wringing ...... Prov. 30:33

B. Used figuratively of:
    Human life .... Job 27:3
God's:
    Power .... Ex. 15:8
    Sovereign control .... 2 Kin. 19:28
    Overindulgence .... Num. 11:20
    National hope (Zedekiah) .... Lam. 4:20
    Something very offensive .... Is. 65:5

Nose jewels
    Worn by women .... Is. 3:21
    Put in swine's snout .... Prov. 11:22

Not-My-People, Not Loved—*symbolic names of
    Hosea's children*
    Lo-Ammi .... Hos. 1:9
    Lo-Ruhamah .... Hos. 1:6

Nothing—*not a thing*
A. Descriptive of:
Something:
    Without payment .... Gen. 29:15
Service without:
    Christ .... John 15:5
    Love .... 1 Cor. 13:3
    Circumcision .... 1 Cor. 7:19
    Flesh .... John 6:63
B. Time of:
    Past .... Neh. 4:15
    Future .... Ps. 33:10
C. Things that will come to:
    Wicked .... Job 8:22
    Wicked counsel .... Is. 8:10
    Babylon .... Rev. 18:17

Nourish—*provide means of growth to*
A. Descriptive of the growth or care of:
    Children .... Acts 7:20, 21
    Animals .... 2 Sam. 12:3
    Plants .... Is. 44:14
    Family .... Gen. 45:11
    Country .... Acts 12:20
B. Figurative of:
    Protection .... Is. 1:2
    Provision .... Ruth 4:15
    Pampering .... James 5:5
    Preparedness .... 1 Tim. 4:6

Novice—*one who is inexperienced; a recent Christian
    convert*
    Bishops, not to be .... 1 Tim. 3:1, 6

Now—*the present time*
A. As contrasted with:
    Old Testament .... John 4:23
    Past .... John 9:25
    Future .... John 13:7, 19
    Two conditions .... Luke 16:25
B. In Christ's life, descriptive of His:
    Atonement .... Rom. 5:11
    Humiliation .... Heb. 2:8
    Resurrection .... 1 Cor. 15:20
    Glorification .... John 13:31

Intercession . . . . Heb. 9:24
Return. . . . . 1 John 2:28
C. In the Christian's life, descriptive of:
Salvation. . . . . .Rom. 13:11
Regeneration . . . . John 5:25
Reconciliation. . . . . .Col. 1:21, 22
Justification. . . . . .Rom. 5:9
Victory . . . . .Gal. 2:20
Worship . . . . John 4:23
Suffering. . . . . 1 Pet. 1:6–8
Hope . . . . .Rev. 12:10
Glorification . . . . .Rom. 8:21, 22; 1 John 3:2
D. Descriptive of the present age as:
Time of:
Opportunity . . . . 2 Cor. 6:2
Evil. . . . . 1 Thess. 2:6
God's:
Greater revelation . . . . Eph. 3:5
Completed redemption. . . . . Col. 1:26, 27
Final dealing with humankind. . . . . . . .Heb. 12:26

Nuisance—*something very irritating*
Descriptive of:
Widow. . . . . Luke 18:2–5

Numbers
Symbolic of:
One—unity . . . . .Deut. 6:4; Matt. 19:6
Two—unity . . . . Gen. 1:27
Two—division. . . . . 1 Kin. 18:21; Matt. 7:13, 14
Three—the Trinity . . . . . Matt. 28:19; 2 Cor. 13:14
Three—resurrection . . . . Hos. 6:1, 2; Matt. 12:40;
Luke 13:32
Three—completion. . . . . 1 Cor. 13:13
Three—testing . . . . .Judg. 7:16
Four—completion . . . . . . .Matt. 13:4–8; John 4:35
Five—incompletion. . . . . .Matt. 25:2; 25:15–20
Six—human testing. . . . . Gen. 1:27, 31; Rev. 13:18
Seven—completion . . . . .Ex. 20:10
Seven—fulfillment . . . . Josh. 6:4
Seven—perfection . . . . .Rev. 1:4
Eighth—new beginning. . . Ezek. 43:27; 1 Pet. 3:20
Ten—completion . . . . Dan. 7:7
Tenth—God's part. . . . . Gen. 14:20; Mal. 3:10
Twelve—God's purpose . John 11:9; Rev. 21:12–17
Forty—testing. . . . . Jon. 3:4; Matt. 4:2
Forty—judgment . . . . .Num. 14:33; Ps. 95:10
Seventy—God's completed purpose . . . .Jer. 25:11;
Dan. 9:24

Numbers, Book of—*a book of the Old Testament*
The census . . . . Num. 1:1–4:49
Cleansing of Levites. . . . . .Num. 8:5–22
The cloud and the tabernacle . . . . . .Num. 9:15–23
The provision of manna . . . . .Num. 11:4–9
The spies. . . . . .Num. 13:1–14:45
The rebellion of Korah . . . . .Num. 16:1–35
The sin of Moses. . . . . .Num. 20:1–13
Aaron's death. . . . . Num. 20:22–29
Balaam and Balak. . . . . .Num. 22:2–24:25
Offerings and feasts. . . . . .Num. 28:1–29:40

Settlements in Gilead . . . . .Num. 32:1–42
Preparation for Canaan . . . . . .Num. 33:50–35:34

Nun—*fish*
1. Father of Joshua, Israel's military
leader. Josh. 1:1; 1 Chr. 7:27
2. Fourteenth letter in the Hebrew
alphabet . . . . .Ps. 119:105–112

Nurse—*one who provides nourishment and protection to*
the young
A. Duties of:
Provide nourishment. . . . . Gen. 21:7
Protect. . . . . 2 Kin. 11:2
Rear "the sons" . . . . .2 Kin. 10:1, 5
B. Figurative of:
Judgment . . . . .Lam. 4:3, 4
Provision. . . . . Num. 11:12
Gentleness . . . . 1 Thess. 2:7

Nuts
Provided as gifts. . . . . Gen. 43:11
Grown in gardens. . . . . Song 6:11

Nymphas—*sacred to the nymphs*
Christian of Laodicea . . . . .Col. 4:15

O

Oak—*a large and strong tree*
A. Uses of:
Place of rest . . . . .1 Kin. 13:14
Place of idolatry . . . . Is. 44:14
For oars. . . . . .Ezek. 27:6
B. Figurative of:
Strength . . . . Amos 2:9
Haughtiness. . . . . Is. 2:11, 13

Oars—*wooden blades used for rowing*
Made of oak. . . . . Ezek. 27:6, 29
Used on galleys . . . . Is. 33:21

Oaths—*solemn promises*
A. Expressions descriptive of:
"As the LORD lives" . . . . 1 Sam. 19:6
"God is witness" . . . . Gen. 31:50
"The LORD be witness". . . . . Jer. 42:5
"God . . . judge between us" . . . . Gen. 31:53
"The LORD make you like" . . . . Jer. 29:22
"I put You" . . . . Matt. 26:63
"I call God as witness" . . . . 2 Cor. 1:23
B. Purposes of:
Confirm covenant . . . . .Gen. 26:28
Insure protection . . . . Gen. 31:44–53
Establish truth . . . . .Ex. 22:11
Confirm fidelity. . . . . .Num. 5:19–22
Guarantee duties . . . . .Gen. 24:3, 4
Sign a covenant. . . . . 2 Chr. 15:12–15
Fulfill promises. . . . . .Neh. 5:12, 13
C. Sacredness of:
Obligatory . . . . .Num. 30:2–16
Maintained even in deception . . . . .Josh. 9:20
Upheld by Christ . . . . .Matt. 26:63, 64

Rewarded . . . . 2 Chr. 15:12–15
Maintained in fear . . . . 1 Sam. 14:24, 26
D. Prohibitions concerning, not:
    In idol's name . . . . Josh. 23:7
    In creature's name . . . . Matt. 5:34–36
    Falsely . . . . Lev. 19:12
    Among Christians . . . . Matt. 5:34

Oaths of God
A. Made in Old Testament concerning:
    Promise to Abraham . . . . Gen. 50:24
    Davidic covenant . . . . 2 Sam. 7:10–16
    Messianic priesthood . . . . Ps. 110:4, 5
B. Fulfilled in New Testament in Christ's:
    Birth. . . . . Luke 1:68–73
    Kingship on David's throne. . . . . Luke 1:32, 33
    Priesthood . . . . Heb. 7:20–28
    See Swearing

Obadiah—*servant of Yahweh*
1. King Ahab's steward . . . . 1 Kin. 18:3–16
2. Descendant of David . . . . 1 Chr. 3:21
3. Chief of Issachar . . . . 1 Chr. 7:3
4. Descendant of Saul . . . . 1 Chr. 8:38
5. Gadite captain . . . . 1 Chr. 12:8, 9
6. Man of Zebulun . . . . 1 Chr. 27:19
7. Prince sent by Jehoshaphat to teach . . . . . 2 Chr. 17:7
8. Levite overseer . . . . 2 Chr. 34:12
9. Leader in the postexilic community . . . . Ezra 8:9
10. Priest who signs the covenant. . . . . Neh. 10:5
11. Levite . . . . 1 Chr. 9:16
    Called Abda. . . . . Neh. 11:17
12. Postexilic gatekeeper . . . . Neh. 12:25
13. Prophet of Judah . . . . Obad. 1

Obadiah, Book of—*a book of the Old Testament*
    Against Edom . . . . Obad. 1–9
    Edom against Judah. . . . . Obad. 10–14
    The day of the Lord . . . . Obad. 15, 16
    Zion's victory. . . . . Obad. 17–21

Obal—*to be bare*
    Descendants of Joktan . . . . Gen. 10:28

Obduracy—*resistance to pleadings of mercy*
Expressed by:
    "Stiff-necked" . . . . Ex. 33:3, 5
    "Uncircumcised" . . . . Lev. 26:41
    "Impenitent" . . . . Rom. 2:5
    "Harden your hearts" . . . . 1 Sam. 6:6
    "Nor will I let" . . . . Ex. 5:1, 2
    "I will not hear". Jer. 22:21
    "Do not seek" . . . . John 5:44
    "Increasingly unfaithful". . . . . 2 Chr. 28:22–25
    "Being past feeling" . . . . Eph. 4:18, 19
    "God gave them up" . . . . Rom. 1:24–28
    "Therefore they could not believe" . . . . John 12:39
    "That cannot cease from sin" . . . . 2 Pet. 2:14
    "They were appointed". . . . . 1 Pet. 2:8
    "Let him be unjust still" . . . . Rev. 22:11
See Hardness of heart; Impenitence

Obed—*servant*
1. Son of Ephlal . . . . 1 Chr. 2:37, 38
2. Son of Boaz and Ruth . . . . Ruth 4:17–22
3. One of David's mighty men . . . . 1 Chr. 11:47
4. Korahite gatekeeper . . . . 1 Chr. 26:7
5. Father of Azariah. 2 Chr. 23:1

Obed-Edom—*servant of Edom*
1. Philistine from Gath; ark of the Lord
    left in his house. . . . . 2 Sam. 6:10–12;
    1 Chr. 13:13, 14
2. Overseer of the storehouse . . . . . . 1 Chr. 26:4–8, 15
3. Levitical musician . . . . 1 Chr. 16:5
4. Guardian of the sacred vessels . . . . 2 Chr. 25:24

Obedience—*submission to authority*
A. Relationship involved:
    God—humans. . . . . Acts 5:29
    Parent—child . . . . Gen. 28:7; Eph. 6:1
    Husband—wife. . . . . 1 Cor. 14:34, 35
    Master—servant. . . . . Eph. 6:5
    Ruler—subject . . . . Titus 1:1; 1 Pet. 2:13, 14
    Leader—follower . . . . Acts 5:36, 37
    Pastor—people . . . . Heb. 13:17
    Humans—nature . . . . James 3:3
    God—nature . . . . Matt. 8:27
    God—demons. . . . . Mark 1:27
B. Spiritual objects of:
    God . . . . Acts 5:29
    Christ. . . . . Heb. 5:9
    Truth . . . . Gal. 5:7
    Faith. . . . . Acts 6:7
C. In the Christian's life:
    Comes from the heart . . . . Rom. 6:17
    Needs testing. . . . . 2 Cor. 2:4
    Aided by the Spirit . . . . 1 Pet. 1:22
    Manifested in Gentiles . . . . Rom. 15:18
    In pastoral relations. . . . . 2 Cor. 7:15
D. Lack of, brings:
    Rejection. . . . . 1 Sam. 15:20–26
    Captivity. . . . . 2 Kin. 18:11, 12
    Death. . . . . 1 Kin. 20:36
    Retribution . . . . 2 Thess. 1:8
E. Examples of:
    Noah . . . . Gen. 6:22
    Abram . . . . Gen. 12:1–4
    Israelites . . . . Ex. 12:28
    Caleb and Joshua . . . . Num. 32:12
    David. . . . . Ps. 119:106
    Asa . . . . 1 Kin. 15:11, 14
    Elijah . . . . 1 Kin. 17:5
    Hezekiah . . . . 2 Kin. 18:6
    Josiah . . . . 2 Kin. 22:2
    Zerubbabel. . . . . Hag. 1:12
    Christ. . . . . Rom. 5:19
    Paul . . . . Acts 26:19
    Christians. . . . . Phil. 2:12

Obedience of Christ, our example
    To death . . . . Phil. 2:5–11

Learned............................Heb. 5:7–10
Submissive ....Matt. 26:39, 42

Obedience to civil government
Meet obligation.................Mark 12:13–17
Of God .... Rom. 13:1–7
Duty................................Titus 3:1
For Lord's sake ....1 Pet. 2:13–17

WORD STUDY   **OBEY,** *hupakouō* (hoop-ak-*oo*-oh). Verb meaning literally "to listen to." In the NT it is used in the sense of "to listen to" one in authority and then submit to that authority, and thus it means "to obey," "to follow," "to be subject to." *Hupakouō* is used with reference to obedience to: parents (Col. 3:20), masters (Eph. 6:5), Christ (Heb. 5:9), the faith (Acts 6:7), the teaching of the apostles (Rom. 6:17), and the gospel (10:16). (Strong's #5219)

Obil—*camel driver*
Ishmaelite in charge of camels ....1 Chr. 27:30

Obituary—*an account of a person's life; a death notice*
Written of Moses ....Deut. 34:1–12

Objectors—*those who oppose something*
A. Argue against God's:
Power............................ Ex. 14:10–15
Provision......................... Ex. 16:2–17
Promises........................Num. 14:1–10
B. Overcome by:
Prophecies cited ....Jer. 26:8–19
Promises claimed ....Acts 4:23–31

Oblivion—*the state of being forgotten*
God's punishment on the wicked........Ps. 34:16

Oboth—*water skins*
Israelite camp .... Num. 21:10, 11; 33:43, 44

Observe—*to keep; to remember*
A. Descriptive of:
Laws..................................Ex. 31:16
Obedience .... Matt. 28:20
Watchfulness.......................Jer. 8:7
False rituals ....Gal. 4:10
B. Blessings of proper:
Material prosperity .... Deut. 6:3
Righteousness .... Deut. 6:25
Elevation........................Deut. 28:1, 13
Lovingkindness ....Ps. 107:43
Christ's presence................... Matt. 28:20
C. Manner of proper:
Carefully.......................... Deut. 12:28
Without change ....Deut. 12:32
Diligently .... Deut. 24:8
Forever ....2 Kin. 17:37
Without preference .... 1 Tim. 5:21

Obstacles—*obstructions*
Eliminated by:
God's help............................ Is. 45:2
Christ's help.......................Is. 49:9–11
Spirit's help........................ Zech. 4:6, 7
Faith..............................Heb. 11:1–40

Obstacles to faith
Human honor .... John 5:44
Haughtiness........................Rom. 11:20
Unbelief .... Heb. 11:6
Doubt ....James 1:6–8

Obstinacy—*stubbornness*
Continuing in sin .... 2 Chr. 28:22, 23
Rejecting counsel .... 1 Kin. 12:12–15
Refusing to change.................Jer. 44:15–27

Obstruct—*to hamper progress*
Attempted .... Ezra 4:1–5
Condemned...................... 3 John 9, 10

Obtain—*to bring into one's possession*
A. Of material things:
Advancement...................... Esth. 2:9–17
B. Of spiritual things:
Favor ....Prov. 8:35
Joy and gladness .... Is. 35:10
Mercy............................Matt. 5:7
Divine help........................ Acts 26:22
Salvation..........................Rom. 11:7
Better resurrection................... Heb. 11:35
Faith..............................2 Pet. 1:1

Occultism—*pertaining to supernatural, especially evil, influences*
A. Forms of:
Astrology .... Is. 47:13
Charming.......................... Deut. 18:11
Spiritism........................... Deut. 18:11
Divination .... Deut. 18:14
Magic............................ Gen. 41:8
Necromancy...................... Deut. 18:11
Soothsaying .... Is. 2:6
Sorcery ....Ex. 7:11; 22:18
Witchcraft .... Deut. 18:10
Wizardry .... Deut. 18:11
B. Attitude toward:
Forbidden..............Deut. 18:10, 11; Jer. 27:9
Punished by death ....Ex. 22:18; Lev. 20:6, 27
Forsaken........................Acts 19:18–20

Ocran—*troubled*
Man of Asher.................... Num. 1:13; 2:27

Oded
1. Father of Azariah the prophet .... 2 Chr. 15:1
2. Prophet of Samaria ....2 Chr. 28:9–15

Odors, sweet
A. Used literally of:
Sacrificial incense.....................Lev. 26:31
Ointment fragrance...................John 12:3
B. Used figuratively of:
New life............................ Hos. 14:7
Prayers.............................Rev. 5:8
Christian service .... Phil. 4:18

Offend, offense
A. Causes of:
Christ...............................Matt. 11:6
Persecution........................ Matt. 24:10

The cross. . . . . 1 Cor. 1:23
B. Causes of, in Christ's:
Lowly position. . . . . .Matt. 13:54–57
Being the Rock . . . . .Is. 8:14
Being the Bread. . . . . John 6:58–66
Being the righteousness of God . . . . Rom. 9:31–33
C. Christians forbidden to give:
In anything . . . . 2 Cor. 6:3
At any time. . . . . Phil. 1:10
See Stumble

Offering of Christ
Of Himself:
Predicted . . . . Ps. 40:6–8
Prepared . . . . .Heb. 5:1–10
Proclaimed. . . . . .Heb. 10:5–9
Purified. . . . . Heb. 9:14
Personalized. . . . . Heb. 7:27
Perfected. . . . . .Heb. 10:11–14
Praised. . . . . Eph. 5:2

Offerings
A. Characteristics of:
Made to God alone. . . . . Ex. 22:20
Limitation of . . . . Heb. 9:9
Prescribed under the Law. . . . . Mark 1:44
B. Thing offered must be:
Perfect. . . . . .Lev. 22:21
Ceremonially clean . . . . .Lev. 27:11, 27
Best. . . . . .Mal. 1:14
C. Offerer must:
Not delay . . . . Ex. 22:29, 30
Offer in righteousness. . . . . Mal. 3:3
Offer with thanksgiving. . . . . Ps. 27:6
D. Classification of:
Private and public . . . . .Lev. 4:1–12
Physical and spiritual . . . . .Lev. 5:1–13
Voluntary and required. . . . . Lev. 1:3
Accepted and rejected. . . . . Judg. 6:17–24
Purified and perverted . . . . Mal. 3:3, 4
Passing and permanent. . . . . Jer. 7:21–23
Typical and fulfilled . . . . .Gen. 22:2, 13

Offerings of the leaders—*by heads, of Twelve Tribes*
1. Six wagons and twelve oxen to transport
tabernacle. . . . . .Num. 7:1–9
2. Dedication gift. . . . . Num. 7:10–89

Office—*a position of trust*
Holders of:
Butler. . . . . .Gen. 40:13
Judge . . . . .Deut. 17:9
Priest . . . . Deut. 26:3
Ministers of song . . . . .1 Chr. 6:32
Gatekeeper. . . . . .1 Chr. 9:22
Tax collector . . . . .Matt. 9:9
Bishop . . . . .1 Tim. 3:1
Treasurer . . . . Neh. 13:13

Officers—*men appointed to rule over others*
A. Descriptive of:
Magistrate . . . . .Luke 12:58
Principal officer . . . . .1 Kin. 4:5, 7

B. Functions of:
Administer justice . . . . Num. 11:16
Offices of Christ
A. As prophet:
Predicted . . . . Deut. 18:18, 19
Fulfilled . . . . .John 6:14; Acts 3:20–23
B. As priest:
Predicted . . . . .Ps. 110:4
Fulfilled . . . . Heb. 5:5–10; 9:11–14, 23–28
C. As king:
Predicted . . . . .Zech. 9:9
Fulfilled . . . . Luke 19:37, 38; Rev. 19:16

Offscouring—*something vile or worthless*
Israel thus described . . . . .Lam. 3:45

Offspring—*issue (physical or spiritual)*
A. Used literally of:
Set apart firstlings . . . . Ex. 13:12; 34:19
Of a donkey you shall redeem. . . . Ex. 13:13; 34:20
Human issue (children) . . . . .Job 5:25
Humankind as created by God. . . . . Acts 17:28, 29
Christ as a descendant of David. . . . . . .Rev. 22:16
B. Used figuratively of:
True believer . . . . Is. 22:24
New Israel. . . . . .Is. 44:3–5
Gentile church. . . . . .Is. 61:9
The church. . . . . Is. 65:23

Og—*giant*
Amorite king of Bashan . . . . Deut. 3:1, 8
Extent of rule. Deut. 3:8, 10
Residences at Ashtaroth and Edrei . . . . .Josh. 12:4
Man of great size. . . . . .Deut. 3:11
Defeated and killed by Israel. . . . . .Num. 21:32–35
Territory of, assigned to Manasseh . . . . Deut. 3:13
Memory of, long remembered. . . . . .Ps. 135:11

Ohad—*powerful*
Son of Simeon . . . . Gen. 46:10

Ohel—*family*
Son of Zerubbabel . . . . .1 Chr. 3:19, 20

Oholah—*tent woman*
Symbolic name of Samaria. . . . . . .Ezek. 23:4, 5, 36

Oil, olive—*a liquid extracted from olives*
A. Features concerning:
Given by God. .Ps. 104:14, 15
Subject to tithing . . . . Deut. 12:17
B. Uses of:
Food. . . . . Num. 11:8
Anointing. . . . . 1 Sam. 10:1
Beautification . . . . Ruth 3:3
Perfumer's ointment . . . . Eccl. 10:1
Illumination . . . Ex. 25:6; 30:26–32; Matt. 25:3–8
C. Types of oil:
Anointing. . . . . .Ex. 25:6
Pure . . . . .Ex. 27:20
Baking. . . . . Ex. 29:23
Pressed . . . . Ex. 29:40
Olive . . . . Ex. 30:24
Precious ointment . . . . .2 Kin. 20:13

Golden. . . . . Zech. 4:12

D. Figurative of:

Prosperity. . . . . Deut. 32:13

Joy and gladness . . . . .Is. 61:3

Wastefulness . . . . Prov. 21:17

Brotherly love . . . . .Ps. 133:2

Real grace. . . . . Matt. 25:4

Holy Spirit . . . . 1 John 2:20, 27

Oil tree

Signifies restoration. . . . . Is. 41:17–20

Ointment—*a salve made of olive oil and spices*

A. Used for holy purpose:

By special prescription

for tabernacle . . . . .Ex. 30:23–25

Misuse of, forbidden . . . . Ex. 30:37, 38

B. Features concerning:

Considered very valuable . . . . .2 Kin. 20:13

Carried or stored in containers. . . . . Matt. 26:7

Can be polluted. . . . . Eccl. 10:1

C. Uses of:

Cosmetic. . . . . Eccl. 9:8

Sign of hospitality . . . . .Luke 7:46

Embalming agent. . . . . Luke 23:55, 56

Sexual attraction . . . . .Is. 57:9

Old—*mature; ancient*

A. Descriptive of:

Age. . . . . Gen. 25:8

Elders. . . . . 1 Kin. 12:6–13

Experienced. . . . . Ezek. 23:43

Ancient times . . . . Mal. 3:4

Old Testament age. . . . . Matt. 5:21–33

Old Testament. 2 Cor. 3:14

Unregenerate nature . . . . .Rom. 6:6

B. Of one's age, infirmities of:

Waning sexual desire. . . . . Luke 1:18

Physical handicaps. . . . . 1 Kin. 1:1, 15

Failing strength . . . . Ps. 71:9

C. Of one's age, dangers of:

Spiritual decline . . . . 1 Kin. 11:4

Not receiving instruction. . . . . Eccl. 4:13

Disrespect toward. . . . . Deut. 28:50

D. Of one's age, blessing of:

God's care. . . . . Is. 46:4

Continued fruitfulness. . . . . .Ps. 92:14

Security of faith .Prov. 22:6

Fulfillment of life's goals . . . . Is. 65:20

Honor . . . . .Lev. 19:32

Grandchildren . . . . Prov. 17:6

Dreams . . . . .Acts 2:17

See Length of life

Old Testament

A. Characteristics of:

Inspired. . . . . .2 Tim. 3:16

Authoritative. . . . . .John 10:34, 35

Written by the Holy Spirit . . . . Heb. 3:7

Uses many figurative expressions . . . Is. 55:1, 12, 13

Written for our admonition. . . . . . . .1 Cor. 10:1–11

Israel now blinded to . . . . .2 Cor. 3:14–16

Foreshadows the New . . . . .Heb. 9:1–28

B. With the New Testament, unified in:

Authorship. . . . . Heb. 1:1

Plan of salvation . . . . 1 Pet. 1:9–12

Presenting Christ

(see Messiah, the). . . . . .Luke 24:25–44

Olive groves

Freely given . . . . .Josh. 24:13

Taken in greed. . . . . 2 Kin. 5:20, 26

Olive tree

A. Used for:

Oil of, many uses (see Oil) . . . . .Ex. 27:20

Temple furniture . . . . .1 Kin. 6:23

Temple construction . . . . 1 Kin. 6:31–33

Booths. . . . . Neh. 8:15

B. Cultivation of:

By grafting. . . . . .Rom. 11:24

Hindered by disease . . . . Deut. 28:40

Failure of, a great calamity. . . . . Hab. 3:17, 18

Poor provided for . . . . Deut. 24:20

Palestine suitable for . . . . .Deut. 6:11

C. Figuratively of:

Peace . . . . Gen. 8:11

Kingship. . . . . .Judg. 9:8, 9

Israel . . . . .Jer. 11:16

The righteous . . . . .Ps. 52:8

Faithful remnant . . . . .Is. 17:6

Gentile believers. . . . . .Rom. 11:17, 24

The church. .Rom. 11:17, 24

Prophetic symbols . . . . Zech. 4:3, 11, 12

Olives, Mount of

A. Described as:

"The Mount of Olives" . . . . Zech. 14:4

"The hill that is east of Jerusalem" . . . . 1 Kin. 11:7

"The Mount of Corruption" . . . . .2 Kin. 23:13

"The mountain" . . . . Neh. 8:15

B. Scene of:

David's flight. . . . . 2 Sam. 15:30

Solomon's idolatry . . . . .2 Kin. 23:13

Ezekiel's vision .Ezek. 11:23

Postexilic festivities. . . . . Neh. 8:15

Zechariah's prophecy . . . . Zech. 14:4

Triumphal Entry. . . . . .Matt. 21:1

Weeping . . . . .Luke 19:37, 41

Great prophetic discourse . . . . Matt. 24:3

Jesus' prayer in Garden

of Gethsemane. . . . . Matt. 26:30, 36;

Mark 14:26, 32

Ascension. . . . . .Acts 1:12

Olympas

Christian in Rome . . . . .Rom. 16:15

Omar—*eloquent*

Grandson of Esau. . . . . Gen. 36:11, 15; 1 Chr. 1:36

Omega—*the last letter in the Greek alphabet*

Descriptive of Christ's

infinity. . . . . Rev. 1:8, 11; 21:6; 22:13

Omen—*a portent; a sign*

    Forbidden......................... Deut. 18:10

    The Lord causes to fail .... Is. 44:25

Omission, sins of

A. Concerning ordinances:

    Moses' neglect of circumcision .... Ex. 4:24–26

    Israel's neglect of the tithe .... Mal. 3:7–12

    Christians neglecting to assemble ..... Heb. 10:25

B. Concerning moral duties:

    Witnessing...................... Ezek. 33:1–6

    Warning.......................... Jer. 42:1–22

    Watchfulness........ Matt. 24:42–51; 26:36–46

Omnipotence—*infinite power*

A. Of God, expressed by His:

    Names ("Almighty, " etc.) .... Gen. 17:1, 2

    Creative word .... Gen. 1:3

  Control of:

    Nature........................... Amos 4:13

    Nations .... Amos 1:1–2:3

    All things .... Ps. 115:3

    Power.......................... Rom. 4:17–24

    Endurance .... Is. 40:28

B. Of Christ, expressed by His power over:

    Disease .... Matt. 8:3

    Unclean spirit .... Mark 1:23–27

    Devil .... Matt. 4:1–11

    Death.......................... John 10:17, 18

    Destiny .... Matt. 25:31–33

C. Of the Holy Spirit, expressed by:

    Christ's anointing....................... Is. 11:2

    Confirmation of the gospel .... Rom. 15:19

Omnipresence—*universal presence of*

    God .... Jer. 23:23, 24

    Christ........................ Matt. 18:20

    Holy Spirit .... Ps. 139:7–12

Omniscience—*infinite knowledge of*

    God .... Is. 40:14

    Christ........................... Col. 2:2, 3

    Holy Spirit .... 1 Cor. 2:10–13

Omri—*Yahweh apportions*

1. Descendant of Benjamin .... 1 Chr. 7:8

2. Judahite .... 1 Chr. 9:4

3. Chief officer of Issachar............. 1 Chr. 27:18

4. King of Israel; made king by Israel's

    army .... 1 Kin. 16:15, 16

    Prevails over Zimri and Tibni.... 1 Kin. 16:17–23

    Builds Samaria .... 1 Kin. 16:24

    Reigns wickedly .... 1 Kin. 16:25–28

    Father of Ahab .... 1 Kin. 16:28

On—*stone*

1. Reubenite leader; joins

    Korah's rebellion .... Num. 16:1

2. City of Lower Egypt; center of sun

    worship....................... Gen. 41:45, 50

    Called Beth Shemesh................. Jer. 43:13

  See Heres

Onam—*vigorous*

1. Horite chief .... Gen. 36:23

2. Man of Judah .... 1 Chr. 2:26, 28

Onan—*strong*

  Second son of Judah; slain for failure

    to consummate union.......... Gen. 38:8–10

WORD STUDY   **ONE**, *'echad* (ehkh-*awd*). The adjective *'echad* is translated in a great number of ways, sometimes as the numeral "one," as in the phrase "the LORD your God, the LORD is one" (Deut. 6:4). At other times it is best translated as "each" or "every." *'Echad* can mean a "certain" person or thing and can also mean "first" and describes the firstborn, for example. It is sometimes used as an indefinite article, "one day" meaning "some day." (Strong's #259)

WORD STUDY   **ONE ACCORD, OF,** *homothumadon* (hom-oth-oo-mad-*on*). The basic idea expressed by the adverb *homothumadon* is unity of purpose (as in Rom. 15:6) or accord (as in unanimous opinion). This word is used in Acts to indicate the unanimity of the early church (1:14; 2:1, 46; 4:24; 5:12; 8:6; 15:25) and the unanimity of those who stand in opposition to the apostles and believers (7:57; 12:20; 18:12; 19:29). (Strong's #3661)

Oneness—*unity*

A. Of Christ, with:

    The Father .... John 10:30

    Christians....................... Heb. 2:11

B. Among Christians of:

    Baptized .... 1 Cor. 12:13

    Union......................... Ezek. 37:16–24

    Headship .... Ezek. 34:23

    Faith........................... Eph. 4:4–6

    Mind .... Phil. 2:2

    Heart .... Acts 4:32

  See Unity of believers

Onesimus—*useful*

  Slave of Philemon converted by Paul

    in Rome .... Philem. 10–17

  With Tychicus, carries Paul's letters to

    Colosse and to Philemon.......... Col. 4:7–9

Onesiphorus—*profit-bearing*

  Ephesian Christian commended for

    his service .... 2 Tim. 1:16–18

Onion—*a bulbous plant used for food*

  Lusted after by Israelites .... Num. 11:5

Only Begotten

Of Christ's:

    Incarnation .... John 1:14

    Godhead.......................... John 1:18

    Mission .... John 3:16, 18; 1 John 4:9

Ono—*strong*

  Town of Benjamin rebuilt by Shemed... 1 Chr. 8:12

  Reinhabited by returnees .... Ezra 2:1, 33

Onycha—*nail; claw; husk*
Ingredient of holy incense .... Ex. 30:34

Onyx—*fingernail (Greek)*
Translation of a Hebrew word indicating
     a precious stone .... Job 28:16; Ezek. 28:13
Found in Havilah .... Gen. 2:11, 12
Placed in high priest's ephod .... Ex. 28:9–20
Gathered by David .... 1 Chr. 29:2

WORD STUDY   **OPEN,** *patach* (paw-*thakh*). The verb meaning "open," *pa-tach,* is used throughout the OT. It can be used in conjunction with windows, doors, mouths, graves, and many other things. Jer. 50:25 talks about God opening up Babylon for destruction. "To open the mouth" can mean "to cry" or "to speak." In Ezek. 3:27 God will open the mouth of the prophet so that the prophet can speak to the people. Giving of one's goods is expressed by the phrase "opening your hand" as in Deut. 15:8. In the story of the Flood, the windows of heaven were opened so that the rain could come down (Gen. 7:11). Another aspect of the term "open" is the meaning "loosen," which can mean "set free" (Ps. 105:20). Someone's bonds can be loosened, and the ground can be loosened by tilling. (Strong's #6605)

Open—*to unfasten; to unlock; to expose*
A. Descriptive of miracles on:
     Womb .... Gen. 30:1, 22
     Earth .... Num. 16:30, 32
     Eyes .... John 9:10–32
     Ears .... Mark 7:34, 35
     Mouth .... Luke 1:64
     Prison doors .... Acts 5:19, 23
     Death .... 2 Kin. 4:35
     Graves .... Matt. 27:52
B. Descriptive of spiritual things:
     God's provision .... Ps. 104:28
     God's bounty .... Mal. 3:10
     Christ's blood .... Zech. 13:1
     Human corruption .... Rom. 3:13
     Spiritual eyesight .... Luke 24:31, 32
     Door of faith .... Acts 14:27
     Opportunity .... 1 Cor. 16:9
     Christ's worthiness .... Rev. 5:2, 8–14

Ophel—*bulge, hill*
South extremity of Jerusalem's eastern
     hill .... Neh. 3:15–27
Fortified by Jotham and Manasseh .... 2 Chr. 27:3
Residence of Nethinim .... Neh. 3:26

Ophir—*rich*
1. Son of Joktan .... Gen. 10:26, 29
2. Land, probably in southeast Arabia, inhabited by
     descendants of 1 .... Gen. 10:29, 30
Famous for its gold .... 1 Chr. 29:4

Ophni—*the high place*
Village of Benjamin .... Josh. 18:24

Ophrah—*hind*
1. Judahite .... 1 Chr. 4:14
2. Town of Benjamin near Michmash ... Josh. 18:21, 23
3. Town in Manasseh; home of Gideon ... Judg. 6:11, 15
     Site of Gideon's burial .... Judg. 8:32

Opportunity—*the best time for something*
A. Kinds of:
     Rejected .... Matt. 23:37
     Spurned .... Luke 14:16–24
     Prepared .... Acts 8:35–39
     Providential .... 1 Cor. 16:9
     For good .... Gal. 6:10
B. Loss of, due to:
     Unbelief .... Num. 14:40–43
     Neglect .... Jer. 8:20
     Unpreparedness .... Matt. 24:50, 51
     Blindness .... Luke 19:41, 42

Oppression—*subjection to unjust hardships*
A. Kinds of:
     Personal .... Is. 38:14
     National .... Ex. 3:9
     Economic .... Mic. 2:1, 2
     Messianic .... Is. 53:7
     Spiritual .... Acts 10:38
B. Those subject to:
     Widows .... Zech. 7:10
     Hired servant .... Deut. 24:14
     Poor .... Ps. 12:5
     Those trusting in human leadership .... Is. 3:5
     Soul .... Ps. 54:3
C. Evils of, bring:
     Guilt .... Is. 59:12, 13
     Reproach .... Prov. 14:31
     Poverty .... Prov. 22:16
     Judgment .... Ezek. 18:12, 13
D. Punishment of:
     God's judgment .... Is. 49:26
     Captivity .... Is. 14:2, 4
     Destruction of .... Ps. 72:4
E. Protection against:
     Sought in prayer .... Deut. 26:7
     Given by the Lord .... Ps. 103:6
     Secured in refuge .... Ps. 9:9
F. Agents of:
     Nations .... Judg. 10:12
     Enemy .... Ps. 42:9; 106:42
     Wicked .... Ps. 55:3
     Humankind .... Ps. 119:134
     Leaders .... Prov. 28:16
     Sword .... Jer. 46:16; 50:16
     Devil .... Acts 10:38
     Rich .... James 2:6

Oracle—*a revelation; a wise saying*
A. Descriptive of the high priest's ephod:
     Source of truth .... 1 Sam. 23:9–12
B. Descriptive of God's Word:
     Received by Israel .... Acts 7:38
     Test of truth .... 1 Pet. 4:11

Oration, orator
Character of:
    Egotistical.........................Acts 12:21–23
    Prejudiced .... Acts 24:1–9
    Inspired..........................Acts 26:1–29

Orchard—*a cultivated garden or park*
    Source of fruits .... Song 4:13
    Source of nuts .... Song 6:11

Orchestra—*group of musicians playing together*
    Instituted by David ....2 Sam. 6:5

Ordain, ordained—*to establish, appoint, set, decree*
A. As appointment to office:
    Prophet...............................Jer. 1:5
B. As appointment of temporal things:
    World order .... Ps. 8:3
Institution of:
    Offering .... Num. 28:6
C. As appointment of eternal things:
    Hidden wisdom .... 1 Cor. 2:7
  See Appoint

Order—*harmony; symmetry; in proper places*
A. As an arrangement in rows:
    Wood for sacrifices .... Gen. 22:9
    Battle formation....................1 Chr. 12:38
    Words logically developed..............Job 33:5
    Consecutive narrative.................. Luke 1:3
    Absence of .... Job 10:22
B. As a classification according to work:
    Priestly service .... 2 Kin. 23:4
    Christ's priesthood...................Ps. 110:4
    Church services..................... 1 Cor. 11:34
    Church officers.......................Titus 1:5
C. Of something prescribed:
    Ritual regulations................... 1 Chr. 15:13
    Church regulations .... 1 Cor. 14:40
    Subjection to ....1 Chr. 25:2, 6
D. Of preparation for death:
    Ahithophel's .... 2 Sam. 17:23
    Hezekiah's ....2 Kin. 20:1
E. Figurative of:
    God's covenant..................... 2 Sam. 23:5
    Believer's life ....Ps. 37:23
    Humankind's ....Ps. 50:21

Ordinances—*regulations established for proper procedure*
A. Descriptive of:
    Ritual observance................... Heb. 9:1, 10
    God's laws .... Is. 24:5
    God's laws in nature ....Jer. 31:35
    Human regulations .... Neh. 10:32
    Human laws........................ 1 Pet. 2:13
    Apostolic messages .... 1 Cor. 11:2
    Jewish legalism .... Eph. 2:15
B. Of the gospel:
    Baptism........................... Matt. 28:19
    Lord's Supper.................. 1 Cor. 11:23–29
    Preaching the Word..................Rom. 10:15

Oreb—*a raven*
1. Midianite prince slain by Gideon .... Judg. 7:25
2. Rock on which Oreb was slain .... Judg. 7:25

Oren—*a fir or cedar tree*
    Judahite............................. 1 Chr. 2:25

Orion—*strong*
    Brilliant constellation ....Job 9:9

Ornaments—*outward adornments of the body*
Figurative of:
    Wisdom's instruction .... Prov. 1:9
    Reproof received.....................Prov. 25:12
    God's provisions................. Ezek. 16:7–14
    Apostasy from God .... Jer. 4:30
See Clothing; Jewels

Orpah—*neck*
    Ruth's sister-in-law.................. Ruth 1:4, 14

Orphans—*children deprived of parents*
    Description of .... Lam. 5:3
    Provision for .... Deut. 24:17, 21
    Job helps .... Job 29:12
    Visitation of, commended .... James 1:27
    Christians not left "orphans" .... John 14:18

Osnapper—*probably the Aramean name for Ashurbanipal, an Assyrian king*
    Called "the great and noble" ....Ezra 4:10

Ostentatious—*vain, ambitious*
Manifested in:
    Boastfulness..................... Luke 18:10–14
    Hypocrisy...................... Matt. 6:1–7, 16
    Conceit .... 2 Sam. 15:1–6
    Egotism.........................Acts 12:20–23

Ostracism—*exclusion of a person from society*
    Accepted...........................Luke 6:22
See Excommunication

Ostrich—*a two-toed, swift, and flightless bird*
    Figurative of cruelty .... Lam. 4:3

Othni—*abbreviation of Othniel*
    Son of Shemaiah..................... 1 Chr. 26:7

Othniel—*God is force*
    Son of Kenaz; Caleb's
        youngest brother ....Judg. 1:13
    Captures Kirjath Sepher; receives Caleb's
        daughter as wife...............Josh. 15:15–17
    First judge of Israel .... Judg. 3:9–11

Ought—*something morally imperative*
A. Of duties not properly done:
    Use of talents...................... Matt. 25:27
    Accusation .... Acts 24:19
    Growth .... Heb. 5:12
B. Of acts wrongly done:
    Worship ....John 4:20, 21
    Death............................. John 19:7
    Wrong behavior .... 2 Cor. 2:3
    Inconsistent speaking .... James 3:10
C. Of moral duties among Christians:
    Witnessing.........................Luke 12:12

Prayer .... Luke 18:1
Service............................ John 13:14
Obedience .... 1 Thess. 4:1
Helping the weak .... Rom. 15:1
Love toward wife .... Eph. 5:28
Proper behavior .... 2 Thess. 3:7
Holy conduct.....................2 Pet. 3:11
Willingness to sacrifice ....1 John 3:16
Love of one another................1 John 4:11
See Must; Necessary, necessity

Outcasts—*dispossessed people*
Israel among the nations .... Ps. 147:2
Israel as objects of mercy .... Is. 16:3, 4
New Israel.......................Jer. 30:17–22

Oven—*a place for baking or cooking*
A. Characteristics of:
   Used for cooking ....Ex. 8:3
   Fuel for, grass........................ Matt. 6:30
   Made on ground .... Gen. 18:6
B. Figurative of:
   Scarcity in famine .... Lev. 26:26
   Lust .... Hos. 7:4, 6, 7
   God's judgments.................... Ps. 21:9
   Effects of famine .... Lam. 5:10

Overcome—*to conquer*
A. Means of, by:
   Wine ....Jer. 23:9
   Fleshly desire.................... 2 Pet. 2:19, 20
   God ....Rom. 8:37
   Believing in Jesus ....1 John 5:5
B. Objects of:
   World........................... John 16:33
   Evil............................. Rom. 12:21
   Satan .... 1 John 2:13, 14
   Evil spirits...........................1 John 4:4
   Two witnesses ....Rev. 11:7
   Evil powers...................... Rev. 17:13, 14
C. Promises concerning, for Christians:
   Eating of the Tree of Life ....Rev. 2:7
   Exemption from the second death.......Rev. 2:11
   Power over the nations ....Rev. 2:26
   Clothed in white garments...............Rev. 3:5
   Made a pillar in God's temple..........Rev. 3:12
   Rulership with Christ ....Rev. 3:21

Overlay—*to spread or place over*
A. Materials used:
   Gold................................ Ex. 26:32
   Bronze.............................Ex. 38:2
   Silver ....Ex. 38:17
B. Objects overlaid:
   Pillar—with gold .... Ex. 26:32
   Board—with gold.................... Ex. 36:34
   Altar—with cedar ....1 Kin. 6:20
   Sanctuary—with gold................1 Kin. 6:21
   Cherubim—with gold................1 Kin. 6:28
   Earthen vessel—with silver dross .....Prov. 26:23
   Images—with silver................... Is. 30:22

Overseer—*a leader or supervisor*
Kinds of:
   Prime minister ....Gen. 39:4, 5
   Managers ....Gen. 41:34
   Elders............................. Acts 20:17, 28

Overthrow—*to throw down; destroy*
Agents of:
   God ....Prov. 21:12
   Evil.................................Ps. 140:11
   Wickedness ....Prov. 11:11
   Evil ruler...........................Dan. 11:41
   Christ.............................. John 2:15

Overwork—*too much work*
   Complaint of Israelites .... Ex. 5:6–21
   Solution of, for Moses .... Ex. 18:14–26

Owe—*an obligation of*
   Financial debt .... Matt. 18:24, 28
   Moral debt .... Philem. 18, 19
   Spiritual debt.......................Rom. 13:8

Owl—*a large-eyed bird of prey*
   Varieties of, all unclean........... Lev. 11:13–17
   Solitary in habit ....Ps. 102:6

Ownership—*title of possession*
A. By people, acquired by:
   Purchase.........................Gen. 23:16–18
   Inheritance........................Luke 15:12
   Covenant .... Gen. 26:25–33
B. By God, of:
   World................................Ps. 24:1
   Souls..............................Ezek. 18:4
   Redeemed.........................1 Cor. 6:19, 20

Ox
A. Uses of:
   Pulling covered carts.................. Num. 7:3
   Plowing............................1 Kin. 19:19
   Food............................... Deut. 14:4
   Sacrifice .... Ex. 20:24
   Means of existence..................... Job 24:3
   Designs in temple....................1 Kin. 7:25
B. Laws concerning:
   To rest on Sabbath ....Ex. 23:12
Not to be:
   Yoked with an ass.................... Deut. 22:10
   Muzzled while treading .... Deut. 25:4
   To be restored ....Ex. 22:4, 9–13
C. Figurative of:
   Easy victory....................... Num. 22:4
   Youthful rashness.....................Prov. 7:22
   Preach the gospel .... Is. 32:20
   Minister's support ....1 Cor. 9:9, 10
D. Descriptive of:
   Great strength......................Num. 23:22
   Very wild and ferocious ....Job 39:9–12
   Frisky in youth ....Ps. 29:6

Ox goad—*spike used to drive oxen*
   As a weapon........................Judg. 3:31

Ozem—*anger*
1. Son of Jesse . . . . 1 Chr. 2:13, 15
2. Descendant of Judah. . . . . 1 Chr. 2:25

Ozni—*gives ear*
Son of Gad and head of a family. . . Num. 26:15, 16
Called Ezbon . . . . Gen. 46:16

P

Paarai—*devotee of Peor*
One of David's mighty men. . . . . 2 Sam. 23:35
Called Naarai . . . . 1 Chr. 11:37

Pacification—*causing anger to rest*
A. Means of:
    Gift. . . . . Prov. 21:14
    Wise man . . . . Prov. 16:14
    Yielding. . . . . Eccl. 10:4
B. Examples of:
    Esau, by Jacob . . . . Gen. 32:11–19
    Lord, toward His people. . . . . Ezek. 16:63
    Ahasuerus, by Haman's death. . . . . Esth. 7:10

Pack animals
Used by Israelites . . . . 1 Chr. 12:40

Padan Aram—*the plain of Aram (Mesopotamia)*
Home of Isaac's wife . . . . Gen. 25:20
Jacob flees to . . . . Gen. 28:2–7
Jacob returns from . . . . Gen. 31:17, 18
Same as Mesopotamia. . . . . Gen. 24:10
People of, called Syrians . . . . Gen. 31:24
Language of, called Aramaic. . . . . 2 Kin. 18:26
See Aramaic

Padon—*ransom*
Head of Nethinim family. . . . Ezra 2:44; Neh. 7:47

Pagan gods
A. Mentioned:
    Molech. . . . . Lev. 18:21
    Chemosh. . . . . Judg. 11:24
    Dagon . . . . Judg. 16:23
    Baal . . . . 2 Kin. 17:16
    Nergal . . . . 2 Kin. 17:30
    Succoth Benoth. 2 Kin. 17:30
    Ashima . . . . 2 Kin. 17:30
    Nibhaz. . . . . 2 Kin. 17:31
    Tartak . . . . 2 Kin. 17:31
    Adrammelech . . . . 2 Kin. 17:31
    Anammelech . . . . 2 Kin. 17:31
    Nisroch . . . . Is. 37:38
    Zeus. . . . . Acts 14:12
    Hermes . . . . Acts 14:12
    Greek Pantheon . . . . Acts 17:16–23
    Diana. . . . . Acts 19:23–37
B. Worship of condemned:
    By apostolic command . . . . 1 Cor. 10:14
    By Law. . . . . Ex. 20:3, 4; Deut. 5:7

Pagiel—*God meets*
Son of Ocran, chief of Asher's tribe. . . . Num. 1:13

Pahath-Moab—*governor of Moab*
Family of postexilic returnees. . . . . Ezra 2:6
Members of, divorced
    foreign wives. . . . . Ezra 10:19, 30
One of, signs covenant . . . . Neh. 10:1, 14
Hashub, one of, helps Nehemiah . . . . Neh. 3:11

Pain—*physical or mental suffering*
A. Kinds of:
    Childbirth . . . . Rev. 12:2
    Physical fatigue. 2 Cor. 11:27
    Physical afflictions. . . . . Job 33:19
    Mental disturbance . . . . Ps. 55:4
B. Characteristics of:
    Affects face . . . . Joel 2:6
    Means of chastening . . . . Job 15:20
    Affects the whole person . . . . Jer. 4:19
    Common to all men . . . . Rom. 8:22
C. Remedies for:
    Balm. . . . . Jer. 51:8
    Prayer . . . . Ps. 25:17, 18
    God's deliverance. . . . . Acts 2:24
    Heaven . . . . Rev. 21:4
D. Figurative of:
    Mental anguish. . . . . Ps. 48:6
    Impending trouble. . . . . Jer. 22:23
    Distressing news. Is. 21:2, 3
    Israel's captivity . . . . Is. 26:17, 18

Paint—*to apply liquid colors*
Applied to a wide house . . . . Jer. 22:14
Used by women. 2 Kin. 9:30
Used especially by prostitutes . . . . . Jer. 4:30; Ezek.
    23:40

Paintings
Of Chaldeans. . . . . Ezek. 23:14
Of animals and idols
    (on a secret wall) . . . . Ezek. 8:7–12

Pair—*two*
Sandals . . . . Amos 2:6
Turtledoves . . . . Luke 2:24
Balances . . . . Rev. 6:5

Palace—*a royal building*
A. Descriptive of:
    King's house. . . . . 2 Chr. 9:11
    Foreign city . . . . Is. 25:2
    Dwellings in Zion. . . . . Ps. 48:3
    Heathen king's residence . . . . Ezra 6:2
B. Characteristics of:
    Place of luxury. . . . . Luke 7:25
    Subject to destruction. . . . . Is. 13:22
C. Figurative of:
    Messiah's temple. . . . . Ps. 45:8, 15
    Divine workmanship. . . . . Ps. 144:12
    Eternal city. . . . . Jer. 30:18

Palal—*judge*
Postexilic laborer . . . . Neh. 3:25

Pale—*deficient in color*
Figurative of:
Shame . . . . Is. 29:22

Palestine (see Canaan, land of)

Palliation of sin—*excusing sin*
A. Manifested by:
Calling bad men good . . . . Mal. 2:17
Describing sin as good . . . . Is. 5:20
Justifying the wicked . . . . Is. 5:23
Encouraging the wicked . . . . Ezek. 13:22
Calling the proud blessed . . . . Mal. 3:13–15
Envying the wicked . . . . Ps. 73:3–15
Supposing God cannot see sin . . . . Ps. 10:11–13
Ignoring reproof .Job 34:5–36
Sinning defiantly . . . . Is. 5:18, 19
Considering God indifferent to evil . . . Zeph. 1:12
Misjudging people . . . . Matt. 11:18, 19
Questioning God's Word . . . . Ezek. 20:49
B. Caused by:
Moral darkness . . . . Matt. 6:23
Human-originated concepts . . . . Matt. 16:3–6
Hypocrisy . . . . .Matt. 23:15–23
Evil heart . . . . Luke 16:15
False teaching . . . . 2 Pet. 2:1–19

Pallu—*distinguished*
Son of Reuben; head of tribal family . . . Gen. 46:9;
Ex. 6:14; Num. 26:5, 8

Palm of the hand
Used literally of:
Priest's hand . . . . Lev. 14:15, 26
Idol's hand . . . . .1 Sam. 5:4
Daniel's hand . . . . Dan. 10:10
Soldier's hand . . . . Matt. 26:67

Palm tree
A. Uses of:
Fruit of, for food . . . . Joel 1:12
Figures of, carved on temple . . . . . . 1 Kin. 6:29–35
Branches of, for booths . . . . .Lev. 23:40–42
Places of, at Elim and Jericho . . . . .Ex. 15:27
Site of, for judgeship . . . . .Judg. 4:5
B. Figurative of:
Righteous . . . . .Ps. 92:12
Beauty . . . . Song 7:7
Victory . . . . John 12:13

Palms, City of
Moabites conquer . . . . Judg. 3:12, 13

Palti—*abbreviation of Paltiel*
1. Benjamite spy . . . . .Num. 13:9
2. Man to whom Saul gives Michal,
David's wife-to-be, in marriage . . . .1 Sam. 25:44

Paltiel—*God has delivered*
1. Prince of Issachar . . . . Num. 34:26
2. Same as Palti 2 . . . . 2 Sam. 3:15

Paltite, the
Native of Beth Pelet . . . . .Josh. 15:27

Home of one of David's
mighty men . . . . 2 Sam. 23:26
Same referred to as the Pelonite . . . . . .1 Chr. 11:27

Pamphylia—*coastal region in South Asia Minor*
People from, at Pentecost . . . . .Acts 2:10
Paul visits . . . . Acts 13:13
John Mark returns home from . . . Acts 13:13; 15:38
Paul preaches in cities of . . . . .Acts 14:24, 25
Paul sails past . . . . .Acts 27:5

Pan—*thin plate*
Offering in . . . . .Lev. 2:5
Cooking . . . . .Lev. 6:21
Pouring . . . . 2 Sam. 13:9

Panic—*fright*
A. Among Israelites:
At the Red Sea . . . . Ex. 14:10–12
Before the Philistines . . . . .1 Sam. 4:10
Of Judah before Israel . . . . .2 Kin. 14:12
B. Among nations:
Egyptians . . . . .Ex. 14:27
Philistines . . . . 1 Sam. 14:22
Syrians . . . . .2 Kin. 7:6, 7
Ammonites and Moabites . . . . 2 Chr. 20:22–25

Paper—*sheet*
Writing material . . . . 2 John 12
See Papyrus

Paphos—*capital of Cyprus*
Paul blinds Elymas . . . . .Acts 13:6–13

Papyrus—*a tall marsh plant growing in the Nile River*
region
Referred to as bulrush in . . . . .Ex. 2:3
Cannot grow without marsh . . . . .Job 8:11
See Paper

Parables—*an earthly story with a heavenly meaning*
A. Purpose of:
Bring under conviction . . . . 2 Sam. 12:1–6
Teach a spiritual truth . . . . Is. 5:1–6
Illustrate a point . . . . Luke 10:25–37
Conceal truth from the
unbelieving . . . . .Matt. 13:10–16
B. In the Old Testament:
Of Jotham (fable) . . . . .Judg. 9:7–15
Of Nathan . . . . 2 Sam. 12:1–4
Of Jehoash (fable) . . . . 2 Kin. 14:9
Of Isaiah . . . . Is. 5:1–7
Of Ezekiel . . . . Ezek. 17:2–10
C. Of Christ, characteristics of:
Numerous . . . . Mark 4:33, 34
Illustrative . . . . Luke 12:16–21
Meaning of:
Self-evident . . . . Mark 12:1–12
Unknown . . . . Matt. 13:36
Explained . . . . .Luke 8:9–15
Prophetic . . . . Luke 21:29–36
D. Of Christ, classification of:
Concerning God's love in Christ:
Lost sheep . . . . .Luke 15:4–7

Lost money...................... Luke 15:8–10
Prodigal son.....................Luke 15:11–32
Hidden treasure .... Matt. 13:44
Pearl of great price ....Matt. 13:45, 46

Concerning Israel:

Barren fig tree................... Luke 13:6–9
Two sons.......................Matt. 21:28–32
Wicked vinedressers ....Matt. 21:33–46

Concerning Christianity (the gospel) in this age:

Unshrunk cloth......................Matt. 9:16
New wine ....Matt. 9:17
Sower.......................... Matt. 13:3–8
Tares ....Matt. 13:24–30
Mustard seed................... Matt. 13:31, 32
Leaven.......................... Matt. 13:33
Dragnet.......................Matt. 13:47–50
Great supper .... Luke 14:16–24
Seed growing secretly ....Mark 4:26–29

Concerning salvation:

House built on the rock ....Matt. 7:24–27
Pharisee and tax collector ....Luke 18:9–14
Two debtors..................... Luke 7:36–50
Marriage of the king's son .... Matt. 22:1–14

Concerning Christian life:

Lamp under a basket.............. Matt. 5:15, 16
Unmerciful servant ....Matt. 18:23–35
Friend at midnight.................Luke 11:5–13
Importunate widow.................Luke 18:1–8
Tower....................... Luke 14:28–35
Good Samaritan................. Luke 10:25–37
Unjust steward ....Luke 16:1–13
Laborers in the vineyard.......... Matt. 20:1–16

Concerning rewards and punishments:

Ten virgins...................... Matt. 25:1–13
Talents.......................Matt. 25:14–30
Minas........................ Luke 19:12–27
Sheep and goats.................Matt. 25:31–46
Master and servant ....Luke 17:7–10
Servants watching ...Mark 13:33–37; Luke 12:36–40
Rich fool....................... Luke 12:16–21
Rich man and Lazarus .... Luke 16:19–31

Paraclete—*called to one's side*

Greek word translated.............John 14:16–18
"Helper" and "Advocate"... John 15:26; 1 John 2:1

Paradise—*an enclosed park similar to the Garden of Eden*

Applied in the New Testament to
heaven.......Luke 23:43; 2 Cor. 12:4; Rev. 2:7

Paradox—*a statement appearing to be untrue or contradictory*

Getting rich by poverty ....Prov. 13:7
Dead burying the dead.............. Matt. 8:22
Finding life by losing it............. Matt. 10:39
Not peace, but a sword ....Matt. 10:34–38
Wise as serpents; harmless as doves ... Matt. 10:16
Hating and loving ....Luke 14:26
Becoming great by serving.......... Mark 10:43
Dying in order to live ....John 12:24, 25
Becoming a fool to be wise........... 1 Cor. 3:18

Parah—*young cow*

City in Benjamin ....Josh. 18:23

Paralytic—*one affected with incapacitation*

Brought to Jesus ....Matt. 9:2; Mark 2:3
Healed by Jesus...........Matt. 4:24; Luke 5:24
Healed by Jesus, through Peter........ Acts 9:33
Healed by Christians...................Acts 8:7

Paramours—*illegal lovers*

Applied to the male lover .... Ezek. 23:20

Paran—*a wilderness region in the Sinaitic peninsula*

Mountainous country.................. Hab. 3:3
Residence of exiled Ishmael.......... Gen. 21:21
Israelites camp in .... Num. 10:12
Headquarters of spies ....Num. 13:3, 26
Site of David's refuge.................1 Sam. 25:1

Parapet—*a low wall to protect the edge of a roof*

For safety .... Deut. 22:8

Parbar—*suburb*

Precinct or colonnade west
of the temple....................1 Chr. 26:18
Same word translated "court"........2 Kin. 23:11

Parched—*roasted, dry*

Grain .... Josh. 5:11; 2 Sam. 17:28

Parchments—*writing material made from animal skin*

Paul sends request for .... 2 Tim. 4:13

Pardon—*to forgive*

A. Objects of our:

Transgressions ....Ex. 23:21
Iniquities ....Ex. 34:9
Backslidings........................ Jer. 5:6, 7

B. God's, described as:

Not granted ....2 Kin. 24:4
Requested..................... Num. 14:19, 20
Abundant............................ Is. 55:7
Gracious, ready to .... Neh. 9:17
Covering all sins.....................Jer. 33:8
Belonging to the faithful remnant........ Is. 40:2

C. Basis of:

Lord's name .... Ps. 25:11
Repentance .... Is. 55:7
Seeking the faith.......................Jer. 5:1

See Forgiveness

Parents—*fathers and mothers*

A. Kinds of:

Faithful (Abraham)...............Gen. 18:18, 19
Neglectful (Moses)................Ex. 4:24–26
Presumptuous (Jephthah) ....Judg. 11:30–39
Holy (Hannah) ....1 Sam. 1:11
Indulgent (Eli)..................1 Sam. 2:22–29
Distressed (David)..............2 Sam. 18:32, 33
Honored (Jonadab) ....Jer. 35:5–10
Forgiving (prodigal son's father) ...Luke 15:17–24
Spiritual (Eunice)...................2 Tim. 1:5

B. Duties toward:

Obedience ....Eph. 6:1
Honor ....Ex. 20:12

Reverence . . . . Lev. 19:3
C. Duties of, toward children:
    Protection . . . . Heb. 11:23
    Training . . . . Deut. 6:6, 7
    Education . . . . Gen. 18:19; Deut. 4:9
    Correction . . . . Deut. 21:18–21
    Provision . . . . 2 Cor. 12:14
D. Sins of:
    Favoritism . . . . Gen. 25:28
    Not restraining children . . . . 1 Sam. 2:27–36
    Bad example . . . . 1 Kin. 15:26
    Provoking . . . . Eph. 6:4
E. Sins against, by children:
    Disobedience . . . . Rom. 1:30
    Cursing . . . . Ex. 21:17
    Mocking . . . . Prov. 30:17
    Disrespect . . . . Gen. 9:21–27

Parmashta—*the very first*
    Haman's son . . . . Esth. 9:9

Parmenas
    One of the seven deacons . . . . Acts 6:5

Parnach
    Zebulunite . . . . Num. 34:25

Parosh—*flea*
1. Head of a postexilic family . . . . Ezra 2:3; 8:3
    Members of, divorced
        foreign wives . . . . Ezra 10:25
    One of, Pedaiah, helps rebuild . . . . Neh. 3:25
2. Chief who seals the covenant . . . . Neh. 10:1, 14

Parricide—*murder of one's father and/or mother*
    Sennacherib's sons guilty of . . . . . . 2 Kin. 19:36, 37

Parshandatha—*inquisitive*
    Haman's son . . . . Esth. 9:7

Part—*a portion of the whole*
    Mary chooses the good . . . . Luke 10:42
    Israel's blindness . . . . Rom. 11:25
    Our knowledge . . . . 1 Cor. 13:9–12

Partake—*to share in*
A. Of physical things:
    Sacrifices . . . . 1 Cor. 10:18
    Suffering . . . . 2 Cor. 1:7
    Benefit . . . . 1 Tim. 6:2
    Human nature . . . . Heb. 2:14
    Discipline . . . . Heb. 12:8
    Bread . . . . 1 Cor. 10:17
B. Of evil things:
    Evil . . . . Eph. 5:3–7
    Demonism . . . . 1 Cor. 10:21
C. Of spiritual things:
    Divine nature . . . . 2 Pet. 1:4
    Christ . . . . Heb. 3:14
    Holy Spirit . . . . Heb. 6:4
    Heavenly calling . . . . Heb. 3:1
    Grace . . . . Phil. 1:7
    Gospel . . . . 1 Cor. 9:23
    Spiritual blessings . . . . Rom. 11:17
    Future glory . . . . 1 Pet. 5:1

Promise of salvation . . . . Eph. 3:6
Holiness . . . . Heb. 12:10
Inheritance . . . . Col. 1:12
Communion . . . . 1 Cor. 10:16, 17
Spiritual things . . . . Rom. 15:27

Parthians—*inhabitants of Parthia*
    Some present at Pentecost . . . . Acts 2:1, 9

> **WORD STUDY**   **PARTIAL, ONE WHO IS,** *prosōpolēptēs* (pros-oh-pol-*aype*-tayce). This noun is based upon the familiar Septuagint expression "to lift (*lambanein*) up the face (*prosōpon*)," in which "face" represents the faculty of seeing. "To lift up the face" means "to show partiality" or "favoritism" (see Luke 20:21; Gal. 2:6). *Prosōpolēptēs*, which means "one who shows partiality," is used only in Acts 10:34 in the NT. (Strong's #4381)

> **WORD STUDY**   **PARTIALITY,** *prosōpolēpsia* (pros-oh-pol-aype-*see*-ah). This noun, which is derived from the expression "to lift up the face" (see the cognate noun at Acts 10:34), is translated as "partiality." The NT makes it clear that God does not show "partiality" (Rom. 2:11; cf. Eph. 6:9) and that believers are not to "hold the faith" with "partiality" (James 2:1). (Strong's #4382)

Partiality—*favoritism*
A. Manifested:
    In marriages . . . . Gen. 29:30
    Among brothers . . . . Gen. 43:30, 34
    Between parents and children . . . . Gen. 25:28
    In social life . . . . James 2:1–4
B. Inconsistent with:
    Household harmony . . . . Gen. 37:4–35
    Justice in law . . . . Lev. 19:15
Favoritism in:
    Ministry . . . . 1 Tim. 5:21
    Restriction of salvation . . . . Acts 10:28–35
C. Consistent with:
    Choice of workers . . . . Acts 15:36–40
    Estimate of friends . . . . Phil. 2:19–22
    God's predestination . . . . Rom. 9:6–24
See Favoritism

Partition—*a dividing wall*
    In the sanctuary . . . . 1 Kin. 6:21
    Between people . . . . Eph. 2:11–14

> **WORD STUDY**   **PARTNER, SHARE IN (PARTAKER),** *metochos* (met-okh-oss). This adjective means "sharing in" or "participating in." Used as a substantive it means "partner" or "companion" (Luke 5:7; Heb. 1:9). The writer of Hebrews uses this adjective five times to strike the theme that his readers are coparticipants, or "sharers," "partners," in the "heavenly calling" (3:1) of Christ (3:14); the Holy Spirit (6:4); and the Lord's discipline (12:8). (Strong's #3353)

Partner—*an associate in*
Crime......................................Prov. 29:24
Business ....Luke 5:7, 10
Christian work ....2 Cor. 8:23; Philem. 17

Partridge—*a wild bird meaning "the caller" (in Hebrew)*
Hunted in mountains ....1 Sam. 26:20
Figurative of ill-gotten riches ....Jer. 17:11

Paruah—*sprouting*
Father of Jehoshaphat, an officer of
Solomon...........................1 Kin. 4:17

Parvaim
Unidentified place providing gold for
Solomon's temple..................2 Chr. 3:6

Parzites
Descendants of Perez ....Num. 26:20

Pasach—*divider*
Asherite..............................1 Chr. 7:33

Pasdammim—*boundary of bloodshed*
Philistines gathered here ....1 Chr. 11:13

Paseah—*lame*
1. Judahite ....1 Chr. 4:12
2. Head of a family of Nethinim ....Ezra 2:43, 49
   One of, repairs walls ....Neh. 3:6
3. A family of temple servants..........Neh. 7:46, 51

Pashur, Pashhur—*free*
1. Official opposing Jeremiah.......Jer. 21:1; 38:1–13
   Descendants of, returnees ....Neh. 11:12
2. Priest who put Jeremiah in jail.........Jer. 20:1–6
3. Father of Gedaliah, Jeremiah's opponent ...Jer. 38:1
4. Priestly family of returnees..............Ezra 2:38
   Members of, divorced foreign wives ...Ezra 10:22
   Spelled Pashur.......................1 Chr. 9:12
5. Priest who signs the covenant...........Neh. 10:3

Passing away—*ceasing to exist*
A. Things subject to:
   Our days.............................Ps. 90:9
   Old things..........................2 Cor. 5:17
   World's fashion......................1 Cor. 7:31
   World's lust ....1 John 2:17
   Heaven and earth.....................2 Pet. 3:10
B. Things not subject to:
   Christ's words ....Luke 21:33
   Christ's dominion ....Dan. 7:14

Passion—*suffering*
A. Descriptive of:
   Christ's sufferings ....Acts 1:3
   Lusts................................Rom. 1:26
B. As applied (theologically) to Christ's sufferings:
   Predicted ....Is. 53:1–12
   Portrayed visibly...................Mark 14:3–8
   Preached............Acts 3:12–18; 1 Pet. 1:10–12

Passover—*a Jewish festival commemorative of the
exodus from Egypt*
A. Features concerning:
   Commemorative of the
   tenth plague ....Ex. 12:3–28

Necessity of blood applied...............Ex. 12:7
   To be repeated annually ....Ex. 12:24–27
B. Observances of:
   At Sinai ....Num. 9:1–14
   At the conquest....................Josh. 5:10–12
   By Christ..........................Matt. 26:18, 19
C. Typical of the Lord's death (the Lord's Supper):
   Lamb without blemish ....1 Pet. 1:19
   One of their own..........Ex. 12:5; Heb. 2:14, 17
   Lamb chosen ....Ex. 12:3; 1 Pet. 2:4
   Slain at God's appointed time..........Ex. 12:6;
   Acts 2:23
   Christ is..............................1 Cor. 5:7
See Lamb of God, the

Password—*a secret word used to identify friends*
Used by Gileadites ....Judg. 12:5, 6

Pastor—*shepherd*
To perfect the saints ....Eph. 4:11, 12
Appointed by God ....Jer. 3:15
Unfaithful ones are punished ....Jer. 22:22
See Shepherd

Pasture—*a place for grazing animals*
A. Used literally of places for:
   Cattle to feed........................Gen. 47:4
   Wild animals to feed ....Is. 32:14
   God's material blessings.............Ps. 65:11–13
B. Used figuratively of:
   Restoration and peace............Ezek. 34:13–15
   True Israel ....Ps. 95:7
   Kingdom of God......................Is. 49:9, 10
   Safety and provision ....Ps. 23:2
   Kingdom of Israel ....Jer. 25:36
   Gospel ....Is. 30:23
C. Of the true Israel (the Church), described as:
   God's people ....Ps. 100:3
   Provided for........................John 10:9
   Purchased..........................Ps. 74:1, 2
   Thankful ....Ps. 79:13
See Shepherd

Patara—*a port of Lycia in Asia Minor*
Paul changes ships here...............Acts 21:1, 2

Path—*a walk; manner of life*
A. Of the wicked:
   Brought to nothing ....Job 6:18
   Becomes dark ....Job 24:13
   Is crooked............................Is. 59:8
   Leads to death.......................Prov. 2:18
   Filled with wickedness ....Prov. 1:15, 16
   Is destructive ....Is. 59:7
   Followed by wicked rulers ....Is. 3:12
   Made difficult by God ....Hos. 2:6
B. Of believers:
   Beset with difficulties.................Job 19:8
   Under God's control ....Job 13:27
   Hindered by the wicked ....Job 30:13
   Enriched by the Lord...................Ps. 23:3
   Upheld by God ....Ps. 17:5
   Provided with light ....Ps. 119:105

Known by God .... Ps. 139:3
Like a shining light .... Prov. 4:18
Directed by God .... Is. 26:7
To be pondered .... Prov. 4:26
No death at the end .... Prov. 12:28
Sometimes unknown................... Is. 42:16
Sometimes seems crooked .... Lam. 3:9
To be made straight................. Heb. 12:13

C. Of righteousness:
Taught by father .... Prov. 4:1, 11
Kept .... Prov. 2:20
Shown to Messiah........... Ps. 16:11; Acts 2:28
Taught to believers..................... Ps. 25:4, 5
Sought by believers .... Ps. 119:35; Is. 2:3
Rejected by unbelieving .... Jer. 6:16; 18:15

D. Of the Lord:
True .... Ps. 25:10
Smooth .... Ps. 27:11
Rich .... Ps. 65:11
Guarded .... Prov. 2:8
Upright .... Prov. 2:13
Living .... Prov. 2:19
Peaceful............................. Prov. 3:17

Pathros—*the Southland*
Name applied to south (Upper)
   Egypt .... Ezek. 29:10–14
Described as a lowly kingdom..... Ezek. 29:14–16
Refuge for dispersed Jews .... Jer. 44:1–15
Jews to be regathered from.............. Is. 11:11

Pathrusim—*the inhabitants of Pathros*
Hamitic people descending from Mizraim
   and living in Pathros .... Gen. 10:14

Patience—*the ability to bear trials without grumbling; perseverance*
A. Of the Trinity:
God, the author of .... Rom. 15:5
Christ, the example of.............. 2 Thess. 3:5
Spirit, the source of .... Gal. 5:22

B. Described as:
Rewarded .... Rom. 2:7
Endured with joy .... Col. 1:11
To be pursued .... 1 Tim. 6:11

C. Is a product of:
Good heart.......................... Luke 8:15
Tribulation......................... Rom. 5:3, 4
Testing of faith .... James 1:3
Hope .... Rom. 8:25
Scriptures .... Rom. 15:4

D. Necessary grace, in:
Times of crises .... Luke 21:15–19
Dealing with a church.............. 2 Cor. 12:12
Opposing evil .... Rev. 2:2
Inheriting God's promises............ Heb. 6:12
Soundness of faith .... Titus 2:2
Waiting for Christ's return .... James 5:7, 8

Patmos—*an Aegean island off the southwestern coast of Asia Minor*
John, banished here, receives the
   Revelation .... Rev. 1:9

Patriarchal age—*the time of Abraham, Isaac, Jacob (between 1900 and 1600 B.C.)*
A. Rulers of:
Kings and princes................ Gen. 12:15–20
Family heads (fathers)............. Gen. 18:18, 19

B. Business of:
Livestock .... Gen. 12:16
Caravans.......................... Gen. 37:28–36
Trading............................ Gen. 23:1–20
Contracts .... Gen. 21:27–30
Business agreements .... Gen. 30:28–34

C. Customs of:
Prevalence of polygamy .... Gen. 16:4
Existence of slavery .... Gen. 12:16
Son's wife, selected by his father...... Gen. 24:1–4
Children given significant names ... Gen. 29:31–35

D. Religion of:
Existence of idolatry .... Gen. 35:1, 2
Worship of God Almighty........ Gen. 14:19–22
God's covenant recognized .... Gen. 12:1–3
Circumcision observed............ Gen. 17:10–14
Headship of father.................... Gen. 35:2
Obedience primary .... Gen. 18:18, 19
Prayers and sacrifices offered .... Gen. 12:8
Blessings and curses pronounced by
   father .... Gen. 27:27–40
True faith believed..... Matt. 15:28; Heb. 11:8–22

Patriarchs—*ancient family, or tribal heads*
Applied, in New Testament, to Abraham, to
   Jacob's sons, and to David........ Acts 7:8, 9;
   2:29; Heb. 7:4

Patriotism—*love of one's country*
Manifested in:
Willingness to fight for one's
   country..................... 1 Sam. 17:26–51
Concern for national survival...... Esth. 4:13–17
Desire for national revival .... Neh. 1:2–11
Loyalty to national leader .... 2 Sam. 2:10
Respect for national leaders....... 2 Sam. 1:18–27

Patrobas
Christian at Rome .... Rom. 16:14

Pattern—*a copy; an example*
A. Of physical things:
Tabernacle .... Heb. 8:5
Temple............................ 1 Chr. 28:11–19

B. Of spiritual things:
Good works .... Titus 2:7
Heavenly originals................... Heb. 9:23
See Example; Example of Christ, the

Pau, Pai—*groaning, bleating*
Edomite town, residence of King Hadar
   (Hadad) .... Gen. 36:39; 1 Chr. 1:50

> **WORD STUDY**

PAY, REWARD, *misthos* (mis-*thoss*). A noun designating the "pay" or "wages" for work done (Matt. 20:8; Luke 10:7), *misthos* is used figuratively to refer to divine recompense or "reward" for an act, either moral or immoral. Jesus distinguishes between the "rewards" for pseudo-righteous acts (Matt. 5:46; 6:1, 2, 5, 16) and the "rewards" given to those who perform truly righteous acts, no matter how small (6:6; 10:41, 42). Paul indicates that spiritual labor or works will merit spiritual "rewards" (1 Cor. 3:8, 14), but stresses that the "wages" for work alone are "debt," not "grace" (Rom. 4:4). Rev. pictures the Last Judgment as the time when the dead will be judged by their work and rewarded accordingly (11:18; 22:12). (Strong's #3408)

Pay—*to give something for something*

Lord's blessing	Prov. 19:17
Punishment	Matt. 5:26
Servitude and forgiveness	Matt. 18:23–35
Sign of righteousness	Ps. 37:21

See Vow

Pe

Seventeenth letter in the Hebrew alphabet	Ps. 119:129–136

> **WORD STUDY**

PEACE, *eirēnē* (eye-*ray*-nay). *Eirene* is a noun meaning "peace," a period marked by the cessation of open and hostile aggression between people and nations (Acts 24:2). It can be used figuratively to refer to "peace" in the sense of "harmony" (Rom. 14:19; Heb. 12:14). Frequently in the NT the meaning of *eirēnē* moves in the direction of the Hebrew word for "peace" (*shalom*) with its nuance of "well-being" and "wholeness." This is the idea behind the formulas of greeting and farewell—"peace to you" (John 20:19, 21); "go in peace" (Luke 7:50; 8:48). As foretold by the prophets (Luke 2:14, 29; cf. 19:38), "peace" will accompany the messianic kingdom, and in the NT "peace" is nearly synonymous with the salvation brought by the Messiah (John 16:33; Acts 10:36; Col. 3:15). (Strong's #1515)

Peace

A. Kinds of:

International	1 Sam. 7:14
National	1 Kin. 4:24
Civil	Rom. 14:19
Domestic	1 Cor. 7:15
Individual	Luke 8:48
False	1 Thess. 5:3
Hypocritical	James 2:16
Spiritual	Rom. 5:1

B. Source of:

God	Phil. 4:7
Christ	John 14:27
Holy Spirit	Gal. 5:22

C. Of Christ:

Predicted	Is. 9:6, 7
Promised	Hag. 2:9
Announced	Is. 52:7

D. Lord's relation to, He:

Reveals	Jer. 33:6
Gives	Ps. 29:11
Establishes	Is. 26:12

E. Among the wicked:

Not known by	Is. 59:8
None for	Is. 48:22

F. Among believers, truths concerning:

Comes through Christ's atonement	Is. 53:5
Results from reconciliation	Col. 1:20
Product of justification	Rom. 5:1
Obtained by faith	Is. 26:3
To be multiplied (through knowledge of God and Christ)	2 Pet. 1:2

G. Among believers, exhortations regarding:

Should live in	2 Cor. 13:11
Should pursue	2 Tim. 2:22

Peacemakers—*those who work for peace*

Christ the great	2 Cor. 5:18–21
Christians become	Matt. 5:9; Rom. 14:19
Rules regarding	1 Pet. 3:8–13

Pearl—*a precious gem found in oyster shells*

A. Used literally of:

Valuable gems	Rev. 18:12, 16
Woman's attire	1 Tim. 2:9

B. Used figuratively of:

Spiritual truths	Matt. 7:6
Kingdom	Matt. 13:45, 46
Worldly adornment	Rev. 17:4
Wonders of heaven's glories	Rev. 21:21

Pedahel—*God saves*

A leader of Naphtali	Num. 34:28

Pedahzur—*the Rock (God) has redeemed*

Father of Gamaliel	Num. 1:10

Pedaiah—*Yahweh redeems*

1. Father of Joel, ruler in David's reign	1 Chr. 27:20
2. Grandfather of Jehoiakim	2 Kin. 23:36
3. Son of Jeconiah	1 Chr. 3:18, 19
4. Postexilic workman	Neh. 3:25
5. Ezra's Levite attendant	Neh. 8:4
6. Man appointed as treasurer	Neh. 13:13
7. Postexilic Benjamite	Neh. 11:7

Peg

Used to hold idols in place	Is. 41:7

Figurative uses of:

Revived nation	Ezra 9:8
Messiah's kingdom	Is. 22:23, 24
Messiah's death	Is. 22:25

Pekah—*opening (of the eye)*

Son of Remaliah; usurps Israel's throne	2 Kin. 15:25–28
Forms alliance with Rezin of Syria against Ahaz	Is. 7:1–9
Alliance defeated; captives returned	2 Kin. 16:5–9

Territory of, overrun by
    Tiglath-Pileser .... 2 Kin. 15:29
Assassinated by Hoshea .... 2 Kin. 15:30

Pekahiah—*Yahweh has opened (the eyes)*
Son of Menahem; king of Israel . . . 2 Kin. 15:22–26
Assassinated by Pekah .... 2 Kin. 15:23–25

Pekod—*visitation*
Aramean tribe during Nebuchadnezzar's
    reign .... Jer. 50:21

Pelaiah—*Yahweh is wonderful*
1. Judahite .... 1 Chr. 3:24
2. Ezra's Levite attendant; reads covenant. . . . Neh. 8:7

Pelaliah—*Yahweh has judged*
Postexilic priest. .... Neh. 11:12

Pelatiah—*Yahweh has freed*
1. Simeonite captain in war with
    Amalekites. .... 1 Chr. 4:42, 43
2. Prince dying while Ezekiel
    prophesies .... Ezek. 11:1–13
3. Descendant of Solomon .... 1 Chr. 3:21
4. One who signs the covenant .... Neh. 10:1, 22

Peleg—*division*
Brother of Joktan .... Gen. 10:25
Son of Eber .... Luke 3:35

Pelet—*(God) has freed*
1. Judahite .... 1 Chr. 2:47
2. Benjamite warrior under David .... 1 Chr. 12:3

Peleth—*swiftness*
1. Reubenite, father of On .... Num. 16:1
2. Judahite .... 1 Chr. 2:33

Pelethites—*perhaps a contraction of Philistines*
David's faithful soldiers during Absalom's and
    Sheba's rebellions. .... 2 Sam. 15:18–22
See Cherethites

Pelican—*the vomiter*
Dwells in wilderness .... Ps. 102:6
Lives in ruins .... Is. 34:11; Zeph. 2:14

Pelonite
Descriptive of two of David's
    mighty men. .... 1 Chr. 11:27, 36

Pen
Figurative of tongue .... Ps. 45:1
False. .... Jer. 8:8
Not preferred. .... 3 John 13

Penalties—*punishment inflicted for wrongdoing*
A. For sexual sins:
    Adultery—death. .... Lev. 20:10
    Incest—death .... Lev. 20:11–14
    Sodomy—destruction. .... Gen. 19:13, 17, 24
B. For bodily sins:
    Drunkenness—exclusion ...... 1 Cor. 5:11; 6:9, 10
    Murder—death. .... Ex. 21:12–15
    Persecution—God's judgment ... Matt. 23:34–36
C. For following heathen ways:
    Human sacrifice—death .... Lev. 20:2–5

Witchcraft—death. .... Ex. 22:18
    Idolatry—death .... Ex. 22:20
D. For internal sins:
    Ingratitude—punished. .... Prov. 17:13
    Pride—abomination .... Prov. 16:5
    Unbelief—exclusion .... Num. 20:12
    Lying—curse .... Jer. 23:10; Zech. 5:3
    Blasphemy—death. .... Lev. 24:14–16, 23

Peninnah—*coral, pearl*
Elkanah's second wife .... 1 Sam. 1:2, 4

Penitence—*state of being sorry for one's sins*
A. Results of:
    Forgiveness. .... Ps. 32:5, 6
    Restoration. .... Job 22:23–29
    Renewed fellowship. .... Ps. 51:12, 13
B. Examples of:
    Job .... Job 42:1–6
    David. .... Ps. 51:1–19
    Josiah. .... 2 Kin. 22:1, 19
    Zacchaeus. .... Luke 19:2–9
    Tax collector .... Luke 18:13
    Thief on the cross. .... Luke 23:39–42
C. Elements:
    Acknowledgment of sin .... Job 33:27, 28;
        Luke 15:18, 21
    Plea for mercy .... Luke 18:13
    Broken heart .... Ps. 34:18; 51:17
    Confession .... 1 John 1:9
See Repentance

Pentecost—*fiftieth (day)*
A. In the Old Testament:
    Called "the Feast of Weeks" .... Ex. 34:22, 23
    Marks completion of
        barley harvest. .... Lev. 23:15, 16
    Called "Feast of Harvest". .... Ex. 23:16
    Work during, prohibited .... Lev. 23:21
    Two loaves presented. .... Lev. 23:17, 20
    Other sacrifices prescribed .... Lev. 23:18
    Offerings given by Levites .... Deut. 16:10–14
    Time of consecration. .... Deut. 16:12, 13
    Observed during Solomon's time . . . 2 Chr. 8:12, 13
See Feasts, Hebrew
B. In the New Testament:
    Day of the Spirit's coming; the formation
        of the Christian church .... Acts 2:1–47
    Paul desires to attend .... Acts 20:16
    Paul plans to stay in Ephesus until. .... 1 Cor. 16:8

Penuel, Peniel—*the face of God*
1. Place east of Jordan; site of Jacob's
    wrestling with angel .... Gen. 32:24–31
    Inhabitants of, slain by Gideon .... Judg. 8:8, 9, 17
    Later refortified by Jeroboam .... 1 Kin. 12:25
2. Judahite .... 1 Chr. 4:4
3. Benjamite. .... 1 Chr. 8:25

Penury—*extreme poverty; destitution*
Widow's gift in, commended. .... Luke 21:1–4

People, God's

Found among Israel .Deut. 7:6
Not limited to Israel . . . . Rom. 2:28, 29
Called the remnant . . . . Is. 11:10, 11, 16
Gentiles included in . . . . .Is. 19:25; 65:1;
   Rom. 15:10, 11
Became such by covenant . . . . Jer. 31:31–34
Secured through the Messiah . . . . .Ezek. 34:22–31
Accomplished by Christ's death . . . . . . Matt. 1:21;
   Luke 1:68, 77
Separated from others . . .2 Cor. 6:16–18; Rev. 18:4
Given a new and better covenant . . . . .Heb. 8:7–13
God's church . . . . 1 Pet. 2:9, 10
All nations included in . . . . .Rev. 5:9; 7:9
God's eternal people . . . . .Rev. 21:3

People of the land—*the conservative element of the*
   population consisting mainly of landholders
The influence of . . . . 2 Kin. 11:13–15
Taxed . . . . .2 Kin. 23:35

Peor—*opening*
1. Mountain of Moab opposite Jericho . . . Num. 23:28
   Israel's camp seen from . . . . Num. 24:2
2. Moabite god called
   Baal of Peor . . . . Num. 25:3, 5, 18
   Israelites punished for worship of . . . . Num. 31:16

Perceive, perception—*knowledge derived through one*
   of the senses
Outward circumstances . . . . .2 Sam. 12:19;
   Acts 27:10
Outward intentions . . . . John 6:15
Intuition . . . . .1 Sam. 3:8; John 4:19
Unusual manifestations . . . . .1 Sam. 12:17, 18;
   Acts 10:34
Spiritual insight . . . . Neh. 6:12; Acts 14:9
God's blessings . . . . Neh. 6:16
Bitter experience . . . . Eccl. 1:17; 3:22
Obvious implication . . . . . Matt. 21:45; Luke 20:19
God's revelation . . . . Gal. 2:9; 1 John 3:16
Internal consciousness . . . . . . Luke 8:46; Acts 8:23

WORD STUDY **PERDITION, DESTRUCTION,** *apōleia* (ap-*oh*-leye-ah). This noun, derived from the verb *apollumi* (see topical word study: "destroy"), means "destruction." It can mean "waste" (Mark 14:4), but the use of *apōleia* in the NT usually refers to personal "destruction," "annihilation," "ruin"—especially as the eternal punishment of the wicked (Matt. 7:13; Rev. 17:8, 11). It is the opposite of salvation (Phil. 1:28) and the end of the enemies of Christ's cross (3:19). The wicked who are destined for "annihilation" are called "sons of perdition" (John 17:12), and the Day of Judgment for them is also the Day of Destruction (2 Pet. 3:7). (Strong's #684)

Perdition—*the state of the damned; destruction*
Judas Iscariot . . . . John 17:12
Lost . . . . Phil. 1:28
Antichrist . . . . 2 Thess. 2:3; Rev. 17:8, 11

Peres—*to split into pieces*
Sentence of doom . . . . Dan. 5:28

Peresh—*dung*
Man of Manasseh . . . . 1 Chr. 7:16

Perez—*a breach*
One of Judah's twin sons
   by Tamar . . . . Gen. 38:24–30
Numbered among Judah's sons . . . . Gen. 46:12
Founder of a tribal family . . . . . . .Num. 26:20, 21
Descendants of, notable
   in later times . . . . 1 Chr. 27:3
Ancestor of David and Christ . . . . . . Ruth 4:12–18

WORD STUDY **PERFECT, MAKE; COMPLETE,** *teleioō* (tel-eye-*ah*-oh). This verb, encountered often in the NT, is used to denote the final intended stage in a process of development. The meaning of *teleioō* is usually captured by translating it as "to complete," "to bring to an end," "to finish," "to bring to its goal," "to bring to its accomplishment," or even "to make perfect." Jesus uses this word to indicate that He must "finish" ("complete") the work of God (John 4:34; cf. 17:4). In instances where *teleioō* implies that an imperfect state has been overcome, as in Heb. 5:9 and 7:28, it is perhaps best to translate it "to make perfect" (1 John 4:12, 17, 18). (Strong's #5048)

Perfection—*the extreme degree of excellence; pure;*
   complete; mature
A. Applied to natural things:
   Day . . . . Prov. 4:18
   Gold . . . . .2 Chr. 4:21
   Weights . . . . Deut. 25:15
   Beauty . . . . Ezek. 28:12
   Offering . . . . .Lev. 22:21
B. Applied to spiritual graces:
   Patience . . . . James 1:4
   Love . . . . Col. 3:14
   Holiness . . . . 2 Cor. 7:1
   Praise . . . . .Matt. 21:16
   Faith . . . . 1 Thess. 3:10
   Good works . . . . Heb. 13:21
   Unity . . . . John 17:23
   Strength . . . . 2 Cor. 12:9
   Peace . . . . Is. 26:3
C. Means of:
   God . . . . .1 Pet. 5:10
   Christ . . . . Heb. 10:14
   Holy Spirit . . . . .Gal. 3:3
   God's Word . . . . 2 Tim. 3:16, 17
   Ministry . . . . Eph. 4:11, 12
   Sufferings . . . . Heb. 2:10
D. Stages of:
   Eternally accomplished . . . . Heb. 10:14
   Objective goal . . . . Matt. 5:48
   Subjective process . . . . 2 Cor. 7:1
   Daily activity . . . . .2 Cor. 13:9
   Present possession . . . . 1 Cor. 2:6
   Experience not yet reached . . . . Phil. 3:12

Descriptive of the completed church... Heb. 11:40

Heaven's eternal standard .... 1 Cor. 13:10–12

Perfume—*a substance producing pleasant scents*

A. Made by:

Apothecary .... Ex. 30:25, 35

Combining:

Various ingredients .... Job 41:31

Olive oil with imported aromatics.... 1 Kin. 10:10

B. Uses of:

Incense and ointment

for tabernacle .... Ex. 30:22–28

Personal adornment.................. Prov. 27:9

Seduction .... Prov. 7:17

C. Figurative of:

Christ's:

Glories.................................. Ps. 45:8

Righteousness and intercession .... Song 3:6

Spiritual prostitution..................... Is. 57:9

Perfumer—*to mix, compound*

Great art .... Ex. 30:25, 35; Eccl. 10:1

Used in tabernacle .... Ex. 30:25, 35

Used in embalming .... 2 Chr. 16:14

A maker of ointment................. Eccl. 10:1

Among returnees .... Neh. 3:8

Perga—*the capital of Pamphylia*

Visited by Paul .... Acts 13:13, 14; 14:25

Pergamos—*a leading city in Mysia in Asia Minor*

One of the seven churches here......... Rev. 1:11

Antipas martyred here .... Rev. 2:12, 13

Special message to .... Rev. 2:12–17

Perida (see Peruda)

Perils—*physical or spiritual dangers*

Escape from, by:

Prayer .... Gen. 32:6–12

Pacifying gifts.................... Gen. 32:13–20

Quick action .... 1 Sam. 18:10, 11

Flight.......................... Matt. 2:12–15

Angel of the Lord .... Acts 12:5–17

Love of Christ .... Rom. 8:35

God .... 2 Cor. 1:10

Perish—*to be destroyed violently*

A. Applied to:

Universe .... Heb. 1:11

Old world .... 2 Pet. 3:6

Animals......................... Ps. 49:12, 20

Vegetation .... Jon. 4:10

Food............................ John 6:27

Gold............................... 1 Pet. 1:7

Human body .... 2 Cor. 4:16

Soul .... Matt. 10:28

B. Safeguards against:

God's:

Power............................ John 10:28

Will .... Matt. 18:14; 2 Pet. 3:9

Providence....................... Luke 21:18

Christ's resurrection .... 1 Cor. 15:18, 19

Repentance .... Luke 13:3, 5

Belief in Christ .... John 3:16

See Lost

Perizzites—*dwellers in the open country*

One of seven Canaanite nations......... Deut. 7:1

Possessed Palestine in Abram's time.... Gen. 13:7

Land of, promised to

Abram's seed.................. Gen. 15:18, 20

Jacob's fear of .... Gen. 34:30

Israel commanded to utterly destroy ... Deut. 20:17

Israel forbidden to intermingle

with.......................... Ex. 23:23–25

Defeated by Joshua.................... Josh. 3:10

Many of, slain by Judah .... Judg. 1:4, 5

Israel intermarries with .... Judg. 3:5–7

Made slaves by Solomon.......... 1 Kin. 9:20, 21

See Canaanites

Perjury—*swearing falsely*

Condemned by the Law .... Lev. 19:12

Hated by God .... Zech. 8:17

Requires atonement.................. Lev. 6:2–7

Brings punishment........ Zech. 5:3, 4; Mal. 3:5

See False witnesses

Permission—*authority to do something*

Granted to Paul..................... Acts 21:40

Perpetual—*lasting forever*

Statute............................... Ex. 27:21

Incense .... Ex. 30:8

Covenant .... Ex. 31:16

Priesthood .... Ex. 40:15

Possession.......................... Lev. 25:34

Desolations .... Ps. 74:3

Pain .... Jer. 15:18

Sleep............................... Jer. 51:39

Perplexity—*a state wherein no way out is seen*

Predicted by Christ .... Luke 21:25

Persecution—*to afflict, oppress, torment*

A. Caused by:

Humankind's sinful nature............. Gal. 4:29

Hatred of God.................... John 15:20–23

Ignorance of God................... John 16:1–3

Hatred of Christ........ 1 Thess. 2:15; Rev. 12:13

Preaching the cross .... Gal. 5:11; 6:12

Godly living............. Matt. 13:21; 2 Tim. 3:12

Mistaken zeal .... Acts 13:50; 26:9–11

B. Christian's attitude under:

Flee from......................... Matt. 10:23

Rejoice in .... Matt. 5:12

Be patient under .... 1 Cor. 4:12

Glorify God in....................... 1 Pet. 4:16

Pray during .... Matt. 5:44

Persecution psalm

Of David.............................. Ps. 69

Perseverance—*steadfastness; persistence*

Elements involved in:

Spiritual growth .... Eph. 4:15

Fruitfulness .... John 15:4–8

God's armor........................ Eph. 6:11–18
Chastening......................Heb. 12:5–13
Assurance.........................2 Tim. 1:12
Salvation......................... Matt. 10:22
Reward ....Gal. 6:9
Faith......................... Heb. 11:1–12:2

Persis—*Persian*
Christian woman in Rome............Rom. 16:12

Persistence in prayer
Need involved ....Luke 11:5–13
Christ's example.....................Luke 22:24
Great intensity of .... Acts 12:5
Results of ....Mark 7:24–30
See Prayer

Personal devotions
A. Prayer:
   In morning......................Ps. 5:3; 119:147
   Three times daily .... Ps. 55:17; Dan. 6:10
   Continually .... 1 Thess. 3:10; 1 Tim. 5:5
B. Study:
   Daily ....Deut. 17:19
   For learning.............. Acts 17:11; Rom. 15:4

Personal work—*seeking to win persons to Christ*
Need of ....John 4:35–38
Model of ....John 4:4–30
Means of........................1 Thess. 1:5, 6
Power of ....John 16:7–11
Methods of....................... 1 Cor. 9:19–22

Persuasion—*inclining another's will toward something*
A. Good, to:
   Worship .... Acts 18:13
   Steadfastness..................... Acts 13:43
   Belief......................... Acts 18:4; 19:8
   Turn from idolatry.................. Acts 19:26
   Trust Jesus .... Acts 28:23
B. Evil, to:
   Unbelief .... 2 Chr. 32:10–19
   Unholy alliance..................... 2 Chr. 18:2
   Fatal conflict.................. 1 Kin. 22:20–22
   Turmoil...........................Acts 14:19
   Error ....Gal. 5:8
C. Objects of:
   Hereafter ....Luke 16:31
   One's faith in God ....Rom. 4:21
   Personal assurance..................Rom. 8:38
   Personal liberty.....................2 Tim. 1:12
   Another's faith ....2 Tim. 1:5

Peruda, Perida—*separated*
One of Solomon's servants whose descendants
   return from exile .... Ezra 2:55; Neh. 7:57

Perverse, perverseness—*willfully continuing
   in sinful ways*
Heart.............................Prov. 12:8
Generation.......................... Phil. 2:15
False doctrine .... Acts 20:30
Comes from the heart................. Prov. 6:14
Issues from the mouth.................Prov. 2:12

Causes strife........................Prov. 16:28
Abomination to God.................Prov. 11:20
Hard way ....Prov. 22:5

Pervert—*to change something from its right use*
A. Evil of, in dealing with:
   Human judgment................... Deut. 24:17
God's:
   Judgment ....Job 8:3
   Word .... Jer. 23:36
   Ways .... Acts 13:10
   Gospel..............................Gal. 1:7
B. Caused by:
   Drink............................ Prov. 31:5
   Worldly wisdom .... Is. 47:10
   Spiritual blindness................Luke 23:2, 14

Pestilence
Fifth Egyptian plague .... Ex. 9:1–16
Used for man's corrections.......... Ezek. 38:22
Precedes the Lord's coming............. Hab. 3:5
Not to be feared ....Ps. 91:5, 6

Pestle—*instrument used for pulverizing*
Figurative of severe discipline........Prov. 27:22

Peter
A. Life of:
Before his call:
   Simon Bar-Jonah..........Matt. 16:17; John 21:15
   Brother of Andrew....................Matt. 4:18
   Married man .... Mark 1:30; 1 Cor. 9:5
   Not highly educated ....Acts 4:13
   Fisherman.........................Matt. 4:18
From his call to Pentecost:
   Brought to Jesus by Andrew .... John 1:40–42
   Named Cephas by Christ.............. John 1:42
   Called to discipleship by Christ .... Matt. 4:18–22
   Mother-in-law healed .... Matt. 8:14, 15
   Called as apostle..................Matt. 10:2–4
   Walks on water..................Matt. 14:28–33
   Confesses Christ's deity .... Matt. 16:13–19
   Rebuked by Jesus ....Matt. 16:21–23
   Witnesses Transfiguration ....Matt. 17:1–8;
     2 Pet. 1:16–18
   Asks important questions .... Matt. 18:21
   Refuses Christ's menial service.....John 13:6–10
   Cuts off high priest's servant's ear...John 18:10, 11
   Denies Christ three times ....Matt. 26:69–75
   Weeps bitterly .... Matt. 26:75
   Runs to Christ's tomb ....John 20:1–8
   Returns to fishing .... John 21:1–14
   Witnesses Christ's ascension......Matt. 28:16–20
   Returns to Jerusalem............... Acts 1:12–14
   Leads disciples .... Acts 1:15–26
From Pentecost onward:
   Explains Spirit's coming
     at Pentecost..................... Acts 2:1–41
   Heals lame man .... Acts 3:1–11
   Pronounces judgment .... Acts 5:1–11
   Heals .... Acts 5:14–16
   Meets Paul ....Acts 9:26; Gal. 1:17, 18

Raises Dorcas ....Acts 9:36–43
Called to Gentiles.................. Acts 10:1–23
Preaches the gospel to Gentiles.... Acts 10:24–46
Explains his action to apostles ...... Acts 11:1–18
Imprisoned—delivered............. Acts 12:3–19
Attends Jerusalem Council .... Acts 15:7–14
Rebuked by Paul for inconsistency ......Gal. 2:14
Commends Paul's writings .... 2 Pet. 3:15, 16
B. His life contrasted before and after Pentecost, once:
Coward; now courageous.....Matt. 26:58, 69–74;
      Acts 2:14–36
Impulsive; now humble.............John 18:10;
      Acts 10:25, 26
Ignorant; now enlightened....... Matt. 16:21, 22;
      Acts 4:13
Deeply inquisitive; now
      submissive.......John 21:21, 22; Acts 11:2–17
Boastful of self; now boastful
      of Christ........ Matt. 26:33, 34; Acts 4:8–12
Timid and afraid; now fearless... Matt. 14:28–31;
      Acts 5:28, 29
C. Significance of:
Often the representative for the
      others ....Matt. 17:24–27
Only disciple personally restored by
      the Lord ....John 21:15–19
Leader in the early church .... Acts 3:12–26
Author of two epistles........ 1 Pet. 1:1; 2 Pet. 1:1

Peter, the Epistles of—*two books of the New Testament*
A. 1 Peter:
God's salvation .... 1 Pet. 1:3–12
Obedience and holiness .... 1 Pet. 1:13–23
Christ the cornerstone .... 1 Pet. 2:4–6
A royal priesthood ....1 Pet. 2:9
Christ's example .... 1 Pet. 2:18–25
Husbands and wives .... 1 Pet. 3:1–7
Partakers of His suffering .... 1 Pet. 4:12–19
Be humble before God.............. 1 Pet. 5:6–10
B. 2 Peter:
Things pertaining to life .... 2 Pet. 1:1–4
Diligent growth .... 2 Pet. 1:5–11
False teachers..................... 2 Pet. 2:1–22
The hope of the Day .... 2 Pet. 3:9, 10

Pethahiah—*Yahweh opens (the womb)*
1. Priest of David's time .... 1 Chr. 24:16
2. Judahite serving as a Persian official ....Neh. 11:24
3. Levite who divorced his
      foreign wife ....Ezra 10:19, 23
Prays with the other Levites .... Neh. 9:4, 5

Pethor—*a town in north Mesopotamia*
Balaam's home.................... Num. 22:5, 7

Pethuel—*God delivers*
Father of Joel the prophet................. Joel 1:1

Petitions—*entreaties for favors*
A. Offered to humans:
Treacherous........................ Dan. 6:7

B. Offered to God:
Favored ....1 Sam. 1:17
Granted.......................... 1 Sam. 1:27

Peulthai—*reward of Yahweh*
Levite doorkeeper ....1 Chr. 26:5

Phanuel—*face of God*
Father of Anna ....Luke 2:36

Pharaoh—*great house*
A. Unnamed ones, contemporary of:
Abram .... Gen. 12:15–20
Joseph .... Gen. 37:36
Moses (the oppression) .... Ex. 1:8–11
Moses (the Exodus) .... Ex. 5–14
Solomon (his father-in-law)....... 1 Kin. 3:1; 9:16
Hadad's friend ....1 Kin. 11:17–20
Hezekiah ....2 Kin. 18:21
B. Named ones:
Shishak .... 1 Kin. 14:25, 26
So .... 2 Kin. 17:4
Tirhakah........................ 2 Kin. 19:9
Necho ....2 Kin. 23:29
Hophra .... Jer. 44:30

Pharisees—*separated ones*
A. Characteristics of:
Jewish sect ....Acts 15:5
Upholders of traditions... Mark 7:3, 5–8; Gal. 1:14
Zealous for Mosaic Law ...... Acts 26:5; Phil. 3:5
Very careful in outward details ......Matt. 23:23;
      Luke 18:11
Rigid in fasting.................Luke 5:33; 18:12
Zealous for Judaism................. Matt. 23:15
Lovers of display................... Matt. 23:5–7
Covetous.......................... Luke 16:14
Cruel persecutors .... Acts 9:1, 2; Phil. 3:5, 6
B. Chief errors of, their:
Outward righteousness........... Luke 7:36–50
Blindness to spiritual things ....John 3:1–10
Emphasis on the ceremonial Law.... Matt. 15:1–9
Perversion of Scripture .... Matt. 15:1, 9
Self-justification before others .....Luke 16:14, 15
Hindering potential believers.......John 9:16, 22
Refusal to accept Christ .... Matt. 12:24–34
C. Christ's description of:
Vipers ....Matt. 12:24, 34
Blind ....Matt. 15:12–14
Hypocrites ....Matt. 23:13–19
Serpents .... Matt. 23:33
Children of the devil...............John 8:13, 44
D. Attitude of, toward Christ, sought to:
Destroy Him .... Matt. 12:14
Test Him.....................Matt. 16:1; 19:3
Entangle Him .... Matt. 22:15
Accuse Him ....Luke 11:53, 54

Pharpar—*haste*
One of the two rivers of Damascus ....2 Kin. 5:12

Phichol
Captain of King Abimelech's
army ....Gen. 21:22, 32

Philadelphia—*brotherly love*
City of Lydia in Asia Minor; church
established here ....Rev. 1:11

Philanthropy
A. Manifested by:
Ethiopian ....Jer. 38:6–13
Samaritan................... Luke 10:30, 33
Roman centurion ....Luke 7:2–5
Pagans......................... Acts 28:2, 7, 10
Christians.......................Acts 4:34–37
B. Precepts concerning:
"Do good to all" ....Gal. 6:10
"Love your enemies" ....Matt. 5:43–48
"Pursue what is good".............. 1 Thess. 5:15
"Lend, hoping for nothing in return" ...Luke 6:35

Philemon—*loving*
Christian at Colosse to whom
Paul writes....................... Philem. 1
Paul appeals to him to receive
Onesimus....................Philem. 9–21

Philemon, the Epistle to—*a book of the*
New Testament
Thanksgiving ....Philem. 4–7
Plea for Onesimus ....Philem. 10–21
Hope through prayer................ Philem. 22

Philetus—*worthy of love*
False teacher .... 2 Tim. 2:17, 18

Philip—*lover of horses*
1. Son of Herod the Great.................Matt. 14:3
2. One of the twelve apostles..............Matt. 10:3
Brought Nathanael to Christ....... John 1:43–48
Tested by Christ ....John 6:5–7
Introduced Greeks to Christ...... John 12:20–22
Gently rebuked by Christ..........John 14:8–12
In the Upper Room ....Acts 1:13
3. One of the seven deacons................Acts 6:5
Called an evangelist.....................Acts 21:8
Father of four prophetesses ....Acts 21:8, 9
Preached in Samaria ....Acts 8:5–13
Led the Ethiopian eunuch
to Christ.....................Acts 8:26–40
Visited by Paul ....Acts 21:8

Philippi—*pertaining to Philip*
City of Macedonia (named after Philip of
Macedon); visited by Paul.... Acts 16:12; 20:6
Paul wrote letter to church of ....Phil. 1:1

Philippians, the Epistle to the—*a book of the*
New Testament
Thanksgiving ....Phil. 1:3–10
Christ is preached..................Phil. 1:12–18
To live is Christ...................... Phil. 1:21
The humility of Christ ....Phil. 2:5–11
Lights in the world.................Phil. 2:12–16
Perseverance .... Phil. 3

Rejoicing in the Lord................Phil. 4:1–13
Appreciation for Philippian
generosity ....Phil. 4:14–19

Philistia—*the country of the Philistines*
"The land of the Philistines".......Gen. 21:32, 34
"The territory of the Philistines"....... Josh. 13:2
Philistia............................... Ps. 60:8

Philistines—*the people of Philistia*
A. History of:
Descendants of Mizraim ....Gen. 10:13, 14
Originally on the island of Caphtor......Jer. 47:4
Israel commanded to avoid ....Ex. 13:17
Not attacked by Joshua..............Josh. 13:1–3
Left to test Israel...................Judg. 3:1–4
Israel sold into hands of ....Judg. 10:6, 7
Delivered from, by Samson ....Judg. 13–16
Defeat Israel....................... 1 Sam. 4:1–11
Take ark to house of Dagon........... 1 Sam. 4; 5
Defeated at Mizpah............... 1 Sam. 7:7–14
Champion, Goliath, killed........ 1 Sam. 17:1–52
David seeks asylum among .... 1 Sam. 27:1–7
Gather at Aphek; Saul and
sons slain by ...... 1 Sam. 29:1; 31:1–13
Often defeated by David .... 2 Sam. 5:17–25
Besieged by Nadab...................1 Kin. 15:27
War against Jehoram.............2 Chr. 21:16, 17
Defeated by Uzziah ....2 Chr. 26:6, 7
Defeated by Hezekiah............... 2 Kin. 18:8
B. Prophecies concerning:
Union against Israel................. Is. 9:11, 12
Punishment pronounced ....Jer. 25:15, 20
Hatred against Israel revenged.... Ezek. 25:15–17
Destruction by Pharaoh .... Jer. 47:1–7
Ultimate decay ....Zeph. 2:4–6

Philologus—*lover of words*
Christian at Rome ....Rom. 16:15

Philosophy
Divisions of ....Acts 17:18
Deception of ....Col. 2:8

Phinehas—*oracle*
1. Eleazar's son; Aaron's grandson...........Ex. 6:25
Slays an Israelite and a Midianite
woman .... Num. 25:1–18
Wonderfully rewarded .... Ps. 106:30, 31
Fights against Midianites..........Num. 31:6–12
Settles dispute over
memorial altar ....Josh. 22:11–32
Prays for Israel...................... Judg. 20:28
2. Younger son of Eli .... 1 Sam. 1:3
Worthless man .... 1 Sam. 2:12–25
Slain by Philistines........... 1 Sam. 4:11, 17
Wife of, dies in childbirth .... 1 Sam. 4:19–22
3. Father of a postexilic priest............. Ezra 8:33

Phlegon—*scorching*
Christian at Rome ....Rom. 16:14

Phoebe—*pure, bright*
Deaconess of the church
at Cenchrea...................Rom. 16:1, 2

Phoenicia—*purple*
Mediterranean coastal region including the cities
of Ptolemais, Tyre, Zarephath and Sidon;
evangelized by early Christians.....Acts 11:19
Jesus preaches here..................Matt. 15:21

Phoenix—*harbor in southern Crete*
Paul was to winter there............Acts 27:12

Phrygia—*a large province of Asia Minor*
Jews from, at Pentecost.............Acts 2:1, 10
Visited twice by Paul..................Acts 16:6

Phygellus—*fugitive*
Becomes an apostate................2 Tim. 1:15

Phylactery—*charm*
Scripture verses placed on the forehead; based
upon a literal interpretation of....Ex. 13:9–16
Condemned by Christ................Matt. 23:5

WORD STUDY   **PHYSICIAN,** *iatros* (eeyaht-*ross*). Noun meaning "physician," one who provides healing services for a fee (see Mark 5:26; Luke 8:43). Jesus uses the word in proverbial sayings (Mark 2:17; Luke 4:23). Paul identifies one of his companions as "Luke the beloved physician" (Col. 4:14). (Strong's #2395)

Physicians—*trained healers*
God the only true...................Deut. 32:39
Practiced embalming ....Gen. 50:2, 26
Job's friends of no value ....Job 13:4
Consulted by Asa ....2 Chr. 16:12
For the sick only ....Matt. 9:12
Proverb concerning, quoted ....Luke 4:23
Payment for services of..............Mark 5:26
Luke, "the beloved" ....Col. 4:14

Pi Beseth—*the house of the goddess Bast*
City of Lower Egypt 40 miles north
of Memphis.....................Ezek. 30:17

Pictures—*drawn or carved representations of life scenes*
Descriptive of idolatrous images .....Num. 33:52

Piece—*part of a larger whole*
Silver ....1 Sam. 2:36
Fig cake..........................1 Sam. 30:12
Money.................... Gen. 33:19; Job 42:11
Fish...............................Luke 24:42

Pierce—*to push a pointed instrument through something*
A. Used literally of:
Nail in Sisera ....Judg. 5:26
Messiah's predicted death ....Ps. 22:16
Christ's death ....John 19:34, 37
B. Used figuratively of:
God's destruction....................Num. 24:8
Egypt's weakness ....2 Kin. 18:21
Harsh words.......................Prov. 12:18
Great conflict of soul..............Job 30:16, 17

God's Word ....Heb. 4:12
Coveted riches...................... 1 Tim. 6:10

Piety—*holy living*
A. Aided by:
God's Word ....2 Tim. 3:14–17
Godly parents ....1 Sam. 1:11
Prayer ....James 5:16–18
Good works ....1 Tim. 5:10
Hope of Christ's return...........Titus 2:11–14
B. Hindered by:
World.............................James 4:4
Flesh.............................. Rom. 8:1–13
Satan ....Luke 22:31
Envying and strife ....1 Cor. 3:1–7
C. Value of:
Profitable now and later .... 1 Tim. 4:8
Safeguard in temptation............Gen. 39:7–9
Rewarded in heaven..................Rev. 14:13
See Holiness of Christians; Sanctification

Pigeon
As a sin offering ....Lev. 12:6
As a burnt offering...................Lev. 1:14
Offered by Mary .... Luke 2:22, 24
See Dove

Pi Hahiroth—*the place of meadows*
Israelite camp before crossing
the Red Sea .... Ex. 14:2, 9; Num. 33:7, 8

Pilate, Pontius
Governor of Judea (A.D. 26–36)........ Luke 3:1
Destroyed Galileans ....Luke 13:1
Jesus brought before .... Matt. 27:2
Washed hands in mock innocency.... Matt. 27:24
Notorious in history .... Acts 3:13; 4:27, 28

Pildash—*steely*
Son of Nahor and Milcah........ Gen. 22:20–22

Pilfering—*stealing*
Forbidden............................Titus 2:10

Pilgrims—*God's people as*
A. Elements involved in:
Forsaking all for Christ .... Luke 14:26, 27, 33
Traveling by faith..................... Heb. 11:9
Faces set toward Zion .... Jer. 50:5
Encouraged by God's promises........ Heb. 11:13
Sustained by God.....................Is. 35:1–10
B. Their journey in this world as:
Pilgrims and strangers .... 1 Pet. 2:11, 12
Lights........................... Phil. 2:15
Salt.................................Matt. 5:13
God's own......................... 1 Pet. 2:9, 10
Chosen out of the world ....John 17:6; 1 Pet. 1:1, 2
See Strangers

Pilha—*plowman*
Signer of the covenant................Neh. 10:24

Pillar—*a column or support*
A. Descriptive of:
Memorial sites....................Gen. 28:18, 22

Woman turned to salt . . . . Gen. 19:26
Altars of idolatry . . . . Deut. 12:3
Supports for a building . . . . Judg. 16:25, 26, 29
Covenant site . . . . Ex. 24:4–8
Miracles . . . . Joel 2:30
Solomon's temple . . . . 1 Kin. 7:21
B. Figurative of:
God's presence . . . . Ex. 33:9, 10
Earth's supports . . . . Job 9:6
God's sovereignty over nations . . . . Is. 19:19
Human legs . . . . Song 5:15
Important persons . . . . Gal. 2:9
Church . . . . 1 Tim. 3:15
True believers . . . . Rev. 3:12
Angel's feet . . . . Rev. 10:1

Pillar of cloud and fire
A. As means of:
Guiding Israel . . . . Ex. 13:21, 22
Protecting Israel . . . . Ex. 14:19, 24
Regulating Israel's journeys . . . . Num. 9:15–23
Manifesting God's glory to Israel . . . Ex. 24:16–18
Manifesting God's presence . . . . Ex. 34:5–8
Communicating with Israel . . . . Ex. 33:9, 10
B. Effect of:
Cause of fear . . . . Ex. 19:9, 16
Repeated in the temple . . . . 1 Kin. 8:10, 11
Long remembered . . . . Ps. 99:7
Recalled with gratitude . . . . Neh. 9:12, 19
Repeated in Christ's transfiguration . . . . Matt. 17:5
C. Figurative of God's:
Wonders . . . . Joel 2:30
Departure from Jerusalem . . . . Ezek. 9:3
Presence among believers . . . . Matt. 18:20

Pillow—*a cushion*
Stone used as . . . . Gen. 28:11, 18
Made of goats' hair . . . . 1 Sam. 19:13, 16
Used on a ship . . . . Mark 4:38

Pilot—*one who guides*
Of Tyre's ships . . . . Ezek. 27:8–29
Shipmaster . . . . Jon. 1:6
Used figuratively . . . . James 3:4

Piltai—*Yahweh delivers*
Priest of Joiakim's time . . . . Neh. 12:12, 17

Pine away—*to waste away*
Jerusalem . . . . Lam. 4:9

Pine trees—*evergreen trees*
Product of Lebanon . . . . Is. 60:13
Used figuratively . . . . Is. 41:19

Pinnacle—*a summit; highest ledge*
Of the temple . . . . Matt. 4:5

Pinon—*darkness*
Edomite chief . . . . Gen. 36:41; 1 Chr. 1:52

Pipe, piper—*a flute*
A. Descriptive of:
Hollow tube . . . . Zech. 4:2, 12
Spiritual discernment . . . . 1 Chr. 14:7

B. Figurative of:
Joyful deliverance . . . . Is. 30:29
Mournful lamentation . . . . Jer. 48:36
Inconsistent reactions . . . . Matt. 11:17
Spiritual discernment . . . . 1 Cor. 14:7

Piram—*indomitable*
Amorite king of Jarmuth . . . . Josh. 10:3

Pirathon—*height*
Town in Ephraim . . . . Judg. 12:15

Pirathonite—*inhabitant of Pirathon*
Descriptive of:
Abdon . . . . Judg. 12:13–15
Benaiah . . . . 2 Sam. 23:30

Pisgah—*a mountain peak in the Abarim range in Moab*
Balaam offers sacrifice upon . . . . Num. 23:14
Moses views Promised Land from . . . . . Deut. 3:27
Site of Moses' death . . . . Deut. 34:1–7
Summit of, called Nebo . . . . Deut. 32:49–52
See Nebo

Pishon—*freely flowing*
One of Eden's four rivers . . . . Gen. 2:10, 11

Pisidia—*a mountainous district in Asia Minor*
Twice visited by Paul . . . . Acts 13:13, 14; 14:24

Pispah—*dispersion*
Asherite . . . . 1 Chr. 7:38

Pit—*a hole*
Figurative of:
Grave . . . . Ps. 30:9
Snare . . . . Ps. 35:7
Harlot . . . . Prov. 23:27
Mouth of strange woman . . . . Prov. 22:14
Destruction . . . . Ps. 55:23
Self-destruction . . . . Prov. 28:10
Hell . . . . Ps. 28:1
Devil's abode . . . . Rev. 9:1, 2, 11
See Abyss

Pitch
Ark covered with . . . . Gen. 6:14
See Asphalt

Pitcher—*an earthenware vessel with handles*
A. Used for:
Water . . . . Gen. 24:16
Protection of a torch . . . . Judg. 7:16, 19
B. Figurative of:
Heart . . . . Eccl. 12:6

Pithom—*mansion of the god Atum*
Egyptian city built by Hebrew slaves . . . . . Ex. 1:11

Pithon—*harmless*
Son of Micah . . . . 1 Chr. 8:35

Pitilessness—*showing no mercy*
Examples of:
Rich man . . . . 2 Sam. 12:1–6
Nebuchadnezzar . . . . 2 Kin. 25:6–21
Medes . . . . Is. 13:18
Edom . . . . Amos 1:11

Heartless creditor.............. Matt. 18:29, 30
Strict religionists .... Luke 10:30–32
Merciless murderers............. Acts 7:54–58
The Lord............................ Zech. 11:6

Pity—*to show compassion*
A. Of God, upon:
    Heathen .... Jon. 4:10, 11
    Israel .... Is. 63:9
    Faithful remnant .... Is. 54:8–10
    Believer .... James 5:11
B. Of humankind:
    Pleaded .... Job 19:21
    Upon the poor .... Prov. 19:17
    Upon children..................... Ps. 103:13
    Encouraged .... 1 Pet. 3:8
  See Compassion; Mercy

Plague—*a severe epidemic*
A. Descriptive of:
    Divine judgment...................... Ex. 9:14
    Leprosy .... Lev. 13:1–59
    Pestilence threatened by God .... Deut. 28:21
    Final judgment .... Rev. 9:20
B. Instances of:
    In Egypt .... Ex. 11:1
    At Kibroth Hattaavah........... Num. 11:33, 34
    At Kadesh......................... Num. 14:37
    At Peor .... Josh. 22:17
Among:
    Philistines......................... 1 Sam. 5:7
    Israelites .... 2 Sam. 24:15
    Sennacherib's soldiers .... Is. 37:36
C. Sent by God:
    Because of sin .... Gen. 12:17
    As final judgments................. Rev. 15:1, 8
D. Remedy against, by:
    Intervention...................... Ps. 106:29, 30
    Prayer and confession .... 1 Kin. 8:37, 38
    Separation .... Rev. 18:4
    Promise............................ Ps. 91:10
    Obedience .... Rev. 22:18

Plain—*a geographically flat area (usually refers to specific regional areas)*
    Dry region .... Num. 22:1; Deut. 3:17; 34:3

Plans—*methods of action*
    Acknowledging God in................ Prov. 3:6
    Considering all possibilities ...... Luke 14:31–33
    Leaving God out.................. Luke 12:16–21
    Not trusting God .... Ps. 52:7
    Evil................................ Ps. 140:2

Plants
    Created by God.................... Gen. 1:11, 12
    Given as food..................... Gen. 1:28, 29

Plants of the Bible
    Anise .... Matt. 23:23
    Bean............................... Ezek. 4:9
    Bramble........................... Judg. 9:14, 15
    Brier.............................. Judg. 8:7, 16

Broom (juniper) .... Ps. 120:4
Calamus .... Song 4:14
Cummin............................ Is. 28:25, 27
Garlic............................. Num. 11:5
Gourd .... 2 Kin. 4:39
Grass .... Ps. 103:15
Henna .... Song 1:14
Hyssop............................. Ex. 12:22
Lily................................ Song 5:13
Mallows............................. Job 30:4
Mandrakes .... Gen. 30:14–16
Mint............................... Matt. 23:23
Mustard .... Matt. 13:31
Myrtle .... Is. 55:13
Rose .... Is. 35:1
Rue................................ Luke 11:42
Saffron............................. Song 4:14
Spelt.............................. Ezek. 4:9
Spikenard .... Song 4:13, 14
Thorn .... Judg. 8:7
Vine of Sodom...................... Deut. 32:32
Wormwood .... Deut. 29:18

Plaster—*building material*
Used on:
    Infested walls .... Lev. 14:42, 48
    Babylon's walls .... Dan. 5:5
  See Lime; Mortar

Platform
    Ezra reads Law from .... Neh. 8:4–8

Platter
    Deep dish or basin .... Matt. 14:8, 11
    In tribal offerings................. Num. 7:13
    Used for a dead man's head .... Matt. 14:8, 11

Play
Used of:
    Music............................. 1 Sam. 16:16–23
    Immoral acts...................... Ex. 32:6
    Dancing .... 2 Sam. 6:5, 21
    Fish............................... Ps. 104:26
    Children .... Is. 11:8
    Beasts............................. Job 40:20

Plead—*to entreat intensely*
A. Asking for judgment against:
    Idolatry........................... Judg. 6:31, 32
    Evil king .... 1 Sam. 24:15
    Ungodly nation.................... Ps. 43:1
B. Asking for protection of:
    Poor .... Prov. 22:23
    Widows........................... Is. 1:17
    Repentant......................... Mic. 7:9

Please—*to satisfy*
A. Applied to God's:
    Sovereignty .... Ps. 115:3
    Election........................... 1 Sam. 12:22
    Method .... 1 Cor. 1:21
    Reactions to Solomon .... 1 Kin. 3:10
    Blessing........................... 2 Sam. 7:29

Purpose.............................Col. 1:19
Creative acts ....1 Cor. 12:18
Will ....Matt. 3:17
B. Applied to the unregenerate's:
Behavior ....Rom. 8:8
Passions..........................Matt. 14:6
Ways ....1 Thess. 2:15
Prejudices........................Acts 12:3
Faithlessness ....Heb. 10:35
C. Applied to the regenerate's:
Faith.............................Heb. 11:5, 6
Calling...........................2 Tim. 2:4
Obedience........................Col. 3:20
Concern for others..............Rom. 15:26, 27
Interaction with others............Prov. 16:7
Example, Christ ....John 8:29

Pleasure—*satisfying the sensations*
A. Kinds of:
Physical..........................Eccl. 2:1–10
Sexual ....Gen. 18:12
Worldly..........................Luke 8:14
Temporary ....Heb. 11:25
Immoral ....Titus 3:3
Spiritual ....Ps. 36:8
Heavenly.........................Ps. 16:11
B. God's, described as:
Sovereign ....Eph. 1:5, 9
Creative..........................Rev. 4:11
In righteousness ....1 Chr. 29:17
Having purpose ....Luke 12:32
Not in evil.........................Ps. 5:4
Not in the wicked.........Ezek. 18:23, 32; 33:11
C. Christian's described as:
Subject to God's will ....2 Cor. 12:10
Inspired by God ....Phil. 2:13
Fulfilled by God ....2 Thess. 1:11
D. The unbeliever's, described as:
Unsatisfying ....Eccl. 2:1
Enslaving ....Titus 3:3
Deadening ....1 Tim. 5:6
Judged ....2 Thess. 2:12

Pledge—*something given for security of a debt*
A. Of material things:
Garments ....Ex. 22:26
Regulations concerning ....Deut. 24:10–17
Evil of ....Job 22:6
Restoration of, sign
  of righteousness...............Ezek. 18:7, 16
Unlawfully held back ....Ezek. 18:12
B. Of spiritual things:
The Holy Spirit in the heart ....2 Cor. 1:22
Given by God......................2 Cor. 5:5
Guarantee of future redemption ....Eph. 1:13, 14
See Borrow; Debt; Lending; Surety

Pleiades—*cluster of many stars*
Part of God's creation.........Job 9:9; Amos 5:8

Plentiful, plenty
A. Of physical things:
Food.............................Gen. 41:29–47
Prosperity........................Deut. 28:11
Productivity......................Jer. 2:7
Rain..............................Ps. 68:9
Water............................Lev. 11:36
B. Of spiritual things:
Souls in need ....Matt. 9:37
C. How to obtain, by:
Industry ....Prov. 28:19
Putting God first ....Prov. 3:9, 10
See Abundance

Plottings
A. Against:
Poor ....Ps. 10:7–11
Prophets ....Jer. 18:18
Persecuted ....Matt. 5:11, 12
B. Inspired by:
Contempt........................Neh. 4:1–8
Hatred...........................Gen. 37:8–20
Devil ....John 13:27
Envy.............................Matt. 27:18
C. Examples of:
Esau against Jacob ....Gen. 27:41–45
Brothers against Joseph ....Gen. 37:17–28
Satan against Job ....Job 1:8–22
Ahab against Naboth ....1 Kin. 21:1–16
Jews against Jeremiah ....Jer. 26:8–15
Haman against the Jews...........Esth. 7:3–6
Chaldeans against Daniel ....Dan. 6:1–8
Jews against Christ ....Matt. 26:1–5;
  John 11:47–53
Jews against Paul ....Acts 23:12–22

Plow, plowing—*to dig up the earth for sowing seed*
A. Used literally of:
Elisha............................1 Kin. 19:19
Forbidden with mixed animals.......Deut. 22:10
Job's servants.....................Job 1:14, 15
B. Used figuratively of:
Proper learning...................Is. 28:24, 26
Wrongdoing.......................Hos. 10:13
Punishment ....Hos. 10:11
Affliction ....Ps. 129:3
Destruction ....Jer. 26:18
Persistent sin ....Job 4:8
Christian labor ....1 Cor. 9:10
Information from a wife.............Judg. 14:18
Constancy in decision...............Luke 9:62
Perverse action ....Amos 6:12

Plowman—*a farmer*
A. Used literally of:
Farming ....Is. 28:24
B. Used figuratively of:
Prosperity........................Amos 9:13
Christian ministry..................1 Cor. 9:10

Plowshares—*the hard part of a plow*
Made into swords . . . . Joel 3:10
Swords made into . . . . Is. 2:4

Plumb line—*a cord with a weight (plummet)*
Figurative of:
Destruction . . . . 2 Kin. 21:13
God's judgment. . . . . Amos 7:7, 8
God's building . . . . Zech. 4:10

Plunder—*spoil*
Silver, gold, and clothing . . . . .Ex. 3:22
Sheep . . . . Num. 31:32
House . . . . Mark 3:27
Camp . . . . .1 Sam. 17:53
See Spoil

Pochereth—*binder*
Descendants of, among
Solomon's servants . . . . . . Ezra 2:57; Neh. 7:59

Pods—*husks of the carob or locust tree*
Fed to swine . . . . .Luke 15:15, 16

Poetry, Hebrew
A. Classified according to form:
Synonymous—repetition of
same thoughts . . . . Ps. 19:2
Progressive—advance of thought
in second line . . . . .Job 3:17
Synthetic—second line adds
something new . . . . .Ps. 104:19
Climactic—the thought climbs
to a climax . . . . .Ps. 121:3, 4
Antithetic—the second line contrasted
with first . . . . Prov. 14:1
Comparative—the "as" compared with
the "so" . . . . .Prov. 10:26
Acrostic—alphabetic . . . . .Ps. 119:1–176
B. Classified according to function:
Didactic (teaching) . . .Deut. 32:1–43; Book of Job
Lyrics . . . . .Ex. 15:1–19; Judg. 5:1–31
Elegies . . . . 2 Sam. 1:17–27
Psalms . . . . .Book of Psalms

Poison
Reptiles . . . . Deut. 32:24
Serpents . . . . Deut. 32:33
Gourd . . . . 2 Kin. 4:39, 40
Hemlock . . . . Hos. 10:4
Waters . . . . .Jer. 8:14
Asps . . . . Ps. 140:3; Rom. 3:13
Cobras . . . . Job 20:16

Politeness—*refined manners*
A. Manifested by:
Kings . . . . .Gen. 47:2–11
Hebrews . . . . Gen. 43:26–29
Romans . . . . .Acts 27:3
Pagans . . . . Acts 28:1, 2
Christians . . . . .Philem. 8–21
B. Counterfeited by:
Trickery . . . . 2 Sam. 20:9, 10
Deceit . . . . 2 Sam. 15:1–6

Hypocrisy . . . . Matt. 22:7, 8
Pride . . . . Luke 14:8–10
Snobbery . . . . .James 2:1–4
Selfishness . . . . 3 John 9, 10
See Courtesy

Politicians—*governmental officials*
A. Evils manifested by:
Ambition . . . . 2 Sam. 15:1–6
Flattery . . . . .Dan. 6:4–15
Indifference . . . . Acts 18:12–16
Avarice . . . . Acts 24:26
Murder . . . . .Matt. 2:16
B. Good manifested by:
Provision . . . . Gen. 41:33–49
Protection . . . . .Neh. 2:7–11
Piety . . . . 2 Chr. 34:1–33
Prayer . . . . 2 Chr. 20:6–12
Praise . . . . 2 Chr. 20:27–29

Pollute—*to defile*
A. Described as something unclean:
Morally . . . . .Num. 35:33, 34
Spiritually . . . . Acts 15:20
B. Means of:
Blood . . . . .Ps. 106:38
Idolatry . . . . Ezek. 20:30, 31
Abominations . . . . .Jer. 7:30
Unregenerate service . . . . Ezek. 44:7
Wickedness . . . . .Jer. 3:1, 2
Contempt of the Lord . . . . Mal. 1:7, 12
See Unclean

Polygamy—*having more than one wife*
A. Caused by:
Barrenness of first wife . . . . .Gen. 16:1–6
Desire for large family . . . . .Judg. 8:30
Political ties with other countries . . . . . . 1 Kin. 3:1
Sexual desire .2 Chr. 11:23
Slavery . . . . Gen. 16:1, 3
B. Contrary to:
God's original Law . . . . Gen. 2:24
Ideal picture of marriage . . . . Ps. 128:1–6
God's commandment . . . . .Ex. 20:14
Relationship between Christ and the
church . . . . .Eph. 5:22–33
C. Productive of:
Dissension . . . . .Gen. 16:1–6
Discord . . . . .1 Sam. 1:6
Degeneracy . . . . .1 Kin. 11:1–4
See Adultery; Family; Fornication; Marriage

Pomegranate—*a small tree bearing an apple-shaped fruit*
Grown in Canaan . . . . Num. 13:23
Ornaments of:
Worn by priests . . . . Ex. 28:33
In temple . . . . 1 Kin. 7:18
Sign of fruitfulness . . . . Hag. 2:19
Used figuratively . . . . Song 4:3

Pond, pool—*a reservoir of water*
A. Used for:
Washing . . . . .1 Kin. 22:38

Water supply . . . . .2 Kin. 20:20
Irrigation . . . . Eccl. 2:6
Healing. . . . . .John 5:2–7

B. Famous ones:
Gibeon. . . . . 2 Sam. 2:13
Hebron . . . . 2 Sam. 4:12
Samaria. . . . . .1 Kin. 22:38
Bethesda. . . . . John 5:2
Siloam . . . . John 9:7
The upper. . . . . .Is. 7:3
The lower . . . . Is. 22:9, 11
The King's . . . . Neh. 2:14

Pontus—*a coastal strip of north Asia Minor*
Jews from, at Pentecost. . . . . Acts 2:5, 9
Home of Aquila . . . . Acts 18:2
Christians of, addressed by Peter. . . . . . .1 Pet. 1:1

WORD STUDY   **POOR,** *'ani* (aw-*nee*). The adjective *'ani* means "poor," "afflicted," or "humble." The poor can be the needy, those with a right to pick up the gleanings in fields as Ruth did. The poor can also be the poor and weak, those who are oppressed by the powerful. Sometimes, the word is used of the poor, weak, afflicted Israel, indicating the pious ones who are afflicted by the wicked who are either from other nations or impious ones within Israel. God is frequently seen to help the poor in some way—for example, saving, delivering, bestowing favor on, or having compassion on. The prophets often express God's displeasure for the way in which the poor of Israel are treated. The term translated "poor" can also mean "humble" or "lowly" as it does in Zech. 9:9, where the coming king is lowly and riding on a donkey. (Strong's #6041)

Poor, poverty
A. Descriptive of:
Needy. . . . . Luke 21:2
Lower classes. . . . . .2 Kin. 24:14
Rebellious. . . . . Jer. 5:3, 4
B. Causes of:
God's sovereignty. . . . . .1 Sam. 2:7
Lack of industry . . . . .Prov. 24:30–34
Love of pleasure . . . . Prov. 21:17
Stubbornness. . . . . .Prov. 13:18
Empty pursuits . . . . Prov. 28:19
Drunkenness. Prov. 23:21
C. Wrong treatment of:
Reproaches God . . . . .Prov. 14:31
Brings punishment. . . . . Prov. 21:13
Brings poverty. . . . . Prov. 22:16
Regarded by God . . . . Eccl. 5:8
Judged by God. Is. 3:13–15
D. Legislation designed for protection of:
Daily payment of wages . . . . .Lev. 19:13
Sharing of tithes with . . . . .Deut. 14:28, 29
Loans to, without interest . . . . Lev. 25:35, 37
Right to glean . . . . .Lev. 19:9, 10
Land of, restored in Jubilee Year. . . . Lev. 25:25–30

Equal participation in feasts . . . . .Lev. 16:11, 14
Permanent bondage of,
    forbidden. . . . . .Deut. 15:12–15
See Needy; Poverty, spiritual

Poor in spirit—*humble, self-effacing*
Promised blessing. . . . . .Matt. 5:3

Poplar tree
Used in deception of Laban. . . . . Gen. 30:37
Pagan rites among . . . . Hos. 4:13
Probably same as "willows" in. . . . . .Lev. 23:40

Popularity—*one's esteem in the world*
Obtained by:
Heroic exploits . . . . .Judg. 8:21, 22
Unusual wisdom. . . . . 1 Kin. 4:29–34
Trickery . . . . 2 Sam. 15:1–6
Outward display. . . . . Matt. 6:2, 5, 16
Success in battle . . . . 1 Sam. 18:5–7

Popularity of Jesus
A. Factors producing, His:
Teaching. . . . . Mark 1:22, 27
Healing. . . . . Mark 5:20
Miracles . . . . .John 12:9–19
Feeding the people. . . . . .John 6:15–27
Compassion. . . . . Matt. 14:13, 14
B. Factors causing decline of:
High ethical standards . . . . .Mark 8:34–38
Foretells His death. . . . . .Matt. 16:21–28
Confrontations with scribes and
    Pharisees . . . . Luke 11:37–54

Population—*the total inhabitants of a place*
Israel's, increased in Egypt. . . . . .Ex. 1:7, 8
Nineveh's, great . . . . .Jon. 4:11
Heaven's, vast .Rev. 7:9

Poratha
One of Haman's sons. . . . . Esth. 9:8

Porch
Portico for pedestrians . . . . John 5:2
Roofed colonnade . . . . .John 10:23

Porcius Festus (see Festus)

Porcupine
Symbolic of devastation . . . . Is. 14:23

Pork—*swine's flesh*
Classified as unclean. . . . . .Lev. 11:7, 8

Port—*a harbor*
Examples of:
At Joppa . . . . Jon. 1:3
Fair Havens . . . . .Acts 27:8
Phoenix. . . . . Acts 27:12
Syracuse . . . . Acts 28:12
Rhegium. . . . . Acts 28:13
Puteoli. . . . . Acts 28:13

Portion—*a stipulated part*
A. Of things material:
Inheritance. .Gen. 48:22
B. Of good things:
Spirit . . . . 2 Kin. 2:9

Lord . . . . Ps. 119:57
Spiritual riches . . . . Is. 61:7
C. Of evil things:
Things of the world . . . . Ps. 17:14
D. Of things eternal:
Punishment of the wicked . . . . Ps. 11:6
See Inheritance

Position—*place of influence*
Sought after by Pharisees . . . . Matt. 23:5–7
James and John request . . . . Mark 10:37
Seeking after, denounced . . . . Luke 14:7–11
Diotrephes, a seeker after . . . . 3 John 9

Possess—*to acquire*
A. Objects of:
Promised Land . . . . Deut. 4:1, 5
Country . . . . Is. 14:21
Spiritual riches . . . . Is. 57:13
Christ . . . . Prov. 8:22
One's:
Soul . . . . Luke 21:19
Own body . . . . 1 Thess. 4:4
B. Of Canaan:
Promised . . . . Gen. 17:8
Under oath . . . . Neh. 9:15
Israel challenged to . . . . Num. 13:30

WORD STUDY	**POSSESSION**, *'achuzzah* (akh-ooz-*zaw*). The noun *'achuzzah,* meaning "possession," comes from a verb meaning "to

grasp." Therefore, something that is seized or grasped is a possession. The term is used especially often in connection with land. In the Jubilee year, land was to be returned to the one who *"owned* the land as a possession," the one whose family had traditionally owned it (Lev. 27:24). Possession often came by right of inheritance (Num. 27:7). The Davidic king, on the other hand, was to be given "the ends of the earth" for a possession (Ps. 2:8). Levitical priests, who were not given any land during the conquest, would receive God as their portion according to Ezek. 44:28. (Strong's #272)

Possible—*that which can exist*
A. Things possible:
All, with God . . . . Matt. 19:26
All, to the believer . . . . Mark 9:23
Peaceful living . . . . Rom. 12:18
B. Things impossible:
Removal of the Cross . . . . Matt. 26:39
Christ's remaining in the grave . . . . Acts 2:24
Removal of sins by animal sacrifice . . . . . Heb. 10:4

Posthumous—*after death*
Mary of Bethany . . . . Matt. 26:13
Abel . . . . Heb. 11:4
All believers . . . . Rev. 14:13

Pot—*a rounded, open-mouthed vessel*
A. Use of:
Cooking . . . . Zech. 14:21
Refining . . . . Prov. 17:3

Container . . . . Ezek. 24:3; Heb. 9:4
B. Figurative of:
Sudden destruction . . . . Ps. 58:9
Impending national destruction . . . . Jer. 1:13
Merciless punishment . . . . Mic. 3:2, 3
Complete sanctification . . . . Zech. 14:20, 21

Potentate—*a mighty one*
Christ the only absolute . . . . 1 Tim. 6:15

Potiphar—*whom Re (the sun-god) has given*
High Egyptian officer . . . . Gen. 39:1
Puts Joseph in jail . . . . Gen. 39:20

Poti-Pherah
Egyptian priest of On
(Heliopolis) . . . . Gen. 41:45–50
Father of Asenath, Joseph's wife . . . . Gen. 46:20

Potsherd—*a fragment of broken pottery*
A. Figurative of:
Weakness . . . . Ps. 22:15
Leviathan's underparts . . . . Job 41:30
B. Uses of:
Scraping . . . . Job 2:8
Scooping water . . . . Is. 30:14

Potsherd Gate—*a gate of Jerusalem*
By Valley of the Son of Hinnom . . . . Jer. 19:2

Potter—*one who makes earthenware vessels*
A. Art of, involves:
Reducing clay to paste . . . . Is. 41:25
Shaping by revolving wheel . . . . Jer. 18:1–4
Molding by hands . . . . Jer. 18:6
B. Figurative of:
Complete destruction . . . . Is. 30:14
God's sovereignty over humankind . . . . . . Is. 64:8
Israel's lack of understanding . . . . Is. 29:16

Potter's field—*burial place for poor people*
Judas's money used for purchase of . . . Matt. 27:7, 8

Poultice—*medicinal material applied to sores or other
lesions*
Figs applied to Hezekiah's boil . . . . Is. 38:21

Pour—*to flow freely from something*
A. Applied to:
Rain from clouds . . . . Amos 9:6
Oil from vessels . . . . Gen. 35:14; 2 Kin. 4:4
Blood from animals . . . . Lev. 8:15
Water from barrels . . . . 1 Kin. 18:33
B. Used figuratively of:
Anointing . . . . Ex. 29:7
Christ's death . . . . Ps. 22:14
Spirit's coming . . . . Joel 2:28, 29
Holy Spirit . . . . Ezek. 39:29
God's:
Wrath . . . . 2 Chr. 34:21, 25
Blessings . . . . Mal. 3:10
Sovereignty . . . . Job 10:9, 10
Prayer and repentance . . . . Lam. 2:19
Extreme emotions . . . . 1 Sam. 1:15

Poverty, spiritual

A. In a bad sense, of spiritual:

Decay................................Rev. 2:9

Immaturity ....1 Cor. 3:1–3

B. Used in a good sense, of:

The contrite...........................Is. 66:2

God's people ....Is. 14:32

C. Caused by:

Hastiness ....Prov. 21:5

Greed...............................Prov. 22:16

Laziness ....Prov. 24:30–34

WORD STUDY — **POWER,** *koach* (koh-*ahkh*). "Power," including capacity and ability, are indicated by the noun *koach*. Power of humans is most often seen as physical strength, of which Samson is the outstanding example. It can also be vigor to procreate, which is a form of strength. When translated "ability," the term can refer to the ability to weep or get wealth or bring forth a child. Power can be the power of a people or a king (Josh. 17:7; Hab. 1:11). Human power is contrasted with God's in Is. 10:13 and Amos 2:14. Is. 40:29 also says that human power is given by God. In at least one instance, the term "power" is used to refer to the strength of angels (Ps. 103:20). God has power in various forms. There is the power to create, to deliver, and to judge. Wisdom is the strength of His mind. The OT also uses the term "power" in connection with animals such as the wild ox, horse, and he-goat. A rare use of the term comes in connection with the soil's strength to produce. (Strong's #3581)

WORD STUDY — **POWER,** *dunamis* (*doo*-nam-is). This noun denotes "power" arising from "strength" or "ability" (equally acceptable translations in Matt. 25:15; 2 Cor. 1:8; 8:3). This "power" may be the result of material externals (e.g., wealth in Rev. 3:8; 18:3), or it may be of divine origin (Acts 1:8). God's "power" is absolute (Matt. 22:29; Rom. 1:16, 20)—hence He is called *Dunamis* (Mark 14:62)—and Christ possesses this divine "power" (2 Pet. 1:3), as does the Holy Spirit (Luke 4:14; Rom. 15:13, 19). Believers are equipped with "power" (Col. 1:11). The word is also used as a designation for powerful beings (Rom. 8:38; 1 Cor. 15:24). (Strong's #1411)

Power of Christ

A. Described as:

Given by God........................ John 17:2

Derived from the Spirit............... Luke 4:14

Delegated to others .... Luke 9:1

Determined by Himself .... John 10:18

B. Manifested as power in:

Creation .... John 1:3, 10

Upholds all things .... Heb. 1:3

Miracles ....Luke 4:36

Healings .... Mark 1:34

Regeneration ....John 5:21–26

Salvation............................ Heb. 7:25

Resurrecting believers..............John 5:28, 29

His return.......................... Matt. 24:30

C. Manifested as authority to:

Forgive sins .... Matt. 9:6, 8

Teach ....Luke 4:32

Lay down His life .... John 10:18

Commission................Matt. 28:18–20

D. Benefits from, to believers:

Life................................ John 17:2

Strength .... Phil. 4:13

Effective service ....1 Tim. 1:12; 2 Tim. 4:17

Perfected in weakness................2 Cor. 12:9

Conquest over temptation .... Heb. 2:18

Glorification ....Phil. 3:20, 21

Power of God

A. Manifested in:

Creation ....Jer. 51:15

Keeps watch on the nations ....Ps. 66:7

Christ's:

Birth.............................. Luke 1:35

Miracles ....Luke 11:20

Resurrection ....2 Cor. 13:4

Exaltation........................ Eph. 1:19, 20

Regeneration ....Eph. 1:19

Sanctification .... Phil. 2:13

Believer's resurrection................ 1 Cor. 6:14

His word ....Heb. 4:12

B. Believer's attitude toward:

Renders praise for .... Ps. 21:13

Sings of .... Ps. 59:16

Talks of ....Ps. 145:11

Power of the Holy Spirit

A. Manifested in Christ's:

Conception.........................Luke 1:35

Ministry ....Luke 4:14

Miracles ....Luke 11:20

Resurrection ....Rom. 1:4

B. Manifested in the believer's:

Regeneration...................... Ezek. 37:11–14

Effective ministry ....Luke 24:49

Power, spiritual

Sources of:

Holy Spirit ....1 Cor. 2:4, 5

Christ.............................1 Cor. 1:24

Gospel............................Rom. 1:16

God's kingdom ....Mark 9:1

God's Word ....Heb. 4:12

New life...........................Eph. 1:19

Powerlessness—*ineffective testimony*

Produced by:

Worldliness ....Gen. 19:14

Unbelief ....Matt. 17:16–20

Practice—*customary habit*

Wicked works ....Ps. 141:4

Ungodliness........................ Is. 32:6

Work evil ....Mic. 2:1

Praetorium—*the governor's official residence*
1. Pilate's, in Jerusalem . . . . Matt. 27:27;
    Mark 15:16; John 18:28
2. Herod's palace at Caesarea . . . . Acts 23:35

PRAISE, *halal* (haw-*lal*). "Praise," which is to boast with words and singing, is indicated by the verb *halal*. One can praise a man or a woman. Usually in the OT, the praise is made to God. The psalmist summons people to praise many times, but does not limit God's praise to humans. Heaven and earth and creatures are also called to praise God. Praise, which included both words and singing, was often carried out during public worship in the sanctuary accompanied by instruments. Praise was also a technical function of Levitical priests, who would be joined by the congregation. This term then carries a special liturgical meaning, especially when used in the imperative phrase "Praise the LORD!"—one of the few that comes to modern worshipers in the Hebrew, "Hallelujah." (Strong's #1984)

PRAISE, *shabach* (shaw-*bakh*). The verb translated "praise," *shabach,* is much less common in the OT than *halal,* which is used repeatedly in Ps. *Shabach* has the implied meaning of pacifying with soothing words. In Ps. 63:3 the psalmist says, "My lips shall praise You." In several cases, the word "praise" implies congratulation or commendation as it does in Eccl. 4:2 where the dead are praised more than the living. The writer of Eccl. also commends enjoyment because there is nothing else that will remain with a person than "to eat, drink, and be merry" (8:15). (Strong's #7623)

PRAISE YAH, *allēlouia* (al-lay-*loo*-eeyah). This expression occurs only four times in the NT (Rev. 19:1, 3, 4, 6). It is the Greek transliteration of the Hebrew liturgical formula *hallu yah,* which means "praise Yahweh" ("yah" is the shortened poetic form), incorporated by Christians into their liturgy. The English transliteration "hallelujah" likely reflects the pronunciation of the expression by early Jewish Christians, while "alleluia" is the spelling found in later Latin manuscripts of the NT. This expression, which can be translated as "praise God," is still used as a liturgical formula in Christian worship. (Strong's #239)

Praise of God
A. Objects of:
　　God Himself . . . . Ps. 139:14
God's:
　　Name. 1 Chr. 29:13; Ps. 99:3
　　Power. . . . . Ps. 21:13
　　Wonders . . . . Ps. 89:5
　　Lovingkindness . . . . Ps. 138:2
　　Works . . . . Ps. 145:4

B. Times of:
　　Daily . . . . Ps. 72:15
　　Continually . . . . Ps. 71:6
　　Seven times daily . . . . Ps. 119:164
　　All the day . . . . Ps. 35:28
　　At midnight . . . . Ps. 119:62; Acts 16:25
　　While I live. . . . . Ps. 146:2

Praise of people
A. Worthy:
　　From another. . . . . Prov. 27:2
For:
　　Faithfulness. . . . . Prov. 31:28
　　Obedience . . . . .Rom. 13:3
　　Works . . . . Prov. 31:31
B. Unworthy for:
　　Wicked . . . . .Prov. 28:4
　　Disorder . . . . 1 Cor. 11:17, 22
　　Self-seeking . . . . John 12:43

Prating—*foolish babbling*
Descriptive of:
　　Fool . . . . .Prov. 10:8, 10
　　Diotrephes . . . . 3 John 10

PRAY, *sha'al* (shaw-*al*). *Sha'al* is a verb that can be translated "pray," "ask," or "inquire." To ask for something from God is to pray. In Jon. 4:8 Jonah prayed for death. Job refused to ask or pray for a curse on the life of another (Job 31:30). One can ask for something as a favor from another person, a temporary borrowing (Ex. 22:13, 14). In the weakest sense, *sha'al* is "to look for," "desire," or "beg" as appears in Prov. 20:4. "To inquire" is to ask for information from someone as Esau did of Jacob's servants in Gen. 32:17. *Sha'al* is used to indicate when someone consults either a deity or an oracle. In Josh. 9:14 the Israelites failed to consult with God before making a treaty with the men of Gibeon. The term is also used in Is. 65:1 as God condemns the people for not seeking Him. (Strong's #7592)

Prayer—*a request to God*
A. Kinds of:
　　Secret. . . . . Matt. 6:6
　　Group . . . . Matt. 18:20
　　Public. . . . . Acts 12:12; 21:5, 6
　　Agreement . . . . Matt. 18:19
B. Parts of:
　　Adoration. . . . . .Dan. 4:34, 35
　　Confession . . . . 1 John 1:9
　　Supplication. . . . . .Acts 1:14; 1 Tim. 2:1–3
　　Intercession . . . . 1 Tim. 2:1–3; James 5:14, 15
　　Thanksgiving . . . . Phil. 4:6
C. Personal conditions of:
　　Purity of heart. .Ps. 66:18, 19
　　Faith. . . . . Matt. 21:22
　　In Jesus' name . . . . John 14:13
　　According to God's will . . . . 1 John 5:14
D. General conditions of:
　　Forgiving spirit. . . . . .Matt. 6:14

Humility and repentance......... Luke 18:10–14
Unity of believers............... Matt. 18:19, 20
Tenacity ....Luke 18:1–8
Persistence ....Luke 11:5–8
Intensity .... Matt. 7:7–11
Confident expectation .... Mark 11:24
Without empty phrases ....Matt. 6:7
Unceasingly.......................1 Thess. 5:17

E. Answers refused, because of:
Sin..................................Ps. 66:18
Selfishness ....James 4:3
Doubt ....James 1:5–7
Lawlessness ....Prov. 28:9
Inhumanity ....Prov. 21:13
Pride .... Luke 18:11, 12, 14
Pretense...........................Mark 12:40

F. Posture for:
Standing............................. Neh. 9:5
Kneeling...........................1 Kin. 8:54
Sitting .... 1 Chr. 17:16–27
Bowing ....Ex. 34:8
Hands uplifted .... 1 Tim. 2:8

Prayer meetings
In the Upper Room .... Acts 1:13, 14
In a house ....Acts 12:5–17
By a river....................... Acts 16:13
On a beach ....Acts 21:5

Prayers of Christ
A. Their nature:
Adoration......................Matt. 11:25–27
Intercession ....John 17:1–26
Thanksgiving ....John 11:41, 42

B. Their great occasions:
At His baptism ....Luke 3:21, 22
Before selecting the apostles ....Luke 6:12–16
When teaching how to pray........ Matt. 6:9–13
At His transfiguration .... Luke 9:28, 29
Following Last Supper ....John 17:1–26
In Gethsemane .... Matt. 26:36–42

C. Their times and places:
Early in morning.....................Mark 1:35
In secret.........................Luke 5:16; 9:18
With others .... Luke 11:1
On mountain..................... Matt. 14:23

Preach, preaching—*proclaiming the gospel*
A. Of the gospel:
Necessity of .... 1 Cor. 9:16
Without charge..................... 1 Cor. 9:18
Extent of, to all ....Col. 1:28
Only one...........................Gal. 1:8, 9
Centers in the Cross................. 1 Cor. 1:23
Preacher's importance in .... Rom. 10:14, 15

B. Attitudes toward:
Accepted..........................Luke 11:32
Rejected .... 2 Pet. 2:4, 5
Not perfected by..................... Heb. 4:2
Perverted .... Gal. 1:6–9
Contentious about ....Phil. 1:15–18

Counted foolishness ....1 Cor. 1:18–21
Ridiculed ....Acts 17:16–18
Not ashamed of.....................Rom. 1:15, 16

Preacher—*one who proclaims publicly*
Author of Ecclesiastes............... Eccl. 1:1, 2
Causes to hear.....................Rom. 10:14
Paul, speaking of himself... 1 Tim. 2:7; 2 Tim. 1:11
Noah, of righteousness ....2 Pet. 2:5

WORD STUDY · **PRECEPT**, *piqud* (pik-*kood*). To oversee or charge is to appoint or give a mandate. The noun *piqud*, coming from the verb that means "oversee," means "that which is appointed, a mandate of God" and is translated "command," "precept," or "statute." The word is always used to refer to a mandate of God, never a human rule. The word is also found only in the Ps., usually in the plural form, and is therefore rather rare. In Ps. 19:8 the psalmist says that the statutes of the Lord are a cause for rejoicing. Ps. 103 tells of God's goodness to those who keep His commandments. The word appears most often in Ps. 119, where the precepts must be understood and be the subject of meditation. (Strong's #6490)

Precepts—*specific charges; commandments*
God's:
Commanded .... Heb. 9:19
Corrupted.......................... Matt. 15:9
Kept...........................Ps. 119:56–69
Sought..........................Ps. 119:40–94
Not forgotten................... Ps. 119:93, 141
Loved...........................Ps. 119:159
Source of understanding .... Ps. 119:100, 104
See Traditions

Precious—*something extremely valuable*
A. Applied to spiritual things:
Wisdom ....Prov. 3:13, 15
One's life...........................1 Sam. 26:21;
2 Kin. 1:13, 14
Redemption of a soul.................... Ps. 49:8
God's thoughts to us ....Ps. 139:17
Death of God's people.................. Ps. 72:14
Christ.............................. Is. 28:16
Christ's blood ....1 Pet. 1:19
Faith................................2 Pet. 1:1
Promises ....2 Pet. 1:4
Trial of faith ....1 Pet. 1:7

B. Applied figuratively to:
Knowledge.......................Prov. 20:15
Sons of Zion........................Lam. 4:2
Rewards ....1 Cor. 3:12–14
Final harvest .... James 5:7
Worldly pomp ....Rev. 17:4
Heaven's glory....................Rev. 21:11, 19

Precious promises
A. To those troubled by:
Doubts........................... Ps. 73:1–28
Afflictions .... Ps. 34:1–22
Persecution...................... Matt. 5:11, 12

Anxiety .... Phil. 4:6
Temptation .... 1 Cor. 10:13
Infirmities ....2 Cor. 12:7–10
Discipline ....Heb. 12:3–13
B. To the sorrowful over:
Death...................... 1 Thess. 4:13–18
Sickness.........................James 5:13–16
Their sins ....Ps. 32:1–11
Disappointment ....Rom. 8:28
C. To those tested by:
World........................ 1 John 2:15–17
Flesh......................... Gal. 5:16–18
Satan ....Luke 22:31, 32
Worry .... Matt. 6:31–34
Sin...........................James 1:12–15
Pride .... 1 Pet. 5:5–7
D. To the active Christian in his:
Giving .... Mal. 3:10
Zeal .... Phil. 4:13
Soul winning ....James 5:20
Fruitfulness ....John 7:38, 39
Graces .... 2 Pet. 1:5–11
Prayers........................... James 5:16
Perseverance ....Gal. 6:9
Watchfulness......................Eph. 6:10–20
Assurance....................... Rom. 8:32–39
Ministry ....Ps. 138:8

Predestination—*God's eternal plan*
A. Described as:
"Purpose"...........................Rom. 8:28
"Prepared beforehand"...............Rom. 9:23
"Foreknowledge" .... Acts 2:23
"Foreknew" ....Rom. 8:29
"Appointed".................. Acts 13:48; 22:10
"Determined" ....Luke 22:22
"Foreseeing"........................Gal. 3:8
"Before time began"................2 Tim. 1:9
B. Determined by God's:
Counsel.......................... Acts 2:23
Foreknowledge .... Acts 2:23
Good pleasure.......... Luke 12:32; 1 Cor. 1:21
Will .... Eph. 1:5, 9, 11
Purpose...........................Eph. 3:11
Power...............Is. 40:10–17; Rom. 9:15–24
C. Expressed toward the believer in:
Election............................Eph. 1:4
Salvation.......................2 Thess. 2:13, 14
Justification.......................Rom. 8:30
Sanctification ....2 Thess. 2:12, 13
Glorification ....Rom. 8:30
Eternal destiny .... Matt. 25:34
See Foreknowledge of God; Elect

Predict—*to foretell*
Astrologers...........................Is. 47:13

Preeminence—*being supreme above all*
A. Of creatures:
Sought by the devil.................Is. 14:12–15
Sought by humankind...............Gen. 3:5, 6

Illustrated by Diotrephes .... 3 John 9, 10
B. Of Christ:
Predicted ....Ps. 45:6, 7
Proclaimed.....................Luke 1:31–33
Visualized........................ Matt. 17:4, 5
Realized ....Col. 1:19
Acknowledged...................... Phil. 2:9, 10

Pregnancy
Safeguards provided .... Ex. 21:22–25
Evidences of........................Luke 1:44
God's call during ....Jer. 1:4, 5; Gal. 1:15

Prejudice—*a biased opinion*
A. Toward others, based on:
Race............................... Acts 19:34
Social position....................James 2:1–4
Jealousy..........................Gen. 37:3–11
B. Toward Christ, based on His:
Lowly origin.......................Mark 6:3
Residence in Galilee .... John 1:46
Race................................ John 4:9
Teaching.......................John 9:16–41
See Bigotry

Premeditation—*deliberate plan to perform an act*
With:
Evil intent....................... Gen. 27:41–45
Good intent .... Luke 14:28–33
Heavenly sanctions ....James 4:13–17

Preparation Day
Evening.......................... Matt. 27:57, 62
Day before Sabbath ......Mark 15:42; Luke 23:54

Prepare—*to make ready*
A. Of spiritual things:
To build an altar.....................Josh. 22:26
God .... Amos 4:12
God's throne .... Ps. 9:7
Heart.............................Ezra 7:10
The way of the Lord........... Is. 40:3; Matt. 3:3
Passover ....Luke 22:8, 9
Spiritual provision .... Ps. 23:5
Service........................... 2 Tim. 2:21
Redeemed people .... Rom. 9:23, 24
Blessings .... 1 Cor. 2:9
B. Of eternal things:
Reward .... Matt. 20:23
Kingdom......................... Matt. 25:34
Heaven ....John 14:2, 3
Heavenly city..............Heb. 11:16; Rev. 21:2
Everlasting fire .... Matt. 25:41

Presbytery—*the Christian eldership acting as a body*
Ordination ascribed to .... 1 Tim. 4:14
See Elders in the church

Presence, divine
Described as:
Majesty ....1 Chr. 16:27
Joyful.............................. Ps. 16:11
Protective ....Ps. 31:20; 91:1–16
Everywhere ....Ps. 139:7

Guide............................ Ex. 33:14, 15
Refreshing ....Acts 3:19

Present, present to—*to offer*
A. As an introduction of:
Joseph's brothers to Pharaoh.......... Gen. 47:2
Joseph to his father ....Gen. 46:29
Dorcas to her friends.................. Acts 9:41
Saul to the apostles.................Acts 9:26, 27
Paul to a governor.................... Acts 23:33
B. Descriptive of the Christian's life as:
Living and holy sacrifice...............Rom. 12:1
Chaste virgin........................ 2 Cor. 11:2
Holy.................................Col. 1:22
Perfect..............................Col. 1:28
Without blemish..................... Eph. 5:27
Resurrected .... 2 Cor. 4:14

Presents—*gifts*
A. Offered to:
Brother .... Gen. 32:13–20
King................................. Is. 39:1
Foreign nation....................... Hos. 10:6
Baby Jesus......................... Matt. 2:1–11
B. Purposes of:
Secure a message...................2 Kin. 8:7–10
Show friendship .... 2 Kin. 20:12, 13
Show obedience ....Ps. 72:10
Show reverence ....Ps. 76:11
See Gifts of humankind

Preservation, God's
A. As manifested over:
World............................... Neh. 9:6
King......................... 2 Sam. 8:6, 14
Animals................................Ps. 36:6
Nation...........................Gen. 45:5, 7
Messiah.............................. Is. 49:8
Apostle .... 2 Tim. 4:18
Believers ....1 Thess. 5:23
Faithful.............................Ps. 31:23
B. Special objects of:
Those who trust Him .... Ps. 16:1
Holy.................................Ps. 86:2
Souls of saints .... Ps. 97:10
Simple .... Ps. 116:6
Those who love Him ....Ps. 145:20
C. Spiritual means of:
Integrity ....Ps. 25:21
Lovingkindness ....Ps. 40:11
Mercy and truth ....Ps. 61:7
Wisdom ....Prov. 4:5, 6
Losing one's life ....Luke 17:33
Prophet ....Hos. 12:13

WORD STUDY   **PRESERVE,** *shamar* (shaw-mar). *Shamar* is a verb seen throughout the OT, meaning "keep," "watch," or "preserve." To keep is to have charge of something, as Adam and Eve had charge of the Garden. It can mean to tend a flock, also. *Shamar* may imply guarding either captives or one's

mouth (Prov. 21:23) and can therefore be used to mean "protect" or "save" (Job 2:6; Prov. 13:3). The watchman of a city is the keeper. The second major meaning of *shamar* is "to retain" as one stores up food (Gen. 41:35). One can also keep something or store it in memory (Prov. 4:21). Keeping can involve celebrating or observing a festival, the Sabbath, or a covenant. There are many references in which God is the one doing the keeping. In those cases God is preserving and protecting as He promises Jacob in Gen. 28:15. Ps. 91:11 is one of the verses quoted by the devil during Jesus' temptation (see Matt. 4:6; Luke 4:10); it says that God "will give His angels charge over you, to keep you," probably one of the most familiar uses of the term. (Strong's #8104)

Pressure—*force exerted*
A. As evil:
Perversion........................... Gen. 19:9
Enticement.........................Judg. 16:16
B. As a good, to:
Hear God's Word..................... Luke 5:1
Get into the kingdom .... Luke 16:16
Attain a goal .... Phil. 3:14

Presumption—*to speak or act without warrant*
A. Manifested in:
Speaking without divine warrant ...Deut. 18:20–22
Acting without God's presence....Num. 14:44, 45
Living without God.............. Luke 12:19–21
Performing functions without
authority ....Num. 16:3–11
Supposing God will not judge sin..... Ps. 73:8–12
Aspiring to divine titles ....Is. 14:12–15
Posing as righteous ....Luke 18:11, 12
Making plans without God ....James 4:13, 14
Self-will............................2 Pet. 2:10
B. Judgment upon:
Defeat ....Is. 37:23–36
Loss of power.......................Judg. 16:20
Quick punishment.................. 2 Sam. 6:6, 7
Rejection.......................1 Sam. 15:3, 9–23
Destruction ....Lev. 10:1, 2

Pretense—*a false or counterfeit profession*
Pharisees condemned for .... Matt. 23:14
Christ preached in truth or .... Phil. 1:18

Prevail—*to get the mastery over*
A. Of physical force:
Waters.......................Gen. 7:18–24
Combat........................... 1 Sam. 17:50
B. Of supernatural force in:
Battle..............................Ex. 17:11
Combat........................ 1 Sam. 17:9, 50
Accomplish much................. 1 Sam. 26:25
Conquest........................... Jer. 20:7
Victory ....Rev. 5:5
Success of Christ's church .... Matt. 16:18, 19

Prevarication—*evasion of truth*
Ananias and Sapphira killed for...... Acts 5:1–10

Solemn warning against . . . . .Col. 3:9

Subject to second death. . . . . .Rev. 21:8

Prey—*that which is taken by attack*

Used figuratively of:

Enemies. . . . . Gen. 49:9

Innocent victims. . . . . Ezek. 22:27

Pride—*a conceited sense of one's superiority*

A. Origin of, in:

Devil . . . . .Is. 14:13–15

Ambition . . . . Dan. 5:20–23

Evil heart . . . . Mark 7:21, 22

World. . . . . .1 John 2:16

Self-righteousness . . . . .Luke 18:11, 12

Worldly power. . . . . Ezek. 16:49, 56

B. Evils of:

Hardens the mind . . . . Dan. 5:20

Produces spiritual decay. . . . . Hos. 7:9, 10

Keeps from real progress . . . . .Prov. 26:12

Hinders coming to God . . . . Ps. 10:4

Issues in self-deception. . . . . Jer. 49:16

Makes people reject God's Word . . . . Jer. 43:2

Leads to ruin . . . . .Prov. 16:18

Hated by the Lord . . . . .Prov. 6:16, 17

Deserving of death. . . . . Rom. 1:28–32

C. Characteristic of:

Wicked . . . . .Ps. 73:6

World rulers. . . . . Hab. 2:4, 5

Last days. . . . . 2 Tim. 3:2

WORD STUDY

PRIEST, *cohen* (koh-*hayn*). There are frequent references throughout the OT to "priests," which translates the noun *cohen*. One of the earliest references is to Melchizedek, a priest/king of Salem who aids Abraham. He becomes a figure of legend and is referred to in other passages (Ps. 110:4). There are also other examples of a king or chief acting as priest (Ex. 2:16; 2 Sam. 8:18). The word can refer to priests serving other gods, such as Baal and Chemosh, so that one can see the word indicates a religious function, not an Israelite position. The most numerous references are to priests serving the true God, YHWH. Among these are Aaronic priests, which include all the males in Aaron's family, Levitical priests sometimes appearing in the phrase "priests and Levites," Zadokite priests who are mentioned by Ezekiel and elsewhere, also, and the most specific position of high priest. The duties of the priests are carefully laid out in the Mosaic Law, and the other references usually occur when telling how some priest went about his duties. (Strong's #3548)

Priest, Levitical

A. Requirements of:

Must be a son of Aaron . . . . .Ex. 29:9

Sanctified to office. . . . . Ex. 29:44

Statute perpetual .Ex. 27:21

No physical blemish. . . . . Lev. 21:17–23

Genealogy of, necessary . . . . Ezra 2:62

B. Duties of:

Keeping the sanctuary . . . . Num. 3:38

Keep lamp burning continually . . . . . Ex. 27:20, 21

Continuing the sacred fire. . . . . Lev. 6:12, 13

Covering furniture when moved . . . .Num. 4:5–15

Burning incense . . . . .Ex. 30:7, 8

Offering sacrifices . . . . .Lev. 1:1–17

Blessing the people. . . . . .Num. 6:23–27

Purifying the unclean . . . . Lev. 15:15–31

Diagnosing leprosy . . . . Lev. 13:2–59

Blowing the trumpets . . . . Num. 10:1–10

Carrying the ark of the covenant. . . . .Josh. 3:6–17

Teaching the Law. . . . . .Lev. 10:11

C. Names of:

Aaron. . . . . .Ex. 31:10

Abiathar . . . . 1 Sam. 23:9

Ahimelech . . . . 1 Sam. 22:11

Amariah . . . . .2 Chr. 19:11

Ananias. . . . . Acts 23:2

Caiaphas. . . . . Matt. 26:3

Eleazar. . . . . Num. 16:39

Eli. . . . . .1 Sam. 1:9

Eliashib . . . . Neh. 3:1

Ezekiel. . . . . .Ezek. 1:3

Ezra . . . . Ezra 7:11, 12

Hilkiah . . . . .2 Kin. 22:4

Jehoiada . . . . 2 Kin. 11:9

Jehozadak. . . . . Hag. 1:1

Joshua . . . . .Zech. 3:1

Maaseiah . . . . .Jer. 37:3

Pashhur. . . . . .Jer. 20:1

Phinehas. . . . . .Josh. 22:30

Sceva . . . . .Acts 19:14

Seraiah . . . . .2 Kin. 25:18

Shelemiah. . . . . Neh. 13:13

Urijah . . . . .2 Kin. 16:10

Zabud . . . . .1 Kin. 4:5

Zacharias . . . . Luke 1:5

Zadok . . . . 2 Sam. 15:27

Zephaniah . . . . .2 Kin. 25:18

See Levites

Priest, Non-Levitical

Believing:

Melchizedek . . . . Heb. 7:1

Christ. . . . . Heb. 3:1

Jethro, priest of Midian . . . . .Ex. 3:1

Pagan:

Poti-Pherah, priest of On . . . . .Gen. 41:45, 50

Mattan (of Baal) . . . . 2 Kin. 11:18

Priesthood of believers

Typical of Israel . . . . .1 Pet. 2:9

Predicted in prophecy. . . . . .Is. 61:6

Including all believers. . . . . .Rev. 1:5, 6

Having access to God . . . . Eph. 2:18

Body as a living sacrifice . . . . .Rom. 12:1

Spiritual sacrifices . . . . .1 Pet. 2:5

Praise and good works . . . . .Heb. 13:15, 16

Deeds of kindness . . . . Phil. 4:18

Priesthood of Christ

A. Superior to Aaron as:

Man; Christ the Son of God .... Heb. 7:28

Sinner; Christ, sinless .... Heb. 7:26, 27

Typical; Christ's the fulfillment....... Heb. 8:1–6

Subject to change; Christ's

unchangeable .... Heb. 7:23, 24

Imperfect; Christ's perfect......... Heb. 7:11, 25

B. Christ as priest:

Satisfies God's justice .... Rom. 3:24–28

Pacifies God's wrath .... Rom. 5:9

Justifies the sinner .... Rom. 5:1

Sanctifies the believer............... 1 Cor. 1:30

Seated at right hand of God............ Heb. 8:1

Mediator of a better covenant.......... Heb. 8:6

Obtained eternal redemption for

believers......................... Heb. 9:12

See High priest

Prince—*a ruler*

A. Descriptive of:

Ruler .... Judg. 5:15

Head or captain .... Ex. 2:14

Noble or volunteer .... Ps. 47:9

Satan .... John 14:30; Eph. 2:2

B. Of the Messiah:

Of David's line .... Ezek. 34:23, 24

Reign of, forever .... Ezek. 37:24, 25

Time of, determined .... Dan. 9:25, 26

Reign of, peaceful...................... Is. 9:6

Author of life........................ Acts 3:15

Exalted to be Savior .... Acts 5:31

Principalities—*rulers*

Created by Christ..................... Col. 1:16

Subject to Christ.................. Eph. 1:20, 21

Beholders of God's redemption .... Eph. 3:10

Overcome by Christ.................... Col. 2:15

Fighting against Christians........... Eph. 6:12

Powerless against Christians.......... Rom. 8:38

Principles—*elementary Christian truths*

To be maintained.................. 1 Tim. 5:21

Christians must go beyond .... Heb. 5:12; 6:1

Print—*a recognizable sign*

On the hands, desired.............. John 20:25

Forbidden........................... Lev. 19:28

Priscilla, Prisca

Wife of Aquila...................... Acts 18:1–3

An instructed Christian .... Acts 18:26

One of Paul's helpers................. Rom. 16:3

Greetings sent from................ 1 Cor. 16:19

Timothy commanded to greet .... 2 Tim. 4:19

Prison—*place of confinement*

A. Place of:

Hard labor .... Judg. 16:21, 25

Confinement......................... Jer. 52:11

Guards.............................. Acts 12:3–6

Stocks .... Acts 16:23, 24

Torture .... Acts 22:24, 25

Execution .... Matt. 14:10

B. Notable occupants of:

Joseph .... Gen. 40:2, 3

Micaiah...................... 1 Kin. 22:26–28

Jeremiah .... Jer. 32:2, 8, 12

Hanani .... 2 Chr. 16:7–10

Zedekiah........................... Jer. 52:11

John the Baptist .... Luke 3:20

Apostles .... Acts 5:18, 19

Peter............................. Acts 12:1–4

Paul .... Acts 16:24

Silas .... Acts 16:25

See Imprisonment

Prisoners—*those confined to jails*

A. Used literally of:

Criminals .... Matt. 27:15, 16

Christians.................... Eph. 4:1; Col. 4:10

B. Used figuratively of:

Gentiles............................. Is. 42:6, 7

Those in spiritual darkness .... Is. 49:9;

Zech. 9:11, 12

Righteous in their need......... Ps. 69:33; 79:11;

146:7, 8

Privileges of believers

Access to God .... Rom. 5:2

Christ's intercession............... Heb. 7:25, 26

Eternal life .... John 17:2, 3

Growth assured...................... 1 Pet. 2:2

Holy Spirit as the Helper ... John 15:26; 16:13–15

Intercession of the Spirit.......... Rom. 8:26, 27

Kinship with Christ................. Heb. 2:10–14

Membership in God's kingdom ..... 1 Cor. 6:9–11

Names written in Book of Life .... Rev. 20:15

Partakers of the divine nature .... 2 Pet. 1:4

Prayers answered .... John 16:23

Reconciled to God .... Rom. 5:10

Suffering with Christ .... Acts 5:41

Trials overcome .... 1 Pet. 1:6–8

Victorious living................. Rom. 8:37–39

Privileges of Israel

A. Consisted of:

Chosen by God .... Deut. 7:6–8

Entrusted with God's revelation ...... Rom. 3:1, 2

Blessings bestowed upon .... Rom. 9:4, 5

Messiah (Christ).................. Acts 2:22–39

Gospel first preached to .... Acts 3:18–26

B. Lost because of:

Unbelief .... Matt. 8:10–12

Spiritual hardness .... John 12:37–40

Spiritual blindness .... John 9:39–41

C. Now given to:

Gentiles........................... Matt. 21:43

Faithful remnant .... Rom. 11:1–7

Church .... 1 Pet. 2:5–10

Prize—*a reward for faithful accomplishment*

A. Described as crown of:

Righteousness...................... 2 Tim. 4:8

Glory .... 1 Pet. 5:4

Life................................ James 1:12

B. Factors involved in obtaining:

Self-control...................... 1 Cor. 9:24–27

Following the rules .... 2 Tim. 2:5

Pressing toward....................... Phil. 3:14

Enduring temptation................ James 1:12

Looking to Jesus.................... Heb. 12:1, 2

Loving His appearing .... 2 Tim. 4:8

Probation—*a period of testing*

A. Factors determining:

God's promises .... Matt. 21:33–43

Specific time .... Dan. 9:24–27

Faith or unbelief... Acts 13:32–48; Rom. 10:1–21

B. None after death:

No change permitted................ Luke 16:26

Judgment final .... Rev. 20:11–15

Destinies eternally fixed............ Matt. 25:46

Prochorus—*leader in a dance*

One of the seven deacons ....Acts 6:5

WORD STUDY

PROCLAIM, *kērussō* (kay-*roos*-oh). This verb means "to proclaim (aloud)," and it was originally used to designate the activity of a herald (*kērux*), whose duty was to make public proclamations on behalf of a government official (e.g., the emperor). *Kērussō* is also used with respect to the religious proclamations of prophets and preachers, and it is sometimes translated as "preach" (Acts 15:21; Gal. 5:11). In the NT *kērussō* usually appears with an object to indicate the content of the proclamation; for example, baptism for the repentance of sins (Luke 3:3); the kingdom of God (Luke 8:1); the gospel (Acts 1:2); and Christ (Acts 8:5; 1 Cor. 15:12). (Strong's #2784)

Proclaim—*to officially announce*

A. Physical objects of:

Idolatrous feast...................... Ex. 32:4, 5

Holy convocation .... Lev. 23:2, 4, 21

Year of Jubilee .... Lev. 25:10

Fast................................2 Chr. 20:3

Release .... Jer. 34:17

Peace .... Is. 52:7

Doom............................ Jer. 4:15, 16

B. Spiritual objects of:

God's name ....Ex. 33:19

God's Word ....Jer. 3:12

Salvation........................... Is. 62:11

Procrastination—*putting off something*

A. Manifested in:

Delaying a decision .... Matt. 19:16–22

Putting other things first......... Luke 9:59–62

Presuming on tomorrow.............. Prov. 27:1

Postponing service...............2 Cor. 8:10–14

Rejecting reproof .... Prov. 29:1

B. Evils of, missing:

Salvation........................... 2 Cor. 6:1

Life's importance .... Eccl. 12:1

God's opportunity .... Jer. 13:16

Prodigal son

Parable concerning ....Luke 15:11–32

Profane—*to act or speak irreverently of holy things; defile*

A. Manifested in:

Breaking God's Law.................. Amos 2:7

Defiling God's house................ Mal. 1:12, 13

Not observing the Sabbath .... Neh. 13:17, 18

Committing abominations .... Mal. 2:10, 11

Idolatry ....Lev. 18:21

Swearing falsely ....Lev. 19:12

Illegal marriages.................Lev. 21:14, 15

Blemished service............... Lev. 21:21–23

Idle words......................... 2 Tim. 2:16

B. Punishment of:

Excommunication ....Lev. 19:8

Death............................Lev. 21:9

Destruction .... Ezek. 28:16

Profession—*to declare one's faith publicly*

Harmful .... 1 Tim. 6:20, 21

Inconsistent........................Titus 1:16

Degrading ....Rom. 1:22

Tragic .... Matt. 7:23

Profit—*gain*

A. Things empty of:

Wickedness ....Prov. 10:2

Riches .... Prov. 11:4

Labor without God .... Eccl. 2:11

Lying words ....Jer. 7:8

World............................. Matt. 16:26

Flesh.............................. John 6:63

Word without faith .... Heb. 4:2

Mere profession ....James 2:14, 16

B. Things full of:

Spiritual gifts........................ 1 Cor. 12:7

Godliness .... 1 Tim. 4:8

Inspired Word.......................2 Tim. 3:16

Good works ....Titus 3:8

Love.............................. 1 Cor. 13:3

Prognosticators—*those who profess to know the future*

Help from, vain..................... Is. 47:13–15

Prohibition—*restraint placed against evil tendencies*

A. Against:

Idolatry...........................1 John 5:21

Drunkenness......................Luke 21:34

Uncleanness...................... Eph. 4:18, 19

Worldliness .... 1 John 2:15–17

B. Based upon:

Sanctity of the body.............. 1 Cor. 6:13–20

New life in Christ...................Col. 3:1–10

God's holiness .... 1 Pet. 1:14–16

WORD STUDY

PROMISE, *epaggelia* (ep-ang-el-*ee*-ah). This noun, originally meaning "announcement," later took on the meaning of "promise," "pledge." In the NT it is always used in the sense of "promise," predominantly with reference to God's promises, such as His "promise" to Abraham (Acts

7:17; cf. Rom. 9:9), the "promise" of the Holy Spirit (Acts 1:4, 5; 2:33, 39; Gal. 3:14), or the "promise" of eternal life (1 John 2:25; cf. Heb. 9:15). (Strong's #1860)

Promises of God

A. Described as:

Never failing . . . . Josh. 23:5–15; 1 Kin. 8:56

Backed by God's oath . . . . .Heb. 6:12–20

Fulfilled on schedule . . . . . . .Acts 7:6, 17; Gal. 4:4

Given to Israel . . . . .Rom. 9:4

Confirmed by Christ . . . . .Rom. 15:8

Kept by faith . . . . .Rom. 4:20, 21; Heb. 11:13–40

Centered in Christ . . . . 2 Cor. 1:20; 2 Tim. 1:1

Exceedingly great . . . . .2 Pet. 1:4

Not slow . . . . 2 Pet. 3:4–13

B. Objects of, for Israel:

Land of Palestine . . . . .Acts 7:5; Heb. 11:9

Davidic kingship . . . . 2 Chr. 6:10–16

Messiah . . . . .Acts 13:23–33

Gospel . . . . Acts 10:43

New heart . . . . .Jer. 31:33

C. Objects of, for Christians:

Holy Spirit . . . . .Luke 24:49

Salvation . . . . Acts 2:39

Kingdom . . . . James 2:5

Life eternal . . . . .Titus 1:2

Crown of life . . . . James 1:12

New earth . . . . .2 Pet. 3:13

See Messiah, the

Promises to believers (see Privileges of believers)

Promotion—*advancement in status*

Deserved . . . . Gen. 41:38–42

Desirable . . . . Prov. 4:8

Divine . . . . .Ps. 75:6, 7

Despicable . . . . Num. 22:17, 37

Property—*material possessions*

Acquired by:

Industry . . . . Gen. 31:36–42

Inheritance . . . . Eccl. 2:21

Purchase . . . . .Gen. 23:7–20

Deception . . . . .1 Kin. 21:1–16

See Ownership

WORD STUDY **PROPHECY,** *prophēteia* (prof-ay-*teye*-ah). This noun, meaning "prophecy," is the designation for the revelation of God's words or plans (either for the present or the future) to others. This word may be used with reference to prophetic activity (Rev. 11:6), to the gift of prophecy or prophesying (Rom. 12:6; 1 Cor. 12:10), or to the utterances of prophets (i.e., the "prophecies" themselves), whether they be Jewish (Matt. 13:14) or Christian (Rev. 1:3; 22:7, 10, 18, 19). (Strong's #4394)

Prophecy—*inspired foretelling of events*

A. Characteristics of:

Given by God . . . . .Is. 41:22, 23

Centered in Christ . . . . Luke 24:26, 27, 44

Inspired by the Spirit . . . . .2 Pet. 1:21

Not of one's own interpretation . . . . 2 Pet. 1:20

Brings blessings . . . . .Rev. 1:3

Always relevant . . . . .Rev. 22:10

Must not be changed by anyone . . . . Rev. 22:18, 19

B. True, based on:

Inspiration . . . . Mic. 3:8

Foreknowledge . . . . Is. 42:9

C. False, evidenced by:

Nonfulfillment . . . . Jer. 28:1–17

Peaceful message . . . . Jer. 23:17–22

Apostasy from God . . . . Deut. 13:1–5

Lying . . . . .Jer. 23:25–34

D. Fulfillment of:

Unconditional . . . . .Ezek. 12:25–28

Sometimes:

Conditional . . . . .Jon. 3:1–10

Dated . . . . Dan. 9:24–27

Nonliteral . . . . Matt. 17:10–12

Unrecognized by Jews . . . . .Acts 13:27–29

Interpretation of, needed . . . . Luke 24:25–44

Often referred to . . . . Matt. 1:22, 23; 2:14–23

WORD STUDY **PROPHET,** *nabi'* (naw-*bee*). One of the words translated "prophet" in the OT is the noun *nabi'.* This term refers to one who is a speaker or spokesman for a deity, not to one who predicts the future, although sometimes a prophet does predict future events. The prophets of God, of which there are several types, are mentioned most often. Prophets could work independently or in bands, a type of guild (1 Kin. 20:35). These men were professional prophets, and the most familiar examples are Nathan and Samuel. After the temple was built, there seems to have been a group of prophets attached to the temple area. Amos claims that he is not a prophet, indicating that he was not a professional prophet but one called out by God for a special task. Isaiah, on the other hand, was a professional prophet. Not all prophets spoke God's word. Sometimes true prophets pointed out the message of false prophets as in Is. 28:7 and Jer. 2:26. At other times, prophets claimed that those men not only carried the occasional false message, but that they were not true prophets ever (see Hos. 4:5). The prophets of other deities are mentioned throughout the OT, but especially in the historic literature where the prophets of Baal and Asherah are common. (Strong's #5030)

Prophetess—*a female prophet*

A. Good:

Miriam . . . . Ex. 15:20, 21

Deborah . . . . .Judg. 4:4, 5

Huldah . . . . 2 Kin. 22:12–20

Isaiah's wife . . . . Is. 8:1–3

Anna . . . . .Luke 2:36

Daughters of Philip . . . . Acts 21:8, 9

Prophecy concerning . . . . .Joel 2:28

B. False:

Women of Judah .Ezek. 13:17

Noadiah	Neh. 6:14
Jezebel	Rev. 2:20

Prophets—*inspired messengers*
A. Described as:

God's servants	Zech. 1:6
God's messengers	2 Chr. 36:15
Holy prophets	Luke 1:70
Holy men	2 Pet. 1:21
Watchmen	Ezek. 3:17
Prophets of God	Ezra 5:2
False	Mark 13:22

B. Message of:

Centered in Christ	Luke 10:24
Interpreted by Christ	Luke 24:27, 44
United in testimony	Acts 3:21, 24
Contains grace and salvation	1 Pet. 1:9–12
Abiding revelation	Matt. 5:17, 18

Prophets, names of

Enoch	Gen. 5:21, 24
Noah	Gen. 9:25–27
Abraham	Gen. 20:1, 7
Jacob	Gen. 49:1
Aaron	Ex. 7:1
Moses	Deut. 18:18
Joshua	1 Kin. 16:34
One sent to Israel	Judg. 6:8–10
One sent to Eli	1 Sam. 2:27–36
Samuel	1 Sam. 3:20
David	Acts 2:25, 30
Nathan	2 Sam. 7:2
Zadok	2 Sam. 15:27
Gad	2 Sam. 24:11–14
Ahijah	1 Kin. 11:29
One of Judah	1 Kin. 13:1
Iddo	2 Chr. 9:29; 12:15
Shemaiah	2 Chr. 12:5, 7, 15
Azariah	2 Chr. 15:1–8
Hanani	2 Chr. 16:7–10
Jehu	1 Kin. 16:1, 7, 12
Elijah	1 Kin. 17:1
Elisha	1 Kin. 19:16
Micaiah	1 Kin. 22:7, 8
Jonah	2 Kin. 14:25
Isaiah	2 Kin. 19:2
Hosea	Hos. 1:1
Amos	Amos 1:1
Micah	Mic. 1:1
Oded	2 Chr. 28:9
Nahum	Nah. 1:1
Joel	Joel 1:1
Zephaniah	Zeph. 1:1
Jeduthun	2 Chr. 35:15
Jeremiah	2 Chr. 36:12, 21
Habakkuk	Hab. 1:1
Obadiah	Obad. 1
Ezekiel	Ezek. 1:3
Daniel	Matt. 24:15
Haggai	Ezra 5:1
Zechariah	Ezra 5:1; Zech. 1:1

Malachi	Mal. 1:1
Zacharias (same as Zechariah)	Luke 1:67
John the Baptist	Luke 7:26–28
Agabus	Acts 11:28
Paul	1 Tim. 4:1
Peter	2 Pet. 2:1, 2
John	Rev. 1:1
Judas	Acts 15:32
Silas	Acts 15:32

Prophets in the New Testament
A. Office of, based upon:

Christ's prophetic office	Deut. 18:15, 18
Old Testament prediction	Joel 2:28; Acts 2:18
Holy Spirit's coming	John 16:7, 13
Divine institution	1 Cor. 12:28

B. Functions of:

Strengthen	Acts 15:32
Define God's will	Acts 13:1–3
Predict the future	Acts 21:10, 11

> **WORD STUDY** **PROPITIATION, EXPIATION,** *hilasmos* (hil-ahs-*moss*). This noun occurs only twice in the NT, and both instances are in 1 John (2:2; 4:10). The basic meaning of *hilasmos* is "propitiation" or "expiation," that is, to appease the wrath caused by offensive actions by means of a sacrificial atonement. Thus, *hilasmos* implies the meaning "sin-offering." Jesus, according to 1 John, offered Himself to God as the "propitiation" for the sins of "the whole world" (2:2). See the cognate noun (Heb. 9:5) and verb (Luke 18:13; Heb. 2:17). (Strong's #2434)

Propitiation—*appeasing or conciliating*
Elements in Christ's:

Dying for others' sins	1 Pet. 1:18, 19
Satisfying God's justice	Rom. 3:25, 26
Reconciling God and humankind	2 Cor. 5:18, 19
Offering believing sinner perfect righteousness	2 Cor. 5:20, 21

Proselyte—*convert to Judaism*
A. Regulations imposed upon:

Circumcision	Gen. 17:13
Observance of the Law	Ex. 12:48, 49
Obedience to the covenant	Deut. 29:10–13
Association with Israel	Ruth 1:16
Separation from heathenism	Ezra 6:21
Participation in feasts	John 12:20–22; Acts 8:27

B. Special significance of:

Typical of Gentile converts	Is. 56:3–8
Concerned about Christ	John 12:20, 21
Among early converts	Acts 6:5
Source of Gentile church	Acts 13:42–46

Prosperity—*a state of material or spiritual bountifulness*
A. Kinds of:

Material	1 Cor. 16:2
National	Ezek. 16:13, 14
Personal	Dan. 6:28

Prostitute—*one engaged in promiscuous sexual activity*

Prostitution (see Harlot)

Protection, divine

Protector, divine

WORD STUDY

PROUD, ARROGANT, *hu per-ēphanos* (hoop-er-*ay*-fan-oss). This adjective is formed from *huper,* "over," and *phainomai,* "to appear" or "to make one's appearance." In the NT *huperēphanos* evokes the unsavory attitude of superiority and means "arrogant," "haughty," "proud." It is cataloged among other vices (Rom. 1:30; 2 Tim. 3:2),

and Jesus uses the cognate noun *huperē-phania,* "arrogance" or "pride," in a list of evil things that "come from within and defile" (Mark 7:22, 23). The "arrogant" are often contrasted to those who are "lowly" or "humble" (*tapeinos),* as in Luke 1:51, 52; James 4:6; and 1 Pet. 5:5. (Strong's #5244)

Proud—*the defiant and haughty*
See Pride

Prove—*to show something to be true*

WORD STUDY

PROVERB, *mashal* (maw-*shawl*). A *mashal* is a "proverb," or "short, pithy saying." Some of the proverbs appear as brief sayings with popular wisdom. These occur in various places in the OT, such as 1 Sam. 10:12 and Ezek. 12:22. The term can be translated "byword," something or someone who is commonly known (as in Ps. 44:14, 15). Proverbs can be part of prophetic figurative discourses as they are in Num. 23:7 and Is. 14:4 or parables used by prophets as in Ezek. 17:2. The most familiar proverbs are those poetic and didactic sayings traditionally ascribed to Solomon and found in the Book of Proverbs. These are generally found in couplets, a two-line form. (Strong's #4912)

Proverb—*a wise saying*

Proverbs, Book of—*a book of the Old Testament*

Proverbs of Agur and Lemuel . . . . . Prov. 30:1–31:9
The worthy woman . . . . Prov. 31:10–31

Providence—*divine guidance of people and things*
A. Described as:
Universal. . . . . Ps. 103:19
Purposive . . . . Gen. 45:5–8
Righteous. . . . . Ps. 145:17
Something mysterious. . . . . Job 11:7–9
Irresistible . . . . Dan. 4:35
B. Manifested, in the world, in God's:
Preserving the world . . . . Neh. 9:6
Providing for His possessions . . . . . . Ps. 104:27, 28
Guiding world events . . . . Acts 17:26, 27
Ruling over the elements . . . . Is. 50:2, 3
Preserving nature. . . . . Gen. 8:22
Ordering one's life . . . . Ps. 75:6, 7
Controlling minute details . . . . Matt. 10:29, 30
C. Attitude of believers toward:
Acknowledge in prosperity . . . . . . 1 Chr. 29:11, 12;
    Prov. 3:6
Humble himself before in
    adversity. . . . . Job 1:21; Ps. 119:75
Remember God's hand . . . . Ps. 37:1–40; 139:10

Province—*a governmental district*
A. Ruled by:
Governors. . . . . Esth. 3:12
Proconsuls . . . . Acts 13:4, 7
Kings. . . . . Esth. 1:1
B. Characteristics of:
Numerous. . . . . Esth. 1:1
Ruled by one man. . . . . Dan. 2:48, 49
Justice perverted in . . . . Eccl. 5:8
People, citizens of. . . . . Acts 23:34
News spreads to . . . . Esth. 9:4
C. Of the Roman Empire:
Achaia . . . . Acts 18:12
Asia . . . . Acts 19:10
Bithynia . . . . Acts 16:7
Cappadocia . . . . Acts 2:9
Cyprus. . . . . Acts 13:4
Egypt . . . . Matt. 2:13
Galatia. . . . . Acts 16:6
Judea . . . . Luke 1:5
Macedonia . . . . Acts 16:12
Pamphylia. . . . . Acts 13:13
Lycia. . . . . Acts 27:5
Syria. . . . . Matt. 4:24

Provision
Provide for own house. . . . . 1 Tim. 5:8
Provide for poor . . . . Is. 58:7

Provoke—*to agitate another's soul*
A. Between people:
Two women . . . . 1 Sam. 1:7
Peoples (nations). . . . . Rom. 10:19
Father and children . . . . Eph. 6:4
B. Causes of, between God and humankind:
Evil. . . . . Deut. 4:25
Sins. . . . . 1 Kin. 16:2

Harlotry . . . . Ezek. 16:26

Prudence—*wisdom applied to practical matters*
A. Characteristics of:
Dwells with wisdom . . . . Prov. 8:12
Observant. . . . . Prov. 14:15
Foresees evil. . . . . Prov. 22:3
Regards reproof . . . . Prov. 15:5
Acts with knowledge. . . . . Prov. 13:16
Crowned with knowledge . . . . Prov. 14:18
Keeps silent . . . . Amos 5:13
B. Descriptive of:
David. . . . . 1 Sam. 16:18
Solomon . . . . 2 Chr. 2:12
Messiah . . . . Is. 52:13
Wife. . . . . Prov. 19:14
Believers . . . . Hos. 14:9
Worldly wise . . . . Matt. 11:25
C. Examples of:
Jacob . . . . Gen. 32:3–23
Joseph . . . . Gen. 41:39–49
Gideon. . . . . Judg. 8:1–3

Prune—*to cut back plants for the purpose of producing*
    more growth
Vineyards. . . . . Lev. 25:3, 4
Figurative of God's care . . . . Is. 5:6; John 15:2
Hooks used for . . . . Is. 2:4; 18:5

 WORD STUDY   **PSALM,** *mizmor* (miz-*mohr*). "Psalm" is the usual translation for the noun *mizmor*, which indicates a melody. The word is derived from the verb, meaning "to make music." The context of the verb shows that the music is intended to praise God. Therefore, "psalm" is a technical designation for a poetic piece intended to be sung as praise to God. The term *mizmor* occurs fifty-seven times in titles to psalms, usually with a personal name or title. These phrases are generally translated "a psalm of David" or "a psalm of Asaph," but could just as well be translated "a psalm for David," and so on, indicating for whom they were written, rather than by whom they were written. Frequently the word "psalm" is preceded or followed by the word "song." The psalms are instrumental music, also, although we do not have the tunes to which they were played. (Strong's #4210)

WORD STUDY   **PSALM,** *psalmos* (psal-*moss*). In the NT this noun refers only to a "song of praise" or "psalm" (Heb. *mizmor*). It can be used with reference to one of the "songs of praise" from the Book of Psalms (as in Luke 20:42; 24:44; Acts 1:20; 13:33). *Psalmos* may also be used as a designation for Christian "songs of praise" (1 Cor. 14:26; Eph. 5:19; Col. 3:16). (Strong's #5568)

Psalm—*a spiritual song*
Some written by David . . . . 2 Sam. 23:1
Prophetic of Christ . . . . Luke 24:44
Used in worship . . . . Ps. 95:2
Used in church . . . . 1 Cor. 14:26

Psalms, Book of—*a book of the Old Testament*

Book I—The Genesis Book

    Concerning Man . . . . Ps. 1–41

Blessed are the righteous . . . . Ps. 1

The holy hill . . . . Ps. 15

God's creation . . . . Ps. 19

Messianic Psalm . . . . Ps. 22

Prayer for God's help . . . . Ps. 28

Book II—The Exodus Book Concerning

    Israel as a Nation . . . . Ps. 42–72

Psalm of longing . . . . Ps. 42

Prayer for cleansing . . . . Ps. 51

Prayer for deliverance . . . . Ps. 70

Book III—The Leviticus Book

    Concerning the Sanctuary . . . . Ps. 73–89

Prayer for restoration . . . . Ps. 80

Book IV—The Numbers Book Concerning

    Israel and the Nation . . . . Ps. 90–106

The Lord reigns . . . . Ps. 93

God's wondrous works . . . . Ps. 105

Book V—The Deuteronomy Book Concerning

    God and His Word . . . . Ps. 107–150

On God's commandments . . . . Ps. 119

Psalm of faithfulness . . . . Ps. 128

God is gracious . . . . Ps. 145

Psalms of praise . . . . Ps. 149; 150

Psaltery—*a musical instrument*

Used in:

Government proclamations . . . . Dan. 3:5, 10

Ptolemais—*a seaport city south of Tyre*

Paul lands at . . . . Acts 21:7

Same as Acco. . . . . Judg. 1:31

Public opinion

Rescues Jonathan . . . . 1 Sam. 14:45

Delays John's death . . . . Matt. 14:1–5

Protects the apostles . . . . Acts 5:26

Makes Saul sin . . . . 1 Sam. 15:24

Increases Pilate's guilt . . . . Matt. 27:21–26

Incites persecution . . . . Acts 12:1–3

Publish—*to proclaim publicly*

Descriptive of:

Message of doom . . . . Jon. 3:7

News of a healing . . . . Mark 1:45

News of deliverance . . . . Mark 5:20

Publius—*common*

Roman official; entertains Paul . . . . . . Acts 28:7, 8

Pudens—*modest*

Believer at Rome . . . . 2 Tim. 4:21

Pul—*strong*

1. King of Assyria; same as Tiglath-Pileser . . . . . 2 Kin. 15:19

2. Country and people in Africa . . . . Is. 66:19

Punishment, everlasting (see Hell; Eternal, everlasting)

Punishments—*penalties inflicted on criminals*

A. Agents of:

State . . . . Rom. 13:1–4

Nation . . . . Josh. 7:25

Prophet . . . . 1 Sam. 15:33

Witnesses . . . . John 8:3–7

Soldiers . . . . Matt. 27:27–35

B. Kinds of (noncapital):

Imprisonment . . . . Matt. 5:25

Fine . . . . Ex. 21:22

Restitution . . . . Ex. 22:3–6

Retaliation . . . . Deut. 19:21

Scourging . . . . Acts 22:25

Bondage . . . . Matt. 18:25

Banishment . . . . Rev. 1:9

Torture . . . . Heb. 11:35

Mutilation . . . . Judg. 1:5–7

C. Kinds of (capital):

Burning . . . . Gen. 38:24

Hanging . . . . Esth. 7:9, 10

Crucifying . . . . Matt. 27:35

Beheading . . . . Mark 6:16, 27

Stoning . . . . Lev. 24:14

Cutting in pieces . . . . Dan. 2:5

Exposing to lions . . . . Dan. 6:16, 24

Killing with the sword . . . . Acts 12:2

See Capital punishment

Punites

Descendants of Puah . . . . Num. 26:23

Punon

Israelite camp . . . . Num. 33:42, 43

Pur—*a lot*

Cast for Jews' slaughter . . . . Esth. 3:7

Origin of Purim . . . . Esth. 9:24–26

Purah—*branch*

Gideon's servant . . . . Judg. 7:10, 11

WORD STUDY	**PURCHASE, BUY,** *agorazō* (og-or-*ahd*-zoh). This verb, literally meaning "to buy"

or "to purchase," occurs frequently in the NT. It is used in this sense to refer to the "purchase" of various things, such as fields (Matt. 13:44) and bread (Mark 6:37). Outside the NT *agorazō* is also used figuratively with respect to the "purchase" of slaves by (or on behalf of) a deity, which resulted in their manumission. This figurative use from the slave market lies behind NT passages in which Christ is said to have paid the price for believers by the shedding of His blood, thereby freeing them from their enslavement to sin and thus redeeming them to God (see 1 Cor. 6:20; 7:23; 2 Pet. 2:1; Rev. 5:9; 14:3). (Strong's #59)

Purchase—*to buy*

A. Used literally of:

Cave . . . . Gen. 49:32

Field . . . . Jer. 32:9–16

Wife . . . . Ruth 4:10

B. Used figuratively of:

Israel's redemption . . . . Ex. 15:16

God's gifts . . . . Acts 8:20

Church . . . . Acts 20:28

Pure, purity—*uncontaminated with dross or evil*

A. Descriptive of:

Chastity ....1 Tim. 5:2

Innocent............................ Acts 20:26

Regenerated........................Titus 1:15

B. Applied figuratively to God's:

Law...............................Ps. 19:8

Word ....Ps. 119:140

Wisdom .... James 3:17

C. Applied figuratively to the believer's:

Heart...............................Ps. 24:4

Mind ....2 Pet. 3:1

Conscience........................ 1 Tim. 3:9

Language .... Zeph. 3:9

Hands .... Job 22:30

D. Applied to the Christian's life:

Source ....Titus 1:15

Command .... 1 Tim. 4:12

Means .... Phil. 4:8

Outward manifestation .... James 1:27

Inward evidence ....1 Tim. 1:5

Goal................................1 John 3:3

Reward ....Matt. 5:8

False...............................Prov. 20:9

E. Applied symbolically to:

New Jerusalem .... Rev. 21:18, 21

Purge—*to cleanse thoroughly*

A. Used, in the Old Testament, ceremonially of:

Cleansing .... Ezek. 20:38

Separation from idolatry ....2 Chr. 34:3, 8

B. Used, in the Old Testament, figuratively of:

Reformation....................... Ezek. 24:13

Regeneration .... Is. 4:4

Sanctification .... Is. 1:25

Forgiveness..........................Ps. 51:7

Consecration ....Is. 6:7

Atonement .... Mal. 3:3, 4

Purification—*ceremonial or spiritual cleansing*

A. Objects of:

Israelites at Sinai.......................Ex. 19:10

Priests at ordination ....Ex. 29:4

Levites at ordination .... Num. 8:6, 7

Offerings ....2 Chr. 4:6

High priest........................ Lev. 16:4, 24

Unclean people .... Lev. 15:2–13

Nazirite after vow ....Acts 21:24, 26

B. Accomplished by:

Sprinkling ....Num. 19:13–18

Washing parts of the body.......... Ex. 30:18, 19

Washing the whole body ....Lev. 8:6

Running water ....Lev. 15:13

C. Figurative of:

Christ's atonement.................... Mal. 3:3

Regeneration ....Acts 15:9

Sanctification .... James 4:8

Obedience .... 1 Pet. 1:22

Purim—*lots*

Jewish festival celebrating being rescued from Haman's plot............... Esth. 9:26–28

Purple

Used in the tabernacle..................Ex. 25:4

Sign of riches ....Luke 16:19

Worn by royalty ....Judg. 8:26

Lydia, seller of....................Acts 16:14

Purposes of God

Characteristics of:

Centered in Christ .... Eph. 3:11; 1 John 3:8

Unknown to the wise................ Is. 19:11, 12

Made known .... Jer. 50:45

Irreversible....................... Jer. 4:28

Planned............................ Is. 23:9

Fulfilled ....Rom. 9:11

Victorious................... 2 Chr. 32:2–22

Certain .... Is. 46:11

Purposes of humankind

A. Good:

Hindered by evildoers..................Ezra 4:5

Known by others .... 2 Tim. 3:10

Permitted ....Dan. 1:8–16

Accomplished .... 1 Kin. 5:5

Determined .... Ps. 17:3

Delayed.......................... Acts 19:21

Not vacillating .... 2 Cor. 1:17

B. Evil:

Known by God .... Jer. 49:30

Designed against the righteous.........Ps. 140:4

Hindered ....Dan. 6:17–23

Purse—*a bag*

One, forbidden .... Prov. 1:14

Pursue—*to go after*

"Enemy said, 'I will'"....................Ex. 15:9

"Shall flee when no one"..............Lev. 26:17

"I will arise and".....................2 Sam. 17:1

"Seek peace and" ....Ps. 34:14

"Blood shall" ....Ezek. 35:6

Put—*foreign bowman*

1. Third son of Ham ....Gen. 10:6

2. Warriors (Libyans) allied with Egypt... Ezek. 27:10

Same as Libyans .... Jer. 46:9

Puteoli—*little wells*

Seaport of Italy .... Acts 28:13

Puthites

Descendants of Caleb ....1 Chr. 2:50, 53

Putiel—*God enlightens*

Father-in-law of Eleazar ....Ex. 6:25

Puvah, Puah—*utterance*

1. Issachar's second son.................. Gen. 46:13

Called Puah; descendants of Punites.......................Num. 26:23

2. Father of Tola, Israel's judge........... Judg. 10:1

Q

Qoph
Nineteenth letter of the Hebrew
    alphabet . . . . Ps. 119:145–152

Quail—*a small bird*
Sent to satisfy hunger . . . . Ex. 16:12, 13
Sent as a judgment . . . . Num. 11:31–34

Quarantine—*restricted in public contacts*
Required of lepers . . . . Lev. 13:45, 46
Miriam consigned . . . . Num. 12:14–16
Imposed under King Azariah . . . . 2 Kin. 15:1–5

Quarrel—*a dispute*
A. Caused by:
    Flesh. . . . . James 4:1, 2
    Hatred. . . . . Mark 6:18, 19
B. Productive of:
    Friction . . . . Matt. 20:20–24
    Separation . . . . Acts 15:37–40
C. Resolved by:
    Gentleness . . . . 2 Tim. 2:24–26
    Forgiveness. . . . . Col. 3:13
    Unity of mind . . . . Phil. 2:3, 4
    Love . . . . Prov. 10:12
    See Contention; Strife

Quartus—*fourth*
Christian at Corinth . . . . Rom. 16:23

Queen—*a king's wife*
A. Applied to:
    Queen regent . . . . 1 Kin. 10:1–13
    Heathen deity . . . . Jer. 44:15–30
    Mystical Babylon . . . . Rev. 18:7
B. Names of:
    Of Sheba . . . . 1 Kin. 10:1
    Vashti. . . . . Esth. 1:9
    Esther . . . . Esth. 5:3
    Candace . . . . Acts 8:27
    Tahpenes . . . . 1 Kin. 11:19
    Of heaven . . . . Jer. 7:18
    Of the South . . . . Matt. 12:42

Quench—*to extinguish*
A. Applied literally to:
    Fire. . . . . Num. 11:2
    Thirst . . . . Ps. 104:11
B. Applied figuratively to:
    Love . . . . Song 8:7
    God's wrath . . . . 2 Kin. 22:17
    Spirit . . . . 1 Thess. 5:19
    Persecution. . . . . Heb. 11:34

Question—*an inquiry*
Asked by:
    The wicked. . . . . . . Matt. 22:16–40; John 18:33–38
    Jesus' disciples . . . . Matt. 18:1–6; Acts 1:6
    Jesus. . . . . Matt. 22:41–45
    Queen of Sheba. . . . . 2 Chr. 9:1, 2

Quietness—*noiselessness*
A. Descriptive of:
    People . . . . Judg. 18:7, 27
    City . . . . 2 Kin. 11:20
    Nation . . . . 2 Chr. 14:1, 5
    Earth . . . . Is. 14:7
B. Realization of:
    Predicted . . . . Is. 32:17, 18
    Comes from God . . . . 1 Chr. 22:9
    Preferred. . . . . Prov. 17:1
    To be sought . . . . 1 Thess. 4:11
    Undeniable. Acts 19:36
    Commanded . . . . 2 Thess. 3:12
    Obtainable . . . . Ps. 131:2
    Very valuable. . . . . 1 Pet. 3:4
    Rewarded . . . . Is. 30:15

Quirinius
Roman governor of Syria . . . . Luke 2:1–4

Quitters, quitting
Unworthy . . . . Luke 9:62
Believers should not be . . . . Gal. 6:9; 2 Thess. 3:13
Press on . . . . Phil. 3:12–14
Continue. . . . . 2 Tim. 3:14

Quiver—*a case for carrying arrows*
A. Used by:
    Hunters. . . . . Gen. 27:3
    Soldiers . . . . Job 39:23; Is. 22:6
B. Figurative of:
    Children . . . . Ps. 127:5
    Messiah. . . . . Is. 49:2

Quotations
A. Introduced by:
    "The Holy Spirit" . . . . Acts 28:25
    "As it is written" . . . . Rom. 15:9
    "The Scripture". . . . . Gal. 3:8
    Old Testament writers . . . . Rom. 10:5–20
B. Purposes of:
    Cite fulfillment. . . . . Matt. 1:22, 23
    Confirm a truth . . . . Matt. 4:4
    Prove a doctrine . . . . Rom. 4:5–8
    Show the true meaning. . . . . Acts 2:25–36

R

Raamah—*trembling*
Son of Cush . . . . Gen. 10:6, 7
Father of Sheba and Dedan . . . . Gen. 10:7
Noted traders. . . . . Ezek. 27:22

Raamiah—*Yahweh has thundered*
Postexilic chief . . . . Neh. 7:7
Same as Reelaiah . . . . Ezra 2:2

Raamses, Rameses—*Ra (Egyptian sun-god) created him*
Treasure city built by Hebrew slaves . . . . . . Ex. 1:11
Jacob's family settles in. . . . . Gen. 47:10, 11

Rabbah—*great*
1. Town of Judah. . . . . Josh. 15:60

2. Capital of Ammon.....................Amos 1:14
   Bedstead of Og here..................Deut. 3:11
   On Gad's boundary..................Josh. 13:25
   Besieged by Joab...................2 Sam. 12:26
   Defeated and enslaved by David...2 Sam. 12:29–31
   Destruction of, foretold..............Jer. 49:2, 3

Rabbi, Rabboni—*my master*
A. Applied to:
   John the Baptist......................John 3:26
   Jesus Christ...................John 3:2; 1:38, 49
B. Significance of:
   Coveted title......................Matt. 23:6, 7
   Forbidden by Christ..................Matt. 23:8
   Expressive of imperfect faith........Mark 14:45;
     John 20:16

Rabbith—*multitude*
   Frontier town of Issachar.............Josh. 19:20

Rabmag—*head of the Magi*
   Title applied to Nergal-Sharezer.....Jer. 39:3, 13

Rabsaris—*head chamberlain*
Title applied to:
   Assyrian officials sent
     by Sennacherib..................2 Kin. 18:17
   Babylonian Nebushasban.............Jer. 39:13
   Babylonian prince.....................Jer. 39:3

Rabshakeh—*head of the cupbearers*
   King of Assyria sent........2 Kin. 18:17; Is. 36:2
   Hezekiah told the words of............Is. 36:22
   Carries message reproaching God.....2 Kin. 19:4

Raca—*a term of insult*
   Use of, forbidden by Christ.......Matt. 5:21, 22

Race, Christian
Requirements of:
   Discipline.....................1 Cor. 9:24–27
   Patience...........................Eccl. 9:11
   Steadfastness..........................Gal. 5:7

Race, human
   Unity of.............................Gen. 3:20
   Divisions of......................Gen. 10:1–32
   Scattering of.....................Gen. 11:1–9
   Bounds of..........................Acts 17:26
   Depravity of.....................Rom. 1:18–32
   Salvation of........................John 3:16

Rachal—*trader*
   City in Judah.....................1 Sam. 30:29

Rachel—*ewe*
   Laban's younger daughter; Jacob's
     favorite wife.................Gen. 29:28–30
   Supports her husband's position....Gen. 31:14–16
   Steals Laban's idols...........Gen. 31:19, 32–35
   Mother of Joseph and Benjamin....Gen. 30:22–25
   Dies in childbirth..............Gen. 35:1, 16–19
   Prophecy concerning, quoted.........Jer. 31:15;
     Matt. 2:18

Rachel, tomb of
   At Bethlehem—first mention of in
     Bible.........................Gen. 35:19, 20

Racial relations
   Salvation is for all...........Eph. 2:11–22; 3:7–9
   All are same in Christ...............Col. 3:9–11

Raddai—*Yahweh has subdued*
   One of David's brothers..........1 Chr. 2:13–15

Radiance in life
Produced by:
   Wisdom...........................Prov. 4:7–9
   Soul winning.......................Dan. 12:3
   Transfiguration.....................Matt. 17:2
   Beholding the Lord.......Ps. 34:5; 2 Cor. 3:7–18
   Loving God's law...................Ps. 119:165

Rafters—*timbers used to support a roof*
   Made of fir.........................Song 1:17

Rage—*raving and violent madness; fury*
A. Descriptive of:
   Sea...............................Luke 8:24
   Anger.............................Dan. 3:13
   Nations..............................Ps. 2:1
B. Caused by:
   Insane madness..................2 Chr. 16:7–10
   Supposed insult.................2 Kin. 5:11, 12
   Jealousy..........................Prov. 6:34
   Insolence against God..........2 Kin. 19:27, 28

Rags—*tattered and spoiled clothing*
   Used as cushions..................Jer. 38:11–13
   Reward of drowsiness.............Prov. 23:21
   Our righteousness like................Is. 64:6

Rahab—*violence*
   Prostitute living in Jericho..............Josh. 2:1
   Concealed Joshua's spies............Josh. 2:1–24
   Spared by invading Israelites.......Josh. 6:17–25
   Included among the faithful..........Heb. 11:31
   Cited as an example................James 2:25
   Ancestress of Christ..................Matt. 1:5

Rahab—*pride, arrogance*
   Used figuratively of Egypt..............Ps. 87:4
   Translated "the proud".................Job 9:13

Raham—*pity*
   Descendant of Caleb.................1 Chr. 2:44

Rain—*water falling from clouds*
A. Features concerning:
   Sent by God.......................Jer. 14:22
   Sent on all mankind.................Matt. 5:45
   Sign of God's goodness............Deut. 28:12
   Controlled by God's decrees......Job 28:26; 37:6
   Withheld because of sin.............Deut. 11:17
   Sent as a result of judgment............Gen. 7:4
   Former and latter.....................Jer. 5:24
   To be prayed for..................1 Kin. 8:35, 36
B. Figurative of:
   God's Word.......................Is. 55:10, 11
   Spiritual blessing.....................Ps. 72:6

> **WORD STUDY** **RANSOM**, *lutron* (*loo*-trahn). This noun, used only in Matt. 20:28 and Mark 10:45, means "price of release" or "ransom." Outside the NT *lutron* is used with reference to the money paid as ransom for the manumission of slaves. Here, it refers to Jesus' death as the "price of release" for many (see also 1 Tim. 2:6). Luke uses the cognates of *lutron* to speak of God's redemption of His people (see 1:68; 2:38; cf. 24:21). A similar idea is expressed in Titus 2:14. (Strong's #3083)

Jephthah's vow . . . . Judg. 11:30–39
Israel's vow against the Benjamites. . . Judg. 21:1–6
Josiah's war against Necho . . . . . . 2 Chr. 35:20–24
Peter's cutting off the ear of Malchus. . . John 18:10

Rationing—*limits prescribed for necessities*
By Joseph, to save Egypt . . . . Gen. 41:35–57

Raven—*a flesh-eating bird*
A. Characteristics of:
Unclean for food. . . . . Lev. 11:15
Solitary in habit . . . . Is. 34:11
Flesh-eating . . . . Prov. 30:17
Black . . . . Song 5:11
B. Special features concerning:
First creature sent from the ark . . . . Gen. 8:7
Elijah fed by . . . . .1 Kin. 17:4–7
Fed by God. . . . . Luke 12:24

Razor—*a sharp instrument used for cutting off hair*
Forbidden to:
Nazirites . . . . Num. 6:1–5
Samson . . . . .Judg. 13:5
Mentioned in Hannah's vow . . . . .1 Sam. 1:11
Used by barbers. .Ezek. 5:1
See Hair; Knife

Readiness—*being prepared for action*
A. Descriptive of:
Being prepared . . . . Matt. 22:4, 8
Being responsive. . . . . .2 Cor. 8:11, 19
B. Objects of:
Willing people. . . . . Luke 1:17
Passover . . . . Luke 22:12, 13
Lord's return . . . . Matt. 24:44
Preaching the gospel . . . . Rom. 1:15

Reading the Bible
A. Blessings of:
Brings repentance. . . . . 2 Kin. 22:8–20
Reminds us of duties . . . . .Neh. 8:12, 13
Produces reformation . . . . .Neh. 13:1–3
Gives knowledge of prophecy . . . . Rev. 1:3
B. Reactions to:
Responsiveness . . . . .Ex. 24:7
Rejection. . . . . .Jer. 36:21–28
Rebellion . . . . Luke 4:16–30
Request for more light. . . . . .Acts 8:29–35
Research . . . . Acts 17:10, 11

Reaiah—*Yahweh has provided for*
1. Reubenite. . . . . 1 Chr. 5:5
2. Founder of Nethinim family . . . . Ezra 2:47
3. Calebite family . . . . 1 Chr. 4:2

Real property
A. Characteristic features of:
Property desired . . . . Gen. 23:4
Price stipulated . . . . Gen. 33:19
Posts erected . . . . Deut. 19:14
Posterity remembered. . . . . Num. 33:54
Publicity required. . . . . .Ruth 4:1–4
Proof documented . . . . .Jer. 32:10–17

B. Unusual examples of:
Monopoly of land established . . . . Gen. 47:20
Sale of, as a prophetic proof . . . . .Jer. 32:6–44
Mark of Beast required . . . . Rev. 13:16, 17

Reaping
A. Provisions concerning :
Areas restricted. . . . . .Lev. 19:9, 10
Times restricted . . . . .Lev. 25:1–11
Sin hinders . . . . Jer. 12:13
B. Figurative of:
Harvest of souls . . . . .John 4:35–38
Trust in God . . . . Matt. 6:26
Gospel age . . . . Amos 9:13–15
Injustice . . . . Matt. 25:26
Payment for services . . . . 1 Cor. 9:11
Blessings . . . . 2 Cor. 9:6
Reward for righteousness. . . . . .Gal. 6:8, 9
Punishment for sin. . . . . Hos. 10:13
Judgment on the world . . . . Rev. 14:14–16
Final judgment . . . . Matt. 13:30–43

Reason—*the faculty by which we think*
A. Faculty of:
Makes people sane . . . . Dan. 4:36
Prepares for salvation . . . . .Is. 1:18
Makes people guilty. . . . . Mark 11:31–33
B. Inadequacy of:
Biased against the truth . . . . Mark 2:6–8
Gospel not explained by . . . 1 Cor. 1:18–31; 2:1–14

Reba—*fourth part*
Midianite chief slain by Israelites . . . . .Num. 31:8;
Josh. 13:21

Rebekah, Rebecca—*loops of a rope*
Daughter of Bethuel; sister of
Laban . . . . .Gen. 22:20–23; 24:29
Becomes Isaac's wife . . . . Gen. 24:15–67
Mother of Esau and Jacob . . . . Gen. 25:21–28
Poses as Isaac's sister . . . . Gen. 26:6–11
Disturbed by Esau's marriages . . . . Gen. 26:34, 35
Causes Jacob to deceive Isaac . . . . . . .Gen. 27:1–29
Urges Jacob to leave home . . . . Gen. 27:42–46
Burial of, in Machpelah . . . . Gen. 49:29–31
Mentioned by Paul. . . . . .Rom. 9:10

Rebellion—*active opposition to authority*
A. Against:
God . . . . Dan. 9:5, 9
God's word. . . . . .Num. 20:24
Davidic kingship . . . . .1 Kin. 12:19
Constituted priesthood. . . . . Num. 17:1–10
Spirit . . . . Is. 63:10
Parents . . . . Deut. 21:18–21
B. Evil of:
Keeps from blessings . . . . Num. 20:24
Increases sin. . . . . Job 34:37
Needs to be confessed . . . . .Dan. 9:4–12
Characterizes a people . . . . Is. 65:2
As sin of witchcraft . . . . 1 Sam. 15:23
See Insurrection

Rebuilding Jerusalem
Permitted by proclamation . . . . Ezra 1:1–4
Opposed . . . . .Ezra 4:1–6; Neh. 4:1–3
Temple. Ezra 5:1, 2; 6:14, 15
Walls . . . . .Neh. 6:15, 16

Rebuke—*to reprimand sharply*
Jesus' power to restrain:
Sea . . . . Matt. 8:26
Demons. . . . . .Matt. 17:18
Fever . . . . .Luke 4:39
Peter. . . . . Mark 8:33

Rebuke for sin
A. Manner of:
Before all. . . . . 1 Tim. 5:20
With long-suffering. . . . . 2 Tim. 4:2
Sharply . . . . .Titus 2:15
With all authority . . . . .Titus 2:15
B. Examples of:
Isaac by Abimelech . . . . Gen. 26:6–11
Laban by Jacob . . . . Gen. 31:36–42
Saul by Samuel . . . . 1 Sam. 13:13
Ahab by Elijah. . . . . .1 Kin. 21:20
Judah by Zechariah . . . . .2 Chr. 24:20
Israel by Ezra. Ezra 10:10, 11
David by God . . . . Ps. 39:11
Peter by Paul . . . . Gal. 2:11–14
Christians by God . . . . Heb. 12:5
Church by Christ .Rev. 3:19

Receive—*to take into one's possession*
A. Good things:
Word . . . . James 1:21
Holy Spirit . . . . Acts 2:38
Christ Jesus . . . . .Col. 2:6
Forgiveness. . . . . Acts 26:18
Petitions . . . . .1 John 3:22
Reward . . . . .1 Cor. 3:8, 14
Eternal life . . . . Mark 10:30
B. Evil things:
Punishment . . . . .Rom. 1:27
Beast's mark. . . . . .Rev. 13:16
Reward for unrighteousness . . . . 2 Pet. 2:13

Rechab—*rider*
1. Assassin of Ishbosheth . . . . .2 Sam. 4:5–7
2. Father of Jehonadab, founder of the
    Rechabites .2 Kin. 10:15–23
    Related to the Kenites. . . . . 1 Chr. 2:55
3. Postexilic ruler . . . . .Neh. 3:14

Rechabites—*descendants of Rechab*
Kenite clan fathered by Rechab and
    believing in the simple life . . . . Jer. 35:1–19

Rechah—*softness*
Place in Judah . . . . 1 Chr. 4:12

Reciprocation—*mutual interchange*
Gentiles to Jews . . . . Rom. 15:27
Students to teachers. . . . . .Gal. 6:6

Recompense—*to pay back in kind*
A. On the righteous:
Even now. . . . . Prov. 11:31
According to one's righteousness. . . . Ps. 18:20, 24
Eagerly expected. . . . . Heb. 10:35
At the resurrection of the just. . . . . . . .Luke 14:14
B. On the unrighteous:
Justly deserved . . . . .Rom. 1:27
Belongs to God only. . . . . Heb. 10:30
Will surely come. . . . . .Jer. 51:56
To the next generation . . . . .Jer. 32:18
Fully at the Second Advent . . . . 2 Thess. 1:6

WORD STUDY **RECONCILE,** *katallassō* (kat-al-*las*-so). Although the verb *katallassō*, meaning "to reconcile," is used with respect to relationships between persons (e.g., between husband and wife, as in 1 Cor. 7:11), it usually refers to the restoration of a broken relationship between God and human beings by means of "the death of His Son" (Rom. 5:10; 2 Cor. 5:18–20). Paul's use of the cognate noun (Rom. 5:11) indicates that God alone effects this "reconciliation," while humans "receive" it. (Strong's #2644)

Reconciliation—*making peace between enemies*
A. Effected on people while:
Helpless. . . . . .Rom. 5:6
Sinners. . . . . .Rom. 5:8
Enemies of God. .Rom. 5:10
God-haters . . . . .Col. 1:21
B. Accomplished by:
God in Christ . . . . 2 Cor. 5:18
Christ's death . . . . .Rom. 5:10
Christ's blood . . . . Eph. 2:13
C. Productive of:
Peace with God. .Rom. 5:1
Access to God . . . . .Rom. 5:2
Union of Jews and Gentiles . . . . Eph. 2:14

Recorder—*high court official*
Records events. . . . . .2 Sam. 8:16
Represents the king . . . . 2 Kin. 18:18
Repairs the temple . . . . .2 Chr. 34:8

Recover—*to restore lost things*
A. Of sickness:
By remedy. . . . . .2 Kin. 20:7
By a miracle . . . . .2 Kin. 5:3–14
Sought from idols. . . . . .2 Kin. 1:2–17
B. Of physical things:
Defeat in war. . . . . .2 Chr. 13:19, 20
Conquered territory. . . . . .2 Sam. 8:3
Captured people . . . . .Jer. 41:16

Recreation—*relaxation and restoration*
Among children, natural . . . . .Zech. 8:5
Among adults, sometimes boring . . . . Eccl. 2:1–11
Lord's place in . . . . .Jer. 33:11
Of the wicked, evil. . . . . .Judg. 16:25

Red—*being red or ruddy*
Blood. . . . . .2 Kin. 3:22

Wine .... Prov. 23:31
Complexion .... Lam. 4:7
Sky .... Matt. 16:2
Dyed rams' skins...................... Ex. 36:19

Red dragon—*another name for Satan*
Seen in John's vision .... Rev. 12:3–17

WORD STUDY

REDEEM, *padah* (paw-*daw*). The verb *padah* is usually translated "redeem," but it also means "liberate" or "free." Someone or something might be redeemed for a price, ransomed, as in Ex. 13:13, where the firstborn sons are to be redeemed from being set aside for God. A person might be freed from violence and death as Jonathan was rescued by the people from being put to death in 1 Sam. 14:45. God can redeem people as He does Israel, liberating them from Egypt (Deut. 7:18) and from exile (Jer. 31:11). The psalmist cries for God to redeem Israel from their troubles in Ps. 25:22. God is also said to redeem individuals, such as Abraham (Is. 29:22) and David (1 Kin. 1:29). (Strong's #6299)

WORD STUDY

REDEEM, *ga'al* (gaw-*awl*). *Ga'al* is a verb, which is translated "redeem"; and it carries the meaning of purchasing or buying back, thus acting as a kinsman. According to the law, if land had to be sold, the closest kinsmen were obligated to buy the land so that it stayed within the family. The closest kinsman (*go'el,* or "redeemer") also had other duties. If a man died without children, the redeemer was supposed to take the widow and raise children with her to be the descendants of the dead man as we see in the story of Ruth. A kinsman was also obligated to redeem from slavery or bondage one who could not free himself. The final duty of the redeemer was to be the blood avenger of one who had been murdered. In poetic contexts, there are passages where God acts as the redeemer, freeing individuals or the entire nation of Israel. In the following passages, God is the Redeemer and the people are the redeemed ones (Is. 35:9; 41:14; 44:6; 51:10). (Strong's #1350)

WORD STUDY

REDEMPTION, *apolutrōsis* (ap-ol-*oo*-troh-sis). This noun originally referred to the "buying back" or the manumission (= "setting free") of a slave or captive by paying a ransom (*lutron*), hence the meaning of "release" or "redemption." In the NT *apolutrōsis* is used figuratively to emphasize the "release" or "redemption" from sin brought about by Christ (see Heb. 9:15). Paul uses the word to indicate the cost of "redemption"—Jesus' blood (Eph. 1:7; Col. 1:14)—and the resulting freedom (Rom. 8:23). (Strong's #629)

Redemption—*deliverance by sacrifice*
A. Defined as deliverance from:
    Curse of the Law...................... Gal. 3:13
    Bondage of the Law .... Gal. 4:5
    Iniquity............................ Titus 2:14

    Destruction .... Ps. 103:4
    Death................................ Hos. 13:14
    Grave................................ Ps. 49:15
    Aimless conduct..................... 1 Pet. 1:18
    Present evil world.................... Gal. 1:4
B. Accomplished by:
    God's power.......................... Deut. 7:8
    Christ's blood .... Eph. 1:7
    God's grace......................... Rom. 3:24, 25
C. Benefits of:
    Forgiveness.......................... Col. 1:14
    Justification........................ Rom. 3:24
    Adoption............................ Gal. 4:4, 5
    God's possession.................... 1 Cor. 6:20
    God's people .... Titus 2:14
    Purification .... Titus 2:14
    Sealing.............................. Eph. 4:30
    Inheritance......................... Heb. 9:15
    Heaven's glory...................... Rev. 14:3, 4

Red heifer (see Heifer)

Red horse—*symbol of war*
Seen in John's vision .... Rev. 6:4

Red Sea—*sea of reeds*
    Locusts destroyed in .... Ex. 10:19
    Divided by God....................... Ex. 14:21
    Crossed by Israel.................... Ex. 14:22, 29
    Egyptians drowned in............... Ex. 15:4, 21
    Boundary of Promised Land........... Ex. 23:31
    Israelites camp by................ Num. 33:10, 11
    Ships built on....................... 1 Kin. 9:26

Reed—*tall grass growing in marshes*
Figurative of:
    Weakness .... Is. 36:6
    Instability.......................... Matt. 11:7
    Davidic line .... Is. 42:3

Refining, spiritual
    By afflictions....................... Is. 48:10
    By fire .... Zech. 13:9
    For a purpose........................ John 15:2
    More precious than gold.............. 1 Pet. 1:7

Reflection—*contemplation on*
    Past................................. Mark 14:72
    Present.............................. Luke 14:31–33
    Future .... Acts 21:12–14

Reformations, religious
Manifested by or in:
    Recovery of the Law .... 2 Kin. 22:8–20
    Resolving to follow the Lord........ Ezra 10:1–17
    Religious zeal for the Lord......... Neh. 13:11–31
    Restoration of judges.............. 2 Chr. 19:1–11

Refresh—*to renew; to restore*
Spiritually:
    In the spirit .... 1 Cor. 16:18
    In the heart .... Philem. 7, 20
    Often needed........................ 2 Tim. 1:16
    Mutual.............................. Rom. 15:32
    Special times .... Acts 3:19

Refused........................... Is. 28:12

Refuge—*a shelter against harm*
Divine:
   In the Lord...........................Ps. 142:5
   From storms...........................Is. 4:5, 6
   Time of trouble........................Ps. 9:9
   Place of protection..................Ps. 91:9, 10
   Always ready..........................Ps. 46:1

Refuge, cities of (see Cities, Levitical)

Refuse—*to reject or decline*
A. Of things, physical:
   Marriage............................Ex. 22:17
   Passage............................Num. 20:21
   King............................... 1 Sam. 16:7
   Display ....Esth. 1:12
   Leader................................Acts 7:35
   Martyrdom ....Acts 25:11
   Fables...............................1 Tim. 4:7
   Adoption......................... Heb. 11:24–26
B. Of things, spiritual:
   Hardness of heart......................Ex. 7:14
   Disobedience........................ Ex. 16:28
   Obedience ....1 Sam. 8:19
   Messiah.............................Ps. 118:22
   Salvation.............................. Is. 8:6
   Shame ....Jer. 3:3
   Repentance .... Hos. 11:5
   Healing.............................Jer. 15:18
   God ....Heb. 12:25

Refuse Gate—*a gate of Jerusalem*
   Nehemiah viewed city from........... Neh. 2:13
   Wall dedicated near.................. Neh. 12:31

Regem—*friend*
   Calebite.............................1 Chr. 2:47

Regem-Melech—*friend of the king*
   Sent in deputation to Zechariah........Zech. 7:2

Regeneration (see Born again; New birth)

Register—*a record of genealogies*
   Priests not recorded in .... Ezra 2:62
   Excluded from priesthood......... Neh. 7:63–65
   Those recorded in...................Neh. 7:5–62

Rehabiah—*Yahweh is wide*
   Grandson of Moses ....1 Chr. 23:17

Rehob—*open place*
1. Two cities of Asher ....Josh. 19:24, 28
   One assigned to Levites .... Josh. 21:31
   Delayed conquest of....................Judg. 1:31
2. Northern city visited by Joshua's
   spies...........................Num. 13:21
   Defeated by David .... 2 Sam. 10:8
3. Father of Hadadezer.................2 Sam. 8:3, 12
4. Signer of the covenant ....Neh. 10:11

Rehoboam—*the people are enlarged*
   Son and successor of Solomon........1 Kin. 11:43
   Refuses reformatory measures .....1 Kin. 12:1–15
   Ten Tribes revolt from .... 1 Kin. 12:16–24

   Tribes of Benjamin and Judah
     remain with....................1 Kin. 12:21
   Has several wives .... 2 Chr. 11:18–21
   Temporary prosperity of .... 2 Chr. 11:5–23
   Lapses into idolatry............. 1 Kin. 14:21–24
   Kingdom of, invaded by Egypt... 1 Kin. 14:25–28
   Humbles himself ....2 Chr. 12:12
   Reigns 17 years ....1 Kin. 14:21
   Death of .... 1 Kin. 14:29–31
   In Christ's genealogy...................Matt. 1:7

Rehoboth—*broad places, streets*
1. Name of a well dug by Isaac .... Gen. 26:22
2. City "by-the-River".................... Gen. 36:37

Rehoboth Ir—*broad places of the city*
   A suburb of Nineveh .... Gen. 10:11

Rehum—*beloved*
1. Persian officer...................... Ezra 4:8–23
2. Postexilic returnee...................... Ezra 2:2
3. Priest who returns with
     Zerubbabel .... Neh. 12:1–7
   Same as Harim .... Neh. 12:15
4. Signer of the covenant .... Neh. 10:25
5. Postexilic Levite.......................Neh. 3:17

Rei—*friendly*
   One of David's faithful officers .... 1 Kin. 1:8

WORD STUDY   **REIGN,** *malak* (maw-*lak*). The verb *malak* means "to be or become king or queen," "to reign." Usually *malak* is used to refer to Hebrew kings; however, it can also refer to the kings of other nations. A king reigns over people or a specific territory that contains those people (1 Sam. 8:9; 12:14). Sometimes God is the subject of the verb, reigning over the nations as He does in Ps. 47:8, 9, or reigning from Mount Zion over a nation created from the lame and outcast as in Mic. 4:7. Is. 32:1 and Jer. 23:5 both speak of the reign of the future Messiah, a time of righteousness and justice. There are only a few references to women reigning. One comes in 2 Kin. 11:3, where Athaliah, the daughter of Jezebel, reigned for a short time in Judah as ruler. The other (Esth. 2:4) refers to the woman who would become queen, which Esther eventually did. (Strong's #4427)

Reign—*to rule over*
A. Descriptive of the rule of:
   Humans .... Gen. 36:31
   God .... Ps. 47:8
   Christ.............................. Rev. 20:4, 6
   Believers ....Rev. 5:10
   Sin...................................Rom. 5:21
   Death............................. Rom. 5:14, 17
   Grace.................................Rom. 5:21
B. Of Christ's rule:
   Predicted .... Is. 32:1
   Described .... Jer. 23:5, 6
   Announced.......................Luke 1:31–33
   Rejected ....Luke 19:14, 27

Fulfilled ....Rom. 15:12
Enthroned ....1 Cor. 15:25
Eternal..........................Rev. 11:15–17

Reject—*to refuse; to disown*
A. Humankind's rejection of:
    God ....1 Sam. 8:7
    God's Word ....1 Sam. 15:23, 26
    God's knowledge .... Hos. 4:6
    Christ..........................Mark 8:31
B. God's rejection of humankind, as:
    Unbeliever ....John 12:48
    Divisive...........................Titus 3:10
    Unfruitful......................... Heb. 6:8
    Reprobate..........................Heb. 12:17

Rejoicing—*being glad*
A. Kinds of:
    Gloating ....Mic. 7:8
    Vindictive........................ Rev. 18:20
    Marital .... Prov. 5:18
    Defiant .... Is. 8:6
    Prophetic .... John 8:56
    Future .... Phil. 2:16
    Rewarded ....Ps. 126:6
    Continual..................... 1 Thess. 5:16
B. Because of:
    God's blessing ....Ex. 18:9
    God's Word ....Jer. 15:16
    Assurance..........................Luke 10:20
    Salvation...................... Luke 15:6–10
    Persecution........................ Acts 5:41
    Reunion of believers .... Phil. 2:28
    Christ's return...................... 1 Pet. 4:13
C. Sphere of, in:
    God's salvation .... Ps. 21:1
    God's protection....................... Ps. 63:7
    God's blessings ....Ps. 106:5
    Lord Himself........................ Hab. 3:18
D. Agents of:
    Heart..............................1 Chr. 16:10
    Soul .... Ps. 35:9
    Earth .... Ps. 97:1
    God's people ....Ps. 118:24
    Believing spirit ....Luke 1:47

Rekem—*friendship*
1. Midianite king slain by Moses ....Num. 31:8
2. Descendant of Caleb...............1 Chr. 2:43, 44
3. City of Benjamin .... Josh. 18:27

Relapse—*to turn back to sin again*
    Danger of, explained ....Heb. 6:4–6

Relatives—*those of near kin*
A. Good derived from:
    Encouragement................... Esth. 4:12–17
    Salvation........................ John 1:40–42
B. Evil derived from:
    Strife ....Gen. 31:1–42
    Persecution........................ Mark 13:12
    Jealousy..........................Gen. 37:3–11

Relief
    In early church ....Acts 4:32–37
    Determined to send.................. Acts 11:29
    Fulfilled at Christ's return.......... 2 Thess. 1:7
    For widows........................1 Tim. 5:16

Religion, false
Characterized by:
    Apostasy......................2 Thess. 2:3, 4
    Backsliding ....Jer. 5:23–31
    Ceremonialism .... Mark 7:3–13
    Display ....Matt. 6:5
    Ease .... 1 Kin. 12:27–31
    Formalism ....2 Tim. 3:5

Remain—*continue; abide*
Used of:
    God's faithfulness .... 2 Tim. 2:13
    One's earthly calling ....1 Cor. 7:20, 24

Remaliah—*whom Yahweh has adored*
    Father of Pekah......................2 Kin. 15:25

Remedy—*a cure*
    Without .... Prov. 6:15
    Right kind ....1 John 1:7

Remember—*to call to mind again*
Aids to:
    Rainbow .... Gen. 9:15, 16
    Covenant ....Ex. 2:24
    Passover ....Ex. 13:3
    Sabbath...........................Ex. 20:8
    Offering .... Num. 5:15
    Son (child) .... 2 Sam. 18:18
    Prophet's presence .... 1 Kin. 17:18
    Book............................ Mal. 3:16
    Lord's Supper.......................Luke 22:19
    Epistle ....2 Pet. 3:1
  See Memories

Remeth—*a high place*
    Frontier town of Issachar.............Josh. 19:21

Remission—*forgiveness*
A. Based upon:
    Christ's death .... Matt. 26:28
    Faith in Christ...................... Acts 10:43
    Repentance ....Mark 1:4
B. Significance of:
    Shows God's righteousness ....Rom. 3:23–26
    Makes salvation real ....Luke 1:77
    Must be preached ....Luke 24:47

Remnant—*what is left over*
A. Used literally of:
    Cloth left over ....Ex. 26:12
    Race left remaining ....Deut. 3:11
    Nation still surviving .... Amos 1:8
B. Used spiritually of the faithful Israel:
    Punished...........................Is. 1:9
    Protected .... Is. 37:31–33
    Scattered..........................Ezek. 5:10
    Gathered..........................Is. 10:20–22
    Repentant........................ Jer. 31:7–9

Forgiven . . . . .Mic. 7:18
Saved . . . . Jer. 23:3–8; Rom. 9:27
Blessing . . . . .Mic. 5:7, 8
Holy . . . . .Zeph. 3:12, 13
Elected. . . . . .Rom. 11:5

Remorse—*distress arising from guilt*
Of a renegade. Matt. 27:3–5
Of a disciple . . . . .Luke 22:62

Remphan—*perhaps the same as Chiun, a pagan*
star-god identified with Saturn
Worshiped by Israelites . . . . Acts 7:41–43

Rend—*to tear apart by force*
Figurative of repentance. . . . . Joel 2:13

Renewal of strength
A. Sources of:
Holy Spirit . . . . .Titus 3:5
Wait for the Lord . . . . Is. 40:31
Cleansing from sin . . . . Ps. 51:10
B. Objects of:
Youthfulness . . . . .Ps. 103:5
Peoples . . . . Is. 41:1–3
Inner self. . . . . 2 Cor. 4:16
New person . . . . .Col. 3:10
Mind . . . . .Rom. 12:2

Renown—*of great reputation*
Man . . . . Gen. 6:4
City . . . . Ezek. 26:17
God . . . . Dan. 9:15
Plant. . . . . Ezek. 34:29

Renunciation—*giving up the right to do something*
Blessings of:
True discipleship .Luke 14:33
True reward . . . . .Mark 10:28–31
Future reward . . . . Luke 18:28–30

| WORD STUDY | **REPENT**, *metanoeō* (met-ahn-ah-*eh*-oh). This verb originally meant "to change one's mind" and later came to mean "to |

feel remorse," "to repent." In the NT the use of *metanoeō* usually implies strongly the notion of turning away, for example, from evil (Acts 8:22; cf. Rev. 9:20, 21) or from sin (especially in the preaching of John the Baptist in Luke 3:3 where the noun form appears). John, Jesus, and the apostles proclaimed the necessity of repentance (Matt. 3:2; 4:17; Mark 1:15; 6:12; Acts 2:38). God's goodness should lead to repentance (Rom. 2:4), for indeed He does not will "that any should perish but that all should come to repentance" (2 Pet. 3:9). (Strong's #3340)

Repentance
A. Described as:
"Turned". . . . . Acts 9:35
"Repent" . . . . Acts 8:22
"Return" . . . . .1 Sam. 7:3
"Conversion" . . . . .Acts 15:3
B. Kinds of:
National . . . . .Joel 3:5–18

Internal . . . . .Ps. 51:10–13
Unavailing . . . . .Heb. 12:16, 17
True . . . . Acts 9:1–20
Insincere . . . . Ex. 9:27–35
C. Derived from gift of:
God . . . . .Acts 11:18
Christ. . . . . .Acts 5:31
Spirit . . . . Zech. 12:10
D. Things leading to:
God's longsuffering . . . . .2 Pet. 3:9
God's goodness . . . . .Rom. 2:4
Conviction of sin . . . . Acts 2:37, 38
E. Productive of:
Life . . . . .Acts 11:18
Remission of sins . . . . .Mark 1:4
New spirit . . . . .Ezek. 18:31
New heart . . . . .Ezek. 18:31
Joy. . . . . Luke 15:7, 10
F. Signs of:
Reformation of life. . . . . .Matt. 3:8
Restitution . . . . Luke 19:8
Godly sorrow . . . . 2 Cor. 7:9, 10
See Conversion

Rephael—*God has healed*
Levite gatekeeper . . . . .1 Chr. 26:7

Rephah—*riches*
Ancestor of Joshua . . . . 1 Chr. 7:25–27

Rephaiah—*Yahweh has healed*
1. Man of Issachar . . . . .1 Chr. 7:2
2. Descendant of Jonathan. . . . . 1 Chr. 9:43
Called Raphah. . . . . .1 Chr. 8:37
3. Simeonite prince . . . . .1 Chr. 4:42, 43
4. Postexilic ruler . . . . .Neh. 3:9
5. Descendant of David. . . . . 1 Chr. 3:21

Rephaim—*giants*
1. Early race of giants in Palestine . . . . .Gen. 14:5
Among doomed nations . . . . Gen. 15:20
See Giants
2. Valley near Jerusalem . . . . .2 Sam. 23:13, 14
Very fertile . . . . .Is. 17:5
Scene of Philistine defeats . . . . 2 Sam. 5:18–22

Rephidim—*rests*
Israelite camp . . . . .Num. 33:12–15
Moses struck rock at . . . . .Ex. 17:1–7
Amalek defeated in . . . . Ex. 17:8–16

Report—*a transmitted account of something*
A. Kinds of:
True . . . . .1 Kin. 10:6
Good . . . . .Prov. 15:30
False . . . . .Ex. 23:1
Defaming . . . . Jer. 20:10
Slanderous . . . . .Rom. 3:8
Evil . . . . 2 Cor. 6:8
B. Good, obtained by:
Fear . . . . Deut. 2:25

Reproach—*something imputed to the discredit of others*

A. Objects of:

God	2 Kin. 19:4–23
God's people	Neh. 6:13
Messiah	Rom. 15:3
Christians	Luke 6:22

B. Agents of:

Enemies	Neh. 4:4
Foolish	Ps. 74:22
Scorner	Prov. 22:10
Satan	1 Tim. 3:7; 5:14, 15

C. Evil causes of:

Unbelief	Jer. 6:10
Idolatry	Ezek. 22:4
Breaking God's Law	Num. 15:30, 31
Sin	Prov. 14:34
Disrespect	Prov. 19:26

D. Good causes of:

Faith in God's promises	Heb. 11:24–26
Living for Christ	1 Pet. 4:14
Suffering for Christ	Heb. 13:13

E. Of God's people:

Permitted by God	Jer. 15:15

Reprobate—*one whose character is utterly bad*

A. Causes of:

Not having Christ	2 Cor. 13:3–5
Rejecting the faith	2 Tim. 3:8
Spiritual barrenness	Heb. 6:7, 8
Lack of discipline	1 Cor. 9:24–27
Rejection by the Lord	Jer. 6:30

B. Consequences of, given up to:

Evil	Rom. 1:24–32
Delusion	2 Thess. 2:11, 12
Blindness	Matt. 13:13–15
Destruction	2 Pet. 2:9–22

Reproof—*sharp criticism*

A. Sources of:

God	Ps. 50:8, 21
Backslidings	Jer. 2:19
God's Word	2 Tim. 3:16
John the Baptist	Luke 3:16, 19

B. Examples of:

Samuel	1 Sam. 13:13
Daniel	Dan. 5:22, 23
John the Baptist	Matt. 3:7–12
Stephen	Acts 7:51
Paul	Gal. 2:11

Reptiles of the Bible

A. Features concerning:

Created by God	Gen. 1:24, 25
Made to praise God	Ps. 148:7, 10
Placed under human power	Gen. 1:26
Classified as unclean	Lev. 11:31–43
Seen in a vision	Acts 10:11–14
Worshiped by pagans	Rom. 1:23
Likeness of, forbidden	Deut. 4:16, 18
Portrayed on walls	Ezek. 8:10

B. List of:

Asp	Rom. 3:13
Chameleon	Lev. 11:30
Cobra	Is. 11:8
Frog	Rev. 16:13
Gecko	Lev. 11:30
Leviathan	Job 41:1, 2
Lizard	Lev. 11:30
Scorpion	Deut. 8:15
Serpents	Matt. 10:16
Viper	Acts 28:3

Reputation—*public esteem; fame*

A. Good:

Wonderful asset	Prov. 22:1
Based on integrity	2 Cor. 8:18–24
Hated by wicked	Dan. 6:4–8
Required of church officials	Acts 6:3
Worthy of trust	Acts 16:2

B. Dangers of:

Universal praise	Luke 6:26
Flattering speech	Rom. 16:18
Worldly friendship	James 4:4
Worldly praise	1 John 4:5, 6
Undue deference toward	Gal. 2:6

Resen—*fortress*

City of Assyria built by Nimrod	Gen. 10:11, 12

Reservoirs—*where water is stored*

Family cisterns	Is. 36:16
Garden pools	Eccl. 2:6

Resh

Twentieth letter of the Hebrew alphabet	Ps. 119:153–160

Resheph—*home*

Descendant of Ephraim	1 Chr. 7:23–25

Residue—*a remnant*

A. Used literally of:

Survivors	Jer. 8:3

B. Used spiritually of:

Faithful remnant	Is. 28:5
Promised seed	Zech. 8:11–13

Resignation—*patient submission to*

Disquieting problem	Josh. 22:9–34
Tragic death	2 Sam. 19:1–8
God's chastening	Job 2:10
Cross	Mark 14:36
Sufferings ahead	Acts 21:11–14
Pain	2 Cor. 12:7–10
Want	Phil. 4:11, 12

Resist—*to stand against*

A. Of evil things:

Sin	Heb. 12:4
Adversaries	Luke 21:15
Proud	James 4:6

B. Of good things:

God's will	Rom. 9:19
Holy Spirit	Acts 7:51
Truth	2 Tim. 3:8

Wisdom ....Acts 6:10
Constituted authority ....Rom. 13:2

Respect—*honor manifested toward the worthy*
A. Wrong kind:
    Favoring the wealthy...............James 2:3, 9
B. Right kind:
    Rejects the proud ....Ps. 40:4
    Toward parents......................Heb. 12:9
    Toward husbands.....................Eph. 5:33
    Toward Christ......................Matt. 21:37
C. On God's part:
    Regards the lowly.....................Ps. 138:6
    Honors His covenant...............2 Kin. 13:23
    Judges justly.........................1 Pet. 1:17
    Shows no partiality ....Acts 10:34

Responsibility—*accountability for one's actions*
A. Shifting of, by:
    Blaming another...................... Gen. 3:12
    Claiming innocency .... Matt. 27:24
    Blaming a people .... Ex. 32:21–24
B. Cannot be excused by:
    Ignorance .... Acts 17:30, 31
    Unbelief ....John 3:18–20
    Previous good .... Ex. 33:12, 13
    One's ancestors.................... Matt. 3:9, 10
C. Is increased by:
    Sight............................. John 9:39–41
    Privilege ....John 15:22, 24
    Opportunity ....Matt. 11:20–24
    Continuance in sin...............Matt. 23:31–35
    Rejection.......................Matt. 10:11–15

WORD STUDY   **REST,** *shabat* (shaw-*bath*). *Shabat* is a verb, translated as "cease," "desist," or "rest." "Cease" is used in various contexts. After the Flood God promised that regular seasons will not cease again (Gen. 8:22), and the daily supply of manna ceased when the people first ate produce of the land of Canaan (Josh. 5:12)."Desist" is usually used in the context of desisting from labor or resting. In Gen. 2 God rested after creating the world. In Ex. 23:10–13 there are laws governing several kinds of rest, one of which is resting on the seventh day, known as the Sabbath, the day of rest. The land is also supposed to be given rest, being sown for six years and allowed to lie fallow on the seventh. (Strong's #7673)

WORD STUDY   **REST,** *anapauō* (an-ap-*ow*-oh). A verb meaning "to (take one's) rest," *anapauō* is used literally with reference to persons who are tired (Mark 6:31) or who are drowsy (14:41), but it can also be used figuratively (1 Pet. 4:14). As a transitive verb *anapauō* means "to cause to rest," "to give (someone) rest" (as in Matt. 11:28; cf. the cognate noun in 11:29). The use of *anapauō* carries the nuance of "to refresh" in 1 Cor. 16:18; 2 Cor. 7:13; and Philem. 7, 20. (Strong's #373)

WORD STUDY   **REST, GIVE,** *nuach* (*noo*-akh). One form of the verb *nuach* is translated "rest." The more commonly used form is to "cause to rest" or "give rest" (Ex. 33:14). The giving of rest can be accomplished in several ways, one of which is to bring the person to a resting place. Another way to give rest is to bring freedom from enemies. A person can also have his or her mind set at rest. Beyond the concept of giving rest, *nuach* can also mean, though less commonly, "to deposit or set something down" (Ezek. 37:1; 40:2); in this sense, it can also be translated "to leave alone" or "abandon." (Strong's #5117)

Rest—*peace and quiet*
A. Descriptive of:
    Physical relaxation.................... Gen. 18:4
    Sinful laziness .... Matt. 26:45
    Confidence........................Hab. 3:16–19
    Completion of salvation ....Heb. 4:3, 8–11
B. Need of:
    Recognized in God's Law.......... Ex. 20:10, 11
    Recognized by Christ ....Mark 6:31
    Longed after .... Ps. 55:6
    Provided for.........................Rev. 6:11
    Enjoyed after death ....Job 3:13, 17; Rev. 14:13
C. Source of, in:
    Christ........................... Matt. 11:28, 29
    Trust .... Ps. 37:7
    Returning to God.................. Is. 30:15
D. Disturbance of, by:
    Sin................................. Is. 57:20
    Rebellion .... Is. 28:12
    Persecution.......................... Acts 9:23
    Anxiety............................2 Cor. 2:13
See Quietness

Restitution—*restoring*
    Of damaged property .... Ex. 22:3–12

Restoration—*renewal of something to its former state*
A. Miraculous, from:
    Death.............................2 Kin. 8:1, 5
    Withered hand ....1 Kin. 13:4, 6; Mark 3:1, 5
    Blindness .... Mark 8:25
    Curse .... Acts 3:21
B. Natural of:
    Man's wife .... Gen. 20:7, 14
    Man's position....................Gen. 40:13, 21
    Land...............................2 Sam. 9:7
    Visit .... Heb. 13:19
    Losses .... Job 42:10
C. Spiritual:
    Joy..............................Ps. 51:11, 12
    Recovery............................Jer. 30:17
    God's blessings ....Joel 2:25
    Christ.............................. Is. 49:6

Restoration of Israel
    Promised in the prophets...............Is. 11:11
    Seen in John's ministry..............Matt. 17:11
    Anticipated by Caiaphas ....John 11:49–52

Questioned by the disciples . . . . .Acts 1:6
Realized at Pentecost. . . . . Joel 2:28–32
Fulfilled in the church . . . . Eph. 2:11–22
Perfected in heaven . . . . Heb. 12:22–28

Restraints, divine
On:
Human wrath . . . . Ps. 76:10
Human designs. . . . . Gen. 11:6, 7
Natural forces . . . . Gen. 8:2
Child bearing . . . . Gen. 16:2
Wicked . . . . .2 Kin. 19:28
Antichrist. . . . . .2 Thess. 2:3–7

Resurrection—*arising from the dead*
A. Doctrine of:
Looked for in faith. . . . . .Job 19:25–27
Taught in Old Testament. . . . . .Is. 26:19;
Dan. 12:2, 3, 13
Denied by Sadducees. . . . . .Matt. 22:23–28;
Acts 23:6, 8
Affirmed by Christ . . . .John 5:28, 29; 6:39, 40, 44
Illustrated by Lazarus . . . . John 11:23–44
Explained away by false teachers . . . . . 2 Tim. 2:18
Questioned by some. . . . . 1 Cor. 15:12
Mocked at by heathen. . . . . Acts 17:32
Proclaimed by Paul . . . . Acts 24:14, 15
B. Accomplished by:
God's power. .Matt. 22:28, 29
Christ. . . . . .John 5:28, 29
Holy Spirit . . . . .Rom. 8:11
C. Proof of, based on:
God's power. . . . . 1 Cor. 6:14
Union with Christ . . . . .Rom. 8:11
Christ's resurrection . . . . 1 Cor. 15:12–56
D. Time of, at:
Last Day . . . . John 6:39–44
Christ's return. . . . . 1 Thess. 4:13–18
Last trumpet .1 Cor. 15:51–55
E. Nature of:
Incorruptible. . . . . 1 Cor. 15:42, 54
Glorious . . . . .1 Cor. 15:43
Spiritual . . . . .1 Cor. 15:44
Transforming . . . . 1 Cor. 15:51
Like angels . . . . Matt. 22:30
Like Christ. . . . . Phil. 3:21
Better. . . . . Heb. 11:35
F. Of the wicked:
Predicted . . . . Dan. 12:2
Described . . . . .John 5:28, 29
Simultaneous. . . . . Acts 24:15

Resurrection of Christ
A. Features concerning:
Foretold in the Psalms. . . . . Ps. 16:10, 11;
Acts 13:34, 35
Presented in prophecy. . . .Is. 53:10–12; 1 Cor. 15:4
Announced by Christ . . . . .Mark 9:9, 10;
John 2:19–22
Proclaimed by the apostles . . . . Acts 2:32; 3:15

B. Accomplished by:
God's power. . . . . Acts 2:24
Christ's power . . . . John 10:18
Spirit's power. . . . . .Rom. 8:11
C. Proven by:
Empty tomb. .John 20:1–9
Angelic testimony . . . . .Matt. 28:5–7
His enemies . . . . Matt. 28:11–15
Many infallible proofs. . . .John 20:20, 27; Acts 1:3
Apostolic preaching. . . . . Acts 1:22; 4:33
Lord's Day (first day of the week) . . . John 20:1, 19;
1 Cor. 16:2
D. Purposes of:
Fulfill scripture. . . . . Luke 24:45, 46
Forgive sins . . . . 1 Cor. 15:17
Justify the sinner . . . . Rom. 4:25; 8:34
Give hope . . . . .1 Cor. 15:18, 19
Make faith real . . . . .1 Cor. 15:14–17
Prove His Sonship . . . . .Ps. 2:7; Rom. 1:4
Set Him on David's throne . . . . .Acts 2:30–32
Insure His exaltation. . . Acts 4:10, 11; Phil. 2:9, 10
Guarantee the coming judgment . . . . . . .Acts 17:31
Seal the believer's resurrection . . . . . . .Acts 26:23;
1 Cor. 15:20, 23
Serve as our High Priest . . . . Heb. 8:1–5
As Mediator of a better covenant. . . . . Heb. 8:6
E. Appearances of, to:
Mary Magdalene .Mark 16:9
Other women. . . . . Matt. 28:9
Two disciples . . . . Luke 24:13–15
Simon Peter . . . . .Luke 24:34
Ten apostles .John 20:19, 24
Eleven apostles . . . . .John 20:26
Apostles at Sea of Tiberias. . . . . John 21:1
Apostles in Galilee. . . . . Matt. 28:16, 17
500 brethren . . . . 1 Cor. 15:6
All the apostles . . . . Luke 24:51; Acts 1:9
Paul . . . . 1 Cor. 15:8
James. . . . . 1 Cor. 15:7

Resurrections of the Bible
Widow's son. .1 Kin. 17:17–22
Shunammite's son . . . . 2 Kin. 4:32–35
Unnamed man. . . . . 2 Kin. 13:20, 21
Jairus's daughter. . . . . .Matt. 9:23–25
Widow's only son . . . . .Luke 7:11–15
Lazarus of Bethany . . . . .John 11:43, 44
Many saints . . . . Matt. 27:52, 53
Dorcas. . . . . .Acts 9:36–40
In symbolism. . . . . Rev. 11:8, 11

Resurrection, spiritual
A. Accomplished by power of:
God . . . . .Eph. 1:19
Christ. . . . . .Eph. 5:14
Holy Spirit . . . . .Ezek. 11:19
B. Features concerning:
Takes place now . . . . John 5:25
Gives eternal life. John 5:24
Delivers from spiritual death . . . . Rom. 6:4, 13
Changes life. . . . . Is. 32:15

Issues in immortality ....John 11:25, 26
Delivers from Satan's power .... Acts 26:18
Realized in new life .... Phil. 3:10, 11
Called "first" .... Rev. 20:5, 6

Retaliation—*returning like for like*
Forbidden........................ Luke 9:54–56
Return good, not evil............ Prov. 25:21, 22
God's responsibility......Prov. 20:22; Rom. 12:19
Christ's teaching on..............Matt. 5:39–44

Retribution—*merited punishment for evil done*
A. Expressed by:
God's wrath ....Rom. 1:18
Lamb's wrath..................... Rev. 6:16, 17
Vengeance .... Jude 7
Punishment ....2 Thess. 1:6–9
Corruption.......................2 Pet. 2:9–22
B. Due to the sinner's:
Sin.............................. Rom. 2:1–9
Evil works........................... Ex. 32:34
Persecution of the righteous .... 2 Thess. 1:6
Rejection of Christ...............Heb. 10:29, 30
C. Deliverance from, by:
Christ............................. 1 Thess. 1:10
God's appointment .... 1 Thess. 5:9

Return
Descriptive of:
Going back home .... Gen. 31:3, 13
Repentance .... 2 Chr. 6:24, 38; Hos. 6:1
Vengeance or retribution .... 1 Kin. 2:33, 44
Christ's advent ....Acts 15:16
Death............................... Gen. 3:19

Reu—*friend*
Descendant of Shem ... Gen. 11:10–21; Luke 3:35

Reuben—*behold a son*
Jacob's eldest son ....Gen. 29:31, 32
Guilty of misconduct; loses
preeminence .... Gen. 35:22
Proposes plan to save
Joseph's life ....Gen. 37:21–29
Offers sons as pledge.................Gen. 42:37
Father of four sons.................Gen. 46:8, 9
Pronounced unstable................Gen. 49:3, 4
Descendants of ....Num. 26:5–11

Reubenites—*descendants of Reuben*
Divided into four tribal families ...Num. 26:5–11
Elizur, warrior....................... Num. 1:5
Census of, at Sinai ....Num. 1:18–21
Census of, at conquest............... Num. 26:7
Place of, in march.................... Num. 2:10
Seek inheritance east of Jordan.....Num. 32:1–42
Blessed by Moses .... Deut. 33:1, 6
Join in war against Canaanites......Josh. 1:12–18
Altar erected by, misunderstood ... Josh. 22:10–34
Criticized by Deborah.............Judg. 5:15, 16
Enslaved by Assyria ....2 Kin. 15:29
12,000 of, sealed........................Rev. 7:5

Reuel—*friend of God*
1. Son of Esau.....................Gen. 36:2–4
2. Moses' father-in-law .... Ex. 2:18
3. Benjamite........................... 1 Chr. 9:8
4. Gadite leader.....................Num. 2:14
Called Deuel ....Num. 7:42, 47

Reumah—*exalted*
Nahor's concubine ....Gen. 22:24

WORD STUDY   **REVEAL, MAKE KNOWN,** *phaneroō* (fahn-er-*ah*-oh). The verb *phaneroō* means "to reveal," "to make known," "to show," "to be revealed," "to become visible." Most of the occurrences of *phaneroō* are to be found in Paul's letters and in John's Gospel and letters, where its use connotes a divine revelation of truth or a supernatural manifestation. It is used especially with reference to God (Rom. 1:19; 2 Cor. 2:14) and Jesus (John 2:11; 7:4), particularly after His resurrection when He appears as Risen Lord (John 21:1, 14). (Strong's #5319)

WORD STUDY   **REVELATION,** *apokalupsis* (ap-ok-*ahl*-oop-sis). The basic idea of this compound noun is to take away (*apo*) a veil or cover (*kalumma*), hence its meaning "uncovering," "revelation," "disclosure," especially with reference to things previously hidden. In the NT *apokalupsis* is used figuratively with respect to the "disclosure" of truths through visions (2 Cor. 12:1; cf. Gal. 1:12). It is used in an eschatological sense to refer to the "disclosure" of the secrets of the last days (1 Pet. 1:7, 13; 4:13; cf. 1 Cor. 1:7; 2 Thess. 1:7)—as the first word of Rev. announces (1:1). (Strong's #602)

Revelation—*an uncovering of something hidden*
A. Source of:
God .... Dan. 2:28–47
Christ.............................. John 1:18
The Spirit........................... 1 Cor. 2:10
Not in humankind.................. Matt. 16:17
B. Objects of:
God .... Matt. 11:25, 27
Christ............................. 2 Thess. 1:7
Man of Sin ....2 Thess. 2:3, 6, 8
C. Instruments of:
Prophets .... 1 Pet. 1:10–12
Daniel .... Dan. 10:1
Christ.............................. Heb. 1:1, 2
Apostles .... 1 Cor. 2:10
Paul ....Gal. 1:16
D. Of the First Advent:
Predicted .... Is. 40:5
Revealed.............................Is. 53:1
Rejected .... John 12:38–41
Of God's righteousness.................. Is. 56:1
Of peace and truth......Jer. 33:6–8; Eph. 2:11–17
E. Time of the Second Advent:
Uncovering........................ Matt. 10:26
Judgment .... Luke 17:26–30

Victory ....2 Thess. 2:3, 6, 8
Glory ....1 Pet. 5:1
Resurrection .... Rom. 8:18, 19
Reward ....1 Cor. 3:13, 14
Glorification ....1 John 3:2
Grace............................. 1 Pet. 1:5, 13
Joy.............................. 1 Pet. 4:13

F. Of divine truth, characteristics of:
God-originated......................Dan. 2:47
Verbal .... Heb. 1:1
In the created world................Ps. 19:1, 2
Illuminative.........................Eph. 1:17
Now revealed...................... Rom. 16:26
Communicating truth................ Eph. 3:3, 4

Revelation, the—*a book of the New Testament*
Vision of the Son of Man .... Rev. 1:9–20
Message to the seven churches ..... Rev. 2:1–3:22
The book of seven seals ....Rev. 4:1–6:17
The judgment ....Rev. 7:1–9:21
The two beasts .... Rev. 13
Babylon doomed............... Rev. 17:1–18:24
The marriage supper.............. Rev. 19:6–10
The judgment of the wicked ...... Rev. 20:11–15
New heaven and new earth .... Rev. 21:1–8
The New Jerusalem .... Rev. 21:9–22:5
Christ's coming................... Rev. 22:6–21

Revenge—*to take vengeance*
A. Manifestation of:
Belongs to God .... Rev. 18:20
Performed by rulers...................Rom. 13:4
Righteously allowed ....1 Kin. 20:42
Pleaded for.......................... Jer. 11:20
Disallowed among people ....Prov. 20:22
Forbidden to disciples.............Luke 9:54, 55
B. Antidotes of:
Overcome by kindness ....1 Sam. 25:30–34
Exhibit love ....Luke 6:35
Bless................................Rom. 12:14
Forbear wrath ....Rom. 12:19
Manifest forbearance ....Matt. 5:38–41
Flee from....................... Gen. 27:41–45
C. Examples of:
Simeon and Levi.....................Gen. 34:25
Joseph .... Gen. 42:9–24
Samson ....Judg. 16:28–30
Joab .... 2 Sam. 3:27, 30
Jezebel..............................1 Kin. 19:2
Ahab .... 1 Kin. 22:26, 27
Haman .... Esth. 3:8–15
Philistines......................... Ezek. 25:15–17
Herodias........................Mark 6:19–24
Jews .... Acts 7:54, 59

Reverence—*a feeling of deep respect, love, awe, and esteem*
Manifested toward:
God ....Ps. 89:7
God's house ....Lev. 19:30
Kings............................. 1 Kin. 1:31

Revile—*to speak of another abusively*
Christ, object of .... Matt. 27:39
Christ, submissive under .... 1 Pet. 2:23
Christians, objects of.................Matt. 5:11
Right attitude toward .... 1 Cor. 4:12
Punishment of....................... 1 Cor. 6:10
False teachers..................... 2 Pet. 2:10–12

Revival—*renewed zeal to obey God*
Conditions for:
Humility............................ 2 Chr. 7:14
Prayer ....2 Chr. 7:14; James 5:16
Broken heart ....Ps. 34:18
Confession ....Ps. 66:18
Repentance .... 2 Cor. 7:10
Turning from sin .... 2 Chr. 7:14; 2 Tim. 2:19
Complete surrender......Acts 9:5, 6; Rom. 12:1, 2

Revive—*to live again more vigorously*
A. Descriptive of:
Renewed strength.....................Gen. 45:27
Refreshment ....Judg. 15:19
Restoration............................ Neh. 4:2
Resurrection ....1 Kin. 17:22
Spiritual renewal......................Ps. 71:20
B. Of the spirit:
Given to the humble ....Is. 57:15
Source of joy...........................Ps. 85:6
Possible even in trouble.................Ps. 138:7
Source of fruitfulness ....Hos. 6:2, 3; 14:7
C. Accomplished by:
God .... 1 Tim. 6:13
Christ..............................1 Cor. 15:45
Holy Spirit .... John 6:63
God's Word ....Ps. 119:25, 50
God's precepts........................Ps. 119:93

Reward of the righteous
A. Described as:
Sure .... Prov. 11:18
Full................................Ruth 2:12
Remembered .... 2 Chr. 15:7
Great .... Matt. 5:12
Open .... Matt. 6:4, 6, 18
B. Obtained by:
Keeping God's commandments........ Ps. 19:11
Sowing righteousness ....Prov. 11:18
Fearing God's commandments.......Prov. 13:13
Feeding an enemy................. Prov. 25:21, 22
Simple service ....Matt. 6:1
Hospitality..................... Matt. 10:40–42
Grace through faith.............. Rom. 4:4, 5, 16
Faithful service.................... Col. 3:23, 24
Seeking God diligently............... Heb. 11:6
C. At Christ's return:
After the resurrection ....Rev. 11:18
Tested by fire......................1 Cor. 3:8–14
According to works .... Rev. 22:12
See Crowns of Christians; Hire; Wages

Reward of the wicked

A. Visited upon:
  Now .... Ps. 91:8
  At the judgment .... 2 Tim. 4:14
B. Measure of:
  By retribution ....Rev. 18:6
  According to the wickedness......... 2 Sam. 3:39
  Plentifully............................Ps. 31:23

Rezeph—*glowing stone*
  Place destroyed by the Assyrians .....2 Kin. 19:12

Rezin

1. King of Damascus; joins Pekah
    against Ahaz .... 2 Kin. 15:37
  Confederacy of, inspires Isaiah's great
    messianic prophecy.............. Is. 7:1–9:12
2. Head of a Nethinim family..............Ezra 2:48

Rezon—*prince*
  Son of Eliadah; establishes Syrian
    kingdom.................... 1 Kin. 11:23–25

Rhegium—*a city of southern Italy*
  Paul's ship arrived at .... Acts 28:13

Rhesa

  Ancestor of Christ .... Luke 3:27

Rhoda—*rose bush*
  Servant girl........................Acts 12:13–16

Rhodes—*an island off the southwest coast of Asia Minor*
  Paul's ship passes by....................Acts 21:1

Rib

  Eve formed of Adam's .... Gen. 2:22

Ribai—*Yahweh strives*
  One of David's mighty men......... 2 Sam. 23:29

Riblah—*fertility*
1. Town on Israel's eastern border ....Num. 34:11
2. Town in the land of Hamath.......... 2 Kin. 23:33
  Headquarters of:
  Pharaoh Necho .... 2 Kin. 23:31–35
  Nebuchadnezzar.............. 2 Kin. 25:6, 20, 21
  Zedekiah blinded here .... Jer. 39:5–7

Rich—*wealthy*
A. Spiritual handicaps of:
  Selfishly satisfied ....Luke 6:24
  Reluctant to leave riches.......... Luke 18:22–25
  Forgetful of God................. Luke 12:15–21
  Indifferent to others' needs .... Luke 16:19–31
  Easily tempted....................... 1 Tim. 6:9
  Hindered spiritually .... Matt. 19:23, 24
  Misplaced trust.....................Prov. 11:28
B. Applied, spiritually, to:
  God .... Eph. 2:4
  Christ.............................. Rom. 10:12
  Christians.......................... James 2:5
  True riches......................... 2 Cor. 8:9
  Good works .... 1 Tim. 6:18
  Worldly people .... Jer. 5:27, 28
  Self-righteous .... Hos. 12:8
  Synagogue of Satan ....Rev. 2:9

Riches, earthly

A. Described as:
  Spiritually valueless...................Ps. 49:6, 7
  Inferior .... Heb. 11:26
  Fleeting............................Prov. 23:5
  Unsatisfying .... Eccl. 4:8
  Hurtful.......................... Eccl. 5:13, 14
  Deceitful......................... Matt. 13:22
  Choking .... Luke 8:14
  Uncertain ....1 Tim. 6:17
  Corrupted........................... James 5:2
B. Proper attitude toward:
  Not to:
  Put first......................... 1 Kin. 3:11, 13
  Be trusted........................... Ps. 52:7
  Set heart upon....................... Ps. 62:10
  Be desired.........................Prov. 30:8
  Not forever........................Prov. 27:24
  Use in giving .... 2 Cor. 8:2
  Remember God's supply.............. Phil. 4:19

Riches, management of

  Reflects spiritual attitude .... Luke 16:10–12
  Demands budget .... Luke 14:28–30

Riches, spiritual

Source of, in:
  God's Law........................... Ps. 119:14
  Divine wisdom ....Prov. 3:13, 14
  Unselfish service..................... Prov. 13:7
  Reverential fear.....................Prov. 22:4
  Fulfillment........................Rom. 11:12
  Christ...........................Col. 1:27
  Assurance...........................Col. 2:2
  Christ's Word ....Col. 3:16

Riddle—*a hidden saying solved by guessing*
  Samson's famous.................. Judg. 14:12–19
  Classed as a parable ....Ezek. 17:2
  Avoided by God .... Num. 12:8

Ridicule (see Mocking)

Right—*that which is just and fair*
A. Things that are:
  God's Law............................ Ps. 19:8
  God's Word .... Ps. 33:4
  God's way ....Ps. 107:7
  Thoughts of the righteous ....Prov. 12:5
  Work of the pure..................... Prov. 21:8
  Obedience to God .... Acts 4:19, 20
  Obedience to parents...................Eph. 6:1
B. Things that are not:
  False riches.........................Jer. 17:11
  Injustice to the poor..................... Is. 10:2
  Human ways ....Prov. 21:2
  Human hearts.......................Ps. 78:37

Righteous—*that which is upright*
A. Applied to:
  God .... John 17:25
  Christ..............................1 John 2:1
  Messiah........................... Is. 53:11

Christians. . . . . Matt. 25:37, 46

B. Blessings of:
Prayers of, heard. . . . . .Prov. 15:29
Safely guarded. .Prov. 18:10
Bold as a lion . . . . .Prov. 28:1
Shine forth. . . . . Matt. 13:43

Righteousness—*uprightness before God*
A. Kinds of:
Created . . . . Eph. 4:24
Legal . . . . Phil. 3:6
Personal . . . . Phil. 3:9
Imputed . . . . Phil. 3:9
Immature. . . . . Heb. 5:13
Actual . . . . Heb. 11:33
Real . . . . .1 John 2:29

B. Of Christ, He:
Is the believer's . . . . .Jer. 33:16
Loves . . . . Heb. 1:9
Judges with. . . . . .Is. 11:4
Is girded with. . . . . .Is. 11:5
Brings in . . . . Is. 46:13
Fulfills all. . . . . .Matt. 3:15
Confers upon believers . . . . .Is. 61:10

Rimmon—*pomegranate*
1. Benjamite. . . . . .2 Sam. 4:2–9
2. Rock near Gibeah . . . . Judg. 20:45–47
Benjamites hide here . . . . Judg. 21:13–23
3. Town in south Judah. . . . . Josh. 15:1, 32
Assigned to Simeon . . . . Josh. 19:7, 8
Mentioned in prophecy. . . . . Zech. 14:10
Called En Rimmon . . . . Neh. 11:29
4. Syrian God (meaning "thunderer")
worshiped by Naaman . . . . 2 Kin. 5:18
5. City of Zebulun . . . . .Josh. 19:13
Levitical city .1 Chr. 6:77
Called Dimnah .Josh. 21:35

Rimmon Perez—*pomegranate of breach*
Israelite camp . . . . Num. 33:19, 20

Ring
A. Article of furniture, for:
Poles of the ark . . . . Ex. 25:12–15
Curtains . . . . Ex. 26:29
Priest's ephod .Ex. 28:23–28
Incense altar . . . . .Ex. 30:4

B. Article of apparel:
Symbol of authority. . . . . .Gen. 41:42
Sealing royal documents. . . . . .Esth. 3:12
Gifts. . . . . .Ex. 35:22
Feminine adornment. . . . . Is. 3:16, 21
Expressive of position . . . . .Luke 15:22
Sign of social status . . . . .James 2:2

Ringleader—*the leader of a mob*
Paul contemptuously called. . . . . Acts 24:5

Rinnah—*ringing cry*
Son of Shimon. .1 Chr. 4:20

Riot—*an unruly mob*
Pacified by town clerk. . . . . .Acts 19:20–41

Riphath—*descendants of Gomer*
Son of Gomer. . . . . Gen. 10:3
Called Diphath . . . . .1 Chr. 1:6

Rise, risen, rising, raised
A. Of resurrection:
Christ's . . . . .Mark 8:31
Believers' (spiritually) . . . . .Col. 2:12
Believers' (physically) . . . . .John 11:23, 24

B. Of Christ's resurrection:
Predicted . . . . Mark 14:28
Fulfilled . . . . Matt. 28:6, 7
Remembered . . . . .John 2:22
Evidenced. . . . . John 21:14
Preached. . . . . .1 Cor. 15:11–15
Misunderstood . . . . Mark 9:9, 10

Rissah—*ruin; rain*
Israelite camp . . . . .Num. 33:21, 22

Rithmah—*broom plant*
Israelite camp . . . . Num. 33:18, 19

Rivalry—*competition*
Between man and neighbor. . . . . Eccl. 4:4

River—*a large stream of water*
A. Uses of:
Water. . . . . .Jer. 2:18
Irrigation . . . . Gen. 2:10
Bathing . . . . .Ex. 2:5
Baptisms . . . . Matt. 3:6
Healing . . . . .2 Kin. 5:10
Hiding place . . . . Ex. 2:2–4
Medium of death sentence. . . . . .Ex. 1:22

B. List of:
Abanah . . . . .2 Kin. 5:12
Arnon . . . . .Josh. 12:1
Chebar. . . . . Ezek. 10:15, 20
Euphrates . . . . Gen. 2:14
Gihon. . . . . Gen. 2:13
Gozan . . . . .2 Kin. 17:6
Hiddekel. . . . . Gen. 2:14
Jabbok . . . . Deut. 2:37
Jordan . . . . .Josh. 3:8
Kanah . . . . .Josh. 16:8
Kishon. . . . . .Judg. 5:21
Nile (Sihor). . . . . .Jer. 2:18
Pharpar. . . . . .2 Kin. 5:12
Pishon . . . . Gen. 2:11
Ulai . . . . .Dan. 8:2, 16

C. Figurative of:
Prosperity of saints . . . . Ps. 1:3
Affliction . . . . .Ps. 124:4
Christ. . . . . Is. 32:1, 2
God's presence . . . . Is. 33:21
Peace . . . . Is. 66:12
Holy Spirit . . . . .John 7:38, 39

Rizia—*delight*
Asherite. . . . . .1 Chr. 7:39

Rizpah—*glowing coal*
Saul's concubine taken by Abner . . . .2 Sam. 3:6–8

Sons of, killed . . . . 2 Sam. 21:8, 9
Grief-stricken, cares for corpses. . . 2 Sam. 21:10–14

Road (see Highway)

Rob, robbery

A. Used literally of:
Plundering . . . . 1 Sam. 23:1
Taking from the poor . . . . .Prov. 22:22
Robbers. . . . . .Judg. 9:25

B. Used figuratively of:
Dishonest riches . . . . Ps. 62:10
Holding back from God . . . . Mal. 3:8, 9
False teachers. . . . . John 10:1, 8
Taking wages. . . . . 2 Cor. 11:8

WORD STUDY　　**ROCK,** *petra* (*pet*-rah). This noun means "rock," and it usually denotes a rock mass of the type from which tombs could be hewn (Matt. 27:60) or that might serve as the foundation for houses (Luke 6:48) or that might not be covered with enough topsoil to support the growth of seed (Luke 8:6). The word figures in a memorable play on words in Matt. 16:18. After Simon Peter affirms that Jesus is the Christ (16:16), Jesus calls him Peter (*petros*) and announces that either the apostles so named or his affirmation will be the rock (*petra*) that will serve as the foundation for His church. (Strong's #4073)

Rock

A. Used for:
Altars. . . . . Judg. 6:20, 26
Idol worship. . . . . .Is. 57:5
Protection. . . . . 1 Sam. 13:6
Shade. . . . . Is. 32:2
Inscriptions . . . . Job 19:24
Executions . . . . 2 Chr. 25:12
Foundations. . . . . Matt. 7:24, 25
Shelter . . . . Job 24:8
Temple. . . . . Matt. 24:1, 2
Tomb . . . . Matt. 27:60

B. Miracles connected with:
Water from. . . . . .Ex. 17:6
Fire from. . . . . .Judg. 6:21
Broken by wind. . . . . 1 Kin. 19:11
Split at Christ's death . . . . Matt. 27:51

C. Figurative of Christ, as:
Refuge. . . . . Is. 32:2
Foundation of the church. . . . . Matt. 16:18
Source of blessings . . . . 1 Cor. 10:4
Stone of stumbling. . . . . .Is. 8:14
Foundation of faith . . . . Matt. 7:24, 25

Rock of Escape
Cliff in the wilderness near Maon . . . 1 Sam. 23:28

Rod—*a staff or stick*

A. Used for:
Sign of authority. . . . . .Ex. 4:17, 20
Egyptians' staffs. .Ex. 7:12
Punishment . . . . .Ex. 21:20

Club . . . . 1 Sam. 14:27
Correction of children . . . . .Prov. 13:24

B. Figurative of:
Christ. . . . . .Is. 11:1
Christ's rule . . . . Ps. 2:9
Authority . . . . Is. 14:5, 29
The gospel . . . . Ps. 110:2

Roebuck—*the deer, gazelle*
In Solomon's provisions . . . . .1 Kin. 4:23

Rogelim—*spies*
Town in Gilead . . . . 2 Sam. 17:27

Rohgah—*tumult*
Asherite. . . . . .1 Chr. 7:34

Romamti-Ezer—*I have raised up help*
Son of Heman .1 Chr. 25:4, 31

Roman
1. Inhabitant of Rome . . . . Acts 2:10
2. Official agent of the Roman
government . . . . .John 11:46–48
3. Person possessing Roman
citizenship . . . . Acts 16:21–38

Romans, the Epistle to the—*a book of the New Testament*
The power of the gospel . . . . .Rom. 1:16
The pagans condemned . . . . Rom. 1:17–32
The Jews condemned. . . . . Rom. 2:1–9
The advantages of the Jews . . . . Rom. 3:1–8
None righteous . . . . Rom. 3:9–20
Righteousness through faith. . . . . . . Rom. 3:21–31
Abraham justified . . . . Rom. 4
The Second Adam . . . . Rom. 5:12–21
On baptism . . . . Rom. 6
The pull of sin. . . . . Rom. 7
The spiritual life. . . . . Rom. 8
The destiny of the Jews. . . . . Rom. 9–11
Life as worship . . . . .Rom. 12:1, 2
Serving the body. . . . . Rom. 12:3–21
Bearing with one another. . . . . Rom. 14, 15
Greetings . . . . Rom. 16:1–24

Rome—*the chief city of Italy*
Jews expelled from. . . . . Acts 18:2
Paul:
Writes to Christians of . . . . .Rom. 1:7
Desires to go to . . . . Acts 19:21
Comes to. . . . . Acts 28:14
Imprisoned in . . . . Acts 28:16

Rooster crowing
Announced the dawn . . . . Mark 13:35
Reminded Peter . . . . .Matt. 26:34, 74

Root—*the part of a plant underground*
Used figuratively of:
Material foundation . . . . .Jer. 12:2
Remnant. . . . . .Judg. 5:14
National existence . . . . Is. 14:30
National source. . . . . Rom. 11:16–18
Source of evil. . . . . 1 Tim. 6:10

Restoration . . . . .2 Kin. 19:30
Spiritual life . . . . Hos. 14:5
Spiritual foundation . . . . Eph. 3:17
Messiah . . . . Is. 11:1, 10

Rose—*a beautiful flower*
Of Sharon . . . . Song 2:1
Desert shall blossom as . . . . .Is. 35:1

Rosh—*head, chief*
1. Benjamin's son . . . . Gen. 46:21
2. Northern people connected with
     Meshech and Tubal . . . . Ezek. 38:2

Rot—*to decay*
A. Used literally of:
     Sickness . . . . .Num. 5:21–27
     Hardwood trees . . . . Is. 40:20
B. Used figuratively of:
     Wicked . . . . Prov. 10:7
     Foolish wife . . . . Prov. 12:4

Rowing—*to navigate a boat with oars*
Against odds . . . . Jon. 1:13
With much labor . . . . Mark 6:48

Royal—*belonging to a king*
A. Used literally of:
     King's children . . . . 2 Kin. 11:1
     Robes of royalty . . . . Esth. 6:8
     City of a king . . . . 2 Sam. 12:26
B. Used spiritually of:
     Israel . . . . Is. 62:3
     The church . . . . .1 Pet. 2:9

Ruby—*a valuable gem (red pearl)*
Very valuable . . . . Prov. 3:15
Wisdom more valuable than . . . . Job 28:18
Good wife above price of . . . . Prov. 31:10
Reddish color . . . . Lam. 4:7

Rudder—*a steering apparatus*
Literally . . . . Acts 27:40
Figuratively . . . . James 3:4

Rudeness—*discourtesy*
Shown toward:
     Christ . . . . .Matt. 26:67, 68
     Paul . . . . Acts 23:2

Rue—*a pungent perennial shrub*
Tithed by Pharisees . . . . Luke 11:42

Rufus—*red-haired*
1. Son of Simon of Cyrene . . . . Mark 15:21
2. Christian of Rome . . . . Rom. 16:13
     Probably the same as 1

Rule—*to govern*
A. Of natural things:
     Sun and moon . . . . Gen. 1:16, 18
     Sea . . . . Ps. 89:9
B. Among people
     Husband over wife . . . . Gen. 3:16
     King over people . . . . Ezra 4:20
     Diligent over the lazy . . . . .Prov. 12:24
     Servant over a son . . . . Prov. 17:2

Rich over poor . . . . Prov. 22:7
Servants over a people . . . . Neh. 5:15
C. Of the Messiah:
     Promised . . . . Zech. 6:13
     Victorious . . . . Ps. 110:2
     Announced . . . . Matt. 2:6
     Established . . . . .Rev. 12:5
     Described . . . . .Rev. 2:27

Ruler—*one who governs*
A. Good characteristics of:
     Upholding the good . . . . .Rom. 13:3
     Believing . . . . Matt. 9:18, 23
     Faithful and wise . . . . Matt. 24:45–47
     Chosen by God .2 Sam. 7:8
B. Bad characteristics of:
     Love human praise . . . . .John 12:42, 43
     Ignorant . . . . .Acts 3:17
     Hostile . . . . Acts 4:26
     Love bribes . . . . Hos. 4:18
C. Respect toward:
     Commanded . . . . Ex. 22:28
     Illustrated . . . . Acts 23:5

Ruler of this world
Satan thus called . . . . John 14:30
To be cast out . . . . John 12:31
Is judged . . . . John 16:11
Source of evil . . . . Eph. 2:2

Rumah—*high place*
Residence of Pedaiah . . . . .2 Kin. 23:36

Run—*to move swiftly*
A. Used literally of:
     Man . . . . Num. 11:27
     Water . . . . .Ps. 105:41
     Race . . . . 1 Cor. 9:24
B. Used figuratively of:
Eagerness in:
     Evil . . . . Prov. 1:16
     Good . . . . Ps. 119:32
     Joy of salvation . . . . Ps. 23:5
     Christian life . . . . Rom. 12:1; 1 Cor. 9:26

Rush—*a cylindrical, often hollow marsh plant*
Cut off from Israel; rendered "bulrush" . . . .Is. 9:14
Signifying restoration . . . . Is. 35:7

Rust—*corrosion of metals*
Destruction of earthly treasures . . . . Matt. 6:19, 20
Of gold and silver . . . . James 5:3

Ruth—*female companion*
Moabitess . . . . Ruth 1:4
Married to Mahlon for 10 years . . . . Ruth 1:4; 4:10
Follows Naomi . . . . .Ruth 1:6–18
In Bethlehem, gleans in Boaz's field . . .Ruth 2:7–23
Marries Boaz . . . . Ruth 4:9–13
Has a son, Obed . . . . .Ruth 4:10, 17
Ancestress of David . . . . Ruth 4:13, 21, 22
Ancestress of Jesus . . . . .Matt. 1:5

Ruth, Book of—*a book of the Old Testament*
Naomi's misfortunes . . . . Ruth 1:1–14

S

Sabachthani—*Why have You forsaken Me?*

| WORD STUDY | **SABAOTH, HOSTS,** *sabaōth* (sab-ah-*ohth*). This noun, which occurs only twice |

in the NT, is the transliteration of the Hebrew word for "army" or "hosts" (*saba'*) in its plural form. Both times it forms part of a name given to God in the OT (Is. 6:3): "Lord of Hosts" or "Lord of (heavenly) armies." This OT characterization of God depicts Him as an avenging God of majesty and might, One who commands a myriad of angels ready to wage His battles. James (5:4) uses this expression to evoke the image of the coming judgment of God the Avenger. In Rom. 9:29 Paul quotes a passage (Is. 1:9) in which the expression occurs. (Strong's #4519)

Sabaoth—*hosts*

Sabbath—*rest*

A. History of:

B. Features concerning:

C. Regulations concerning:

Sabbath day's journey—*about 3,100 feet*

Sabbatical year—*a rest every seventh year*

A. Purpose of:

B. Allusions to, in history, in:

C. Spiritual significance of:

Sabeans—*descendants of Sheba*

Sabtah

Sabtechah

Sacar—*hired*

Sachiah—*fame of Yahweh*

Sackcloth—*a coarse fabric made of goat's hair*

A. Worn by:

B. Expressive of:

C. Symbolic of:

Sacrament (see Baptism, Christian; Lord's
   Supper)

Sacred places

Sacrifice, sacrifices

A. Requirements of:

By appointed priests . . . . 1 Sam. 2:28
In faith . . . . Gen. 4:4
In obedience . . . . 1 Sam. 15:22
B. Perversion of, in offering:
To demons . . . . 1 Cor. 10:20
To idols . . . . 2 Chr. 34:25
Defective animals. . . . . Mal. 1:13, 14
Without respect . . . . 1 Sam. 2:29
C. Inadequacy of:
Could not atone for sins . . . . Ps. 40:6;
  Heb. 10:1–4
Limited to legal purification . . . . Heb. 9:13, 22
D. Figurative of:
Christ's sacrifice . . . . 1 Cor. 5:7
Prayer . . . . Ps. 141:2
Worship . . . . 1 Pet. 2:5
Righteousness . . . . Ps. 51:19
E. Of Christ to:
Redeem from the Curse . . . . Gal. 3:13
Secure our redemption . . . . Matt. 20:28
Reconcile God and humankind . . . . Rom. 5:10

Sacrilege—*profaning holy things*
A. Done by:
Defaming God's name . . . . 2 Kin. 18:28–35
Profaning the Sabbath . . . . Neh. 13:15–21
Debauching holy things . . . . John 2:14–16
B. Those guilty of:
People . . . . 1 Sam. 6:19
Pagans . . . . Dan. 5:1–4
Priests . . . . Lev. 10:1–7
Pharisees . . . . Matt. 23:16–22

Saddle—*cloth or leather seat for a rider*
Balaam's . . . . Num. 22:21

Sadducees—*followers of Zadok*
Rejected by John . . . . Matt. 3:7
Tested Jesus . . . . Matt. 16:1–12
Silenced by Jesus . . . . Matt. 22:23–34
Did not believe in resurrection of
 the dead . . . . Mark 12:18
Antagonized by teaching of
 resurrection . . . . Acts 4:1, 2
Opposed apostles . . . . Acts 5:17–40

Safe, safety—*dwelling without fear or harm*
A. False means of:
Wickedness . . . . Job 21:7–9, 17
Folly . . . . Job 5:2–4
False hope . . . . 1 Thess. 5:3
B. True means of:
Lord . . . . Ps. 4:8
Lord's protection . . . . Deut. 33:12
Apostolic admonition . . . . Phil. 3:1

Saffron—*a variety of crocus; used as a perfume or medicine*
Figurative of the bride . . . . Song 4:14

Sail—*an expanse of material used to catch the wind and propel a sailing ship*
Figurative of:
Enemies' weakness . . . . Is. 33:23

The pride of Tyre . . . . Ezek. 27:7

Sailors—*mariners; seamen*
Skilled . . . . 1 Kin. 9:27
Fearful . . . . Jon. 1:5
Cry bitterly . . . . Ezek. 27:8–36
Storm-tossed . . . . Acts 27:18–31

Saints—*God's redeemed people*
A. Descriptive of:
Old Testament believers . . . . Matt. 27:52
Christians . . . . Acts 9:32, 41
Christian martyrs . . . . Rev. 16:6
Those present with Christ at His
 return . . . . 1 Thess. 3:13
B. Their weaknesses, subject to:
Needs . . . . Rom. 12:13; 2 Cor. 9:1, 12
Persecution . . . . Dan. 7:21, 25
C. Their duty to:
Keep God's Word . . . . Jude 3
Grow spiritually . . . . Eph. 4:12
Avoid evil . . . . Eph. 5:3
Judge world . . . . 1 Cor. 6:1, 2
Pray for others . . . . Eph. 6:18
Minister to others . . . . Heb. 6:10
D. God's protection of, He:
Forsakes them not . . . . Ps. 37:28
Gathers them . . . . Ps. 50:5
Keeps them . . . . 1 Sam. 2:9
Counts them precious . . . . Ps. 116:15
Intercedes for them . . . . Rom. 8:27
Will glorify them . . . . 2 Thess. 1:10

Salamis—*a town of Cyprus*
Paul preaches here . . . . Acts 13:4, 5

Salcah—*wandering*
City in Bashan . . . . Deut. 3:10

Salem—*peace*
Jerusalem's original name . . . . Gen. 14:18
Used poetically . . . . Ps. 76:2

Salim—*completeness*
Place near Aenon . . . . John 3:23

Sallai—*rejecter*
1. Benjamite chief . . . . Neh. 11:8
2. Priestly family . . . . Neh. 12:20
Called Sallu . . . . Neh. 12:7

Sallu—*contempt*
Benjamite family . . . . 1 Chr. 9:7
See Sallai 2

Salma—*clothing*
Son of Hur . . . . 1 Chr. 2:50, 51

Salmon
Father of Boaz . . . . Ruth 4:20, 21
Ancestor of Christ . . . . Matt. 1:4, 5

Salome—*feminine of Solomon*
1. Among ministering women . . . . Mark 15:40, 41
Visits empty tomb . . . . Mark 16:1
2. Herodias's daughter (not named in
 the Bible) . . . . Matt. 14:6–11

SALT, *halas* (*hahl-oss*). *Halas* is a noun meaning "salt." Salt is used as a seasoning, a preservative, and a fertilizer. Jesus uses "salt" in a figure (Luke 14:34) to describe the spiritual qualities He desires of His disciples, although there is debate about which of the uses of salt He had in mind. See also Col. 4:6. (Strong's #217)

Salt

A. Uses of:

Seasoning:

Food.................................Job 6:6
Sacrifice ....Lev. 2:13
Rubbed on infants at birth............Ezek. 16:4
Making land unproductive ....Judg. 9:45

B. Miracles connected with:

Lot's wife becomes pillar of..........Gen. 19:26
Elisha purified water with ....2 Kin. 2:19–22

C. Figurative of:

God's everlasting covenant ....Num. 18:19
Barrenness and desolation...........Deut. 29:23
Good influence......................Matt. 5:13
Peace in the heart...................Mark 9:50
Wise speech..........................Col. 4:6
Final judgment ....Mark 9:49
Reprobation........................Ezek. 47:9, 11

Salt, City of

City in the wilderness of Judah........Josh. 15:62

Salt Sea

Old Testament name for the
Dead Sea ....Gen. 14:3; Num. 34:3, 12

Salt, Valley of—*a valley south of the Dead Sea*

Site of:

David's victory ....2 Sam. 8:13
Amaziah's victory ....2 Kin. 14:7

Salu—*restored*

Simeonite prince...................Num. 25:14

SALVATION, *sōtēria* (so-tay-*ree*-ah). This noun originally meant "deliverance (from)" or "preservation (in)" dangerous or threatening circumstances (see Luke 1:71; Acts 27:34). Outside the NT it was also used to denote "salvation," which true religion bestows. In the NT it is used in this sense only in association with God's work (Luke 1:69, 77) through Jesus Christ (Acts 4:12) as Savior (*sōtēr*) and His redemptive act of delivering humanity from everything that might lead to eternal death—for example, sin—or from the judgment that might lead to that fate (see 2 Cor. 7:10; Eph. 1:13; Phil. 1:28; 2 Tim. 2:10; Heb. 5:9). This "salvation" is experienced in the present (Luke 19:9, 10) but will be consummated in the future when the Lord comes again (Rom. 13:11; Heb. 9:28; 1 Pet. 1:5). (Strong's #4991)

Salvation

A. Descriptive of:

National deliverance ....Ex. 14:13

Deliverance from enemies ....2 Chr. 20:17
Messiah.............................Matt. 1:21

B. Source of, in:

God's grace......................... Eph. 2:5, 8
God's love..........................Rom. 5:8
God's mercy........................Titus 3:5
Christ alone .... Acts 4:12
Cross .... 1 Cor. 1:18

C. History of:

Promised to Adam.................... Gen. 3:15
Announced to Abram ....Gen. 12:1–3
Revealed to the prophets .... 1 Pet. 1:10–12
Longed for by the saints ....Ps. 119:81, 174
Promised to Gentiles............... Is. 45:21, 22
To be realized in the Messiah .... Is. 59:16, 17
Seen in Christ's birth..............Luke 1:69, 77
Christ, the author..................... Heb. 5:9
Appeared to all people.................Titus 2:11
Proclaimed to Israel................Zech. 9:9
Accomplished on the cross.......... John 3:14, 15
Preached through the gospel............Eph. 1:13
Rejected by Israel .... Acts 13:26–46
Extended to Gentiles............... Acts 28:28
This age, day of....................... 2 Cor. 6:2
God's longsuffering in ....2 Pet. 3:9
Final, nearer each day ....Rom. 13:11
Consummated in the Second Advent ... Heb. 9:28
Praise for, in heaven.................... Rev. 7:10

D. Requirements of:

Confession ....Acts 2:21; Rom. 10:10
Repentance ....Mark 1:15
Faith.............................John 3:14–18
Regeneration ....John 3:3–8
Holy Scripture......................2 Tim. 3:15
Believe.............................Rom. 10:9

E. Negative blessings of, deliverance from:

Sin................................Matt. 1:21
Satan's power......................Heb. 2:14, 15
Wrath ....Rom. 5:9
Eternal death....................... John 3:16, 17

F. Positive blessings of:

Chosen to .... 2 Thess. 2:13
Appointed to .... 1 Thess. 5:9
Kept unto ....1 Pet. 1:5
Rejoiced in .... 1 Pet. 4:13
To be worked out .... Phil. 2:12

G. Temporal aspects of:

Past................................. Eph. 2:8
Present............................. 1 Cor. 1:18
Future .... Heb. 9:28

Samaria—*watchtower*

1. Capital of Israel ....1 Kin. 16:24–29
Built by Omri.................... 1 Kin. 16:23, 24
Israel's "crown of pride" .... Is. 28:1
Besieged twice by Ben-Hadad..... 1 Kin. 20:1–22
Miraculously saved .... 2 Kin. 6:8–23
Worshipers of Baal destroyed ..... 2 Kin. 10:1–28
Taken captive; people of, exiled .... 2 Kin. 17:6

Threatened with divine judgment..... Is. 28:1–4;
    Amos 3:11, 12
Repopulated with foreigners..... 2 Kin. 17:24–41
2. Name of northern kingdom ....1 Kin. 21:1
3. District of Palestine in
    Christ's time .... Luke 17:11–19
Preaching in, forbidden by Christ ..... Matt. 10:5
Preaching of gospel in, commanded ......Acts 1:8
Churches established there ....Acts 9:31
Paul preached there ....Acts 15:3

Samaritans—*inhabitants of Samaria*
Of mixed blood and defiled
    religion.................... 2 Kin. 17:24–41
Seek alliance with Jews.............. Ezra 4:1–4
Jews did not associate with .... John 4:9
Christ and the Samaritan woman ... John 4:5–42
Story of "the Good Samaritan".... Luke 10:30–37
Jesus heals a Samaritan leper......Luke 17:11–19
A town of, rejects Jesus .... Luke 9:52–55
Beliefs of............................ John 4:25
Converts among .... Acts 8:5–25

Samek
Fifteenth letter of the Hebrew
    alphabet................... Ps. 119:113–120

Samgar-Nebo—*be gracious, Nebo*
Prince of Nebuchadnezzar.............. Jer. 39:3

Samlah—*a garment*
Edomite king.................... Gen. 36:36, 37

Samos—*an island off the coast of Lydia*
Visited by Paul .... Acts 20:15

Samothrace—*an island in the Aegean Sea*
Visited by Paul ....Acts 16:11

Samson—*sunlike*
A. Life of:
Judge from tribe of Dan ....Judg. 13:2, 5
Birth of, predicted .... Judg. 13:3–7
God's Spirit moves him........... Judg. 13:24, 25
Desired a Philistine wife............Judg. 14:1–9
Posed a riddle .... Judg. 14:10–14
Betrayed, kills 30 men........... Judg. 14:15–20
Enticed by Delilah, loses strength ... Judg. 16:4–20
Blinded and bound.................Judg. 16:21
Destroyed over 3,000 in
    his death.........Judg. 16:22–31; Heb. 11:32
Listed as a man of faith.............. Heb. 11:32
B. Character of:
Weaknesses:
Attracted to foreign women ....Judg. 14:1–4;
    16:1; 16:4
Takes revenge ....Judg. 15:1–8
Disregard for his Nazirite vow ......Judg. 13:4, 5;
    14:8, 9; 16:19
Strengths:
Dependence on God ....Judg. 15:18, 19
Repentance that restored .... Judg. 16:28–31

Samuel—*name of God (a godly name)*
A. Life of:
Born in answer to Hannah's prayer . 1 Sam. 1:5–21
Before birth, dedicated to God as a
    Nazirite .... 1 Sam. 1:11, 22
Brought to Shiloh; reared by Eli ...1 Sam. 1:24–28
His mother praised God for........ 1 Sam. 2:1–10
The child Samuel called by God.... 1 Sam. 3:2–10
Delivered God's rebuke to Eli..... 1 Sam. 3:11–18
Recognized as a prophet.......... 1 Sam. 3:20, 21
Became a circuit judge .... 1 Sam. 7:15–17
Called Israel to repentance .... 1 Sam. 7:3–6
Samuel's sons rejected by Israel; they
    ask for a king .... 1 Sam. 8:1–6
Anointed Saul as king .... 1 Sam. 10:1
Advised Saul God had rejected
    him as king ....1 Sam. 13:13, 14; 15:28
Anointed David as king .... 1 Sam. 16:13
Woman of En Dor calls up spirit of; he foretells
    Saul's defeat and death....... 1 Sam. 28:11–20
Lamented in death.................1 Sam. 25:1
B. Ministry of:
Served as priest.................1 Sam. 2:11, 18;
    1 Chr. 6:1, 28
Served as prophet, seer .... 1 Sam. 3:19–21
Served as judge .... 1 Sam. 7:15–17
Organized gatekeepers .... 1 Chr. 9:22; 26:28
Inspired as a writer..................1 Chr. 29:29
Inspired as a prophet.................. Acts 3:24
Faithful to God................. Heb. 11:32–34
Industrious in service ....1 Chr. 9:22
Devout in life........................Jer. 15:1
Powerful in prayer ....Ps. 99:6

Samuel, Books of—*two books of the Old Testament*
A. 1 Samuel:
Birth of Samuel................. 1 Sam. 1:19–28
Hannah's song.................... 1 Sam. 2:1–10
The ark captured .... 1 Sam. 4:1–11
The ark returned .... 1 Sam. 6:1–21
Saul chosen as king .... 1 Sam. 9:1–27
Saul anointed..................... 1 Sam. 10:1–27
Saul against the Philistines .... 1 Sam. 13:1–4
Saul is rejected................... 1 Sam. 15:10–31
David is anointed .... 1 Sam. 16:1–13
David and Goliath ....1 Sam. 17:23–58
Jonathan's love .... 1 Sam. 19:1–7
Saul against David ....1 Sam. 23:6–29
David spares Saul .... 1 Sam. 24:1–8; 26:1–16
The medium of En Dor........... 1 Sam. 28:7–25
David against the Amalekites..... 1 Sam. 30:1–31
Death of Saul................... 1 Sam. 31:1–13
B. 2 Samuel:
David's lament .... 2 Sam. 1:17–27
David anointed as king............ 2 Sam. 2:1–7
The ark in Zion................... 2 Sam. 6:1–19
David plans the temple .... 2 Sam. 7:1–29
The kingdom expands .... 2 Sam. 8:1–18
David and Bathsheba .... 2 Sam. 11:1–27
Nathan rebukes David .... 2 Sam. 12:1–12

David repents .... 2 Sam. 12:13, 14
David's child dies.............. 2 Sam. 12:15–23
Amnon and Tamar.............. 2 Sam. 13:1–19
The mighty men................ 2 Sam. 23:8–39
David takes a census .... 2 Sam. 24:1–25

Sanballat—*Sin (the moon-god) has given life*
Influential Samaritan .... Neh. 2:10
Opposes Nehemiah's plans .... Neh. 4:7, 8
Seeks to assassinate Nehemiah........Neh. 6:1–4
Fails in intimidation ....Neh. 6:5–14
His daughter marries Eliashib, the
    high priest ....Neh. 13:4, 28

WORD
STUDY

SANCTIFICATION, *hagiasmos* (hag-ee-ahs-*moss*). This noun is derived from the verb *hagiazō*, which has as its basic idea the act of setting aside things for ritual purposes and thus making them holy, or the act of separating persons from moral or ritual defilement and thus making them holy. *Hagiasmos* therefore can be translated as "sanctification" or "consecration" or "holiness." God effects "sanctification" (Rom. 6:22)—the state of being made holy—through His Spirit (2 Thess. 2:13) and His Anointed One, Jesus (1 Cor. 1:30). In some passages the result of being made holy by God carries with it the sense of moral "holiness" (1 Thess. 4:3, 7; 1 Tim. 2:15; Heb. 12:14). Sometimes the distinction between *hagiasmos* as the act and *hagiasmos* as the result is blurred. (Strong's #38)

Sanctification—*growing in holiness*
Produced by:
    God ....1 Thess. 5:23
    Christ............................... Heb. 2:11
    Holy Spirit ....1 Pet. 1:2
    Truth......................... John 17:17, 19
    Christ's blood .... Heb. 9:14
    Prayer .... 1 Tim. 4:4, 5
    Believing spouse..................... 1 Cor. 7:14
See Godliness; Holiness of Christians; Piety

Sanctimoniousness—*assumed and pretended holiness*
    Condemned by Christ.................Matt. 6:5

Sanctuary (see Most Holy Place; Tabernacle)

Sand
Figurative uses of:
    One's posterity .... Gen. 22:17
    Weight................................Job 6:3
    Large number of people .... Josh. 11:4
    God's thoughts toward us ....Ps. 139:17, 18

Sandals, shoe—*leather strapped to the feet*
A. Characteristics of:
    Some considered worthless .... Amos 2:6
    Used for dress occasions.............Luke 15:22
    Worn as adornment................... Song 7:1
    Worn out after a journey ....Josh. 9:5, 13
    Preserved supernaturally .... Deut. 29:5
    Worn by Christ's disciples ....Mark 6:9

B. Symbolism of:
    Taking on—readiness for a journey .....Ex. 12:11
    Putting off—reverence before God....... Ex. 3:5;
      Josh. 5:15
    Want of—mourning .... 2 Sam. 15:30
    Giving to another—manner of attestation
      in Israel........................ Ruth 4:7, 8
    To unloose another's—act of homage... Luke 3:16
C. Figurative of:
    Protection and provision .... Deut. 33:25
    Preparation for service .... Eph. 6:15
    Alertness............................. Is. 5:27

Sanhedrin (see Council)

Sanitation and hygiene
A. Laws relating to:
    Dead bodies.....................Lev. 11:24–40
    Contagion...................... Num. 9:6, 10
    Leprosy .... Lev. 13:2–59
    Menstruation................... Lev. 15:19–30
    Women in childbirth................ Lev. 12:2–8
    Man's discharge .... Lev. 15:2–18
B. Provisions for health:
    Washing .... Deut. 23:10, 11
    Burning........................Num. 31:19–23
    Isolation ....Lev. 13:2–5, 31–33
    Destruction ....Lev. 14:39–45
    Covering excrement..............Deut. 23:12, 13

Sanity, spiritual
    Young men urged to....................Titus 2:6
    Accomplished by Christ...............Luke 8:35
    Illustrated by Paul's change........ Acts 26:11, 25

Sansannah—*palm branch*
    Town in south Judah.................. Josh. 15:31

Sap—*the living fluid of woody plants*
    Lord's trees full of ....Ps. 104:16

Saph—*basin*
    Philistine giant ....2 Sam. 21:18
    Called Sippai ....1 Chr. 20:4

Sapphira—*beautiful*
    Wife of Ananias ....Acts 5:1
    Struck dead for lying............... Acts 5:1–11

Sapphire—*a precious stone*
    Worn by high priest...................Ex. 28:18
    John's vision........................Rev. 21:19

Sarah, Sarai—*princess*
    Half sister and wife of Abram..... Gen. 11:29–31;
      20:11–13
    Represented as Abram's sister.....Gen. 12:10–20;
      20:1–13
    Barren .... Gen. 11:30
    Gave Abram her maid............... Gen. 16:1–3
    Promised a son .... Gen. 17:15–21; Rom. 9:9
    Gave birth to Isaac................. Gen. 21:1–8
    Responsible for Hagar's and Ishmael's
      departure.....................Gen. 21:8–21
    Lived 127 years .... Gen. 23:1

Died at Kirjath Arba . . . . Gen. 23:2
Buried by Abraham at Machpelah . . . . . Gen. 23:19
Example of submission . . . . 1 Pet. 3:6

Saraph—*burning*
Descendant of Judah . . . . 1 Chr. 4:22

Sarcasm—*a biting taunt, mock*
A. Purposes of, to:
Recall injustice . . . . Judg. 9:7–19
Remind of duty neglected . . . . 1 Sam. 26:15
Mock idolaters. 1 Kin. 18:27
Deflate pride . . . . 1 Kin. 20:10, 11
Warn of defeat. . . . . 2 Kin. 14:8–12
B. Uttered by:
Friend . . . . Job 11:2–12
Enemies. . . . . Neh. 4:2, 3
Persecutors. . . . . Matt. 27:28, 29
Apostle . . . . Acts 23:1–5
God . . . . Jer. 25:27

Sardis—*the chief city of Lydia in Asia Minor*
One of the seven churches . . . . Rev. 1:11

Sardites
Descendants of Sered . . . . Num. 26:26

Sardius—*a precious stone*
Used in "breastplate". . . . . Ex. 28:15–17
In the Garden of Eden. . . . . Ezek. 28:13
Worn by priest. . . . . Ex. 28:17

Sardonyx—*a precious stone*
In John's vision . . . . Rev. 21:19, 20

Sargon—*the constituted king*
King of Assyria . . . . Is. 20:1

Sarid—*survivor*
Village of Zebulun . . . . Josh. 19:10, 12

Sarsechim
Prince of Nebuchadnezzar . . . . Jer. 39:3

WORD STUDY
SATAN, *satan* (saw-*tawn*). *Satan* is the noun translated "adversary" or "Satan." The adversaries can be human as in Num. 22:22 and 1 Sam. 29:4. At times God is the adversary of humans (1 Kin. 11:14). The superhuman adversary, or Satan, is seen in only three passages in the OT, the most familiar of which is Job 1 and 2. In these passages Satan is the adversary who obstructs or accuses. There is some question whether the Satan is a role being played by a supernatural being or whether the title refers to a particular being. In any case, the Satan is not all-powerful and is subject to God's rebuke. (Strong's #7854)

Satan—*adversary*
A. Names of (see Devil)
B. Designs of, to:
Undo God's work . . . . Mark 4:15
Make people turn away from God . . . . . . Job 2:4, 5
Instigate evil . . . . John 13:2, 27
Secure humankind's worship . . . . Luke 4:6–8;
2 Thess. 2:3, 4

C. Character of:
Deceiver . . . . Rev. 12:9
Father of lies . . . . John 8:44
Adversary . . . . 1 Pet. 5:8
Tempter . . . . Matt. 4:3
D. Methods of:
Disguises himself . . . . 2 Cor. 11:14
Insinuates doubt. . . . . Gen. 3:1
Misuses Scripture . . . . Matt. 4:6
Uses schemes . . . . 2 Cor. 2:11
Afflicts believers . . . . Luke 13:16
E. Judgment upon:
Bound . . . . Mark 3:27
Cast out. . . . . John 12:31
Judged . . . . John 16:11
Bruised . . . . Rom. 16:20
Assigned to hell. . . . . Matt. 25:41

Satiate(d)—*to be satisfied*
Scorners and fools shall be . . . . Prov. 1:22, 31
The sword shall be . . . . Jer. 46:10
Israel was not. Ezek. 16:28

Satire—*exposing problems to ridicule*
Jesus' devastating use of . . . . Matt. 23:1–33

Satisfaction—*that which completely fulfills*
A. Of physical things:
Sexual pleasures . . . . Prov. 5:19
Bread of heaven. . . . . Ps. 105:40
Long life . . . . Ps. 91:16
B. Of spiritual things, God's:
Mercy. . . . . Ps. 90:14
Presence . . . . Ps. 17:15
C. Of things empty of:
Labor . . . . Is. 55:2
Sinful ways . . . . Ezek. 16:28, 29
Persecution. . . . . Job 19:22

Satrap—*protector of the land*
Officials appointed over the
kingdom. . . . . Dan. 6:1

Saul—*asked (of God)*
1. Son of Kish; first king of Israel. . . . . . . 1 Sam. 9:1, 2
From tribe of Benjamin. . . . . 1 Sam. 9:1, 2
Seeks his father's donkeys . . . . 1 Sam. 9:3–14
Meets Samuel . . . . 1 Sam. 9:16–27
Prophesies as sign. . . . . 1 Sam. 10:7, 11
Anointed as king . . . . 1 Sam. 10:1–16
Victories and family . . . . 1 Sam. 14:47–52
Fights against Philistines; becomes
jealous of David . . . . . 1 Sam. 17:1–58; 18:6–13
Promises his daughter
to David . . . . 1 Sam. 18:14–30
Seeks to murder David . . . . 1 Sam. 19:1–24
Pursues David . . . . 1 Sam. 23:1–28
His life spared by David . . . . 1 Sam. 26:1–25
Seeks out medium . . . . 1 Sam. 28:1–14
Samuel's spirit predicts defeat and
death. . . . . 1 Sam. 28:15–20
Defeated, commits suicide. . . . . 1 Sam. 31:1–6

Men of Jabesh Gilead reclaim his
    body .... 1 Sam. 31:11, 12
    Burial of ....1 Sam. 31:13
    David's lament over............. 2 Sam. 1:17–27
    Sin of, exposed.................... 2 Sam. 21:1–9
2. King of Edom .... Gen. 36:37

WORD STUDY   **SAVE,** *yasha'* (yaw-*shah*). "To be saved" or "liberated" is a passive form of the verb *yasha'*. In this form, people are saved from external evils. Usually God is the one saving people. In a few of the references, God's people are saved in battle, which means that they were victorious, not just saved from being killed. The active form of the verb, meaning "deliver" or "save," occurs within the context of evils or troubles. Humans can save others as is seen especially in Judg. where heroic men rescued Israel from trouble time after time. God saved the people as a whole, pious ones, the king, His servants, and so on. Only in Ezek. is God said to save humans from moral trouble (Ezek. 36:29; 37:23). The noun form of this verb, meaning "savior," is *Yeshua,* which comes to us as "Jesus" or "Joshua." (Strong's #3467)

WORD STUDY   **SAVE,** *sōzō* (*sohd*-zoh). The basic meaning of this verb is "to save," "to keep from harm," "to preserve," "to rescue." It appears often in the NT and with a variety of meanings. For instance, *sōzō* can be used in the sense of "to deliver" from danger (Matt. 10:22) and death (e.g., "rescue" from drowning; Matt. 14:30), or "to save" from disease (e.g., "heal"; Mark 5:34). Frequently, however, *sōzō* is used with reference to divine salvation from eternal death (Matt. 1:21; Luke 19:10; John 3:17; 12:47; Acts 16:31) or with reference to that which leads to such salvation, such as grace (Acts 15:11; Eph. 2:5), faith (1 Cor. 15:2), hope (Rom. 8:24). (Strong's #4982)

WORD STUDY   **SAVE NOW,** *hōsanna* (ho-san-*nah*). This word appears in the accounts of Jesus' triumphant entry into Jerusalem (Matt. 21:9, 15; Mark 11:9, 10; John 12:13). *Hōsanna* is the Greek transliteration of the Aramaic form of the Hebrew expression meaning "Help" or "Save, I pray." This expression, taken from a messianic psalm (Ps. 118:25, 26) read during the Feast of Passover, became part of a liturgical formula familiar to all the devout in Israel. This acclamation was part of the liturgy in the feasts of Passover and Tabernacles, but the waving of palm branches occurred only during the latter. (Strong's #5614)

Savior—*one who saves*
Applied to:
    God ....Ps. 106:21
    Christ..................................2 Tim. 1:10

Savior, Jesus as
A. Characteristics of:
    Only............................... Acts 4:10, 12

    Complete ....Col. 2:10
    Powerful.......................... Col. 1:12–18
    Authoritative...................... John 10:18
    Universal.......................... 1 Tim. 4:10
    Loving..............................Titus 3:4
    Merciful ....Titus 3:5
B. Announcement of, by:
    Prophets .... Is. 42:6, 7
    Angels .... Matt. 1:20, 21
    John the Baptist .... John 1:29
    Christ...................... John 12:44–50
    Peter................................Acts 5:31
    Paul ....1 Tim. 1:15
    John ....1 John 4:14
C. Office of, involves His:
    Becoming man .... Heb. 2:14
    Perfect righteousness................. Heb. 5:8, 9
    Perfect obedience................. Rom. 5:19, 20
    Dying for us...................... 1 Pet. 1:18–20
D. Saves us from:
    Wrath ....Rom. 5:9
    Sin.................................John 1:29
    Death.........................John 11:25, 26

Saw—*a toothed tool*
For cutting:
    Stones .... 1 Kin. 7:9
    Wood...............................Is. 10:15
    For torture ....1 Chr. 20:3

Scab
    Disqualifies an offering .... Lev. 22:21, 22
    Priest observes..................... Lev. 13:6–8
    Israel threatened with............... Deut. 28:27

Scabbard—*a sheath*
    For God's Word ....Jer. 47:6

Scandal—*something disgraceful*
In:
    Priesthood .... 1 Sam. 2:22–24
    Family.......................... 2 Sam. 13:1–22

Scapegoat—*a goat of departure*
    Bears sin away..................... Lev. 16:8–22
    Typical of Christ.................. Is. 53:6, 11, 12

Scarlet—*a brilliant crimson*
A. Literal uses of, for:
    Tabernacle .... Ex. 26:1, 31, 36
    Identification .... Gen. 38:28, 30
B. Symbolic uses of:
    Royalty .... Matt. 27:28
    Prosperity.......................... 2 Sam. 1:24
    Conquest......................... Nah. 2:3
    Deep sin ....Is. 1:18

Scatter—*to disperse abroad*
A. Applied to:
    Nations .... Gen. 11:8, 9
    Christians.........................Acts 8:1, 4
B. Caused by:
    Sin................................1 Kin. 14:15, 16
    Persecution.........................Acts 11:19

Scepter—*a royal staff*
   Sign of authority.......................Esth. 4:11
   Of Judah's tribe.......................Gen. 49:10
   Promise concerning.................Num. 24:17
   Fulfilled in Christ ....Heb. 1:8

Sceva
   Jewish priest at Ephesus ....Acts 19:14
   Father of seven sons..................Acts 19:14

Schemes of Satan
   Known by Christians .... 2 Cor. 2:11
   Warnings against............. 2 Cor. 11:3, 13–15
   Armor provided against .... Eph. 6:11
   World falls before.................. Rev. 13:1–18

Schism—*a division within a body*
   Prohibition concerning..............1 Cor. 12:25
   Translated "pulls away" ....Matt. 9:16

Scholars—*men reputed for learning*
   Numbered by David..............1 Chr. 25:1, 7, 8
   God's judgment against .... Mal. 2:12
   Moses, an expert.................... Acts 7:22
   Gamaliel, famous as .... Acts 5:34

School—*an institution of learning*
   Home...........................Deut. 6:6–10
   Temple..........................1 Chr. 25:7, 8
   In Ephesus .... Acts 19:1, 9
   Levites, teachers of.................2 Chr. 17:7–9
   Best subjects of .... Is. 50:4

Schoolmaster—*a tutor*
   Applied to the Mosaic Law .... Gal. 3:24, 25

Science—*exact knowledge*
A. Implied reference to:
   Architecture.....................2 Chr. 2:1–18
   Astronomy .... Gen. 15:5
   Biology .... Ps. 139:13–16
   Engineering ....Gen. 6:14–16
   Medicine............................Ps. 103:3
   Meteorology......................Job 38:22–38
   Surveying .... Ezek. 40:5, 6
B. Significance of, to:
   Manifest God's existence.............Ps. 19:1–6
   Prove God's prophecies................Jer. 25:12
   Illustrate heaven's glory .... Rev. 21:9–23
   Point to Christ as source of ....Col. 2:2, 3

Scoffers
   Wicked .... Prov. 9:7
   Unwilling to take rebuke .... Prov. 9:7, 8
   Incorrigible ....Prov. 15:12
   Abomination......................Prov. 24:9

Scorners—*arrogant disdainers of others*
   Classified among fools ....Prov. 1:22
   Manifested in the last days ....2 Pet. 3:3
   Will be judged......................Prov. 19:29

Scorpion—*an eight-legged creature having a poisonous tail*
A. Used literally of:
   Desert creatures ....Deut. 8:15
   Poisonous creatures..................Luke 10:19

B. Used figuratively of:
   Heavy burdens ....1 Kin. 12:11
   Agents of the Antichrist.......... Rev. 9:3, 5, 10

Scourging—*punishment by whipping; flogging*
   For immorality ....Lev. 19:20
   Forty blows........................ Deut. 25:1–3
   Of Christ .....Matt. 27:26; Mark 15:15; John 19:1
   Of Christians...................... Matt. 10:17
   Thirty-nine lashes ....2 Cor. 11:24
   Of apostles..................Acts 5:40; Gal. 6:17

Scribe's knife—*a knife used to sharpen reed pens*
   Used by Jehoiakim on Jeremiah's
     scroll ....Jer. 36:23–28

Scribes—*experts in legal matters*
A. Employment of:
   Transcribers of legal contracts .... Jer. 32:12
   Keepers of records ....Jer. 36:25, 26
   Advisors in state affairs ....1 Chr. 27:32
   Custodians of draft records..........2 Kin. 25:19
   Collectors of temple revenue........2 Kin. 12:10
   Teacher of the Law............... Ezra 7:6, 10, 12
B. Characteristics of, in New Testament times, their:
   Righteousness external.............. Matt. 5:20
   Teaching without authority.......... Matt. 7:29
   Desired notoriety .... Luke 20:46, 47
C. Their attitude toward Christ:
   Accusing Him of blasphemy .... Mark 2:6, 7
   Seeking to accuse .... Luke 6:7
   Questioning His authority..........Luke 20:1, 2
   Desiring to kill Him ....Luke 22:2
D. Christ's attitude toward:
   Exposes them....................Matt. 23:13–36
   Condemns them .... Luke 20:46, 47
   Calls them hypocrites .... Matt. 15:1–9

Scriptures—*God's revelation*
A. Called:
   Word of God .... Heb. 4:12
   Word of truth .... James 1:18
   Oracles of God ....Rom. 3:2
   Word ....James 1:21–23
   Holy Scriptures.....................Rom. 1:2
   Sword of the Spirit .... Eph. 6:17
   Scriptures of the prophets .... Rom. 16:26
B. Described as:
   Authoritative.....................1 Pet. 4:11
   Inspired..........................2 Tim. 3:16
   Effectual in life .... 1 Thess. 2:13
   Truth ....Ps. 119:160
   Perfect .... Ps. 19:7
   Sharp .... Heb. 4:12
   Pure ....Prov. 30:5
C. Inspiration of, proved by:
   External evidence...................Heb. 2:1–4
   Internal nature .... 2 Tim. 3:16, 17
   Infallibility.......................John 10:35
   Fulfillment of prophecy .... John 5:39, 45–47
D. Understanding of, by:
   Spirit's illumination...............1 Cor. 2:10–14

Searching .... John 5:39
Reasoning.......................... Acts 17:2
Comparing..................... 2 Pet. 1:20, 21
Human help..................... Acts 17:10–12
E. Proper uses of:
Regeneration .... 1 Pet. 1:23
Salvation..........................2 Tim. 3:15
Producing life .... John 20:31
Searching our hearts .... Heb. 4:12
Spiritual growth .... Acts 20:32
Sanctification .... John 17:17
Illumination ....Ps. 119:105
Keeping from sin ....Ps. 119:9, 11
Defeating Satan .... Eph. 6:16, 17
Proving truth..................... Acts 18:28
F. Misuses of, by:
Satan .... Matt. 4:6
Hypocrites ....Matt. 22:23–29
False teachers...................... 2 Cor. 2:17
Unlearned.........................2 Pet. 3:16
G. Positive attitudes toward:
Let dwell in richly.....................Col. 3:16
Search daily ....Acts 17:11
Hide in the heart .... Ps. 119:11
Love...................... Ps. 119:97, 113, 167
Delight in .... Ps. 1:2
Receive with meekness .... James 1:21
Teach to children ....Deut. 11:19
Obey .... James 1:22
Read...........................Deut. 17:19
H. Negative attitudes toward, not to:
Add to or subtract from .... Deut. 4:2
Handle deceitfully.....................2 Cor. 4:2
Twist ....2 Pet. 3:16
Invalidate by traditions .... Mark 7:9–13
I. Fulfillment of, cited to show:
Christ's:
Mission .... Luke 4:16–21
Death.....................Luke 24:27, 44–47
Rejection.......................Acts 28:25–29
Resurrection ....Acts 2:24–31
Spirit's descent ....John 14:16–21
Faith..............................Rom. 4:3
J. Distortion of:
Condemned .... Prov. 30:5, 6; Rev. 22:18–20
Predicted .... 2 Tim. 4:3, 4
K. Memorization of:
Keeps from sin .... Ps. 119:11
Gives understanding.................Ps. 119:130
Facilitates prayer .... John 15:7

Scriptures, devotional readings
A. For personal needs:
Comfort .... Ps. 43:1–5; Rom. 8:26–28
Courage............... Ps. 46:1–11; 2 Cor. 4:7–18
Direction .... Heb. 4:16; James 1:5, 6
Peace .... Ps. 4:1–8; Phil. 4:4–7
Relief............... Ps. 91:1–16; 2 Cor. 12:8–10
Rest ....Matt. 11:28–30; Rom. 8:31–39

Temptation .... Ps. 1:1–6; 1 Cor. 10:6–13;
James 1:12–16
B. For instruction:
Sermon on the Mount .... Matt. 5:1–7:29
Prayer ....Matt. 6:5–15; Phil. 4:6, 7
Golden Rule..........................Matt. 7:12
Great Commandment.......... Matt. 22:36–40
Great Commission.............Matt. 28:18–20
Salvation..........................John 3:1–36
Good Shepherd....................John 10:1–18
Spiritual fruit......... John 15:1–17; Gal. 5:22, 23
Guilt...............................Rom. 8:1
Righteousness .... Rom. 3:19–28
Justification....................... Rom. 5:1–21
Christian service ....Rom. 12:1–21; 13:1–14
Stewardship............... 2 Cor. 8:1–24; 9:1–15
Love ....1 Cor. 13:1–13
Regeneration .... Eph. 2:1–10
Christ's exaltation ....Phil. 2:5–11
Resurrection .... 1 Thess. 4:13–18
Judgment .... Rev. 20:10–15
New heaven and earth....... Rev. 21:1–27; 22:1–5

Scriptures, distortion of
Condemned......................Prov. 30:5, 6
Turning to fables .... 2 Tim. 4:3, 4
By unlearned .... 2 Pet. 3:15–17
God will punish ....Rev. 22:18–20

Scroll—*a papyrus or leather roll (book)*
Applied to the heavens .... Is. 34:4
Sky split apart like a....................Rev. 6:14
Called a book...........................Ps. 40:7
State documents written on.............Ezra 6:2
Scripture written on....................Is. 8:1

Scum—*the residue of dirt*
Used figuratively ....Ezek. 24:6–12

Scythians—*natives of Scythia*
In the Christian church ....Col. 3:11

Sea—*a large body of water*
A. Described as:
Created by God....................... Acts 4:24
Deep................................Ps. 68:22
Turbulent and dangerous................ Ps. 89:9
All rivers run into..................... Eccl. 1:7
Bound by God's decree ....Jer. 5:22
Manifesting God's works......... Ps. 104:24, 25
B. List of, in the Bible:
Great Sea (Mediterranean) ....Ezek. 47:10
Salt or Dead Sea .... Gen. 14:3
Red Sea ....Ex. 10:19
Sea of Galilee (Chinnereth)......... Num. 34:11
Adriatic............................ Acts 27:27
C. Figurative of:
Extension of the gospel..................Is. 11:9
Righteousness .... Is. 48:18
False teachers........................ Jude 13

Sea gull
Listed as unclean ....Lev. 11:13, 16

Sea, cast metal
    Vessel in the temple . . . . 1 Kin. 7:23

Sea of glass
    Before the throne of God . . . . .Rev. 4:6

Seal—*instrument used to authenticate ownership*
A. Used literally to:
    Guarantee business deals . . . . Jer. 32:11–14
    Ratify covenants . . . . Neh. 10:1
    Insure a prophecy . . . . Dan. 9:24
    Protect books . . . . Rev. 5:2, 5, 9
    Lock doors . . . . Matt. 27:66
B. Used figuratively of:
    Ownership of married love . . . . Song 4:12; 8:6
    Hidden things . . . . Is. 29:11
    God's witness to Christ . . . . John 6:27
    Believer's security . . . . 2 Cor. 1:22
    Assurance . . . . Eph. 4:30
    God's ownership of His people . . . . Rev. 7:3–8

Seamstress—*a dressmaker*
    Dorcas known as . . . . .Acts 9:36–42

Search—*to make intensive investigation*
A. Applied literally to:
    Lost article . . . . Gen. 31:34–37
    Records . . . . Ezra 4:15, 19
    Child . . . . .Matt. 2:8
    Scriptures . . . . John 5:39
    Enemy . . . . 1 Sam. 23:23
B. Applied figuratively to:
    Human heart . . . . .Ps. 139:1, 23
    Understanding . . . . Prov. 2:4
    Conscience . . . . .Prov. 20:27
    Self-examination .Judg. 5:16

Season—*a period of time*
A. Descriptive of:
    Period of the year . . . . Gen. 1:14
    Revealed times . . . . 1 Thess. 5:1
    Right time . . . . .Deut. 11:14
B. Of the year:
    Guaranteed by God . . . . Gen. 8:22
    Proof of God's providence . . . . .Acts 14:17
    Indicated by the moon . . . . .Ps. 104:19

Seat—*a place of authority*
A. Descriptive of:
    Inner court . . . . .Ezek. 8:3
    Assembly . . . . Matt. 23:6
B. Figurative of:
    God's throne . . . . Job 23:3
    Association with evil . . . . Ps. 1:1
    Satanic power . . . . .Rev. 13:2

Seba
    Cush's oldest son . . . . Gen. 10:7
See Sabeans

Secacah—*thicket*
    Village of Judah . . . . .Josh. 15:1, 61

Sechu—*observatory*
    Village near Ramah . . . . 1 Sam. 19:22

Second
A. Descriptive of:
    Next in order . . . . Gen. 1:8
    Repetition . . . . .1 Kin. 18:34
    Second Advent . . . . Heb. 9:28
B. Used figuratively and spiritually of:
    Christ . . . . .1 Cor. 15:47
    Finality . . . . .Titus 3:10
    New covenant . . . . Heb. 8:7
    Death . . . . .Rev. 2:11

Second chance
    None in hell . . . . Luke 16:23–31

Second coming of Christ
A. Described as:
Day of:
    The Lord . . . . 1 Thess. 5:2
    Lord Jesus . . . . 1 Cor. 5:5
    God . . . . .2 Pet. 3:12
    That Day . . . . 2 Thess. 1:10
    Last Day . . . . .John 12:48
B. Purposes of, to:
    Fulfill His Word . . . . John 14:3
    Raise the dead . . . . 1 Thess. 4:13–18
    Destroy death . . . . .1 Cor. 15:25, 26
    Gather the elect . . . . Matt. 24:31
    Judge the world . . . . Matt. 25:32–46
    Glorify believers . . . . .Col. 3:4
    Reward God's people . . . . Matt. 16:27
C. Time of:
    Unknown to us . . . . Matt. 24:27, 36
    After the gospel's proclamation
        to all . . . . Matt. 24:14
    After the rise of the Antichrist . . . . .2 Thess. 2:2, 3
    At the last trumpet . . . . .1 Cor. 15:51, 52
    In days like Noah's . . . . .Matt. 24:37–47
D. Manner of:
    In the clouds . . . . Matt. 24:30
    In flaming fire . . . . 2 Thess. 1:7, 8
    With the angels . . . . Matt. 25:31
    As a thief . . . . .1 Thess. 5:2, 3
    In His glory . . . . Matt. 25:31
E. Believer's attitude toward, to:
    Wait for . . . . 1 Cor. 1:7
    Look for . . . . .Titus 2:13
    Be ready for .Matt. 24:42–51
    Love . . . . 2 Tim. 4:8
    Be busy until . . . . Luke 19:13–18
    Pray for . . . . Rev. 22:20

Secret disciples
    Among Jewish leaders . . . . .John 12:42
    Fearful of Jewish disfavor . . . . .John 19:38

Secret prayer
    Commended by Christ . . . . Matt. 6:6
Practiced by:
    Christ . . . . .Mark 1:35
    Peter . . . . Acts 10:9

Secret things

Known by God . . . . Deut. 29:29

See Mystery

Secrets—*things unknown to others*

To be kept. . . . . Prov. 25:9

Sign of faithfulness . . . . Prov. 11:13

Those who expose, condemned . . . . Prov. 20:19

Sects of Christ's time

Pharisees. . . . . Acts 15:5; 26:5

Sadducees. . . . . Acts 5:17

Herodians. . . . . Matt. 22:16

Christians described as. . . . . Acts 24:5, 14

Secundus—*second*

Thessalonian Christian . . . . Acts 20:4

Security of the saints

A. Expressed by:

"Shall never perish" . . . . John 10:28

"None of them is lost" . . . . John 17:12

"Kept by the power of God" . . . . 1 Pet. 1:5

B. Guaranteed by:

Spirit's sealing. 2 Cor. 1:21, 22

Christ's intercession. . . . . Rom. 8:34–39

God's power. . . . . Jude 24

See Assurance

Sedition—*attack upon an established government*

Miriam and Aaron, against Moses . . . Num. 12:1–13

Paul accused of, by Jews a

nd Tertullus . . . . Acts 24:1–9

Seducers—*those who lead others astray*

A. Agents of:

Evil leaders. . . . . 2 Kin. 21:9

B. Characteristics of:

Lead to evil. . . . . Rev. 2:20

Preach false message . . . . Ezek. 13:9, 10

Seed—*the essential element of transmitting life*

A. Descriptive of:

One's ancestry. . . . . Gen. 12:7

Messianic line . . . . Gen. 21:12

Christ. . . . . Gal. 3:16, 19

B. Figurative of true believers:

Born of God. . . . . 1 Pet. 1:23

Abraham's true children. . . . . Gal. 3:29

Children of promise. . . . . Rom. 9:7, 8

Including Israel's faithful. . . . . Rom. 9:29

C. Sowing of, figurative of:

God's Word . . . . Matt. 13:3, 32

Spiritual blessings. . . . . 1 Cor. 9:11

Christ's death . . . . John 12:24

Christian's body . . . . 1 Cor. 15:36–49

Seeking—*trying to obtain*

A. Things of the world:

Material things . . . . Matt. 6:32

One's life. . . . . Luke 17:33

One's selfish interest . . . . Phil. 2:21

Pleasing others . . . . Gal. 1:10

One's own glory . . . . John 7:18

B. Things of the Spirit:

True wisdom . . . . Prov. 2:4

God's kingdom . . . . Matt. 6:33

Another's benefit . . . . 2 Cor. 12:14

Peace . . . . 1 Pet. 3:11

Heavenly country. Heb. 11:14

WORD
STUDY

SEER, *ro'eh* (roh-*ay*). The noun *ro'eh* is an early term for "prophet" and is usually translated "seer." The term is used to refer to Samuel in 1 Sam. 9. In other references, such as those in Chr., the term is considered an archaism by most scholars, an older word with most of the same connotations as the later word usually translated "prophet." David the king asked Zadok the priest if he was not also a seer, one who gives a word from God (2 Sam. 15:27). In Is. 30:10 the seers are a separate class from the prophets, although they do have prophetic visions (Is. 28:7). (Strong's #7203)

Seers—*prophets*

Amos . . . . Amos 7:12

Asaph. . . . . 2 Chr. 29:30

Gad. . . . . 2 Sam. 24:11

Heman. . . . . 1 Chr. 25:5

Samuel. . . . . 1 Sam. 9:19

Zadok . . . . 2 Sam. 15:27

Iddo . . . . 2 Chr. 9:29

Hanani . . . . 2 Chr. 16:7

Jeduthun. . . . . 2 Chr. 35:15

Segub—*exalted*

1. Son of Hiel. . . . . 1 Kin. 16:34

2. Son of Hezron. . . . . 1 Chr. 2:21, 22

Seir—*hairy; shaggy*

1. Mt. Seir . . . . Gen. 14:6

Home of Esau . . . . Gen. 32:3

Mountain range of Edom. . . . . Gen. 36:21

Horites dispossessed by Esau's

descendants. Deut. 2:12

Refuge of Amalekite remnant. . . . . 1 Chr. 4:42, 43

Desolation of. . . . . Ezek. 35:15

2. Landmark on Judah's boundary . . . . Josh. 15:10

Seirah—*rough*

Ehud's refuge. . . . . Judg. 3:26

Seize—*to take or keep fast, hold*

Used of:

Darkness. . . . . Job 3:6

Inheritance being taken . . . . Matt. 21:38

Sela

Place in Edom . . . . 2 Kin. 14:7

Selah

Musical term found in Psalms. . . . . Ps. 3:2

Found in . . . . Hab. 3:3, 9, 13

Seled—*exultation*

Judahite. . . . . 1 Chr. 2:30

Seleucia—*a city on the seacoast of Syria*

Paul and Barnabas embark from . . . . Acts 13:4

Self-abasement

Jacob, before Esau ....Gen. 33:3–10

Moses, before God......................Ex. 3:11

Roman, before Christ ....Luke 7:7–9

Christ, true example of.............Phil. 2:5–8

Self-acceptance—*having the proper attitude toward oneself*

A. By Christians, based on:

Planned before birth by God....... Ps. 139:13–16

Workmanship of God.................Ps. 138:8; Eph. 2:10

Christ has provided life ....John 10:10

God's desire for human fellowship ..... John 17:3

God's love............................Rom. 5:8

Living epistle of God.................2 Cor. 3:2

Complete in Christ ....Col. 2:10

Chosen by God ....1 Pet. 2:9

B. Hindered by false attitudes:

Looking on outward appearance ..... 1 Sam. 16:7

Questioning God's direction............. Is. 45:9

Doubting God's grace.............2 Cor. 12:9, 10

Self-condemnation

Caused by one's:

Heart..............................1 John 3:20

Conscience..........................John 8:7–9

Sins............................... 2 Sam. 24:17

Mouth .... Job 9:20

Evil works......................... Matt. 23:31

WORD STUDY

SELF-CONTROL, *egkrateia* (eng-*krat-eye*-ah). This noun means "self-control," especially with respect to matters pertaining to sexual activity, as is indicated by the cognate verb (*egkrateuomai*) in 1 Cor. 7:9 and the antonym (*akrasia*) in 7:5. *Egkrateia* may also be used in the more general sense of "self-disciplined," as it is in conjunction with "righteousness" (Acts 24:25) and the dedication of athletes (1 Cor. 9:25). It is listed among other virtues as a "fruit of the Spirit" (Gal. 5:23), and the cognate adjective describes one of many qualifications of a bishop (Titus 1:8). (Strong's #1466)

Self-control

A. Origin of:

Brought about by Christ............... Luke 8:35

Christian grace ....2 Pet. 1:6

B. Elements involved in:

Ruling one's spirit.......Prov. 16:32; Col. 3:14–17

Soberness ....Rom. 12:3

Control of the body ....1 Cor. 9:27

C. Hindered by:

Fleshly lusts ....1 Pet. 2:11

Tongue ....Ps. 39:1, 2

Drink.............................. Prov. 23:29–35

Sexual sins ....1 Thess. 4:3, 4

Unclean spirit .... Mark 5:2–16

Self-expressionism ....Prov. 25:28

Self-control, lack of—*uncontrolled indulgence of the passions*

A. Expressed in:

Unbridled sexual morals......... Ex. 32:6, 18, 25

Abnormal sexual desires.......... 2 Sam. 13:1–15

Unnatural sexual appetites .... Gen. 19:5–9; Rom. 1:26, 27

B. Sources of:

Lust .... 1 Pet. 4:2, 3

Satan .... 1 Cor. 7:5

Apostasy..........................2 Tim. 3:3

Self-deception

A. Factors contributing to:

Scoffers........................... 2 Pet. 3:3, 4

Worldliness ....Matt. 24:48–51

False teaching ....1 Thess. 5:3

B. Examples of:

Babylon........................... Is. 47:7–11

Jewish women ....Jer. 44:16–19

Jewish leaders ....John 8:33, 41

Self-denial

A. Expressed by:

"Denying"...........................Titus 2:12

"No longer should live"................1 Pet. 4:2

"Does not forsake"................Luke 14:33

"Take his cross" ....Matt. 10:38

"Crucified the flesh"...................Gal. 5:24

"Put off"............................. Eph. 4:22

"Put to death" ....Col. 3:5

B. Objects for:

Appetite ....Prov. 23:2

Sinful pleasures...................Heb. 11:25, 26

Worldly ambitions...............Matt. 16:24–26

C. Willingness to, manifested by:

Judah..............................Gen. 44:33

Moses.............................. Ex. 32:32

Paul ....Acts 20:22–24

D. Commended as:

Christian duty.....................Rom. 12:1, 2

Rewardable .... Luke 18:28–30

Self-exaltation

A. Manifested by:

Satan ....Is. 14:12–15

Antichrist..........................2 Thess. 2:4

Wicked ....Ps. 73:9

B. Evils of, seen in:

Self-abasement .... Matt. 23:12

Pride ....Prov. 16:18

C. Antidotes for:

Humility..........................Prov. 15:33

Christ's example ....Phil. 2:5–8

See Pride

Self-examination

A. Purposes of, to:

Test one's faith ....2 Cor. 13:5

Prepare for the Lord's Supper .... 1 Cor. 11:28–32

Prove one's work.......................Gal. 6:4

Test all things ....1 Thess. 5:21

Avoid judgment....................1 Cor. 11:28
B. Means of:
  God Himself ....Ps. 26:2
  God's Word .... Heb. 4:12
  Christ's example...................Heb. 12:1, 2

Selfishness—*loving one's self first*
A. Exemplified in:
  Self-love.......................... 2 Tim. 3:2
  Self-seeking .... Phil. 2:21
B. Avoidance of, by:
  Seeking the good of others..........1 Cor. 10:24
  Putting Christ first .... Phil. 1:21, 22
  Manifesting love...................1 Cor. 13:5
C. Examples of:
  Nabal.......................... 1 Sam. 25:3, 11
  Haman ....Esth. 6:6
  James and John ....Mark 10:35–37
  Solomon .... Eccl. 2:10, 11
  Rich fool...................... Luke 12:16–21
  Rich man .... Luke 16:19–25
D. Consequences of:
  Poverty ....Prov. 23:21
  Sin................................. Rom. 13:13, 14
  Loss of spirituality.................Gal. 5:16, 17

Self-righteousness
A. Described as:
  Objectionable ....Deut. 9:4–6
  Self-condemned .... Job 9:20
  Unprofitable .... Is. 57:12
  Like filthy rags .... Is. 64:6
  Offensive .... Is. 65:5
  External ....Matt. 23:25–28
  One-sided.........................Luke 11:42
  Boastful..........................Luke 18:11, 12
  Insufficient .... Phil. 3:4–9
B. Condemned because it:
  Cannot make pure ....Prov. 30:12
  Cannot save .... Matt. 5:20
  Rejects God's righteousness ....Rom. 10:3
C. Examples of:
  Saul............................1 Sam. 15:13–21
  Young man......................Matt. 19:16–20
  Lawyer......................... Luke 10:25, 29
  Pharisees.........................Luke 11:39

Self-will—*stubbornness*
A. Manifested in:
  Presumption .... Num. 14:40–45
  Unbelief .... 2 Kin. 17:14
  Evil heart ....Jer. 7:24
  Disobeying parents ....Deut. 21:18–20
  Pride ....Neh. 9:16, 29
  Stubbornness........................Is. 48:4–8
  Rejecting God's messengers .... Jer. 44:16
  Resisting God's Spirit ....Acts 7:51
  False teaching ....2 Pet. 2:10
B. Sin of, among Christians:
  Illustrated..................... Acts 15:36–40
  Warned against....................Heb. 3:7–12

C. Examples of:
  Simeon and Levi...................Gen. 49:5, 6
  Israelites ....Ex. 32:9
  Saul............................1 Sam. 15:19–23
  David.......................... 2 Sam. 24:4
  See Pride

Semachiah—*Yahweh supports*
  Levite gatekeeper ....1 Chr. 26:7

Semei—*Greek form of Shimei*
  In Christ's ancestry ....Luke 3:26

Senaah—*thorny*
  Family of returnees .... Ezra 2:35; Neh. 7:38

WORD STUDY   **SEND,** *apostellō* (ap-oss-*tel*-loh). Verb meaning "to send," "to send away," which is used frequently and in a variety of contexts in the NT. It can be used with other verbs to show that a particular action has been done by someone at the direction of another; in such cases it functions like the auxiliary verb "have" (e.g., Mark 6:17: "he had John arrested"). *Apostellō* is used especially with reference to the "sending" of the disciples by Jesus (Matt. 10:5; Mark 3:14; Luke 9:2; John 4:38)—hence their designation as "apostles" (cf. the cognate noun *apostolōs*)—and God's "sending" of Jesus on His divine mission (Matt. 15:24; Luke 9:48), particularly in the Gospel of John (3:17, 34; 5:36, 38; 6:29, 57). (Strong's #649)

Seneh—*thornbush*
  Sharp rock between Michmash and
    Gibeah .... 1 Sam. 14:4, 5

Senir—*mount of light*
  Amorite name of Mount Hermon ....Deut. 3:9
  Noted for firs.........................Ezek. 27:5

Sennacherib—*Sin (moon-god) multiplied brothers*
  Assyrian king (705–681 B.C.); son and
    successor of Sargon II............2 Kin. 18:13
  Death of, by assassination .... 2 Kin. 19:36, 37

Senses—*the faculties of feeling*
  Described figuratively..............Eccl. 12:3–6
  Used by Isaac.....................Gen. 27:21–27
  Impaired in Barzillai............2 Sam. 19:32–35
  Use of, as evidence .... John 20:26–29
  Proper use of .... Heb. 5:14

Senses, spiritual
  Taste ....Ps. 34:8
  Sight...............................Eph. 1:18
  Hearing.............................Gal. 3:2
  Smell .... Phil. 4:18

Sensual—*fleshly*
Descriptive of:
  Unregenerate........................... Jude 19
  Worldly wisdom .... James 3:15
  Same as "natural"..................... 1 Cor. 2:14
  Rebellious against God................Rom. 8:7

Sensualist—*one who satisfies the physical senses*
Illustrated by:
    Nabal . . . . 1 Sam. 25:36
    Rich fool . . . . Luke 12:16–21

Senuah (see Hassenuah)

Seorim—*barley*
    Name of a priestly division . . . . 1 Chr. 24:1–8

Separating courtyard—*the temple yard*
    Of Ezekiel's temple . . . . .Ezek. 41:12

Separation—*setting apart from something*
A. As a good act from:
    Unclean. . . . . .Lev. 15:31
    Evil workers . . . . Num. 16:21
    Heathen filthiness . . . . Ezra 6:21
    Pagan intermarriages . . . . .Ezra 9:1, 2
    Foreigners. . . . . Neh. 13:3
    Wine . . . . .Num. 6:2–6
B. As an evil act by:
    False teachers. .Luke 6:22
    Separatists . . . . Jude 19
    Whisperers. . . . . .Prov. 16:28
    Gossipers . . . . Prov. 17:9
C. As descriptive of:
    God's judgment. Deut. 29:21
    God's sovereignty. . . . . Deut. 32:8
    Israel's uniqueness . . . . Lev. 20:24
    Choice of the Levites. . . . . Num. 8:14
    Nazirite vow . . . . .Num. 6:2–6
    Christian obedience . . . . 2 Cor. 6:17
    Union with Christ . . . . Rom. 8:35, 39
    Christ's purity. . . . . Heb. 7:26
    Final separation . . . . Matt. 25:32

Sephar—*numbering*
    Place on Joktan's boundary . . . . Gen. 10:30

Sepharad
    Place inhabited by exiles. . . . . .Obad. 20

Sepharvaim—*an Assyrian city*
    People of, sent to Samaria . . . . .2 Kin. 17:24, 31

Serah—*abundance*
    Daughter of Asher . . . . . . .Gen. 46:17; Num. 26:46

Seraiah—*Yahweh has prevailed*
1. David's secretary . . . . 2 Sam. 8:17
    Called Sheva, Shisha, and Shavsha . . .2 Sam. 20:25;
        1 Kin. 4:3; 1 Chr. 18:16
2. Son of Tanhumeth. . . . . 2 Kin. 25:23
3. Son of Kenaz . . . . 1 Chr. 4:13, 14
4. Simeonite. . . . . 1 Chr. 4:35
5. Chief priest . . . . Jer. 52:24, 27
6. Postexilic leader . . . . Neh. 12:1, 12
7. Signer of the covenant. . . . . .Neh. 10:2
8. Postexilic priest . . . . .Neh. 11:11
9. Officer of King Jehoiakim. . . . . .Jer. 36:26
10. Prince of Judah; carries Jeremiah's
    prophecy to Babylon . . . . Jer. 51:59, 61

SERAPHIM, *seraphim* (sehr-aw-*fim*). *Seraphim* is a plural noun used infrequently in the OT. The same word is used in Is. 6:2, 6 and Is. 14:29 and a few other places. In the first instance, the reference is obviously to angelic beings, having six wings and human hands and voices, who surround the Lord. The second use is more common but still unusual, referring to a serpent, flying serpent, or dragon. Both uses come from the word meaning "burn"; in the case of the serpents, presumably the poison burns. For the angelic beings, perhaps there is something in their appearance that suggests fire. Seraphim and cherubim are often associated with each other today, although there is not a single passage in the OT where they are mentioned together. (Strong's #8314)

Seraphim—*burning ones*
    Type of angels . . . . Is. 6:1, 2

Sered—*deliverance*
    Son of Zebulun; founder of Sardites . . . Gen. 46:14

Sergius Paulus
    Roman proconsul of Cyprus converted
      by Paul . . . . Acts 13:7–12

Sermon on the Mount
    Preached by Christ. . . . . .Matt. 5–7
    Those blessed . . . . Matt. 5:3–12
    Salt and light . . . . Matt. 5:13–16
    The law fulfilled. . . . . Matt. 5:17–20
    On anger. . . . . Matt. 5:21–26
    On adultery and divorce. . . . . Matt. 5:27–32
    Oaths. . . . . .Matt. 5:33–37
    Love your enemies . . . . .Matt. 5:38–48
    The religious life. . . . . .Matt. 6:1–4; 6:5–15
    How to pray . . . . Matt. 6:16–18
    Undivided devotion. . . . . Matt. 6:19–34
    Judging others. Matt. 7:1–6
    Encouragement to pray. . . . . Matt. 7:7–12
    Entering the kingdom. . . . . .Matt. 7:13–23
    Two foundations. . . . . .Matt. 7:24–27

Serpents
A. Characteristics of:
    Pierced by God . . . . Job 26:13
    Cunning . . . . Gen. 3:1
    Some poisonous . . . . Num. 21:6
    Live on rocks, walls, etc. . . . . .Prov. 30:19
    Cursed by God . . . . Gen. 3:14, 15
B. Miracles connected with:
    Aaron's rod turned into. . . . . .Ex. 7:9, 15
    Israelites cured by looking at. . . . . . . Num. 21:6–9;
      John 3:14, 15
    Power over, given to apostles. . . . . .Mark 16:18
    Healing from bite of . . . . .Acts 28:3–6
C. Figurative of:
    Intoxication. .Prov. 23:31, 32
    Wisdom . . . . Matt. 10:16
    Malice . . . . .Ps. 58:3, 4
    Unexpected evil . . . . Eccl. 10:8

Enemies............................... Is. 14:29
Christ.............................John 3:14–16
Satan .... Rev. 20:2
Dan's treachery..................... Gen. 49:17
Sting of wine ....Prov. 23:31, 32
Wickedness of sinners................Ps. 58:3, 4

Serug—*branch*
Descendant of Shem .... Gen. 11:20–23
In Christ's ancestry ....Luke 3:35

Servant—*one who serves others*
A. Descriptive of:
Slave................................. Gen. 9:25
Worshiper of God.....................1 Sam. 3:9
Messenger of God .... Josh. 1:2
Messiah............................... Is. 42:1
Follower of Christ .... 2 Tim. 2:24
B. Applied distinctively to:
Prophets ....Zech. 1:6
Messiah.............................Zech. 3:8
Moses............................. Mal. 4:4
Christians...........................Acts 2:18
Glorified saints......................Rev. 22:3
See Slave

WORD STUDY **SERVE,** *'abad* (aw-*bahd*). The verb *'abad* is translated "work" or "serve." It has several variations within that meaning. It can be used to indicate someone who is laboring as Adam tilled the ground in Gen. or labor as the opposite of rest in the commandment to rest from labor on the seventh day. The word can also be used when someone works for another as Jacob worked for Laban for seven years to marry Rachel, and animals can be said to work. In Ex. 1:14, when the Israelites were made to serve the Egyptians as slaves, the same word is used. The meaning "serve" is seen when certain individuals work for their own chief or king as in Judg. 9. It can also be used when a king or nation pays tribute to another. Service for God is indicated by offerings as in Is. 19:21 and Ex. 3:12. Service to other gods is mentioned in many places, such as in Deut. 7:16 and the historical books. (Strong's #5647)

WORD STUDY **SERVE,** *douleuō* (dool-*yoo*-oh). This verb, from which is derived the noun "slave" (*doulos*), can be used to indicate relationship. In such usage it means "to be a slave," "to be subjected," as in Gal. 4:25 ("be in bondage"). *Douleuō* can also be used to show action, in which case it means "to perform the duties of a slave," even when it is rendered into English less forcefully as "to serve," as in Luke 15:29; 16:13. It is used figuratively in the expression "to serve God" (Matt. 6:24) or "Christ" (Rom. 14:18), where God and Christ are conceived of as "Lord" or "Master" (*kurios*) and the believer as "slave" (*doulos*). *Douleuō* is also used figuratively in other senses (Rom. 6:6; 16:18; Phil. 2:22). (Strong's #1398)

WORD STUDY **SERVICE,** *leitourgia* (leye-toorg-*ee*-ah). *Leitourgia* is a noun meaning "service." Outside the NT it denotes an individual's voluntary service to the state, but in the NT it always carries a religious connotation. It is used to refer to a person's "service" as priest (Luke 1:23; cf. Heb. 8:6). *Leitourgia* sometimes designates other kinds of "service": for example, Epaphroditus's "service" to Paul on behalf of the Philippians (2:30) and Paul's own service to the Philippians (2:17). It is also used with reference to the Corinthians' gift to the poor Christians in Jerusalem (2 Cor. 9:12). The En glish word for the Christian worship "service"—"liturgy"—is derived from this word. (Strong's #3009)

Service to God
A. Requirements of:
Fear .... Ps. 2:11
Upright walking .... Ps. 101:6
Absolute loyalty .... Matt. 6:24
Regeneration.........................Rom. 7:6
Fervency............................Rom. 12:11
Humility............................ Acts 20:19
Love ....Gal. 5:13
B. Rewards of:
Divine honor ....John 12:26
Acceptance before God...............Rom. 14:18
Inheritance............................Col. 3:24
Eternal blessedness ....Rev. 7:15; 22:3

WORD STUDY **SET FREE, LIBERATE,** *eleutheroō* (el-yoo-ther-*ah*-oh). Meaning "to free" or "to set free," this verb is used literally to refer to the emancipation of slaves. In the NT it is used figuratively in a religious sense. Jesus announces that truth—but above all, the Son—will "set free" believers (John 8:32, 36). Paul declares himself "set free" from sin and death (Rom. 8:2), that believers are "set free" from sin (6:18, 22), and in the anticipated and future glory (8:18) creation itself will be "set free" from corruption (8:21). Paul also uses this verb and its cognates to speak of being set free from the Mosaic Law (Rom. 8:21; Gal. 5:1). (Strong's #1659)

Seth—*appointed*
Third son of Adam.................... Gen. 4:25
His genealogy ....Gen. 5:6–8
In Christ's ancestry ....Luke 3:38

Sethur—*hidden*
Asherite spy ....Num. 13:2, 13

Setting—*woven together*
For precious stones worn by the high
    priest...............................Ex. 28:11
Corded chains on filigree.......... Ex. 28:13, 14
Same Hebrew word translated "woven"...Ps. 45:13

Seven—*one more than six*
A. Of social customs:
Serving for a wife ....Gen. 29:20, 27

Brevity.............................Ps. 102:11
Change ....James 1:17
Death.............................Matt. 4:16
Types.............................Col. 2:17
Old Testament period................ Heb. 10:1

Shadrach
Hananiah's Babylonian name........Dan. 1:3, 7
Deported by Nebuchadnezzar ....Dan. 1:6, 7
Refused defiling food ....Dan. 1:8–20
Refused to bow to image ....Dan. 3:8–18
Cast into the fiery furnace.........Dan. 3:19–23
Delivered by God ....Dan. 3:24–28
Promoted by Nebuchadnezzar ......Dan. 3:29, 30

Shageh—*wandering*
Father of one of David's mighty men...1 Chr. 11:34

Shaharaim—*double dawn*
Benjamite.........................1 Chr. 8:8–11

Shahazimah—*heights*
Town of Issachar ....Josh. 19:17, 22

Shake—*to move violently*
A. Descriptive of:
Thunder ....Ps. 77:18
Earthquakes........................ Acts 4:31
Fear ....Matt. 28:4
B. Used figuratively of:
Fear .... Is. 14:16
Second Advent ....Heb. 12:26, 27
Rejection................... Luke 9:5; Acts 18:6

Shalisha—*a third part*

Shallecheth—*a casting out*
Gate of Solomon's temple............1 Chr. 26:16

Shallum—*recompense*
1. King of Israel.....................2 Kin. 15:10–15
2. Husband of Huldah .... 2 Kin. 22:14
3. Judahite ....1 Chr. 2:40, 41
4. Simeonite.......................... 1 Chr. 4:25
5. Father of Hilkiah..................1 Chr. 6:12, 13
6. Naphtali's son.....................1 Chr. 7:13
7. Family of gatekeepers ....Ezra 2:42
8. Father of Jehizkiah ....2 Chr. 28:12
9. One who divorced his foreign wife ......Ezra 10:24
10. Another who divorced his foreign wife...Ezra 10:42
11. Son of Hallohesh ....Neh. 3:12
12. Jeremiah's uncle.......................Jer. 32:7
13. Father of Maaseiah ....Jer. 35:4

Shalmai—*Yahweh is recompenser*
Head of a family of Nethinim.......... Ezra 2:46

Shalman
Contraction of Shalmaneser ....Hos. 10:14

Shalmaneser—*Shulmanu (a god) is chief*
Assyrian king ....2 Kin. 17:3

Shama—*He (God) has heard*
Son of Hotham ....1 Chr. 11:44

Shamariah—*Yahweh has kept*
Son of Rehoboam................2 Chr. 11:18, 19

Shame—*a feeling of guilt*
A. Caused by:
Rape........................... 2 Sam. 13:13
Defeat ....2 Chr. 32:21
Folly..............................Prov. 3:35
Idleness..........................Prov. 10:5
Pride ....Prov. 11:2
A wicked wife ....Prov. 12:4
Lying ....Prov. 13:5
Stubbornness......................Prov. 13:18
Haste in speech....................Prov. 18:13
Mistreatment of parents............Prov. 19:26
Evil companions...................Prov. 28:7
Juvenile delinquency..............Prov. 29:15
Nakedness .... Is. 47:3
Idolatry..........................Jer. 2:26, 27
Impropriety .... 1 Cor. 11:6
Lust .... Phil. 3:19
B. Of the unregenerate:
Hardened in........................Jer. 8:12
Pleasure in .... Rom. 1:26, 27, 32
Vessels of.........................Rom. 9:21
Glory in.......................... Phil. 3:19
C. In the Christian life, of:
Former life ....Rom. 6:21
Sinful things .... Eph. 5:12
Improper behavior..............1 Cor. 11:14, 22
In gospel of Christ no ....Rom. 1:16

Shamer (see Shemer)

Shamgar—*cupbearer*
Judge of Israel; struck down 600
Philistines ....Judg. 3:31

Shamhuth—*desolation*
Commander in David's army ....1 Chr. 27:8

Shamir—*a sharp point*
1. Town in Judah.................... Josh. 15:1, 48
2. Town in Ephraim...................... Judg. 10:1
3. Levite ....1 Chr. 24:24

Shamma—*astonishment*
Asherite..........................1 Chr. 7:36, 37

Shammah—*waste*
1. Son of Reuel...................... Gen. 36:13, 17
2. Son of Jesse ....1 Sam. 16:9
Called Shimea.....................1 Chr. 2:13
3. One of David's mighty men ....2 Sam. 23:11
Also called Shammoth the Harorite...1 Chr. 11:27

Shammai—*celebrated*
1. Grandson of Jerahmeel.............1 Chr. 2:26, 28
2. Descendant of Caleb..............1 Chr. 2:44, 45
3. Descendant of Judah.................. 1 Chr. 4:17

Shammoth—*waste*
One of David's mighty men..........1 Chr. 11:27

Shammua—*renowned*
1. Reubenite spy .... Num. 13:2–4
2. Son of David ....2 Sam. 5:13, 14

3. Levite ....Neh. 11:17
4. Postexilic priest ....Neh. 12:1, 18

Shamsherai—*sunlike*
    Son of Jeroham ....1 Chr. 8:26, 27

Shapham—*youthful*
    Gadite ....1 Chr. 5:12

Shaphan—*prudent, shy*
    Scribe under Josiah ....2 Kin. 22:3
    Takes Book of the Law to Josiah... 2 Kin. 22:8–10
    Is sent to Huldah for interpretation ...2 Kin. 22:14
    Assists in repairs of temple ....2 Chr. 34:8
    Father of notable son...........Jer. 36:10–12, 25

Shaphat—*he has judged*
1. Simeonite spy ....Num. 13:2–5
2. Son of Shemaiah.....................1 Chr. 3:22
3. Gadite chief.......................1 Chr. 5:11, 12
4. One of David's herdsmen............ 1 Chr. 27:29
5. Father of the prophet Elisha ....1 Kin. 19:16, 19

Shaphir—*glittering*
    Town of Judah........................Mic. 1:11

Sharai—*Yahweh is deliverer*
    Divorced his foreign wife..........Ezra 10:34, 40

Sharar—*firm*
    Father of Ahiam ....2 Sam. 23:33

Sharezer, Sherezer—*protect the king*
1. Son of Sennacherib ....Is. 37:37, 38
2. Sent to Zechariah concerning fasting...Zech. 7:1–3

Sharon—*plain*
1. Coastal plain between Joppa and
    Mt. Carmel ....1 Chr. 27:29
    Famed for roses......................Song 2:1
    Inhabitants turn to the Lord.......... Acts 9:35
2. Pasture east of the Jordan .... 1 Chr. 5:16

Sharonite—*an inhabitant of Sharon*
    Shitrai called ....1 Chr. 27:29

Sharp—*having a keen edge; biting*
A. Descriptive of:
    Stone ....Ex. 4:25
    Knives.............................Josh. 5:2, 3
    Plowshare.....................1 Sam. 13:20, 21
    Rocks............................. 1 Sam. 14:4
    Arrows............................. Is. 5:28
    Razor................................Ps. 52:2
B. Used to compare a sword with:
    Tongue .... Ps. 57:4
    Adulteress........................... Prov. 5:4
    Mouth .... Is. 49:2
    God's Word .... Heb. 4:12
C. Figurative of:
    Deceitfulness........................Ps. 52:2
    Falsehood..........................Prov. 25:18
    Contention .... Acts 15:39
    Severe rebuke......................2 Cor. 13:10
    Christ's conquest .... Rev. 14:14–18

Sharuhen—*abode of pleasure*
    Town of Judah assigned to Simeon ... Josh. 19:1, 6

Called Sharaim.....................Josh. 15:36
Called Shaaraim...................1 Chr. 4:31

Shashai—*whitish*
    Divorced his foreign wife.........Ezra 10:34, 40

Shashak—*assaulter*
    Benjamite.........................1 Chr. 8:14, 25

Shaul—*asked (of God)*
1. Son of Simeon....................... Gen. 46:10
    Founder of a tribal family .... Num. 26:13
2. Kohathite Levite .... 1 Chr. 6:24

Shave—*to cut off the hair*
A. Used worthily to express:
    Accommodation..................... Gen. 41:14
    Cleansing ....Lev. 14:8, 9
    Commitment...................Deut. 21:10–13
    Mourning..........................Job 1:18–20
    Sorrow...............................Jer. 41:5
B. Used unworthily to express:
    Defeat of a Nazirite ....Judg. 16:19
    Contempt .... 2 Sam. 10:4
    Unnaturalness.....................1 Cor. 11:5, 6

Shaveh—*plain*
    Valley near Salem; Abram meets king
    of Sodom here................. Gen. 14:17, 18

Shaveh Kiriathaim—*plain of Kiriathaim*
    Plain near Kiriathaim inhabited by
    the Emim......................... Gen. 14:5

Shavsha, Shisha—*nobility*
    David's secretary ....1 Chr. 18:14, 16
    Serves under Solomon also ....1 Kin. 4:3

Sheal—*asking*
    Divorced his foreign wife............. Ezra 10:29

Shealtiel—*I have asked God*
    Son of King Jeconiah and father
    of Zerubbabel.......... 1 Chr. 3:17; Ezra 5:2

Sheariah—*Yahweh has esteemed*
    Descendant of Saul ....1 Chr. 9:44

Shear-Jashub—*a remnant shall return*
    Symbolic name given to Isaiah's son ....Is. 7:3

Sheba—*seven; an oath*
1. City in territory assigned to Simeon ....Josh. 19:1, 2
2. Benjamite insurrectionist .... 2 Sam. 20:1–22
3. Descendant of Cush through Raamah....Gen. 10:7
4. Descendant of Shem .... Gen. 10:28
5. Grandson of Abraham and Keturah......Gen. 25:3
6. Gadite chief........................ 1 Chr. 5:13
7. Land of, occupied by Sabeans,
    famous traders ....Job 1:15; Ps. 72:10
    Queen of, visits Solomon; marvels at
    his wisdom ....1 Kin. 10:1–13
    Mentioned by Christ .... Matt. 12:42

Shebah—*seven; an oath*
    Name given to a well and town
    (Beersheba) ....Gen. 26:31–33

Shebaniah—*Yahweh has returned me*
1. Levite trumpeter .... 1 Chr. 15:24
2. Levite; offers prayer and
    signs covenant.................... Neh. 9:4, 5
3. Levite who signs covenant.............Neh. 10:12
4. Priest who signs covenant ....Neh. 10:4

Shebarim—*breakings*
    Place near Ai .... Josh. 7:5

Shebat
    Eleventh month of the Hebrew year .....Zech. 1:7

Sheber—*breaking*
    Son of Caleb.........................1 Chr. 2:48

Shebna—*perhaps an abbreviation of Shebaniah*
    Treasurer under Hezekiah.............. Is. 22:15
    Demoted to position of scribe.........2 Kin. 19:2
    Man of pride and luxury; replaced
        by Eliakim.....................Is. 22:19–21

Shebuel—*God is renown*
1. Son of Gershon...................... 1 Chr. 23:16
2. Son of Heman....................... 1 Chr. 25:4

Shecaniah, Shechaniah—*Yahweh has dwelt*
1. Descendant of Zerubbabel .... 1 Chr. 3:21, 22
2. Postexilic returnee....................... Ezra 8:5
3. Descendant of Aaron .... 1 Chr. 24:11
4. Priest............................... 2 Chr. 31:15
5. Divorced his foreign wife.............Ezra 10:2, 3
6. Father of Shemaiah ....Neh. 3:29
    Probably same as number 1
7. Postexilic priest....................... Neh. 12:3, 7
8. Father-in-law of Tobiah ....Neh. 6:18

Shechem—*shoulder*
1. Son of Hamor; seduces Dinah, Jacob's
    daughter........................Gen. 34:1–26
    Deceived and killed by Levi
        and Simeon ....Gen. 34:13–18, 25, 26
2. Son of Gilead; founder of a
    tribal family.......................Num. 26:31
3. Son of Shemida.........................1 Chr. 7:19
4. Ancient city of Ephraim.................Gen. 33:18
    Abram camps near .... Gen. 12:6
    Jacob buys ground here............Gen. 33:18, 19
    Inhabitants of, slaughtered by Simeon
        and Levi..................... Gen. 34:25–29
    Becomes city of refuge ....Josh. 20:7
    Joseph buried here ....Josh. 24:32
    Joshua's farewell address here.......Josh. 24:1, 25
    Center of idol worship............. Judg. 9:1, 4–7
    Town destroyed .... Judg. 9:23, 45
    Jeroboam made king here..........1 Kin. 12:1–19
    Name of, used poetically ....Ps. 108:7

Shed—*to pour out*
A. Descriptive of:
    Blood................................. Gen. 9:6
    Holy Spirit ....Titus 3:6
B. As applied to blood, indicative of:
    Justifiable execution .... Gen. 9:6
    Unjustifiable murder................. Gen. 37:22

    Unacceptable sacrifice ....Lev. 17:1–5
    Attempted vengeance .... 1 Sam. 25:31, 34
    Unpardonable ....2 Kin. 24:4
    Abomination.....................Prov. 6:16, 17
    Heinous crime......................... Is. 59:7
    New covenant .... Matt. 26:28
    Martyrdom .... Acts 27:20

Shedeur—*shedder of light*
    Reubenite leader.................... Num. 1:5

Sheep—*a domesticated animal*
A. Characteristics of:
    Domesticated .... 2 Sam. 12:3
    Gentle ....Jer. 11:19
    Defenseless........................... Mic. 5:8
    Needful of care .... Ezek. 34:5
    Respond only to shepherd's voice.....John 10:2–5
B. Uses of, for:
    Food............................. 1 Sam. 25:18
    Milk............................... 1 Cor. 9:7
    Clothing .... Prov. 31:13
    Presents......................... 2 Sam. 17:29
    Tribute .... 2 Kin. 3:4
    Sacrifice .... Gen. 4:4
C. Uses of, in Levitical system as:
    Burnt offering ....Lev. 1:10
    Sin offering ....Lev. 4:32
    Trespass offering ....Lev. 5:15
    Peace offering ....Lev. 22:21
D. Needs of:
    Protection......................... Job 30:1
    Shepherd.......................John 10:4, 27
    Fold .... John 10:1
    Pastures............................. Ex. 3:1
    Water........................Gen. 29:8–10
    Rest .... Ps. 23:1, 2
    Shearing .... 1 Sam. 25:2, 11
E. Figurative of:
    Innocent........................... 2 Sam. 24:17
    Wicked .... Ps. 49:14
    Jewish people........................... Ps. 74:1
    Backsliders....................... Jer. 50:6
    Lost sinners .... Matt. 9:36
    Christians....................John 10:1–16
    Christ............................. John 1:29
    Church .... Acts 20:28
  See Lamb; Lamb of God

Sheepbreeder
    Mesha, king of Moab................. 2 Kin. 3:4

Sheepfold—*shelter*
A. Used literally:
    Enclosure for flocks................. Num. 32:16
B. Used figuratively:
    Entrance to, only by Christ .... John 10:1

Sheep Gate—*a gate of the restored Jerusalem*
    Repaired .... Neh. 3:32
    Dedicated.......................Neh. 12:38, 39

Sheepshearers
  Employed by Judah .... Gen. 38:12
  Many employed by Nabal......... 1 Sam. 25:7, 11
  Used figuratively .... Is. 53:7

Sheerah—*blood relationship*
  Daughter of Ephraim; builder
    of cities........................ 1 Chr. 7:24

Sheets
  Large piece of cloth .... Acts 11:5

Sheharaiah—*Yahweh is the dawn*
  Benjamite .... 1 Chr. 8:26

Shekel—*a Jewish measure (approximately .533 oz.)*
A. As a weight:
  Standard of, defined .... Ex. 30:13
  Used in weighing .... Josh. 7:21
  See Weights and measures
B. As money:
  Used in currency.................... 1 Sam. 9:8
  Fines paid in.................... Deut. 22:19, 29
  Revenues of the sanctuary paid in..... Neh. 10:32

Shekinah—*a word expressing the glory and presence of God*
A. As indicative of God's presence:
  In nature.......................... Ps. 18:7–15
  In the exodus from Egypt.......... Ex. 13:21, 22
  At Sinai .... Ex. 24:16–18
  In tabernacle .... Ex. 40:34–38
  Upon the mercy seat .... Ex. 25:22
  In the wilderness .... Num. 9:15–23; 10:11–36
  In the temple .... 2 Chr. 7:1–3
  In Ezekiel's vision of the temple..... Ezek. 43:4, 5
B. Illustrated by Christ in His:
  Divine nature...................... Col. 2:9
  Incarnation .... Luke 1:35
  Nativity........................... Luke 2:9
  Manifestation to Israel .... Hag. 2:9; Zech. 2:5
  Transfiguration .... 2 Pet. 1:17
  Ascension .... Acts 1:9
  Transforming us by His Spirit .... 2 Cor. 3:18; 4:6
  Return............................ Matt. 24:44
  Eternal habitation with saints.......... Rev. 21:3
C. Accompanied by:
  Angels .... Is. 6:1–4
  Cloud............................. Num. 9:15–23
  Fire.............................. Heb. 12:18–21
  Earthquake .... Hag. 2:21

Shelah—*sprout; request*
1. Son of Arphaxad...................... 1 Chr. 1:18
2. Son of Judah .... Gen. 38:1–26
  Founder of the Shelanites........... Num. 26:20
3. Pool at Jerusalem .... Neh. 3:15

Shelemiah—*friend of Yahweh*
1. Father of Hananiah................... Neh. 3:30
2. Postexilic priest .... Neh. 13:13
3. Father of Irijah................... Jer. 37:13
4. Gatekeeper .... 1 Chr. 26:14
  Called Meshelemiah .... 1 Chr. 9:21
5. Ancestor of Jehudi................... Jer. 36:14

6. Son of Abdeel .... Jer. 36:26
7. Father of Jehucal...................... Jer. 37:3

Sheleph—*drawn out*
  Son of Joktan; head of a tribe .... 1 Chr. 1:20

Shelesh—*might*
  Asherite............................ 1 Chr. 7:35

Shelomi—*at peace*
  Father of an Asherite prince .... Num. 34:27

Shelomith, Shelomoth—*peaceful*
1. Daughter of Dibri; her son
    executed .... Lev. 24:10–23
2. Chief Levite of Moses......... 1 Chr. 23:18; 24:22
3. Gershonites in David's time .... 1 Chr. 23:9
4. Descendant of Moses, had charge of
    treasuries .... 1 Chr. 26:25
5. Son or daughter of King Rehoboam... 2 Chr. 11:20
6. Daughter of Zerubbabel............. 1 Chr. 3:19
7. Family who went with Ezra .... Ezra 8:10

Shelumiel—*at peace with God*
  Simeonite warrior.................... Num. 1:6

Shem—*name; renown*
  Oldest son of Noah .... Gen. 5:32
  Escapes the Flood.................... Gen. 7:13
  Receives a blessing .... Gen. 9:23, 26
  Ancestor of Semitic people .... Gen. 10:22–32
  Ancestor of:
  Abram .... Gen. 11:10–26
  Jesus .... Luke 3:36

Shema—*report; rumor*
1. Reubenite .... 1 Chr. 5:8
2. Benjamite head.................... 1 Chr. 8:12, 13
3. Ezra's attendant .... Neh. 8:4
4. City of Judah...................... Josh. 15:26
5. Son of Hebron..................... 1 Chr. 2:43

Shemaah—*fame*
  Father of two of David's warriors...... 1 Chr. 12:3

Shemaiah—*Yahweh has heard*
1. Father of Shimri..................... 1 Chr. 4:37
2. Reubenite .... 1 Chr. 5:4
3. Levite who helped move the ark..... 1 Chr. 15:8, 12
4. Scribe in David's time................ 1 Chr. 24:6
5. Son of Obed-Edom .... 1 Chr. 26:4, 6, 7
6. Prophet of Judah .... 1 Kin. 12:22–24
  Explains Shishak's invasion as divine
    punishment................... 2 Chr. 12:5–8
  Records Rehoboam's reign........... 2 Chr. 12:15
7. Levite teacher under Jehoshaphat ...... 2 Chr. 17:8
8. Levite in Hezekiah's reign........ 2 Chr. 29:14, 15
9. Levite treasurer.................. 2 Chr. 31:14, 15
10. Officer of Levites in Josiah's reign .... 2 Chr. 35:9
11. Father of Urijah .... Jer. 26:20
12. False prophet .... Jer. 29:24–28
13. Father of Delaiah .... Jer. 36:12
14. Descendant of David .... 1 Chr. 3:22
15. Keeper of the East Gate
    under Nehemiah .... Neh. 3:29

16. Merarite Levite living in Jerusalem.... 1 Chr. 9:14
17. Son of Adonikam .... Ezra 8:13
18. Leading man under Ezra .... Ezra 8:16
19. Priest who divorced his foreign wife....Ezra 10:21
20. Man who divorced his foreign wife..... Ezra 10:31
21. Prophet hired by Sanballat .... Neh. 6:10–14
22. Priest who signs covenant ....Neh. 10:1, 8
23. Participant in dedication service...... Neh. 12:34
24. Postexilic priest .... Neh. 12:35
25. Levite musician .... Neh. 12:36

Shemariah—*Yahweh keeps*
1. Mighty man of Benjamin.............. 1 Chr. 12:5
2. Son of Rehoboam................. 2 Chr. 11:18, 19
3. Divorced his foreign wife...........Ezra 10:31, 32

Shemeber—*splendor of heroism*
King of Zeboiim...................... Gen. 14:2

Shemed—*destruction*
Son of Elpaal .... 1 Chr. 8:12

Shemer, Shamer—*guard*
1. Sells Omri hill on which Samaria
    is built...................... 1 Kin. 16:23, 24
2. Levite .... 1 Chr. 6:46
3. Asherite .... 1 Chr. 7:30, 34

Shemida—*fame of knowing*
Descendant of Manasseh; founder of
    the Shemidaites .... Num. 26:29, 32

Sheminith—*eighth*
Musical term .... 1 Chr. 15:21

Shemiramoth—*fame of the highest*
1. Levite musician in David's time.... 1 Chr. 15:18, 20
2. Levite teacher under Jehoshaphat...... 2 Chr. 17:8

Shemuel—*name of God*
1. Grandson of Issachar .... 1 Chr. 7:1, 2
2. Representative of Simeon .... Num. 34:20

Shen—*tooth; a pointed rock*
Rock west of Jerusalem............... 1 Sam. 7:12

Shenazzar
Son of Jeconiah .... 1 Chr. 3:18

Shepham—*nakedness*
Place near the Sea of Galilee .... Num. 34:11

Shephatiah—*Yahweh judges*
1. Benjamite warrior .... 1 Chr. 12:5
2. Son of David .... 2 Sam. 3:4
3. Simeonite chief....................... 1 Chr. 27:16
4. Son of King Jehoshaphat .... 2 Chr. 21:2
5. Opponent of Jeremiah .... Jer. 38:1
6. Descendant of Judah....................Neh. 11:4
7. Servant of Solomon whose descendants
    return from exile .... Ezra 2:57

Shepher—*beauty*
Israelite encampment .... Num. 33:23

Shepherd—*one who cares for the sheep*
A. Duties of, toward his flock:
    Defend.....................1 Sam. 17:34–36
    Water.......................Gen. 29:2–10

Give rest to..........................Jer. 33:12
Know.............................John 10:3–5
Number............................Jer. 33:13
Secure pasture for............... 1 Chr. 4:39–41
Search for the lost... Ezek. 34:12–16; Luke 15:4, 5
B. Good, described as:
    Faithful...................... Gen. 31:38–40
    Fearless ....1 Sam. 17:34–36
    Unselfish........................ Luke 15:3–6
    Considerate ....Gen. 33:13, 14
    Believing........................ Luke 2:8–20
C. Bad, described as:
    Unfaithful .... Ezek. 34:1–10
    Cowardly ....John 10:12, 13
    Selfish .... Is. 56:11, 12
    Ruthless ....Ex. 2:17, 19
    Unbelieving..................... Jer. 50:6
D. Descriptive of:
    God ....Ps. 78:52, 53
    Christ..................John 10:11; Heb. 13:20
    Joshua ....Num. 27:16–23
    David.........................2 Sam. 5:2
    Judges .... 1 Chr. 17:6
    National leaders ....Jer. 49:19
    Cyrus................................. Is. 44:28
    Church elders ....1 Pet. 5:2

Shepherd, Jesus the Good
A. Described prophetically in His:
    Prophetic position (teaching) .... Is. 40:10, 11
    Priestly position (sacrifice) ....Zech. 13:7;
      Matt. 26:31
    Kingly position (ruling) ....Ezek. 37:24; Matt. 2:6
B. Described typically as:
    Good ....John 10:11, 14
    Chief ....1 Pet. 5:4
    Great .... Heb. 13:20
    Gentle .... Is. 40:11
    One who separates..............Matt. 25:31–46

Shepho—*unconcern*
Son of Shobal.......................Gen. 36:23

Sherebiah—*Yahweh has sent burning heat*
1. Levite family returning with Ezra .... Ezra 8:18
2. Levite who assists Ezra...................Neh. 8:7

Sheresh—*root*
Grandson of Manasseh.............. 1 Chr. 7:16

Sheshach—*(probably a cryptogram)*
Symbolic of Babylon .... Jer. 25:26

Sheshai—*whitish*
Descendant of Anak .... Num. 13:22
Driven out by Caleb.................. Josh. 15:14
Destroyed by Judah ....Judg. 1:10

Sheshan—*whitish*
Jerahmeelite.................... 1 Chr. 2:31–35

Sheshbazzar—*sin (the moon-god) protect the father*
Prince of Judah .... Ezra 1:8, 11

Shethar—*star*
Persian prince . . . . Esth. 1:14

Shethar-Boznai—*starry splendor*
Official of Persia. . . . . Ezra 5:3, 6

Sheva—*self-satisfying*
1. Son of Caleb. 1 Chr. 2:43, 49
2. David's scribe . . . . .2 Sam. 20:25

Shibboleth—*stream, or ear of corn*
Password. . . . . .Judg. 12:5, 6

Shicron—*drunkenness*
Town of Judah. . . . . Josh. 15:11

Shield—*a protective armor*
A. Uses of:
Protection. . . . . .2 Chr. 14:8
Treasures in war . . . . 1 Kin. 14:25, 26
Riches . . . . .2 Chr. 32:27
Ornamenting public buildings . . . . . . .1 Kin. 10:17
B. Figurative of:
God's:
Protection. . . . . .Ps. 33:20
Favor . . . . Ps. 5:12
Salvation. . . . . .Ps. 18:35
Truth. . . . . Ps. 91:4
Faith. . . . . Eph. 6:16
Rulers . . . . Ps. 47:9

Shiggaion—*a musical term*
Plural form:
Shigionoth . . . . Hab. 3:1

Shihor—*black; turbid*
Name given to the Nile. . . . . Is. 23:3
Israel's southwestern border . . . . .Josh. 13:3

Shihor Libnath—*turbid stream of Libnath*
Small river in Asher's territory . . . . . . .Josh. 19:26

Shilhi—*Yahweh has sent*
Father of Azubah . . . . .1 Kin. 22:42

Shilhim—*missiles*
Town in south Judah . . . . .Josh. 15:1, 32

Shillem—*compensation*
Son of Naphtali. . . . . .Gen. 46:24

Shiloah—*sent*
A pool of Jerusalem, figurative of God's
protection . . . . Is. 8:6
See Siloam

WORD STUDY — **SHILOH**, *shiloh* (shee-*loh*). The noun *shiloh* literally means "tranquil," but is not used in that way. In the blessing of Jacob to Judah (Gen. 49:10) is found the extremely problematic phrase "until Shiloh comes." This passage obviously refers to a Judean leader, usually understood to be a coming Messiah. However, the question remains whether this messiah is a tribal leader, a Davidic king, or a future messiah. Since the sixteenth century, Christians have associated this passage with Christ. Shiloh is also a place-name for the city in Israel where the ark of the covenant rested from the time of Joshua,

shortly after the entry into the land, until the time of Samuel. (Strong's #7886, 7887)

Shiloh
1. Town of Ephraim. . . . . Judg. 21:19
Center of religious worship . . . . .Judg. 18:31
Canaan divided here . . . . .Josh. 18:1, 10
Benjamites seize women here . . . . . Judg. 21:19–23
Ark of the covenant taken from . . . . 1 Sam. 4:3–11
Site of Eli's judgeship. . . . . 1 Sam. 4:12–18
Lord revealed Himself to Samuel in . . . 1 Sam. 3:21
Home of Ahijah . . . . .1 Kin. 14:2, 4
Punishment given to . . . . Jer. 7:12–15
2. Messianic title. . . . . .Gen. 49:10

Shiloni—*a Shilonite*
Father of Zechariah. . . . . Neh. 11:5

Shilonite
Native of Shiloh .1 Kin. 11:29

Shilshah—*might*
Asherite. . . . . .1 Chr. 7:36, 37

Shimea, Shimeah—*He (God) has heard*
1. Gershonite Levite. . . . . 1 Chr. 6:39
2. Merarite Levite. . . . . 1 Chr. 6:30
3. Brother of David . . . . .2 Sam. 13:3
4. Son of David . . . . 1 Chr. 3:1, 5
5. Benjamite. . . . . 1 Chr. 8:1, 32
Called Shimeam . . . . .1 Chr. 9:38

Shimeath—*report*
Ammonitess. . . . . .2 Kin. 12:21

Shimeathites
Family of scribes. .1 Chr. 2:55

Shimei, Shimi—*renowned*
1. Son of Gershon. . . . . Ex. 6:17
2. Son of Merari . . . . 1 Chr. 6:29
3. Simeonite. . . . . .1 Chr. 4:24–27
4. Levite . . . . 1 Chr. 6:42
5. Benjamite family head . . . . 1 Chr. 8:21
6. Gershonite family head . . . . 1 Chr. 23:7, 9
7. Levite musician in David's time. . . . . 1 Chr. 25:3, 17
8. Overseer of vineyards under David. . . . 1 Chr. 27:27
9. Benjamite; insults David . . . . 2 Sam. 16:5–13
Pardoned, but confined . . . . .2 Sam. 19:16–23
Breaks parole; executed
by Solomon . . . . 1 Kin. 2:39–46
10. Faithful follower of Solomon . . . . .1 Kin. 1:8
11. Levite; assists in purification . . . . .2 Chr. 29:14–16
12. Levite treasurer in Hezekiah's
reign. . . . . .2 Chr. 31:12, 13
13. Benjamite ancestor of Mordecai . . . . Esth. 2:5
14. Brother of Zerubbabel . . . . 1 Chr. 3:19

Shimeon—*hearing*
Divorced his foreign wife. . . . . Ezra 10:31

Shimon—*trier*
Judahite family. .1 Chr. 4:1, 20

Shimrath—*guarding*
Benjamite. . . . . 1 Chr. 8:21

Shimri—*vigilant*
1. Father of Jediael . . . . 1 Chr. 11:45
2. Merarite Levite . . . . 1 Chr. 26:10
3. Levite; assists in purification . . . . 2 Chr. 29:13

Shimrith—*vigilant*
Moabitess . . . . .2 Chr. 24:26

Shimron—*watching*
1. Son of Issachar . . . . Gen. 46:13
2. Town of Zebulun . . . . .Josh. 11:1

Shimron Meron—*guard of lashing*
Town conquered by Joshua . . . . .Josh. 12:20

Shimshai—*sunny*
Scribe opposing the Jews . . . . Ezra 4:8–24

Shin
Twenty-first letter of the Hebrew
alphabet . . . . Ps. 119:161–168

Shinab—*king of Admah*
Fought against Chedorlaomer . . . . Gen. 14:1, 2

Shinar—*the region around Babylon*
Original home of Noah's sons . . . . Gen. 10:10
Tower built here . . . . .Gen. 11:2–9
Amraphel, king of . . . . Gen. 14:1, 9
Home of the remnant Jews . . . . .Is. 11:11

Shine—*to radiate with light*
A. Used literally of:
Sun . . . . Job 31:26
Moon . . . . .Job 25:5
Stars . . . . Joel 3:15
Earth . . . . Ezek. 43:2
Moses' face . . . . .Ex. 34:29–35
Christ's face . . . . .Matt. 17:2
Angels . . . . Acts 12:7
Glorified Christ . . . . .Acts 9:3
Christ's return . . . . .Luke 17:24
B. Applied figuratively to:
God's blessing . . . . Num. 6:25
God's Word . . . . .2 Pet. 1:19
Christ's first advent . . . . .Is. 9:2; John 1:5
Gospel . . . . 2 Cor. 4:4
Believer's life . . . . Prov. 4:18; Matt. 5:16
Regeneration . . . . 2 Cor. 4:6
Believer's glory . . . . Dan. 12:3; Matt. 13:43

Shion—*ruin*
Town of Issachar . . . . Josh. 19:19

Shiphi—*abundant*
Simeonite . . . . .1 Chr. 4:37

Shiphmite—*a native of Siphmoth*
Zabdi called . . . . .1 Chr. 27:27

Shiphrah—*beauty*
Hebrew midwife . . . . .Ex. 1:15

Shiphtan—*judicial*
Ephraimite . . . . .Num. 34:24

Ships—*vessels designed for use on water*
A. Uses of:
Fishing . . . . .John 21:3–8

Travel . . . . Jon. 1:3
Cargoes . . . . .Acts 27:3, 10, 38
War . . . . .Num. 24:24
Commerce . . . . .Ps. 107:23
B. Parts of:
Figurehead . . . . Acts 28:11
Skiff . . . . .Acts 27:16–32
Anchor . . . . .Acts 27:29, 40
Rudder . . . . Acts 27:40
Cables . . . . .Acts 27:17
Ropes . . . . Acts 27:32
Sails . . . . Is. 33:23
Oars . . . . .Ezek. 27:6
C. Notable ones:
Ark . . . . Gen. 7:17, 18
Jonah's . . . . .Jon. 1:3, 4
Of Tarshish . . . . Is. 23:1, 14
Paul's . . . . .Acts 27:1–44

Shipwreck—*a wreck of a sea-going vessel*
Paul in three . . . . .2 Cor. 11:25
Figurative of apostasy . . . . .1 Tim. 1:19

Shisha—*distinction*
Father of Solomon's scribes . . . . 1 Kin. 4:3
Called Shavsha . . . . .1 Chr. 18:16

Shitrai—*Yahweh is deciding*
Sharonite overseer of David's herds . . .1 Chr. 27:29

Shiza—*splendor*
Reubenite . . . . .1 Chr. 11:42

Shoa—*rich*
Race or tribe against Israel . . . . Ezek. 23:23

Shobab—*returning*
1. Son of Caleb . . . . 1 Chr. 2:18
2. Son of David . . . . 2 Sam. 5:14

Shobach—*expansion*
Commander of the Syrian army . . . 2 Sam. 10:16–18
Spelled Shophach . . . . .1 Chr. 19:16, 18

Shobai—*glorious*
Head of a family of gatekeepers . . . . Ezra 2:42

Shobal—*flowing*
1. Son of Seir; a Horite chief . . . . .Gen. 36:20–29
2. Judahite, son of Caleb and ancestor of
the people of Kirjath Jearim . . . . . 1 Chr. 2:50, 52

Shobek—*forsaking*
Signer of Nehemiah's sealed
covenant . . . . .Neh. 10:24

Shobi—*Yahweh is glorious*
Ammonite who brings food to
David . . . . 2 Sam. 17:27, 28

Shoe (see Sandals)

Shoham—*beryl or onyx*
Merarite Levite . . . . .1 Chr. 24:27

Shomer—*keeper, watchman*
Asherite . . . . .1 Chr. 7:30, 32

Short—*not long; brief*
A. Descriptive of:
  Life....................................Ps. 89:47
  Time of the devil on earth............Rev. 12:12
  Gospel age ....1 Cor. 7:29
B. Expressive of God's:
  Plan ....Rev. 22:6
  Provision............................. Is. 59:1, 2
  Tribulation......................Matt. 24:21, 22

Short measure
  Abomination........................ Mic. 6:10

Shoulder
A. Used for:
  Carrying burdens....................... Is. 46:7
  Supporting clothes.................... Ex. 12:34
B. Figurative of:
  Notable persons .... Ezek. 24:4, 5
  Destruction ....Ezek. 29:7
  Servitude .... Is. 10:27
  Rebellion ....Zech. 7:11
  Messianic authority..................... Is. 9:6
  Security........................... Deut. 33:12
  Twelve Tribes .... Ex. 28:10–12

WORD STUDY	**SHOUT,** *teru'ah* (ter-oo-*aw*). The noun *teru'ah*, which is usually translated "shout," can indicate various types of loud cries. In some instances the shout is a war-cry as it is in Josh. 6:5, 20. At other times it indicates a blast on a horn to start a march (Num. 10:5). This blast was to be given on the Day of Atonement (Lev. 25:9) and on the first day of the seventh month (Lev. 23:24). In some instances the loud cry is one of alarm (Jer. 20:16). Frequently the shout is a shout of joy in a religious setting. In these cases the shout is part of public worship as in Job 33:26. In Ps. shouting is part of the musical service in worship (Ps. 33:3; 47:6). (Strong's #8643)

Shout, Shouted
A. Occasions of, in:
  Conquest......................Josh. 6:5, 16, 20
  Choosing a king .... 1 Sam. 10:24
  Sound of singing....................Ex. 32:17, 18
  Laying foundation of the temple ... Ezek. 3:11–13
  Christ's second coming............ 1 Thess. 4:16
B. In spiritual things:
  At creation .... Job 38:7
  In the Messiah's arrival...............Zech. 9:9

Shovel
1. Used for removing ashes .... Ex. 27:3
2. Winnowing tool.......................Is. 30:24

Showbread—*bread of Your face*
A. Provisions concerning:
  Provided by the people ....Lev. 24:8
  Prepared by the Levites...............1 Chr. 9:32
  Presented to the Lord ....Lev. 24:7, 8
  Provided for priests only... Lev. 24:9; Matt. 12:4, 5

B. Table of:
  Placed in holy place .... Ex. 26:35; Heb. 9:2
  Made of acacia....................Ex. 25:23–28
  Carried by Kohathite Levites ..... Num. 4:4, 7, 15
  High priest...................... Num. 4:7, 8, 16
C. Symbolic of:
  Twelve Tribes .... Ex. 28:10–12
  Christ...............................John 6:48
  Church .... 1 Cor. 10:17

Showers—*sudden outpourings*
A. Used literally of rain:
  Withheld ....Jer. 3:3
  Predicted ....Luke 12:54
  Requested...................... Zech. 10:1
  Blessing........................... Ps. 65:10
  See Rain
B. Used figuratively of:
  God's Word .... Deut. 32:2
  God's wrath.................... Ezek. 13:11, 13
  Messiah's advent....................... Ps. 72:6
  Gospel.......................... Ezek. 34:25, 26
  Remnant...........................Mic. 5:7

Shua, Shuah, Shuhah—*prosperity*
1. Son of Abraham by Keturah..........Gen. 25:1, 2
2. Father of Judah's wife.............. Gen. 38:2, 12
3. Descendant of Judah............... 1 Chr. 4:1, 11
4. Daughter of Heber................... 1 Chr. 7:32

Shual—*jackal*
1. Asherite .... 1 Chr. 7:30, 36
2. Region raided by a
     Philistine company ....1 Sam. 13:17

Shubael, Shebuel
1. Levite, son of Amram .... 1 Chr. 24:20
2. Levite, son of Heman .... 1 Chr. 25:4

Shuham—*depression*
  Son of Dan ....Num. 26:42
  Called Hushim ....Gen. 46:23
  Head of the Shuhamites.........Num. 26:42, 43

Shuhite—*a descendant of Shuah*
  Bildad called; a descendant of Abraham by
     Keturah .... Gen. 25:1–4; Job 2:11

Shulamite—*a native of Shulem*
  Shepherd's sweetheart................. Song 6:13

Shumathites
  Family of Kirjath Jearim ....1 Chr. 2:53

Shunammite—*a native of Shunem*
1. Abishag, David's nurse called........ 1 Kin. 1:3, 15
2. Woman who cared for Elisha ....2 Kin. 4:8–12

Shunem—*uneven*
  Border town of Issachar .... Josh. 19:18

Shuni—*fortunate*
  Son of Gad .... Gen. 46:16

Shuppim—*serpent*
  Levite gatekeeper ....1 Chr. 26:16

Shur—*fortification*
- Wilderness in south Palestine.........Gen. 16:7
- Israel went from Red Sea to............Ex. 15:22
- On Egypt's border ....1 Sam. 15:7
- Hagar flees to ....Gen. 16:7

Shushan—*a city of Elam*
- Residence of Persian monarchs.........Esth. 1:2
- Located on river Ulai..................Dan. 8:2
- Court of Ahasuerus here ....Esth. 1:2, 5

Shut—*to close securely*

A. Applied literally to:
- Ark.................................Gen. 7:16
- Door.............................Gen. 19:6, 10
- Animals...........................Dan. 6:22
- Court................................Jer. 33:1
- Prison ....Acts 26:10

B. Applied figuratively to:
- God's mercies ....Ps. 77:9
- Finality of salvation................ Matt. 25:10
- Spiritual blindness.....................Is. 6:10
- Awe.................................Is. 52:15
- Heaven's glory.........................Is. 60:11
- God's Word ....Jer. 20:9
- Vision ....Dan. 12:4
- Secret prayer .... Matt. 6:6
- Christ's sovereignty ....Rev. 3:7, 8

Shuthelah
1. Son of Ephraim; head of a family... Num. 26:35, 36
2. Ephraimite....................... 1 Chr. 7:20, 21

Shuttle—*a weaving tool*
- Our days swifter than ....Job 7:6

Siaha, Sia—*assembly*
- Family of returning Nethinim ..... Ezra 2:43, 44; Neh. 7:47

Sibbechai
- One of David's mighty men..........1 Chr. 11:29
- Slays a Philistine giant ....2 Sam. 21:18
- Commander of a division............1 Chr. 27:11

Sibmah, Shibmah—*balsam*
- Town of Reuben ....Num. 32:3, 38
- Famous for wines .... Is. 16:8, 9

Sibraim—*double hope*
- Place in north Palestine ....Ezek. 47:16

Sick, Sickness—*the state of being unwell*

A. Caused by:
- Age................................Gen. 48:1, 10
- Accident ....2 Kin. 1:2
- Wine .... Hos. 7:5
- Sins................................. Mic. 6:13
- Despondency.......................Prov. 13:12
- Prophetic visions ....Dan. 8:27
- Love................................ Song 2:5
- God's judgment.................. 2 Chr. 21:14–19

B. Healing of, by:
- Figs..............................2 Kin. 20:7
- Miracle ....1 Kin. 17:17–23

- Prayer ....James 5:14, 15
- God's mercy.......................Phil. 2:25–30
- Laying on of hands...............Mark 16:17, 18; Acts 5:12, 15, 16

See Diseases; Healing

Sickle—*an instrument for cutting grain*
- Literally.............................. Deut. 16:9
- Figuratively .... Mark 4:29; Rev. 14:14–19

Siddim, Valley of
- Valley of bitumen pits near the Dead Sea ....Gen. 14:3, 8, 10

Sidon—*fishery*
- Canaanite city 20 miles north of Tyre .... Gen. 10:19
- Israel's northern boundary ....Josh. 19:28
- Canaanites not expelled from.........Judg. 1:31
- Israelites oppressed by ....Judg. 10:12
- Solomon worshiped goddess of....... 1 Kin. 11:5
- Elijah sent to region of .... 1 Kin. 17:9
- Judgments pronounced on............. Is. 23:12
- Israelites sold as slaves by.............Joel 3:4–6
- People from, hear Jesus............... Luke 6:17
- Visited by Jesus..................... Matt. 15:21
- Paul visits at........................Acts 27:3

Siege of a city—*a military blockade*

A. Methods employed in:
- Supplies cut off ....2 Kin. 19:24
- Ambushes laid.......................Judg. 9:34
- Battering rams used..................Ezek. 4:2
- Arrows shot ....2 Kin. 19:32

B. Suffering of:
- Famine .... 2 Kin. 6:26–29
- Pestilence ....Jer. 21:6

C. Examples of:
- Jericho............................ Josh. 6:2–20
- Jerusalem .... 2 Kin. 24:10, 11

See War

Sieve, sift—*screen*

Used figuratively of:
- God's judgment..................... Amos 9:9
- Satan's temptation ....Luke 22:31

 WORD STUDY   **SIGN,** *'ot* (*oht*). A "sign" or "signal" is indicated by the noun *'ot*. A sign can be a token, an indication that this person or thing is set apart in some way. The blood of the Passover on the doorposts was a sign to the death angel to leave the inhabitants of the house. At times there were signs or omens promised by prophets to show people that the events predicted would happen (1 Sam. 10:7; Is. 8:18). Frequently the sign was a miracle, which pledged divine presence. The word *'ot* can also be used to describe memorials, such as the stones from the Jordan that were stacked up to commemorate the crossing (Josh. 4:6). Signs were part of covenants, showing that the participants were committed to the treaty. Two of the best-known covenant signs are the rainbow and circumcision. (Strong's #226)

> **WORD STUDY**

SIGN, PORTENT, *sēmeion* (say-meye-on). The noun *sē meion* literally means "sign." A *sēmeion*, in the most general sense, can be a "(distinguishing) mark" or "indication" by which something is known (as the "mark" or "sign" of circumcision in Rom. 4:11). *Sēmeion* can be used to refer to a "sign" of warning (Luke 11:29, 30), a previously agreed upon "signal" (Matt. 26:48), or an "indication" of things to come (Matt. 24:3). Frequently *sēmeion* refers to an unusual event that lies outside the bounds of the ordinary, especially a "wonder" or "miracle" of divine origin performed by God, Jesus, or their devotees (Matt. 12:38f.; John 2:11; 6:26; Acts 2:22; 8:13)—or one of demonic origin (Mark 13:22; 2 Thess. 2:9; Rev. 13:13). Unusual and frightening occurrences in the skies are interpreted as "portents" of the last days (Luke 21:11, 25; Acts 2:19; Rev. 12:1, 3). (Strong's #4592)

Sign—*an outward token having spiritual significance*

A. Descriptive of:
- Heavenly bodies .... Gen. 1:14
- Rainbow ....Gen. 9:12–17
- Circumcision....................... Gen. 17:11
- Blood...............................Ex. 12:13
- God's wonders.......................... Ps. 65:8
- Covenant ....Rom. 4:11
- Miracles .... Deut. 26:8
- Memorial .... Num. 16:38
- Symbolic act...........................Is. 8:18
- Witness .... Is. 19:19, 20
- Outward display.......................John 4:48
- God's power....................... Ps. 78:42, 43
- Satan's power......................2 Thess. 2:9

B. Purposes of, to:
- Authenticate a prophecy.............Deut. 13:1; 1 Sam. 2:31, 34
- Strengthen faith .... Judg. 6:17; Is. 7:11
- Recall God's blessings........... Josh. 24:15–17
- Confirm God's Word ....2 Kin. 19:28, 29; Heb. 2:4
- Affirm a promise .... 2 Kin. 20:5, 9–11
- Confirm a prophecy............... 1 Kin. 13:3–5

C. Concerning Christ in His:
- Nativity............................Luke 2:12
- Ministry ....John 20:30; Acts 2:22
- Resurrection .... Matt. 12:38–40

D. Value of:
- Discounted as such................. Matt. 16:1–4
- Demanded unnecessarily..............John 6:30
- Demonstrated by apostles ....Acts 5:12
- Displayed by Paul...................Rom. 15:19

E. In prophecy, concerning:
- Christ's first advent .... Is. 7:11, 14; Matt. 1:21–23
- Christ's second advent............ Matt. 24:3, 30
- Antichrist..........................2 Thess. 2:9
- End.................................Rev. 15:1

F. As assurance of:
- God's presence ....Ex. 3:12

- Judgment upon sin.................. Num. 17:10
- Goodness .... Ps. 86:17
- Genuineness .... 2 Thess. 3:17

See Token

Signify—*to make known by signs*

A. Concerning people:
- Peter's death........................ John 21:19

B. Concerning predicted events:
- Christ's death ....John 12:33
- Gospel age ....Rev. 1:1

Sihon—*bold*
- Amorite king residing at Heshbon .... Num. 21:26–30
- Victorious over Moabites........ Num. 21:26–30
- Ruler of five Midianite princes........Josh. 13:21
- Refused Israel's request for passage....................Deut. 2:26–28
- Defeated by Israel...... Num. 21:21–32; Deut. 1:4
- Territory of, assigned to Reuben and Gad ....Num. 32:1–38
- Victory over, long celebrated..........Deut. 31:4

Silas, Silvanus—*wooded*
- Leader in the Jerusalem church .... Acts 15:22
- Christian prophet.................... Acts 15:32
- Sent on a mission ....Acts 15:22–35
- Became Paul's companion ....Acts 15:36–41
- Roman citizen.....................Acts 16:25–39
- Paul commended his work at Corinth ... 2 Cor. 1:19
- Called Silvanus .... 1 Thess. 1:1
- Associated in Paul's writings......... 2 Thess. 1:1
- Peter's helper ....1 Pet. 5:12

Silence—*the lack of noise*

A. Kinds of:
- Will of God .... 1 Pet. 2:15; Rev. 8:1
- Troubled............................. Jer. 20:9

B. Virtue of:
- Suitable time for .... Eccl. 3:7
- Commanded ....1 Cor. 14:34
- Sign of prudence....................Prov. 21:23
- Sign of wisdom ....Prov. 17:28
- Sign of reverence......................Hab. 2:20

C. Forbidden to God's:
- Watchmen .... Is. 62:6
- Messengers........................Acts 5:27–42
- Praisers ....Ps. 30:12

D. Considered as:
- Blessing............................. Zech. 2:13
- Curse ....1 Sam. 2:9
- Judgment ....Jer. 8:14

E. Of God:
- Broken in judgment................... Ps. 50:3
- Misunderstood by humans ....Ps. 50:21, 23

F. Of Christ:
- Predicted .... Is. 53:7

Before:
- Sinners............................. John 8:6
- High priest....................Matt. 26:62, 63

WORD STUDY — **SIN**, *hamartia* (ham-ar-*tee*-ah). *Hamartia* is a noun meaning "sin." In the NT a "sin" is any act that violates or transgresses the religious or moral law of God or the way of righteousness (1 John 3:4; 5:17). In the Gospel of John "sin" is regarded as a condition (state) or an inherent flaw in character (8:21, 24; 9:34, 41; 19:11). Paul conceives of "sin" as a power that came into the world (Rom. 5:12), rules the world (5:21; 6:14), enslaves human beings (6:17, 20) and controls them (7:17, 20). In Heb. "sin" is viewed as a power that deceives and destroys, which can be overcome only by sacrifice (3:13; 5:1; 9:23ff.). (Strong's #266)

Omission of known duty .... James 4:17
Not from faith...................... Rom. 14:23
Thought of foolishness............... Prov. 24:9
B. Sources of, in:
Satan .... John 8:44
Human heart.................... Matt. 15:19, 20
Lust .... James 1:15
Adam's transgression.............. Rom. 5:12, 16
Natural birth......................... Ps. 51:5
C. Kinds of:
National .... Prov. 14:34
Personal .... Josh. 7:20
Secret............................. Ps. 90:8
Presumptuous...................... Ps. 19:13
Open .... 1 Tim. 5:24
Shameless.......................... Is. 3:9
Youthful .... Ps. 25:7
Public.......................... 2 Sam. 24:10, 17
Unforgivable .... Matt. 12:21, 32; John 8:24
Of ignorance .... Lev. 4:2
Willful.............................. Heb. 10:26
D. Consequences of, among the unregenerate:
Blindness .... John 9:41; 2 Cor. 4:3, 4
Servitude .... John 8:34
Death............................... Rom. 6:23
E. God's attitude toward:
Withholds Abimelech from........... Gen. 20:6
Punishes for....................... Ex. 32:34
Provides a fountain for .... Zech. 13:1
Blots out .... Is. 44:22
Casts away .... Mic. 7:19
Forgives............................. Ex. 34:7
Remembers no more .... Jer. 31:34
F. Christ's relationship to:
Free of .... 1 John 3:5
Knew no .... 2 Cor. 5:21
Makes people conscious of........ John 15:22, 24
Died for our .... 1 Cor. 15:3
As an offering for .... Is. 53:10; Heb. 9:28
Substitutionary........... Is. 53:5, 6; Matt. 26:28
Takes it away .... John 1:29
Saves His people from................ Matt. 1:21
Has power to forgive .... Matt. 9:6
Makes propitiation for .... Heb. 2:17
Purges our .... Heb. 1:3
Cleanses us from.................... 1 John 1:7, 9
Washes us from...................... Rev. 1:5
G. Regenerate must:
Acknowledge........................ Ps. 32:5
Confess .... Ps. 51:3, 4
Be sorry for........................ Ps. 38:18
Not serve........................... Rom. 6:6
Not obey........................... Rom. 6:6, 12
Subdue............................. Rom. 6:14–22
Lay aside........................... Heb. 12:1
Resist.............................. Heb. 12:4
Keep from.......................... Ps. 19:13
Repent of .... Acts 17:30

H. Helps against:
Use God's Word .... Ps. 119:11
Guard the tongue................... Ps. 39:1
Walk in the Spirit.................. Rom. 8:1–14
Avoid evil companions .... 1 Tim. 5:22
Confess to the Lord .... 1 John 1:8, 9
Exercise love....................... 1 Pet. 4:8
Go to the Advocate .... 1 John 2:1

Sin—*the moon-god*
1. Wilderness between the Red Sea
   and Sinai............................ Ex. 16:1
2. City of Egypt..................... Ezek. 30:15, 16

Sinai, Mount—*also known as Mt. Horeb*
Major events that occurred at:
Israel camped here .... Ex. 19:1, 2
God appears to Israel.............. Ex. 19:11–20
Elders of Israel go up .... Ex. 24:1, 9
Law given to Moses .... Ex. 19:20; 20:1–17
Moses allowed to see God's glory.... Ex. 24:16–18
Israel worships gold calf .... Ex. 32:1, 4, 8
Law given to Moses again........... Ex. 34:1–28
Elijah encouraged by God .... 1 Kin. 19:8
See Horeb

Sincerity—*freedom from deceit; genuineness*
A. Descriptive of:
God's Word .... 1 Pet. 2:2
Faith............................... 1 Tim. 1:5
Believer's love .... 2 Cor. 8:8, 24
B. Should characterize:
Young men........................ Titus 2:6, 7
Worship .... John 4:23, 24
Preaching .... 2 Cor. 2:17
Believers' life .... 2 Cor. 1:12
Public relationships .... Judg. 9:16, 19
C. Examples of:
Nathanael.......................... John 1:47
Christ............................. 1 Pet. 2:22
Paul .... 1 Thess. 2:3–5

Singed—*burnt hair*
Miraculously saved from being........ Dan. 3:27

Singers—*those who make music with voice*
Leaders of........................ 1 Chr. 25:2–6
Under teachers .... 1 Chr. 15:22, 27
Mixed .... 2 Chr. 35:15, 25

Singing—*uttering words in musical tones*
A. Descriptive of:
Birds............................. Ps. 104:12
Trees .... 1 Chr. 16:33
Believers .... Eph. 5:19
Redeemed......................... Rev. 5:9
Morning stars .... Job 38:7
B. Occasions of:
Times of:
Victory .... Ex. 15:1, 21
Revelry .... Ex. 32:18
Imprisonment..................... Acts 16:25
Joy............................... James 5:13

Lord's Supper...................... Matt. 26:30

C. Manner of, with:

Thanksgiving .... Ps. 147:7

Joy................................. Ps. 27:6

Gladness............................ Jer. 31:7

Spirit .... 1 Cor. 14:15

Grace.............................. Col. 3:16

D. Objects of:

God's:

Power.............................. Ps. 59:16

Mercies .... Ps. 89:1

Righteousness....................... Ps. 51:14

New song .... Rev. 14:3

Sinim, Sinites—*people in the far east*

1. Canaanite people................ Gen. 10:15–18

2. Distant land from which people will
   return .... Is. 49:7–12

Sink—*to go down under something soft*

Used literally of:

Ax head............................ 2 Kin. 6:5, 6

Stone .... 1 Sam. 17:49

Army .... Ex. 15:4, 5, 10

Boat .... Luke 5:7

Man .... Matt. 14:30

Sinlessness (see Holiness of Christ; Perfection)

Sinners—*those who are unregenerate*

A. Descriptive of:

Wicked city .... Gen. 13:13

Race............................... 1 Sam. 15:18

Wicked Israelites .... Amos 9:8, 10

One under conviction .... Luke 5:8; 18:13

Human race........................ Rom. 5:8, 19

B. Characteristics of:

Hostile to God...................... Jude 15

Scheme wickedly .... Ps. 26:9, 10

Easily ensnared.................... Eccl. 7:26

Can entice the righteous............. Prov. 1:10

Law made for....................... 1 Tim. 1:9

Conscious of sin .... Luke 18:13

Able to repent .... Luke 15:7, 10

Able to be converted .... James 5:20

In need of cleansing............... James 4:8

C. Punishment of:

Pursued by evil.................... Prov. 13:21

Overthrown by evil .... Prov. 13:6

Wealth of, acquired by the just....... Prov. 13:22

Sorrow given to.................... Ezek. 18:20

Will be punished .... Prov. 11:31

Will be consumed................... Ps. 104:35

D. Christ's relationship to:

Came to call....................... Luke 5:32

Friend of.......................... Luke 7:34

Receives such...................... Luke 15:1, 2

Endures hostility from .... Heb. 12:3

Separate from .... Heb. 7:26

Came to save .... 1 Tim. 1:15

Sion—*elevated*

Name given to all or part of

Mt. Hermon .... Deut. 4:48

See Zion

Siphmoth—*fruitful*

David shares spoils with........ 1 Sam. 30:26–28

Sippai—*Yahweh is preserver*

Philistine giant .... 1 Chr. 20:4

Called Saph .... 2 Sam. 21:18

Sirah—*turning aside*

Well near Hebron................... 2 Sam. 3:26

Sirion—*coat of mail*

Sidonian name for Mt. Hermon .... Deut. 3:9

Sisera—*meditation*

1. Canaanite commander of Jabin's army;
   slain by Jael .... Judg. 4:2–22

2. Ancestor of postexilic Nethinim...... Ezra 2:43, 53

Sismai—*Yahweh is distinguished*

Judahite........................... 1 Chr. 2:40

Sister

A. Descriptive of:

Female relative .... Gen. 24:30–60

Women of the same tribe............ Num. 25:18

B. Features concerning:

Protected by:

Brothers .... Gen. 34:13–31

Laws.............................. Lev. 18:9–13, 18

Friction between.................. Luke 10:39, 40

Loved by Jesus.................... John 11:5

C. Figurative of:

Samaria and Jerusalem .... Ezek. 23:1–49

Christian.......................... Matt. 12:50

Christian woman .... Rom. 16:1

Church .... 2 John 13

Sistrum—*a musical instrument*

A part of worship .... 2 Sam. 6:5

Sit

A. Descriptive of:

Judge .... Ex. 18:13, 14

Priest .... Zech. 6:13

King.............................. Deut. 17:15, 18

God .... Ps. 2:4

Messiah........................... Ps. 110:1

B. Purposes of, to:

Eat .... Matt. 26:20, 21

Rest .... John 4:6

Mourn............................ Neh. 1:4

Teach............................. Matt. 26:55

Transact business................. Matt. 9:9

Beg .... Luke 18:35

Learn .... Mark 5:15

Ride .... Matt. 21:5

Worship .... Acts 2:2

C. Figurative of Christ's:

Taking His rightful place in heaven ..... Heb. 1:3

Rule .... Matt. 19:28
Judgment .... Matt. 25:31

Sitnah—*enmity*
Well dug by Isaac near Gerar .... Gen. 26:21

Sivan
Third month of the Jewish and
     Babylonian year .... Esth. 8:9

Skeptical—*characterized by doubts*
Thomas, the doubter............ John 20:24–28

Skilled—*those possessing special abilities*
A. Required of:
     Soldiers .... 1 Chr. 5:18
     Craftsmen .... 2 Chr. 2:7, 14
     Musicians .... 2 Chr. 34:12
B. Obtained by:
     Spirit's help......................... Ex. 31:2–5
     God's Word .... Ps. 119:98–100
     Lord's help ....Ps. 144:1

Skin—*the outer covering of a body*
A. Of animals, used for:
     Clothing .... Gen. 3:21
     Deception......................... Gen. 27:16
     Coverings ....Ex. 26:14
     Bottles .... Josh. 9:4
B. Of humankind:
     Diseased .... Lev. 13:1–46
     Sign of race........................ Jer. 13:23

Skull—*skeleton of the head*
Abimelech's crushed by a woman....... Judg. 9:53
Jezebel's left by dogs .... 2 Kin. 9:30–37
They brought Him to a place called ... Mark 15:22
Another name for Golgotha .... Matt. 27:33
     See Golgotha

Sky—*the expanse of the heaven*
A. Place of:
     Stars............................... Heb. 11:12
     Expanse............................Job 37:18
     Weather changes .... Matt. 16:2, 3
     Thunder ....Ps. 77:17
B. Figurative of:
     God's abode........................ Ps. 18:11
     Righteousness .... Is. 45:8
     Ultimate judgment.....................Jer. 51:9

Slander—*a malicious statement*
A. Described as:
     Destructive .... Prov. 11:9
     Deceitful............................Ps. 52:2
     Deluding.........................Prov. 10:18
     Devouring .... Prov. 16:27–30
B. Hurled against:
     Joseph ....Gen. 39:14–19
     David............................ 2 Sam. 10:3
     Jews .... Ezra 4:7–16
     Christ.........................Matt. 26:59–61
     Paul .... Acts 24:5, 6
     Stephen............................Acts 6:11
     Christians......................... 1 Pet. 2:12

C. Hurled against the righteous by:
     Devil .... Job 1:9–11
     Revilers............................1 Pet. 3:16
     Hypocrites .... Prov. 11:9
     False leaders........................ 3 John 9, 10
D. Charged against Christ as:
     Winebibber ....Matt. 11:19
     Blasphemer........................Matt. 9:3
     Demonized....................John 8:48, 52
     Rebel .... Luke 23:5
     Insurrectionist ....Luke 23:2
E. Christians:
     Warned against....................Titus 3:1, 2
     Must endure..................... Matt. 5:11, 12
     Must lay aside .... Eph. 4:31

Slave, slavery—*a state of bondage*
A. Acquired by:
     Purchase .... Gen. 17:12
     Voluntary service .... Ex. 21:5, 6
     Birth............................. Ex. 21:2–4
     Capture...................... Deut. 20:11–14
     Debt................................ 2 Kin. 4:1
     Arrest.......................... Ex. 22:2, 3
     Inheritance........................Lev. 25:46
     Gift........................... Gen. 29:24, 29
B. Rights of:
     Sabbath rest ....Ex. 20:10
     Share in religious feasts .... Deut. 12:12, 18
     Membership in covenant ....Gen. 17:10–14
     Refuge for fugitive.............. Deut. 23:15, 16
     Murder of, punishable.................Ex. 21:12
     Freedom of, if maimed .... Ex. 21:26, 27
     Entitled to justice .... Job 31:13–15
C. Privileges of:
     Entrusted with missions............Gen. 24:1–14
     Advice of, heeded .... 1 Sam. 9:5–10
     Marriage in master's house .... 1 Chr. 2:34, 35
     Rule over sons .... Prov. 17:2
     May become heir ....Gen. 15:1–4
     May secure freedom.................. Ex. 21:2–6
D. State of, under Christianity:
     Union "in Christ".....................Gal. 3:28
     Treatment of with justice............... Eph. 6:9
     Duties of, as pleasing God .... Eph. 6:5–8
     No longer slaves to sin................. Rom. 6:6

Sleep—*a state of complete or partial unconsciousness*
A. Descriptive of:
     Slumber..........................Prov. 6:4, 10
     Desolation .... Jer. 51:39, 57
     Unregeneracy .... 1 Thess. 5:6, 7
     Death........................... John 11:11–14
     Spiritual indifference .... Matt. 25:5
     Prophetic vision .... Dan. 8:18
B. Beneficial:
     When given by God................Ps. 3:5; 127:2
     While trusting God.................... Ps. 4:8
     While obeying parents .... Prov. 6:20–22
     When following wisdom .... Prov. 3:21–24
     To the working person .... Eccl. 5:12

After duty is done. . . . . .Ps. 132:1–5
During a pleasant dream . . . . .Jer. 31:23–26
C. Condemned:
When excessive. . . . . Prov. 6:9–11
During harvest . . . . .Prov. 10:5
In times of danger . . . . Matt. 26:45–47
D. Inability to:
Caused by worry. . . . . Dan. 2:1
Produced by insomnia. . . . . Esth. 6:1
Brought on by overwork. . . . . Gen. 31:40

Sling—*an instrument for throwing stones*
A. Used by:
Warriors . . . . .Judg. 20:16
David. .1 Sam. 17:40–50
B. Figurative of:
God's punishment . . . . 1 Sam. 25:29
Foolishness. . . . . .Prov. 26:8

Slothfulness, sluggard—*laziness*
A. Sources of, in:
Excessive sleep. . . . . Prov. 6:9–11
Laziness . . . . .Prov. 19:15, 24
Indifference. . . . . .Judg. 18:9
Desires. . . . . Prov. 21:25
Fearful imaginations. . . . . .Prov. 22:13
B. Way of:
Brings hunger . . . . .Prov. 19:15
Leads to poverty. . . . . .Prov. 20:4
Produces waste . . . . Prov. 18:9
Causes decay . . . . Eccl. 10:18
Results in forced labor. . . . . .Prov. 12:24
C. Antidotes of, in:
Faithfulness. . . . . .Matt. 25:26–30
Fervent spirit. .Rom. 12:11
Following the faithful. . . . . Heb. 6:12

Small—*little in size; few in number*
A. Applied to God's:
Choice . . . . Num. 16:5, 9
Faithful remnant . . . . .Is. 1:9
B. Applied to human:
Sin. . . . . Ezek. 16:20
Unconcern . . . . Zech. 4:10

Smith—*a metal worker*
Blacksmith. . . . . 1 Sam. 13:19, 20
Worker in iron. . . . . Is. 44:12
Tubal-Cain, first. . . . . Gen. 4:22
Demetrius, silversmith . . . . .Acts 19:24–27
Alexander, coppersmith . . . . 2 Tim. 4:14

Smoke
A. Resulting from:
Destruction . . . . Gen. 19:28
God's presence . . . . Is. 6:4
God's vengeance. . . . . .Is. 34:8–10
Babylon's end. . . . . Rev. 14:8–11
World's end . . . . .Is. 51:6
B. Figurative of:
Our life . . . . .Ps. 102:3
Spiritual distress. . . . . .Ps. 119:83

Something offensive . . . . Is. 65:5
Spirit's advent . . . . .Joel 2:29, 30
Smyrna—*a city of Iona in Asia Minor*
One of the seven churches . . . . Rev. 1:11
Snail
Creature with a spiral tail. . . . . .Ps. 58:8
Snake charmer
Alluded to. . . . . .Ps. 58:4, 5
Snares—*traps*
A. Uses of:
Catch birds. . . . . .Prov. 7:23
B. Figurative of:
Pagan nations .Josh. 23:12, 13
Idols. . . . . .Judg. 2:3
God's representative . . . . .Ex. 10:7
Words . . . . Prov. 6:2
Wicked works . . . . Ps. 9:16
Fear of people .Prov. 29:25
Immoral woman. . . . . Eccl. 7:26
Christ. . . . . Is. 8:14, 15
Sudden destruction . . . . .Luke 21:34, 35
Riches . . . . 1 Tim. 6:9, 10
Devil's trap. . . . . 2 Tim. 2:26

> **WORD STUDY**   **SNATCH, SEIZE,** *harpazō* (har-*pod*-zoh). Meaning "to snatch," "to seize," *harpazō* usually involves taking something away suddenly, vehemently, or forcefully. It can be used in the sense of "to steal" or "to take away" animals (John 10:12) or property. *Harpazō* can also mean "to snatch," "to take away forcefully" (Matt. 13:19; John 6:15; 10:28), and sometimes with such suddenness that no resistance is offered (Acts 8:39; 2 Cor. 12:2; 1 Thess. 4:17). The meaning of *harpazō* in Matt. 11:12 is difficult, but it probably means something like "seize for oneself" or "steal (plunder)." (Strong's #726)

Sneezed
Seven times . . . . .2 Kin. 4:35
Snow—*frozen crystallized flakes of water*
A. Characteristics of:
Comes in winter .Prov. 26:1
Sent by God . . . . .Job 37:6
Waters the earth. Is. 55:10
Melts with heat . . . . Job 6:16, 17
Notable event during. . . . . 2 Sam. 23:20
B. Whiteness illustrative of:
Leprosy. . . . . .Ex. 4:6
Converted sinner . . . . .Ps. 51:7; Is. 1:18
Nazirite's purity . . . . .Lam. 4:7
Angel. . . . . Matt. 28:3
Risen Christ. . . . . .Rev. 1:14
So
Egyptian king . . . . .2 Kin. 17:4
Soap
Figuratively in. . . . . Mal. 3:2

Sober, sobriety

A. Described as:

Sanity. . . . . 2 Cor. 5:13

Soberness (not drunk). . . . . 1 Tim. 3:2, 11

Temperate nature. . . . . Titus 1:8

Humble mind . . . . Rom. 12:3

Moral rectitude. . . . . Titus 2:12

Self-control. . . . . 1 Cor. 7:9; Gal. 5:23

B. Incentives to, found in:

Lord's return . . . . 1 Thess. 5:1–7

Nearness of the end . . . . 1 Pet. 4:7

Satan's attacks. . . . . 1 Cor. 7:5

C. Required of:

Christians. . . . . 1 Thess. 5:6, 8

Church officers. . . . . 1 Tim. 3:2, 3

Wives of church officers. . . . . 1 Tim. 3:11

Aged men . . . . Titus 2:2

Young women . . . . Titus 2:4

Young men . . . . Titus 2:6

Women . . . . 1 Tim. 2:9

Children . . . . 1 Tim. 2:15

Evangelists. . . . . 2 Tim. 4:5

See Temperance

Sociability—*friendly relations in social gatherings*

A. Manifested in:

Family life . . . . John 12:1–9

National life. . . . . Neh. 8:9–18

Church life. . . . . Acts 2:46

B. Christian's kind, governed by:

No fellowship with evil. . . . . 2 Cor. 6:14–18

Righteous living . . . . Titus 2:12

Honesty in all things. . . . . Col. 3:9–14

Socialism (see Communism, Christian)

Socoh, Sochoh—*thorn*

1. Town in south Judah. . . . . Josh. 15:1, 35

Where David killed Goliath . . . . . . 1 Sam. 17:1, 49

2. Town in Judah's hill country . . . . Josh. 15:1, 48

Sodi—*an acquaintance*

Father of the Zebulunite spy . . . . Num. 13:10

Sodom—*burnt*

A. History of:

Located in Jordan plain . . . . Gen. 13:10

Became Lot's residence . . . . Gen. 13:11–13

Wickedness of, notorious. . . . . Gen. 13:13

Plundered by Chedorlaomer . . . . Gen. 14:9–24

Abram rescues Lot . . . . Gen. 14:13–16

Abraham interceded for . . . . Gen. 18:16–33

Destroyed by God . . . . Gen. 19:1–28

Lot sent out of . . . . Gen. 19:29, 30

B. Destruction of, illustrative of:

God's wrath . . . . Deut. 29:23

Sudden destruction . . . . Lam. 4:6

Total destruction . . . . Jer. 49:18

Future judgment. . . . . Matt. 11:23, 24

Example to the ungodly . . . . 2 Pet. 2:6

C. Sin of, illustrative of:

Shamelessness. . . . . Is. 3:9

Persistence in wrongdoing. . . . . Jer. 23:14

Sexual perversion . . . . Jude 7

D. Figurative of:

Wickedness . . . . Deut. 32:32

Jerusalem . . . . Is. 1:9, 10

Judah. . . . . Ezek. 16:46–63

Sodomite—*a male cult prostitute*

Prohibition of . . . . Deut. 23:17, 18

Prevalence of, under Rehoboam. . . . . . 1 Kin. 14:24

Asa's removal of . . . . 1 Kin. 15:11, 12

Jehoshaphat's riddance of. . . . . 1 Kin. 22:46

Josiah's reforms against . . . . 2 Kin. 23:7

Result of unbelief. . . . . Rom. 1:27

Soil—*dirt*

It was planted in good. . . . . Ezek. 17:8

Uzziah loved it. 2 Chr. 26:10

Sold

Descriptive of:

Purchase. . . . . Matt. 26:9

Slavery. . . . . Ps. 105:17

Bondage to sin. . . . . Rom. 7:14

Soldiers—*military agents of a nation*

A. Duties of:

Subdue riots. Acts 21:31–35

Guard prisoners . . . . Acts 12:4–6

B. Good characteristics of:

Obedience . . . . Matt. 8:9

Devotion. . . . . Acts 10:7

Valor . . . . 2 Chr. 13:3

C. Bad characteristics of:

Cowardice . . . . Deut. 20:8

Discontent and violence . . . . Luke 3:14

Rashness. . . . . Acts 27:42

Bribery . . . . Matt. 28:12

Irreligion. . . . . John 19:2, 3, 23

D. Figurative of:

Christians. . . . . 2 Tim. 2:4

Christian workers. . . . . Phil. 2:25

Spiritual armor . . . . Eph. 6:10–18

Solitude—*aloneness*

For:

Adam, not good . . . . Gen. 2:18

Prayer, good. . . . . Matt. 6:6; 14:23

Rest, necessary . . . . Mark 6:30, 31

Solomon—*peace*

A. Life of:

David's son by Bathsheba. . . . . 2 Sam. 12:24

Name of, significant . . . . 1 Chr. 22:9

Anointed over opposition. . . . . 1 Kin. 1:5–48

Received dying instruction

from David . . . . 1 Kin. 2:1–10

Purged his kingdom of corrupt

leaders. . . . . 1 Kin. 2:11–46

Prayer of, for wisdom . . . . 1 Kin. 3:1–15

Exhibited wise judgment . . . . 1 Kin. 3:16–28

Organized his kingdom . . . . 1 Kin. 4:1–28

Fame of, worldwide . . . . 1 Kin. 4:29–34

Built the temple. . . . . 1 Kin. 5; 6

Dedicated the temple .... 1 Kin. 8:22–66
Built personal palace .... 1 Kin. 7:1–12
Lord reappeared to .... 1 Kin. 9:1–9
Strengthened his kingdom .... 1 Kin. 9:10–28
Received queen of Sheba .... 1 Kin. 10:1–13
Encouraged commerce .... 1 Kin. 10:14–29
Fell into polygamy and idolatry ..... 1 Kin. 11:1–8
God warned him .... 1 Kin. 11:9–13
Adversaries arose against him ... 1 Kin. 11:14–40
Reign and death .... 1 Kin. 11:41–43

B. Positive features of:
Chooses an understanding heart .... 1 Kin. 3:5–9
Exhibits sound judgment .... 1 Kin. 3:16–28
Excels in wisdom .... 1 Kin. 4:29–34
Great writer .... 1 Kin. 4:32
Writer of psalms .... Ps. 72 (Title); 127 (Title)

C. Negative features of:
Loves luxury .... Eccl. 2:1–11
Marries pagans .... 1 Kin. 11:1–3
Turns to idolatry .... 1 Kin. 11:4–8
Enslaves Israel .... 1 Kin. 12:1–4

> **WORD STUDY**
> **SON, ONLY,** *yachid* (yaw-*kheed*). The adjective *yachid* is literally translated "only" or "only one." This word is usually used in the substantive form and translated "only one," meaning "only son." This is the way the word is used to describe Isaac's relationship with Abraham, "your son, your only *son*" (Gen. 22:2). The term is used in this same way in Jer. 6:26, Amos 8:10, and Zech. 12:10. In a few other cases, "my only one" refers to "my life" as a precious possession (Ps. 22:20, 21; 35:17). This word indicates that which is solitary or isolated. (Strong's #3173)

> **WORD STUDY**
> **SON,** *ben* (*bayn*). *Ben* is the noun used to indicate a male child. Sons were the way in which a father's name lived on into the future and were treasured because of this. The word "son" appears in the phrase "son of his mother," indicating someone who is a brother. The word can also be used to indicate cousins. "My son," while sometimes expressing a true father-son relationship, can also be used as a term of endearment or kindness. Eli used the phrase in addressing Samuel when he was a boy. God calls Israel "My sons" in several places, indicating a relationship. The "sons of gods" were supernatural beings. The word "sons" is used frequently with a name to express a line of descent, such as the sons of Lot or sons of Edom. The plural of "son" can mean children and include both sons and daughters except in Josh. 17:2 where the text specifies "male children." *Ben* is used in compound names, the best known of which is Benjamin ("Son of the Right Hand"). (Strong's #1121)

Son

A. Descriptive of:
Male child .... Gen. 4:25, 26
Grandson .... Gen. 29:5
Disciple .... Prov. 7:1

One destined to a certain end .... John 17:12
Messiah .... Is. 7:14
Angels .... Job 1:6

B. Characteristics of, sometimes:
Jealous .... Judg. 9:2, 18
Quite different .... Gen. 9:18–27
Disloyal .... Luke 15:25–30
Unlike their father .... 2 Sam. 13:30–39
Spiritually different .... Gen. 25:22–34
Rebellious .... Deut. 21:18–21

C. Admonitions addressed to, concerning:
Instruction .... Prov. 1:8
Sinners .... Prov. 1:10–19
Wisdom .... Prov. 3:13–35
Correction .... Prov. 3:11, 12
Immorality .... Prov. 5:1–23
Life's dangers .... Prov. 6:1–35

Son-in-law—*a daughter's husband*
Sinful .... Gen. 19:14
Believing .... Mark 1:29, 30

Son of God—*a title indicating Christ's deity*
A. Descriptive of Christ as:
Eternally begotten .... Ps. 2:7; Heb. 1:5
Messianic King .... Ps. 89:26, 27
Virgin-born .... Luke 1:31–35
Trinity-member .... Matt. 28:19
Priest-King .... Heb. 1:8; 5:5, 6
Intercessor .... Rom. 8:34

B. Witnesses of, by:
Father .... Matt. 17:5
Demons .... Mark 5:7
Satan .... Matt. 4:3, 6
Men .... Matt. 16:16
Christ Himself .... John 9:35–37
His resurrection .... Rom. 1:1–4
Christians .... Acts 2:36
Scriptures .... John 20:31
Inner witness .... 1 John 5:10–13

C. Significance of, as indicating:
Cost of humankind's
    reconciliation .... Rom. 5:6–11
Greatness of God's love .... John 3:16
Sin of unbelief .... Heb. 10:28, 29
Worship due Christ .... Rev. 4:11
Dignity of human nature ..... Rom. 8:3; Heb. 2:14
Humanity of Christ .... Gal. 4:4
Pattern of glorification ..... Rom. 8:29; Phil. 3:21
Destruction of Satan .... 1 John 3:8
Uniqueness of Christ .... Heb. 1:5–9

D. Belief in Christ as:
Derived from the Scriptures .... John 20:31
Necessary for eternal life .... John 3:18, 36
Source of eternal life .... John 6:40
Foundation of the faith .... Acts 9:20
Affirmation of deity .... 1 John 2:23, 24
Illustrated .... John 11:14–44

E. Powers of Christ as, to:
Have life in Himself .... John 5:26
Reveal the Father .... Matt. 11:27

Glorify the Father .... John 17:1
Do the Father's works .... John 5:19, 20
Redeem humankind .... Gal. 4:4, 5
Give freedom..................... John 8:36
Raise the dead.................... John 5:21, 25
Judge people...................... John 5:22

Son of Man—*a self-designation of Christ*
A. Title of, applied to:
    Ezekiel.......................... Ezek. 2:1, 3, 6
    Daniel .... Dan. 8:17
    Messiah........................... Dan. 7:13
Christ:
    By Himself....................... Matt. 8:20
    By Stephen ....Acts 7:56
    In John's vision ....Rev. 1:13
B. As indicative of Christ's:
    Self-designation .... Matt. 16:13
    Humanity........................Matt. 11:19
    Messiahship.....................Luke 18:31
    Lordship........................ Matt. 12:8
    Sovereignty .... Matt. 13:41
    Obedience .... Phil. 2:8
    Suffering........................Mark 9:12
    Death........................... Matt. 12:40
    Resurrection .... Matt. 17:9–23
    Regal power .... Matt. 16:28
    Return..........................Matt. 24:27–37
    Glorification ....Heb. 2:6–10
C. Christ's powers as, to:
    Forgive sins .... Matt. 9:6
    Save people....................... Luke 19:10
    Redeem people .... Matt. 20:28
    Rule His church ....Col. 1:17, 18
    Reward people........... Matt. 16:27; 19:28

Song of Solomon—*a book of the Old Testament*
The bride and the bridegroom ....Song 1
Song of the bride..................Song 2:8–3:5
Song of the bridegroom ....Song 4:1–15
The bride meditates...............Song 4:16–6:3
The bridegroom appeals............Song 6:4–7:9
Lovers united....................Song 7:10–8:14

Songs
A. Described as:
    New ....Rev. 5:9
    Spiritual ....Eph. 5:19
B. Uses of, as:
    Witness.......................Deut. 31:19–22
    Torment .... Ps. 137:3
    March .... Num. 21:17, 18
    Processional......................1 Chr. 13:7, 8
C. Expressive of:
    Triumph ....Judg. 5:12
    Physical joy.......................Gen. 31:27
    Spiritual joy ....Ps. 119:54
    Deliverance .... Ps. 32:7
    Hypocrisy.......................Amos 5:23
    Derision .... Ps. 69:12

D. Figurative of:
    Passover (the Lord's Supper) .... Is. 30:29;
        Matt. 26:26–30
    Messiah's advent................... Is. 42:10
    Gospel age .... Is. 26:1, 2
    Praise and thanksgiving.... Neh. 12:46; Ps. 69:30

Songwriter
Solomon, famous as.................1 Kin. 4:32

Sonship of believers
A. Evidences of, seen in:
    New nature....................... 1 John 3:9–12
    Possession of the Spirit .... Rom. 8:15–17
    Chastisement.....................Heb. 12:5–8
B. Blessedness of, manifested in:
    Regeneration .... John 1:12
    Adoption.........................Gal. 4:5, 6
    Glorification .... Rom. 8:19–21

Soothsayer—*a diviner, fortune-teller*
Among Philistines .... Is. 2:6
At Babylon ....Dan. 2:27
At Philippi .... Acts 16:12, 16
Unable to interpret.................. Dan. 4:7
Forbidden in Israel.................... Mic. 5:12
See Divination

Sopater—*of sound parentage*
One of Paul's companions .... Acts 20:4

Sophereth—*writer, scribe*
Descendants of Solomon's servants..... Neh. 7:57

Sorcerers—*supposed possessors of supernatural powers*
A. Prevalence of, in:
    Assyria...........................Nah. 3:4, 5
    Egypt............................. Ex. 7:11
    Babylon...........................Is. 47:9–13
    Palestine ....Acts 8:9–24
    Last days..........................Rev. 9:21
B. Punishment of, described:
    Legally..........................Deut. 18:10–12
    Prophetically .... Mal. 3:5
    Symbolically ....Rev. 21:8
See Divination; Magic, magician

WORD STUDY   **SORCERY, MAGIC,** *pharmakeia* (far-mak-*eye*-ah). This noun, meaning "sorcery" or "magic," is used to designate the practice of magic in which potions are concocted as a means of attaining something desirable. The cognate noun *pharmakon* means "poison," "(magic) potion," "medicine," "remedy, or "drug," which suggests that this type of magic was practiced for both evil ends (to poison) and good ends (to remedy illness). It is listed in a catalog of vices (Gal. 5:20). The author of Rev. associates *pharmakeia* with demon worship, idolatry, and other evils (9:21), and identifies it as the means by which "Babylon" deceived the world (18:23). (Strong's #5331)

Sorcery—*the practice of magic*
Forbidden in Israel................. Deut. 18:10

Condemned by the prophets . . . . Mic. 5:12
Practiced by Manasseh . . . . 2 Chr. 33:6
Work of the flesh . . . . Gal. 5:20

Sore
Result of plague . . . . Lev. 13:42, 43

Sorek—*a choice vine*
Valley, home of Delilah. . . . . Judg. 16:4

Sorrow—*grief*
A. Kinds of:
Hypocritical. . . . . Matt. 14:9
Unfruitful. . . . . Matt. 19:22
Temporary . . . . John 16:6, 20–22
Continual . . . . Rom. 9:2
Fruitful . . . . 2 Cor. 7:8–11
Christian. . . . . 1 Thess. 4:13
B. Caused by:
Sin. . . . . Gen. 3:16, 17
Death. . . . . John 11:33–36
Drunkenness . . . . Prov. 23:29–35
Love of money. . . . . 1 Tim. 6:10
Apostasy . . . . Ps. 16:4
Persecution. . . . . Esth. 9:22
Hardship of life. Ps. 90:10
Knowledge . . . . Eccl. 1:18
Distressing news. . . . . Acts 20:37, 38
C. Of the righteous:
Not like the world's . . . . 1 Thess. 4:13
Sometimes intense . . . . Ps. 18:4, 5
Seen in the face . . . . Neh. 2:2–4
None in God's blessings . . . . Prov. 10:22
Shown in repentance . . . . 2 Cor. 7:10
To be removed. . . . . Is. 25:8
None in heaven . . . . Rev. 21:4
Shall flee away. . . . . Is. 51:11
See Grief

Sosipater—*saving a father*
Kinsman of Paul . . . . Rom. 16:21

Sosthenes—*of sound strength*
1. Ruler of the synagogue at Corinth . . . . . . Acts 18:17
2. Paul's Christian brother. . . . . 1 Cor. 1:1

Sotai—*Yahweh is turning aside*
Head of a family of servants . . . . Ezra 2:55

WORD
STUDY

SOUL, LIFE, *psuchē* (psoo-*khay*). This noun appears often in the NT and is usually translated "soul." The fundamental meaning refers to the "life-principle" that animates the body of earthly creatures (animal or human). When the *psuchē* leaves the body, death occurs (Luke 12:20). The word can refer to "(earthly) life" (Mark 10:45). The *psuchē* is envisioned as the seat and center of a person's inner life—objectivized as the "self" (Luke 12:19)—or a person's emotions and feelings (Matt. 26:38). The *psuchē* is thought to transcend the earthly body after death (Matt. 10:28). *Psuchē* can also be used figuratively to refer to a "living being" (1 Cor. 15:45) or "souls" (= persons; Acts 2:41). (Strong's #5590)

WORD
STUDY

SOUL, PERSON, *nephesh* (neh-*fesh*). *Nephesh* is a noun meaning "soul" or "person." At times it means the inner being as distinct from flesh (Is. 10:18). This inner being departs from the body at death (Gen. 35:18; Jer. 15:9). *Nephesh* can indicate a living being where life resides in the blood. This would explain the prohibition against eating blood. Numerous times the term is used to mean "life" of either animals or humans; for example, Ex. 21:23 says, "If *any* harm follows, then you shall give life for life." In poetic usage, the soul is the person, so that the phrase "my life" means "me." *Nephesh* can also be used to indicate appetites, as in Eccl. The soul is seen as the seat of emotions over 150 times in the OT. (Strong's #5315)

Soul—*the immaterial part of human beings*
A. Descriptive of:
People . . . . Acts 2:41, 43
Sinner . . . . James 5:20
Emotional life . . . . 1 Sam. 18:1, 3
Spiritual life. Ps. 42:1, 2, 4
Disembodied state . . . . Rev. 6:9; 20:4
B. Characteristics of:
Belongs to God . . . . Ezek. 18:3, 4
Possesses immortality. . . . . Matt. 10:28
Most vital asset. . . . . Matt. 16:26
Leaves body at death . . . . Gen. 35:18
C. Abilities of, able to:
Believe. . . . . Heb. 10:39
Love God . . . . Luke 10:27
Sin. . . . . Mic. 6:7
Prosper . . . . 3 John 2
Survive death. Matt. 10:28
D. Duties of, to:
Keep itself. . . . . Deut. 4:9
Seek the Lord. . . . . Deut. 4:29
Love the Lord . . . . Deut. 6:5
Serve the Lord. Deut. 10:12
Store God's Word. . . . . Deut. 11:18
Keep God's Law . . . . Deut. 26:16
Obey God. . . . . Deut. 30:2, 6, 10
Get wisdom . . . . Prov. 19:8
E. Enemies of, seen in:
Fleshly lusts . . . . 1 Pet. 2:11
Evil environment . . . . 2 Pet. 2:8
Sin. . . . . Lev. 5:4, 15, 17
Adultery . . . . Prov. 6:32
Evil people . . . . Prov. 22:24, 25
Ignorance . . . . Prov. 8:36
Hell . . . . Prov. 23:14
F. Of the righteous:
Kept by God. . . . . Ps. 121:7
Vexed by sin . . . . 2 Pet. 2:8
Subject to authorities. . . . . Rom. 13:1
Purified by obedience . . . . 1 Pet. 1:22
Not allowed to famish. . . . . Prov. 10:3
Restored . . . . Ps. 23:1, 3
Enriched . . . . Prov. 11:25

Satisfied . . . . Prov. 13:25
Reign with Christ. . . . . Rev. 20:4
G. Of the wicked:
Desires evil. . . . . Prov. 21:10
Delights in abominations. . . . . Is. 66:3
Has nothing. . . . . Prov. 13:4
Required. . . . . Luke 12:19, 20
To be punished . . . . Rom. 2:9

Soul winning
Importance of . . . . James 5:20
Christ's command . . . . Matt. 4:19
Our reward. . . . . Dan. 12:3

Sound (see Sober)

Sound doctrine
A. Manifested in:
Heart's prayer . . . . Ps. 119:80
Speech . . . . 2 Tim. 1:13
Righteous living . . . . 1 Tim. 1:10
B. Need of:
For exhortation. . . . . Titus 1:9
For the faith. . . . . Titus 1:13
Denied by some. . . . . 2 Tim. 4:3

Sour grapes—*not yet mature*
Used proverbially . . . . Jer. 31:29, 30

Sowing—*scattering seed*
A. Restrictions upon, regarding:
Sabbath year . . . . Lev. 25:3–22
Mingled seed . . . . Lev. 19:19
Weather . . . . Eccl. 11:4, 6
B. Figurative of evil things:
Iniquity. . . . . Job 4:8
Wind . . . . Hos. 8:7
Discord . . . . Prov. 6:14, 19
Strife . . . . Prov. 16:28
False teaching . . . . Matt. 13:25, 39
Sin. . . . . Gal. 6:7, 8
C. Figurative of good things:
God's Word . . . . Is. 55:10
Reward . . . . 2 Cor. 9:6, 10
Gospel. . . . . Matt. 13:3, 4, 37
Gospel messengers. . . . . John 4:36, 37
Resurrection . . . . 1 Cor. 15:36–44
Eternal life . . . . Gal. 6:7–9

Spain—*a country in southwest Europe*
Paul desires to visit. . . . . Rom. 15:24, 28

Sparrow—*a small bird*
Value of. . . . . Matt. 10:29, 31

Spearmen—*infantry men with spears*
One of, pierces Christ's side. . . . . John 19:34
Paul's military escort. . . . . Acts 23:23, 24

Special—*something separated to one's own use*
A. Applied literally to:
Israel (God's own) . . . . Ex. 19:5;
Deut. 7:6
Treasure (Solomon's own) . . . . Eccl. 2:8
Translated "jewels" . . . . Mal. 3:17

B. Applied figuratively to:
True Israel . . . . Ps. 135:4
Christian. . . . . Titus 2:14
The church. . . . . 1 Pet. 2:9

Speck—*a small particle*
Used in contrast to a beam. . . . . Matt. 7:3, 5

Speckled
Spotted (of goats) . . . . Gen. 30:32–39
Colored (of birds) . . . . Jer. 12:9

Speech—*the intelligible utterance of the mouth*
A. Of the wicked, consisting of:
Lies. . . . . Ps. 58:3
Cursing . . . . Ps. 59:12
Enticements. . . . . Prov. 7:21
Blasphemies. . . . . Dan. 7:25
Earthly things . . . . John 3:31
Deception. . . . . Rom. 16:18
B. Of the righteous, consisting of:
God's righteousness. . . . . Ps. 35:28
Wisdom . . . . 1 Cor. 2:6, 7
God's Word . . . . Ps. 119:172
Truth. . . . . Eph. 4:25
Mystery of Christ. . . . . Col. 4:3, 4
Sound doctrine . . . . Titus 2:1, 8
Boldness . . . . Phil. 1:4

Speed—*to hasten*
"Let Him make" . . . . Is. 5:19
"They shall come with" . . . . Is. 5:26

Spending—*paying out money or service for things*
A. Wastefully, on:
Harlots . . . . Luke 15:30
B. Wisely:
In Christ's service. . . . . 2 Cor. 12:15

Spices—*aromatic vegetable compounds*
A. Uses of:
Food. . . . . Song 8:2
Incense . . . . Ex. 30:34–38
Fragrance . . . . Song 4:10
B. Features concerning:
Used as presents . . . . Gen. 43:11
Objects of commerce . . . . Gen. 37:25
Tokens of royal favor. . . . . 1 Kin. 10:2
Stored in the temple. . . . . 1 Chr. 9:29
Sign of wealth . . . . 2 Kin. 20:13

Spider
Web of, figurative of:
Insecurity. . . . . Is. 59:5
Godless. . . . . Job 8:14

Spies—*secret agents of a foreign government*
A. Purpose of, to:
Search out Canaan. . . . . Num. 13:1–33
Prepare for invasion. . . . . Josh. 2:1–21
Search out new land. . . . . Judg. 18:2–17
Make false charges. . . . . Luke 20:20
B. Men accused of, falsely:
Jacob's sons . . . . Gen. 42:9–34
David's servants . . . . 2 Sam. 10:3

Spikenard

    Used as a perfume .... Song 1:12

    Mary uses it in anointing Jesus........ Mark 14:3;
    John 12:3

Spill—*to flow forth*

    Water........................... 2 Sam. 14:14

    Wine .... Luke 5:37

Spinning—*twisting fibers together to form cloth*

    Work done by women .... Ex. 35:25

    Sign of industry..................... Prov. 31:19

    As an illustration .... Matt. 6:28

WORD STUDY   **SPIRIT,** *ruach* (roo-*akh*). "Breath," "wind," and "spirit" are three different ways in which the noun *ruach* can be translated. The choice of word is sometimes very difficult as it is in Gen. 1:2 where traditionally it is the Spirit of God hovering over the water. Any of the three could just as easily be used. In other cases the choice is more clear-cut. At times the word means "breath of the mouth or nostrils" and is seen especially as a sign of life (Gen. 6:17 and others). "Wind" can be the wind of heaven, or a north wind, east wind, storm wind, and so on. Wind can also imply vanity or emptiness as it does in Job 7:7 or Eccl. 1:14. "Spirit" is that which breathes quickly in animation or agitation, as in a state of temper. "Spirit" can also be the Spirit of God, which inspires prophetic actions, gives power and gifts. (Strong's #7307)

Spirit—*an immaterial being*

A. Descriptive of:

    Holy Spirit .... Gen. 1:2

    Angels .... Heb. 1:7, 14

    Humankind's immaterial nature...... 1 Cor. 2:11

    Evil...........................1 Sam. 16:14–23

    Believer's immaterial nature .... 1 Cor. 5:3, 5

    Controlling influence .... Is. 29:10

    Inward reality .... Rom. 2:29

    Disembodied state .... Heb. 12:23; 1 Pet. 3:19

B. Characteristics of, in humankind:

    Center of emotions................... 1 Kin. 21:5

    Source of passions .... Ezek. 3:14

    Cause of volitions (will) .... Prov. 16:32

    Subject to divine influence .... Deut. 2:30;
    Is. 19:14

    Leaves body at death .... Eccl. 12:7;
    James 2:26

    See Soul

Spirit, Holy (see Holy Spirit)

Spirit of Christ

A. Descriptive of the Holy Spirit as:

    Dwelling in Old Testament prophets 1 Pet. 1:10, 11

    Sent by God......................... Gal. 4:6

    Given to believers.................... Rom. 8:9

    Supplying believers .... Phil. 1:19

    Producing boldness .... Acts 4:29–31

    Commanded .... Eph. 5:18

B. Christ's human spirit (consciousness), of His:

    Perception .... Mark 2:8

    Emotions .... Mark 8:12

    Life............................... Luke 23:46

Spirits, discerning

A. Described as:

    Spiritual gift....................... 1 Cor. 12:10

    Necessary .... 1 Thess. 5:19–21

B. Tests of:

Christ's:

    Deity .... 1 Cor. 12:3

    Humanity......................... 1 John 4:1–6

    Christian fellowship .... 1 John 2:18, 19

WORD STUDY   **SPIRITUAL,** *pneumatikos* (pnyoo-maht-ik-*oss*). This adjective, derived from the noun for "spirit" (*pneuma*), means "pertaining to the spirit" or "spiritual." Paul uses the word mainly to refer to "that which is caused by" or "filled with the (divine) spirit" (e.g., "understanding" in Col. 1:9) or to "that which pertains to" or "corresponds to the (divine) spirit" (e.g., "gifts" in Rom. 1:11); but *pneumatikos* can also refer to the "spirit-forces of evil" (Eph. 6:12). *Pneumatikos* may be used as a substantive for a "Spirit-filled person" (see 1 Cor. 14:37; cf. Gal. 6:1); it can also refer to "those who possess spiritual gifts" (1 Cor. 12:1; 14:1). The resurrection body is "spiritual," that is, it belongs to the supernatural, not the "natural," order of existence (1 Cor. 15:44; cf. 15:46). (Strong's #4152)

Spiritual—*the holy or immaterial*

A. Applied to:

    Gifts .... 1 Cor. 12:1

    Law................................ Rom. 7:14

    Things............................. Rom. 15:27

    Christians........................... 1 Cor. 3:1

    Resurrected body .... 1 Cor. 15:44–46

    Evil forces.......................... Eph. 6:12

B. Designating, Christians:

    Ideal state.......................... 1 Cor. 3:1

    Discernment .... 1 Cor. 2:13–15

    Duty.............................. Gal. 6:1

    Manner of life .... Col. 3:16

Spiritual gifts (see Gifts, spiritual)

Spirituality—*a holy frame of mind*

    Source of.......................... Gal. 5:22–26

    Expression of..................... 1 Cor. 13:1–13

    Growth in......................... 2 Pet. 1:4–11

    Enemies of .... 1 John 2:15–17

Spite—*an injury prompted by contempt*

    Inflicted upon Christ .... Matt. 22:6

WORD STUDY   **SPITEFULLY TREAT,** *hubrizō* (hoo-brid-zoh). A verb meaning "to treat in an arrogant or spiteful manner," "to mistreat," "to insult," *hubrizō* can refer to insolent and abusive verbal behavior. Jesus predicts that He will receive abusive insults (Luke 18:32), and He is accused of meting out such treatment (11:45). The word also applies to abusive physical behavior (Matt. 22:6; Acts 14:5). Paul suffers spiteful maltreatment at Philippi (1 Thess. 2:2; but see the cognate noun at 1 Tim. 1:13). (Strong's #5195)

Spitting, spittle
A. Symbolic of:
Contempt..........................Num. 12:14
Rejection..........................Matt. 26:67
Uncleanness.........................Lev. 15:8
B. Miraculous uses of, to heal:
Dumb man......................Mark 7:33–35
Blind man......................Mark 8:23–25
Man born blind....................John 9:6, 7

Spoil—*loot or plunder*
Cattle.............................Josh. 8:2
Silver and gold.......................Nah. 2:9
See Plunder

Spokesman—*one who speaks for others*
Aaron deputed to be ....Ex. 4:14–16

Sponge—*a very absorbent sea fossil*
Full of vinegar, offered to Christ.....Matt. 27:48

Spot, spotless
A. Descriptive of:
Blemish on the face....................Job 11:15
Imperfection of the body..............Song 4:7
Mixed colors....................Gen. 30:32–39
Leopard's body markings.............Jer. 13:23
B. Figuratively ("spotless") of:
Christ's death........................1 Pet. 1:19
Believer's perfection.................2 Pet. 3:14
Glorified church......................Eph. 5:27
Obedience..........................1 Tim. 6:14

Springtime—*the season of nature's rebirth*
Symbolically described............Song 2:11–13

Sprinkle
A. Used literally of:
Water..............................Num. 8:7
Oil................................Lev. 14:16
B. Of blood, used in:
Passover..........................Ex. 12:21, 22
Sinaitic covenant.........Ex. 24:8; Heb. 9:19, 21
Sin offering..........................Lev. 4:6
New covenant.......................Heb. 12:24
C. Used figuratively of:
Regeneration......................Heb. 10:22
Purification..........................1 Pet. 1:2

Square—*having four equal sides*
Altar...............................Ex. 27:1
Breastplate.......................Ex. 39:8, 9
City of God.........................Rev. 21:16

Stab—*to pierce with a knife*
Asahel by Abner.................2 Sam. 2:22, 23
Abner by Joab......................2 Sam. 3:27
Amasa by Joab.....................2 Sam. 20:10

Stachys—*head of grain*
One whom Paul loved.................Rom. 16:9

Staff—*a long stick or rod*
A traveler's support.................Gen. 32:10
A military weapon.....................Is. 10:24

Stairs, winding
Part of Solomon's temple..............1 Kin. 6:8

Stalls—*quarters for animals*
40,000 in Solomon's time............1 Kin. 4:26

Stammerer—*one who stutters*
Of the gospel age.....................Is. 32:1, 4

Stars
A. Features concerning:
Created by God.......................Gen. 1:16
Ordained by God........................Ps. 8:3
Set in the expanse....................Gen. 1:17
Follow fixed ordinances..........Jer. 31:35, 36
Named by God........................Ps. 147:4
Established forever.................Ps. 148:3, 6
Of vast numbers.....................Gen. 15:5
Manifest God's power.................Is. 40:26
Of different proportions.............1 Cor. 15:41
Very high..........................Job 22:12
B. Worship of:
Forbidden..........................Deut. 4:19
Punished.........................Deut. 17:3–7
Introduced by Manasseh.............2 Kin. 21:3
Condemned by the prophets............Jer. 8:2; Zeph. 1:4, 5
C. List of, in Bible:
The Bear.............................Job 9:9
Mazzaroth..........................Job 38:32
Orion...............................Job 9:9
Pleiades.............................Job 9:9
Chambers of the south................Job 9:9
Of Bethlehem....................Matt. 2:2, 9, 10
D. Figurative of:
Christ's:
First advent.......................Num. 24:17
Second advent......................Rev. 22:16
Angels............................Rev. 1:16, 20
Judgment.........................Ezek. 32:7
False security........................Obad. 4
Glorified saints.....................Dan. 12:3
Apostates............................Jude 13

State—*established government*
A. Agents of:
Under God's control..............Dan. 4:17, 25; John 19:10, 11
Sometimes evil..................Mark 6:14–29
Sometimes good.....................Neh. 2:1–9
Protectors of the law..............Rom. 13:1–4
B. Duties of Christians to:
Pray for...........................1 Tim. 2:1, 2
Pay taxes to....................Matt. 22:17–21
Be subject to.....................Rom. 13:5, 6
Resist (when evil).................Acts 4:17–21

Stature—*the natural height of the body*
A. Used physically of:
    Giants . . . . Num. 13:32
    Sabeans . . . . Is. 45:14
B. Significance of:
    Normal, in human growth . . . . Luke 2:52
    Cannot be changed . . . . Matt. 6:27
    Not indicative of greatness . . . . 1 Sam. 16:7
    In spiritual things . . . . Eph. 4:13

WORD STUDY

STATUTE, *choq* (*khohk*). A "statute" is something that is prescribed and is designated by the noun *choq*. At times the word is used for a prescribed task or portion, such as the portion due to priests from offerings (Lev. 6:11, 18), which has a positive implication. The prescribed area of the sea or heaven, on the other hand, has a slightly negative or limiting meaning. Most often the term is used for an enactment or decree from either God or humans. It can be a specific decree (such as the statute regarding Passover in Ex. 12:14), a law of nature, or a more general law. There are many enactments or statutes of law in the OT, especially the civil laws given by God. The term *choq* is used many times in reference to these, especially in the law codes in the Pentateuch or referring to those codes (Lev. 10:11; Ps. 50:16; Amos 2:4). (Strong's #2706)

Statute of limitation
    Recognized in the Law . . . . Deut. 15:1–5, 9

Steadfastness—*firm, persistent, and determined in one's endeavors*
A. In human things, following a:
    Person . . . . Ruth 1:18
    Leader . . . . Jer. 35:1–19
    Principle . . . . Dan. 1:8
B. In spiritual things:
    Enduring chastisement . . . . Heb. 12:7
    Bearing persecution . . . . Rom. 8:35–37
    Maintaining perseverance . . . . Heb. 3:6, 14
    Stability of faith . . . . Col. 2:5; Heb. 2:1–4
    Persevering in service . . . . 1 Cor. 15:58
    Resisting Satan . . . . 1 Pet. 5:9
    Defending Christian liberty . . . . Gal. 5:1
C. Elements of, seen in:
    Having a goal . . . . Phil. 3:12–14
    Discipline . . . . 1 Cor. 9:25–27
    Run the race . . . . Heb. 12:1, 2
    Never give up . . . . Rev. 3:10, 21

Stealing—*taking another's property*
    Common on earth . . . . Matt. 6:19
Forbidden in:
    Law . . . . Ex. 20:15
    Gospel . . . . Rom. 13:9
    Christians not to do . . . . Eph. 4:28
    Excludes from heaven . . . . 1 Cor. 6:9, 10
    None in heaven . . . . Matt. 6:20

Stephanas—*crowned*
    Corinthian Christian . . . . 1 Cor. 1:16

    First convert of Achaia . . . . 1 Cor. 16:15
    Visits Paul . . . . 1 Cor. 16:17

Stephen—*wreath or crown*
    One of the seven deacons . . . . Acts 6:1–8
    Accused falsely by Jews . . . . Acts 6:9–15
    Spoke before the Jewish Sanhedrin . . . Acts 7:2–53
    Became first Christian martyr . . . . . . Acts 7:54–60
    Saul (Paul) involved in death of . . . . Acts 7:58

Stew—*a thick vegetable soup*
    Price of Esau's birthright . . . . Gen. 25:29–34
    Eaten by Elisha's disciples . . . . 2 Kin. 4:38–41
    Ordinary food . . . . Hag. 2:12

Steward, stewardship—*a trust granted for profitable use*
A. Descriptive of:
    One over Joseph's household . . . . Gen. 43:19
    Curator or guardian . . . . Matt. 20:8
    Manager . . . . Luke 16:2, 3
    Management of entrusted duties . . . . . . 1 Cor. 9:17
B. Duties of, to:
    Expend monies . . . . Rom. 16:23
    Serve wisely . . . . Luke 12:42
C. Of spiritual things, based on:
    Lord's ownership . . . . Ps. 24:1, 2; Rom. 14:8
    Our redemption . . . . 1 Cor. 6:20
    Gifts bestowed upon us . . . . Matt. 25:14, 15;
      1 Pet. 4:10
    Offices given to us . . . . Eph. 3:2–10; Titus 1:7
    Faithful in responsibilities . . . . Luke 16:1–3

Stewardship, personal financial
Basic principles:
    Settling accounts . . . . Rom. 14:12
    God's ownership . . . . Ps. 24:1; Rom. 14:7, 8
    Finances and spirituality
      inseparable . . . Matt. 19:16–22; Luke 16:10–13;
      1 Cor. 6:20; 2 Cor. 8:3–8
    Needs will be provided . . . . Matt. 6:24–34;
      Phil. 4:19
    Content with what God provides . . . . Ps. 37:25;
      1 Tim. 6:6–10; Heb. 13:5
    Righteousness . . . . Prov. 16:8; Rom. 12:17
    Avoid debt . . . . Prov. 22:7; Rom. 13:8
    Do not be a cosigner . . . . Prov. 6:1–5; 22:26
    Inheritance uncertain . . . . Prov. 17:2; 20:21
    Proper priority . . . . Matt. 6:19–21, 33
    Prosperity is from God . . . . . Deut. 29:9; Ps. 1:1–3;
      3 John 2
    Saving . . . . Prov. 21:20
    Laziness condemned . . . Prov. 24:30, 31; Heb. 6:12
    Giving is encouraged . . . . Mal. 3:10–12;
      Prov. 3:9, 10; 2 Cor. 9:6–8

Sticks—*pieces of wood*
    Gathering on Sabbath
      condemned . . . . Num. 15:32–35
    As fuel for cooking . . . . 1 Kin. 17:10–12
    Miracle producing . . . . 2 Kin. 6:6
    Two become one . . . . Ezek. 37:16–22
    Viper in bundle of . . . . Acts 28:3

Stiff-necked—*rebellious; unteachable*

A. Indicative of Israel's rebelliousness at:

Sinai.................................Ex. 32:9

Conquest......................... Deut. 9:6, 13

Captivity...........................2 Chr. 36:13

B. Remedies of, seen in:

Circumcision (regeneration) .... Deut. 10:16

Yielding to God ....2 Chr. 30:8

Still

A. Indicative of:

God's voice.........................1 Kin. 19:12

God's presence ....Ps. 139:18

Fright...............................Ex. 15:16

Fixed character ....Rev. 22:11

Peace ....Jer. 47:6

Quietness .... Num. 13:30

B. Accomplished by:

God ....Ps. 107:29

Christ............................. Mark 4:39

Submission...........................Ps. 46:10

Meditating...........................Ps. 4:4

Stinginess—*lack of generosity; miserly*

A. Characteristics of:

Choosing selfishly ....Gen. 13:5–11

Living luxuriantly ....Amos 6:4–6

Showing greediness ....John 12:5, 6

Withholding God's tithe .... Mal. 3:8

Unmerciful toward the needy ...... Zech. 7:10–12

B. Punishment of, brings:

Poverty .... Prov. 11:24, 25

A curse............................Prov. 11:26

Revenge............................Prov. 21:13

The closing of God's kingdom .... Luke 18:22–25

Stink, stench—*a foul smell*

A. Caused by:

Dead fish ....Ex. 7:18, 21

Corpse............................ John 11:39

Wounds.............................Ps. 38:5

B. Figurative of:

Hell .... Is. 34:3, 4

Stir up

A. Of strife, etc., by:

Wrath .... Prov. 15:18

Hatred............................Prov. 10:12

Grievous words......................Prov. 15:1

Unbelief .... Acts 13:50

Agitators.......................... Acts 6:12

Kings.............................Dan. 11:2, 25

B. Of good things:

Generosity .... Ex. 35:21, 26

Repentance .... Is. 64:7

Ministry ....2 Tim. 1:6

Memory ....2 Pet. 1:13

C. Of God's sovereignty in:

Fulfilling His word ....2 Chr. 36:22; Ezra 1:1

Accomplishing His purpose....Is. 13:17; Hag. 1:14

Stocks—*blocks of wood*

Instrument of punishment............Job 33:11;
Acts 16:19, 24

Stoics—*pertaining to a colonnade or porch*

Sect of philosophers founded by Zeno
around 308 B.C. ....Acts 17:18

Stones—*rocks*

A. Natural uses of:

Weighing ....Lev. 19:36

Knives ....Ex. 4:25

Weapons.....................1 Sam. 17:40–50

Holding water ....Ex. 17:1–7

Covering wells...................... Gen. 29:2

Covering tombs..................... Matt. 27:60

Landmarks......................... Deut. 19:14

Writing inscriptions ....Ex. 24:12

Buildings .... Matt. 24:1, 2

Missiles.............................Ex. 21:18

B. Religious uses of:

Altars............................ Ex. 20:25

Grave.............................Josh. 7:26

Memorial ....Josh. 4:20

Witness......................... Josh. 24:26, 27

Inscriptions .... Deut. 27:4, 8

Idolatry.............................Lev. 26:1

C. Figurative of:

Reprobation...................... 1 Sam. 25:37

Contempt .... 2 Sam. 16:6, 13

Christ's rejection....................Ps. 118:22

Christ as foundation .... Is. 28:16

Desolation ....Jer. 51:26

Unregeneracy ....Ezek. 11:19

Christ's advent ....Dan. 2:34, 35

Conscience........................ Hab. 2:11

Insensibility........................Zech. 7:12

Gentiles...........................Matt. 3:9

Christ as head .... Matt. 21:42–44

Good works .... 1 Cor. 3:12

Christians...........................1 Pet. 2:5

Spirit's witness......................Rev. 2:17

See Rock

Stones, precious

Agate ....Ex. 28:19

Amethyst ....Rev. 21:20

Beryl..............................Rev. 21:20

Chalcedony ....Rev. 21:19

Chrysolite.........................Rev. 21:20

Crystal.............................Rev. 22:1

Diamond............................Jer. 17:1

Emerald............................Ex. 28:17

Jasper..............................Rev. 4:3

Jacinth.............................Ex. 28:19

Onyx .... Gen. 2:12

Ruby............................. Prov. 3:15

Sapphire .... Job 28:6, 16

Sardius............................Rev. 4:3

Sardonyx..........................Rev. 21:20

Topaz............................. Job 28:19

Stoning—*a means of executing criminals*

A. Punishment inflicted for:

Sacrificing children . . . . Lev. 20:2–5

Divination . . . . Lev. 20:27

Blasphemy . . . . Lev. 24:15–23

Sabbath-breaking. . . . . .Num. 15:32–36

Apostasy. . . . . Deut. 13:1–10

Idolatry . . . . Deut. 17:2–7

Juvenile rebellion . . . . Deut. 21:18–21

Adultery . . . . Deut. 22:22

B. Examples of:

Achan . . . . Josh. 7:20–26

Adoram. . . . . .1 Kin. 12:18

Naboth . . . . .1 Kin. 21:13

Zechariah. . . . . 2 Chr. 24:20, 21

Stephen . . . . .Acts 7:59

Paul . . . . .Acts 14:19

Prophets . . . . Heb. 11:37

Storehouses—*places for storing things*

A. Descriptive of:

Barns . . . . Deut. 28:8

Warehouses . . . . Gen. 41:56

Temple. . . . . Mal. 3:10

B. Used for storing:

Grain. . . . . .2 Chr. 32:28

The tithe. . . . . Mal. 3:10

Stork—*a large, long-legged, migratory bird*

Nesting of. . . . . .Ps. 104:17

Migration of. . . . . .Jer. 8:7

Ceremonially unclean. . . . . Lev. 11:19

Storm—*a violent upheaval of nature*

A. Described as:

Grievous. . . . . Ex. 9:23–25

Sent by God . . . . .Josh. 10:11

Destructive . . . . Matt. 7:27

B. Effects of, upon:

Israelites . . . . Ex. 19:16, 19

Philistines. . . . . .1 Sam. 7:10

Mariners. . . . . .Jon. 1:4–14

Animals. . . . . Ps. 29:3–9

Disciples . . . . Mark 4:37–41

Soldiers and sailors . . . . .Acts 27:14–44

Nature. . . . . .Ps. 29:3, 5, 8

Strangers—*foreigners living among the Jews*

A. Descriptive of:

Non-Jews . . . . Ex. 12:48

Foreigners. . . . . Matt. 17:25

Transients. . . . . .Luke 24:18

B. Positive laws, to:

Love them. . . . . .Lev. 19:34

Relieve them . . . . .Lev. 25:35

Provide for them. . . . . Deut. 10:18

Share in leftovers . . . . .Deut. 24:19–22

Treat fairly. . . . . Deut. 24:14, 17

Share in religious festivals . . . . Deut. 16:11, 14

Hear the law. . . . . Deut. 31:12

See Foreigners

Stratagem—*a plan designed to deceive an enemy*

Joshua's famous. .Josh. 8:1–22

Gibeonites' trickery. . . . . .Josh. 9:2–27

Hushai's successful . . . . 2 Sam. 17:6–14

Gideon's three hundred . . . . .Judg. 7:1–25

Straw—*the stalk of wheat or barley*

Used for animals. . . . . .Gen. 24:25, 32

Used in making bricks . . . . Ex. 5:7–18

Eaten by a lion. . . . . .Is. 11:7

Something worthless. . . . . .Job 41:27–29

Stray animals

Must be returned . . . . .Ex. 23:4

Saul's pursuit of . . . . 1 Sam. 9:3–5

Streets—*principal thoroughfares*

A. Uses of:

Display . . . . .Matt. 6:5

Teaching. . . . . .Luke 13:26

Parades . . . . .Esth. 6:9, 11

Proclamations. . . . . .Neh. 8:3–5

B. Dangers of, from:

Fighting . . . . .Josh. 2:19

Prostitutes . . . . Prov. 7:6–23

Wicked . . . . Ps. 55:11

Assault. . . . . Judg. 19:15–26

Strength, strengthen—*resident power*

A. Kinds of:

Physical. . . . . .Prov. 20:29

Constitutional. . . . . .Ps. 90:10

Hereditary . . . . Gen. 49:3

Angelic . . . . .Ps. 103:20

Military. . . . . Dan. 2:37

Spiritual . . . . .Ps. 138:3

Super-human. . . . . Judg. 16:5, 6, 19

Divine . . . . Is. 63:1

B. Dissipation of, by:

Iniquity . . . . Ps. 31:10

Hunger . . . . .1 Sam. 28:20, 22

Sexual looseness . . . . Prov. 31:3

Age. . . . . Ps. 71:9

Visions. . . . . Dan. 10:8, 16, 17

C. Increase of:

From:

God . . . . Is. 41:10

Christ. . . . . 2 Tim. 4:17

Spirit . . . . Eph. 3:16

Brothers . . . . .Luke 22:32

By:

Wisdom . . . . Eccl. 7:19

Waiting on the Lord . . . . Is. 40:31

Lord's grace . . . . 2 Cor. 12:9

Strife—*conflicts between people*

A. Sources of, in:

Hatred. . . . . .Prov. 10:12

Perverseness. . . . . .Prov. 16:28

Transgression . . . . Prov. 17:19

Scorner . . . . .Prov. 22:10

Anger. . . . . .Prov. 29:22

Flesh. . . . . Gal. 5:19–21

B. Actual causes of, seen in:
  Self-seeking . . . . .Luke 22:24
  Dispute between people . . . . .Gen. 13:7–11
  Contentious man . . . . .Prov. 26:21
  Being carnal. . . . . 1 Cor. 3:3
C. Avoidance of, by:
  Love . . . . .Prov. 10:12
  Being slow to anger . . . . .Prov. 15:18
  Simplicity of life . . . . Prov. 17:1
  See Contention; Quarrel

Strike—*afflict; attack*
A. Descriptive of:
  Plagues . . . . .Ex. 3:20
  Miracle . . . . .Ex. 17:5, 6
  God's punishments . . . . Deut. 28:22–28
  Death. . . . . 2 Sam. 4:6, 7
  Fear . . . . Dan. 5:6
  Slapping . . . . .John 18:22
B. Of divine punishment, upon:
  Christ. . . . . Is. 53:4, 8
  Sinners. . . . . .Prov. 7:23
  World. . . . . Ps. 110:5
  Rebellious. . . . . Is. 14:6
  Israel . . . . Is. 30:26
  Philistines. . . . . 1 Sam. 5:6, 9
  Pagan nation . . . . .2 Chr. 14:12
  King's house. 2 Chr. 21:5–19
C. Used messianically of Christ's:
  Scourging. . . . . Is. 50:6
  Bearing our sins . . . . Is. 53:4
  Death. . . . . Zech. 13:7
  Judgment . . . . .Is. 11:4

Stripes—*used in scourging*
  Limit of. . . . . Deut. 25:1–4
  Because of sin . . . . .Ps. 89:32
  Upon the Messiah, healing . . . Is. 53:5; 1 Pet. 2:24
  Uselessness of, on a fool . . . . Prov. 17:10
  Paul's experience with. . . . . Acts 16:23, 33;
    2 Cor. 11:23

Striving, spiritual
  To enter the narrow gate. . . . . .Luke 13:24
  Against sin . . . . Heb. 12:4
  With divine help. .Col. 1:29
  In prayer . . . . Rom. 15:30
  For the faith of the gospel . . . . Phil. 1:27

Stroke—*a blow*
  With an ax . . . . Deut. 19:5
  With a sword . . . . Esth. 9:5

Strong drink (see Drunkenness)

Stronghold—*fortress*
  David captured .2 Sam. 5:7, 9
  The Lord is. . . . . Nah. 1:7

Studs—*ornaments*
  Of silver . . . . Song 1:11

Study—*intensive intellectual effort*
  Of the Scriptures. . . Acts 17:10, 11; 2 Tim. 3:16, 17

Stumble—*to trip on some obstacle*
A. Occasions of, found in:
  Strong drink. . . . . Is. 28:7
  God's Word . . . . .1 Pet. 2:8
  Christ. . . . . Rom. 9:32, 33
  Christ crucified. 1 Cor. 1:23
  Christian liberty. 1 Cor. 8:9
B. Avoidance of, by:
  Following wisdom . . . . .Prov. 3:21, 23
  See Offend, offense

Suah—*sweepings*
  Asherite. . . . . .1 Chr. 7:36

Subjection—*the state of being under another's control*
A. Of domestic and civil relationships:
  Servants to masters . . . . .1 Pet. 2:18
  Citizens to government. . . . . Rom. 13:1–6
  Children to parents . . . . 1 Tim. 3:4
  Wives to husbands . . . . Eph. 5:24
  Younger to elder . . . . .1 Pet. 5:5
B. Of spiritual relationships:
  Creation to sin. . . . . Rom. 8:20, 21
  Demons to the disciples . . . . .Luke 10:17, 20
  Believers to the gospel. . . . . 2 Cor. 9:13
  Christians to one another . . . . .1 Pet. 5:5
  Christians to God. . . . . Heb. 12:9
  Creation to Christ . . . . Heb. 2:5, 8
  Church to Christ. . . . . Eph. 5:24
  Christ to God . . . . 1 Cor. 15:28

Subjugation—*the state of being subdued by force*
  Physical force. . . . . 1 Sam. 13:19–23
  Spiritual power . . . . Mark 5:1–15

Submission—*humble obedience to another's will*
  Each other . . . . Eph. 5:21
  Husbands . . . . Eph. 5:22
  Rulers . . . . 1 Pet. 2:13
  Elders. . . . . .1 Pet. 5:5
  Christian leaders . . . . Heb. 13:17
  God . . . . James 4:7

Substitution—*replacing one person or thing for another*
  Ram for the man. . . . . Gen. 22:13
  Offering for the offerer. . . . . Lev. 16:21, 22
  Levites for the firstborn . . . . .Num. 3:12–45
  Christ for the sinner . . . . . . .Is. 53:4–6; 1 Pet. 2:24

Success—*accomplishment of goals in life*
A. Rules of:
  Put God first . . . . .Matt. 6:32–34
  Follow the Book .Josh. 1:7–9
  Seek the goal . . . . Phil. 3:13, 14
  Never give up. . . . . .Gal. 6:9
  Do all for Christ . . . . .Phil. 1:20, 21
B. Hindrances of, seen in:
  Disobedience. . . . . .Heb. 4:6, 11
  Enemies. . . . . .Neh. 4:1–23
  Sluggishness. .Prov. 24:30–34
  Love of the world . . . . Matt. 16:26

Succoth—*booths*
  1. Place east of the Jordan. . . . . .Judg. 8:4, 5

Jacob's residence here . . . . Gen. 33:17

2. Israel's first camp. . . . . Ex. 12:37

Succoth Benoth—*tabernacles of girls*
Idol set up in Samaria
    by Babylonians . . . . 2 Kin. 17:30

Suchathites
Descendants of Caleb . . . . 1 Chr. 2:42, 55

Suck—*to give milk to offspring*
Characteristics of:
True among animals . . . . 1 Sam. 7:9
Normal for human mothers. . . . . Job 3:12
Figurative of Israel's restoration. . . . . Is. 60:16
Figurative of wicked . . . . Job 20:16

Suffering—*afflicted; in pain*
Need prayer in . . . . James 5:13

Suffering for Christ
Necessary in Christian living . . . . 1 Cor. 12:26;
    Phil. 1:29
Blessed privilege . . . . Acts 5:41
Never in vain . . . . Gal. 3:4
After Christ's example . . . Phil. 3:10; 1 Pet. 2:20, 21
Of short duration . . . . 1 Pet. 5:10
Not comparable to heaven's glory . . . . . Rom. 8:18;
    1 Pet. 4:13

Sufferings of Christ
A. Features concerning:
Predicted . . . . 1 Pet. 1:11
Announced. . . . . Mark 9:12
Explained . . . . Luke 24:26, 46
Fulfilled . . . . Acts 3:18
Witnessed. . . . . 1 Pet. 5:1
Proclaimed. . . . . Acts 17:2, 3
B. Benefits of, to Christ:
Preparation for priesthood . . . . Heb. 2:17, 18
Learned obedience. . . . . Heb. 5:8
Way to glory. . . . . Heb. 2:9, 10
C. Benefits of, to Christians:
Brought to God. 1 Pet. 3:18
Our:
Sins atoned. . . . . Heb. 9:26–28
Example . . . . 1 Pet. 2:21–23
Fellowship . . . . Phil. 3:10
Consolation . . . . 2 Cor. 1:5–7

Suicide—*self-murder*
A. Thought of, induced by:
Life's weariness. . . . . Job 3:20–23
Life's vanity . . . . Eccl. 2:17
Anger. . . . . Jon. 4:3, 8, 9
B. Brought on by:
Hopelessness . . . . Judg. 16:29, 30
Sin. . . . . 1 Kin. 16:18, 19
Disappointment . . . . 2 Sam. 17:23
Betrayal of Christ. . . . . Matt. 27:3–5
C. Other features concerning:
Desired by some . . . . Rev. 9:6
Attempted but prevented . . . . Acts 16:27, 28
Imputed to Christ. . . . . John 8:22

Satan tempts Christ to . . . . Luke 4:9
D. Principles prohibiting, found in:
Body's sacredness . . . . 1 Cor. 6:19
Prohibition against murder . . . . Ex. 20:13
Faith's expectancy . . . . 2 Tim. 4:6–8, 18

Sukkiim
African people in Shishak's army . . . . . . 2 Chr. 12:3

Summer
Made by God. . . . . Ps. 74:17
Sign of God's covenant . . . . Gen. 8:22
Time of:
Fruit harvest . . . . 2 Sam. 16:1, 2
Sowing and harvest . . . . Prov. 6:6–8
Figurative of: Industry . . . . Prov. 10:5
Opportunity . . . . Jer. 8:20

Sun
A. Characteristics of:
Created by God. . . . . Gen. 1:14, 16
Under God's control . . . . Ps. 104:19; Matt. 5:45
"Rules the day" . . . . Gen. 1:16
Necessary for fruit. . . . . Deut. 33:14
Given for light. . . . . Jer. 31:35
Made for God's glory. . . . . Ps. 148:3
No need for, in New Jerusalem . . . . Rev. 21:23
Overexposure to, can cause:
Scorching . . . . Jon. 4:8
Sunstroke . . . . 2 Kin. 4:18, 19
B. Miracles connected with:
Stands still . . . . Josh. 10:12, 13
Shadows of, turned back. . . . . 2 Kin. 20:9–11
Darkening of, at Crucifixion. . . . . . Luke 23:44–49
Going down at noon . . . . Amos 8:9
C. Worship of:
Forbidden. . . . . Deut. 4:19
By Manasseh . . . . 2 Kin. 21:3, 5
By Jews . . . . Jer. 8:2
D. Figurative of:
God's presence . . . . Ps. 84:11
Earth's sphere of action . . . . Eccl. 1:3, 9, 14
God's Law. . . . . Ps. 19:4–7
Future glory. . . . . Matt. 13:43
Christ's glory. . . . . Matt. 17:2

Sunday (see First day of the week)

Sundial—*an instrument for telling time*
Miracle of. . . . . Is. 38:8

Sunstroke—*stricken by sun's heat*
Child dies of. 2 Kin. 4:18–20

Superstition—*gullible ideas based on fancy or fear*
A. Causes of, in wrong views of:
God . . . . 1 Kin. 20:23
Holy objects. . . . . 1 Sam. 4:3
God's providence . . . . Jer. 44:15–19
B. Manifestations of, in:
Seeking illogical causes. . . . . Acts 28:4
Ignorance of the true God . . . . Acts 17:22
Perverting true religion . . . . Mark 7:1–16

Supper (see Lord's Supper)

Sur—*turning aside, entrance*
    Name given to a gate . . . . .2 Kin. 11:6
    Called "Gate of the Foundation" . . . . . .2 Chr. 23:5

Sure—*something trustworthy*
A. Descriptive of divine things:
    God's Law. . . . . Ps. 19:7
    New covenant . . . . Acts 13:34
God's:
    Prophecies . . . . .2 Pet. 1:19
    Promises . . . . .Rom. 4:16
B. Applied to the believer's:
    Calling and election. . . . . .2 Pet. 1:10
    Faith. . . . . .John 6:69
    Dedication . . . . Neh. 9:38
    Confidence in God's Word . . . . Luke 1:1
    Reward . . . . Prov. 11:18

Surety—*one who guarantees another's debt*
A. Descriptive of:
    Guarantee. . . . . Gen. 43:9
    Our Lord. . . . . Heb. 7:22
B. Features concerning:
    Risks involved in. . . . . Prov. 11:15
    Warning against. .Prov. 6:1–5

Surname—*a family name*
A. Descriptive of:
    Simon Peter . . . . Acts 10:5, 32
    John Mark . . . . Acts 12:12, 25
    Judas Iscariot. . . . . .Luke 22:3
    Judas Barsabas. . . . . Acts 15:22
    Joses Barnabas. . . . . Acts 4:36
    James and John Boanerges. . . . . .Mark 3:17
B. Figurative of God's:
    Call of Gentiles. . . . . Is. 44:5
    Sovereignty over kings . . . . Is. 45:4

Susanna—*lily*
    Believing woman ministering
        to Christ. . . . . .Luke 8:2, 3

Susi—*horseman*
    Manassite spy . . . . Num. 13:11

Suspicion—*doubt of another's intent*
A. Kinds of:
    Unjustified. . . . . Josh. 22:9–31
    Pretended. . . . . .Gen. 42:7–12
    Unsuspected .John 13:21–28
B. Objects of:
    Esau by Jacob. .Gen. 32:3–12
    Jeremiah by officials . . . . Jer. 37:12–15
    Jews by Haman. .Esth. 3:8, 9
    Mary by Joseph . . . . Matt. 1:18–25
    Peter after Jesus' arrest . . . . Matt. 26:69–74

WORD STUDY **SUSTAIN,** *kul* (*kool*). The verb *kul* can mean "sustain" in the sense of bearing up under as it does in Amos 7:10 when Amaziah says the land cannot bear the words of Amos. There is a similar setting in Jer. 10:10. *Kul* can also

mean to "nourish" or supply those things necessary for life (Gen. 45:11; Ruth 4:15). In some contexts it means "contain" as it does when 2 Chr. 2:5, 6 says heaven cannot contain God. This same sense is used for something holding liquid or for someone holding in anger (Jer. 6:11). A person can also support or can endure sickness. (Strong's #3557)

Sustenance—*means of sustaining life*
    Israel by the Lord . . . . Neh. 9:21
    Elijah by ravens and a widow. . . . . . . .1 Kin. 17:1–9
    Believer by the Lord. . . . . Ps. 3:5

Swaddling—*bandages, wrappings*
    Figurative of Jerusalem. . . . . Ezek. 16:3, 4
    Jesus wrapped in. . . . . .Luke 2:7

Swallow—*a long-winged, migratory bird*
    Nesting in the sanctuary . . . . Ps. 84:3
    Noted for chattering . . . . Is. 38:14

Swallow—*to engulf; to overwhelm*
A. Applied miraculously to:
    Aaron's rod. . . . . .Ex. 7:12
    Red Sea . . . . .Ex. 15:12
    Earth . . . . Num. 16:30–34
    Great fish . . . . .Jon. 1:17
B. Applied figuratively to:
    God's judgments. . . . . Ps. 21:9
    Conquest. . . . . .Jer. 51:34, 44
    Captivity. . . . . Hos. 8:7, 8
    Sorrow. . . . . 2 Cor. 2:7
    Resurrection . . . . Is. 25:8

WORD STUDY **SWEAR,** *shaba'* (shaw-*bah*). The verb *shaba'* literally means "to seven oneself," that is, "to swear by something seven times" or "to swear by seven of something." The shortened meaning, which appears in the OT, is simply "to swear" or "to take an oath." There are many instances in which humans swear an oath; for example, Abraham swears an oath to Abimelech that he will deal justly with him in the future (Gen. 21:24). Human swearing can also be an imprecation or curse as seems to be the case in Ps. 102:8, which speaks of the psalmist's enemies swearing an oath against him. Various places in the OT describe God's taking an oath. Frequently the oath begins with the phrase "I swear by Myself." Often the oaths are in connection with the land God has promised to give to Israel. God can either take an oath (Ex. 13:11; Deut. 2:14) or promise by oath to do something (Gen. 50:24; Mic. 7:20). (Strong's #7650)

Swearing—*taking an oath*
A. Kinds of:
    Proclamatory. . . . . .Ex. 17:16
    Protective . . . . Gen. 21:23
    Personal . . . . 1 Sam. 20:17
    Purificatory . . . . Neh. 13:25–30
    Promissory . . . . .Luke 1:73
    Prohibited. . . . . James 5:12

B. Of God, objects of:

God's purpose......................Is. 14:24, 25

God's covenant.......................Is. 54:9, 10

God's greatness.......................Heb. 6:13

Messianic priesthood ....Heb. 7:21

See Oaths

Sweat—*perspiration*

Penalty of sin......................Gen. 3:18, 19

Cause of, avoided ....Ezek. 44:18

Of Jesus, in prayer ....Luke 22:44

Sweet—*that which is pleasing to the taste*

A. Descriptive, literally, of:

Water...............................Ex. 15:25

Honey ....Judg. 14:18

Incense ....Ex. 25:6

B. Descriptive, figuratively, of:

God's Law.............................Ps. 19:10

God's Word ....Ps. 119:103

Spiritual fellowship ....Ps. 55:14

Meditation...........................Ps. 104:34

Pleasant words.......................Prov. 16:24

Sleep.................................Prov. 3:24

Christians............................2 Cor. 2:15

Christian service .... Eph. 5:2

Swim—*to propel oneself in water by natural means; to float on a liquid*

Miraculously, of iron..................2 Kin. 6:6

Naturally, of people ....Acts 27:42, 43

Figuratively, of tears ....Ps. 6:6

Swine—*hogs*

A. Features concerning:

Classed as unclean ....Lev. 11:7, 8

Eating of, abominable...................Is. 65:4

Caring of, a degradation..............Luke 15:16

Herd of, drowned.................Matt. 8:30–32

B. Figurative of:

Abominable things .... Is. 65:4

False teachers........................2 Pet. 2:22

Indiscreet woman....................Prov. 11:22

Reprobate...........................Matt. 7:6

Sword—*a weapon of war*

A. Described as:

Having hilt and blade ....Judg. 3:22

Worn in a sheath.....................1 Sam. 17:51

Fastened at the waist................2 Sam. 20:8

B. Used for:

Defense........................Luke 22:36, 38

Fighting in war ....Josh. 6:21

Executing criminals................1 Sam. 15:33

Suicide............................Acts 16:27

C. Figurative of:

Divine retribution .... Deut. 32:41

Divine victory.......................Josh. 5:13

God's judgment......................1 Chr. 21:12

An adulteress.......................Prov. 5:3, 4

Anguish of soul.......................Luke 2:35

Civil authority......................Rom. 13:4

God's Word .... Eph. 6:17

Sycamore—*a fig-bearing tree (not the same as the American sycamore)*

Overseers appointed to care for ......1 Chr. 27:28

Abundant in Palestine ....1 Kin. 10:27

Amos, a gatherer of .... Amos 7:14

Zacchaeus climbs up ....Luke 19:4

Sychar

City of Samaria; Jesus talks to

woman near....................John 4:5–39

Syene—*seven*

An Egyptian city.............. Ezek. 29:10; 30:6

Symbols—*a thing or act representing something spiritual*

A. Of things:

Names............................. Is. 7:3, 14

Numbers.............................Rev. 13:18

Garments ....Zech. 3:3–9

Metals ....1 Cor. 3:12

Animals............................Dan. 7:1–8

B. Of acts (gestures):

Tearing:

Mantle......................... 1 Sam. 15:27, 28

Garment...................... 1 Kin. 11:30–32

Curtain .... Matt. 27:51

Wearing a yoke ....Jer. 27:2–12

Buying a field.......................Jer. 32:6–15

Piercing the ear.......................Ex. 21:6

Surrendering the shoe.................. Ruth 4:7

Going naked ....Is. 20:2, 3

C. Of spiritual truths:

Bow—God's covenant..............Gen. 9:12, 13

Circumcision—God's covenant.... Gen. 17:1–14; Rom. 4:11

Passover—Christ ....Ex. 12:3–28; 1 Cor. 5:7

Rock—Christ ....1 Cor. 10:4

Blood sprinkled—Christ's blood ....Ex. 12:21, 22; 1 Pet. 1:18, 19

Bronze serpent—Christ... Num. 21:8, 9; John 3:14

Lamb—Christ........................ John 1:29

Bread and wine—the new covenant.... Matt. 26:26–28; 1 Cor. 11:23–29

Sympathy—*a feeling shared in common with another person*

A. Manifested in:

Bearing others' burdens ...... Gal. 6:2; Heb. 13:3

Expressing sorrow ....John 11:19–33

Offering help in need .... Luke 10:33–35

Helping the weak .... Acts 20:35

B. Expressed by:

Servant for a prophet................. Jer. 38:7–13

King for a king .... 2 Sam. 10:2

A maid for a general.................2 Kin. 5:1–4

Old man for a king...............2 Sam. 19:31–39

Pagan for a Jew ....Dan. 6:18–23

Synagogue—*a Jewish assembly*

A. Organization of:

Under elders.......................Luke 7:3–5

Ruler in charge .... Mark 5:22

Attendant..........................Luke 4:17, 20

Chief seats of, coveted............... Matt. 23:6
Expulsion from ....John 9:22, 34
B. Purposes of, for:
Prayer ....Matt. 6:5
Reading Scripture .... Acts 13:15
Hearing expositions.............. Acts 13:14, 15
Discipline...........................Acts 9:2
C. Christ's relation to:
Teaches often in .... John 18:20
Worships in .... Luke 4:16–21
Performs miracles in .... Matt. 12:9, 10
Expelled from .... Luke 4:22–30

Syntyche—*fortunate*
Philippian woman exhorted by Paul..... Phil. 4:2

Syracuse—*a city of Sicily*
Visited by Paul .... Acts 28:12

Syria—*the high land*
News of Jesus went into .... Matt. 4:24
Governed by Romans ....Luke 2:2

Syrians—*the Arameans*
Descendants of Aram, Shem's son ..... Gen. 10:22
Related to the Hebrews.............. Deut. 26:5
Intermarriage of,
    with Hebrews .... Gen. 24:4, 10–67
Called Syrians .... 2 Sam. 10:11
Speak Aramaic .... Dan. 2:4
Idolatrous.......................... 2 Kin. 5:18
Subdued by David .... 2 Sam. 8:11–13
Elijah anointed king over........... 1 Kin. 19:15
Army of, routed..................... 2 Kin. 7:5–7
Joined Israel against Jerusalem........ 2 Kin. 16:5
Taken captive by Assyria .... 2 Kin. 16:9
Destruction of, foretold .... Is. 17:1–3
Governed by Romans .... Luke 2:2
Gospel preached to............... Acts 15:23, 41

Syro-Phoenician—*an inhabitant of Phoenicia*
Daughter of, freed of demon ...... Mark 7:25–31

Syrtis Sands
Endangers Paul's ship .... Acts 27:17

System—*an orderly method of procedure*
Orderly writing........................ Luke 1:3
Governing people................... Ex. 18:13–27
Church government.................. Acts 6:1–7
Priestly ministry....................Luke 1:8, 9
Giving .... 1 Cor. 16:1, 2

T

Taanach, Tanach—*sandy*
Canaanite city conquered by Joshua ... Josh. 12:21
Assigned to Manasseh................ Josh. 17:11
Assigned to Kohathite Levites .... Josh. 21:25
Canaanites not expelled from...... Josh. 17:12, 13
Site of Canaanite defeat .... Judg. 5:19–22

Taanath Shiloh—*approach to Shiloh*
City of Ephraim ....Josh. 16:5, 6

Tabbaoth—*rings*
Ancestor of a Nethinim family........ Ezra 2:43

Tabbath—*extension*
Refuge of Midianites.................Judg. 7:22

Tabel—*God is good*
Persian official ....Ezra 4:7
Father of a puppet-king put forth by Rezin
    and Pekah ....Is. 7:1, 6

Taberah—*burning*
Israelite camp; fire destroys
    many here .... Num. 11:1–3

Tabernacle
A. Descriptive of:
Moses' administrative office......... Ex. 33:7–11
Structure erected at Sinai........Ex. 40:2, 35–38
Portable shrine containing an idol...... Acts 7:43
Tent prepared for the ark
    by David.................... 1 Chr. 16:1–43
Heavenly prototype..........Heb. 8:2, 5; 9:11, 24
Holy city..............................Rev. 21:3
B. Sinaitic, constructed:
By divine revelation............Ex. 25:8; Heb. 8:5
By craftsmen inspired by the Spirit ....Ex. 31:1–11
Out of contributions willingly
    supplied .... Ex. 25:1–9
For the manifestation of God's glory .... Ex. 25:8;
    29:42, 43
In two parts—holy place and
    Most Holy .... Ex. 26:33, 34; Heb. 9:2–7
With surrounding court................Ex. 40:8
Within a year's time.................. Ex. 40:2, 17
C. Furnishings of:
Courtyard:
Curtains, linen (exterior boundary) .. Ex. 36:8–13
Curtains of goats' hair.............. Ex. 36:14–18
Ram skin and badger skin coverings.....Ex. 36:19
Screen .... Ex. 36:37, 38
Altar of burnt offering .... Ex. 38:1–7
Bronze laver..........................Ex. 38:8
Holy Place:
Table of showbread .... Ex. 37:10–14
Utensils of gold.......................Ex. 37:16
Gold lampstand .... Ex. 37:17–22
Lamps and utensils of gold.......... Ex. 37:23, 24
Altar of incense.................... Ex. 37:25–28
Most Holy Place:
Veil, with design of cherubim .... Ex. 36:35
Ark of the Testimony .... Ex. 37:1–5
Mercy seat with two cherubim .... Ex. 37:6–9
D. History of:
Set up at Sinai .... Ex. 40:1–38
Sanctified and dedicated .... Ex. 40:9–16
Glory of the Lord fills ....Ex. 40:34–38
Moved by priests and Levites ....Num. 4:1–49
Camped at Gilgal .... Josh. 5:10, 11
Set up at Shiloh .... Josh. 18:1
Israel's center of worship .... Judg. 18:31;
    1 Sam. 1:3, 9, 24

Ark of, taken by Philistines .... 1 Sam. 4:1–22
Worship not confined to. ..... 1 Sam. 7:1, 2, 15–17
Located at Nob during Saul's reign. . . 1 Sam. 21:1–6
Moved to Gibeon .... 1 Kin. 3:4
Ark of, brought to Jerusalem by
    David .... 2 Sam. 6:17
Brought to the temple by Solomon . . . 1 Kin. 8:1, 4, 5
E. Typology of, seen in:
    Christ. .... John 1:14
    God's household. .... Eph. 2:19
    Believer. .... 1 Cor. 6:19
    Heaven .... Heb. 9:23, 24
F. Typology of, seen in Christ:
    Lampstand—His enlightening us .... Rev. 1:13
    Sacred bread—His sustaining us .... John 6:27–59
    Altar of incense—His intercession
        for us. .... John 17:1–26; Heb. 7:25
    Veil—His flesh .... Heb. 10:20
    Ark (wood and gold)—His humanity
        and deity .... John 1:14

Tabernacles, Feast of (see Feasts, Hebrew)

Table
A. Descriptive of:
    Article of furniture .... Matt. 15:27
    For showbread. .... Heb. 9:2
B. Figurative of:
    God's provision. .... Ps. 23:5
    Intimate fellowship .... Luke 22:30
    Lord's Supper. .... 1 Cor. 10:21

Tablet
A. Descriptive of:
    Small writing board. .... Luke 1:63
    Stone slabs .... Ex. 24:12
B. Figurative of:
    Christian's heart. .... 2 Cor. 3:3
    Human heart. .... Prov. 3:3

Tabor—*mountain height*
1. Mountain on borders of Zebulun and
        Issachar. .... Josh. 19:12, 22
    Great among mountains. .... Jer. 46:18
    Scene of rally against Sisera...... Judg. 4:6, 12, 14
2. Town of Zebulun .... 1 Chr. 6:77
3. Terebinth of, near Ramah .... 1 Sam. 10:3

Tabrimmon—*Rimmon is good*
    Father of Ben-Hadad. .... 1 Kin. 15:18

Tachmonite—*wise*
    Descriptive of one of David's
        mighty men. .... 2 Sam. 23:8
    Same as Hachmonite in .... 1 Chr. 11:11

Tackle—*ropes, cord, line*
    Ship's ropes. .... Is. 33:23
    All of a ship's removable gear .... Acts 27:19

Tactfulness—*the knack of knowing the right thing to do*
    or say
A. Manifested in:
    Appeasing hatred. .... Gen. 32:4, 5, 13–21
    Settling disputes. .... 1 Kin. 3:24–28

Obtaining one's wishes .... Esth. 5:1–8; 7:1–6
B. Illustrated by Christ, in:
    Rebuking a Pharisee .... Luke 7:39–50
    Teaching humility .... Mark 10:35–45
    Forgiving a sinner. .... John 8:1–11
    Rebuking His disciples .... John 21:15–23

Tadmor—*palm tree*
    Trading center near Damascus. .... 2 Chr. 8:4
    A desert town .... 1 Kin. 9:18

Tahan—*encampment*
    Ephraimite; founder of the
        Tahanites. .... Num. 26:35; 1 Chr. 7:25

Tahath—*station*
1. Kohathite Levite .... 1 Chr. 6:24
2, 3. Two descendants of Ephraim. .... 1 Chr. 7:20
4. Israelite encampment .... Num. 33:26, 27

Tahpanhes, Tehaphnehes
    City of Egypt; refuge of fleeing Jews. .... Jer. 2:16;
        44:1; Ezek. 30:18

Tahpenes—*royal wife*
    Egyptian queen. .... 1 Kin. 11:19, 20

Tahrea—*flight*
    Descendant of Saul .... 1 Chr. 9:41
    Called Tarea .... 1 Chr. 8:33, 35

Tahtim Hodshi
    Place visited by census-taking Joab . . . 2 Sam. 24:6

Tailoring—*the art of making clothes*
    For Aaron's garments .... Ex. 39:1

WORD STUDY   **TAKE UP, LIFT UP,** *airō* (*heye*-roh). This verb, which means "to lift up," "to take up," "to pick up," is often used literally in the NT with reference to actual objects (Matt. 9:6; John 8:59). It may also be used figuratively to refer to "lifting up" one's eyes in prayer (John 11:41) or "lifting" (= raising) one's voice (Luke 17:13). In some instances the meaning of *airō* implies "lifting up" but the emphasis is on "to take," in the sense of "to carry" (Luke 9:3) or "to carry away" (John 20:2, 13, 15). In some idiomatic expressions *airō* means "to take away," as in "remove" (John 1:29), sometimes with the connotation of force (Luke 11:22) or injustice (Luke 6:29)—even by killing (John 19:15). (Strong's #142)

Tale
    Nonsensical talk. .... Luke 24:11

Talebearer—*one who gossips*
    Reveals secrets. .... Prov. 11:13
    Injures character. .... Prov. 18:8
    Creates strife .... Prov. 26:20

Talent (see Jewish measures)
    Of gold .... Ex. 37:24
    Of silver .... 2 Kin. 5:5, 22, 23
    Of bronze .... Ex. 38:29
    Of iron. .... 1 Chr. 29:7
    Parable of .... Matt. 25:14–30

Talitha, cumi—*"Little girl, arise"*
　　Jairus's daughter thus addressed ...... Mark 5:41

Talk—*verbal communication between persons*
A. Described as:
　　Divine ....Ex. 33:9
　　Deceitful.............................Job 13:7
　　Proud................................1 Sam. 2:3
　　Troublemaking......................Prov. 24:2
　　Idle................................Titus 1:10
　　Foolish.............................. Eph. 5:4
B. Of good things, God's:
　　Law.................................Deut. 6:7
　　Judgment ....Ps. 37:30, 31
　　Righteousness......................Ps. 71:24
　　Power..............................Ps. 145:11

Talmai—*plowman*
1. Son of Anak driven out by Caleb ....Josh. 15:14
2. King of Geshur whose daughter, Maacah,
　　becomes David's wife .... 2 Sam. 3:3

Talmon—*oppressor, violent*
　　Levite gatekeeper .... 1 Chr. 9:17
　　Descendants of, return from exile ...... Ezra 2:42
　　Members of, become temple
　　　gatekeepers .... Neh. 11:19

Tamah—*combat*
　　Family of Nethinim.................. Ezra 2:53

Tamar—*palm tree*
1. Wife of Er and mother of Perez and
　　Zerah by Judah ....Gen. 38:6–30
　　Ancestress of tribal families ......Num. 26:20, 21
2. Absalom's sister ....2 Sam. 13:1–32
3. Absalom's daughter..................2 Sam. 14:27
4. Place south of the Dead Sea........... Ezek. 47:19

Tamarisk tree
　　Planted by Abraham .... Gen. 21:33
　　Saul was under .... 1 Sam. 22:6

Tambourine—*a musical instrument*
　　A part of worship ....2 Sam. 6:5

Tammuz—*a Babylonian god*
　　Mourned by women of Jerusalem.......Ezek. 8:14

Tanhumeth—*consolation*
　　Father of Seraiah ....2 Kin. 25:23

Tanner—*dresser of hides*
Simon, the:
　　Peter lodges with ....Acts 10:5, 6, 32

Tapestry—*hand-woven coverings*
Symbolic of:
　　Licentiousness....................... Prov. 7:16
　　Diligence............................Prov. 31:22

Taphath—*a drop*
　　Daughter of Solomon .... 1 Kin. 4:11

Tappuah—*apple*
1. Town of Judah.................... Josh. 15:1, 34
2. Town of Ephraim.................... Josh. 16:8, 9
3. Son of Hebron..................... 1 Chr. 2:43

Taralah—*power of God*
　　City of Benjamin ....Josh. 18:21, 27

Tares—*the bearded darnel, a poisonous grass*
　　Sown among wheat .... Matt. 13:24–40

Tarpelites
　　People transported to Samaria by the
　　　Assyrians.........................Ezra 4:9

Tarry—*to delay*
　　Divine visitation...................... Hab. 2:3
　　Spirit's coming.......................Luke 24:49
　　Christ's return...................... Heb. 10:37

Tarshish, Tharshish
1. Son of Javan and great-grandson
　　of Noah............................Gen. 10:4
2. City at a great distance from Palestine......Jon. 1:3
　　Ships of, noted in commerce .... Ps. 48:7
3. Benjamite............................1 Chr. 7:10
4. Persian prince ....Esth. 1:14

Tarsus—*the capital of the Roman province of Cilicia*
　　Paul's birthplace..................... Acts 21:39
　　Saul sent to........................... Acts 9:30
　　Visited by Barnabas.................. Acts 11:25

Tartak—*hero of darkness*
　　Deity worshiped by the Avites ....2 Kin. 17:31

Tartan—*the title of Assyria's commander*
　　Sent to fight against Jerusalem.......2 Kin. 18:17

Taskmaster—*a foreman*
　　Over sons of Israel .... Ex. 1:11

Tassel
　　On Israelites' garments......... Num. 15:38–40

WORD STUDY

TASTE, *ta'am* (taw-ahm). *Ta'am* is a verb meaning to "taste" or "perceive." When the word is translated as "taste," it can mean to eat a quantity of food as it does in 1 Sam. 14:24, where the people were forbidden by Saul to taste any food for a specific time, or it can refer to the sense of taste (Job 12:11; 34:3). The word can be used in a figurative context to mean "perceive." In Prov. 31:18 the good wife "perceives that her merchandise *is* good." Quite literally, this says that she tastes her merchandise. Perhaps she tastes the grain to inspect its quality. Ps. 34:8 says, "Oh, taste and see that the LORD *is* good." This is an invitation to experience and therefore perceive God's goodness. (Strong's #2938)

Taste
A. Of divine things:
　　God's Word ....Ps. 119:103
　　Lord...................................Ps. 34:8
　　Heavenly gift.......................... Heb. 6:4
B. Of material things:
　　Honey .... 1 Sam. 14:29, 43
　　Manna...............................Ex. 16:31
　　Food .... 1 Sam. 14:24
　　Wine .... John 2:9
　　Vinegar .... Matt. 27:34

Tattenai
　　Persian governor opposing the Jews ... Ezra 5:3, 6

Tattooing—*marking the skin indelibly*
　　Forbidden by God .... Lev. 19:28

Tau
　　Twenty-second letter in the Hebrew
　　　alphabet .... Ps. 119:169–176

Taunt—*a scornful glee*
　　Goliath against David .... 1 Sam. 17:43, 44
　　David against Abner .... 1 Sam. 26:14–16
　　Rabshakeh against the Jews ...... 2 Kin. 18:28–35
　　Soldiers and people against
　　　Christ .... Matt. 27:28–41

Taxes—*money, goods, or labor paid to a government*
A. Derived from:
　　People's possessions .... 1 Sam. 8:10–18
　　Poor .... Amos 5:11
B. Paid by:
　　Forced labor .... Deut. 20:11; 1 Kin. 5:13–17
　　Foreigners .... 1 Chr. 22:2
　　All people .... 2 Sam. 8:6, 14
　　All except Levites .... Ezra 7:24
　　Christians .... Rom. 13:6, 7
C. Used for:
　　Sanctuary .... Ex. 30:11–16
　　King's household .... 1 Kin. 4:7–19
　　Tribute to foreign nations .... 2 Kin. 15:17–22
　　Authorities .... Rom. 13:6, 7
D. Abuses of:
　　Lead to rebellion .... 1 Kin. 12:1–19
　　Burden people with debts .... Neh. 5:1–13
　　Bring enslavement .... Neh. 9:36, 37

Tax collectors—*those engaged in tax collecting*
A. Features concerning:
　　Collector of taxes .... Matt. 9:9; Luke 5:27
　　Often guilty of extortion .... Luke 3:12, 13
　　Classed with lowest
　　　sinners .... Matt. 9:10, 11; 21:31, 32
　　Thomas and Matthew, the .... Matt. 10:3
　　"Thank You that I am not like" .... Luke 18:11
　　"Like a heathen and a" .... Matt. 18:17
B. Spiritual attitude of:
　　Often conscientious .... Luke 19:2, 8
　　Often hospitable .... Luke 5:29
　　Received John's beliefs .... Matt. 21:32
　　Listened to Jesus .... Luke 15:1
　　Conscious of their sins .... Luke 18:13, 14
C. Jesus' association with:
　　Many sat with Him .... Mark 2:15
　　"Why do you eat with" .... Luke 5:30
　　A friend of .... Matt. 11:19; Luke 7:34

> **WORD STUDY**　**TEACH,** *yarah* (yaw-*raw*). The verb *yarah* has two meanings, which are difficult to connect. The first is to "throw" or "shoot." Within this meaning come the passages that say something about shooting arrows, casting lots, or God's throwing the Egyptian army into the sea. The second

meaning is to "direct," "teach," or "instruct." One can teach a handicraft, or a father can instruct a son (Prov. 4:4). There is teaching in the way, which means teaching the appropriate way of life (1 Sam. 12:23; Ps. 25:8; Prov. 4:11). Teaching can be the authoritative teaching of the priests regarding ceremonial matters as it is in Deut. 33:10 and Ezek. 44:23. At times God is the teacher of humans (Ps. 27:11; 119:102; Is. 28:26). Hab. 2:18 talks about idols as teachers of lies. (Strong's #3384)

> **WORD STUDY**　**TEACH, DISCIPLE,** *mathēteuō* (mahht-ayt-*yoo*-oh). When this verb is used intransitively, it means "to be" or "become a pupil" or "disciple," as in Matt. 13:52; 27:57. When it is used as a transitive verb, *mathēteuō* means "to make a disciple of" or "to teach someone," as in Matt. 28:19; Acts 14:21. The familiar cognate noun meaning "disciple" (or "pupil," "learner"), *mathētēs*, is derived from the verb *manthanō,* which means "to learn" (Rom. 16:17). (Strong's #3100)

Teacher—*the Greek equivalent of the Hebrew word "rabbi" (meaning "my master")*
　　Instructed in song .... 1 Chr. 25:1
　　Come from God .... John 3:2
　　To the Gentiles .... 2 Tim. 1:11

Teaching, teachers
A. Those capable of:
　　Parents .... Deut. 11:19
　　Levites .... Lev. 10:11
　　Ancestors .... Jer. 9:14
　　Disciples .... Matt. 28:19, 20
　　Older women .... Titus 2:3
　　Nature .... 1 Cor. 11:14
B. Significance of:
　　Combined with preaching .... Matt. 4:23
　　Divine calling .... Eph. 4:11
　　Necessary for bishops .... 1 Tim. 3:2
　　Necessary for the Lord's
　　　servants .... 2 Tim. 2:24–26
　　From house to house .... Acts 20:20
　　By sharing .... Gal. 6:6
C. Authority of, in divine things:
　　Derived from Christ .... Matt. 28:19, 20
　　Empowered by the Spirit .... John 14:26
　　Taught by the Lord .... Is. 54:13
　　Originates in revelation .... Gal. 1:12
D. Objects of, in divine things, concerning:
　　God's way .... Ps. 27:11
　　God's path .... Ps. 25:4, 5
　　God's Law .... Ps. 119:12, 26, 66
　　God's will .... Ps. 143:10
　　Holiness .... Titus 2:12
　　Spiritual truths .... Heb. 8:11, 12
E. Perversion of, by:
　　False prophets .... Is. 9:15
　　False priests .... Mic. 3:11
　　Traditionalists .... Matt. 15:9

False teachers...................... 1 Tim. 4:1–3
Judaizers..............................Acts 15:1
False believers .... 2 Tim. 4:3, 4

Tear, Torn
A. Used literally of:
Garments .... Ezra 9:3, 5
Clothing .... Esth. 4:1
Rocks............................ Matt. 27:51
Flesh..............................Matt. 7:6
B. Used figuratively of:
Destruction .... Hos. 13:8
Dissolution of the old covenant ...... Mark 15:38

Tears
A. Kinds of:
Agonizing..............................Ps. 6:6
Rewarded ....Ps. 126:5
Repentant....................Luke 7:38, 44
Insincere........................... Heb. 12:17
Intense.........................Heb. 5:6–8
Woman's........................... Esth. 8:3
B. Caused by:
Remorse .... Gen. 27:34
Approaching death .... 2 Kin. 20:1–5
Oppression...........................Eccl. 4:1
Defeat .... Is. 16:9
Affliction and anguish .... 2 Cor. 2:4
Christian service .... Acts 20:19, 31

Tebah—*slaughter*
Son of Nahor ....Gen. 22:24

Tebaliah—*Yahweh has immersed*
Merarite Levite.....................1 Chr. 26:11

Tebeth—*the name of the Hebrew tenth month*
Esther becomes queen in ....Esth. 2:16, 17

Teeth, tooth
A. Used for:
Eating .... Num. 11:33
Showing hatred...................... Acts 7:54
B. Figurative of:
Destruction ....Job 4:10
Holding on to life.....................Job 13:14
God's chastening ....Job 16:9
Escaped by the "skin of my teeth" ...... Job 19:20
Judgment .... Ps. 3:7
Hatred.............................. Ps. 35:16
Persecution.......................... Ps. 57:4
Corporate guilt................ Jer. 31:29, 30
Greediness .... Dan. 7:5, 7, 19
Starvation........................... Amos 4:6
Hired prophets ....Mic. 3:5
Remorse ....Matt. 13:42, 50

Tehinnah—*grace*
Judahite.............................1 Chr. 4:12

Tekel—*weighed*
Descriptive of Babylon's judgment...... Dan. 5:25

Tekoa—*firm, settlement*
Ashhur the father of ....1 Chr. 2:24; 4:5

Fortress city of Judah ....2 Chr. 20:20
Home of a wise woman......... 2 Sam. 14:2, 4, 9
Fortified by Rehoboam............. 2 Chr. 11:6
Home of Amos .... Amos 1:1

Tekoite—*an inhabitant of Tekoa*
Ikkesh thus called .... 2 Sam. 23:26
Among postexilic workmen.........Neh. 3:5, 27

Tel Abib—*hill of grain*
Place in Babylonia ....Ezek. 3:15

Telah—*fracture*
Ephraimite...........................1 Chr. 7:25

Telaim—*little lambs*
Saul assembles his army here..........1 Sam. 15:4

Telassar—*hill of Asshur*
People of Eden inhabit ..... 2 Kin. 19:12; Is. 37:12

Telem—*a lamb*
1. Town in south Judah................. Josh. 15:24
2. Divorced his foreign wife..............Ezra 10:24

Tel Harsha—*mound of the craftsman's work*
Babylonian town...................... Neh. 7:61

Tel Melah—*hill of salt*
Place in Babylonia .... Ezra 2:59

Tema—*sunburnt*
1. Son of Ishmael ....Gen. 25:15
Descendants of Abraham............. 1 Chr. 1:30
Troops of ....Job 6:19
2. Remote from Palestine..................Jer. 25:23
On trade route through Arabia....... Is. 21:13, 14

Teman—*the south*
1. Grandson of Esau; chief of Edom ... Gen. 36:11, 15
2. Another chief of Edom................ Gen. 36:42
3. Tribe in northeast Edom .... Gen. 36:34
Judgment pronounced against .... Amos 1:12
God appears from...................... Hab. 3:3

Temanite—*an inhabitant of Teman*
Job's friend, Eliphaz.................. Job 42:7, 9

Temeni—*fortunate*
Son of Ashhur ....1 Chr. 4:5, 6

Temperance
A. Needed in:
Eating ....Prov. 23:1–3
Sexual appetites .... 1 Cor. 7:1–9
All things .... 1 Cor. 9:25–27
B. Helped by:
Self-control........................Prov. 16:32
God's Spirit ....Gal. 5:23
Spiritual growth ....2 Pet. 1:6
C. In the use of wine, total recommended by:
Solomon .... Prov. 23:31–35
Angel .... Judg. 13:3–5
Nazirite vow .... Num. 6:2, 3
First, among Rechabites............. Jer. 35:1–10
See Self-control; Sober, sobriety

Tempests—*terrible storms*

A. Literal uses of:

At Sinai ....Heb. 12:18–21
Jonah's ship tossed by ....Jon. 1:4–15
Calmed by Christ.................Matt. 8:23–27
Paul's ship destroyed by ....Acts 27:14–20

B. Figurative of:

Destructiveness........................ Is. 28:2
God's wrath ....Jer. 30:23
God's chastening ....Job 9:17
Furious troubles ....Ps. 55:8
God's judgments......................Ps. 83:15
Hell's torments .... Ps. 11:6
Raging destructiveness...............2 Pet. 2:17
Destruction by war .... Amos 1:14

Temple, Herod's

Zacharias received vision in......... Luke 1:5–22
Infant Jesus greeted here by Simeon
    and Anna..................... Luke 2:22–39
Jesus visited at age 12 .... Luke 2:42–52
Jesus visited and cleansed..........John 2:15–17
Amount of time to construct,
    specified..................... John 2:19, 20
Jesus taught in........................John 8:20
Jesus cleansed again............. Matt. 21:12–16
Jesus spoke parables in .... Matt. 21:23–46
Jesus exposes Pharisees in .... Matt. 23:1–39
Destruction of, foretold .... Matt. 24:1, 2
Veil of, torn at Christ's death........ Matt. 27:51;
    Heb. 10:20
Christians worshiped here............. Acts 2:46
Apostles taught here .... Acts 3:1–26
Paul accused of profaning ....Acts 21:20–30

Temple, Solomon's

A. Features regarding:

Site of, on Mt. Moriah..........2 Sam. 24:18–25
Conceived by David................ 2 Sam. 7:1–3
Building of, forbidden to David ... 1 Chr. 22:5–16
David promised a greater house .... 2 Sam. 7:4–29
Pattern of, given to Solomon
    by David..................... 1 Chr. 28:1–21
Provisions for, given to Solomon ...1 Chr. 29:1–19
Supplies furnished by Hiram........1 Kin. 5:1–18
Construction of, by Solomon .... 2 Chr. 3; 4
Dedication of, by Solomon.............2 Chr. 6
Seven years in building............... 1 Kin. 6:38
No noise in building .... 1 Kin. 6:7
Date of building ....1 Kin. 6:1, 37, 38
Workmen employed in ....1 Kin. 5:15–17

B. History of:

Ark brought into....................1 Kin. 8:1–9
Filled with God's glory............1 Kin. 8:10, 11
Treasures taken away .... 1 Kin. 14:25, 26
Repaired by Jehoash .... 2 Kin. 12:4–14
Treasures of, given to Arameans by
    Jehoash.....................2 Kin. 12:17, 18
Treasures of, given to Assyrians by
    Ahaz ....2 Kin. 16:14, 18
Worship of, restored by Hezekiah . 2 Chr. 29:3–35

Treasures of, given by Hezekiah to
    Assyrians................... 2 Kin. 18:13–16
Desecrated by Manasseh's idolatry . 2 Kin. 21:4–7
Repaired and purified by Josiah... 2 Kin. 23:4–12
Plundered and burned by
    Babylonians.................. 2 Kin. 25:9–17

Temple, spiritual

A. Descriptive of:

Christ's body ....John 2:19, 21
Believer's body .... 1 Cor. 6:19
The church.......................1 Cor. 3:16, 17
Apostate church .... 2 Thess. 2:4

B. Believers as, described as:

Indwelt by God...................... 2 Cor. 6:16
Indwelt by Christ .... Eph. 3:17, 18
Indwelt by the Spirit .... Eph. 2:21, 22
Priests ....1 Pet. 2:5
Offering spiritual sacrifices........Heb. 13:15, 16

Temple, Zerubbabel's

By the order of Cyrus .... Ezra 1:1–4
Temple vessels restored for .... Ezra 1:7–11
Worship of, restored .... Ezra 3:3–13
Work of rebuilding hindered......... Ezra 4:1–24
Building of, completed .... Ezra 6:13–18
Inferiority of ....Ezra 3:12

Temple tax

Levied yearly upon all Jews ....Matt. 17:24–27

Temporal—*for a short time*

Things that are seen .... 2 Cor. 4:18

Temporal blessings

A. Consisting of:

Rain............................... Matt. 5:45
Seedtime and harvest .... Gen. 8;22
Food and clothes.................. Luke 12:22–31
Prosperity......................... Deut. 8:7–18
Children .... Ps. 127:3–5
Preservation of life.............. 2 Tim. 4:16–18
Providential guidance..... Gen. 24:12–14, 42–44

B. God's supply of:

Promised........................Prov. 3:9, 10
Provided .... Neh. 9:15
Prayed for ....Matt. 6:11
Acknowledged......................Ps. 23:1–5
Explained .... Deut. 8:2, 3
Contingent upon obedience ....Mal. 3:7–11;
    Matt. 6:25–34
Object of praise.....................Ps. 103:1–5

WORD STUDY

TEMPT, *nasah* (naw-*saw*). *Nasah* is a verb, sometimes translated "tempt"; but in modern English "test" or "try" are better understandings of the meaning. A sword can be tested or tried. In Dan. 1:12 Daniel and his friends were tested after eating the food they chose instead of the rich food of the king. *Nasah* can mean "to attempt" or "to try to do" something as Eliphaz attempts to reason with Job in Job 4:2. In the sense of testing or proving, God tests humans as He did Abraham when

Abraham was supposed to offer Isaac as a sacrifice (Gen. 22:1) or as He tested Israel in the wilderness (Ex. 15:25). At times it is said that Israel tests or tempts God as they did when they demanded water from Moses (Ex. 17:2). Ahaz refused to test God when he was offered a chance to do so (Is. 7:12). (Strong's #5254)

| WORD STUDY | **TEMPT, TEST,** *peirazō* (peye-*rahd*-zoh). The verb *peirazō* means "to try," "to attempt" (Acts 16:7), or, more commonly, |

"to try," "to make trial of," "to put to the test" (in order to discover what kind of person someone is). The latter use can be positive (2 Cor. 13:5) or negative (Matt. 22:18, 35). God (Heb. 11:17) and Jesus (John 6:6) put humans to the test, thereby giving them the opportunity to prove themselves true, and some of these trials are painful (1 Cor. 10:13). However, the devil puts humans—even Jesus (Matt. 4:1)—to the test in order to entice them to sin (1 Cor. 7:5; 1 Thess. 3:5); thus *peirazō* can be used as substantive to designate "the tempter" (Matt. 4:3). To test God (Acts 15:10; Heb. 3:9), Christ (1 Cor. 10:9), or the Spirit (Acts 5:9) usually leads to disaster. (Strong's #3985)

Temptation—*a testing designed to strengthen or corrupt*
A. Of God:
　　Forbidden . . . . .Matt. 4:7
　　By Israel . . . . Ps. 78:18–56; Heb. 3:9
　　Not possible . . . . James 1:13
B. Of Christ:
By:
　　The devil. . . . . Matt. 4:1–10
　　Jewish leaders . . . . .Matt. 16:1
　　His disciples. . . . . Matt. 16:23
　　Like us, but without sin . . . . Heb. 4:15
　　Design of. . . . . Heb. 2:18
C. Of Satan, against:
　　Job . . . . Job 1:6–12
　　David. . . . . 1 Chr. 21:1
　　Joshua . . . . Zech. 3:1–5
　　Jesus. . . . . .Luke 4:1–13
　　Ananias and Sapphira. . . . . Acts 5:1–3
　　Christians. . . . . 1 Cor. 7:5
D. Of Christians:
By:
　　Lust . . . . .James 1:13–15
　　Riches . . . . 1 Tim. 6:9
　　Liability to . . . . .Gal. 6:1
　　Warnings against . . . . Matt. 26:41
　　Prayer against . . . . Matt. 6:13
　　Limitation of . . . . .1 Cor. 10:13
　　Deliverance from .2 Pet. 2:9

Temptress—*female tempter*
　　Eve . . . . Gen. 3:6
　　Potiphar's wife. . . . . .Gen. 39:1–19
　　Delilah. . . . . .Judg. 16:6–20
　　Jezebel. . . . . 1 Kin. 21:7
　　Job's wife. . . . . .Job 2:9

　　Adulteress. . . . . Prov. 7:5–27
　　Herodias's daughter (Salome) . . . . . .Mark 6:22–29

Ten Commandments
A. Features concerning:
　　Given at Sinai . . . . Ex. 20:1–17
　　Written on stone. . . . . .Ex. 24:12
　　Written by God. . . . . .Ex. 31:18
　　First stones broken. . . . . .Ex. 32:19
　　Another copy given . . . . .Ex. 34:1
　　Put in the ark. . . . . Deut. 10:1–5
　　Called a covenant. . . . . Ex. 34:28
　　Given in a different form . . . . Deut. 5:6–21
　　The greatest of these . . . . .Matt. 22:35–40;
　　　　Rom. 13:8–10
B. Allusions to, in Scripture:
　　First . . . . Acts 17:23
　　Second. . . . . 1 Kin. 18:17–40
　　Third. . . . . .Matt. 5:33–37
　　Fourth . . . . Jer. 17:21–27
　　Fifth. . . . . .Deut. 21:18–21; Eph. 6:1–3
　　Sixth. . . . . .Num. 35:16–21
　　Seventh . . . . .Num. 5:12–31; Matt. 5:27–32
　　Eighth . . . . Matt. 19:18
　　Ninth. . . . . .Deut. 19:16–21
　　Tenth . . . . .Rom. 7:7

Tender—*soft; compassionate*
A. Used of physical things:
　　Animal . . . . Gen. 18:7
　　Grass . . . . 2 Sam. 23:4
　　Son . . . . Prov. 4:3
　　Women . . . . Deut. 28:56
B. Used of spiritual things:
　　Messiah. . . . . Is. 53:2
　　Compassion. . . . . Eph. 4:32
　　God's mercy. . . . . Luke 1:78
　　Human heart. .2 Kin. 22:19
　　Christ's return. Matt. 24:32
　　Babylon's destruction . . . . .Is. 47:1

Tenderness—*expressing a feeling or sympathy*
　　Shown toward the young . . . . Gen. 33:13
　　Expressed toward an enemy. . . . . . 1 Sam. 30:11–15
　　Illustrated by a Samaritan . . . . Luke 10:33–36
　　Manifested by a father . . . . .Luke 15:11–24

Tens of the Bible
A. Descriptive of:
　　Brothers . . . . Gen. 42:3
　　Cubits . . . . .Ex. 26:16
　　Pillars and sockets . . . . .Ex. 27:12
　　Commandments. Ex. 34:28
　　Shekels. . . . . .Num. 7:14
　　Years . . . . Ruth 1:4
　　Loaves . . . . .1 Sam. 17:17
　　Tribes. . . . . .1 Kin. 11:31, 35
　　Degrees . . . . 2 Kin. 20:9–11
　　Virgins. . . . . Matt. 25:1–13
　　Talents. . . . . Matt. 25:28
　　Lepers . . . . .Luke 17:11–19
　　Pieces of money. . . . . Luke 19:12–27

Horns....................................Rev. 12:3

B. Expressive of:

Representation .... Ruth 4:2

Intensity.............................. Num. 14:22

Sufficiency........................... Neh. 4:12

Magnitude .... Dan. 1:20

Remnant............................. Amos 5:3

Completion ....Dan. 7:7, 20, 24

Perfection..................... Luke 19:16–24

Tentmaker

The occupation of:

Aquila and Priscilla................ Acts 18:2, 3

Paul .... Acts 18:2, 3

Tents—*movable habitations*

A. Used by:

People .... 1 Chr. 17:5

Shepherds........................... Is. 38:12

Armies............................. 1 Sam. 13:2

Rechabites ....Jer. 35:7, 10

Women ....Gen. 24:67

Maidservants....................... Gen. 31:33

B. Features concerning:

Fastened by cords..................... Is. 54:2

Door provided...................... Gen. 18:1

Used for the ark .... 2 Sam. 7:1–6

C. Figurative of:

Shortness of life .... Is. 38:12; 2 Cor. 5:1

Heavens............................. Is. 40:22

Enlarging .... Is. 54:2

Terah—*duration; wandering*

1. Father of Abram.......................Gen. 11:26

Idolater ....Josh. 24:2

Dies in Haran ....Gen. 11:25–32

2. Israelite encampment ....Num. 33:1, 27

Teraphim—*household idols*

Laban's, stolen by Rachel ....Gen. 31:19–35

Used in idolatry .... Hos. 3:4

Terebinth tree

A. Uses of:

Landmarks.......................Judg. 6:11, 19

Burial place .... Gen. 35:8

B. Figurative of:

Judgment .... Is. 1:29, 30

Teresh—*dry*

King's official .... Esth. 2:21

Terrestrial—*belonging to the earth*

Spoken of bodies.................... 1 Cor. 15:40

Terror—*extreme fear*

A. Caused by:

Lord's presence .... Heb. 12:21

Fear .... Job 9:34

Death.............................. Job 24:17

War ....Ezek. 21:12

Fright.............................Luke 24:37

Persecutors.........................1 Pet. 3:14

B. Sent as means of:

Protection.......................... Gen. 35:5

Punishment ....Lev. 26:16

C. Safeguards against, found in:

God's promise........................ Ps. 91:5

God's plan .... Luke 21:9

Tertius—*third*

Paul's scribe .... Rom. 16:22

Tertullus—*diminutive of Tertius*

Orator who accuses Paul .... Acts 24:1–8

Test—*something that manifests a person's real character*

A. Kinds of:

Hard, given to Solomon ....1 Kin. 10:1–3

Physical...................... 1 Sam. 17:38, 39

Supernatural .... Ex. 7–11

Spiritual ....Dan. 6:1–28

National .... Ex. 32:1–35

B. Purposes of, to:

Test obedience..............Gen. 3:1–8 ; 22:1–18

Learn God's will....................Judg. 6:36–40

Accept good diet....................Dan. 1:12–16

Refute Satan's claims................Job 1:6–22

Destroy idolatry .... 1 Kin. 18:22–24

C. Descriptive of:

Testing physically....... 1 Sam. 17:39; Luke 14:19

Testing morally....................... John 6:6

Showing something to be true .....Gen. 42:15, 16

D. Objects of, among Christians:

Faith............................... 2 Cor. 13:5

Abilities........................... 1 Tim. 3:10

Testament—*a will or covenant*

Descriptive of a person's will........Heb. 9:15–17

WORD STUDY   **TESTIMONY, PROOF,** *marturion* (mar-*too*-ree-on). *Marturion* is a noun and means "testimony" or "proof." In addition to spoken statements in a courtroom setting (perhaps imagined in Matt. 10:18; Mark 13:9), a *marturion* may consist of actions or circumstances (Matt. 8:4; Mark 1:44; 6:11; Luke 5:14; 9:5; 21:13). *Marturion* is also used with reference to the proclamation of the gospel (Acts 4:33; 1 Cor. 1:6; 2:1; 2 Thess. 1:10; 2 Tim. 1:8). The use of *marturion* in the Septuagint to refer to the "tabernacle" or "tent of witness" is echoed in Acts 7:44. (Strong's #3142)

Testimony—*witness borne in behalf of something*

A. Necessary elements of, seen in:

Verbal expression ....2 Sam. 1:16

Witnesses .... Neh. 13:15; John 8:17

B. Means of:

Prophets ....Acts 10:42, 43

Friends .... 3 John 12

Jews .... Acts 22:12

Messengers.......................Acts 20:21, 24

Song............................... Deut. 31:21

Our sins........................... Is. 59:12

C. Reaction to:

Believed........................... 2 Thess. 1:10

Confirmed .... 1 Cor. 1:6

D. Purpose of, to:
    Establish the gospel . . . . Acts 10:42
    Prove Jesus was the Christ . . . . .Acts 18:5
    Lead to repentance . . . . Acts 20:21
    Qualify for office . . . . .1 Tim. 3:7

Tests of faith
By:
    Difficult demands . . . . Gen. 12:1, 2
    Severe trials . . . . .Job 1:6–22
    Prosperity of the wicked . . . . Ps. 73:1–28
    Hardships . . . . .2 Cor. 11:21–33

Teth
    Ninth letter in the Hebrew
       alphabet . . . . Ps. 119:65–72

Tetrarch—*a ruler over a fourth part of a kingdom*
    Applied to Herod Antipas . . . . .Matt. 14:1

Thaddaeus—*breast*
    One of the twelve disciples . . . . .Mark 3:18

Thahash—*porpoise, dolphin*
    Son of Nahor . . . . Gen. 22:24

> **WORD STUDY**   **THANK,** *yadah* (yaw-*daw*). The verb *yadah* can mean "to throw," but also can mean to "give thanks," "laud," or "praise." Humans can praise other humans. In the blessing of Jacob, Judah is told that his brothers will praise him (Gen. 49:8). Usually, however, the phrase is part of ritual worship of God. People are told to thank or praise the name of God in Is. 25:1. In Ps. there are frequent instructions to praise God. Sometimes *yadah* is addressed directly to God, "praise You." In a rare use, 1 Kin. 8:33 says that Israel will "confess the name" of God as part of their repentance. (Strong's #3034)

Thankfulness—*gratitude for blessings*
A. Described as:
    Spiritual sacrifice . . . . Ps. 116:17
    Duty . . . . 2 Thess. 2:13
    Unceasing . . . . .Eph. 1:16
    Spontaneous . . . . Phil. 1:3
    In Christ's name . . . . Eph. 5:20
    God's will . . . . 1 Thess. 5:18
    Heaven's theme . . . . Rev. 7:12
B. Expressed for:
    Food . . . . .John 6:11, 23
    Wisdom . . . . Dan. 2:23
    God's goodness and mercy . . . . .1 Chr. 16:34
    Converts . . . . 1 Thess. 1:2
    Prayer answered . . . . John 11:41
    Victory . . . . 1 Cor. 15:57
    Salvation . . . . 2 Cor. 9:15
    Lord's Supper . . . . 1 Cor. 11:24
    Changed lives . . . . 1 Thess. 2:13
C. Expressed by:
    Healed Samaritan . . . . .Luke 17:12–19
    Righteous . . . . .Ps. 140:13

> **WORD STUDY**   **THANKS, GIVE,** *eucharisteō* (yoo-khar-is-*teh*-oh). Verb meaning "to give thanks," "to render" or "return thanks." In the NT this verb is used to express thanks to Father God (as in Acts 28:15; 1 Cor. 14:18; cf. Rom. 1:21; 1 Thess. 5:18), with two exceptions (Luke 17:16; Rom. 16:4). *Eucharisteō* is frequently used with reference to giving thanks before meals (Acts 27:35), a custom Jesus is shown practicing regularly (Matt. 15:36; Mark 8:6; Luke 22:17, 19; John 6:11; cf. 1 Cor. 11:24). The cognate noun *eucharistia* ("thanksgiving") is used to refer to a prayer of "thanksgiving" (1 Cor. 14:16) and, in later tradition, to the Lord's Supper. (Strong's #2168)

> **WORD STUDY**   **THANKSGIVING,** *todah* (toh-*daw*). *Todah* is a noun, translated "thanksgiving," derived from the verb *yadah*, meaning "thank." In some instances praise was given to the Lord by acknowledging and abandoning sin. This is seen in the story of Achan, when Joshua urges him to "give glory to the Lord God of Israel, and make confession to Him" (Josh. 7:19). Most often, however, thanksgiving is given to God in songs of liturgical worship. Examples of places where this specific term is used include Ps. 26:7, Ps. 42:4, 5, and Jon. 2:10. Sometimes thanksgiving is expressed by a choir and procession, such as the one described in Neh. 12:31. There is also thanksgiving given with the thank offering in Lev. 7:12 and Amos 4:5. (Strong's #8426)

Theater—*a place of public assembly*
    Paul kept from entering . . . . Acts 19:29–31

Thebez—*brightness*
    Fortified city near Shechem . . . . Judg. 9:50–55

Theft, thief—*the act and agent of stealing*
A. Kinds of:
    Imputed . . . . .Gen. 44:1–17
    Improbable . . . . Matt. 28:11–13
    Real . . . . Acts 5:1–3
B. Characteristics of:
    Done often at night . . . . .Jer. 49:9
    Comes unexpectedly . . . . .Luke 12:39
    Purpose of, to steal . . . . John 10:10
    Window used by . . . . John 10:1
C. Objects of:
    Idol . . . . .Gen. 31:19–35
    Food . . . . .Prov. 6:30
    Traveler . . . . Luke 10:30, 36
    Money . . . . John 12:6
D. Evil of:
    Condemned . . . . Ex. 22:1–12
    Punished . . . . .Josh. 7:21–26
    Inconsistent with truth . . . . .Jer. 7:9, 10
    Defiles a person . . . . Matt. 15:19, 20
    Excludes from heaven . . . . 1 Cor. 6:10
    Not to be among Christians . . . . Eph. 4:28
See Stealing

Theocracy—*government by God*
Evident under Moses.................. Ex. 19:3–6
Continued under Joshua............Josh. 1:1–8
Rejected by Israel.................. 1 Sam. 8:4–9
To be restored ....Is. 2:2–4; 9:6, 7

Theophany—*an appearance of God*
A. Of God:
At Sinai........................... Ex. 24:9–12
In the tabernacle...................Ex. 40:34–38
In the temple ....1 Kin. 8:10, 11
To Isaiah............................. Is. 6:1–9
B. Of Christ as "the Angel," to:
Abraham.......................Gen. 18:1–8
Jacob .... Gen. 31:11, 13
Moses..........................Ex. 3:1–11
Joshua ....Josh. 5:13–15
Israel ....Judg. 2:1–5
Gideon.......................... Judg. 6:11–24
Manoah........................ Judg. 13:2–25
Shadrach, Meshach, Abed-Nego .... Dan. 3:28
Paul ....Acts 27:23, 24
C. Of Christ, as incarnate, in:
Nativity..........................John 1:14, 18
His:
Resurrected form .... John 20:26–29
Ascended form .... Acts 7:55, 56
Return in glory ....Rev. 1:7, 8
Glorified form.................... Matt. 17:1–9

Theophilus—*beloved of God*
Luke addresses his writings to .... Luke 1:3;
Acts 1:1

Thessalonians, the Epistles to the—*two books of the New Testament*
A. 1 Thessalonians:
Commendation..................1 Thess. 1:2–10
Paul's apostolic ministry ....1 Thess. 2:1–20
Timothy as envoy................1 Thess. 3:1–10
The quiet life..................1 Thess. 4:11, 12
The Second Coming .... 1 Thess. 4:13–18
Sons of light, not darkness........1 Thess. 5:4–7
Christian conduct .... 1 Thess. 5:12–24
B. 2 Thessalonians:
Encouragement in suffering ......2 Thess. 1:3–12
The Man of Sin................. 2 Thess. 2:3–10
Steadfastness...................2 Thess. 2:15–17
Maintaining order ....2 Thess. 3:1–15

Thessalonica—*an important city of Macedonia (modern Salonika)*
Paul preaches in .... Acts 17:1–13
Paul writes letters to churches of ..... 1 Thess. 1:1

Theudas—*God-giving*
Leader of an unsuccessful revolt .... Acts 5:36

Thirst—*a craving for water*
A. Caused by:
Wilderness drought.....................Ex. 17:3
Unbelief ....Deut. 28:47, 48
Siege.............................2 Chr. 32:11

Travels............................2 Cor. 11:27
Extreme pain.......................John 19:28
Flame.............................Luke 16:24
B. Figurative of:
Salvation............................Is. 55:1
Righteousness.......................Matt. 5:6
Holy Spirit ....John 7:37–39
Serving Christ..................Matt. 25:35–42
C. Satisfaction of:
By a miracle ....Neh. 9:15, 20
Longed for .... Ps. 63:1
In Christ alone .... John 6:35
Final invitation.....................Rev. 22:17
Perfectly fulfilled............Is. 49:10; Rev. 7:16

Thirty mighty men, the
Served David.................... 1 Chr. 12:1–40

Thirty pieces of silver—*bribe of Judas*
Price of slave ....Ex. 21:32
Given to Judas....................Matt. 26:14–16
Buys field .... Matt. 27:3–10

Thistle—*spiny weeds*
Obnoxious among wheat .... Job 31:40

Thomas—*twin*
Apostle of Christ .... Matt. 10:3
Ready to die with Christ............. John 11:16
In need of instruction ....John 14:1–6
Not present when Christ appears ... John 20:19–24
States terms of belief.................John 20:25
Christ appears again and
convinces him......... John 20:26–29; 21:1, 2
In the Upper Room ....Acts 1:13

Thongs—*leather straps*
Used to bind Paul..................... Acts 22:25

Thorn—*a plant with sharp projections on its stems*
A. Used literally of:
Earth's produce...................... Gen. 3:18
Land under judgment .... Is. 34:13
Christ's crown .... John 19:2
B. Used figuratively of:
Unbelief ....Is. 32:13–15
Judgments .... Hos. 2:6
Pain ....Prov. 26:9
False prophets .... Matt. 7:15, 16
Agent of Satan.......................2 Cor. 12:7
Barrenness .... Matt. 13:7, 22

> **WORD STUDY**
>
> **THOUGHT, OPINION,** *dialog ismos* (dee-al-og-is-*moss*). This noun—derived from the verb *dialogizomai*, which means "to consider," "to ponder," "to reason" (especially in one's own mind or heart, as in Mark 2:6, 8; Luke 12:17), or "to argue" (Mark 8:16, 17)—may be translated in a variety of ways. It can refer to "thought" (Luke 2:35; 6:8), "reasoning" (Luke 5:22), "designs" (= evil machinations, as in Matt. 15:19; Mark 7:21), or "opinion" (perhaps a legal technical term for "decision," as in James 2:4). *Dialogismos* may also be used

with reference to "doubts" (Luke 24:38), an "argument" (Luke 9:46), or a "dispute" (Phil. 2:14). (Strong's #1261)

Thought—*the reasoning of the mind*
A. Of the wicked, described as:
　　Evil................................. Gen. 6:5
　　Abominable........................Prov. 15:26
　　Sinful............................... Is. 59:7
　　Devoid of God....................... Ps. 10:4
　　Futile............................. Rom. 1:21
　　Known by God ....1 Cor. 3:20
　　In need of repentance .... Acts 8:22
B. Of the believer:
　　Comprehended by God............. 1 Chr. 28:9;
　　　　Ps. 139:2
　　Captivated by Christ.................2 Cor. 10:5
　　Criticized by God's Word............. Heb. 4:12
　　In need of examination...............Ps. 139:23
C. Of God:
　　Not like humankind's................ Is. 55:8, 9
　　To believer, good ....Ps. 139:17

Thousand years
　　As one day ....2 Pet. 3:8
　　Millennial reign .... Rev. 20:1–7

Thread
　　Refused by Abram ....Gen. 14:23
　　Tied to hand ....Gen. 38:28
　　Lips like scarlet....................... Song 4:3

Threatenings—*menacing actions or words against another*
A. Purposes of, to:
　　Silence a prophet...................1 Kin. 19:1, 2
　　Hinder a work.......................Neh. 6:1–14
　　Hinder the gospel................... Acts 4:17, 21
B. Exemplified by:
　　Jehoram against Elisha...............2 Kin. 6:31
　　Jews against Christians................ Acts 4:29
　　Saul against Christians..................Acts 9:1

Threshing—*separating kernels of grain by force*
A. Characteristics of:
　　Done by a stick .... Is. 28:27
　　Done by cartwheels ....Is. 28:27, 28
　　By the feet of cattle .... Hos. 10:11
B. Figurative of:
　　God's judgments.....................Jer. 51:33
　　Minister's labor....................1 Cor. 9:9, 10

Threshold
　　Will shake .... Amos 9:1
　　Descriptive of Nineveh's fall.......... Zeph. 2:14

Throat—*the front part of the neck*
　　Glutton's warning.....................Prov. 23:2
　　Thirsty one .... Ps. 69:3
　　Source of evil.......................... Ps. 5:9

Throne—*the seat and symbol of regal authority*
A. Of human rulers:
　　Under God's sovereignty ....Dan. 5:18–21

Established on righteousness..........Prov. 16:12
Upheld by mercy.....................Prov. 20:28
Subject to:
　　Succession........................2 Chr. 6:10, 16
　　Termination.......................Jer. 22:4–30
B. Of God:
　　Resplendent in glory .... Is. 6:1–3
　　Relentless in power ....Dan. 2:44
　　Ruling over all.................. Dan. 4:25, 34, 35
　　Righteous in execution...............Ps. 9:4, 7, 8
　　Regal throughout eternity .... Rev. 22:1, 3
C. Of Christ:
　　Based upon the Davidic
　　　　covenant.................... 2 Sam. 7:12–16
　　Of eternal duration ....Ps. 89:4, 29, 36;
　　　　Dan. 7:13, 14
　　Explained in its nature .... Is. 9:6, 7
　　Symbolized in its functions .... Zech. 6:12, 13
　　Promised to Christ.................Luke 1:31–33
　　Christ rises to possess .... Heb. 8:1
　　Christ now rules from............. Eph. 1:20–22;
　　　　1 Pet. 3:20–22
　　Shares with the Godhead.......... Rev. 5:12–14
　　Shares with believers.......Luke 22:30; Rev. 3:21
　　Judges humankind from............ Matt. 25:31

Thumb—*first fingers of human hand*
　　Anointing of, as an act
　　　　of consecration................. Lev. 8:23, 24
　　As an act of purification..... Lev. 14:14, 17, 25, 28
　　Cutting off of, an act of subjugation...Judg. 1:6, 7

Thunder—*the sound that follows a flash of lightning*
A. Supernaturally brought:
　　Upon the Egyptians................. Ex. 9:22–34
　　At Sinai............................Ex. 19:16
　　Against the Philistines ....1 Sam. 7:10
　　At David's deliverance .... 2 Sam. 22:14, 15
B. Figurative of:
God's:
　　Power............................. Job 26:14
　　Control ....Ps. 104:7
　　Majesty ....Rev. 4:5
　　Visitations of judgment ....Rev. 11:19

Thyatira—*an important town in the Roman province of Asia*
　　Residence of Lydia....................Acts 16:14
　　One of the seven churches .... Rev. 2:18–24

Tibhath—*slaughter*
　　Town in the kingdom of Zobah ....1 Chr. 18:8

Tibni—*intelligent*
　　Son of Ginath .... 1 Kin. 16:21, 22

Tidal—*splendor*
　　King allied with Chedorlaomer ...... Gen. 14:1, 9

Tidings
A. Descriptive of:
　　Joyful............................. Gen. 29:13
　　Good .... 1 Kin. 1:42
　　Evil................................. Ps. 112:7

B. Of salvation:
Out of Zion . . . . Is. 40:9
By a person . . . . Is. 41:27
By an angel . . . . .Luke 2:8–18
See News

Tiglath-Pileser—*my trust is in the god Ninib*
Powerful Assyrian king who invades
Samaria . . . . .2 Kin. 15:29

Tikvah—*hope*
1. Father-in-law of Huldah . . . . 2 Kin. 22:14
Called Tokhath .2 Chr. 34:22
2. Father of Jahaziah . . . . Ezra 10:15

Tile
Earthen roof . . . . Luke 5:19

Tiller—*a farmer*
Man's first job . . . . Gen. 2:5
Sin's handicap on . . . . Gen. 4:12
Industry in, commended . . . . Prov. 12:11

Tilon—*scorn*
Son of Shimon . . . . .1 Chr. 4:20

Timaeus—*highly prized*
Father of Bartimaeus . . . . Mark 10:46

Timbrel—*a small hand drum*
Used in:
Entertainment . . . . Gen. 31:27
Worship . . . . .Ps. 81:1–4

> **WORD STUDY**
> **TIME (quality of)**, *kairos* (keye-*ross*). *Kairos* is a noun meaning "time," but with emphasis on a specific point or period of time. It is used in idiomatic expressions, such as "until (another) time" (–for awhile) in Luke 4:13; see others in Acts 12:1 and Eph. 6:18. *Kairos* is often used to denote "the right (proper, favorable) time" (as in Matt. 24:25; John 7:6) or, in an idiomatic expression, "opportunity" (Gal. 6:10). With qualifying phrases *kairos* is used to define a specific period of time—for example, harvest (Matt. 13:30)—or to indicate why a period of time is set apart—for example, the time of fulfillment (Mark 1:15; Luke 1:20); the time of the Gentiles (Luke 21:24). *Kairos* is one of the main eschatological terms used in the NT to denote "the time of crisis," "the last times" (Luke 21:8; Eph. 1:10; 1 Pet. 1:5; Rev. 1:3; 22:10), or "messianic times" (Matt. 16:3; Acts 3:19). (Strong's #2540)

> **WORD STUDY**
> **TIME (quantity of, that is, lapse, span)**, *chronos* (khron-*oss*). This noun, meaning "time," describes a "period of time" in general, especially in phrases like "a long time" (Matt. 25:19) or "a little while" (John 7:33). *Chronos* can also be used with certain verbs to denote the period of time when something is to occur (Matt. 2:7; Luke 1:57; Acts 7:17) or when something is complete (Gal. 4:4). The plural of *chronos* appears in expressions to specify a rather long period of time, even an eternal period before earthly time (2 Tim. 1:9; Titus 1:2). This word

can also be used as an eschatological term (Acts 1:7; 1 Thess. 5:1; 1 Pet. 1:20). (Strong's #5550)

Time—*a measurable period*
A. Computation of, by:
Years . . . . Gen. 15:13
Months . . . . .1 Chr. 27:1
Weeks . . . . .Dan. 10:2
Days . . . . Gen. 8:3
Moments . . . . .Ex. 33:5
Sundial . . . . 2 Kin. 20:9–11
B. Events of, dated by:
Succession of families . . . . .Gen. 5:1–32
Lives of great men . . . . Gen. 7:6, 11
Succession of kings . . . . 1 Kin. 11:42, 43
Earthquakes . . . . Amos 1:1
Important events (the Exodus) . . . . 1 Kin. 6:1
Important emperors . . . . Luke 3:1
C. Periods of, stated in years:
Bondage in Egypt . . . . .Acts 7:6
Wilderness wanderings . . . . .Deut. 1:3
Judges . . . . .Judg. 11:26
Captivity . . . . Dan. 9:2
Seventy weeks (490 years) . . . . Dan. 9:24–27
D. Sequence of prophetic events in, indicated by:
"The time is fulfilled"
(Christ's advent) . . . . .Mark 1:15
"The fullness of the time"
(Christ's advent) . . . . .Gal. 4:4
"The times of the Gentiles"
(the gospel age) . . . . .Luke 21:24
"The day of salvation" (the gospel age) . . . 2 Cor. 6:2
"In the last days" (the gospel age) . . . . . . .Acts 2:17
"In the last days"(the time
before Christ's return) . . . 2 Tim. 3:1; 2 Pet. 3:3
"The last day"
(Christ's return) . . . . John 6:39, 54; 12:48
"New heavens" (eternity) . . . . .2 Pet. 3:13
E. Importance of, indicated by:
Shortness of life . . . . .Ps. 89:47
Making the most of it . . . . .Eph. 5:16
Purpose of, for salvation . . . . 2 Pet. 3:9, 15
Uncertainty of . . . . Luke 12:16–23
Our goal, eternity . . . . Heb. 11:10, 13–16
God's plan in . . . . Acts 14:15–17
F. For everything:
To give birth, to die . . . . .Eccl. 3:1–8, 17

Timidity—*lack of courage*
Nicodemus . . . . John 3:1, 2
Joseph of Arimathea . . . . John 19:38
Certain people .John 9:18–23

Timna, Timnah—*restraint*
1. Concubine of Eliphaz . . . . Gen. 36:12, 22
2. Chief of Edom . . . . Gen. 36:40

Timnah—*allotted portion*
1. Town of Judah . . . . .Josh. 15:10
Assigned to Dan . . . . Josh. 19:40, 43
Captured by Philistines . . . . .2 Chr. 28:18
2. Town in Judah's hill country . . . . .Josh. 15:57

Timnath Serah—*extra portion*
Village in Ephraim's hill country . . . . . . Josh. 19:50
Place of Joshua's burial . . . . Josh. 24:29, 30
Called Timnath Heres . . . . .Judg. 2:9

Timnite—*an inhabitant of Timnah*
Samson thus called. . . . . .Judg. 15:6

Timon—*deeming worthy*
One of the seven deacons . . . . Acts 6:1–5

Timothy—*revere God*
A. Life of:
Of mixed parentage . . . . Acts 16:1, 3
Faith of, from childhood . . . . .2 Tim. 1:5; 3:15
Becomes Paul's companion . . . . Acts 16:1–3
Ordained by the presbytery . . . . 1 Tim. 4:14
Left behind at Troas . . . . .Acts 17:14
Sent by Paul to Thessalonica . . . . .1 Thess. 3:1, 2, 6
Rejoined Paul at Corinth . . . . Acts 18:1–5
Preached Christ to Corinthians . . . . . . 2 Cor. 1:19
Sent by Paul into Macedonia . . . . Acts 19:22
Sent by Paul to Corinth. . . . . 1 Cor. 4:17
Returned with Paul to Jerusalem . . . . . Acts 20:1–5
With Paul in Rome . . . . Phil. 1:1; 2:19, 23
Set free. . . . . Heb. 13:23
Left at Ephesus by Paul. . . . . .1 Tim. 1:3
Paul summoned him to Rome . . . 2 Tim. 4:9, 11, 21
B. Character of:
Devout from childhood . . . . .2 Tim. 3:15
Faithful in service . . . . Phil. 2:22
Beloved by Paul. . . . . 1 Tim. 1:2, 18
Follows Paul's way . . . . 1 Cor. 4:17
In need of instruction . . . . 1 Tim. 4:12–16
Of sickly nature . . . . 1 Tim. 5:23
Urged to remain faithful . . . . 1 Tim. 6:20, 21
Emotional. . . . . .2 Tim. 1:4

Timothy, the Epistles to—*two books of the New Testament*
A. 1 Timothy:
Toward true doctrine . . . . 1 Tim. 1:3–7
Paul's ministry . . . . 1 Tim. 1:12–17
Christ, the Mediator . . . . 1 Tim. 2:5, 6
Instructions to women . . . . 1 Tim. 2:9–15
Church officials . . . . 1 Tim. 3:1–13
The good minister . . . . 1 Tim. 4:6–16
Fight the good fight. . . . . 1 Tim. 6:11–21
B. 2 Timothy:
Call to responsibility . . . . 2 Tim. 1:6–18
Call for strength . . . . 2 Tim. 2:1–13
Against apostasy. . . . . 2 Tim. 3:1–9
The Scriptures called inspired . . . . 2 Tim. 3:14–17
Charge to Timothy . . . . 2 Tim. 4:1–8
Paul's personal concerns. . . . . 2 Tim. 4:9–18

Tin—*a metal obtained by smelting*
Used in early times. . . . . Num. 31:22
Brought from Tarshish . . . . .Ezek. 27:12

Tiphsah—*passage; crossing*
1. Place designating Solomon's northern
boundary . . . . 1 Kin. 4:24

2. Unidentified town attacked by
Menahem . . . . 2 Kin. 15:16

Tiras
Son of Japheth . . . . Gen. 10:2

Tirathites
Family of scribes. . . . . .1 Chr. 2:55

Tirhakah—*the king of Cush (Nubia)*
Opposes Sennacherib . . . . 2 Kin. 19:9

Tirhanah—*kindness*
Son of Caleb. 1 Chr. 2:42, 48

Tiria—*foundation*
Son of Jehallelel. . . . . 1 Chr. 4:16

Tirzah—*delight*
1. Zelophehad's youngest daughter . . . . . . .Num. 26:33
2. Town near Samaria . . . . Josh. 12:24
Seat of Jeroboam's rule . . . . 1 Kin. 14:17
Israel's kings rule here down
to Omri . . . . 1 Kin. 16:6–23
Famous for its beauty . . . . Song 6:4

Tishbite—*an inhabitant of Tishbe*
Elijah thus called . . . . 1 Kin. 17:1

Tithes—*the tenth of one's income*
Given by Abraham to Melchizedek. . . Heb. 7:1, 2, 6
Promised by Jacob . . . . .Gen. 28:22
Belongs to the Lord . . . . Lev. 27:30–33
Given to Levites . . . . .Num. 18:21–24
Given by Levites to priests . . . . .Num. 18:25–28
Taken to temple . . . . Deut. 12:5–19
Rules regarding. . . . . .Deut. 14:22–29
Honesty in, required . . . . .Deut. 26:13–15
Of animals, every tenth . . . . Lev. 27:32, 33
Recognition of, by Jews. . . . . .Neh. 13:5, 12
Promise regarding . . . . Mal. 3:7–12
Pharisaic legalism on, condemned. . .Luke 18:9–14

Titles—*appellations of honor*
Condemned by Christ. . . . . Matt. 23:1–10

Tittle—*a mark distinguishing similar letters*
Figurative of minute requirements . . . . .Matt. 5:18
See Jot

Titus
Greek Christian and Paul's companion . . .Titus 1:4
Sent by Paul to Corinth. . . . . .2 Cor. 7:13, 14
Organized Corinthian relief fund . . . 2 Cor. 8:6–23
Met Paul in Macedonia. . . . . .2 Cor. 7:6, 7
Accompanied Paul to Crete. . . . . .Titus 1:5
Sent by Paul to Dalmatia . . . . 2 Tim. 4:10

Titus, the Epistle to—*a book of the New Testament*
Qualifications of an elder . . . . Titus 1:5–9
Against false teachings. . . . . Titus 1:10–16
Domestic life . . . . Titus 2:1–10
Godly living. . . . . Titus 3:3–8

Tizite
Description of Joha, David's
mighty man. . . . . .1 Chr. 11:45

Tob—*good*
    Jephthah's refuge east of the Jordan . .Judg. 11:3, 5

Tobadonijah—*good is Lord Yahweh*
    Levite teacher . . . . 2 Chr. 17:7, 8

Tobiah—*Yahweh is good*
1. Founder of a postexilic family . . . . .Ezra 2:60
2. Ammonite servant; ridiculed the Jews. . . .Neh. 2:10

Tobijah—*Yahweh is good*
1. Levite teacher . . . . .2 Chr. 17:7, 8
2. Came from Babylon . . . . .Zech. 6:10, 14

Tochen—*a measure*
    Town of Simeon . . . . .1 Chr. 4:32

Toe—*the terminal part of the foot*
    Aaron's, anointed . . . . Ex. 29:20
    Of captives, amputated. . . . . .Judg. 1:6, 7
    Of an image . . . . .Dan. 2:41, 42
    Man with six . . . . 2 Sam. 21:20

Togarmah
    Northern country inhabited by descendants of
        Gomer . . . . Gen. 10:3

Toi
    King of Hamath; sends embassy to
        salute David . . . . 2 Sam. 8:9–12

Token—*a visible sign*
    Guarantee. . . . . Josh. 2:12, 18, 21
    See Sign

Tola—*worm; scarlet*
1. Son of Issachar and family head. . . . . . . Gen. 46:13
2. Son of Puah; a judge of Israel . . . . Judg. 10:1

Tolad—*begetter*
    Simeonite town. .1 Chr. 4:29
    Called Eltolad . . . . Josh. 19:4

Tolerance—*an attitude of patience toward opposing*
        views
A. Approved in dealing with:
    Disputes among brothers . . . . .Mark 9:38–40
    Weaker brother. . . . . Rom. 14:1–23
    Repentant brother . . . . .2 Cor. 2:4–11
B. Condemned in dealing with:
    Sin. . . . . .1 Cor. 5:1–13
    Evil. . . . . .2 Cor. 6:14–18
    Sin in ourselves . . . . .Mark 9:43–48
    Error . . . . 2 John 10, 11

Tomb—*a place of burial*
    John's body placed in. . . . . .Mark 6:25–29
    Christ's body placed in Joseph's. . . Matt. 27:57–60;
        John 19:41, 42
    Figurative of hypocrisy. . . . . Matt. 23:27

Tongue—*the organ of speech*
A. Descriptive of:
    Speech . . . . .Ex. 4:10
    The physical organ. . . . . .Judg. 7:5
    Externalism . . . . .1 John 3:18
    People or race . . . . Is. 66:18
    Spiritual gift. . . . . 1 Cor. 12:10–30

    Submission. . . . . Is. 45:23
B. Kinds of:
    Backbiting . . . . .Prov. 25:23
    As of fire . . . . .Acts 2:3
    Deceitful. . . . . Mic. 6:12
    Double. . . . . 1 Tim. 3:8
    False. . . . . .Ps. 120:3
    Flattering . . . . .Prov. 6:24
    Gentle . . . . .Prov. 25:15
    Just. . . . . .Prov. 10:20
    Lying . . . . Prov. 21:6
    Muttering. . . . . Is. 59:3
    New . . . . .Mark 16:17
    Perverse. . . . . .Prov. 17:20
    Powerful. . . . . .Prov. 18:21
    Prideful. . . . . .Ps. 12:3, 4
    Sharpened. . . . . .Ps. 140:3
    Slow . . . . .Ex. 4:10
    Stammering. . . . . Is. 33:19
    Wholesome . . . . .Prov. 15:4
    Wise. . . . . .Prov. 15:2
C. Characteristics of:
    Small but important . . . . James 3:5
    Untamable . . . . .James 3:6–8
    Source of trouble. . . . . .Prov. 21:23
    Means of sin. . . . . Ps. 39:1
    Known by God . . . . .Ps. 139:4
D. Proper employment of, in:
Speaking:
    God's righteousness. . . . . .Ps. 35:28
    Wisdom . . . . .Ps. 37:30
    God's Word . . . . .Ps. 119:172
    Keeping from evil. . . . . .Ps. 34:13
    Singing praises .Ps. 126:2
    Kindness. . . . . .Prov. 31:26
    Confessing Christ. . . . . Phil. 2:11
    See Slander

Tongues, speaking in
A. At Pentecost:
    Opposite of Babel. . . . . .Gen. 11:6–9
    Sign of the Spirit's coming . . . . Acts 2:3, 4
    External manifestation. . . . . .Acts 2:4–6
    Meaning of, interpreted by Peter . . . .Acts 2:14–40
B. At Corinth:
    Spiritual gift. . . . . 1 Cor. 12:8–10, 28–30
    Interpreter of, required. . . . . .1 Cor. 14:27, 28
    Love superior to . . . . .1 Cor. 13:1–13
    Subject to abuse . . . . 1 Cor. 14:22–26

Tools of the Bible
    Anvil . . . . .Is. 41:7
    Awl. . . . . Deut. 15:17
    Ax. . . . . .1 Chr. 20:3
    Bellows . . . . Jer. 6:29
    Compass. . . . . Is. 44:13
    Refining pot. . . . . Prov. 17:3
    Fleshhook. . . . . 1 Sam. 2:13
    Fork . . . . .Ex. 27:3
    Furnace. . . . . Prov. 17:3
    Goad . . . . 1 Sam. 13:21

Engraving tool.........................Ex. 32:4
Hammer...............................Ps. 74:6
Inkhorn.............................Ezek. 9:2
Knife............................... Gen. 22:6
Mattock .... 1 Sam. 13:21
Ox goad..........................Judg. 3:31
Firepans...........................Ex. 27:3
Plane .... Is. 44:13
Plowshare........................... Is. 2:4
Plumb line .... Amos 7:8
Pruning hook........................ Is. 2:4
Razor............................. Num. 6:5
Saw.............................. 2 Sam. 12:31
Shovel ....Ex. 27:3
Sickle .... Deut. 16:9
Wheel .... Eccl. 12:6

Topaz—*a precious stone*
Used in breastplate....................Ex. 39:10
Of great value .... Job 28:19
In Eden .... Ezek. 28:13
In New Jerusalem.................. Rev. 21:2, 20

Tophel—*lime; cement*
Israelite camp ....Deut. 1:1

Tophet—*altar*
Place of human sacrifice in the
    Valley of Hinnom .... Jer. 7:31, 32

Torment—*to suffer unbearable pain*
A. Kinds of:
  Physical............................ Matt. 8:6
  Eternal............................ Rev. 20:10
  Internal...........................2 Pet. 2:7, 8
B. Means of:
  Official .... Matt. 18:34
  Persecutors......................... Heb. 11:35
  Fear ....1 John 4:18
  Flame...................... Luke 16:23–25
  God .... Rev. 14:9–11
  Human soul........................Job 19:2

Touch—*contact between two things*
A. Kinds of:
  Unclean..........................Lev. 5:2, 3
  Angelic .... 1 Kin. 19:5, 7
  Queenly...........................Esth. 5:2
  Cleansing ....Is. 6:7
  Healing..........................Matt. 8:3
  Sexual .... 1 Cor. 7:1
  Satanic............................1 John 5:18
B. Purposes of, to:
  Purify ....Is. 6:7
  Strengthen .... Dan. 10:10–18
  Harm.............................. Zech. 2:8
  Heal........................... Mark 5:27–31
  Receive a blessing................... Mark 10:13
  Restore to life .... Luke 7:14
  Manifest faith .... Luke 7:39–50

Towel—*a cloth used in drying*
Used by Christ..................... John 13:4, 5

Tower of the Ovens—*a tower of Jerusalem*
Rebuilt by Nehemiah .... Neh. 3:11

Tower of the Hundred
Restored by Eliashib .... Neh. 3:1

Towers
A. Purposes of, for:
  Protection......................... Matt. 21:33
  Watchmen .... 2 Kin. 9:17
  Safe-guarding people........... 2 Chr. 26:10, 15
B. Partial list of:
  Babel .... Gen. 11:4, 9
  David............................. Song 4:4
  Lebanon .... Song 7:4
  Penuel ....Judg. 8:17
  Shechem .... Judg. 9:40, 47, 49
  Siloam .... Luke 13:4

Trachonitis—*hilly land*
Volcanic region southeast of Damascus... Luke 3:1

Trade and transportation
A. Objects of, such as:
  Gold...............................1 Kin. 9:28
  Timber ....1 Kin. 5:6, 8, 9
  Hardwood ....1 Kin. 10:11, 12
  Spices..........................1 Kin. 10:10, 15
  Property ....Ruth 4:3, 4
  Slaves ....Joel 3:6
B. Means of, by:
  Wagons ....Gen. 46:5, 6
  Cows ....1 Sam. 6:7, 8
  Rafts ....1 Kin. 5:7–9
  Camels............................1 Kin. 10:1, 2
  Donkeys ....Num. 22:21–33
  Horses...........................1 Kin. 20:20
  Caravans......................... Gen. 37:25–36
C. Centers of, in:
  Tyre .... Ezek. 27:1–36
  Jerusalem ....Neh. 13:15–21

Trades and crafts
Baker .... Gen. 40:1
Brickmakers......................... Ex. 5:7
Carpenter..........................Is. 41:7
Engineers .... Gen. 11:3, 4
Farmers .... Ps. 104:13–15
Fishermen........................Matt. 4:18–22
Gatekeeper....................... 2 Sam. 18:26
Lawyers........................... Luke 5:17
Millers............................Ex. 11:5
Physician..........................Col. 4:14
Smiths .... Is. 44:12
Watchman .... 2 Sam. 18:26
See Arts and crafts in the Bible

Trade, spiritual
Buying the truth.....................Prov. 23:23
Value of wisdom .... Prov. 2:2–4
Above gold in value .... Ps. 119:72, 127
Without price ....Is. 55:1
True gold, from Christ ....Rev. 3:18

Traditions—*precepts passed down from past generations*

A. Jewish, described as:

Commandments of men............. Matt. 15:9

Rejection of God's Word .... Mark 7:8, 9

Productive of hypocrisy .... Mark 7:6, 7

Inconsistent with Christ................Col. 2:8

B. Christian, described as:

Inspired by the Spirit.............John 15:26, 27

Handed down by apostles ....2 Thess. 3:6, 7

Based on eyewitnesses............. 2 Pet. 1:16, 19

Classed as Scripture.......1 Tim. 5:18; 2 Pet. 3:16

Once for all delivered .... Jude 3

Consisting of fundamental truths...1 Cor. 15:1–3

Originating with Christ........... Matt. 28:20;
1 Cor. 11:1–23

Train

Trailing robe ....Is. 6:1

Traitor—*one who betrays a trust*

Descriptive of:

Judas .... Luke 6:16

End-time people .... 2 Tim. 3:4

WORD STUDY **TRANCE, AMAZEMENT,** *ekstasis* (ek-*stahs-iss*). In the NT this noun for "being beside oneself" refers to a state of "amazement" (Mark 5:42; Acts 3:10), "astonishment," or "terror" (associated with trembling and fear in Mark 16:8; cf. Luke 5:26). *Ekstasis* can also refer to a state in which consciousness is suspended, in which case it is translated as "trance" (Acts 10:10; cf. 22:17). The basic meaning of the cognate verb *existēmi* is "to lose (or be driven out of) one's senses" (said of Jesus in Mark 3:21). (Strong's #1611)

Trance—*a somnolent state*

Peter's on a housetop................. Acts 10:10

Transfiguration—*a radical change in appearance of*

Moses'...........................Ex. 34:29–35

Christ's, on a high mountain....... Matt. 17:1–13

Christ's, remembered .... 2 Pet. 1:16–18

Stephen's............................Acts 6:15

WORD STUDY **TRANSGRESSION,** *pesha'* (peh-*shaw*). "Transgression" is the translation of the noun *pesha'*, which comes from the verb meaning "rebel." Transgressions can be made against other individuals, as is indicated by Jacob's speech in Gen. 31:36. Nation can also transgress against nation. Amos describes the brutalities of nations against others in the oracles against nations in Amos 1. Most frequently there are transgressions against God. Various prophets are told to speak to the people of Israel regarding their transgressions and these transgressions are not specified (Is. 58:1; Ezek. 21:24, 29; Mic. 1:5). At times the transgression is recognized by the sinner, who knows it and turns from it. God deals with transgression in one of two ways, either punishing the transgressor, or forgiving, pardoning, and covering the sin. (Strong's #6588)

WORD STUDY **TRANSGRESSION,** *parabasis* (par-*ahb-ahs-iss*). The noun *parabasis* is derived from the verb *parabainō*, which literally means "to go aside," "to turn aside." In the Septuagint it is used figuratively and frequently in the sense of "to transgress" in conjunction with the nouns "law" and "commandment." Thus, *parabasis* is used to signify "transgression" of state, moral, or religious law. This is the sense in which it is used when particular mention is made of the Mosaic Law (Rom. 2:23; 4:15; Gal. 3:19). It can also be used to refer generally to "transgression" (Rom. 4:15; Heb. 2:2). (Strong's #3847)

Transgression—*a violation of God's law*

A. Described as:

Personal ....1 Tim. 2:14

Public...............................Rom. 5:14

Political..............................Esth. 3:3

Premeditated.....................Josh. 7:11–25

B. Caused by:

Deception..........................1 Tim. 2:14

Law................................Rom. 4:15

Sin................................1 John 3:4

Wine .... Hab. 2:5

Idolatry............................1 Chr. 5:25

Intermarriage .... Ezra 10:10, 13

Fear of the people................. 1 Sam. 15:24

C. Productive of:

Powerlessness ....Judg. 2:20–23

Unfaithfulness .... 1 Chr. 9:1

Death............................1 Chr. 10:13

Destruction .... Ps. 37:38

Curse .... Is. 24:5, 6

D. Punishment of, by:

Defeat ....2 Chr. 12:1–5

Disease .... 2 Chr. 26:16–21

Captivity............................ Neh. 1:8

Affliction ....Ps. 107:17

Death in hell .... Is. 66:24

E. Reaction to, by:

Further disobedience ....Num. 14:41–45

Covering up ....Job 31:33

Repentance .... Ezra 9:4–7

F. Forgiveness of:

Difficult ....Josh. 24:19

Out of God's mercy ....Ex. 34:7

By:

Confession ....Ps. 32:1, 5

Removal ....Ps. 103:12

Blotting out ....Is. 44:22

G. Christ's relation to:

Wounded for our .... Is. 53:5

Stricken for our...................... Is. 53:8

Made intercession for .... Is. 53:12

Was a Redeemer for............. Rom. 11:26, 27

Died for our .... Heb. 9:15

See Sin

Transitory—*passing quickly away*
A. Descriptive of human:
    Life .... Ps. 39:4, 5
    Pleasures .... Is. 47:8, 9
    Plans .... Luke 12:16–21
B. Caused by:
    World's passing away .... 1 John 2:15–17
    Our mortality .... Ps. 90:3–12
    Impending future world .... 2 Cor. 4:17, 18

Translations—*physical transportation to heaven*
    Enoch .... Heb. 11:5
    Elijah .... 2 Kin. 2:1–11
    Christians .... 1 Thess. 4:16, 17

Treachery—*pretending friendship in order to betray*
A. Manifested by:
    Woman .... Judg. 4:18–21
    People .... Josh. 9:3–15
    King .... 2 Sam. 11:14, 15
    Son .... 2 Sam. 13:28, 29
    Enemy .... Esth. 3:8–15
    Disciple .... Matt. 26:47–50
B. Accompanied by:
    Deceit .... Gen. 34:13–31
    Soothing words .... Judg. 9:1–5
    Professed favor .... 1 Sam. 18:17–19
    Pretense .... Dan. 6:1–8

Treason—*betrayal of one's country*
A. Instances of:
    Rahab against Jericho .... Josh. 2:1–24
    Israelites against Rehoboam ..... 1 Kin. 12:16–19
    Absalom against David .... 2 Sam. 15:1–14
    Sheba against David .... 2 Sam. 20:1–22
    Athaliah against Judah .... 2 Kin. 11;
    2 Chr. 22:10–12
B. Characterized by:
    Conspiracy .... 1 Kin. 16:9–11, 20
    Giving secrets .... 1 Sam. 30:15, 16
    Dispute .... 2 Sam. 3:6–21
    Jealousy .... Num. 12:1–11
    See Conspiracy; Treachery

Treasure—*something valuable stored away*
A. Descriptive of:
    Places for storing archives .... Ezra 5:17
B. Figurative of:
    Earth's productive capacity .... Ps. 17:14
    Wisdom .... Prov. 2:4
    People of God .... Ex. 19:5
    Humankind's spiritual possibilities .. Matt. 12:35
    New life in Christ .... 2 Cor. 4:6, 7
    Christ as the divine depository .... Col. 2:3, 9
    Future rewards .... Matt. 6:19, 20

Treasurer—*a custodian of public funds*
Under:
    David, Ahijah .... 1 Chr. 26:20
    Solomon, Jehiel .... 1 Chr. 29:7, 8
    Hezekiah, Shebna .... Is. 22:15
    Cyrus, Mithredath .... Ezra 1:8

    Candace, the Ethiopian eunuch .... Acts 8:27
    At Corinth, Erastus .... Rom. 16:23

Treasury
    Gifts for temple kept here .... Luke 21:1
    Storehouses .... 1 Kin. 7:51

Tree
A. Characteristics of:
    Created by God .... Gen. 1:11, 12
    Of fixed varieties .... Gen. 1:12, 29
    Can be grafted .... Rom. 11:24
    Subject to God's judgments .... Hag. 2:17, 19
B. Used for:
    Shade .... Gen. 18:4
    Burial sites .... Gen. 35:8
    Food .... Deut. 20:19, 20
    Cross .... Acts 5:30
    Buildings .... 1 Kin. 5:10
    Idolatry .... Is. 44:14, 17
    Fuel .... Is. 44:15, 16, 19
C. List of, in Bible:
    Acacia .... Ex. 36:20
    Algum .... 2 Chr. 2:8
    Almond .... Gen. 30:37
    Aloe .... Ps. 45:8
    Apple .... Song 2:3
    Box .... Is. 41:19
    Broom .... 1 Kin. 19:4, 5
    Cedar .... 1 Kin. 10:27
    Chestnut .... Gen. 30:37
    Citron .... Rev. 18:12
    Cypress .... Is. 44:14
    Ebony .... Ezek. 27:15
    Fig .... Deut. 8:8
    Fir .... 2 Sam. 6:5
    Mulberry .... 2 Sam. 5:23
    Myrtle .... Is. 41:19
    Nut .... Song 6:11
    Oak .... Is. 44:14
    Oil .... Is. 41:19
    Olive .... Judg. 9:9
    Palm .... Ex. 15:27
    Pine .... Is. 41:19
    Pomegranate .... Deut. 8:8
    Poplar .... Hos. 4:13
    Sycamore .... Amos 7:14
    Tamarisk .... Gen. 21:33
    Terebinth .... Hos. 4:13
    Willow .... Is. 44:4
D. Figurative of:
    Righteous .... Ps. 1:1–3
    Believer's life .... Prov. 11:30
    Wisdom .... Prov. 3:18
    Basic character .... Matt. 7:17–19
    Continued prosperity .... Is. 65:22
    Judgment .... Luke 23:31
    Eternal life .... Rev. 22:14
    Covenant .... Rom. 11:24

Tree of Knowledge

In the Garden of Eden	Gen. 2:9
God forbids eating of	Gen. 2:16, 17
Eve is deceived and eats	Gen. 3:6
Adam eats of	Gen. 3:6
Causes their eyes to be opened	Gen. 3:7
God enacts their penalty	Gen. 2:16, 17

Tree of Life

In Eden	Gen. 2:9
In New Jerusalem	Rev. 22:1, 2

Tremble—*to shake with fear*

A. Expressive of:

Deep concern	Gen. 27:33
Fear	Mark 16:8
Filial trust	Is. 66:2, 5
Apprehension	1 Sam. 16:4
Infirmity	Eccl. 12:3
Obedience	Phil. 2:12

B. Applied to:

People	Dan. 6:26
Earth	Ps. 97:4
Nations	Is. 64:2
Heart	Deut. 28:65
Flesh	Ps. 119:120
Servants	Eph. 6:5
Christians	1 Cor. 2:3
Demons	James 2:19

C. Caused by:

Physical change	Luke 8:47
Earthquake	Acts 16:29

Trials—*hardships that try our faith*

A. Characteristics of:

Some very severe	2 Cor. 1:8–10
Cause of, sometimes unknown	Job 1:7–22
Sometimes physical	2 Cor. 12:7–10
Endurable	1 Cor. 10:13
Rewardable	Matt. 5:10–12

B. Design of, to:

Test faith	Gen. 22:1–18
Purify faith	Mal. 3:3, 4; 1 Pet. 1:6–9
Increase patience	James 1:3, 4, 12
Bring us to a better place	Ps. 66:10–12
Chasten us	Is. 48:10
Glorify God	1 Pet. 4:12–16

WORD STUDY   **TRIBE,** *matteh* (mat-*teh*). The noun *matteh* can be translated in two ways, both derived from the verb meaning "to stretch out." First, the word can mean "rod" or "staff." The staff is a familiar object carried by shepherds in the OT. Moses also carried a rod (Ex. 4:2). The second translation derives from the first. A "tribe" was originally a company of people led by a chief who carried a staff. The word "tribe" occurs many times in the OT, usually specifically indicating the tribes of Israel. Num. and Josh. include the most frequent uses of the word. The noun *shebet* has the same basic meanings. (Strong's #4294)

Tribes of Israel

Twelve in number	Gen. 49:28
Descended from Jacob's sons	Gen. 35:22–26
Jacob forecasted future of	Gen. 49:3–27
Moses foretold future of	Deut. 33:6–29
Numbered	Num. 1:44–46
Camped by standards	Num. 2:2–31
Canaan divided among	Josh. 15–19
Names of, engraven	Ex. 39:14
United until Rehoboam's rebellion	1 Kin. 12:16–20
Returned after exile	Ezra 8:35
Typical of Christians	James 1:1
Names on gates of New Jerusalem	Rev. 21:12

WORD STUDY   **TRIBULATION, AFFLICTION,** *thlipsis* (*thlips*-iss). *Thlipsis* is a noun meaning literally "pressing," "pressure." In the Septuagint and NT, it is used solely in a figurative sense to mean "oppression," "affliction," or "tribulation" when the source of distress is external circumstance—such as persecution (Acts 11:19), the pangs of childbirth (John 16:21), or other physical suffering (Col. 1:24). It is also used figuratively with respect to mental or spiritual "affliction" (2 Cor. 2:4; Phil. 1:16). The "great tribulation" is to be understood eschatologically as a period of great distress during the last days (Rev. 7:14; cf. Matt. 24:21, 29; Mark 13:19, 24). (Strong's #2347)

Tribulation—*a state or time of great affliction*

A. Descriptive of:

Afflictions	1 Sam. 10:19
Persecutions	1 Thess. 3:4
Severe testings	Rev. 2:10, 22

B. Christian's attitude toward:

Must expect	Acts 14:22
Glory in	Rom. 5:3
Overcome	Rom. 8:35–37
Patient in	Rom. 12:12
Joyful in	2 Cor. 7:4
Don't lose heart	Eph. 3:13

Tribute—*a tax imposed upon a subjugated nation*

Imposed by Jews	Ezra 4:20
Imposed upon Jews	Ezra 4:13
Levied upon Israelites	2 Kin. 23:33
Christ settles question concerning	Matt. 22:17–21
Paul's admonition concerning	Rom. 13:6, 7

Trickery—*use of guile or deceit*

By Gibeonites	Josh. 9:3–16
By Saul	1 Sam. 28:7–10
By Amnon	2 Sam. 13:1–33
Christians, beware of	Eph. 4:14

Trinity, the

A. Revealed in the Old Testament:

At Creation	Gen. 1:1–3, 26
In the personality of the Spirit	Is. 40:13; 48:16

By:

Divine angel	Judg. 13:8–23

Personification of Wisdom .... Prov. 8:22–31
Threefold "Holy" ....Is. 6:3
Aaronic benediction .... Num. 6:24–27
B. Revealed in the New Testament:
At Christ's baptism .... Matt. 3:16, 17
In:
Christ's teaching...............John 14:26; 15:26
Baptismal formula .... Matt. 28:19
Apostolic benediction.............. 2 Cor. 13:14
Apostolic teaching................... Gal. 4:4–6

Triumphal entrance—*Jesus' entry into Jerusalem on the last week of His earthly ministry*
Prophesied ....Zech. 9:9
Fulfilled .... Matt. 21:2–11

Troas—*a seaport city near Troy*
Paul received vision here .... Acts 16:8–11

Trogyllium—*a seaport city of Asia Minor*
Paul's ship tarried here .... Acts 20:15

Troops—*a group of soldiers*
Placed in fortified cities .... 2 Chr. 17:2
Came together and camped............Job 19:12

Trophimus—*nourishing*
One of Paul's companions .... Acts 20:4

WORD STUDY

TROUBLE, *'amal* (aw-*mawl*). "Trouble," "labor," and "toil" are three related words that are all translations of the noun *'amal.* "Trouble" can be sorrow, which is usually because of one's own suffering. This meaning appears throughout Job and Ps. and in Jer. 20:18. Trouble can also be the troublemaking done to others as it is in Ps. 7:16, Prov. 24:2, and Hab. 1:13. The meanings "toil" and "labor" occur only in late Hebrew passages and appear often in Eccl. (see, for example, 2:10; 3:13). This meaning also appears in at least two psalms (105:44; 107:12). (Strong's #5999)

WORD STUDY

TROUBLE, DISTURB, *tarassō* (tar-*ahs*-soh). With reference to water, this verb means "to shake together," "to stir up" (as in John 5:4, 7). Elsewhere in the NT it is used figuratively of mental and spiritual agitation or confusion, in which case it is translated as "to stir up," "to disturb," "to unsettle," "to throw into confusion" (Acts 17:8, 13). *Tarassō* can also be used with reference to the confusion caused by false teaching (Acts 15:24; Gal. 1:7; 5:10). *Tarassō* also carries with it the meaning "to be troubled" (as is Jesus in John 11:33; 12:27; 13:21; cf. 14:1, 27), often with the sense of "to be frightened" or "terrified," especially by disturbing events (Matt. 14:26; Luke 1:12; 24:38). (Strong's #5015)

Trouble—*that which causes concern or distress*
A. Kinds of:
Physical, of nature ....Ps. 46:3
Mental................................ Dan. 5:9
Spiritual, of the wicked................. Is. 57:20
Spiritual, of the righteous .... Ps. 77:3

National .... Jer. 30:7
Domestic..........................Prov. 11:29
B. Caused by:
Misdeeds of sons.....................Gen. 34:30
Mysterious dream .... Dan. 2:1, 3
Unexpected news .... 1 Sam. 28:21
Sin................................. Josh. 7:25
Evil spirits............... 1 Sam. 16:14, 15
Enemies..............................Ezra 4:4
Physical malady ....Job 4:5
God's:
Withdrawal .... Ps. 30:7
Wrath ....Ps. 78:49
Our sins............................. Ps. 38:4–6
The mouth ....Prov. 21:23
Angel visitant ....Luke 1:12, 29
Wars, etc. ....Mark 13:7
Trials .... 2 Cor. 7:5
Affliction .... 2 Thess. 1:7
C. God's help to His saints in, to:
Hide.............................. Ps. 27:5
Deliver.................. Ps. 50:15; 2 Cor. 1:8–10
Help .... Ps. 46:1
Attend .... Ps. 91:15
Revive .... Ps. 138:7
Comfort .... 2 Cor. 7:5, 6

Truce—*a temporary cessation of warfare*
With good results................ 2 Sam. 2:25–31

True—*that which agrees with the facts*
A. Applied to:
God .... John 17:3
Christ...........................Rev. 3:7, 14
God's judgments.......................Rev. 16:7
Believer's heart .... 2 Cor. 6:8
Worshipers.......................... John 4:23
B. Christ as proof of:
Given by others.....................John 5:32, 33
Based upon testimony..............John 8:13–18
Recognized by many .... John 10:41
See Truth

Trumpet—*a wind musical instrument*
A. Features concerning:
Instrument of music .... 1 Chr. 13:8
Made of ram's horn .... Josh. 6:4
B. Uses of, in Israel, to:
Signal God's presence .... Ex. 19:16, 19
Regulate marchings...............Num. 10:2, 5, 6
Call assemblies .... Num. 10:2, 3, 7
Announce a feast .... Lev. 23:23–25
Gather the nation.....................Judg. 3:27
Alert against an enemy............Neh. 4:18, 20
Herald a new king .... 1 Kin. 1:34–41
Hail a religious event.................1 Chr. 13:8
Assist in worship................. Neh. 12:35–41
C. Uses of, at Christ's return, to:
Herald Christ's coming.............. Matt. 24:31
Signal prophetic events....... Rev. 8:2, 6, 13; 9:14
Raise the dead..................... 1 Thess. 4:16

Trust—*to put one's confidence in*

A. Not to be placed in:

Weapons.............................Ps. 44:6

Wealth...............................Ps. 49:6, 7

Leaders ....Ps. 146:3

Humankind..........................Jer. 17:5

Works ....Jer. 48:7

One's own righteousness ....Ezek. 33:13

B. To be placed in:

God's:

Name...............................Ps. 33:21

Word ....Ps. 119:42

Christ.............................Matt. 12:17–21

C. Benefits of:

Joy.................................. Ps. 5:11

Deliverance ....Ps. 22:4, 5

Triumph ....Ps. 25:2, 3

God's goodness.....................Ps. 31:19

Mercy...............................Ps. 32:10

Provision...........................Ps. 37:3, 5

Blessedness.........................Ps. 40:4

Safety..............................Ps. 56:4, 11

Usefulness ....Ps. 73:28

Guidance ....Prov. 3:5, 6

Inheritance.........................Is. 57:13

WORD STUDY	**TRUTH,** *'emet,* (eh-*met*). The noun *'emet,* translated "truth," "reliability," or "firmness,"* can be used to modify other nouns

so that there is a reliable or sure way (Gen. 24:48) or a sure reward (Prov. 11:18). It can also indicate "stability" and occurs with this intent in the phrase "peace and truth" (Esth. 9:30; Is. 39:8). "Faithfulness" can be a human characteristic, indicating a faithful man or one who walks in faithfulness. Reliability and faithfulness are also attributes of God. "Truth" can be a spoken truth (Jer. 9:4, 5) or testimony. In Mal. 2:6 truth is a divine instrument allied to justice. Truth can also be a body of religious or ethical knowledge as it is in Dan. 8:12. (Strong's #571)

Truth—*that which agrees with final reality*

A. Ascribed to:

God's Law.....................Ps. 119:142–160

Christ..............................John 14:6

Holy Spirit ....John 14:17

God's Word ....John 17:17, 19

Gospel.............................Gal. 2:5, 14

B. Effects of, to:

Make free ....John 8:31, 32

Sanctify...........................John 17:17–19

Purify ....1 Pet. 1:22

Establish ....Eph. 4:15

C. Wrong attitudes toward, to:

Change into a lie...................Rom. 1:25

Disobey............................Rom. 2:8

Walk contrary to ....Gal. 2:14

Love not ....2 Thess. 2:10

Believe not ....2 Thess. 2:12

Be destitute of....................1 Tim. 6:5

Never come to ....2 Tim. 3:7

Resist..............................2 Tim. 3:8

Turn from..........................2 Tim. 4:4

D. Right attitudes toward, to:

Speak..............................Eph. 4:25

Walk in ....3 John 3, 4

Declare ....Acts 26:25

Worship in ....John 4:23, 24

Come to............................1 Tim. 2:4

Believe and know ....1 Tim. 4:3

Handle accurately ....2 Tim. 2:15

Obey ....1 Pet. 1:22

Be established ....2 Pet. 1:12

Truthfulness—*abiding by the truth*

Commanded ....Ps. 15:2

Exemplified by Levi.................Mal. 2:6

Should characterize Christians........Eph. 4:25

Tryphena—*delicate*

Woman at Rome commended by Paul...Rom. 16:12

Tryphosa—*dainty*

Woman at Rome commended by Paul...Rom. 16:12

Tsadde

Eighteenth letter of the Hebrew
alphabet...................Ps. 119:137–144

Tubal

1. Son of Japheth........................Gen. 10:2

2. Tribe associated with Javan and
Meshech...............Is. 66:19; Ezek. 27:13

In Gog's army ....Ezek. 38:2, 3

Punishment of....................Ezek. 32:26, 27

Tubal-Cain—*Tubal, the smith*

Son of Lamech.....................Gen. 4:19–22

Tumors

Threatened as a curse ....Deut. 28:27

Inflicted upon Philistines ....1 Sam. 5:6–12

Tumult—*a confused uproar*

Against:

God ....Is. 37:29

Christ..............................Matt. 27:24

Paul ....Acts 19:29, 40

Paul pleads innocent of..............Acts 24:18

Tunic—*an outer garment*

Christ's, seamless...................John 19:23

Makers of:

God—for Adam and Eve ....Gen. 3:21

Jacob—for Joseph....................Gen. 37:3

Dorcas—for wearing.................Acts 9:39

Turban—*a headdress*

Worn by the high priest ....Ex. 28:36–39

Inscription "Holiness to the Lord"
worn on ....Ex. 39:28–31

Worn by Aaron for anointing and on
Day of Atonement..............Lev. 8:9; 16:4

Uncovering of, forbidden..........Lev. 21:10–12

Removal of, because of sin..........Ezek. 21:26

Symbolic restoration of.............Zech. 3:5

Turtledove—*a dove or pigeon*

Migratory bird	Song 2:12
Term of affection	Ps. 74:19
Offering of the poor	Lev. 12:2, 6–8; Luke 2:24

Twelve

Angels	Rev. 21:12
Apostles	Rev. 21:14
Baskets	John 6:13
Bronze bulls	Jer. 52:20
Brothers	Gen. 42:32
Cakes	Lev. 24:5
Cities	1 Chr. 6:63
Cubits	1 Kin. 7:15
Foundations	Rev. 21:14
Fruits	Rev. 22:2
Gates	Rev. 21:12
Golden pans	Num. 7:86
Governors	1 Kin. 4:7
Hours	John 11:9
Legions of angels	Matt. 26:53
Lions	1 Kin. 10:20
Male goats	Ezra 8:35
Men	Josh. 3:12
Months	Dan. 4:29
Officers	1 Kin. 4:7
Oxen	2 Chr. 4:15
Patriarchs	Acts 7:8
Pearls	Rev. 21:21
Pieces	1 Kin. 11:30
Pillars	Ex. 24:4
Princes	Gen. 17:20
Rods	Num. 17:2
Silver bowls	Num. 7:84
Sons of Jacob	Gen. 35:22
Springs	Num. 33:9
Stars	Rev. 12:1
Stones	1 Kin. 18:31
Thousand	2 Sam. 17:1
Thrones	Matt. 19:28
Tribes	Luke 22:30
Wells	Ex. 15:27
Years of age	Luke 2:42

Twins of the Bible

Esau and Jacob	Gen. 25:24–26
Perez and Zerah	Gen. 38:27–30

Two

Lights	Gen. 1:16
Angels	Gen. 19:1
Tablets of stone	Ex. 34:1, 4
Goats	Lev. 16:7, 8
Spies	Josh. 2:1, 4
Wives	1 Sam. 1:2
Women	1 Kin. 3:16–28
Evils	Jer. 2:13
Masters	Matt. 6:24
Witnesses	Matt. 18:16
People agreeing	Matt. 18:19, 20
Commandments	Matt. 22:40

Thieves	Matt. 27:38
Mites	Luke 21:2
Covenants	Gal. 4:24
Become one	Eph. 5:31
Hard-pressed from both directions	Phil. 1:23

Tychicus—*chance happening*

Asian Christian and companion	Acts 20:4
Carried Paul's letter to Colossians	Col. 4:7
Carried letter to Ephesians	Eph. 6:21, 22
Accompanied Onesimus to his master	Col. 4:7
Later sent to Ephesus by Paul	2 Tim. 4:12

Types, typology—*divine illustration of truth*
May be:

Ceremony—Passover	1 Cor. 5:7
Event—wilderness journeys	1 Cor. 10:1–11
Institution—priesthood	Heb. 9:11
Person—Adam	Rom. 5:14
Thing—veil	Heb. 10:20

Tyrannus—*tyrant*

Paul teaches in his school	Acts 19:9

Tyre—*a seaport city 25 miles south of Sidon*

Ancient city	Josh. 19:29
Noted for commerce	Ezek. 27:1–36
King of, helped Solomon	1 Kin. 5:1–10
Denounced by prophets	Joel 3:4–6
Fall of predicted	Ezek. 26:1–21; Amos 1:9, 10
Jesus visited	Matt. 15:21–28

U

Ucal—*I am strong*

Proverbs addressed to	Prov. 30:1

Uel—*will of God*

Divorced his foreign wife	Ezra 10:34

Ulai—*a river of Elam near Shushan*

Scene of Daniel's visions	Dan. 8:2–16

Ulam—*first; leader*

Manassite	1 Chr. 7:16, 17

Ulla—*burden*

Descendant of Asher	1 Chr. 7:30, 39

Ummah—*association*

Asherite town	Josh. 19:24, 30

Unbelief

A. Caused by:

Sin	John 16:9
Satan	John 8:43–47
Evil heart	Heb. 3:12
Honor from one another	John 5:44
Not belonging to Christ	John 10:26
Judicial blindness	John 12:37–40

B. Manifested in:

Questioning God's Word	Gen. 3:1–6; 2 Pet. 3:4, 5
Turning from God	Heb. 3:12
Questioning God's power	Ps. 78:19, 20

Hating God's messengers.......... Acts 7:54, 57
Resisting the Spirit................. Acts 7:51, 52
Discounting evidence ....John 12:37
Opposing the gospel ....1 Thess. 2:14–16
Rejecting Christ ....John 12:48; 16:9

C. Consequences of, seen in:
Hindering miracles .... Matt. 13:58
Exclusion from blessings ....Heb. 3:15–19
Condemnation ....John 3:18, 19
Rejection...........................Rom. 11:20
Judgment ....John 12:48
Death.............................John 8:24, 25
Destruction ....2 Thess. 1:8, 9
God's wrath ....John 3:36

D. Those guilty of, described as:
Stiff-necked ....Acts 7:51
Uncircumcised ....Jer. 6:10
Blinded .... Eph. 4:18
Rebels .... Num. 17:10

Unbelievers—*those who reject Christ*
Condemnation of....................Mark 16:16
Intermarriage with Christians,
    forbidden.....................2 Cor. 6:14, 15

Uncertainties—*things which may or may not happen*
A. Caused by:
Unknown future...................... Prov. 27:1
Divine providence ....James 4:13–17
Our lack of knowledge ....John 21:18–23
B. Need not affect our:
Assurance...........................1 Cor. 9:26
Trust in God .... Rom. 4:19–21
Plans ...., Acts 21:11–15

Uncharitableness—*a critical spirit*
Condemning others...Matt. 7:1–4; James 4:11, 12
Passing false judgments .... Luke 7:39
Assuming superior holiness......... John 8:1–11
Not forgiving readily.............Luke 15:25–32;
    2 Cor. 2:6–11
Imputing evil to others.......... 1 Sam. 1:14–17

Uncircumcised—*not circumcised, spiritually impure*
A. Descriptive of:
Gentiles.............................Gal. 2:7
Unregenerate state....................Col. 2:13
Unregenerate Jews and Gentiles...... Jer. 9:25, 26
B. State of, in the Old Testament, excludes from:
Passover .... Ex. 12:48
Land...............................Josh. 5:6, 7
Sanctuary........................ Ezek. 44:7, 9
Holy city .... Is. 52:1
C. State of, in the New Testament:
Has no spiritual value ....Gal. 5:6
Need not be changed.............. 1 Cor. 7:18, 19
Explained .... Rom. 2:25–29

WORD STUDY   **UNCLEAN,** *tame'* (taw-may). *Tame'* is an adjective, describing that which is ethically or religiously unclean. Isaiah claims that his lips are unclean in the vision of Is. 6. A closely related and more common use of the term is to indicate that which is ritually impure. People could be unclean for a wide variety of reasons, from coming in contact with a dead person to bearing children; and these things are carefully spelled out in the legal codes. Animals are divided into those that are clean and may be eaten and those that are unclean and, therefore, to be avoided. Pigs are the animal most often thought of as unclean. At times it is not the item that has an unclean nature, but contact with another thing that passes uncleanness (Lev. 11:35). Houses, food, and offerings can all be unclean; and aliens are generally considered unclean. (Strong's #2931)

Unclean—*that which is defiled*
A. Descriptive of:
Men and women........Lev. 15:1–33; Deut. 23:10
Not of the Lord.......................... Is. 52:1
Person ....Eph. 5:5
Sons of Israel ....Lev. 16:16
B. Transformation of, by:
Purification .... Is. 6:5–7
Separation .... 2 Cor. 6:17
Knowledge in Jesus ....Rom. 14:14
Prayer .... 1 Tim. 4:3–5
See Clean; Pollute; Sanitation and hygiene

Unconditional surrender
Required by Christ............... Luke 14:26, 27
As sacrifice...........................Rom. 12:1

Undefiled—*untainted*
Such persons are blessed................ Ps. 119:1
Christ is............................... Heb. 7:26
Describes marriage act .... Heb. 13:4
Applied to true religion.,,,,,,,,,,,,James 1:27
Our inheritance thus called............1 Pet. 1:4

WORD STUDY   **UNDERSTAND,** *bin* (been). The verb *bin* means to "understand" or "discern." One can perceive with the senses: the eyes (Job 9:1; Prov. 2:7), the ears (Job 13:1), and touch (Ps. 58:9). *Bin* usually means "to understand" or "to know with the mind." Job's friend uses the word in this way as he encourages Job to "gain understanding." The word implies observing or marking and giving heed to the things one hears. In Jer. 49:7 God remarks on the lack of wisdom and insight in Edom. In Ps. 119:34 and other places, the word is used in a form that means "to give understanding," or "to cause to understand," which is usually translated "teach." (Strong's #995)

WORD STUDY   **UNDERSTANDING,** *sunesis* (soon-ehs-iss). Usually translated as "intelligence," "acuteness," "insight," "understanding" (see Mark 12:33; Luke 2:47; 1 Cor. 1:19), this noun is used to designate the "faculty of comprehension." *Sunesis* is also used with reference to "insight" or "understanding" granted to believers by God, described in Col. 1:9 as "spiritual"; see also Eph. 3:4; Col. 2:2; 2 Tim. 2:7. (Strong's #4907)

Understanding—*knowing things in their right relationship*
A. Means of, by:
God's:
    Gift........................... 1 Kin. 3:9–12
    Revelation ....Rom. 1:20
    Word .... Ps. 119:104, 130
    Books...........................Dan. 9:2, 23
    Holy Spirit ....Ex. 31:3
    Christ...........................1 John 5:20
    Prayer .... Ps. 119:34–125
    Departing from evil............. Job 28:28
    Faith............................. Heb. 11:3
    Enlightening ....Eph. 1:18
    Interpretation ....Neh. 8:2–13
    Explanation ....Luke 24:45
    Reproof..........................Prov. 15:32
    Later event .... Ps. 73:17
B. Limitations on, by:
    Unbelief .... John 8:43
    Unregeneracy .... Eph. 4:18
    Spiritual blindness.................... Is. 6:9, 10
    Judicial punishment................. Is. 44:18, 19
    Difficulties.......................2 Pet. 3:16

Unfruitfulness—*not producing good fruit*
A. Caused by:
    Unfaithfulness .... Is. 5:1–7
    Worldliness ....James 4:1–4
    Negligence .... Luke 19:20–27
B. Punished by:
    God's judgments.....................Matt. 3:10
Rejection:
    Now ....John 15:2, 4, 6
    Hereafter .... Heb. 6:8

Ungodliness, ungodly—*the morally corrupt*
A. Described as:
    Prospering in the world................Ps. 73:12
    Growing worse .... 2 Tim. 2:16
    Perverting God's grace .... Jude 4
    Abounding in the last days .... Jude 18
    Christ died for.......................Rom. 5:6
B. Judgments upon, by:
    Flood .... 2 Pet. 2:5, 6
    Law.................................1 Tim. 1:9
    God's decree .... Jude 4
    God's revelation ....Rom. 1:18
    Christ's return.....................Jude 14, 15
    World's end ....2 Pet. 3:7
    Final judgment ....Ps. 1:4–6

Unintentionally—*without premeditation*
    Concerning an innocent killer ...... Josh. 20:3–5

Union
Of:
    Godhead.......................John 17:21, 22
    Christ and believers.................John 15:1–7
    God and humankind.............. Acts 17:28, 29
    Humankind...................... Acts 17:26

    Satan and the unsaved................John 8:44
    Believers in prayer .... Matt. 18:19, 20
See Oneness

Union with Christ
A. Compared to:
    Head and the body................. Eph. 4:15, 16
    Marriage bond.....................Eph. 5:23, 30
    Building .... Eph. 2:21, 22
    Parts of the body............. 1 Cor. 12:12, 27
    Vine and branches ....John 15:4, 5
    Food and the body ....John 6:56, 57
B. Illustrated in the "togethers":
    Crucified ....Rom. 6:6
    Buried ....Rom. 6:4
    Made alive .... Eph. 2:5
    Sitting .... Eph. 2:6
    Suffering.........................Rom. 8:17
    Reigning......................... 2 Tim. 2:12
    Glorified.........................Rom. 8:17
C. Manifested in, oneness:
    Of mind......................... 1 Cor. 2:16
    Of spirit......................... 1 Cor. 6:17
    In suffering .... Phil. 3:10
    In worship ....1 Cor. 10:16, 17
    In ministry.......................2 Cor. 5:18–21

Unity of believers
A. Based upon:
    Indwelling Spirit............. 1 Cor. 3:16, 17; 6:19
    New birth.......................... 2 Cor. 5:17
    Union with Christ .... 2 Cor. 13:5
B. Expressed by oneness of:
    Mind ....1 Pet. 3:8
    Unity of Spirit ....Ps. 133:1–3
    Faith.............................Eph. 4:4–6
    Fellowship ....Acts 2:42–47
    Concern .... 1 Cor. 12:25, 26
C. Consistent with such differences as:
    Physical........................... 1 Pet. 3:1–7
    Social.............................Eph. 6:5–9
    Mental......................... 1 Cor. 1:26–29

Unjust
Described as:
    Abomination.......................Prov. 29:27
    Recipient of God's blessings .... Matt. 5:45
    Christ died for.......................1 Pet. 3:18

Unknown god
    Altar to .... Acts 17:22, 23

Unleavened bread
    Used in the Passover... Ex. 12:8–20; Mark 14:1, 12
    Typical of Christians................ 1 Cor. 5:7, 8

Unmercifulness—*lacking mercy*
    Shown by Simeon and Levi .... Gen. 34:25–31
    By Pharaoh........................ Ex. 5:4–19
    By creditor ....Matt. 18:28–30

Unni—*answering is with Yahweh*
    Levite musician.................... 1 Chr. 15:18

Unpardonable sin
   Sin not forgivable . . . . . Matt. 12:31, 32; Luke 12:10

Unrest—*a state of agitation*
   Of the nations . . . . Luke 21:25, 26
   Of the wicked . . . . Is. 57:20
   Remedy given by Christ . . . . Matt. 11:28
   Antidote for . . . . Phil. 4:7

Unrighteousness—*wickedness*
A. Attitude toward, by the wicked, they:
   Suppress the truth in . . . . Rom. 1:18
   Are filled with . . . . Rom. 1:29
   Obey it . . . . Rom. 2:8
   Love the wages of . . . . 2 Pet. 2:15
   Take pleasure in . . . . 2 Thess. 2:12
   Receive the wages of . . . . 2 Pet. 2:13
   Shall not inherit the kingdom . . . . 1 Cor. 6:9
B. Relation of believers toward:
   They are cleansed from . . . . 1 John 1:9
   God is merciful toward their . . . . Heb. 8:12
   Must not fellowship with . . . . 2 Cor. 6:14
   All the world guilty . . . . Rom. 3:1–20

Unselfishness—*not putting self first*
A. Christ, an example of, in His:
   Mission . . . . John 6:38
   Suffering . . . . Matt. 26:39, 42
   Concern . . . . John 19:26, 27
   Death . . . . Phil. 2:5–8
B. In the believer, prompted by:
   Christ's example . . . . Phil. 2:3–8
   Love . . . . 1 Cor. 13:4, 5
   Concern . . . . 1 Cor. 10:23–33
   Christian service . . . . Phil. 2:25–30
   Sacrifice . . . . Rev. 12:11
C. Examples of:
   Abram . . . . Gen. 13:8–12
   Moses . . . . Num. 14:12–29
   Gideon . . . . Judg. 8:22, 23
   Jonathan . . . . 1 Sam. 18:4
   David . . . . 1 Chr. 21:17
   Nehemiah . . . . Neh. 5:14–19
   Daniel . . . . Dan. 5:17
   Christians . . . . Acts 4:34, 35
   Paul . . . . 1 Cor. 9:19–23
   Onesiphorus . . . . 2 Tim. 1:16–18

Untempered mortar—*whitewash*
   Figurative of false prophets . . . . Ezek. 13:10, 14

Unwittingly—*without premeditation*
   Concerning an innocent killer . . . . . . Josh. 20:3–5

Unworldliness—*a heavenly frame of mind*
A. Negatively expressed in, not:
   Loving the world . . . . 1 John 2:15–17
   Fellowshipping with evil . . . . 2 Cor. 6:14–18
   Mixing in worldly affairs . . . . 2 Tim. 2:4
B. Positively expressed in:
   Seeking God's kingdom first . . . . Matt. 6:33, 34
   Living for Jesus . . . . Gal. 2:20
   Becoming a living sacrifice . . . . Rom. 12:1, 2

Having a heavenly mind . . . . Col. 3:1, 2
Looking for Jesus . . . . Titus 2:11–15
Looking to Jesus . . . . Heb. 12:1, 2

Unworthiness—*not being fit; lacking merit*
A. Caused by a sense of:
   Failure . . . . Gen. 32:10
   Social difference . . . . 1 Sam. 18:18, 23
   Sin . . . . Luke 15:19, 21
   Inferiority . . . . John 1:27
B. Examples of:
   Moses . . . . Ex. 4:10
   Centurion . . . . Matt. 8:8
   Peter . . . . Luke 5:8
   Paul . . . . 1 Cor. 15:9

Upharsin—*and divided*
   Interpreted by Daniel . . . . Dan. 5:5, 25, 28

Uphaz
   Unidentified place of fine gold . . . . Jer. 10:9

Upper room—*chamber, usually built on a roof*
   Ahaziah fell from . . . . 2 Kin. 1:2
   Ahaz's . . . . 2 Kin. 23:12
   Disciples prepared for Christ . . . . . Mark 14:14–16
   Dorcas placed in . . . . Acts 9:36, 37
   Paul preached in . . . . Acts 20:7, 8

Uprightness—*character approved by God*
A. Descriptive of:
   God's nature . . . . Is. 26:7
   Man's state . . . . Eccl. 7:29
   The devout . . . . Job 1:1, 8
B. Of God, manifested in His:
   Works . . . . Ps. 111:8
   Judgments . . . . Ps. 119:137
   Delights . . . . 1 Chr. 29:17
C. Blessings of, for saints:
   Temporal blessings . . . . Ps. 84:11
   Lord's blessings . . . . Ps. 11:7
   Prosperity . . . . Prov. 14:11
   Deliverance . . . . Prov. 11:3, 6, 11
   Salvation . . . . Ps. 7:10
   God's presence . . . . Ps. 140:13
   Light in darkness . . . . Ps. 112:4
   Answered prayer . . . . Prov. 15:8
   Righteousness . . . . Ps. 36:10
   Joy . . . . Ps. 32:11
   Glory . . . . Ps. 64:10
   Final dominion . . . . Ps. 49:14
D. Attitude of wicked toward, they:
   Are devoid of . . . . Hab. 2:4
   Leave the path of . . . . Prov. 2:13
   Hate . . . . Prov. 29:10
   Persecute . . . . Ps. 37:14
   Laugh to scorn . . . . Job 12:4

Ur—*flame*
   Father of Eliphal . . . . 1 Chr. 11:35
   Called Ahasbai . . . . 2 Sam. 23:34

Ur of the Chaldeans
   City of Abram's early life .....Gen. 11:28–31; 15:7
   Located in Mesopotamia by Stephen ... Acts 7:2, 4

Urbanus—*polite*
   Christian..........................Rom. 16:9

Uri—*an abbreviation of Urijah*
1. Father of Bezalel.....................1 Chr. 2:20
2. Father of Geber ....1 Kin. 4:19
3. Divorced his foreign wife..............Ezra 10:24

Uriah—*Yahweh is light*
1. Hittite and one of David's warriors....2 Sam. 23:39
   Condemned to death by David....2 Sam. 11:1–27
2. Priest..................................Ezra 8:33

Uriel—*God is light*
1. Kohathite Levite ....1 Chr. 6:22, 24
2. Man of Gibeah ....2 Chr. 13:2

Urijah—*Yahweh is light*
1. High priest in Ahaz's time.........2 Kin. 16:10–16
2. Postexilic priest ....Neh. 3:4, 21
3. Prophet in Jeremiah's time ....Jer. 26:20–23
4. Stands with Ezra ....Neh. 8:4

Urim and Thummim—*lights and perfections*
   Placed in the breastplate of the high
      priest............................Ex. 28:30
   Method of consulting God..........Num. 27:21;
   1 Sam. 14:3–37
   Use of, confined to priests ....Deut. 33:8
   Answer by, refused..................1 Sam. 28:6

WORD STUDY   **USELESS, WORTHLESS,** *mataios* (maht-eye-oss). The adjective *mataios* describes that which is "empty," "useless," "worthless," "futile." In the NT *mataios* is used with reference to religious beliefs or practices that are void of meaning, truth, or worth (see Titus 3:9; 1 Pet. 1:18). The term is applied directly to the Christian faith, which is useless if one cannot control one's tongue (James 1:26), and which is empty and worthless "if Christ is not risen" (1 Cor. 15:17). (Strong's #3152)

Usurpation—*seizing authority illegally*
A. Methods of, by:
   Intrigue........................2 Sam. 15:1–12
   Defying God's Law ....1 Sam. 13:8–14
   Changing God's worship ....2 Kin. 16:10–17
   Conspiracy...................1 Kin. 15:27, 28
   Assuming dictatorial rights..........3 John 9, 10
B. Consequences of, seen in:
   Defeat and death ....2 Kin. 11:1–6
   Another conspiracy ....2 Kin. 15:10–15
   Defeat and conditional
      forgiveness....................1 Kin. 1:5–53
C. Spirit of, manifested in:
   Human transgression ....Gen. 3:1–7
   Satan's fall ....Is. 14:12–14
   Antichrist's desire ...2 Thess. 2:3, 4; Rev. 13:1–18

Utensils, kitchen
   Bowls..............................Amos 6:6

   Platter ....Matt. 14:11
   Jar.................................1 Kin. 17:12
   Cup and dish ....Matt. 23:25
   Fleshhooks.....................1 Sam. 2:13, 14
   Iron pan ....Ezek. 4:3
   Kettle (pot).......................1 Sam. 2:14
   Kneading bowls.....................Ex. 8:3
   Millstones.........................Is. 47:2
   Pan................................Lev. 2:5

Uthai—*Yahweh is help*
1. Judahite ....1 Chr. 9:4
2. Postexilic returnee....................Ezra 8:14

Uz—*firmness*
1. Descendant of Shem ....Gen. 10:23
2. Descendant of Seir....................Gen. 36:28
3. Place in south Edom; residence of Job ......Job 1:1

WORD STUDY   **UTTERANCE, ORACLE,** *massa'* (mas-saw). *Massa',* translated "utterance," is a noun used often to describe prophetic utterances. Isaiah begins many of his oracles against foreign nations with "the burden [oracle] against." In Hab. 1:1 *massa'* means "a revelation." Jer. 23 uses the term to begin utterances of the Lord. It is also used (2 Kin. 9:25; Zech. 9:1; 12:1) to refer to specific messages given by God. Prov. 31:1 begins to repeat or proclaim the utterances of King Lemuel's mother, the single reference to utterances that were not from God. (Strong's #4853)

Uzai—*hoped for*
   Father of Palal........................Neh. 3:25

Uzal
   Son of Joktan........................Gen. 10:27

Uzza, Uzzah—*strength*
1. Son of Shimei ....1 Chr. 6:29
2. Descendant of Ehud ....1 Chr. 8:7
3. Head of a returning temple servant
     family ....Ezra 2:49
4. Name of a garden..............2 Kin. 21:18, 26
5. Son of Abinadab struck down for touching the ark
    of the covenant..................2 Sam. 6:3–11

Uzzen Sheerah—*top of Sheerah*
   Town built by Sheerah, Ephraim's
     daughter........................1 Chr. 7:24

Uzzi—*my strength*
1. Descendant of Aaron ....1 Chr. 6:5, 51
2. Descendant of Issachar ....1 Chr. 7:1–3
3. Son of Bela............................1 Chr. 7:7
4. Levite overseer ....Neh. 11:22
5. Postexilic priest ....Neh. 12:19, 42

Uzzia—*my strength is Yahweh*
   One of David's mighty men..........1 Chr. 11:44

Uzziah—*my strength is Yahweh*
1. Kohathite Levite ....1 Chr. 6:24
2. Father of Jehonathan ....1 Chr. 27:25

3. King of Judah, called
   Azariah................... 2 Kin. 14:21; 15:1–7
   Reigned 52 years...................2 Kin. 15:1, 2
   Reigned righteously...............2 Chr. 26:4, 5
   Conquered the Philistines........ 2 Chr. 26:6–8
   Strengthened Jerusalem ....2 Chr. 26:9
   Developed agriculture..............2 Chr. 26:10
   Usurped priestly function; stricken
        with leprosy................. 2 Chr. 26:16–21
   Life of, written by Isaiah .... 2 Chr. 26:22, 23
   Earthquake in the days of .... Amos 1:1
   Death of, time of Isaiah's vision...........Is. 6:1
4. Priest who divorced his foreign wife...Ezra 10:19, 21
5. Judahite ....Neh. 11:4

Uzziel—*God is my strength*
1. Levite, son of Kohath and family head ...Ex. 6:18, 22
2. Son of Bela............................1 Chr. 7:7
3. Simeonite captain ....1 Chr. 4:41–43
4. Levite musician .... 1 Chr. 25:3, 4
5. Levite assisting in Hezekiah's
        reforms ....2 Chr. 29:14–19
6. Goldsmith working on Jerusalem's wall ...Neh. 3:8

V

Vagabond—*an aimless wanderer*
   Curse on Cain ....Gen. 4:12, 14
   Curse upon the wicked ....Ps. 109:10

Vain—*empty; useless*
A. Applied to physical things:
   Beauty ....Prov. 31:30
   Life.................................. Eccl. 6:12
   Adornment............................ Jer. 4:30
   Healing............................. Jer. 46:11
   Protection...................... 1 Sam. 25:21
   Safety................................ Ps. 33:17
   World's creation .... Is. 45:18, 19
B. Applied to spiritual things:
   Idolatry ....Acts 14:15
   Serving God........................ Mal. 3:14
   Babblings .... 2 Tim. 2:16
C. Applied to possibilities:
   God's grace........................ 1 Cor. 15:10
   Christ's death ....Gal. 2:21
   Scriptures .... James 4:5
   Faith............................1 Cor. 15:2–17
   Worship .... Is. 45:19
   Labor .... 1 Thess. 3:5
   Reception .... 1 Thess. 2:1, 2
   Sufferings...........................Gal. 3:4
   See Futile

Vajezatha—*son of the atmosphere*
   One of Haman's sons.................. Esth. 9:9

Valley Gate
   Entrance into Jerusalem.............. Neh. 2:13

Valley of dry bones
   Vision of Ezekiel.................. Ezek. 37:1–14

Valley, the King's
   A valley near Jerusalem............Gen. 14:17–20
   Site of Absalom's monument........ 2 Sam. 18:18

Vaniah—*Yahweh is praise*
   Divorced his foreign wife............. Ezra 10:36

Various—*of all kinds*
   Colors ....Ezek. 17:3
   Diseases...........................Luke 4:40
   Doctrines .... Heb. 13:9
   Lusts...............................Titus 3:3
   Miracles .... Heb. 2:4
   Times.............................. Heb. 1:1
   Trials .... James 1:2
   Washings .... Heb. 9:10

Vashti—*beautiful woman*
   Queen of Ahasuerus, deposed and
        divorced...................... Esth. 1:9–22

Veal
   Prepared for King Saul .... 1 Sam. 28:21–25

Vegetables—*plants grown for food*
   Part of God's creation .... Gen. 1:11, 12
   Controversy regarding .... Rom. 14:1–23
   Preferred by Daniel ....Dan. 1:12, 16

Veil, the sacred
A. Features regarding:
   Made by divine command .... Ex. 26:31, 32
   Used to separate the holy and
        Most Holy .... Ex. 26:33
   Means of concealing the divine Person ...Ex. 40:3
   In the temple also.................... 2 Chr. 3:14
   Torn at Christ's death .... Matt. 27:51
B. Entrance through:
   By the high priest alone .... Heb. 9:6, 7
   On Day of Atonement only .... Heb. 9:7
   Taking blood........................ Heb. 9:7
C. Figurative of:
   Old Testament dispensation .... Heb. 9:8
   Christ's flesh ....Heb. 10:20
   Access now into God's presence... Heb. 10:19–22

Veil—*head covering*
A. Literal uses of:
   For modesty........................Gen. 24:65
   For adornment ....Is. 3:19
   To conceal identity................... Gen. 38:14
   To soften the divine glory of God ...Ex. 34:33–35
B. Figurative of:
   Coming of the Lord................... Is. 25:7
   Turning to the Lord...............2 Cor. 3:14–16

Vengeance—*retribution as a punishment*
A. Belonging to God, as:
   Judgment upon sin................Jer. 11:20–23
   Right not to be taken
        by humankind ....Ezek. 25:12–17; Heb. 10:30
   Set time........................... Jer. 46:9, 10
B. Visitation of, by God, at:
   Nation's fall .... Jer. 51:6, 11, 36
   Christ's first coming ....Is. 35:4–10

Jerusalem's destruction..............Luke 21:22
Sodom's destruction ....Jude 7
Christ's return.....................2 Thess. 1:8
See Revenge

Ventriloquism—*appearing to speak from another source*
From the dust .... Is. 29:4

Verdict—*a judicial decision*
Unjustly rendered................ Luke 23:13–26
Pronounced by hypocrites ....John 8:1–11

Vermilion—*a brilliant red color*
Ceiling painted with ....Jer. 22:14

Vessels—*hollow utensils for holding things*
A. Made of:
Wood or stone..........................Ex. 7:19
Gold and silver .... Dan. 5:2
Clay ....Rom. 9:21
Bronze.......................... Ezra 8:27
B. Of the tabernacle:
Under care of Levites............. Num. 3:31, 32
Carried away into Babylon..........2 Chr. 36:18
Belshazzar uses in feast...............Dan. 5:1–4
Returned to Jerusalem .... Ezra 1:7–11
C. Figurative of:
Humankind.................... Rom. 9:21–23
Human weakness................... 2 Cor. 4:7
Believers .... 2 Tim. 2:20, 21
Person's body or wife............... 1 Thess. 4:4
Chosen person........................Acts 9:15

Vex—*to irritate*
Caused by nagging..................Judg. 16:16
See Harass; Distress

Vicarious suffering of Christ
A. Expressed in Old Testament, by:
Types..........................Gen. 22:7, 8, 13
Explicit prophecies......Is. 53:1–12; Acts 8:32–35
B. Expressed in the New Testament, by:
John the Baptist ....John 1:29
Christ Himself .... Mark 10:45
Peter........................... 1 Pet. 1:18, 19
John ....1 John 3:16
Paul ....Gal. 2:20
Hebrews .... Heb. 2:9, 17

Victory—*attaining the mastery over*
A. Of Christ:
Promised.........................Ps. 110:1–7
Accompanied by suffering...........Is. 53:10–12
By resurrection ....Acts 2:29–36
By His return.................... Rev. 19:11–21
B. Of Christians:
Through Christ.................... Phil. 4:13
By the Holy Spirit...........Gal. 5:16, 17, 22, 25
Over:
Flesh............................. Gal. 5:16–21
World.............................1 John 5:4
Satan ....James 4:7

Vigor in old age
Moses at 120 .... Deut. 34:7

Caleb at 85 ....Josh. 14:10–13
Jehoiada at 130 ....2 Chr. 24:15, 16

Vileness—*the state of physical or moral corruption*
Used of:
Something insignificant................ Job 40:4
Human corruption...................Judg. 19:24
See Rotten; Filthy

Village—*a settlement*
Of the Samaritans ....Luke 9:52

Vine, vineyard
A. Features regarding:
Grown by Noah..................... Gen. 9:20
Native of Palestine....................Deut. 6:11
Reaping of, by poor ....2 Kin. 25:12
Fruit of, God's gift ....Ps. 107:37
Pruning of, necessary ....Lev. 25:3, 4
Dead branches burned ....John 15:5, 6
B. Enemies of:
Hail and frost ....Ps. 78:47
Foxes .... Song 2:15
Boars ....Ps. 80:13
Thieves ....Jer. 49:9
Stones ....Is. 5:2
Sloth............................ Prov. 24:30, 31
C. Laws concerning:
Care of, exempts from military
service......................... Deut. 20:6
Diverse seed forbidden in............ Deut. 22:9
Neighbors may eat of............... Deut. 23:24
No cultivation of, during
Sabbatical year.....................Ex. 23:11
Second gathering of, forbidden........Lev. 19:10
New, five years' waiting .... Lev. 19:23–25
Nazirites forbidden to eat of .... Num. 6:3, 4
Rechabites forbidden to plant.........Jer. 35:7–9
Not to be mortgaged .... Neh. 5:3, 4
D. Figurative of:
Jewish nation......................... Is. 5:1–7
Growth in grace .... Hos. 14:7
Purifying afflictions .... John 15:1, 2
Peacefulness.......................1 Kin. 4:25
Worthlessness ....John 15:2, 6
Fruitful wife........................Ps. 128:3
God's kingdom .... Matt. 20:1–16

Vinedresser
Poor made to be ....2 Kin. 25:12

Vinegar—*wine or strong drink fermented*
Figurative of agitation ....Prov. 25:20
Hard on teeth ....Prov. 10:26
Forbidden to Nazirites .... Num. 6:3
Offered to Christ in mockery ....Ps. 69:21

Viper—*a deadly snake*
Figurative of spiritual transformation .....Is. 11:8
Figurative of Dan's treachery .... Gen. 49:17
Jewish leaders compared to ....Matt. 3:7
Paul bitten by.....................Acts 28:3–5

WORD STUDY **VIRGIN,** *betulah* (beth-oo-*law*). *Betulah* is a noun, indicating a "virgin." The word describes a girl who is living in her father's house, generally apart from men. The legal codes include several references to virginity, generally explaining what to do if a girl's virginity is lost: Ex. 22:16; Lev. 21:3, 14; Deut. 22:19. The term also appears in the description of Rebekah in Gen. 24:16. In a number of places, especially in Is. and Jer., a nation is personified as a virgin who is turning away from the correct path. (Strong's #1330)

WORD STUDY **VIRGIN,** *parthenos* (par-*then*-oss). *Parthenos* means "virgin," that is, a chaste woman who has had no intercourse with a man. This noun is used in the Septuagint to translate the Hebrew *'almah,* meaning a "young woman" of marriageable age who, according to Jewish tradition, is not to have had sexual relations prior to marriage (see Luke 1:34; 2:36). Thus, *parthenos* is used in the quotation of the messianic prophecy (Matt. 1:23). Luke uses the term for the Blessed Virgin Mary (1:27) and for the daughters of Philip (Acts 21:9). Paul uses it for "virgins" who are admitted to the office of widows (1 Cor. 7:25f.). In Rev. 14:4 it is used as a masculine substantive to designate a "chaste (or celibate) man." (Strong's #3933)

Virgin—*a woman untouched sexually*
Penalty for seduction of . . . . Deut. 22:28, 29
Parable of ten. Matt. 25:1–13
Specifications regarding. . . . . 1 Cor. 7:28–38
Christ born of . . . . Luke 1:26–35
Figurative of Christians . . . . Rev. 14:4

Virgin conception
Prophesied . . . . Is. 7:14
Christ conceived of Holy Spirit. . . . . . . Matt. 1:18;
　Luke 1:26–35
Born of virgin . . . . Matt. 1:19–25

WORD STUDY **VIRTUE,** *aretē* (ar-*et*-ay). The noun *aretē,* meaning "excellence," is used in the NT only in the sense of "moral excellence" or "virtue" (Phil. 4:8; 2 Pet. 1:3, 5). The meaning of *aretē* in 1 Pet. 2:9 is difficult to ascertain. Given the practice of translating the Hebrew *tehillah* ("praise") with *aretē,* it may mean "praises." However, the later meaning "manifestation of divine power" is equally possible (and perhaps also at 2 Pet. 1:5). (Strong's #703)

WORD STUDY **VISION,** *chazon* (khaw-*zohn*). A "vision," *chazon* is the noun derived from the verb for "to see." Generally the word is used in poetic material. Some visions were those seen in an ecstatic state. Many visions were seen in the night, although they differed from dreams (Mic. 3:6). Visions were a form of divine communication that could be sought. In 1 Chr. 17:15 we read that David received his instructions from God in a vision. Not all visions were to be trusted, some being false, deliberately given to the

people even though there was no message from God (Jer. 14:14). The term "vision" is used in the title of several of the prophetic books: Is., Obad., and Nah. (Strong's #2377)

Visions—*divine revelations*
A. Characteristics of:
　Understandable. . . . . Dan. 7:15–19
　Authenticated by divine glory. . . . . . . Ezek. 8:1–4
　Personal and phenomenal . . . . Dan. 10:7–9
　Prophetic . . . . Dan. 9:23–27
　Dated and localized. . . . . Ezek. 1:1–3
　Causes trembling and dread . . . . Dan. 10:7–17
　Meaning of, interpreted . . . . Dan. 9:21–24
　Absence of, tragic. . . . . Prov. 29:18
　Performances of, sure . . . . Ezek. 12:21–28
　Proof of messianic times. . . . . . . Joel 2:28; Acts 2:17
　Imitated by false prophets . . . . Jer. 14:14
B. Productive of:
　Guidance . . . . Gen. 46:2–5
　Direction . . . . Acts 16:9, 10
　Encouragement. . . . . Acts 18:9, 10
　Warning . . . . Is. 21:2–6
　Judgment . . . . 1 Sam. 3:15–18
　Action for the Lord . . . . Acts 26:19, 20
C. Objects of, revealed in:
　Israel's future. . . . . Gen. 15:1–21
　Succession of world empires . . . . Dan. 7:1–8
　Ram . . . . Dan. 8:1–7, 20
　Expanding river . . . . Ezek. 47:1–12
　Throne of God . . . . Rev. 4:1–11

Visit, visitation—*to go to see a person*
Descriptive of:
　Going to a person. . . . . Acts 15:36
　God's care. . . . . Ps. 65:9
　God's purposed time. . . . . Luke 19:44

Voice of God, the
A. Importance of:
　Must be obeyed. . . . . Gen. 3:1–19
　Disobedience to, judged . . . . Jer. 42:5–22
　Obedience to, the essence of true
　　religion. . . . . 1 Sam. 15:19–24
　Obedience to, rewarded . . . . Gen. 22:6–18
　Sign of the covenant. . . . . Josh. 24:24, 25
B. Heard by:
　Adam. . . . . Gen. 3:9, 10
　Moses. . . . . Ex. 19:19
　Israel . . . . Deut. 5:22–26
　Samuel. . . . . 1 Sam. 3:1–14
　Elijah . . . . 1 Kin. 19:12, 13
　Isaiah . . . . Is. 6:8–10
　Ezekiel. Ezek. 1:24, 25; 2:1
　Christ. . . . . Mark 1:11
　Peter, James, and John. . . . . Matt. 17:1, 5
　Paul . . . . Acts 9:4, 7
　John . . . . Rev. 1:10–15

Vomit—*to discharge with force or violence*
A. Used literally of:
　Dog. . . . . Prov. 26:11

One who eats in excess .... Prov. 25:16
Drunken man .... Is. 19:14
Great fish .... Jon. 2:10
B. Used figuratively of:
    False teaching .... 2 Pet. 2:22
    Judgment .... Jer. 48:25, 26
    Riches .... Job 20:15

Vophsi—*rich*
    Naphtalite spy .... Num. 13:14

Vow—*a voluntary pledge to fulfill an agreement*
A. Objects of one's:
    Life .... Num. 6:1–21
    Children .... 1 Sam. 1:11–28
    Possessions .... Gen. 28:22
    Gifts .... Ps. 76:11
B. Features concerning:
    Must be voluntary .... Deut. 23:21, 22
    Must be uttered .... Deut. 23:23
    Once made, binding .... Eccl. 5:4, 5
    Benefits of, sometimes included ... Gen. 28:20–22
    Invalidity of, specified .... Num. 30:1–16
    Abuse of, condemned .... Matt. 15:4–6
    Rashness in, condemned .... Prov. 20:25
    Perfection in, required .... Lev. 22:18–25
    Wickedness of some .... Jer. 44:25

Voyage—*an extended trip*
    Paul's to Rome .... Acts 27:10

Vulture—*a carrion-eating bird of prey*
    Classed as unclean .... Lev. 11:13, 18

W

Wafers—*thin cakes of flour*
    Often made with honey .... Ex. 16:31
    Used in various offerings .... Ex. 29:2; Lev. 2:4

Wages, hire—*payments for work performed*
A. Principles governing payment of:
    Must be paid promptly .... Deut. 24:14, 15
    Withholding of, forbidden .... James 5:4
B. Paid to such classes as:
    Soldiers .... 2 Sam. 10:6
    Fishermen .... Mark 1:20
    Shepherds .... John 10:12, 13
    Masons and carpenters .... 2 Chr. 24:12
    Farm laborers .... Matt. 20:1–16
    Male prostitutes .... Deut. 23:18
    Wet nurses .... Ex. 2:9
    Ministers .... 1 Cor. 9:4–14
    Teachers .... Gal. 6:6, 7
    Gospel messengers .... Luke 10:7
C. Figurative of:
    Spiritual death .... Rom. 6:23
    Unrighteousness .... 2 Pet. 2:15
    Reward .... John 4:36
See Hire

Wailing—*crying out in constant mourning*
A. Caused by:
    King's decree .... Esth. 4:3
    City's destruction .... Ezek. 27:31, 32
    God's judgment .... Amos 5:16, 17
    Girl's death .... Mark 5:38–42
    Christ's return .... Rev. 1:7
    Hell's torments .... Matt. 13:42, 50
B. Performed by:
    Women .... Jer. 9:17–20
    Prophets .... Mic. 1:8
    Merchants .... Rev. 18:15, 19
See Mourning

Waist
A. Used literally of:
    Hips .... Gen. 37:34; Ex. 28:42
B. Used figuratively of:
    Commitment to spiritual truth .... Eph. 6:14

> **WORD STUDY**   **WAIT,** *qavah* (kaw-*vaw*). The verb *qavah* is translated "wait" and means "to wait hopefully" or "to look eagerly" for something. In Is. 5:7, Is. 59:9, 11, and Jer. 8:15, the prophets warn of a time to come when the people of Israel will look to God for good things, such as blessings and peace. This implies that in the coming time there will be a lack of blessings and peace. In Job and a few of the psalms, *qavah* is used of a person in the middle of unpleasant circumstances who hopes for better times to come (Job 3:9; 6:19). The word can be used to mean "lie in wait for," which implies the intent to do wrong to someone as it does in Ps. 56:6, 7 and 119:95. (Strong's #6960)

Waiting on the Lord
A. Agents of:
    Creatures .... Ps. 145:15
    Creation .... Rom. 8:19, 23
    Gentiles .... Is. 51:5
    Christians .... 1 Cor. 1:7
B. Manner of:
    With the soul .... Ps. 62:1, 5
    With quietness .... Lam. 3:25, 26
    With patience .... Ps. 40:1
    With courage .... Ps. 27:14
    All the day .... Ps. 25:5
    Continually .... Hos. 12:6
    With great hope .... Ps. 130:5, 6
    With crying .... Ps. 69:3
C. Objects of God's:
    Salvation .... Is. 25:9
    Law .... Is. 42:4
    Protection .... Ps. 33:20
    Pardon .... Ps. 39:7, 8
    Food .... Ps. 104:27
    Kingdom .... Mark 15:43
    Holy Spirit .... Acts 1:4
    Son .... 1 Thess. 1:10
D. Blessings attending, described as:
    Spiritual renewal .... Is. 40:31

Not be ashamed . . . . Ps. 69:6

Inherit the land. .Ps. 37:9, 34

Something unusual . . . . Is. 64:4

Unusual blessing. . . . . Luke 12:36, 37

Walk of believers

A. Stated negatively, not:

In darkness. . . . . John 8:12

After the flesh . . . . .Rom. 8:1, 4

As Gentiles. . . . . Eph. 4:17

In craftiness. . . . . 2 Cor. 4:2

In sin . . . . Col. 3:5–7

In disorder . . . . .2 Thess. 3:6, 11

B. Stated positively:

In the light . . . . .1 John 1:7

In the truth . . . . 3 John 3, 4

In Christ. . . . . .Col. 2:6

In the Spirit . . . . Gal. 5:16, 25

In love . . . . Eph. 5:2

As children of light . . . . Eph. 5:8

As Christ walked .1 John 2:6

After His commandments. . . . . .2 John 6

By faith . . . . 2 Cor. 5:7

In good works . . . . Eph. 2:10

Worthy . . . . .Eph. 4:1

Worthy of the Lord . . . . Col. 1:10

Worthy of God . . . . 1 Thess. 2:12

Circumspectly. . . . . .Eph. 5:15

In wisdom. . . . . Col. 4:5

Pleasing God . . . . 1 Thess. 4:1

Wall—*a rampart or partition*

A. Used for:

Shooting arrows from . . . . 2 Sam. 11:24

Observation. . . . . 2 Sam. 18:24

B. Unusual events connected with:

Woman lives on. Josh. 2:15

Jericho's, falls by faith . . . . .Josh. 6:5, 20

Saul's body fastened to . . . . 1 Sam. 31:10, 11

Woman throws stone from . . . . . . 2 Sam. 11:20, 21

27,000 killed by. . . . . .1 Kin. 20:30

Son sacrificed on. . . . . 2 Kin. 3:27

Warning inscribed on . . . . Dan. 5:5, 25–28

Paul escapes through. . . . . Acts 9:25

C. Figurative of:

Defense. . . . . 1 Sam. 25:16

Protection. . . . . .Ezra 9:9

Great power . . . . .Ps. 18:29

Peacefulness. . . . . .Ps. 122:7

Self-sufficiency . . . . Prov. 18:11

Powerlessness .Prov. 25:28

Salvation. . . . . Is. 26:1

God's kingdom . . . . Is. 56:5

Heaven . . . . .Is. 60:18–21

Spiritual leaders . . . . Is. 62:6

God's messengers . . . . Jer. 1:18, 19

Protection. . . . . .Zech. 2:5

Hypocrisy. . . . . Acts 23:3

Ceremonial law. Eph. 2:14

New Jerusalem . . . . Rev. 21:12–19

D. Of Jerusalem:

Built by Solomon . . . . 1 Kin. 3:1

Broken down by Jehoash . . . . .2 Kin. 14:13

Destroyed by Babylonians . . . . .2 Chr. 36:19

Seen at night by Nehemiah . . . . .Neh. 2:12–18

Rebuilt by returnees . . . . Neh. 6:1, 6, 15

Dedication of. . . . . Neh. 12:27–47

Wallow—*to roll about in an ungainly manner*

In:

Blood . . . . 2 Sam. 20:12

Vomit. . . . . Jer. 48:26

Ashes . . . . Jer. 6:26

Mire . . . . 2 Pet. 2:22

On the ground. . . . . Mark 9:20

Wandering—*roaming about*

A. Descriptive of:

Hagar's travels. Gen. 21:14

Israel's wilderness travels . . . . Num. 32:13

God's pilgrims. . . . . .Heb. 11:37, 38

Captivity. . . . . Hos. 9:17

Joseph in the field. . . . . Gen. 37:15

Early saints. . . . . Heb. 11:38

B. Figurative of:

Apostasy. . . . . Ps. 119:10

Dissatisfaction .Prov. 27:8

Hopelessness . . . . Jude 13

Wanderer—*one who moves about aimlessly*

Curse on Cain .Gen. 4:12, 14

Curse on the wicked . . . . .Ps. 109:10

Professional exorcists called . . . . Acts 19:13

Want—*to lack*

A. Caused by:

Hastiness . . . . .Prov. 21:5

Greed. . . . . .Prov. 22:16

Sloth. . . . . Prov. 24:30–34

Debauchery . . . . Dan. 5:27

B. Provision against, by:

Trusting the Lord. . . . . Ps. 23:1

God's plan . . . . .Jer. 33:17, 18

See Lack

Wantonness—*lustful behavior*

In suggestive movements . . . . .Is. 3:16

Characteristic of doctrinal laxity. . . . . . .2 Pet. 2:18

Unbecoming to a Christian . . . . .Rom. 13:13

War—*armed conflict between nations*

A. Caused by:

Sin. . . . . James 4:1, 2

God's judgments. . . . . 2 Sam. 12:10

God's decree . . . . Ex. 17:16

B. Regulations concerning:

Consultation of:

Urim . . . . 1 Sam. 28:6

Ephod . . . . 1 Sam. 30:7, 8

Prophets . . . . 1 Kin. 22:7–28

Troops mustered. . . . . .Judg. 3:27

Some dismissed. . . . . .Deut. 20:5–8

Spies dispatched . . . . Num. 13:17

WORD
STUDY

WAY, *derek* (deh-*rek*). The noun *derek* can mean "way," "road," "journey," or "manner." There are many places where the term indicates a road or path. In Gen. 16:7, after Hagar fled from Sarai, the angel of the Lord found her on the way to Shur. In 1 Sam. 15:18 the term means "mission" or "journey." *Derek* can mean "in the direction of" or "toward," and the people are told to pray "toward the city" (2 Chr. 6:34). Amos 4:10 uses the term to mean "in the manner or habit" of the Egyptians. "Ways" can be the undertakings of life; the disobedient ones are told that their ways will not prosper (Deut. 28:29). "Ways" can also be moral actions, especially those commanded by the Lord. In a positive context, Samuel is going to teach the people "the good and the right way" (1 Sam. 12:23). More often, the people are seen clinging to their stubborn ways, which include following other gods. (Strong's #1870)

Walk in .... Deut. 8:6
Remember ....Deut. 8:2
Know................................. Ps. 67:2
Teach to transgressors.................. Ps. 51:13
Rejoice in .... Ps. 119:14

B. God's attitude toward, He:

Knows................................ Ps. 1:6
Is acquainted with .... Ps. 139:3
Delights in ....Ps. 37:23
Leads us in ....Ps. 139:24
Teaches.............................Ps. 25:9, 12
Makes known .... Ps. 103:7
Makes perfect .... Ps. 18:32
Blesses..............................Prov. 8:32

C. With reference to our way:

Acknowledge Him in.................. Prov. 3:6
Commit to the Lord.................... Ps. 37:5
Makes prosperous .... Josh. 1:8
All before God. ....Ps. 119:168
Teach me............................Ps. 143:8

Ways of humankind

Described as:

Perverse before God .... Num. 22:32
Hard................................Prov. 13:15
Abomination....................... Prov. 15:9
Not good..........................Prov. 16:29
Dark................................ Prov. 2:13

Weak, weakness

A. Kinds of:

Political............................2 Sam. 3:1
Physical.............. Judg. 16:7, 17; 2 Cor. 11:30
Spiritual .... Is. 35:3
Moral...................2 Sam. 3:39; Rom. 8:26

B. Caused by:

Fasting..............................Ps. 109:24
Discouragement .... Neh. 6:9
Sin............................ 1 Cor. 11:26–30
Discouraging preaching................ Jer. 38:4
Conscientious doubts .... Rom. 14:1–23

C. Victory over, by:

Christ............................2 Cor. 13:3, 4
Grace..........................2 Cor. 12:9, 10
Faith.............................Heb. 11:33, 34

D. Our duty toward, to:

Bear ....Rom. 15:1
Support..................Acts 20:35; 1 Cor. 9:22
Not become a stumbling block .... 1 Cor. 8:9

E. Our duties with reference to:

Pleasure in ....2 Cor. 12:10
Help those afflicted with ....Rom. 15:1

WORD STUDY **WEALTH,** *mammōnas* (mahm-moh-*noss*). This noun is the Greek transliteration of the Aramaic word meaning "wealth," "property." Jesus contrasts "unrighteous wealth" to "genuine" or "true" wealth (Luke 16:9, 11) and then personifies "mammon" as a rival god (Luke 16:13; cf. Matt. 6:24). (Strong's #3126)

Wealth—*riches*

A. Descriptive of:

Material possessions ....Gen. 34:29

B. Advantages of:

Given by God..................... Deut. 8:18, 19
Source of security.................... Prov. 18:11
Adds friends ....Prov. 19:4

C. Disadvantages of:

Produces self-sufficiency ....Deut. 8:17
Leads to conceit ....Job 31:25
Subject to loss ....Prov. 13:11
Lost by dissipation................. Prov. 5:8–10
Cannot save..........................Ps. 49:6, 7
Must be left to others.................. Ps. 49:10

See Riches, earthly

Wean—*to accustom a child to independence from the mother's milk*

Celebrated .... Gen. 21:8
Figurative of spiritual rest .... Ps. 131:2

Weapons, spiritual

Against:

World—faith..........................1 John 5:4
Satan—armor of God .... Eph. 6:11–17
Flesh—the Spirit.................... Gal. 5:16–25

Weary—*to become tired*

A. Caused by:

Journeys .... John 4:6
Ritualism ....Is. 1:14
Study .... Eccl. 12:12
Anxiety........................... Gen. 27:46
Words .... Mal. 2:17
Not speaking......................... Jer. 20:9
Too frequent visits .... Prov. 25:17

B. Overcome by:

Waiting on the Lord ....Is. 40:30, 31
Appropriate word..................... Is. 50:4
God's promise........................ Is. 28:12
Persevering faith......................Gal. 6:9
Promised ruler........................ Is. 32:1, 2
Looking to Jesus....................Heb. 12:2, 3

Weather

Proverb concerning .... Job 37:9–11
Under divine control............ 1 Sam. 12:16–19
Signs of .... Luke 12:54–57

Weaving—*uniting threads to produce cloth*

Men endowed in art of ....Ex. 35:35
Performed by worthy woman ......Prov. 31:13, 19
Figurative of life's shortness ....Job 7:6

See Spinning

Wedding (see Marriage)

Wedge of gold

Stolen by Achan ....Josh. 7:20, 21

Weeds

Wrapped around Jonah's head .... Jon. 2:5

Week—*seven days*

Origin of, early .... Gen. 2:1–3

Used in dating events . . . . Gen. 7:4, 10
One, length of mourning . . . . Gen. 50:10
Part of ceremonial law. . . . . Ex. 13:6, 7
Seventy, prophecy of . . . . Dan. 9:24
Christ arose on first day of. . . . . Matt. 28:1
Christians worship on first day of . . . . . Acts 20:7;
    1 Cor. 16:2
    See Pentecost

Weeks of years
Seven . . . . Lev. 25:8
Seventy . . . . Jer. 25:11; Dan. 9:2

Weeping—*intense crying*
A. Kinds of:
Rebellious. . . . . Num. 11:4–20
Hypocritical. Judg. 14:16, 17
Sincere. . . . . 1 Sam. 20:41
Exhausting. . . . . 1 Sam. 30:4
Secret. . . . . Jer. 13:17
Permanent . . . . Matt. 8:12
Bitter . . . . Matt. 26:75
Divine . . . . John 11:35
Sympathetic. . . . . Rom. 12:15
B. Caused by:
Despair . . . . Gen. 21:16
Death. . . . . Gen. 50:1
Love . . . . Gen. 29:11
Joy of reunion . . . . Gen. 33:4
Loss of child. . . . . Gen. 37:35
Restraint of joy . . . . Gen. 42:24
Hearing God's Word. . . . . Neh. 8:9
C. Cessation of:
After a child's death. . . . . 2 Sam. 12:21–23
In the morning . . . . Ps. 30:5
In eternity . . . . Is. 65:19
After seeing the Lord. . . . . John 20:11–18

Weights and measures
A. Monies of the Bible:
Bekah. . . . . Ex. 38:26
Gerahs. . . . . Ex. 30:13
Mite . . . . Mark 12:42
Denarii . . . . Matt. 18:28
Daric . . . . 1 Chr. 29:7
Drachma. . . . . Ezra 2:69
Pieces of silver. . . . . Matt. 26:15
Shekel . . . . Ex. 30:24
Shekels of gold. . . . . 1 Chr. 21:25
Shekels of silver. . . . . 2 Sam. 24:24
Silver . . . . 2 Chr. 21:3
Talents. . . . . Matt. 18:24
Talents of bronze . . . . 1 Chr. 29:7
Talents of gold. . . . . 1 Chr. 29:4
Talents of iron. . . . . 1 Chr. 29:7
Talents of silver. . . . . 1 Chr. 29:4
B. Distance or length measurements:
Acre . . . . 1 Sam. 14:14
Cubit . . . . Gen. 6:15
Fathom . . . . Acts 27:28
Finger . . . . Jer. 52:21
Miles . . . . Luke 24:13

Hand-breadth . . . . Ex. 25:25
Measuring rod. . . . . Ezek. 40:3
Pace . . . . 2 Sam. 6:13
Span. . . . . Ex. 28:16
Sabbath day's journey . . . . Acts 1:12
C. Liquid measures:
Bath . . . . 1 Kin. 7:26
Kor. . . . . Ezek. 45:14
Gallons . . . . John 2:6
Hin. . . . . Ex. 29:40
Homer. . . . . Ezek. 45:11
Kab. . . . . 2 Kin. 6:25
Log . . . . Lev. 14:10
D. Dry measures:
Kab. . . . . 2 Kin. 6:25
Ephah . . . . Ex. 16:36
Homer. . . . . Lev. 27:16
Log . . . . Lev. 14:10
Omer . . . . Ex. 16:16
Gerah. . . . . Ex. 30:13
Mina . . . . 1 Kin. 10:17
E. Weight measures:
Beka. . . . . Ex. 38:26
Shekel . . . . 2 Sam. 14:26
Talents. . . . . Ex. 38:27

Welcome—*to receive with gladness*
A. Extended to:
Returning brother . . . . Gen. 33:1–11
Father . . . . Gen. 46:29–34
Hero. . . . . 1 Sam. 18:6, 7
Prodigal son. Luke 15:20–32
Messiah. . . . . Matt. 21:6–10
B. Circumstances attending:
Courtesies offered . . . . Gen. 18:1–8
Discourtesies shown . . . . 2 Sam. 10:1–5
Fear expressed. . . . . 1 Sam. 16:4, 5
Fellowship denied . . . . 2 John 10, 11

Wells—*pits dug for water*
A. Features concerning:
Women come to, for water. . . . . Gen. 24:13, 14;
    John 4:7
Surrounded by trees. . . . . Gen. 49:22
Often very deep . . . . John 4:11
Covered with large stone . . . . Gen. 29:2, 3
Sometimes cause strife . . . . Gen. 21:25
B. Names of:
Beer . . . . Num. 21:16–18
Beer Lahai Roi. Gen. 16:14
Beersheba . . . . Gen. 21:30, 31
Bene Jaakan . . . . Deut. 10:6
Esek . . . . Gen. 26:20
Jacob . . . . John 4:6
Rehoboth . . . . Gen. 26:22
Sitnah . . . . Gen. 26:21
C. Figurative of:
Salvation. . . . . Is. 12:3
False teaching . . . . 2 Pet. 2:17
One's wife. . . . . Prov. 5:15
The Holy Spirit. John 4:10

Whale

    Created by God . . . . Gen. 1:21
    See Great fish

Wheat—*a cereal grass used for food*
A. Features concerning:
    Grown in Egypt . . . . .Ex. 9:32
    Grown in Palestine . . . . 1 Kin. 5:11
    Made into bread . . . . .Ex. 29:2
    Used in trade . . . . .Ezek. 27:17
    Harvested . . . . .Ruth 2:23
    Threshed . . . . .Judg. 6:11
    Gathered . . . . Matt. 3:12
    Harvesting of, celebrated . . . . Ex. 34:22
B. Figurative of:
    Spiritual blessings . . . . Ps. 81:16
    Christians . . . . Matt. 3:12
    Christ's death . . . . .John 12:24
    Resurrection . . . . 1 Cor. 15:37

Wheel—*a circular frame*
A. Used on:
    Carts . . . . Is. 28:27, 28
    Threshing instrument . . . . .Prov. 20:26
    Chariots . . . . Nah. 3:2
    The Lord's throne . . . . Ezek. 10:1–22
B. Figurative of:
    Future things . . . . Ezek. 1:15–28
    Punishment . . . . .Prov. 20:26
    Cycle of nature ("course") . . . . James 3:6
    God's sovereignty . . . . Ezek. 10:9–19

Whelp—*offspring of certain animals*
Figurative of:
    Judah . . . . Gen. 49:9
    Dan . . . . Deut. 33:22
    Babylonians . . . . .Jer. 51:38

Whirlwind—*a great storm or tempest*
A. Used literally of:
    Elijah's translation . . . . 2 Kin. 2:1
    Its fury . . . . .Is. 17:13
B. Used figuratively of:
    Sudden destruction . . . . Prov. 1:27
    God's anger . . . . .Jer. 23:19
    God's might . . . . Nah. 1:3

Whisperer—*a gossiper*
    Separates chief friends . . . . .Prov. 16:28

Whistle—*meaning to call, allure, or entice*
Applied to:
    Nations . . . . Is. 5:26
    Egypt and Assyria .Is. 7:18
    Israel . . . . Zech. 10:8

White (see Colors)

> **WORD STUDY**
>
> **WICKED,** *rasha'* (raw-*shaw*). The adjective usually translated "wicked," is the word *rasha'*. The term normally describes one guilty of crime, the opposite of righteous. *Rasha'* is used this way in many passages, including Ex. 2:13, Deut. 25:2, and Prov. 17:23. Frequently the wicked

person is guilty of hostility to God or toward God's people, so that there are "wicked" enemies rather than just enemies. Specific uses of the term are applied to Pharaoh (Ex. 9:27), Babylon (Is. 13:11), and the Chaldeans (Hab. 1:4). The term can also mean one who is guilty of a sin as it does in Num. 16:26 and in Mal. 3:18 where the sin involved is not serving the Lord. This meaning is rare in the earliest preexilic literature and appears mainly in Ps., Ezek., and the wisdom literature. (Strong's #7563)

Wicked, the
A. Satan as "the Wicked One":
    Unregenerate belong to . . . . Matt. 13:38
    Snatches away the good seed . . . . Matt. 13:19
    World lies in . . . . .1 John 5:19
    Christians can overcome . . .Eph. 6:16; 1 John 2:13
B. Descriptive of:
    Sodomites . . . . Gen. 13:13
    Egyptians . . . . .Ex. 9:27
    Athaliah . . . . .2 Chr. 24:7
    Haman . . . . Esth. 7:6
    Apostates . . . . 1 Cor. 5:13
    Pharisees . . . . .Matt. 22:15–18
C. State of, described as:
    Desiring evil . . . . .Prov. 21:10
    Having no peace . . . . Is. 48:22
    Pouring out evil . . . . .Prov. 15:28
    Refusing judgment . . . . Prov. 21:7
    Cruel in their mercies . . . . .Prov. 12:10
    Like the troubled sea . . . . Is. 57:20
    Far from God . . . . .Prov. 15:29
    Offering abominable sacrifice . . . . Prov. 15:8
    Way is like darkness . . . . Prov. 4:19
    Forsaking the law . . . . .Prov. 28:4
D. God's attitude toward:
    Sorry He made humankind . . . . Gen. 6:5, 6
    Will not justify . . . . .Ex. 23:7
    Will punish . . . . Ps. 75:8
    Will overthrow . . . . Prov. 21:12
    Their thoughts abominable to . . . . . . .Prov. 15:26
    God hates . . . . Ps. 11:5
E. Punishment of:
    Shortened life . . . . .Prov. 10:27
    Soon destroyed . . . . .Ps. 37:35, 36
    Driven away . . . . .Prov. 14:32
    Slain by evil . . . . .Ps. 34:21
    His lamp put out .Job 21:17
    His triumph short . . . . Ps. 37:10
    His name put out forever . . . . Ps. 9:5
    Silent in the grave . . . . Ps. 31:17
    God rains fire on . . . . Ps. 11:6
    Cast into hell . . . . .Ps. 9:17
    Consumed . . . . Ps. 37:20
    Will die . . . . Prov. 11:7
    In the resurrection, judgment . . . . Acts 24:15
F. Attitude of believers toward:
    Wonder about their prosperity . . . . .Ps. 73:3
    Concerned about their triumph . . . . . . .Ps. 94:3, 4
    Will not sit with . . . . Ps. 26:5

Must not envy . . . . .Prov. 24:19
Will triumph over . . . . Ps. 58:10

Wickedness—*all forms of evil*
A. Humankind's relationship to:
Not profited by . . . . .Prov. 10:2
Not established by .Prov. 12:3
Sells self to . . . . 1 Kin. 21:25
Strengthens self in . . . . Ps. 52:7
Refuses to turn from . . . . Jer. 44:5
Inside humankind . . . . Luke 11:39
Among all. . . . . Jer. 44:9
Will fall by . . . . Prov. 11:5
Driven away. . . . . .Prov. 14:32
B. God's punishment of, seen in:
Driving out other nations. . . . . Deut. 9:4, 5
Shiloh's destruction. . . . . .Jer. 7:12
Judah's punishment. . . . . .Jer. 1:16
Destruction of food supply . . . . Ps. 107:33, 34
Causing the Flood . . . . .Gen. 6:5–7
Death of men. . . . . .Judg. 9:56
Destroying the evildoers . . . . .Ps. 94:23
C. Attitude of the righteous toward:
Wash from heart. .Jer. 4:14
Struggle against . . . . Eph. 6:12
Fear to commit . . . . Gen. 39:9
Not to dwell in. . . . . .Ps. 84:10
Pray for end of. . . . . Ps. 7:9
Confession of. . . . . 1 Kin. 8:47

Wick-trimmers
Used for trimming wicks in lamps. . . . . . .Ex. 37:23
Trays used to catch snuff of lamps. . . . . . .Ex. 25:38

Widow—*a woman who has outlived her husband*
A. Provision of, for:
Remarriage. . . . . .Rom. 7:3
Food. . . . . .Deut. 24:19–21
Protection. . . . . Is. 1:17, 23
Vows of . . . . Num. 30:9
Garment . . . . Deut. 24:17
B. Mistreatment of, by:
Children . . . . .1 Tim. 5:4
Neglect . . . . .Acts 6:1
Scribes. . . . . Mark 12:40
Creditors. . . . . 2 Kin. 4:1
Princes. . . . . Is. 1:23
Judges . . . . Is. 10:1, 2
C. Protection of, by:
God . . . . .Ex. 22:22–24
Law. . . . . Deut. 24:17
Pure religion . . . . .James 1:27
Honor . . . . .1 Tim. 5:3
D. Examples of:
Naomi . . . . .Ruth 1:20, 21
Woman of Tekoa . . . . 2 Sam. 14:4, 5
Woman of Zarephath . . . . 1 Kin. 17:9, 10
Anna . . . . .Luke 2:36, 37
"A certain poor widow" . . . . .Luke 21:2, 3
"A persistent widow". . . . . Luke 18:2–5

Wife—*a married woman*
A. Described as:
"A helper comparable to him". . . . . . .Gen. 2:18, 20
"The crown of her husband". . . . . .Prov. 12:4
"A good thing". .Prov. 18:22
"The weaker vessel". . . . . .1 Pet. 3:7
"The wife of your youth". . . . . Mal. 2:14, 15
"Your companion" . . . . Mal. 2:14
B. Duties of, to:
Submit to husband. . . . . 1 Pet. 3:5, 6
Reverence her husband. . . . . Eph. 5:33
Love her husband. . . . . .Titus 2:4
Learn from her husband. . . . . 1 Cor. 14:34, 35
Be trustworthy .Prov. 31:11, 12
Love her children . . . . .Titus 2:4
Be chaste. . . . . .Titus 2:5
Be homemakers. . . . . .Titus 2:5
C. Duties of husband toward, to:
Love . . . . Eph. 5:25, 28
Honor . . . . .1 Pet. 3:7
Provide for . . . . .1 Tim. 5:8
Instruct. . . . . 1 Cor. 14:35
Protect. . . . . 1 Sam. 30:1–19
Not divorce . . . . 1 Cor. 7:11
D. Relationship with her husband, to be:
Exclusive. . . . . Prov. 5:15–17, 20
Satisfying . . . . .Prov. 5:18, 19
Mutually agreeable . . . . 1 Cor. 7:1–5
Undefiled . . . . Heb. 13:4
E. Special temptations of:
Disobedience. . . . . .Gen. 3:1–19
Unfaithfulness . . . . John 4:17, 18
Contentiousness . . . . .Prov. 19:13
F. Types of:
Disobedient—Eve . . . . .Gen. 3:1–8
Obedient—Sarah . . . . 1 Pet. 3:5, 6
Worldly—Lot's . . . . .Gen. 19:26
Humble—Manoah's . . . . Judg. 13:22, 23
Prayerful—Hannah. . . . . 1 Sam. 1:1–15
Prudent—Abigail. . . . . .1 Sam. 25:3, 14–35
Criticizing—Michal . . . . 2 Sam. 6:15, 16
Unscrupulous—Jezebel . . . . .1 Kin. 21:5–15
Modest—Vashti . . . . .Esth. 1:11, 12
Courageous—Esther. . . . . .Esth. 4:16, 17
Foolish—Job's wife . . . . Job 2:7–10
Cruel—Herodias . . . . .Matt. 14:3–12
Righteous—Elizabeth. . . . . .Luke 1:5, 6
Lying—Sapphira. . . . . Acts 5:1–10

Wilderness—*a desolate place*
A. Descriptive of:
Israel's wanderings. . . . . .Ex. 16:1
Desolate place . . . . Matt. 3:1, 3
Desolation . . . . Jer. 22:6
B. Characterized by:
Wild creatures. . . . . .Deut. 8:15
No water. . . . . .Deut. 8:15
Being "great and terrible". . . . . .Deut. 1:19
Being uninhabited . . . . .Ps. 107:4, 5

C. Israel's journey in, characterized by:

God's provision.........................Deut. 2:7

God's guidance.........................Ps. 78:52

God's mighty acts.....................Ps. 78:15, 16

Israel's provoking God ....Ps. 78:17–19, 40

Israel's sin..............................Heb. 3:7–19

Testings.................................Deut. 8:2

D. Significant events in:

Hagar's flight ....Gen. 16:6–8

Israel's journeys ....Ps. 136:16

John's preaching ....Matt. 3:1–12

Jesus' temptation ....Matt. 4:1

Jesus' miracle....................Matt. 15:33–38

Moses' serpent........................John 3:14

Wild ox

Of great strength ....Num. 23:22

Very wild and ferocious ....Job 39:9–12

Frisky in youth ....Ps. 29:6

Willingness

A. On God's part, to:

Exercise mercy....................2 Kin. 8:18, 19

Rule sovereignly ....Dan. 4:17

Save humankind...........1 Tim. 2:4; 2 Pet. 3:9

B. On Christ's part, to:

Do God's will.......................Heb. 10:7, 9

Submit to the Father ....John 8:28, 29

Reveal the Father ....Matt. 11:27

Heal people ....Matt. 8:2, 3

Die ....Mark 14:36

C. On humankind's part, to:

Do Satan's will......................John 8:44

Refuse salvation ....John 5:40

Pervert the truth.......................2 Pet. 3:5

Follow evil ....Mark 15:15

Persecute the righteous..............Matt. 2:13

D. On the believer's part, to:

Be saved...........................Rev. 22:17

Follow Christ......................Matt. 16:24

Live godly.........................2 Tim. 3:12

Give ....2 Cor. 8:3–12

Die ....2 Cor. 5:8

Will of God

A. Defined in terms of:

Salvation............................2 Pet. 3:9

Salvation of children ....Matt. 18:14

Belief in Christ ....Matt. 12:50

Everlasting life ....John 6:39, 40

Thanksgiving ....1 Thess. 5:18

Sanctification ....1 Thess. 4:3

B. Characteristics of:

Can be:

Known...............................Rom. 2:18

Proved..............................Rom. 12:2

Done .... Matt. 6:10

Sovereign over:

Nations ....Dan. 4:35

Individuals.........................Acts 21:14

C. God's power in doing, seen in:

Predestination....................Rom. 9:18–23

Sovereignty ....Dan. 4:35

Humankind's salvation ....1 Tim. 2:4

Believer's salvation....................James 1:18

Redemption...........................Gal. 1:4

D. Believer's relationship to, seen in:

Calling..............................1 Cor. 1:1

Regeneration ....James 1:18

Sanctification ....Heb. 10:10

Transformation......................Rom. 12:2

Instruction..........................Ps. 143:10

Prayers.............................1 John 5:14

Submission..........................Acts 21:14

Whole life............................1 Pet. 4:2

Daily work ....Eph. 6:6

Travels...............................Rom. 1:10

Plans ....James 4:13–15

Suffering............................1 Pet. 3:17

Perfection............................Col. 4:12

Will, human (see Freedom; Liberty, spiritual)

Willow—*a tree*

Booths made of..................Lev. 23:40, 42

Grows beside brooks ....Job 40:22

Harps hung on ....Ps. 137:2

See Poplar tree

WORD STUDY   **WIND, SPIRIT,** *pneuma* (*pnyoo*-mah). Noun meaning "blowing," "breathing," and thus "wind," as well as "the breathing out of air," "blowing," "breath," and thus "(life-)spirit," "soul." The NT uses the word in a variety of ways. *Pneuma* can refer to: the "life-spirit" that animates the human body (Matt. 27:50; Luke 8:55); the "spirit" as the immaterial part of human personality, in contrast to the "flesh," *sarx* (2 Cor. 7:1); the seat of human insight, feeling, and will (Mark 8:12); or independent and immaterial beings, such as evil "spirits" (Matt. 12:43). However, the most frequent use of *pneuma* in the NT is with reference to the Divine Spirit as the "Spirit of God" (1 Cor. 2:11) or "the Lord" (Luke 4:18). This Spirit is called the "Holy Spirit" (Matt. 12:32) because of His heavenly origin and divine nature. (Strong's #4151)

Wind—*movement of the air*

A. Characteristics of:

Movement of, significant.........Luke 12:54, 55

Cannot be seen ....John 3:8

Sometimes destructive ....Job 1:19

Dries the earth ....Gen. 8:1

Often accompanies rain ....1 Kin. 18:44, 45

Makes sea rough......................Ps. 107:25

Drives ships ....Acts 27:7, 13–18

Drives chaff away ....Ps. 1:4

Possesses weight......................Job 28:25

B. God's relation to, He:

Creates ....Amos 4:13

Sends ....Ps. 147:18

Brings out of His treasures............Ps. 135:7
Gathers.............................Prov. 30:4
Controls.............................Ps. 107:25

C. Directions of, from:
East ....Jer. 18:17
West................................Ex. 10:19
North...............................Prov. 25:23
South ....Acts 27:13
All directions.......................Ezek. 37:9

D. Miracles connected with:
Flood subsided by....................Gen. 8:1
Locust brought and taken by........Ex. 10:13, 19
Red Sea divided by...................Ex. 14:21
Quail brought by ....Num. 11:31
Rain brought by .... 1 Kin. 18:44, 45
Mountains broken by ....1 Kin. 19:11
Jonah's ship tossed by ....Jon. 1:4
Christ calms.......................Matt. 8:26

E. Figurative of:
Empty speech ....Job 8:2
Empty boasting.....................Prov. 25:14
Vanity ....Eccl. 5:16
Calamity............................Is. 32:2
God's discipline ....Hos. 13:15
God's judgment......................Jer. 22:22
Dispersion ....Ezek. 5:10
Ruin................................Hos. 8:7
Holy Spirit ....Acts 2:2
False teaching ....Eph. 4:14

Windows of heaven
Descriptive of:
Judgment rendered "opened" ....Gen. 7:11
Unbelief ....2 Kin. 7:2, 19
Blessings ....Mal. 3:10

Wine
A. Kinds of:
New ....Luke 5:37–39
Old................................Luke 5:39
Fermented ....Num. 6:3
Refined ....Is. 25:6

B. Features concerning:
Made from grapes....................Gen. 40:11
Mixed ....Prov. 23:30
Kept in bottles......................Jer. 13:12
Kept in wineskins....................Matt. 9:17

C. Used by:
Noah ....Gen. 9:20, 21
Melchizedek ....Gen. 14:18
Isaac...............................Gen. 27:25
Esther ....Esth. 5:6
Jesus.............................John 2:1–11
Timothy ....1 Tim. 5:23

D. Uses of, as:
Offering ....Lev. 23:13
Drink..............................Gen. 27:25
Festive drink ....Esth. 1:7
Disinfectant........................Luke 10:34
Drug .... Mark 15:23
Medicine..........................1 Tim. 5:23

E. Evil effects of:
Leads to violence ....Prov. 4:17
Mocks a person......................Prov. 20:1
Makes poor .... Prov. 23:20, 21
Bites like a serpent ....Prov. 23:31, 32
Impairs the judgment ....Prov. 31:4, 5
Inflames the passions ....Is. 5:11
Enslaves the heart...................Hos. 4:11

F. Intoxication from, falsely charged to:
Hannah........................1 Sam. 1:12–16
Jesus..............................Matt. 11:19
Apostles ....Acts 2:13

G. Uses of, in:
Offering ....Num. 15:4–10
Miracle ....John 2:1–10
Lord's Supper....................Matt. 26:27–29

H. Figurative of:
God's wrath .... Ps. 75:8
Wisdom's blessings ....Prov. 9:2, 5
Gospel..............................Is. 55:1
Christ's blood ....Matt. 26:27–29
Fornication.........................Rev. 17:2

See Drunkenness; Temperance

Winepress—*a machine for extracting the juice from grapes*
Used literally .... Neh. 13:15
Figurative of appointed time........... Joel 3:13

Wings—*the locomotive appendages on flying creatures*
A. Used literally of:
Flying creatures .... Gen. 1:21
Cherubim........................... Ex. 25:20

B. Used figuratively of:
God's mercy......................... Ps. 57:1
Protection........................Luke 13:34
Place of rejoicing................... Ps. 63:7
Strength .... Is. 40:31
Healing............................ Mal. 4:2

Winking the eye
Hate............................... Ps. 35:19
Evil..............................Prov. 6:12, 13

Winnow—*to toss about*
A. Used literally of:
Fork for winnowing grain .... Is. 30:24

B. Used figuratively of judgments:
God's............................. Is. 30:24
Nation's............................Jer. 51:2
Christ's .... Matt. 3:12

Winter—*the coldest season of the year*
Made by God......................... Ps. 74:17
Continuance of, guaranteed .... Gen. 8:22
Time of snow .... 2 Sam. 23:20
Hazards of travel during............. 2 Tim. 4:21

WORD STUDY | **WIPE AWAY, ERASE,** *exaleiphō* (eks-al-*eye*-foh). Verb meaning "to wipe away" or "to wipe out," "to erase." *Exaleiphō* is used metaphorically by the author of Rev. in an image depicting the end of human sorrow (tears are "wiped away"; 7:17; 21:4). It is also used to describe the practice of "wiping away" or "erasing" the writing in a document, such as names "from the Book of Life" (Rev. 3:5). *Exaleiphō* can also carry the sense "to remove," "to destroy," "to obliterate," "to blot out" a written record, which voids its effects. This is the meaning of *exaleiphō* with reference to the sins of humans who repent (Acts 3:19; cf. Col. 2:14). (Strong's #1813)

Wipe—*to clean or dry*

A. Used literally of:

Dust removal	Luke 10:11
Feet dried	John 13:5

B. Used figuratively of:

Jerusalem's destruction	2 Kin. 21:13
Tears removed	Rev. 7:17

WORD STUDY **WISDOM,** *chokmah* (khohk-*maw*). "Wisdom" is the usual translation of the noun *chokmah*. The word can indicate skill in war or in technical work. Wisdom can be seen in a person's administration. Solomon's wisdom included this ability to administer well. In Is. 11:2 the prophet states that the Messiah will have this ability. Wisdom is also shrewdness. In a rather humorous passage, Job 39:17 says that God deprived the ostrich of wisdom. Wisdom is most often seen in the OT in ethical and religious terms. Wisdom is an attribute of God and is sometimes personified and seen as acting in cre-ation (Prov. 8:22–31). For humans the fundamental property of wisdom is a fear of God. This wisdom is something to be sought from God. There are many passages in Job and Prov., as well as a few in Ps., where this use may be seen. (Strong's #2451)

WORD STUDY **WISDOM,** *sophia* (sof-*ee*-ah). Noun meaning "wisdom," commonly used in the NT to refer to an intellectual or spiritual faculty of discernment, insight, understanding, or judgment. Jesus manifests "wisdom" (Matt. 13:54; Mark 6:2), even as a child (Luke 2:40, 52). God's "wisdom" is revealed in His creation (1 Cor. 1:21) and in His designs for the salvation of His creatures (Rom. 11:33; Eph. 3:10, 11). Christ indeed is "the wisdom of God" (1 Cor. 1:24, 30). Earthly or natural "wisdom" is contrasted to the "wisdom" God imparts (1 Cor. 1:17–20), which is a spiritual gift (12:8). (Strong's #4678)

Wisdom—*knowledge guided by understanding*

A. Sources of, in:

The Spirit	Ex. 31:3
The Lord	Ex. 36:1, 2
God's Law	Deut. 4:6
Fear of the Lord	Prov. 9:10
The righteous	Prov. 10:31

B. Ascribed to:

Workmen	Ex. 36:2
Women	Prov. 31:26
Bezalel	Ex. 31:2–5
Joseph	Acts 7:9, 10

Moses	Acts 7:22
Joshua	Deut. 34:9
Huram (Hiram)	1 Kin. 7:13, 14
Solomon	1 Kin. 3:16–28
Children of Issachar	1 Chr. 12:32
Ezra	Ezra 7:25
Daniel	Dan. 1:17
Magi	Matt. 2:1–12
Jesus	Luke 2:52
Stephen	Acts 6:3, 10
Paul	2 Pet. 3:15

C. Described as:

Discerning	Gen. 41:33
Technical skill	Ex. 28:3
Common sense	2 Sam. 20:14–22
Mechanical skill	1 Kin. 7:14
Understanding	Prov. 10:13, 23
Military ability	Is. 10:13
Commercial industry	Ezek. 28:3–5

D. Value of:

Gives happiness	Prov. 3:13
Benefits of, many	Prov. 4:5–10
Keeps from evil	Prov. 5:1–6
Better than rubies	Prov. 8:11
Above gold in value	Prov. 16:16
Should be acquired	Prov. 23:23
Excels folly	Eccl. 2:13
Gives life	Eccl. 7:12
Makes strong	Eccl. 7:19
Better than weapons	Eccl. 9:18
Insures stability	Is. 33:6
Produces good fruit	James 3:17

E. Limitations of:

Cannot save us	1 Cor. 1:19–21
Cause of self-glory	Jer. 9:23
Can pervert	Is. 47:10
Nothing, without God	Jer. 8:9
Can corrupt	Ezek. 28:17
Of this world, foolishness	1 Cor. 3:19
Earthly, sensual	James 3:15
Gospel not preached in	1 Cor. 2:1–5

F. Of believers:

Given by Christ	Luke 21:15
Gift of the Spirit	1 Cor. 12:8
Given by God	Eph. 1:17
Prayed for	Col. 1:9
Means of instruction	Col. 1:28
Lack of, ask for	James 1:5

Wisdom of Christ

Predicted	Is. 11:1, 2
Realized	Luke 2:52
Displayed	Matt. 13:54
Perfected	Col. 2:3
Imputed	1 Cor. 1:30

Wisdom of God

A. Described as:

Universal	Dan. 2:20
Infinite	Ps. 147:5
Unsearchable	Is. 40:28

Mighty............................ Job 36:5

Perfect...........................Job 37:16

B. Manifested in:

Creation ....Ps. 104:24

Nature.........................Job 38:34–41

Sovereignty ....Dan. 2:20, 21

The church....................... Eph. 3:10

Witchcraft—*the practice of sorcery*

Forbidden in Israel................ Deut. 18:9–14

Used by Jezebel......................2 Kin. 9:22

Condemned by the prophets.......... Mic. 5:12

Practiced by Manasseh ....2 Chr. 33:6

Suppressed by Saul............... 1 Sam. 28:3, 9

Work of the flesh ....Gal. 5:20

See Divination

Wither—*to dry up*

A. Caused by:

God's judgment...................... Is. 40:7, 24

Christ's judgment............... Matt. 21:19, 20

No root .... Matt. 13:6

Heat................................ James 1:11

B. Applied literally to:

Ear of grain .... Gen. 41:23

Gourd ....Jon. 4:7

Man's hand......................Luke 6:6, 8

Witnessing—*bearing testimony to something*

A. Elements of, seen in:

Public transaction ....Ruth 4:1–11

Signing a document...............Jer. 32:10–12

Calling witnesses ....Lev. 5:1

Requiring two witnesses..............1 Tim. 5:19

Rejection of false witnesses ....Prov. 24:28

B. Material means of, by:

Heap of stones................... Gen. 31:44–52

Song........................... Deut. 31:19–21

Altar.........................Josh. 22:26–34

Works .... John 10:25

Sign (miracles)........................ Heb. 2:4

C. Spiritual means of, by:

God's Law......................... Deut. 31:26

Gospel .... Matt. 24:14

Father .... John 5:37

Conscience.......................Rom. 2:15

Holy Spirit ....Rom. 8:16

D. Christ as object of, by:

John the Baptist .... John 1:7, 8, 15

His works .... John 5:36

Father .... John 8:18

Himself.......................... John 8:18

Holy Spirit ....John 15:26, 27

His disciples........................ John 15:27

Prophets .... Acts 10:43

E. Of Christians to Christ:

Chosen .... Acts 10:41

Commissioned ....Acts 1:8

Empowered .... Acts 4:33

Confirmed....................... Heb. 2:3, 4

F. Objects of Christ's:

Resurrection .... Acts 2:32

Saviorhood....................... Acts 5:31, 32

Life................................ Acts 1:21, 22

Mission ....Acts 10:41–43

Sufferings..........................1 Pet. 5:1

See Testimony

Wolf—*a doglike animal*

A. Characteristics of:

Ravenous ....Gen. 49:27

Nocturnal............................Jer. 5:6

Sheep-eating .... John 10:12

B. Figurative of:

False prophets.....................Matt. 7:15

Gospel transformation ....Is. 11:6

Woman—*the female sex*

A. Described as:

Beautiful...........................2 Sam. 11:2

Wise........................... 2 Sam. 20:16

Widow.......................1 Kin. 17:9, 10

Evil................................Prov. 6:24

Foolish............................Job 2:10

Gracious .... Prov. 11:16

Excellent.......................Prov. 12:4

Contentious....................... Prov. 21:19

Adulterous ....Prov. 30:20

Prominent ....Acts 17:12

Gullible.......................... 2 Tim. 3:6

Holy............................1 Pet. 3:5

B. Work of:

Kneading meal .... Gen. 18:6

Drawing water.................Gen. 24:11, 13, 15

Tending sheep...................... Gen. 29:6

Making cloth....................Prov. 31:13, 19

Caring for the household .... Prov. 31:27; 1 Tim. 5:14

Serving as queen......................Esth. 2:17

Judging Israel ....Judg. 4:4, 5

Leading an army....................Judg. 4:6–9

Bearing children....................1 Tim. 2:15

Counseling king..................1 Sam. 28:8–23

Selling purple cloth goods ....Acts 16:14

Acting as hostess to church .... Philem. 2

Midwifery.......................Ex. 1:15, 16

Providing religious training for children .... Prov. 31:1; 2 Tim. 1:5; 3:15

Prophesying.....................Luke 2:36, 37

C. Rights of, to:

Marry...........................1 Cor. 7:36

Hold property ....Num. 27:6–11

Make vows ....Num. 30:3–9

D. Position of, in relation to man:

Created from man ....Gen. 2:21–25

Made to help man..................Gen. 2:18, 20

Glory of man ....1 Cor. 11:7–9

Becomes subject to man .... Gen. 3:16

E. Position of, in spiritual things:

Insight of, noted ....Judg. 13:23

Prayer of, answered .... 1 Sam. 1:9–28

Understanding of, rewarded ......1 Sam. 25:3–42
Faith of, brings salvation .... Luke 7:37–50
Made equal in Christ................Gal. 3:28
Labor of, commended............... Phil. 4:2, 3
Faith of, transmitted ....2 Tim. 1:5

F. Good traits of:
Obedience .... 1 Pet. 3:5–7
Concern for children................. Ex. 2:2–10
Loyalty ....Ruth 1:14–18
Desire for children................ 1 Sam. 1:9–28
Modesty .... Esth. 1:10–12
Industry .... Prov. 31:10–31
Complete devotion................ Luke 7:38–50
Tenderness.......................John 11:20–35

G. Bad traits of:
Inciting to evil....................... Gen. 3:6, 7
Crafty .... Prov. 7:10
Fond of adornments..................Is. 3:16–24
Self-indulgent .... Is. 32:9, 11
Led away........................... 2 Tim. 3:6

H. Prohibitions concerning, not to:
Wear man's clothing .... Deut. 22:5
Have head shaved.................1 Cor. 11:5–15
Usurp authority .... 1 Tim. 2:11–15
Be unchaste .... 1 Pet. 3:1–7

I. Christ's dealing with:
Receives support from...............Luke 8:1–3
Forgives........................John 8:3–11
Delivers from demons............Mark 7:25–30
Heals ....Matt. 9:20–22
Teaches ....Luke 10:39
Born of ....Gal. 4:4
Visits ....Luke 10:38
Anointed by........................ Mark 14:3, 8
Appears to .... Matt. 28:5, 9; Mark 16:9

Womb—*the uterus*

A. God's control over, to:
Close .... Gen. 20:18
Open .... Gen. 29:31
Fashion us in ....Job 31:15
Separate and call....................Gal. 1:15
Cause to conceive.................... Luke 1:31
Make alive .... Rom. 4:19–21

B. Babe inside:
Grows mysteriously................... Eccl. 11:5
Known by God .... Ps. 139:13–16
Lame ....Acts 3:2
Leaps ....Luke 1:41, 44

C. Humankind coming from:
Different.........................Gen. 25:23, 24
Consecrated.......................Judg. 13:5, 7
Naked ....Job 1:21
Helpless.........................Ps. 22:9, 10
Sustained .... Ps. 71:6
Estranged .... Ps. 58:3

Women of the Bible, named

Abi, wife of Ahaz ....2 Kin. 18:1, 2
Abigail
(1) wife of Nabal................1 Sam. 25:3

(2) sister of David..............1 Chr. 2:15, 16
Abihail, wife of Abishur.............1 Chr. 2:29
Abijah, wife of Hezron ....1 Chr. 2:24
Abishag, nurse of David............1 Kin. 1:1–3
Abital, David's wife .... 2 Sam. 3:2, 4
Achsah, daughter of Caleb........... Josh. 15:16
Adah
(1) a wife of Lamech .... Gen. 4:19
(2) Canaanite wife of Esau.......... Gen. 36:2
Ahinoam
(1) wife of Saul .... 1 Sam. 14:50
(2) a Jezreelitess, wife of David... 1 Sam. 25:43
Anah, daughter of Zibeon .... Gen. 36:2
Anna, an aged widow ....Luke 2:36, 37
Apphia, a Christian of Colosse........ Philem. 2
Asenath, wife of Joseph .... Gen. 41:45
Atarah, wife of Jerahmeel ....1 Chr. 2:26
Athaliah, mother of Ahaziah ....2 Kin. 8:26
Azubah
(1) first wife of Caleb .... 1 Chr. 2:18
(2) daughter of Shilhi .... 1 Kin. 22:42
Baara, wife of Shaharaim..............1 Chr. 8:8
Basemath
(1) daughter of Elon .... Gen. 26:34
(2) third wife of Esau............. Gen. 36:2, 3
Bathsheba, wife of David .... 2 Sam. 11:3, 27
Bernice, sister of Agrippa............. Acts 25:13
Bilhah, Rachel's handmaid ....Gen. 29:29
Bithiah, daughter of a pharaoh........1 Chr. 4:18
Candace, a queen .... Acts 8:27
Chloe, woman of Corinth .... 1 Cor. 1:11
Claudia, Christian of Rome......... 2 Tim. 4:21
Cozbi, Midianite slain...........Num. 25:15–18
Damaris, woman of Athens........... Acts 17:34
Deborah
(1) Rebekah's nurse .... Gen. 35:8
(2) judge...........................Judg. 4:4
Delilah, Philistine woman..........Judg. 16:4, 5
Dinah, daughter of Jacob..........Gen. 30:19, 21
Dorcas, called Tabitha .... Acts 9:36
Drusilla, wife of Felix .... Acts 24:24
Eglah, one of David's wives ....2 Sam. 3:5
Elizabeth, mother of John the
Baptist ....Luke 1:5, 13
Elisheba, wife of Aaron.................Ex. 6:23
Ephah, concubine of Caleb ....1 Chr. 2:46
Ephrath, mother of Hur ....1 Chr. 2:19
Esther, a Jewess who became queen
of Persia ....Esth. 2:16, 17
Eunice, mother of Timothy...........2 Tim. 1:5
Euodia, a laborer with Paul .... Phil. 4:2
Eve, first woman..................... Gen. 3:20
Gomer, wife of Hosea .... Hos. 1:2, 3
Hagar, Sarai's maid .... Gen. 16:1
Haggith, wife of David............. 2 Sam. 3:2, 4
Hammoleketh, mother of Ishhod ..... 1 Chr. 7:18
Hamutal, daughter of Jeremiah ......2 Kin. 23:31
Hannah, mother of Samuel .... 1 Sam. 1:20
Hazelelponi, in genealogies of Judah ...1 Chr. 4:1–3

Helah, one of the wives of Ashhur . . . . . . 1 Chr. 4:5
Hephzibah, mother of Manasseh . . . . . . 2 Kin. 21:1
Herodias, sister-in-law of Herod . . . . Matt. 14:3–6
Hodesh, wife of Shaharaim . . . . 1 Chr. 8:8, 9
Hoglah, a daughter of Zelophehad . . . Num. 26:33
Huldah, a prophetess . . . . 2 Kin. 22:14
Hushim, a Moabitess . . . . 1 Chr. 8:8–11
Iscah, daughter of Haran . . . . Gen. 11:29
Jael, wife of Heber . . . . Judg. 4:17
Jecholiah, wife of Amaziah . . . . 2 Kin. 15:1, 2
Jedidah, mother of Josiah . . . . 2 Kin. 22:1
Jehoaddan, wife of Joash . . . . 2 Kin. 14:1, 2
Jehosheba, daughter of Joram . . . . 2 Kin. 11:2
Jemimah, Job's daughter . . . . Job 42:12, 14
Jerioth, wife of Caleb . . . . 1 Chr. 2:18
Jerusha, daughter of Zadok . . . . 2 Kin. 15:33
Jezebel, wife of Ahab . . . . 1 Kin. 16:30, 31
Joanna, wife of Chuza . . . . Luke 8:3
Jochebed, mother of Moses . . . . Ex. 6:20
Judith, daughter of Beeri . . . . Gen. 26:34
Julia, Christian woman of Rome . . . . . . Rom. 16:15
Keren-Happuch, Job's daughter . . . . Job 42:14
Keturah, second wife of Abraham . . . . . . Gen. 25:1
Keziah, daughter of Job . . . . Job 42:14
Leah, wife of Jacob . . . . Gen. 29:21–25
Lois, grandmother of Timothy . . . . 2 Tim. 1:5
Lo-Ruhamah, daughter of Gomer . . . . . Hos. 1:3–6
Lydia, first Christian convert in
    Europe . . . . Acts 16:14
Maacah, Maachah
    (1) daughter of Nahor . . . . Gen. 22:23, 24
    (2) daughter of Talmai . . . . 2 Sam. 3:3
    (3) granddaughter of Abishalom . . . 1 Kin. 15:2
    (4) grandmother of Asa . . . . 1 Kin. 15:9, 10
    (5) concubine of Caleb . . . . 1 Chr. 2:48
    (6) wife of Machir . . . . 1 Chr. 7:16
    (7) wife of Jeiel . . . . 1 Chr. 8:29; 9:35
Mahalath
    (1) wife of Esau . . . . Gen. 28:9
    (2) granddaughter of David . . . . 2 Chr. 11:18
Mahlah, daughter of Zelophehad . . . . Num. 26:33
Mara, another name for Naomi . . . . Ruth 1:20
Martha, friend of Christ . . . . Luke 10:38–41
Mary
    (1) mother of Jesus . . . . Matt. 1:16
    (2) Mary Magdalene . . . . Matt. 27:56–61
    (3) Mary, sister of Martha . . . . . . Luke 10:38, 39
    (4) Mary, wife of Clopas . . . . John 19:25
    (5) Mary, mother of Mark . . . . Acts 12:12
    (6) a Christian at Rome . . . . Rom. 16:6
Matred, mother-in-law of Hadar . . . . . . Gen. 36:39
Mehetabel, daughter of Matred . . . . Gen. 36:39
Merab, King Saul's eldest daughter . . . 1 Sam. 14:49
Meshullemeth, wife of Manasseh . . . 2 Kin. 21:18, 19
Michal, daughter of King Saul . . . . . . 1 Sam. 14:49
Milcah
    (1) daughter of Haran . . . . Gen. 11:29
    (2) daughter of Zelophehad . . . . Num. 26:33

Miriam
    (1) sister of Moses . . . . Ex. 15:20
    (2) disputed daughter of Ezrah . . . . . 1 Chr. 4:17
Naamah
    (1) daughter of Lamech . . . . Gen. 4:19–22
    (2) wife of Solomon . . . . 1 Kin. 14:21
Naarah, one of the wives of Ashhur . . . . 1 Chr. 4:5
Naomi, wife of Elimelech . . . . Ruth 1:2
Nehushta, daughter of Elnathan . . . . . . 2 Kin. 24:8
Noadiah, a false prophetess . . . . Neh. 6:14
Noah, daughter of Zelophehad . . . . Num. 26:33
Oholah . . . . Ezek. 23:4
Oholibah . . . . Ezek. 23:4
Orpah, sister-in-law of Ruth . . . . Ruth 1:4
Peninnah, one of the wives
    of Elkanah . . . . 1 Sam. 1:1, 2
Persis, convert of early church . . . . Rom. 16:12
Phoebe, a deaconess . . . . Rom. 16:1, 2
Priscilla, wife of Aquila . . . . Acts 18:2
Puah, a midwife . . . . Ex. 1:15
Rachel, wife of Jacob . . . . Gen. 29:28
Rahab, aid to Israel's spies . . . . Josh. 2:1–3
Reumah, mother of Tebah . . . . Gen. 22:24
Rhoda, a girl . . . . Acts 12:13
Rizpah, concubine of Saul . . . . 2 Sam. 3:7
Ruth, daughter-in-law of Naomi . . . . . . Ruth 1:3, 4
Salome, wife of Zebedee . . . . Matt. 27:56;
    Mark 15:40
Sapphira, wife of Ananias . . . . Acts 5:1
Sarah, (Sarai) wife of Abraham
    (Abram) . . . . Gen. 11:29
Serah, daughter of Asher . . . . Gen. 46:17
Sheerah, daughter of Beriah . . . . 1 Chr. 7:23, 24
Shelomith
    (1) daughter of Dibri . . . . Lev. 24:11
    (2) daughter of Zerubbabel . . . . 1 Chr. 3:19
Shimeath, mother of Zabad . . . . 2 Chr. 24:26
Shimrith, mother of Jehozabad . . . . . . 2 Chr. 24:26
Shiphrah, a midwife . . . . Ex. 1:15
Shua, daughter of Heber . . . . 1 Chr. 7:32
Susanna, ministered to Jesus . . . . Luke 8:3
Syntyche, convert of church at Philippi . . . Phil. 4:2
Tabitha, same as Dorcas . . . . Acts 9:36
Tahpenes, queen of Egypt . . . . 1 Kin. 11:19
Tamar
    (1) daughter-in-law of Judah . . . . Gen. 38:6
    (2) a daughter of David . . . . 2 Sam. 13:1
    (3) daughter of Absalom . . . . 2 Sam. 14:27
Taphath, one of Solomon's daughters . . . 1 Kin. 4:11
Timna, concubine of Eliphaz . . . . Gen. 36:12
Tirzah, one of daughters of
    Zelophehad . . . . Num. 26:33
Tryphena, convert at Rome . . . . Rom. 16:12
Tryphosa, convert at Rome . . . . Rom. 16:12
Vashti, wife of Ahasuerus . . . . Esth. 1:9
Zebudah, mother of Jehoiakim . . . . 2 Kin. 23:36
Zeresh, wife of Haman . . . . Esth. 5:10
Zeruah, a widow . . . . 1 Kin. 11:26
Zeruiah, mother of Joab . . . . 2 Sam. 17:25

Zibiah, mother of Jehoash . . . . 2 Kin. 12:1
Zillah, wife of Lamech . . . . Gen. 4:19
Zilpah, Leah's handmaid . . . . Gen. 29:24
Zipporah, wife of Moses . . . . Ex. 2:21

WORD STUDY	**WONDER,** *teras* (*ter*-ahs). Noun mean-

ing "portent," "omen," "wonder." It is used especially of events or occurrences that evoke a sense of wonder and are regarded as terrifying "portents" (Matt. 24:24; Mark 13:22). In the NT *teras* appears together with "sign" (*sēmeion),* as in Acts 2:19, particularly with reference to the mighty works of Jesus and His apostles (John 4:48; Acts 2:22, 43). See also 2 Cor. 12:12 and Heb. 2:4. (Strong's #5059)

Wonderful—*full of wonder; unusually good*
A. Ascribed to:
    Human love . . . . 2 Sam. 1:26
    Lord's works . . . . Ps. 78:4
    Mysterious things . . . . Prov. 30:18
    Lord's Law . . . . Ps. 119:18
    Lord's testimonies . . . . Ps. 119:129
    Lord's knowledge . . . . Ps. 139:6
    Our being . . . . Ps. 139:14
    Messiah's name . . . . Is. 9:6
B. Descriptive of the Lord's work, as:
    Numerous . . . . Ps. 40:5
    Transmitted . . . . Ps. 78:4
    Remembered . . . . Ps. 111:4
    Praised . . . . Is. 25:1

WORD STUDY	**WONDROUS THING, DO A,** *pala'*

(paw-*law*). The verb *pala'* means "to be surpassing or extraordinary." Another form of the verb means "to do a hard thing." In Lev. 27:2 and Num. 6:2, the word is used to describe one making a hard vow. Yet another form of the verb means "to make wonderful." This form of the word is used of God and describes His action in sending the plagues (Deut. 28:59). God's counsel is described as wonderful, also (Is. 28:29). In Judg. 13:19 the term is used to describe God working wonders. (Strong's #6381)

Wonders—*miraculous works*
A. Performed by:
    God . . . . Heb. 2:4
    Moses and Aaron . . . . Ex. 11:10
    Christ . . . . Acts 2:22
    Apostles . . . . Acts 2:43
    Jesus' name . . . . Acts 4:30
    Stephen . . . . .Acts 6:8
    Paul and Barnabas . . . . Acts 14:3
    Paul . . . . 2 Cor. 12:12
B. Places of:
    Egypt . . . . Acts 7:36
    Land of Ham . . . . .Ps. 105:27
    Canaan . . . . Josh. 3:5
    Deep . . . . Ps. 107:24
    Heaven . . . . Dan. 6:27
    Among the peoples . . . . Ps. 77:14

C. Described as:
    Numerous . . . . .Ex. 11:9
    Great . . . . .Acts 6:8
    Mighty . . . . Dan. 4:3
D. Humankind's reactions to:
    Did not remember . . . . Neh. 9:17
    Forgetful of . . . . .Ps. 78:11, 12
    Not understanding . . . . .Ps. 106:7
    Not believing . . . . .Ps. 78:32
    Inquiring about . . . . .Jer. 21:2
E. Believer's attitude toward, to:
    Remember . . . . .1 Chr. 16:9, 12
    Declare . . . . Ps. 71:17
    Give thanks for . . . . .Ps. 136:1, 4
    Consider . . . . .Job 37:14

Wood
A. Descriptive of:
    Part of a tree . . . . Num. 19:6
    Forest . . . . .Josh. 17:15, 18
B. Place of:
    Animals . . . . .2 Kin. 2:24
    Fortresses . . . . 2 Chr. 27:4
C. Used for:
    Fire . . . . 1 Kin. 18:23–38
    Carts . . . . .1 Sam. 6:14
    Weapons . . . . Num. 35:18
    Ships . . . . Gen. 6:14
    Palanquin . . . . Song 3:9
    Musical instruments . . . . 1 Kin. 10:12
    Buildings . . . . 1 Kin. 6:15–33
    Tabernacle furniture . . . . Ex. 25:9–28
    Platform . . . . Neh. 8:4
    Gods . . . . .Is. 37:19

Woodcutters
    Gibeonites . . . . .Josh. 9:17–27
    Classed with "water carriers" . . . . . . .Josh. 9:21, 23
    Sent to Solomon . . . . 2 Chr. 2:10

Woof—*the threads crossing the warp of a woven*
    garment
    Inspection of, for leprosy . . . . Lev. 13:48–59

Wool—*the soft hair of sheep*
    Inspection of, for leprosy . . . . Lev. 13:47–59
    Mixture of, forbidden . . . . Deut. 22:11
    Used as a test . . . . .Judg. 6:37
    Valuable article of trade . . . . .Ezek. 27:18
    Figurative of whiteness . . . . .Is. 1:18

WORD STUDY	**WORD,** *'imrah* (ihm-*raw*). The noun

'imrah means "word" and comes from the verb that means "to say." This term appears in poetic contexts and indicates an utterance or speech. In Gen. 4:23 Lamech says, "Listen to my speech," when he has an announcement to make. Isaiah says, "Hear my speech" (Is. 28:23). There are other places where this word is used by the speaker to refer to his own saying, and at times the sayings or words are the words of God. In Deut. 33:9 (part of the blessing of Moses), *'imrah* means the commands and promises of

God that are part of the covenant. In 2 Sam. 22:31 and Ps. 12:6, 7, the words of God (probably also meaning a combination of commands and promises) are proven and pure. (Strong's #565)

> **WORD STUDY**

WORD, *dabar* (daw-*bawr*). The noun *dabar,* which is translated "word," is used frequently throughout the OT. Sometimes the "word" is a speech or saying, being the sum of the spoken thing. When discussing human speech, this "word" can be a description, a command, a message or report, advice, or a request. God's words, which are divine communication in various forms, are referred to as *dabar* several hundred times. "The word of the LORD came to" is one of the common phrases. *Dabar* is used in contexts that refer to God's remembering or acting on His word. At times it is used for a section of the spoken thing so that a "word" is a sentence or the words of a song, records, or the title of writings (Eccl. 1:1). This meaning can also refer to divine commands, such as the Ten Words (Ex. 34:28). Although this meaning is less frequent, there are a number of times when "word" can mean a matter or affair, the thing about which one speaks, such as business, acts, events, or judicial cases. (Strong's #1697)

> **WORD STUDY**

WORD, *logos* (*log*-oss). This noun has several meanings, but the central one is "word." *Logos* may be used with reference to: "speaking" (2 Cor. 8:7); a "speech" (Acts 15:32); a question (Matt. 21:24); the "matter" or subject under discussion (Acts 15:6); a "report," "story," or "account" (Luke 5:15); or, in a special sense, to God's revelation of His word or command (John 8:55; Rom. 3:4; 9:6, 9, 28) through Christ and the apostles (John 17:14; Acts 4:29, 31). *Logos* may be used to refer to the "computation," "reckoning," or settlement of accounts (Matt. 25:19; Rom. 14:12), or in the expanded sense to a "reason" or "motive" (Matt. 5:32; Acts 10:29). A special use of *logos* can be found in John 1:1, 14 (cf. 1 John 1:1), where the *logos* is the divine "Word" of God, personified and identified as a particular Person, Jesus. This use of *logos* may mean that Jesus is the expression of God's revelation, or it may mean that Jesus is the "reason" (organizing principle) behind the cosmos. (Strong's #3056)

Word of God

A. Called:

B. Descriptive of:

C. Described as:

D. Compared to:

E. Agency of, to:

F. Proper attitude toward, to:

G. In the believer's life, as:

H. Prohibitions concerning, not to be:

Used deceitfully . . . . 2 Cor. 4:2

Altered . . . . Rev. 22:18, 19

Words—*intelligible sounds or signs*

A. Described as:

Acceptable . . . . Eccl. 12:10

Lying and corrupt. Dan. 2:9

Persuasive . . . . 1 Cor. 2:4

Inexpressible . . . . 2 Cor. 12:4

Empty . . . . Eph. 5:6

Flattering . . . . 1 Thess. 2:5

Wholesome . . . . 1 Tim. 6:3

B. Power of, to:

Stir up wrath . . . . Prov. 15:1

Wound. . . . . .Prov. 26:22

Sustain. . . . . Is. 50:4

Determine destiny . . . . Matt. 12:36, 37

WORD STUDY   **WORK, BE AT,** *energeō* (en-erg-*eh*-oh). Verb meaning "to work," "to be at work," "to operate," "to be effective," "to produce." This verb is used to identify the agent—personal or impersonal—responsible for certain events or effects. For instance, it is used with reference to the working of miracles or the activity of powerful supernatural forces or beings (Matt. 14:2; Mark 6:14; Gal. 3:5; Eph. 3:20). *Energeō* is used to show the effect or the working of: the passions (Rom. 7:5), death (2 Cor. 4:12), consolation (2 Cor. 1:6), faith (Gal. 5:6), prayer (James 5:16). The word is often used to describe the activity of God among believers (Eph. 1:11; 2:2; 3:20; Gal. 2:8; Phil. 2:13; 1 Thess. 2:13). (Strong's #1754)

Work, Christ's

A. Defined as:

Doing God's will. John 4:34

Limited in time. . . . . John 9:4

Incomparable . . . . John 15:24

Initiated by God . . . . John 14:10

Finished in the Cross. . . . . John 17:4

B. Design of, to:

Attest His mission . . . . John 5:36

Encourage faith. . . . . John 14:11, 12

Judge the world. . . . . John 15:24

Provide abundant life . . . . John 10:10

Provide salvation . . . . Acts 4:10–12

Work, the Christian's

A. Agency of, by:

God . . . . Phil. 2:13

Spirit . . . . 1 Cor. 12:11

God's Word . . . . 1 Thess. 2:13

Faith. . . . . .Gal. 5:6

B. Characteristics of:

Designed for God's glory . . . . .Matt. 5:16

Divinely called . . . . Acts 13:2

Produces eventual glory . . . . 2 Cor. 4:17

Subject to examination. . . . . .Gal. 6:4

Final perfection in . . . . Heb. 13:21

C. God's regard for, will:

Reward . . . . .Jer. 31:16

Perfect. . . . . Phil. 1:6

Not forget. . . . . Heb. 6:10

See Labor, spiritual

Work, physical

Required of Christians . . . . .2 Thess. 3:7–14

Nehemiah's zeal .Neh. 6:1–4

Paul's example. . . . . Acts 18:1–3

See Labor, physical

Works, God's

A. Described as:

Perfect. . . . . Deut. 32:4

Awesome. . . . . .Ps. 66:3

Incomparable . . . . .Ps. 86:8

Honorable and glorious . . . . Ps. 111:3

Marvelous. . . . . .Ps. 139:14

Righteous . . . . Ps. 145:17

Unusual. . . . . Is. 28:21

Great and marvelous . . . . .Rev. 15:3

B. Manifested in:

Creation . . . . Gen. 1:1–3

Heavens. . . . . Ps. 8:3

Deeps . . . . .Ps. 107:24

Regenerate people . . . . Is. 19:25

C. God's attitude toward:

Rejoice in . . . . .Ps. 104:31

Made known to His people . . . . Ps. 111:6

His mercies over . . . . Ps. 145:9

Glorified in . . . . Is. 60:21

D. Believer's attitude toward, to:

Consider . . . . Ps. 8:3

Behold . . . . .Ps. 46:8

Meditate upon. . . . . .Ps. 77:12; 143:5

Triumph in. . . . . Ps. 92:4

Declare . . . . .Ps. 107:22

Praise God for . . . . .Ps. 145:4, 10

Pray for revival of . . . . Hab. 3:2

E. Unbeliever's attitude toward:

Not regarding . . . . Ps. 28:5

Forgetting. . . . . Ps. 78:11

Not believed. . . . . Acts 13:41

Works, good

A. Considered negatively, they cannot:

Justify . . . . Rom. 4:2–6

Determine God's election . . . . .Rom. 9:11

Secure righteousness . . . . Rom. 9:31, 32

Substitute for grace . . . . .Rom. 11:6

B. Considered positively:

Reward for . . . . .1 Cor. 3:13–15

Created for . . . . Eph. 2:10

Prepared for . . . . 2 Tim. 2:21

Equipped for . . . . .2 Tim. 3:17

Works, Satan's (see Satan)

Works, the unbeliever's

A. Described as:

Wicked . . . . .Col. 1:21

Done in darkness . . . . Is. 29:15

Abominable . . . . Ps. 14:1

Deceitful. . . . . Prov. 11:18

Evil................................ John 7:7
Unfruitful........................Eph. 5:11

B. God's attitude toward, will:

Never forget........................ Amos 8:7
Reward..........................Prov. 24:12
Bring to judgment .... Rev. 20:12, 13

C. Believer's relation to:

Cast off..........................Rom. 13:12
Have no fellowship with...............Eph. 5:11
Be delivered from.................. 2 Tim. 4:18

 WORLD, ORDER, *kosmos* (*kos*-moss). Noun meaning "adornment" (as in 1 Pet. 3:3) or "order." In philosophical and religious usage, *kosmos* is used for the "world" as the sum of the here and now, thus the "(orderly) universe" (Matt. 24:21; 25:34). Although this is the predominant usage in the NT, a wide range of nuances is evident. *Kosmos* may refer to: the planet we inhabit (Mark 16:15); the habitation of humankind (1 Cor. 5:10); "earth" in contrast to heaven (John 3:17; 16:28); the world as the whole of humankind (Matt. 5:14; 18:7; Rom. 3:6; 5:12), especially believers loved by God (John 6:33, 51); the scene of earthly joys, possessions, cares, and suffering (Luke 9:25; 1 Cor. 7:33f.); or everything that belongs to the "world" that is hostile to God and ruled by the devil (John 12:31). (Strong's #2889)

World

A. God's relation to, as:

Maker .... Jer. 10:12
Possessor...........................Ps. 24:1
Redeemer .... John 3:16
Judge ,,,,,,,,,,,,,,,,,,,,,,,,,,,,,,,,Ps. 96:13

B. Christ's relation to, as:

Maker .... John 1:10
Sin-bearer........................... John 1:29
Savior...............................John 12:47
Life...........................John 6:33, 51
Light .... John 8:12
Judge ....Acts 17:31
Overcomer........................ John 16:33
Reconciler........................ 2 Cor. 5:19

C. Christian's relation to:

Light of ....Matt. 5:14
Not of .... John 17:14, 16
Chosen out of .... John 15:19
Tribulation in .... John 16:33
Sent into by Christ................ John 17:18
Not conformed to....................Rom. 12:2
Crucified to ....Gal. 6:14
To live soberly.....................Titus 2:12
Unspotted from ....James 1:27
Overcomers of....................1 John 5:4, 5
Denying desires of ....Titus 2:12

D. Dangers of, arising from:

Wisdom .... 1 Cor. 3:19
Love of............................ 2 Tim. 4:10
Friendship ....James 4:4
Corruptions........................2 Pet. 1:4

Lusts........................... 1 John 2:15–17
False prophets ....1 John 4:1
Deceivers ....2 John 7

E. In the plan of redemption:

Elect chosen before ....Eph. 1:4
Revelation made before .... Matt. 13:35
Sin's entrance into ....Rom. 5:12
Its guilt before God ....Rom. 3:19
Original revelation to ....Rom. 1:20
God's love for .... John 3:16
Christ's mission to .... John 12:47
Spirit's conviction of .... John 16:8
Gospel preached in................. Matt. 24:14
Reconciliation of .... 2 Cor. 5:19
Destruction of.......................2 Pet. 3:7
Final judgment of...................Acts 17:31
Satan deceives ....Rev. 12:9

Worm—*a soft-bodied, slender, creeping animal*

A. Ravages of:

On bread......................... Ex. 16:15, 20
On plants .... Jon. 4:7
On the body....................... Acts 12:23
In the grave .... Job 24:19, 20
In hell .... Mark 9:44–48

B. Figurative of:

Insignificance ....Job 25:6
Messiah...............................Ps. 22:6

Wormwood—*a bitter-tasting plant*

Figurative of:

Idolatry........................... Deut. 29:18
Adultery .... Prov. 5:4
God's judgments....................Jer. 9:15
Symbol of doom ....Rev. 8:11

Worry (see Cares, worldly)

WORSHIP, *shachah* (shaw-khaw). The verb, translated "worship," and meaning "bow down," is *shachah*. A person bows down before a superior or a monarch to show respect (Gen. 23:7; Ruth 2:10; 1 Kin. 1:31). People bowed down before God in worship as Moses did on Mt. Sinai when God came to inscribe the tablets (Ex. 34:8). Humans also bowed before angels in a theophany if they recognized the angel as such (Josh. 5:14). There are references to bowing before other gods, although the Ten Commandments explicitly forbid this behavior (Ex. 20:5). Is. 2:20 says that in the day of the Lord people will throw away the idols that they have made to worship. And in Is. 44:15 the foolishness of worshiping a god made of wood, which could be burned for a cooking fire, is pointed out rather ironically. (Strong's #7812)

WORSHIP, *proskuneō* (pros-koo-*neh*-oh). Noun used to designate the act of obeisance, which involves falling down or bowing before kings, deities, or masters and kissing their feet, the hem of their garment, or the ground. *Proskuneō* can be translated as "to (fall down and) worship," "to do obeisance to," "to prostrate oneself before," "to do reverence to." In the NT *proskuneō* is used for the reverence of a slave toward his master (Matt. 18:26), Cornelius toward Peter (Acts 10:25), but it is used especially with reference to the worship of God (Matt. 4:10; 1 Cor. 14:25; Rev. 7:11), of Jesus as Messianic King (Matt. 2:2, 8, 11), and the Risen Lord (Matt. 28:9, 17). However, *proskuneō* also refers to the worship of idols (Acts 7:43), and demonic beings (Luke 4:7; Rev. 9:20; 13:12, 15). (Strong's #4352)

Worship—*an act of reverence*
A. Of God:
- Defined........................... John 4:20–24
- Commanded ....1 Chr. 16:29
- Corrupted...........................Rom. 1:25
- Perverted ....2 Kin. 21:3, 21
- Debated........................ 1 Kin. 18:21–39

B. Of Christ, by:
- Angels .... Heb. 1:6
- Magi............................. Matt. 2:1, 2, 11
- Men .... John 9:30–38
- Women .... Matt. 15:25
- Disciples .... Matt. 28:17
- Heavenly choir ....Rev. 4:11
- Twenty-four elders......................Rev. 4:10
- Everyone .... Phil. 2:10

C. Of wrong objects, such as:
- "Sun or moon or any of the host of heaven"...........................Deut. 17:3
- Other gods ....Ex. 34:14
- Demons........................ Deut. 32:17
- Creatures ....Rom. 1:25
- Images...........................Dan. 3:5–18
- Humans ....Acts 10:25, 26
- Antichrist........................ Rev. 13:4–13

D. Of wrong objects, by:
- Israel ....2 Kin. 21:3, 21
- Pagans...............................Rom. 1:25
- Professing Christians ....Col. 2:18
- World........................ 2 Thess. 2:3–12

Worthiness—*qualities due honor or merit*
A. Of Christ:
- For more glory......................... Heb. 3:3
- To open the book .... Rev. 5:2, 4
- To receive worship .... Rev. 5:9–14

B. Of believers, for:
- Provisions...................... Matt. 10:10
- Discipleship .... Matt. 10:37
- Their calling ....Eph. 4:1
- Suffering........................... Acts 5:41
- Their walk ....Col. 1:10
- Honor ....1 Tim. 6:1
- The kingdom...................... 2 Thess. 1:5

Worthless—*useless, despicable*
- Sacrifice ....Is. 1:13
- Religion........................... James 1:26
- Vile things ....1 Sam. 15:9
- See Futile

Wound—*to injure*
A. Of physical injury, by:
- God .... Deut. 32:39
- Battle..............................1 Sam. 31:3
- Adultery .... Prov. 6:32, 33
- Robbers...................... Luke 10:30, 34
- Evil spirit ....Acts 19:16

B. Of spiritual injury, by:
- God's punishment .... Jer. 30:14
- Drunkenness..................... Prov. 23:29, 30
- Adultery .... Prov. 6:32, 33
- Sin.................................Is. 1:6

> **WORD STUDY** **WRATH,** *thumos* (thoo-*moss*). Noun meaning "anger," "wrath," "rage," which emphasizes the intense passion of this emotion. In the NT it is used for the "wrath" of humans (Luke 4:28; Eph. 4:31; Heb. 11:27), of Satan (Rev. 12:12), and outbursts of "anger" (2 Cor. 12:20; Gal. 5:20). In Rev. *thumos* is used mostly for the holy and just "wrath" of God against wickedness, which leads to judgment (14:10; 15:1, 7; 16:1). (Strong's #2372)

Wrath of God
A. Described as:
- Anger........................Num. 32:10–13
- Prolonged............................Ps. 90:9
- Great ....Zech. 7:12
- Willing ....Rom. 9:22
- Revealed ....Rom. 1:18
- Stored up.......................... Rom. 2:5–8
- Abiding............................. John 3:36
- Accomplished .... Rev. 6:16, 17

B. Caused by:
- Apostasy....................... 2 Chr. 34:24, 25
- Sympathy with evil.................. Lev. 10:1–6
- Unfaithfulness ....Josh. 22:20
- Provocations ....2 Kin. 23:26
- Fellowship with evil............... 2 Chr. 19:2
- Mockery ....2 Chr. 36:16
- Idolatry...........................Ps. 78:58, 59
- Intermarriage ....Ezra 10:10–14
- Profaning the Sabbath .... Neh. 13:18
- Speaking against God.............. Ps. 78:19–21

C. Effects of, seen in:
- The Flood...........................Gen. 6:5–7
- Sodom's destruction ....Gen. 19:24, 25
- Egypt's army's destruction............Ex. 15:4, 7
- Great plague .... Num. 11:33
- Israel's wanderings...............Num. 32:10–13
- Withholding of rain..................Deut. 11:17
- Destruction of a people............. 1 Sam. 28:18
- Trouble ....Ps. 90:7
- Death................................Ps. 90:9
- Jerusalem's destruction........... Luke 21:23, 24
- Punishments of hell...................Rev. 14:10
- Final judgments ....Rev. 19:15
- Israel's captivity ....2 Chr. 36:16, 17

D. Deliverance from, by:
- Atonement .... Num. 16:46

WRITE, *katab* (kaw-*thab*). *Katab* is a verb used frequently in the OT and is translated "write." It can refer to the action of writing something, such as a book or a letter. The tablets of the Ten Commandments were inscribed by the finger of God (Ex. 31:18). More often *katab* occurs when somebody writes on or in a tablet, roll, or book. Jeremiah says that God will give a new covenant, which will be written on the hearts of people (Jer. 31:33). Less frequent uses include writing something down, describing it in writing, as in Josh. 18:4. In Is. 10:19 and Neh. 12:22, the term is used meaning "enroll" or "make a record." Job uses *katab* to mean "decree" (Job 13:26). (Strong's #3789)

Write, writing, written
A. Purposes of, to:
B. Unusual:
C. Of the Bible as written, involving its:
D. Figurative of:

Y

 YAH, *Yah* (yaw). *Yah* is the name of God in contracted form, coming from the tetragrammaton *YHWH*. This divine name is pronounced "Yahweh," not as "Jehovah," which comes from scribal insertions in the text that served as reminders not to speak the most holy name. The contracted form appears in early poetic texts, such as Ex. 15:2, Ex. 17:16, Is. 26:4, and Is. 38:11. In Ps. the contracted name is frequently used with the imperative form of the word "praise" to say "praise the LORD." This combination is used in modern settings in the Hebrew, *halleluyah*. *Yah* is also part of many biblical names that end in *-iah* or *-yah*. This is supposed to show the allegiance to God of the one so named. (Strong's #3050)

Yah—*a poetic form of Yahweh*

Years, thousand

Yield—*to produce; to surrender*
A. Used literally of:
B. Used figuratively of:

Yod

Yoke—*a frame uniting animals for work*
A. Used literally on:
B. Used figuratively of:

 YOU HAVE FORSAKEN ME, *sabachthani* (sahb-ahk-thahn-ee). This is the Greek transliteration of an Aramaic verb, which is the equivalent of the Hebrew verb *'azabtani,* meaning "you have forsaken me" (see Ps. 22:1). This word appears only in Matt. 27:46 and Mark 15:34 as part of Jesus' cry of anguish from the cross. (Strong's #4518)

Young men

A. Characteristics of, seen in:

Unwise counsel . . . . 1 Kin. 12:8–14

Godly fervor . . . . 1 John 2:13, 14

Passion . . . . .Prov. 7:7–23

Strength . . . . .Prov. 20:29

Impatience . . . . .Luke 15:12, 13

B. Special needs of:

God's Word . . . . Ps. 119:9

Knowledge and discretion . . . . Prov. 1:4

Encouragement . . . . .Is. 40:30, 31

Full surrender . . . . .Matt. 19:20–22

Soberness . . . . .Titus 2:6

Counsel . . . . 1 John 2:13, 14

Youth—*the early age of life*

A. Evils of, seen in:

Sin . . . . Ps. 25:7

Lusts . . . . 2 Tim. 2:22

Enticements . . . . .Prov. 1:10–16

Self-will . . . . .Luke 15:12, 13

B. Good of, seen in:

Enthusiasm .1 Sam. 17:26–51

Children . . . . .Ps. 127:3, 4

Hardships . . . . .Lam. 3:27

Godly example . . . . 1 Tim. 4:12

Z

Zaanan—*rich in flocks*

Town in west Judah .Mic. 1:11

Zaanannim

Border point of Naphtali . . . . Josh. 19:32, 33

Zaavan—*unquiet*

Son of Ezer . . . . .Gen. 36:27

Zabad—*gift*

1. Descendant of Judah . . . . 1 Chr. 2:3, 36

2. Ephraimite . . . . 1 Chr. 7:20, 21

3. One of Joash's murderers . . . . 2 Chr. 24:26

Called Jozachar . . . . .2 Kin. 12:21

4. Son of Zattu . . . . .Ezra 10:27

5. Son of Hashum . . . . .Ezra 10:33

6. Son of Nebo . . . . .Ezra 10:43

Zabbai—*(God) has given*

1. Man who divorced his foreign wife . . . . . .Ezra 10:28

2. Father of Baruch . . . . .Neh. 3:20

Zabbud—*given (by God)*

Postexilic returnee . . . . .Ezra 8:14

Zabdi—*(God) has given*

1. Achan's grandfather . . . . .Josh. 7:1, 17, 18

2. Benjamite . . . . 1 Chr. 8:1, 19

3. One of David's officers . . . . 1 Chr. 27:27

Zabdiel—*God has given*

1. Father of Jashobeam . . . . 1 Chr. 27:2

2. Postexilic official . . . . .Neh. 11:14

Zabud—*bestowed*

Son of Nathan . . . . 1 Kin. 4:5

Zaccai—*probably a contraction of "Zechariah"*

Head of a postexilic family . . . . .Ezra 2:9

Zacchaeus—*pure*

Wealthy tax collector converted to

Christ . . . . .Luke 19:1–10

Zaccur, Zacchur—*remembered*

1. Father of the Reubenite spy . . . . Num. 13:2, 4

2. Simeonite . . . . .1 Chr. 4:24, 26

3. Merarite Levite . . . . 1 Chr. 24:27

4. Gershonite Levite; a son of Asaph . . . 1 Chr. 25:2, 10

5. Signer of the covenant . . . . Neh. 10:1, 12

6. A treasurer under Nehemiah . . . . .Neh. 13:13

Zacharias

Father of John the Baptist . . . . .Luke 1:5–17

Zadok—*righteous*

1. Descendant of Aaron . . . . 1 Chr. 24:1–3

Copriest with Abiathar . . . . 2 Sam. 20:25

Loyal to David . . . . .2 Sam. 15:24–29

Gently rebuked by David . . . . 2 Sam. 19:11–14

Remained aloof from Adonijah's

usurpation . . . . 1 Kin. 1:8–26

Commanded by David to anoint

Solomon . . . . 1 Kin. 1:32–45

Replaced Abiathar . . . . .1 Kin. 2:35

Sons of, faithful . . . . Ezek. 48:11

2. Priest, the son or grandson of Ahitub . . . 1 Chr. 6:12

3. Jotham's maternal grandfather . . . .2 Kin. 15:32, 33

4. Postexilic workman, son of Baana . . . . .Neh. 3:4

5. Postexilic workman, son of Immer . . . . . . .Neh. 3:29

6. Ancestor of Christ . . . . Matt. 1:14

Zaham—*foul*

Son of Rehoboam . . . . .2 Chr. 11:18, 19

Zair—*little*

Battle camp in Edom . . . . .2 Kin. 8:21

Zalaph—*caper plant*

Father of Hanun . . . . .Neh. 3:30

Zalmon—*dark*

1. One of David's mighty men . . . . .2 Sam. 23:28

2. Mount near Shechem . . . . Judg. 9:48

Zalmonah—*shady*

Israelite camp .Num. 33:41, 42

Zalmunna—*deprived of shade*

Midianite king . . . . Judg. 8:4–21

Zamzummim—*murmurers*

Race of giants . . . . Deut. 2:20, 21

Same as the Zuzim . . . . Gen. 14:5

Zanoah—*rejected*

1. Town in south Judah . . . . Josh. 15:1, 34

2. Town of Judah . . . . Josh. 15:56

Zaphnath-Paaneah—*revealer of secrets*

Name given to Joseph by Pharaoh . . . . . Gen. 41:45

Zaphon—*concealed*

Town of Gad east of the Jordan . . . Josh. 13:24, 27

Zarephath

Town of Sidon where Elijah restores
widow's son........1 Kin. 17:8–24; Luke 4:26

Zaretan—*cooling*

Town near Jezreel.........Josh. 3:16; 1 Kin. 4:12
Huram worked near..................1 Kin. 7:46

Zattu—*lovely*

Founder of a postexilic family .... Ezra 2:2, 8
Members of, divorced foreign
wives.....................Ezra 10:18, 19, 27
Signs covenant......................Neh. 10:1, 14

Zayin

Seventh letter in the Hebrew
alphabet......................Ps. 119:49–56

Zaza—*projection*

Jerahmeelite.........................1 Chr. 2:33

WORD
STUDY
ZEAL, JEALOUSY, *zēlos* (*dzay*-loss).
This noun is derived from the verb *zēloō*,
which means "to strive," "to desire," "to
exert oneself earnestly," "to be deeply concerned about,"
"to manifest zeal," "to be filled with jealousy (or envy)
toward someone." Used in a positive sense, *zēlos* means
"zeal," "ardor," "earnestness" (Rom. 10:2; 2 Cor. 9:2;
Phil. 3:6). Used in a negative sense, it means "jealousy,"
"envy" (Acts 5:17; 1 Cor. 3:3). As a plural noun in the
negative sense ("jealousies"), it probably denotes the
various forms and manifestations of envy (Rom. 13:13;
2 Cor. 12:20; Gal. 5:20). (Strong's #2205)

Zeal—*intense enthusiasm for something*

A. Kinds of:
Divine.....................................Is. 9:7
Glorious .... Is. 63:15
Wrathful......................Ezek. 5:13
Stirring .... 2 Cor. 9:2
Intense.......................... 2 Cor. 7:11
Boastful.......................... Phil. 3:4, 6
Ignorant .... Rom. 10:2, 3
Righteous......................John 2:15–17
Sinful.......................... 2 Sam. 21:1, 2
B. Manifested in concern for:
Lord's sake .... Num. 25:11, 13
Others' salvation......................Rom. 10:1
Missionary work................ Rom. 15:18–25
Reformation of character............ 2 Cor. 7:11
Desire for spiritual gifts .... 1 Cor. 14:12
Doing good works.................Titus 2:14
C. Illustrated in Paul's life by his:
Desire to reach the Jews .... Rom. 9:1–3; 10:1
Determination to evangelize all... 1 Cor. 9:19–23
Willingness to lose all things for
Christ.........................Phil. 3:4–16
Plan to minister to unreached
places ....Rom. 1:14, 15
Support of himself................2 Cor. 11:7–12
D. Other examples of:
Moses.......................... Ex. 32:19–35

Phinehas........................Num. 25:7–13
Joshua .... Josh. 24:14–16
Gideon........................ Judg. 6:11–32
David......................1 Sam. 17:26–51
Elijah ....1 Kin. 19:10
Jehu ....2 Kin. 9:1–37
Josiah .... 2 Kin. 22:1–20
Ezra ....Ezra 7:10
Nehemiah......................Neh. 4:1–23
Peter and John......................Acts 4:8–20
Timothy ....Phil. 2:19–22
Epaphroditus......................Phil. 2:25–30
Epaphras......................... Col. 4:12, 13

Zealot—*zealous one*

Applied to Simon, the Cananite; a party of
fanatical Jews ....Luke 6:15

WORD
STUDY
ZEALOUS, BE, *qana'* (kaw-*naw*). *Qana'* is
a verb meaning "be jealous" or "be zealous." It appears in Num. 5:14 to describe a
man jealous of his wife. The word can also indicate
when one person is envious of another as it does in Gen.
30:1 where Rachel, who had no children, was envious of
Leah because she did have. More often the word indicates zeal. In Num. 11:29 Moses asks Joshua if he is
zealous for him. Sometimes people are zealous for God
as in 1 Kin. 19:10 where Elijah tells God that he has
been zealous for Him. At times it is God who is zealous
as can be seen in Zech. 1:14. (Strong's #7065)

Zebadiah—*Yahweh has bestowed*

1, 2. Two Benjamites .... 1 Chr. 8:1, 15, 17
3. Benjamite warrior among David's
mighty men .... 1 Chr. 12:1–7
4. One of David's commanders.......... 1 Chr. 27:7
5. Korahite Levite.................... 1 Chr. 26:1, 2
6. Levite teacher under Jehoshaphat...... 2 Chr. 17:8
7. Officer of Jehoshaphat .... 2 Chr. 19:11
8. Postexilic returnee......................Ezra 8:8
9. Priest who put away his foreign wife.....Ezra 10:20

Zebah—*victim; sacrifice*

King of Midian killed by Gideon.... Judg. 8:4–28

Zebaim—*gazelles*

Native place of Solomon's slaves..... Ezra 2:55, 57

Zebedee—*Yahweh is gift*

Galilean fisherman; father of James
and John...................... Matt. 4:21, 22

Zebina—*purchased*

Priest who put away his foreign wife... Ezra 10:43

Zeboiim

One of five cities destroyed with Sodom
and Gomorrah .... Gen. 10:19

Zeboim—*hyenas*

1. Valley in Benjamin............... 1 Sam. 13:16–18
2. City of Judah..........................Neh. 11:34

Zebudah—*given*

Mother of Jehoiakim................2 Kin. 23:36

Zemirah—*song*
Grandson of Benjamin . . . . 1 Chr. 7:6, 8

Zenan—*place of flocks*
Town in Judah. . . . . .Josh. 15:21, 37

Zenas—*gift of Zeus*
A lawyer . . . . .Titus 3:13

Zephaniah—*hidden of Yahweh*
1. Ancestor of Samuel . . . . 1 Chr. 6:33, 36
2. Author of Zephaniah . . . . Zeph. 1:1
3. Priest and friend of Jeremiah during
    Zedekiah's reign. . . . . Jer. 21:1
4. Father of a certain Josiah in Zechariah's
    time . . . . .Zech. 6:10

Zephaniah, Book of—*a book of the Old Testament*
Coming judgment . . . . .Zeph. 1:2–18
Call to repentance . . . . Zeph. 2:1–3
The nations judged . . . . .Zeph. 2:4–15
Jerusalem is blessed . . . . .Zeph. 3:9–20

Zephath—*watchtower*
Canaanite town destroyed by Simeon and
    Judah . . . . .Judg. 1:17
See Hormah

Zephathah
Valley near Mareshah . . . . .2 Chr. 14:10

Zepho, Zephi—*watch*
Grandson of Esau and a
    chief of Edom . . . . . Gen. 36:15, 19; 1 Chr. 1:36

Zephon—*watching*
Son of Gad and tribal head . . . . Num. 26:15
Called Ziphion . . . . Gen. 46:16

Zer—*rock*
City assigned to Naphtali. . . . . .Josh. 19:32, 35

Zerah—*dawning*
1. Son of Reuel and chief of
    Edom. . . . . Gen. 36:17, 19; 1 Chr. 1:44
2. Son of Judah . . . . Num. 26:20
    Ancestor of Achan . . . . .Josh. 7:1–18
3. Son of Simeon and tribal head . . . . . Num. 26:12, 13
    Called Zohar . . . . Gen. 46:10
4. Gershomite Levite. . . . . .1 Chr. 6:20, 21, 41
5. Ethiopian general defeated by
    King Asa. . . . . .2 Chr. 14:8–15

Zerahiah—*Yahweh is appearing*
1. Ancestor of Ezra. . . . . .Ezra 7:1, 4, 5
2. Son of Pahath-Moab . . . . .Ezra 8:4

Zered—*willow bush*
Brook and valley crossed by Israel . . . . Num. 21:12

Zereda, Zeredah—*the fortress*
1. City of Ephraim; birthplace
    of Jeroboam. 1 Kin. 11:26
2. City in the Jordan Valley . . . . 2 Chr. 4:17
    Same as Zaretan in. . . . . .1 Kin. 7:46

Zererah
Town in the Jordan Valley . . . . .Judg. 7:22
Same as Zaretan . . . . .1 Kin. 7:46

Zeresh—*golden*
Wife of Haman. . . . . .Esth. 5:10, 14

Zereth—*splendor*
Judahite. . . . . 1 Chr. 4:5–7

Zereth Shahar—*the splendor of dawn*
City of Reuben .Josh. 13:19

Zeror—*bundle*
Benjamite . . . . .1 Sam. 9:1

Zeruah—*smitten; leprous*
Mother of King Jeroboam I . . . . .1 Kin. 11:26

Zerubbabel—*seed of Babel*
Descendant of David. . . . . 1 Chr. 3:19
Leader of Jewish exiles . . . . Neh. 7:6, 7
Restores worship in Jerusalem . . . . Ezra 3:1–8
Rebuilds the temple. . . . . Zech. 4:1–14
Prophecy concerning. . . . . Hag. 2:23
Ancestor of Christ . . . . . . Matt. 1:12, 13; Luke 3:27

Zeruiah—*balm*
Half sister of David . . . . 1 Chr. 2:16
Mother of Joab, Abishai, and Asahel . . . .2 Sam. 2:18

Zetham—*olive tree*
Gershonite Levite. . . . . .1 Chr. 23:7, 8

Zethan—*olive tree*
Benjamite . . . . .1 Chr. 7:6, 10

Zethar—*sacrifice*
One of the seven eunuchs of
    King Ahasuerus . . . . Esth. 1:10

Zia—*the trembler*
Gadite . . . . .1 Chr. 5:11, 13

Ziba—*plant*
Saul's servant. . . . . .2 Sam. 9:9
Befriends David . . . . 2 Sam. 16:1–4
Accused of deception by
    Mephibosheth . . . . 2 Sam. 19:17–30

Zibeon—*hyena*
Son of Seir and a clan chief . . . . .Gen. 36:20, 21

Zibia—*gazelle*
Benjamite and household head. . . . . . .1 Chr. 8:8, 9

Zibiah—*gazelle*
Mother of King Jehoash . . . . .2 Kin. 12:1

Zichri—*famous*
1. Kohathite Levite . . . . Ex. 6:21
2, 3, 4. Three Benjamites. . . . . .1 Chr. 8:19, 23, 27
5. Son of Asaph . . . . 1 Chr. 9:15
6. Descendant of Moses . . . . 1 Chr. 26:25
7. Reubenite . . . . 1 Chr. 27:16
8. Judahite . . . . .2 Chr. 17:16
9. Mighty man in Pekah's army . . . . 2 Chr. 28:7
10. Benjamite. . . . . .Neh. 11:9
11. Postexilic priest . . . . .Neh. 12:17

Ziddim—*sides*
City of Naphtali . . . . .Josh. 19:35

Ziha
Head of a Nethinim family . . . . Ezra 2:43

Ziklag—*winding*
　　City on the border of Judah........Josh. 15:1, 31
　　Assigned to Simeon ....Josh. 19:1, 5
　　Held by David.....................1 Sam. 27:6
　　Overthrown by Amalekites.......1 Sam. 30:1–31
　　Occupied by returnees ....Neh. 11:28

Zillah—*shadow*
　　One of Lamech's wives ....Gen. 4:19–23

Zillethai—*shadow of Yahweh*
　　1. Benjamite...........................1 Chr. 8:20
　　2. Manassite captain ....1 Chr. 12:20

Zilpah—*a drop*
　　Leah's maid ....Gen. 29:24
　　Mother of Gad and Asher ....Gen. 30:9–13

Zimmah—*counsel*
　　Gershonite Levite.............1 Chr. 6:20, 42, 43

Zimran—*antelope*
　　Son of Abraham and Keturah........Gen. 25:1, 2

Zimri—*pertaining to an antelope*
　　1. Grandson of Judah ....1 Chr. 2:3–6
　　　　Called Zabdi ....Josh. 7:1–18
　　2. Simeonite prince slain by
　　　　　　Phinehas.....................Num. 25:6–14
　　3. Benjamite..........................1 Chr. 8:1, 36
　　4. King of Israel for seven days........1 Kin. 16:8–20
　　5. Place or people otherwise unknown ......Jer. 25:25

Zin—*lowland*
　　Wilderness through which the Israelites
　　　　passed..........................Num. 20:1
　　Border of Judah and Edom ....Josh. 15:1–3

Zina—*abundance*
　　Son of Shimei.......................1 Chr. 23:10

Zion—*fortress*
　　A. Used literally of:
　　　　Jebusite fortress captured by David...2 Sam. 5:6–9
　　　　Place from which Solomon brings
　　　　　　the ark ....2 Chr. 5:2
　　　　Area occupied by the temple ....Is. 8:18
　　B. Used figuratively of:
　　　　Israel as a people of God.............2 Kin. 19:21
　　　　God's spiritual kingdom................Ps. 125:1
　　　　Eternal city.....................Heb. 12:22, 28
　　　　Heaven ....Rev. 14:1

Zior—*smallness*
　　Town of Judah.......................Josh. 15:54

Ziph—*refining place*
　　1. Town in south Judah.................Josh. 15:24
　　2. City in the hill country of Judah ....Josh. 15:55
　　　　David hides from Saul in wilderness
　　　　　　here ....1 Sam. 23:14, 15
　　3. Son of Jehallelel ....1 Chr. 4:16

Ziphah—*lent*
　　Son of Jehallelel.....................1 Chr. 4:16

Ziphites—*inhabitants of Ziph*
　　Betray David ....1 Sam. 23:19–24

Ziphron—*beautiful top*
　　Place in north Palestine ....Num. 34:9

Zippor—*sparrow*
　　Father of Balak ....Num. 22:4, 10

Zipporah—*bird*
　　Daughter of Jethro; wife of
　　　　Moses ....Ex. 2:18, 20–22; 18:1–6

Zithri—*my protection*
　　Grandson of Kohath ....Ex. 6:18, 22

Ziv—*splendor, bloom*
　　Second month of the Jewish year ....1 Kin. 6:1

Ziz—*brightness*
　　Pass leading from Dead Sea to
　　　　Jerusalem......................2 Chr. 20:16

Ziza—*brightness*
　　1. Simeonite leader................1 Chr. 4:24, 37, 38
　　2. Son of Rehoboam.................2 Chr. 11:18–20

Zizah
　　Gershonite Levite..............1 Chr. 23:7, 10, 11
　　Same as Zina ....1 Chr. 23:10

Zoan
　　City in Lower Egypt...............Num. 13:22
　　Place of God's miracles............Ps. 78:12, 43
　　Princes resided at ....Is. 30:2, 4
　　Object of God's wrath..............Ezek. 30:14

Zoar—*little*
　　Ancient city of Canaan originally named
　　　　Bela............................Gen. 14:2, 8
　　Spared destruction at
　　　　Lot's request ....Gen. 19:20–23
　　Seen by Moses from Mt. Pisgah .....Deut. 34:1–3
　　Object of prophetic doom ....Is. 15:5

Zobah
　　Syrian kingdom; wars against Saul ..1 Sam. 14:47

Zobebah—*the affable*
　　Judahite............................1 Chr. 4:1, 8

Zohar—*gray*
　　1. Father of Ephron the Hittite.............Gen. 23:8
　　2. Son of Simeon.......................Gen. 46:10

Zoheleth—*serpent*
　　Stone near En Rogel...................1 Kin. 1:9

Zoheth—*proud*
　　Descendant of Judah...............1 Chr. 4:1, 20

Zophah—*potbellied jug*
　　Asherite......................1 Chr. 7:30, 35, 36

Zophar—*chirper*
　　Naamathite and friend of Job ....Job 2:11

Zophim—*watchers*
　　Field on the top of Mt. Pisgah........Num. 23:14

Zorah—*hornet*
　　Town of Judah.....................Josh. 15:1, 33
　　Inhabited by Danites.............Josh. 19:40, 41

Place of Samson's birth
  and burial . . . . Judg. 13:24, 25; 16:30, 31
Inhabited by returnees . . . . Neh. 11:25, 29

Zorathite
Native of Zorah. . . . . 1 Chr. 4:2
Descendants of Caleb . . . . 1 Chr. 2:50, 53

Zorite
Same as Zorathite. . . . . 1 Chr. 2:54

Zuar—*small, little*
Father of Nethanel. . . . . Num. 1:8

Zuph—*honeycomb*
1. Ancestor of Samuel . . . . 1 Chr. 6:33, 35

2. Region in Judah . . . . 1 Sam. 9:4–6

Zur—*rock*
1. A Midianite leader. . . . . Num. 25:15, 18
2. Son of Jeiel. . . . . 1 Chr. 8:30; 9:35

Zuriel—*God is a rock*
Merarite Levite. . . . . Num. 3:35

Zurishaddai—*the Almighty is a rock*
Father of Shelumiel . . . . Num. 7:36, 41

Zuzim—*prominent; giant*
Tribe east of the Jordan . . . . Gen. 14:5
Probably same as Zamzummim . . . . Deut. 2:20